Well-Being

Well-Being:
The Foundations of
Hedonic Psychology

Daniel Kahneman,
Ed Diener, and
Norbert Schwarz   EDITORS

RUSSELL SAGE FOUNDATION
NEW YORK

The Russell Sage Foundation

The Russell Sage Foundation, one of the oldest of America's general purpose foundations, was established in 1907 by Mrs. Margaret Olivia Sage for "the improvement of social and living conditions in the United States." The Foundation seeks to fulfill this mandate by fostering the development and dissemination of knowledge about the country's political, social, and economic problems. While the Foundation endeavors to assure the accuracy and objectivity of each book it publishes, the conclusions and interpretations in Russell Sage Foundation publications are those of the authors and not of the Foundation, its Trustees, or its staff. Publication by Russell Sage, therefore, does not imply Foundation endorsement.

Library of Congress Cataloging-in-Publication Data

Well-Being: the foundations of hedonic psychology / Daniel Kahneman, Ed Diener,
  and Norbert Schwarz, editors.
    p. cm.
    Includes bibliographical references and index.
    ISBN 0-87154-424-5
1. Quality of life. 2. Pleasure. 3. Suffering. I. Kahneman,
Daniel. II. Diener, Ed. III, Schwarz, Norbert, Dr. phil.
BF637.C5F68 1999
152.4'2—dc21   98-32295
                     CIP

RUSSELL SAGE FOUNDATION
112 East 64th Street, New York, New York 10021
10 9 8 7 6 5 4 3 2 1

Contents

Acknowledgments

WE ARE GRATEFUL to the Russell Sage Foundation and to its president, Dr. Eric Wanner, for their exceptionally generous support of this project. The foundation supported the conference at which draft versions of the chapters were presented. Its support in the preparation of manuscripts and the collection of reviews of individual chapters also greatly helped us in our editorial task. The support of the foundation was based on the hope that this volume would promote the integration of diverse strands of research in the study of enjoyment and well-being and make the results of this research accessible to social scientists and ultimately to students and policymakers. We can only hope that the foundation's expectations will be met.

The able staff of the Woodrow Wilson School of Public and International Affairs at Princeton University took responsibility for the administration of the conference. We appreciate their help.

The Langfeld Fund of the Department of Psychology at Princeton University supported an initial workshop on issues of well-being, which led directly to the planning of this volume.

Kris Eaton at the University of Illinois carried out the difficult task of assembling the volume, with great organizational skill, unfailing good cheer, and considerable patience for the weaknesses of authors and editors.

We wish to thank the following individuals who provided insightful reviews and suggestions to chapter authors: Julian Barling, Jonathan Brown, Charles Carver, Margaret Clark, Martin Daly, Paul DiMaggio, Robert Emmons, Randy Gallistel, Ian Gotlib, Richard Gracely, Jerome Kagan, Richard Koestner, George Koob, Joseph LeDoux, George Loewenstein, Colin Martindale, Sandra Murray, Randolph Nesse, Jerry Parrott, Ira Roseman, Ruut Veenhoven, David Watson, Timothy Wilson, Hans Wittchen, and Albert Wu.

DANIEL KAHNEMAN
ED DIENER
NORBERT SCHWARZ

Preface

Daniel Kahneman, Ed Diener, and Norbert Schwarz

OUR AIM IN editing this book was not at all modest: we hoped to announce the existence of a new field of psychology. Hedonic psychology—that could be its name—is the study of what makes experiences and life pleasant or unpleasant. It is concerned with feelings of pleasure and pain, of interest and boredom, of joy and sorrow, and of satisfaction and dissatisfaction. It is also concerned with the whole range of circumstances, from the biological to the societal, that occasion suffering and enjoyment. Although the adjective "hedonic" is often used to refer solely to pleasure, hedonic psychology covers the full spectrum from the pleasant to the unpleasant, consistent with a definition of "hedonics" in Webster's New Universal Unabridged Dictionary, (1989) as a "branch of psychology that deals with pleasurable and unpleasurable states of consciousness." We apply the term even more broadly, to include levels of psychological analysis other than states of consciousness.

Enjoyment and suffering have attracted far less systematic research than many other psychological functions, such as attention or memory. The neglect of hedonics is obvious in the index sections of introductory textbooks: there are a few pages about pain, a mention of pleasure centers and the pleasure principle, but little else. There are typically no entries at all for happiness or well-being. This pattern does not reflect the importance of the topics in people's lives, but it does reflect the history of the dominant themes of modern psychology.

First there was behaviorism, then there was the cognitive revolution, and the study of hedonics could not thrive under either of these intellectual regimes. Feelings were explicitly rejected as a legitimate object of study in the behavioristic philosophy of science, and they were of little interest in the information-processing approach. Research on hedonics never actually ceased, but its results could not be elegantly described in the dominant theoretical language of the day. As a consequence, this research was relegated to peripheral regions, where small communities of investigators focused on different aspects of hedonics and developed separate dialects in which to speak about their particular problems. Students of the pleasures of food and of the pains of arthritis have had no common framework and little to say to each other, students of mood and well-being did not appear to be aware of the mutual relevance of their work, and the physiology and psychology of hedonic states were studied separately.

Another characteristic of past research is the remarkable accentuation of the negative. Textbooks that do not mention pleasure or well-being at all devote many pages to the clinical phenomena of anxiety and depression. This negative focus is due to many causes; the eternal fascination with the abnormal and the professional concerns of clinical psychologists are certainly part of the story. It is also relevant that the determinants of negative affective states are often associated with considerable urgency, and that the physiological and behavioral manifestations of these states are often obvious and dramatic; for these and other reasons, pain avoidance provides explanations of behavior that are often more compelling than explanations in terms of pleasure-seeking.

Our aim is to bring these threads together to facilitate an integrative view of hedonic experiences in all their instantiations. The hedonic psychology of the future, as we imagine it, will analyze the full range of evaluative experience, from sensory pleasure to creative ecstasy, from fleeting anxiety to long-term depression, from misery to joy. It will also address the determinants of these experiences, from the genetic to the societal, and from the biochemical to the cultural. Researchers will inevitably specialize, but they will be aware of their place in the broader picture and alert to the possibility of instructive parallels between phenomena in different domains.

We have tried to anticipate future developments by featuring some new approaches and by emphasizing some distinctions that have often been blurred in past research. The new approaches we

feature involve the collection of measures of hedonic experiences over time rather than total reliance on global retrospective evaluations, based
on the memory of past experiences. The study of
on-line measures of experience and real-time physiological measurements is in its infancy as this collection goes to press. We believe, however, that
there will be increasing use of such indices in the
future, and that they will eventually define the
standard for accurate measurement of the pleasures and pains of individual life, and for a more
objective measurement of overall well-being.

The distinction between real-time experience
and global retrospective evaluations raises new
questions, which have not yet attracted the attention they deserve. How do global evaluations of an
aspect of life, or of life as a whole, relate to the
actual pleasures and pains that an individual has
experienced over time? How accurate are these
retrospective evaluations? Related questions can be
raised about the accuracy of people's predictions
of their future pleasures and pains, and about their
intuitive understanding of the rules of hedonic
psychology. An ability to predict future tastes and
experiences is central to the economic model of
rational choice that provides the foundation for
much of the theorizing in the social sciences and
for many policy applications. Pursuing one's own
self-interest requires appropriate predictions of the
likely short-term and long-term hedonic consequences of different courses of action, but the
question of how people arrive at these predictions
has hardly been addressed in psychological research. The evidence available suggests that people
may not have the ability to predict their future
tastes and hedonic experiences with the accuracy
that the economic model requires.

THE SCOPE OF HEDONIC PSYCHOLOGY

The question of what makes for a good life can be
studied at many different levels. Starting at the top
of figure P.1, we note that any evaluation of quality of life is embedded in the cultural and social
context of both the subject and the evaluator. Alternative views of what constitutes a good life
must be part of the analysis. In particular, the serious student of well-being soon discovers that
quality of life cannot be reduced to the balance of
pleasure and pain, or to assessments of subjective
life-satisfaction; other values contribute to the
judgment. Moreover, objective characteristics of a
society, like poverty, infant mortality, crime rate, or

FIGURE P.1   Levels in the Analysis of the
Quality of Life

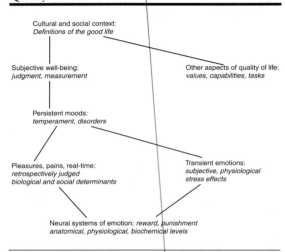

pollution, figure prominently at this level. Though
these qualifications are important, the experience
of pleasure and the achievement of a subjective
sense of well-being remain at the center of the
story.

Subjective well-being, at the next level down,
involves a component of judgment and comparisons with ideals, aspirations, other people, and
one's own past. Several decades ago, social scientists began large-scale investigations of individuals'
satisfaction with their lives and with their society.
One of the robust findings of this research was
that the correlations between global judgments of
the quality of life and objective conditions of living are often quite low. Leaders in this field, such
as Frank Andrews, Angus Campbell, Norman
Bradburn, and Gerald Gurin, emphasized, as we
do, the need for assessments of the positive aspects
of life, including pleasant emotions. Our selection
of chapters for this book belongs to this tradition,
but it also departs from the past in several ways—
perhaps most importantly in our emphasis on subjective and on physiological measures of ongoing
hedonic experience as an essential supplement to
global judgments of life.

One level below global well-being we find
mood states, which are characterized by their persistence and by their loose connection to particular
events. There are large individual differences in
people's characteristic mood, which clearly should
be assigned substantial weight in assessing their
well-being. Next we encounter affective states that
are more closely related to the current situation.

These include the many varieties of pleasures and pains, and transient emotional states. Each of these affective responses has multiple aspects beyond the subjective experience of the moment: there is a cognitive coding of the present, and a retrospective coding of past affect; there are both transient physiological and chemical changes and permanent adaptations.

The next level of reduction involves neural systems and the biochemistry of hormones and neurotransmitters that regulate the motivational systems with which affective responses at all levels are associated. One of the important lessons of recent years is that the physiological and biochemical levels of analysis are characterized by the prevalence of opponent systems and complex feedback loops, with effects that often appear paradoxical, such as the familiar "runner's high." And it is probably at these levels that the main keys to the understanding of addictions, anhedonia, and depression will be found.

This overview of levels of analysis suggests that an understanding of the higher levels will often require careful consideration of lower ones. However, there are also important influences that travel the other way. Among the most dramatic are the almost complete suppression of pain in some war-wounded and in some states of exaltation and the well-documented effects of mental states on physiological responses. We hope that collecting treatments of the different levels of analysis in a single volume will contribute to research that traces the connections between these levels. Equally important, it may contribute to an understanding of questions that arise at several levels, and may have related answers in all. One such question is the nature of the relation between positive and negative affect: is this a single bipolar dimension, where factors that produce one kind of affect can cancel the effects of factors that operate in the opposite direction? Or should we understand positive and negative affect as separate attributes of experience? This question can be raised at the level of self-reported affect, but it can also be raised at the biochemical levels, where pleasure and pain appear to be mediated by different neurotransmitters.

A related multi-level question concerns the apparent asymmetry between the relative potencies of pain and pleasure. In the context of decision research, the overweighing of negative consequences has been called loss aversion; does this phenomenon have a counterpart at the various levels of hedonic experience? Another general question concerns adaptation. This label has

sometimes been applied to negative feedback loops in the intracellular environment, and it has also been used to explain why the mean level of satisfaction with income hardly changed over a fifteen-year period in which mean income nearly doubled. Are there important commonalities in adaptation processes at different levels? Are there general characteristics of stimuli to which adaptation is easy or rapid? We believe that the pursuit of cross-level analogies is likely to yield useful hypotheses for future research, and we hope that bringing together discussions of these levels under a single cover will advance that process.

Cross-cutting this organization by levels of analysis, there is an organization by causes and contexts. It is useful to know the circumstances under which people are most likely to experience well-being or misery. For example, what is to be made of the finding that people experience many of their happiest moments in the presence of friends, whereas more intimate family relations are often loaded with substantial ambivalence? And what is the impact of insecurity about the future (for example, for people with no health insurance) on well-being? Issues like these have rarely been addressed in psychological research, but their investigation is likely to contribute to our basic understanding of hedonic experience as well as to psychology's relevance to society.

POLICY RELEVANCE

Our hope is that hedonic psychology will be relevant to policy. We recognize, with a large degree of humility, that scientific understanding in this field is currently woefully inadequate to provide a strong underpinning for national policies. We believe, however, that in the decades to come there will be much greater success in understanding hedonics, and that principles will emerge that can be used by policy makers. We are particularly hopeful that a scientific understanding of hedonic experience will allow for the development of valid hedonic indicators that reflect the pleasantness of life in the everyday experiences of people. At present, economic indicators hold the most sway in policy circles. Yet, the economic approach is limited in several ways. First, it focuses on those aspects of life that can be traded in the marketplace. Thus, desirable goods such as love, mental challenge, and stress are given little consideration. As people reach what Ronald Inglehart has labeled a "post-materialist" level in which basic physical needs are met, they become increasingly concerned with fulfillment in less materialistic realms. Second, the economic view presupposes that individuals will choose the greatest amount of utility for themselves; yet a great deal of evidence now contradicts this proposition. Third, economics assesses variables that are only indirect indicators of something else—of subjective fulfillment. What is not known is whether people are becoming happier or less happy, and in what situations people experience the most enduring pleasures. To this end, we propose that nations should begin monitoring pleasure and pain through on-line experience recording among samples of respondents to complement existing social indicators, and to provide a more direct assessment of the final outcome about which people are most concerned.

Fortunately, there have already been major advances in the field of hedonic psychology. The neural areas related to pleasure, pain, and to specific emotions are understood with increasing clarity, as are the hormonal underpinnings of hedonic phenomena. Scientists are accumulating increasing knowledge of affect—of mood and emotion—that promises to shed light on the long-term aspects of pleasant experience. We are beginning to understand factors such as adaptation that can strongly influence pleasurable and unpleasurable feelings, and the personality correlates of pleasant experiences are receiving increasing empirical attention. Thus, despite our relatively modest degree of understanding, progress in the science of hedonics has been made in the last several decades.

The following chapters present overviews of the knowledge accumulated thus far about hedonics. Our advice to authors was to make the chapters accessible to educated lay readers. Our selection of topics was based on the idea that hedonics can be understood well only through an approach that brings together understanding at all levels of analysis. Although there are several glaring omissions in the book, we believe that most important topics are covered. And we hope that reading this volume will bring to each reader a degree of pleasure.

Part I

How Can We Know Who Is Happy? Conceptual and Methodological Issues

1   Objective Happiness

Daniel Kahneman

An assessment of a person's objective happiness over a period of time can be derived from a dense record of the quality of experience at each point-instant utility). Logical analysis suggests that episodes should be evaluated by the temporal integral of instant utility. Objective happiness is defined by the average of utility over a period of time. The concept of instant utility must be rich enough to support its role in the assessment of happiness. A purely hedonic concept will not be adequate. The brain constructs a running affective commentary, which evaluates the current state on a Good/Bad (GB) dimension. The commentary has physiological and behavioral manifestations. Although "Good" and "Bad" appear to be mediated by separate systems that can be active concurrently, the description of each moment by a single GB value remains useful. The GB dimension has a natural zero point, "neither pleasant nor unpleasant," which retains its hedonic significance across contexts and permits a measurement of the relative frequencies and durations of positive and negative affect. Comparisons to expectations are an important source of pleasure and pain, but routine experiences are not necessarily affectively neutral. Adaptation to new circumstances has been attributed to a "hedonic treadmill," which reduces the hedonic effect of changes. Some of the evidence for a hedonic treadmill may be due to a satisfaction treadmill, in which the standards that people apply to declare themselves satisfied change. People often assess the well-being effects of states by using the affective value of transitions to these states. Such judgments ignore adaptation. Attempts to estimate the effect of changed circumstances on well-being are susceptible to a focusing illusion in which the weight of the new circumstance is exaggerated. Inferences from preferences to actual hedonic experience are risky. The imbalance of responses to losses and to gains is perhaps more pronounced in decisions than in experience. Retrospective evaluations of episodes give special weight to Peak Affect and End Affect and are insensitive to the duration of episodes. These characteristics of evaluation can yield absurd preferences.

Questions about satisfaction with life domains or general happiness are answered by applying heuristics, which are associated with particular biases.

HOW HAPPY WAS HELEN IN MARCH? A question is raised in a conversation between two psychologists about a common friend: "How happy was Helen in March?" In the context of an informal conversation, this question would usually be understood and answered with little difficulty. If we know Helen well and saw her often in March, we probably believe we know whether she was happy then, we almost certainly believe that *she* knows whether she was happy then, and with even greater certainty we believe that she knew it then. We also expect our answer to be understood more or less as intended. But we retain this confidence only so long as we remain in the role of intuitive judges in an informal conversation. As soon as we take on the scientific role, we are no longer sure of what the question means, or of the kind of information that we need in order to answer it. The aim of this chapter is to narrow the gap between lay knowledge and professional ignorance. I explore a concept of *objective happiness,* which is an attempt to specify what an objective observer would need to know in order to determine how happy Helen was in March, and the rules for using that knowledge.

A BOTTOM-UP APPROACH TO THE ANALYSIS OF WELL-BEING

The utterances "I am enjoying this experience and would like it to continue," "Last evening was fun," "I am satisfied with my job," and "I am very happy" all refer to a favorable state of being. All imply a positive value on a broad dimension that will here be labeled GB (for Good/Bad) to avoid the overly intellectual connotation of the commonly used term "evaluation." The four variants of the GB dimension differ in the level of integration to which they refer.

1. Being pleased or distressed is an attribute of experience at a particular moment. I will label this attribute *instant utility*, borrowing the term "utility" from Bentham (1789/1948).[1] Instant utility is best understood as the strength of the disposition to continue or to interrupt the current experience.
2. *Remembered utility* is the global evaluation that is retrospectively assigned to a particular past episode or to a situation in which similar experiences recur. This global evaluation can be expressed in words such as "liked it" and "hated it" or in emotional responses of fear or eager anticipation when a recurrence is likely.
3. Satisfaction questions refer to more inclusive domains of life, such as family life or work.
4. At the highest level of integration we find dimensions such as happiness, or well-being, which encompass all domains of life.

The goal of this chapter is to advance our understanding of the higher level of integration. We want to understand and to be able to assess Helen's happiness. The perspective of the present chapter is bottom-up. It takes the instant utility of the moment as the basic unit of analysis and seeks an objective and normatively justified definition of "true" well-being that is based mainly on information about instant utility.[2] An assessment of Helen's objective happiness in March should be made on the basis of the relevant aspects of her life during that month by applying definite rules to summarize this information in a single value. Helen's own judgment of how happy she was in March is viewed as a fallible estimate of her objective well-being. This conception does not deny the significance of Helen's evaluation of her life. Her thoughts about whether she is currently happy or depressed are themselves causes of pleasure and pain and can be significant if they are frequent and emotionally arousing. In the present framework, however, what Helen thinks about her happiness matters to her "true" or objective well-being only to the extent that her thoughts affect the pleasantness or unpleasantness of particular moments in her life.

Figure 1.1 illustrates the basic approach in an elementary case. The figure presents records of the pain reported by two patients undergoing colonoscopy (Redelmeier and Kahneman 1996). The patients were prompted every sixty seconds to report the intensity of their current pain. They were to use a scale where 10 was "intolerable pain" and 0 was "no pain at all." Later the patients evaluated the experience as a whole, compared it to other unpleasant experiences, and made a hypothetical

FIGURE 1.1   Pain Intensity Reported by Two Colonoscopy Patients

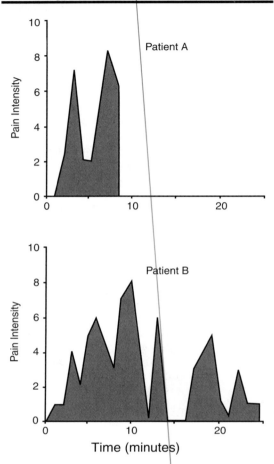

Source: Redelmeier and Kahneman 1996, 4. Reprinted with permission from the International Association for the Study of Pain.

choice between a repeat colonoscopy and a barium enema. We wish to use these data to answer questions such as: "How bad was Patient A's overall experience of colonoscopy?" "Who had the worse experience, Patient A or Patient B?" The approach to these questions (developed in the next section) accepts the patients' ratings of instantaneous pain as valid but does not take their global assessments of the experience at face value. As will be shown later in the chapter, the retrospective evaluations of patients are suspect because they are liable to biases of memory and to a process of evaluation that sometimes violates elementary logical rules. Instead of relying on the patients' judgments, we identify prescriptive principles that should govern the evaluation of episodes. These principles are then applied to evaluate the profiles of particular episodes, such as those illustrated in figure 1.1. The individual's own retrospective evaluation of the experience (its *remembered utility*) is viewed as a fallible estimate of this constructed evaluation, which is called the *total utility* of the episode (Kahneman, Wakker, and Sarin 1997).

This chapter extends the idea of bottom-up construction of global evaluations to levels of integration higher than brief episodes, including judgments of satisfaction with life domains and overall happiness. We distinguish two notions of happiness, or well-being (the two terms are used interchangeably in this chapter). *Subjective happiness* is assessed by asking respondents to state how happy they are. *Objective happiness* is derived from a record of instant utility over the relevant period. The relation between subjective and objective happiness is precisely analogous to the relation between the remembered utility and the total utility of episodes. Like the total utility of a colonoscopy, Helen's objective happiness in the month of March is to be derived according to appropriate rules from a record of her instant utility during that month.

Objective happiness, of course, is ultimately based on subjective data: the Good/Bad experiences of moments of life. It is labeled objective because the aggregation of instant utility is governed by a logical rule and could in principle be done by an observer with access to the temporal profile of instant utility (Kahneman, Wakker, and Sarin 1997). Objective happiness is not to be confused with objective good fortune, which is an assessment of the circumstances of someone's life. All combinations of levels of good or bad fortune, objective happiness or misery, and subjective happiness or misery are possible, and all are probably quite common.

The goals of this chapter are to identify some of the logical and technical problems that need to be solved to turn the measurement of objective happiness into a practical possibility; to identify some of the biases that affect individuals' global judgments of their experiences; and to present an account of the bottom-up approach that is sufficiently clear to advance the discussion of how this approach should be modified, or perhaps to identify fatal flaws that should cause it to be abandoned.

A LOGIC FOR OBJECTIVE HAPPINESS

The conceit of this chapter is that an observer could evaluate Helen's objective happiness in March on the basis of a continuous record of her status on the Good/Bad dimension, along the lines of figure 1.1. This approach is hardly new. More than a century ago, the economist Francis Edgeworth (1881) wrote of using a "hedonimeter" in just this way. A natural way to use such a record is to define the total utility experienced during an interval of time by the temporal integral of instant utility. The temporal integration idea was formulated by Edgeworth (1881), more recent statements of it can be found in Parfit (1984), Broome (1991), and Parducci (1995), and it is invoked implicitly or explicitly in utilitarian analyses (Glover 1990).

The core idea that leads to temporal integration is straightforward, and the colonoscopy example can be used to illustrate it. Obviously, there are two ways of making a painful medical procedure worse: by increasing the level of pain, or by making the procedure longer. Thus, an equivalence can be established between changes of pain intensity and of duration. Furthermore, because duration is measured on a ratio scale in physical units, it is possible in principle to rescale pain intensity in terms of duration.

Kahneman, Wakker, and Sarin (1997) investigated the logical conditions that would justify the temporal integral of instant utility as a measure of the total utility of outcomes. The theory is concerned with profiles of instant utility, such as those illustrated in figure 1.1, that are produced by a subject recording her experiences. Stringent assumptions about the subject's ratings of instant utility are made: these ratings must contain all the relevant information required for its temporal integral to be a plausible measure of the total utility of an extended period. It is also assumed that the scale has a stable and distinctive zero point ("neither good nor bad," "neither approach nor avoid"), and that the measurement of positive and negative deviations from zero is ordinal. The subject's ratings correctly order experiences by the intensity of Good or Bad, but the intervals between ratings may be arbitrary: a pain rating of 7 is reliably worse than a rating of 6, but the interval between 7 and 6 need not be psychologically equivalent to the interval between 3 and 2.

In addition to the subject, the theory involves an observer, who is knowledgeable about the subject's use of the scale. The observer and the subject may be the same person. The observer's task is to make comparative judgments about utility profiles. These judgments, if they satisfy some rather innocuous axioms,[3] effectively determine the equivalence between the original utility scale and duration. At least in principle, this trade-off can then be used to rescale the reports made by the subject. For example, suppose that the observer judges that one minute of pain at level 7 is as bad as two minutes of pain at level 6. According to the theory, this judgment implies that the original reports of pain should be rescaled, assigning level 7 a value that is twice as high as the value assigned to level 6. If the observer's judgments obey the axioms, the theory asserts that a consistent rescaling is possible, yielding a ratio scale for instant utility that is calibrated by its relation to duration. The rescaling procedure is a close cousin of the method used in medical research to estimate Quality-Adjusted Life Years (QALYs) by establishing equivalences between years of survival in normal health and years of survival at some lower level of health (Weinstein, Fineberg, et al. 1980).

The formal analysis describes a theoretical possibility, not a practical procedure. Its contribution is to clarify the logic that applies to the evaluation of profiles of instant utility. It is important to note that the rule of temporal integration may not apply to the original profiles. It applies only after a rescaling that incorporates a judgment about the equivalence of intensity and duration. Independent of whether or not it is implemented by rescaling instant utility, the principle of temporal integration highlights the importance of duration. The principle is consistent with the intuition that it is imprudent to seek short and intense pleasures that are paid for by prolonged mild distress. The theory also provides an intuitively appealing account of cases in which the consumption of memories matters. It suggests, for example, that the evaluation of the global utility of a safari in Kenya should properly include subsequent episodes of slide-showing and story-telling.

Utility profiles can be used to describe brief episodes, as illustrated by figure 1.1, or longer periods, such as the month of March for Helen. Two families of cases can be distinguished. In some, such as colonoscopies and Caribbean cruises, duration is a relevant characteristic of the outcome that is to be evaluated. It makes sense to say that one cruise is better than another because it is longer. In such cases, as implied by the definition of total utility, the temporal integral of the rescaled profile (the area under the curve) is the appropriate index with which to compare outcomes that vary in duration. In other cases, the duration of the profile is arbitrary: it does not make sense to say that the month of March was better than the first week of March because it was longer. To compare profiles of this type for periods of different length, the appropriate index is the average height of the rescaled profile. Thus, the objective happiness of Helen in March should be measured by the average of the instant utility that she experienced during that period, after appropriate rescaling.

The conception of instant utility is severely constrained by its proposed role in the definitions of total utility and of objective happiness. The concept of what it is that makes a moment good or bad must be sufficiently rich for integration and averaging to be plausible. Philosophical discussions of the measurement of well-being (for a useful introduction, see Brock 1993) remind us of the common intuition that the evaluation of happiness is in part a moral judgment, which invokes a conception of the good life. A physiological indicator that responds strongly to the pleasures of food and sex but shows only a minuscule response to music would be rejected as a measure of instant utility, both on such philosophical grounds and because it would fail to correspond to the intuitions of music lovers about what makes them happy.[4]

What should a concept of instant utility include? The hedonic quality of current sensory experience is the first candidate, of course, but it is not sufficient. The pleasures and pains associated with anticipation of future experience and with remembering the past must surely be counted (Elster and Loewenstein 1992). Other pleasures (and pains) of the mind are to be included as well (Kubovy, this volume). In particular, the measure of instant utility must allow for states of "flow" (Csikszentmihalyi 1990) in which one is so involved in an experience or activity that hedonic value fades into the background of experience. More generally, the index of instant utility should be adequately sensitive to involvement in tasks and activities (Cantor and Sanderson, this volume). And, of course, the notion of a GB value for a moment must be closely related to an assessment of mood, which is interpreted as reflecting the current balance between resources and demands (Morris, this volume). To capture common intuitions about well-being, an adequate measure should also distinguish between activities that have a promotion focus or a prevention focus (Higgins, Grant, and Shah, this volume) and between situations that vary in the extent of personal control (Peterson, this volume).

The diversity of Good and Bad states is intimidating, and the task of constructing a ratio scale measure of instant utility that can be applied to all these states is formidably difficult and perhaps intractable. However, the study of objective happiness can be pursued usefully with much weaker measurements of instant utility. As discussed later, it is not particularly difficult to distinguish good, bad, and neutral moments, and distinguishing a few categories of intensity among good and bad states is probably no harder. And as a first approximation, it makes sense to call Helen "objectively happy" if she spent most of her time in March engaged in activities that she would rather have continued than stopped, little time in situations she wished to escape, and—very important because life is short—not too much time in a neutral state in which she would not care either way. This is the essence of the approach proposed here.

THE GOOD/BAD DIMENSION

The bottom-up construction of objective happiness from a record of momentary experience requires that each moment be uniquely characterized by a value on the Good/Bad dimension. Two separate assumptions are involved: that the brain continuously constructs an affective or hedonic commentary on the current state of affairs, and that this commentary is adequately summarized by a single value. The first assumption has a fair amount of support; the second is clearly an oversimplification, but perhaps a tolerable one. The two assumptions are discussed in turn in this and in the following section.

The pervasiveness of the GB dimension was noted long ago. Frijda (1986) writes: "According to Wundt (1903), Titchener (1908) and others, 'feelings' are a basic, irreducible kind of mental element. . . . They presuppose the presence of sensations, that is, they presuppose some object the feeling is about. They have the property of subjectivity. They are experienced in one's own subjective response, rather than as asserting a property of the object. They are evaluative. They imply acceptance or nonacceptance of the stimulus or of the experience itself" (179). Frijda cites a participant in an introspective study of pleasant and unpleasant fragrances (Young 1927): "When I say 'pleasant,' it doesn't stand for anything more than I would smell it more if I could." As these quotations from psychological classics illustrate, the GB dimension has two aspects: it involves both an attribute of subjective experience and an action tendency: to go on or to stop.

The idea that evaluation on a Good/Bad dimension occurs continuously and automatically was later developed in several important bodies of research. In their reviews of the literature, Bargh (1997) and Zajonc (1997) both noted the relevance of early studies of the semantic differential (Osgood, Suci, and Tannenbaum 1957), which showed that most stimuli evoke distinctly positive or negative values on a factor of evaluation (marked by the scales "good-bad," "beautiful-ugly," "kind-cruel"). Zajonc (1980, 1997) and Bargh (1997) describe strong experimental evidence for the proposition that every stimulus evokes an affective evaluation, and that this evaluation can occur outside of awareness. As indicated by the famous subtitle of his essay ("Preferences Need No Inferences"), Zajonc (1980) suggested further that evaluation is at least partly independent of the cognitive processing of information about the stimulus. He later argued (Zajonc 1997) that this claim is supported by the discovery of a direct neural pathway that mediates some emotions and bypasses the systems that normally serve conscious processing of information (LeDoux and Armony, this volume).

Lang (1995) has reported studies of the interactive effects of concurrent stimuli, which provide strong support for the existence of a common mechanism that evaluates stimuli as good or bad, pleasant or threatening. Thus, the magnitude of the blink evoked by a burst of loud noise is potentiated in the presence of aversive pictures (for example, poisonous snakes, aimed guns) and apparently inhibited in the presence of pleasing pictures (for example, happy babies, appetizing food). The generality of the evaluative process is also supported by an experiment (Bargh et al. 1996) in which the prior presentation of any positively evaluated word (such as *water*) was found to facilitate selectively the rapid pronunciation of any other positively evaluated word (such as *Friday*).

The close and immediate link between the GB dimension and tendencies to approach or avoid has been demonstrated in several experiments. For example, Bargh (1997) describes a replication of a striking study (Solarz 1960) in which subjects were instructed to eliminate a word from the screen by moving a lever. Half of the subjects pulled the lever toward themselves, half pushed it away. Subjects were relatively faster in pulling a lever toward themselves (approach) in response to an attractive stimulus, and relatively faster in pushing the lever away (avoidance) when the word was aversive. Other demonstrations of the links between affective evaluation and movements that express approach or avoidance have been described by Cacioppo, Priester, and Berntson (1993) and by Förster and Strack (1996).

Several physiological correlates of evaluation have been identified (see Ito and Cacioppo, this volume; Davidson 1992, 1994). These include subtle electromyographic changes in facial muscles—with zygomatic activity indicating positive affect and corrugator activity indicating negative affect. In a series of important experiments, Davidson and his colleagues (for a review, see Davidson 1992) have found that differences in the activation of the anterior regions of the left and right cortices are correlated with the quality of experience. Starting in infancy (Davidson and Fox 1989), a predominance of left-sided anterior activation is associated with positive states, whereas a predominance of right-sided activation indicates negative affect. At a still more basic level, there are discussions of specific neural pathways that deal with the computation of overall reward value (see Shizgal, this volume) and specific neurotransmitters that appear to be involved in the control of approach/avoidance tendencies (Hoebel, this volume).

All these lines of evidence, from the introspective to the biochemical, point to the existence of a continuous evaluative process, which manifests itself in physiological responses at several levels, in expressions of affect and in an immediate propensity to approach or to avoid. The continuous Good/Bad commentary is not necessarily conscious. When it is conscious, it is experienced as pleasure or distress, with a corresponding acceptance or rejection of the stimulus. The notions of acceptance and rejection imply that the GB commentary is associated with a disposition to respond both emotionally and instrumentally to an unexpected interruption of an experience: the interruption of a pleasurable activity will elicit frustration and may evoke resistance; the interruption of a painful state will be accepted with relief. The GB commentary has multiple physiological and behavioral manifestations that are potentially available for continuous measurement. The prospects for useful measurement of the momentary GB value are examined in greater detail in subsequent sections.

IS THERE ONE GB VALUE AT A TIME?

The discussion so far has presupposed that any moment of time can be characterized by a particular value of the GB dimension—positive, neutral, or negative. Doubts would be cast on this assumption by finding that an evaluation can be both Good and Bad at the same time, or by finding that major manifestations of the GB dimension can be dissociated.

The Good and the Bad regions of the GB dimension are subjectively distinguished by different qualities of experience. They also appear to be mediated by different mechanisms (Cacioppo and Berntson 1994). Approach and avoidance are associated with different neurotransmitters (Hoebel, this volume), reward and punishment with distinct neural pathways (Gray 1994), and positive and negative affect with differential lateral activity in the anterior cortex (Davidson 1992, 1994). There is also ample evidence that approach and avoidance tendencies can occur simultaneously or in rapid alternation, generating internal conflict. Furthermore, studies of individual differences suggest that the frequency and intensity of good and bad affect are independent rather than negatively correlated (Diener and Emmons 1985). Cacioppo and Berntson (1994) concluded, from this and other evidence, that evaluation is better described as bivalent than as bipolar (see also Ito and Cacioppo, this volume).

The bivalent nature of the Good/Bad system is not necessarily incompatible with the notion that most moments can be usefully characterized by a single value on a bipolar Good/Bad dimension. A bivalent system yields a bipolar dimension if the separate mechanisms that mediate Good and Bad are mutually inhibitory or reciprocally innervated (Lang 1995) or if the relevant output of the system is the difference between the levels of activity of the two mechanisms (for example, Davidson 1992). Lang's studies of the effects of pleasant pictures on the startle reflex demonstrate the inhibitory connection. Davidson (1992) suggested that the brain may compute both the sum and the difference of the levels of activity in the separate systems that mediate positive and negative affect. He proposed that the GB value corresponds to the difference, and that emotional arousal corresponds to the summed activity in the two systems.

In summary, it appears that most moments of experience can be adequately characterized by a single summary value on the GB dimension. This summary is crude or misleading in some cases: experiences such as those of a straining runner or a spectator watching a tragedy call for more differentiated descriptions. Even in such cases, however, it is usually possible to locate the moment on the Good or on the Bad side of neutral, by applying the additional criterion of whether an interruption would be welcome or resisted. Would the runner be relieved by an announcement that the race is canceled? Would the spectator welcome the unexpected termination of the performance?

The bipolar nature of the Good/Bad dimension raises some difficult questions. The first such question concerns the relation between pleasure and diminishing pain. Imagine, for example, that you are out in the country during a cold night, inadequately dressed for the torrential rain, your clothes soaked.[5] A stinging cold wind completes your misery. As you wander around you run into a large rock that provides some shelter from the fury of the wind. The event is certainly associated with a reduction of pain. Cabanac (1992) would call the experience of that moment intensely pleasurable, because he believes that the function of pleasure is to indicate the direction of a biologically significant change. However, the experience could also be described as a composite of pleasure and pain, or perhaps as a succession of affective events in which pleasurable relief is quickly followed by a return of (diminished) distress. There is little hope of resolving this problem by introspection, but good reason to believe that the relation between diminishing pain and pleasure will eventually be clarified by studies of relevant brain activity.

Another instructive example, discussed in Kahneman (1992), is the response to a much-wanted salary increase that turns out to be smaller than expected. Casual introspection suggests that, if you expected a raise of $3,000 and received less, any intermediate amount involves both a gain and a loss; there is no intermediate value for which the affective response is neutral. A possible resolution is that this situation resembles familiar examples of bi-stable perceptual organization, such as the Necker cube or Leeper's picture of the wife/mother-in-law. The Necker cube is never seen in two orientations at once, but the orientations dominate in alternation. The perception of a bi-stable figure is best described statistically, by specifying the rate of alternation and the relative proportion of time in which each of the percepts dominates. A similar type of description may prove useful in many situations of affective bivalence and ambivalence.

Observations of hypnotic dissociation reported by Hilgard (1977) suggest that incompatible affective processes can occur in parallel and in relative isolation from each other. Subjects in Hilgard's laboratory were sometimes instructed to maintain a "hidden observer" who would "know what is going on" and who could be reached by tapping the subject's shoulder. In one of the demonstrations, a hypnotized subject was instructed to suck a lemon, which was to be experienced as a delicious orange. As expected, the subject sucked the lemon with every evidence of delight, but when his shoulder was touched he instantly clapped his hand to his mouth, crying, "You have squirted acid in my mouth!" Any simple description of such an experience will be arbitrary to some extent.

Studies of hypnotic analgesia suggest that the hypnotic instruction has its strongest effects on reports of subjective experience and on expressive movements that are under voluntary control. Hilgard states: "The indicators that are essentially *involuntary* (italics in original) have seldom shown consistent reduction under hypnotic analgesia. A subject who is perfectly comfortable and at ease through suggested hypnotic analgesia may still show a rise in heart rate or blood pressure" (Hilgard and Hilgard 1975, 75; see also Berridge, this volume). These observations raise questions about the interpretation of other instances of top-down control of pain (Melzack and Wall 1965). There are well-documented reports of severely wounded soldiers reporting no pain at all during continued fighting and through their evacuation. A compelling film, which often causes observers to feel faint, shows a trepanation operation performed with a blunt-appearing stone on the skull of an awake, impassive member of an African tribe. Do such feats of pain control represent a true reduction of pain or only the inhibition of some of its manifestations? (see Eich et al., this volume; Hilgard 1977).

TOWARD A COMMON METRIC OF GB VALUE

The references to a single GB dimension in this discussion assume that eating a ripe cherry and watching one's favorite team win the pennant share the important attribute of Goodness, and that arthritic pains and pangs of guilt are both Bad. The project of assessing objective happiness from a record of GB values requires methods of measurement that permit comparisons of GB values across contexts.

An obvious objection to the idea of a common GB metric is that there can be no meaningful comparison of intensity between experiences that differ in their quality. A particular instance of that problem was directly addressed in an important program of research on pain (Melzack 1983; see Eich et al., this volume). The findings confirmed both the existence of qualitative differences between experiences of pain and the possibility of applying a single scale of global intensity to different kinds of pain. The McGill Pain Questionnaire (MPQ) (Melzack, 1983) consists of twenty separate sets of adjectives that represent different qualities of pain, or different attributes of the experience. The categories are divided into four groups: sensory, affective, evaluative, and miscellaneous. The adjectives are ordered by intensity within each set, and the patient responds to each adjective by indicating whether it applies. For example, scale 1 consists of the labels "Flickering, Quivering, Pulsing, Throbbing, Beating, Pounding." Another sensory scale (7) consists of "Hot, Burning, Scalding, Searing." One of the evaluative scales (16) includes "Annoying, Troublesome, Miserable, Intense, Unbearable." The questionnaire also includes a set of adjectives that describe overall Present Pain Intensity (PPI): "No pain, Mild, Discomforting, Distressing, Horrible, Excruciating."

The exemplary methodology that Melzack and his collaborators applied to develop the MPQ could in principle be extended to other domains. They collected adjectives that are frequently used to describe pain and required judges to group them into sets that could be ordered by intensity, using psychometric methods to select descriptors that represent distinct values on each underlying scale. Finally, they had patients complete the questionnaire and investigated various ways of generating an overall score from the separate scales. A very encouraging result was obtained: a simple sum of ranks across scales yielded a scale that was highly correlated with the PPI measure. This finding sustains the more general hope that it may be possible to measure different kinds of GB experiences on a common scale, without intolerable distortion or loss of information.

Now consider the task of measuring Helen's GB experience during the month of March. Obviously, it is not possible to obtain from her a continuous record of her instant utility. However, the techniques of experience sampling (Stone, Shiffman, and DeVries, this volume) can be used to achieve a useful estimate. Helen might be probed at irregular intervals by a beeper mounted in a special watch, which also displays a scale on which she can select a value that describes the GB value of the moment. To support the measurement of her objective happiness by the average of instant utility, Helen would be required to apply the scale to an extraordinarily broad range of situations and stimuli: embarrassment and a stubbed toe, a gourmet dish and a joke.

Devising a scale that can be applied to many types of stimuli is not difficult. For example, Helen could surely rate qualitatively diverse experiences on a scale anchored, say, on the adjectives "intolerable" and "thrilling."[6] The key question is whether she would be able to use the scale consistently across contexts, thus ensuring that a given rating, say, "Quite Good," corresponds to the same instant utility. To achieve this goal, Helen should be instructed to evaluate her current subjective experience, not the current stimulus. Judging stimuli induces a strong tendency to relate each object to its most natural frame of reference: just as the adjective "tall" does not mean the same thing when applied to a child and to an adult, "quite good" does not have the same hedonic meaning when applied to a breakfast omelette and to a gourmet dish. This tendency can be overcome, however, and there is much evidence of people's ability to adjust their use of scales as required by instructions and by circumstances (Parducci 1995). It is therefore likely that Helen could eventually learn to make GB ratings that reflect the attribute of experience that is shared by good moments of various kinds.

Is there a way to confirm that the GB scale is used appropriately? An economist might wish to anchor the scale in consequential choices, so that GB ratings correspond to preferences. An individual who assigns the same ratings to moments of two different experiences should be equally willing to accept these moments. Unfortunately, single moments are not meaningful units of choice; significant outcomes are normally extended over time and particular moments cannot be segregated. As we shall see later, there are other reasons to reject preferences as the final criterion for the value of experiences.

A more promising approach to the validation of subjective reports of GB values—and more generally, to the measurement of this dimension—may emerge from research on the neuropsychology and psychophysiology of affect (Davidson 1994; Ito and Cacioppo, this volume). It is conceivable, if not likely, that a composite physiological measure of the GB response could eventually be constructed, and that this measurement would be quite highly correlated with subjective experience of pleasure and distress. Continuous records of affective state could possibly be derived from non-invasive measures of localized brain activity, eventually leading to accurate assessments of well-being over time. The movement from science fiction to practical application is likely to be rapid in this domain.

DOES THE GB DIMENSION HAVE A ZERO POINT?

The question we consider next is whether the zero point of the GB scale ("neither good nor bad") retains the same interpretation as circumstances change in any particular domain, such as food quality, income, or health, and across different domains of experience.

Suppose that Helen's financial circumstances have recently changed for the better, and that her eating habits have changed accordingly. She has graduated from hamburgers and canned tuna to filet mignon and rare tuna steak. Helen's ranking of these items has not changed: even in her days of poverty she preferred tuna steak to tuna salad. However, her talk of food suggests that she now derives less pleasure from food of any given quality: she indicates reduced enjoyment of both superb salad and mediocre steak. In particular, the quality of the food that she labels "neither pleasant nor unpleasant" has also shifted: she now attaches this label to items that she would have called "quite pleasurable" earlier. How are we to interpret what has happened to Helen's hedonic experience of food? Is Helen on a "hedonic treadmill" (Brickman and Campbell 1971; Frederick and Loewenstein, this volume) that completely negates the effect of her improved circumstances?

To interpret Helen's changing hedonic response to food, we compare it to two standard psychological experimental demonstrations: color aftereffects and absolute judgment of length. Imagine a color perception experiment, conducted in two sessions. On each trial of the first session, the subject is initially exposed to strong green light, then to an adjustable mixture of green and red lights. The subject's task is to describe various mixtures on a scale ranging from intense red, through reddish, "neither red nor green" (or white), greenish, and intense green. The second session is similar to the first except for the initial phase of each trial, in which the subject is now exposed to intense red light. A color aftereffect will be observed: the proportion of red light in the mixture that is described as "white" will be much higher in the second session than in the first.

Now consider a two-session experiment in which the subject is exposed to lines of differing length, which are to be described on a scale that ranges from "very long," through "neither long nor short," to "very short." In the first session the subject is exposed to lines ranging from three to twenty millimeters. In the second session, the lines range from ten to fifty millimeters. A context effect will be observed: a line that is described as "neither long nor short" in the first session will be judged "short" or "very short" in the second.

We now consider two questions that are central to the argument of this chapter. Is there an essential difference between the processes that give rise to shifting scales of judgment in the two experiments? If there is a difference, which of the two provides a better model for Helen's changing attitude to food?

Because of the behavioristic tradition of scaling research, the context effects observed in the two experiments are commonly considered similar, if not identical. Both experiments are examples of the oddly labeled absolute judgment task, and standard treatments of this task do not distinguish them (Birnbaum 1982; Helson 1964; Parducci 1995). In fact, the color and length experiments differ in three important aspects.

1. One difference between the two experiments is in the nature of the scales: the scale of length is unipolar, and "short" is roughly equivalent to "not very long"; in contrast, the hue dimension defined by red and green is bipolar, with different sensory qualities on either side of a zero point that is itself distinctive—either "white" or "neither red nor green." The bipolar scale is linked to two distinct mechanisms, which are selectively sensitive to red and green light and linked by an opponent process. A similar structure is found in the temperature sense, a bipolar dimension in which different systems mediate the response to cold and to heat.

2. The similar results observed in the color and length experiments are produced by different processes: color adaptation reflects a change in the sensory mechanism, whereas the context effect observed in size judgments is driven by the requirements of effective communication. Parducci's range-frequency theory (described in the context of an analysis of happiness in Parducci, 1995) explains how respondents adapt their use of the set of labels to the distribution of observations in a way that tends to optimize the informativeness of stated judgments. This is also what people do in adapting labels to categories, as in the familiar example of a large mouse climbing up the trunk of a small elephant.

3. A compelling difference between the experiments is phenomenologically obvious but surprisingly neglected in the scaling literature: subjects in the color experiment will report that the light mixtures that they called

"white" in the two sessions actually looked alike, whereas the lines they called "neither long nor short" looked quite different. In the length experiment, subjects learn to attach new labels to the unchanging experience of any given stimulus, but in the color experiment it is the experience that changes.[7]

A corollary of these differences is that the neutral value of the scale is appropriately labeled a perceptual zero point in the case of color, but not in the case of length. We are now ready for the question of whether the Good/Bad dimension is more like color or more like length. The answer is unequivocal: in all the aspects listed, the hedonic dimension resembles color more than it resembles size. Like the red-green scale, the hedonic scale is bipolar: pain or distress differs qualitatively from pleasure. There is also evidence for distinct mechanisms that mediate positive and negative affect (see earlier discussion in "Is There One GB Value at a Time"; Cacioppo and Berntson 1994). Finally, hedonic adaptation can be observed without requiring the subject to communicate anything, by observing behaviors of approach and avoidance. Returning to Helen's changing food consumption, the example of the color aftereffect suggests that the hedonic experience of foods that Helen labels (or otherwise treats as) "neither pleasing nor aversive" remains the same as her consumption changes. As Helen adapts to her improving circumstances, however, improving food quality is required to produce this constant experience. This type of adaptation is properly labeled a "hedonic treadmill" (Brickman and Campbell 1971).

Another indication that the zero point of the GB scale is neither arbitrary nor labile is that some experiences never change their sign. Parducci (1995) has noted that there is no context in which cutting oneself shaving will be a pleasant experience. Of course, an individual who normally cuts himself three times every morning might be pleased to observe at the end of a shave that he has cut himself only once—but this is a context-dependent evaluation of the shave as a whole, not an immediate response to the nick of the blade.

The preceding section discussed the ambitious goal of achieving a quantitative measure of the GB dimension that would allow comparisons across contexts. The arguments reviewed in the present section suggest that useful measurements of objective happiness could still be obtained even if precise quantitative measurement of GB values remains elusive. We have concluded that most ex-

periences can be classified as Good, Bad, or neutral with little difficulty and that the neutral affective experience retains the same meaning even when the stimuli that produce it change. It also appears reasonable to assume that the neutral point of the scale is interpersonally comparable, because approach and avoidance have the same meaning for different people (Kahneman and Varey 1991). The intrapersonal stability and interpersonal comparability of the neutral affective experience guarantee the feasibility of at least a crude measurement of the GB dimension. As noted earlier, the relative amounts of time that Helen spent on either side of the GB zero point, or at zero, provide important information about her objective happiness (for similar views, see Diener, Sandvik, and Pavot [1991] and Parducci [1995]).

NORMS AND STANDARDS

The preceding section distinguished between comparison processes in judgment and in perception. The judgment that a line is long or short arises from an explicit comparison of the current line to a relevant set of stimuli previously experienced. Changing the comparison set changes the judgment, but not the perception of the current stimulus. However, perception itself is also inherently comparative. The perception of a particular mixture of wavelengths as reddish or greenish can be seen as arising from an implicit comparison of the current stimulus to a "memory" of prior stimulation. The adaptation level for hue or temperature is such a memory. Changes in the adaptation level for these modalities are accompanied by changes in perception, as indicated by the possibility of matching experiences (of "white" or "warm") across adapting contexts. We concluded that the zero point of the GB scale is perceptual, and that genuine changes of taste are possible, causing the same stimulus to produce different hedonic experiences and different stimuli to produce identical GB values.

Judgmental comparisons are hardly irrelevant to hedonic life. Indeed, such comparisons are often the *cause* of significant pleasure and pain. The following discussion of the affective consequences of comparison draws on norm theory (Kahneman and Miller 1986). The central idea of norm theory is that reality is continuously experienced in a context of relevant counterfactual alternatives, as each stimulus evokes representations of what it could have been and was expected to be. These representations provide a norm to which the evoking stimulus is automatically compared. On most occasions, of course, the stimulus matches its norm and is accordingly experienced as normal. A stimulus that differs sharply from its norm is perceived as surprising or novel. An important tenet of norm theory is *emotional amplification*: the emotional response to abnormal events is enhanced, relative to the response to the same events when they are normal and expected.

Emotional amplification implies that novel events elicit especially strong Good/Bad values. For example, suppose that the newly affluent Helen has switched to a new cereal, which she likes much better than the one she had consumed for a long time. For the first few mornings, the norm that is evoked by the experience of the new cereal mainly consists of memories of the inferior cereal. The positive deviation of present reality from the norm that it evokes surely enhances the pleasure of consuming the new cereal. However, the special pleasure derived from abnormality will inevitably disappear, as the norm gradually changes to reflect Helen's new routine. In the terms introduced in the preceding section, the disappearance of the novelty component of pleasure is a genuine hedonic adaptation. It affects the experience itself, not merely the descriptive labels that would be used to describe it. However, the elimination of novelty pleasure does not imply that the experience of eating cereal is no longer pleasurable. Comparison is not the only source of pleasure, and normality does not imply affective neutrality.

Novelty is only one of several ways in which comparisons induce affect. Comparisons to what might have been can cause counterfactual emotions, such as regret and frustration, guilt and envy (Kahneman and Miller 1986; Roese and Olson 1995). The intense pains and pleasures of comparing oneself to others are central to the lives of many people (Wheeler and Miyake 1992). Comparisons to normative standards and to aspiration levels are particularly important in the context of well-being research, where questions about satisfaction are commonly asked. Satisfaction and the GB dimension are related in two distinct ways. First, high GB values yield satisfaction. Second, the judgment that one is satisfied is an occasion for pleasure as well as a consequence of pleasure. However, the zero point on the satisfaction-dissatisfaction scale ("neither satisfied nor dissatisfied") does not necessarily correspond to a neutral GB value. A gourmet may enjoy a dish that is quite tasty, but not fully satisfactory.

THE HEDONIC TREADMILL

In a landmark essay, Brickman and Campbell (1971) explored the implications of Helson's adaptation level theory for human happiness and for planning the good society. They developed the deeply troubling notion of a "hedonic treadmill": if people adapt to improving circumstances to the point of affective neutrality, the improvements yield no real benefits. Subsequent observations of the apparent lack of effect of increasing real income on satisfaction with income and with other domains of life (Duncan 1975; Easterlin 1974) appeared to provide strong support for the hypothesis of a hedonic treadmill. Perhaps the most dramatic evidence for this hypothesis was the finding by Brickman, Coates, and Janoff-Bulman (1978) that lottery winners were not particularly happy and that paraplegics were much less unhappy than most readers would have anticipated. The distinction between pleasures and comforts that Tibor Scitovsky (1976) developed in his famous book *The Joyless Economy* draws much of its intuitive appeal from the same source. In contrast to pleasures, which are arousing experiences, comforts ultimately produce no significant hedonic experience at all. Related developments include Parducci's psychophysical theory of happiness (Parducci 1968, 1995) and Tversky and Griffin's (1991) endowment/contrast model, in which any pleasant stimulus reduces the pleasure associated with subsequent stimuli of the same kind.

The hedonic treadmill hypothesis and the cluster of findings and ideas surrounding it have been very influential (Frederick and Loewenstein, this volume) because of their links with the familiar themes of the relativity of happiness and the futility of the rat race, and because of the doubts they cast on the welfare consequences of economic progress. However, this seductive idea must be interpreted with caution. For example, a radical version of the treadmill concept might suggest that an experience that is routine and fully expected must become affectively neutral. As noted earlier, however, normality does not imply affective neutrality. Breakfast is almost always pleasant even when thoroughly routinized, and shaving cuts will remain unpleasant even for an inept shaver who cuts himself every morning. The extreme interpretation of the treadmill idea cannot be maintained.

A weaker version of the treadmill hypothesis may suffice to sustain the most provocative implication of Brickman and Campbell's (1971) analysis, that increases in standard of living do little to improve the human lot, at least above a threshold of adequate per-capita income (see Diener and Suh, this volume). For example, the idea that pleasure is tightly linked to need reduction suggests that different ways of satisfying the same need could eventually yield similar GB values. If this idea is correct, Helen will always derive pleasure from breakfast because she comes to it hungry, but she will ultimately derive no more pleasure from a superior cereal than from an inferior brand.

Another version of the treadmill idea was developed by Headey and Wearing (1992), who argued that the hedonic quality of particular experiences and overall well-being are subject to homeostatic processes that tend to restore a similar distribution of GB values—not necessarily neutral—under varying circumstances. They reviewed evidence that individuals exposed to life-altering events ultimately return to a level of well-being that is characteristic of their personality, sometimes by generating good or bad outcomes that restore this characteristic level. There is other support for the view that happiness—probably both in its objective and subjective varieties—is a personality trait with a large heritable component (Diener and Lucas, this volume). Each individual may be on a personal treadmill that tends to restore well-being to a predetermined set point after each change of circumstances.

The hedonic treadmill hypothesis assumes that a change in objective circumstances causes a predictable change in the GB value of stimuli. Two mechanisms that produce treadmill-like results were illustrated earlier by Helen's response to an improvement in the quality of her food. One suggestion was that adaptation to more palatable food can move the location of the hedonic zero point without altering the palatability ordering, in analogy to color adaptation effects. This mechanism is true hedonic adaptation. The other observation was that changing circumstances yield pleasures and pains that are linked specifically to the contrast between the new circumstances and previous expectations. The amplifying effects of novelty on hedonic experience must eventually disappear as a new routine is established.

A SATISFACTION TREADMILL

We next consider the possibility of a mechanism that could produce treadmill-like effects without any change in hedonic experience. This mechanism is best labeled a "satisfaction treadmill": it involves a change in the relation between the distribution of GB values and the scales on which individuals report satisfaction and subjective happiness. Consider an individual whose circumstances have changed because of an increase in income or because of a crippling accident. The new circumstances yield a new distribution of Good and Bad experiences in many domains of life. One possible response to this change is to alter the standard by which overall satisfaction with each of these domains is judged: the paraplegic may declare himself satisfied with a leaner diet of pleasure than he required before the accident, and the individual whose income has risen may require a more favorable distribution of GB values to report the same satisfaction as before.

Brickman and Campbell (1971) derived the hedonic treadmill from Helson's (1964) notion of adaptation level. The satisfaction treadmill can be derived from another familiar notion: the aspiration level, which defines a boundary between satisfactory and unsatisfactory achievements. The classic observation about aspiration levels is that they are highly correlated both with real and with expected achievements, though aspirations are generally somewhat higher than expectations (Irwin 1944). It is a commonplace that people's aspiration level for income is moderately higher than their actual income, and research confirms that current income is the single most important determinant of the income that is considered satisfactory (van Praag and Frijters, this volume).

The satisfaction treadmill that is relevant here would operate on the distribution of GB values, not on income as such. The hypothesis is that, as in the case of income, improved circumstances could cause people to require ever more frequent and more intense pleasures to maintain the same level of satisfaction with their hedonic life. In the terms that were introduced earlier, the satisfaction treadmill causes subjective happiness to remain constant even when objective happiness improves.

Of course, hedonic adaptation and changes of aspiration level may both occur. Observed adaptation to new circumstances is the joint effect of the two mechanisms. The relative contributions of the two types of treadmill effects can be studied adequately only by assessing objective happiness. It is remarkable that the necessary research was not done during the first twenty-five years after the formulation of the hedonic treadmill hypothesis—probably because of the absence of a clear distinction between subjective and objective happiness.

As a consequence, the issues raised by Brickman and Campbell (1971) are still unresolved.

The question of whether observed treadmill effects should be attributed to hedonic adaptation or to rising aspirations has important implications for the issues of public policy with which Brickman and Campbell were concerned. The assumption of their analysis was that policies that improve people's circumstances are futile unless they yield an improvement in satisfaction and in subjective happiness. In the present framework, however, it is objective happiness that matters. Policies that improve the frequencies of good experiences and reduce the incidence of bad ones should be pursued even if people do not describe themselves as happier or more satisfied. The recognition that aspiration levels adjust and that people will never be fully satisfied does not mean that they cannot be made (objectively) happier. The implication of this analysis is that the goal of policy should be to increase measures of objective well-being, not measures of satisfaction or subjective happiness.

THE PREDICTED UTILITY OF STATES: EVALUATION BY CHANGES

Duration is a basic and often neglected dimension in the evaluation of the utility of particular outcomes and in the more inclusive assessment of well-being. Pleasure and pain are characteristics of single moments, and instant utility is therefore attached to slices through the stream of experience. However, all hedonically significant outcomes—from the drilling of a tooth to a love affair—are extended over time. Furthermore, the outcomes that are generally considered most significant to well-being are relatively stable states, of wealth, health, employment, or family status. As we will see, however, the task of evaluating such temporally extended outcomes is quite difficult and unnatural.

A thought experiment will place the difficulty of evaluating extended episodes in a broader perspective. Consider an observer in a vision experiment who is exposed on each of a series of trials to an illuminated panel. The trials vary in duration. The luminance of the panel varies both within each trial and across trials. Now consider three tasks that the observer might be assigned:

1. "Assign a value to the current brightness of the panel." This is a standard psychophysical task that requires matching the intensity of a perceptual experience to a value on a scale.
2. "Assign a value to the brightness of the panel on the last trial." This question can also be answered with little difficulty, by visualizing a representative moment of the experience and by assessing the brightness associated with that moment.
3. "Assign a value to the total brightness that you experienced on this trial." This task appears difficult and unnatural, because the total brightness experienced over time is not a quantity for which a perceptual representation is available. Informal observations on tasks of this type suggest that many observers will base their answer primarily on the brightness of the representative moment.

The example highlights two general principles: perception is about the attributes of current events and objects; judgment tasks that require integration of perceptual experience over time are difficult. Both principles apply to evaluations of the utility of temporally extended episodes. Like brightness, the GB value (or instant utility) is an attribute of a moment of experience. Like the total brightness experienced over a trial, the total utility of an episode has no direct perceptual representation and is not easily evaluated. However, there is an important difference between brightness and utility: an inability to evaluate total brightness is probably of little significance to individual adjustment, but an inability to assess the total utility of temporally extended outcomes can be much more important if it causes people to make choices that do not maximize their experienced utility.

The next three sections explore a general hypothesis—labeled *evaluation by moments*—according to which people evaluate the utility of temporally extended outcomes and states by retrieving or constructing a representative moment and evaluating the utility of that moment. The temporal dimension of experience is not directly included in the representations that are evaluated. As a result, the subjective utilities of temporally extended outcomes and states depart systematically from the logic of evaluation, according to which the total utility of an episode is the product of average instant utility and duration (Kahneman, Wakker, and Sarin 1997).

The hypothesis of evaluation by moments must be supplemented by more specific hypotheses concerning the selection or construction of the representative moment. The rules that govern this representation appear to depend on temporal perspective. When an episode or a state is considered *ex ante,* the initial moment of the episode and the transition to the new state dominate the evaluation. Thus, an evaluation of the subjective utility of changes dominates both the predicted utility and the decision utility of episodes and periods. Other moments are likely to be most salient, however, when the utility of an episode is considered *ex post.* As will be shown, the evidence suggests that the instant utilities of the end of the episode and of its affective peak often dominate its remembered utility.

The hypothesis that people evaluate the utility of future states by evaluating the transitions to these states helps answer a question about the most famous article in the well-being literature. Why did the study of paraplegics and lottery winners by Brickman, Coates, and Janoff-Bulman (1978) become an instant classic and why has it retained its status? The answer is that the main result of this study violates a powerful intuition that paraplegics are utterly miserable, and that this intuition reflects a failure to distinguish appropriately between the state of *being* a paraplegic and the event of *becoming* a paraplegic. The focus on the tragedy of the transition to the paraplegic state is inevitably associated with neglect of the processes of adaptation that were discussed in the preceding section.

To test this hypothesis about the lay theory of well-being, Kahneman and Schkade (1998) asked subjects to evaluate the effect of different features of a new location on well-being. A control group evaluated the features separately (for example, a short and easy commute, or a commute that is long and hard). Several experimental groups were told that a family unexpectedly had to move between two locations that differed in this feature, and they were asked to assess the impact of the new feature on the family's well-being. Separate groups were assigned different temporal perspectives. One group evaluated the impact of the new feature "in anticipation of the move," another "in the first few months after the move," and another group "in the third year." Two additional groups evaluated the impact of the new feature "overall in the first five years," with one of these groups specifically reminded that "when you think about these features, please take a minute to imagine how their influence might change over the years." There were twenty-four pairs of features, which the subjects were instructed to evaluate independently.

The mean ratings of the impact of features on well-being were predicted quite accurately ($R = .99$) by a simple linear combination of the separate values of the original and of the new feature:

$$V(X \rightarrow Y) = 0.47 \ V(Y) - 0.23 \ V(X)$$

As expected, this formula reflects the intuition that the contrast with the preceding state affects well-being in a new situation. Quite reasonably, it appears that the direct contribution of the new state is more important than this contrast effect. The equation provides a plausible representation of the response to a change of circumstances.

It should be self-evident that a contrast effect is unlikely to retain its intensity forever. However, the surprising result of the study was that the same formula fit the data for all experimental groups equally well, regardless of temporal perspective. There was no significant indication that the respondents spontaneously realized that the earlier state of affairs would be more important to current well-being in the first few months after a move than three years later. The findings support the hypothesis that people use an estimate of the hedonic impact of a *change* as a proxy for the evaluation of the impact of a new state.

The errors of predicted utility that are produced by the heuristic of evaluating states by moments are generally reinforced by a systematic overweighting of the distinctive aspects of the new state, an effect that has been labeled the *focusing illusion* (Schkade and Kahneman 1998). Gradual shifts of attention are important mechanisms of adaptation to new situations: as time passes, a paraplegic or a bereaved person certainly spends more and more of his or her day attending to aspects of life other than the tragedy. Schkade and Kahneman noted that this aspect of adaptation is particularly difficult to incorporate into predictions of well-being. Consider the questions, "How miserable would you be as a paraplegic?" or, "How happy would you be in California?" It is natural to answer these questions by focusing on the distinctive aspects of life as a paraplegic or in California. However, such a focus inevitably fails to represent the actual experience of people who have had time to adapt and to redirect their attention to other aspects of life. Thus, the impact of any significant new circumstance on well-being is likely to be overestimated when attention is focused on it.[8] Schkade and Kahneman illustrated this by a study that compared the anticipated and the actual effects on well-being of living in California or in the Midwest. The results indicated no difference in the self-reported well-being of students in the two regions (although the Californians were much more satisfied with their climate). However, residents of both the Midwest and California agreed in predicting greater happiness for Californians, probably because they exaggerated the weight of region-specific experiences in everyday life.

The focusing illusion is not a mere artifact in the measurement of well-being; it can have real consequences in people's lives. Some people may be so persuaded that moving to California would increase their well-being that they will actually move there, although it is far from certain that their prediction of the ultimate outcome will prove correct. More generally, an individual may become fixated on the belief that some change will have important consequences for the quality of life, and this belief may then acquire motivating force. Such a fixation of attention could be the origin of many passions, in both the private and the public domains. If the present analysis is correct, of course, most of these passions are built on an illusion.

THE DECISION UTILITY OF CHANGES: GAINS AND LOSSES

The weight that is assigned to the desirability of an outcome in the context of a decision is called its *decision utility*. Decision utilities are inferred from choices and are used to explain choices. Much of the research on decision-making and on utility has been conducted in a rational and behavioristic tradition, which focuses on observable choices and shuns subjective notions such as experienced utility. It is implicitly assumed in this tradition that the experienced utility of outcomes can be inferred from their decision utility, because rational decision-makers surely know what they will like. In this and the following section, we raise doubts about this inference (see also Berridge, this volume). We also show that the hypothesis of evaluation by moments applies to decision utility, where the relevant moment is the transition from one state to another.

Outcomes can usually be represented and evaluated either as changes or as states. For example, the outcome of a financial transaction can be stated in terms of the amount that was gained or lost (a change of wealth) or in terms of the individual's state of wealth immediately after the transaction. Ever since Bernoulli's classic statement of expected utility theory (1738/1954), standard economic analyses of decision-making have assumed that people evaluate their options by

the states of wealth that they could yield. Bernoulli's analysis was a tour de force that anticipated both Weber and Fechner by more than a hundred years. However, his analysis of decision-making was psychologically wrong in a crucial respect: contrary to its main assumption, people do not usually think of outcomes in terms of levels of wealth or income. The analysis that Bernoulli proposed would be valid only if past outcomes did not matter at all—but, of course, they do. Indeed, the utility of a given level of wealth or income depends on the reference to which it is compared: an income of $60,000 does not have the same utility for individuals who recently had incomes of $40,000 or $80,000.

An analysis of risky choice called prospect theory (Kahneman and Tversky 1979, 1984) took a position that is diametrically opposed to the tradition of explaining decisions by attitudes to wealth. In prospect theory, the carriers of decision utility are gains and losses relative to a reference level, which is often the status quo. In this theory, a given state can be assigned quite different utilities depending on the state that preceded it, and quite different states can be assigned approximately the same utility if they represent the same change relative to the reference level.

The centerpiece of prospect theory is the value function for gains and losses of money (illustrated in figure 1.2), and the critical feature of this function is that it is steeper in the domain of losses than in the domain of gains. The differential sensitivity to losses and to gains is called loss aversion. The coefficient of loss aversion is the ratio of the slopes of the value function in the two domains. Figure 1.2 illustrates a value function in which the coefficient is 2.5. The coefficient of loss aversion

FIGURE 1.2   A Typical Value Function

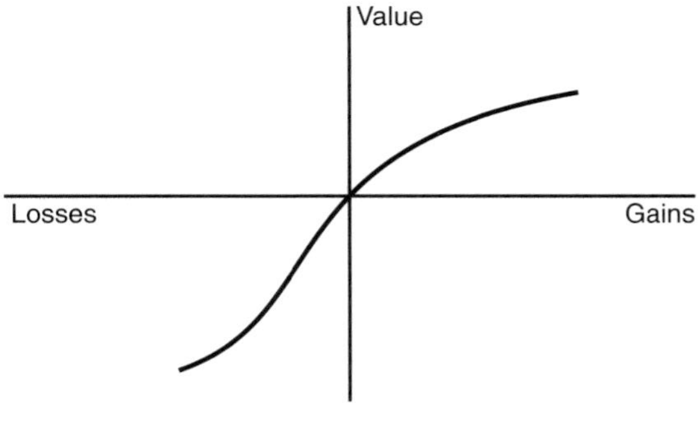

FIGURE 1.3   Multiple Reference Points for the Choice Between A and D

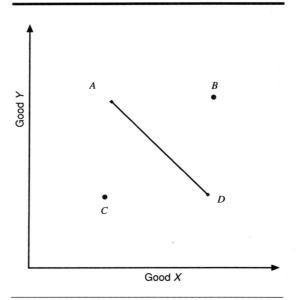

can be estimated, for example, by offering participants a bet on the toss of a coin: they can either lose $10 or win $X. The factor by which X must exceed $10 provides an approximate measure of loss aversion. The median value in a classroom demonstration is rarely far from $25.

The coefficient of loss aversion can also be estimated from a comparison of the monetary value that subjects attach to the same object in different situations. In a standard classroom demonstration of this effect, the object is a decorated coffee mug. There are two experimental conditions. (1) Some subjects are given a mug and asked to indicate the minimal amount that would induce them to give it up. (2) Other subjects are given a choice between a mug and an amount of money and asked to indicate the minimal amount of money that they would prefer to a mug. In a typical result, subjects in condition 1 valued the mug at $7.12, whereas the median subject in condition 2 switched to a preference for money at $3.50 (Kahneman, Knetsch, and Thaler 1991). This result can be explained by referring to figure 1.3. To read the figure, assume that Good X is money and Good Y is the mug. The same choice (between points A and D) is evaluated from point A in condition 1, and from point C in condition 2. The difference between the states of "having a mug" and "not having a mug" is evaluated as a positive change ("getting a mug") from C, and as a negative change ("giving up a mug") from A. In both cases, the value of this difference is matched to the value of a monetary gain (Good X). Because "giving up" is evaluated on the steep limb of the value function, the gain required to offset it is larger, by a factor of about two.

It is tempting to assume that the properties of decision utility reflect the actual experience of outcomes. Two inferences from figure 1.2 are particularly inviting: (1) the GB value of the reference point is zero; (2) loss aversion reflects a differential sensitivity to pain and to pleasure. Unfortunately, both inferences are dubious.

Prospect theory assigns a value of zero to the reference point that separates positive from negative outcomes. Because the reference point is often the status quo, the theory may appear to incorporate an extreme version of the hedonic treadmill idea, but this inference is unwarranted.[9] The function of figure 1.2 represents the *decision utility* of the gains and losses associated with possible outcomes of the decision at hand; it is silent about the *experienced utility* of the reference situation. Thus, prospect theory is entirely compatible with the conclusion reached earlier (in the discussion of breakfast cereals and shaving cuts) that a state of affairs can be normal without being hedonically neutral.

Another tempting inference from figure 1.2 is that the different slopes of the value function in the positive and in the negative domains reflect differences in the relative sensitivity to pain and to pleasure. However, this inference is also unwarranted. There are two possible interpretations of loss aversion, and they are not mutually incompatible. Loss aversion could represent either a general priority of negative over positive affect in hedonic experience or a deeply ingrained conservative tendency in decision-making. Evidence about the relative importance of the two effects is scarce. However, a psychophysical experiment by Galanter (1992) suggests that the asymmetry between pains and pleasures could well be much smaller in experience than in decisions. Galanter applied the technique of direct magnitude scaling to positive and negative events, including gains and losses of money. He found that the scaled value of gains and losses was a power function of the amount gained or lost. Although there was a difference between the responses to gains and to losses, it was quite small: in a typical experiment the exponents were .54 and .58, respectively, for gains and for losses. This difference would not account for the extensive loss aversion observed in choice experiments.

The three major conclusions of this discussion of decision utility are that (1) the hypothesis that changes are evaluated as proxies for states holds in the context of decision-making; (2) there is a pronounced asymmetry in the weighting of gains and losses in decisions, but the extent to which loss aversion is also found in experience is not yet known; and (3) more generally, inferences from decision utility to experienced utility should be made with great caution. The next section provides further arguments for the latter conclusion.

REMEMBERED UTILITY: EPISODES AND MOMENTS

Consider the following two questions: "How do you feel right now?" and, "How did you feel last night?" Under normal circumstances, we treat answers to these questions with the same easy confidence. Upon reflection, however, the two questions differ greatly in their cognitive demands, and there is a corresponding difference in the authority that should be attached to the answers they evoke. Generating an answer to the retrospective question involves two operations that are not required for the reporting of current feelings: retrieval of a record of GB values from memory, and an act of integrative evaluation that summarizes that record by a single descriptive response.

Earlier discussion ("A Logic for Objective Happiness") proposed temporal integration as the normative principle that should guide the evaluation of a (suitably measured) profile of GB values. However, the hypothesis of evaluation by moments implies that people are unlikely to follow the integration rule, because the temporal integral of momentary sensations is not directly available to conscious awareness. Indeed, several studies have shown that people's intuitive evaluations of their own experiences and of the experiences of others deviate sharply from temporal integration. The participants in these studies generally provided a real-time record of their experience during an episode and later provided a global evaluation of the entire episode, or indicated a choice of which of several episodes they would rather repeat. The situations studied included painful medical procedures, including the colonoscopy study from which figure 1.1 was drawn (Redelmeier and Kahneman 1996); short

plotless films of pleasant subjects, such as low-level flying over an African landscape, or of unpleasant subjects, such as an amputation (Fredrickson and Kahneman 1993); immersion of one hand in cold water (Kahneman et al. 1993); and aversive sounds of varying loudness and duration (Schreiber and Kahneman 1998). All these studies share several important features: the participant is essentially passive during a relatively brief episode in which the valence of the experience does not change and the main task is simply to endure the experience and (for some subjects) to evaluate it in real time. The conclusions should not be extended beyond this range of situations.[10]

The retrospective evaluations and choices observed in these studies generally conformed to a simple rule of Peak-End evaluation. Global retrospective evaluations were well predicted by an average of the peak affective response recorded during the episode (in the case of aversive episodes, the worst moment) and of the End value, recorded just before the termination of the episode. For example, in the study from which figure 1.1 is drawn, the correlations between the average of Peak and End ratings and several measures of the patients' global evaluations of their colonoscopy experience ranged from .56 to .67 (Redelmeier and Kahneman 1996). In the study by Fredrickson and Kahneman (1993), subjects were exposed to short films that varied substantially in both duration and affective impact. The mean correlations (within-S) between global evaluations and the Peak-End average were .78 for pleasant films and .69 for unpleasant films. The same rule applies to observers: the physicians who administered the procedures also rated the patient's overall experience according to the Peak-End rule (Redelmeier and Kahneman 1996). Finally, the average of Peak and End discomfort accounted for 93 percent of the systematic variance in an experiment in which subjects rated the total aversiveness of a profile of experience allegedly provided by other people (Varey and Kahneman 1992).

A significant corollary of Peak-End evaluation is duration neglect. Duration was a factor in all the studies mentioned so far, and in others in the same series, but this variable had little or no effect on retrospective global evaluations. In the colonoscopy study, for example, the duration of the procedures varied widely across patients: the mean was twenty-three minutes, and the standard deviation (SD) was thirteen minutes. With Peak and End partialled out, however, duration was not a significant predictor of subsequent global evaluations. Similar results were reported by Fredrickson and Kahneman (1993) in a study of emotionally arousing films. In other studies, the effects of duration were significant but small (Schreiber and Kahneman 1998; Varey and Kahneman 1992, experiment 2). These findings are compatible with the idea of evaluation by moments: people apparently construct and evaluate a representative moment and use the evaluation of this moment as a proxy for the evaluation of the entire episode. Duration is effectively deleted from this representation, in which the Peak and the End are given special weight. Duration neglect is not restricted to human subjects: Mowrer and Solomon (1954) observed that the fear of rats exposed to electric shock depended on the intensity of the shock, not on its duration. Shizgal (this volume) described similar results for electric stimulation of the "pleasure centers" in the rat brain.

The third finding of the studies with human subjects is a robust violation of monotonicity: the retrospective global evaluation of an aversive episode can actually be improved by extending it, provided that the increment yields a lower average of Peak and End values. The participants in an experiment reported by Kahneman and his colleagues (1993) were exposed to two trials of a cold-pressor situation. In the short trial, the subject kept one hand in water at fourteen degrees Celsius for sixty seconds. In the long trial, the immersion lasted a total of ninety seconds. Water temperature was kept at fourteen degrees Celsius for the first sixty seconds, at which point (unbeknownst to the subject) the experimenter caused the temperature of the water to rise gradually from fourteen degrees to fifteen degrees Celsius over the next thirty seconds. Seven minutes after the second trial, the subject was called in for another trial, informed that one of the two previous procedures would be repeated exactly, and given a choice of whether the first or the second trial should be repeated. The robust result of this study is that about 65 percent of participants chose to repeat the long rather than the short trial. The percentage was 80 percent in a subgroup of participants whose real-time ratings indicated a pronounced decline of pain during the last thirty seconds of the long trial.

The results of the cold-water experiment were confirmed and extended in a study using loud aversive sounds as stimuli (Schreiber and Kahneman 1998). Subjects were exposed to pairs of sounds in immediate succession and asked which of the two sounds they would rather hear repeated

in a subsequent phase of the experiment. For example, one of the pairs of stimuli that the subjects heard was ten seconds of an unpleasant sound at seventy-eight decibels, then the same sound followed by four additional seconds at a lower intensity (sixty-six decibels). There was a significant preference for repeating the long sounds in such pairs. In a clinical experiment by Katz, Redelmeier, and Kahneman (1996), half of a large group of patients undergoing a colonoscopy were randomly assigned to a condition in which the procedure was briefly extended after the examination was complete, without informing the patient. The colonoscope was left stationary during the added period (about one minute), causing mild discomfort but less pain than many patients had experienced earlier. The prolongation of the colonoscopy, though distinctly unpleasant, yielded a highly significant improvement in subsequent global evaluations of the procedure. A clinical application of such an intervention could be justified if it increased patients' willingness to undergo further colonoscopies when their treatment required it.

The simplest account of this set of results is that subjects form a global evaluation of episodes by the Peak-End rule. As this rule implies, an added period of diminishing pain causes most subjects to retain a more favorable memory of the entire episode. When given a choice, subjects prefer to repeat the trial associated with the less aversive memory. Thus, the remembered utility of past episodes determines the decision utility of repeating them. These results illustrate a general fact of life: except for acts that escape current pain (removing a hand from a flame), the sovereign masters that determine what people will do are not pleasure and pain, but fallible memories of pleasure and pain. The only utility that people (and other organisms) can learn from personal experience to maximize is the utility that they store in memory. Where retrospective evaluations distort actual experience, subsequent preferences are governed by the distorted evaluation, not by the experience.

In the context of measurement of well-being, these results convey a discouraging message: retrospective evaluations of experiences are likely to provide erroneous estimates of the "true" total utility of past experiences. Consequently, Helen's retrospective assessments of the quality of her life cannot be assumed to be valid representations of her objective happiness. However, the analysis also suggests alternatives to methods that rely on global evaluations of the past. One suggestion has already been mentioned on several occasions: because immediate

reports of the quality of experience avoid the difficulties of memory and of integration, experience-
sampling methods have significant advantages and
should be used whenever possible (Stone et al., this
volume).

Experience-sampling studies are cumbersome
and expensive, however, and this method will
never fully replace retrospective judgments. It will
therefore be necessary to develop methods of
probing memory that follow the basic principle of
human engineering: only ask people to do what
they can do well. For example, consider the task of
evaluating how happy Helen was yesterday. Helen
will probably be able to divide the day into meaningful segments, to estimate the duration of each
of these segments with fair accuracy, and to evaluate the average GB value of each segment. The
average experienced utility of the entire day is easily derived from these judgments by weighting the
average utility of each segment by its duration—
an operation that Helen is unlikely to perform
well on her own. As this speculative example illustrates, new methods for the assessment of happiness should build on detailed studies of the
strengths and weaknesses of evaluative memory.

HEURISTICS AND BIASES IN SATISFACTION AND HAPPINESS

People have ready-made answers to many questions about themselves: they know their name,
their address, and their party affiliation. But they
do not generally know how happy they are, and
they must construct an answer to that question
whenever it is raised. As they do with other complex questions that must be answered quickly, people are likely to apply simplifying heuristics to the
happiness question. As is the case for other simplifying heuristics, the heuristics of satisfaction and
subjective happiness are inevitably associated with
characteristic biases. There are two general ways of
confirming judgmental biases and the heuristics
that cause them (Kahneman and Tversky 1996).
One method is to compare judgments to true
value. In the present context, this method would
require comparisons of subjective happiness to independent assessments of objective happiness. An
easier way to establish bias is by showing that a
judgment is affected by a factor that is normatively
irrelevant. Schwarz and Strack (this volume) offer
many examples of the latter approach.

Variants of the availability heuristic are natural
candidates for answering questions such as, "How

satisfied are you with your housing?" or "How
happy are you?" or, "How important is this aspect
of life to your well-being?" Satisfaction questions
can be answered by sampling memories of recent
evaluative thoughts or by retrieving and evaluating
relevant incidents, which are then compared to a
standard or aspiration level. Judgments of satisfaction that are derived in this manner will be overly
influenced by recent events and by events that are
especially memorable (Tanur 1992). The more
general happiness question can also be answered
by sampling domains of life and assessing their status. This heuristic yields a bias toward domains
that are the focus of current attention, perhaps because satisfaction in these domains is especially
high or low.

An earlier section argued that the neutral point
of the scale of momentary affect is truly neutral
and subjectively distinctive, but this argument
does *not* extend to judgments of satisfaction or
happiness. The argument was that "neither pleasant nor unpleasant," like "white" or "neither
warm nor cold," refers to a distinctive experience
at a particular moment. The neutral affective point
was said to be determined by a process of hedonic
adaptation, which resembles other cases of sensory
or perceptual adaptation. In contrast, satisfaction
judgments typically refer to a broad domain of life
rather than to a single experience, and the anchor
of a satisfaction scale is a standard of acceptability
or aspiration level, not an adaptation level. The
standard for the judgment of happiness is not obvious at all. Most people describe themselves as
happy (Diener and Diener 1996), but the meaning of this finding is unclear because the phrase
"neither happy nor unhappy" has a distinctly negative connotation.

Other heuristics are at work in judgments of
happiness. Schwarz and Strack (this volume) review evidence of large effects of current mood—
and even of current weather—on self-reports of
subjective happiness. They suggest that the results
confirm the role of a "How do I feel" heuristic in
individuals' judgments of their happiness (see
Schwarz and Clore [1996] for a review). The interpretation is supported by the remarkable finding that the effect of bad weather on reported happiness is reduced or eliminated by drawing the
respondent's attention to the weather: this manipulation causes the subject to make a correct attribution of current mood to the weather and
reduces the misattribution of current mood to
general happiness.

Reports of subjective happiness are highly susceptible to manipulations that attract attention to particular domains of life. In a well-known example, Strack, Martin, and Schwarz (1988) presented the following two questions consecutively in a survey administered to students: "How happy are you?" and, "How many dates did you have last month?" The correlation between these questions varied with the order in which they appeared. The correlation was .12 when the general happiness question came first, but when the dating question came first the correlation rose to .66. Two important conclusions can be drawn from this finding, which has been replicated many times with diverse populations and in a variety of life domains (Schwarz and Strack, this volume). First, people evidently compute an answer to the subjective happiness question on the fly, instead of retrieving a prepared answer from memory. Second, respondents appear to anchor their report of well-being on their satisfaction with any significant life domain to which attention has been drawn. As in the examples of the focusing illusion discussed in an earlier section, selective attention to a significant domain of life produces substantial overweighting of this domain in reports of overall subjective well-being.

In the present framework, the optimal source of data for the assessment of objective well-being would be a continuous record of GB values over time. Although records of affect at the needed level of detail will remain rare for a long time, the adoption of such records as an idealized criterion for the evaluation of well-being has both conceptual and methodological implications. The focus of methodological analyses of self-reported satisfaction and happiness (Schwarz and Strack, this volume) will surely change if these analyses treat reports of subjective happiness as fallible estimates of an objective "true" score. If there is a true score, the operational task becomes the development of practical methods that yield reliable and unbiased measurements of that score. The assumption that objective happiness is well defined and can be measured could be useful in guiding research, even if it is overly optimistic.

CONCLUDING COMMENT

The present is fleeting, but memories and evaluations of the past endure and populate the mind. When they think about their lives, therefore, people have nothing to work with but memorized assessments and assessments of memories. The central claim of this chapter has been that the scientific study of enjoyment and suffering need not be subject to the same constraint. Real-time measures of experience can be obtained, stored without error, and aggregated to yield a measure of objective well-being that is anchored in the reality of present experience, not in fallible reconstructions and evaluations of the past.

The conception of objective well-being suggests a complex agenda of research, both methodological and substantive. First, there is much to be learned about the various types of real-time measures and how they relate to each other. A second task is to develop methods that minimize the biases of retrospective assessments in order to achieve a measurement of objective happiness that is at once valid and efficient. A combination of methods will eventually be available to characterize the objective well-being of individuals and groups, to determine the true nature of adaptation to new circumstances, to assess enjoyment and suffering in different settings, and to provide a criterion for the evaluation of economic and social policy.

NOTES

1. The term "utility" has multiple meanings. Later in the chapter we discuss the concept of *decision utility,* which links utility to choices and preferences rather than to the experience of outcomes.
2. Parducci (1995) offers a similar definition of happiness as "a theoretical summation over separate momentary pleasures and pains" (11).
3. The axioms are: (1) the global utility of a utility profile is not affected by concatenation with a neutral utility profile; (2) increases of instant utility do not decrease the global utility of a utility profile; (3) in a concatenation of two utility profiles, replacing one profile by another with a higher global utility increases the global utility of the concatenation. Peter Wakker has proved the following theorem: "These three axioms hold if and only if there exists a nondecreasing ('value') transformation function of instant utility, assigning value 0 to 0, such that global utility orders utility profiles according to the integral of the value of instant utility over time."
4. Other moral issues relate to the sources of experienced utility. For example, there may be objections to describing Helen as happy if she was maintained in an uncharacteristically euphoric state by mood-altering drugs, if her most significant experiences were delightful hallucinations, or if she lives under such constrained and impoverished circumstances that she has not acquired the normal set of wishes and aspirations (Dasgupta 1993; Sen 1993).
5. The example is Michel Cabanac's.
6. This scale probably incorporates a cultural bias. As several authors have noted (Higgins 1997; Higgins, Grant and Shah, this volume; Russell 1980; Warr, this vol-

ume) Good and Bad states differ on a dimension of arousal. In Warr's terms, the pleasant states are joy and serenity, the unpleasant states are depression and anxiety. A scale anchored on "thrilling" and "intolerable" implicitly assigns higher value to joy than to serenity.

7. It is also possible to preadapt the two eyes simultaneously to different colors. Preadaptation is followed by a display in which two circles of light are seen next to each other, one of which is shown to the left eye and the other to the right eye. Different mixtures of red and green produce an impression of white in the two patches, depending on the color to which each eye was adapted. No high-level cognitive process is involved.

8. Schwarz and Strack discuss subtle manipulations of mood attribution in which directing attention to an aspect of the current situation that affects mood (for example, the weather) may reduce the effect of the current situation on judged happiness. There is no contradiction between these findings and the focusing illusion, which arises when attention is drawn to significant domains of life.

9. The inference described here as unsound is one I have made in the past. It led me to be insufficiently critical of the hedonic treadmill hypothesis in previous writings (Kahneman and Varey [1991]).

10. The evaluation of episodes of goal-directed activity could well follow a different rule. The affect experienced when the goal is achieved or given up may be much more important to retrospective evaluations than the affect experienced while the activity was going on (Carmon and Kahneman 1996).

REFERENCES

Bargh, J. A. (1997). The automaticity of everyday life. In R.S. Wyer, Jr. (Ed.), *Advances in social cognition* (vol. 10). Mahwah, N.J.: Erlbaum.

Bargh, J. A., Chaiken, S., Raymond, P., and Hymes, C. (1996). The automatic evaluation effect: Unconditional automatic attitude activation with a pronunciation task. *Journal of Experimental Social Psychology, 32*(1), 104–28.

Bentham, J. (1948). *An introduction to the principle of morals and legislation*. Oxford: Blackwell. (Originally published in 1789)

Bernoulli, D. (1954). Exposition of a new theory on the measurement of risk. *Econometrica, 22,* 23–36. (Originally published in 1738).

Birnbaum M. H. (1982). Controversies in psychological measurement. In B. Wegener (Ed.), *Social attitudes and psychophysical measurement* (pp. 401–85). Hillsdale, N.J.: Erlbaum.

Brickman, P., and Campbell, D. T. (1971). Hedonic relativism and planning the good society. In M. H. Apley (Ed.), *Adaptation-level theory: A symposium* (pp. 287–302). New York: Academic Press.

Brickman, P., Coates, D., and Janoff-Bulman, R. (1978). Lottery winners and accident victims: Is happiness relative? *Journal of Personality and Social Psychology, 37,* 917–27.

Brock, D. (1993). Quality-of-life measures in health care and medical ethics. In M. C. Nussbaum and A. Sen (Eds.), *The quality of life* (pp. 95–132). Oxford: Clarendon.

Broome, J. (1991). *Weighing goods*. Oxford: Blackwell.

Cabanac, M. (1992). Pleasure: The common currency. *Journal of Theoretical Biology, 155,* 173–200.

Cacioppo, J. T., and Berntson, G. G. (1994). Relationships between attitudes and evaluative space: A critical review with emphasis on the separability of positive and negative substrates. *Psychological Bulletin, 115,* 401–23.

Cacioppo, J. T., Priester, J. R., and Berntson, G. G. (1993). Rudimentary determinants of attitudes: II. Arm flexion and extension have differential effects on attitudes. *Journal of Personality and Social Psychology, 65,* 5–17.

Carmon, Z., and Kahneman, D. (1996). The experienced utility of queuing: Experience profiles and retrospective evaluations of simulated queues. Working paper. Durham, N.C.: Fuqua School of Business, Duke University.

Csikszentmihalyi, M. (1990). *Flow: The psychology of optimal experience*. New York: Harper and Row.

Dasgupta, P. (1993). *An inquiry into well-being and destitution*. Oxford: Clarendon.

Davidson, R. J. (1992). Anterior cerebral asymmetry and the nature of emotion. *Brain and Cognition, 6,* 245–68.

———. (1994). On emotion, mood, and related affective constructs. In P. Ekman and R. Davidson (Eds.), *The nature of emotion* (pp. 51–55). New York: Oxford University Press.

Davidson, R. J., and Fox, N.A. (1989). Frontal brain asymmetry predicts infant response to maternal separation. *Journal of Abnormal Psychology, 98,* 127–31.

Diener, E., and Diener, C. (1996). Most people are happy. *Psychological Science, 7,* 181–85.

Diener, E., and Emmons, R. A. (1985). The independence of positive and negative affect. *Journal of Personality and Social Psychology, 50,* 1031–38.

Diener, E., Sandvik, E., and Pavot, W. (1991). Happiness is the frequency, not the intensity, of positive versus negative affect. In F. Strack, M. Argyle, and N. Schwarz (Eds.), *Subjective well-being* (pp. 119–40). New York: Pergamon Press.

Duncan, O. (1975). Does money buy satisfaction? *Social Indicators Research, 2,* 267–74.

Easterlin, R. A. (1974). Does economic growth improve the human lot? Some empirical evidence. In P. A. David and M. W. Reder (Eds.), *Nations and Households in Economic Growth* (pp. 89–125). New York: Academic Press.

Edgeworth, F. Y. (1967). Mathematical psychics: An essay on the application of mathematics to the moral sciences. New York: M. Kelly (Originally published in 1881).

Elster, J., and Loewenstein, G. (1992). Utility from memory and anticipation. In J. Elster and G. Loewenstein (Eds.), *Choice over time* (pp. 213–24). New York: Russell Sage Foundation.

Förster, J., and Strack, F. (1996). Influence of overt head movements on memory for valenced words: A case of conceptual-motor compatibility. *Journal of Personality and Social Psychology, 71,* 421–30.

Fredrickson, B. L., and Kahneman, D. (1993). Duration neglect in retrospective evaluations of affective episodes. *Journal of Personality and Social Psychology, 65,* 45–55.

Frijda, N. (1986). *The emotions.* Cambridge: Cambridge University Press.

Galanter, E. (1992). Utility functions for nonmonetary events. *American Journal of Psychology, 103,* 449–70.

Glover, J. (1990). *Utilitarianism and its critics.* New York: Macmillan.

Gray, J. A. (1994). Three fundamental emotion systems. In P. Ekman and R. Davidson (Eds.), *The nature of emotion* (pp. 243–47). New York: Oxford University Press.

Headey, B., and Wearing, A. (1992). *Understanding happiness: A theory of subjective well-being.* Melbourne: Longman Cheshire.

Helson, H. (1964). *Adaptation level theory: An experimental and systematic approach to behavior.* New York: Harper and Row.

Higgins, E. T. (1997). Beyond pleasure and pain. *American Psychologist, 52,* 1280–1300.

Hilgard, E. (1977). *Divided consciousness: Multiple controls in human thought and action.* New York: Wiley.

Hilgard, E. R., and Hilgard, J. R. (1975). *Hypnosis in the relief of pain.* Los Altos, Calif.: William Kaufmann.

Irwin, F. W. (1944). The realism of expectations. *Psychological Review, 51,* 120–26.

Kahneman, D. (1992). Reference points, anchors, norms, and mixed feelings. *Organizational Behavior and Human Decision Processes, 51,* 296–312.

Kahneman, D., Fredrickson, B. L., Schreiber, C. A., and Redelmeier, D. A. (1993). When more pain is preferred to less: Adding a better end. *Psychological Science, 4,* 401–5.

Kahneman D., Knetsch J. L., and Thaler R. H. (1991). The endowment effect, loss aversion, and status quo bias. *Journal of Economic Perspectives. 5,* 193–206.

Kahneman, D., and Miller, D. (1986). Norm theory: Comparing reality to its alternatives. *Psychological Review, 93,* 136–53.

Kahneman, D., and Schkade, D. (1998). Predicting the well-being effect of new circumstances: Changes are proxies for states. Working paper. Princeton, N.J.: Princeton University.

Kahneman, D., and Tversky, A. (1979). Prospect theory: An analysis of decisions under risk. *Econometrica, 47,* 313–27.

———. (1984). Choices, values, and frames. *American Psychologist, 39,* 341–50.

———. (1996). On the reality of cognitive illusions: A reply to Gigerenzer's critique. *Psychological Review, 103,* 582–91.

Kahneman, D., and Varey, C. (1991). Notes on the psy-

chology of utility. In J. Elster and J. E. Roemer (Eds.), *Interpersonal comparisons of well-being* (pp. 127–63). New York: Cambridge University Press.

Kahneman, D., Wakker, P. P., and Sarin, R. (1997). Back to Bentham? Explorations of experienced utility. *Quarterly Journal of Economics, 112,* 375–405.

Katz, J., Redelmeier, D. A., and Kahneman, D. (1996). Memories of painful medical procedures (abstract). Fifteenth annual scientific meeting of the American Pain Society, Washington (November 14–17, 1996).

Lang, P. (1995). The emotion probe: Studies of motivation and attention. *American Psychologist, 50,* 372–85.

Melzack, R. (1983). The McGill Pain Questionnaire. In R. Melzack (Ed.), *Pain measurement and assessment.* New York: Raven Press.

Melzack, R., and Wall, P. D. (1965). Pain mechanisms: A new theory. *Science, 150,* 971–79.

Mowrer, O. H., and Solomon, L. N. (1954). Contiguity versus drive-reduction in conditioned fear: The proximity and abruptness of drive reduction. *American Journal of Psychology, 67,* 15–25.

Osgood, C., Suci, G., and Tannenbaum, P. (1957). *The measurement of meaning.* Urbana: University of Illinois Press.

Parducci, A. (1968). The relativism of absolute judgments. *Scientific American, 219,* 84–90.

———. (1995). *Happiness, pleasure, and judgment: The contextual theory and its applications.* Hillsdale, N.J.: Erlbaum.

Parfit, D. (1984). *Reasons and persons.* Oxford: Oxford University Press.

Redelmeier, D., and Kahneman, D. (1996). Patients' memories of painful medical treatments: Real-time and retrospective evaluations of two minimally invasive procedures. *Pain, 116,* 3–8.

Roese, N. J., and Olson, J. M. (Eds.) (1995). *What might have been: The social psychology of counterfactual thinking.* Mahwah, N.J.: Erlbaum.

Russell, J. A. (1980). A circumplex model of affect. *Journal of Personality and Social Psychology, 39,* 1161–78.

Schkade, D. A., and Kahneman, D. (1998). Does living in California make people happy? A focusing illusion in judgments of life satisfaction. *Psychological Science, 9,* 340–46.

Schreiber, C. A., and Kahneman, D. (1998). Beyond the peak-end hypothesis: Exploring the relation between real-time displeasure and retrospective evaluation. Working paper. Princeton University.

Schwarz, N., and Clore, G. L. (1996). Feelings and phenomenal experiences. In T. E. Higgins, and A. W. Kruglanski (Eds.), *Social psychology: Handbook of basic principles* (pp. 433–65). New York: Guilford.

Scitovsky, T. (1976). *The joyless economy: The psychology of human satisfaction.* New York: Oxford University Press.

Sen, A. K. (1993). Capability and well-being. In M.C. Nussbaum and A. K. Sen (Eds.), *The quality of life* (pp. 30–53). Oxford: Clarendon.

Solarz, A. (1960). Latency of instrumental responses as a function of compatibility with the meaning of eliciting verbal signs. *Journal of Experimental Psychology, 59,* 239–45.

Strack, F., Martin, L., and Schwarz, N. (1988). Priming and communication: Social determinants of information use in judgments of life satisfaction. *European Journal of Social Psychology, 18,* 429–42.

Tanur, J. M. (Ed.). (1992). *Questions about questions: Inquiries into the cognitive bases of surveys.* New York: Russell Sage Foundation.

Tversky, A., and Griffin, D. (1991). Endowment and contrast in judgments of well-being. In F. Strack, M. Argyle, and N. Schwarz (Eds.), *Subjective well-being: An interdisciplinary perspective* (pp. 101–18). Oxford: Pergamon Press.

Varey, C., and Kahneman, D. (1992). Experiences extended across time: Evaluation of moments and episodes. *Journal of Behavioral Decision Making, 5,* 169–86.

Weinstein. M. C., and Fineberg, H. V. (1980). *Clinical decision making.* Philadelphia: W. B. Saunders.

Wheeler, L., and Miyake, K. (1992). Social comparisons in everyday life. *Journal of Personality and Social Psychology, 62,* 760–73.

Young, P. T. (1927). Studies in affective psychology. *American Journal of Psychology, 38,* 157–93.

Zajonc, R. B. (1980). Feeling and thinking: Preferences need no inferences. *American Psychologist, 35,* 151–75.

———. (1997). Emotions. In D. T. Gilbert, S. T. Fiske, and Lindzey, G. (Eds.), *Handbook of social psychology* (4th ed., pp. 591–632). New York: Oxford University Press.

2 Ecological Momentary Assessment

Arthur A. Stone, Saul S. Shiffman, and Marten W. DeVries

The purpose of this chapter is to describe the significant problems with standard retrospective questionnaires and interviews that challenge the validity of such reports. Information emerging from cognitive science investigations highlights processes that can affect recall when we attempt to remember and/or summarize past experiences. Only rarely do self-report assessments take this information into account. We argue that one alternative method for collecting accurate data is to target multiple, immediate reports from people in their typical environments. Many examples of such studies are presented to document the detailed, dynamic information that such data collection methodologies afford. We expect that Ecological Momentary Assessment (EMA) methods will be used more commonly in the future and will provide new insights into daily life.

A VAST AMOUNT OF behavioral science research, especially psychological research, is conducted each year using self-report questionnaire and interview methodologies. Collecting information by having people report on their attitudes, current feelings, state of their mental health, opinions about various matters, and scores of other topics has proved useful and practical and has the virtue of a high degree of face validity. Despite these strengths and the overall acceptance of the methods, we argue that recent research indicates there are many potential problems with the self-report method as it is currently implemented. Methods of collecting information that do not rely on people's ability to summarize their thoughts and feelings over substantial time periods provide an alternative. With "momentary" methods, individuals are asked to report on what is happening at the moment in their typical environment.

The Experience Sampling Method (ESM) was developed as a way to study individuals' experiences in their natural environment by means of signaled random assessments. Each assessment entailed the completion of a brief questionnaire. Assessments were typically completed several times a day for many days. In 1994 Stone and Shiffman introduced another term, Ecological Momentary Assessment (EMA), which was intended to capture not only experience but all phenomena measured on a momentary basis in subjects' natural environment (Stone and Shiffman 1994). In particular, technological advances have allowed a number of physiological tests to be measured on an ambulatory basis. (Several are discussed later.) The two terms denote the same fundamental notions of examining momentary phenomena in the natural environment, and paying particular attention to the timing of measurements, though the focus of ESM is somewhat narrower than that of EMA.

We first present a brief history of the developments leading up to the advent of momentary reporting strategies. A summary of research highlighting retrospective recall biases, one of the main reasons for moving to momentary reports, is next presented. This is followed by a brief section about the potential uses of EMA, and the chapter concludes with descriptions of several EMA studies.

HISTORICAL PERSPECTIVE

The development of experience sampling was a response to a number of currents within psychology and medical and social science research. From a research perspective, experience sampling grew out of the dissatisfaction with the increasingly demonstrated inability of people to provide accurate retrospective information about their daily behavior and experience (discussed more fully later). Clinically, the need to move toward ecologically valid information that went beyond interviews and key informant approaches, as well as beyond laboratory tests, became pressing.[1] The shortcoming in clinical research was that patients and their symptoms were inadequately understood in the context of daily community life, and therefore the places and social contexts were not available for clinical reasoning. At the University of Chicago, landmark studies in adolescents (Csikszentmihalyi and Larson 1984) and optimal experience or "flow" (Csikszentmihalyi 1994) took on the challenge of studying normal states of consciousness in everyday life in order to understand the interactions between the states of optimal and aversive experience.

Other direct antecedents of ESM came from developmental psychology (Barker 1978), ethology (Hinde 1992), sociology (Szalai, Converse, and Feldheim 1972), and anthropology (Gross 1984). In the ethnography of Malinowski (1935), the use of time budgeting and sampling in order to detect societal patterns and regularities was already evident. Time observations formed the basis of biological and ethological research with animals during the middle of this century. Systematic time observation techniques in naturalistic field studies with humans soon followed animal studies (Chapple 1970; Monroe and Monroe 1971). The Kansas School of Ecological Research, for example, pioneered the use of time allocation observational techniques in investigating the behavioral settings of importance to the socialization of children (Barker 1978). These studies were later extended cross-culturally (Whiting and Whiting 1975; Monroe and Monroe 1971) as ethology and ethnography began to influence one another in the 1970s. In clinical psychiatry, such approaches were applied by Reynolds (1965) and McGuire and Polsky (1979) in studying psychiatric disorders in clinical settings and in the behavioral monitoring of the institutionalized mentally retarded (Nelson 1977). In medicine, ambulatory blood pressure monitoring (ABPM) has become a valuable tool for the evaluation of the borderline hypertension patient (Pickering et al. 1985; Weber and Drayer 1984). Ambulatory monitoring provides a glimpse of the circulatory system in dynamic action viewed from within the pattern of the patient's familiar daily life (Egeren and Madarasmi 1992).

A key ancestor of these approaches was the time budget survey. A good example of this research tradition is the International Time Budget Study. This massive undertaking obtained 25,000 twenty-four-hour diaries in twelve countries and represented more then 640,000 events. Information was gathered on what people did, when and for how long they did it, where it took place, and in what social context. It provided information about the frequency, duration, and sequence of circumstances in events (Szalai, Converse, and Feldheim 1972) and demonstrated time use variations that differentiated populations on the basis of cultural, political, class, occupational, or personal factors

(Stone and Nicolson 1987). Another influence on the development of experience sampling was the research on circadian rhythm. This research evolved from early work by Wada (1922)—who described rhythmicity in gastric motility—to later detailed explorations of cyclical rapid eye movements during different stages of sleep (Kleitman 1963). These investigators (Kripke 1983) had sought a comparable rhythmicity cycle of arousal and behavior in the waking person but found instead the profound influence of zeitgebers (daily environmental time setters) and contextual influences on a variety of biological and behavioral measures (Minors and Waterhouse 1981; Monk et al. 1990).

ESM researchers responded to the need to investigate these dynamic daily influences on behavior and mental state. They took the first steps in seeking a degree of ecological validity (Bronfenbrenner 1979) of phenomena already described or discovered in the laboratory or clinic. ESM provided a means to move beyond case vignettes and gather empirical data on essentially subjective experience with a precision that had previously been available only in biomedicine. ESM was a next logical step to take in these investigations since we cannot experimentally manipulate important social variables in the natural environment in order to produce the human behavior we wish to study, as in the laboratory. We must therefore opportunistically use available natural experience in the context of daily life to come to an understanding of the actual dynamic processes of human well-being and suffering.

ECOLOGICAL MOMENTARY ASSESSMENT

We now provide a more formal definition of EMA. There are three characteristics that define it (Stone and Shiffman 1994). First, subjects are studied in the environment they typically inhabit. This requirement of EMA is in contrast to laboratory-based studies in which subjects respond to various tasks in circumstances considerably different from those they are usually in. In a similar manner, data collected in a clinician's office are (for most people) atypical of their usual environment. At issue is the ecological validity of the measurements because environmental characteristics may affect the responses of individuals, both behavioral and physiologic. A good example is the phenomenon of white-coat hypertension: blood pressures are elevated when taken by medical personnel (who are typically attired in a white lab coat). EMA maximizes ecological validity by allowing respondents to provide data in their normal environment.

Second, EMA depends on data collection about momentary or near-immediate states to avoid retrospective distortion of data. There is considerable evidence supporting this central element of EMA. Given the importance of this issue, we devote the next section to a discussion of several of the more important retrospective biases.

Third, the typical EMA sampling strategy—many momentary collections per day—has two purposes: to ensure a reasonable characterization of the phenomena, and to enable the researcher to examine fluctuations of phenomena over time. By repeated sampling, phenomena are evaluated over a number of environmental, social, and psychological conditions, providing a view reflecting the impact of the environment and person in the conditions that are typical for them. Various methods of combining or aggregating data may be employed to characterize EMA information. The notion of repeated sampling also allows the investigator to view the dynamic course of phenomena over time. For example, the diurnal cycles of environmental, social, psychological, and biological states may be examined with the technique. Circaseptian, monthly, and other longer rhythms may also be fruitfully explored with EMA. However, the reader should note that repeated samples are not necessarily required for an EMA design. It is possible to imagine a study design that samples only a single momentary point from many, many subjects. Although the within-person feature of the design is lost and the design becomes very inefficient, many questions could nevertheless be examined with such a study.

BIASES INHERENT IN CURRENT SELF-REPORT METHODS

Cognitive scientists and survey researchers have been at the forefront of efforts to examine the limitations of self-report data. We will not attempt a thorough summary of this large literature (the interested reader is referred to Schwarz and Sudman's [1994] book on autobiographical memory) but rather will highlight some of the most pertinent findings. It is important to acknowledge at the outset that the phenomenon of forgetting past experiences is not a simple linear function of time. If it were, adjustments could presumably be incorporated into recall assessments, correcting for the

time expired since the experience. Instead, a number of much more complex processes affect the quality of recalled information.

When subjects are asked to summarize experience over an interval, research suggests that more recent experiences have a greater influence on recall than more distant ones (Schwarz and Sudman 1994). For example, it is likely that the experience of a particularly pleasant day on the day before an assessment of an entire week's mood will bias the weekly rating in a positive direction. Another phenomenon affecting recall of particular events is called "effort-after-meaning" (Brown and Harris 1978). For example, if the degree of stressfulness were assessed immediately after an individual argues with his job supervisor, it would be very high. However, suppose that the supervisor reports the next day that the argument has made him see the employee in a new, more positive light. A week later, when the employee is asked about the argument, he may rate it as only mildly stressful because the events following the argument were positive. Thus, recall of experiences can be influenced by later experiences.

Apart from the impact of recent events and effort-after-meaning, little is known about how people summarize experiences over a period of time. Researchers and clinicians often ask patients to report pain for a given period, for instance, over the last week or month. We usually do not give much thought to the question of how patients summarize their pain over a certain period, but we must be assuming something about the meaning of these reports—probably that they represent an average of experience over the time period. Apart from the issue of whether people are even capable of cognitively computing the average of their pain experiences, there are a number of alternative ways they may be summarizing their experiences. Perhaps their retrospective recall is based entirely on the frequency of intensely painful episodes, or even on the severity of the most painful episode of the entire period. Alternatively, it may be that variability of pain is what influences recall. The point is that there is currently little information about summary processes, and how people do it could have implications for both research and medical practice. Kahneman and his colleagues used continuous assessments of pain and pleasure to explore these processes (Redelmeier and Kahneman 1996). They found that recall of pain and pleasure was most strongly related to a combination of the peak experience during the interval and the most recent experience. An EMA study addressing this question is presented later in the chapter. Unfortunately, individuals may vary in their methods of summarizing experiences, although we know of no data supporting this possibility.

Several studies have shown that a person's state at the time of assessment influences recall. Subjects experiencing high levels of negative affect at recall, for instance, may have better access to memories of negatively valenced events. This process is acknowledged in the depression literature (see Salovey et al. [1994] for a discussion of recall of pain), but the work has had minimal impact on our understanding of the recall process.

Autobiographical memory work has also highlighted the strategies that people use to remember particular events and the dates of their occurrence (for a review, see Schwarz and Sudman 1994). A well-known and heavily researched example is called "telescoping": events are recalled as having occurred more recently than objective dating indicates. Considerable evidence also exists that people use counting strategies for reporting on infrequent events, but estimation strategies when it comes to recalling frequent events. Discoveries of heuristic strategies have provided insights for improving survey designs and interviews (Bradburn and Shevell 1987). For example, people often use particularly salient events, with known dates of occurrence, as a point of comparison for dating other events. Based on this information, some surveys include explicit identification of salient dates to enhance this comparison process and thus improve event dating. Nevertheless, substantial concerns about recalled information remain. The approach discussed in the remainder of the chapter minimizes recall bias by using assessments of phenomena as they occur—that is, momentary assessment.

EMA AS A TOOL FOR THE BEHAVIORAL AND MEDICAL SCIENCES

Before presenting a number of examples of EMA research, we discuss the potential of the EMA methodology for the behavioral and medical sciences.

Because EMA reduces recall bias, use of the technique may generate new and, perhaps, surprising results where data have previously been collected with retrospective methods. Many psychological traits are assessed by asking individuals to rate themselves on some characteristic, for instance, how happy, how talkative, or how outgo-

ing they are. Retrospective and/or summarizing strategies may affect a person's report of these traits. EMA assessments of the same phenomenon may yield different results because these biases are reduced. One of the studies described later shows that two different methods of assessing how well people cope with stressful events vary depending on the time frame of the assessments.

A natural application for EMA is the study of the dynamics of everyday phenomena. One appealing aspect is the ability to examine processes with multiple, momentary assessments. Fluctuations in environmental or psychological variables could, for example, be used as predictors of outcomes. Given the correlational nature of the data, a powerful technique for analyzing questions with EMA data takes advantage of the prospective reports. By computing lagged variables, predictions of outcomes at time 2 may be made from variables collected at time 1 or earlier. This may improve an investigator's confidence in the temporal relationships among study variables.

While these are very positive attributes of the method, we must also mention a number of its limitations. Because EMA studies are often burdensome to participants, the duration of time individuals are willing to participate may be limited, and indeed, it may be difficult to collect a representative sample of individuals willing to participate. The latter point may have serious implications for the generalizability of findings produced by EMA studies. A recent study by Litt and Cooney (1998) demonstrated particularly low reliability. However, we must point out that EMA studies incorporating many assessments per day have been successful over a period of several weeks, and participants from whom one might expect poor compliance (drug abusers, for instance) have generated surprisingly good data. Another issue concerns the possible reactive arrangements that frequent signaling and questionnaire completion could invoke. For example, could asking chronically ill patients frequently about pain alter their pain levels? While there is some evidence that this is not a major problem (Cruise et al. 1996), additional work needs to be completed regarding this question.

In addition to the burden for study participants, a considerable financial commitment is required to conduct an EMA study, especially one that utilizes the highest level of technological innovation, the palmtop computer. There are advantages to computerizing data collection, but these are accompanied by a host of technical and logistical issues pertaining to the technology. Finally, proper analysis of EMA data presents numerous challenges for the investigator (see Schwartz and Stone 1998).

All of these points should go into a carefully considered decision to employ an EMA design. For some research questions, there is simply no alternative, but when more traditional methods would suffice, the investigator needs to weigh judiciously the pros and cons of the methods available.

CURRENT EMA RESEARCH IN THE BEHAVIORAL SCIENCES

We now move on to a consideration of selected studies using EMA as the primary mode of data analysis. This is not a comprehensive review of the EMA literature—that would be far too long for this chapter. Rather, we have chosen to present a diverse array of studies, many done by ourselves and our colleagues. A brief description of the research questions addressed by the study is followed by an account of selected results, emphasizing the unique findings allowed by the use of EMA. Data are presented on pain and symptoms in chronic disease, determinants of smoking behavior, psychiatric symptoms, situational determinants of mood, mood and minor events, coping with stressful experiences, physiological and behavioral variables, and ambulatory blood pressure and heart rate.

Pain and Symptoms in Chronic Disease Patients

Several investigations have examined pain in chronic disease patients, including those with diagnoses of rheumatoid arthritis, chronic fatigue syndrome, and fibromyalgia. Measuring pain with EMA techniques appears particularly appropriate given the variable and, for some patients, episodic pattern of pain experience. Clinicians have recognized the utility of momentary assessments of pain and often incorporate pain diaries into patient assessments. There are important differences, however, between diaries and EMA protocols in how patients are signaled to report their pain and in the schedules for reporting. Using diaries, patients may rate their pain on a regular schedule (hourly, three times a day, or when they perceive a change in their pain). In contrast, EMA utilizes random or near-random assessment intervals to minimize patient expectations about the signaling, to ensure that regular environmental events (such as meals)

are not entrained to the recording schedule, and to minimize difficult cognitive decisions, such as when to report a "change" in pain intensity.

Stone and his colleagues (Stone et al. 1995, 1996) examined the pain experiences of thirty-four rheumatoid arthritic (RA) patients over a one-week period. Patients were signaled seven times a day by a preprogrammed wristwatch and rated their pain on a 0-10-point scale. On the eighth day, patients had a scheduled appointment with their rheumatologist, who at that time rated their overall level of pain for the past week; patients also rated their pain for the preceding week. These ratings allowed a comparison of the retrospective assessment with various combinations of EMA data.

Many different ways of summarizing the forty-nine EMA pain reports were explored, including the average, mode, minimum, maximum, range, and variability, the average for each of the seven days, the average across all seven mornings, all seven afternoons, and all seven evenings, and a combination of peak and most recent pain. Investigators and clinicians may suspect that the retrospective reports represent average pain—a perfectly reasonable assumption—and results showed that average EMA ratings accounted for about 50 percent of the variance. However, other EMA statistics accounted for significantly more variance. The maximum pain level reported throughout the week, the 90th percentile, reports for day 6, morning pain, and the peak-recency statistic all were significantly better predictors of retrospective pain. These data may be interpreted as supporting the idea that retrospective pain reports are not simple averages of the pain experiences but reflect particular memory processes (emphasizing the influence of extreme pain experiences and recent pain). An interesting, yet somewhat disturbing, issue that should be explored in future research is the possibility that different patients use different heuristics in summarizing their pain. We also suspect that these findings generalize to affective states and to well-being.

Prior to the completion of this study, little was known about the diurnal patterns of pain in this patient group. Clinicians generally thought that pain was worse in the morning than at other times of the day, and this diurnal cycle was found in our study. Of particular interest, though, was the observation that only 50 percent of the group exhibited this pattern; no distinct patterns were common to the remaining. This finding highlights the importance of within-person data in the identification of individual differences. A second interesting result was the association between pain and the stressful events reported at each beep. There was a clear monotonic relationship between the degree of stressfulness and the pain level, confirming prior stress-pain associations derived from an end-of-day study of RA patients (Affleck et al. 1992). We also note that there have been similar EMA studies of fibromyalgia (Affleck et al. 1996) and chronic fatigue syndrome (Stone et al. 1994) patients.

Asthma symptomatology has also been examined with EMA techniques. Our laboratory studied thirty asthmatics and the effects of a tape-recorded relaxation intervention on symptoms and pulmonary function (Smyth, Soefer, et al., in press). For many years ambulatory devices have been available to measure peak expiratory flow (PEF), a measure of lung capacity closely associated with pulmonary function. A patient carries the small device and, at signaled intervals, records PEF by exhaling deeply into the device. Subjects in this study were signaled five times a day at random intervals (within blocks of time over the day to ensure representation of all parts of the day) for about ten consecutive days (the control period), after which they began daily listening to a tape-recorded relaxation intervention and were followed for about another ten days. At each signal, patients recorded their asthma symptoms, mood, and situation and took a PEF reading. (Subjects also took a saliva sample for other biochemical assays not discussed here.)

Results showed an effect of the intervention: compared to the stable pattern of symptoms and PEF over the control period, a clear shift to an increased level of PEF and decreased level of symptoms was found after the intervention. Furthermore, analyses indicated not only a level shift across the intervention days, but a change in slope over those days toward progressively less symptomatology. Additional analyses indicated a stress-pulmonary association: lung function worsened with minor daily stressors.

Determinants of Smoking and Craving for Cigarettes

An especially comprehensive line of EMA research on cigarette smoking has been done by Shiffman and his colleagues. Smoking is in many respects ideally suited to study by EMA methods: it is frequent, easily discriminable, and thought to be linked to a variety of environmental and internal stimuli (for instance, others smoking,

mood). Relapse episodes are also linked to internal states and environmental circumstances (Shiffman et al. 1996); relapse tends to occur under conditions of emotional upset, alcohol consumption, and exposure to smoking cues. While there are self-report questionnaires that assess these linkages, these measures may not be valid (Shiffman 1993). The sheer frequency of smoking (a pack-a-day smoker smokes 7,300 times per year) makes it implausible that smokers would be able to encode and process information about their smoking in order to provide faithful summaries of their smoking patterns.

In one study, Shiffman used a computerized self-monitoring of smoking supplemented by random EMA assessments to evaluate the situational and emotional correlates of smoking in two groups of smokers: heavy (and presumably dependent) smokers, and light smokers who were not nicotine-dependent (called "chippers") (Shiffman 1997). The most striking finding was that chippers' smoking was much more stimulus-bound— that is, much more closely associated with environmental and emotional stimuli. Interestingly, the particular stimuli that control chippers' smoking were idiosyncratic, differing among individual chippers. This finding is consistent with models of addiction and demonstrates the utility of intensive within-subject assessment for idiographic analyses.

Shiffman has also applied EMA methods to the study of relapse. Because most smoking cessation efforts end in relapse, the need to understand relapse and its antecedents is urgent. One approach has been to gather data on the characteristics of situations in which recent ex-smokers first reinitiate smoking. Such data have typically been collected retrospectively (see, for instance, O'Connell and Martin 1987), and without any control for the base rate of the relevant variables. To determine what aspects of the lapse situation are unique, Shiffman and his colleagues (1996) contrasted the characteristics of lapse situations against two standards of comparison: an episode of temptation (when the urge to smoke was intense, but the person did not lapse) and to a randomly selected moment. Both comparison situations were selected from the few days preceding the index lapse episode. Lapse situations were marked by negative affect, presence of smoking cues, and alcohol consumption. In most respects, temptation situations were intermediate between lapse situations and randomly sampled situations. However, lapses were more likely when subjects reported having failed to attempt a coping response.

Prior analyses of lapses and temptation episodes had been conducted as contrasts between lapse episodes—necessarily collected from smokers who lapsed—and temptation episodes—usually collected from smokers who maintained abstinence. Thus, the analyses confounded between- and within-subject (situational) variance. By making use of intensive within-subject EMA assessment, these analyses isolated situational influences on temptation and relapse and demonstrated their importance.

Shiffman and his colleagues also demonstrated how momentary EMA assessments could be aggregated into larger units. To assess the influence of craving on relapse, multiple EMA assessments were aggregated into daily averages. One goal of the analysis was to assess the natural history of craving over time. Clinical lore, based on smokers' global accounts of the process, suggested that craving increased initially after cessation, subsequently returning to normal. However, summaries of daily craving, based on multiple daily EMA assessments per subject, showed that craving generally did not increase after cessation. Instead, craving was found to decrease steadily after subjects stopped smoking. The data also confirmed that smokers' experience of abstinence was punctuated by periodic episodes of severe craving. These episodes decreased in frequency over time. Whereas smokers often report that craving seems to be constantly present during the early days of abstinence, the data showed that even this period is marked by episodic upsurges in craving, which are associated with particular situational provocations (Shiffman et al. 1997a). Further analyses examined whether craving on a given day predicted the risk of relapse on the subsequent day. The focus of the analysis was on dynamic changes in craving. Whereas it is relatively well known that individuals who experience more craving are more vulnerable to relapse, the focus here was on whether dynamic, day-to-day changes in craving predict day-to-day changes in relapse risk. The analysis demonstrated that relapse risk could indeed be predicted from such dynamic data, even after individual differences in nicotine dependence and craving had been accounted for. Interestingly, Shiffman and his colleagues (1997a) found that craving reports obtained first thing in the morning (just after the smoker woke up) were the most robust predictors of relapse risk, exceeding the power of more global daily averages. This finding illustrates the importance of timing and sampling in assessment.

Psychiatric Symptoms

ESM studies in Maastricht, the Netherlands, have intensively studied the lives of individuals experiencing stress and psychopathology (DeVries 1992; Van Eck, Nicolson, et al. 1996; Delespaul 1995). Subjects experiencing schizophrenia, stress, anxiety, depression, drug abuse, trauma, and pain contributed more than 100,000 days of ESM data. These studies used a standard six-day sampling format with ten semirandom signals per day asking about symptoms, mental state, and context. Four basic questions were asked of the subjects with the goal of recontextualizing psychiatric diagnoses (DeVries 1997): (1) What do people with or without mental disorders actually do throughout the day? (2) What do they experience cognitively and emotionally in this period? (3) What are the specific effects of setting on their mental state? (4) What are the time patterns of symptoms and mental states—that is, onset, episode, and recovery?

In Maastricht, experience-sampling data are incorporated into a multimethod, experimental ethnographic approach that links ESM to other methods and levels of data, such as the epidemiologic survey, target sampling (snowball sampling, for instance), focus groups, and social network analyses, and to experiments in the natural environment (DeVries 1997). With these methods, research has been focused on clarifying the behavioral and contextual aspects of psychiatric disorders for both refining diagnoses and tailoring treatments to the needs of individuals and specific populations. Compliance with ESM, except for melancholia in the elderly and acute psychoses, has been extraordinarily good. The large number of such studies has led to interesting findings. They have demonstrated that drug craving is related to mood and social context (Kaplan 1992). Anxiety with episodes of panic was found to be episodic and dynamic; depression was seen as a highly variable disorder over the course of the day and found to have a different form and context for males and females; responders to antidepressant treatment had clearly different motivational, emotional, and time budget profiles after treatment; and schizophrenic, auditory, and visual hallucinations are relatively short in duration, approximately two hours, and are not triggered by environmental stimuli (Delespaul 1995).

Other targets of our ESM research are a large study of the elderly, a drug abuse study examining both the detox and intox contexts, and studies into treatment effects and the relationship of stress to symptoms in manic depression as well as schizophrenia, with the goal of providing a better description of mental disorders for use in treatment and the development of therapies. These last studies are also aimed at deriving new, less labor-intensive methods to use over a wide variety of contexts to assess these new aspects of psychiatric disorders.

Situational Determinants of Mood

Mood is a pervasive concept in the behavioral sciences: it may be conceptualized as a general indicator of functioning and is associated with well-being; is itself closely linked to psychiatric disorders; and is often viewed as a mediational pathway to physiological systems associated with somatic health (Stone 1995). Although some ways of thinking about mood consider it as a relatively stable measure with little within-subject variation, other conceptualizations focus on its transitory nature. Especially with regard to the latter view, EMA studies of mood and other behavioral variables offer the potential to understand more fully the dynamic interplay of situation and affect. Furthermore, measurement issues relating to mood may be particularly pertinent to the assessment of suffering. EMA should be a useful method for gaining insight into the stability of the construct and into its psychological and situational determinants.

One study demonstrated the importance of considering situational factors for interpreting mood data (Stone et al. 1996). We examined the diurnal cycle of mood as well as the diurnal cycle of activities (for instance, working, watching TV, eating) and settings (at home, in car, at work, and so on). Most moods did indeed evidence a diurnal cycle, as did most of the activities. Interestingly, when patterns of mood were examined after activities and settings had been statistically controlled, some moods lost their diurnal cycle (happiness) whereas others retained it (tiredness). What, then, does an end-of-day mood reflect? And why are some moods seemingly less determined by situation? We believe that EMA methods have opened the door to discovering and understanding phenomena such as these.

In another study, Penner and her colleagues (1994) used momentary mood, collected from cigarette smokers as part of a smoking study, to analyze individual differences in the moment-to-moment variability of mood. Strikingly, they found that such variability itself showed stable individual differences. The study showed that these differences could not be accounted for by response styles but appeared to represent true individual differences in the volatility of mood. Analysis of within-subject variability particularly lends itself to study by EMA methods, since multiple assessments are available for each individual.[2]

Capturing Mood and Minor Events

Many studies have used daily diaries to summarize subjects' experience over an entire day (for example, Stone, Neale, and Shiffman 1993). However, even summarizing a single day's experience requires substantial cognitive processing, which can introduce bias into the resulting data. For example, research suggests that, because of its salience, subjects' most recent experience may have the greatest influence on their daily summaries. To assess this effect, we correlated subjects' end-of-day summaries of stress with their momentary mood in three-hour blocks successively more distant from the time the daily summary was completed (Shiffman, unpublished).

As hypothesized, end-of-day summaries were quite sensitive to the most recent emotional experience. Particularly on days when salient negative events occurred, the daily summary seemed to be almost entirely controlled by recent experience. More distant experience (such as the first three hours of the day) seemed to be completely ignored in these daily summaries. Thus, daily summaries cannot substitute for momentary assessment in capturing daily experience.

Conversely, another study showed that EMA measures could capture momentary variations in experience. In this study, subjects monitored their momentary experience using palmtop computers. At the end of each day, they also reported (retrospectively) any minor positive or negative events they had experienced (such as having a pleasant dinner or waiting in traffic), including the time of the event. We contrasted EMA assessments collected during positive-event periods with those from negative-event periods, often within a single day. The analysis showed that EMA mood and activity data could distinguish the small within-day variations associated with such minor events.

Coping with Stressful Situations

Coping with stressful situations has long been thought to be a core process in behavioral medicine and in social psychology, one that theoretically mediates the negative impact of stress. A very influential approach to measuring coping was developed by several investigators in the 1970s. It asks participants to describe a recent stressful event (usually one that occurred within the last month), to rate several qualities of the stressor (such as the degree of threat), and finally, to indicate which of a long list of strategies were employed to cope with the stressor. One obvious concern about this assessment procedure is the potential for retrospective bias to influence the reports. As a step in the direction of reducing bias and enabling examination of the dynamics of coping, some researchers developed end-of-day methods of measuring coping (Stone and Neale 1984, for example). However, at least one study has indicated that even daily reports may not be very accurate (Ptacek et al. 1994).

Stone, Schwartz, Neale, Shiffman, Marco, and their colleagues (1998) have used palmtop computers to explore EMA methods of measuring stress and coping. In our first study, one hundred community residents who reported high levels of work stress or marital stress in a telephone screening interview were studied intensively for two and a half days. Approximately every forty minutes subjects were signaled to report any stressors that were either occurring at the moment or were on their minds. When they answered affirmatively, subjects were presented with a series of questions about how they were coping with the problem. During a debriefing session following daily participation, subjects completed a retrospective questionnaire about the most stressful problem they had encountered during the previous two and a half days. Concurrently, a research assistant uploaded the momentary data and created a printout of each problem reported. After completing the retrospective questionnaire, which contained the same coping questionnaires that were programmed in the computer, the research assistant and the subject identified the momentary assessments that corresponded to the problem mentioned in the retrospective questionnaire. In this way, a direct comparison between momentary and retrospective reports could be made.

Without going into too much detail, we found that there was only modest correspondence between momentary and retrospective reports (Stone et al. 1998). Discrepancies were found in both commissions and omissions, and surprisingly, there were no strong person factors (individual differences) that predicted those discrepancies. Additionally, we attempted to identify specific coping items that were particularly high in discrepancies, but no clear pattern emerged. Other analyses of

these data have provided new insights about coping. For example, it appears that in the face of stressful work events, coping efforts offer little in the way of modifying momentary mood (Marco et al. in press). This was quite a surprising finding given the central position of coping in the stress-mood link. While there are a number of potential explanations for the finding, it nevertheless gives us pause and highlights the new kinds of findings that may emerge from EMA studies. We have also examined the idea of constructing trait measures on the basis of EMA data (Schwartz et al., in press). Rather than depend on subjects to evaluate the stability of their own behaviors—a dubious task, as we have previously discussed—we evaluated stability from multiple momentary reports from subjects about their coping efforts. This new measure was not associated with the typical trait measure of coping, again suggesting the new light that EMA sheds on this area of study. We doubt that this finding will be limited to coping and wonder how new ways of measuring traits will play out in other fields of behavioral science.

Data from the Shiffman group concerning smoking relapse episodes illustrate another EMA approach to assessing coping, using EMA methods to collect qualitative, narrative coping data rather than structured assessments (questionnaires). It has been suggested that success in smoking cessation depends on subjects' ability to cope skillfully with tempting situations. However, relatively little is known about how people actually cope with such situations. Moreover, using closed-ended queries to collect data on coping poses two significant challenges. First, it requires that subjects be able to characterize their coping according to meaningful categories that are often quite abstract. This has proved to be a difficult challenge. Second, even if smokers could be taught to use a coding system, teaching them such a system is itself an intervention: repeatedly presenting a list of categories amounts to reminding subjects of their coping options.

To circumvent these challenges, O'Connell and her colleagues (1987) elected to collect coping data as open-ended narratives. Besides carrying a palmtop computer, subjects in this study also carried a small tape recorder. They completed a structured assessment on the computer, and when they reported an episode of temptation, they were directed to talk into the tape recorder, describing how they had coped with the episode. Their open-ended narratives were later reviewed and coded into categories. Analysis showed that coping varied with situational variables as well as personal characteristics. For example, subjects who had previously tried and failed to quit smoking reported relying less on cognitive coping strategies.

Physiological Processes and Behavioral Variables

Developments in biochemical assay technologies have made it possible to measure a number of hormones in saliva. Techniques for conveniently collecting saliva in test tube–like devices are also available. The combination of the collection methods and assays has made it possible to refine our understanding of behavioral-hormonal interactions in ecologically valid studies. The specific investigations we cite to demonstrate EMA used to examine biobehavioral questions concern the hypothalamic-pituitary-adrenal axis and its major end-product, cortisol. This hormone is involved in a number of the body's metabolic and inflammatory systems and is often thought of as one of the two major stress hormones.

In Maastricht, van Eck and her colleagues (van Eck, Berkhof, et al. 1996) examined the association between salivary cortisol and many variables representing the psychosocial environment. Ninety-seven adults were signaled ten times a day for five consecutive days, and stressful events, mood, and more stable personal characteristics (perceived stress, trait anxiety, depression) were measured. As half of the participants were selected because they had high levels of perceived stress, it was possible to examine cortisol in high- and low-stress individuals. Neither overall level nor diurnal cycle of cortisol differed in those with high- versus low-stress levels. Regarding momentary variables, negative mood was associated with higher levels of cortisol, but positive affect was not. Stressful daily events also increased cortisol levels, and events that were continuing at the time of the assessment exerted an even greater effect. Surprisingly, considering the theoretical basis of the research, the content of the stressor or its appraisal was not related to cortisol production. Analyses also indicated that stressful events' effects on cortisol were largely mediated through mood alterations.

In addition to the natural observation aspect of the study just described, van Eck had subjects participate in a laboratory stress reactivity protocol (van Eck, Nicolson, et al. 1996). Participants were exposed to a speech task that has been shown to elicit moderate levels of stress, and saliva for cortisol assays was collected during the task. An important finding from these analyses was that cortisol reactivity to the laboratory task was not associated with a reactivity measure derived from the natural observation study. This finding has serious implications for interpreting results from laboratory experiments, which are often intended to represent typical, everyday response patterns of subjects.

A similar study was run at Stony Brook (Okenfels et al. 1995). The primary question addressed in this investigation was whether individuals under chronic stress would have different levels of cortisol secretion compared with those not under stress. The literature is conflicting regarding this question: some studies show increased secretion, some show decreased secretion, and others show no difference at all. In this study, chronic stress was defined as being unemployed for at least six months. A number of family, financial, and interpersonal problems are associated with unemployment, qualifying it as a chronic stressor. Sixty unemployed community residents and sixty employed community residents took EMA recordings of their mood, stress levels, and situations (where they were, who they were with, and so on) seven times a day for two consecutive days. Twenty minutes after each EMA recording a sample of saliva was taken with a salivette, a small test tube–like device containing a cotton wad that is placed in the mouth for two minutes.

As in the previously discussed study, no evidence was found for a different overall level of cortisol secretion in the two groups. However, there was a significant difference in the diurnal cycle of cortisol secreted over the day. Cortisol has a distinct diurnal cycle: values are highest upon awakening and decrease dramatically throughout the day. Chronically stressed individuals exhibited higher morning cortisol levels and lower evening levels than control subjects (Okenfels et al. 1995). This finding may help to explain the contradictory results from prior studies (both increases and decreases in cortisol were observed depending on the time of day studied) and suggests a dysregulation of the hypothalamic-pituitary-adrenal axis in these subjects. Additional analyses confirmed the findings from the study of van Eck, Nicolson, and their colleagues (1996): daily stressful events were associated with higher cortisol levels (Smyth, Okenfels, et al. 1997).

Ambulatory Blood Pressure and Heart Rate in Paramedics

Jamner and his colleagues (Jamner et al. 1991; Goldstein, Jamner, and Shapiro 1992) have investigated situational effects on cardiovascular (CV) functioning by monitoring a small group of paramedics over two days. The investigators hypothesized that various degrees of psychological stress engendered by stressful situations would be associated with CV functioning. Furthermore, they speculated that two personality traits, cynical hostility and social desirability, would moderate subjects' responses to environmental conditions. During each of the days, an ambulatory monitor recorded CV parameters every twenty minutes (with some variability in the exact timing of assessments). Every two hours subjects were signaled by a countdown timer to complete a brief assessment of mood, anxiety symptoms, and situational characteristics. Two days were studied: a typical workday and a non-workday. During the former, situations were classified according to activity: on-scene at an emergency, riding ambulance to the scene of the emergency, waiting at the base station for a call, and sleeping.

Evidence was obtained supporting the hypothesized associations. CV function varied systematically according to situations: blood pressure and heart rate were highest on the scene and lowest during sleep. Hostility moderated some of the associations between situations and CV functioning, but not uniformly. Subjects high in cynical hostility had higher blood pressure than those with a low level of hostility. Interestingly, CV function did not vary much between workdays and nonworkdays.

Because heart rate and blood pressure are highly variable and responsive to environmental input, assessment of these parameters in subjects' natural environment has been considered essential for obtaining valid estimates of blood pressure. It is thought that some people are more reactive to stress, and investigators in this area have also been interested in assessing how subjects' blood pressure varies across environmental contexts. Kamarck, Shiffman, and their collaborators used EMA methods to examine some of the psychosocial determinants of blood pressure during daily life (Kamarck et al. 1998a, 1998b). In this study, 120 healthy community adults were followed over a six-day period, with cardiovascular and diary assessments taken every 45 minutes during the waking day. The assessments were cued either by the inflation of the blood pressure cuff or (if the subject missed that cue) by a palmtop computer, which also recorded all self-report responses. An average of 109 assessments were available on each person over this period. The data showed that negative affect (feeling sad, anxious, angry, or generally upset) and arousal (feeling alert and not tired) were independent predictors of fluctuations in cardiovascular activity during daily life, even after adjustments for posture, activity, recent food or drug consumption, and temperature (Kamarck et al., 1998a, 1998b). Interestingly, the data showed significant and independent lag effects of negative affect as well, suggesting that the effects of negative mood on cardiovascular responses persist over a 45-minute period. Some of the unique prognostic significance of ambulatory blood pressure may lie in its susceptibility to psychosocial determinants. If so, EMA methods may be uniquely suited for exploring the significance of these effects.

CONCLUSION

EMA methods provide the researcher and clinician with methods for investigating experiences, behaviors, and physiological processes with little concern that such reports are biased by retrospective recall. It also affords the opportunity to investigate the dynamic interplay over time among these variables. The methods are relatively new, and much information is required before they can be fully accepted by the scientific community. Some continuing concerns are: participants' reactions to repeated assessments, the reactive nature of the task, issues in the analysis of repeated measurement data, and the relationship of momentary information to other forms of self-report data. We nevertheless eagerly await studies addressing these questions and expect EMA to take a significant place among the tools available to behavioral science and medical researchers and clinicians.

NOTES

1. This was due in large part to information provided by studies that used diary approaches in clinical settings during the 1960s (Meyer and Haggerty 1962). These early studies created a growing awareness that lifestyle and stress significantly influenced both individual and family health and disease.
2. Obviously, this sort of EMA study demands enormous effort, one that could not be justified if the same information could be garnered from simple self-report questionnaires. In the smoking literature, there is a long history of questionnaire assessment of smoking patterns (Shiffman 1988). Therefore, it seems important to determine whether such "smoking typology" questionnaires contain the same information as the EMA data. Shiffman and his colleagues (in press) correlated smoking typology questionnaires and EMA data. The correlations hover close to zero. Thus, questionnaires cannot substitute for EMA data.

Prior to this, most of the literature on smoking relapse episodes relied on recall of such episodes, collected retrospectively at follow-up, usually months after the target event. Subjects might well be able to recall these episodes, since they are significant life events with relatively distinctive properties. To determine whether such recall could accurately capture the details of relapse episodes, Shiffman and his colleagues (1977b) compared recalled reports of relapse episodes with real-time EMA recordings. The correspondence was found to be modest, with correlations averaging 0.32. Moreover, other data suggested that even some of this modest correspondence was actually due to "schematic recall"—that is, the ability to reconstruct the episode from general knowledge about such occasions as a class, rather than from specific recollection of material encoded at the time of the experience.

REFERENCES

Affleck, G., Urrows, S., Tennen, H., and Higgins, P. (1992). Daily coping with pain from rheumatoid arthritis: Patterns and correlates. *Pain, 51,* 221–29.

Affleck, G., Urrows, S., Tennen, H., Higgins, P., and Abeles, M. (1996). Sequential daily relations of sleep, pain intensity, and attention to pain among women with fibromyalgia. *Pain, 68,* 363–68.

Barker, R. G. 1978. *Habitats, environments and human behavior: Studies in the ecological psychology and eco-behavioral science of the Midwest Psychological Field Station: 1947–1972.* San Francisco: Jossey-Bass.

Bradburn, N. M., and Shevell, S. K. (1987). Answering autobiographical questions: The impact of memory and inference on surveys. *Science, 236,* 157–61.

Bronfenbrenner, U. (1979). *The ecology of human development.* Cambridge, Mass.: Harvard University Press.

Brown, G. W., and Harris, T. (1978). *Social origins of depression: A study of psychiatric disorder in women.* New York: Wiley.

Chapple, E. D. (1970). *Culture and the biological man: Explanations in behavioral anthropology.* New York: Holt, Rinehart and Winston.

———. (1987). Validity and reliability of the Experience Sampling Method. *Journal of Nervous and Mental Disease, 175,* 526–36.

Cruise, C. E., Broderick, J., Porter, L., Kaell, A. T., and Stone, A. A. (1996). Reactive effects of diary self-assessment in chronic pain patients. *Pain, 67,* 253–58.

Csikszentmihalyi, M. (1994). *Flow: The Psychology of Optimal Experience.* New York: HarperCollins.

Csikszentmihalyi, M., and Larson, R. (1984). *Being adolescent: Conflict and growth in the teenage years.* New York: Basic.

Delespaul, P. A. E. G. (1995). *Assessing schizophrenia in daily life: The Experience Sampling Method.* Maastricht: University of Limburg.

DeVries, M. W. (Ed.). (1992). *The experience of psychopathology: Investigating mental disorders in their natural settings.* Cambridge: Cambridge University Press.

———. (1997). Recontextualizing psychiatry: Toward ecologically valid mental health research. *Transcultural Psychiatry, 34,* 185–218.

Egeren, L. F. van, and Madarasmi, S. (1992). Blood pressure and behavior: Mood, activity, and blood pressure in daily life. In M. W. DeVries (Ed.), *The experience of psychopathology: Investigating mental disorders in their natural settings* (pp. 240–52). Cambridge: Cambridge University Press.

Goldstein, I., Jamner, L., and Shapiro, D. (1992). Ambulatory blood pressure and heart rate in healthy male paramedics during a workday and a non-workday. *Health Psychology, 11,* 48–54.

Gross, D. R. (1984). Time allocation: A tool for the study of cultural behavior. *American Review of Anthropology, 13,* 519–58.

Hinde, R. A. (1992). Developmental psychology in the context of other behavioral sciences. *Developmental Psychology, 28,* 1018–29.

Jamner, L., Shapiro, D., Goldstein, I., and Rozanne Hug, B. (1991). Ambulatory blood pressure and heart rate in paramedics: Effects of cynical hostility and defensiveness. *Psychosomatic Medicine, 53,* 393–406.

Kamarck, T. W., Shiffman, S., Smithline, L., Goodie, J., Paty, J. A., Gnys, M., and Jong, J. (1998a). Effects of task strain, social conflict, and emotional activation on ambulatory cardiovascular activity: Daily life consequences of recurring stress in a multiethnic adult sample. *Health Psychology, 17,* 17–29.

Kamarck, T. W., Shiffman, S., Smithline, L., Goodie, J. L., Thompson, H. S., Ituarte, J. J., Pro, V., Paty, J. A., Kassel, J. S., Gnys, M., and Perz, W. (1998b). The diary of ambulatory behavioral states: A new approach to the assessment of psychosocial influences on ambulatory cardiovascular activity. In D. S. Krantz and A. Baum (Eds.), *Technology and methods in behavioral medicine* (pp. 163–94). Mahwah, N.J.: Erlbaum.

Kaplan, C. D. (1992). Drug craving and drug use in the daily life of heroin addicts. In M. W. DeVries (Ed.), *The experience of psychopathology: Investigating mental disorders in their natural settings* (pp. 193–218). Cambridge: Cambridge University Press.

Kleitman, N. (1963). *Sleep and wakefulness.* 2nd ed. Chicago: University of Chicago Press.

Kripke, D. F. (1983). Phase advance theories for affective illnesses. In T. Wehr and F. Goodwin (Eds.), *Circadian rhythms in psychiatry: Basic and clinical studies.* Pacific Grove, Calif.: Boxwood.

Litt, M. D., and Cooney, N. L. (1998). Ecological Momentary Assessment (EMA) with treated alcoholics: Methodological problems and potential solutions. *Health Psychology, 17,* 48–52.

Malinowski, B. (1935). *Coral gardens and their magic: Soil tilling and agricultural rites.* Vol. 1. Bloomington: Indiana University Press.

Marco, C. A., Schwartz, J. E., Neale, J. M., Shiffman, S., and Stone, A. A. (in press). Do appraisals of daily problems and how they are coped with moderate mood in everyday life? *Journal of Counseling and Clinical Psychology.*

McGuire, M. T., and Polsky, R. H. (1979). Behavioral changes in hospitalized acute schizophrenics: An ethological perspective. *Journal of Nervous and Mental Disease, 167,* 651–57.

Meyer, E., and Haggerty, R. T. (1962). Streptococcal infections in families: Factors altering individual susceptibility. *Pediatrics, 29,* 539–49.

Minors, D. S., and Waterhouse, J. M. (1981). *Circadian rhythms and the human.* Bristol, Eng.: Wright and Sons.

Monk, T. H., Flaherty, J. F., Frank, E., Hoskinson, K., and Kupfer, D. J. (1990). The social rhythm metric: An instrument to quantify the daily rhythms of life. *Journal of Nervous and Mental Disease, 178,* 120–26.

Monroe, R. H., and Monroe, R. L. (1971). Household density and infant care in an East African society. *Journal of Social Psychology, 83,* 9–13.

Nelson, R. O. (1977). Assessments and therapeutic functions of self-monitoring. In M. Hersen, R. M. Eisler, and P. Miller (Eds.), *Progress in behavior modification* (vol. 5, pp. 3–41). New York: Academic Press.

O'Connell, K. A., and Martin, E. J. (1987). Highly tempting situations associated with abstinence, temporary lapse, and relapse among participants in smoking cessation programs. *Journal of Consulting and Clinical Psychology, 55,* 367–71.

Okenfels, M. C., Porter, L., Smyth, J., Kirschbaum, C., Hellhammer, D. H., and Stone, A. A. (1995). The effect of chronic stress associated with unemployment on salivary cortisol: Overall cortisol levels, diurnal rhythm, and acute stress reactivity. *Psychosomatic Medicine, 57,* 460–67.

Penner, L. A., Shiffman, S., Paty, J. A., and Fritzsche, B. A. (1994). Individual differences in intraperson variability in mood. *Journal of Personality and Social Psychology, 66,* 712–21.

Pickering, T. S., Harshfield, G. A., Devereux, R. B., and Laragh, J. H. (1985). What is the role of ambulatory blood pressure monitoring in the management of hypertensive patients? *Hypertension, 7,* 171–77.

Ptacek, J., Smith, R., Espe, K., and Raffety, B. (1994). Limited correspondence between daily coping reports and retrospective coping recall. *Psychological Assessment, 6,* 41–49.

Redelmeier, D., and Kahneman, D. (1996). Patients' memories of pain medical treatments: Real-time and retrospective evaluations of two minimally invasive procedures. *Pain, 66,* 3–8.

Reynolds, T. D. (1965). Fluctuations in schizophrenic behavior. *Medical Annals of the District of Columbia, 34,* 520–49.

Salovey, P., Sieber, W. J., Jobe, J. B., and Willis, G. B. (1993). The recall of physical pain. In N. Schwarz and S. Sudman (Eds.), *Autobiographical memory and the validity of retrospective reports* (pp. 89–106). New York: Springer-Verlag.

Schwartz, J. E., Neale, J. M., Marco, C. A., Shiffman, S., and Stone, A. A. (in press). Are there really trait-like ways of coping? *Journal of Personality and Social Psychology.*

Schwartz, J. E., and Stone, A. A. (1998). Data analysis for EMA studies. *Health Psychology, 17,* 6–16.

Schwarz, N., and Sudman, S. (1994). *Autobiographical memory and the validity of retrospective reports.* New York: Springer-Verlag.

Shiffman, S. (1988). Behavioral assessment. In D. M. Donovan and G. A. Marlatt (Eds.), *Assessment of addictive behaviors: Behavioral, cognitive, and physiological procedures* (pp. 139–81). New York: Guilford.

———. (1993). Assessing smoking patterns and motives. *Journal of Consulting and Clinical Psychology, 61,* 732–42.

———. (1997). Individual differences in nicotine addiction: The case of tobacco "chippers." In D. Malin (Chair), *Research models of nicotine dependence: Data from laboratory and research clinic.* Plenary symposium presented at the annual meeting of the Society for Research on Nicotine and Tobacco, Nashville (June).

———. (in press). Real-time self-report of momentary states in the natural environment: Computerized ecological momentary assessment. In A. A. Stone, J. Turkkan, J. Jobe, C. Bachrach, H. Kurtzman, and V. Cain (Eds.), *The science of self-report: Implicates for research and practice.* Mahwah, N.J.: Erlbaum.

Shiffman, S., Engberg, J., Paty, J. A., Perz, W., Gnys, M., Kassel, and Hickcox, M. (1997a). A day at a time: Predicting smoking lapse from daily urge. *Journal of Abnormal Psychology, 106,* 104–16.

Shiffman, S., Hufford, M., Hickcox, M. Paty, J. A., Gnys, M., and Kassel, J. D. (1997b). Remember that? A comparison of real-time versus retrospective recall of smoking lapses. *Journal of Consulting and Clinical Psychology, 65,* 292–300.

Shiffman, S., Paty, J. A., Gnys, M., Kassel, J. D., and Hickcox, M. (1996). First lapses to smoking: Within subjects analysis of real time reports. *Journal of Consulting and Clinical Psychology, 64,* 366–79.

Smyth, J. M., Okenfels, M. C., Gorin, A. A., Catley, D., Porter, L. S., Kirschbaum, C., Hellhammer, D. H., and Stone, A. A. (1997). Individual differences in the diurnal cycle of cortisol. *Psychoneuroendocrinology, 22,* 89–105.

Smyth, J., Okenfels, M., Port, L., Kirschbaum, C., Hellhammer, D. H., and Stone, A. A. (1998). Stressors and mood measured on a momentary basis are associated with salivary cortisol secretion. *Psychoneuroendocrinology, 23,* 353–70.

Smyth, J., Soefer, M. H., Hurewitz, A., and Stone, A. A. (in press). The effect of tape-recorded relaxation training on well-being, symptoms, and peak expiratory flow in adult asthmatics. *Psychology and Health.*

Stone, A. A. (1995). Measures of affective response. In S. Cohen, R. Kessler, and L. Gordon (Eds.), *Measuring stress: A guide for health and social scientists* (pp. 148–71). New York: Cambridge University Press.

Stone, A. A., Broderick, J. B., Kaell, A. T., and Porter, L. (1995). Retrospective reports of pain do not correspond well to momentary reports of pain over one week in rheumatoid arthritis patients. *Arthritis and Rheumatism, 38,* S227 (abstract).

Stone, A. A., Broderick, J. B., Porter, L. S., Krupp, L., Gyns, M., Paty, J., and Shiffman, S. (1994). Fatigue and mood in chronic fatigue syndrome patients: Results of a momentary assessment protocol examining fatigue and mood levels and diurnal patterns. *Annals of Behavioral Medicine, 16,* 228–34.

Stone, A. A., and Neale, J. M. (1984). A new measure of daily coping: Development and preliminary results. *Journal of Personality and Social Psychology, 46,* 892–906.

Stone, A. A., Neale, J. M., and Shiffman, S. (1993). How mood relates to stress and coping: A daily perspective. *Annals of Behavioral Medicine, 15,* 8–16.

Stone, P. J., and Nicolson, N. A. (1987). Infrequently occurring activities and contexts in time use data. *Journal of Nervous and Mental Diseases, 175,* 519–25.

Stone, A. A., Schwartz, J. E., Neale, J. M., Shiffman, S., Marco, C. A., Hickcox, M., Paty, J., Porter, L. S., and Cruise, L. J. (1998). How accurate are current coping assessments? A comparison of momentary versus end-of-day reports of coping efforts. *Journal of Personality and Social Psychology, 74,* 1670–80.

Stone, A. A., and Shiffman, S. (1994). Ecological Momentary Assessment (EMA) in behavioral medicine. *Annals of Behavioral Medicine, 16,* 199–202.

Stone, A. A., Smyth, J. M., Pickering, T., and Schwartz, J. (1996). Daily mood variability: Form of diurnal patterns and determinants of diurnal patterns. *Journal of Applied Social Psychology, 26,* 1286–1305.

Szalai, A., Converse, P., Feldheim, P., et al. (1972). *The use of time.* The Hague: Mouton.

Van Eck, M., Nicolson, N., Berkhof, H., and Sulon, J. (1996). Individual differences in cortisol responsiveness to a laboratory speech task and their relationship to responses to stressful daily events. *Biological Psychiatry, 43,* 69–84.

Van Eck, M., Berkhof, H., Nicolson, N., and Sulon, J. (1996). The effects of perceived stress, traits, mood states, and stressful events on salivary cortisol. *Psychosomatic Medicine, 58,* 447–58.

Wada, T. (1922). An experimental study of hunger and its relation to activity. *Archives Psychology Monographs, 8,* 1–65.

Weber, M. A., and Drayer, J. M. (1984). *Ambulatory blood pressure monitoring.* Darmstadt: Steinkopf.

Whiting, B., and Whiting, J. (1975). *Children of six cultures.* Cambridge, Mass.: Harvard University Press.

3 Measurement Issues in Emotion Research

Randy J. Larsen and Barbara L. Fredrickson

We open this chapter on measurement issues with the recommendation that researchers construct a working definition of emotion(s) that best fits their research agenda prior to selecting measures. We then discuss issues that cut across all types of emotion measurement, such as timing and context, as well as reliability and validity. Next, we provide a selective review of specific measurement techniques, touching on self-reports of subjective experience, observer ratings, facial measures, autonomic measures, brain-based measures, vocal measures, and responses to emotion-sensitive tasks. Our aim in this selective review is to highlight some specific strengths, weaknesses, and measurement issues associated with different types of emotion measures. Finally, because emotions are only probablistically linked to emotion measures, we also recommend that, to the extent possible, researchers collect and cross-reference multiple measures of emotion.

EXPERIENCES OF psychic pain and pleasure, and the limitless variations on this hedonic theme, define the domain of emotions. The content of a person's emotional life strongly influences his or her judgments of the quality of that life. In addition, a person's emotional engagement with the "stuff" of life defines the "wantability" and utility of that stuff for building quality into life, for deciding to do one thing instead of another, and for being satisfied with the outcomes of his or her choices. To be sure, quality of life goes far beyond just feeling more pleasant than unpleasant emotions in one's life over time. Nevertheless, as pointed out in the preface to this book, we can approach an understanding of quality of life by considering some of its lower-level components and building blocks, such as emotions.

How might the study of emotions help in understanding quality of life? We have space to give only a few examples. One question concerns the relation between pleasure and pain, between the positive and negative emotions. Are the conditions that give rise to pleasant emotions simply the opposite of those that produce unpleasant emotions?

Can circumstances that bring about pleasantness cancel unpleasant states, and vice versa? Should we think of pleasure and pain as end points on a continuum, or as completely separate and independent dimensions? Emotions can be thought of as both inputs into processes that contribute to quality of life and as outcomes that provide feedback as to how those processes are working. Another line of inquiry concerning quality of life would address the habituation of emotional responses. Good and bad things happen to everyone. And we know that people habituate to the good and the bad at different rates. Are there ways to potentiate habituation to unpleasant events, and ways to slow habituation to positive events? Do different components of the emotional response (such as bodily reactions and subjective feelings) habituate differently? Another emotional topic useful in understanding quality-of-life concerns situational and individual differences in emotional responding. For example, what are the conditions under which most people are likely to experience joy or suffering? Why is it that many episodes of joy and happiness occur in the context of a pending tragedy that has been averted? Similar questions may be applied to individual differences. Why is it that some people are easily made anxious and fearful, whereas others are less vulnerable to these unpleasant emotions? People differ in their thresholds for evoking emotions as well as in the magnitude of their emotional responses to the same events. Because emotions contribute to quality of life, understanding these individual and situational differences in emotional responding may contribute to understanding quality of life.

These few research questions should make it clear that there are many lines of inquiry about emotions that may be important in understanding quality-of-life. Empirical inquiry requires measurement, and so the editors of this book asked us to address the assessment of emotions. This is a daunting task, even if we were to simply list, in how-to fashion, all the different ways emotions have been measured in the research literature. We have chosen instead to focus more on measurement issues than on specific measures per se. Although we review some specific measurement techniques, our review is not meant to be exhaustive. Instead we cover examples that are meant to be illustrative and that we use as vehicles for discussing the strengths, weaknesses, and implications of certain techniques for assessing emotions. Let us first, however, address some issues that should be considered before turning to specific techniques.

PROLEGOMENA TO MEASUREMENT ISSUES

What, exactly, is an emotion? Emotion researchers do not fully agree on the answer to this basic question (compare, Ekman and Davidson 1994). In fact, Kleinginna and Kleinginna (1981) identified over ninety different definitions. Yet this does not mean that research on emotions is stalled at the starting gates, haggling over definitions. It does mean, however, that researchers should begin by articulating their own *working definition of emotion(s)* in planning and communicating their work. We recommend this step for two reasons. First, it can limit the possible misinterpretations of your results. Second, and perhaps more critically, it can make choosing among various emotion measures an easier task. Working definitions are appropriate because they imply revision and refinement over time as new findings about the nature of emotion inevitably emerge.

Our own working definition of emotions draws from a systems perspective, identifying emotions as multifaceted processes that unfold over time. Emotions are manifest in multiple channels, and the channels themselves are loosely coupled and interact in a complex way (Venables 1984). These channels span both psychological and physiological domains, including subjective experience, facial action, central and peripheral nervous system activation, cognitive or information-processing changes, and behavioral action tendencies. In the ideal case, charting emotions entails assessing organized changes across these multiple components simultaneously. Data streams obtained from these multiple domains may converge on the underlying construct of emotion and increase confidence that we can fathom its presence and magnitude. Yet even with multiple, synchronized measures, the underlying psychological construct of "emotion" remains some inferential steps away from the more tangible data it can produce. In other words, we view an emotion as an inferred construct and caution against purely operational (or reductionistic) definitions of emotion. The term "emotion" carries surplus meaning beyond any set of emotion measures.

Other issues researchers need to consider in constructing working definitions are whether they conceptualize emotions as (a) discrete and/or dimensional (b) states and/or traits and (c) event-related and/or diffuse (for discussions of these issues, see Frijda, this volume; Lazarus 1991; Morris, this volume). While the latter two of these issues may impinge primarily on the expected intensity and duration of emotion experiences, the first issue can impinge directly on emotion measurement. Discussions about whether emotions operate as two or three general dimensions, or as seven or more separate and distinct categories of experience, go back more than one hundred years (Darwin 1872/1965) and continue to this day (for reviews, see Izard 1993; Lazarus 1991). One widely espoused dimensional view of emotion is represented by the circumplex model (Russell 1980; Watson and Tellegen 1985; for a review, see Larsen and Diener 1992). This model posits that emotions conform to a circular or radex arrangement with the coordinates of this circular space representing valence and arousal: emotions that are similar to each other (for instance, anger, distress) are close to each other on the circumference of the circle, whereas emotions that are so-called opposites (for example, happiness, sadness) are 180 degrees away from each other. In contrast, proponents of discrete views (Ekman 1992; Izard 1977; Lazarus 1991) hold that dimensional views often blur meaningful distinctions between adjacent emotions (for example, fear versus anger versus disgust). More recently, research by Feldman-Barrett (1995; in press) suggests that individuals reliably differ in whether they describe their affective states as discrete or as dimensional. The measurement issue embedded within this dialogue concerns specificity: while measures that fit the discrete emotions views can be reduced to a dimensional arrangement post hoc, the converse is rarely possible. For this reason, researchers should consider a priori whether distinctions between specific negative or positive emotions are likely to have an impact on their theoretical and empirical agenda.

In sum, *whether* and *how* the measurement issues and types of emotion measures discussed in this chapter apply to any given research agenda follows from the working definition of emotion(s) adopted within that research agenda. For this reason, we recommend that those embarking on emotions research first consider what they take emotions to be.

MEASUREMENT ISSUES

Before turning to descriptions of specific domains of measurement, we discuss a series of issues that cut across all types of emotion assessment. In addition to discussing the traditional measurement issues of reliability and validity, we also discuss the issues surrounding timing and context that can be particularly vexing in emotion research.

Timing

Emotions take time. They are dynamic processes that unfold, linger, and then dissipate over time—sometimes gradually, other times rapidly. Moreover, emotions involve a cascade of different response systems, and each may have its own time of onset and duration. For instance, if you were to be startled by a sudden loud noise, like a car horn, you would blink your eyes in about forty milliseconds, your heart rate would begin to accelerate in about five hundred milliseconds, your sweat glands would become active after two to three seconds, and a hormonal response might occur minutes later. Emotions also change in character depending on the temporal vantage point from which they are viewed. In real time, for instance, emotions can implicate multiple physiological systems, whereas in retrospect, these same bodily changes become less evident, often dropping out of measurement range altogether. Likewise, an open empirical question is whether perhaps in real time the subjective experience of emotions may be quite nuanced, best represented by specific emotion terms, whereas in retrospect, a single valance dimension (good-bad) may adequately represent this same experience (see Kahneman, this volume).

One critical measurement issue is how to isolate the targeted emotion episode. When does it start and when does it end? Identifying these moments with precision can greatly increase researchers' chances of observing emotion-related changes. Imprecision at this stage can, in effect, dilute the targeted emotional episode within a wash of emotion-irrelevant moments (Levenson 1988).

A second critical measurement issue is how to ensure that purported measures of emotion have sufficient *temporal resolution* to capture the dy-namic aspects of the concept under study. Some markers of emotion—for example, an increase in cardiac output—might span only a minute or less. The subjective experience of emotional arousal, however, might last much longer. Thus, readings of cardiac output taken once every fifteen minutes have only a remote chance of capturing an emotion-related change, whereas self-report measures taken in that same time span might successfully capture some of the emotional effect. If working definitions identify the targeted emotion concept as a quick-changing state, then measures should be appropriately fine-grained, exhibiting a temporal resolution that is smaller (ideally much smaller, to provide reliable aggregate measures) than the expected duration of the emotion-related change.

A third issue concerns the *temporal proximity* of emotion measures to the emotion experience. Measures obtained on-line or *during* an emotion experience are perhaps feasible more often than is recognized. This is certainly true for measures obtained from video records and through physiological recording devices, but perhaps no less so for measures obtained via self-report (see discussion later in the chapter). Emotion measures obtained concurrently with emotion experience maximize validity and accuracy (with the exception of measures extracted at the cost of disrupting the emotion experience). When concurrent measures are not feasible or practical, lagged measures that minimize the latency between emotion experience and emotion measurement should be sought. Except when memory for emotion is the target of study, the shorter the latency, the better the measure (Levenson 1988).

Context

Emotions occur within the broader psychological context of subjective and bodily experience. Other features of this context can no doubt impinge upon emotion measurement. A study aimed at inducing a specific emotion in all participants (anger or sadness, for instance) may find that the success of the induction depends on contextual factors that vary from individual to individual, such as ambient mood (for example, irritable or depressed mood), emotion-related personality traits (for example, hostility or pessimism), recent life events (such as perceived personal injustices or losses), or preexisting arousal (did the participant just drink four cups of coffee?). Diurnal, circadian, and circaseptum influences on mood might also alter emotion experience. If the researchers' aim is to create a comparable emotional state across all participants, then contextual influences such as these might be considered noise. There are two defenses against "noise-producing" constructs: hold constant or limit nuisance variance, or measure it. Success at the first strategy comes with familiarity in a research area and good experimental design. Success at the second strategy allows researchers to determine which participants might be extreme outliers in terms of ambient mood or recent life events, and/or how emotion-related personality traits covary with the phenomena under study. Yet one researcher's noise is another researcher's data: the extent to which neighboring aspects of subjective experience, such as emotions, moods, traits, and nonspecific arousal, influence one another is the target of study for several research programs.

Reliability

Many researchers think of measurement reliability as a high test-retest correlation. As a measurement concept, reliability in fact refers to the degree to which observed scores reflect the "true" amount of the construct being measured. Because we never have access to "true" scores, we can only estimate reliability. For certain psychological constructs, a test-retest correlation is a good estimate of reliability. Test-retest is an appropriate way to estimate reliability for between-subjects constructs (traits), where the variance of interest is between participants and we assume there will be little or no meaningful within-participant variance. Intelligence is a good example of a between-subject construct: we assume that, for any single individual, intelligence is stable and not easily changed, at least not over a few weeks or months. As such, reliable measures of intelligence demonstrate high test-retest correlations.

Emotion, however, is more typically construed as a within-subject construct (a state), and we assume that it may change quickly and frequently within any single individual. To complicate matters, emotion can be a between-subjects construct as well, where the variance of interest might be differences between individuals in their responses to identical emotion-provoking events. Because emotion is a complicated state-trait construct, we cannot use simple test-retest correlations as estimates of measurement reliability.

A second way to estimate reliability is through internal consistency estimates, such as coefficient alpha, or odd-even item composite correlations. These are actually measures of item homogeneity:

they assess the degree to which the various items are measuring the same underlying construct (though alpha is, in part, inflated by scale length) (compare, Clark and Watson 1995). Because many self-report emotion measures are factor-analytically constructed, internal consistency or item homogeneity is built in during the scale construction process. Internal consistency analysis is thus one way to estimate reliability, and it works equally well for both state and trait measures. However, internal consistency estimates of reliability work only for multi-item scales. Single-item measures, which are very popular in emotion research, simply cannot be examined in terms of internal consistency.

What, then, is the researcher using single-item measures to do? One approach is to bypass reliability concerns altogether and focus instead on concerns about validity. This is reasonable because measurement reliability (in the sense of the proportion of variance in the observed scores that is attributable to true score variance) sets the upper bound on validity correlations. In other words, a measure cannot correlate with external validity criteria higher than it can correlate with itself. As such, valid measures are de facto reliable. Clearly, a researcher who passes up reliability concerns treads on thin ice. Nevertheless, strong evidence for validity, with multiple converging methods and replicated patterns of association, can add credibility to the claim that a particular measure is reliable.

Reliability is most important in interpreting failures to refute the null hypothesis. For example, if a study is completed and no predicted effects are found, three obvious reasons must be entertained: the theory is wrong, the measures used are not reliable, or some auxiliary conditions of the study were not met (for more detailed discussion, see Meehl 1978). If a study fails and the researcher is confident that the measures used are reliable, then the researcher must question the theory or look for something that might have gone wrong with the procedures (including data management and analysis). It is precisely in such circumstances (null findings) that reliability evidence is crucial.

Validity

Emotions, we have argued, are theoretical constructs that are only probabilistically linked to observable indicators. As such, the term "emotion" has surplus meaning: even though it may be represented by many different measures, emotion is not equivalent, nor can it be reduced to, any single measure. This underscores the importance of construct validity in understanding the scientific meaning of emotion terms (Cronbach and Meehl 1955).

In construct validity, meaning is given to a scientific term (such as "emotion") by the nomological network of assertions in which that term appears. Our theories and measurement models guide us in building a network of associations around the construct of emotion. In construct validation, theory testing and measurement development proceed in tandem. Each link in the network adds to the scientific meaning of the term. Some links refer to positive associations (convergent validity), and some refer to negative or null associations (discriminant validity). In addition, some links specify the conditions under which emotions are likely to be evoked (predictive validity).

The total collection of relationships built up around the construct of "emotion," or around specific emotions, creates a mosaic of research findings. When enough pieces of the network are in place, we "get the picture." That is, when enough information is available about what something is, what it isn't, and what it predicts, we begin to have the feeling that we "understand" it. This is not to say that our understanding of an emotion is complete at this point. Construct validity is always unfinished, and things are always "true until further notice." Nevertheless, even though there are always new links to be added to the network of associations surrounding a construct, there comes a point where we reach some consensual agreement about the scientific meaning of a construct, such as an emotion.

Again, because emotions implicate multiple channels or component systems (for example, facial action, autonomic activity, subjective experience, action tendencies), the question arises about whether we should expect strong convergence among measures of these different components. Most researchers hold the view that components of emotion are loosely coupled systems that interact in a complex way (see Frijda, this volume). Clearly, the various response systems have multiple tasks beyond indexing emotions. For instance, the autonomic nervous system responds to metabolic demands and maintains the delicate balance of homeostasis, facial muscles are used for communication and eating, and conscious experience follows the streams of thought. Although emotions may bring the disparate component systems into some synchronization, total convergence among measures is neither expected nor required for con-

struct validity. In fact, discrepancies between component measures can represent challenges to existing theories and may provide insights into how emotion systems work. Moreover, for some researchers, discrepancies between component measures of emotion are used to index emotional dissociation or repression (see Bonanno et al. 1995; Newton and Contrada, 1992).

Perhaps the strongest evidence for validity is when the theory of the particular emotion can be used to generate predictions about the conditions under which that emotion will be evoked, or the type of persons for whom that emotion will be most easily evoked. Couple this with measurement theory and knowledge of specific measures of emotion, and very specific predictions may be generated. We turn now to a consideration of specific measures in the emotions domain.

TYPES OF EMOTION MEASURES

Self-Reports of Subjective Experience

Self-report measures of emotion are widely used and form a broad range of assessment instruments. These measures rely on participants not only to experience their emotions but also to reflect accurately their phenomenal awareness through the use of rating scales or adjective checklists. Proponents of self-report assume that participants are in a privileged position to monitor, assess, and integrate information about their own emotions. Through self-report measures, the participant has the opportunity to express, in some integrated and standardized format, a good deal of information that only he or she has access to.

Although there are a great many instruments, substantial similarities can be found among them. Rather than conduct an exhaustive review, we instead concentrate on a few exemplars and highlight common measurement themes and issues. Additional instruments are reviewed in MacKay (1980) and Stone (1995).

Single-Item Measures   A technique with a good deal of face validity is simply to ask research participants to rate how they are/were feeling on a single emotional construct. That construct might be a global affective dimension ("How unpleasant are you feeling?") or a specific emotion ("How angry do you feel?"). And the response scale might be unipolar ("not at all angry" to "extremely angry") or bipolar ("unpleasant" to "pleasant"). Response options are often Likert-type scales, with five-, seven-, or nine-point formats. The advantages of single-item measures are that they are simple to construct, easily understood by participants, and brief to administer. Plus, virtually any emotion term can anchor a single-item scale, making this self-report technique indispensable for researchers targeting specific, discrete emotions (Ekman, Friesen, and Ancoli 1980; Gross and Levenson 1993). The disadvantages are the same as those encountered whenever measurement is extremely brief: concerns about the ratio of error variance to true variance, representativeness, domain specificity, and sampling error. Despite these disadvantages, single-item measures are very popular in the experimental and survey literatures, where brevity is important.

An important variant on this technique is to make the response scale a visual analog of the digits representing response options. Such Visual Analog Scales (VAS) typically present the participant with a horizontal line separating two opposing adjectives. Participants are asked to place a mark on the line describing how they are/were feeling along that dimension. Researchers have also used VAS methods with unipolar response options; the line is anchored with "not at all" to "extremely much" for a specific emotion construct (sad, for instance). A related technique is to make the question itself an analog of the construct being assessed. For example, the participant might be presented with a series of five cartoon faces, going from a neutral expression on one face to an extreme frown on another, and he or she is asked to circle the face that most represents how she or he is/was feeling. This has the advantage of being useful with participants for whom adjectives might not be meaningful, such as very young children or participants from different linguistic cultures.

A recent single-item questionnaire measure, called the Affect Grid, has been introduced by Russell and colleagues (Russell, Weiss, and Mendelsohn 1989). Based on the circumplex model of emotion (Larsen and Diener 1992; Russell 1980; Watson and Tellegen 1985), the Affect Grid is composed of a nine-by-nine matrix. Emotion adjectives are placed at the midpoints of each side of the grid, as well as at the four corners. These adjectives are (starting in the high-arousal, pleasant quadrant, and proceeding clockwise) excitement, pleasantness, relaxation, sleepiness, depression, unpleasantness, stress, and high arousal. Participants are instructed to place a check within the cell of the grid that best reflects how they are/were feel-

ing along the pleasantness and arousal dimensions. The developers of this scale report that its performance is similar to that of other longer and more cumbersome measures of pleasure and arousal. In addition, Russell and his colleagues (1989) report that this measure is sensitive to manipulations designed to alter participants' levels of pleasantness and arousal. One advantage of this measure is that it may be administered many times without fatigue.

Multiple-Item Measures Representing a large class of assessment instruments, the majority of multi-item measures consist of lists of adjectives describing emotional states. Some measures are checklists: the participant is instructed to simply check all those emotions that he or she is/was feeling. Other measures are rating tasks: the participant is instructed to rate each adjective for the degree to which he or she is/was feeling that particular emotion. The numerous multi-item instruments are essentially variations on these response themes; differences have to do primarily with response scales, the number and nature of the emotion adjectives, the scoring and scale names, and the instructions that accompany the self-report tasks.

One of the first adjective rating scales formally constructed was the 130-item Mood Adjective Check List (MACL) (Nowlis and Green 1957). Despite the name, the MACL is not literally a checklist: the participant is asked to rate how he or she felt at the time the emotion adjective was read on the following scale: "definitely felt it," "slightly," "cannot decide," "definitely not." Based on factor analytic studies, thirty-six items were selected for a short form of the MACL (Nowlis 1965). Scoring results in twelve factor scores: aggression, anxiety, surgency, elation, concentration, fatigue, social affection, sadness, skepticism, egotism, vigor, and nonchalance. Other researchers propose a simple positive-negative valence scale scoring (Stone 1981). The MACL has not become a widely used measure, perhaps because it was never published in a journal format or by a test publisher. The original version (Nowlis and Green 1957) was in an unpublished naval technical report, and the later shortened version (Nowlis 1965) appeared in a chapter in an edited book (Tomkins and Izard 1965).

A subsequent affect checklist has since eclipsed the MACL in popularity: Zuckerman and Lubin's (1965) Multiple Affect Adjective Check List (MAACL). It is very similar to the MACL in length: the MACL has 130 items, and the MAACL has 132. Moreover, many of the items are the same on the two inventories. Despite these similarities, the MACL has languished whereas the MAACL went on to become the most widely used self-report emotion assessment instrument in the psychological literature (Larsen and Sinnett 1991). Perhaps the critical ingredient to the MAACL's success was that it was distributed by Educational and Industrial Testing Service (EITS), a professional test publisher. It comes with a user manual, complete with annotated references, developmental history, psychometric properties, scoring keys, and multiple answer sheets. Other reasons for its popularity might be the checklist format, which makes administering the MAACL much faster than the MACL. And finally, the MAACL has only three subscales, compared to twelve on the MACL. The parsimony associated with the more global scales is probably appealing to many, although more specific scales have their uses as well. The three scale scores on the MAACL are depression, anxiety, and hostility. These three scales are highly intercorrelated and appear to lack discriminant validity. Gotlib and Meyer (1986) factored the original MAACL items and reported two factors, which they labeled positive and negative affect, consistent with the labels proposed by Watson and Tellegen (1985) a few years earlier.

In 1985 Zuckerman and Lubin published a revised version of the Multiple Affect Adjective Check List (MAACL-R). The revision mainly concerns the scoring format, which now allows for several pleasant emotion scores as well as global positive and negative affect and sensation-seeking. While the new scoring format appears better in some respects (it conforms to more recent factor analytic studies of emotion ratings), the new format is not without problems. For example, table 10 in the MAACL-R manual reports that the sensation-seeking scale has a coefficient alpha of .09 in a large (over one thousand) sample.

This is a good point at which to pause and take up the issue of response formats. The MAACL and its revision are in the form of checklists: the subject merely indicates the presence or absence of a particular emotion by checking a box. Some researchers have argued that checklists are particularly susceptible to response sets and other forms of nonrandom error. Almost three decades ago, Bentler (1969) argued against using checklists in psychometric assessment. More recently, Green, Goldman, and Salovey (1993) demonstrated that checklist mood assessments contain significant

nonrandom error, and, "like Bentler (1969) before us, we advise caution when researchers analyze data obtained with a checklist format" (1036). A related issue concerns nonbalanced or asymmetric Likert response options, which were popular on early mood assessment inventories. Research on this issue is adequately reviewed by Mackay (1980) and will not be repeated here.

In 1967 Thayer published the Activation-Deactivation Adjective Check List (A-D ACL). Based on his own theory of activation, arousal, and affect, the A-D ACL contains adjectives that primarily refer to valenced arousal states, such as energetic, lively, active, sleepy, tired-tense, clutched-up, fearful-jittery, calm, quiet, and at rest. Participants rate the adjectives on a four-point scale, from "definitely do not feel" to "definitely feel." There are several factor-analytic-based scoring strategies, although the most widely used strategy results in two scores: energetic arousal (which is high-arousal positive affect) and tense arousal (which is high-arousal negative affect). Research with the A-D ACL is reviewed in Thayer (1986).

In 1977 Izard introduced the multi-item Differential Emotions Scale (DES) aimed at assessing multiple discrete emotions. Respondents are asked to rate (on a five-point scale) how much they are/were experiencing various discrete emotions by rating clusters of three emotion words (for example, scared/fearful/afraid, angry/irritated/annoyed, glad/happy/joyful). The original DES has since been modified to distinguish between self-conscious emotions (Mosher and White 1981).

One of the more recent introductions in this long line of mood adjective rating scales is the Positive Affect Negative Affect Schedule (PANAS) (Watson, Clark, and Tellegen 1988). The PANAS is based on the circumplex model of affect (Russell 1980; Watson and Tellegen 1985; Larsen and Diener 1992). Of the eight potential scores derivable from the circumplex model, the PANAS focuses on two positive affect (PA) (high-arousal pleasant), and negative affect (NA) (high-arousal unpleasant). The PANAS contains ten items on each of the two scales. The items are mood adjectives and are rated on a five-point scale, labeled as "not at all or slight," "a little," "moderately," "quite a bit," and "very much." The PA and NA scales were constructed to be uncorrelated, and conforming with the theoretical model positing the independence of positive and negative affect, they generally are.

Much of the work with the PANAS has been correlational, and the scales correlate with external variables in ways that imply validity. For example, extraversion correlates with frequent reports of PA, and neuroticism correlates with frequent reports of NA. Few studies have used the PANAS in experimental research. Larsen and Ketelaar (1991) used the PANAS in an experiment wherein pleasant and unpleasant moods were induced using guided imagery techniques. They found that the positive induction increased PA but did not lower NA, and that the negative induction increased NA but did not lower PA. This differential sensitivity to positive and negative emotion inductions supports the construct validity of the PANAS. The PANAS has not been free from criticism, however. The reader may refer to Larsen and Diener (1992) for a discussion of potential problems and misinterpretations of the circumplex model and of the PANAS as a measure of that model.

Adding the Temporal Dimension to Self-Reports Self-report measures of emotions, whether single-item or multiple-item, require research participants to report *globally* on an emotional episode that extended over time. For instance, researchers might ask, "How pleasant or unpleasant was your visit to the dentist?" or, ". . . your experience of childbirth?" or, "How much fear did you feel while watching this film?" This measurement strategy is often used without recognizing that the mental processes respondents must invoke to supply these global self-reports can introduce distortion and measurement error. Specifically, providing a global self-report implicates both memory processes (respondents recall the targeted episode) and aggregation processes (respondents in some manner combine their multiple and often varied momentary experiences into an overall report). Both of these mental processes may obscure or misrepresent dynamic changes in emotion as experienced over time. For instance, Fredrickson and Kahneman have documented that people's global reports for extended emotional episodes draw highly from the momentary affect experienced at the most intense and final moments of the episode (called the peak-end rule; see Kahneman, this volume), with the duration of the emotional experience largely neglected (Fredrickson and Kahneman 1993; Kahneman et al. 1993; for related issues, see Thomas and Diener 1990).

REAL-TIME RATINGS One way to circumvent some of the problems inherent in global reports is to collect real-time ratings of emotion. In recent years, several such techniques have been developed. The general strategy across these techniques

is to collect self-reports of subjective experience on a moment-by-moment basis, either *on-line* as the emotion is first experienced or *retrospectively* as the temporal dimension of the original episode is "replayed" while real-time momentary self-reports are collected. A sample of momentary self-report measures is described later.

Conceptually, the most basic real-time self-report measure can be viewed as a single-item measure (as described earlier) with a temporal dimension added. Using either a rotating dial or a sliding meter, respondents are instructed to adjust a pointer as often as necessary so that it always reflects how they are feeling each moment throughout an extended episode. Several researchers have described continuous "rating dials" of this sort (Fredrickson and Kahneman 1993; Fredrickson and Levenson, in press; Gottman and Levenson 1985; Bunce, Larsen, and Cruz 1993). Like single-item measures more generally, rating dials may use either bipolar ("very negative" to "very positive") or unipolar verbal anchors ("no sadness at all" to "extreme sadness") and either Likert-type or visual analog scales.

In addition to capturing the ebb and flow of emotional experience over time, continuous rating dials also automate data acquisition. The dial itself is connected to a potentiometer or rheostatic resistor that controls the voltage output from a common nine-volt battery (much like a dimmer switch controls the amount of electricity going to a lighting fixture). The electrical output from the dial is then monitored by an analog-to-digital (A/D) data-acquisition device to record continuously respondents' self-reports. Properly calibrated, the amount of electricity at the recording output is a direct representation of the respondent's moment-by-moment self-report.

When the demands of an experimental protocol are low (for example, viewing emotional film clips), research participants can use a rating dial to provide continuous self-reports of emotion "on-line" during the actual emotional episode (Fredrickson and Kahneman 1993; Fredrickson and Levenson, in press). In contexts where such on-line measurement would be too cumbersome or disruptive (for example, during actual social interaction), participants can use a rating dial to provide continuous, *retrospective* self-reports of their emotional experience, so long as the temporal dimension of the original experience is "replayed" during the rating procedure. In studies of emotions in marital interaction, for instance, Gottman and Levenson (1985) obtained continuous self-reports of emotion experience using a video-recall technique. In an initial session, they had married couples discuss an area of conflict in their marriage while their conversation and nonverbal displays were recorded on video and each spouse's autonomic reactions were recorded with physiological sensors. In subsequent individual sessions (again with video and physiological recording), spouses each independently viewed the videotape of their conversation and used a bipolar rating dial to indicate how positive or negative they were feeling each moment *during the actual interaction*. Validating this video-recall technique, Gottman and Levenson (1985) reported that each spouse's autonomic activity during the later rating session patterned that evident during the actual marital interaction, suggesting that viewing the videotaped conversation was sufficient to re-create (to some degree) the affect experienced during the original episode.

One drawback of the momentary self-report measures described thus far is that they limit self-reports to just one or two dimensions. Certainly it is *technically* feasible to create a whole bank of rating dials, perhaps one to reflect each of several discrete emotional states (anger, fear, sadness, disgust, attraction/love, enjoyment, contentment, and so on—akin to adding a temporal dimension to Ekman's [1992] various single-item scales or Izard's [1977] DES). The limiting factor, however, would be the respondent's ability to track the ebb and flow of multiple discrete emotions simultaneously, in real time. One way around this obstacle would be to collect self-reports for multiple emotions using multiple iterations of the video-recall technique. Such a strategy, however, would no doubt push the limits of participants' cooperation and/or induce fatigue.

A more reasonable way around this obstacle is to use a hybrid technique, introduced by Rosenberg and Ekman (1994) and called "cued review," which derives partially from Gottman and Levenson's (1985) video recall technique. In cued review, participants are instructed to stop the video replay at moments when they remember having felt an emotion during the original episode. They then use a multiple-item emotion report form to rate what they remember feeling at that precise moment. For example, Rosenberg and Ekman collected Likert-type ratings for eight emotion terms: anger, contempt, disgust, embarrassment, fear, happiness, sadness, and surprise. After completing a given rating form, participants then restarted the video and, whenever they remember having felt a

change in emotion (in either degree or type) during the original episode, they stopped the playback again and completed another emotion report form for that moment. This procedure was then repeated for the entire emotion episode. Because the emotion report forms can contain separate ratings for multiple, discrete emotions, the cued-review technique uncouples momentary self-reports from unidimensional scales or two-dimensional circumplex models. The resulting self-report data, although momentary, are neither continuous nor equally spaced. Providing validity for this technique, Rosenberg and Ekman found that momentary reports of specific emotions obtained through cued review coincided in time with facial indications of the same specific emotions.

Advantages to these automated techniques include the ease of administration, the on-line nature of the recording, the ability to record continuously for long time periods, and the lack of data entry concerns (provided the output is read by computerized A/D equipment). The major disadvantage is the need for specialized equipment and the fact that the participant is literally tied down by the device (though this could change if radio telemetry or on-board memory could accompany a rating device that the participant could carry during the reporting period). Moreover, it seems likely that continuously monitoring the participant's emotions may lead to a form of fatigue or be so intrusive that it actually alters his or her emotions. These issues remain open questions for researchers.

Evaluation of Self-Report Methods   Self-report methods are perhaps the most efficient and easiest techniques for measuring emotions. Even so, they rely on the assumption that research participants are both *able* and *willing* to observe and report on their own emotions. Often fused with the assumption that participants are able to report their emotions is the corollary assumption that self-reports are in fact the *best* source of information about an individual's emotional experience. Each of these assumptions, however, can be questioned. For example, if some emotional episodes are either outside of phenomenal awareness or not represented in working memory, participants will be unable to perceive or recognize the feeling state accurately and, as a consequence, unable to provide accurate self-reports. Of course, some would question whether an unperceived emotion is an emotion at all. Without fully entering the debate about the existence of unconscious emotions, it seems possible that a person might "have" an emotion in a nonverbal channel (for example, autonomic activation or action tendency) yet never label that experience and hence not perceive it as an emotion at all (Tranel and Damasio 1985). Moreover, some persons may repress emotional experiences, resulting in biased or incomplete memory for emotions (Newton and Contrada 1992). There is some evidence that the repressive coping style works by preventing emotions from being encoded into memory (Cutler, Bunce, and Larsen 1996). Certainly, using measures in addition to self-report would be important in these instances.

Other issues underlying the assumption that participants are able to observe and report on their emotions are more practical. Certain populations, for various reasons, may have meager comprehension of semantic information. Very young children are one example. Other populations, like the very old, may not have the concentration or attention span to complete a lengthy self-report measure like the MAACL. Responses to self-report questionnaires may not provide accurate estimates of emotional states in such samples. Measurement accuracy may be similarly jeopardized when rating scales are used with participants whose principal language is not the one in which the instrument is presented. Translation is always questionable, given cultural variation in the experience, comprehension, and linguistic expression of emotion. Cultural psychologists have further argued that some cultures have emotions, or emotion terms, that are not identifiable in other cultures (see, for example Mesquita and Frijda 1992). For all of these reasons, self-report scales should be brief and easy to comprehend, and researchers should attend to cultural, demographic, and contextual factors that might compromise accurate responding.

Turning to the second assumption—that participants are *willing* to report on their emotions— the main issue is one of response sets, where responses to items may contain noncontent variance. That is, the participants' responses might reflect something that is not contained in the questionnaire itself. The most frequently discussed response set is socially desirable responding: the participant responds to the items in a manner that creates a positive impression or makes him or her appear to possess mostly positive attributes. People may be motivated to deny undesirable attributes or emotions and to endorse positive ones. One way to control social desirability responding is to measure it using a social desirability measure (for example, the Marlowe-Crowne scale)

and partial it out in statistical analyses. Some researchers, however, question this approach (Diener, Smith, and Fujita 1995), primarily on the basis of the validity of social desirability measures.

A different response set is extreme responding: a participant may be motivated to use scale end points or large numbers in describing his or her emotions. While some researchers have written about this, the few studies done on extreme responding on emotional trait questionnaires have not found much evidence that this is a problem (Larsen and Diener 1987). Other researchers have argued that even a small amount of extreme responding can introduce systematic distortions that particularly affect the covariance structure of a set of ratings (Bentler 1969). The effect of extreme responding would be to attenuate negative correlations between polar opposite terms. A recent discussion and demonstration of correlated error in affect ratings is provided by Green, Goldman, and Salovey (1993). These authors demonstrate the utility of multiple measures of emotion— something we also recommend—in accounting for random and nonrandom (response bias) measurement error.

Another potential problem with self-report concerns the effects of repeated assessments. One issue is measurement reactivity, the idea that the actual process of measurement alters the thing being measured. Administering an emotion adjective rating scale multiple times may in fact create or alter the emotional state of interest. A second issue is measurement independence. Researchers often want to assess emotion frequently during an experiment, especially in within-subject designs. Ideally, each measurement occasion is independent from the last. The only way to achieve this in a repeated-measures experiment would be to remove the previous experience with the self-report items from the participant's memory prior to each new assessment. Because this is not possible, one potential effect of repeated emotion measurement is stereotypic responding (Stone 1995): participants settle into a response profile that does not change much across the assessment occasions. This can be assessed by examining standard deviations across assessment occasions.

Observer Ratings of Emotion

With sufficient information available, virtually any self-report measure described in the previous section might also be collected from a third-person perspective. Such observer reports might be obtained from "expert" observers of the target person's emotional experiences (such as a spouse, best friend, or therapist) or simply from strangers without any special training. The key is to provide the observer-rater with emotion-relevant information about the target person's experience—written accounts, audiotaped or transcribed dialogue, video recordings or photographs of facial behavior, or some combination of these data. Upon reviewing these data, observers make judgments about the likely emotional state of the target person (including type and/or intensity) either globally or at a particular moment. It is critical to note, however, that observer reports like these represent *social attributions* about a target person's emotional state and should be cross-validated against other emotion measures. Like attribution processes more generally, attributions about emotion are constrained by the information available or biased by an observer's self-serving tendencies. (This is perhaps most true when an observer-rater has a close relationship with the target person.)

A conceptually related method of obtaining observer reports is to use specially trained observers to code emotions. One example of this method is the Specific Affect Coding System (SPAFF) developed by Gottman and his colleagues to study emotions in marital interaction (Krokoff, Gottman, and Hass 1989; Gottman 1993). This system separates the emotion evident in marital exchanges into specific positive and negative categories. The SPAFF positive affect categories are interest, affection, humor, validation, and excitement/joy. The SPAFF negative affects are anger, belligerence, domineering, contempt, disgust, tension/fear/worry, sadness, whining, and defensiveness. Similar to observers without special training making attributions about emotions, when making emotion ratings SPAFF coders consider a gestalt of information, including verbal content, voice tone, context, facial expression, gestures, and body movement. This is what makes the SPAFF a "cultural informants" coding system rather than a physical features coding system (for example, Ekman and Freisen's [1978] Facial Action Coding System [FACS], described later). What sets SPAFF coders apart from other observers is (a) their special training in recognizing important physical markers of emotion in the face and voice, and (b) the pace of their coding. Although Gottman has divised an "Affect Wheel" to use the SPAFF system in real-time interactions, more commonly SPAFF requires microanalyses of video recordings—six to ten hours of coding for each fifteen minutes of dyadic interaction.

A key advantage of observer reports is that they are often unobtrusive and can track naturalistic social exchanges. And when no special training is required of observers, they are also inexpensive and fast measures. Gottman (1993) argues that gestalt approaches to coding emotions circumvent the assumption hidden within physical features coding systems (such as FACS) that different emotion components or channels combine additively to create emotional meaning. Among the disadvantages of observer coding systems like SPAFF is the intensive training required of the coders. Moreover, SPAFF has been developed specifically to study marital interactions and may not suit other types of interactions, like those between friends or coworkers or intergenerational relationships. Studying emotions in these other interpersonal contexts may require new codes altogether.

Other recent studies have shown the utility of using relatively untrained informants to provide observer reports. For example, Watson and Clark (1991) asked subjects to sign up for their study with some friends or acquaintances. Among well-acquainted peers, they found mostly significant correlations between self-report and peer-reported emotions—for example, .52 for sadness, .49 for positive affect, .40 for fear, and .31 for hostility. Similar untrained peers were used by Diener, Smith, and Fujita (1995) and Lucas, Diener, and Suh (1996), with similar convergence results. Such findings bolster the view that, although emotions are thought to be private, there is nevertheless a public aspect that can be tapped through trained and even untrained observers.

Facial Measures of Emotion

Coding Systems   One of the most comprehensive and widely used systems for coding emotion in the face is the Facial Action Coding System (FACS) (Ekman and Friesen 1975, 1978). The FACS consists of forty-six anatomically based "action units" (AUs). Each AU refers to a specific observable change in the face. For example, AU 1 raises the inner brows, AU 9 wrinkles the nose, and AU 12 raises the outer lip corners. The system describes all possible movements in the skin of the face observable to the naked eye. There is an extensive training and certification system for learning the FACS (contact the Human Interaction Lab at the University of California at San Francisco). This self-paced training program involves learning about the muscular and appearance basis of each AU, extensive exposure to the forty-six AUs and their combinations in photos and videotape, instructions for producing the AUs with one's own face, and rules for specifying minimal changes for scoring and combining AUs. It requires about forty hours of initial training to achieve acceptable reliability (Ekman and Friesen 1975).

Facial coding is useful in measuring emotion to the extent that overt, spontaneous facial changes accompany people's emotional responses. Yet because facial muscles are also enervated by the voluntary nervous system, observable facial action is not simply a direct readout or "expression" of underlying emotional states. Emotion-related facial actions, for instance, may be controlled through inhibition, exaggeration, or masking. Nevertheless, FACS has been very useful in studies of emotion. For example, FACS codes can reliably distinguish so-called genuine smiles ("Duchenne smiles"), which are spontaneous expressions of positive emotion, from so-called deceptive smiles "non-Duchenne smiles"), which are often deliberate attempts to appear as if positive emotion is being felt when it is not (Ekman, Friesen, and O'Sullivan, 1988). A recent edited volume describes a range of research programs in which FACS has been a critical ingredient (Ekman and Rosenberg 1997).

Full use of the FACS provides exhaustive real-time description of facial action. It also demands a lot of time and effort. For example, FACS-scoring videotaped faces requires about one hour of coding for each minute of videotape (depending, of course, on the density of facial action). For many research questions less fine-grained codings of facial expressions may be reasonable, and several researchers (including Ekman and his colleagues) have developed selective, emotion-specific, and/or global systems for coding facial action (for example, EMFACS [Emotion FACS]—see Fridlund, Ekman, and Oster, 1987; MAX [for Maximally Discriminative Facial Movement Coding System] by Izard 1979; for global coding systems, see Gross and Levenson 1993; Kring and Neale 1996).

Electromyography Facial measures of emotion may also be obtained using physiological measures of muscle contractions. The neural activation of the striated muscles in the face (and elsewhere in the body) produce muscle action potentials that can be detected using electromyography (EMG). EMG recordings are obtained using two electrodes placed over the muscle bundle of interest. The electrical signal given off by the muscle during contraction is on the order of a few to a few hundred microvolts, though facial muscle contrac-

tions in typical lab settings rarely exceed eighty microvolts. The amount of electrical activity detected over the muscle is directly related to the number of motoneuronal pools involved in the contraction. Detailed descriptions of facial electromyographic technique may be found in Cacioppo and Tassinary (1990).

The muscles typically assessed using EMG are the corrugator supercilia (responsible for the furrowed brow that occurs with many unpleasant emotions) and the zygomaticus major (responsible for pulling the corner of the mouth back and up, toward the ear). Other muscles, such as those responsible for wrinkling the nose during disgust, are also sometimes assessed. Evidence for the validity of facial EMG suggests that this is an effective technology for assessing both the valence and intensity of affective responses (Cacioppo et al. 1986). Moreover, EMG techniques can assess neuromuscular actions that are too small to generate visible changes in the face (Cacioppo et al. 1986). As such, EMG may be more sensitive to emotion in the face than is FACS, albeit in many fewer locations. Such sensitivity has a downside, however, in that electrical signals from sites other than the muscle of interest may also be detected during EMG assessments. Researchers interested in measuring emotions with facial EMG should seek training in electophysiological measurement and/or collaborators with appropriate expertise.

Autonomic Measures of Emotion

Emotions are often closely tied to urges to act in specific ways, be it to strike out against a competitor, escape imminent danger, or be near a loved one. Many emotion theorists view the link between emotions and action tendencies as part and parcel of the definition of emotions (Frijda 1988; Lazarus 1991), and arguably, it is this association that makes emotions "embodied" (Lazarus 1991), evident in both somatic nervous system activity and, when emotions are intense and/or prolonged, in autonomic nervous system (ANS) activity (Cacioppo et al. 1993).

Although a wide range of theorists have tried to describe the precise relationships between emotions and ANS activity, these can be distilled into those who argue that distinct emotions are associated with distinct ANS activity (for example, Averill 1969; Levenson, Ekman and Friesen 1990) and those who argue that distinct emotions are associated with undifferentiated ANS activity (for example, Cannon 1927; Mandler 1975; Schacter and Singer 1962). Although empirical support for autonomic specificity across emotions has been observed in multiple studies and in multiple laboratories, the cumulative data are mixed and therefore remain inconclusive (for reviews, see Cacioppo et al. 1993; Levenson 1992; Zajonc and McIntosh 1992).

Psychophysiological Inference   The state of the science, then, does not support the use of autonomic measures (used singly or in combination) to index or infer specific emotions. That is, we cannot distinguish anger from fear, or disgust from anger (or any emotion from any other emotion), solely using autonomic measures. Moreover, even though emotions (when sufficiently intense) reliably yield ANS changes, neither can we distinguish emotional states from non-emotional states solely using autonomic measures. As Cacioppo and Tassinary (1990) put it: "When a physiological event differentiates the presence versus absence of a particular psychological element, one may infer the *absence* of this psychological element given the nonoccurrence of the physiological event, but one cannot infer anything about the *presence* of the psychological element given the occurrence of the physiological event" (24). This is so because ANS activity can (and does) index a range of psychological events, including but certainly not limited to emotions. These include attentional states, such as orienting to novel stimuli (Graham and Clifton 1966; Lacey et al. 1963), anticipated or actual somatic activity (Obrist et al. 1970), respiration (Porges, 1995), as well as individual differences (Levenson, 1983).

At present, then, how can autonomic measures be used to index emotions? The answer is simple: in combination with other (non-ANS) measures of emotion. In other words, the same caveat that we have applied to all other measures discussed in this chapter also applies to autonomic measures: any single measure of emotion is imperfect and incomplete. Researchers can be more confident about the presence of an emotion to the extent that multiple measures provide independent and converging evidence of that emotion.

Fruitful Autonomic Measures   Of the dozens of different autonomic measures that have been used to measure emotions over the last several decades, some have been more fruitful than others. One set of measures indexes *electrodermal* activity (skin conductance is currently the accepted and most reliable measure), another set of measures index *respiratory* activity, and perhaps the broadest set of measures index *cardiovascular* activity. Within this last and largest set, measures range from gross, end-organ responses (for example, heart rate, diastolic and systolic blood pressure) to measures of the various underlying hemodynamic processes responsible for these end-organ responses (such as cardiac output, stroke volume, and total peripheral resistance; interested readers should see Sherwood [1993] and Sherwood et al. [1990] for information on impedance cardiography). Still other measures link respiratory to cardiovascular activity (for example, Respiratory Sinus Arrhythmia [RSA], a purported measure of cardiac vagal tone; Grossman, van Beek, and Wientjes 1990; Porges 1995). Researchers interested in incorporating autonomic measures into their empirical projects should seek out special training and/or experienced collaborators.

In addition to issues of theory and inference, there are many practical issues to keep in mind when considering the use of autonomic measures. First, autonomic measures vary widely in how invasive they are. By consequence, some autonomic measures might elicit emotions in and of themselves. On the less invasive end are measures of pulse rate and skin conductance that simply require that sensors be placed on a participant's fingers. Impedance cardiography, by contrast, uses band electrodes that circle a participant's neck and chest in several locations. To have these sensors attached, participants must disrobe partially, a requirement that is likely to elicit subjective reactions. Measures of blood pressure are often invasive in another way: most use pressurized cuffs on either the upper arm or the finger. The pressure in these cuffs can draw attention and sometimes even pain, which, again, can elicit emotional reactions in and of itself. Invasiveness of this sort certainly complicates emotion measurement. Second, autonomic measures have typically greatly restricted participants' mobility simply because autonomic signals are carried by wires that connect sensors to amplifiers and recording devices (for example, computers). Because lengthy wires and body movement can sometimes increase measurement noise, participants are often on a rather short tether, being required to remain seated and largely immobile. While ambulatory autonomic monitors have been available for some time, their reliability does not yet match laboratory-based measures and may still be subject to movement artifacts. And third, the temporal resolution of various autonomic measures varies widely. Although autonomic measures are increasingly available on a continuous basis, some measures (for example, RSA, impedance cardiography) require somewhat longer durations for reliable measurement (perhaps one minute), epochs that may be longer than the duration of any given emotion episode (see earlier discussion of timing).

Brain-Based Measures of Emotion

In the last decade or so, researchers have begun to refine neurophysiological measures of emotion. Scalp-recorded brain electrical activity, or electroencephalogram (EEG), can index patterns of anterior asymmetries that distinguish specific emotion states as well as individual differences in affective style (for a review, see Davidson 1993). For instance, Davidson and his colleagues have demonstrated that approach-related positive emotions are associated with left anterior activation whereas withdrawal-related negative emotions are associated with right anterior activation. Other, more localized measures of emotion-related changes in the brain are on the horizon as well, including PET scans and functional MRI (see, for example, Lang et al. 1998). Many of the same inferential and measurement issues discussed with respect to autonomic measures of emotion also apply to measures of brain activity. Again, researchers interested in measuring emotion-related changes in the brain should seek out special training and/or experienced collaborators.

Vocal Measures of Emotion

Although most information conveyed by vocalization derives from verbal content (language use), voice stylistics (such as pitch, loudness, tone, quality, timing) can convey much information about a speaker's emotional state because vocalization is a *bodily* process sensitive to emotion-related changes in the broader bodily context (for example, muscle tension, respiration rate, and blood pressure). As such, changes in a speaker's emotional state often yield quite noticeable changes in voice stylistics.

Emotion-related vocal changes have been assessed using both low-tech and high-tech means. The low-tech path is to listen (with or without special training) to audiotaped speech samples and evaluate them on emotional terms. The high-tech path is to have these same audiotapes digitized and analyzed by electro-acoustic equipment and/ or digital computers that decompose the speech sound waves into a set of acoustic parameters. We describe each of these measurement techniques in turn.

Several "decoding" studies have tested the abilities of untrained listeners to recognize correctly or infer speakers' emotional states (for an early review, see Scherer 1986; van Bezooijen 1984). Typically, these studies ask actors to read standard or meaningless sentences in manners that convey specific emotional states, such as anger, fear, disgust, joy, sadness, even contempt, pride, love, and jealousy. These speech samples (sometimes content-filtered) are then played for naive listeners who must choose the intended emotional state from a list of forced-choice alternatives. After correcting for chance guessing and sampling error, recognition rates across these studies are about 50 percent, which is four to five times what would be expected by chance (Pittam and Scherer 1993). Recognition rates across cultures (and languages) remain higher than chance, consistent with the claim of universal vocal patterns of emotion (van Bezooijen, Otto, and Heenan 1984). Nonetheless, some emotions are easier to recognize than others: sadness and anger are best recognized, whereas disgust, contempt, and joy are least recognized (Pittam and Scherer 1993; van Bozooijen et al. 1983). Moreover, analyzing confusions in these decoding studies reveals that the arousal level of a speaker's emotional state is better transmitted by vocal cues than is the evaluative component (positivity or negativity) (Apple and Hecht 1982; van Bozooijen et al. 1983).

Listener ratings of vocal emotion have been particularly useful in research on the emotional trait of hostility, perhaps because many people may be unwilling or unable to identify themselves as hostile on self-report instruments (for information on the Interpersonal Hostility Assessment Technique, or IHAT, see Barefoot 1992; Haney et al. 1996). Strikingly, hostility assessed through the voice has been shown to relate better to adverse health outcomes than hostility assessed through self-report (Barefoot et al. 1994).

Comparing low-tech and high-tech means of detecting vocal expressions of emotion, Scherer (1986) has noted a paradox: "Whereas judges seem to be rather accurate in decoding emotional meaning from vocal cues, researchers in psychoacoustics and psychophonetics have so far been unable to identify a set of vocal indicators that reliably differentiate a number of discrete emotions" (143–44). Among the set of acoustic parameters typically gathered using high-tech means are (a) fundamental frequency, or F_0 (the rate at which the vocal folds vibrate, perceived as overall voice pitch); (b) minute perturbations in F_0 (two indices—"jitter" and "shimmer"—assess cycle-to-cycle variations in the frequency and amplitude, respectively, of F_0); (c) intensity (energy values indexed in decibels, perceived as loudness); and (d) speech rate or tempo (for a more complete listing of acoustic parameters, see Scherer 1986). In digitally analyzed emotional speech, these acoustic parameters tend to covary and cluster into two types: one pattern combines high and variable F_0, high intensity, and fast tempo and marks the high-arousal emotions such as joy, anger, and fear. A second pattern combines low and stable F_0, low intensity, and slow tempo and marks the low-arousal emotions such as sadness, boredom, and contempt. To date, then, high-tech acoustical analyses effectively identify the arousal level associated with different emotional states, even when emotions are quite mild (for an excellent example, see Bachorowski and Owren 1995). Even so, these high-tech measures fall short of identifying the particular emotions experienced. Perhaps most notably, positive and negative emotional states often remain undistinguished. Scherer (1986; see also Pittam and Scherer 1993) has argued, however, that given untrained listeners' abilities to infer speakers' specific emotional states, patterns across acoustic parameters ought to distinguish between discrete emotions—in theory. Empirical support for Scherer's claim is still lacking.

When considering whether to pursue vocal measures of emotion, researchers should keep the following in mind. First, vocal indicators of emotion are not always present. Unlike facial and autonomic measures, voice is not a continuous variable for the simple reason that people do not speak continuously. Second, positive and negative emotions often go undistinguished by sound-wave analyses and are even sometimes confused by human raters. Vocal measures, then, are perhaps best used in conjunction with other measures of emotion. And third, much like the face and self-report, the voice can reflect both emotional/physiological "push" and sociocultural "pull" effects (Scherer 1989). That is, beyond reflecting internal physiological states, vocalization also reflects ritualized communication patterns, impression management, and coping styles. Disentangling push effects from pull effects is rarely an easy task.

Vocal measures of emotion are perhaps most useful either when voice is only one strand of the emotion-related data available (for example, audiotaped interviews, perhaps via telephone) or when the experimental situation disallows more invasive or obtrusive bodily measures (for example, physi-

ological sensors on the skin, visible video cameras). Certainly, high-tech vocal measures will advance in step with the currently building knowledge about the acoustic parameters associated with emotional speech. Once again, training and/or expert collaborators are recommended for sound-wave analysis.

Emotion-Sensitive Tasks

A variety of tasks have been shown to be sensitive to affective states. These emotion-sensitive tasks can be defined as tasks on which response or performance differences are, at least in part, a function of emotional state (Mayer 1986; Mayer and Bremer 1985; Mayer, Mamberg, and Volanth 1988). While many of these emotion-sensitive tasks started out as independent and dependent variables in experimental paradigms, many are now used as manipulation checks. That is, many researchers see the links between these tasks and emotions as reliable enough to use responses to these tasks as indicators that an emotion has been induced through some manipulation.

Cognitive Appraisals   Many emotion researchers hold that emotions result when individuals appraise the meaning of a particular situation or event in certain ways. Different emotions are distinguished by different appraisals. For example, if an individual perceives that she was wrongly treated by someone, and she makes the further appraisal that the other did so *willingly*, the resulting emotion is likely to be anger. Moreover, a relatively small set of appraisal dimensions (eight or ten) are thought to account for a large proportion of emotional experiences. This appraisal model implies that one way to measure emotions is to measure cognitive appraisals of specific situations or events. Smith and Ellsworth (1985; 1987) identified a series of cognitive appraisal dimensions that distinguish between specific emotions. Because appraisals target people's interpretations of *situations*, they circumvent some of the problems associated with self-reports of subjective experience. As such, measuring a person's appraisals of a situation may indirectly reveal his or her emotional state. For example, if a subject said that some hurtful event was caused by someone else on purpose, then we might infer that he or she is angry.

Action Tendencies   Many lines of research have converged on a central notion that some form of action tendency (sometimes called action readiness, action disposition, or behavioral activation) is a central component of emotional experience. Physiological reactions (such as increased heart rate in fear) are often seen as preparatory for action readiness (the tendency to flee that comes with fear). Other specific action tendencies are associated with other specific emotions (such as withdrawal and sadness or striking out and anger; see Fridja [this volume] for a more detailed discussion of action tendencies). The probability of participants engaging in such actions, or saying that they would like to engage in such actions, has been related to specific affective states (Frijda, Kuipers, and ter Schure 1989; see also Fredrickson et al., in press).

A related judgment task is to ask participants how much they would like to engage in various behaviors, such as talk with a good friend, engage in some exercise, or have a pleasant meal. Teasdale, Taylor, and Fogarty (1980) have used this task and found it sensitive to depressed mood. This task supposedly works because sadness is related to the action tendency to withdraw. A related concept is that, when depressed, people often lose interest in activities that formerly gave them pleasure. Depressed mood is thought to be associated with depressed psychomotor function. As such, tasks involving coordinated psychomotor movements should be sensitive to sadness or unpleasant affective states. Writing speed, for example, is a popular psychomotor task thought to be influenced by depressed mood. Velten (1968) used this task as a non-self-report measure of affect in the validation study of his "Velten mood induction procedure." Participants' writing speed was significantly slower after reading the depression Velten statements, compared to writing speed following the elation Velten statements. Other psychomotor tasks that have been used in emotion research include letter cancellation and smooth pursuit motor tasks. Performance speed is most often the variable sensitive to depressed emotional state, and the effect appears unipolar (for example, pleasant moods do not necessarily increase psychomotor speed).

Performance Measures One category of emotion-sensitive performance measures consists of various judgment tasks. One popular judgment task is to have participants make probability estimates of the likelihood of various good and bad events. For example, participants may be asked the probability of being killed in a tornado, dying in an airplane crash, or contracting cancer in their lifetime. It has been shown that persons in un-

pleasant emotional states overestimate the probability of such bad events (Johnson and Tversky 1983). Moreover, the events do not have to be self-referential to be sensitive to affective states (Cunningham 1988). Ketelaar (1989) showed that people in a good mood also overestimate the probability of pleasant events, such as the probability of the economy improving over the next year, or the probability of a good friendship lasting an entire life.

Several theoretical explanations for why such judgments should be sensitive to mood have been offered (see, for example, Mayer 1986). Chief among these are mood-congruent recall effects, spreading activation models, and category boundary shifts. When using such tasks to assess affective states, it is important that participants understand probability ratings. Providing an example or two is helpful (for example, "The probability of tossing a coin and having it land heads up is 50 percent"). Some questions might be phrased in terms of "what percent of the population . . ." Because percentages are often skewed, some data transformation may be in order. Also, because some participants have no idea about percentages but will nevertheless provide estimates, it may be advantageous to normalize data within participants across probability estimates.

Another useful performance task is to ask participants to generate associations to positive, neutral, and negative stimuli. For example, write down as many words as come to mind in sixty seconds when you hear each of the following stimulus words: happy, disappointed, generous, destroy, peace, pain, and so on. Mayer and Bremer (1985) showed that performance on this task correlates with naturally occurring mood. Ketelaar (1989) showed that such a word association task correlates with self-reported mood following pleasant or unpleasant mood inductions. Seidlitz and Diener (1993) used a variation on this task: participants were asked to recall as many happy experiences from their lives as they could in a given time period. Participants higher on trait happiness recalled more pleasant experiences, in the same time period, than participants lower on trait happiness. Teasdale and his colleagues (Teasdale and Fogarty 1979; Teasdale and Russell 1983) have also demonstrated that temporary emotion inductions influence recall of pleasant and unpleasant events in predictable ways.

A second category of performance measures involves information-processing parameters. Reaction times in lexical decision tasks, for example, have been shown to be sensitive to affective states (Challis and Krane 1988). The participant's task here is to judge whether a string of letters presented on the computer screen represents a word or a nonword. On each trial, the letters that come on the screen represent a nonword, an emotion word (for instance, *anger*), or a neutral word (such as *house*). Participants in positive affective states are quicker and sometimes more accurate at judging positive words as words than participants in neutral states, and vice versa for unpleasant moods (Niedenthal and Setterlund 1994).

A variation that also involves information-processing is to present participants with incomplete word stems and ask them to add letters to complete the word. Word stems are selected so that they can be completed as an emotion term or as a neutral term. For example, ANG＿＿ could be completed as ANGER, ANGLE, ANGEL, or ANGLO. A related technique is the use of homophones (words that sound alike but have different meanings). With this technique, the subject hears the word (*die* or *dye,* for example) and is asked to write it. Participants in an unpleasant mood are more likely to write or complete the word stems in a manner congruent with their mood (Halberstadt, Niedenthal, and Kushner 1995).

Startle Potentiation Another emotion-sensitive task relies on a very simple behavior—the startle reflex. The startle is characterized by a rapid shutting of the eyes (blink), pulling the chin down, and a rapid inhalation. It is a defensive response, and its protective value (shutting the eyes) is obvious. The startle reflex is also easy to elicit through the application of a sudden and loud acoustic stimulus. Because it is a reflex, it is not easily controlled, although like many reflexes, adaptation occurs with repeated stimulation.

Startle potentiation refers to an increase in the startle response brought about by an emotional state (Vrana, Spence, and Lang 1988). For example, if a person is in an aversive or unpleasant state when the startle stimulus is emitted, the startle blink will be faster and stronger than if the participant were in a neutral emotional state. If a person were already anxious, an augmented defensive response makes evolutionary sense. Researchers typically measure the muscle contraction responsible for the blink during the startle response. They can then score the blink for latency (time from the startle sound to the onset of the muscle contraction) as well as for magnitude (the force of the muscle contraction producing the blink).

The researcher most responsible for developing this technique in humans is Peter Lang (see, for example, Lang, Bradley, and Cuthbert 1990). Lang has demonstrated startle potentiation for unpleasant emotions, as well as a slowing-down of the startle during positive emotions, compared to neutral states. This effect had been well documented in animals for decades. Christopher Patrick has studied individual differences in startle potentiation, with an emphasis on psychopaths (Patrick 1994; Patrick, Cuthbert, and Lang 1994). Psychopaths are thought to be deficient in fear and other self-regulating negative emotions. Patrick's research shows that psychopaths do not show the expected pattern of startle potentiation to fear or anxiety stimuli, even though they do show the expected slowing of startle during positive emotions found in normal samples.

The strengths of the startle potentiation technique are that it is a nonverbal, nonvoluntary, and extremely fast measure of internal affective state. This measure, however, appears limited to assessing the pleasantness-unpleasantness or approach-avoidance dimension of affective state. In addition, the laboratory equipment and expertise necessary to employ this technique represent a heavy cost to the researcher. Nevertheless, this emotion measure appears promising, and researchers who think they might benefit from employing this technique should consider training and/or collaborating with a psychophysiologist who is set up to analyze eyeblinks.

CONCLUSIONS

Emotion measures come in many forms and, in our opinion, should be used in many forms. Perhaps most important, no single emotion measure can serve as the "gold standard" for other emotion measures. Each measurement type has its strengths and its weaknesses, and each in isolation provides only an incomplete picture of emotion processes. So, to the extent that emotions invoke changes across numerous channels or component systems, data streams from those various channels should be collected in synchrony. Cross-referencing multiple measures of emotion increases researchers' chances of pinpointing emotions and discerning their precursors and effects.

In this chapter, we have reviewed the many classics of emotion measurement, alongside some relatively new, cutting-edge measures. When choosing and employing these measures, researchers should consider the various issues underlying emotion measurement discussed throughout this chapter. With an appreciation of these measurement issues, researchers should feel comfortable adding novel, theoretically derived measures to the mix of those that they collect. Any list of valid emotion measures will surely need updating with time as new links are added to the network of associations surrounding the construct of emotion.

REFERENCES

Apple, W., and Hecht, K. (1982). Speaking emotionally: The relation between verbal and vocal communication of affect. *Journal of Personality and Social Psychology, 42,* 864–75.

Averill, J. R. (1969). Autonomic response patterns during sadness and mirth. *Psychophysiology, 5,* 399–414.

Bachorowski, J., and Owren, M. J. (1995). Vocal expression of emotion: Acoustic properties of speech are associated with emotional intensity and context. *Psychological Science, 6,* 219–24.

Barefoot, J. C. (1992). Recent developments in the measurement of hostility. In H. S. Friedman (Ed.), *Hostility, coping, and health* (pp. 13–31). Washington, D.C.: American Psychological Association.

Barefoot, J. C., Patterson, J. C., Haney, T. L., Cayton, T. G., Hickman, J. R., and Williams, R. B. (1994). Hostility in asymptomatic men with angiographically confirmed coronary artery disease. *American Journal of Cardiology, 74,* 439–42.

Bentler, P. M. (1969). Semantic space is (approximately) bipolar. *Journal of Psychology, 71,* 33–40.

Bonanno, G. A., Keltner, D., Holen, A., and Horowitz, M. J. (1995). When avoiding unpleasant emotions might not be such a bad thing: Verbal-autonomic response dissociation and mid-life conjugal bereavement. *Journal of Personality and Social Psychology, 69,* 975–89.

Bunce, S. C., Larsen, R. J., and Cruz, M. (1993). Individual differences in the excitation transfer effect. *Personality and Individual Differences, 15,* 507–14.

Cacioppo, J. T., Klein, D. J., Berntson, G. G., and Hatfield, E. (1993). The psychophysiology of emotion. In M. Lewis and J. M. Haviland (Eds), *Handbook of emotions* (pp. 119–42). New York: Guilford.

Cacioppo, J. T., Petty, R. E., Losch, M. E., and Kim, H. S. (1986). Electromyographic activity over facial muscle regions can differentiate the valence and intensity of affective reactions. *Journal of Personality and Social Psychology, 50,* 260–68.

Cacioppo, J. T., and Tassinary, L. G. (1990). Inferring psychological significance from physiological signals. *American Psychologist, 45,* 16–28.

Cannon, W. B. (1927). The James-Lange theory of emotions: A critical examination. *Psychological Review, 38,* 281–95.

Challis, B. H., and Krane, R. V. (1988). Mood induction and the priming of semantic memory in a lexical decision task: Asymmetric effects of elation and depression. *Bulletin of the Psychonomic Society, 26,* 309–12.

Clark, L. A., and Watson, D. (1995). Constructing validity: Basic issues in objective scale development. *Psychological Assessment, 7* (special issue: Methodological issues in psychological assessment research), 309–19.

Cronbach, L. J., and Meehl, P. (1955). Construct validity in psychological tests. *Psychological Bulletin, 52,* 281–302.

Cunningham, M. R. (1988). What do you do when you're happy or blue? Mood, expectancies, and behavioral interest. *Motivation and Emotion, 12,* 309–31.

Cutler, S. E., Bunce, S. C., and Larsen, R. J. (1996). Repressive coping style and its relation to daily emotional experience and remembered emotional experience. *Journal of Personality, 64,* 379–405.

Darwin, C. (1872/1965). *The expression of the emotions in man and animals.* Chicago: University of Chicago Press.

Davidson, R. J. (1993). The neuropsychology of emotion and affective style. In M. Lewis and J. M. Haviland (Eds.), *Handbook of emotions* (pp. 143–54). New York: Guilford.

Diener, E., Smith, H., and Fujita, F. (1995). The personality structure of affect. *Journal of Personality and Social Psychology, 69,* 130–41.

Ekman, P. (1992). An argument for basic emotions. *Cognition and Emotion, 6,* 169–200.

Ekman, P., and Davidson, R. (1994). *The nature of emotion.* New York: Oxford University Press.

Ekman, P., and Friesen, W. (1975). *Unmasking the face.* Englewood Cliffs, N.J.: Prentice-Hall.

———. (1978). *Facial Action Coding System.* Palo Alto, Calif.: Consulting Psychologists Press.

Ekman, P., Freisen, W. V., and Ancoli, S. (1980). Facial signs of emotional experience. *Journal of Personality and Social Psychology, 39,* 1125–34.

Ekman, P., Friesen, W. V., and O'Sullivan, M. (1988). Smiles when lying. *Journal of Personality and Social Psychology, 54,* 414–20.

Ekman, P., and Rosenberg, E. L. (Eds.) (1997). *What the face reveals: Basic and applied studies of spontaneous facial expressions using the Facial Action Coding System (FACS).* New York: Oxford University Press.

Feldman, L. (1995). Variations in the circumplex structure of emotion. *Personality and Social Psychology Bulletin, 21,* 806–17.

Feldman-Barrett, L. (in press). Discrete emotions or dimensions: The role of valence focus and arousal focus. *Cognition and Emotion.*

Fredrickson, B. L., and Kahneman, D. (1993). Duration neglect in retrospective evaluations of affective episodes. *Journal of Personality and Social Psychology, 65,* 45–55.

Fredrickson, B. L., and Levenson, R. W. (in press). Positive emotions speed recovery from the cardiovascular sequelae of negative emotions. *Cognition and Emotion.*

Fredrickson, B. L., Roberts, T., Noll, S. M., Quinn, D. M., and Twenge, J. M. (in press). That swimsuit becomes you: Sex differences in self-objectification, restrained eating, and math performance. *Journal of Personality and Social Psychology.*

Fridlund, A. J., Ekman, P., and Oster, H. (1987). Facial expressions of emotion. In A. W. Siegman and S. Feldstein (Eds.), *Nonverbal behavior and communication* (2nd ed., pp. 143–223). Hillsdale, NJ: Lawrence Erlbaum.

Frijda, N. H. (1988). The laws of emotion. *American Psychologist, 43,* 349–58.

Frijda, N. H., Kuipers, P., and ter Schure, E. (1989). Relations among emotion, appraisal, and emotional action readiness. *Journal of Personality and Social Psychology, 57,* 212–29.

Gotlib, I., and Meyer, J. (1986). Factor analysis of the Multiple Affect Adjective Check List: A separation of positive and negative affect. *Journal of Personality and Social Psychology, 50,* 1161–65.

Gottman, J. M. (1993). Studying emotion in social interaction. In M. Lewis and J. M. Haviland (Eds.), *Handbook of emotions* (pp. 475–87). New York: Guilford.

Gottman, J. M., and Levenson, R. W. (1985). A valid measure for obtaining self-report of affect. *Journal of Consulting and Clinical Psychology, 53,* 151–60.

Graham, F. K., and Clifton, R. K. (1966). Heart rate change as a component of orienting response. *Pschological Bulletin, 65,* 305–20.

Green, D. P., Goldman, S. L., and Salovey, P. (1993). Measurement error masks bipolarity in affect ratings. *Journal of Personality and Social Psychology, 64,* 1029–41.

Gross, J. J., and Levenson, R. W. (1993). Emotional suppression: Physiology, self-report, and expressive behavior. *Journal of Personality and Social Psychology, 64,* 970–86.

Grossman, P., Van Beek, J., and Wientjes, C. (1990). A comparison of three quantification methods for estimation of respiratory sinus arrhythmia. *Psychophysiology, 27,* 702–14.

Halberstadt, J. B., Niedenthal, P. M., and Kushner, J. (1995). Resolution of lexical ambiguity by emotional state. *Psychological Science, 6,* 278–82.

Haney, T., Maynard, K. E., Houseworth, S. J., Scherwitz, L. W., Williams, R. B., and Barefoot, J. C. (1996). The Interpersonal Hostility Assessment Technique: Description and validation against the criterion of coronary artery disease. *Journal of Personality Assessment, 66,* 386–401.

Izard, C. E. (1977). *Human emotions.* New York: Plenum Press.

Izard, C. E. (1979). *Emotions in personality and psychopathology.* New York: Plenum.

Izard, C. E. (1993). Four systems for emotion activation: Cognitive and noncognitive processes. *Psychological Review, 100,* 68–90.

Johnson, E. J., and Tversky, A. (1983). Affect, generalization, and the perception of risk. *Journal of Personality and Social Psychology, 45,* 21–31.

Kahneman, D., Fredrickson, B. L., Schreiber, C. A., and Redelmeier, D. A. (1993). When more pain is preferred to less: Adding a better end. *Psychological Science, 4,* 401–5.

Ketelaar, T. (1989). Examining the circumplex model of affect in the domain of mood-sensitive tasks. Master's thesis, Purdue University.

Kleinginna, P. R., and Kleinginna, A. M. (1981). A categorized list of emotion definitions, with suggestions for a consensual definition. *Motivation and Emotion, 5,* 345–79.

Kring, A. M., and Neale, J. M. (1996). Do schizophrenic patients show a disjunctive relationship among expressive, experiential, and psychophysiological components of emotion? *Journal of Abnormal Psychology, 105,* 249–57.

Krokoff, L. J., Gottman, J. M., and Hass, S. D. (1989). Validation of a global rapid couples interaction scoring system. *Behavioral Assessment, 11,* 65–79.

Lacey, J. I., Kagan, J., Lacey, B. C., and Moss, H. A. (1963). The visceral level: Situational derterminants and behavioral correlates of automatic response patterns. In P. H. Kapp (Ed.), *Expression of the emotions in man* (pp. 161–96). New York International Universities Press.

Lang, P. J., Bradley, M. M., and Cuthbert, B. N. (1990). Emotion, attention, and the startle reflex. *Psychological Review, 97,* 377–95.

Lang, P. J., Bradley, M. M., Fitzsimmons, J. R., Cuthbert, B. N., Scott, J. D., Moulder, B., and Nangia, V. (1998). Emotional arousal and activation of the visual cortex: An fMRI analysis. *Psychophysiology, 35,* 199–210.

Larsen, R. J., and Diener, E. (1987). Affect intensity as an individual difference characteristic: A review. *Journal of Research in Personality, 21,* 1–39.

———. (1992). Problems and promises with the circumplex model of emotion. *Review of Personality and Social Psychology, 13,* 25–59.

Larsen, R. J., and Ketelaar, T. (1991). Personality and susceptibility to positive and negative emotional states. *Journal of Personality and Social Psychology, 61,* 132–40.

Larsen, R. J., and Sinnett, L. (1991). Meta-analysis of manipulation validity: Factors affecting the Velten mood induction procedure. *Personality and Social Psychology Bulletin, 17,* 323–34.

Lazarus, R. S. (1991). *Emotion and adaptation.* New York: Oxford University Press.

Levenson, R. W. (1983). Personality research and psychophysiology: General considerations. *Journal of Research in Personality, 17,* 1–21.

———. (1988). Emotion and the autonomic nervous system: A prospectus for research on autonomic specificity. In H. L. Wagner (Ed.), *Social psychophysiology and emotion: Theory and clinical applications* (pp. 17–42). Chichester, Eng.: Wiley.

———. (1992). Autonomic nervous system differences among emotions. *Psychological Science, 3,* 23–27.

Levenson, R. W., Ekman, P., and Friesen, W. V. (1990). Voluntary facial action generates emotion-specific autonomic nervous system activity. *Psychophysiology, 27,* 363–84.

Lucas, R. E., Diener, E., and Suh, E. (1996). Discriminant validity of well-being measures. *Journal of Personality and Social Psychology, 71,* 616–28.

MacKay, C. J. (1980). The measurement of mood and psychophysiological activity using self-report techniques. In I. Martin and P. Venables (Eds.), *Techniques in psychophysiology* (pp. 501–62). New York: Wiley.

Mandler, G. (1975). *Mind and emotion.* New York: Wiley.

Mayer, J. D. (1986). How mood influences cognition. In N. E. Sharkey (Ed.), *Advances in cognitive science* (pp. 290–314). Chichester, Eng.: Ellis Horwood.

Mayer, J. D., and Bremer, D. (1985). Assessing mood with affect-sensitive tasks. *Journal of Personality Assessment, 49,* 95–99.

Mayer, J. D., Mamberg, M. M., and Volanth, A. J. (1988). Cognitive domains of the mood system. *Journal of Personality, 56,* 453–86.

Meehl, P. E. (1978). Theoretical risks and tabular asterisks: Sir Karl, Sir Ronald, and the slow progress of soft psychology. *Journal of Consulting and Clinical Psychology, 46,* 806–34.

Mesquita, B., and Frijda, N. H. (1992). Cultural variations in emotions: A review. *Psychological Bulletin, 112,* 179–204.

Mosher, D. L. and White, B. B. (1981). On differentiating shame and shyness. *Motivation and Emotion, 5,* 61–74.

Newton, T. L., and Contrada, R. J. (1992). Repressive coping and verbal-autonomic response dissociation: The influence of social context. *Journal of Personality and Social Psychology, 62,* 159–67.

Niedenthal, P. M., and Setterlund, M. B. (1994). Emotion congruence in perception. *Personality and Social Psychology Bulletin, 20,* 401–11.

Nowlis, V. (1965). Research with the Mood Adjective Check List. In S. S. Tomkins and C. E. Izard (Eds.), *Affect, cognition, and personality* (pp. 352–89). New York: Springer.

Nowlis, V., and Green, R. (1957). *The experimental analysis of mood.* Technical report, contract no. Nonr-668(12). Washington, D.C.: Office of Naval Research.

Obrist, P. A., Webb, R. A. Sutterer, J. R., and Howard, J. L. (1970). The cardiac-somatic relationship: Some reformulations. *Psychophysiology, 6,* 569–87.

Patrick, C. J. (1994). Emotion and psychopathy: Startling new insights. *Psychophysiology, 31,* 319–30.

Patrick, C. J., Cuthbert, B. N., and Lang, P. J. (1994). Emotion in the criminal psychopath: Fear image processing. *Journal of Abnormal Psychology, 103,* 523–34.

Pittam, J., and Scherer, K. R. (1993). Vocal expression and communication of emotion. In M. Lewis and J. M. Haviland (Eds.), *Handbook of emotions* (pp. 185–97). New York: Guilford.

Porges, S. W. (1995). Cardiac vagal tone: A physiological index of stress. *Neuroscience and Biobehavioral Reviews, 19,* 225–33.

Rosenberg, E. L., and Ekman, P. (1994). Coherence between expressive and experiential systems in emotion. *Cognition and Emotion, 8,* 201–29.

Russell, J. A. (1980). A circumplex model of affect. *Journal of Personality and Social Psychology, 39,* 1161–78.

Russell, J. A., Weiss, A., and Mendelsohn, G. A. (1989). The Affect Grid: A single-item scale of pleasure and arousal. *Journal of Personality and Social Psychology, 57,* 493–502.

Schacter, S., and Singer, J. E. (1962). Cognitive, social, and physiological determinants of emotional state. *Psychological Review, 69,* 379–99.

Scherer, K. R. (1986). Vocal affect expression: A review and a model for future research. *Psychological Bulletin, 99,* 143–65.

———. (1989). Vocal correlates of emotional arousal and affective disturbance. In H. L. Wagner and A. Manstead (Eds.), *Handbook of social psychophysiology* (pp. 165–97). Chichester, Eng.: Wiley.

Scherer, K. R., Banse, R., Wallbott, H. G., and Goldbeck, T. (1991). Vocal cues in emotion encoding and decoding. *Motivation and Emotion, 15,* 123–48.

Seidlitz, L., and Diener, E. (1993). Memory for positive versus negative life events: Theories for the difference between happy and unhappy persons. *Journal of Personality and Social Psychology, 64,* 654–63.

Sherwood, A. (1993). Use of impedance cardiography in cardiovascular reactivity research. In J. Blascovich and E. S. Katkin (Eds.), *Cardiovascular reactivity to psychological stress and disease* (pp. 157–99). Washington, D.C.: American Psychological Association.

Sherwood, A., Allen, M. T., Fahrenberg, J., Kelsey, R. M., Lovallo, W. R., and van Doornen, L. J. P. (1990). Committee Report: Methodological guidelines for impedance cardiography. *Psychophysiology, 27,* 1–23.

Smith, C. A., and Ellsworth, P. C. (1985). Patterns of cognitive appraisal in emotion. *Journal of Personality and Social Psychology, 48,* 813–38.

———. (1987). Patterns of appraisal and emotion related to taking an exam. *Journal of Personality and Social Psychology, 52,* 475–88.

Stone, A. A. (1981). The association between perceptions of daily experiences and self- and spouse-rated mood. *Journal of Research in Personality, 15,* 510–22.

———. (1995). Measures of affective response. In S. Cohen, R. Kessler, and L. Gordon (Eds.), *Measuring stress: A guide for health and social scientists* (pp. 148–71). New York: Cambridge University Press.

Teasdale, J. D., and Fogarty, S. J. (1979). Differential effects of induced mood on retrieval of pleasant and unpleasant events from episodic memory. *Journal of Abnormal Psychology, 88,* 248–57.

Teasdale, J. D., and Russell, M. L. (1983). Differential effects of induced mood on the recall of positive, negative, and neutral words. *British Journal of Clinical Psychology, 22,* 163–71.

Teasdale, J. D., Taylor, R., and Fogarty, S. J. (1980). Effects of induced elation-depression of the accessibility of memories of happy and unhappy experiences. *Behavior Research and Therapy, 18,* 339–46.

Thayer, R. E. (1967). Measurement of activation through self-report. *Psychological Reports, 20,* 663–78.

———. (1986). Activation-Deactivation Adjective Check List: Current overview and structural analysis. *Psychological Reports, 58,* 607–14.

Thomas, D. L. and Diener, E. (1990). Memory accuracy in the recall of emotions. *Journal of Personality and Social Psychology, 59,* 291–97.

Tomkins, S. S., and Izard, C. E. (1965). *Affect, cognition, and personality: Empirical studies.* New York: Springer.

Tranel, D., and Damasio, A. R. (1985). Knowledge without awareness: An autonomic index of facial recognition by prosopagnosics. *Science, 228,* 1453–54.

Van Bezooijen, R. (1984). *The characteristics and recognizability of vocal expression of emotions.* Dordrecht, the Netherlands: Foris.

Van Bezooijen, R., Otto, S. A., and Heenan, T. A. (1983). Recognition of vocal expressions of emotion: A three-nation study to identify universal characteristics. *Journal of Cross-cultural Studies, 14,* 387–406.

Velten, E. (1968). A laboratory task for the induction of mood states. *Behavior Research and Therapy, 6,* 473–82.

Venables, P. H. (1984). Arousal: An examination of its status as a concept. In M. G. H. Coles, J. R. Jennings, & J. A. Stern (Eds.), *Psychophysiological perspectives* (134–42). New York: Van Nostrand Reinhold.

Vrana, S. R., Spence, E. L., and Lang, P. J. (1988). The startle probe response: A new measure of emotion? *Journal of Abnormal Psychology, 97,* 487–91.

Watson, D., and Clark, L. A. (1991). Self- versus peer ratings of specific emotional traits: Evidence of convergent and discriminant validity. *Journal of Personality and Social Psychology, 60,* 927–40.

Watson, D., Clark, L. A., and Tellegen, A. (1988). Development and validation of brief measures of positive and negative affect: The PANAS scales. *Journal of Personality and Social Psychology, 54,* 1063–70.

Watson, D., and Tellegen, A. (1985). Toward a consensual structure of mood. *Psychological Bulletin, 98,* 219–35.

Zajonc, R. B. and McIntosh, D. N. (1992). Emotions research: Some promising questions and some questionable promises. *Psychological Science, 3,* 70–74.

Zuckerman, M., and Lubin, B. (1965). *The Multiple Affect Adjective Check List.* San Diego: Educational and Industrial Testing Service.

———. (1985). *Manual for the Multiple Affect Adjective Check List—Revised.* San Diego: Educational and Industrial Testing Service.

4 Reports of Subjective Well-Being: Judgmental Processes and Their Methodological Implications

Norbert Schwarz and Fritz Strack

The cognitive and communicative processes underlying individuals' reports of happiness and satisfaction with their lives as a whole are reviewed in this chapter. Reports of subjective well-being (SWB) do not reflect a stable inner state of well-being. Rather, they are judgments that individuals form on the spot, based on information that is chronically or temporarily accessible at that point in time, resulting in pronounced context effects. The way in which accessible information about an individual's life influences the judgment depends on how it is used. Information that is used in forming a mental representation of the individual's life as a whole or of some extended episode results in assimilation effects, such as higher reports of SWB when a happy rather than sad event comes to mind. Information that is used in forming a standard of comparison results in contrast effects. In this case, the individual's life looks bland by comparison to a happy event. The variables that determine assimilation or contrast effects are identified. Given that the same event can increase or decrease an individual's judgment of SWB, depending on its use in the construal of the individual's life or of a standard, the relationship between objective events and subjective evaluations is necessarily weak. Hence, SWB cannot be predicted on the basis of objective circumstances, unless one takes the construal processes into account. In addition to information about his or her own past, present, or future, the individual may use information about others' lives in assessing the quality of his or her life. Although people often feel better when they compare themselves to others who are less well off, the specific outcome again depends on the specific nature of the mental construal. Individuals may simplify the complexities of evaluating their lives by drawing on their feelings at the time of judgment as a source of information. Hence, they report higher SWB when in a good rather than bad mood (and finding a dime is sufficient to increase temporarily one's life satisfaction). Moods are more likely to affect judgments of general SWB than judgments of specific life domains. As a result, a particularly happy event in domain X may increase an individual's satisfaction with his or her life as a whole but decrease satisfaction with the specific domain by way of contrast. Such divergent influences decrease the relationship between global SWB and domain satisfaction. Public reports of SWB are often inflated owing to self-presentation concerns. Methodological implications are discussed.

MUCH OF WHAT we know about individuals' subjective well-being (SWB) is based on self-reports of happiness and life satisfaction. Since the groundbreaking studies of Bradburn (1969), Andrews and Whithey (1976), and Campbell, Converse, and Rodgers (1976), hundreds of thousands of survey respondents around the world have been asked questions like, "Taking all things together, how would you say things are these days—would you say that you are very happy, pretty happy, or not too happy?" or, "How satisfied are you with your life as a whole these days? Are you very satisfied, satisfied, not very satisfied, not at all satisfied?" Questions of this type are intended to assess the subjective quality of life in an attempt to monitor the subjective side of social change. These *subjective social indicators* supplement measures of the objective standard of living, which have long dominated welfare research in the social sciences.

As Angus Campbell (1981) noted, the "use of these measures is based on the assumption that all the countless experiences people go through from day to day add to . . . global feelings of well-being, that these feelings remain relatively constant over extended periods, and that people can describe them with candor and accuracy" (23). These assumptions have increasingly been drawn into question, however, as the empirical work has progressed. First, the relationship between individuals' experiences and objective conditions of life and their subjective sense of well-being is often weak and sometimes counterintuitive. Most objective life circumstances account for less than 5 percent of the variance in measures of SWB, and the combination of the circumstances in a dozen domains of life does not account for more than 10 percent (Andrews and Whithey 1976; Kammann 1982; for a review, see Argyle, this volume). Second, measures of SWB have low test-retest reliabilities, usually hovering around .40, and not exceeding .60 when the same question is asked twice during the same one-hour interview (Andrews and Whithey 1976; Glatzer 1984). Moreover, these measures are extremely sensitive to contextual influences. Thus, minor events, such as finding a dime (Schwarz 1987) or the outcome of soccer games (Schwarz et al. 1987), may profoundly affect reported satisfaction with one's life as a whole. Most important, however, the reports are a function of the research instrument and are strongly influenced by the content of preceding questions, the nature of the response alternatives, and other "technical" aspects of questionnaire design (Schwarz and Strack 1991a, 1991b).

Such findings are difficult to reconcile with the assumption that subjective social indicators directly reflect stable inner states of well-being (Campbell 1981) or that the reports are based on careful assessments of one's objective conditions in light of one's aspirations (Glatzer and Zapf 1984). Instead, the findings suggest that reports of SWB are better conceptualized as the result of a judgment process that is highly context-dependent. This chapter reviews what is known about *how* persons determine whether they are happy with their lives as a whole or not. Our focus is on evaluations of one's life as a whole or of some extended episode of one's life, rather than the evaluation of single events (which is addressed in other chapters in this volume; see, for example, Kahneman). As will become apparent later, contextual influences do often have an opposite impact on evaluations of a specific event versus evaluations of an extended episode. A particularly dreadful event, for example, makes more moderate events look good by comparison (Parducci 1995), yet it decreases the evaluation of the episode of which it is a part (Strack, Schwarz, and Gschneidinger 1985). We note such discrepancies where appropriate but primarily focus on how people evaluate their "life as a whole," as survey questions ask them to do. Similarly, our review does not address how differences in personality may influence the judgmental processes of interest here (but see

the chapters in this volume by Cantor and Sanderson; Diener and Lucas; and Higgins, Grant, and Shah).

A PREVIEW

Not surprisingly, individuals may draw on a wide variety of information when asked to assess the subjective quality of their lives. Ross, Eyman, and Kishchuck (1986) explored the range of information used by asking respondents how they arrived at a judgment of SWB. They observed that explicit references to one's momentary affective state accounted for 41 to 53 percent of the reasons that various samples of adult Canadians provided for their reported well-being, followed by future expectations (22 to 40 percent), past events (5 to 20 percent), and social comparisons (5 to 13 percent). The experimental literature confirms the relevance of these different sources of information, and we address them in turn.

We first explore the impact of information about one's own life, such as past events or expectations about the future. This review indicates that the same event may increase as well as decrease general life satisfaction, depending on how information bearing on the event is used in forming a judgment. Next, we address the role of comparisons of one's own lot with the lot of others. Although people generally tend to feel better when they compare themselves to others who are worse off, the dynamics of social comparison are more complicated than early theorizing and common sense would suggest. Following these discussions of intra- and interindividual comparisons, we turn to the influence of temporary mood states and address how one's momentary feelings may override the impact of other information relevant to one's life. Finally, we integrate these processes in a judgment model of SWB before we turn to an assessment of the methodological implications for survey research into SWB.

USING INFORMATION ABOUT ONE'S OWN LIFE: INTRAINDIVIDUAL COMPARISONS

Comparison-based evaluative judgments require a mental representation of the object of judgment, commonly called a *target*, as well as a mental representation of a relevant *standard* to which the target can be compared. The chosen standard may be *intraindividual* (for example, a previous state of one's life or one's expectations) or *interindividual* (the situation of close others or a relevant reference group). The outcome of the comparison process depends on (a) which information is used in constructing (b) the target or (c) the standard (Schwarz and Bless 1992a). We first address which of the many aspects of one's life are likely to be used in forming a judgment.

Which Information Is Used?

When asked, "Taking all things together, how would you say things are these days?" respondents are ideally assumed to review the myriad of relevant aspects of their lives and to integrate them into a mental representation of their life as a whole. In reality, however, individuals rarely retrieve all information that may be relevant to a judgment. Instead, they truncate the search process as soon as enough information has come to mind to form a judgment with sufficient subjective certainty (Bodenhausen and Wyer 1987). Hence, the judgment is based on the information that is most *accessible* at that point in time. In general, the accessibility of information depends on the recency and frequency of its use (for a review, see Higgins 1996). Information that has just been used—for example, to answer a preceding question in the questionnaire—is particularly likely to come to mind later on, although only for a limited time. This *temporarily accessible* information is the basis of most context effects in survey measurement and results in variability in the judgment when the same question is asked at different times (see Schwarz and Strack 1991b; Strack 1994a; Sudman, Bradburn, and Schwarz 1996, chs. 3 to 5; Tourangeau and Rasinski 1988). Other information, however, may come to mind because it is used frequently—for example, because it relates to the respondent's current concerns (Klinger 1977) or life tasks (Cantor and Sanderson, this volume). Such *chronically accessible* information reflects important aspects of respondents' lives and provides for some stability in judgments over time.

Accessibility

As an example, consider experiments on question order. Strack, Martin, and Schwarz (1988) observed that dating frequency was unrelated to students' life satisfaction when a general satisfaction question preceded a question about the respondent's dating frequency, $r = -12$. Yet reversing the question order increased the correlation to

$r = .66$. Similarly, marital satisfaction correlated with general life satisfaction $r = .32$ when the general question preceded the marital one in another study (Schwarz, Strack, and Mai 1991). Yet reversing the question order again increased this correlation to $r = .67$. Findings of this type indicate that preceding questions may bring information to mind that respondents would otherwise not consider. If this information is included in the representation that the respondent forms of his or her life, the result is an assimilation effect, as reflected in increased correlations. Thus, we would draw very different inferences about the impact of dating frequency or marital satisfaction on overall SWB, depending on the order in which the questions are asked.

Theoretically, the impact of a given piece of accessible information increases with its extremity and decreases with the amount and extremity of other information that is temporarily or chronically accessible at the time of judgment (see Schwarz and Bless 1992a). To test this assumption, Schwarz, Strack, and Mai (1991) asked respondents about their job satisfaction, leisure time satisfaction, and marital satisfaction prior to assessing their general life satisfaction, thus rendering a more varied set of information accessible. In this case, the correlation between marital satisfaction and life satisfaction increased from $r = .32$ (in the general-marital satisfaction order) to $r = .46$, yet this increase was less pronounced than the $r = .67$ observed when marital satisfaction was the only specific domain addressed.

In light of these findings, it is important to highlight some limits for the emergence of question-order effects. First, question-order effects of the type discussed here are to be expected only when answering a preceding question increases the temporary accessibility of information that is not chronically accessible anyway. We would assume, for example, that respondents who are currently undergoing a divorce would consider their marriage independent of whether it was addressed in a preceding question or not. Second, the impact of information rendered accessible by preceding questions decreases with the amount and extremity of competing information. Hence, chronically accessible current concerns would limit the size of any emerging effect, and the more they do so, the more extreme the implications of these concerns are. This implies that question-order effects should be relatively small for respondents who are preoccupied with a current concern, but rather sizable for respondents who are not. If so, the differential size of context effects may cloud actual differences in SWB. Unfortunately, data bearing on these possibilities are not available. Finally, information may be rendered temporarily accessible by other fortuitous events, such as what happens to be in the news (Iyengar 1987). From a methodological point of view, such influences are less problematic than the impact of question order. Most fortuitous events affect only a small subset of the sample, in particular when data collection extends over several weeks, as is typical for surveys. Question order, however, affects most members of the sample, thus introducing systematic bias.

Conversational Norms

Complicating things further, information rendered accessible by a preceding question may not always be *used*. In daily conversations, speakers are supposed to provide information that is new to the recipient, rather than to reiterate information that the recipient already has (Grice 1975; for more detailed discussions, see Schwarz 1994, 1996; Strack 1994b). Having just answered a question about her marriage, for example, a respondent may therefore assume that a subsequent question about her life in general pertains to new aspects of her life, much as if it were worded, "Aside from your marriage, how's the rest of your life?" Whether the general question is interpreted in this way or not depends on whether it is assigned to the same conversational context as the more specific question.

Partially Redundant Questions   In the above studies (Strack et al. 1988; Schwarz et al. 1991), the conversational norm of nonredundancy was evoked by a joint lead-in that informed respondents that they would now be asked two questions pertaining to their well-being. Following this lead-in, they first answered the specific question (about dating frequency or marital satisfaction) and subsequently reported their general life satisfaction. In this case, the previously observed correlations of r = .66 between dating frequency and life satisfaction, or r = .67 between marital satisfaction and life satisfaction, dropped to r = .15 and .18, respectively. Thus, the same question order resulted in dramatically different correlations, depending on the elicitation of the conversational norm of nonredundancy. Consistent with this interpretation, a reworded version of the general question "Aside from your marriage, which you already told us about, how satisfied are you with other aspects

of your life?" resulted in a similar correlation with marital satisfaction, r = .20 (Schwarz et al. 1991). Again, we would draw very different substantive conclusions from the obtained data, depending on question order and the presence or absence of a joint lead-in that assigns both questions to the same conversational context.

The Redundancy of Highly Similar Questions   In the earlier examples, a general question was rendered partially redundant when preceded by a more specific one that addressed a subset of the relevant information. The same logic, however, also applies to cases in which several highly similar questions are presented. Strack, Schwarz, and Wänke (1991) asked respondents to report their happiness as well as their satisfaction with life. When both questions were introduced as the last and first question of two different questionnaires, presented by two different researchers, both reports correlated r = .96. Moreover, respondents' mean happiness ratings (M = 8.0) did not differ from their mean satisfaction ratings (M = 8.2), suggesting that they did not differentiate between these concepts. Presumably, they assumed that two different researchers were asking the same thing in somewhat different words. When both questions where presented by the same researcher, however, one after the other in the same questionnaire, the correlation dropped to r = .75, and respondents reported higher happiness (M = 8.2) than satisfaction (M = 7.4). Thus, assigning both questions to the same conversational context elicited a differentiation because the two questions would otherwise have been redundant—Why would the same researcher ask both questions if they were not supposed to tap different aspects? These processes may underlie apparent inconsistencies in the relationship between reports of happiness and satisfaction and their respective predictors in different studies and may contribute to low test-retest reliabilities when the same question is reiterated within a short time span.

Summary

Judgments are based on the subset of potentially applicable information that is chronically or temporarily accessible at the time. Accessible information, however, may not be used when its repeated use would violate conversational norms of nonredundancy. Next, we turn to the different ways in which accessible information may influence a judgment.

MENTAL CONSTRUALS OF ONE'S LIFE AND A RELEVANT STANDARD: WHAT IS, WAS, WILL BE, AND MIGHT HAVE BEEN

The way in which chronically or temporarily accessible information about one's life affects the judgment depends on how it is *used* (Schwarz and Bless 1992a; Strack 1992). Suppose that an extremely positive (or negative) life event comes to mind. If this event is included in the temporary representation of the target "my life now," it results in a more positive (negative) assessment of SWB, reflecting an *assimilation effect*, as observed in an increased correlation in the studies discussed earlier. However, the same event may also be used in constructing a standard of comparison, resulting in a *contrast effect*: compared to an extremely positive (negative) event, one's life in general may seem relatively bland (or pretty benign). These opposite influences of the same event are sometimes referred to as endowment (assimilation) and contrast effects (Tversky and Griffin 1991). To understand the respective conditions of their emergence, we need to understand how individuals *use* accessible information.

The variables that determine the use of information in constructing standards and targets can be conceptualized in terms of several broad decisions a respondent has to make (for detailed discussions, see Schwarz and Bless 1992a; Strack 1992). The most important one is whether the information "belongs to," or is representative of, the target category (for our current purposes, "my life now"). Information that bears on a different episode of one's life, for example, or that seems extreme and unusual, will not be used in forming a representation of the target, thus making it available for constructing a standard.

What Is, Was, and Will Be: Is the Information Representative of My Life?

Information about one's life, such as specific life events, will be used in constructing a representation of one's current life only when it seems representative of the target. If the event is categorized as pertaining to a different episode of one's life, or as being unusual, it will serve as a standard of comparison, as a few examples may illustrate.

Temporal Distance   Strack, Schwarz, and Gschneidinger (1985, Experiment 1) asked respondents to report either three positive or three negative recent life events, thus rendering these events tem-

TABLE 4.1   Subjective Well-Being: The Impact of Valence of Event and Time Perspective

	Valence of Event	
	Positive	Negative
Time perspective		
Present	8.9	7.1
Past	7.5	8.5
Category boundary		
Not salient	8.7	7.4
Salient	6.2	8.2

Source: Top panel adapted from Strack et al. (1985, Experiment 1). Copyright 1985 by the American Psychological Association. Bottom panel from Schwarz and Hippler (unpublished data).
Notes: For the mean score of happiness and satisfaction questions, the range is 1 to 11, with higher values indicating reports of higher well-being.

porarily accessible. As shown in the top panel of table 1, these respondents reported higher current life satisfaction after they recalled three positive rather than negative *recent* events. Other respondents, however, had to recall events that happened at least five years before. These respondents reported higher current life satisfaction after recalling negative rather than positive *past* events. This indicates that respondents included accessible recent events in the representation formed of their current lives but used distant events as a standard of comparison (see also Dermer et al. 1979; Tversky and Griffin 1991).

These experimental results are consistent with correlational data (Elder 1974) indicating that U.S. senior citizens, the "children of the Great Depression," are more likely to report high subjective well-being the more they suffered under adverse economic conditions when they were adolescents. The accumulation of negative experiences during childhood and adolescence presumably established a baseline against which all subsequent events could only be seen as an improvement. Portraying the other side of the coin, Runyan (1980) found that the upwardly mobile recollected their childhood as less satisfying than did the downwardly mobile, presumably because they used their current situation in evaluating their past.

Chunking the Stream of Life: Category Boundaries
Whereas the use of life events was determined by their temporal distance in the above studies, other variables may similarly influence how the stream of life is chunked into discrete units. One of these variables is the salience of relevant transition

points. For example, Schwarz and Hippler asked first-year students to report a positive or negative event that "happened two years ago." As shown in the second panel of table 1, this again resulted in an assimilation effect on current life satisfaction. Other students, however, were subtly alerted to a major role transition, namely, their change from high school to university status. Specifically, they were asked to report a positive or negative event that "happened two years ago, *that is, before you came to the university.*" These respondents reported lower life satisfaction after recalling a positive rather than a negative event, indicating that their identification of the event as a "high school" event resulted in its use as a standard of comparison.

Similarly, thinking about positive or negative events that might happen in the future resulted in assimilation effects on current life satisfaction (Strack, Schwarz, and Nebel unpublished data). Yet reminding the student respondents that they would meanwhile have left the university again reversed the pattern, resulting in a contrast effect. Hence, positive expectations about the future can increase as well as decrease current SWB, depending on their use in the judgment process.

Extremity   Similarly, extreme events may seem unusual and not representative of how one's life is going in general. They may therefore be excluded from the representation formed and serve as standards of comparison. If so, extreme and unusual events are likely to result in contrast effects, at least after some time has passed (thus providing temporal distance) and their immediate emotional impact (to be addressed later) has waned. Although such exclusion processes have been observed in other domains of judgment (Herr, Sherman, and Fazio 1983; Herr 1986; for a discussion, see Schwarz and Bless 1992a, 230–31), the relevant studies in the domain of SWB are limited to evaluations of specific other events in people's lives, not evaluations of their lives as a whole.

Category Width: Judgments of Specific Events Versus Life as a Whole   Importantly, a highly positive (negative) event is likely to affect judgments of other specific events and judgments of one's life as a whole in opposite directions. This suggests that the event can be included in the representation formed of one's life in general (a "wide" target category), resulting in assimilation effects. However, it cannot be included in the representation formed of another specific event (a "narrow" target category), and hence it serves as a standard of

comparison, resulting in contrast effects. In an initial test of the impact of category width, Schwarz and Bless (1992b) had respondents think about a politician who was involved in a scandal (say, Richard Nixon). This decreased judgments of the trustworthiness of politicians in general, reflecting that the exemplar could be included in the representation formed of the group. However, it increased judgments of the trustworthiness of all other individual politicians assessed, reflecting that a given exemplar cannot be included in the representation of other exemplars—after all, Bill Clinton is not Richard Nixon, and compared to Richard Nixon, Bill Clinton looks fine.

Consistent with this notion, thinking about a negative (positive) event *decreased* (increased) reported satisfaction with one's life as a whole in the examples reviewed earlier, unless the temporal distance of the event or the salience of the category boundary elicited its exclusion from the representation formed. In contrast, Parducci (1995; see also Smith, Diener, and Wedell 1989) observed that an extreme negative (positive) event *increased* (decreased) satisfaction with subsequent modest events (see Kahneman, this volume, for a more detailed discussion). Thus, the occasional experience of extreme negative events facilitates the enjoyment of the modest events that make up the bulk of our lives, whereas the occasional experience of extreme positive events reduces this enjoyment (for an extensive review, see Parducci 1995).

Hence, what we conclude about the impact of extreme events on individuals' subjective well-being will often depend on the measure we use. When we draw on self-reports of satisfaction with life as a whole (a "wide" category), we are likely to observe assimilation effects because the extreme event will be included in the representation formed, unless its exclusion is triggered by one of the variables discussed earlier. Accordingly, we would conclude that the experience of extreme positive events increases, and the experience of extreme negative events decreases, overall life satisfaction. As an alternative, however, we may draw on moment-to-moment measures of hedonic experience, as suggested by Parducci (1995) (and others), who proposed that happiness is "the balance of pleasure over pain" (9). This approach is based on evaluations of specific hedonic events, which are likely to show contrast effects. Accordingly, we would conclude that individuals had better avoid extremely positive experiences because they reduce the overall balance of pleasure over pain, whereas occasional negative experiences enhance this balance (for recommendations on which experiences we should seek or avoid, see Parducci 1995). Given that both sets of findings are reliably replicable, self-assessments of general well-being and measures of moment-to-moment hedonic experience are likely to diverge under many conditions.

Summary　In combination, the reviewed research illustrates that the same life event may affect judgments of SWB in opposite directions, depending on its use in the construction of the target "my life now" and of a relevant standard of comparison. It therefore comes as no surprise that the relationship between life events and judgments of SWB is typically weak. Today's disaster can become tomorrow's standard, making it impossible to predict SWB without a consideration of the mental processes that determine the use of accessible information. Whereas the results of our experimental manipulations illustrate the power of these processes, we know little about how people spontaneously parse the stream of life events into discrete chunks. Exploring this issue provides a promising avenue for future research at the interface of autobiographical memory and social judgment.

What Might Have Been: Counterfactuals

So far, we have seen that the way people think about *actual* outcomes may influence their judgments of SWB (as well as their momentary mood, to be addressed in a later section). In a different line of research, it has been observed that the mental construction of *fictitious* outcomes may have similar effects.

Assume that for some trivial reason a person misses the plane for which she had a reservation, and then learns that this very plane has fatally crashed. Although everybody who was not on the plane has reason to be relieved, this person is more likely to experience relief because she had *almost* been a victim. Conversely, assume a car driver has to endure a long wait at a construction site and misses an important business appointment. This driver may experience anger and self-blame if he focuses on the possibility that he *would have* arrived in time had he not deviated from his usual route to work. In both cases, *what might have been* serves as a standard that influences the assessment of the actual event.

The antecedents and consequences of our construals of "what might have been" (Roese and Olson 1995a) have been investigated in a research program on counterfactual thinking (Kahneman and Miller 1986; Miller, Turnbull, and McFarland 1990; Roese 1997; Roese and Olson 1995b; Wells and Gavanski 1989). This work is based on the insight that when outcomes deviate from norms or expectancies, people construct the normative outcome as an alternative (Kahneman and Miller 1986). The likelihood of this construction depends on the ease with which an actual abnormal event can be mentally converted into the counterfactual normative outcome. If only a minor aspect of the actual outcome needs to be altered, counterfactual thinking is more likely than if some fundamental components need to be changed. For example, our lucky passenger should be more likely to see herself as a potential victim of the plane crash if the change of reservation was a spontaneous decision, made immediately before boarding the plane, than if it was a deliberate action taken several days earlier. As a consequence, more relief would be experienced in the former than in the latter case.

Counterfactual thinking can influence affect and subjective well-being in several ways (see Roese 1997; Roese and Olson 1995b). First, the mental construction of the normative outcome provides a *standard of comparison* against which the actual outcome can be evaluated, resulting in contrast effects. This is more likely the easier it is to construct the counterfactual. For example, winners of Olympic bronze medals reported being more satisfied than silver medalists (Medvec, Madey, and Gilovich 1995), presumably because for winners of bronze medals, it is easier to imagine having won no medal at all (a "downward counterfactual"), while for winners of silver medals, it is easier to imagine having won the gold medal (an "upward counterfactual"). As a further consequence of this comparison, bronze medalists can be expected to experience more joy, while silver medalists may be more likely to experience disappointment.

Second, counterfactual thinking may suggest specific *causal implications* that influence judgments and affective experiences (Roese 1997). As observed in numerous studies (for a review, see Weiner 1985), causal attributions determine specific emotions. It is therefore not surprising that different explanations of why the abnormal outcome occurred, rather than its normative alternative, may elicit different reactions. For example, a surprising failure is more likely to raise hope for future improvement if it is attributed to transient circumstances rather than to stable personality characteristics (Boninger, Gleicher, and Strathman 1994).

Finally, our feelings may be influenced by the very act of *explaining* the abnormal outcome. Specifically, counterfactual thinkers may ruminate about the cause of the abnormal event and mentally try to undo what has happened. Continuous thoughts of "if only . . ." and "why me . . ." may dominate the person's cognitive activity and lead to self-pity and depression (see Martin and Tesser 1989). Such a prevalence of counterfactual rumination may result from two related aspects of counterfactual reasoning. On the one hand, counterfactual thinking is most likely when the normative outcome is easily constructed; hence, the counterfactual may intrude on people's thinking whenever the abnormal outcome comes to mind. At the same time, the superficial aspects of an abnormal event that elicit its counterfactual alternative are rarely the best candidates for a causal explanation. Thus, by directing attention to the normative outcome, aspects of the abnormal event deny themselves as plausible causes.

In summary, judgments of SWB can be profoundly influenced by mental constructions of what might have been. Hence, the impact of a given event will be more pronounced the easier it is to imagine that things could have turned out otherwise.

Direction of Comparison

So far, we have reviewed different intraindividual standards of comparison—pertaining to what is, was, will be, or might have been—and focused on the processes that determine whether a given piece of information is used in forming a representation of the target or of the standard. Next, we need to consider an additional, and somewhat counterintuitive, complication. On logical grounds, we should assume that comparing X to Y results in the same outcome as comparing Y to X. For example, when our present situation (X) is better than our past situation (Y), we should be pleased no matter whether we compare the present to the past or the past to the present. Yet the specific information we actually draw on is likely to differ in these two cases, resulting in different outcomes.

This possibility is suggested by Tversky's (1977; Tversky and Gati 1978) research into similarity judgments and has recently been confirmed for comparison processes (Dunning, Madey, and Parpal 1995; Wänke, Schwarz, and Noelle-Neumann

FIGURE 4.1   Asymmetries in Feature Comparison

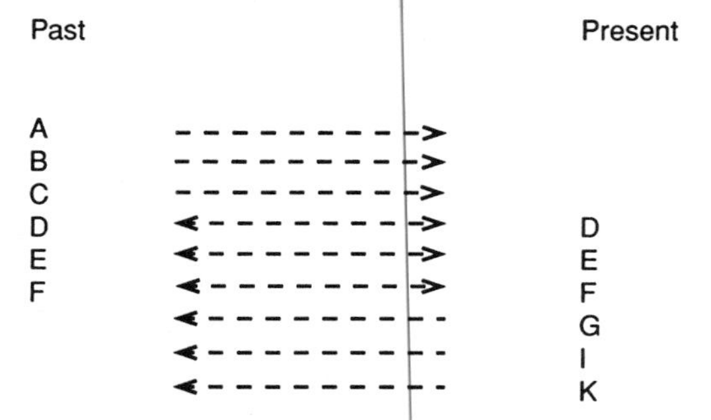

1995; Schwarz, Wänke, and Bless 1994). Suppose, for example, that a respondent's representation of the past includes features A through F, as shown in figure 4.1, whereas her representation of the present includes features D through K.

According to Tversky's (1977) model of similarity judgments, a comparison of the past to the present would involve the respondent's assessment of whether features A through F are also part of the present. The features G through K, which are part of the present but not of the past, are likely to receive little attention in this case. Conversely, a comparison of the present to the past would be based on the features D through K. However, the features A through C, which characterize the past but not the present, would go largely unnoticed. As a result, the outcome of the comparison process would differ, depending on whether we compared the past to the present or the present to the past.

Such judgmental asymmetries are particularly pronounced when the to-be-compared targets are represented in differential detail (Srull and Gaelick 1984; Tversky 1977). For example, Dunning et al. (1995) suggested that people may possess a rich array of information about the present that they may have forgotten about the past. If so, our representation of the present would include a larger set of unique features than our representation of the past. Hence, we should detect more unique features when comparing the present to the past, rather than the past to the present, and thus conclude that more change has occurred in the former than in the latter. Dunning, Madey, and Parpal's (1995) results confirmed this prediction.

While such findings alert us to the impact of differences in question wording (for a methodological discussion, see Wänke et al. 1995), they also suggest some troublesome (but as yet untested)

implications for the comparisons we are likely to make spontaneously. Of course, in making our own spontaneous assessments, we may, in principle, use either direction of comparison. In most cases, however, our spontaneous attempts to assess the quality of life are likely to be triggered by some current problem. If so, the current problematic situation is in the focus of our attention, making it likely that we compare the current situation to some previous (or counterfactual) state of affairs, rather than vice versa. Owing to the logic of the comparison process, the outcome of this enterprise is bound to be negative: chances are that our current problem is not a feature of our past. Other problems that we had in the past, however, are unlikely to be considered because the consideration of features of the past is constrained by the features that make up our representation of the present. Accordingly, the problems of the past may escape our attention, contributing to the impression that the past was the time of the "good old days" (for a more detailed discussion, see Schwarz et al. 1994).

The Outcome of Comparisons: The Differential Impact of Losses and Gains

Finally, let us turn to the outcomes of the comparisons we make. Whichever of the above standards we use, the comparison may tell us that our actual situation either falls short of the chosen standard or exceeds it. Unfortunately, the former observation is likely to have a more pronounced impact on judgments of SWB than the latter, reflecting a general tendency to give more weight to perceived losses than to gains. This is particularly likely when we make intraindividual comparisons across time, but it has also been observed for comparisons with others (Brandstätter 1998). As described in Kahneman and Tversky's (1979) prospect theory, the value function for losses is steeper than the value function for gains. Hence, gains and losses of an equal magnitude may not result in "zero net change." Rather, the steeper value function for losses implies, for example, that a $100 increase in rent, which constitutes a loss relative to the reference point of one's previous rent, has a higher impact on one's subjective sense of economic well-being than an apparently equivalent pay raise of $100, constituting a gain relative to one's previous income. As a result, the net effect of both changes would not be neutral but negative. Accordingly, the gains must far exceed the losses to result in an overall sense of improvement, and relatively large

improvements may be offset by comparatively smaller losses.

Again, however, the specific outcome is likely to depend on the mental representations formed. If the wording of the judgment task induces respondents to balance their separate mental accounts (Thaler 1985) for rent and income prior to evaluation of the net result, they may indeed perceive zero change. Thus, the parsing of reality into different chunks is again likely to affect the judgmental outcome, as we have seen in the preceding discussion (see Schwarz et al. 1994).

What Gets Lost: Duration Neglect

In combination, the discussion in the preceding sections suggests that nearly any aspect of one's life can be used in constructing representations of one's "life now" or a relevant standard, resulting in many counterintuitive findings. Sometimes, however, the surprises do not result from what is used in which way, but from what is neglected.

Common sense suggests that misery that lasts for years is worse than misery that lasts only for a few days. Hence, the evaluation of a given episode should depend not only on the episode's hedonic valence but also on its duration. Recent research suggests, however, that people may largely neglect the duration of the episode, focusing instead on two discrete data points, namely, its most intense hedonic moment ("peak") and its ending (Fredrickson and Kahneman 1993; Varey and Kahneman 1992). Hence, episodes whose worst (or best) moments and endings are of comparable intensity are evaluated as equally (un)pleasant, independent of their duration (for a more detailed discussion, see Kahneman, this volume).

Although the available data are restricted to episodes of short duration, it is tempting to speculate about the possible impact of duration neglect on the evaluation of more extended episodes. If duration neglect applies to extended episodes, we may expect, for example, that three years of economic hardship may not seem much worse in retrospect than one year, provided that the peak and end values of both episodes are comparable. In addition, we may speculate that the level of hardship at points other than the peak and the end may prove irrelevant as well. By the same token, the degree of variation within an episode should prove largely irrelevant when the changes occur gradually and are not marked by salient events. On the other hand, if the changes are pronounced, or are marked by some salient event, the episode may be broken down into a series of shorter episodes, with each one having its own peak and end. Moreover, retrospective evaluations should crucially depend on the hedonic value experienced at the end of the respective episode. Thus, a period of ten years of scarcity may benefit from some improvement in the final year to a much larger extent than the relative durations would seem to justify, whereas a decline at the end may cloud longer periods of relative well-being. Assuming some variation over time, the hedonic value of the end of the episode is likely to depend on the specific boundary chosen, which may be a function of other, rather fortuitous events, including the context provided in the research situation. Accordingly, not only may the choice of category boundaries determine what we include in the representation of the respective episode, as discussed earlier, but the chosen end of the episode may also determine what will be given special weight in evaluating the episode as a whole. Unfortunately, the limited data available do not yet allow us to assess these possibilities.

Summary

As our selective review illustrates, judgments of SWB are not a direct function of one's objective conditions of life and the hedonic value of one's experiences. Rather, they crucially depend on the information that is accessible at the time of judgment and how this information is used in constructing mental representations of the to-be-evaluated episode and a relevant standard. This standard may reflect previous states of affairs (what was), expectations about the future (what will be), counterfactual alternatives (what might have been), or the lot of others (to be addressed later). As we have seen repeatedly, how individuals parse the stream of life into discrete units determines whether the event is included in the episode, resulting in an assimilation effect, or excluded from the episode, resulting in a contrast effect. Moreover, the direction of comparison chosen, or suggested by the wording of the question, influences which features are likely to be considered. One feature that is likely to be neglected in retrospective evaluations is the duration of the episode, reflecting reliance on a peak-and-end rule. Finally, the perception that one's current situation falls short of the standard is likely to have a more pronounced impact than the perception that it exceeds the standard to the same degree, reflecting that losses loom larger than gains.

As a result of these construal processes, judg-ments of SWB are highly malleable and difficult to predict on the basis of objective conditions. Hence, it is not surprising that the relationship between the objective conditions of life and their subjective evaluation is weak and often counterintuitive. Theoretically, we may expect that this relationship is more pronounced, and more straightforward, in a person who is preoccupied with a current concern, such as a severe illness. This concern would presumably be chronically accessible in memory and would hence come to mind independent of whether it has been addressed in preceding questions. Moreover, it would be likely to be included in the representation formed of one's current situation, reflecting its numerous links to other aspects of daily life. Even under these conditions, however, the current concern may be deliberately disregarded, for example, when its repeated consideration would violate norms of conversational conduct. Moreover, the evaluation would still shift as a function of the standard of comparison used, as research into social comparison illustrates. We turn to this work next.

USING INFORMATION ABOUT OTHERS: SOCIAL COMPARISONS

Obviously, the range of potentially relevant standards is not restricted to those aspects of one's own life that pertain to what was, will be, or might have been, all of which may serve as *intraindividual* standards. Rather, *interindividual standards* provided by information about others' lives may have similarly pronounced effects on judgments of SWB. In this section, we address different interindividual standards and the determinants of their use in real life and in research situations.

Choosing Comparison Others: Downward, Upward, and Lateral Comparisons

Not surprisingly, we may feel better about our lives when we compare ourselves to others who are less well off (a *downward comparison*) than when we compare ourselves to others who are better off (an *upward comparison*). In fact, the more people assume that their own living conditions are better than those of others, the more satisfaction they report (see Campbell et al. 1976; Carp and Carp 1982), although such correlational findings do not unequivocally bear on the causal role of comparison processes. However, the causal impact of comparison processes has been well supported in laboratory experiments that exposed respondents to relevant comparison standards, further illustrating that respondents are likely to draw on whatever information is most accessible at the time of judgment (for reviews, see Miller and Prentice 1996; Wills 1981; Wood 1989). For example, Strack and his colleagues (1990) observed that the mere presence of a handicapped confederate was sufficient to increase reported SWB under self-administered questionnaire conditions, presumably because the confederate served as a salient standard of comparison. Consistent with this accessibility principle, numerous studies found that temporarily accessible standards can override chronically accessible standards (for a review, see Miller and Prentice 1996). For example, most people are presumably very familiar with societal standards of physical attractiveness. Nevertheless, exposing research participants to photographs of highly attractive women has been found to decrease women's self-assessments of their own physical attractiveness (Cash, Cash, and Butters 1983), as well as men's satisfaction with the attractiveness of their romantic partner (Kendrick and Gutierres 1980).

However, recent naturalistic studies suggest a more complicated picture (for a review, see Taylor, Wayment, and Carrillo 1996). Under unconstrained conditions, respondents may engage in downward, upward, or lateral comparisons; moreover, the impact of any comparison standard may change over time and affect different dependent variables in different ways. These complications suggest that self-initiated social comparisons may serve a variety of different functions.

Self-Assessment　First, social comparisons may serve a self-assessment function, as initially proposed by Festinger (1954), who assumed that assessments of one's own abilities and outcomes are best served by comparisons with similar others (lateral comparisons). Specifying what exactly determines whether another is sufficiently similar to serve as a relevant comparison other has been one of the vaguest points of social comparison theory—and indeed, the accessibility principle illustrated earlier guarantees that relatively dissimilar, but highly salient, others may often be chosen. In general, however, "given a range of possible persons for comparison, someone who should be close to one's own performance or opinion, given his standing on characteristics related to and predictive of performance or opinion, will be chosen for comparison" (Goethals and Darley 1977,

265). This "related attributes" hypothesis is empirically well supported (for a review, see Miller and Prentice 1996), although it is often difficult to specify a priori which attributes will be considered "relevant and predictive."

Self-Enhancement　Second, social comparisons may serve a self-enhancement function, which is most easily satisfied by downward comparisons with someone who is less well off (Wills 1981), as seen in Strack and his colleagues' (1990) finding that the mere presence of a handicapped confederate may increase reports of SWB. Note, however, that such downward comparisons should be comforting only when we can assume that the other's unfortunate state does not provide a glimpse at our own future. A person who has been diagnosed as HIV-positive, for example, may derive little comfort from exposure to a person with advanced AIDS. Hence, the outcome of downward comparisons depends on the perceived mutability and controllability of the relevant outcome, as well as the time frame employed and the individual's sense of self-esteem (see Major, Testa, and Bylsma 1991; Taylor et al. 1996). If the outcome is mutable and controllable, and one's own self-esteem suggests one has the necessary skills, downward comparisons do indeed increase an individual's sense of SWB. If the outcome is uncontrollable, or one perceives a lack of relevant skills, downward comparisons may be comforting only in the short term and in fact may elicit a sense of despair about the likely future development. Much as we have seen for the impact of information about one's own life, it is not the information about the other's situation per se that determines the outcome, but the use of this information in constructing representations of one's own present or future situation and a relevant standard.

Moreover, researchers may have overestimated the prevalence of downward comparisons, as Taylor, Wayment, and Carrillo (1996) noted. Although people typically report that they are better off than others, even under very unfortunate circumstances (Taylor and Brown 1988), more detailed investigations suggest that these reports may be based on comparisons with manufactured *hypothetical others* rather than on comparisons with actual individuals (Taylor, Wood, and Lichtman 1983), with whom contact is often avoided (Taylor and Lobel 1989).

Self-Improvement　As a third function, social comparisons may serve *self-improvement* goals, which are best satisfied by upward comparisons with individuals who are better off and whose success may provide relevant performance information. Early research concluded that the potential for long-term self-improvement comes at the price of short-term dissatisfaction because the upward comparison highlights one's own shortcomings (Morse and Gergen 1970; Salovey and Rodin 1984). Confirming this conclusion, Wayment, Taylor, and Carrillo (1994) observed in a longitudinal study that college freshmen who engaged in upward comparisons felt worse over the short term. Four months later, however, these freshmen were better adjusted to college life than those who did not engage in upward comparisons, suggesting a positive long-term effect of the actual self-improvement facilitated by upward comparisons.

Moreover, the impact of upward comparisons depends on how close and similar the comparison other is and on how self-relevant one considers the respective performance dimension (Tesser 1988; for a recent review, see Tesser and Martin 1996). If a close and similar other, such as a good friend, outperforms us on a self-relevant attribute, the comparison results in dissatisfaction and withdrawal from the friend. If the attribute is not self-relevant, however, we may take pleasure in the friend's achievement. Finally, highly dissimilar others may not be perceived as relevant comparison standards and may hence not pose a particular threat, independent of the self-relevance of the crucial attribute. We conjecture that this differential impact of similar and dissimilar others reflects, in part, the processes we discussed in the section on counterfactuals: the more similar the other is, the easier it is to imagine that we might have obtained a similar outcome, yet we didn't.

Affiliation   As a final function, social comparisons may serve affiliative needs, as initially proposed by Schachter (1959). Recent naturalistic studies (for example, Helgeson and Taylor 1993; Taylor and Lobel 1989; Ybema and Buunk 1995) suggest that "people may compare themselves with others sharing a similar fate not only to evaluate their own emotional experiences, but also to create the experience of social bonding and comfort that arise from the observation of a shared fate" (Taylor et al. 1996, 5). These comforts may mitigate the otherwise expected impact of evaluative comparisons.

Summary   As this discussion indicates, the impact of social comparison processes on SWB is more complex than early research suggested. As far as judgments of global SWB are concerned, we can expect that exposure to someone who is less well off will usually result in more positive—and to someone who is better off in more negative—assessments of one's own life. However, information about the other's situation will not always be used as a comparison standard. Rather, relevant information about the other's situation may enter the representation of one's own future, for example, resulting in assimilation rather than contrast effects. We therefore emphasize that knowing *who* individuals compare themselves to does not allow us to predict the impact of the comparison other on individuals' sense of SWB unless we know *how* this information is used in the relevant mental construals.

Standards Provided by the Social Environment

So far, our discussion of social comparison processes has had a distinctly individualistic and volitional flavor, focusing on who we choose as comparison others. This perspective needs to be complemented by a consideration of the influence of more stable aspects of our social environment.

First, our degree of freedom may often be more constrained than experimental research suggests, and our immediate *social environment* may force standards upon us that are difficult to ignore. This has been most consistently observed in research that addressed the impact of students' standing within their school on their sense of self-esteem. Students with a given level of performance on standardized tests have higher self-esteem when they are at a low-quality school, where many students do poorly, rather than at a high-quality school, where many students do well (Bachman and O'Malley 1986; Marsh 1993; Marsh and Parker 1984). Although these findings may in part reflect that these students are likely to receive differential acknowledgment from their teachers, they also indicate that it is difficult to escape the norm provided by one's environment by pursuing self-enhancement through the choice of comparison others who are doing less well. In a similar vein, Morawetz (1977) observed that citizens of a community with a relatively equal income distribution reported higher well-being than citizens of a community with an unequal income distribution, although the latter's absolute level of income was higher. This finding at the community level is consistent with Easterlin's (1974) conclusion that increasing levels of income within a given country are not related to increasing reports of life satisfaction. Instead, Easterlin's findings suggested that the effect of income is largely relative, increasing one's sense of well-being if one earns more than others (but see Diener and Suh, this volume, for a review of the contradictory evidence bearing on this hypothesis). As a final example, Seidman and Rapkin (1983) found that the usually observed increase in the prevalence of mental illness during an economic downturn was most pronounced in heterogeneous communities, where the recession did not affect everyone equally. In combination, these findings illustrate the power of highly accessible standards provided by one's immediate environment. Such standards presumably limit individuals' freedom in pursuing the comparison goals discussed earlier. If so, we may be most likely to see differential construals of comparison standards when the judgment pertains to an attribute for which one's environment provides a range of comparison others with widely different standings, as is typical for the health-related research reviewed in the preceding section. In contrast, judgments that pertain to attributes on which one's social environment is homogeneous (as in the earlier examples of unemployment and income) may be less open to differential construal processes.

Second, an individual's position in the social structure may influence which comparison others he or she deems relevant, as suggested by reference group theory (Hyman and Singer 1968). For example, Runciman (1966) noted that British workers' strong sense of social class constrained the range of jobs they considered relevant in making income comparisons to a larger degree than was the case for American workers, at least in the 1960s. Thus, self-categorizations with regard to class or other relatively stable social attributes may constrain the range of comparison others to members of the same, or closely related, categories. Importantly, these self-categorizations are likely to change in cases of social mobility, resulting in changes in the comparison group deemed relevant. Such changes in the comparison standard may lead to decreased satisfaction despite improved objective circumstances (see Frederick and Loewenstein, this volume). Several researchers suggested, for example, that objective improvements in women's situation in the workforce did not result in increased satisfaction because they were accompanied by an increase in the legitimacy of comparisons with men, who are still doing better (Elster 1983; Walster, Walster, and Berscheid 1978).

Finally, socially shared norms may replace specific comparison groups or individuals as relevant standards, implying, for example, that every citizen is entitled to certain outcomes. Although perceptions of entitlement are themselves a function of social comparisons (see Major 1994), they may obliterate the need for specific comparison others once they are formed.

In combination, these examples draw attention to the possibility that salient comparison standards in one's immediate environment, as well as socially shared norms, may constrain the impact of fortuitous temporary influences. At present, the interplay of chronically and temporarily accessible standards on judgments of SWB has received little attention. The complexities that are likely to result from this interplay provide a promising avenue for future research.

Interindividual Standards Implied by the Research Instrument

Finally, we extend our look at the influences of the research instrument by addressing a frequently overlooked source of temporarily accessible comparison information. In many studies, researchers assess respondents' experiences, their objective conditions of living, or the frequency with which they engage in a certain behavior, by asking them to check the proper answer on a list of response alternatives provided to them. As an example, table 4.2 shows different response alternatives presented as part of a question about daily television consumption (Schwarz et al. 1985).

As numerous studies have indicated (for a review, see Schwarz 1996, ch. 5), respondents assume that the list of response alternatives reflects the researcher's knowledge of the distribution of the behavior: they assume that the "average" or "usual" behavioral frequency is represented by values in the middle range of the scale, and that the extremes of the scale correspond to the extremes of the distribution. Accordingly, they use the range of the response alternatives as a frame of reference in estimating their own behavioral frequency, resulting in different estimates of their own behavioral frequency, as shown in table 4.2. More important for our present purposes, they further extract comparison information from their own location on the scale. Checking "two and a half hours" on the low-frequency scale suggests that one's own television consumption is above average, whereas checking the same television consumption on the high-frequency scale suggests it is

TABLE 4.2   Reported Daily Television Consumption and Leisure Time Satisfaction as a Function of Response Alternatives

Low-Frequency Alternatives (Percentage)		*High-Frequency Alternatives (Percentage)*	
Reported daily television consumption			
Up to half an hour	11.5	Up to 2 1/2h	70.4
Half an hour to one hour	26.9	2 1/2h to 3h	22.2
One hour to one and a half hours	26.9	3h to 3 1/2h	7.4
One and a half hours to two hours	26.9	3 1/2h to 4h	0.0
Two hours to two and a half hours	7.7	4h to 4 1/2h	0.0
More than two and a half hours	0.0	More than 4 1/2h	0.0
Leisure time satisfaction			
	9.6		8.2

Source: Adapted from Schwarz et al. (1985, Experiment 2). Reprinted with permission from The University of Chicago Press.

below average. Hence, respondents in this study reported lower satisfaction with the variety of things they do in their leisure time when the low-frequency scale suggested they watch more television than others than when the high-frequency scale suggested they watch less—despite the fact that the former respondents reported watching less television to begin with (see table 4.2).

Similar findings have been obtained with regard to the frequency of physical symptoms and health satisfaction (Schwarz and Scheuring 1992), the frequency of sexual behaviors and marital satisfaction (Schwarz and Scheuring 1988), and various consumer behaviors (Menon, Raghubir, and Schwarz 1995). In combination, they illustrate that response alternatives convey highly salient comparison standards that may profoundly affect subsequent evaluative judgments. Researchers are therefore well advised to assess information about respondents' behaviors or objective conditions in an open-response format, thus avoiding the introduction of comparison information that respondents would not draw on in the absence of the research instrument.

Summary

In summary, the use of interindividual comparison information follows the principle of cognitive accessibility that we have highlighted in our discussion of intraindividual comparisons. Individuals often draw on the comparison information that is rendered temporarily accessible by the research instrument or the social context in which they form the judgment, although chronically accessible standards may attenuate the impact of temporarily accessible information. Despite this caveat, the se-

lection of comparison standards is not solely determined by relatively stable attributes of the respondant that may be expected to change only slowly over time, such as reference group orientation (Hyman and Singer 1968; Runciman 1966), adaptation level (Brickman and Campbell 1971), or aspiration level (Michalos 1985). Rather, individuals construct a relevant social comparison standard based on the information that is most accessible at the time of judgment. Moreover, these constructions may reflect different goals, including self-assessment, self-enhancement, self-improvement, or affiliation. Which of these goals is being pursued at a given point in time is likely to be itself context-dependent, rendering general predictions difficult.

THE IMPACT OF MOOD STATES

In the preceding sections, we considered how respondents use information about their own lives or the lives of others in comparison-based evaluation strategies. However, judgments of well-being are a function not only of what one thinks about but also of how one *feels* at the time of judgment. A wide range of experimental data confirms this intuition. Finding a dime on a copy machine (Schwarz 1987), spending time in a pleasant rather than an unpleasant room (Schwarz et al. 1987, Experiment 2), or watching the German soccer team win rather than lose a championship game (Schwarz et al. 1987, Experiment 1) all resulted in increased reports of happiness and satisfaction with one's life as a whole.

Two different processes may account for these observations. On the one hand, it has been shown that moods may increase the accessibility of mood-congruent information in memory (for reviews, see Blaney 1986; Bower 1981; Morris, this volume; Schwarz and Clore 1996). That is, individuals in a happy mood are more likely to recall positive information from memory, whereas individuals in a sad mood are more likely to recall negative information. Hence, thinking about one's life while in a good mood may result in a selective retrieval of positive aspects of one's life, and therefore in a more positive evaluation.

On the other hand, the impact of moods may be more direct. People may assume that their momentary well-being at the time of judgment is a reasonable and parsimonious indicator of their well-being in general. Hence, they may base their evaluation of their life as a whole on their feelings at the time of judgment and may evaluate their well-being more favorably when they feel good rather than bad. In doing so, laypeople follow the same logic as psychologists who assume that one's mood serves as a "barometer of the ego" (Jacobsen 1957) that reflects the overall state of the organism (Ewert 1983) and the countless experiences one goes through in life (Bollnow 1956). In fact, when people are asked how they decide whether they are happy or not, most of them are likely to refer explicitly to their current affective state, saying, for example, "Well, I feel good" (Ross et al. 1986).

Experimental evidence supports this assumption. For example, Schwarz and Clore (1983, Experiment 2) called respondents on sunny or rainy days and assessed reports of SWB in telephone interviews. As expected, respondents reported being in a better mood, and being happier and more satisfied with their life as a whole, on sunny rather than on rainy days. Not so, however, when respondents' attention was subtly drawn to the weather as a plausible cause of their current feelings. In one condition, the interviewers pretended to call from out of town and asked as a private aside, "By the way, how's the weather down there?" Under this condition, respondents interviewed on rainy days reported being as happy and satisfied as respondents interviewed on sunny days. In addition, a measure of current mood, assessed at the end of the interview, was not affected by the attention manipulation, indicating that the weather question did not affect respondents' current mood itself but only their inferences based upon it. Accordingly, the mood measure was more strongly correlated with reported SWB when the weather was not mentioned than when it was mentioned.

These and related findings (see Keltner, Locke, and Audrain 1993; Schwarz 1987; Schwarz and Clore 1983, Experiment 1) demonstrate that respondents use their affective state at the time of judgment as a parsimonious indicator of their well-being in general, unless the informational value of their current mood is called into question. Moreover, the discounting effects (Kelley 1972) obtained in these studies rule out an alternative explanation based on mood-congruent retrieval. According to this hypothesis, respondents may recall more negative information about their life when in a bad mood rather than a good mood, and may therefore base their evaluation on a selective sample of data. Note, however, that the impact of a selective database should be independent of respondents' attributions for their current mood. Attributing one's current mood to the weather discredits only the informational value of one's current mood itself, not the evaluative implications of any positive or negative events one may recall. Inferences based on selective recall should therefore be unaffected by salient explanations for one's current feelings. Thus, the reviewed data demonstrate that moods themselves may serve informative functions according to a "How do I feel about it?" heuristic, a hypothesis that has received considerable support in different domains of judgment (for a review, see Schwarz and Clore 1996).

When Do People Rely on Their Mood Rather Than on Other Information?

The observation that individuals may evaluate their well-being either on the basis of (intra- or interindividual) comparisons or on the basis of their momentary feelings raises an obvious question. Under which conditions will they rely on one rather than the other source of information?

General Life Satisfaction Versus Specific Life Domains   On theoretical grounds, we may assume that people are more likely to use the simplifying strategy of consulting their affective state the more burdensome it would be to form a judgment on the basis of comparison information. Note in this regard that evaluations of general life satisfaction pose an extremely complex task that requires a large number of comparisons along many dimensions with ill-defined criteria and the subsequent integration of the results of these comparisons into one composite judgment. Evaluations of specific life domains, on the other hand, are often less complex. In contrast to judgments of general life satisfaction, comparison information is usually available for judgments of specific life domains, and criteria for evaluation are well defined. An attempt to compare one's income or one's "life as a whole" with that of colleagues aptly illustrates the difference. For these reasons, judgments of domain satisfaction may be more likely to be based on inter- and intraindividual comparisons, whereas judgments of one's life as a whole may be based on one's momentary feelings. Supporting this reasoning, the outcome of the 1982 championship games of the German national soccer team affected respondents' general life satisfaction, but not their satisfaction with work and income (Schwarz et al. 1987, Experiment 1).

If judgments of general well-being are based on respondents' affective state, whereas judgments of domain satisfaction are based on comparison processes, it is conceivable that the same event may influence evaluations of one's life as a whole and evaluations of specific domains in opposite directions. For example, an extremely positive event in domain *X* may induce good mood, resulting in reports of increased global SWB. However, the same event may also increase the standard of comparison used in evaluating domain *X*, resulting in judgments of decreased satisfaction with this particular domain. Again, experimental evidence supports this conjecture. In one study (Schwarz et al. 1987, Experiment 2), students were tested in either a pleasant or an unpleasant room, namely, a friendly office or a small, dirty laboratory that was overheated and noisy, with flickering lights and a bad smell. As expected, participants reported lower general life satisfaction in the unpleasant room than in the pleasant room, in line with the moods induced by the experimental rooms. In contrast, they reported higher housing satisfaction in the unpleasant than in the pleasant room, consistent with the assumption that the rooms served as salient standards of comparison.

In summary, the same event may influence judgments of general life satisfaction and judgments of domain satisfaction in opposite directions, reflecting that the former judgment is based on the mood elicited by the event whereas the latter is based on a comparison strategy. This differential impact of the same objective event further contributes to the weak relationships between global and specific evaluations, as well as measures of objective circumstances, that we addressed earlier.

The Relative Salience of Mood and Competing Information   Finally, we return to the impact of re-

called life events on judgments of SWB. In the section on intraindividual comparison processes, we mentioned that the same event may result in assimilation as well as contrast effects, depending on whether it is used to construct a representation of the target or a standard. These processes are further complicated by the degree to which the recall task is emotionally involving. In the absence of emotional involvement, the impact of recalled events follows the mental construal logic described earlier. If recalling a happy or sad life event elicits a happy or sad mood at the time of recall, however, respondents are likely to rely on their feelings rather than on recalled content as a source of information. This overriding impact of current feelings is likely to result in mood-congruent reports of SWB, independent of the mental construal variables discussed earlier.

The best evidence for this assumption comes from experiments that manipulated the emotional involvement that subjects experienced while thinking about past life events. In one experiment (Strack et al. 1985, Experiment 2), subjects were asked either to give a short description of only a few words or to provide a vivid account of one to two pages in length. In another study (Strack et al. 1985, Experiment 3), subjects had to explain "why" the event occurred, or "how" the event proceeded. Explaining why the event occurred or providing a short description did not affect subjects' current mood, whereas "how" descriptions and vivid reports resulted in pronounced mood differences between subjects who reported positive and negative experiences.

Table 4.3 shows the results. When no pronounced mood state was induced, subjects reported higher SWB after recalling negative rather

TABLE 4.3   Subjective Well-being: The Impact of Style of Thinking

	Valence of Event	
	Positive	Negative
Detailed description	9.1	7.9
Short description	6.8	8.4
"How" description	8.2	6.3
"Why" description	7.8	8.9

Source: Copyright 1985 by the American Psychological Association. Adapted from Strack et al. (1985, Experiments 2 and 3).
Note: For the mean score of happiness and satisfaction questions, the range is 1 to 11, with higher values indicating reports of higher well-being.

than positive past events, thus replicating the contrast effects discussed earlier (see table 4.1). When the recall task did induce a pronounced mood state, on the other hand, mood had an overriding effect: in that case, subjects who had to describe negative past events reported lower well-being than subjects who had to describe positive past events, replicating the mood effects found in other studies. Subsequent experiments by Clark and her colleagues (Clark and Collins 1993; Clark, Collins, and Henry 1994) provided conceptual replications of these findings.

In combination with the research reviewed in the section on information about one's own life, these studies demonstrate that the impact of an event is a joint function of its hedonic quality, variables that govern the use of information in mental construals of the target and standard (such as the event's temporal distance or salient category boundaries), and the person's emotional involvement while thinking about the event. That the relationship between objective events and subjective well-being is as weak as the subjective indicator literature has demonstrated is therefore not surprising. Knowing the hedonic quality of an event does not allow a prediction of its impact on reported well-being in the absence of knowledge about other judgmental variables.

REPORTING THE JUDGMENT

Once respondents have formed a judgment, either based on their mood or based on a comparison process, they need to communicate it to the researcher. Self-presentation and social desirability concerns may arise at the reporting stage, and respondents may *edit* their private judgment before they communicate it (for a more detailed discussion, see Strack and Martin 1987; Sudman et al. 1996, ch. 3). In general, social desirability influences are more pronounced in face-to-face interviews than in telephone interviews and are of least concern under the confidential conditions of self-administered questionnaires (for a review, see DeMaio 1984). Consistent with this generalization, Smith (1979) observed in a meta-analysis that higher well-being is reported in face-to-face interviews than in mail surveys.

Experimental research confirmed this finding (Strack et al. 1990) and indicated that self-presentation effects are moderated by interviewer characteristics. Specifically, respondents reported higher well-being in personal interviews than in self-administered questionnaires. Moreover, this difference was more pronounced when the interviewer was of the opposite sex but was not obtained when the interviewer was severely handicapped. Respondents apparently hesitated to tell someone in an unfortunate condition how great their own life was. In contrast, when the handicapped confederate did not serve as an interviewer but was present in the room as another research participant filling out his own questionnaire, his presence did increase subjects' reported SWB, presumably because the handicapped confederate served as a salient standard of comparison.

In summary, the available research indicates that public reports of SWB may be more favorable than respondents' private judgments. On the other hand, individual differences in social desirability show a weak relationship with measures of SWB ($r = .20$) (see Diener 1984). In combination, this suggests that respondents' editing of their reports is more strongly affected by characteristics of the interview situation than by individual differences between respondents.

A JUDGMENT MODEL OF SUBJECTIVE WELL-BEING

Figure 4.2 summarizes the processes reviewed in this chapter. If respondents are asked to report their happiness and satisfaction with their "life as a whole," they are likely to base their judgment on their current affective state; doing so greatly simplifies the judgmental task. If the informational value of their affective state is discredited, or if their affective state is not pronounced and other information is more salient, they are likely to use a comparison strategy. This is also the strategy that is likely to be used for evaluations of less complex specific life domains.

When using a comparison strategy, individuals draw on the information that is chronically or temporarily most accessible at that point in time: whatever comes to mind first, and is relevant to the judgment at hand, is most likely to be used, unless the conversational context renders the use of information that has already been "given" inadequate. Whether information that comes to mind is used in constructing a representation of the target "my life now" or a representation of a relevant standard depends on the variables that govern the use of information in mental construal (Schwarz and Bless 1992a; Strack 1992). Information that is included in the representation of the target results

FIGURE 4.2   A Judgment Model of Subjective Well-Being

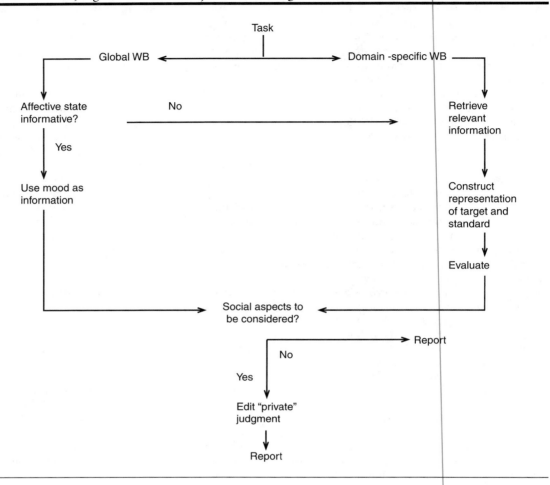

in assimilation effects, whereas information that is used in constructing a standard results in contrast effects. Hence, the same information may influence judgments in opposite directions, depending on its use in mental construal.

If the accessibility of information is due to temporary influences, such as preceding questions in a questionnaire, the obtained judgment is unstable over time and a different judgment will be obtained in a different context. On the other hand, if the accessibility of information reflects chronic influences—such as current concerns or life tasks, or stable characteristics of the social environment—the judgment is likely to be less context-dependent. The size of context-dependent assimilation effects increases with the amount and extremity of the temporarily accessible information that is included in the representation of the target, and it decreases with the amount and extremity of chronically accessible information. Conversely, the size of context-dependent contrast effects increases with the amount and extremity of the temporarily accessible information used in constructing a standard, and it decreases with the amount and extremity of chronically accessible information that enters this representation.

Finally, after having formed a judgment on the basis of comparisons or on the basis of their affective state, respondents have to report their judgment to the researcher. At this stage, they need to format their answer according to the response alternatives provided by the researcher, and they may or may not edit their report to conform to social expectations, depending on the nature of the situation.

METHODOLOGICAL IMPLICATIONS

Our review emphasizes that reports of well-being are subject to a number of transient influences. Like other social judgments, they are best considered constructions in response to particular questions posed at a particular time. Although the information that respondents draw on reflects the reality in which they live, which aspects of this reality they consider and how they use these aspects in forming a judgment is profoundly influenced by features of the research instrument.

Implications for Survey Research

The reviewed findings have profound methodological implications. First, the obtained reports of SWB are subject to pronounced question-order effects because the content of preceding questions influences the temporary accessibility of relevant information. Moreover, questionnaire design variables, like the presence or absence of a joint lead-in to related questions, determine how respondents use the information that comes to mind. As a result, mean reported well-being may differ widely, as seen in many of the reviewed examples. Moreover, the correlation between an objective condition of life (such as dating frequency) and reported SWB can run anywhere from $r = -.1$ to $r = .6$, depending on the order in which the same questions are asked (Strack et al. 1988), suggesting dramatically different substantive conclusions.

Second, the impact of information that is rendered accessible by preceding questions is attenuated the more the information is chronically accessible (see Schwarz and Bless 1992a). Hence, a preceding question about the respondent's health is likely to affect respondents with minor or no health problems to a larger degree than respondents with severe health problems; the latter would be likely to think of their health concerns independent of the preceding question. Accordingly, the same question may affect different subsets of a sample to different degrees.

Third, the stability of reports of SWB over time (that is, their test-retest reliability) depends on the stability of the context in which they are assessed. The resulting stability or change is meaningful when it reflects the information that respondents spontaneously consider because the same, or different, concerns are on their mind at different points in time. It is potentially misleading, however, when it indicates that the research instrument is drawing attention to the same or different aspects of the respondent's life. In the former case, the influence of the research instrument may cloud the impact of actual changes in other domains of respondents' lives; in the latter case, it may suggest changes where none have occurred by ensuring that respondents draw on different aspects at different points in time.

Fourth, in contrast to influences of the research instrument, influences of respondents' mood at the time of judgment are less likely to result in systematic bias. The fortuitous events that affect one respondent's mood are unlikely to affect the mood of many others. An exception to this rule are events of national importance, such as the outcome of major international sports events (Schwarz et al. 1987), which may affect a larger segment of the population. Even the impact of these events, however, is unlikely to last for the whole duration of data collection, which usually extends over several days, if not weeks, for large-scale surveys. Hence, mood effects are likely to introduce random variation, whereas instrument effects introduce systematic bias relative to a population that has not been exposed to the instrument, but to which the findings are to be generalized.

Fifth, as our review indicates, there is no reason to expect strong relationships between the objective conditions of life and subjective assessments of well-being under most circumstances. To begin with, many aspects are not considered when making a judgment, although they would have a pronounced impact if they were. Moreover, even if considered, the same information can drive the judgment in different directions, depending on how it is used in the construal of targets and standards. As we have seen repeatedly, today's tragedy can be tomorrow's standard, depending on the variables that determine its use in mental construal. Our analysis does allow us, however, to circumscribe the conditions under which strong relationships should be observed.

Specifically, strong *positive relationships* between a given objective aspect of life and judgments of SWB are likely to emerge when most respondents include the relevant aspect in the representation that they form of their life and do not draw on many other aspects. This is most likely to be the case when (a) the target category is wide ("my life as a whole") rather than narrow (a more limited episode, for example); (b) the relevant aspect is highly accessible; and (c) other information that may be included in the representation of the target is relatively less accessible. These conditions were satisfied, for example, in the Strack, Martin, and Schwarz (1988) dating frequency study, in which a question about dating frequency rendered this information highly accessible, resulting in a correlation of $r = .66$ with evaluations of the respondent's life as a whole. Yet, as this example illustrates, we would not like to take the emerging correlation seriously when it reflects only the impact of the research instrument, as indicated by the fact that the correlation was $r = -.1$ when the question order was reversed.

Similarly, strong *negative relationships* between a given objective aspect of life and judgments of SWB are likely to emerge when most respondents use the relevant aspect in constructing a standard of comparison and do not draw on many other aspects in forming this representation. This is most likely to be the case when (a) the target category is narrow (for example, a relatively short episode of the respondent's life) rather than wide ("my life as a whole"); (b) the relevant aspect is highly accessible; and (c) other information that may be used in constructing a standard is relatively less accessible. These conditions would be satisfied, for example, in a follow-up study of previously unemployed workers who are asked to report on their previous episode of unemployment and subsequently evaluate their current SWB.

When the instrument does not guide respondents' thought processes, however, different respondents are likely to draw on different information and to use the same information in different construals, resulting in the weak relationships between objective conditions and subjective evaluations that are typically obtained in survey research into SWB. These weak relationships are therefore a natural consequence of the complexity of the underlying judgmental processes—and the occasional observation of strong relationships is cause for methodological suspicion.

Finally, it is worth noting that the context effects reviewed in this chapter limit the comparability of results obtained in different studies. Unfortunately, this comparability is a key prerequisite for many applied uses of subjective social indicators, in particular their use in monitoring the subjective side of social change over time (for examples, see Campbell 1981; Glatzer and Zapf 1984).

If we want to avoid misinterpretations of method effects as substantive effects in this as well as other areas of psychological and social research, we need to learn more about the cognitive processes that underlie the reports that our respondents provide. Perhaps the recent collaboration of survey methodologists and psychologists will advance our knowledge of these important aspects of social research (for reviews of the current state of this field, see Schwarz, Groves, and Schuman 1998; Sudman et al. 1996).

Which Measures Are We to Use?

By now, most readers have probably concluded that there is little to be learned from self-reports of global well-being. Although these reports do reflect subjectively meaningful assessments, what is being assessed, and how, seems too context-dependent to provide reliable information about a population's well-being, let alone information that can guide public policy (but see Argyle, this volume, for a more optimistic take). As an alternative approach, several researchers have returned to Bentham's (1789/1948) notion of happiness as the balance of pleasure over pain (for examples, see Kahneman, this volume; Parducci 1995). Rather than asking respondents to provide a global assessment of SWB, such an approach would rely on moment-to-moment measures of hedonic experience. While the hedonic experiences assessed by these measures are themselves dependent on the context provided by respondents' other life experiences (see Parducci 1995), reporting one's momentary hedonic state poses a less formidable task than providing an evaluation of one's life as a whole. Such momentary reports can be assessed with experience sampling methods (Stone, Shiffman, De Vries, this volume; Csikszentmihalyi and Wong 1991; for a methodological review, see Hormuth 1986), such as beepers that remind respondents at randomly chosen times to report their current affective state. Such measures are unlikely to correlate well with global reports of SWB, as Parducci (1995, 13) noted because the same event is likely to affect evaluations of other specific events and evaluations of extended episodes in opposite directions, as discussed earlier. To what extent measures of momentary hedonic state are likely to show strong and meaningful relationships with objective conditions of living is difficult to determine at the present stage of affairs, yet optimism seems warranted (see Kahneman, this volume). However, experience sampling methods are considerably more expensive than the relatively cheap option of asking respondents to provide global assessments of their lives as a whole. Hence, considerable methodological effort needs to be invested before the use of these measures in large-scale representative studies can be justified.

REFERENCES

Andrews, F. M., and Whithey, S. B. (1976). *Social indicators of well-being: Americans' perceptions of life quality.* New York: Plenum.

Bachman, J., and O'Malley, P. (1986). Self-concepts, self-esteem, and educational experiences: The frog pond revisited (again). *Journal of Personality and Social Psychology, 50,* 35–46.

Bentham, J. (1948). *An introduction to the principles of morals and legislation.* New York: Hafner. (Originally published in 1789)

Blaney, P. H. (1986). Affect and memory: A review. *Psychological Bulletin, 99,* 229–46.

Bodenhausen, G. V., and Wyer, R. S. (1987). Social cognition and social reality: Information acquisition and use in the laboratory and the real world. In H. J. Hippler, N. Schwarz, and S. Sudman (Eds.), *Social information processing and survey methodology* (pp. 6–41). New York: Springer-Verlag.

Bollnow, O. F. (1956). *Das Wesen der Stimmungen* (The nature of moods). Frankfurt: Klostermann.

Boninger, D. S., Gleicher, F., and Strathman, A. (1994). Counterfactual thinking: From what might have been to what may be. *Journal of Personality and Social Psychology, 67,* 297–307.

Bower, G. H. (1981). Mood and memory. *American Psychologist, 36,* 129–48.

Bradburn, N. M. (1969) *The structure of psychological well-being.* Chicago: Aldine.

Brandstätter, E. (1998). *Ambivalente Zufriedenheit: Der Einfluss sozialer Vergleiche.* (Ambivalent satisfaction: The impact of social comparisons). Muenster: Waxmann.

Brewer, M. B. (1988). A dual process model of impression formation. In T. K. Srull and R. S. Wyer (Eds.), *Advances in Social Cognition, 1,* 1–36. Mahwah, NJ: Erlbaum.

Brickman, P., and Campbell, D. T. (1971). Hedonic relativism and planning the good society. In M. H. Appley (Ed.), *Adaptation-level theory* (pp. 215–31). New York: Academic Press.

Brickman, P., Coates, D., and Janoff-Bulman, R. (1978). Lottery winners and accident victims: Is happiness relative? *Journal of Personality and Social Psychology, 36,* 917–27.

Campbell, A. (1981). *The sense of well-being in America.* New York: McGraw-Hill.

Campbell, A., Converse, P. E., and Rodgers, W. L (1976). *The quality of American life.* New York: Russell Sage Foundation.

Carp, F. M., and Carp, A. (1982). Test of a model of domain satisfaction and aging. *Research on Aging, 4,* 503–22.

Cash, T. F., Cash, D. W., and Butters, J. W. (1983). "Mirror, mirror, on the wall": Contrast effects in self-evaluation of physical attractiveness. *Personality and Social Psychology Bulletin, 9,* 351–58.

Clark, L. F., and Collins, J. E. (1993). Remembering old flames: How the past affects assessment of the present. *Personality and Social Psychology Bulletin, 19,* 399–408.

Clark, L. F., Collins, J. E., and Henry, S. M. (1994). Biasing effects of retrospective reports on current self-assessments. In N. Schwarz and S. Sudman (Eds.), *Autobiographical memory and the validity of retrospective reports* (pp. 291–304). New York: Springer-Verlag.

Csikszentmihalyi, M., and Wong, M. M. (1991). The situational and personal correlates of happiness: A cross-national comparison. In F. Strack, M. Argyle, and N. Schwarz (Eds.), *Subjective well-being: An interdisciplinary perspective* (pp. 193–212). Oxford: Pergamon.

DeMaio, T. J. (1984). Social desirability and survey measurement: A review. In C. F. Turner and E. Martin (Eds.), *Surveying subjective phenomena* (vol. 2, pp. 257–81). New York: Russell Sage Foundation.

Dermer, M., Cohen, S. J., Jacobsen, E., and Anderson, E. A. (1979). Evaluative judgments of aspects of life as a function for vicarious exposure to hedonic extremes. *Journal of Personality and Social Psychology, 37,* 247–60.

Diener, E. (1984). Subjective well-being. *Psychological Bulletin, 235,* 542–75.

Dunning, D., Madey, S. F., and Parpal, M. (1995). Frames and counterfactual thought: On comparing the "road taken" to hypothetical alternatives and the past. In N. J. Roese and J. M. Olson (Eds.), *What might have been: The social psychology of counterfactual thinking.* Mahwah, N.J.: Erlbaum.

Easterlin, R. A. (1974). Does economic growth improve the human lot? Some empirical evidence. In P. A. David and M. W. Reder (Eds.), *Nations and households in economic growth* (pp. 98–125). New York: Academic Press.

Elder, G. H. (1974). *Children of the Great Depression.* Chicago: University of Chicago Press.

Elster, J. (1983). *Sour grapes.* New York: Cambridge University Press.

Ewert, O. (1983). Ergebnisse und Probleme der Emotionsforschung (Finding problems in emotial research). In H. Thomae (Ed.), *Theorien und Formen der Motivation. Enzyklopädie der Psychologie,* Series C, Part IV, Vol. 1. Gottingen: Hogrefe.

Festinger, L. (1954). A theory of social comparison processes. *Human Relations, 7,* 117–40.

Fredrickson, B. L., and Kahneman, D. (1993). Duration

neglect in retrospective evaluations of affective episodes. *Journal of Personality and Social Psychology, 65,* 45–55.

Glatzer, W. (1984). Lebenszufriedenheit und alternative Masse subjektiven Wohlbefindens (Life-satisfaction and alternative measures of SWB). In W. Glatzer and W. Zapf (Eds.), *Lebensqualität in der Bundesrepublik* (Quality of life in Germany). Frankfurt: Campus.

Glatzer, W., and Zapf, W. (1984). Lebensqualität in der Bundesrepublik (Quality of life in Germany). In W. Glatzer and W. Zapf (Eds.), *Lebensqualität in der Bundesrepublik.* (Quality of life in Germany). Frankfurt: Campus.

Goethals, G. R., and Darley, J. M.(1977). Social comparison theory: An attributional approach. In J. M. Sulls and T. A. Wills (Eds.), *Social comparison* (pp. 59–278). Washington, D.C.: Halstead.

Grice, H. P. (1975). Logic and conversation. In P. Cole and J. L. Morgan (Eds.), *Syntax and semantics,* vol. 3, *Speech acts* (pp. 41–58). New York: Academic Press.

Helgeson, V. S., and Taylor, S. E. (1993). Social comparisons and adjustment among cardiac patients. *Journal of Applied Social Psychology, 23,* 1171–95.

Herr, P. M. (1986). Consequences of priming: Judgement and behavior. *Journal of Personality and Social Psychology, 51,* 1106–1115.

Herr, P. M., Sherman, S. J., and Fazio, R. H. (1983). On the Consequences of priming: Assimilation and contrast effects. *Journal of Experimental Social Psychology, 19,* 323–40.

Higgins, E. T. (1996). Knowledge: Accessibility, applicability, and salience. In E. T. Higgins and A. Kruglanski (Eds.), *Social psychology: Handbook of basic principles* (pp. 133–68). New York: Guilford.

Hormuth, S. E. (1986). The sampling of experiences in situ. *Journal of Personality, 54,* 262–93.

Hyman, H. H., and Singer, E. (Eds.). (1968). *Readings in reference group theory and research.* New York: Free Press.

Iyengar, S. (1987). Television news and citizens' explanations of national affairs. *American Political Science Review, 81,* 815–31.

Jacobsen, E. (1957). Normal and pathological moods: Their nature and function. In R. S. Eisler, A. F. Freud, H. Hartman, and E. Kris (Eds.), *The psychoanalytic study of the child* (pp. 73–113). New York: International University Press.

Kahneman, D., and Miller, D. T. (1986). Norm theory: Comparing reality to its alternatives. *Psychological Review, 93,* 136–53.

Kahneman, D., and Tversky, A. (1979). Prospect theory: An analysis of decision under risk. *Econometrica, 47,* 363–91.

Kammann, R. (1982). Personal circumstances and life events as poor predictors of happiness. Paper presented at the annual convention of the American Psychological Association, Washington, D.C. (August).

Kelley, H. H. (1972). *Causal schemata and the attribution process.* Morristown, N.J.: General Learning Press.

Keltner, D., Locke, K. D., and Audrain, P. C. (1993). The influence of attributions on the relevance of negative feelings to satisfaction. *Personality and Social Psychology Bulletin, 19,* 21–29.

Kendrick, D. T., and Gutierres, S. (1980). Contrast effects and judgments of physical attractiveness: When beauty becomes a problem. *Journal of Personality and Social Psychology, 38,* 131–40.

Klinger, E. (1977). *Meaning and void.* Minneapolis: University of Minnesota Press.

Major, B. (1994). From social inequality to personal entitlement: The role of social comparison, legitimacy appraisals, and group membership. In M. Zanna (Ed.), *Advances in experimental social psychology* (vol. 26, pp. 293–355). San Diego: Academic Press.

Major, B., Testa, M., and Bylsma, W. H. (1991). Responses to upward and downward social comparisons: The impact of esteem-relevance and perceived control. In J. Suls and T. A. Wills (Eds.), *Social comparison: Contemporary theory and research* (pp. 237–60). Hillsdale, N.J.: Erlbaum.

Marsh, H. W. (1993). Academic self-concept: Theory, measurement, and research. In J. Suls (Ed.), *Psychological perspectives on the self* (vol. 4, pp. 1–26). Hillsdale, N.J.: Erlbaum.

Marsh, H. W., and Parker, J. W. (1984). Determinants of student self-concept: Is it better to be a relatively large fish in a small pond even if you don't learn to swim as well? *Journal of Personality and Social Psychology, 47,* 213–31.

Martin, L. L., and Tesser, A. (1989). Toward a motivational and structural theory of ruminative thought. In J. S. Uleman and J. A. Bargh (Eds.), *Unintended thought* (pp. 306–26). New York: Guilford.

Medvec, V. H., Madey, S. F., and Gilovich, T. (1995). When less is more: Counterfactual thinking and satisfaction among Olympic medalists. *Journal of Personality and Social Psychology, 69,* 603–10.

Menon, G., Raghubir, P., and Schwarz, N. (1995). Behavioral frequency judgments: An accessibility-diagnosticity framework. *Journal of Consumer Research, 22,* 212–28.

Michalos, A. (1985). Multiple discrepancies theory. *Social Indicators Research, 16,* 347–413.

Miller, D. T., and Prentice, D. A. (1996). The construction of norms and standards. In E. T. Higgins and A. W. Kruglanski (Eds.), *Social psychology: Handbook of basic principles* (pp. 799–829). New York: Guilford.

Miller, D. T., Turnbull, W., and McFarland, C. (1990). Counterfactual thinking and social perception: Thinking about what might have been. In M. P. Zanna (Ed.), *Advances in experimental social psychology* (vol. 23, pp. 305–31). New York: Academic Press.

Morawetz, D. (1977). Income distribution and self-rated happiness: Some empirical evidence. *Economic Journal, 87,* 511–22.

Morse, H., and Gergen, K. J. (1970). Social comparison, self-consistency, and the concept of the self. *Journal of Personality and Social Psychology, 36,* 148–56.

Parducci, A. (1995). *Happiness, pleasure, and judgment: The contextual theory and its applications.* Hillsdale, N.J.: Erlbaum.

Roese, N. J. (1997). Counterfactual thinking. *Psychological Bulletin, 121,* 133–48.

Roese, N. J., and Olson, J. M. (Eds.). (1995a). *What might have been: The social psychology of counterfactual thinking.* Mahwah, N.J.: Erlbaum.

Roese, N. J., and Olson, J. M. (1995b). Counterfactual thinking: A critical overview. In N. J. Roese and J. M. Olson (Eds.), *What might have been: The social psychology of counterfactual thinking* (pp. 1–55). Mahwah, N.J.: Erlbaum.

Ross, M., Eyman, A., and Kishchuck, N. (1986). Determinants of subjective well-being. In J. M. Olson, C. P. Herman, and M. Zanna (Eds.), *Relative deprivation and social comparison* (pp. 78–103). Hillsdale, N.J.: Erlbaum.

Runciman, W. G. (1966). *Relative deprivation and social justice.* London: Routledge and Kegan Paul.

Runyan, W. M (1980). The life satisfaction chart: Perceptions of the course of subjective experience. *International Journal of Aging and Human Development, 11,* 45–64.

Salovey, P., and Rodin, J. (1984). Some antecedents and consequences of social comparison jealousy. *Journal of Personality and Social Psychology, 47,* 780–92.

Schachter, S. (1959). *The psychology of affiliation.* Stanford, Calif.: Stanford University Press.

Schwarz, N. (1987). *Stimmung als Information: Untersuchungen zum Einfluß von Stimmungen auf die Bewertung des eigenen Lebens* (Mood as information on the impact of moods on evaluations of one's life). Heidelberg: Springer-Verlag.

———. (1994). Judgment in a social context: Biases, shortcomings, and the logic of conversation. In M. Zanna (Ed.), *Advances in experimental social psychology* (vol. 26, pp. 123–62). San Diego: Academic Press.

———. (1996). *Cognition and communication: Judgmental biases, research methods, and the logic of conversation.* Hillsdale, N.J.: Erlbaum.

Schwarz, N., and Bless, H. (1992a). Constructing reality and its alternatives: Assimilation and contrast effects in social judgment. In L. L. Martin and A. Tesser (Eds.), *The construction of social judgment* (pp. 217–45). Hillsdale, N.J.: Erlbaum.

———. (1992b). Scandals and the public's trust in politicians: Assimilation and contrast effects. *Personality and Social Psychology Bulletin, 18,* 574–79.

Schwarz, N., and Clore, G. L. (1983). Mood, misattribution, and judgments of well-being: Informative and directive functions of affective states. *Journal of Personality and Social Psychology, 45,* 513–23.

———. (1996). Feelings and phenomenal experiences. In E. T. Higgins and A. Kruglanski (Eds.), *Social psychology: A handbook of basic principles* (pp. 433–65). New York: Guilford.

Schwarz, N., Groves, R., and Schuman, H. (1998). Survey methods. In S. Fiske, D. Gilbert, and G. Lind-

zey (Eds.), *Handbook of social psychology* (4th ed., vol. 1, 143–79). New York: McGraw Hill.

Schwarz, N., Hippler, H. J., Deutsch, B., and Strack, F. (1985). Response categories: Effects on behavioral reports and comparative judgments. *Public Opinion Quarterly, 49,* 388–95.

Schwarz, N., and Scheuring, B. (1988). Judgments of relationship satisfaction: Inter- and intraindividual comparisons as a function of questionnaire structure. *European Journal of Social Psychology, 18,* 485–96.

———. (1992). Selbstberichtete Verhaltens- und Symptomhäufigkeiten: Was Befragte aus Anwortvorgaben des Fragebogens lernen (Frequency reports of psychosomatic symptoms: What respondents learn from response alternatives.) *Zeitschrift für Klinische Psychologie, 22,* 197–208.

Schwarz, N., and Strack, F. (1991a). Evaluating one's life: A judgment model of subjective well-being. In F. Strack, M. Argyle, and N. Schwarz (Eds.), *Subjective well-being: An interdisciplinary perspective* (pp. 27–47). Oxford: Pergamon.

———. (1991b). Context effects in attitude surveys: Applying cognitive theory to social research. In W. Stroebe and M. Hewstone (Eds.), *European Review of Social Psychology* (vol. 2, pp. 31–50). Chichester: Wiley.

Schwarz, N., Strack, F., Kommer, D., and Wagner, D. (1987). Soccer, rooms, and the quality of your life: Mood effects on judgments of satisfaction with life in general and with specific life domains. *European Journal of Social Psychology, 17,* 69–79.

Schwarz, N., Strack, F., and Mai, H. P. (1991). Assimilation and contrast effects in part-whole questions sequences: A conversational logic analysis. *Public Opinion Quarterly, 55,* 3–23.

Schwarz, N., Wänke, M., and Bless, H. (1994). Subjective assessments and evaluations of change: Some lessons from social cognition research. In M. Hewstone and W. Stroebe (Eds.), *European Review of Social Psychology* (vol. 5, pp. 181–210). Chichester: Wiley.

Seidman, E., and Rapkin, B. (1983). Economics and psychosocial dysfunction: Toward a conceptual framework and prevention strategies. In R. D. Feiner, L. A. Jason, J. N. Moritsugu, and S. S. Farber (Eds.), *Preventive psychology* (pp. 175–98). New York: Pergamon.

Smith, R. H., Diener, E., and Wedell, D. H. (1989). Intrapersonal and social comparison determinants of happiness: A range-frequency analysis. *Journal of Personality and Social Psychology, 56,* 317–25.

Smith, T. W. (1979). Happiness. *Social Psychology Quarterly, 42,* 18–30.

Srull, T. K., and Gaelick, L. (1984). General principles and individual differences in the self as an habitual reference point: An examination of self-other judgments of similarity. *Social Cognition, 2,* 108–21.

Strack, F. (1992). The different routes to social judgments: Experiential versus informational strategies. In L. L. Martin and A. Tesser (Eds.), *The construction of social judgments* (pp. 249–76). Hillsdale, N.J.: Erlbaum.

———. (1994a). *Zur Psychologie der standardisierten Befragung* (The psychology of standardized interviews). Heidelberg: Springer-Verlag.

———. (1994b). Response processes in social judgment. In R. S. Wyer and T. K. Srull (Eds.), *Handbook of social cognition* (2nd ed., vol. 1, pp. 287–322). Hillsdale, N.J.: Erlbaum.

Strack, F., and Martin, L. (1987). Thinking, judging, and communicating: A process account of context effects in attitude surveys. In H. J. Hippler, N. Schwarz, and S. Sudman (Eds.), *Social information processing and survey methodology* (pp. 123–48). New York: Springer-Verlag.

Strack, F., Martin, L. L., and Schwarz, N. (1988). Priming and communication: Social determinants of information use in judgments of life satisfaction. *European Journal of Social Psychology, 18,* 429–42.

Strack, F., Schwarz, N., Chassein, B., Kern, D., and Wagner, D. (1990). The salience of comparison standards and the activation of social norms: Consequences for judgments of happiness and their communication. *British Journal of Social Psychology, 29,* 303–14.

Strack, F., Schwarz, N., and Gschneidinger, E. (1985). Happiness and reminiscing: The role of time perspective, mood, and mode of thinking. *Journal of Personality and Social Psychology, 49,* 1460–69.

Strack, F., Schwarz, N., and Wänke, M. (1991). Semantic and pragmatic aspects of context effects in social and psychological research. *Social Cognition, 9,* 111–25.

Sudman, S., Bradburn, N., and Schwarz, N. (1996). *Thinking about answers: The application of cognitive processes to survey methodology.* San Francisco: Jossey-Bass.

Taylor, S. E., and Brown, J. D. (1988). Illusion and well-being: A social psychological perspective on mental health. *Psychological Bulletin, 103,* 193–210.

Taylor, S. E., and Lobel, M. (1989). Social comparison activity under threat: Downward evaluation and upward contacts. *Psychological Review, 96,* 569–75.

Taylor, S. E., Wayment, H. A., and Carrillo, M. (1996). Social comparison, self-regulation, and motivation. In R. M. Sorrentino and E. T. Higgins (Eds.), *Handbook of motivation and cognition* (vol. 3, pp. 3–27). New York: Guilford.

Taylor, S. E., Wood, J. V., and Lichtman, R. R. (1983). It could be worse: Selective evaluation as a response to victimization. *Journal of Social Issues, 39,* 19–40.

Tesser, A. (1988). Toward a self-evaluation maintenance model of social behavior. In L. Berkowitz (Ed.), *Advances in experimental social psychology* (vol. 21, pp. 181–227). New York: Academic Press.

Tesser, A., and Martin, L. L. (1996). The psychology of evaluation. In E. T. Higgins and A. W. Kruglanski (Eds.), *Social psychology: Handbook of basic principles* (pp. 400–432). New York: Guilford.

Thaler, R. H. (1985). Mental accounting and consumer choice. *Marketing Science, 4,* 199–214.

Tourangeau, R., and Rasinski, K. A. (1988). Cognitive processes underlying context effects in attitude measurement. *Psychological Bulletin, 103,* 299–314.

Tversky, A. (1977). Features of similarity. *Psychological Review, 84,* 327–52.

Tversky, A., and Gati, I. (1978). Studies of similarity. In E. Rosch and B. B. Lloyd (Eds.), *Cognition and categorization* (pp. 81–98). Hillsdale, N.J.: Erlbaum.

Tversky, A., and Griffin, D. (1991). On the dynamics of hedonic experience: Endowment and contrast in judgments of well-being. In F. Strack, M. Argyle, and N. Schwarz (Eds.), *Subjective well-being* (pp. 101–18). Oxford: Pergamon.

Varey, C., and Kahneman, D. (1992). Experiences extended across time: Evaluation of moments and episodes. *Journal of Behavioral Decision Making, 5,* 169–95.

Walster, E., Walster, G. W., and Berscheid, E. (1978). *Equity theory and research.* Boston: Allyn and Bacon.

Wänke, M., Schwarz, N., and Noelle-Neumann, E. (1995). Asking comparative questions: The impact of the direction of comparison. *Public Opinion Quarterly, 59,* 347–72.

Wayment, H. A., Taylor, S. E., and Carrillo, M. (1994). The motivational and performance implications of upward and downward comparisons. University of California at Los Angeles. Unpublished paper.

Wells, G. L., and Gavanski, I. (1989). Mental simulation of causality. *Journal of Personality and Social Psychology, 49,* 1460–69.

Weiner, B. (1985). An attributional theory of achievement motivation and emotion. *Psychological Review, 89,* 548–73.

Wills, T. A. (1981). Downward comparison principles in social psychology. *Psychological Bulletin, 90,* 245–71.

Wood, J. V. (1989). Theory and research concerning social comparisons of personal attributes. *Psychological Bulletin, 106,* 231–48.

Ybema, J. F., and Buunk, B. P. (1995). The effects of social comparison direction and social comparison dimension upon affect and identification among disabled individuals. *British Journal of Social Psychology, 34,* 279–92.

5 Wouldn't It Be Nice? Predicting Future Feelings

George Loewenstein and David Schkade

The mechanics of hedonics (that is, what makes people happy) are only half the picture; the other half is the question of whether people are aware of these mechanics and can apply them to their own lives. All decisions involve predictions of future tastes or feelings. The quality of the decision depends critically on the accuracy of these predictions. While the majority of predictions of feelings are probably reasonably accurate, there appear to be many situations in which people make systematic prediction errors. This chapter focuses on when and why such errors occur. Measuring the accuracy of predictions of feelings requires contrasting people's predictions of how they will feel in a certain situation with the feelings they ultimately do experience in that situation. This structure poses significant methodological challenges for researchers, because of both the difficulty of measuring feelings and the intertemporal character of the phenomenon. Studies of predictions of tastes and feelings have appeared in several widely scattered literatures and have addressed a great variety of topics. The different examples of mispredictions of tastes and feelings in our review point to at least three different, but interrelated, mechanisms as major sources of errors in predicting feelings:

1. People often hold incorrect intuitive theories about the determinants of happiness, which in turn lead to errors when predictions are based on them.

2. Different considerations may be salient when predicting future feelings than those that actually influence experienced feelings.

3. When in a "cold" state people often have difficulty imagining how they would feel or what they might do if they were in a "hot" state—for example, angry, hungry, in pain, or sexually excited. It may also be the case that, when in a hot state, people frequently have difficulty imagining that they will inevitably cool off eventually. Such "hot/cold empathy gaps" can lead to errors in predicting both feelings and behavior.

Learning from experience does not seem to offer a broad cure for prediction errors because intuitive theories are often resistant to change, memories of experience are often themselves biased or incomplete, and experiences rarely repeat themselves often enough to make diagnostic patterns noticeable.

IN THE BEACH BOYS song "Wouldn't It Be Nice," an adolescent laments parental oppression, which stands in the way of the anticipated bliss of marriage to his sweetheart. If his wishes came true, would he be as happy as he believes? Or do his parents know something about his future preferences that he doesn't? George Bernard Shaw might have sided with the parents, noting as he did that "there are two tragedies in life. One is to lose our heart's desire. The other is to gain it."

The book in which this chapter appears is mostly about the mechanics of hedonics—what makes people happy. But this is only half the picture; the other half is whether people are aware of these mechanics and can apply them to their own lives. As March (1978) noted in a seminal article, all decisions involve predictions of future tastes or feelings. Getting married involves a prediction of one's long-term feelings toward one's spouse; returning to school for an advanced degree involves predictions about how it will feel to be a student as well as predictions of long-term career preferences; buying a car involves a prediction of how it would feel to drive around in different cars. In each of these examples, the quality of the decision depends critically on the accuracy of the prediction; errors in predicting feelings are measured in units of divorce, dropout, career burnout, and consumer dissatisfaction.

The accuracy of people's predictions of their own feelings is important not only for individual well-being but also, increasingly, for public policy.[1] Recent decades have seen an expansion of attempts to base public policies on measurements of public values. The best known of these efforts is Oregon's experiment in health-care rationing, but attempts to base public policy on public values have been made in many other areas as well, such as transportation safety and environmental policy.[2] Measurement of public values typically involves surveys in which respondents are asked to predict how they would feel if they were in health conditions or environmental states different from the ones they are in. The meaningfulness of the measured values, and the optimality of the policies based on them, therefore depend in part on the accuracy of predictions of feelings.

Undoubtedly, the great majority of predictions of feelings are reasonably accurate. People know they will feel bad if they lose their job, get rejected by a lover, or fail an examination; that they will be stressed on the first few days of a new job; and that they will experience a post-jog "high." There do, however, appear to be many situations in which people systematically mispredict their own future feelings. Besides marrying too young, there is shopping for groceries on an empty stomach; professing love during moments of lust; believing that one can "eat just one chip"; deciding during the winter to vacation in the south during the summer; and believing one could live the "good life" if one's income were only 10 percent higher.

In this chapter, we address the question of when and why such errors in predicting feelings occur. In the following section, we discuss some methodological issues associated with studying predictions of feelings. Next, we review findings from diverse studies that have examined the accuracy of such predictions. We then discuss three different sources of prediction errors that, in combination, can account for a large fraction of such errors. Finally, we discuss the implications for decision-making and social policy of the fact that people do make systematic errors in predicting their own feelings.

ON STUDYING PREDICTIONS OF FEELINGS

To measure the accuracy of predictions of feelings, it is necessary to contrast people's predictions of how they will feel in a certain situation with the feelings they ultimately do experience in that situation. This task poses significant challenges to researchers, because of both the difficulty of measuring feelings and the intertemporal nature of the phenomenon. In attempting to overcome these obstacles, researchers have employed a variety of research designs and measurement approaches.

Research Design Issues

There are many different research designs that can be used to compare predicted against actual feelings. Of these, the best is typically a prospective longitudinal study. To study the accuracy of expectant parents' predictions of how much they will enjoy parenting, for example, we might ask them, prior to the birth of their first child, to predict on a 0 to 100-point "happiness" scale how happy they will feel at some point following the birth of their child—say, on the child's first birthday. When the child's first birthday arrives, the parents are then asked to report, on the same scale, how happy they actually feel. There are, however, several problems with such a prospective longitudinal design.

First, it is feasible only for short- and medium-term phenomena that are predictable. It is impractical for studying the predicted and actual impacts of events that can't be predicted by the researcher (for example, major earthquakes, except in areas where they are extremely frequent), and it is also impractical for studying predictions of reactions to long-term processes, such as global climate change.

A second problem relates to scaling. The way in which people interpret scales can change over time, owing either to self-norming (see Frederick and Loewenstein, this volume) or other effects such as maturation. For example, if parenting produces either extreme emotional highs or extreme lows, parents may change their notion of what it means to be either extremely happy or extremely unhappy so that the anchor points on the 0 to 100-point happiness scale may have different meanings to them before and after experiencing the joys or miseries of parenting.

Third, people's actual feelings at the time being predicted may be influenced by their predictions in a number of different ways. The act of making a prediction, for example, can artificially increase the salience of prior expectations, leading to an amplification of contrastive emotions such as regret and elation. Thus, parents who explicitly predicted that parenting would be an unremitting joy might feel worse when reporting that it is in fact a mixed bag than they would have if they had not made such a prediction. Alternatively, and perhaps most commonly, a prediction can become a self-fulfilling prophecy (see, for example, Jones 1977), through a variety of mechanisms that have been discussed in the psychology literature. Finally, it is possible that people may avoid the effort of introspectively exploring their current feelings and instead simply report their prior predictions.

All three of these problems associated with having people make explicit predictions are eliminated by conducting a between-subject study in which one group's predictions are contrasted with a different group's actual reports. However, the between-subject design has much lower statistical power and precludes a variety of interesting analyses, such as examining correlates of prediction errors. (Errors can't be directly measured because each subject provides only a prediction *or* an experience.) Perhaps the best design, then, is a mixed between/within hybrid in which half of the subjects make a prediction and half do not, then all report their actual happiness (for examples, see Loewenstein and Adler 1995; Rachman and Eyrl 1989).

Other research designs are possible as well. Some researchers have conducted retrospective studies in which people are asked how they currently feel and are also asked to recall how they expected to feel at some point in the past. For example, Suedfeld and his colleagues (1982) asked inmates in long-term solitary confinement to report their current feelings and also to recall how they had expected to adjust when they were first placed in solitary confinement. The major problem with this design is that people's memories of how they expected to feel are likely to be distorted powerfully by how they actually feel (the "hindsight bias"), most likely in a bias-attenuating fashion. That is, they are likely to remember erroneously that they expected to feel as they actually feel. On the other hand, people may have quite a good memory for disconfirmed expectations (see, for example, Hastie 1984; Mandler 1975).

Another possibility is a cross-sectional design in which one group of subjects, who face some type of event, are asked to predict how it will affect them, while another group, who have already experienced matched events, are asked how it has affected them. Loewenstein and Frederick (1997) employed such a design to study the predicted and actual (that is, self-reported) impact on subjective well-being (SWB) of a variety of long-term environmental events (for example, the deterioration of fish stocks) and nonenvironmental events (such as weight gain). Some subjects were asked to predict how the event would affect their well-being in the next ten years, and others were asked whether the event had happened in the last ten years and to report how it had affected their well-being. Schkade and Kahneman (1998) used a similar design to contrast the self-reported well-being of college students in California with predictions of

well-being made by students in the Midwest (and vice versa). This design suffers, of course, from a number of limitations. First, it can be difficult to match the prospective and retrospective events. Second, as noted earlier, retrospective reports are notoriously inaccurate. For studying long-term effects in a study of limited duration, however, this may be the only practical design.

Measuring Feelings

The most straightforward way to assess the accuracy of predictions of feelings is to measure both the predictions and the feelings on the same scale. Thus, in the parenting example discussed earlier, both predicted and actual happiness were to be measured on a 0 to 100-point "happiness scale." Subjective ratings of this type may not do justice to the feelings they are intended to measure for two reasons: because feelings are multidimensional while single rating scales are unidimensional; and because feelings are, by their very nature, "hot," whereas the respondent is probably in a "cold" state when making a prediction of future feelings. For either or both of these reasons, an individual who predicts that parenting will produce a happiness rating of 70 and then subsequently reports a happiness level of 70 might nonetheless feel that she had not correctly predicted how she would feel about parenting.

The problem of multidimensionality complicates the task of measuring predicted and actual happiness, but it can, at least in principle, be solved through the use of multidimensional scales. In such scales, people either rate themselves (or their predictions) on a variety of different affective dimensions or check off a variety of adjectives that describe how they currently feel (Melzack 1975; Niven and Brodie 1995). The major problems with such scales is that they are difficult to work with statistically and rarely yield a consistent and easily interpretable pattern across scales. Whereas with a monodimensional scale, bias can be measured simply with a t-test, measuring difference on multiple dimensions is more difficult, owing in part to the need to look for changes in the configuration of means across dimensions, and in part to reduced statistical power.

The problem associated with the hot/cold discrepancy is more knotty and, to our knowledge, has not been discussed in the literature on prediction of feelings. It has, however, received some attention in the literature on memory for pain. Many studies of pain memory ask subjects to rate the pain they are experiencing at a particular point in time, on either a unidimensional or multidimensional scale, and then later to report their memory of the pain on the same scale. The majority of these studies have concluded that memory for pain is relatively accurate—even though most people believe that their own memory for pain is poor. One possible explanation for this discrepancy is that intuitions about memory for pain and studies of memory for pain deal with different aspects of pain memory. Morley (1993), for example, distinguishes between three possible variants of memory for pain: sensory reexperiencing of the pain; remembering the sensory, intensity, and affective qualities of the pain without reexperiencing it; and remembering the circumstances in which the pain was experienced. While most studies of pain memory have focused on the second, it seems likely that people are referring to the first when they report poor memory for pain.[3] Generalized to other types of feelings, such as anger, happiness, or sadness, there is a real risk that "cold" paper-and-pencil ratings fail to capture the "hot" dimensions of feeling states.

The pitfalls of relying on such paper-and-pencil ratings is illustrated by a study of memory for pain conducted by Read and Loewenstein (1995). They included two types of measures of pain memory: conventional ratings of the intensity, and other dimensions of, pain; and willingness to accept pain for payment, a decision-based measure that involved giving subjects the option of holding their hand in ice water for different lengths of time (one, three, and five minutes) in exchange for different payment amounts (one dollar, three dollars, and five dollars). Some subjects had just experienced a sample of the ice water, some had experienced it one week earlier, and some had never experienced it. Pain *ratings* did not differ significantly between the three groups, but willingness to incur pain in exchange for payment differed markedly: it was highest for the group that had not experienced the pain sample and lowest for those who had just experienced it. Whether the decision-based measure of pain memory tapped into the hot dimension of pain memory or for some other reason, it clearly measured some aspect of pain that the paper-and-pencil ratings failed to capture.

Other studies have not measured feelings directly at all but rather have measured tastes or preferences at different points in time before an experience. Under certain conditions, inconsistencies in preferences at different points in time could

constitute errors of prediction. For example, Simonson (1990) asked subjects to select snacks they would eat one or more weeks later and then, when the time of consumption arrived, asked them again which snack they would prefer. By comparing these two sets of preferences, he was able to identify a systematic discrepancy in preferences over time. While preferences do not directly measure feelings, even when assessed close in time to the experience, the prediction of preferences and the forecasting of feelings are closely related tasks.

EMPIRICAL RESEARCH ON PREDICTIONS OF FEELINGS

Our review of this widely scattered literature is organized around five broad domains in which predicted feelings have been studied: feelings toward objects (that is, tastes); changed life circumstances (for example, predictions of subjective well-being); changes in health status (for example, the pain or outcome of medical procedures); behavior under temptation or duress (for example, craving or social pressure); and other phenomena.

Feelings Toward Objects

Several studies have examined various processes relating to changes in tastes—feelings toward objects—such as satiation and ownership effects. Kahneman and Snell (1990, 1992), in the first study that explicitly focused on predictions of feelings, had subjects consume a portion of ice cream or plain yogurt while listening to music on eight consecutive days. At the beginning of the experiment, they asked subjects to predict how they would feel about the experience over time, and then to rate the experience during each of the eight sessions. The subjects who ate the ice cream correctly predicted satiation—that they would enjoy the ice cream less over time. However, the subjects who ate the plain yogurt also expected to like it less over time but in fact liked it more (or—for those subjects who considered eating plain yogurt an aversive experience—disliked it less). The most striking finding, however, was the near-zero correlation between individual subjects' anticipated and actual reactions to the experience. Subjects' feelings *did* change substantially over time, but they had little idea, at the outset, about how they would change.

While Kahneman and Snell observed generally

inaccurate, but not strongly biased, predictions of tastes, Simonson (1990) observed what could be interpreted as a significant bias. Students in a class chose one snack from among six snack types to be consumed in three successive class sessions. In the "simultaneous choice" condition, subjects chose all three snacks on the first day of the study. That is, on the first day they chose the snack they would eat during that class and during the following two classes. In the "sequential choice" condition, students chose each snack on the same day it was to be consumed. Simonson observed that students chose substantially more variety when all the choices were bracketed together (the simultaneous choice condition) than when they were bracketed individually (in the sequential choice condition). He termed the difference the "diversification bias." In a series of studies that extended Simonson's findings, Read and Loewenstein (1995) replicated the diversification bias result, ruled out a variety of artifactual explanations, and showed that in simultaneous choice subjects ended up regretting having opted to change snacks in the second and third weeks—consistent with the notion that they mispredicted their own tastes.

Loewenstein and Adler (1995) studied people's predictions of how attached they would become to objects they were endowed with, and also observed a significant bias in people's predictions of their own future feelings. Research on the "endowment effect" (Thaler 1980) has shown that people tend to become attached to objects they are endowed with, even if they would not have desired the object particularly had they not been endowed with it. In a typical demonstration of the effect (see, for example, Kahneman, Knetsch, and Thaler 1990), one group of subjects (sellers) are endowed with an object and given the option of trading it for various amounts of cash; another group (choosers) are not given the object but are given a series of choices between getting the object and getting various amounts of cash. Although the objective wealth position of the two groups is identical, as are the choices they face, endowed subjects hold out for significantly more money than those who are not endowed. In one study, Loewenstein and Adler informed some subjects that they would be endowed with an object and asked them to predict the price at which they would sell the object back to the experimenter once they were endowed. These subjects, and others who did not make a prediction, were then endowed with the object and given the opportunity to sell it back to the experimenter. Subjects

who were not yet endowed substantially underpredicted their own postendowment selling prices. In a second experiment, selling prices were elicited from subjects who were actually endowed with an object and from others who were told they had a 50 percent chance of getting the object. Selling prices were substantially higher for the former group, and the valuations of subjects who were not sure of getting the object were indistinguishable from buying prices of subjects who did not have the object.

Changed Life Circumstances

From a decision-making perspective, one of the most important issues is whether people can predict the impact on their own SWB of life circumstances that are under their control. For example, many people play the lottery, presumably with the idea that it would make them happy to win. According to Brickman, Coates, and Janoff-Bulman (1978), however, this outcome cannot be taken for granted. They asked lottery winners and an informally matched control group a series of questions about past, present, and future happiness. The lottery group ($n = 22$) consisted of people who had recently (within the previous year) won between $50,000 and $1,000,000 in the Illinois state lottery. Lottery winners rated their happiness at 4.0 on a 5-point scale, but the control group rated its happiness at nearly the same level—3.82 on the same scale. Brickman and his colleagues also interviewed a "victim" group consisting of twenty-nine people who had suffered a debilitating accident within the last year that had left them paraplegic or quadriplegic. Although accident victims rated their current happiness at 2.96 on the same 5-point scale, which was significantly lower than did the control group, many people find the difference in the two groups' self-rated well-being to be surprisingly small, given the extremity of the debilities. Brickman and his colleagues did not ask people to predict their own experience utilities beforehand, since lottery winners and paraplegics cannot be identified beforehand, but it seems likely that both groups would have overestimated the impact of these outcomes on their own self-rated well-being.

Schkade and Kahneman (1998) found no difference in self-reported well-being between students at California and midwestern universities, despite large differences in satisfaction with their respective climates. However, when rating the well-being of another student similar to themselves, students predicted large differences across regions in both overall well-being and in satisfaction with the climate. Thus, while students apparently focused on the difference in climate satisfaction, and perceived it accurately, they overextended this observation to conclude that they would be much happier in California, despite the fact that individuals who already live in the two regions report the same overall well-being.

Loewenstein and Frederick (1997) had some subjects predict how various personal and environmental changes would affect their well-being over the next decade, while other subjects evaluated how matched changes had affected their well-being over the last decade. Some of the changes were environmental (levels of local air pollution, rain forest destruction, restriction of sport-fishing due to pollution, and recovery of certain endangered species); some were social (increase in number of coffee shops and cafés, increase in number of television channels and selection of videotapes, reduced risk of nuclear war, and increased risk of AIDS); and some were personal (change in free time, development of pain-causing chronic health condition, change in household income, and increase in body weight). There were significant problems in matching changes retrospectively and prospectively. For example, everyone could be asked to predict how gaining weight would affect their well-being, but the actual (reported) impact of weight gain could be elicited only from the subset of subjects who had in fact gained weight in the prior decade.[4] However, despite the noise introduced by these problems, a clear general pattern emerged from the data: people expected future changes to affect their overall well-being much more than they believed that matched changes in the past had affected their well-being. Viewed retrospectively, it seems, people recognize the relatively minor impact on well-being of specific narrow changes in their circumstances, but they lack the ability to put such changes into perspective when they contemplate them prospectively.

In a study of long-term reactions to noise, Weinstein (1982) reported evidence consistent with overprediction of adaptation. He interviewed people living adjacent to a newly opened highway spur four months and sixteen months after its opening. Subjects became increasingly pessimistic about their ability to adjust to the noise, as if they had overestimated that ability to begin with. At the four-month interview, 21 percent were not annoyed by the noise, 44 percent thought they would eventually adjust, and 30 percent thought

they would not adjust. Sixteen months after the opening, however, only 16 percent were not annoyed, 26 percent still thought they might adjust in the future, and 52 percent thought they would not adjust.

In the study by Suedfeld and his colleagues that was mentioned earlier (1982), the researchers observed what appears to be underprediction of adaptation on the part of prisoners placed in solitary confinement (SC):

> Several of the prisoners indicated that when they had first gone into SC they were afraid that serious mental or physical deterioration would occur, but in general this expectation was not borne out. Similarly, fears of being unable to adjust to the situation were unjustified. The first 72 hours were quite difficult for many prisoners, but the adjustment after that made SC quite tolerable. (330)

Gilbert and his colleagues (1997) studied assistant professors' forecasts of how they would feel at various points in time after their tenure decision; the investigators compared these forecasts to the self-reported well-being of others whose tenure decision had been made in the past. The sample frame consisted of all assistant professors who were considered for tenure in the liberal arts college of a major university over a ten-year period, and it was divided into three categories: current assistants, those whose decision was five or fewer years before, and those whose decision was more than five years before. Current assistants predicted that they would be much happier during the first five years after a positive decision, but that this difference would dissipate or disappear during the subsequent five years (that is, they expected to adapt eventually). Surprisingly, there was no significant difference in reported well-being between those who had and had not received tenure in either the first five or the next five years afterward. Overall, assistant professors predicted that they would be less happy during the first five years after being turned down than they actually were. They also predicted that they would be more happy with tenure during these five years than those who received tenure actually were (albeit significant only at $p < .12$). No such estimation errors were observed for the second five-year period following the tenure decision.

Changes in Health Status

Much of the research on predictions of feelings comes from the field of health. Medical providers are especially interested in this issue, in part because they would like to know whether patients grant informed consent to medical procedures with a realistic appreciation of what they are getting into (for a discussion of this issue, see Ubel and Loewenstein 1997).

After describing to sixty-six laryngeal cancer patients the types of outcomes they might expect from the radiation therapy they were about to undergo, Llewelyn-Thomas, Sutherland, and Thiel (1993) elicited from them predictions of how they would feel after four weeks of radiation therapy, contingent on different objective outcomes. Following completion of the therapy, patients described their actual end-of-therapy state and assigned a utility to it. Actual and predicted feelings were measured using direct utility rating scales and time trade-off measures of utility. The researchers found that the utility ratings were remarkably close to the values predicted prior to therapy.[5] Rachman and Eyrl (1989) similarly found that people suffering from chronic headaches were relatively accurate in predicting the intensity of future headaches, and, moreover, that they tended to revise their expectations of future pain in an adaptive fashion—raising them following an underprediction, and lowering them following an overprediction.

Other studies in the medical domain, however, have revealed systematic errors in predictions of future feelings. Rachman (1988), for example, summarizes a large number of studies showing that people tend to overpredict their own level of fear in a situation. This is true of phobics (see, for example, Rachman and Lopatka 1986) and patients with panic disorder (Rachman, Lopatka, and Levitt 1988), but also of normal subjects. For example, Rachman (1983) found that military trainees undergoing a course of parachuting significantly overpredicted the level of fear they would experience on the final and most difficult jump of their training course (see also McMillan and Rachman 1988). Kent (1985) interviewed forty-four dental patients immediately before, immediately after, and three months following a dental appointment. On average, subjects overpredicted the degree of pain they would experience, and perhaps not surprisingly, this tendency was particularly strong for subjects who were anxious about the appointment. The mean expected level of pain was 16.5 on a 100-centimeter visual analog pain scale, and the reported actual level of experienced pain was 9.0. The correlation between expected and experienced pain was .16.[6] Arntz, van Eck, and Heijmans (1990) similarly observed a strong tendency to overpredict the pain of dental treatment.

In contrast to studies that have observed overprediction of pain, at least two studies have found underprediction of pain. Interestingly, both of these studies used behavioral measures rather than subjective ratings, suggesting that the two methods may yield systematically different conclusions. Christensen-Szalanski (1984) found that a majority of expectant women stated a desire and intention not to use anesthesia during childbirth but reversed their prior decision when they went into labor, as if they had previously underestimated the intensity of the pain they would experience. The reversal of preference occurred among not only women giving birth for the first time but also those who had previously experienced the pain of childbirth. Read and Loewenstein (1995) observed a striking difference in the willingness to submit to cold pressor pain in exchange for payment between people who had and had not experienced a sample of the pain, as if those who had not experienced the pain underestimated its intensity.

Another set of studies has compared how people expect to react and actually do react to good or bad *news* about disease prognoses, as opposed to disease states themselves. Intuitively, one might think that facing a $p < 1$ chance that one has a disease would not be as bad as knowing for sure that one has the disease. Analogously, one might assume that confirmation of one's terror of having a disease would be devastating. Indeed, this belief seems to deter people from getting tested (or examining themselves) for diseases such as Huntington's disease (Mastromauro, Myers, and Berkman 1987) and breast cancer (Kash et al. 1992). However, several studies have found little distress among those who learn that they have, or are at increased risk of having, diseases such as Huntington's disease (Brandt et al. 1989; Wiggins et al. 1992). The finding that people resist getting such news but do not seem extremely adversely affected when they do get it is suggestive of, but does not actually demonstrate, an error in predicting feelings.

To address the issue of prediction accuracy more explicitly, Sieff, Dawes, and Loewenstein (in press) conducted a study in which people who came to a clinic to get tested for HIV predicted how they would feel approximately five weeks after obtaining the test result. Subjects completed a survey consisting of twenty-one mood inventory items based on how they would expect to feel in five weeks if they obtained a negative (favorable) result and a second identical survey based on how they would expect to feel if they obtained a positive (unfavorable) result. The study was intended to permit within-subject comparisons of expected and subsequently reported affect, but a very low rate of HIV-positive results precluded such a comparison for those with positive results. As an imperfect remedy to this problem, the researchers recruited, through advertisements in local newspapers, a comparison group who had received positive HIV test results in the previous four to ten weeks. Consistent with the notion that people underpredict their own robustness in the face of bad news, subjects who made predictions, on average, predicted greater misery from a positive test result than those who tested positive for HIV reported actually feeling.[7] A within-subject analysis of people who obtained negative test results similarly revealed that people anticipated greater elation following a favorable test result than they actually ended up experiencing.

In a *New York Times* article, Kolata (1997) reported on differences between healthy and sick persons' attitudes toward "heroic measures" to extend the lives of the terminally ill. Many healthy Americans state that they do not want to die in a nursing home or hospital or, worse yet, an intensive-care unit, but 90 percent of dying patients, most of whom die in acute-care hospitals, view favorably the care they receive. In one study (Slevin et al. 1990, cited in Kolata 1997), different groups of respondents were asked whether they would accept a grueling course of chemotherapy if it would extend their lives by three months. No radiotherapists said that they would accept the chemotherapy, only 6 percent of oncologists, and 10 percent of healthy people; but 42 percent of current cancer patients say they would. Another study (Danis et al. 1996) found that 58 percent of patients with serious illnesses said that when death was near they would want treatment, even if it prolonged life by just a week. Even after they had been subjected to the most advanced medical technology and seen little long-term benefit, a majority of families of patients who died were willing to undergo the intensive-care experience again. Danis comments that "the whole premise on which advanced directives [such as living wills] is based is that you want a person to articulate what their wishes are so that you can act on them at a future time, but that presumes that the wishes you express today will be applicable at a time when your health is really different" (quoted in Kolata 1997). It is possible, of course, that healthy people realize that their preferences will change but nevertheless want to impose their healthy preferences on their future sick selves. However, it seems likely that the willingness of the healthy to forgo life-extending treatments if they should become sick reflects, in part, an error in predictions of future feelings.

One possible type of prediction error that could contribute to healthy persons' underprediction of their own future desire for heroic measures is an underestimation of the quality of life of a sick person. There is very substantial evidence of such underestimation. In one study of 126 elderly outpatients with five common chronic diseases (arthritis, ischemic heart disease, chronic pulmonary disease, diabetes mellitus, and cancer), Pearlman and Uhlmann (1988) found that patients generally rated their quality of life to be slightly worse than "good, no major complaints," but their physicians rated their quality of life as significantly worse, a pattern that was consistent across all five medical conditions. Sackett and Torrance (1978) compared kidney dialysis patients' evaluations of their own quality of life (measured using the time trade-off method) with evaluations made by members of the general population; for five different kidney dialysis scenarios (for example, three months of hospital dialysis), the general public rated the scenarios as worse than did those who were actually experiencing them. Boyd and his colleagues (1990) compared self-assessments of quality of life (based on diverse measures) made by patients who had received colostomy for rectal cancer with assessments of postcolostomy quality of life made by four "proxy" groups (surgeons specializing in rectal cancer, two groups of healthy subjects, and patients with rectal cancer who had received radiotherapy but not colostomy). All four of the proxy groups rated the patients' quality of life as worse than the patients did.

These disparities may, in part, reflect a difference in patients' and nonpatients' assessments of patients' functional status. Patients' reports of their own functional status are generally far superior to assessments made by proxies, and especially by caretakers (Magaziner et al. 1988; Rubenstein et al. 1984; although, see Epstein et al. 1989).

Behavior Under Temptation/Duress

One special category of situation in which people predict their own feelings is the attempt by people who are in a "cold" state to predict how they will behave in a "hot" state—for example, in the face of some type of temptation or powerful influence on their behavior (see Loewenstein 1996a, in press). The recovering alcoholic, for example, must decide whether he can safely attend the office Christmas party, and persons considering a visit to Las Vegas might well ask themselves whether they can keep their gambling under control. Likewise, people who hear about acts of savagery and bravery during the Holocaust often wonder how they would have behaved in that situation, or how they will behave if they encounter a similar situation in the future. Research findings in this domain present a highly consistent pattern: people tend to overestimate the strength of their own willpower and to underestimate the influence on their behavior of being in a hot state.

Social Influences   Two studies point to a general tendency to underestimate the impact of social influences on one's own behavior. Milgram (1965) conducted a piggyback study to his famous electric shock experiment in which subjects were asked to predict what they would do if they participated in the experiment (but did not know about it). Most subjects did not think that they would have succumbed to the pressure to shock, despite their awareness that a substantial majority of subjects delivered what they believed were powerful shocks. In a closely related study, Wolosin, Sherman, and Cann (1975) showed that subjects underpredicted their own vulnerability to social pressures to conform.

Sexual Desire   Any reader of fiction will find noncontroversial the notion that people often underpredict the power of their own sexual desires. People go on dates planning to refrain from having sex, engage in foreplay with the expectation of using a condom at the next stage, and initiate sex with the plan to "interrupt" prior to the critical moment. As Gold (1993) found in interviews with gay men about their attempts to practice safe sex, however, such resolutions often break down in the "heat of the moment." Daum (1996) exposes the foolishness of admonitions to practice safe sex in a *New York Times Magazine* article titled "Safe-Sex Lies."

Loewenstein, Nagin, and Paternoster (1997) hypothesized that male youths would estimate a higher likelihood of committing date rape when they were sexually aroused than when they were not aroused. They randomly assigned undergraduate males to view sexually arousing or nonarousing photographs and exposed them to a vivid first-person scenario in which their "date" asked them to stop. Aroused subjects reported substantially higher likelihoods of behaving in a sexually aggres-

sive fashion than nonaroused subjects, a finding that is consistent with the prediction that nonaroused subjects would have a difficult time imagining what they might do if they were aroused.

Drug Craving   An important prediction for anyone contemplating recreational drug use, including use of cigarettes and alcohol, is the risk of getting addicted. This prediction is likely to hinge, in turn, on the individual's perception of the intensity of the craving they will experience if they consume the drug for a period then attempt to stop. Loewenstein (1996a, in press) argues that underestimation of such craving is one important factor contributing to drug addiction and presents scattered supportive evidence. Lynch and Bonnie (1994), for example, report results from a longitudinal study in which high school students were asked whether they expected to be smoking cigarettes in five years. Among respondents who were occasional smokers (less than one cigarette per day), only 15 percent predicted that they might be smoking in five years, but five years later 43 percent were in fact smoking. Only 32 percent of those who smoked at least one pack a day expected to still be smoking in five years, but five years later 70 percent still smoked one pack or more per day.[8] To our knowledge, no one has specifically studied the relationship between the predicted and actual intensity of craving.

Curiosity   Loewenstein, Prelec, and Shatto (1996) conducted studies that point to a general tendency for people to underpredict the influence of curiosity on their own behavior (see also Loewenstein 1994). In one representative study, subjects attempted to answer ten geography questions (selected from a group of eleven) and were given a choice between receiving the answers to the questions or getting an attractive candy bar. Half the subjects were first presented with a sample geography question randomly chosen from the group of eleven and were asked to choose between the answers versus the candy bar *before* they attempted to answer the remaining ten questions. The other half were simply given the ten questions and then given the answer/candy bar choice. Subjects who made the choice prior to attempting to answer the questions were significantly more likely to opt for the candy bar, as if they underestimated the curiosity they would experience. In a subsequent experiment, the same researchers included a condition in which subjects were asked to predict what they would choose, rather than actually choosing, prior to answering the questions. Subjects in this condition underestimated their own subsequent likelihood of opting for the answers.

The Urge to Spend   Ausubel (1991) noted that large numbers of credit card users expect to maintain a zero credit balance but fail to do so—apparently underestimating their own future desire to spend. This self-forecasting error can explain the failure of competition between card issuers to drive down credit card interest rates; consumers who expect to maintain zero card balances will not care about credit card interest rates.

Hunger   It is a commonplace that shopping on an empty stomach leads to overshopping. However, to our knowledge, there is only one study showing this effect. Nisbett and Kanouse (1968) asked shoppers who were entering a supermarket to predict what they would buy and also to tell them when they last ate. Shoppers were then observed as they went through the checkout line to see if they had purchased more than they had planned or expected to. For normal-weight shoppers, the researchers observed a positive correlation between overshopping—that is, buying more than planned—and hunger as measured by when the shopper had last eaten. Surprisingly, no such relationship was observed for overweight shoppers. The finding for the former group could be interpreted as a type of prediction error induced by hunger.

Other Phenomena

Other types of prediction errors have been documented that don't fit neatly into one of the above categories. Mitchell and his colleagues (1996) studied the expectations, actual reports, and recollections of happiness of tourists on a European tour, students who went home for Thanksgiving vacation, and students who took a three-week bicycle trip. Respondents tended to make slightly overoptimistic predictions of their own happiness during the event and also tended to recall themselves as having enjoyed the event slightly more than they actually seem to have.[9]

Nichols and his colleagues (1994) conducted an experiment based on Ellen Langer's concept of the "illusion of control" in which students who participated in a lottery were either given a number to bet on or allowed to choose a number and then given the opportunity to sell the ticket back to the experimenter. Consistent with Langer's

findings, selling prices were higher when subjects chose their own numbers. However, when another group of subjects was presented with the experimental design and asked to predict how choosing the number would affect selling prices, these subjects predicted that there would be no difference between the two conditions. Although these researchers did not study self-predictions in this domain, it seems highly likely that subjects would have similarly underpredicted the difference in their own selling prices in the two conditions.

Finally, Tat, Cunningham, and Babakus (1988) observed that consumers are quite sensitive to rebate offers when making purchases, but that very few ultimately send in the forms required to obtain the rebate. It seems logical to infer from this finding that consumers overestimate, at the time of purchase, their own likelihood of redeeming the coupon in the future.

SOURCES OF ERROR IN THE PREDICTION OF FEELINGS

The different examples of mispredictions of tastes and feelings just discussed point to at least three different, but interrelated, mechanisms as major sources of error in predicting feelings. First, people often hold incorrect intuitive theories about the determinants of happiness. For example, it is commonly believed that women are happier when married, and men when single—contrary to observed patterns. Such an incorrect intuitive theory could lead to errors in predicting marital happiness, both by women and by men. Second, different considerations may be salient when predicting future feelings than the considerations that actually influence experienced feelings. Anticipation of a visit to Disney World, for example, is likely to be dominated by images of exciting rides and encounters with Disney characters, while the reality is more likely to be characterized by long waits in line, stifling temperatures, money worries, and domestic disputes (Sutton 1992). Lastly, people seem to have difficulty predicting the impact of drives and emotions such as hunger, pain, and anger. Practicing unsafe sex contrary to one's vows and self-expectations is a classic example of such underprediction.

Inadequate Intuitive Theories

How do people make predictions of feelings? Intuitive theories of well-being would seem to be essential to this task. When it comes to recalling past feelings, it is well established that people often rely on intuitive theories to reconstruct a plausible rendition of the past rather than on actual personal experience (Ross 1989). For example, women's recollections of their own menstrual pain correspond more closely to their personal theories about the time course and intensity of such pain than to their own diary ratings (McFarland, Ross, and DeCourville 1989). If intuitive theories play such a role in *memory* for feelings, when people actually have relevant past experience to draw upon, inevitably they must play an even more important role when it comes to *predictions* of feelings. Indeed, when it comes to predicting their own tastes for and feelings toward novel experiences, people have little more to go on than their own intuitive theories of hedonics. The role of theory in both memory and anticipation is illustrated by the commonly held belief that people tend to become more rigid in their political views as they age. This belief causes young people to exaggerate the degree to which they changed their views in the past *and* leads them to predict that they will become more rigid in their views in the future. In fact, evidence from longitudinal studies of political beliefs does not support the notion that people tend to become more rigid politically as they age (Marcus 1986; Ross 1989).

Intuitive theories of hedonics are extremely diverse. People have theories about what types of activities make them happy or unhappy (for example, good food, human relationships, money, sleep, sex, intoxicants); about how their current experiences will affect their future tastes (satiation, addiction, taste formation); and about serial correlation between moods at different points in time (for example, theories about mood swings and monthly and yearly cycles). Moreover, people differ both in what makes them happy and in the intuitive theories they hold about what makes them happy—greatly complicating research on the accuracy of such intuitions. Even social scientists disagree in often fundamental ways about the determinants of well-being, and prevailing views often change dramatically over time, as illustrated, for example, by the rise and fall of the perceived importance of social comparisons for personal well-being over the last half-century (for the latest historical development, see Diener and Fujita 1996). Few studies have tried to elicit such theories, perhaps because the lack of scholarly consensus makes it impossible to judge their accuracy. Snell, Gibbs, and Varey (1995) attempted to get around the problem posed by the lack of consensus among researchers by eliciting the respon-

dents' intuitions about hedonic processes that the authors considered noncontroversial. These included classical conditioning effects, the Weber/Fechner law, opponent processes, adaptation, mere exposure, and cognitive dissonance effects. Respondents, it turned out, were aware of some processes, such as classical conditioning and the Weber/Fechner law, but not others, such as mere exposure effects.

In a survey that mainly examined perceptions of income inequality, Loewenstein (1996b) asked visitors to Pittsburgh International Airport to rank from most important (1) to least important (5) a list of "things that might be important when it comes to making people happy." Subjects were then asked to go through the list again and "distribute 100 points between the different factors to indicate how important each is relative to the others." The list, ranks, and importance ratings (leaving out the category "other") were as follows:

Item	Mean Rank	Mean Points
Family life	1.7	37
Friends	2.4	22
Satisfying job	2.5	26
High income	3.6	15

Ranking the importance of different factors is in theory difficult since importance ratings should logically depend on the expected variance of a particular item (Goldstein and Mitzel 1992). Nevertheless, it is interesting to note that "high income" ranked, and was rated, below all other items in importance. The lack of importance that subjects place on income relative to other categories seems roughly consistent with findings from the literature on SWB that downplay the importance of income (see, for example, Diener et al. 1993; Easterlin 1995; Lykken and Telligen 1996). On the other hand, the downplaying of income as a source of happiness in these rankings and ratings seems somewhat inconsistent with the effort that people put into securing a high income relative to other goals. This contradiction offers another case in which ratings and behavioral measures would lead a researcher to different conclusions.

A number of the prediction errors summarized in the previous section could be explained on the basis of theory inadequacy. For example, the failure to anticipate the impact of ownership on their preferences (Loewenstein and Adler 1995) can be explained by the fact that people are simply not aware of the endowment effect. Indeed, social scientists have themselves only recently discovered the effect, despite considerable research by cognitive dissonance theorists on the effects of choosing objects. The finding of Nichols and colleagues (1994) that people fail to anticipate Ellen Langer's "illusion of control" effect can similarly be explained by the fact that most people are unaware of the effect. Indeed, this is, in effect, the explanation offered by the authors: "Folk psychology includes no information about the Langer Effect, so predictors get it wrong" (19).

Gilbert and his colleagues (1997) theorized that the errors they observed in affective predictions about negative events resulted from subjects' lack of awareness of the potency of their "psychological immune system" (the ability to transform, invent, or ignore information) in mitigating or even eliminating negative affect. In addition to the two studies about changes in romantic relationships and tenure mentioned earlier, they performed exit interviews at a polling station in the 1994 Texas gubernatorial election, asking people who had just voted how happy they were overall, their evaluations of the two candidates (George Bush Jr. and Ann Richards), and how they would feel if their candidate won or lost. Richards supporters (mostly Democrats) predicted that they would be much less happy if Bush won (the eventual result) and that his winning would not affect their evaluation of him, while Bush supporters expected no difference on either measure. These same voters were called back one month later and asked the same questions. There was no change in overall happiness for either group, but Richards supporters' evaluation of Bush had improved significantly (although they still liked him less than did his supporters). The authors interpreted this improvement as evidence that the psychological immune system was at work to reduce negative affect, an effect that Richards supporters were apparently unaware of at the time they voted.[10] Two additional experiments further investigated this hypothesis by examining the effects of false negative feedback. Subjects expected negative feedback from both more and less reliable sources to have the same effect on their well-being, but they actually felt better later if the feedback came from the less reliable source. The authors argued that feedback from a fallible source was more easily rationalized or discounted by the psychological immune system than subjects believed beforehand. Their overall theme, then, is that when making forecasts about their affective reactions to negative events,

people are largely unaware of or do not focus on their ability to mitigate or eliminate negative affect. Such unawareness of the power of adaptation (Loewenstein and Frederick 1997) could also help to explain the pervasive underestimation by healthy persons of the chronically ill person's quality of life (Boyd et al. 1990; Pearlman and Uhlmann 1988; Sackett and Torrance 1978).

Other prediction errors can be attributed to people's tendency to overapply the theories they do hold. The diversification bias demonstrated by Simonson (1990) can be explained in such terms. People have a (correct) theory that, if they eat the same snack repeatedly in one sitting, they will come to like it less. However, when faced with a situation in which the snack will be consumed only once a week, they overapply the theory, exaggerating the impact of satiation, which would in fact be very weak in such a situation. Consistent with this interpretation, Read and Loewenstein (1995) found that when the salience of the time intervals between class meetings was increased by first asking subjects to say what snacks they would choose if all were to be consumed immediately, *then* asking them to choose snacks for three successive class meetings, the discrepancy between sequential and simultaneous choice was significantly reduced. The many studies by Rachman and his colleagues showing overprediction of fear seem similarly to reflect the exaggerated application of a correct intuitive theory. Snake phobics, for example, know that they are extremely afraid of snakes, but perhaps because their own phobia is highly salient to them, they tend to exaggerate the frequency and intensity of such feelings of fear.

Finally, in some situations people may fail to recognize boundary conditions that limit the applicability of a particular intuitive theory. Thus, for example, there is evidence that people don't adapt to noise, at least in some circumstances (see Frederick and Loewenstein, this volume), but don't recognize that they won't adapt. Given the ubiquitousness of adaptation, it hardly seems surprising that people aren't aware of the few exceptions to the rule.

Differential Salience

One of the authors was recently camping with a friend in the wilds of Alaska. In one of many games of Scrabble they played during the trip, the author's friend played the word *fungo* (a practice ball hit to a fielder by a baseball coach). Unfamiliar with the word, and lacking a dictionary, the author disallowed it, and they both resolved to look it up upon returning to civilization (and at the time fully expected to do so). On the same trip, they decided to obtain a fish book when they got home to determine what type of fish they had been catching and eating. Of course, both the Scrabble game and fish were much less salient when they got back to civilization; the fish remains unidentified, and the Scrabble word was not looked up until it was recalled while working on this chapter. Clearly, the salience of different issues, events, and attributes often changes over time, and such shifts in salience can result in errors of prediction. Can anything systematic be said about what types of features tend to be salient when making predictions, as opposed to when actually experiencing events?

The notion of differential salience has received considerable attention in recent literature. Gillovich and Medvec (1995), for example, argue that when people think about events in the present or immediate past, they tend to regret acts of commission—things they did that they wish they hadn't done, such as things they said to people that they shouldn't have. When they contemplate their more distant past, however, they tend to regret omissions—things they didn't do that they should have. This pattern can be interpreted as a change of salience that occurs with the passage of time. For example, the prospect of the pain of rejection may be very salient to a boy who is considering asking a girl on a date, but years later that pain seems trivial relative to the memory of never having worked up the courage to ask her out. Similarly, the time that would be required to learn a foreign language seems prohibitively costly from today's perspective, but five years from now our failure to learn a foreign language will be more salient than the time that was saved by not doing so. Several ideas closely related to differential salience have been discussed in various papers by Kahneman and his colleagues in their studies of memory for extended experiences. For example, they have argued that when people look back on extended episodes, the peak and the end of the episode tend to be highly salient, while the duration of the experience does not (see, for example, Fredrickson and Kahneman 1993; Kahneman et al. 1993; Varey and Kahneman 1992).

One general rule seems to be that people place disproportionate emphasis on whatever their attention is directed toward. As Loewenstein and Frederick (1997) comment in explaining their findings, "perhaps, when a respondent's attention is focused on a particular type of change—e.g., in opportunities for fishing—they exaggerate its overall importance." Schkade and Kahneman (1998) refer to this phenomenon as the "focusing illusion" and argue that it explains their finding that people's predictions exaggerate the impact of climate on SWB.[11]

Kahneman and Schkade (1998) ran another study that makes the point even more explicitly. They asked large samples of subjects how various features of a new location would affect the well-being over time of a couple who unexpectedly had to move there. In the within-subject condition, subjects were asked to rate the impact on the couple's well-being of each feature both during the first few months after the move and during the third year after the move. In the between-subject conditions, subjects were asked only about one time period, ranging from "before the move" to "overall, for the first five years." Subjects in the within condition did not expect much change in the couple's well-being over the first three years, although they did predict changes if a simple story about the feature could easily be evoked. For example, it is initially thrilling to escape from a location where "you live near an obnoxious relative who often insists on coming over for dinner," but the thrill fades after three years. The between-subject conditions produced no differences across time periods. When their attention was drawn to the impact of adaptation in the within-subject design, subjects sometimes provided predictions that reflected a belief in adaptation, but when their attention was not so directed in the between-subject design, their predictions did not appear to take adaptation into account.

Differential salience can also result from changes in points of comparison that occur with the passage of time. Such shifts can produce such prediction errors as the tendency to exaggerate one's own likelihood of sending in a rebate coupon (Mitchell et al. 1996). A two-dollar rebate from a six-dollar purchase of underwear seems large at the time of making the purchase, but decoupled from the six dollars, the two-dollar rebate seems trivial days later when it comes time to mail in the coupon. Predictions of future feelings inevitably involve some type of stylized representation of future events. Mental images of future vacations and holidays, for example, typically do not include features such as rain, mosquitoes, and rude service-people, which may help to explain the failure to predict the negative affect often experienced during the trips (Mitchell et al. 1996). Similarly, images of winning the lottery do not typically include unwanted media attention or doubts about the motives of friends who suddenly become friendlier (Brickman et al. 1978), and images of paralysis do not include new hobbies, interests, and personal relationships that people develop to cope with disability.

Finally, if social scientists during the last half-century have exaggerated the importance of social comparison for SWB, as Diener and Fujita (1996) argue, this exaggeration could similarly be attributed to differential salience. For most persons, social comparisons are periodically sources of profound misery. The tendency to infer from this that they are an important cause of SWB may be due to the failure to take into account the infrequency with which such feelings of misery from social comparison are actually experienced.

Hot/Cold Empathy Gap

As discussed in Loewenstein (1996a), when in a "cold" state people often have difficulty imagining how they would feel or what they might do if they were in a "hot" state—for example, angry, hungry, in pain, or sexually excited. It may also be the case that, when in a hot state, people frequently have difficulty imagining that they will inevitably cool off. Both of these types of hot/cold empathy gaps lead to errors in predicting both feelings and behavior.

The source of hot/cold empathy gaps may be closely related to the measurement problem associated with measuring hot emotions with cold paper-and-pencil ratings. People may not be able to predict how they will behave under the influence of drives and emotions because our ability to conjure up such drives and emotions is highly constrained. Except under exceptional circumstances, memory for emotions, drive states, and other "visceral factors" (Loewenstein 1996a) appears to be qualitatively different from other forms of memory. Human memory seems to be well suited to storing visual images, words, and semantic meaning, but ill suited to storing information about visceral sensations. Visual recall, for example, activates brain systems that are involved in visual perception (Kosslyn et al. 1993). To imagine a visual scene is, in a very real sense, to "see" the scene again. The same is true for music and words: one can render a tune in one's head or articulate a word without producing any externally audible sound. Memory for visceral states, on the other hand, seems to correspond mainly to Morley's first notion of memory—remembering the circum-

stances under which the feeling was experienced. Thus, Scarry (1985) notes that descriptions of pain rarely describe the pain itself but instead tend to focus on the external agent of pain ("It feels as though a hammer is coming down on my spine"), or on the objective bodily damage associated with the pain ("It feels as if my arm is broken at each joint and the jagged ends are sticking through the skin") (15). Fienberg, Loftus, and Tanur (1985) conclude their review of the literature on memory for pain with the question: "Is it pain that people recall or is it really the events such as injuries and severe illnesses?" (592).

All of the errors in predicting feelings classified under the heading "behavior under temptation/duress" can be understood as consequences of hot/cold empathy gaps. Pregnant women may eschew anesthesia, for example, because the pain of childbirth does not seem "real" to them until they actually experience it. People underpredict the shock they would give in the Milgram experiment (Milgram 1965) and overestimate how honorably they would have behaved in Nazi Germany because they are not actually experiencing the coercive forces that would be operational in the situation. Similarly, people who are not sexually excited underestimate the impact of such excitement (Gold 1993, 1994; Loewenstein, Nagin, and Paternoster 1997); people who are not craving drugs underestimate the force of such craving (Lynch and Bonnie 1994; Loewenstein 1999); people who are not curious underestimate the force of curiosity (Loewenstein et al. 1996a); and people who are not in a shopping situation underestimate the "urge to splurge" (Hoch and Loewenstein 1991) that they will experience when they enter a shopping mall (Ausubel 1991). Other findings can also be plausibly attributed to hot/cold empathy gaps. For example, the person who cavalierly signs a living will may be underestimating the intensity of the emotions that are induced by the prospect of imminent death and people who are not endowed with an object may underestimate the intensity of the feeling of attachment induced by owning it.

Other Mechanisms

Other work calling into question the accuracy of taste predictions includes a theoretical analysis of what Harrison and March (1984) call "postdecisional surprises." The basic idea is that if a decision-maker estimates the desirability of choice items, if those estimates are a combination of the true average value and an error term, and if the alternative with the highest expected return is chosen, then the chosen option will also on average be one with a positive error term. Thus, the actual desirability of a chosen good will tend to be lower than its predicted desirability, and realized satisfaction will fall below anticipated satisfaction. The postdecisional surprise phenomenon is a one-person analog of the better-known "winner's curse" whereby the person who purchases an item in an auction is likely to be the one who most overestimated its value (Bazerman and Samuelson 1983). To our knowledge, there have been no empirical tests of expectations inflation.

Discussion

In this chapter, we have surveyed and proposed several mechanisms to account for errors in predicting future feelings. A great diversity of such errors have indeed been documented. However, as we mentioned in the introduction, it would be foolish to conclude from the length of the list that people typically mispredict their own feelings. While people might judge poorly whether dinner or a movie will make a more enjoyable evening out, they clearly understand that a trip to the dentist would be decidedly inferior to either.[12] A decision-making system that gets these large distinctions right might perform at a high level despite inconsistencies within smaller categories. The great disproportion of studies that find biases and errors in predictions of feelings probably reflects the fact that most researchers test for prediction accuracy in domains where they expect to find errors.

Nevertheless, it would be a mistake to conclude that errors in predicting feelings are uninteresting or unimportant. Although errors may be rare, they can also be momentous when they occur: experimenting with crack because you think you can resist your own future craving, marrying "on the rebound" or while in the thrall of transient passion, blurting out an unfortunate remark because you are sure you will forever feel the anger that you feel in the present, or committing suicide because you are convinced that you will never feel happy again, are only a few examples of the significant consequences that can result from errors in predicting feelings.

Limitations on Learning from Experience Why are these errors in predicting feelings not corrected as people learn from personal experience? Although people do, sometimes, respond to their errors by appropriately adjusting subsequent predic-

tions (see, for example, Hoch and Loewenstein 1989; Rachman and Eyrl 1989), a variety of mechanisms apparently impede such learning from experience. First, considerable research suggests that the intuitive theories that drive predictions are resistant to correction based on individual experience. The resistance of theories to empirical observation is in part due to the confirmation bias—the tendency to focus on theory-confirming evidence (see Klayman and Ha 1987) and to ignore or denigrate the evidentiary value of discordant observations (Lord, Ross, and Lepper 1979).

Second, even when theories do change with experience, the memories of experience on which these changes are based may themselves be biased. For example, as documented in numerous experiments conducted by Fischhoff (1975, 1982) and others (Marcus, 1986), there is a tendency to forget one's own past predictions and to recall oneself as having predicted whatever is known to have occurred. If people don't remember what they originally predicted when an outcome is realized, they will be unaware of, and thus unable to correct for, prediction errors. Similarly, the previously mentioned tendency to remember extended experiences in terms of the peak and the end, and to deemphasize duration, leaves only a very limited representation of the experience to be processed (Kahneman 1994).

Third, self-correction of predictions requires repeated observation of errors, but situations rarely repeat themselves exactly. If a person underpredicts his own hunger on one occasion, his sex drive on another, and his curiosity on a third, is it likely that he will draw any connection between these three events? Even if hunger is the operational drive state in all three instances, the circumstances may be sufficiently different in each case to disguise the repetitive nature of the error. More broadly, Kleinmuntz and Schkade (1993) argue that the dissimilarity in criteria for success across situations inhibits learning about the accuracy of judgment and decision strategies.

What Can Be Done to Help?

The evidence we have reviewed, which shows that people make systematic errors in predicting their own future feelings and preferences, raises the question of whether paternalistic interventions would be justified. For example, suppose a doctor knows from experience that people will remember a painful medical procedure more positively if a medically unnecessary period of diminishing pain is added at the end of the procedure. Should the doctor go ahead with this extra pain, on behalf of the patient's future well-being, even though the patient would probably reject the option beforehand? Should governments ignore current fears of global warming since people will be happier than they think because they underestimate adaptation? On the one hand, numerous paternalistic policies that are already in place—for example, social security, prohibitions against suicide, criminalization of narcotics use, and consumer protection clauses—reflect a recognition by policy-makers that people make mistakes in predicting their own feelings and preferences. On the other hand, our understanding of hedonic prediction errors is far too preliminary to justify further paternalistic interventions. In any case, given the risk of "slippery slopes," such policies should be implemented only under dire circumstances.

Perhaps educational interventions could help for certain types of prediction errors, such as those caused by theory inadequacy. Educational interventions designed to help people predict how they will feel are currently largely limited to the domain of medicine. Researchers concerned with the question of whether patients are really giving *informed* consent to medical procedures have begun to develop sophisticated decision aids using modern technologies such as interactive videodisks, the value of which is the subject of current research (for a discussion of this general issue, see Agre, Kurtz, and Krauss 1994; Hopper et al. 1994; Ubel and Loewenstein 1997). The educational approach would seem to be least promising for errors that result from hot/cold empathy gaps, whose very existence suggests a resistance to cognitive interventions.[13] On the other hand, education about hot/cold empathy gaps could be partially effective if decision-makers use this knowledge to avoid situations in which the dangerous temptations might occur. Successful educational interventions may require the possibility of direct experience and highly structured feedback.

CONCLUDING COMMENTS

In closing, it is probably worth returning to, and questioning, the initial premise of this essay, which is, as expressed by March (1978), that "all decisions involve predictions of future tastes or feelings." In fact, as Langer (1989) and others have pointed out, many decisions involve little conscious deliberation. People decide based on rules (Anderson 1987; Prelec 1991), habits (Ronis,

Yates, and Kirscht 1989), and gut feelings (Damasio 1994), none of which involve explicit predictions of future feelings. The most common source of experiential surprises could therefore be the *absence* of an explicit prediction in the first place.

Indeed, there may be some situations in which making explicit predictions of future decisions, whether accurate or inaccurate, leads to worse decision outcomes. For example, when one of the authors of this chapter cooks for his family, he has the bad habit of making, and announcing, optimistic predictions of the quality of the meal ("Prepare yourself for a *delicious* meal!"). To judge by the ensuing quality of the food on these occasions, it is a big mistake to make, or at least to broadcast, such predictions. Despite counterexamples of this type, however, we suspect that in a wide range of situations explicit prediction of tastes improves the quality of decision-making (see, for example, Frisch and Jones 1993). In many decision contexts, the only thing worse than mispredicting one's tastes may be not to predict them at all.

We thank Ed Diener, Donna Harsch, Daniel Kahneman, John Miller, Peter Ubel, and Timothy Wilson for helpful comments and suggestions, and we gratefully acknowledge support to Loewenstein from the Center for Integrated Study of the Human Dimensions of Global Change at Carnegie Mellon University (NSF grant SBR# 9521914) and to Schkade from the Graduate School of Business Faculty Research Committee at the University of Texas.

NOTES

1. In addition to serving as important inputs into decision-making, predictions of future feelings are important for other reasons as well. Anticipation is an important source of pleasure and pain in its own right (Bentham 1789/1948; Elster and Loewenstein 1992; Loewenstein 1987; Tiger 1979); people who expect to feel good in the future typically feel good in the present, and negative expectations similarly induce immediate negative affect. Anticipations are also an important determinant of postdecision feelings such as regret and disappointment (Gillovich and Medvec 1995; Loomes and Sugden 1982) because people naturally compare how they feel in a situation with how they expected to feel.

2. In the environmental arena, the "contingent valuation" method has been used to measure public values for different environmental amenities; these measurements are then used as inputs into decisions about allocating government spending and siting and development decisions, as well as for guidance in litigation involving environmental damage, such as oil or chemical spills.

3. Morley (1993) conducted a study in which subjects were asked to recall a pain event and then were asked questions designed to measure, for that event, the extent of the three variants of pain memory dimensions. When asked questions about the second type of pain memory, 59 percent were able to recall at least some aspect of the pain sensation, while the remaining 41 percent reported that they had no recall of the pain sensation at all and were thus unable to rate the vividness of their pain experience. For example, one subject reported, "I remember the pain getting worse and worse, but I can't remember what the pain felt like at all." Not a single subject reported actually reexperiencing the pain. Strongman and Kemp (1991) found that spontaneous accounts of pain tended to fit Morley's first variant of pain memory—remembering the circumstances in which the pain was experienced: "Overwhelmingly, the descriptions were of 'objective' details of the events rather than of the feelings of the respondents" (195).

4. This creates potential selection effects since it is possible that the people who allow themselves to gain weight are those who are least bothered by doing so.

5. A weakness of the study is that subjects' evaluations of their objective state may have been influenced by how they felt subjectively. That is, they may have said to themselves, "I feel bad, and therefore my health state must be unfavorable." This type of confounding would attenuate or eliminate any bias that was present.

6. Kent (1985) also found that memories for pain three months after the appointment were more highly correlated with predicted ($r = .49$) than with actual reported ($r = .42$) pain. On average, people remembered the pain as having been 17.9 on the visual analog scale—quite close to the predicted value of 16.5.

7. Given the noncomparability of the groups, however, the results for positive tests must be treated with skepticism.

8. There is also anecdotal evidence pointing to an underprediction of the intensity of craving. Seeburger (1993), for example, in a recent book on addiction, comments that the motivation to stay off a drug "lasts as long as the memory of the undesirable consequences stays strong. But . . . before long, the memory of the pain that one brought on oneself through the addiction begins to pale in comparison to the anticipation of the satisfaction that would immediately attend relapse into the addiction" (152). Osiatynski (1992) refers to the alcoholic's rocky road in coming to appreciate the power of addiction to alcohol: "After hitting bottom and achieving sobriety, many alcoholics must get drunk again, often not once but a few times, in order to come to believe and never forget about their powerlessness" (128). O'Brien and his colleagues (1988) report that patients undergoing cocaine addiction treatment "often return home after a period of brief treatment feeling well and confident that they will not resume drug use. They are usually surprised to suddenly feel craving, withdrawal, or even 'high' when they encounter people or places associated with their prior drug use" (18).

9. Unfortunately, Mitchell and his colleagues (1996) seem to have screened subjects for their positive expectations, thus opening their results to interpretation as regression to the mean.

10. An alternative interpretation is that Bush ended up doing a better job than his opponents had anticipated.

11. The focusing illusion has ramifications that go beyond predictions of future feelings. For example, Strack, Martin, and Schwarz (1988) asked students a question about their overall well-being and then a question about how many dates they had been on recently, or vice versa. When the overall SWB question was asked first, the correlation between the two responses was only .12, but it rose dramatically to .66 when the dating question was asked first. Apparently, asking about dates first focused subjects' attention on that aspect of their lives and increased its perceived importance. The focusing illusion is also related to research on "meta-memory" that shows that people tend to overestimate the likelihood that they will remember whatever happens to be on their mind at a particular time.

12. We thank Ed Diener for suggesting this example.

13. Many different types of interventions have been attempted to help people in a cold state imagine what it would be like to be in a hot state. For example, recent driver's education tools include a cart into which the student is strapped. The cart rolls down a short incline, gathering speed, and hits a rubber barrier, providing the occupant with the bodily sensations accompanying a five-mile-per-hour collision. Now several auto companies are competing to produce realistic drunken driving simulators. By introducing time delays in response to the steering wheel and control pedals, such simulators seek to make salient the loss of control that accompanies drunkenness. Similarly, the "scared straight" program introduced in New Jersey, and since implemented elsewhere, brought juvenile delinquents to a maximum-security prison for a field trip where they were harassed by inmates and verbally abused by guards. All of these interventions seem premised on the view that knowledge of abstract consequences is insufficient to deter undesirable behavior; individuals need to experience the consequence and the emotions associated with it. Unfortunately, the effect of such interventions has typically been found to be weak and short-lived, or even counterproductive. In most cases, it seems, the emotions induced by the program fade quickly, and the impact on behavior along with them.

REFERENCES

Agre, P., Kurtz, R. C., and Krauss, B. J. (1994). A randomized trial using videotape to present consent information for colonoscopy. *Gastrointestinal Endoscopy, 40*, 271–76.

Anderson, J. R. (1987). Skill acquisition: Compilation of weak-method problem solutions. *Psychological Review, 94*, 192–210.

Arntz, A., van Eck, M., and Heijmans, M. (1990). Predictions of dental pain: The fear of any expected evil is worse than the evil itself. *Behaviour Research and Therapy, 26*, 207–23.

Ausubel, L. M. (1991). The failure of competition in the credit card market. *American Economic Review, 81*, 50–81.

Bazerman, M., and Samuelson, W. F. (1983). "I won the auction but I don't want the prize." *Journal of Conflict Resolution, 27*, 618–34.

Bentham, J. (1789/1948). *Introduction to the Principles and Morals of Legislation.* London: University of London Athlone Press.

Boyd, N. F., Sutherland, H. J., Heasman, K. Z., Tritchler, D. L., and Cummings, B. J. (1990). Whose utilities for decision analysis? *Medical Decision Making, 10,* 58–67.

Brandt, J., Quaid, K. A., Folstein, S. E., Garber, P., et al. (1989). Presymptomatic diagnosis of delayed onset disease with linked DNA markers: The experience in Huntington's disease. *Journal of the American Medical Association 261*(21), 3108–14.

Brickman, P., Coates, D., and Janoff-Bulman, R. (1978). Lottery winners and accident victims: Is happiness relative? *Journal of Personality and Social Psychology, 36,* 917–27.

Christensen-Szalanski, J. J. J. (1984). Discount functions and the measurement of patients' values: Women's decisions during childbirth. *Medical Decision Making, 4,* 47–58.

Damasio, A. R. (1994). *Descartes' error: Emotion, reason, and the human brain.* New York: Putnam.

Danis, M., Mutran, E., Garrett, J. M., Stearns, S. C., Slifkin, R. T., Hanson, L., Williams, J. F., and Churchill, L. R. (1996). A prospective study of the impact of patient preferences on life-sustaining treatment and hospital cost. *Critical Care Medicine, 24,* 1811–17.

Daum, M. (1996). Safe-sex lies. *New York Times Magazine,* January 21, 32–33.

Diener, E., and Fujita, F. (1996). Social comparisons and subjective well-being. In B. Buunk and R. Gibbons (Eds.), *Health, coping, and social comparison.* Hillsdale, N.J.: Erlbaum.

Diener, E., Sandvik, E., Seidlitz, L., and Diener, M. (1993). The relationship between income and subjective well-being: Relative or absolute? *Social Indicators Research, 28,* 195–223.

Easterlin, R. A. (1995). Will raising the incomes of all increase the happiness of all? *Journal of Economic Behavior and Organization, 27,* 35–47.

Elster, J., and Loewenstein, G. (1992). Utility from memory and anticipation. In J. Elster and G. Loewenstein (Eds.), *Choice over Time* (pp. 213–34). New York: Russell Sage Foundation.

Epstein, A. M., Hall, J. A., Tognetti, J., Son, L. H., and Conant, Jr., L. (1989). Using proxies to evaluate quality of life: Can they provide valid information about patients' health status and satisfaction with medical care? *Medical Care, 27,* S91–98.

Fienberg, S. E., Loftus, E. F., and Tanur, J. M. (1985). Recalling pain and other symptoms. *Health and Society, 63,* 582–97.

Fischhoff, B. (1975). Hindsight . . . foresight: The effects of outcome knowledge on judgment under uncertainty. *Journal of Experimental Psychology: Human Perception and Performance, 1,* 288–99.

———. (1982). For those condemned to study the past: Heuristics and biases in hindsight. In D. Kahneman, P. Slovic, and A. Tversky (Eds.), *Judgment under uncertainty: Heuristics and biases* (pp. 335–54). New York: Cambridge University Press.

Fredrickson, B., and Kahneman, D. (1993). Duration neglect in retrospective evaluations of affective episodes. *Journal of Personality and Social Psychology, 65,* 45–55.

Frisch, D., and Jones, S. K. (1993). Assessing the accuracy of decisions. *Theory and Psychology, 3,* 115–35.

Gilbert, D. T., Pinel, E. C., Wilson, T. D., Blumberg, S. J., and Wheatley, T. (1997). Immune neglect: A source of durability bias in affective forecasting. Working paper. Cambridge, Mass.: Department of Psychology, Harvard University.

Gillovich, T., and Medvec, V. (1995). The experience of regret: What, when, and why. *Psychological Review, 102,* 379–95.

Gold, R. (1993). On the need to mind the gap: On-line versus off-line cognitions underlying sexual risk-taking. In D. Terry, C. Gallois, and M. McCamish (Eds.), *The theory of reasoned action: Its application to AIDS preventive behavior* (pp. 227–52). New York: Pergamon Press.

———. (1994). Why we need to rethink AIDS education for gay men. Plenary address to the Second International Conference on AIDS' impact: Biopsychosocial aspects of HIV infection. Brighton, Eng., July 7–10.

Goldstein, W. M., and Mitzel, H. C. (1992). The relative importance of relative importance: Inferring other people's preferences from relative importance ratings and previous decisions. *Organizational Behavior and Human Decision Processes, 52,* 382–415.

Harrison, J. R., and March, J. G. (1984). Decision making and postdecision surprises. *Administrative Science Quarterly, 29,* 26–42.

Hastie, R. (1984). Causes and effects of causal attribution. *Journal of Personality and Social Psychology, 46,* 44–56.

Hoch, S., and Loewenstein, G. (1989). Outcome feedback: Hindsight and information. *Journal of Experimental Psychology: Learning, Memory and Cognition, 15,* 605–19.

———. (1991). Time-inconsistent preferences and consumer self-control. *Journal of Consumer Research, 17,* 492–507.

Hopper, K. D., Zajdel, M., Hulse, S., Yanidis, N. R., TenHave, T. R., Labuski, M. R., Houts, P. S., Brensinger, C. M., and Hartman, D. S. (1994). Interactive method of informing patients of the risks of intravenous contrast media. *Radiology, 192,* 67–71.

Jones, R. A. (1977). *Self-fulfilling prophecies: Social, psychological and physiological effects of expectations.* Hillsdale, N.J.: Erlbaum.

Kahneman, D. (1994). New challenges to the rationality assumption. *Journal of Institutional and Theoretical Economics, 150,* 18–36.

Kahneman, D., Fredrickson, B., Schreiber, C. M., and Redelmeir, D. (1993). When more pain is preferred to less: Adding a better end. *Psychological Science, 4,* 401–5.

Kahneman, D., Knetsch, J., and Thaler, R. (1990). Experimental tests of the endowment effect and the Coase theorem. *Journal of Political Economy, 98,* 1325–48.

Kahneman, D., and Schkade, D. (1998). Ex ante evaluation of temporally extended outcomes: changes as proxies for states. Unpublished paper. Princeton University.

Kahneman, D., and Snell, J. (1990). Predicting Utility. In R. M. Hogarth (Ed.), *Insights in decision making: A tribute to Hillel J. Einhorn* (pp. 295–310). Chicago: University of Chicago Press.

———. (1992). Predicting a changing taste: Do people know what they will like? *Journal of Behavioral Decision Making, 5,* 187–200.

Kash, K. M., Holland, J. C., Halper, M. S., and Miller, D. G. (1992). Psychological distress and surveillance behaviors of women with a family history of breast cancer. *Journal of the National Cancer Institute, 84,* 24–30.

Kent, Gerry (1985). Memory of dental pain. *Pain 21,* 187–94.

Klayman, J., and Ha, Y.-W. (1987). Confirmation, disconfirmation, and information in hypothesis testing. *Psychological Review, 94,* 211–28.

Kleinmuntz, D. N., and Schkade, D. A. (1993). Information displays in decision making. *Psychological Science, 4,* 221–27.

Kolata, G. (1997). Living wills aside, the dying cling to hope. *New York Times,* January 15.

Kosslyn, S. M., Alpert, N. M., Thompson, W. L, Maljkovic, V., Weise, S. B., Chabris, C. F., Hamilton, S. E., Rauch, S. L., and Buonanno, F. S. (1993). Visual mental imagery activates topographically organized visual cortex: PET investigations. *Journal of Cognitive Neuroscience, 5,* 263–87.

Langer, E. (1989). *Mindfulness.* Reading, Mass.: Addison-Wesley.

Llewelyn-Thomas, H., Sutherland, H., and Theil, E. (1993). Do patients' evaluations of a future health state change when they actually enter that state? *Medical Care, 31*(11), 1002–12.

Loewenstein, G. (1987). Anticipation and the valuation of delayed consumption. *Economic Journal, 97,* 666–84.

———. (1994). The psychology of curiosity: A review and reinterpretation. *Psychological Bulletin, 116,* 75–98.

———. (1996a). Out of control: Visceral influences on behavior. *Organizational Behavior and Human Decision Processes, 65,* 272–92.

———. (1996b). Explaining public indifference to income inequality. Paper presented to MacArthur Foundation meeting on inequality. Cambridge, Mass., May 3.

———. (1999). A visceral account of addiction. In J. Elster and O. J. Skog (Eds.), *Getting hooked: Ratio-*

nality and addiction (pp. 235–64). Cambridge: Cambridge University Press.

Loewenstein, G., and Adler, D. (1995). A bias in the prediction of tastes. *Economic Journal, 105,* 929–37.

Loewenstein, G., and Frederick, S. (1997). Predicting reactions to environmental change. In M. Bazerman, D. Messick, A. Tenbrunsel, and K. Wade-Benzoni (Eds.), *Environment, ethics, and behavior* (pp. 52–72). San Francisco: New Lexington Press.

Loewenstein, G., Nagin, D., and Paternoster, R. (1997). The effect of sexual arousal on predictions of sexual forcefulness. *Journal of Crime and Delinquency, 34,* 443–73.

Loewenstein, G., Prelec, D., and Shatto, C. (1996). Hot/cold intrapersonal empathy gaps and the prediction of curiosity. Working paper. Pittsburgh: Carnegie-Mellon University.

Loomes, G., and Sugden, R. (1982). Regret theory: An alternative to rational choice under uncertainty. *Economic Journal, 92,* 805–24.

Lord, C. G., Ross, L., and Lepper, M. R. (1979). Biased assimilation and attitude polarization: The effects of prior theories on subsequently considered evidence. *Journal of Personality and Social Psychology, 37,* 2098–2119.

Lykken, D., and Telligen, A. (1996). Happiness is a stochastic phenomenon. *Psychological Science, 7,* 186–89.

Lynch, B. S., and Bonnie, R. J. (1994). Toward a youth-centered prevention policy. In B. S. Lunch and R. J. Bonnie (Eds.), *Growing up tobacco-free: Preventing nicotine addiction in children and youths* (pp. 3–25). Washington, D.C.: National Academy Press.

Magaziner, J., Simonsick, E. M., Kashner, T. M., Hebel, J. R., (1988). Patient-proxy response comparability on measures of patient health and functional status. *Journal of Clinical Epidemiology, 41,* 1065–74.

Mandler, G. (1975). *Mind and emotion.* New York: Wiley.

March, J. (1978). Bounded rationality, ambiguity, and the engineering of choice. *Bell Journal of Economics, 9,* 587–608.

Marcus, G. B. (1986). Stability and change in political attitudes: Observe, recall, and "explain." *Political Behavior, 8,* 21–44.

Mastromauro, C., Myers, R. H., and Berkman, B. (1987). Attitudes toward presymptomatic testing in Huntington's disease. *American Journal of Medical Genetics, 26,* 271–82.

McFarland, C., Ross, M., and DeCourville, N. (1989). Women's theories of menstruation and biases in recall of menstrual symptoms. *Journal of Personality and Social Psychology, 57,* 522–31.

McMillan, T., and Rachman, S. (1988). Fearlessness and courage in novice paratroopers undergoing training. *Personality and Individual Differences, 9,* 373–78.

Melzack, R. (1975). The McGill Pain Questionnaire:

Major properties and scoring methods. *Pain, 1,* 277–99.

Milgram, S. (1965). *Obedience to authority.* New York: Harper and Row.

Mitchell, T. R., Thompson, L., Peterson, E., and Cronk, R. (1996). Temporal adjustments in the evaluation of events: The "rosy view." Working paper. Seattle: University of Washington.

Morley, S. (1993). Vivid memory for "everyday" pains. *Pain, 55,* 55–62.

Nichols, S., Stich, S., Leslie, A., and Klein, D. (1994). Varieties of off-line simulation. In P. Carruthers (Ed.), *Theories of theories of mind.* New York: Cambridge University Press.

Nisbett, R. E., and Kanouse, D. E. (1968). Obesity, hunger, and supermarket shopping behavior. *Proceedings of the Annual Convention of the American Psychological Association, 3,* 683–84.

Niven, C. A., and Brodie, E. E. (1995). Memory for labor pain: Context and quality. *Pain, 64,* 387–92.

O'Brien, C. P., Childress, A. R., Arndt, I. O., McLellan, A. T., Woody, G. E., and Maany, I. (1988). Pharmacological and behavioral treatments of cocaine dependence: Controlled studies. *Journal of Clinical Psychiatry, 49,* 17–22.

Osiatynski, W. (1992). *Choroba kontroli* (The disease of control). Warszawa: Instytut Psychiatrii i Neurologii.

Pearlman, R. A., Uhlmann, R.F. (1988). Quality of life in chronic diseases: Perceptions of elderly patients. *Journal of Gerontology, 43,* M25–30.

Prelec, D. (1991). Values and principles: Some limitations on traditional economic analysis. In A. Etzioni and P. Lawrence (Eds.), *Socioeconomics: Toward a new synthesis* (pp. 131–45). New York: M. E. Sharpe.

Rachman, S. (1983). Fear and fearlessness among trainee parachutists. *Advances in Behaviour Research and Therapy, 4,* 153–60.

———. (1988). Panics and their consequences. In S. Rachman and J. Maser (Eds.), *Panic: Psychological perspectives* (pp. 259–303). Hillsdale, N.J.: Erlbaum.

Rachman, S., and Eyrl, K. (1989). Predicting and remembering recurrent pain. *Behaviour Research and Therapy, 27*(6), 621–65.

Rachman, S., and Lopatka. (1986). Accurate and inaccurate predictions of pain. *Behaviour Research and Therapy, 26,* 291–96.

Rachman, S., Lopatka, C., and Levitt, K. (1988). Experimental analyses of panic. *Behaviour Research and Therapy, 26,* 33–40.

Read, D., and Loewenstein, G. F. (1995). Diversification bias: Explaining the discrepancy in variety-seeking between combined and separated choices. *Journal of Experimental Psychology: Applied, 1,* 34–49.

———. (in press). Enduring pain for money: Decisions based on the perception and memory of pain. *Journal of Behavioral Decision Making.*

Ronis, D. L., Yates, J. F., and Kirscht, J. P. (1989). Attitudes, decisions, and habits as determinants of repeated behavior. In A. R. Pratkanis, S. J. Breckerler, and A. G. Greenwald (Eds.), *Attitude, structure, and function* (pp. 213–39). Hillsdale, N.J.: Erlbaum.

Ross, M. (1989). Relation of implicit theories to the construction of personal histories. *Psychological Review, 96,* 341–57.

Rubenstein, L. Z., Schairer, C., Wieland, G. D., Kane, R. (1984). Systematic biases in functional status assessment of elderly adults: Effects of differential data sources. *Journal of Gerontology, 39,* 686–91.

Sackett, D. L., Torrance, G. W. (1978). The utility of different health states as perceived by the general public. *Journal of Chronic Diseases, 31,* 697–704.

Scarry, E. (1985). *The body in pain.* Oxford: Oxford University Press.

Schkade, D., and Kahneman, D. (1998). Does living in California make people happy? A focusing illusion in judgments of life satisfaction. *Psychological Science, 9,* 340–46.

Seeburger, F. F. (1993). *Addiction and responsibility: An inquiry into the addictive mind.* New York: Crossroads Press.

Sieff, E. M., Dawes, R. M., and Loewenstein, G. F. (in press). Anticipated versus actual responses to HIV test results. *American Journal of Psychology.*

Simonson, I. (1990). The effect of purchase quantity and timing on variety-seeking behavior. *Journal of Marketing Research, 32,* 150–62.

Slevin, M. L., Plant, H., Lynch, D., Drinkwater, J., Gregory, W. M. (1988). Who should measure quality of life, the doctor or patient? *British Journal of Cancer, 57,* 109–12.

Snell, J., Gibbs, B. J., and Varey, C. (1995). Intuitive hedonics: Consumer beliefs about the dynamics of liking. *Journal of Consumer Psychology, 4,* 33–60.

Strack, F., Martin, L. L., and Schwarz, N. (1988). Priming and communication: Social determinants of information use in judgments of life satisfaction. *European Journal of Social Psychology, 18,* 429–42.

Strongman, K. T., and Kemp, S. (1991). Autobiographical memory for emotion. *Bulletin of the Psychonomic Society, 29,* 195–98.

Suedfeld, P., Ramirez, C., Deaton, J., and Baker-Brown, G. (1982). Reactions and attributes of prisoners in solitary confinement. *Criminal Justice and Behavior, 9,* 303–40.

Sutton, R. I. (1992). Feelings about a Disneyland visit: Photography and reconstruction of bygone emotions. *Journal of Management Inquiry, 1,* 278–87.

Tat, P., Cunningham, W. A., and Babakus, E. (1988). Consumer perceptions of rebates. *Journal of Advertising Research, 28,* 45–50.

Thaler, R. (1980). Toward a positive theory of consumer choice. *Journal of Economic Behavior and Organization, 1,* 39–60.

Tiger, L. (1979). *Optimism: The biology of hope.* New York: Simon & Schuster.

Ubel, P., and Loewenstein, G. (1997). The role of decision analysis in informed consent: Choosing between intuition and systematicity. *Social Science and Medicine, 44,* 647–56.

Varey, C., and Kahneman, D. (1992). Experiences extended across time: Evaluation of moments and episodes. *Journal of Behavioral Decision Making, 5,* 169–86.

Weinstein, N. D. (1982). Community noise problems: Evidence against adaptation. *Journal of Environmental Psychology, 2,* 87–97.

Wiggins, S., Whyte, P., Huggins, M., Adam, S., et al. (1992). The psychological consequences of predictive testing for Huntington's disease. *New England Journal of Medicine 327*(20), 1401–5.

Wolosin, R. J., Sherman, S. J., and Cann, A. (1975). Predictions of own and other's conformity. *Journal of Personality, 43,* 357–78.

Part II

Feeling Good or Bad: Pleasures and Pains; Moods and Emotions

6 Preadaptation and the Puzzles and Properties of Pleasure

Paul Rozin

Sensory pleasures derive primarily from the contact senses that cover the body surface and the body apertures. It is proposed that, by the processes of preadaptation and increased accessibility, the subjective and expressive aspect of this pleasure system is, in later evolution and development, extended to a wider range of pleasure elicitors, including aesthetic and mastery pleasures. Many basic principles of hedonic systems may be studied in the more primitive sensory pleasure system. These include the properties of context dependence and the mappings between remembered, experienced, and anticipated pleasures. Pleasure in the food domain is specifically considered, including the elicitors of pleasure, the role of context, and the acquisition of likes and dislikes (hedonic changes). Special attention is paid to hedonic reversals, in which innately negative sensory hedonic responses become positive (for example, the case of chili pepper). It is argued that on the appraisal side, basic sensory pleasures are qualitatively different from aesthetic pleasures (such as music), but that both feed into the same subjective and expressive system. Some basic features of sensory pleasures are listed.

THE HUMAN BODY is physically defined by a sheath of skin, penetrated by seven holes. The sheath and holes are a veritable playground of pleasure and pain. Virtually all of the sensation-localizable pleasures we have, and many of the pains, are generated along this surface. Most sensations that come to us from this perforated sheath are hedonically tinged. The apertures, the salient points of entry and egress from the body—the mouth, nostrils, and genital and anal openings—are foci of affect, perhaps because of their critical and ambiguous (inside or outside of the body?) positions (Rozin et al., 1995). The aperture exception to this principle is the external auditory canals, but these are the only apertures not involved in material ex-

changes between the outside and inside of the body.

The notion that the "contact" senses (skin, taste, and smell) differ from the others in their close link to affect dates at least from Charles Sherrington (1906) and was elaborated in detail by Leonard Troland (1928). (The sense of smell holds an anomalous position as a "contact" sense. In some ways, it is an exteroceptor, detecting properties of objects in the outside world. However, it resembles taste and skin senses in two important ways: in the experience of flavor, the sense of smell is reporting on substances in contact with the body, and like taste, the stimulus itself [that is, its molecules] is actually incorporated in smelling [Rozin 1982a].)

Troland (1928) divides sensory inputs into the body into beneceptive (beneficial), nociceptive (harmful), and neutroceptive (neutral). The nociceptive systems include pain, negative signals from "stressed" organs, such as empty lungs or a full bladder, and certain chemical inputs such as bitter tastes and repugnant odors. The beneceptive system includes erotic and a range of gustatory and olfactory stimulation. Troland leaves touch out of this system, but it seems to me touch is principally beneceptive, particularly as it pertains to contact-comfort. Troland's neutroceptive system includes our two major sensory inputs, vision and audition, and touch as well. The neutroceptive inputs, as a rule, are informative rather than directly evaluative.

Troland is aware that these are only approximations, but they are in fact good approximations. He notes a clear correlation between sense modality and affective "loading," while recognizing that the same input channel can carry both nociceptive and beneceptive inputs (as when low salt levels are pleasant, and high salt levels are unpleasant). He summarizes his view by the claim that the nociceptive and beneceptive systems are reporting, by and large, on the state of the organism, whereas the neutroceptive systems are reporting on the state of the environment.

We can add to Troland's conception that while the surface and aperture inputs signal both positive and negative affect, the internal, evaluative inputs indicate primarily that something is wrong, that is, they give rise almost entirely to pain (from the viscera, joints, or muscles). In a way, this can be interpreted to mean that for the body interior the normal state is neutral and only malfunction is signaled. From the perspective of the body interior, "no news is good news." For receptors that line the interface between the body and the world, good news is transmitted as well as bad news; the neutral state is a midpoint. Good news often has behavioral and survival implications (approach) over and above neutral news.

The functional and direct link between the contact (surface and aperture) and visceral senses and survival is too clear to require comment. It is the premise of this chapter that hedonic experiences originate in these systems, both phylogenetically and ontogenetically. Insofar as nonhuman animals have a conscious "pleasure" experience, we presume that it is closely related, via sensory systems, to basic needs, such as maintaining adequate nutrients, oxygen, and temperature, avoiding bodily harm, and encouraging social contact and reproduction.

Our previous analysis of the emotion of disgust (Rozin, Haidt, and McCauley 1993; Rozin, Haidt, McCauley, and Imada 1997) provides evidence that disgust began, both phylogenetically and ontogenetically, as part of a food rejection system. In evolution and development, the expressive and output side of this system remains more or less intact, while the domain of elicitors expands, depending on the culture and historical time, to include reminders of our animal nature (such as gore and death), contact with most other human beings, and certain types of moral offenses. We identify the process through which this occurs as preadaptation in the domain of cultural evolution. In biological evolution, preadaptation involves the co-opting of a structure or system involved for one function to another function (Mayr 1960; Bock 1959), and is a major force in large changes in evolution. An appropriate example is the human mouth, evolved for food and fluid intake and air input and output, and co-opted in later human evolution as a vocal output. The tongue and teeth, critical for speech production, evolved for purposes of handling food.

In cultural evolution, through socialization, the range of elicitors that tap into a basic biological system can be extended. As this process occurs ontogenetically, whether programmed biologically or by culturally prescribed experience, systems initially limited in their inputs become more widely used and generalized. This process, in development, I have called increased accessibility (Rozin 1976). The same type of analysis holds for food itself (Rozin 1996): a nutritive and sensory pleasure function expands to include the social, moral, and metaphorical domains.

Along the same lines, our pleasure system may have its origin in, and derive its basic character from, the fundamental life-protecting inputs from the skin surface and apertures. If so, to understand both the function of pleasure and its nature, examination of its primitive roots would seem to be an opportune strategy. That is the approach taken in this chapter.

This inquiry into the fundamental nature and function of pleasure focuses on the food system, which is a very appropriate choice, on the following grounds:

1. The food (nutrient procurement) system is one of the most basic and fundamental of all biological/behavioral systems

2. The relevant behaviors (unlike sex) are exercised very frequently.

3. Food is the only biologically based system that has its own dedicated emotion (disgust) and its own dedicated sense modality (taste).

4. Given that the apertures seem to be foci for pleasure, it is of note that the food system is heavily involved with holes. It lays claim to one of the holes (the mouth), invokes two more intimately in detecting and experiencing food (the nostrils), and provides the materials that "supply" the two excretory holes.

5. Unlike many of the other "primitive" biological systems, such as the needs for air and appropriate temperatures, the food system relies heavily on experience and hence becomes highly elaborated in human cultures. Indeed, some of the greatest cognitive demands facing the human omnivore have to do with finding an adequate food supply (for extensions of this argument, see Rozin 1996).

6. The wide range of food metaphors in English testifies to the foundational (preadaptive) role of the food system. That is, we use food terminology to describe many aspects of our lives, as when I say, "I hope this article is in good taste," or, "I will soon get to the meat of this chapter," or, "I hope the reader can stomach my approach and digest my arguments" (for

a full discussion of metaphor in this context, see Lakoff and Johnson 1980.

7. I have been studying this system in one way or another (from its biological to its cultural aspects) for most of my research career, so I have the relevant information at hand.

Even if the ideas about preadaptation and accessibility fail to hold up with respect to the food system, we can rest assured that we will be at least setting out to understand one of the major sources of pleasure for the human race, and the aspect of life that commands more of our currency (across all cultures) than any other. So this is not like a *Drosophila* or *E. coli* model system, which depends almost entirely on its generality.

I have argued that the food system is a foundation system, and that many preadaptations for general human systems originate in adaptations to making optimal food choices (Rozin 1996). There is also evidence that at least some cognitive abilities emerge first, in human children, in the context of food choice problems (Siegal 1996). When food is the focus, children are more inclined to behave in an adult, logical manner in dealing with the issues of contamination, distinguishing appearance from reality, and distinguishing lies from mistakes.

Much of this chapter is a presentation of what we know about pleasure in the food system of humans. But first, as an appetizer, I want to raise some fundamental issues about the nature of pleasure and some of the basic questions any student of pleasure must face. In my discussion of pleasure and food, I refer to these basic issues. In the final section, I summarize what we know about pleasure and evaluate the extent to which what we learn about food can be applied in other pleasure domains, particularly to that special domain of exquisite positive affect, music.

PLEASURE PRELIMINARIES

Our Ignorance About Pleasure

We know very little about pleasure from a natural science perspective. Few have tried to answer the basic questions. Pleasure has been of great interest to lay folk, philosophers, and Wilhelm Wundt, the founder of experimental psychology. In the middle of this century, Paul Thomas Young (see, for example, Young 1948, 1959, 1961) devoted much of his distinguished career to the study of affective processes in animals, and J. G. Beebe-Center

(1932) did much the same for humans. Both tried to create a science based on pleasure. The emphasis on pleasure by both introspectionists and psychoanalysts, the two bêtes noires of behaviorism, relegated pleasure to a minor place in the behaviorist psychology of the mid-twentieth century. And the pleasure-laden apertures, dear to the heart of Freud, were perhaps for this very reason pushed aside as foci of concern in the middle and late twentieth century. One might almost say there was a reaction formation to the study of apertures and pleasure.

The idea was that pleasure is either very difficult or impossible to measure, and anyway, it might be an epiphenomenon, with no significance for understanding behavior. It could be translated into terms like reinforcement, changed probability of response, or utility without any loss (see critical discussion in Kahneman, Wakker, and Sarin 1997). From our current perspective, neither the measurement problems (which can be solved in many ways on the model of the very successful field of psychophysics) nor the easy substitutability of behavior for mental events are substantial arguments.

As of 1919, Edward Titchener complains: "The reason then, that our descriptive psychology of emotion is schematic rather than analytical is, simply, that experimental psychology has so far found neither the time nor the courage to take emotion into the laboratory" (471–72).

The Definition of Pleasure

According to the first of many definitions in the *Oxford English Dictionary*, pleasure is: "1.a. The condition of consciousness or sensation induced by the enjoyment or anticipation of what is felt or viewed as good or desirable."

In the long list of *Oxford* definitions, it is striking that none refer to the dimension of pleasure, used frequently in American conversation and modern psychology (for example, in scales of pleasantness). Thus, pleasure, pleasantness, and happiness all stand for both a state of affairs and a dimension that they anchor. Note that the opposite end of the dimension is the negated form of the positive term (displeasure, unpleasant, unhappy). One can invoke opposites for these words (aversion/pain, aversiveness/painfulness, or sad) but none of these words can be negated to generate the positive. ("Unaversive," "unpained," and, "unsad" don't sound right.) In English, it is quite reasonable to ask someone, "How pleasant was this?" and reasonable answers include: "very," "extremely unpleasant," and "50-50." One study of how these evaluative terms are treated in many different languages with respect to the asymmetries in both negation and naming of the dimension confirms that English is representative (Rozin, Berman, and Royzman 1999).

We will adopt a simple definition of pleasure: "a positive experienced state that we seek and that we try to maintain or enhance." Similarly, pain (or aversion) is "a negative experienced state that we avoid and that we try to reduce or eliminate."

These problems with the word *pleasure* may cause some to use the more precise but less familiar word *hedonic* or even Jeremy Bentham's (1789/ 1948) *utility*. I will continue to use the familiar word *pleasure* here, but will sometimes use the word *hedonic* to refer to the dimension.

The Types of Pleasure

There is no shortage of taxonomies of pleasure. Aristotle mentions two different aspects of pleasure: "Desire being appetite for what is pleasurable." (*De Anima*, 59); and "Pleasure perfects the activity" (*Nichomachean Ethics*, 595).

Karl Duncker (1941) deals with types of pleasure systematically in a thoughtful discussion of the nature of pleasure. He asks whether the object of pleasure is the wine, the drinking of the wine, or the sensory experience of drinking the wine. That is, respectively, the object, the communication with the object, or the experience of communication with the object. In the case of wine, the answer is clearly the last, the experience of the flavor. There is no such thing as free-floating pleasure; it must be "attached" to something. But that something need not be a sensory experience. Duncker develops a rich taxonomy at this point, and I will abbreviate and modify it here. There are three types of pleasures: sensory, aesthetic, and accomplishment pleasures. Sensory pleasures are tightly tied to sensory input and hence are physically localizable: we experience the pleasure of good food in our mouth. Aesthetic pleasures are more abstract, and not physically localizable, but linked to sensory input. Accomplishment pleasures derive from achieving something of value through mastery. (Some aesthetic pleasures may also involve mastery.) Duncker emphasizes the importance of such pleasures in terms of frequency and salience and describes this type of pleasure as hormic: "Hormism, then, is the theory that pleasure occurs when a conation, i.e., some striving for an object or goal, is being successful, while displea-

sure occurs when a conation is being frustrated" (392).

The focus of this chapter is on sensory pleasure because I suspect it is the most primitive and least complex. Also, in the phylogenetic or ontogenetic frame, it may be the anlage from which other types of pleasure are elaborated. Bentham (1789/ 1948) gives sensory pleasure a special, fundamental place. He holds that physical pleasure may operate independent of other pleasures (moral, political, and religious) and must be included in each of the other three. In short, he holds for the primacy of sensory (physical) pleasure.

The Temporal Frame of Pleasure

According to Aristotle: "What is pleasant is the activity of the present, the hope of the future, and the memory of the past" (*Nicomachean Ethics* Book 9, ch. 7). That is, at any point in time there are three temporal frames for pleasure. Troland (1928) sounds the same note, identifying three domains of pleasure: hedonism of the future, the present, and the past.

The attention of experimentally oriented students of pleasure has been almost entirely on the on-line, present experience of pleasure. However, in recent years Daniel Kahneman and his colleagues (Kahneman and Snell 1992; Kahneman et al. 1993; Kahneman et al. 1997; Frederickson and Kahneman 1993) have developed an analysis of pleasure (called utility by these authors) that incorporates the temporal frame. This distinction is also stressed by Jon Elster and George Loewenstein (1992) in their discussion of backward and forward consumption. The distinctions are between experienced (on-line, present) pleasure, remembered pleasure, and anticipated pleasure. Kahneman and his colleagues make a critical point: the mapping functions between experienced and either remembered or anticipated pleasure are complex and may be non-monotonic. For Kahneman, experienced pleasure is on-line and momentary, like brightness, and hence a sort of primitive. Integrated pleasure (the "experienced" pleasure of episodes) is a mentally constructed entity, which is accessed and/or reconstructed in remembered and anticipated pleasure. Experienced pleasure and pain, on this view, function to influence or guide the behavior of the moment; anticipated and remembered pleasure may guide ongoing behavior, but they also may participate in decisions and evaluations of future courses of action. Of course, a remembered pleasure may be sufficiently vivid to function in many ways as an experienced pleasure.

In terms of real life, most pleasure may come from memory or anticipation, as opposed to on-line experience. The few seconds of experienced pain at a typical visit to the dentist are dwarfed by the displeasure of anticipation and by the frequent, frightful recalls of the experience after the fact. Although it may be most convenient to measure on-line pleasure, these measurements leave out a good part of the experience of pleasure. And it is critical to note that sensory pleasures remain sensory and localized in both memory and anticipation. We think we taste that delicious (or hopefully delicious) meal as we remember or savor it. The new line of work on pleasure from Kahneman and his associates opens up the temporal domain of pleasure, provides us with some experimental paradigms to explore it, and establishes an important theoretical and experimental agenda for an experimental hedonics.

One or Two Dimensions

In much of lay and experimental psychology, at least in the English-speaking world, the pleasure dimension is taken for granted. People easily use the hedonic dimension (for example, the nine-point scale anchored by "dislike extremely" and "like extremely"). However, these results indicate only that people are capable of combining or integrating experiences of varying hedonic qualities. There is abundant evidence that both people and animals can have simultaneous negative and positive hedonic experiences. Terms such as "bittersweet" applied to chocolate, or the simultaneous or near-simultaneous facial and bodily expression of pleasure and aversion in humans and laboratory rats (Berridge and Grill 1983), argue for co-occurrence. These behaviors are more easily interpreted as due to a simultaneous activation of two palatability dimensions than as a reflection of a neutral palatability. When increases in the magnitude of aversive responses are produced by increasing the bitterness of taste mixtures, there is not necessarily a reciprocal decrease in ingestive responses (Berridge and Grill 1983). This asymmetry supports the hypothesis of independent palatability dimensions. In the human domain, psychometric measures of positive and negative affect (as with the Positive Affect Negative Affect Scale [PANAS] are uncorrelated over short or long periods (Watson, Clark, and Tellegen 1988).

Christian Ruckmick (1925), in arguing for two dimensions of pleasure almost seventy-five years ago, notes that the pleasure/displeasure opposition is more logical than psychological. Hot and cold are opposites, but there is both psychological and physiological evidence that these two sensations are mediated by separate systems. The same may be true of pleasures. We should certainly not take for granted that pleasure is unidimensional.

The Purpose of Pleasure

It is easy to assign a function to pleasure as a guide for behavior: we behave so as to increase pleasure and remove pain (aversion). Such a function maps well onto the pleasures of eating or sex, and the avoidance of hunger for food or air or of extremes of temperature. Michel Cabanac (1971, 1985) has made this explicit and shows that in a number of systems, including temperature and food, pleasure covaries with departure from ideal physiological values, a phenomenon he calls alliesthesia.

Both instrumental and Pavlovian learning paradigms provide ways to accomplish the same ends without invoking the mental state of pleasure. Why not maintain the "easier" solution of just having mechanisms for increasing and decreasing the probability of behaviors? What Kahneman describes as "decision utility weighting" seems to do the job. This reasonable concern about the function of pleasure may be misplaced.

Although the decision utility account is more satisfying for behaviorally oriented scientists, it does not follow that such a solution is easier to instantiate in an actual organism: mother nature did not design animals and people so that they would be easy for psychologists to study (or hard for them to study either). Furthermore, there may actually be advantages to the experiential representation of utility.

First, even if pleasure is an epiphenomenon, some noncausal readout of the integrated utility function, it may be a powerful and useful indicator of the nature of that function. Second, pleasure as a mental event may function in the mental calculus of choice and decision-making. However, I must confess that none of the reasons I am about to propose are terribly convincing.

As systemwide experiences—that is, occupants of consciousness—hedonic experiences allow for translation into systemwide responses. In this sense, the general representation of hedonic state might function the way epinephrine functions as a hormone: it allows for a systemwide activation.

If the conscious system makes explicit and considered decisions, then the hedonic reports it receives become an appropriate condensed datum, in terms that influence conscious function.

To function well in any particular cultural context, humans have to learn a wide range of behaviors, values, beliefs, and so on. The investment of these values with affect, insofar as this is congruent with the cultural values, makes it easy for someone to function in the culture. That is, a properly enculturated person likes what his or her culture values, and dislikes what the culture shuns. Such a solution reduces conflict, allowing more time and energy for other life and social functions. Cultural values imply many positive as well as negative feelings. I have suggested elsewhere (Rozin 1982b) that these demands may account for the fact that humans have a strong proclivity to develop very strong, lifelong likings for all kinds of objects and activities. This may be a hedonic adaptation to culture; such strong acquired likes (outside of the human social domain) are very uncommon, so far as we know, in nonhuman animals.

Since humans plan for their future and use their past as a guide to their future, the instantiation of a salient, integrative representation of past and future experiences, that is, a remembered or anticipated and integrated hedonic value, may be a convenient shorthand for decision-making on-line (Kahneman et al. 1997). That is, the integrated affective memory or anticipation may be just what is needed to make sensible decisions now. If this is so, then there is substantial adaptive value in our mental representation of remembered and anticipated pleasure (utility).

These considerations are meant merely to raise the important issue of the function of hedonic experience. That function is still uncertain. Furthermore, certain features of hedonic experience, such as its presence or absence in particular activities, are extremely hard to explain functionally. An example discussed later concerns the fact that nausea produces food dislikes (a hedonic change), while other types of distress after eating produce avoidance but not dislike.

The Importance of Pleasure

How important is pleasure, and particularly sensory pleasure, in mental life? This has been a subject of dispute. From ancient Greece we have the opposed Epicurean and Stoic philosophies.

Perhaps the most famous quote, and the strongest position, comes from Jeremy Bentham (1789/1948): "Nature has placed mankind under the governance of two sovereign masters, *pain* and *pleasure*. It is for them alone to point out what we ought to do, as well as to determine what we shall do." And, later: "they govern us in all we do, in all we say, in all we think" (1).

It would seem fair to say that hedonic factors are clearly an important, that is to say, salient, and frequent part of human life. The normative side of this had best be left for others to discuss.

The importance of pleasure, especially sensory pleasure, no doubt varies across time and place. It is a feature of many of the philosophies from the Far East and South Asia that sensory pleasure is not very important, and that happiness comes from rising above it. For example, one of the sayings in the *Dhammapada*, the Buddhist prayer book, is "212. From pleasure comes grief, from pleasure comes fear; he who is free from pleasure neither sorrows nor fears" (34) (Babbitt 1936). These supposed differences refer, of course, not just to the experience of pleasure but to its motivational role, and the salience and frequency of remembered and anticipated pleasure in mental life. While it is clear that for Americans doing what is pleasant is a major part of living a successful life, this seems to be less the case for, among others, Hindus in India. Pleasure seems less important, and duty and tradition more important, in daily Hindu life. For example, in a questionnaire given to college students in the United States and India, 34 percent of Indian subjects and only 12 percent of Americans agreed with the statement "Whether or not an outcome of an action will be pleasant or unpleasant for me is not an important consideration." On the other hand, in evaluating the statement "Do your duty above all else," 86 percent of Hindu Indians expressed agreement, in contrast to 45 percent of Americans (Rozin, Grant, and Puhan 1997).

FOOD: PLEASURES AND AVERSIONS

The Framework of Food Choice

Human beings are quintessential omnivores or generalists. They consider almost anything as a possible food. They share this status with such other worthy species as rats and cockroaches. The generalist strategy has the advantage of lack of dependence on the availability of any particular food; blights or competitors are not usually serious threats for generalists. But being a generalist entails problems as well. Many potential foods are toxic, and the multiple nutrient requirements of animals place constraints on acceptable mixtures and amounts of different foods. Basically, generalists learn what to eat, and this learning is produced, in large part, by delayed feedback from the consequences of ingestion (for a detailed treatment, see Rozin and Schulkin 1990). The momentary and medium-term health rewards of finding and consuming a nutritious food are great, as are the dangers of consuming something toxic. As a result, it is not surprising that a great deal of affect is invested in the process of food selection.

Pleasure and Food

Food is one of the major sources of pleasure for human beings. In different parts of the world, at different times, it is also a source of distress either because of a lack of food or a surfeit. It is not surprising that the major champion of hedonics in animal psychology, Paul Thomas Young (1948, 1959, 1961), focused on food choice, and sweetness in particular, in his research on rats. Carl Pfaffman (1960), in his important paper "The Pleasures of Sensation," chooses food and taste as the model system. Other leading investigators of food choice, including Eliot Stellar (1974), Michele Cabanac (1971), Herbert Meiselman (1996), David Booth (1994), John Blundell (1980), Barbara Rolls (Rolls et al. 1986), Rose Marie Pangborn (1980), and Richard Shepherd (1989), have devoted attention to the pleasure dimension. In the hands of all of these investigators and others, hedonic scaling of foods is a commonplace activity. (For broad reviews of food consumption and choice, see the edited volumes Barker [1982] and Capaldi [1996]; and Meiselman and MacFie 1996.)

Pleasure and the Gustatory System

There is abundant evidence for sensory pleasure in the food system. Pfaffman (1960) lays out the case that the gustatory sensory inputs are substantially correlated with hedonic variables (figure 6.1). The sweet system is innately hedonically positive for rats and humans. When small amounts of stimulus are used (forestalling satiation), gustatory afferent discharge and hedonic response increase with stimulus intensity. For bitter tastes, increases in afferent input covary monotonically with decreases in liking. For salty tastes, the relation is not monotonic. While the afferent discharge increases with concentration, the hedonic function rises at low concentrations, and then falls to unpleasant with

higher concentrations (all of these results are determined by hedonic ratings in humans and by short-term preference tests and/or analysis of facial and bodily gestures in rats [see, for example, Grill and Norgren 1978]). In all cases, and for sour tastes as well, there is a distinct functional relation between stimulus intensity and hedonic response.

The functional value of the salt, sweet, and bitter systems is obvious. Sweet signals calories (via fruit) in nature, salt is a dietary essential but may be harmful at high levels, and there is a substantial correlation between bitter taste and toxicity in nature.

Jacob Steiner (1979; for confirmation with more objective techniques, see Rosenstein and Oster 1988) has demonstrated aversions to bitter and high levels of sour in human infants, and preferences (using facial expressions) for sugar. Humans probably also have an innate liking for the fatty texture (correlated in the real world with caloric value) and innate aversions for even low levels of irritating stimuli. Of course, fattiness and irritation are not transmitted by the taste system, narrowly conceived, but are food-relevant mouth sensations. Oddly, the biological significance of avoidance of sour (high-acid) or irritant foods (such as chili pepper or ginger) foods is not clear, since harmful concentrations of either of these stimulants do not exist in nature.

Hedonic response to mixtures of tastes is not predictable from algebraic combinations of hedonic ratings of the components. A particularly relevant example, for humans, is the complex palatability relationship between sweetness and fat. There is clearly an optimal combination, and it is far from maximal levels of each (Drewnowski and Greenwood 1983).

While much of the taste-related literature has explored solutions of pure chemicals and their combinations, real-world eating involves foods and beverages that are extremely complex in their gustatory and other oral and flavor properties. Rose Marie Pangborn (1980) pioneered the study of hedonic values in more complex stimuli (such as lemonade) and also demonstrated the wide degree of individual variation. For example, some people show monotonically increasing palatability with sugar concentration (depending on the vehicle); others, with the same vehicle, may show an inverted U or even a monotonically declining function (for a general review of sensory hedonic aspects of food choice, see Cardello, 1996).

The non-additivity of hedonic effects is abundantly clear when real foods are involved. For example, sugar may accentuate the palatability of

FIGURE 6.1   Pleasure Judgments in Relation to the Concentration of Taste Solutions

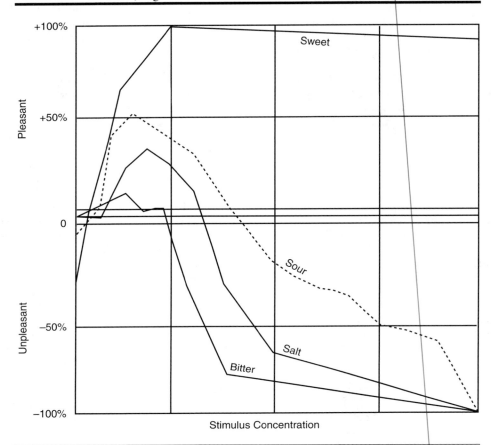

Source: Pfaffman 1960, 261.

Notes: The preponderance of "pleasant" or "unpleasant" judgments in relation to the concentration of taste solution. The ordinate gives percentage "pleasant" minus percentage "unpleasant." The abscissa is proportional to concentration, the full length of the baseline standing for 40 percent cane sugar, 1.12 percent tartaric acid, 10 percent sodium chlorine, and .004 percent quinine sulphate (by weight).

breakfast cereal, for Americans, but reduce the palatability of steak.

A Psychological Taxonomy of Foods

People eat foods, not nutrients (or pure substance solutions), so a psychological taxonomy of foods should not look at all like a nutritional classification. April Fallon and I (Rozin and Fallon 1980; Fallon and Rozin 1983) developed a psychological taxonomy of foods for Americans, by a process of interview and questionnaire. We believe the taxonomy that emerged holds for all cultures, although the foods that fall into the various categories will vary across cultures.

We begin with the set of all possible foods, then divide them, for any person, into accepted and rejected items. The results of the research indicate that acceptance or rejection can be motivated by three factors (see table 6.1): sensory-affective reasons (liking or disliking the sensory properties), anticipated consequences of ingestion (satiation, illness, and so on), and ideational reasons (knowledge of the nature or origin of the food). Only the first reason directly generates sensory pleasure (or displeasure).

The three reasons, alone or in combination, generate a set of relatively pure categories of rejection or acceptance. For rejection, there are four major categories.

TABLE 6.1   Psychological Food Taxonomy

Dimension	Distaste	Danger	Inappro-priate	Disgust	Good taste	Beneficial	Appro-priate	Transvalued
Sensory/ affective	—			(−)	+			(+)
Antici-pated conse-quences		—		(−)		+		(+)
Ideational			—	—			+	+
Examples	beer chili spinach	allergy foods carcino-gens	grass sand	feces insect rotted foods	saccharine favorite foods	medicine healthy foods	ritual foods	leavings of heroes, loved ones, or deities

Source: Modified from Fallon and Rozin, 1983.
Note: Sign in parentheses indicates a statistical, but not a necessary relation, between a dimension and a food category.

Distastes are rejections based primarily on sensory properties. These include rejection of bitter foods and foods like broccoli or lima beans for those who reject them. Most within-culture individual differences in food choice result from differences in sensory/affective response.

Dangers are rejections based on anticipated negative consequences, short- or long-term. Rejection of tobacco, allergy foods, or fattening foods (for some) would fall under this category.

Inappropriates are rejections based on ideational grounds. The items in question are not considered a food, or edible, by the culture. Most objects in the world fall into this category, such as paper, pencils, rocks, and grass.

Disgust involves complex motivations. Disgusting entities are always rejected because of their nature or origin (ideational). However, they are virtually always thought to taste bad (distaste) by virtue of their ideational origin, and they are often perceived as dangerous. Disgust constitutes the strongest affective reaction to foods (for more on disgust in the food domain, see Rozin and Fallon 1987).

With respect to pleasure, note that two of the categories, distaste and disgust, involve negative reactions to the sensory properties of the foods, whereas the other two (danger and inappropriate) involve a more cognitively based rejection.

On the positive side, there are comparable categories, though the ideational categories have little import in most Western cultures. The major contrast is between good tastes and beneficials, the former being, once again, an example of sensory pleasure.

Of course, many foods do not fall neatly into one of these categories. Milk is both a good taste

and beneficial for most Americans. But many foods do fall naturally into one of the categories.

Context Dependence

Experimental psychology has generally adopted an abstractive, elementaristic approach to the analysis of phenomena, including pleasure. The interaction term of Analyses of Variance (ANOVAS) is the major concession to the fundamental gestalt ideas of contextual influence. Thus, in the history of studies of pleasure in the food domain, the work is dominated by the use of simple tastants in aqueous solution and rarely by combinations of these, or by more general contextual change. Yet, for any layperson, the roles of context in food pleasure are enormous, such that almost any food could be judged pleasant or not in some context. We divide contextual influences into three types: simultaneous internal, simultaneous external, and successive external (for a full discussion of context effects, see Rozin and Tuorila 1993).

Simultaneous Internal Context   The principal internal state related to pleasure interpretations of food is hunger. Cabanac (1971, 1985), in particular, has demonstrated that the pleasantness of simple food stimuli is a function of food deprivation (hunger). His concept of alliesthesia captures that idea: "A given stimulus can induce a pleasant or unpleasant sensation depending on the subject's internal state." Cabanac invokes this idea to account for the adaptive value of pleasure. There is minimal work on how hunger may differentially affect the pleasure of different foods. (Perhaps, for example, desserts are more resistant to hunger decrease than other types of foods.) Other internal states, such as nausea, clearly influence the hedonic evaluation of foods.

Simultaneous External Context   Events simultaneous with the experience of a target food stimulus have major effects on the reported hedonic value of that stimulus. There are a wide variety of taste or flavor interactions, internal as it were, to the target stimulus. These effects are sensory, perceptual, and cognitive and include taste interactions (Rozin and Tuorila 1993; Bartoshuk and Gent 1984) and culturally induced preferences (for example, salt taste is appropriate in some contexts [meats in the United States] and not in others [desserts in the United States]).

Construals of the nature and origin (ideational issues) of a potential food may dominate its sensory qualities. Subjects will rate the same odor as very unpleasant if they think it is from cat feces and as very pleasant if they think it comes from cheese. A buttermilk drinker will dislike the flavor and odor of what is construed as buttermilk if informed that it is actually spoiled milk (that is, spoiled in an unintentional way, as opposed to the intentional "spoiling" of buttermilk).

At the level of normal eating, where individual foods (spinach, or spinach soufflé) are the "units," there are a variety of cultural rules of "appropriateness" that determine acceptable (and hence pleasant) combinations. This idea has been developed by Howard Schutz (1989). Thus, in American culture, steak and ice cream are not eaten together and offer an unpleasant prospect. Similarly, occasions dictate the appropriateness of certain foods, so that for most Americans dry cereal is presumably liked more for breakfast than for dinner.

Successive External Context   There are two extremely important aspects of successive or temporal context. One refers to the recent food experience environment of a person. The other refers to the interplay of remembered, experienced, and anticipated pleasures.

As with sensory phenomena, there is a great deal of adaptation in sensory pleasure. Some of this stems directly from sensory adaptation, which is extensive in the olfactory and some of the oral somatosensory (for example, irritation) systems. In a sense, the sensory pleasure system is doubly sensitive to sequence; the receptor input itself shows adaptation, and the central processes that "generate" pleasure are also inclined to adapt or habituate and to be sensitive to temporal context. Pleasure systems, like sensory systems, tend to be sensitive to change and to adapt to baselines. Harry Helson's (1964) ideas about adaptation level apply here, particularly as modernized and formalized by Allen Parducci (1995). Parducci has shown that the strong tendencies of humans to adjust to baselines and distribute evaluations in accordance with the range and frequencies of experiences shown in sensory systems also hold for the hedonic/happiness dimensions.

However, range-frequency effects do not account for the simplest of all exposure sequences—repeated responses to the same stimulus. Here, adaptation or habituation seems to occur. At least under some conditions (including moderately palatable foods and frequent exposures over periods of minutes to hours), repeated exposures to an already familiar food produce a nonpermanent decline in liking for that food. This phenomenon, originally described in animals by David Katz (1937) and Jacques LeMagnen (1956), has been studied extensively in the laboratory, with human subjects, by Barbara Rolls and her colleagues (Rolls et al. 1986). It is appropriately called sensory-specific satiety. The effect is usually modest in size and has been measured in terms of both reduced intake and reduced ratings of liking. One reason that sensory-specific satiety is very sensitive to the particular local conditions is that it is opposed by another basic process, the mere exposure effect (discussed later in the chapter), which generally produces increased liking with exposure.

A second basic temporal contextual feature, observed in the food as well as other systems, is the affective primacy effect. Under an as-yet-unspecified range of conditions, other things being equal, two primacy relations may hold: the stimuli at the beginning of a sequence are more potent in overall hedonic effect than those same stimuli at the end; the earlier in a small set of food stimuli will yield a more positive hedonic response. Norman Anderson and Ann Norman (1964) read the names of six foods/dishes to subjects and asked them to rate their liking for a meal composed of these foods in the specified order. Subjects rated meals that began with three liked foods, followed by three disliked foods, higher than meals presented in the reverse order. In paired comparisons involving actual sampling of either food or beverage products, Michael Dean (1980) found, with an appropriately counterbalanced design, that the item sampled first tends to be preferred. The resilience and size of affective primacy effects in the food domain have yet to be determined.

My own experience in talking to eaters suggests

that scaling and framing effects are very important in determining the pleasures of consuming a specific dish or meal. For example, in establishing the range of judgment, people have framing options with respect to unusual experiences. Having had a superb experience of a great red wine, some find that the subsequent very good wines pale in quality; they have anchored their scale with a very rare and high-quality experience. Others seem able to frame such very special culinary experiences "out of bounds" and are not so negatively affected following a great experience.

Most of humanity consumes most of its foods in the form of meals. Meals are culturally prescribed eating bouts, and they often include multiple dishes. The order of dishes is often culturally prescribed. More than one dish may be available at any given point in a meal. If so, individuals have some options as to how to temporally structure their own meals. Thus, a survey of American college students (Rozin 1998) indicates that faced with a typical main course of two to four items, some people complete their favorite item first, then finish each of the other items in turn. Others also eat one food at a time, saving the best for last, and still others systematically rotate through the available foods. About half of the respondents do not subscribe to any of these patterns and report no habitual pattern of which they are aware. Each of these patterns presumably generates different experienced and remembered pleasure.

There has been very little research on the experienced pleasure of meals made up of diverse food items. John Rogozenski and Howard Moskowitz (1982) obtained ratings of five-course meals (on a questionnaire) and modeled them with some success from weighted ratings of the individual foods made on a different questionnaire. The issue of remembered utility (pleasure) for meals has not been addressed, nor has the issue of hedonic contrast within a series of sampled foods or a meal. Along the lines suggested by Kahneman's experimental hedonics, it would presumably be possible to arrange a meal sequence (both the order of dishes and the style of consumption) that would maximize remembered pleasure.

The domain of food and eating is dominated by remembered and anticipated pleasures. The dinner reservation at a fine restaurant is an opportunity to savor for weeks (or months—or years for Girardet!) an experience that will last but a few hours. And the memories of a great, distinctive meal last a lifetime and fuel the anticipation of a return to the same site. (Unfortunately, regression to the mean usually intervenes.) This is the other side of the nasty visit to the dentist's office, where a few seconds of experienced pain gives rise to mountains of anxious anticipation and negative memories that are bad out of proportion to the actual experience in the dentist's chair.

Furthermore, meals are social events, in which eating is typically interposed with conversation perhaps about sports and politics and the like in the United States, and more likely about the food itself and the pleasure it induces in France. We have recently documented major differences in attitudes to food and eating in the French versus Americans: Americans tend to worry that they will eat too much of a really good meal, and the French tend to just anticipate it positively (Rozin, Fischler, et al. in press). So the general social context of a meal and cultural attitudes to eating will also strongly influence the sensory pleasure induced by the food. And of course, when it comes to fine cuisine, the line between sensory pleasure and aesthetics is often blurred.

The Acquisition or Change of Hedonic Value of Foods

Acquisition of Likes (Good Tastes) and Dislikes (Distastes)   The catalog of innately liked tastes/flavors is very limited: there are biases toward liking sweet tastes and fatty textures, and biases toward avoiding irritation, bitterness, and strong tastes and flavors. In contrast to taste, the olfactory domain, while intensely "hedonic," comes with no innately hedonically valenced sensations (Bartoshuk 1991).

Almost everything an adult likes and dislikes is at least partly an acquired taste (distaste). What causes some things to become good tastes and others beneficials, or some things distastes and others dangers?

Research on acquired likes and dislikes focuses on humans because direct measures of pleasure can be obtained only from humans. However, principles borrowed from animal psychology, particularly the psychology of learning, have informed this work. Furthermore, the possibility of a parallel to human sensory pleasure in animals has allowed for tentative generalizations. The development of expressive facial/gestural measures of rat responses to food by Harvey Grill and Ralph Norgren (1978) provided a tool that licensed stronger inferences about experienced pleasure in laboratory animals.

The most robust procedure for producing hedonic change in humans emerged directly from studies of taste aversions in the animal laboratory. The pairing of a preferred taste with any of a variety of negative events, including X-radiation and nausea-inducing drugs, led to a robust aversion (decrease in preference). These phenomena were known in the animal literature for a long time before 1966, when the classic demonstrations of John Garcia and his colleagues showed that aversions were learned with a long delay between conditioned stimulus (CS) and unconditioned stimulus (US) (reviewed in Garcia, Hankins, and Rusiniak 1974). The animal literature alone could not demonstrate that conditioned taste aversions involve a hedonic change—that the food CS now "tasted bad," that is, was an acquired distaste.

A number of questionnaire studies on humans (initially by Garb and Stunkard 1974) demonstrated by retrospective report a parallel phenomenon in humans, in which it was clear that illness following a food (especially a novel food) led to an acquired distaste for the food. Subsequent laboratory experiments on humans (for example, Bernstein 1978) confirmed this.

The next two steps in establishing taste aversion learning as the quintessential example of experimentally induced hedonic change were taken by my student, Marcia Pelchat, in her doctoral dissertation. A retrospective questionnaire indicated that only USs that had a nausea component reliably produced acquired distastes. Other negative consequences following ingestion, such as lower gut problems, or allergy symptoms such as skin eruptions or respiratory distress produced dangers (that is, avoidance), but not distastes (figure 6.2) (Pelchat and Rozin 1982). Nausea appeared to be the magic bullet that produced distastes.

This analysis was extended to laboratory rats, using Grill and Norgren's (1978) analysis of facial and bodily gestures associated with consumption of bitter and other aversive solutions. Assuming that these expressions indicated distaste, Pelchat and her collaborators (1983) monitored these responses in rats after Pavlovian pairings of sweet tastes with a variety of USs. The results were extremely clear, and very supportive of the nausea-distaste link. Sweet avoidance responses produced with intragastric lithium chloride, a substance that produces nausea in animals and humans, reliably induce aversion gestures (such as a gape) when the CS solution is offered post-conditioning. Strong avoidance (danger categorization) but rare aversion expressions occur when the US is either electric shock to the foot or intragastric lactose, which produces lower rather than upper gut dis-

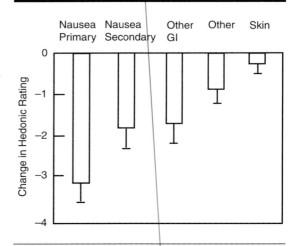

FIGURE 6.2   Relation of Human Taste Aversions to Negative Events

Source: Pelchat and Rozin 1982, 345.

Notes: Taste aversions in humans as a function of type of negative event. Subjects self-reported on experiences in which ingestion of a food was followed by a negative event. The food in question was rated on a 1 (extremely unpleasant) to 9 (extremely pleasant) scale for before and after the event. Subjects also indicated features of the negative event, designating one of these as the primary feature. The mean change in liking (rating-after minus rating-before) is presented as a function of type of negative event. Negative events are characterized, on the abscissa, as "Nausea primary" (nausea or vomiting is the primary feature), "Nausea secondary" (nausea or vomiting is a nonprimary feature), "Other GI" (gastrointestinal symptoms other than nausea or vomiting are primary), "Other" (items that did not fit in any of the other categories, such as respiratory distress, cardiovascular problems, systemic shock, or reception of very upsetting news, such as the death of a loved one), and "Skin" (skin symptoms, usually allergenic, such as rashes).

tress (figure 6.3) (for related findings see Parker 1982).

These nausea "magic bullet" experiments establish a Pavlovian pathway for hedonic change. The change is dramatic, occurs in one trial, and is the best experimental and real-world example of acquired hedonic change. Our recent evidence indicates that for both human taste aversions and phobias (with frightening USs) there are many occasions when the appropriate pairings occur in real life but hedonic changes do not occur (Rozin, Wrzesniewski, and Byrnes 1998). We do not yet know what contextual conditions promote or retard this type of hedonic change, but the novelty of the CS is surely important.

A second problem raised by the taste aversion studies has to do with the adaptive value of hedonic change, and of hedonic responses them-

FIGURE 6.3   Orofacial Responses of Poisoned Rats to Sucrose: Relation of Taste Aversions in Rats to Negative Events

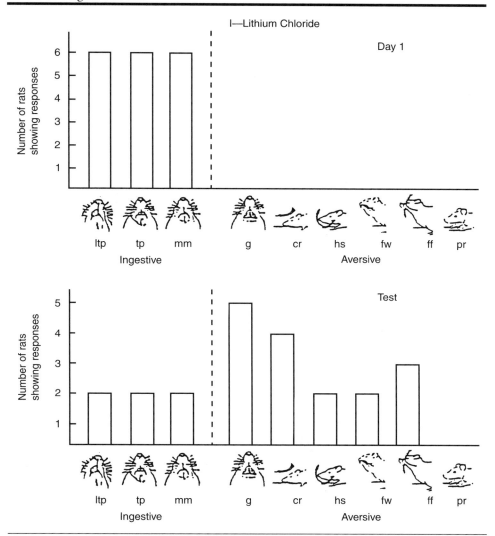

Source: Pelchat, Grill, Rozin, and Jacobs (1983). Copyright 1983 the American Psychological Association.

Notes: Orofacial responses of rats before and after exposure to pairings between sucrose ingestion and one of three negative events: (I) intragastric lithium chloride (LiCl) believed to induce nausea; (II) electric shock; (III) intragastric intubation of lactose, which induces lower gastrointestinal symptoms (such as cramps in humans) and diarrhea, but little nausea. Graphs show the number of rats (five or six per group, as indicated) who display the indicated behavior. The three positive followed by six negative orofacial responses are designated on the abscissa. ltp = lateral tongue protrusions, tp = tongue protrusions, mm = mouth movements, g = gape, cr = chin rub, hs = head shaking, fw = face washing, ff = forelimb flailing, pr = paw rubbing.

(*Figure continued on p. 122.*)

selves. Nausea USs lead to hedonic changes, and most other USs do not. Why? What is the adaptive value of endowing nausea with a qualitatively different (hedonic) change as opposed to other events including gut pain? We don't know and suspect that the answer to this question may tell us something about the functions of hedonic systems.

Taste aversions are an example of Pavlovian procedures that induce hedonic change. The general process has been called evaluative conditioning. It

FIGURE 6.3   *Continued*

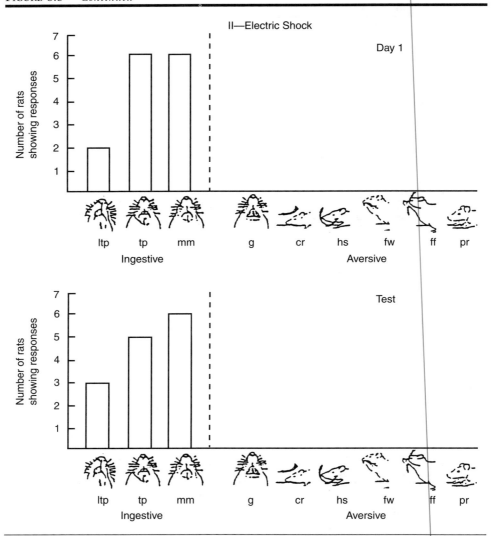

was originally described and named as a laboratory phenomenon by Irene Martin and A. B. Levey (1978), using visual stimuli of neutral and negative or positive valence as CSs and USs, respectively. Evaluative conditioning has been studied systematically by a group of Belgian psychologists under the leadership of Frank Baeyens. Both positive and negative evaluative conditioning have been demonstrated, using visual (Baeyens et al. 1988, 1991), olfactory (Todrank et al. 1995), and taste/flavor stimuli (Zellner et al. 1983; Baeyens et al. 1990; for a review of Pavlovian conditioning with respect to changes in food preferences, see Rozin and Zellner 1985).

Taste aversion learning seems somewhat atypical of other examples of evaluative conditioning. It occurs very rapidly, is a robust effect, and is not strongly resistant to extinction. Evaluative conditioning usually requires multiple trials, is a modest-sized effect, and is surprisingly resistant to extinction (Baeyens et al. 1988, 1991). In the food domain, aside from nausea-based taste aversions, the two major evaluative conditioning effects demonstrated prior to 1995 were increases in liking for flavors paired with a sugar US (Zellner et al. 1983) and decreases in liking for flavors paired with a disliked US (Baeyens et al. 1990).

Evaluative conditioning is one of the two well-documented models of hedonic change for foods and other stimuli. It is very likely that many common acquired likes, such as for coffee, occur

FIGURE 6.3 *Continued*

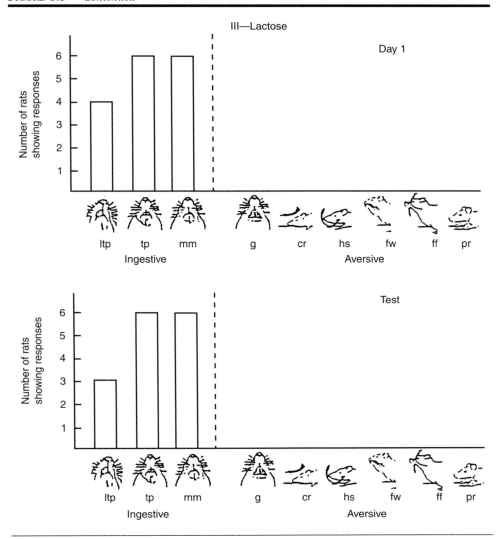

through a procedure like evaluative conditioning. When first introduced, coffee is often made very sweet, and the strong taste is softened with milk or cream. For many people, after many such experiences, the coffee flavor alone becomes liked, in the absence of milk or sugar.

Internal USs (such as relief of hunger) also function in evaluative conditioning (although we all know many highly nutritive foods that we don't like). There are surprisingly few studies on humans of satiation-induced liking, but David Booth and his collaborators have produced one empirical demonstration of enhanced liking, when the sub-

ject is trained and tested hungry, for a flavor associated with substantial caloric repletion (Booth, Mather, and Fuller 1982).

In the real world, it is likely that the most powerful US is social, perhaps the appearance of a respected other enjoying (or detesting) a particular event or food. Recently, Baeyens and his colleagues (Baeyens et al. 1996) have reported the first laboratory demonstration of a hedonic shift with a social US. Adult subjects watched videotapes in which a demonstrator person sampled various beverages in distinctive glasses and indicated pleasure or displeasure facially. Beverages varied in color, and the glass shapes also varied. One of the glass shapes (with or without a "foot") was contingently paired with expressed pleasure, the other with expressed displeasure. Subjects showed a relative increase in liking for the glass shape paired with the pleasure expression. This is just the beginning of what should be some major investigations of hedonic shift in a social Pavlovian framework. Sylvan Tomkins (1963) raises the interesting possibility that observations of emotional expressions in others induces the parallel emotion in the observer. This internal representation can then serve as the US for evaluative conditioning.

The second well-documented mechanism for hedonic shift is mere exposure, a phenomenon that occurs in both animals and humans. As Robert Zajonc (1968) has forcefully shown from research covering a wide domain of stimuli and situations, exposure, in and of itself, tends to promote liking. This is a modest-sized effect that operates over a broad range of stimuli and conditions. It is limited by boredom effects resulting from high levels of exposure and/or very frequent exposure, but the basic effect is substantial and important (for a recent review of conditions that increase or reduce mere exposure effects, see Bornstein 1989). Mere exposure effects have been demonstrated in the laboratory with foods by Patricia Pliner (1982) and Leann Birch and Diane Marlin (1982), among others.

There are no doubt other pathways to hedonic change in the food domain, but none have been well documented. A variety of possible channels of social influence, besides Pavlovian conditioning, are likely to produce changes. Prominent among these are perceptions that respected others like or dislike a food, or value it in some other way (for reviews, see Birch 1987; Rozin and Vollmecke 1986). The literature in social psychology on intrinsic value (for example, Lepper 1983; Deci and Ryan 1985) offers evidence about what promotes and deters hedonic change. According to the "minimal sufficiency" principle, overt reward for consumption of a food may ultimately decrease the liking for it, while more subtle approval may promote liking or discourage a decrease in liking. Applications of this idea to the food domain have been reported (see, for example, Birch et al. 1982).

The Acquisition of Disgust   The aversion to disgusting entities is based on ideational factors. We might find a food quite tasty and then, hearing that it was seal meat, find the taste repulsive. Because disgust is so strong and specific, it offers the prospect of being a natural arena in which to discover some general principles of hedonic shift (Rozin and Fallon 1987). Disgusting entities are so powerful that they are contaminants: contact between a disgusting item and an otherwise edible item renders that item inedible, and disgusting. Thus, one way to transfer negative affect to an object is to touch it to an already disgusting object. This affective route is captured in the sympathetical magical law of contagion, "once in contact, always in contact" (for a review, see Rozin and Nemeroff 1990).

Feces is a universal disgust substance. This reaction seems to be acquired, perhaps at least in part in the process of toilet training. It may be that affective displays by parents and others in the presence of feces help to endow feces with its powerful negative affective properties, but we really do not know how this process occurs. Disgust, as a powerful negative-affective force, becomes a principal instrument of socialization; a very effective way to enforce a cultural prohibition is to make the act or object disgusting.

Disgust is also a quintessential example of an affective-cognitive link, in which a cognition (for example, of a particular origin) produces a major hedonic shift. Discovery of the contents of an attractive-looking food morsel, or of the way a food animal was killed, can rapidly generate disgust.

We have been exploring some of these hedonic shifts in the context of the emergence of vegetarianism. It seems that disgust toward meat is promoted if a person holds to the immorality of killing animals, as opposed to the position that meat is just unhealthy (Rozin, Markwith, and Stoess 1997). That is, the involvement of a negative moral issue promotes the development of disgust, and disgust may further reinforce the negative moral response. Indeed, cross-culturally, disgust is an emotion that represents what the culture in question finds to be offensive. In the frame of pre-adaptation discussed earlier, disgust provides a prime example of how a food rejection system becomes co-opted and released by a wide range of meanings and elicitors, including death and a variety of moral violations (Rozin, Haidt, and McCauley 1993; Rozin, Haidt, et al. 1997).

The Reversal of Innate Aversions   Human beings frequently, and uniquely, come to like objects and situations that innately give rise to fear or aversion. Roller-coaster riding and sad or horror movies are salient instances. The food domain is replete with examples: innately aversive oral experiences such as coffee, beer, spirits, wine, tobacco, high levels of salt, carbonated beverages, and irritant spices (for example, chili pepper, black pepper, ginger) are among the most preferred foods and drinks on the planet. The irritant and bitter (or other strong) properties of these foods successfully deter other mammals from ingesting them, but humans have found pleasure where others find pain.

Hedonic reversals may be particularly informative, since the hedonic changes that occur are so large. There are almost no good examples of acquisition of likes for innately unpalatable substances in any nonhuman mammal. Extensive exposure of rats, in the food context, to either bitter tastes (Warren and Pfaffman 1958) or irritant sensations, such as chili pepper (Rozin, Gruss, and Berk 1979) does not induce a positive preference, or even any permanent reduction of aversion. Unlike their human owners, the animals in a Mexican village who regularly eat chili pepper on food in the garbage do not come to like it (reviewed in Rozin 1990). The only positive cases (presented and reviewed in Rozin and Kennel 1983) are a few pet primates and one pet dog, all of whom consumed "hot" food in the company of humans and developed actual likes for piquant foods.

We initiated studies of the acquisition of a liking for chili pepper as an example of hedonic reversal (reviewed in Rozin 1990). Chili pepper seemed like a good model system, since chili peppers are the most widely consumed spice in the world (well over one billion eager users), and they are neither harmful nor addictive, unlike some other innately unpalatable foods.

The situation, in brief, is as follows (for more details, see Rozin 1990). Chili peppers contain a set of chemicals called capsaicins, which cause irritation of mucus membranes; they cause pain. The peppers are actually harmless; the irritation is a sensory phenomenon, and any tissue damage that results from high levels of capsaicin on a sensitive surface results not directly from the stimulus but from the body's response to it.

The oral irritation produced by chilies is innately aversive. The evidence indicates that those who come to like chili pepper receive roughly the same neural signal from their mouths as those who do not. That is, the change is not peripheral; the same central input, once judged to be negative and painful, becomes pleasant after some substantial experience, often spreading over months or years. It is the very same sensory features of irritation that initially promote rejection, that later become attractive.

The strength of the attraction to the trigeminally mediated oral irritation experience is indicated by the wholesale adoption of chili peppers, especially in tropical Africa and Asia, when these became available after the discovery of the Americas by the European explorers of the fifteenth and sixteenth centuries.

Mexican children come to like the burn of chilies sometime between four and seven years of age. This happens rather naturally in the course of eating with their families, observing their older family members eating and enjoying chilies and being offered mildly seasoned foods by their parents (Rozin and Schiller 1980). The hedonic reversal associated with chili pepper is "surface-specific." Getting to like the burn in one's mouth does not cause one to like the burn in one's eyes. We do not know whether exposure of only one part of the mouth to chili pepper would cause only that part to "like it."

The mechanism of the chili pepper hedonic reversal (or any other reversal) is not known. Mere exposure, evaluative conditioning, and a variety of social conditions already cited as promoting liking are present. But there are two other mechanisms of the hedonic reversal that require, as a precondition, an initial aversion.

First is the idea of opponent processes (Solomon 1980). According to this attractive view, the body achieves homeostasis, in part, by canceling out any departure from an optimal position (an A process) by generating an opposite, countervailing departure (B process). The opponent concept is embellished with three additional assumptions: (1) with exercise, the B process becomes larger in magnitude; (2) with exercise, the B process shows a more rapid onset and a much longer time course, which extends well beyond the termination of the stimulus-bound A process; (3) the changes described in (1) and (2) occur only when the A process is reinstigated before the prior B process has disappeared. The dynamics of the system are illustrated in figure 6.4. Solomon uses opiate addiction as a model system. By the opponent analysis, tolerance occurs because the building B process reduces the effect of the A process (assumption 1). Withdrawal follows from the second assumption; as the A process dissipates, what remains is a large, sluggish B process, which produces symptoms opposite to those induced by the A process.

The opponent model is about more than hedonic change, but it certainly encompasses hedonic change. For the case of chili peppers, the pain discomfort of the oral burn is the A process,

FIGURE 6.4   Opponent Process Theory

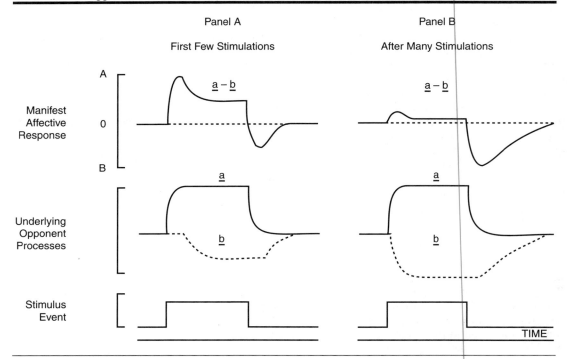

Panel A

First Few Stimulations

Panel B

After Many Stimulations

Manifest
Affective
Response

Underlying
Opponent
Processes

Stimulus
Event

TIME

Source: Solomon 1980, 700. Copyright 1980 the American Psychological Association.
Notes: Schematic representation of opponent process theory. Panel A represents the balance of A and B responses for the first few exposures. Panel B represents the A and B responses after repeated exposures. The manifest response is the summation of the two underlying processes.

and a hypothetical compensating "pleasure" B process is generated in the brain. Over many experiences, the B process would come to dominate the A process. (In the original model, it was not assumed that the B process can dominate the A process while the A process is near its peak.) Thus, pain becomes pleasure, and there is a pleasant afterglow. The opponent model tracks the process of getting to like chili pepper rather well. However, there is minimal evidence for the opponent processes model other than that it tracks the sequence of either opiate addiction or chili liking. For example, there are no signs of a positive afterglow (B process) following an early negative hedonic experience with chili pepper (Rozin, Ebert, and Schull 1982).

The opponent model stands as an interesting, unproven account of hedonic changes. A second version of the hypothesis, put forth by Siegel (1977) and Schull (1979), holds that the B process, rather than being an innately determined part of the system, is a conditioned compensatory response. Siegel has accumulated evidence for the existence of such compensatory conditioning processes in drug addiction in both rats and humans.

Either opponent model requires multiple experiences in order to generate the full-blown opponent response. Normally when one encounters a hedonically negative situation, one subsequently avoids it. The multiple experiences, for drug addiction or chili use, are created by social pressures (from addicted companions or family members, respectively). Why else would one continue to assault one's mouth with something that burns?

For the case of chili pepper and other initially painful experiences, it is natural to assume that the B process is instantiated by the secretion of brain endorphins. Oversecretion of these, as a result of the augmenting B process, would be a natural channel for converting pain to pleasure. We have tried to demonstrate such effects with chili pepper, but with results that are only suggestive (see discussion in Rozin 1990).

The final model for hedonic reversal is what we call benign masochism (Rozin and Schiller 1980; Rozin 1990). It holds that the whole range of human pleasures that derive from negative emotions or aversions is based directly upon the experience of negative sensations and experiences. We may come to enjoy our body's negative responses to situations when we realize that there is no, or minimal, actual danger. In the case of the roller coaster, our body is scared, and sympathetically activated, but we know we are safe. Similarly for our crying in sad movies, and the burn we feel with chili pepper. Our mouth is saying, "Get this out of here," but we know it is safe. This type of enjoyment of constrained risk is related to Zuckerman's (1979) sensation-seeking. One appeal of the benign masochism model—mind-over-matter or -body model—is that it is the only one that neatly explains why hedonic reversals are common in humans but very rare in animals. (Can you imagine cats lining up to get on roller coasters or to do recreational parachute jumping?) The evidence for this model, in the domain of chili pepper, is that (1) the peak burn intensity preference for chili likers is often just below the level they claim is overtly painful and negative, and (2) many chili likers enjoy the body's defensive reaction to high levels of chili pepper: sweating, nose running, and eyes tearing (Rozin 1990).

Daniel Berlyne (1971) suggests a similar account for the many human hedonic reversals, or what I call the human proclivity to "play with fire." He assembles some quotes from major thinkers on this point. A. Doring (1890) suggests that there is pleasure in the inhibition of an aversion system, and that it is one of the properties of aesthetic systems. Closest to the mark of benign masochism is Edmund Burke's (1757) account of the sublime: "When we have an idea of pain and danger, without being actually in such circumstances" (quoted in Berlyne 1971, 94). Immanuel Kant (1790/1966) contributes a similar idea: the dynamically sublime "must be represented as exciting fear." It is identified as "might that has no dominion over us." Kant explains further that "there accompanies the reception of an object as sublime a pleasure, which is only possible through the medium of pain" (quoted in Berlyne 1971, 94). We presume that if there is truth in these accounts, it may be limited to *Homo sapiens*. They may all be linked to our enjoyment of arousal, within limits (Berlyne 1971).

PRINCIPLES OF PLEASURE: A COMPARISON OF THE DOMAINS OF FOOD AND MUSIC

We can agree that:

1. Pleasure is a subjective (mental) experience.
2. Pleasure is a salient part of mental life.

3. Pleasure has a motivating function: we seek to maintain it or induce it, and to avoid its "opposite," pain.
4. Pleasures exist in three temporal frames: remembered, experienced, and anticipated.
5. There is something in common (at least items 1 through 4) for all the pleasures we experience, from a very wide domain of elicitors and activities.
6. There are at least three types of pleasures: sensory, aesthetic, and mastery.

Now we shall consider differences between two very different types of pleasures.

Differences Between Food and Music as Pleasures

Even for elaborated culinary experiences, the pleasures of food have a sensory quality, a palatability. We experience the pleasure as coming from the mouth, even as some of the experiences we have result from "palate training." Many of the pleasures of eating seem to involve little cognitive processing.

The pleasures of music are not localizable. They are not in our ear; they are generally not like the soothing sound of ocean waves at the shore. Stimulus "analysis" seems to be much more a part of music appreciation than of food appreciation. Chocolate and Mozart are not equally complex, and they are not complex in the same way. In the terminology proposed by Kubovy (this volume), chocolate is a pleasure of the body, and music a pleasure of the mind.

The most psychologically appealing account of the enjoyment of music comes from Leonard Meyer (1956). He holds an implication/realization model. As we listen to Mozart, we internalize the stylistic structure, develop expectations for the music, and get pleasure when they are realized. Until we have sufficient exposure to get a sense of the style, we cannot fully enjoy the music. On the other hand, a new piece of a familiar style fits our expectations in general but violates them in detail. It is the partial match that is pleasurable, and the lack of a complete match that keeps us from being bored. William Gaver and George Mandler (1987) build on Meyer's formulation, placing relatively more emphasis on the development of schemas of the musical structure, and less attention than Meyer on the importance of innate gestalt principles in providing the structure. Gaver and Mandler argue that discrepancy between the music and the schema is arousing, and that when this discrepancy is rather small and resolvable, there is the pleasure of a match energized by the arousal produced by the slight mismatch.

There is a serious problem with the Meyer formulation. Why do we continue to enjoy the same piece of music year after year? We know what is going to happen; we don't have expectations, we have knowledge. Meyer handles this problem in two ways: (1) in different performances, the music is actually subtly different; (2) because memory is less than perfect, we still get expectation/realization pleasure after many hearings. A much more satisfactory solution, and one that is of great psychological interest, comes from Meyer's former student, Eugene Narmour (1991).

Narmour holds that there are a set of innate expectations for sequences of auditory inputs. For example, we expect patterns to continue (a reasonable assumption about the world). We expect repetitions to continue, and we expect rising short intervals to be followed by more rising intervals. However, we expect a large change in tonality to be followed by a "corrective" movement, headed toward the original note. Narmour holds that these innate expectations are unbidden and unchangeable. This bottom-up expectation system has superimposed upon it a top-down, acquired style expectation system of the sort Meyer postulated. The result is that modest violations of innate expectations by composers continue to produce the arousal or tension that prevents boredom. And it is this tension resolution that would seem to be at least some of the source of the aesthetic pleasure of music. Such a formulation does not seem to capture anything of the pleasures of eating, even in the most exalted culinary contexts.

Appreciation of the spatial and temporal array of sensations produced by an excellent dish or wine requires experience, directed attention, and some familiarity and expectation with respect to the genre. Sensory pleasures can be complex and can seep into the cognitive domain. But the trained palate, it would seem, does not produce its pleasure principally by expectation and realization. Note that exquisite culinary experiences can well be assigned to aesthetic pleasures, but not to the same root cause as musical aesthetic pleasures. There seems, in the extremes, to be a qualitative difference between the pleasure derived from chocolate, building on a complex interplay of some innately pleasant textural, aromatic, and taste sensations, and the pleasure of Mozart. The Mozart is made up of sound "units" of no particular appeal; it is all in the sequence. But, of course, chocolate may be a poor representative of foods; it offers complexity but has innate appeal. Perhaps wine, an acquired taste, is a better example. Even

here, however, though the pleasures may be aesthetic in some sense, they are tightly tied to the exact form of the stimulus.

The pleasures of the wine connoisseur and the lover of Mozart probably both include a touch of mastery pleasure (described as virtuosity by Kubovy, this volume)—the realization through experience, in both cases, of a rich structure of harmonies and sequences. The wine or music grows in appeal, perhaps from an initially unpleasant response. The Narmour bottom-up and top-down view parallels the benign masochism account of reversing innate aversions. In both cases, the accounts posit an interplay and opposition between an innate system that cannot be denied and an acquired, more sophisticated system that reinterprets or reevaluates.

Imagine a Mozartian symphony of sensations played out in the mouth, or on the skin. A gustatory theme, followed by systematic variations of the temporal sequence, tempo, and sensation qualities. Could this result in the type of aesthetic pleasure that we experience in music? We could surely mimic some of the structure of music. It may be that specifics of the auditory system, particularly tonality and the relations built into it, are essential for the type of structure that gives rise to the musical experience. Perhaps it is the fundamentally and deeply sequential nature of auditory input, illustrated so well in language, with the many brain adaptations to process it, that form a precondition for the musical aesthetic experience. An alternative account of pleasures of the mind (Kubovy, this volume) focuses on the necessary condition of an experience of a sequence of emotions. This criterion has much to recommend it but, like those offered here, founders on the classification of pleasures such as those derived from massage, wine, or the complex change of sensations of temperature, taste, texture, and flavor that accompany consuming a bite of ice cream.

We do not know whether a subtle aesthetic appreciation of food could ever be established in a nonhuman. Similarly, there is no evidence for an acquired liking for music in any nonhuman, in contrast to the ubiquity of music and musical pleasure in humans. We have no idea what the adaptive value of listening to music is. One possibility is that the enjoyment of music is a by-product of an organism built to be motivated to detect structure in the world, a clearly adaptive feature.

We can tentatively conclude that the aesthetic pleasures of music and the usually more sensory pleasures of food differ considerably in those processes that mediate between perception and the ultimate pleasure experience. However, a sense of mastery may intrude into both experiences, sometimes nurtured by rising above an initial bewildered or aversive response to the stimulus.

Some Preliminary Principles of Pleasure

In this section, I offer a very preliminary set of principles about pleasure that may characterize sensory pleasures. If sensory pleasures are a model for others, such possible principles may have a wider domain.

1. Sensory pleasure (especially culinary and sexual) is extremely context-dependent. The context includes both the internal and the external (including social) environment.
2. In general, high levels of stimulation are negative, and often, middle levels are most pleasing. This probably links directly to the "Wundt curve," suggesting maximal hedonic effect for moderate levels of arousal.
3. Most sensory pleasure is experienced in the remembered or anticipated domains, as opposed to the online (experienced) domain.
4. Remembered pleasure departs from experienced pleasure and is much more sensitive to state changes. Thus, remembered pleasures show duration neglect and overemphasis on peaks, onset, and offset (Kahneman, Wakker, and Sarin 1997). There are probably also major order effects.
5. There are many positive-negative asymmetries:
   a. the body surface provides most of the positive hedonic inputs and many of the negative inputs.
   b. The body interior provides almost exclusively negative inputs.
   c. Most hedonically tinged sensory inputs are positive, but the negative inputs may be more salient.
6. Familiarity and complexity play important roles in adaptation and habituation to stimulation, but parts of the sensory pleasure system, especially those having to do with pain and some positive skin sensations, show remarkably little hedonic habituation.
7. Combinations of sensory pleasures do not obey any simple, hedonic algebra. This may result from large temporal context effects, limited attention, and specific interactions. As Duncker (1941) points out, it is not clear what we would even want to say about the pleasure of listening to Beethoven while eating our favorite food (and having a massage).
8. There is a large effect of experience on sensory pleasures. Hedonic shifts and reversals are common, and they may be very localized, so that only one patch of skin shows a change even though the effects are surely not at the periphery.

Preadaptation: Pleasure from Sugar to Mozart

I began this chapter with the suggestion that the various hedonic experiences are important and puzzling from a functional point of view. I suggested that the subjective and expressive side of the hedonic system may be quite similar across the different types of pleasures: sensory, aesthetic, and mastery. The principle of preadaptation suggests that the subjective and expressive system that originated for sensory pleasures is co-opted as the output system for the more complex mastery and aesthetic pleasures. Whatever the function and advantages of a salient subjective representation of sensory pleasures, the representation is there and can serve the same functions for more elaborated pleasures. This "model," then, holds for conservatism of the output side, with an expanding range and complexity of elicitors.

If this is so, then one can make some predictions about the neural representation of the various pleasures. In particular, one might predict that these very different types of pleasures (viewed from the input side) funnel together somewhere into a common neural substrate. A common neurochemical mediator, in the endorphin and/or dopamine systems, might be implicated. If that were true, and the phylogenetic and ontogenetic priority of the sensory pleasure system could be demonstrated, then the preadaptation and accessibility hypothesis would have much more force.

The preparation of this chapter was supported by a National Institutes of Drug Abuse (NIDA) grant (R21–DA10858–0). Thanks to Daniel Kahneman for helpful comments.

REFERENCES

Anderson, N. H., and Norman, N. (1964). Order effects in impression formation in four classes of stimuli. *Journal of Abnormal and Social Psychology, 69,* 467–71.

Aristotle. (1965). *De anima.* Translated by R. D. Hicks. New York: Putnam.

Aristotle. (1934). *Nicomachean ethics,* Translated by H. Rackham. Cambridge, Mass.: Harvard University Press.

Babbitt, I. (1936). *The Dhammapada.* Translated from the Pali with an essay on Buddha and the Occident. New York: New Directions.

Baeyens, F., Crombez, G., van den Bergh, O., and

Eelen, P. (1988). Once in contact always in contact: Evaluative conditioning is resistant to extinction. *Advances in Behaviour Research and Therapy, 10* (4), 179–99.

Baeyens, F., Eelen, P., van den Bergh, O., and Crombez, G. (1990). Flavor-flavor and color-flavor conditioning in humans. *Learning and Motivation, 21,* 434–55.

———. (1991). Human evaluative conditioning: Acquisition trials, presentation schedule, evaluative style, and contingency awareness. *Behaviour Research and Therapy, 30,* 133–42.

Baeyens, F., Kaes, B., Eelen, P., and Silverans, P. (1996). Observational evaluative conditioning of an embedded stimulus element. *European Journal of Social Psychology, 26,* 15–28.

Barker, L. M. (1982). *The psychobiology of human food selection.* Westport, Conn.: AVI.

Bartoshuk, L. M. (1991). Taste, smell, and pleasure. In R. C. Bolles (Ed.), *The hedonics of taste* (pp. 15–28). Hillsdale, N.J.: Erlbaum.

Bartoshuk, L. M., and Gent, J. F. (1984). Taste mixtures: An analysis of synthesis. In *Taste, olfaction, and the central nervous system* (pp. 210–32). New York: Rockefeller University Press.

Beebe-Center, J. G. (1932). *The psychology of pleasantness and unpleasantness.* New York: Van Nostrand.

Bentham, J. (1948). *Principles of morals and legislation.* New York: Hafner. (Originally published in 1789)

Berlyne, D. E. (1971). *Aesthetics and psychobiology.* New York: Appleton-Century-Crofts.

Bernstein, I. L. (1978). Learned taste aversions in children receiving chemotherapy. *Science, 200,* 1302–3.

Berridge, K. C., & Grill, H. J. (1983). Alternating ingestive and aversive consummatory responses suggest a two-dimensional analysis of palatability in rats. *Behavioral Neuroscience, 97,* 221–31.

Birch, L. L. (1987). The acquisition of food acceptance patterns in children. In R. Boakes, D. Popplewell, and M. Burton (Eds.), *Eating habits* (pp. 107–30). Chichester, Eng.: Wiley.

Birch, L. L., Birch, D., Marlin, D. W., and Kramer, L. (1982). Effects of instrumental eating on children's food preferences. *Appetite, 3,* 125–34.

Birch, L. L., and Marlin, D. W. (1982). I don't like it; I never tried it: Effects of exposure on two-year-old children's food preferences. *Appetite, 3,* 77–80.

Blundell, J. (1980). Hunger, appetite, and satiety: Constructions in search of identities. In M. Turner (Ed.), *Nutrition and life style* (pp. 21–41). London: Applied Sciences Publishers.

Bock, W. J. (1959). Preadaptation and multiple evolutionary pathways. *Evolution, 13,* 194–211.

Booth, D. A. (1994). *Psychology of nutrition.* London: Taylor & Frances.

Booth, D. A., Mather, P., and Fuller, J. (1982). Starch content of ordinary foods associatively conditions human appetite and satiation, indexed by intake and eating pleasantness of starch-paired flavors. *Appetite, 3,* 163–84.

Bornstein, R. F. (1989). Exposure and affect: Overview and meta-analysis of research, 1968–1987. *Psychological Bulletin, 106,* 265–89.

Burke, E. A. (1757). *A philosophical inquiry into the origin of our ideas of the sublime and beautiful.* London: Dodsley.

Cabanac, M. (1971). Physiological role of pleasure. *Science, 173,* 1103–7.

———. (1985). Preferring for pleasure. *American Journal of Clinical Nutrition, 42,* 1151–55.

Capaldi, E. D. (Ed.). (1996). *Why we eat what we eat: The psychology of eating.* Washington, D.C.: American Psychological Association.

Cardello, A. (1996). The role of the human senses in food acceptance. In H. L. Meiselman and H. J. H. MacFie (Eds.), *Food choice, acceptance, and consumption* (pp. 1–82). London: Blackie Academic and Professional.

Dean, M. L. (1980). Presentation order effects in product taste tests. *Journal of Psychology, 105,* 107–10.

Deci, E. L., and Ryan, R. M. (1985). *Intrinsic motivation and self-determination in human behavior.* New York: Plenum Press.

Doring, A. (1890). Die aesthetischen Gefuhle. *Zeitschrift fur die Psychologie der Sinnesorgane, 1,* 161–86.

Drewnowski, A., and Greenwood, M. R. C. (1983). Cream and sugar: Human preferences for high-fat foods. *Physiology and Behavior, 30,* 629–33.

Duncker, K. (1941). On pleasure, emotion, and striving. *Philosophy and Phenomenological Research, 1,* 391–430.

Elster, J., and Loewenstein, G. (1992). Utility from memory and anticipation. In G. Loewenstein and J. Elster (Eds.), *Choice over time* (pp. 213–34). New York: Russell Sage Foundation.

Fallon, A. E., and Rozin, P. (1983). The psychological bases of food rejections by humans. *Ecology of Food and Nutrition, 13,* 15–26.

Frederickson, B. L., and Kahneman, D. (1993). Duration neglect in retrospective evaluation of affective episodes. *Journal of Personality and Social Psychology, 65,* 45–55.

Garb, J., and Stunkard, A. J. (1974). Taste aversions in man. *American Journal of Psychiatry, 131,* 1204–7.

Garcia, J., Hankins, W. G., and Rusiniak, K. W. (1974). Behavioral regulation of the *milieu interne* in man and rat. *Science, 185,* 824–31.

Gaver, W. W., and Mandler, G. (1987). Play it again, Sam: On liking music. *Cognition and Emotion, 1,* 259–82.

Grill, H. J., and Norgren, R. (1978). The taste reactivity test: I. Oro-facial responses to gustatory stimuli in neurologically normal rats. *Brain Research, 143,* 263–79.

Helson, H. (1964). *Adaptation-level theory.* New York: Harper and Row.

Kahneman, D., Fredrickson, B. L., Schreiber, C. A., and Redelmeier, D. A. (1993). When more pain is preferred to less: Adding a better end. *Psychological Science, 4,* 401–5.

Kahneman, D., and Snell, J. (1992). Predicting a change in taste: Do people know what they will like? *Journal of Behavioral Decision Making, V,* 187–200.

Kahneman, D., Wakker, P. P., and Sarin, R. (1997). Back to Bentham? Explorations of experienced utility. *Quarterly Journal of Economics, 112,* 375–405.

Kant, I. (1914). *Critique of judgment.* Translated by F. M. Miller. London: Macmillan. (Originally published in German, 1790).

Katz, D. (1937). *Animals and men: Studies in comparative psychology.* London: Longmans.

Lakoff, G., and Johnson, M. (1980). *Metaphors we live by.* Chicago: University of Chicago Press.

LeMagnen, J. (1956). Hyperphagie provoquée chez le rat blanc par altération du mécanisme de satiété périphérique. *Comptes Rendus Societé de Biologie, 150,* 32.

Lepper, M. R. (1983). Social control processes and the internalization of social values: An attributional perspective. In E. T. Higgins, D. N. Ruble, and W. W. Hartup (Eds.), *Social cognition and social development* (pp. 294–330). New York: Cambridge University Press.

Levey, A. B., and Martin, I. (1983). Cognitions, evaluations, and conditioning: Rules of sequence and rules of consequence. *Advances in Behavior Research and Therapy, 4,* 181–95.

Martin, I., and Levey, A. B. (1978). Evaluative conditioning. *Advances in Behavior Research and Therapy, 1,* 57–102.

Mayr, E. (1960). The emergence of evolutionary novelties. In S. Tax (Ed.), *Evolution after Darwin,* vol. 1, *The evolution of life* (pp. 349–82). Chicago: University of Chicago Press.

Meiselman, H. L. (1996). The contextual basis for food acceptance, food choice, and food intake: The food, the situation, and the individual. In H. L. Meiselman and H. J. H. MacFie (Eds.), *Food choice, acceptance, and consumption* (pp. 239–63). London: Blackie Academic and Professional.

Meiselman, H. L. and MacFie, H. J. H. (Eds.). (1996). *Food choice, acceptance, and consumption.* London: Blackie Academic and Professional.

Meyer, L. (1956). *Emotion and meaning in music.* Chicago: University of Chicago Press.

Narmour, E. (1991). The top-down and bottom-up systems of musical implication: Building on Meyer's theory of emotional syntax. *Music Perception, 9,* 1–26.

Pangborn, Rose-Marie. (1980). A critical analysis of sensory responses to sweetness. In P. Koivistoinen and L. Hyvonen (Eds.), *Carbohydrate sweeteners in foods and nutrition* (pp. 87–110). London: Academic Press.

Parducci, A. (1995). *Happiness, pleasure, and judgment: The contextual theory and its applications.* Mahwah, N.J.: Erlbaum.

Parker, L. A. (1982). Nonconsummatory and consummatory behavioral CRs elicited by lithium- and amphetamine-paired flavors. *Learning and Motivation, 13,* 281–303.

Pelchat, M. L., and Rozin, P. (1982). The special role of nausea in the acquisition of food dislikes by humans. *Appetite, 3,* 341–51.

Pelchat, M. L., Grill, H. J., Rozin, P., and Jacobs, J. (1983). Quality of acquired responses to tastes by *Rattus norvegicus* depends on type of associated discomfort. *Journal of Comparative Psychology, 97,* 140–53.

Pfaffman, C. (1960). The pleasures of sensation. *Psychological Review, 67,* 253.

Pliner, P. (1982). The effects of mere exposure on liking for edible substances. *Appetite, 3,* 283–90.

Rogozenski, J. E., Jr., and Moskowitz, H. R. (1982). A system for the preference evaluation of cyclic menus. *Journal of Food Service Systems, 2,* 139–61.

Rolls, B. J., Hetherington, M., Burley, V. J., and van Duijvenvoorde, P. M. (1986). Changing hedonic responses to foods during and after a meal. In M. A. Kare and J. G. Brand (Eds.), *Interaction of the chemical senses with nutrition* (pp. 247–68). New York: Academic Press.

Rosenstein, D., and Oster, H. (1988). Differential facial responses to four basic tastes in newborns. *Child Development, 59,* 1555–68.

Rozin, P. (1976). The evolution of intelligence and access to the cognitive unconscious. In J. A. Sprague and A. N. Epstein (Eds.), *Progress in psychobiology and physiological psychology* (vol. 6, pp. 245–80). New York: Academic Press.

———. (1982a). "Taste-smell confusions" and the duality of the olfactory sense. *Perception and Psychophysics, 31,* 397–401.

———. (1982b). Human food selection: The interaction of biology, culture, and individual experience. In L. M. Barker (Ed.), *The psychobiology of human food selection* (pp. 225–54). Westport, Conn.: AVI.

———. (1990). Getting to like the burn of chili pepper: Biological, psychological, and cultural perspectives. In B. G. Green, J. R. Mason, and M. L. Kare (Eds.), *Chemical irritation in the nose and mouth* (pp. 231–69). New York: Marcel Dekker.

———. (1996). Towards a psychology of food and eating: From motivation to model to morality to metaphor. *Current Directions in Psychological Science, 5,* 18–24.

———. (1998). Unpublished data. University of Pennsylvania.

Rozin, P., Berman, L., and Royzman, E. (1999). Positivity bias in 17 languages. Unpublished manuscript. University of Pennsylvania.

Rozin, P., Ebert, L., and Schull, J. (1982). Some like it hot: A temporal analysis of hedonic responses to chili pepper. *Appetite, 3,* 13–22.

Rozin, P., and Fallon, A. E. (1980). Psychological categorization of foods and non-foods: A preliminary taxonomy of food rejections. *Appetite, 1,* 193–201.

———. (1987). A perspective on disgust. *Psychological Review, 94,* 23–41.

Rozin, P., Fischler, C., Imada, S., Sarubin, A., and Wrzesniewski, A. (In press). Attitudes to food and the role of food in life: Cultural comparisons that enlighten the diet-health debate. *Appetite.*

Rozin, P., Grant, H., and Puhan, B. (1997). Some fundamental value differences between Hindu Indians and Americans. University of Pennsylvania. Unpublished paper.

Rozin, P., Gruss, L., and Berk, G. (1979). The reversal of innate aversions: Attempts to induce a preference for chili peppers in rats. *Journal of Comparative and Physiological Psychology, 93,* 1001–14.

Rozin, P., Haidt, J., and McCauley, C. R. (1993). Disgust. In M. Lewis and J. Haviland (Eds.), *Handbook of emotions* (pp. 575–94). New York: Guilford.

Rozin, P., Haidt, J., McCauley, C. R., and Imada, S. (1997). The cultural evolution of disgust. In H. M. Macbeth (Ed.), *Food preferences and taste: Continuity and change* (pp. 65–82). Oxford: Berghahn.

Rozin, P., and Kennel, K. (1983). Acquired preferences for piquant foods by chimpanzees. *Appetite, 4,* 69–77.

Rozin, P., Markwith, M., and Stoess, C. (1997). Moralization: Becoming a vegetarian, the conversion of preferences into values, and the recruitment of disgust. *Psychological Science, 8,* 67–73.

Rozin, P., and Nemeroff, C. J. (1990). The laws of sympathetic magic: A psychological analysis of similarity and contagion. In J. Stigler, G. Herdt, and R. A. Shweder (Eds.), *Cultural psychology: Essays on comparative human development* (pp. 205–32). Cambridge: Cambridge University Press.

Rozin, P., Nemeroff, C., Horowitz, M., Gordon, B., and Voet, W. (1995). The borders of the self: Contamination sensitivity and potency of the mouth, other apertures and body parts. *Journal of Research in Personality, 29,* 318–40.

Rozin, P., and Schiller, D. (1980). The nature and acquisition of a preference for chili pepper by humans. *Motivation and Emotion, 4,* 77–101.

Rozin, P., and Schulkin, J. (1990). Food selection. In E. M. Stricker (Ed.), *Handbook of behavioral neurobiology,* vol. 10, *Food and water intake* (pp. 297–328). New York: Plenum.

Rozin, P., and Tuorila, H. (1993). Simultaneous and temporal contextual influences on food choice. *Food Quality and Preference, 4,* 11–20.

Rozin, P., and Vollmecke, T. A. (1986). Food likes and dislikes. *Annual Review of Nutrition, 6,* 433–56.

Rozin, P., Wrzesniewski, A., and Byrnes, D. (1998). The elusiveness of evaluative conditioning. *Learning and Motivation, 28,* 423–36.

Rozin, P., and Zellner, D. A. (1985). The role of Pavlovian conditioning in the acquisition of food likes and dislikes. *Annals of the New York Academy of Sciences, 443,* 189–202.

Ruckmick, C. A. (1925). The psychology of pleasantness. *Psychological Review, 32,* 362–83.

Schull, J. (1979). A conditioned opponent theory of Pavlovian conditioning and habituation. In G. Bower (Ed.), *The psychology of learning and motivation* (vol. 13, pp. 57–90). New York: Academic Press.

Schutz, H. G. (1989). Beyond preference: Appropriateness as a measure of contextual acceptance of food. In D. M. H. Thomson (Ed.), *Food acceptability* (pp. 115–34). Essex, Eng.: Elsevier Applied Science Publishers.

Shepherd, R. (1989). Factors influencing food preferences and choice. In R. Shepherd (Ed.), *Handbook of the psychophysiology of human eating* (pp. 3–24). Chichester, Eng.: Wiley.

Sherrington, C. (1906). *The integrative action of the nervous system.* London: Constable.

Siegal, M. (1996). Becoming mindful of food. *Current Directions in Psychological Science, 4,* 177–81.

Siegel, S. (1977). Learning and psychopharmacology. In M. L. Jarvik (Ed.), *Psychopharmacology in the practice of medicine* (pp. 59–70). New York: Appleton-Century-Crofts.

Solomon, R. L. (1980). The opponent process theory of acquired motivation. *American Psychologist, 35,* 691–712.

Steiner, J. E. (1979). Human facial expressions in response to taste and smell stimulation. In H. W. Reese and L. P. Lipsitt (Eds.), *Advances in child development and behavior* (vol. 13, pp. 257–95). New York: Academic Press.

Stellar, E. (1974). Brain mechanisms in hunger and other hedonic experiences. *Proceedings of the American Philosophical Society, 118,* 276–82.

Titchener, E. B. (1919). *Textbook of psychology.* New York: Macmillan.

Todrank, J., Byrnes, D., Wrzesniewski, A., and Rozin, P. (1995). Odors can change preferences for people in photographs: A cross-modal evaluative conditioning study with olfactory USs and visual CSs. *Learning and Motivation, 26,* 116–40.

Tomkins, S. (1963). *Affect imagery, consciousness.* Vol. II. *The negative affects.* New York: Springer-Verlag.

Troland, L. T. (1928). *The fundamentals of human motivation.* New York: Van Nostrand.

Warren, R. P., and Pfaffman, C. (1958). Early experience and taste aversion. *Journal of Comparative and Physiological Psychology, 52,* 263–66.

Watson, D., Clark, L. A., and Tellegen, A. (1988). Development and validation of brief measures of positive and negative affect: The PANAS scale. *Journal of Personality and Social Psychology, 54,* 1063–70.

Young, P. T. (1948). Appetite, palatability, and feeding habit: A critical review. *Psychological Bulletin, 45,* 289–320.

———. (1959). The role of affective processes in learning and motivation. *Psychological Review, 66,* 104–25.

———. (1961). *Motivation and emotion: A survey of the determinants of human and animal activity.* New York: Wiley.

Zajonc, R. B. (1968). Attitudinal effects of mere exposure. *Journal of Personality and Social Psychology, 9* (part 2), 1–27.

Zellner, D. A., Rozin, P., Aron, M., and Kulish, C. (1983). Conditioned enhancement of humans' liking for flavors by pairing with sweetness. *Learning and Motivation, 14,* 338–50.

Zuckerman, M. (1979). *Sensation seeking: Beyond the optimal level of arousal.* Hillsdale, N.J.: Erlbaum.

7 On the Pleasures of the Mind

Michael Kubovy

Pleasures of the mind are different from pleasures of the body. There are two types of pleasures of the body: tonic pleasures and relief pleasures. Pleasures of the body are given by the contact senses and by the distance senses (seeing and hearing). The distance senses provide a special category of pleasure. Pleasures of the mind are not emotions; they are collections of emotions distributed over time. Some distributions of emotions over time are particularly pleasurable, such as episodes in which the peak emotion is strong and the final emotion is positive. The idea that all pleasurable stimuli share some general characteristic should be supplanted by the idea that humans have evolved domain-specific responses of attraction to stimuli. The emotions that characterize pleasures of the mind arise when expectations are violated, causing autonomic nervous system arousal and thereby triggering a search for an interpretation. Thus, pleasures of the mind occur when an individual has a definite set of expectations (usually tacit) and the wherewithal to interpret the violation (usually by placing it in a narrative framework). Pleasures of the mind differ in the objects of the emotions they comprise. There is probably a small number of categories of objects of emotions that we share with other mammals. I discuss two: the unknown (giving rise to curiosity) and skill (giving rise to virtuosity), two others being nurturing and sociality. There is also a uniquely human category of objects of emotion: suffering.

Don't make it a matter of course, but as a remarkable fact, that pictures and fictitious narratives give us pleasure, occupy our minds.
—Wittgenstein 1958, §524

IT IS EASIER to point to pleasures of the mind than to define them. Imagine you're ending a magnificent meal with good friends at Troisgros with the celebrated *jeu de pommes*—Granny Smith apple tartlets, topped with caramelized confectioners' sugar and covered with a sauce of warmed acacia honey, calvados, and lemon juice (Lang 1988, 31) accompanied by a Coteau du Layon (Loire) sweet chenin blanc.[1]

Now remove the elements that made this a marvelous experience, except for the food. You eat the same dessert alone at home, on your everyday dishes, without having anticipated the delectable food or wine. What you have lost are pleasures of the mind. I do not wish to imply that you have lost *all* the pleasures of the mind or that the pleasures that remain are just pleasures of the body.

We can take the opposite tack, as the following anecdote suggests:

> My friend, a French painter and Resistance fighter, was put in a concentration camp by the Nazis. Every evening during his long incarceration, he and two or three of his fellow prisoners . . . entirely by means of conversation and gestures . . . dressed for dinner in immaculate white shirts that did not exist, and placed, at times with some difficulty because of the starched material that wasn't there, pearl or ruby studs and cuff links in those shirts. . . . They drank Châteauneuf-du-Pape throughout the meal and Château d'Yquem with the dessert pastry. . . . There were certain restaurants they did not patronize a second time because the lobster had been overcooked. . . . On the evenings that they saw themselves as men of letters, they quoted from the great poets while they dined. (Boyle 1985, 88)

We have removed the food; what we have *retained* are pleasures of the mind.

The notion of pleasures of the mind goes back to Epicurus (341–270 B.C.E.) who regarded pleasures of the mind as superior to pleasures of the body because they were more varied and durable.[2] As Cabanac (1995) remarks, these pleasures have been neglected by contemporary psychology. Their scope and their differentiation from other pleasures and from emotions need to be explored and eventually specified.

As we embark on our exploration, we must avoid being too restrictive. You might identify the pleasures of the mind with aesthetic pleasures—

the pleasures of listening to music, hearing poetry, or attending a play. But what you or I have learned to call aesthetic pleasures may not be universal. Some cultures, such as the BaAka pygmies, do not make a distinction between listening to music, performing it, and dancing to it.[3] Other cultures, such as certain Bedouin societies, have forms of poetry that cannot be interpreted unless it is known who recited the poem and under what circumstances (Abu-Lughod 1986). You might identify the pleasures of the mind with intellectual pleasures—the pleasures of hearing about a new discovery or a brilliant theory. But many cultures do not have the kinds of intellectual exploration that were institutionalized during the Renaissance in Europe.

As soon as we move beyond the restrictive categories of the aesthetic and intellectual pleasures of modern Western cultures, can we exclude pleasurable activities such as playing backgammon and gardening? We are faced with an embarrassment of riches. We don't know where to stop: should we include bird-watching, collecting stamps, and flirting? The answer to all of these is yes, for reasons that will become clear as my argument unfolds.

This chapter consists of three sections. In the first, I offer a definition of the pleasures of the mind, first by distinguishing them from pleasures of the body, and then by clarifying the relation between pleasures of the mind and emotions. I conclude the first section with my conjecture that all pleasures of the mind consist of sequences of emotions (in which moods and pleasures of the body may play a role). This is the heart of my thesis, and I ask the reader to keep it in mind as I develop my argument. In the second section, which deals with the ecology of pleasures of the mind, I analyze the situations and stimuli that give rise to pleasures of the mind. Here I suggest that different pleasures of the mind provide different temporal patterns and different intensities of emotions. I conclude the chapter with further differentiation of the pleasures of the mind. I suggest that they differ in the objects of their emotions.

Defining the Pleasures of the Mind

Pleasures of the Mind and Pleasures of the Body

We begin by exploring the distinction between pleasures of the mind and pleasures of the body, bearing in mind that we may come across cases that are difficult to classify.[4] As the dining example suggests, many pleasures of the mind are closely tied to pleasures of the body, because they amplify them or involve elements that are pleasures of the body.

The main sources of bodily pleasure are our sheath of skin and the holes in it—the nostrils, the mouth, the genitals, the urethra, and the rectum—that engage in material exchanges with the environment. These sources give us two kinds of pleasures of the body. In the first kind, the sources of pleasure for the skin and its orifices are specific stimuli, such as caresses, sweet foods, flowery aromas, or sexual stimulation.[5] The second kind of pleasure of the body stems from the fact that orifices are also valves. The orifices allow us to rapidly—at times explosively—evacuate or expel foreign objects or bodily fluids. As a result, we experience sudden and pleasurable relief from internal sources of discomfort or tension by sneezing, belching, micturating. Having an orgasm, even though not caused by irritants, is not dissimilar: a gradual increase in tension is ended suddenly with great pleasure.[6]

I call pleasures of the body of the first kind *tonic pleasures* because they are relatively extended in time. They are often called *positive hedonic states*. I call pleasures of the body of the second kind *relief pleasures* because they follow a prior tension or discomfort. In contrast to the tonic pleasures, they are relatively brief. In this respect, sexual pleasures are unique: they involve both tonic pleasures (such as caresses) and relief pleasures (such as the orgasm).[7] Table 7.1 compares the tonic and relief pleasures. (The skin is excluded because it doesn't afford relief pleasures.)

We not only need to show that pleasures of the mind have a standing separate from pleasures of the body but must also answer the question: Don't all pleasures of the body require mind? To be sure, awareness accompanies pleasures, and pleasures can have meanings beyond the immediate experience. For example, when primates groom each other, they are not only giving each other pleasures of the body but also reassuring and appeasing each other: "Grooming . . . is the social cement of primates" (Jolly 1985, 207). That assertion does not imply, however, that when you have a pleasure of the body you are necessarily having a pleasure of the mind. Nevertheless, I suspect that for humans most tonic pleasures of the body are embedded in pleasures of the mind. In contrast, bodily relief pleasures may not occur frequently in pleasures of the mind, although analogous pleasures—such as relief from tension or resolution of

TABLE 7.1   Comparison of Two Types of Pleasures of the Body

Source	Tonic Pleasures	Pains or Discomforts	Relief Pleasures
Nostrils	Aromas	Irritation (for example, horseradish, dust), disgusting odors (for example, rotting eggs)	Sneeze
Mouth	Good flavors	Burn, distastes (bitter), disgusts (rotting food)	Spit, cough, belch
Genitals	Sexual pleasure	Sexual tension	Orgasm
Urethra	?	Full bladder	Micturition
Rectum	Sexual pleasure	Full bowel, flatulence	defecation, passing gas

suspense—are a central feature of pleasures of the mind.

As they become more dynamic and complex, we may be tempted to think of tonic pleasures of the body as pleasures of the mind. The tonic pleasures of the body, as we have defined them, involve objects or substances coming in contact with the body (the senses involved—smell, taste, and touch—are sometimes called contact senses) and relatively unitary experiences. But consider the following description: "This wine has a wonderful ripe nose that is full, rich, complex and intensely peppery and spicy. In the mouth, this wine was quite soft and round . . . with great extraction, balance and harmony. The finish is long and dignified."[8] If we used complexity or heterogeneity as a criterion of pleasures of the mind, we might say that this was a description of a pleasure of the mind. I do not think, however, that it will serve our purposes to make either complexity or variability criteria of pleasures of the mind. As I spell out later, the distinction between them does not rest on the simplicity, the brevity, or the absence of change of pleasures of the body. Rather, the difference is that pleasures of the mind are sequences of emotions. The sequence of experiences caused by the taste of wine may be a sequence of hedonic states, but not a sequence of emotions.

The so-called distance senses—hearing and seeing—can also give us pleasures of the body. Up to this point, we have discussed pleasures of the body that involve the contact senses. We must consider, however, sounds and sights we call attractive, pleasant, or harmonious—beautiful landscapes, graceful bodies, soothing harmonies, felicitous color combinations. I say that these are pleasures of the body because although they produce hedonic states, they do not provide emotions.

The role of the distance senses in giving us pleasure is complex because even though they can give rise to hedonic states, they are also important vehicles for the communication of pleasure. They do so by conveying and triggering emotions. For hu-

mans, the two most important vehicles of emotions are tone of voice and facial expression, transmitted, respectively, through hearing and seeing. Most forms of art[9] are conveyed by hearing and seeing. However, the sensory vehicle of a pleasure of the mind does not necessarily tie the pleasure to that sense. There is no more reason to call the pleasure we get from hearing a joke an auditory pleasure than there is to say that reading a poem gives us visual pleasure—disregarding the occasional shaped poem (Hollander 1975).

Furthermore, much that is received through other channels can modulate emotions conveyed by a distance sense. For instance, non-auditory knowledge affects our response to music. I listened to Smetana's beautiful tone poem *Vltava* with new emotions when I was told that it was composed soon after the composer went deaf (I felt compassion and admiration) and that it vividly depicts various parts of the river's course (I experienced curiosity).[10]

Finally, many pleasures of the mind are compound: they involve several senses. A film offers us sights, a sound track, and spoken dialogue; although it is in principle possible that the pleasure we get from a film can be captured by talking about the pleasures we get from each of these sources separately, it is unlikely. The pleasure it gives us is postsensory: it creates suspense, satisfies our curiosity, instructs (Burke 1973; Koubovi 1992), and moves us.

Having made some progress in differentiating pleasures of the body from pleasures of the mind, we turn to the differences between the pleasures of the mind and emotions.

Pleasures of the Mind and Basic Emotions

Although there is controversy in the literature on emotion, Ekman's (1992, 1994) view of the basic emotions (such as anger, fear, sadness, disgust, happiness) is a good point of departure: "(1) There are a number of separate emotions which differ from one another in important ways. (2) Evolution played an important role in shaping both the unique and the common features which these emotions display as well as their current function" (1994, 170). The left-hand column of table 7.2 summarizes Ekman's eight features of emotions; the right-hand column shows that in most ways pleasures of the mind differ from basic emotions.

How can the pleasures of the mind be so different from the basic emotions? As I pointed out earlier, although the pleasures of the mind are complex, their complexity does not go to the heart of the difference. Rather, basic emotions are different from pleasures of the mind because emotions are *constituents* of pleasures of the mind.

CONJECTURE 1: The pleasures of the mind are collections of emotions distributed over time.

This formulation is reminiscent of Kahneman's work (this volume). He proposes a "bottom-up approach to well-being, in which the criterion variable [a person's assessment of her well-being] is a function . . . of the distribution of affective states over time." He summarizes the evidence in favor of a *peak-end evaluation rule*. "The participants in these studies . . . provided a real-time record of their experience during an episode . . . and later provided a global evaluation of the entire episode. . . . Global retrospective evaluations were well predicted by a simple average of the *peak* affective response recorded during the episode (in the case of aversive episodes, the worst moment) and of the *end* value, recorded just before the episode ended."

More generally, episodes in human life—important social transitions especially—have (or are described by people retelling them as having) a constant temporal structure, as Ruble and Seidman (1996) show. As they point out, a person starts out in a so-called *prior state*, consisting of concepts and schemata about her relation with her environment, in the light of which she interprets the events of her life. There comes a moment, which they call the *onset*, at which her relation with her context is disrupted. The new state of affairs requires a period of *change*, during which she tries to adjust to it or to reconstruct it. Either path leads her to a final phase of this transition, *equilibrium*. In reconstructing an episode in a person's life, one inevitably divides the constituent events into *kernels*—events that entail choices and are consequences of earlier kernels—and *satellites* that may fill in, elaborate, or complete the kernel (Chatman 1978). Each of these kernels gives rise to emotions. When a kernel event presents itself, we feel *suspense* which is accompanied by *fear* and *hope*; when the choice has been made, we may experience *surprise* accompanied by *disappointment* or *elation*. If the person emerges triumphant from the challenge, she will cherish the episode as a pleasure of the mind (for a demonstration of the peak-end rule in dramatic presentations, see Zillmann, Hay, and Bryant 1975). Thus, some episodes in human life provide sequences of emotions that are pleasures of the mind, some that are neutral, and some that may be called *displeasures of the mind*.

TABLE 7.2   Features of Emotions and Pleasures of the Mind

Emotions . . .	Pleasures of the Mind . . .
have a distinctive universal signal (such as a facial expression).	do not have a distinctive universal signal.
are almost all present in other primates.	at least some of them may be present in other primates.
are accompanied by a distinctive physiological response.	are not accompanied by a distinctive physiological response.
give rise to coherent responses in the autonomic and expressive systems.	do not give rise to coherent responses.
can develop rapidly and may happen before one is aware of them.	are relatively extended in time.
are of brief duration (on the order of seconds).	are usually not of brief duration.
are quick and brief; they imply the existence of an automatic appraisal mechanism.	even though neither quick nor brief, may be generated by an automatic appraisal mechanism.
are quick, brief, and involve automatic appraisal; therefore, their occurrence is unbidden.	are generally voluntarily sought out.

As Elias and Dunning (1986) illustrate, cultures have invented institutions that provide opportunities for pleasures of the mind:

> It may not be easy to find a clear consensus with regard to the characteristics of plays or symphonies which provide a high and low degree of audience satisfaction, although the difficulties may not be insuperable even in the case of concerts in spite of the greater complexity of the problems. With regard to sports-games such as football [soccer], the task is simple. If one follows the game regularly one can learn to see, at least in broad outline, what kind of game figuration provides the optimum enjoyment: it is a prolonged battle between teams that are matched in skill and strength. It is a game which a large crowd of spectators follows with mounting excitement, produced not only by the battle itself but also by the skill displayed by the players. It is a game which sways to and fro, in which the teams are so evenly matched that first one, then the other scores and the determination of each to score the decisive goal grows as time runs out. The tension of the play communicates itself visibly to the spectators. Their tension, their mounting excitement in turn communicates itself back to the players and so on until the tension reaches a point where it can just be borne and contained without getting out of hand. If, in this manner, the excitement approaches a climax, and if then suddenly one's own team scores the decisive goal so that the excitement resolves itself in the happiness of triumph and jubilation, that is a great game which one will remember and about which one will talk for a long time—a really enjoyable game. (86–87)

Consider the pleasures of the mind we get from works of art that unfold over time.[11] Take, for example *narratives*. "Every narrative . . . a structure with a content plane (called 'story') and an expression plane (called 'discourse')" (Chatman 1978, 146). Many stories have a structure that parallels the *prior state, onset, change,* and *equilibrium* pattern of episodes in a human life. They begin with an *exposition,* introduce a *complication,* and end with a *dénouement* and thus can provide sequences of emotions similar to those provided by episodes in human life (Brooks and Warren 1979).

> Just as in ordinary circumstances an emotional response is the product of a perceived situation which is apprehended by the individual as promising or threatening, so the expressiveness of the imaginative work arises, at least in part, from the fact that it provides a dramatic representation of an action of which the evoked emotion is the expressive counterpart (Aiken 1955, 390).

The purpose of discourse is to add emotions to those provided by the story. Consider just one example from Chatman (1978). In Hawthorne's "Rappacini's Daughter," we read: "The youth might have taken Baglioni's opinions with many grains of allowance had he known that there was a professional warfare of long continuance between him and Dr. Rappacini." Chatman comments on this passage: "Giovanni could have discounted Baglioni's opinions, but he did not because he was ignorant of his rivalry with Rappacini. The narrator tells us in so many words what could have happened and did not" (226). As a result of the way in which the story is presented, what is not a kernel for Giovanni becomes one for us. The author (via the narrator) has planted a question in our minds: Will Giovanni see through Baglioni? As a result of this device, which is part of the discourse rather than the story, we are in an emotional state, suspense.

In brief, all works of art, and more generally all pleasures of the mind—from roller-coaster rides to gardening—derive their pleasurability from the sequence of emotions they bring about.

> CONJECTURE 2: The pleasures of the mind are collections of emotions distributed over time whose global evaluation depends on the intensity of the peak emotion and favorability of the end.

A brief reconsideration of the experience of a fine wine (like the description of the 1992 Jean-Louis Chave Hermitage quoted earlier) may clarify what I have said up to this point. The experience shares some features with pleasures of the mind: it resembles them insofar as it is complex, consisting of a sequence of pleasurable sensations. But the experience is not a pleasure of the mind because it does not give rise to a sequence of emotions. If an enologist were to report that the taste of a wine is accompanied by a series of emotions, then it would be a candidate for a pleasure of the mind. It is more likely, however, that an evening of wine-tasting, with its good wines and bad wines, with its anticipations and surprises, with its debates and disagreements, would count as a pleasure of the mind.

In the remaining two sections of this chapter, I address two questions about the pleasures of the mind (inspired by Shweder's [1991, ch. 6] cross-cultural analysis of emotion). The first is the *eco-*

logical question: How do certain stimuli give rise to sequences of emotions? The second is the *taxonomic* question: How do pleasures of the mind differ other than by the sequence of the emotions they produce?

THE ECOLOGICAL QUESTION

Up to now I have emphasized the role of sequences of emotions as constituents of pleasures of the mind. I have already sketched part of my answer to the ecological question: the stimuli and activities that give rise to pleasures of the mind are those activities that give rise to certain patterned sequences of emotions. But I do not believe that this is the whole answer. Some stimuli are in themselves pleasurable, but they do not by themselves produce sequences of emotions. What is their role in the pleasures of the mind?

The role of pleasant and attractive stimuli seems to be the creation of a *context* for the generation of pleasures of the mind. When you describe a pleasure of the mind to someone, emotions are not the only mental states you refer to. You may also refer to *moods* (happy versus sad) and *levels of arousal* (excited versus calm). Moods and levels of arousal differ from emotions in an important way: they are not intentional, that is, they are not focused on objects. But moods and levels of arousal are related to emotions. Moods share at least one property with emotions: they both involve affect. For instance, a good mood is a state of unfocused pleasant feeling, which produces a general proclivity to see the positive (see Frijda 1993; Morris, this volume). Furthermore, levels of arousal are inextricable consequences of moods and emotions. So it is likely that levels of arousal and moods are facilitators of sequences of emotions.

Pleasurable Stimuli

Even though levels of arousal and moods do not have objects, they can be affected by stimuli: background music, soothing colors, the babbling of a brook, the chirping of birds, the aroma of a freshly mowed lawn, the scent of a delicate perfume—these are stimuli that we like; they tend to reduce arousal and improve our mood.[12] I call these *pleasures of the distance senses* to make it clear that such pleasures do not count as pleasures of the mind.

Traditional psychological approaches to the relation between stimuli and pleasures of the mind have been narrower in scope than the one I am proposing. Two approaches have been tried. The first was formulated by Fechner in a paper on preferences for the proportions of rectangles, which is said to have founded the discipline of experimental aesthetics (Boring 1950). He asked: What properties should stimuli of a certain category possess to make people prefer them over other stimuli of the same category? For instance, are rectangles whose proportions approximate the Golden Mean[13] more pleasing than other rectangles? The second approach originated with Berlyne, who thought that arousal is the key to the appeal of stimuli. Since it is beyond the scope of this chapter to discuss both approaches, I have chosen to discuss Berlyne's.

Berlyne's Approach: Preference for Intermediate Levels of Complexity　In the late 1950s Berlyne revived ideas first proposed some eighty years earlier by Wundt (1874) and embarked on an influential research program whose aim was to found a psychological aesthetics on the premise that the hedonic value of stimuli is maximal at intermediate levels of arousal.

Arousal is a general state of the organism that affects the vigor and organization of its behavior, between sleep and disorganization at one extreme and frenzy at the other. It can be affected by internal influences (drugs, hormones, and deprivation levels) or by external influences (the sight or smell of food, or painful stimuli). The foundation of Berlyne's theory (1960, 1967, 1971) is the so-called Wundt curve (figure 7.1). The curve follows

FIGURE 7.1　The Wundt Curve

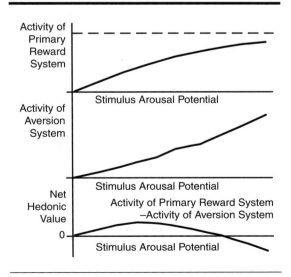

Source: Adapted From Berlyne 1971, figures 8.3 and 8.4.

from several propositions about brain systems that control hedonic processes:

1. There are in the brain two antagonistic systems involved in the regulation of pleasure: a primary reward system and an aversion system.
2. Any stimulus has arousal potential; that is, it can increase the activity of these two systems.
3. The greater the intensity of a stimulus, the greater its arousal potential, and the greater the activity of the two systems.
4. The mathematical functions that relate the amount of activity in the two systems to stimulus arousal potential are different: the primary reward system is activated more effectively by weak stimuli than is the aversion system, but the reverse is true for strong stimuli.
5. The net hedonic value of a stimulus is given by the difference between the activity of the two systems (Berlyne, 1974; Francès 1970, 1971; Frank 1959; Jones, Wilkinson, and Braden 1961; Molès 1966; Schneirla 1959).

It is thus a theory of the pleasures of the mind. The reader may wish to consult Martindale, Morre, and Borkum (1990) for an excellent overview of this line of research.

As Berlyne's ideas evolved, he and others came to identify stimulus arousal potential with complexity, defined in information-theoretic terms. As an example of the sort of research his ideas inspired, consider an experiment by Dorfman and McKenna (1966). They showed one hundred women sixty pairs of patterns resembling the one shown in figure 7.2. Each pattern consisted of a number of tiles (4, 16, 36, 64, 100, or 144) whose color—green or white—was determined randomly. The patterns were of the same size, but they differed in the number of tiles they comprised.

After the data were collected, Dorfman and McKenna grouped the participants into 6 classes, according to the number of tiles in the patterns they tended to prefer. (Twelve percent of the participants were excluded from the analysis because their preferences were ambiguous.) The data (figure 7.3) show that each class of participant had a single-peaked preference for a certain amount of uncertainty.

Results such as these were taken to imply that each person has a single-peaked preference for objects possessing differing degrees of complexity; that is, the further the complexity of objects departs from some optimum, the less appealing they are.

FIGURE 7.2   A Pattern Based on a Twelve-by-Twelve Matrix of White or Green Tiles

Source: Dorfman and McKenna 1966, figure 1.
Note: Black tiles signify green tiles.

Berlyne's approach suffers from three problems. First, it incorrectly considers complexity to be a measurable characteristic of single stimuli. Second, its claim that we prefer intermediate levels of complexity is theoretically weak and empirically unfounded. Third, it does not capture the phenomenology of pleasures of the mind; it represents an inappropriately reductionistic oversimplification of the pleasures of the mind.

Berlyne mistakenly thought that complexity is a measurable characteristic of single stimuli. Kahneman and Miller (1986), building on Garner's (1962, 1970) insights, have shown that "each stimulus selectively recruits its own alternatives and is interpreted in a rich context of remembered and constructed representations of what it could have been, might have been, or should have been" (136).

"Good [that is, simple] patterns have few alternatives," as Garner's title (1970) suggests. When John looks at a Mondrian and says that his four-year-old niece could have done as well, he is saying that the painting is simple because he is comparing it to few alternatives. He may think that all the artist could have done differently was to fail to stay within the lines or use different primary colors. John does not consider the many choices Mondrian faced in the placement of rectangles and boundary lines and in the balance of forms. On the other hand, John may admire the landscape painting taught on television because it in-

FIGURE 7.3   Number of Tiles Preferred by Six Classes of Participants in Dorfman and McKenna (1966) Experiment

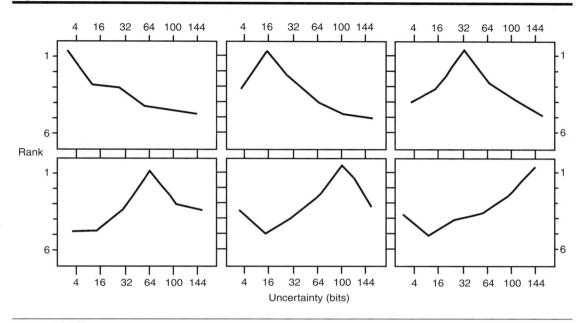

Source: Adapted from Dorfman and McKenna (1966), figure 2.

volves many strokes of the paintbrush. To him, each stroke seems to be the result of a choice. If he realized that this painting actually has few alternatives, that he is watching the application of a few painterly tricks, applied according to simple rules of thumb, he might reconsider his judgment.

Thus, complexity is a property of the structure of an imagined set of alternatives to the object. A person's construal of the set to which an object belongs determines her judgment of the object's complexity.

Despite Berlyne's misconstrual of complexity, he was, in a sense, right: we are not entertained either by a blank wall or by random noise; both boredom and overload are unpleasant. One can always find a range of similar stimuli such that the simplest is too simple and the most complex is too complex. In that sense, we prefer intermediate levels of complexity,[14] and in that sense, the Wundt curve and Berlyne's theory are trivially true. But we need no experiments to realize that Berlyne's theory cannot be true for *any* individual and *any* set of stimuli: show me a set of ten random patterns varying between one million and ten million elements; I will surely judge all of them to be too complex to be pleasurable.

Keeping in mind that people assess the com-

plexity of a stimulus with respect to the set to which it belongs, consider a collection of paintings by Rothko. The dimensions along which these paintings vary are not given; they must be discovered, or perhaps invented. Some viewers may focus on form, others may focus on colors, and yet others may focus on brush strokes. An individual's interest in and knowledge of the ways in which the set varies determines how the complexity of its constituent stimuli will be judged. People's interests and knowledge are more fundamental to their preferences than is complexity. This is what Martindale and his collaborators (Martindale and Moore 1989; Martindale et al. 1990) found: content has a much greater effect on preference than does complexity. In fact, they and Walker (1981) have shown that complexity does not predict preference well at all and that preference is not even a single-peaked function of complexity.

Berlyne's approach suffers from a third, even more serious, deficiency. It does not capture the *phenomenology* of pleasures of the mind. His concepts of arousal and complexity leave out the two fundamental features of pleasures of the mind: emotions and their temporal organization. His theory ignores the all-important emotional dynamics of pleasures of the mind. If my conjecture is true, namely, that all pleasures of the mind consist of patterned sequences of emotions, then complexity should be relevant to pleasures of the mind only insofar as it contributes to the generation of emotions.

A Better Approach to Pleasurable Stimuli: The Naturalization of Beauty   Let us think of beauty as the property we attribute to objects that give rise to pleasures of the distance senses. It is a commonplace of folk psychology that beauty is in the eye of the beholder. Scholars in the humanities (and probably many social scientists) hold a more subtle view, namely, that beauty is a social construction (Turner 1991). Berlyne's position minimized the role of subjectivity and the effect of culture. He proposed a *general mechanism* to account for what makes stimuli appealing. A general mechanism is one that is present in all humans, regardless of culture and individual differences within the culture. The search for such general mechanisms appeals to the reductionistic bent of psychology: whatever can be naturalized, that is, attributed to universal characteristics of the mind, should be naturalized.

Even though Berlyne's approach was appealing because he was trying to naturalize beauty, he was mistaken in how he tried to do so. Contemporary psychology has amassed considerable evidence that behaviors previously thought to be governed by general-purpose processing rules are in fact controlled by specialized modules (Cosmides and Tooby 1994; for an example of this hotly debated topic, see Shapiro and Epstein, 1998; Tooby and Cosmides 1998).

The contemporary project of naturalizing beauty relies on the idea that we have evolved domain-specific responses to stimuli that make a difference to our reproductive success. Each of these specific responses is an *evolved psychological mechanism*, defined by Buss (1996) as:

A set of processes inside an organism that (1) exists in the form it does because it (or other mechanisms that reliably produce it) solved a specific problem of individual survival or reproduction recurrently over human evolutionary history; (2) takes only certain classes of information or input, where input (a) can be either external or internal, (b) can be actively extracted from the environment or passively received from the environment, and (c) specifies to the organism the particular adaptive problem it is facing; and (3) transforms that information into output through a procedure (e.g., a decision rule) where output (a) regulates physiological activity, provides information to other psychological mechanisms, or produces manifest action, and (b) solves a particular adaptive problem. (8)

Two examples of responses to stimuli to which we may have evolved domain-specific preferences—and therefore provide pleasures of the distance senses—are landscapes and faces.

A sample of North Americans were shown photographs of five types of landscapes (Balling and Falk 1982; Orians and Heerwagen 1992). While viewing these photographs, they were asked to rate how much they would like to "live in" or "visit" an East African savanna, three types of forest (tropical, deciduous, or coniferous), or a desert. Children (modal age eight) preferred the East African savanna over the other four (even though no animals or water were shown in any of the pictures). According to Orians and Heerwagen (1992), these data (particularly the preferences of young children) are consistent with the idea that our preferences for landscapes are the manifestation of an evolved psychological mechanism shaped during the Pleistocene Epoch.[15] These preferences are adaptive because they attract us to environments that provide food, water, protection from natural hazards, and freedom from predators or parasites. I cite this research not because it is particularly convincing, but because it is an example of what interesting research on the topic of hard-wired pleasures of the distance senses might be like.

Another—more persuasive—example of domain-specific preferences is drawn from Johnston and Franklin (1993), who studied preferences for women's faces. They created a computer program that allowed observers to manipulate the features of composite female faces. They first obtained the participants' ratings (on a 10-point scale) of thirty randomly generated composite faces. They interpreted these numbers as ratings of fitness. They then took the fittest face and probabilistically combined its features with one of the remaining twenty-nine faces (with a likelihood proportional to each face's fitness), to produce two new composite faces. The observer was then allowed to improve these faces by manipulating the position of the hair, nose, mouth, or chin and changing the interpupil distance. Then the observer rated the beauty of the resulting composite face. If either face was rated fitter than the least fit face in the current population of thirty faces, then it replaced that face. This process was repeated until the participant gave a composite face a score of 10.

This experimental procedure generated forty faces. An average face formed from these "perfect" composites was quite different from an average formed from sixty-eight photographs of the local student population. Anthropometric growth curves allow us to estimate the age of a young woman from the relative size of her lower jaw (roughly speaking). By this measure, Johnston and Franklin (1993) estimated the age of the average "perfect" composite to be 11, whereas they estimated the age of the average of the local faces to be 18. (Their true mean age was 19.9.) However, when new observers were asked to estimate the age of the women depicted in the two average pictures, the age they assigned to the average of local faces was 27.4, whereas they thought that the age of the average "perfect" composite was 24.9. Now it so happens that 25 is about the age of maximum female fertility, and it is also the age that mates say is the ideal age for their long-term mate (Buss 1989). Noting that the growth of the lower jaw in females is controlled by adrenal androgens, Johnston and Franklin (1993) speculate: "A beautiful female face is that of a 25 year old female who has been less influenced by puberal androgens . . . and may [therefore] have an even higher fertility than the average 25 year old female" (196–97).

Even if we establish with certitude that some of our pleasures of the distance senses are based on evolved psychological mechanisms, what is considered beautiful or attractive cannot be explained without taking into account the powerful effects of culture. How else to account for the pervasive but culture-specific modifications of the body, such as foot-binding?

What is the "beauty-generating mechanism" through which culture works? Zajonc (1968) asked North American observers to rate how well they liked Chinese ideographs, after they had seen each either zero, one, two, five, ten, or twenty-five times (for two seconds each time). The more times they saw an ideograph, the more they liked it. In reviewing this "mere exposure" effect, Tesser and Martin (1996) conclude that "liking can be shaped without conscious awareness," and indeed, that it "may be stronger when the subjects are unaware of exposure than when they are aware" (403). The automaticity of the growth of liking and its independence from awareness are suggestive of a hard-wired mechanism. So even though

not all our preferences are based on evolved psychological mechanisms, the mere exposure effect may be a manifestation of an evolved psychological mechanism that generates pleasures of the distance senses, and perhaps some pleasures of the body (such as a taste for certain spices). There are undoubtedly other mechanisms for the development of preferences, the foremost among them being classical conditioning. But their discussion is beyond the scope of this chapter.

The Generation of Emotion in Pleasures of the Mind

In the first part of this chapter, I suggested that pleasures of the mind consist of sequences of emotions. In the second part of this chapter, I complicated this position by discussing the role of pleasures of the distance senses in the pleasures of the mind. I now turn to the question of how activities that we consider pleasures of the mind give rise to emotions. I investigate this question using two examples: music and humor.

Music   My explanation (a mere sketch, to be sure) of how music can give rise to sequences of emotions is based on Mandler's cognitive theory of emotions (Berscheid 1983; Dowling and Harwood 1986; Mandler 1984) and Maus's theory of narrative and music (Maus 1988, 1991, 1997). Its outline is this: (a) Whenever a musical event occurs, you interpret it in terms of your current schematic expectations. If the event is ambiguous, you interpret it in terms of the schema that comes most quickly to your mind. (b) If the musical event violates your expectations, your autonomic nervous system is aroused. (c) Because of this arousal, you search for an interpretation of the source of the violation of your expectation. (d) Your interpretation is based on your tendency to hear music as a narrative, and it can produce an emotional response.

About the time Berlyne was developing his theory, Meyer (1956, 1973) was developing an approach that has—in contrast—fared well. It is a theory about how tonal music pleases us. Fiske (1996) summarizes the theory well:

> During the course of a musical work listeners create on-going expectations about what particular tonal-rhythmic events are likely to occur "next" in the piece. The expected next-event is based upon

the cumulation of events that have occurred in the piece so far. If this expected event is delayed or fails to occur at all, then emotional arousal will be stronger than it would be if the event had occurred as predicted. . . . For a piece to be meaningful, the composer must tread a thin line between absolute predictability of musical events and the fulfillment of predictability versus absolute unpredictability through the frustration, inhibition, and avoidance of expected events. (19, 107)

In Meyer's (1956) words: "Affect or emotion-felt is aroused when an expectation activated by the musical stimulus situation is temporarily inhibited or permanently blocked" (31).

In its most recent incarnation, Meyer's theory has been developed by Narmour (1990, 1992) in a monumental treatise on his implication-realization model. Narmour's theory is both broader than Meyer's and narrower. It is broader because it is far more explicit as a theory of music perception and as a theory of the formation and fulfillment of expectancies. For instance, Narmour conjectures that many of our musical expectations are the consequence of the bottom-up operation of universal (and perhaps innate) gestalt principles such as grouping by proximity, similarity, and symmetry. It is narrower than Meyer's theory because it does not explicitly address the issue of emotion or pleasure.[16]

The expectancy component of Meyer's theory has been tested empirically, thanks to the precision of Narmour's theory. Schellenberg (1996) has reported data that support Narmour's theory. He also successfully applied the theory to earlier data on the formation of expectancy in music (Carlsen 1981; Unyk and Carlsen 1987).

Expectancies are probably formed by *implicit learning*, a process whereby people learn rules (a) without having been told that what they are trying to memorize is governed by rules, and (b) without realizing that they are learning the rules. For instance, participants in an experiment by Reber (1993) were randomly assigned to two groups. Members of one group were asked to memorize sets of four strings of letters generated by the "grammar" represented in figure 7.4; the members of the other group were asked to memorize sets of four strings of the same letters in random order. Both groups made the same number of errors before they committed the strings to memory, but only for the first and second sets (about eighteen and eight, respectively). After that, the mem-

FIGURE 7.4   Reber's (1993) Artificial Grammar and the Eight Strings It Generates

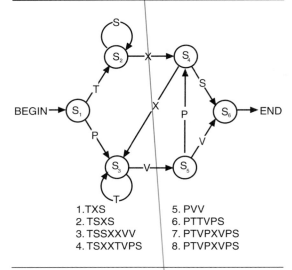

1. TXS
2. TSXS
3. TSSXXVV
4. TSXXTVPS
5. PVV
6. PTTVPS
7. PTVPXVPS
8. PTVPXVPS

Source: Reber 1993.
Notes: Reber's artificial grammar can be learned implicitly. To generate a letter, you move from one "state" (S_1, S_2, . . . S_6) to another. When you are in a given state (the *source state*, say, S_3), you may go only to states (the *target states*, such as S_3, which generates a T, and S_5, which generates a V) that are connected with the source state by an arrow directed toward the target state.

bers of the group that learned the random strings ceased to improve, whereas the performance of members of the group that learned the rule-governed strings gradually improved until, by the seventh set, they made, on the average, fewer than three errors. Although subjects did become aware of some of the rules they were using, they were unable to articulate all the rules. In other words, some of their learning was implicit or tacit.

A newcomer to Reber's tasks would find his artificial grammars easier to articulate than a musically uneducated listener can express the rules that govern a piece of music. And yet—as Schellenberg (1996), Krumhansl (1990), and others have shown—they do form expectancies.

Let us suppose that your knowledge of a piece of music grows in two ways: tacitly, a process of which you are not directly aware, and explicitly, a process of which you become aware as your ability to sing the music—or at least sing along with it—grows. Your tacit knowledge triggers expectations automatically and uncontrollably. (Bharucha 1994] calls this *schematic expectation;* Dowling and Harwood, [1986] call it a *schema*.) The Stroop effect is an example of this sort of process: suppose the letters RED were printed in blue and you were asked to name the color of the ink. Suppose that on another occasion you were asked to perform the same task with the letters DOG printed in blue. You would involuntarily read either string of letters as a word, even though you had not been asked to do so. Because RED is a color name, it would give rise to internal processes that interfere with your saying "blue," thus slowing down your response, whereas the processes triggered by DOG would not.

According to Mandler's theory, you do not experience an emotion until you have found the source of a physiological arousal. The Meyer-Narmour theory provides us with the arousal component of the emotion, but not with its object. Maus (1997) quotes an analysis of the slow movement of Mozart's Symphony No. 39:

> The second violins initiate a new exchange in their darkest tones, reinforced in their darkness by the cellos and double basses and by a pulsating E-flat pedal tone in the violas. The first violins respond, alone in their treble. . . . The first violins strain to break away from their E-flat mooring. The dialogue has taken on an air of urgency and anxiety. On their third try the first violins succeed in breaking away and immediately become frisky in their new freedom. The lower strings abandon their seriousness (have they meant it?) and join in the spirit of the first violins, contributing staccato punctuation while the first violins replace the dots with rests to lighten their iambic rhythm. (Treitler 1989, 205)

Maus believes that a common strategy for listening combines emotional ascription (for example, to take "on an air of urgency and anxiety") with other attributions of action (for example, "the first violins succeed in breaking away") and psychological states ("become frisky in their new freedom"). It is this narrative interpretation of music that allows us to understand the final stage of the generation of emotion in music (the finding of an object of the emotion) as we might understand the generation of emotion in response to any narrative.

But what happens to our emotional responses when we have heard the music more than once? This is a problem that has received considerable attention in the aesthetic literature but has not been discussed much in the psychological literature. Bever (1987) believes and Jackendoff (1989)

concurs that because the emotions should not survive beyond one listening, Meyer's approach collapses.

> The central assumption of the arousal theory of aesthetics cannot explain how one could possibly enjoy a melody the second time, never mind the thousandth time, since the expected tone sequence is the actual tone sequence once the melody has been memorized. It is striking how theorists in the optimal-arousal school deal with this simple fact—generally they argue that our memory is mercifully short, so we keep forgetting what we have heard and are able to be re-surprised by it afresh to *juuuuuuuust* the right degree. (319)

Bever's criticism is valid only if at least one of the following claims is true: (a) expectancies are controlled by explicit memory, or (b) our tendency to perceive music in narrative terms decreases as we become familiar with it. We have seen earlier that the first of these two claims is probably false. Your conscious familiarity with the melodic line of a specific piece of music goes through several stages. There is a stage at which you know the line well enough to hum along, that is, when prompted by the performance you can hum a few bars, but you are stymied from time to time. Your ability to reproduce the melodic line is confined to the more predictable parts of the melody. At a later stage, you might know the melody so well that you can hum it from beginning to end without prompting. (Bharucha [1994] calls this *veridical expectation*.) At that point, if Bever were right, pleasure would vanish. But perhaps your conscious knowledge of the melodic line has outstripped the ability of the implicit learning system, which is strongly bound to rules it has acquired over the years. The tacit system, operating automatically, may still be generating expectations that are temporarily thwarted, then eventually resolved, just as Meyer described. This system may be a source of pleasure even when you are in a choir singing Handel's *Messiah* or doing karaoke to the Beatles' "Eleanor Rigby." Perhaps when even our schematic expectations have reached the point where the piece does not defeat them, we tire of the piece. (For a similar account, see Jackendoff [1989], 240–45.) As to the second claim, does our tendency to ascribe agency, sentience, and emotionality to a piece of music decrease as we become more familiar with it? I do not know of any empirical research on the topic. However, I conjecture that the opposite is true. The tendency probably *grows* as the music becomes more familiar, thus reinforcing our ability to construe the music as providing objects of emotion.

In summary, the Meyer-Narmour theory, supplemented with a theory of tacit expectancies and narrative interpretation, could account for the pleasures of the mind we get from listening to music repeatedly.

Humor   Our second example of how activities can create patterns of emotions concerns humor. The most comprehensive current theory of humor is that of Wyer and Collins (1992), which draws on insights from the work of Suls (1972, 1977) and Apter (1982). It is based on the very same assumptions as Mandler's theory, which I summarized earlier.

Suppose you walk into a movie theater after the film has begun. On the screen you see a man sitting at a desk and staring at a blank sheet of paper. He pats the pockets of his jacket, and you assume that he's looking for a pen; you're interpreting the action in terms of preexisting concepts and schemata. The man's action is ambiguous; he could be looking for a cigarette, but the desk and the paper make the pen-search schema come to mind more quickly than the cigarette-search schema. You are now expecting the man to produce a pen, or to discover that he has none. To your surprise, he brings out a cigarette lighter. You look for a different set of concepts and schemata that fit the current and past events: you wonder whether he's planning to burn the sheet of paper.

The crux of the theory is this: if the reinterpretation paints a more mundane or less desirable picture of the protagonist or the event (a process that Apter [1982] and Wyer and Collins, [1992] call *diminishment*), then you will find the event to be humorous. Although you were surprised by the lighter, the reinterpretation does not involve diminishment.

As soon as he pulls out the lighter, the protagonist quickly slams it against the sheet of paper, crushing a fly that you glimpse briefly before it disappears under the lighter. You chuckle, and wonder whether what you thought was going to be a *film noir* is actually a spoof of one.

The assumptions of the Apter/Wyer theory of humor are similar to the assumptions of our theory of emotion in music. They share the idea that we get pleasure from the violation of expectations followed by a return to a stable state. So how does a joke differ from a piece of music? (This is not the opening line of a joke.) Is the level of abstraction

at which I am answering the question not too high? I think not. I think that there are two parts to the answer: one part involves the sequence of emotions produced by the two; the other has to do with an aspect of the pleasures of the mind we have not yet discussed, to which we will turn in the next section.

With respect to emotions, humor and music differ in emotional pacing and emotional intensity. Telling a joke may take a minute or two, after which the punch line causes the listeners to reinterpret the situation rapidly and radically. If the reinterpretation involves diminishment, the joke is successful, and the audience laughs. A piece of music (tonal music, that is) reaches a cadence (a return to a resting point, literally a "fall," from the Latin *cadere*) roughly two or three times a minute and usually does not involve a radical reconceptualization of what was just heard.

Work to Be Done on the Ecological Question

We need an ethology of emotional patterns generated by activities that give us pleasures of the mind. To do so, we could, for example, have sports fans watch videos of games and collect their categorizations of their moment-to-moment emotional states and their ratings of the intensity of these states. We could also collect the commentaries of experts on what is at stake in the moment-to-moment progress of the game. We do not yet know how to characterize the emotional pacing and emotional intensity (together they might be called the *emotional rhythm*) of different pleasures of the mind. Novels, as a group, are likely to have different emotional rhythms from sports events (even though both are heterogeneous categories). Caring for children surely has a unique emotional rhythm: calm some of the time, punctuated by unpredictable and sometimes overwhelming crises, ending with what kind of adult the child grows to be. We would probably find systematic differences in parents' retrospective assessments of how much pleasure they got from raising a child, and we probably could discover a few ideal child-rearing pleasures of the mind. Caring for pets is a pleasure of the mind that has some of the same features as child-rearing, but on a smaller time scale.

The ethology of pleasures of the mind is, of course, complicated by individual differences in preferences for emotional rhythms. A good example is the personality dimension of sensation-seeking, reviewed by Green (1997, 390, 399–404).

THE TAXONOMIC QUESTION: THE OBJECTS OF EMOTION

We have dealt at some length with the role of emotions in the pleasures of the mind. It is unlikely, however, that people seek particular pleasures of the mind just on the basis of their emotional rhythm. Suppose that it were possible to create two pleasures of the mind with similar emotional rhythms. What would be the best way to distinguish them?

We have seen that emotions are intentional: they are *about* something; they have an *object*. When you are enjoying a pleasure of the mind, the emotions you experience are about events. In fact, philosophers classify emotions as a species of *propositional attitude:* a state of mind whose content is a *proposition,* or an *assertion* about the world. To say that you are afraid of the dog is to say something about your state of mind vis-à-vis a certain dog. So fear is a propositional attitude. To believe, to hope, to doubt, are propositional attitudes (Scheffler 1991). So in addition to being differentiated by their emotional rhythms, pleasures of the mind differ with respect to the contents of their propositional attitudes, that is, the objects of their emotions.

I will discuss two categories of objects of emotion (OOE) that are present to varying degrees in most pleasures of the mind: curiosity and virtuosity. Both of these are rooted in our animal natures and based on evolutionary adaptation. There are certainly other categories, such as nurturing and sociality, which I will briefly touch on later.

The Unknown: Curiosity

To be curious means that you get pleasure from learning something that you did not previously know. So the OOE we are dealing with is the unknown. Curiosity is not limited to humans but has its roots in animal behavior. The behaviorists did not understand this: from Watson's behaviorist manifesto (1913) until Hull's death in 1952, American psychology was dominated by the image of a satisfied, sleeping, sated animal and by the belief that drive reduction was the fundamental principle of motivation. This was thoroughly disproved by showing that rats will work to drink a non-nutritive solution of saccharin in water (Sheffield and Roby 1950), and that male rats will work to obtain access to a female in heat even if they are not allowed to ejaculate (Sheffield, Wulff, and Backer 1951).

Moreover, the notion of animals that sleep as much as possible does not apply to animals that have evolved complex foraging strategies (Krebs and Inman 1994; Ollason and Lamb 1995; Real 1994). Curiosity evolved from the need to search for food. But curiosity has a long-term adaptive function that goes beyond foraging. Bell (1991) reports, for instance, that animals often explore immediately after feeding and often explore more when satiated than when hungry.

Curiosity implies preference for an environment that can satisfy it. Indeed, many species of mammals, when offered the choice between environments of varying complexity, choose—or even work to obtain—the richer environment (Dember, Earl, and Paradise 1957; Havelka 1956; Hebb and Mahut 1955). Surveys of this literature, which burgeoned in the 1950s and 1960s, may be found in Kreitler and Kreitler's *Psychology of the Arts* (1972, ch. 1, notes 13 and 14) and in Loewenstein (1994).

There is little doubt about the insatiable curiosity of human beings, documented so thoroughly by Shattuck (1996). In our species, curiosity can extend to the contents of our own minds or someone else's. Under these circumstances, propositional attitudes apply to other propositional attitudes. For instance, when I *believe* that I am *remembering* a phone number correctly, the object of my belief (a propositional attitude) is directed toward my remembering (also a propositional attitude) a phone number (the object of the second propositional attitude). Following Scheffler (1991), we say that a *cognitive emotion* is an emotion that rests on a supposition relating to the contents of a person's propositional attitudes (beliefs, predictions, expectations) and bears on its epistemological status (for instance, confirmation). He proposes two such emotions that are familiar to scientists but widespread in entertainment as well. The *joy of verification* is characteristic of much puzzle-solving, and the *feeling of surprise* is a feature much sought after in the mystery genre.

Virtuosity

By virtuosity I mean the pleasure we have when we feel we are doing something well. We say, for example, that an act is performed with virtuosity if it is difficult for most people to do but is carried out with ease and economy. Tightrope-walking and performing lightning mental arithmetic are two examples. However, virtuosity as a source of pleasure does not require that the achievement be extraordinary. We think of our own acts as exhibiting virtuosity when we can perform them when we once could not, even if our skill is no greater than that of others. We then experience the pleasures afforded by virtuosity relative to our previous lack of ability. Sudnow (1978, 1979), for example, describes the feelings of achievement over a period of six years during which he learned to improvise jazz on the piano.

As with curiosity, virtuosity can also be traced back to animal behavior. Anecdotes (Hearne 1987, 1991, 1993) suggest that many domesticated animals enjoy working. Hearne (1987), paraphrasing an animal trainer she admires, writes:

> He says that there are motivations more powerful than instinct, including the instinct to play games. Dogs, he says, *like people,* get the greatest satisfactions from doing something that is difficult well. But he is not so foolish as to suggest that difficulty in the abstract . . . is a motivator. . . . A dog who is track-sure is, most of all, undistractible. Pheasants may explode under her nose, or her worst enemy may offer to fight, she may become footsore, hot, cold or lonely, but if she has a true handler she will keep tracking. (87)

Pryor (1991) writes: "I have seen a dolphin, striving to master an athletically difficult trick, actually refuse to eat its 'reward' fish until it got the stunt right" (346). And finally, an anecdote from Jolly (1985): "The psychologist D. O. Hebb was once testing a chimpanzee on oddity problems when he ran out of banana slices. He noticed that the chimpanzee had been hoarding, rather than eating the rewards, so he took a chance at continued testing. The chimp not only solved his problems but rewarded Hebb with a slice of banana. He ended 22 slices to the good." (409)[17]

Such animals do not "misbehave." The behaviors they learned do not drift toward the fixed action patterns they performed when untrained (Breland and Breland 1961). This suggests that they are doing something for which they are well suited, doing it consistently, and with determination (see D'Amato's [1974, 95–97] discussion of "the work ethic in animals and children").

It is not only domesticated animals that show such tenacity. Consider a rhesus monkey who in the wild leaps over and over again, varying where and how, but persisting in his repetition of the same act. Simpson (1976) has called the repetition of similar actions "projects." Such patterns of behavior are often thought of as play because they

appear to be circumscribed in time and they do not satisfy an immediate need.

The projects of two animals can become coordinated if they are compatible. Mitchell and Thompson (1991) have shown how one animal can engage in its project while offering another the opportunity to engage in another project. For instance, one dog's project may be chasing while the other's is running away, or one chimpanzee may play tickle-the-other while playing avoid-tickles-from-the-other.

From an evolutionary perspective, play evolved to get individuals to practice skills they need to survive. For instance, rough-and-tumble play appears to be an exercise in hunting, avoiding predators, and within-species fighting (Bekoff and Byers 1981; Fagen 1974, 1978, 1981; Konner 1975, 1977; Symons 1974, 1978a, 1978b). The evolutionary perspective does not tell us what process ensures that the individual will engage in play. This, I submit, is the function of pleasures of virtuosity. The pleasures of virtuosity make us want to do things well, and hence we play in order to achieve this pleasure, which gives us skills we need to survive.

The projects of animals at play mentioned in the preceding paragraph are a good example. All of us have experienced the pleasure of a chase. The chaser's anticipation of the pounce grows as she closes in on the pursued, but the emotion changes to momentary disappointment when the pursued dodges a lunge, leading to redoubled efforts on the part of the chaser, and so on. This little episode of play has the required features of a pleasure of the mind: it consists of a sequence of emotions, against the background of a mood of friendliness. At least one object of these emotions is virtuosity—success in a physical activity that requires skill.

Csikszentmihalyi's (1975, 1989) work on *flow,* which may be described as an attempt to develop a theory of the pleasures of the mind,[18] has particular bearing on my discussion of virtuosity. Csikszentmihalyi (1990) describes flow:

> One of the main forces that affects consciousness adversely is psychic disorder [or psychic entropy]—that is, information that conflicts with existing intentions, or distracts us from carrying them out. . . . The opposite state from the condition of psychic entropy is optimal experience. When the information that keeps coming into awareness is congruent with goals, psychic energy flows effortlessly. There

is no need to worry, no reason to question one's adequacy. But whenever one does stop to think about oneself, the evidence is encouraging: "You are doing all right." . . . We have called this state the *flow experience*, because this is the term many of the people we interviewed used in their descriptions of how it felt to be in top form. (36, 39–40)

"Being in top form" captures well the experiences Csikszentmihalyi equates with flow. Here are two of his examples: (1) Rico has a repetitive job on an assembly line, but he does not get bored because he approaches his task the way an athlete approaches a competition: he challenges himself to improve the speed of his performance, and when he does well, the experience is enthralling. (2) Pam is a young lawyer who sometimes spends hours in the library; her concentration is such that she skips meals and doesn't notice the passage of time.

Csikszentmihalyi (1990, 48–67) lists eight properties of enjoyment, two of which I interpret as features of virtuosity, and two of which I consider to be features of all pleasures of the mind. (Unfortunately, I can do no more than mention the latter two here.) The four properties are shown in table 7.3.

As I have characterized virtuosity, I have made it clear that it is a pleasure that is present only in animals that play. It is a pleasure that is functional in altricial species that do not come into the world fully equipped to perform whatever tasks they need for survival. The more learning the young of the species needs to do, the greater its pleasure from virtuosity. In contrast, curiosity is a far more primitive pleasure (although the human form of reflexive curiosity has no apparent evolutionary antecedent); it emerged out of foraging far earlier in evolutionary time than did play.

Work to Be Done on the Taxonomic Question

I have only scratched the surface of the taxonomic question. There is much work to be done on the role of curiosity and virtuosity in the pleasures of the mind. But I have not even touched on two important issues regarding the taxonomic question. The first is the existence of other evolutionarily important categories of OOEs. I have given some thought to two likely categories: the pleasures of nurture and the pleasures of belonging to a social group. The former may contribute not only to pleasures that involve child-rearing but to any activity that requires taking care of living things, such as gardening, nursing, or teaching. The latter may contribute to activities that involve social interactions, essentially variants of primate grooming and human gossip (Dunbar 1996; Levin and Arluke 1987).

The second important taxonomic issue is the existence of what might be called *negative pleasures of the mind*, which are unique to humans. These are pleasures whose function is to relieve the psychological suffering that is our fate. Two kinds of suffering may be palliated through pleasures of the mind: *mundane suffering* and *existential suffering*. Mundane suffering consists of psychological pains such as shame and guilt (Schneider 1977/1992; Lewis 1993), whereas existential suffering consists of fears of death and related concerns (Becker 1973; Solomon, Greenberg, and Pyszczynski 1971). Whether each of these categories gives rise to a different set of pleasures, and what particular OOEs are involved, are open questions. It is likely that some spiritual pleasures are related to these forms of suffering and are thus negative pleasures. It is also likely that pleasures of the mind whose OOE arouses disgust or depicts violence belong to the category of negative pleasures.

TABLE 7.3   Reinterpretation of Four Features of Flow

Category	Features	Reinterpretation
Nature of the activity	Neither too easy nor too hard (49–53) Has goals (54–56) Gives feedback (56–58)	Features of activities that offer opportunity to acquire virtuosity
Effect of the activity	We feel in control (59–62)	Effect of acquiring virtuosity
Nature of our involvement in the activity	We immerse ourselves in it (53–54)	Precondition of all pleasures of the mind
Effects of the activity	Makes us forget ourselves (58–59, 62–66) Time slows down (66–67)	Effects of all pleasures of the mind

Source: Csikszentmihalyi (1990). The page numbers refer to this text.

Conclusions

The pleasures of the mind present numerous research problems that touch on cognition, personality theory, and social psychology; anthropology and primatology; philosophy; and literary and music theory. I have proposed a research framework that characterizes the pleasures of the mind by claiming that they are delimited (but not necessarily continuous) experiences that we seek out and cherish, they involve sequences of emotions, and they differ from each other in three ways: the emotions they consist of, their temporal organization, and the objects of these emotions.

I am grateful to many for suggestions on this chapter: Felice Bedford, Marcel Franciscono, Renate Franciscono, Mitchell Green, Jon Haidt, Angeline Lillard, Colin Martindale, Paul Rozin, Arthur Schulman, Judith Shatin, Timothy Wilson, Daniel Wegner, and Dan Willingham. I also am grateful to Tom Bever for inviting me to give a lecture on this work at the University of Arizona in 1997, an experience that led me to rethink certain aspects of this project.

Notes

1. You may substitute whatever gastronomic joy you wish. I chose this restaurant because, according to http://www.eurogourmet.com/rest/rindex.html (accessed August 17, 1997), it gets the highest marks from Michelin and Gault-Millau.
2. According to Epicurus, the highest pleasure is the pleasure of tranquillity, which is to be obtained by the removal of unsatisfied wants. The way to do this is to eliminate all but the simplest wants.
3. For instance: "Among BaAka (central African pygmies) . . . not moving, singing, or clapping or at least commenting socially in an active way means one is not 'there'" (M. Kisliuk, personal communication, June 19, 1997).
4. This section owes a great deal to Paul Rozin (this volume).
5. For my present purposes, I exclude from these material exchanges drinking, sniffing, snorting, eating, or inhaling substances that alter moods, perception, or behavior by acting on the central nervous system.
6. How the female orgasm fits into this scheme—whether it involves a physiological analog to ejaculation—is a matter of debate (see, for example, Alzate 1985).
7. Relief pleasures should not be confused with the emotional *opponent processes* that occur after the removal of emotionally charged stimuli (Mauro 1988; Sandvik, Diener, and Larsen 1985; Solomon 1980; Solomon and Corbit 1974). A discussion of the relation between opponent processes and relief pleasures would be profitable but beyond the scope of this chapter.

8. A description of a 1992 Jean-Louis Chave Hermitage from the Northern Rhône, found at http://www.inter-axus.com/pages/wrhone92.html (accessed July 1, 1997).
9. The visual, graphic, plastic, decorative, and performing arts, to which we can add music and architecture.
10. At http://ourworld.compuserve.com/homepages/R_Behringer/smetmol.htm (accessed November 28, 1997) R. Behringer quotes Smetana's description: "The work depicts the course of the river Vltava, beginning from the two small sources, the cold and the warm Vltava, the joining of both streams into one, then the flow of the Vltava through forests and across meadows, through the countryside where festivals are just being celebrated; by the light of the moon a dance of water nymphs; on the nearby cliffs proud castles, mansions and ruins rise up; the Vltava swirls in the St. John's rapids, flows in a broad stream as far as Prague, the Vyšehrad [the oldest building in Prague] appears, and finally the river disappears in the distance as it flows majestically into the Elbe."
11. Even the immobility of painting does not mean that our experience of it is static. Indeed, the search for a temporal pattern in the scanning of pictures is one of the motivations for recording the eye movements of viewers (Gandelman 1986; Kristjanson and Antes 1989; Molnar 1976–77; Sprinkart 1987; Zangemeister, Sherman, and Stark 1995). Also keep in mind that not all works of visual art are immobile (for example, the paintings of Agam, which change as you walk past them).
12. But the mood-altering properties of these stimuli may become ineffective when we are depressed. For example, consider William Styron's account of his depression "My . . . beloved home for thirty years, took on for me . . . an almost palpable quality of ominousness" (quoted in Frijda 1993, 384).
13. The proportion is $\phi = (1 + \sqrt{5})/2 = 1.618 \ldots$, which is the solution of the quadratic equation $\phi^2 - \phi - 1 = 0$ (Kappraff 1991, §1.6, 1.7, and ch. 3).
14. Bever (1987, p. 317) calls this "the 'goldilocks' theory of aesthetic experience—what humans like must not be too intense, not too weak, but *juuuuuust* right" (317).
15. The Pleistocene epoch was a geochronological period that began about 1.6 million years ago and ended about 10,000 years ago, consisting of a succession of glacial and interglacial climatic periods. By the mid-Pleistocene, *Homo sapiens* had evolved in Africa.
16. But even Meyer does not flesh out his argument about emotion.
17. I am grateful to my colleague, Charles L. Fry Jr., for bringing this anecdote to my attention.
18. I do not present it as such because its scope is narrower than my view of the pleasures of the mind, as becomes clear from the following summary.

References

Abu-Lughod, L. (1986). *Veiled sentiments: Honor and poetry in a Bedouin society.* Berkeley: University of California Press.

Aiken, H. D. (1955). Some notes concerning the aesthetic and the cognitive. *Journal of Aesthetics and Art Criticism, 13,* 390–91.

Alzate, H. (1985). Vaginal eroticism: A replication study. *Archives of Sexual Behavior, 14,* 529–37.

Apter, M. J. (1982). *The experience of motivation: The theory of psychological reversals.* San Diego: Academic Press.

Balling, J. D., and Falk, J. H. (1982). Development of visual preference for natural environments. *Environment and Behavior, 14,* 5–28.

Becker, E. (1973). *The denial of death.* New York: Free Press.

Bekoff, M., and Byers, J. (1981). A critical analysis of the ontogeny and phylogeny of mammalian social and locomotor play: An ethological hornet's nest. In K. Immelman (Ed.), *Behavioral development* (pp. 296–337). Cambridge: Cambridge University Press.

Bell, W. J. (1991). *Searching behaviour: The behavioural ecology of finding resources.* London: Chapman and Hall.

Berlyne, D. E. (1960). *Conflict, arousal, and curiosity.* New York: McGraw-Hill.

———. (1967). Arousal and reinforcement. In D. Levine (Ed.), *Nebraska symposium on motivation 1967* (pp. 1–110). Lincoln: University of Nebraska Press.

———. (1971). *Aesthetics and psychobiology.* New York: Appleton-Century-Crofts.

——— (Ed.) (1974). *Studies in the new experimental aesthetics: Steps toward an objective psychology of aesthetic appreciation.* Washington, D.C.: Hemisphere.

Berscheid, E. (1983). Emotion. In H. H. Kelley (Ed.), *Close relationships* (pp. 110–68). San Francisco: Freeman.

Bever, T. G. (1987). The aesthetic basis for cognitive structures. In M. Brand and R. Harnish (Eds.), *The representation of knowledge and belief* (pp. 314–56). Tucson: University of Arizona Press.

Bharucha, J. J. (1994). Tonality and expectation. In R. Aiello and J. A. Sloboda (Eds.), *Musical perceptions* (pp. 213–39). New York: Oxford University Press.

Boring, E. G. (1950). *A history of experimental psychology.* 2nd ed. Englewood Cliffs, N.J.: Prentice-Hall.

Boyle, K. (1985). *Words that must somehow be said.* San Francisco: North Point Press.

Breland, K., and Breland, M. (1961). The misbehavior of organisms. *American Psychologist, 16,* 661–64.

Brooks, C., and Warren, R. P. (1979). *Modern rhetoric.* 4th ed. New York: Harcourt Brace Jovanovich.

Burke, K. (1973). Literature as equipment for living. In *The philosophy of literary form* (3rd ed., pp. 293–304). Berkeley: University of California Press.

Buss, D. M. (1989). Sex differences in human mate preferences: Evolutionary hypotheses tested in 37 cultures. *Behavioral and Brain Sciences, 12,* 1–49.

———. (1996). The evolutionary psychology of human social strategies. In E. T. Higgins and A. W. Kruglanski (Eds.), *Social psychology: Handbook of basic principles* (pp. 3–38). New York: Guilford.

Cabanac, M. (1995). What is sensation? In R. Wong

(Ed.), *Biological perspectives on motivated activities* (pp. 399–418). Norwood, N.J.: Ablex.

Carlsen, J. C. (1981). Some factors which influence melodic expectancy. *Psychomusicology, 1,* 12–29.

Chatman, S. (1978). *Story and discourse: Narrative structure in fiction and film.* Ithaca, N.Y.: Cornell University Press.

Cosmides, L., and Tooby, J. (1994). Origins of domain specificity: The evolution of functional organization. In L. Hirschfeld and S. Gelman (Eds.), *Mapping the mind* (pp. 85–116). New York: Cambridge University Press.

Csikszentmihalyi, M. (1975). *Beyond boredom and anxiety.* San Francisco: Jossey-Bass.

———. (1989). The dynamics of intrinsic motivation. In R. Ames and C. Ames (Eds.), *Handbook of motivation theory and research* (vol. 3, pp. 45–71). New York: Academic Press.

———. (1990). *Flow: The psychology of optimal experience.* New York: Harper & Row.

D'Amato, M. R. (1974). Derived motives. *Annual Review of Psychology, 25,* 83–106.

Dember, W. N., Earl, R. W., and Paradise, N. (1957). Response by rats to differential stimulus complexity. *Journal of Comparative and Physiological Psychology, 50,* 514–18.

Dorfman, D. D., and McKenna, H. (1966). Pattern preference as a function of pattern uncertainty. *Canadian Journal of Psychology, 20,* 143–53.

Dowling, W. J., and Harwood, D. L. (1986). *Music cognition.* Orlando, Fla.: Academic Press.

Dunbar, R. (1996). *Grooming, gossip, and the evolution of language.* Cambridge, Mass.: Harvard University Press.

Ekman, P. (1992). An argument for basic emotions. *Cognition and Emotion, 6,* 169–200.

———. (1994). All emotions are basic. In P. Ekman and R. J. Davidson (Eds.), *The nature of emotion: Fundamental questions* (pp. 15–19). New York: Oxford University Press.

Elias, N., and Dunning, E. (1986). The quest for excitement in leisure. In N. Elias and E. Dunning (Eds.), *Quest for excitement: Sport and leisure in the civilizing process* (pp. 63–90). Oxford: Basil Blackwell.

Fagen, R. M. (1974). Selective and evolutionary aspects of animal play. *American Naturalist, 108,* 850–58.

———. (1978). Evolutionary biological models of animal play behavior. In G. Burghardt and M. Bekoff (Eds.), *The development of behavior: Comparative and evolutionary aspects* (pp. 385–404). New York: Garland STPM Press.

———. (1981). *Animal play behavior.* New York: Oxford University Press.

Fiske, H. E. (1996). *Selected theories of music perception.* Lewiston, N.Y.: Edwin Mellen.

Francès, R. (1970). Intèrêt et préférence esthéthique pour les stimuli de complexité variable. Étude comparative. *La Recherche, 70,* 207–24.

———. (1971). Les choix et les jugements esthétiques. *Journal de Psychologie, 46,* 553–61.

Frank, H. (1959). *Informationsästhetik.* Quickborn, Germany: Schnelle.

Frijda, N. H. (1993). Moods, emotion episodes, and emotions. In M. Lewis and J. M. Haviland (Eds.), *Handbook of emotions* (pp. 381–403). New York: Guilford.

Gandelman, C. (1986). The "scanning" of pictures. *Communication and Cognition, 19,* 3–26.

Garner, W. R. (1962). *Uncertainty and structure as psychological concepts.* New York: Wiley.

———. (1970). Good patterns have few alternatives. *American Scientist, 58,* 3442.

Green, R. G. (1997). Psychophysiological approaches to personality. In R. Hogan, J. Johnson, and S. Briggs (Eds.), *Handbook of personality psychology* (pp. 387–414). San Diego: Academic Press.

Havelka, J. (1956). Problem-seeking behavior in rats. *Canadian Journal of Psychology, 10,* 91–97.

Hearne, V. (1987). *Adam's task: Calling the animals by name.* London: Heinemann.

———. (1991). *Bandit: Dossier of a dangerous dog.* New York: HarperCollins.

———. (1993). *Animal happiness.* New York: Harper Perennial.

Hebb, D. O., and Mahut, H. (1955). Motivation et recherche du changement perceptif chez le rat et chez l'homme. *Journal de Psychologie Normale et Pathologique, 48,* 209–21.

Hollander, J. (1975). The poem in the eye. In *Vision and resonance: Two senses of poetic form* (pp. 245–87). New York: Oxford University Press.

Jackendoff, R. (1989). *Consciousness and the computational mind.* Cambridge, Mass.: MIT Press.

Johnston, V. S., and Franklin, M. (1993). Is beauty in the eye of the beholder? *Ethology and Sociobiology, 14,* 183–99.

Jolly, A. (1985). *The evolution of primate behavior.* 2nd ed. New York: Macmillan.

Jones, A., Wilkinson, H. J., and Braden, I. (1961). Information deprivation as a motivational variable. *Journal of Experimental Psychology, 62,* 126–37.

Kahneman, D., and Miller, D. T. (1986). Norm theory: Comparing reality to its alternatives. *Psychological Review, 93* (2), 136–53.

Kappraff, J. (1991). *Connections: The geometric bridge between art and science.* New York: McGraw-Hill.

Konner, M. S. (1975). Relations among infants and juveniles in comparative perspective. In M. Lewis and L. A. Rosenblum (Eds.), *Friendship and peer relations* (pp. 99–129). New York: Wiley.

———. (1977). Evolution of human behavior development. In P. H. Liederman and S. Tulkin (Eds.), *Culture and infancy: Variations in human experience* (pp. 69–109). New York: Academic Press.

Koubovi, D. (1992). [Bibliotherapy: Literature, education, and mental health]. Jerusalem: Magness Press. (Published in Hebrew)

Krebs, J. R., and Inman, A. J. (1994). Learning and foraging: Individuals, groups, and populations. In L. A. Real (Ed.), *Behavioral mechanisms in evolutionary biology* (pp. 46–65). Chicago: University of Chicago Press.

Kreitler, H., and Kreitler, S. (1972). *Psychology of the arts.* Durham, N.C.: Duke University Press.

Kristjanson, A. F., and Antes, J. R. (1989). Eye movement analysis of artists and non-artists viewing paintings. *Visual Arts Research, 15,* 21–30.

Krumhansl, C. L. (1990). *Cognitive foundations of musical pitch.* New York: Oxford University Press.

Lang, J. H. (Ed.). (1988). *Larousse gastronomique.* New York: Crown.

Levin, J., and Arluke, A. (1987). *Gossip: The inside scoop.* New York: Plenum Press.

Lewis, M. (1993). Self-conscious emotions: Embarrassment, pride, shame, and guilt. In M. Lewis and J. M. Haviland (Eds.), *Handbook of emotions* (pp. 563–73). New York: Guilford.

Loewenstein, G. (1994). The psychology of curiosity: A review and reinterpretation. *Psychological Bulletin, 116,* 75–98.

Mandler, G. (1984). *Mind and body.* New York: Norton.

Martindale, C., and Moore, K. (1989). Relationship of musical preference to collative, ecological, and psychological variables. *Music Perception, 6* (4), 431–46.

Martindale, C., Morre, K., and Borkum, J. (1990). Aesthetic preference: Anomalous findings for Berlyne's psychobiological theory. *American Journal of Psychology, 103* (1), 58–80.

Mauro, R. (1988). Opponent processes in human emotions? An experimental investigation of hedonic contrast and affective interactions. *Motivation and Emotion, 12,* 333–418.

Maus, F. E. (1988). Music as drama. *Music Theory Spectrum, 10,* 56–73.

———. (1991). Music as narrative. *Indiana Theory Review, 11,* 1–34.

———. (1997). Narrative, drama, and emotion in instrumental music. *Journal of Aesthetics and Art Criticism, 53,* 293–303.

Meyer, L. B. (1956). *Emotion and meaning in music.* Chicago: University of Chicago Press.

———. (1973). *Explaining music.* Berkeley: University of California Press.

Mitchell, R., and Thompson, N. (1991). Projects, routines and enticements in dog-human play. In P. P. G. Bateson and P. H. Klopfer (Eds.), *Perspectives in ethology,* vol. 9, *Human understanding and animal awareness* (pp. 189–216). New York: Plenum Press.

Molès, A. (1966). *Information theory and aesthetic perception.* Urbana: University of Illinois Press.

Molnar, F. (1976–77). [Temporal aspects of spatial arts]. *Bulletin de Psychologie, 30,* 739–45. (Published in French)

Narmour, E. (1990). *The analysis and cognition of basic melodic structures: The implication-realization model.* Chicago: University of Chicago Press.

———. (1992). *The analysis and cognition of melodic complexity: The implication-realization model.* Chicago: University of Chicago Press.

Ollason, J. G., and Lamb, A. E. (1995). The meaninglessness of foraging behavior. In N. S. Thompson (Ed.), *Behavioral design* (pp. 279–96). New York: Plenum Press.

Orians, G. H., and Heerwagen, J. H. (1992). Evolved responses to landscapes. In J. H. Barkow, L. Cosmides, and J. Tooby (Eds.), *The adapted mind: Evolutionary psychology and the generation of culture* (pp. 555–79). New York: Oxford University Press.

Pryor, K. (1991). The domestic dolphins. In K. Pryor and K. S. Norris (Eds.), *Dolphin societies: Discoveries and puzzles* (pp. 345–47). Berkeley: University of California Press.

Real, L. A. (1994). Information processing and the evolutionary ecology of cognitive architecture. In L. A. Real (Ed.), *Behavioral mechanisms in evolutionary biology* (pp. 99–132). Chicago: University of Chicago Press.

Reber, A. S. (1993). *Implicit learning and tacit knowledge: An essay on the cognitive unconscious.* New York: Oxford University Press.

Ruble, D. N., and Seidman, E. (1996). Social transitions: Windows into social psychological processes. In E. T. Higgins and A. W. Kruglanski (Eds.), *Social psychology: Handbook of basic principles* (pp. 799–829). New York: Guilford.

Sandvik, E., Diener, E., and Larsen, R. J. (1985). The opponent process theory and affective reactions. *Motivation and Emotion, 9,* 407–18.

Scheffler, I. (1991). In praise of the cognitive emotions. In *In praise of the cognitive emotions and other essays in the philosophy of education* (pp. 3–17). New York: Routledge.

Schellenberg, E. G. (1996). Expectancy in melody: Tests of the implication-realization model. *Cognition, 58,* 75–125.

Schneider, C. D. (1992). *Shame, exposure, and privacy.* New York: Norton. (Originally published in 1977)

Schneirla, T. C. (1959). An evolutionary and developmental theory of biphasic processes underlying approach and withdrawal. In M. R. Jones (Ed.), *Nebraska symposium on motivation* (vol. 7, pp. 1–42). Lincoln: University of Nebraska Press.

Shapiro, L., and Epstein, W. (1998). Evolutionary psychology meets cognitive psychology: A more selective perspective. *Mind & Language, 13,* 171–94.

Shattuck, R. (1996). *Forbidden knowledge: From Prometheus to pornography.* New York: St. Martin's Press.

Sheffield, F. D., and Roby, T. B. (1950). Reward value of a non-nutritive sweet taste. *Journal of Comparative and Physiological Psychology, 43,* 471–81.

Sheffield, F. D., Wulff, J. J., and Backer, R. (1951). Reward value of copulation without sex drive reduction. *Journal of Comparative and Physiological Psychology, 44,* 3–8.

Shweder, R. A. (1991). *Thinking through cultures: Expeditions in cultural psychology.* Cambridge, Mass.: Harvard University Press.

Simpson, M. J. A. (1976). The study of animal play. In P. P. G. Bateson and R. A. Hinde (Eds.), *Growing points in ethology* (pp. 385–400). New York: Cambridge University Press.

Solomon, R. (1980). The opponent-process theory of acquired motivation: The costs of pleasure and the benefits of pain. *American Psychologist, 8,* 691–712.

Solomon, R., and Corbit, R. (1974). An opponent-process theory of motivation: Temporal dynamics of affect. *Psychological Review, 81,* 119–45.

Solomon, S., Greenberg, J., and Pyszczynski, T. (1971). Terror management theory of self-esteem. In C. R. Snyder and D. R. Forsyth (Eds.), *Handbook of social and clinical psychology: The health perspective* (pp. 21–40). New York: Pergamon Press.

Sprinkart, P. (1987). [Saccadic eye movements in aesthetic perception]. *Rivista di Psicologia dell'Arte, 8,* 19–37. (Published in Italian)

Sudnow, D. (1978). *Ways of the hand: The organization of improvised conduct.* New York: Knopf.

———. (1979). *Talk's body: A meditation between two keyboards.* New York: Knopf.

Suls, J. M. (1972). Two-stage model for the appreciation of jokes and cartoons: Information-processing analysis. In J. H. Goldstein and P. E. McGhee (Eds.), *The psychology of humor* (pp. 81–100). San Diego: Academic Press.

———. (1977). Cognitive and disparagement theories of humor: A theoretical and empirical synthesis. In A. J. Chapman and H. C. Foot (Eds.), *It's a funny thing, humor* (pp. 41–45). Elmsford, N.Y.: Pergamon Press.

Symons, D. A. (1974). Aggressive play and communication in rhesus monkeys (*Macaca mulatta*). *American Zoologist, 14,* 317–22.

———. (1978a). *Play and aggression: A study of rhesus monkeys.* New York: Columbia University Press.

———. (1978b). The question of function: Dominance and play. In E. O. Smith (Ed.), *Social play in primates* (pp. 193–230). New York: Academic Press.

Tesser, A., and Martin, L. (1996). The psychology of evaluation. In E. T. Higgins and A. W. Kruglanski (Eds.), *Social psychology: Handbook of basic principles* (pp. 400–32). New York: Guilford.

Tooby, J., and Cosmides, L. (1998). Evolutionizing the cognitive sciences: A reply to Shapiro and Epstein. *Mind & Language, 13.*

Treitler, L. (1989). *Music and the historical imagination.* Cambridge, Mass.: Harvard University Press.

Turner, F. (1991). *Beauty: The value of values.* Charlottesville: University Press of Virginia.

Unyk, A. M., and Carlsen, J. C. (1987). The influence of expectancy on melodic perception. *Psychomusicology, 7,* 3–23.

Walker, E. L. (1981). The quest for the inverted U. In H. I. Day (Ed.), *Advances in intrinsic motivation and aesthetics* (pp. 39–70). New York: Plenum Press.

Watson, J. B. (1913). Psychology as the behaviorist views it. *Psychological Review, 20,* 158–77.

Wittgenstein, L. (1958). *Philosophical investigations.* 3rd ed. Translated by G. E. M. Anscombe, Englewood Cliffs, N.J.: Prentice-Hall.

Wundt, W. M. (1874). *Grunzüge der physiologischen Psychologie.* Leipzig: Engelmann.

Wyer, R. S., Jr., and Collins, J. E. (1992). A theory of humor elicitation. *Psychological Review, 99,* 663–88.

Zajonc, R. B. (1968). Attitudinal effects of mere exposure. *Journal of Personality and Social Psychology, 9* (monograph supplement 2, part 2), 1–28.

Zangemeister, W. H., Sherman, K., and Stark, L. (1995). Evidence for a global scanpath strategy in viewing abstract compared with realistic images. *Neuropsychologia, 33,* 1009–25.

Zillmann, D., Hay, T. A., and Bryant, J. (1975). The effect of suspense and resolution on the appreciation of dramatic presentations. *Journal of Research in Personality, 9,* 307–23.

8 Questions Concerning Pain

Eric Eich, Ian A. Brodkin, John L. Reeves, and Anuradha F. Chawla

What would interested nonspecialists most want to know about pain? What would be most important for them to know? From this perspective, this chapter examines eight questions—some conceptual in nature (for example, how is pain defined?), others methodological (how is pain measured?), and still others oriented toward issues of practical significance (how do changes in weather affect pain perception?). In developing answers to these questions, our goals are cogency and conciseness, not completeness. Much more thorough and detailed accounts are available in the publications cited throughout this chapter and in the standard reference texts edited by Bonica (1990a), Bromm and Desmedt (1995), Sicuteri et al. (1992), Sinatra et al. (1992), Turk and Melzack (1992), and Wall and Melzack (1994). Issues relating specifically to the management of clinical pain are reviewed broadly by Scarfing (1994) and discussed in detail by Gatchel and Turk (1996).

WHAT IS PAIN? The most obvious question to ask about pain has long been considered one of the hardest to answer. Indeed, many of this century's leading pain specialists either despaired of ever devising a suitable definition or insisted that pain is undefinable (see Bonica 1990a). Thus, Lewis (1942) allowed that "I am so far from being able satisfactorily to define pain . . . that the attempt could serve no useful purpose" (V), while Beecher (1959) asserted that "lexicographers, philosophers and scientists have none of them succeeded in defining pain" (5).

Much of the difficulty that attends the problem of defining pain reflects the perplexing, often paradoxical, nature of pain itself. As Melzack and Wall have remarked:

> Pain has obvious sensory qualities, but it also has emotional and motivational elements. It is usually caused by intense, noxious stimulation, yet it sometimes occurs spontaneously without apparent cause. It normally signals physical injury, but it sometimes fails to occur even when extensive areas of the body have been seriously injured; at other times it persists after all the injured tissues have healed and becomes a crippling problem that may require urgent, radical treatment. (1982, 9)

Despite these complexities, and notwithstanding the disheartening views of Lewis and Beecher, many researchers and clinicians have persisted in their efforts to develop a definition of pain that would be acceptable to most, if not all, concerned parties. Their persistence has paid off: it is now possible to point to a general definition of pain that has gained widespread, though not universal, acceptance in a relatively short time. Here we refer to the definition, published in 1979 by the International Association for the Study of Pain (IASP), which states that pain is *an unpleasant sensory and emotional experience associated with actual or potential tissue damage, or described in terms of such damage* (IASP Subcommittee on Taxonomy, 1979).

Simple as it sounds, the IASP definition is significant in three respects. First, the definition breaks with the centuries-old tradition of conceptualizing pain strictly as a sensory response to noxious stimulation—a process termed "nociception" by Sherrington (1906). Instead, the IASP definition implies that pain is more properly understood as a psychological state, a subjective experience, or, more simply, a perception. Elaborating on this shift in emphasis, the noted neurophysiologist Allan Basbaum observes that:

> Pain is not just a stimulus that is transmitted over specific pathways but rather a complex perception, the nature of which depends not only on the intensity of the stimulus but on the situation in which it is experienced and, most importantly, on the affective or emotional state of the individual. Pain is to somatic stimulation as beauty is to a visual stimulus. It is a very subjective experience. (cited in Morris 1994, 18)

Second, the IASP definition acknowledges that pain is a multidimensional rather than a unitary construct; that is, pain is an experience associated not only with sensory attributes such as intensity, duration, and location, but also with emotional feelings, including anxiety, annoyance, and depression (see Craig 1994; Price and Harkins 1992).

Third, by allowing that pain can be *either* associated with *or* described in terms of tissue damage, the IASP definition accommodates the astonishing fact that physical injury is neither a necessary nor a sufficient condition for the subjective experience of pain. Amplifying this point, Melzack and Wall note that:

> The link between pain and injury seems so obvious that it is widely believed that pain is always the result of physical damage and that the intensity of pain we feel is proportional to the severity of injury. In general, this relationship between injury and pain holds true: a pinch of a finger usually produces mild pain while a door slammed on it is excruciating; a small cut hurts a little, while a laceration can be agonizing. However, there are many instances in which the relationship fails to hold up. For example, about 65% of soldiers who are severely wounded in battle and 20% of civilians who undergo major surgery report feeling little or no pain for hours or days after the injury or incision (Beecher 1959). In contrast, no apparent injury can be detected in about 70% of people who suffer from chronic low back pain (Loeser 1980). Clearly, the link between injury and pain is highly variable: injury may occur without pain, and pain without injury. (1982, 15)

Earlier we remarked that the IASP definition has gained widespread but not universal acceptance since its publication in 1979. One criticism is that the definition does not apply to living organisms (including human infants, demented adults, and nonhuman primates) who are incapable of expressing their subjective experience of pain through verbal self-report (Anand and Craig 1996). Also, while it is clear that pain is "unpleasant," the qualities of this state are complex and comprise multiple dimensions that have yet to be determined (Melzack and Wall 1982). Nonetheless, even the sternest critics agree that the IASP definition (1) represents a marked improvement over prior formulations, (2) enhances communication among pain specialists (no small feat, given that pain science subsumes such diverse specialities as anesthesiology, neurology, psychiatry, and psychophysics), and (3) opens the door to areas of research that might otherwise have remained closed (such as cultural, religious, and personality differences in the experience and expression of pain; see Chapman and Turner 1990). Accordingly, many specialists regard the IASP definition as one of the most important advances that have been made in the field of pain within the last twenty years.

HOW DOES ACUTE PAIN DIFFER FROM CHRONIC PAIN?

A second recent development of major significance has been the realization that chronic pain is a distinct medical entity that differs from acute pain along several dimensions, including time course. As a rule, acute pain appears in close association with tissue injury, inflammation, or a disease process, and it disappears with healing; in contrast, chronic pain persists beyond the usual course of an acute disease or a reasonable time for an injury to heal. Thus, whereas in acute pain the pain is a symptom of disease, in chronic pain the pain itself is the disease (see Fine and Hare 1990; Sternbach 1974).

Emotional reactions represent another point of departure between acute and chronic pain. Though people suffering acute pain understandably worry about their prospects for full recovery, their anxiety abates once proper diagnosis and treatment begin. For people with chronic pain, however, the pattern is different—and more distressing. According to Fordyce and Steger:

> The initial anxiety associated with the pain experience persists and may eventually evolve into a feeling of helplessness and despair as the pain persists in spite of the health system's attempts to alleviate it. Without relief, the patient suffering from chronic pain begins to feel fatigued by constant pain and the relatively small amounts of sleep which result. In addition, he or she feels hopeless and frustrated, and cannot see an end to the suffering. With continuation of this scenario, the patient becomes increasingly frustrated and angry at the health care system or his or her immediate family, since no one has been able to provide a "cure" for the pain. Also by this time, typically it has been suggested that the pain may not be "real" and psychotherapy may be the only answer. To a person perceiving almost constant daily pain these suggestions are not anxiety-reducing. (1979, 130)

Fordyce and Steger further argue that although a strict focus on tissue damage can be an effective orientation in the treatment of acute pain, such a unidimensional approach often proves problematic in dealing with chronic pain. In part, this is because many chronic pain complaints (especially those involving the lower back) cannot be traced to an identifiable organic insult or injury. More important, however, is the fact that chronic pain patients have to learn how to live with their illness, month after month, year after year; thus, over time, both their public expression and their private experience of pain become more dependent on environmental, cognitive, and social influences, and less dependent on nociceptive input (see Fine and Hare 1990). Indeed, so great are the differences between chronic and acute pain that medical treatments well suited to the latter are often unsatisfactory for the former. As an example, Shealy and Maurer (1974) found that transcutaneous nerve stimulation was 80 percent effective in cases of acute pain, but only 25 percent effective in cases of chronic pain.

One other difference between acute and chronic pain merits mention. As Bonica (1990a) has pointed out, acute pain due to internal disease has the vital function of warning the individual that something is wrong, and it often prompts the person to seek professional aid and to modify temporarily his or her normal activities so as to promote healing. In contrast, pain in its chronic, persistent form serves *no* biologic function. Instead, it is, to borrow Bonica's piquant phrase, a "malefic force that often imposes severe emotional, physical, economic, and social stresses on the patient and on the family, and is one of the most costly health problems for society" (19).

We will revisit the distinction between acute and chronic pain later in the chapter. Here we focus more generally on, first, the physiological mechanisms by which pain is perceived, and then on the psychometric methods by which pain is measured.

WHAT MECHANISMS UNDERLIE PAIN PERCEPTION?

Throughout the twentieth century, two general theories of pain mechanisms have been especially influential in shaping the course of both basic research and clinical applications. The first, *specificity theory*, proposes the existence of a specific pain system that projects messages from pain receptors in the skin via a pain pathway in the spinal cord to a pain center in the brain.

Though specificity theory was formally developed in the nineteenth century by Müller, Von Frey, and other notable neurophysiologists (see

Bonica 1990b; Melzack and Wall 1982), its conceptual origins are traceable to René Descartes' *Treatise of Man*, posthumously published in 1664. This work contains a number of oft-reproduced illustrations, the most famous of which is the kneeling individual depicted in figure 8.1. Descartes wrote:

> If fire *A* is near foot *B*, the particles of this fire (which move very quickly, as you know) have force enough to displace the area of skin that they touch; and thus pulling the little thread *cc*, which you see to be attached there, they simultaneously open the entrance to the pore *de* where this thread terminates [in the brain]; just as, pulling on one end of a cord, one simultaneously rings a bell which hangs at the opposite end.
>
> Now the entrance of the pore or small conduit *de*, being thus opened, the animal spirits from cavity *F* enter and are carried through it—part into the muscles that serve to withdraw this foot from the fire, part into those that serve to turn the eyes and head to look at it, and part into those that serve to advance the hands and bend the whole body to protect it. (1664/1972, 34–35)

To the scientifically sophisticated and technologically minded reader of today, Descartes' ideas

FIGURE 8.1   Descartes' Concept of the Specific Pain Pathway

Source: Descartes, 1664/1972, 35.

are certain to seem quaint, outmoded, even comically simplistic. Yet as Morris has astutely observed:

> This rope-pull model of pain, however primitive, is a direct precursor of the standard medical model developed from Cartesian principles in the mid-19th century and (in many quarters) still going strong. Doctors and researchers adhering to the medical model talk about nociception and endorphins rather than about filaments and animal spirits, but the basic idea is unchanged. They view pain as strictly the result of an internal mechanism that sends a signal from the site of tissue damage to the brain. Most people in the Western world grow into adulthood believing in some version of this Cartesian picture. (1994, 12)

Specificity theory—as originally described by Descartes or as formally detailed much later by Müller, Von Frey, and others—has two big problems. One pertains to the distinction between *physiological specialization* and *psychological specificity.* According to Melzack and Wall:

> Consider the proposition that the skin contains "pain receptors." To say that a receptor responds only to intense, noxious stimulation of the skin is a physiological statement of fact; it says that the receptor is specialized to respond to a particular kind of stimulus. To call a receptor a "pain receptor," however, is a psychological assumption: it implies a direct connection from the receptor to a brain center where pain is felt [as depicted in Descartes' kneeling figure], so that stimulation of the receptor must always elicit pain and only the sensation of pain. (1965, 971)

The problem here is that the assumption of a one-to-one relation between pain perception and the intensity of the stimulus is flatly refuted by the fact, noted earlier, that injury may occur without pain, and pain without injury (see Melzack and Wall 1982).

The second problem with specificity theory is evident upon realizing what is lacking in Descartes' drawing. As Morris has remarked:

> Notice how he—or at least his illustrator—suspends the human figure in a limbo outside time or space. There is literally almost no ground to stand on. The diagram cannot tell us whether the kneeling figure is aristocrat or commoner, French or English, Christian or Jew, even, perhaps, male or female. The calculated blankness probably reflects a desire to situate scientific truth in an abstract or universal realm beyond the irrelevant historical accidents of a specific time and place. But the vagueness of the drawing is exactly the point. Descartes, in this early version of the medical model, gives us pain in a vacuum. (1994, 12–13)

But pain no more exists in a vacuum than it ensues from a fixed, direct-line communication system from the skin to the brain. Instead of simply being a sensation born of bottom-up processing, pain—like any other perception (see Coren and Ward 1989)—is strongly influenced by top-down processes that reflect a broad array of psychological, social, and cultural factors.

Partly as a reaction against specificity theory, Melzack and Wall (1965) introduced the *gate control theory.* illustrated in figure 8.2. The theory is founded on five key propositions:

1. The transmission of nerve impulses from afferent fibers in the skin to spinal cord *transmission (T) cells,* which relay sensory signals to the brain, is modulated by a neural gating mechanism located in the *substantia gelatinosa (SG)*—a gelatinous area of short, densely packed nerve fibers that runs the length of the spinal cord.
2. The gating mechanism is affected by the relative amount of activity in *large-diameter (L)* and *small-diameter (S) fibers:* whereas activity in *L* fibers tends to inhibit transmission (closes the gate), activity in *S* fibers tends to facilitate transmission (opens the gate).
3. The *SG* gating mechanism is influenced by nerve impulses that descend from the brain.
4. A specialized system of large-diameter, fast-conducting fibers—the *central control trigger*—activates selective cognitive processes that then influence, by way of descending fibers, the modulating properties of the *SG.*
5. When the output of the *T* cells exceeds a critical level, it activates the *action system*—those neural areas that underlie the complex, sequential patterns of behavior and experience that are characteristic of pain. (For more detail, see Melzack and Wall 1982, 226–33.)

Though it is hard to overstate the impact that gate control theory had on pain research and therapy, it is easy to understand why the theory proved so influential. For one thing, gate control was the first—and arguably, still the best—model for understanding the dynamic interplay between bottom-up (nociceptive) and top-down (cognitive) processes in the experience of pain. Over the last thirty years, gate control theory has provided a

FIGURE 8.2   Schematic Diagram of the Original Gate Control Theory of Pain

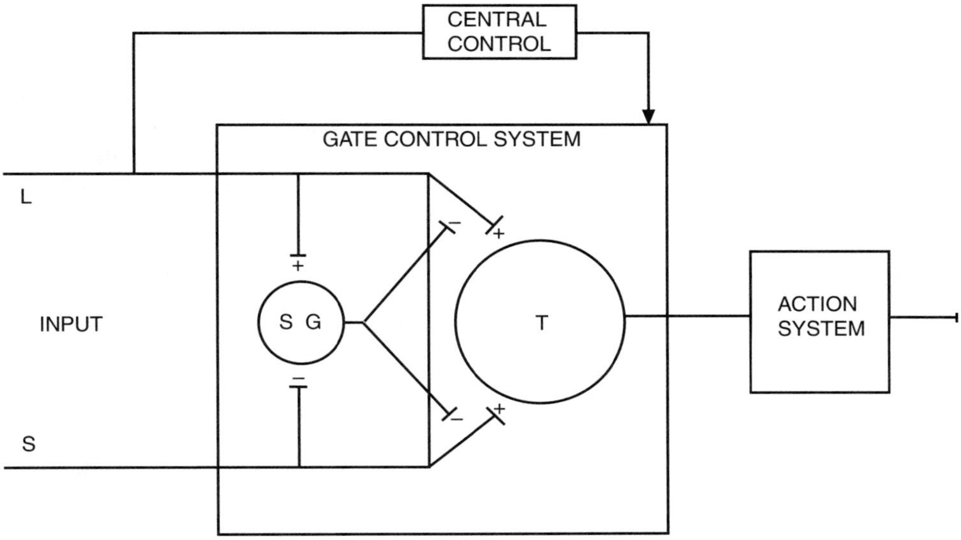

Source: Melzack and Wall 1982, 226. Reprinted with permission from the authors.
Notes: L = large-diameter fibers; S = small-diameter fibers; + = excitation;— = inhibition. L and S fibers project to the substantia gelatinosa (SG) and central transmission (T) cells. The inhibitory effect exerted by the SG on afferent fiber terminals is increased by activity in L fibers (closing the gate) and decreased by activity in S fibers (opening the gate). The central control trigger is represented by a line running from L fibers to the central control mechanisms; these mechanisms, in turn, project back to the gate control system. The T cells project to the action system.

framework for research that has identified a host of physical, emotional, and cognitive conditions (for example, extent of tissue damage, anxiety, depression, focusing on the pain, boredom) that appear to either open the gate, and hence potentiate pain, or close the gate, and hence diminish pain (for example, counterstimulation through heat or massage, relaxation training, and stress inoculation techniques).

Gate control theory also helps explain many commonplace pain experiences. For instance, an attentive parent is often able to quiet a crying child who has bumped her head on a table (activating S fibers that are preferentially responsive to noxious or potentially noxious stimulation) by gently "kissing the boo-boo" (activating L fibers that carry information about harmless stimuli like touching or rubbing). Alternatively, even severe injuries sustained in the heat of intense athletic activity may not be perceived as painful as long as the participant's concentration remains fixed on the game. From a clinical perspective, gate control theory has provided valuable insights into pathological conditions, including deafferentation pain

syndromes caused by a variety of lesions to or diseases of the peripheral and/or central nervous system (see Casey 1991; Nashold and Ovelmen-Levitt 1991).

In addition to giving rise to a variety of new neurophysiological, pharmacological, and psychological treatments (see Abram 1993; Brown 1992; Turk 1996), gate control theory has helped establish a new model for understanding chronic pain. In contrast to the enduring *biomedical* model's emphasis on chronic pain as a disease resulting from "objective" anatomic or physiologic pathology, the newer *biopsychosocial* model focuses on illness—a subjective state or self-attribution that results from a complex interaction of biological, psychological, and societal variables (see Morris 1994; Turk 1996).

Since its introduction in 1965, gate control theory has undergone several revisions in an attempt to accommodate new psychological and physiological knowledge (see Melzack and Casey 1968; Melzack 1993). Though several specific aspects of the theory have been challenged in the past (see Nathan 1976) and remain contentious today (see

Wall 1996), gate control theory still provides a coherent framework for many clinical observations, and it continues to spur research and to stimulate interest in both the psychological and the physiological factors involved in the experience of pain.

How Is Pain Measured?

As noted earlier, pain research has been dominated until recently by the concept of pain as a purely sensory experience (Melzack and Katz 1992). The pain experience was thought to reflect directly the degree of tissue damage or disease present and the corresponding activation of specialized nerve endings or nociceptors. Thus, the pain experience was seen as reflecting a linear transmission of nociceptive information from the point of injury to the brain. However, as has already been stressed, pain is much more than a purely sensory experience initiated by nociceptive stimulation. Rather, nociceptive information enters a dynamic nervous system that is the substrate of the individual's current and past psychosocial and experiential history, where it undergoes significant transformation (Melzack and Wall 1982). Since the time of Beecher (1959), systematic investigations and clinical observation have shown the pain experience to be significantly influenced by psychosocial context (Kerns and Jacob 1992), the meaning of the pain to the individual (Beecher 1959), the patient's cultural background (Melzack and Wall 1982), and the individual's beliefs and coping resources (Williams and Keefe 1991). Pain is also dramatically influenced by one's emotional status, particularly with respect to levels of anxiety and depression (Sternbach 1974, 1977). Clearly, pain is not the simple end-product of a linear sensory transmission system; rather, it is a complex perceptual experience involving interactions between ascending and descending systems (Melzack and Katz 1992). As a result, individual experiences of pain may vary widely.

Pain has been used to describe experiences ranging from a fractured finger to a broken heart. One patient suffering from back pain may communicate the experience as burning, deep, and aching, while another may describe the pain as frightening, depressing, and devastating, even though the extent of tissue pathology is apparently identical. The same pain, but very different communications. In the former scenario, the descriptors are indicative of a physiologically based sensory experience, while in the latter the descriptors describe the distasteful dimension of pain we call suffering, or the affective experience. Moreover, one patient may continue to pursue gainful employment while the other may stay in bed, showing different behavioral responses to the pain.

Individual differences in the pain experience are not only personal but also involve an astonishingly complex interaction of sensory, affective, and evaluative qualities. In an extension of the original gate control theory, Melzack and Casey (1968) proposed a model of pain composed of three psychological dimensions. In addition to the sensory-physiological dimension, which occupied the attention of earlier research and clinical practice, they proposed that pain also consists of motivational-affective and cognitive-evaluative dimensions, each subserved by physiologically specialized systems of the brain. The multidimensional model of pain is widely accepted in both experimental and clinical settings.

There are no biological markers available at the present time to indicate the presence or degree of pain. Thus, like depression and anxiety, pain must be inferred from the subject's or patient's verbal communications and behaviors. Since pain is not directly observable, how is it measured? Obviously, quantification of pain is critically important in order to assess outcome and make clinical judgments.

The rest of this section provides a brief overview of some of the more frequently used methods for measuring pain, with the focus on clinical settings. Some of the psychophysical and psychophysiological methodologies used in experimental pain research, and to a lesser degree in clinical practice, will not be discussed here but are reviewed in Turk and Melzack's (1992) excellent edited series on pain measurement. The primary forms of pain measurement used by clinicians with humans experiencing pain have been verbal pain descriptors, visual analog scales, numerical rating scales, and measurement of pain behaviors.

Verbal Rating Scales

Since the experience of pain is most frequently communicated verbally, it is not surprising that a significant proportion of pain measurement approaches have involved the use of verbal pain descriptors. Categorical scales, consisting of verbal descriptors or Verbal Rating Scales (VRS), have been widely employed in research and clinical settings (Seymour 1982). The earliest attempts to quantify pain using VRS focused only on the sensory dimension of pain by scaling pain intensity. Patients were asked to choose a descriptor that best characterized their pain from a list of adjectives representing pain intensity and presented in the order of pain severity. For example, one commonly used VRS employs the following descriptors: no pain = 0, mild pain = 1, moderate pain = 2, and severe pain = 3. The number of descriptors may vary. Although simple to use, this form of VRS has been criticized. The data correspond to ordinal- but not ratio-level measurement; hence, assumptions about the intervals between the adjectives reflecting equal magnitudes or increments are impossible. Four-point scales, such as the VRS example given here, can distort the true magnitude differences that may occur as a result of an intervention. For example, Jenson and Karoly (1992) point out that a change from severe (3) to moderate (2) pain on the VRS may represent a 10 percent change in pain or a 50 percent change, depending on the perceived interval of the words on the list. Therefore, questions about the relative magnitude of treatment effects are not possible, and in actuality, one is left only with a rough estimation of pain intensity. The earliest uses of the VRS also failed to measure the affective dimension of pain.

More recent VRS scales have evolved significantly. They now attempt to measure not just the sensory/intensity dimension of pain but affective and evaluative dimensions as well. Some VRS also use sophisticated psychophysical methodology to derive ratio-level scale values for the verbal pain descriptors.

The first real attempt to scale pain as a multidimensional experience was prompted by the gate control theory. The McGill Pain Questionnaire (MPQ) was designed to measure the sensory, affective, and evaluative dimensions of pain (Melzack 1975; Melzack and Torgerson 1971). The MPQ consists of a list of twenty sets of words that describe pain. Patients are told to choose a word from each relevant set consisting of two to six pain descriptors that are rank-ordered with respect to intensity. A numerical value assigned to each descriptor corresponds to its rank order in the respective set. Some of the sets represent sensory-physiological qualities, others are affective-motivational, and one is cognitive-evaluative in nature. A total MPQ score is derived by summing the rank-order value of the chosen descriptors. Similar scores for each of the three dimensions are also calculated, as well as a total number of words chosen. The MPQ continues to be one of the most

widely used instruments and has been translated into several languages. The MPQ has been shown to be sufficiently sensitive to detect the effects of many interventions designed to reduce clinical pain (Melzack and Katz 1992). In addition, the MPQ has been shown to have powerful diagnostic value for a number of pain syndromes (Dubisson and Melzack 1976).

Gracely and his colleagues (see Gracely 1989, 1994) have used cross-modality matching techniques (CMM) to derive ratio-level scale values for pain descriptors. CMM, developed by Stevens (1975), has a long history in the psychophysical scaling of vision, taste, and somatosensory modalities (Price and Harkins 1992). CMM methodology involves matching the perceived intensity of a stimulus (the pain descriptor) proportionately to a quantifiable scale, such as hand-grip force, brightness of light, loudness of a tone, or length of a line. For example, a subject is instructed to squeeze a hand-grip dynamometer, then the loudness of a tone is adjusted to correspond to the magnitude of any verbal pain descriptor, such as "very intense," "weak," and so forth. The scores derived from the hand-grip dynamometer and tone loudness are plotted on a log-log scale to produce a numerical value or magnitude estimation for each descriptor. In this way, meaningful statements can be made about the relative magnitudes of different pain descriptors. In addition, scales have been derived that independently measure both sensory and affective dimensions of pain. Though CMM scales have desirable psychometric properties, they are time-consuming and tedious to develop. Different scales have to be developed for different pain conditions, since standardized descriptor lists have not yet been produced. Research also suggests that CMM-derived pain scores may correlate highly with those obtained using ranking methods, which are much easier to derive. Ease of scale construction and use are critically important for clinical applications.

Visual Analog Scale

Another pain measurement technique that has gained popularity and widespread use in research and clinical settings is the Visual Analog Scale (VAS) (Huskisson 1983; Scott and Huskisson 1976). The VAS and its many variants are perhaps the most widely used pain scaling instruments in pain research and clinical practice. A VAS is a horizontal straight line, usually ten centimeters in length and anchored at each end by the extremes of the experience being measured. For example, in pain research the VAS may be anchored by "no pain" on the left and "most intense pain imaginable" on the right. Pain is signified by placing a mark somewhere on the line representing the magnitude of the experience being measured. A score is derived by measuring the distance in centimeters from "no pain" to the mark placed on the horizontal line. The VAS may have specific points along the line delineating adjectives or numbers, although this practice has been criticized on the grounds that it changes the psychometric properties of the instrument (Huskisson 1983). The VAS has advantages that make it a most desirable instrument. First, it is easy to administer. Second, by changing the descriptors anchoring the ends of the scale, one is able to measure the affective as well as other dimensions of pain and pain-related behavior. Price and his associates (Price 1988; Price et al. 1983) have shown that the VAS can reliably differentiate the sensory and affective dimensions of pain. Third, scores derived from the VAS may be treated as a ratio level and are therefore amenable to statements regarding relative magnitudes of the dimensions being measured. Fourth, the VAS demonstrates sensitivity to treatment effects (Price and Harkins 1992; Turner 1982). The VAS, however, is difficult for many patients to comprehend, especially the elderly, and it is also time-consuming to score.

Numerical Rating Scales

Numerical Rating Scales (NRS) have also been used extensively in clinical settings. They rate pain intensity on a 0 ("no pain") to 10 or 100 ("pain as bad as it could be") continuum. NRS may be presented in various formats and have properties similar to those of the VAS. They are easier to comprehend and score than the VAS. Though this scale has face validity, research is lacking as to its ability to differentiate pain dimensions and show sensitivity to treatment effects (Jenson and Karoly 1992). Patients also have a tendency to remember numbers and to recall the memory of the number rather than the experience.

Pain Behavior

Pain is always communicated through observable behaviors. Pain vocalizations (such as moaning, sighing, crying), as well as physical behaviors (posturing, limping) and facial expressions (grimacing), are frequently observed in relationship to pain. Verbal and nonverbal expressions of pain have been termed "pain behaviors" (see Fordyce 1976, 1988). Many patients may exhibit maladaptive patterns of behavior such as excessive pain verbalizations and somatic preoccupation, as well as a sedentary and restrictive lifestyle and overdependence on medications, family, and the health care system. The extent to which a patient engages in pain behaviors also influences clinical decision-making regarding additional assessment and treatment interventions. Pain behaviors are therefore important not only as a target for clinical intervention but as a subject of measurement themselves (see Keefe and Dunsmore 1992).

Fordyce (1976) pioneered strategies for assessing pain behaviors. He used patient diaries to record major activities performed and amount of time engaged in these activities while sitting, standing and walking, and reclining. The ratings were charted every hour of the waking day along with the patient's corresponding pain rating on a 0 to 10 numerical rating scale. Subsequent research has provided strong support for the role of psychosocial context in eliciting and maintaining pain behaviors independent of the degree of underlying pathophysiology. For example, Block, Kremer, and Gaylor (1980) found that chronic back pain sufferers exhibited many more pain behaviors in the presence of an overly solicitous spouse than in the presence of a neutral observer. Also, White and Sanders (1986) found that by merely attending to a pain patient's discussions about pain, subsequent pain ratings increased significantly. This emphasizes the importance of how pain behaviors may be controlled by their consequences. As Keefe and Williams (1992) have pointed out, the construct of pain behavior is a key component in social learning models of chronic pain (Fordyce 1976).

Keefe and his colleagues (for a review, see Keefe and Williams 1992) have developed sophisticated techniques to observe and measure multiple categories of pain behaviors simultaneously using rating scales and videotaped sampling methodology. They devised specific behavioral categories that have proven useful in determining treatment strategies and assessing outcome. They videotape patients, and specific pain behaviors are measured and categorized while the patient engages in a predetermined sequence of positions (sitting, standing, and reclining) and movements, including pacing (walking) and shifting (moving from one position to another). For example, the most frequent pain behavior categories observed in patients with osteoarthritis are guarding, active rubbing of joints (primarily the knee), unloading the joint, rigidity with movement, and repetitive joint flexion. Chronic back pain patients tend to grimace, guard their movements, rub themselves, and sigh. These categories of pain behaviors have been shown to be relatively independent of depression and to correlate well with several subjective measures of pain intensity (Keefe and Gil 1986). Investigators are now starting to focus not only on the patient's pain behaviors but also on the behaviors of others occupying the patient's psychosocial space (Romano et al. 1992). While assessing pain behaviors is free of the biases inherent in inferring pain from subjective self-report, it is a complicated way of routinely assessing clinical pain and requires trained observers and equipment.

Not only have the scaling techniques of pain measurement become increasingly sophisticated, but these scales have been critically important in advancing research on clinical outcome as well as in enhancing our understanding of basic pain mechanisms.

How Accurate Is Memory for Pain?

Memory for pain plays a prominent role in medical practice. In addition to providing patients with an incentive for seeking professional aid and advice, retrospective reports of pain affect both the diagnosis and the treatment they receive. Moreover, clinicians routinely rely on changes between past and present pain complaints to evaluate the effects of therapy. For these reasons, it is important to ask: What factors affect the accuracy of memory for pain?

One factor is the presence or absence of pain at the time of attempted retrieval. Evidence from several sources suggests that prior episodes of pain are remembered as more severe than they actually were when the intensity of present pain is high, but as less severe when present pain intensity is low (see, for example, Eich et al. 1985; Salovey et al. 1993; Smith and Safer 1993). Thus, present pain intensity appears to exert an assimilative effect on memory for prior pain intensity, such that ratings of the latter are attracted to or displaced toward ratings of the former.

A second significant factor is the duration of the retention interval. By several accounts (for example, Erskine, Morley, and Pearce 1990; Kent 1985), memory for acute pain, like memory for other discrete episodes or events, becomes poorer with the passage of time. Whether memory for a particular

episode of pain "decays" at the same rate as does memory for other kinds of episodic information (such as the emotion one experienced at some specific moment in the past) is an open issue, as is whether different forms of acute pain follow different forgetting functions.

Though issues of a similar sort could be profitably pursued in connection with chronic pain, they may prove more difficult to answer in a clear-cut manner. Part of the problem here is that chronic pain is just that—chronic—and so what happens today (vis-à-vis pain-related experiences and behaviors) is correlated with what will happen in the future and with what has happened in the past. Consequently, when asked to recall the contents of a pain diary they maintained for several weeks or even months, chronic pain patients may respond by reconstructing the past based on their readily accessible knowledge of recent pain experiences and behaviors. Provided that their pain condition has not changed markedly in the meantime, the patients' memory may appear to be very accurate—even though they may be unable to consciously remember the actual data with any degree of confidence, clarity, or completeness. Thus, long-term memory for chronic pain, in contrast to acute pain, may be more a matter of "knowing" than of "remembering" (see Erskine et al. 1990; Tulving 1985).

Two additional factors that may determine the accuracy of pain memory are the type and dimension of pain under investigation. As noted earlier, it is now considered a truism that pain is not a monolithic construct, and that it is useful, for both empirical and theoretical purposes, to differentiate pain in terms of its type (chronic rheumatoid pain versus acute labor pain, for instance) and in terms of its dimension (for example, affective versus sensory). Though there are some preliminary data to suggest that the accuracy of memory depends on both pain type and pain dimension, neither factor has been explored in a rigorous, systematic manner (see Bryant 1993; Erskine et al. 1990).

In designing future studies of these factors, it may be helpful to draw on allied psychophysical research concerning memory for other kinds of subjective states, such as thirst or fear, or memory for other sorts of sensory stimuli, such as taste or color. As an example, Bartleson (1960) had subjects retrieve from memory the image of a named object (such as a field of grass or a box of sand). The subjects then decided which of over nine hundred color chips best matched the object's remembered color. Bartleson compared these "remembered colors" to normative data reflecting the average hue, saturation, and brightness of the corresponding objects.

The result was that nearly every remembered color shifted in the direction of the dominant or most impressive chromatic attribute of the object in question. Thus, grass was remembered as being greener than it actually is, bricks as more red, and the sky as more blue. It would be interesting to know whether the same applies to memory for pain. Do people remember severe sunburns as being hotter and stiffer than they really were, and knife cuts as deeper and sharper, even though they retain an accurate impression of the overall intensity of the pain associated with either injury?

Throughout the section, the focus of discussion has been on how varying retention intervals or other factors affect the accuracy of memory for pain. In a sense, this account is misleading, for what people actually remember, with more or less accuracy, is not pain per se but rather their cognitive experience of pain. Mercifully, most people can recall the sensory, intensity, and affective qualities of a previous episode of pain without actually reexperiencing it (see Morley 1993; Wright and Morley 1995). However, case studies of individuals who have undergone surgical removal of a limb suggest that physical sensations of pain can be relived even in the absence of the original nociceptive input. Such "somatosensory memories" (Katz and Melzack 1990) are a hallmark of the fascinating and frightful phenomenon of phantom limb pain, discussed in the next section.

WHAT IS PHANTOM LIMB PAIN?

The mystery of the pain perceived in a limb that has been removed as a result of an accident or a disease remains unsolved. This chronic pain state is rather easy to diagnose, remarkably difficult to treat, and requires a lot of personal strength on the part of the person afflicted with it. Commonly, sensory attributes of the phantom's pain (for example, location, intensity, and duration) are described as being similar or even identical to characteristics of the pain that was felt in the limb prior to its amputation. The experience of phantom limb pain can be accompanied by a unique set of tactile, visual, auditory, and olfactory sensations. Phantom limb pain has been reported in as many as 80 percent of amputees, sometimes in association with post-traumatic stress disorder; however, research to date has revealed no consistent rela-

tions between the presence or absence of a pre-amputation psychological or psychiatric disease and post-amputation limb pain (Katz and Melzack 1990).

It is currently thought that two connected but dissociable neural systems interact to generate memories serving as a basis for a variety of phantom limb experiences (see Katz 1993; Melzack 1995). The longer and the more continuous the barrage of nociceptive signals from the peripheral somatosensory system into the spinal cord and the brain, the more likely is the involvement of the relevant portion of the sympathetic nervous system controlling various nonvoluntary autonomic vegetative functions. These events combine to sensitize a sensory neuronal circuit for the formation of the memory of pain. This somatosensory memory is reinforced by the cognitive memory component, which contains information about the personal meaning and context of the pre-amputation experience.

The most promising clinical approach to the prevention of phantom limb pain is "preemptive analgesia"—chemical denervation of the to-be-amputated limb achieved by administering regional anesthesia (epidural, spinal, or nerve plexus blockade using narcotics and local anesthetics) for one or two days prior to surgery. An additional benefit appears to be gained if the surgery is performed under a combination of regional and general anesthesia. This strategy allows for maximal abolition of both the sensory and cognitive components of the pain memory, without which phantom limb pain cannot exist.

DO CHANGES IN WEATHER AFFECT THE PERCEPTION OF PAIN?

Many patients with arthritis or other chronic pain conditions, including phantom limb, report that their pain is influenced by changes in the weather. Though a recent study by Jamison, Anderson, and Slater (1995) lends credibility to this claim, it also adds a new, surprising twist to the perceived relation between weather changes and pain complaints.

Participants in the study conducted by Jamison and his colleagues were 558 patients attending chronic pain programs in three meteorologically distinct regions of the United States: a warm, dry climate (San Diego, California), a warm, wet climate (Nashville, Tennessee), and a cold, wet climate (Boston or Worcester, Massachusetts). All patients completed a questionnaire designed to assess which, if any, weather conditions they felt most affected their pain.

The results showed that the majority (68 percent) of all patients believed that changes in the weather influenced their pain. Though cold and damp conditions were considered to affect pain the most, the perceived impact of weather on pain was unrelated to regional climate. Thus, contrary to the common belief that chronic pain is worsened by living in a cold, wet climate, Boston and Worcester patients did not report higher pain scores, higher pain frequencies, or a greater influence of weather on pain than did their counterparts in San Diego and Nashville. In fact, the greatest sensitivity to seasonal changes was reported by patients residing in San Diego, a city known for its pleasant year-round climate.

Though the explanation for this counterintuitive result is unclear, one possibility is that "the body establishes an equilibrium in relation to the local climate so that changes in weather trigger an increase in pain regardless of the prevailing meteorologic conditions" (Jamison et al. 1995, 313)—an idea that calls to mind Brickman, Coates, and Janoff-Bulman's (1978) finding that, over time, people who have experienced either a stunning success (like winning the lottery) or a singular tragedy (like becoming paraplegic) tend to revert to their original level of happiness or sadness. Whatever the explanation, the finding that pain reports are influenced more by relative than by absolute changes in weather further underscores the importance of psychological as opposed to nociceptive factors in the experience of chronic pain.

LIFE WITHOUT PAIN?

Life without pain may sound like an attractive and worthy pursuit, but a close examination of such a goal may surprise the reader. The current working definition of pain—an unpleasant sensory and emotional experience associated with actual or potential tissue damage, or described in terms of such damage—suggests that there are at least two ways to abolish pain. The first solution could lie in becoming profoundly insensate at the periphery of one's sensory domain, while the other could lie in becoming unable to discriminate between pleasure and pain, owing to altered central processing—a state tantamount to becoming emotionally and cognitively inert.

Readers who live with or care for people who,

after years of poorly controlled diabetes mellitus, developed peripheral polyneuropathy may have seen some of the possible ramifications of the first suggestion. The permanent loss of a normal ability to perceive sensations from the feet and hands has profoundly adverse consequences for life and living. These patients are unable to tell the temperature of the water they use and often are unaware of having a cut, a skin breakdown, or an infection, about their feet. Consequently, even the most mundane activities of daily living become a constant threat to their health. Moreover, these patients routinely require numerous hospitalizations for the treatment of injuries that have progressed to a stage where amputation is often the only viable option. There is no doubt that the loss of ability to feel pain results in major changes in these people's life-style that eventually compromises the quality of their very existence.

Some examples of altered central processing (obtundation) are an unconscious coma, psychosis, and similarly abnormal states of perception and cognition. Few if any individuals would consider this approach to be a solution to the problem of the pain-triggered reduction in the quality of their lives.

In the context of this chapter, such abstractions as a pain-free life and living with pain should be examined along the empirical and sequentially causative axis of nociception, disability, and suffering. A total protection against nociceptive stimulation, occurring in either the absence or presence of an identifiable tissue injury, can be ensured only in an extremely protected and sheltered environment where the means to enjoy the pursuit of personal happiness through active living and recreation would be significantly more limited than those currently available to many people. Most people readily accept the risks of short-term pain, which often results from such a pursuit, as long as it does not have any prolonged adverse consequences. Therefore, the identification of the factors and interventions that decrease the likelihood of an acute physical or mental distress becoming either a disabling pain or a painful disability is an important research goal of the medical and socioeconomic sciences.

Generally, in terms of the nature and magnitude of ensuing disability, (1) personal motivation carries the greatest impact on those with lesser injuries, but it is the extent of the (2) initial damage and (3) the sophistication of the available medical expertise that frequently have the greatest impact on the eventual outcome of the more seriously injured. Other important determinants of post-recovery disability are the (4) familial/societal support resources and (5) preexisting individual psychological attributes. For any given individual, the particular combination of these five factors, whether compounded by post-injury pain or not, influences not only the scale of the ensuing physical disability but also the degree of perceived personal (psychological, emotional, spiritual) suffering resulting from it, and therefore, principally determines the quality of that person's life after an injury.

The pursuit of a fulfilling, conscious life without pain, with the concurrent loss of the ability to experience the pleasures of life, is more likely to frustrate a person than to eliminate the pains of living. An improved pain-related quality of life appears to be more achievable by focusing individual and societal resources on limiting the escalation of the mental and physical disability and the person's sense of suffering, both of which may be complicated by recalcitrant pain syndromes, than by attempting to convert life into a pain-free existence. While life as we know and enjoy it is not possible without pain, the challenge for society in general, and science in particular, is to minimize the consequences of the latter on the quality of the former.

Preparation of this chapter was aided by grants to the first author from the (American) National Institute of Mental Health (R01-MH48502) and the (Canadian) Natural Sciences and Engineering Research Council (37335).

References

Abram, S. E. (1993). Advances in chronic pain management since gate control. *Regional Anesthesia, 18,* 66–81.

Anand, K. J. S., and Craig, K. D. (1996). New perspectives on the definition of pain (ediorial). *Pain, 67,* 3–6.

Bartleson, C. J. (1960). Memory colors of familiar objects. *Journal of the Optical Society of America, 50,* 73–77.

Beecher, H. K. (1959). *Measurement of subjective responses.* New York: Oxford University Press.

Block, A. R., Kremer, E. F., and Gaylor, M. (1980). Behavioral treatment of chronic pain: Variables affecting treatment efficacy. *Pain, 8,* 367–75.

Bonica, J. J. (1990a). Definitions and taxonomy of pain. In J. J. Bonica (Ed.), *The management of pain* (2nd. ed., vol. 1, pp. 18–27). Philadelphia: Lea and Febiger.

Bonica, J. J. (1990b). History of pain concepts and therapies. In J. J. Bonica (Ed.), *The management of pain* (2nd. ed., vol. 1, pp. 2–17). Philadelphia: Lea and Febiger.

Brickman, P., Coates, D., and Janoff-Bulman, R. (1978). Lottery winners and accident victims: Is happiness relative? *Journal of Personality and Social Psychology, 35,* 917–27.

Bromm, B., and Desmedt, J. E. (Eds.). (1995). *Advances in pain research and therapy,* vol. 22, *Pain and the brain.* New York: Raven Press.

Brown, R. E. (1992). Transcutaneous electrical nerve stimulation for acute and postoperative pain. In R. S. Sinatra, A. H. Ord, B. Ginsberg, and L. M. Preble (Eds.), *Acute pain: Mechanisms and management* (pp. 379–89). St. Louis: Mosby.

Bryant, R. A. (1993). Memory for pain and affect in chronic pain patients. *Pain, 54,* 347–51.

Casey, K. L. (Ed.). (1991). *Pain and central nervous system disease.* New York: Raven Press.

Chapman, C. R., and Turner, J. A. (1990). Psychologic and psychosocial aspects of acute pain. In J. J. Bonica (Ed.), *The management of pain* (2nd. ed., vol. 1, pp. 122–32). Philadelphia: Lea and Febiger.

Coren, S., and Ward, L. M. (1989). *Sensation and perception.* 3rd. ed. San Diego: Harcourt Brace Jovanovich.

Craig, K. D. (1994). Emotional aspects of pain. In P. D. Wall and R. Melzack (Eds.), *Textbook of pain* (pp. 261–74). Edinburgh: Churchill Livingstone.

Descartes, R. (1972). *Treatise of man.* French text with translation and commentary by Thomas Steele Hall. Cambridge, Mass.: Harvard University Press. (Originally published in 1664)

Dubisson, D., and Melzack, R. (1976). Classification of clinical pain descriptions by multiple group discriminant analysis. *Experimental Neurology, 51,* 480–87.

Eich, E., Reeves, J. L., Jaeger, B., and Graff-Radford, S. B. (1985). Memory for pain: Relation between past and present pain intensity. *Pain, 23,* 375–79.

Erskine, A., Morley, S., and Pearce, S. (1990). Memory for pain: A review. *Pain, 41,* 255–65.

Fine, P. G., and Hare, B. D. (1990). Introduction to chronic pain. *Problems in Anesthesia, 5,* 553–60.

Fordyce, W. E. (1976). *Behavioral methods for chronic pain and illness.* St. Louis: Mosby.

———. (1988). Pain and suffering: A reappraisal. *American Psychologist, 43,* 276–82.

Fordyce, W. E., and Steger, C. C. (1979). Chronic pain. In O. F. Pomerleau and J. P. Brady (Eds.), *Behavioral medicine: Theory and practice* (pp. 125–53). Baltimore: Williams and Wilkins.

Gatchel, R. J., and Turk, D. C. (Eds.). (1996). *Psychological approaches to pain management.* New York: Guilford.

Gracely, R. H. (1989). Pain psychophysics. In C. R. Chapman and J. D. Loeser (Eds.), *Advances in pain research and therapy*, vol. 12, *Issues in pain measurement* (pp. 211–29). New York: Raven Press.

———. (1994). Studies of pain in normal man. In P. D. Wall and R. Melzack (Eds.), *Textbook of pain* (pp. 315–36). Edinburgh: Churchill Livingstone.

Huskisson, E. C. (1983). Visual analogue scales. In R. Melzack (Ed.), *Pain measurement and assessment* (pp. 33–37). New York: Raven Press.

IASP Subcommittee on Taxonomy. (1979). Pain terms: A list with definitions and notes on usage. *Pain, 6,* 247–52.

Jamison, R. N., Anderson, K. O., and Slater, M. A. (1995). Weather changes and pain: Perceived influence of local climate on pain complaint in chronic pain patients. *Pain, 61,* 309–15.

Jenson, M. P., and Karoly, P. (1992). Self-report scales and procedures for assessing pain in adults. In D. C. Turk and R. Melzack (Eds.), *Handbook of pain assessment* (pp. 135–51). New York: Guilford.

Katz, J. (1993). The reality of phantom limbs. *Motivation and Emotion, 17,* 147–79.

Katz, J., and Melzack, R. (1990). Pain "memories" in phantom limbs: Review and clinical observations. *Pain, 43,* 319–36.

Keefe, F. J., and Dunsmore, J. (1992). Pain behavior: Concepts and controversies. *APS Journal, 1,* 92–100.

Keefe, F. J., and Gil, K. M. (1986). Behavioral concepts in the analysis of chronic pain. *Journal of Consulting and Clinical Psychology, 54,* 776–83.

Keefe, F. J., and Williams, D. A. (1992). Assessment of pain behaviors. In D. C. Turk and R. Melzack (Eds.), *Handbook of pain assessment* (pp. 275–92). New York: Guilford.

Kent, G. (1985). Memory for dental pain. *Pain, 21,* 187–94.

Kerns, R. D., and Jacob, M. C. (1992). Assessment of the psychosocial context in the experience of pain. In D. C. Turk and R. Melzack (Eds.), *Handbook of pain assessment* (pp. 235–53). New York: Guilford.

Lewis, T. (1942). *Pain.* London: Macmillan.

Loeser, J. D. (1980). Low back pain. In J. J. Bonica (Ed.), *Pain* (pp. 363–77). New York: Raven Press.

Melzack, R. (1975). The McGill Pain Questionnaire: Major properties and scoring methods. *Pain, 1,* 277–99.

———. (1993). Pain: Past, present, and future. *Canadian Journal of Psychology, 47,* 615–29.

———. (1995). Phantom-limb pain and the brain. In B. Bromm and J. E. Desmedt (Eds.), *Advances in pain research and therapy*, vol. 22, *Pain and the brain* (pp. 73–81). New York: Raven Press.

Melzack, R., and Casey, K. L. (1968). Sensory, motivational, and central control determinants of pain: A new conceptual model. In D. Kenshalo (Ed.), *The skin senses* (pp. 423–39). Springfield, Ill.: Charles C. Thomas.

Melzack, R., and Katz, J. (1992). The McGill Pain Questionnaire: Appraisal and current status. In D. C.

Turk and R. Melzack (Eds.), *Handbook of pain assessment* (pp. 152–60). New York: Guilford.

Melzack, R., and Torgerson, W. S. (1971). On the language of pain. *Anesthesiology, 34,* 50–59.

Melzack, R., and Wall, P. D. (1965). Pain mechanisms: A new theory. *Science, 150,* 971–79.

———. (1982). *The challenge of pain.* Harmondsworth, Eng.: Penguin Books.

Morley, S. (1993). Vivid memory for "everyday" pains. *Pain, 55,* 55–62.

Morris, D. B. (1994). What we make of pain. *Wilson Quarterly* (Fall), 8–26.

Nashold, B. S., and Ovelmen-Levitt, J. (Eds.). (1991). *Advances in pain research and therapy.* vol. 19, *De-afferentation pain syndromes.* New York: Raven Press.

Nathan, P. W. (1976). The gate control theory of pain: A critical review. *Brain, 99,* 123–58.

Price, D. D. (1988). *Psychological and neural mechanisms of pain.* New York: Raven Press.

Price, D. D., and Harkins, S. W. (1992). The affective-motivational dimension of pain: A two-stage model. *APS Journal, 1,* 229–39.

Price, D. D., McGrath, P. A., Rafi, A., and Buckingham, B. (1983). The validation of Visual Analogue Scales as ratio scale measures for chronic and experimental pain. *Pain, 17,* 45–56.

Romano, J. M., Turner, J. A., Friedman, L. S., Bulcroft, R. A., Jensen, M. P., Hops, H., and Wright, S. F. (1992). Sequential analysis of chronic pain behaviors and spouse responses. *Journal of Consulting and Clinical Psychology, 60,* 777–82.

Salovey, P., Smith, A. F., Turk, D. C., Jobe, J. B., and Willis, G. B. (1993). The accuracy of memory for pain: Not so bad most of the time. *APS Journal, 2,* 184–91.

Scarfing, E. P. (1994). *Health psychology.* 2nd ed. New York: Wiley.

Scott, J., and Huskisson, E. C. (1976). Graphic representation of pain. *Pain, 2,* 175–84.

Seymour, R. A. (1982). The use of pain scales in assessing the efficacy of analgesics in post-operative dental pain. *European Journal of Clinical Pharmacology, 23,* 441–44.

Shealy, C., and Maurer, D. (1974). Transcutaneous nerve stimulation for control of pain. *Surgery and Neurosurgery, 2,* 45–47.

Sherrington, C. S. (1906). *Integrative action of the nervous system.* New York: Scribner's.

Sicuteri, F., Terenius, L., Vecchiet, L., and Maggi, C. A. (Eds.). (1992). *Advances in pain research and therapy*, vol. 20, *Pain versus man.* New York: Raven Press.

Sinatra, R. S., Ord, A. H., Ginsberg, B., and Preble, L. M. (Eds.). (1992). *Acute pain: Mechanisms and management.* St. Louis: Mosby Year Book.

Smith, W. B., and Safer, M. A. (1993). Effects of present pain level on recall of chronic pain and medication use. *Pain, 55,* 355–61.

Sternbach, R. A. (1974). *Pain patients: Traits and treatments*. New York: Academic Press.

———. (1977). Psychological aspects of chronic pain. *Clinical Orthopedics, 129,* 150–55.

Stevens, S. S. (1975). *Psychophysics: Introduction to its perceptual, neural, and social prospects*. New York: Wiley.

Tulving, E. (1985). Memory and consciousness. *Canadian Journal of Psychology, 25,* 1–12.

Turk, D. C. (1996). Biopsychosocial perspective on chronic pain. In R. J. Gatchel and D. C. Turk (Eds.), *Psychological approaches to pain management* (pp. 3–32). New York: Guilford.

Turk, D. C., and Melzack, R. (Eds.). (1992). *Handbook of pain assessment*. New York: Guilford.

Turner, J. A. (1982). Comparison of group progressive-relaxation training and cognitive-behavioral group therapy for chronic low back pain. *Journal of Consulting and Clinical Psychology, 50,* 757–65.

Wall, P. D. (1996). Comments after thirty years of the gate control theory. *Pain Forum, 5,* 12–22.

Wall, P. D., and Melzack, R. (Eds.). (1994). *Textbook of pain*. Edinburgh: Churchill Livingtone.

White, B., and Sanders, S. H. (1986). The influence of patients' pain intensity ratings on antecedent reinforcement of pain talk or well talk. *Journal of Behavior Therapy and Experimental Psychiatry, 17,* 155–59.

Williams, D. A., and Keefe, F. J. (1991). Pain beliefs and the use of cognitive-behavioral coping strategies. *Pain, 46,* 185–90.

Wright, J., and Morley, S. (1995). Autobiographical memory and chronic pain. *British Journal of Clinical Psychology, 34,* 255–65.

9　The Mood System

William N. Morris

A review of discussions of the mood concept reveals divergent opinions as to what moods are, especially in terms of their relationship to emotions. In an effort to identify the nature of mood, I reviewed research on the influence of mood on memory, judgment, and self-focused attention. Converging across experimental and correlational methodologies and across clinical and nonclinical populations, I found that elated and depressed moods are generally associated with mood-congruent memory and judgment, and that bad moods increase self-focus. Based on this evidence and a consideration of apparent antecedents of mood, I conclude that mood has the attributes of an "evolved psychological mechanism," as described by Buss (1995). Specifically, mood appears to be sensitive to a particular class of input, namely, the adequacy of resources given current levels of demand. Positive and negative disparities activate the mood system, causing it to influence other psychological systems in such a way as to maintain homeostatic balance between perceived resources and demands. I consider this conception of mood in relation to current and future areas of inquiry such as the influence of mood on information processing, self-regulation of mood, and whether affective states such as anxiety and irritability qualify as moods. I conclude that the intimate connection between mood and subjective well-being follows from the idea that mood is a feeling-based predictor of the near-term prospects of pleasure and pain.

AT THEIR EXTREMES, moods produce uniquely complex and powerful states that afford great pleasure or pain. In her recent memoir of manic-depressive illness, Kay Jamison (1995) vividly portrays both.

> Depression is awful beyond words or sounds or images. . . . It bleeds relationships through suspicion, lack of confidence and self-respect, inability to enjoy life, to walk or talk or think normally, the exhaustion, the night terrors, the day terrors. There is nothing good to be said for it except that it gives you the experience of how it must be to be old, to be old and sick, to be dying; to be slow of mind; to be lacking in grace, polish, and coordination; to be ugly; to have no belief in the possibilities of life, the pleasures of sex, the exquisiteness of music, or the ability to make yourself and others laugh. (p. 217) Yet no matter how dreadful (such) moods . . . have been, they have always been offset by the elation and vitality of others; and whenever a mild and gentlish wave of brilliant and bubbling manic enthusiasm comes over me, I am transported by a pungent scent into a world of profound recollection—to earlier, more intense and passionate times. (211)

Though Jamison is referring to moods that are outliers on the mood continuum, they share with their more mundane and manageable cousins the family resemblance that marks the mood system, namely, their capacity to influence behavior by producing feelings and thoughts regarding one's resourcefulness. In good moods, most goals seem possible of attainment; in bad moods, few do. I believe it is the registration of these changing prospects that produces the suffering and enjoyment associated with mood.

In this chapter, I intend to review what we know about moods: where they come from, how they influence us and, in turn, how we influence or manage them. I believe that the pattern of findings that will emerge from this review is consistent with the speculations of early mood theorists who believed that mood operates as a cue in a self-regulatory system that controls goal-directed behavior. Because moods signal the adequacy of available resources given the level of demands that are impinging (Morris 1992), they constitute a feeling-based prediction about the likelihood of success of goal-directed behavior in the near term (Batson, Shaw, and Oleson 1992). Thus, the pain of depression is due to the inability to envision the experience of rewarding outcomes in the immediately foreseeable future. This suggests an intimate connection between mood and subjective well-being.

A Brief Modern History of the Mood Concept

Currently, psychologists appear to mean one of two things when they use the term "mood." Some (for example, Forgas 1995; Izard 1993) regard mood as an attenuated form of emotion. Others (for example, Batson et al. 1992; Davidson 1994) see mood as a distinctive affective construct with a function that is different from emotion. The rather sharp differences between these two positions can be better understood in the context of a brief historical consideration of how the mood concept has evolved.

An early view was offered by Ruckmick (1936). He considered mood to be "a degenerated or decayed type of emotion" with the following characteristics.

> A mood has only the general affective tone and some of the bodily symptoms in common with emotion. Otherwise it stands in direct contrast to the typical emotion. . . . It is not sudden but usually long drawn out, lasting sometimes for hours, occasionally for days. It has no particular cognitive element. We are often at a loss to say toward whom or what it is directed. By the same token it does not generally seize the whole of consciousness. . . . It does not lend itself to any definite action. Biologically its function is hard to determine. Positively one might state that it is probably more allied to physiological conditions than to direct experience. But certainly many moods are occasioned through . . . experience—a series of mishaps during the day, a stroke of luck in many enterprises, a gay evening with many pleasures. (72–73)

Remarkably, sixty years later, many psychologists would agree almost wholly with these observations.

The first person to focus on moods as a major topic of systematic research was Vincent Nowlis. Best remembered for creating the Mood Adjective Check List, Nowlis can also be credited with the notion that moods are functional. In an early statement, Nowlis and Nowlis (1956) defined mood as "an intervening variable or predispositional factor that is a source of information or discriminable stimuli to the organism, about the current functioning characteristics of the organism" (352).

The Nowlises went on to suggest that moods operate both below and above the threshold of awareness. In the former case, moods have a direct predispositional effect, changing the probability of actions, whereas in the latter, mood operates as a cue, the recognition of which triggers self-regulatory behavior.

Though Nowlis's views were most prominent, other well-known psychologists of the time espoused similar ideas about mood. For example, Edith Jacobsen, a psychodynamicist, called moods the "barometers of the ego" (1957), and Karl Pribram (1970) described them as "monitors" that reflect appraisal of life circumstances.

Despite some degree of consensus about the nature of moods, interest waned and little systematic research followed. There seem to be two likely reasons. First, early research on mood mostly depended on self-report measures, which went out of favor during the 1960s because of their vulnerability to problems such as role demand and experimenter expectancy effects. Second, the cognitive psychology revolution was on the immediate horizon, leading psychologists to turn away from affect.

Interestingly and ironically, the very success of cognitive psychology revived interest in mood, but now because of mood's effect on cognitive processes, especially memory. During the early 1970s, altruism and prosocial behavior was a major research focus in an increasingly cognitive social psychology, and one active area of investigation was the relationship between affective states and helping behavior. In an influential paper, Isen and her colleagues (1978) proposed that the effects of mood on helping might be due to the thoughts that mood brings to mind. In two studies, Alice Isen and her colleagues demonstrated that good moods create a positive bias in memory and judgment.

Later, Gordon Bower (1981) would offer a more formal model of the relation between affective states and memory, and it continues to guide research today. The fundamental idea endorsed by both Isen and Bower was that memory might be organized as a network of "nodes" whose proximity depends in part on the degree to which they are associated in experience. If one adds the assumption of spreading activation, that is, stimulation of a given node produces excitation that spreads to nearby nodes, it follows that moods produce mood-congruent memory because, in life, feeling good tends to be associated with positive events, and feeling bad with negative events.

The success of the early studies on mood and processes of memory and judgment shifted interest toward mood in its own right (for an early review, see Clark and Isen 1982), apart from its influence on helping behavior. A key feature of mood, according to Isen, is its subtlety. Unlike emotions, which she regarded as "interruptive," moods often go largely unnoticed, Isen thought, and as a result, they can broadly affect how we react to whatever is in focal attention at the time.

Also stimulating interest in mood was Zajonc's controversial proposal (1980) that affective systems are at least partly independent of those associated with cognitive processes and that the affective systems have primacy because they are more sensitive to low-intensity stimuli. This implies that affect can be aroused without our knowing the cause because "knowing" is an accomplishment of the cognitive system. This conclusion is important to an understanding of mood because if there is one thing that all commentators have agreed on, it is that moods are diffuse, global, and pervasive as compared to emotions (Morris 1989). The power of Zajonc's contention is that it could explain why this was so. Specifically, because affect can arise without awareness of the inducing event, the feeling would be unaccompanied by the cognitive structure and action tendencies typically provided by appraisal. Indeed, on these grounds, Russell and Woudzia (1986) suggested that Zajonc's notions were of special relevance to mood.

Though both Isen and Zajonc recognized that affect need not be mild in order to be global, diffuse, and pervasive or unarticulated, their research uniformly created feeling states through the use of low-impact manipulations such as free gifts (Isen et al. 1978) and the presentation of sad and happy faces (Murphy and Zajonc 1993). Given the success of these and other studies at demonstrating that mild manipulations influenced a wide range of cognitive processes and behavior (much of this work will be discussed later in this chapter), it is understandable that some psychologists concluded that the mildness of the affect was an essential or defining property (for example, see Sedikides 1995) in order for it to be global, diffuse, and pervasive—in other words, mood. Such a conclusion represented a clear break with early mood theorists who thought moods, like emotions, could vary from mild to intense.

Though such studies made it appear that we often dysfunctionally misattribute feelings to the wrong sources, the ideas of Zajonc were firmly based in a functional approach to affect that helped to legitimize a different way of thinking about mood. Whereas Isen and Bower saw mood as a not necessarily functional by-product of the way in which cognitions are organized, Zajonc's approach is friendly to the idea that specific affective systems might have evolved to accomplish particular objectives—a key feature of many recent discussions of the nature of mood (for example, Batson et al. 1992; Davidson 1994; Frijda 1994; Morris 1992).

Currently, then, advocates of the "little emotion" view of mood, mostly social psychologists, continue to press their view and have been active in research that continues to expand the sorts of cognitive processes that are influenced by low-level affect manipulations. Meanwhile, though the list of those who see mood as having a function distinct from emotion is expanding, there is little agreement about what that function is. For example, Davidson (1994) says that moods exist to bias cognition while emotions bias action. Batson, Shaw, and Oleson (1992) contend that moods inform us of temporary fluctuations in the likelihood of occurrence of future pleasurable and painful events whereas emotions are the result of present hedonically relevant events. Frijda (1994) argues that whereas both mood and emotion are sources of information to the person, they differ in what they signal, emotions indicating reactions to specific affectively important events and mood being a cue to one's current "global state of action readiness" and/or "evaluation of the life situation."

How are we to evaluate these divergent claims? Most of the existing efforts at distinguishing between mood and emotion (for a collection of such distinctions, see Ekman and Davidson 1994) rely on anecdote and opinion. I believe we can do better. Though the definition of hypothetical constructs must rest to some degree on assumption, data and theory can combine to provide shape to what cannot be directly seen. It is to the task of assembling data relevant to understanding the nature of mood that I now turn.

WHAT WE KNOW FROM RESEARCH ABOUT MOOD

Given the disagreements over what moods are, it follows that operational definitions would diverge as well. Thus, what some investigators call mood is seen by others as something else. For example, when Sedikides (1995) wished to study the effect of "mood" on self-conceptions, he asked his subjects to imagine that a friend had been seriously burned or had won a Caribbean cruise. Such a manipulation would not be regarded as a mood manipulation by those who see mood as a response to the circumstances of the self (for example, Lazarus 1994; Morris 1992).

A similar sort of problem arises in studies that simply try to measure "mood" and correlate it with something else. If moods are nothing more than mild or residual emotions, they can be measured with self-report instruments containing representative affects such as "irritated," "sad," "anxious," and "elated." Are these all "moods"? The experimental and clinical literature on mood is heavily focused on a depressed-elated or sad-happy continuum. Later in this chapter, I will consider the extent to which affective states such as anxiety and irritability can be viewed as moods, but for the time being it must be regarded as an open question. To the extent, then, that everyday moods are measured as combinations of more specific positive or negative affects, it may well be that the measured states are quite different from those produced in the laboratory and those observed in clinical settings.

My solution to the question of whether any given study is really about mood or about some other type of affect is to depend upon converging operations. Specifically, I am prepared to assume that when experimental, correlational, and clinical studies of mood converge on the same kind of finding, it is likely that the induced or measured state is qualitatively the same, and also that the process linking the state to a consequence is similar. Though this strategy temporarily reduces the number of different kinds of cognitive and behavioral results that can be attributed to mood, it enhances my confidence that the discovered relationships are both reliable and, importantly, about mood. This sort of strategy, if successful, permits the establishment of a "beachhead"—a firm ground from which theory may emerge that will direct us to expect yet other kinds of findings about mood, which can then be sought in the literature. I believe that there are, in fact, three literatures that demonstrate this property of convergence across manipulated and measured mood, of both the everyday and the clinical variety: mood-congruent memory, mood-congruent perception and judgment, and the effect of mood on self-focused attention.

Mood-Congruent Memory

Through a confluence of events, the possibility that mood might bias memory in such a way as to make mood-congruent thoughts come to mind

has been a major research focus for over twenty-five years among specialties ranging from clinical and experimental psychopathology to social and cognitive psychology. The attention of those interested in abnormal affective processes was stimulated by cognitive theories of depression, especially Beck (1967), who supposed that unfavorable life circumstances, such as the loss of a parent, tend to produce a vulnerability to think about subsequent stressful life events in negative or "depressogenic" ways. These negative schemata purportedly guide explanations for current situations and prevent the adoption of schema-inconsistent beliefs. It wasn't long before other, related theories emerged. Not all of these theories assumed that depressed mood *causes* negative thoughts to come to mind, but all required measurements of the association between mood and memory, and so a lot of data were collected.

As for social psychologists, they were stimulated by Isen's work as well as by the ideas of Zajonc and Bower (the latter being especially influential among cognitive psychologists). Momentum was also supplied as the pendulum that had swung away from affect toward cognition during the late 1960s and early 1970s started to swing back.

As research accumulated, reviews began appearing at a heavy pace (for example, Blaney 1986; Clore, Schwarz, and Conway 1994; Matt, Vazquez, and Campbell 1992; Morris 1989; Sedikides 1992a). In general, these reviews are complementary in that they use different rules for inclusion and exclusion. For example, Matt, Vazquez, and Campbell (1992) excluded all studies in which the to-be-recalled material was self-relevant, whereas Sedikides's (1992a) review considered nothing but the recall of such items. My effort here will be to identify areas of agreement across these various reviews.

The best place to begin, I think, is the review by Matt, Vazquez, and Campbell (1992) because, unlike the others, it employed the technique of meta-analysis to discipline the conclusion-drawing process. Matt and his colleagues selected published studies between 1975 and 1988 in which the to-be-recalled items were verbal materials (for example, nouns, adjectives, sentences, idea units) introduced by the researcher—that is, studies involving personal memories and other self-generated materials were excluded. The degree of mood-congruent recall was assessed in five categories: normal nondepressed, subclinically depressed, clinically depressed, induced depressed, and induced elated.

one dying of a disease, judgments of their own vulnerability to disease should be enhanced more than judgments about other negative events because thoughts related specifically to disease are primed. However, in a series of studies reported by Johnson and Tversky (1983), reading about someone dying of disease increased judgments of vulnerability to disease and nondisease sources of mortality (such as car accidents) just as much as it made other negative events, such as divorce, seem more likely. Similar results have been reported by Kavanagh and Bower (1985). Such results are consistent with the view that feelings, not thoughts, are the principal determinants of these judgments.

Finally, a third line of work initiated by Martin and his colleagues (1993) also bolsters the mood-as-information approach. Their idea is that the influence of mood on a decision depends on how one frames the decision question. For example, if one is engaged in a task while in a good mood and has been given a stop-rule that says, "You may stop whenever you feel satisfied with your performance," the mood-as-information approach predicts early stopping because good mood may be perceived as a sign of satisfaction. On the other hand, if subjects are told to stop when they no longer enjoy the task, sad subjects should stop sooner than happy ones. Martin and his colleagues found exactly such results, and they have since been conceptually replicated and extended in studies by Hirt and his colleagues (1996) and by Sanna, Turley, and Mark (1996).

A different approach has been taken by Forgas (1995), who argues that the relationship between mood and judgment depends on the nature of the strategy that subjects use to make judgments. Forgas identifies four strategies:

1. The direct access strategy, based on direct retrieval of preexisting, crystallized judgments
2. The motivated processing strategy, employed when the computation of a judgment is guided by a specific motivation
3. The heuristic processing strategy, used when judges seek to construct a judgment using various shortcuts
4. The substantive processing strategy, adopted when judges need to engage in the selective, constructive processing of the available information and rely on a variety of learning, associative, and memory processes (1995, 60)

The choice of strategy is supposedly determined by aspects of the judge, the judgment task, and the situation. Strategy tends to determine the likelihood and degree of mood congruence, according to Forgas, with the greatest amount occurring in cases of substantive processing, in which reliance on mood-congruent memory would be greatest. Mood-congruent judgments would also be expected when the heuristic processing strategy is used, as suggested by the mood-as-information approach. On the other hand, Forgas predicted that mood-congruent judgment would not occur in cases where the direct access or motivated processing strategies were used.

Forgas is to be credited for his attempt to integrate the mood-as-information and mood-congruent memory retrieval explanations for mood-congruent judgment, but in my opinion, his analysis does not accommodate the existing literature well. For example, motivated judgments are not supposed to be susceptible to mood, and yet Sedikides's review (1992a) of studies in which mood was manipulated and self-relevant judgments measured found consistent support for mood-congruent judgments across both happy and sad moods. Judgments of self are clearly motivated judgments, and so Forgas cannot easily explain what Sedikides found. Similarly, judgments that have already been arrived at, the so-called direct access case, are said to be relatively impervious to mood. How, then, can one explain the early findings of Isen and her colleagues (1978) showing that judgments about the performance of one's car and television are influenced by mood?

These failures to substantiate predictions of the model as to when there will be a *lack* of mood congruence are critical since, as Schwarz and Clore (1996) point out, most data in the literature demonstrate mood congruence and can be explained without reference to the Forgas typology of judgment strategy. It remains to be seen whether subsequent data will be more supportive.

In conclusion, there is clear and consistent evidence that mood influences judgments of various sorts, and this evidence easily passes the test of convergence across experimental and correlational studies. There are two main exceptions to mood congruence that have occurred with any frequency. First, as I found in my review of the mood-congruent memory literature, a number of researchers fail to find the full measure of mood congruence in the case of negative mood. For example, Moretti and her colleagues (1996) reported that nondysphoric subjects, when provided with positive and negative social reactions directed at them, rated the positive responses as more informative, but subclinically and clinically dysphoric groups rated positive and negative reactions as equally informative. Such results are consistent with the idea of "depressive realism" (Alloy and Abramson 1988), implying that the self-enhancement often found among normal good-mood subjects is lacking among the depressed.

The second consistent failure to find mood-congruent judgments occurs in studies (reviewed by Schwarz and Clore 1996) that manipulate the apparent source of mood so as to discredit its relevance to the target of judgment. Clearly such studies are important because they support the mood-as-information approach and suggest a general way to discover when mood is directly influencing judgments by serving as a source of information, as opposed to the indirect influence of biased memory processes.

Mood and Self-Focused Attention

The last of the well-documented consequences of mood is its effect on attention toward the self. More specifically, it has been repeatedly shown that dysphoric mood is related to higher levels of attention to one's own thoughts and feelings. This result has been demonstrated in a variety of experiments in which mood was manipulated (Greenberg and Pyszczynski 1986; Salovey 1992; Sedikides 1992b; Wood, Saltzberg, and Goldsamt 1990), in correlational studies of nondisturbed populations (Csikszentmihalyi and Figurski 1982; Larsen and Cowan 1988; Wood, Saltzberg, Neale, et al. 1990), and among depressed college students and the clinically depressed (for a review, see Ingram 1990).

The effects of good mood on focus of attention have been inconsistent. Salovey (1992, Study 1) found that both good and bad mood heightened attention to self, but neither Sedikides (1992b) nor Wood, Saltzberg, and Goldsamt (1990, Study 2) found a good-mood effect, and in fact, in the latter study, an internal analysis found a significant negative relationship with better mood being associated with less self-focus.

Curiously, this literature has developed quite independently of the literature on mood-congruent memory and judgment. The major impetus behind the work has been the model of self-regulatory processes proposed by Carver and Scheier (1981). The basic unit in this model is a negative feedback loop that functions to reduce discrepancies between the present state of the organism and some standard or reference value. Such a model might envision negative affect as the central means whereby the system meets its objective. As Wood, Saltzberg, and Goldsamt (1990) put it, "Affect

may warn that something is wrong and that one must attend to the self in order to surmount the failure or to adjust one's standards" (900). Of course, this is precisely what some mood theorists have supposed one distinctive function of mood to be—the provision of information about the self (see, for example, Nowlis and Nowlis 1956; Morris 1992).

In some respects, these ideas and data would also seem relevant to the mood-as-information approach offered by Schwarz and Clore, although they have not discussed the self-focus literature, to my knowledge (nor do the self-focus researchers discuss the mood-as-information idea). In fact, their comments about the effect of mood bear a striking similarity to those of Wood and her colleagues just quoted; specifically, they observe that "negative affective states would inform individuals that their current situation is problematic" (Schwarz and Clore 1996, 446), and they use this idea to explain a variety of results in the literature that suggest that subjects in bad moods work more diligently, processing information more completely in laboratory tasks than do those in a good mood. The difference is that Schwarz and Clore are theorizing about cases where subjects *conclude or decide* something based upon affect, whereas Wood and her colleagues assume that the feelings *initiate* a decision-making process that requires closer examination of self-relevant information.

From my perspective, whether moods influence decisions or initiate self-examination is likely to be a function, in part, of the intensity of the mood. Moods that are low in intensity can influence a wide range of judgments because they do not attract attention or attributional activity on arising and thus are susceptible to misattribution, as the Schwarz and Clore review shows. However, the fact remains that the very same manipulation, the autobiographical recollection technique, has dominated in the study both of mood-congruent judgment (see, for example, Schwarz and Clore 1983, Study 1; Wright and Mischel 1982) and of mood and self-focus (Salovey 1992, Study 1; Wood, Saltzberg, and Goldsamt 1990, Study 1) and so it seems unlikely that self-focus research produces more intense moods. Rather, I suspect that the kind of result obtained in laboratory experiments is mostly determined by what the subjects are asked to do while they are in the mood that was induced. Asking for judgments will interfere with self-focused attention unless the judgments are about internal states or thoughts. Clearly our understanding of mood would benefit if these literatures and paradigms could be better integrated than they currently are.

What Do These (and Other) Data Tell Us About the Nature of Mood?

Summarizing, it appears that bad mood, whether experimentally induced or measured in its "normal" or clinically significant forms, is associated with poorer access to positive memories and heightened access to negative memories, although the latter finding is not obtained quite as consistently. Judgments are mood-congruent as well, except when attention is drawn to an ostensible mood source that is unrelated to the object of judgment. Likewise, positive mood is associated with plentiful evidence of mood-congruent memory and judgment with fewer exceptions than is the case for bad mood. If one were to assume that, overall, manipulated and measured moods are equally strong in their positive and negative manifestations, it would appear that negative moods are less robust causal agents, at least with respect to memory and judgment. If so, this may be due to negative mood being less stable because it is an undesirable state that subjects resist, thereby weakening its influence; alternatively, negative mood may be more likely to attract attention at or near onset, thereby reducing its ability to influence seemingly unrelated objects of judgment (cf. Schwarz and Clore 1983). As for self-focused attention, negative mood is reliably associated with more of it across a large number of studies of differing kinds, but there is little evidence that good mood has any consistent effect on self-focus.

Taken together, these results suggest a number of conclusions about the nature of mood. First, these data help us rule out the idea that moods are "little emotions." Though the decision to consider the three different kinds of research designs—experimental, correlational studies of everyday mood, and studies of clinically significant mood—was undertaken as a way of demonstrating convergent validity, the fact that the exercise was successful in finding similar results across these boundaries strongly implies that moods in mild laboratory manifestations are qualitatively similar to normal everyday moods and the intense moods that are associated with dysfunction and disorder. Indeed, I have previously presented other evidence of this similarity (Morris 1989, 1992) by comparing the symptoms designated by the American Psychiatric Association (1994) as indicative of depressive and manic episodes with the correlates and/or consequences of everyday or manipulated depressed or euphoric mood. For the large majority of the symptoms, laboratory evidence suggests an everyday equivalent. For example, depressed subjects typically report a loss of interest in previously pleasurable activities. Normal subjects induced into a depressed mood show a similar disinterest (Velten 1968). Likewise, the heightened speed of speech that is such a striking feature of mania has been found, though at reduced levels, among normal people in elated moods (Hale and Strickland 1976). Indeed, these kinds of results suggest that differentiating between normal and disordered mood requires more than the blithe assumption that the latter is syndromal since the former appears to be as well.

If moods are not little emotions, what are they? The most important clue derives from the self-focus findings. In their general review of the effect of feelings on various kinds of information-processing tasks, Schwarz and Clore (1996) observe that "negative feelings focus attention on problematic features of the situation" (454). In the case of emotion, it has long been assumed that this focus is directed outward at the provoking stimulus (see, for example, Easterbrook 1959). The fact that bad mood promotes self-focus implies that moods refer distinctively to something about the self, just as Jacobsen (1957), Nowlis and Nowlis (1956), and I (Morris 1992) have supposed. In addition, it seems worth noting that since focal attention is thought to be limited, directing attention toward self means that attention outward is reduced. This implies a concurrent reduction in active involvement in the environment.

As for mood-congruent memory and judgment, both would seem likely to influence action tendencies as well, though it must be admitted that mood-behavior relationships have not been studied as well as mood-cognition relationships. When mood is bad, pessimism reigns. Though the evidence comes largely from self-reports rather than from direct observations of behavior, it appears that people in bad moods have lowered expectations of success whereas those in good moods become more optimistic (see, for example, Cunningham 1988; Johnson and Tversky 1983). Cunningham reports that the preferred activities of subjects in manipulated depressed moods were sitting and thinking, being alone, and taking a nap. Taken together, then, the apparent consequences of bad mood seem designed to cause one to reflect on thoughts and feelings, which, in turn, at least temporarily discourage active involvement in the pursuit of environmental goals. By contrast, good moods seem to maintain or even increase investment in vigorous, outwardly directed action. Cunningham's good-mood subjects were most interested in social, prosocial, vigorous, and leisure activities.

The overall pattern of findings appears consistent with the idea that depression has the function of encouraging conservation of resources. For example, Thayer (1989) suggests the following somewhat more general explanation for why we experience moods: "I view the subjective states as signal systems of resources and depletions, and of danger or safety. They register in conscious awareness the state of the whole body at any point in time and provide a continuing indication of readiness for action or of the need for rest and recuperation" (64).

The view that mood reflects the adequacy of our resources fits nicely with a variety of findings regarding the antecedents of mood. Consider, for example, the findings showing that moods display within-day rhythms in both normal and disordered populations. The best evidence of within-day mood rhythms in normals comes from a study by Clark, Watson, and Leeka (1989), who surveyed the moods of a large sample of college students seven times a day for a week. These investigators found that positive feelings of an activated sort— for example, feeling excited, proud, enthusiastic, and so forth—rose sharply from early morning until midday and then remained constant until 9:00 P.M., after which they fell sharply. Further analysis showed that the noon to 9:00 P.M. plateau was an artifact of averaging across subjects whose peak positive affects occurred equally across the noon, 3:00 P.M., 6:00 P.M., and 9:00 P.M. measurements. No such rhythms were found for activated negative feelings such as irritability, jitteriness, and upset. Low levels of activated positive feelings early and late in the day among the clinically depressed have not been directly measured but can be inferred from reports showing that peak depression also occurs at these two times (Morris 1992), since a lack of positive feelings is the signature of depressive affect.

In addition to diurnal rhythms in mood, survey data reported by Kasper and her colleagues (1989) show seasonal mood shifts in a randomly selected sample of household members. Respondents reported feeling worst mainly in the winter months, with a smaller peak in the summer. These findings correspond to evidence showing the highest levels of seasonal affective disorder (SAD) during the winter, with a second, smaller peak occurring during the summer (Oren and Rosenthal 1992).

Why are moods of a depressive sort worst during the early morning and late in the day and during the winter months? The answer I would propose is that those are the most likely times when we regularly feel less activated. Rhythmic changes in the availability of energy and accompanying perceptions of feelings of activation make sense from an adaptive point of view. Human beings are relatively less equipped to be active at night, because we have poor night vision, and during winter, because the days are cold and short; moreover, sources of food would be relatively unavailable during the winter. Thus, it would be adaptive to experience the impetus to goal-directed activities less at these times than at others. This is exactly what I believe the mood system has evolved to do for us.

A similar explanation can be offered for findings showing a relationship between mood and other determinants of feelings of energy. For example, in a recent study, Gold and her colleagues (1995) employed a hyperinsulinemic glucose clamp procedure to study the effects of acute hypoglycemia on the moods of normal (nondiabetic) subjects. The clamp enabled Gold and her colleagues to precipitate and maintain diabetic-like levels of blood sugar in volunteer subjects. Findings showed that compared to placebo control periods, subjects with induced hypoglycemia reported an increase in what the authors referred to as *tense tiredness* (see Thayer 1989). Tense tiredness consists of the simultaneous presence of high levels of *tense arousal* and low levels of *energetic arousal*. Many other findings testify to the importance of energy as a determinant of mood. For example, Thayer (1987) has shown that both sugar snacks and exercise can produce mood change, and there are plentiful examples of ill health adversely affecting mood (Cohen and Rodriguez 1995).

In some ways, of course, such results seem quite unremarkable. Blood sugar levels became unusually low, and so it seems quite "natural" that one would feel tired. The same kind of criticism might be leveled at the Clark, Watson, and Leeka (1989) findings showing diurnal changes in positive mood. Again, it could be argued that it is unsurprising to find subjects feeling less "energetic" and "alert" in the early morning and late evening given the likely heavy dependence of such feelings on biological processes, which are known to be rhythmic. But it must be remembered that subjects also reported feeling less "proud" and less "enthusiastic" at these times. Similarly, why did subjects with low blood sugar experience high levels of jitteriness and tension? After all, they were fully informed about the nature of the study, so there was little reason to worry about the effects they were feeling. I think both sets of results suggest that there is a functional correspondence between biology and psychology. Specifically, moods tend to be in line with one's biological readiness to engage in potentially costly, goal-directed activity because such a correspondence is generally advantageous.

Of course, not all resources are related to the body, though these may be of great importance to mood. The idea that moods are triggered, more generally, by an assessment of the adequacy of all goal-relevant resources helps to explain why moods also often follow in the wake of emotion. From my perspective, basic emotions, like moods, can be considered adaptive. Elsewhere (Morris 1992) I have suggested that they promote adaptive responses to unexpected environmental events perceived to be either harmful or beneficial. Activation of the sympathetic nervous system prepares one to respond quickly and vigorously to a sudden demand, whether an opportunity or a threat. Instigation of telltale facial expressions signals nearby friends, family, or coworkers who may be able to assist us in taking advantage or defending ourselves. These activated states of emotion are thought by many to simply decay, causing us to pass through a period of attenuated affect widely equated with mood. Thus, it is thought that sadness turns into depression, anger becomes irritation, and fear fades to anxiety. However, evidence suggests that this pattern is far from reliable.

Consider the case of bereavement where grief, an extreme form of sadness, is expected to give way to a period of depression prior to a return to normalcy and health. This pattern is regarded as sufficiently normative that the depression, even though it may reach full syndromal status, is not considered diagnosable as a "disorder" until at least two months have passed (American Psychiatric Association 1994). However, depression need not follow grief. In a well-known study of the bereavement process, Brown and Harris (1978) have shown that the availability of someone who provides a bereaved spouse with a close, confiding relationship prevents the "conversion" of grief into depression.

Similarly, although stressful life events are, by definition, unpleasant, their mood effects may be quite limited because the increased demands that produce stress can be offset by challenge-induced changes in activation, as Thayer (1989) has suggested. It is only when demands exceed available resources that one might expect mood to deteriorate. In fact, stress that is successfully managed confirms the adequacy of one's resources and may even boost mood. Perhaps this helps to explain the otherwise modestly puzzling results reported by both DeLongis, Folkman, and Lazarus (1988) and Bolger and his colleagues (1989). In both of these studies, married-couple respondents completed some weeks' worth of end-of-day diaries designed to assess the occurrence of stressful life events and affect. Although respondents rated their affect as more negative than normal on days during which stressful life events were reported, the mood of respondents was actually higher on the days *following* days containing a stressful life event than it was on the average of all days not containing such an event. One interpretation of such findings is that a contrast effect is at work. Alternatively, and more compatible with the current formulation, I would argue that the negative affect reported on days during which stressful life events occurred was mostly emotion, that is, directly associated with the perceived cause and generative of targeted responses. The heightened positive affect on the succeeding days seems more likely to be good mood that is due to the effect of successful coping on the assessment of self-related resources.

Of course, not all tests of the adequacy of one's resources produce passing grades and the positive mood that may follow. Whereas it is to be expected that the average married couple can cope with what the average day dishes out, more severe tests are likely to defeat a higher proportion of victims, leaving depression as a result. A fairly striking confirmation of this and of the dynamics involved can be found in data reported by Norris and Kaniasty (1995). These authors reviewed the literature looking at the effects of received social support on the well-being of persons subjected to stressful life events and found that "only a handful of studies . . . have revealed beneficial effects of support receipt." Indeed, as they pointed out, "a greater number of studies have revealed no effects or, worse, positive associations between receipt of support and psychological distress" (498). On the other hand, *perceived* social support is consistently associated with better maintenance of well-being subsequent to such events.

Norris and Kaniasty offer what they call the "social support deterioration deterrence" model to account for these results. According to the model, the problem with much of the actual support provided to people in times of need is that it is too little, too late, or even irrelevant to actual need. Given this eventuality, the loss associated with the stressful life event is compounded by the realization that one's social support network is ineffectual. Because social support networks constitute a key resource to help people cope with life's demands, it follows from my theory that a substantial mood effect would ensue. If, on the other hand, the network performs well in a time of need, well-being would be maintained because one would not perceive a deterioration in one's social support network.

Norris and Kaniasty tested their model on data gathered subsequent to two natural disasters, Hurricane Hugo, a category 4 hurricane that devastated North and South Carolina in 1989, and Hurricane Andrew, which struck southern Florida in 1992 and, at the time, became the most costly natural disaster to strike the United States. The key variables measured in both longitudinal studies included an index of the *scope of disaster exposure,* which included assessments of the degree to which respondents experienced injury, perceived threat to life, financial loss, and personal loss (that is, loss of items having more sentimental than financial value); a measure of the amount of *social support received,* including tangible, emotional, and informational support; a measure of *perceived social support;* and a measure of *psychological distress.* Distress was operationalized differently in the two studies, but each had a standardized depression scale, either as its main measure (Hugo) or as its only measure (Andrew). Variables were measured at two points in time, twelve and twenty-four months after Hugo, and six and twenty-eight months after Andrew.

Interestingly, the direct effect linking the scope of disaster exposure to distress (that is, depressive mood) was small and obtained only in the data most proximal to the disaster. The more reliable effect of disaster exposure on distress was an indirect result of a two-component process in which disaster exposure reduced the perception of social support, leading, in turn, to psychological distress, measured as depressive mood. I consider the scope of disaster exposure measure to be an index of loss, and as such a direct determinant of the likely emotional response to these hurricane events. Thus, what would arguably be the best predictor of emotion—loss—turns out to be a relatively poor predictor of mood, here depression. Instead, depression in hurricane victims was largely determined by the grade they assigned to their social support network. People whose social support networks failed to live up to expectation felt diminished and depressed, believing that they had fewer resources than they previously thought.

More generally, the results from these studies involving life stressors and affect suggest to me that though moods and emotions may both be instigated by the same event, they are different processes that respond to different aspects of the episode and different needs of the organism. Basic emotions consist of a collection of reactions including physiological, motoric, and attentional changes, all of which are designed to promote our ability to deal optimally with situations that are important and unexpected. Because emotions suggest some degree of a lack of preparedness for a biologically important event, each occurrence of emotion has the potential to reveal or test the adequacy of the means we have for dealing with the world. This is why moods often follow emotions but need not. The mood consequence depends critically on what we find out about ourselves once the emotion-inducing circumstance subsides. Confirmation of resources promotes good mood and the optimism that attends it. Disconfirmation leads to bad mood, pessimism, and, importantly, self-focus. The capacity of the mood system to attract attention is critically important as a means of facilitating the rebuilding of resources to a more satisfactory level.

Other social scientists have theorized about the importance of resources for affect and well-being. For example, Hobfoll (1989) defines resources as "those objects, personal characteristics, conditions, or energies that are valued by the individual or that serve as a means for attainment of these objects, personal characteristics, conditions, or energies" (516). Hobfoll argues that loss of resources, or the threat of same, produces stress that motivates efforts to minimize further loss. When not under stress, Hobfoll suggests, people strive to generate surplus resources in order to protect against possible future loss. I find much to agree with in Hobfoll's analysis, though I differ with him somewhat on the issue of surplus resources. Though people may attempt to squirrel away extra resources as part of a strategic plan generated by some other psychological mechanism, I believe that the mood mechanism instigates the spending of "surplus resources" by stimulating optimism, which, in turn, should promote new "investments." Thus, I see mood as a homeostatic mechanism, promoting conservation when resources are low and expenditure when they are high (cf. Emmons 1991).

The relationship between resources, affect, and subjective well-being has been the subject of an important study by Diener and Fujita (1995). These researchers obtained estimates of the degree to which their college student subjects were seen by friends and family members as endowed with twenty-one different resources that Diener and Fujita regarded as instrumental in achieving goals. Examples included money, good looks, self-confidence, intelligence, and good health. Moods and a measure of global subjective well-being (SWB) were measured daily for fifty-two days, and life satisfaction, also considered a measure of SWB, was measured at the beginning and end of the study. In addition, all subjects were asked to indicate their fifteen major goals and to rate the relevance of each of the twenty-one resources to obtaining these goals.

Diener and Fujita found generally small relationships between informants' ratings of *individual* resources and subjects' ratings of mood and SWB. However, when resource ratings were summed across all twenty-one resources, slightly more than 25 percent of the variance in the two SWB measures could be accounted for, a substantial relationship given that the resource ratings came from informants, not the subjects themselves. The relationships between summed resources and the daily positive and negative mood ratings were also significant. Further analyses showed that even better predictability of SWB from resources could be obtained by taking account of the fit between the resources an individual was judged as having and the specific goals he or she had. Those subjects who were judged as having the resources that they themselves saw as relevant to the goals that were most important to them had the highest level of SWB. These latter results are consistent with the idea that level of resources is not, in itself, the best predictor of mood. Rather, it is the disparity between available resources and existing demands that is the mood trigger (Morris 1992).

In conclusion, I would argue that the evidence I have reviewed about mood, most of which passes the test of being convergently confirmed across experimental-correlational and normal mood–clinical mood boundaries, suggests that mood has the properties that Buss (1995) associates with "evolved psychological mechanisms." Such mechanisms must have three basic attributes, according to Buss: they must solve a specific problem of individual survival (or reproduction); they must take only certain classes of input that specify to the organism the particular problem it is facing; and finally, they must transform that input through a procedure (such as a decision rule) into output that changes physiological activity, provides information to other psychological mechanisms, or directly influences behavior that results in solving the adaptive problem. Mood solves a problem for us by providing continuous monitoring of the availability of resources necessary for meeting current demands. The input, which consists of information coming from within (the body) and without (the environment), is transformed into feelings (good mood and bad mood) by a decision rule that involves the assessment of resource adequacy. The resulting moods can directly or indirectly influence behavior or attract attention (mostly in the negative case), leading to reassessment of goals or the decision to recruit added resources, thus eliminating any disparities between available resources and demands. The adaptiveness of this system rests on the assumption that goal-directed behavior is more likely to succeed when one possesses ample resources, whereas conservation of existing resources or recruitment of new ones works better than continued striving for a goal when our resources are relatively low.

OLD ISSUES AND NEW DIRECTIONS IN THE STUDY OF MOOD

Space does not permit me much additional discussion, but three topics demand at least brief consideration. First, a relatively large literature concerned with the effects of mood on information processing is beginning to coalesce. I would like to make some comments about the shape that literature is taking. Second, some progress has been made on self-regulation of mood since I last reviewed that literature (Morris 1989), so I would like to update what I think we know now. And finally, much of the literature on mood assumes that moods are adequately described as being of two kinds: good and bad. However, two areas of inquiry, one on the dimensional structure of self-reported affect and the other on the relationship between depression and anxiety, suggest otherwise. Hanging in the balance is whether my analysis of mood can be extended to anxiety and irritability, and so I would like to conclude with some remarks about possible movement forward in that area.

The Effects of Mood on Information Processing

Given the rather impressively consistent and interesting results that emerged from studies looking at the influence of affect on memory and judgment, it is hardly surprising to find this work being extended across a variety of cognitive tasks. Unfortunately, this work has attracted little attention thus far from researchers studying either everyday mood and its correlates or clinically significant mood. As a consequence, I am unable to apply the converging operations approach to these findings in order to ferret out reliable mood effects. Nonetheless, some order has been found amid the chaos by Schwarz and Clore (1996) in their recent review of this literature, though doing so required limiting their consideration of information-processing tasks to those that the authors deemed "sufficiently well understood to allow at least limited inferences" (448). These included the processing of persuasive messages, person perception, and stereotyping. Excluded were studies looking at the influence of affect on information processing during learning tasks, organization of information into meaningful units, and logical problem-solving, areas in which, according to Schwarz and Clore, the findings were considerably less consistent.

The most frequent result among those who have studied the influence of affect on persuasion, stereotyping, and person perception is that depressed subjects are more likely to engage in systematic information processing than subjects who are in a good mood; the latter seem to prefer to use heuristic devices such as stereotypes (see, for example, Bodenhausen 1993) or scripts (Bless et al. 1996). What is puzzling about such results is that they are seemingly inconsistent with findings, from other tasks, that suggest that bad mood leads to reduced effort (see, for example, Hertel and Hardin 1990; Lassiter, Koenig, and Apple 1996). However, it is possible that these findings are compatible. Perhaps bad mood reduces *both* the use of heuristics and effort expenditure. In tasks for which heuristics are available, bad-mood subjects must get along without them, requiring more systematic processing. Why would bad-mood subjects resist the use of heuristics? According to Schwarz and Clore (1996), bad mood signals danger, possibly discouraging shortcuts and promoting full processing of the available information. Al-

ternatively, bad mood seems more likely to attract attention and attributional activity (Schwarz and Clore 1983), and to the extent that many judgmental heuristics are feeling-based (cf. Damasio 1994), bad-mood subjects may be more likely to recognize that such means are at least temporarily unreliable.

Of what relevance are these findings to the theory of mood that I've offered here? Evidence suggesting that bad mood undermines confidence—one way to construe the most reliable effect to emerge from this literature—is supportive, though it must be admitted that one could take the opposite stance by noting that bad-mood subjects are putting forth what seems to be greater effort.

Self-Regulation of Mood

During the 1980s the idea that people regulated their mood emerged from two separate literatures, each of which seemed to show an asymmetry between the effects of good and bad mood. First, whereas positive mood seemed generally to facilitate helping, bad mood did not always reduce helping (for a review, see Carlson and Miller 1987), and in fact, the research of Cialdini and his colleagues showed increases in helping due to bad mood under circumstances suggesting that the helping was undertaken to improve mood (see, for example, Manucia, Baumann, and Cialdini 1984). Second, despite the generally firm evidence of mood-congruent memory, occasional failures were reported, and they were all of a certain kind, namely, while good mood was reliably associated with improved recall of positive memories, bad mood did not always enhance the recall of negative material. A popular explanation for these results was that of "mood repair" (see, for example, Isen 1985): people in bad moods were pictured as actively resisting the remembering of negative items so as to prevent a further deterioration of their moods. However, this explanation suffered because no evidence had surfaced that showed bad-mood subjects recalling more positive memories; they simply failed to remember more negative ones. If one is going to improve one's mood by selective remembering, why not do it right?

Since then, however, such a demonstration has been made, although it was limited to nonlaboratory conditions. Parrot and Sabini (1990) tried to make the case that mood-congruent results are favored in the laboratory, where subjects may perceive a demand to produce them, whereas in the natural environment their only motive is to improve their mood. This seems unlikely in view of the findings of Mayer, McCormick, and Strong (1995) showing robust mood-congruent memory obtained in survey data. More generally, I would expect that mood repair processes would be better predicted by measures of individual differences. A persuasive example has been reported by Smith and Petty (1995). These authors found that negative mood produced mood-congruent memory among subjects with low self-esteem but not in subjects whose self-esteem was high. In fact, the more negative the mood of their high-self-esteem subjects, the more positive were their recollections.

However, the best evidence, in my opinion, of self-regulation of mood came from two other research areas. First, there is the important work of Hull and his colleagues on the effects of alcohol. It is clear that alcohol reliably improves self-reported mood (Hull and Bond 1986), although the effect is short-lived with the longer-term relationship reversed (Aneshensel and Huba 1983). Hull (1981) has suggested that alcohol improves mood because it interferes with the self-relevant thoughts that maintain bad moods. In a pair of studies, Hull, Levenson, Young, and Sher (1983) had subjects consume either alcohol or a placebo beverage, after which they were asked to give short speeches. The speeches were coded for the presence of self-focused statements and first-person pronouns. Alcohol significantly reduced the number of each. Hull and Young (1983) found that subjects given failure feedback consumed more of an alcoholic beverage in a bogus "taste test" that followed *only if they were high in private self-consciousness,* a dispositional measure of the tendency to be self-focused. Taken together, these two papers support Hull's hypothesis.

The other major set of findings demonstrating self-regulation of mood comes from the vast literature demonstrating that most people are motivated to think well of themselves, leading them to take credit for positive information about self while denying or distorting negative information (for a review, see Kunda 1990). Great weight is added to these results if one includes the literature on cognitive dissonance (Festinger 1957), which is still alive and going strong (Aronson 1992). Dissonance research establishes well the conclusion that people who believe that they have freely, and with foreknowledge of the likely consequences, behaved in a way that can be construed as impugning good qualities such as intelligence or good moral standards are motivated to alter their cognitions so as to make such an implication less credible. Dissonance certainly seems to have mood-like characteristics. It is induced by events that imply a diminished resource, namely, self-esteem (Steele, Spencer, and Lynch 1993); it certainly appears to be global and diffuse in that it is readily misattributable to other sources (Cooper and Fazio 1984); and it affects a broad variety of cognitions, perceptions, and behaviors rather than being targeted at a specific object. Most important in the current context, Elliot and Devine (1994) have shown that, subsequent to a standard induced-compliance dissonance manipulation, subjects report increased feelings of psychological discomfort and that these feelings return to baseline levels after subjects are provided with an opportunity to endorse a dissonance-reducing attitude change.

The fact that people appear to self-regulate bad mood by distorting negative self-relevant information and by drinking alcohol, which may work because it permits one to ignore more readily such information, raises two important questions for a functional analysis. First, if bad mood constitutes an important signal to self about the adequacy of resources, aren't these commonly employed ways of "killing the messenger" likely to have negative consequences down the road? The answer to this question is being hotly debated (though not with regard to the use of alcohol, which, as I indicated earlier, seems deleterious in the long run). Specifically, in a much-cited paper, Taylor and Brown (1988) have suggested that mood-enhancing distortions promote good mental health. This idea has stimulated counterargument and a variety of intriguing data suggesting exactly the opposite (see, for example, Colvin, Block, and Funder 1995). Second, the idea that people contrive to silence their moods begs the question of how we accomplish the self-deception that appears to be involved (see Lockard and Paulhus 1988). I suspect that both issues will provide fruitful areas of investigation for some time to come.

How Many "Kinds" of Mood Are There?

Especially among researchers who subscribe to the "little emotion" view of mood, there is an uneasy recognition that virtually all mood research employs manipulations targeted at a happy-sad dimension. Consequently, one finds occasional mention of the need to consider whether other "moods," such as anxiety or irritability, would produce comparable effects. Similar concerns can be found among those who do correlational studies using measures of self-reported mood because, although many negative affects are highly correlated with each other (Watson and Clark 1984), it is also clear that these states have distinctive features (Watson and Clark 1992).

The latter results emerge from an extensive literature indicating that self-reported affect is best fit by two broad bipolar dimensions, either positive and negative affect (Watson and Tellegen 1985) or arousal and pleasantness (Russell 1980). Using arousal and pleasantness as the basic dimensions produces four quadrants of affect: activated pleasant, activated unpleasant, unactivated pleasant, and unactivated unpleasant, within which individual "mood" terms tend to cluster together (Reisenzein 1994). This implies that a minimum of two kinds of positive and negative mood exist.

The idea that momentary mood reflects disparities between perceived resources and demands can be expanded to accommodate this degree of differentiation of the mood space. To do so, one must assume not only that the valence of mood is determined by the adequacy of available resources but that the degree of activation is associated with the kind of demand that is active. Specifically, if the current goal is to obtain some reward, inadequate resources will produce what Higgins (1987) describes as "dejection-related" affect, whereas the very same inadequacy will produce "agitation-related" feeling states when avoidance of a negative or punishing outcome is the goal. (I restrict my discussion here to negative affects because there is much more data and discussion to draw upon, but it should be understood that a similar analysis could be made of the positive affects.) However, because inadequate resources expose one to both kinds of negative outcomes, it also follows that depression, a dejection-related affect, and anxiety, an agitation-related one, would be associated over time. The data indicate this quite clearly. Comorbidity of anxiety and depression is substantial among clinical populations (Judd and Burrows 1992), and in normal ranges, tendencies toward depression and anxiety reside together as central features of the negative affectivity construct (Watson and Clark 1984).

All of this raises the question as to whether the effects of anxiety on memory, judgment, and attention are like those associated with depression. The relevant data, though relatively sparse on the topic of anxiety, have been reviewed by Mathews and MacLeod (1994). These authors concluded that anxiety does produce mood-congruent judgments but that memory and attention are differentially influenced, with anxiety promoting vigilance and better encoding of negative stimuli (little evidence of this was found among depressives) and depression more reliably influencing memory in mood-congruent directions than does anxiety. As for self-focus and anxiety, Ingram (1990) concluded that there is a positive association, though most of the evidence came from studies correlating dispositional measures. In addition, virtually all of the studies reviewed by Mathews and MacLeod measured rather than manipulated anxiety. Thus, the strong conclusions I could reach about the consequences of depression are not possible here.

All in all, though, these few data seem at least compatible with the analysis presented earlier. Because both depression and anxiety are presumed to reflect the perception of inadequate resources, self-focused attention and conservative judgments that promote identification, remedial building, and/or protection of relevant resources make sense. The relation between anxiety and enhanced processing of negative stimuli in the environment follows because punishment is most likely to come from without; vigilance could promote successful passive avoidance. Mood-congruent memory seems more appropriate in the case of depression since there the object is to discourage temporarily further expenditures of already low levels of resources in fruitless efforts to obtain some reward. Because appetitive behavior is more likely to emanate from some internally generated plan, it would be more readily influenced by an expectancy-generating mechanism such as memory.

More valuable than post hoc explanations would be additional data comparable to those I reviewed earlier. Studies that manipulate anxiety would be especially valuable at this point. Researchers following that path would do well to emulate the laboratory studies of dejected affect, which have mostly avoided manipulations of depression-inducing events in favor of instructions designed to get subjects to access the mood states directly. To the extent that anxiety is produced by the mood system, it, too, should be global, diffuse, and pervasive and should often be the *aftermath* of an event that threatens punishment, especially one that somehow reveals or makes salient a deficiency in resources. However, producing such an event in the laboratory would be ill advised because the direct effects would be emotion, not mood, and they would also be subject to the counterinfluence of coping mechanisms.

Perhaps this explains findings reported by Constans and Mathews (1993), who made students anxious by introducing the prospect of taking an examination and then asked for likelihood estimates of various negative events. Constans and Mathews found that "anxious" subjects showed heightened estimates of the likelihood of failing exams but not of other negative events such as being robbed. This evidence of specificity is inconsistent with the global effects of mood manipulations on judgments as reported by Johnson and Tversky (1983) and Kavanagh and Bower (1985). Indeed, Constans and Mathews (1993, Study 1) also found such global effects when they manipulated mood by asking subjects to imagine a series of positive or negative events. They concluded from these data that global effects are due to interference that is caused by using multiple stimuli to produce mood. I consider this unlikely given that Johnson and Tversky used an account of a single event to produce mood and repeatedly found global effects on risk judgments. My explanation of the specificity effect found by Constans and Mathews is that subjects informed of an unanticipated exam initially experience emotion, not mood. Fear, like other emotions, would be expected to produce a narrow focus on the specific threatening event. A better way to study the effect of an anxious *mood* on judgment or any other psychological process or behavior would be to ask subjects to try to recall a time when they felt generally apprehensive about their ability to fend off a variety of punishing circumstances, or perhaps the investigator could give subjects a list of generally accepted "symptoms" of anxiety and invite them to role-play such feelings, as is done in the Velten (1968) procedure.

Finally, the other frequently mentioned negative "mood" is irritability, but even less relevant information exists about it. Anecdotally, of course, feeling irritable is presumed to facilitate the likelihood of angry responses and aggression, and it is the most frequently mentioned exemplar of an attribute often associated with mood, namely, that it changes the threshold for emotional responding (see, for example, Ekman 1994). Though a few scattered investigations have induced low levels of anger and measured some aspect of memory, attention, or judgment, the evidence is too spotty to review. However, there is a promising development on the antecedent side. If irritability is to be subsumed under the heading of negative mood, it must be shown to follow events that lead to a perception of inadequate resources. In a provocative review, Baumeister, Smart, and Boden (1996) mustered a variety of evidence that suggests that aggression is most likely to occur among individuals with unstable high self-esteem in response to feedback that threatens their positive self-image. Baumeister and his colleagues believe that such feedback directly leads to anger and aggression, and that would certainly be an appropriate analysis in cases where hostility is directed at the source of the feedback. However, hostile actions are often "displaced" onto other targets and occur with no obvious provocation. In such cases, irritable mood following in the wake of the threatening event may be a better explanation, especially if it can be shown that aggression helps to restore a sense of adequacy.

MOOD AND SUBJECTIVE WELL-BEING

Summarizing, based on the evidence that I have reviewed, I believe that the mood system serves us by assessing the adequacy of our current resources and producing feelings capable of influencing goal-directed activity. It is, I think, an ancient system, shared with every organism whose reward-seeking and punishment-avoiding behaviors are sufficiently complex and flexible that they can vary as a function of its currently available assets. If I am on the right track in characterizing the mood system this way, then it follows that mood can be a major determinant of subjective well-being because what it tells us is nothing short of the prospects for pleasure and pain.

And yet, it is well to remember that the mood system appears to be a homeostatic mechanism, the success of which is suggested by the fact that the average mood of the average person is mildly positive (Diener 1984). With mood mostly out of mind, operating quietly in the background (Morris 1989), it may appear to be a less influential determinant of subjective well-being than cognitively based construals about our progress toward major life goals . . . at least until we recognize our ultimate dependence on feelings, including mood, in charting the very path toward those goals (cf. Zajonc 1980; Damasio 1994).

REFERENCES

Alloy, L. B., and Abramson, L. Y. (1988). Depressive realism: Four theoretical perspectives. In L. B. Alloy (Ed.), *Cognitive processes in depression* (pp. 223–65). New York: Guilford.

American Psychiatric Association. (1994). *Diagnostic and statistical manual of mental disorders.* 4th ed. Washington, D.C.: American Psychiatric Association.

Aneshensel, C. S., and Huba, G. J. (1983). Depression, alcohol use, and smoking over one year: A four-wave longitudinal causal model. *Journal of Abnormal Psychology, 92,* 119–33.

Aronson, E. (1992). The return of the repressed: Dissonance theory makes a comeback. *Psychological Inquiry, 3,* 303–11.

Batson, C. D., Shaw, L. L., and Oleson, K. C. (1992). Differentiating affect, mood, and emotion: Toward functionally based conceptual distinctions. *Review of Personality and Social Psychology, 13,* 294–326.

Baumeister, R. F., Smart, L., and Boden, J. M. (1996). Relation of threatened egotism to violence and aggression: The dark side of high self-esteem. *Psychological Review, 103,* 5–33.

Beck, A. T. (1967). *Depression: Clinical, experimental, and theoretical aspects.* New York: Hoeber.

Blaney, P. H. (1986). Affect and memory: A review. *Psychological Bulletin, 99,* 229–46.

Bless, H., Schwarz, N., Clore, G. L., Golisano, V., Rabe, C., and Wolk, M. (1996). Mood and the use of scripts: Does a happy mood really lead to mindlessness? *Journal of Personality and Social Psychology, 71,* 665–79.

Bodenhausen, G.V. (1993). Emotions, arousal, and stereotypic judgments. In D. M. Mackie and D. L. Hamilton (Eds.), *Affect, cognition, and stereotyping* (pp. 13–37). San Diego: Academic Press.

Bolger, N., DeLongis, A., Kessler, R. C., and Schilling, E. A. (1989). Effects of daily stress on negative mood. *Journal of Personality and Social Psychology, 57,* 808–18.

Bower, G. H. (1981). Mood and memory. *American Psychologist, 36,* 129–48.

Bower, G. H., and Mayer, J. D. (1989). In search of mood-dependent retrieval. *Journal of Social Behavior and Personality, 4,* 133–68.

Bower, G. H, Monteiro, K., and Gilligan, S. G. (1978). Emotional mood as a context for learning and recall. *Journal of Verbal Learning and Verbal Behavior, 17,* 573–87.

Brown, G. W., and Harris, T. (1978). *Social origins of depression: A study of psychiatric disorder in women.* New York: Free Press.

Buss, D. M. (1995). Evolutionary psychology: A new paradigm for psychological science. *Psychological Inquiry, 6,* 1–30.

Carlson, M., and Miller, N. (1987). Explanation of the relation between negative mood and helping. *Psychological Bulletin, 102,* 91–108.

Carver, C. S., and Scheier, M. F. (1981). *Attention and self-regulation: A control-theory approach to human behavior.* New York: Springer-Verlag.

Clark, L. A., Watson, D., and Leeka, J. (1989). Diurnal variation in the positive affects. *Motivation and Emotion, 13,* 205–34.

Clark, M. S., and Isen, A. M. (1982). Toward understanding the relationship between feeling states and social behavior. In A. H. Hastorf and A. M. Isen (Eds.), *Cognitive social psychology* (pp. 73–108). New York: Elsevier.

Clore, G. L., Schwarz, N., and Conway, M. (1994). Affective causes and consequences of social information processing. In R. S. Wyer and T. K. Srull (Eds.), *Handbook of social cognition* (2nd ed., vol. 1, pp. 323–418). Hillsdale, N.J.: Erlbaum.

Cohen, S., and Rodriguez, M. S. (1995). Pathways linking affective disturbances and physical disorders. *Health Psychology, 14,* 374–80.

Colvin, C. R., Block, J., and Funder, D. C. (1995). Overly positive self-evaluations and personality: Negative implications for mental health. *Journal of Personality and Social Psychology, 68,* 1152–62.

Constans, J. I., and Mathews, A. M. (1993). Mood and the subjective risk of future events. *Cognition and Emotion, 7,* 545–60.

Cooper, J., and Fazio, R. H. (1984). A new look at dissonance theory. In L. Berkowitz (Ed.), *Advances in experimental social psychology* (vol. 17, pp. 229–66). New York: Academic Press.

Csikszentmihalyi, M., and Figurski, T. J. (1982). Self-awareness and aversive experience in everyday life. *Journal of Personality, 50,* 15–28.

Cunningham, M. R. (1988). What do you do when you're happy or blue? Mood, expectancies, and behavioral interest. *Motivation and Emotion, 12,* 309–32.

Damasio, A. R. (1994). *Descartes' error: Emotion, reason, and the human brain.* New York: Grosset/Putnam.

Davidson, R. J. (1994). On emotion, mood, and related affective constructs. In P. Ekman and R. J. Davidson (Eds.), *The nature of emotion: Fundamental questions* (pp. 51–55). New York: Oxford.

DeLongis, A., Folkman, S., and Lazarus, R. S. (1988). The impact of daily stress on health and mood: Psychological and social resources as mediators. *Journal of Personality and Social Psychology, 54,* 486–95.

Diener, E. (1984). Subjective well-being. *Psychological Bulletin, 95,* 542–75.

Diener, E., and Fujita, F. (1995). Resources, personal strivings, and subjective well-being: A nomothetic and idiographic approach. *Journal of Personality and Social Psychology, 68,* 926–35.

Easterbrook, J. A. (1959). The effects of emotion on cue utilization and the organization of behavior. *Psychological Review, 66,* 183–200.

Eich, E. (1995). Searching for mood dependent memory. *Psychological Science, 6,* 67–75.

Ekman, P. (1994). Moods, emotions, and traits. In P. Ekman and R. J. Davidson (Eds.), *The nature of emotion: Fundamental questions* (pp. 56–58). New York: Oxford.

Ekman, P., and Davidson, R. J. (1994). *The nature of emotion: Fundamental questions.* New York: Oxford.

Elliot, A. J., and Devine, P. G. (1994). On the motivational nature of cognitive dissonance: Dissonance as psychological discomfort. *Journal of Personality and Social Psychology, 67,* 382–94.

Emmons, R. A. (1991). Personal strivings, daily life events, and psychological and physical well-being. *Journal of Personality, 59,* 453–72.

Festinger, L. (1957). *A theory of cognitive dissonance.* Evanston, Ill.: Row-Peterson.

Forgas, J. P. (1995). Mood and judgment: The Affect Infusion Model (AIM). *Psychological Bulletin, 117,* 39–66.

Frijda, N. H. (1994). Varieties of affect: Emotions and emotion episodes, moods, and sentiments. In P. Ekman and R. J. Davidson (Eds.), *The nature of emotion: Fundamental questions* (pp. 59–67). New York: Oxford.

Gold, A. E., MacLeod, K. M., Frier, B. M., and Deary, I. J. (1995). Changes in mood during acute hypoglycemia in healthy participants. *Journal of Personality and Social Psychology, 68,* 498–504.

Greenberg, J., and Pyszczynski, T. (1986). Persistent high self-focus after failure and low self-focus after success: The depressive self-focusing style. *Journal of Personality and Social Psychology, 50,* 1039–44.

Hale, W. H., and Strickland, B. R. (1976). Induction of mood states and their effect on cognitive and social behaviors. *Journal of Consulting and Clinical Psychology, 44,* 155.

Hertel, P. T., and Hardin, T. S. (1990). Remembering with and without awareness in a depressed mood: Evidence of deficits in initiative. *Journal of Experimental Psychology: General, 119,* 45–59.

Higgins, E. T. (1987). Self-discrepancy: A theory relating self and affect. *Psychological Review, 94,* 319–40.

Hirt, E. R., Melton, R. J., McDonald, H. E., and Harackiewicz, J. M. (1996). Processing goals, task interest, and the mood-performance relationship: A mediational analysis. *Journal of Personality and Social Psychology, 71,* 245–61.

Hobfoll, S. E. (1989). Conservation of resources: A new attempt at conceptualizing stress. *American Psychologist, 44,* 513–24.

Hull, J. G. (1981). A self-awareness model of the causes and effects of alcohol consumption. *Journal of Abnormal Psychology, 90,* 586–600.

Hull, J. G., and Bond, C. F. J. (1986). Social and behavorial consequences of alcohol consumption and expectancy: A meta-analysis. *Psychological Bulletin, 99,* 347–60.

Hull, J. G., Levenson, R. W., Young, R. D., and Sher, K. J. (1983). The self-awareness reducing effects of alcohol consumption. *Journal of Personality and Social Psychology, 44,* 461–73.

Hull, J. G., and Young, R. D. (1983). Self-consciousness, self-esteem, and success-failure as determinants of alcohol consumption in male social drinkers. *Journal of Personality and Social Psychology, 44,* 1097–1109.

Ingram, R. E. (1990). Self-focused attention in clinical disorders: Review and a conceptual model. *Psychological Bulletin, 107,* 156–76.

Isen, A. M. (1985). Asymmetry of happiness and sadness in effects on memory in normal college students: Comment on Hasher, Zacks, Sanft, and Doren. *Journal of Experimental Psychology: General, 114,* 388–91.

Isen, A. M., Shalker, T. E., Clark, M. S., and Karp, L. (1978). Positive affect, accessibility of material in memory, and behavior: A cognitive loop? *Journal of Personality and Social Psychology, 36,* 1–12.

Izard, C. E. (1993). Four systems for emotion activation: Cognitive and noncognitive processes. *Psychological Review, 100,* 68–90.

Jacobsen, E. (1957). Normal and pathological moods: Their nature and functions. In R. S. Eisler, A. F. Freud, H. Hartmann, and E. Kris (Eds.), *The psychoanalytic study of the child* (pp. 73–113). New York: International University Press.

Jamison, K. R. (1995). *An unquiet mind.* New York: Knopf.

Johnson, E. J., and Tversky, A. (1983). Affect, generalization, and the perception of risk. *Journal of Personality and Social Psychology, 45,* 20–31.

Judd, F. K., and Burrows, G. D. (1992). Anxiety disorders and their relationship to depression. In E. S. Paykel (Ed.), *Handbook of affective disorders* (2nd ed., pp. 77–87). New York: Guilford.

Kasper, S., Wehr, T. A., Bartko, J. J., Gaist, P. A., and Rosenthal, N. E. (1989). Epidemiological findings of seasonal changes in mood and behavior. *Archives of General Psychiatry, 46,* 823–33.

Kavanagh, D. J., and Bower, G. H. (1985). Mood and self-efficacy: Impact of joy and sadness on perceived capabilities. *Cognitive Therapy and Research, 9,* 507–25.

Kunda, Z. (1990). The case for motivated reasoning. *Psychological Bulletin, 108,* 278–98.

Larsen, R. J., and Cowan, G. S. (1988). Internal focus of attention and depression: A study of daily experience. *Motivation and Emotion, 12,* 237–50.

Lassiter, G. D., Koenig, L. J., and Apple, K. J. (1996). Mood and behavior perception: Dysphoria can increase and decrease effortful processing of information. *Personality and Social Psychology Bulletin, 22,* 794–810.

Lazarus, R. (1994). The stable and the unstable in emotion. In P. Ekman and R. J. Davidson (Eds.), *The nature of emotion: Fundamental questions* (pp. 79–85). New York: Oxford.

Lockard, J. S., and Paulhus, D. L. (1988). *Self-deception: An adaptive mechanism?* Englewood Cliffs, N.J.: Prentice-Hall.

Manucia, G. K., Baumann, D. J., and Cialdini, R. B. (1984). Mood influences on helping: Direct effects or side effects? *Journal of Personality and Social Psychology, 46,* 357–64.

Martin, L. L., Ward, D. W., Achee, J. W., and Wyer, R. S. (1993). Mood as input: People have to interpret the motivational implications of their moods. *Journal of Personality and Social Psychology, 64,* 317–26.

Mathews, A., and MacLeod, C. (1994). Cognitive approaches to emotion and emotional disorders. *Annual Review of Psychology, 45,* 25–50.

Matt, G. E., Vazquez, C., and Campbell, W. K. (1992). Mood-congruent recall of affectively toned stimuli: A meta-analytic review. *Clinical Psychology Review, 12,* 227–55.

Mayer, J. D., McCormick, L. J., and Strong, S. E. (1995). Mood-congruent memory and natural mood: New evidence. *Personality and Social Psychology Bulletin, 21,* 736–46.

Moretti, M. M., Segal, Z. V., McCann, C. D., Shaw, B. F., Miller, D. T., and Vella, D. (1996). Self-referent versus other-referent information processing in dysphoric, clinically depressed, and remitted depressed subjects. *Personality and Social Psychology Bulletin, 22,* 68–80.

Morris, W. N. (1989). *Mood: The frame of mind.* New York: Springer-Verlag.

———. (1992). A functional analysis of the role of mood in affective systems. *Review of Personality and Social Psychology, 13,* 256–93.

Murphy, S. T., and Zajonc, R. B. (1993). Affect, cognition, and awareness: Affective priming with optimal and suboptimal stimulus exposures. *Journal of Personality and Social Psychology, 64,* 723–39.

Norris, F. H., and Kaniasty, K. (1995). Received and perceived social support in times of stress: A test of the social support deterioration deterrence model. *Journal of Personality and Social Psychology, 71,* 498–511.

Nowlis, V., and Nowlis, H. H. (1956). The description and analysis of mood. *Annals of the New York Academy of Sciences, 65,* 345–55.

Oren, D. A., and Rosenthal, N. E. (1992). Seasonal affective disorders. In E. S. Paykel (Ed.), *Handbook of affective disorders* (2nd ed., pp. 551–68). New York: Guilford.

Parker, E. S., Birnbaum, I. M., and Noble, E. P. (1976). Alcohol and memory: Storage and state-dependency. *Journal of Verbal Learning and Verbal Behavior, 15,* 691–702.

Parrott, W. G., and Sabini, J. (1990). Mood and memory under natural conditions: Evidence for mood-incongruent recall. *Journal of Personality and Social Psychology, 59,* 321–36.

Peters, R., and McGee, R. (1982). Cigarette smoking and state-dependent memory. *Psychopharmacology, 76,* 232–35.

Pribram, K. H. (1970). Feelings as monitors. In M. Arnold (Ed.), *Feelings and emotions* (pp. 41–53). New York: Academic Press.

Reisenzein, R. (1994). Pleasure-arousal theory and the intensity of emotions. *Journal of Personality and Social Psychology, 67,* 525–39.

Ruckmick, C. A. (1936). *The psychology of feeling and emotion.* New York: McGraw-Hill.

Ruehlman, L. S., West, S. G., and Pasahow, R. J.

(1985). Depression and evaluative schemata. *Journal of Personality, 53,* 46–92.

Russell, J. A. (1980). A circumplex model of affect. *Journal of Personality and Social Psychology, 39,* 1161–78.

Russell, J. A., and Woudzia, L. (1986). Affective judgments, common sense, and Zajonc's thesis of independence. *Motivation and Emotion, 10,* 169–84.

Salovey, P. (1992). Mood-induced self-focused attention. *Journal of Personality and Social Psychology, 62,* 699–707.

Sanna, L. J., Turley, K. J., and Mark, M. M. (1996). Expected evaluation, goals, and performance: Mood as input. *Personality and Social Psychology Bulletin, 22,* 323–35.

Schwarz, N., and Clore, G. L. (1983). Moods, misattribution, and judgments of well-being: Informative and directive functions of affective states. *Journal of Personality and Social Psychology, 45,* 513–23.

———. (1996). Feelings and phenomenal experiences. In E. T. Higgins and A. W. Kruglanski (Eds.), *Social psychology: Handbook of basic principles* (pp. 433–65). New York: Guilford.

Sedikides, C. (1992a). Changes in the valence of self as a function of mood. *Review of Personality and Social Psychology, 14,* 271–311.

———. (1992b). Mood as a determinant of attentional focus. *Cognition and Emotion, 6,* 129–48.

———. (1995). Central and peripheral self-conceptions are differentially influenced by mood: Tests of the differential sensitivity hypothesis. *Journal of Personality and Social Psychology, 69,* 759–77.

Smith, S. M., and Petty, R. E. (1995). Personality moderators of mood congruency effects on cognition: The role of self-esteem and negative mood regulation. *Journal of Personality and Social Psychology, 68,* 1092–1107.

Steele, C. M., Spencer, S. J., and Lynch, M. (1993). Self-image resilience and dissonance: The role of affirmational resources. *Journal of Personality and Social Psychology, 64,* 885–96.

Taylor, S. E., and Brown, J. D. (1988). Illusion and well-being: A social psychological perspective on mental health. *Psychological Bulletin, 103,* 193–210.

Thayer, R. E. (1987). Energy, tiredness, and tension effects of a sugar snack vs. moderate exercise. *Journal of Personality and Social Psychology, 52,* 119–25.

———. (1989). *The biopsychology of mood and arousal.* New York: Oxford.

Velten, E. J. (1968). A laboratory task for the induction of mood states. *Behaviour Research and Therapy, 6,* 473–82.

Watson, D., and Clark, L. A. (1984). Negative affectivity: The disposition to experience aversive emotional states. *Psychological Bulletin, 96,* 465–90.

———. (1992). Affects separable and inseparable: On the hierarchical arrangement of the negative affects. *Journal of Personality and Social Psychology, 62,* 489–505.

Watson, D., and Tellegen, A. (1985). Toward a consensual structure of mood. *Psychological Bulletin, 98,* 219–35.

Weingartner, H., Miller, H., and Murphy, D. L. (1977). Mood-state-dependent retrieval of verbal associations. *Journal of Abnormal Psychology, 86,* 276–84.

Wood, J. V., Saltzberg, J. A., and Goldsamt, L. A. (1990). Does affect induce self-focused attention? *Journal of Personality and Social Psychology, 58,* 899–908.

Wood, J. V., Saltzberg, J. A., Neale, J. M., Stone, A. A., and Rachmiel, T. B. (1990). Self-focused attention, coping responses, and distressed mood in everyday life. *Journal of Personality and Social Psychology, 58,* 1027–36.

Wright, J., and Mischel, W. (1982). Influence of affect on cognitive social learning person variables. *Journal of Personality and Social Psychology, 43,* 901–14.

Wyer, R. S. J., and Srull, T. K. (1986). Human cognition in its social context. *Psychological Review, 93,* 322–59.

Zajonc, R. B. (1980). Feeling and thinking: Preferences need no inferences. *American Psychologist, 35,* 151–75.

10 Emotions and Hedonic Experience

Nico H. Frijda

This chapter presents an analysis of emotions in terms of the components of affect, action readiness, autonomic arousal, and cognitive activity changes. The total emotional response patterns include emotion regulation and the individual's response to his or her own emotion (here called the emotion's "significance"). The chapter also discusses emotional experience—viewed as combined awareness of all components—and such major emotion aspects as intensity and duration, both of which turn out to be rather complex notions. Emotion space is described as dimensional, categorical, and multicomponential. All three aspects are regarded as viable, though not equivalent, representations. Several functions of emotion are distinguished, as well as functional consequences of emotions, notably consequences for social interaction and the content of social relationships. The latter in particular make emotions an essential aspect of human functioning.

EMOTIONS ARE AN essential ingredient in the shaping of subjective well-being and the experienced quality of life. Well-being and experienced quality of life are emotional notions; they imply affect that is at emotion's core. Moreover, the degree of well-being and judgment of quality are likely to be influenced by the number, and perhaps the duration and intensity, of pleasant and unpleasant emotions. For these reasons, understanding emotions is an important concern in the study of well-being and the quality of life.

THE NATURE OF EMOTIONS

What we call emotions are responses to significant events that consist of several components belonging to the domains of subjective experience, behavior, and physiological reaction. These components tend to be only loosely connected. The occurrence of one of them is not always accompanied by the others; a feeling of fear is not always accompanied by physiological upset or a tendency to flee, for instance. As a consequence, different components can be considered criterial, and conceptions and definitions of emotion differ accordingly. Emotions have been defined as states of emotional feeling (Johnson-Laird and Oatley 1989) or as feeling states involving positive or negative affective valence (Ortony, Clore, and Collins 1988). Alternatively, they have been defined as states of autonomic arousal (for example, Mandler 1984; Schachter and Singer 1962) or as changes in the activation of action dispositions (Frijda 1986; Lang 1995). Which component is considered criterial determines which phenomena are considered emotions and which are not. If affective valence is considered criterial, surprise is not an emotion; surprise can be pleasant or unpleasant, or even neutral. (It was not an emotion for Spinoza [1677/1989] or for Ortony et al. [1988], but it is in many other theories.) If action disposition is considered criterial, sheer liking (as in "I like this odor") is not an emotion (most emotion theorists would indeed exclude it), but desire would be. (It was for Spinoza, but it is for only a few current theorists, such as Frijda [1986] and Panksepp [1982].)

Views of emotion also differ deeply with regard to their functional interpretation. Emotions have been regarded primarily as disruptions or disturbances. Kant considered them "sicknesses of the mind" (see Pott, in press); Hebb (1949) also treated them that way. The disruptiveness has been explained by viewing emotions as caused by events to which the organism cannot adapt (Hebb 1949) or as the outputs of an old evolutionary, obsolete mechanism. Such a view is obviously opposite to the view that emotions have adaptive functions, even in current society (Damasio 1994); indeed, I think that seemingly irrational emotions like desire for revenge may be regarded as rational (Frank 1988).

Another far-reaching difference in perspective concerns the appropriate level of description of the emotional phenomena. Emotions have been treated just as state changes of the organism (changes in autonomic arousal state or feeling state), and thus as intra-organismic events. They have also been discussed as an individual's perceptions of the subject-environment relationship or as changes in such relationships. Emotions have been viewed as attitudes (Bull 1951), as modes of appraisal in person-event transactions (Lazarus 1991), and as changes in current motivation or in readiness for given kinds of action or interaction (Frijda 1986; Lang 1984, 1995; Plutchik 1980). Finally, they have been interpreted as mechanisms for dictating goal shifts, that is, as commands for shifts in the individual's currently prominent goal, thus relegating them to a role in the provisions for control of behavior (Frijda 1986; Oatley 1992; Simon 1967). The various interpretations may all at times apply. It makes a considerable difference, however, whether the emphasis falls upon the nature of emotions as function disturbances, as intrapsychic state changes, as interpersonal events, or as control shift mechanisms.

The relatively loose connection between components precludes a deterministic definition of emotions and forces a disjunctive one. Emotion may be defined as the response to a significant event, consisting of elements from one or more of the components of experience, behavior, and physiological reaction. However, two phenomena recur in attempts at definition and appear criterial for the use of the emotion concept, or of its older cousins "passion" and "affection"; they may even be the reasons why the very concepts came into existence. The two phenomena delimit response domains that largely but not entirely overlap. One is the occurrence of changes in the control of behavior and thought. Sometimes an external event or thought causes ongoing behavior and thought to be interrupted and new behavior and thought to take control, and to do so in imperative fashion. In other words, there are experiential and behavioral phenomena that give the impression of being involuntary, of being "passive," and to "affect" the subject. I have termed this phenomenon "control precedence" (Frijda 1986). The other phenomenon concerns the special nature of emotional experience.

EMOTIONAL EXPERIENCE

Emotional experience has been analyzed in essentially two ways. One has been to reduce emotional experience to other kinds of experience, notably body awareness and cognitions. In older efforts, feelings of pleasure and pain were regarded as variants of kinesthetic sensations (see Arnold [1960] for that history). A more recent version was the Schachter-Singer theory (Schachter and Singer 1962): emotional experience was interpreted as the feeling coming from one's state of autonomic arousal, combined with cognitions of what might have caused that state. Introspective and experimental evidence (see Arnold 1960; Reisenzein 1983) render this theory implausible. The second approach views emotional experience as being, at least in part, a kind of experience of its own. Experiences are felt as emotional only, or primarily (depending upon definition) when they contain such an irreducible experience, usually combined with cognitions and body feelings. One variant of that approach posits a small set of such irreducible emotional qualia, pretty much like the qualia of color experience (red, yellow, green, and blue) (Izard 1977; Johnson-Laird and Oatley 1989). The qualia are thought of as basic emotions. Evidence for such qualia (and for which emotions would correspond to a quale) is restricted to the evidence for basic and universal facial expressions, and to certain language phenomena (Johnson-Laird and Oatley 1989). The evidence is obviously indirect and appears to be rather weak (Reisenzein 1995; Wierzbicka, 1992). Even the presumed basic emotions are not irreducible, but can be analyzed and described like any other emotion (Frijda, Kuipers, and Terschure 1989; Shaver et al. 1987; Wierzbicka 1992).

Current investigation seems to favor the theorizing by Wundt (1902), who argued that the only irreducible qualia are the feelings of pleasure and pain, which I will be referring to as "affect."

Experiences considered to be "emotions" thus usually or always (depending upon one's definition) contain affect. They usually, or always, have affective valence. They share these qualia with other experiences not usually considered "emotions," notably moods and certain sensory experiences, like sweet tastes and foul smells. One aspect that sets them apart is that emotions involve an object. Emotions are "intentional states": they are felt to be "about" something—a person, object, or event—and they involve a particular relationship to that object (Ryle 1949). This may well be the main aspect that distinguishes emotions from moods. One may know what caused one's mood, but feeling and behavioral impulse are not directed toward or away from the causal object. (The major aspect differentiating emotions from sensory affect, and from non-emotional states, is the experience of a shift in control precedence. Only when a sweet taste makes one stop doing what one did and dwell upon one's tasting would it be considered an emotion of enjoyment.)

Emotional experience usually consists of much more than affect and a sense of a shift in control precedence. It contains awareness of the emotional object and further cognitions regarding that object; those cognitions are often referred to as "appraisal" (Lazarus 1991). It also contains awareness of changes in action readiness (Frijda 1986). It is most notably appraisal and the awareness of action readiness that define experiences as those of particular emotions such as joy, anger, or nostalgia. Experience may further contain feedback from the physiological reactions and from facial expressions ("facial feedback," for example, Izard 1977), as well as containing those cognitions that I later refer to as the emotion's "significance."

Not all emotional experiences are full-blown. Not every emotional experience is articulate, includes all components, and can be labeled with a specific emotion name. Feelings of "being excited," "moved," or "disturbed" are cases in point.

I describe the components of emotions in more detail after discussing how emotions are aroused.

EMOTION ANTECEDENTS

There are a number of events that elicit emotions in most people in most cultures. They include achievement of desired goals after uncertainty, reunion with intimates, threat of physical harm, permanent loss of a spouse or child, rejection from the group, and willful interference by someone else (Mesquita, Frijda, and Scherer 1997). Also, there exist certain stimuli (for example, angry faces, foul smells, pain) or stimulus constellations (such as familiarity [Zajonc 1980]) that very generally appear capable of evoking positive or negative affect or of influencing other affective processes (Öhman 1993). They suggest universal human sensitivities. However, the array of events that elicit emotions is considerably more varied than those mentioned and appears to call for analysis at a deeper level than that of specific types of event.

Hence the endeavors to link the emotion elicitation to more general principles. One such principle is that of conditioning: emotions are aroused by innate reinforcers or by conditioned signals for the advent of such reinforcers (Mowrer 1960). Although probably a correct formulation at some abstract level, this principle would seem to be too abstract to provide much insight. Somewhat closer to the phenomena is the principle that emotions reflect the life history of an individual's concerns. Phrased a bit more formally: emotions are elicited primarily by events or contingencies considered relevant to the actual or expected achievement of or harm to major goals, motives, and values (Frijda 1986; Lazarus 1991, Roseman, Wiest, and Swartz 1994; Scherer 1984). Closely similar are the formulations that view emotion elicitors as events or contingencies that signal goal- or plan-achievement contingencies (Oatley 1992), represent the (non)fulfillment of expectations (Hebb 1949; Mandler 1984), or define a subclass of elicitors as offenses to or conformity with norms (Ortony et al. 1988). The word *contingency* is added to include situations of extended duration such as poverty, oppression, or abandonment after the death of a loved one. The events mentioned elicit emotions (and not merely liking or dislike) only when they involve some difficulty in dealing with them, or when dealing with them goes faster or slower than expected (Carver and Scheier 1990).

Two classes of elicitors have to be either added or distinguished in the more encompassing formulation. One is confrontation with events that impinge upon the individual's affective sensitivities, that is, confrontation with aversive or pleasant stimuli and with objects or persons with affective valence (Ortony et al. 1988). They evoke emotions (and again, not merely liking or dislike) when the individual is incapable of dealing with them directly or of using the opportunity they offer. More interesting is the distinction of the second class of elicitors: events, actions, and contingencies that involve an individual's unimpeded or impeded functioning. Illustrations are movement restraint as a cause of anger (Stenberg, Campos, and Emde 1983) and the execution of activities as causes of "flow" experience (Csikszentmihalyi and Csikszentmihalyi 1988). Enjoyment generally is the emotion resulting either from perceiving a fit object for some concern or from the successful exercise of some of one's capabilities when such success is not taken for granted (function pleasure) (Bühler 1930). It can be argued that all elicitors can be subsumed under the heading of events involving impeded or unimpeded functioning. Impeded or unimpeded functioning, relevance to concerns, and affective valence may be three sides of the same coin (Frijda 1986; and see the subsection on affect later in the chapter.)

The conditions for the elicitation of different emotions have been described in various ways that, on close scrutiny, are highly similar. All include sets of variables from the context in which the affectively relevant stimulus acts upon the subject. The sets of variables have been described in terms of the actual or the expected increase or decrease of a positive or negative reinforcer (Mowrer 1960); description along these lines has been extended to include whether the outcomes of these constellations depend upon the subject's response (Gray 1987). Sadness, in this framework, is caused by the actual decrease of a positive reinforcer when decrease is response-independent, and anxiety by an expected increase in a negative reinforcer that is response-dependent. Lazarus (1991) describes the antecedents of major emotions as "core relational themes"; the universal event types mentioned earlier are exemplars. Core relational themes include reasonable progress toward the realization of a goal, irrevocable loss, threat, and demeaning offense. Events representing different core relational themes would lead to different emotions: to happiness, sadness, fear, and anger, respectively.

The themes can be fairly easily translated into a more differentiated, flexible, and general descriptive system, that of "appraisal variables" (Lazarus 1991), with some gain in generality. "Demeaning offense" can be analyzed into "unpleasant event caused by someone else's blameworthy intent." Several proposals of sets of appraisal variables have been made (Frijda et al. 1989; Lazarus 1991; Ortony et al. 1988; Roseman, Antoniou, and Jose 1996; Smith and Ellsworth 1985; Smith and Lazarus 1993); there is a great deal of overlap between these various proposals (Scherer 1988). The variables include affective valence, motivational congruence, expectedness, coping potential, uncertainty, causation (by someone else, by the self, or by events), and norm compatibility. There is some evidence that these variables might be cross-culturally valid (Frijda et al. 1995; Mauro, Sato, and Tucker 1992; Scherer 1997).

It is hypothesized, by Lazarus as well as by others (for example, Ortony et al. 1988; Roseman et al. 1996; Scherer, Walbott, and Summerfield 1986; Smith and Ellsworth 1985), that different emotions (as defined by subjective or behavioral response components, as described later) are elicited by different patterns of these appraisal variables, or by different core relational themes. The appraisal patterns are thought to consist in part of properties of the eliciting event, to the extent that these are picked up by the individual, and in part

of properties added to the event by the expectations, interpretations, schemas, and thoughts that the individual brings to it.

Evidence on which appraisal variables might be relevant in eliciting the various emotions, and on which appraisal patterns lead to which emotions, is largely derived from self-reports on emotion antecedents and emotional experience. Considering those self-reports as evidence for actual emotion antecedents would appear unjustified, because these data do not allow distinctions between antecedents and the semantics of the emotion labels or the contents of the emotional experiences (Frijda 1993; Parkinson 1995). Some experimental evidence exists for the causal role of some of the appraisal variables (or their stimulus sources), such as controllability, predictability, and coping potential in determining emotion (see, for example, Glass and Singer 1972; Seligman 1975). Also, analysis of eliciting events shows solid support for the Mowrer and Gray contingencies: for instance, a loss of positive events as well as an increase in negative events causes negative emotion, and irretrievable loss or uncontrollable aversiveness causes apathy (Seligman 1975). Beyond that, the evidence for their role in determining specific emotion is as yet modest. Unexpectedness has been shown to determine major parameters of surprise (Meyer et al. 1991); appraisals of anticipated effort influence heart rate (Smith 1989) and skin conductance level (Pecchinenda and Smith 1996); and appraised goal obstruction correlates with facial corrugator activity (Smith 1989). The role of animate agency in anger elicitation appears from the direction of most angry behavior, even when elicited by hypothalamic stimulation (Hess 1957). So, although the experimental evidence is modest, it has begun to accumulate. The hypothesis that different emotions (as defined by independent criteria such as mode of action readiness) are caused by different appraisals is a plausible one. It is capable of explaining the emergence of the various emotions. The sequencing of different emotions within an emotion episode is also easily explained by shifts in attention for potential appraisal variables. On the other hand, the question remains whether the appraisal patterns are necessary conditions for the arousal of the various emotions (Frijda 1993).

In the elicitation of emotion, cognitive variables play a major role. Most emotions are aroused by events that are relevant to one of an individual's concerns, but only on condition that that relevance has in some way been appraised as such. Cognitive processes are also vital in the determination of which emotion is aroused by a given event, because this largely depends upon the individual's expectations, appraisal of difficulties in and possibilities for dealing with the event, and assessments of causal agency, controllability, and the like. All this forms the substance of the "cognitive appraisal theories" of emotion, that of Lazarus (1991) being probably the most representative and influential contemporary version. These theories make a major contribution to understanding emotions in that they give an account of the degree to which emotions are elicited by the meaning assigned to the eliciting events, rather than to the properties of the events per se. They provide insight into the intra-individual variations in the emotions aroused by a given kind of event: which information is or is not picked up by an individual, which associations or expectations are activated, which meanings are attached, and which concerns alerted, may vary from moment to moment depending upon context and upon variations in the individual's coping potential. The cognitive approach also provides insight into individual and cultural differences in emotion; since goals and values differ, so will the meaning attached to a given event (Lutz 1988; Markus and Kitayama 1991; Mesquita et al. 1997).

That cognitive variables play an important role in emotion arousal primarily means that information and its processing play an important role. The processes involved are highly varied, however, in level and complexity (Leventhal and Scherer 1987). They range from direct and automatic stimulus effects over simple associations or conditioning to the confirmation or disconfirmation of expectancies and the arousal or non-arousal of memory traces (for the role of unexpectedness in surprise, see Meyer et al. 1991; for the affective effects of familiarity, see Zajonc 1980). They range further to the involvement of cognitive schemas and complex comparison or inference processes, as illustrated by the arousal of jealousy in Othello by a lost handkerchief, and by the importance of counterfactual scenarios in the arousal and intensity of regret (Landman 1993; Gilovich and Medvec 1995) or, generally, the role of comparisons with what has been, what might have been, what others have, and what one feels justified in having in emotions like sadness, disappointment, anger, and envy. (For the role of what is felt to be justified in envy, for example, see Smith et al. [1994].) Appraisal variables like causal agency and coping potential may also operate through elementary processes, such as perceived causality and the simple failure of intended actions, as well as through elab-

orate inferences. By and large, most cognitive processes in emotion elicitation can be assumed to operate automatically, as is evident from emotion arousal by the mere presentation of stimuli (such as familiar stimuli [Zajonc 1980], names of affectively valenced entities [Bargh 1997], and slides of affectively laden stimuli [Lang 1995]). Affect can be aroused by such stimuli even if presented below the threshold of awareness (Murphy and Zajonc 1993; Fox 1996; Esteves, Dimberg, and Öhman 1994), and stimuli so presented may influence affective ratings of other stimuli or cause physiological response when these had earlier been conditioned to them.

COMPONENTS OF EMOTIONS

Emotion components can be distinguished in several ways. The following distinctions are those that I consider useful for describing emotions as well as for understanding the possible implications for well-being.

Affect

"Affect" here primarily refers to hedonic experience, the experience of pleasure or pain. Such experience may appear as a distinct feeling, as in suffering and happiness, but it also may appear only in the guise of a perceived property of events or stimulus objects ("pleasant stimulus," "horrible sight," "shocking news"). However, affect may also be used as a hypothetical construct that is meaningful, quite apart from the subject's conscious awareness, to explain phenomena of approach and avoidance (for example, wriggling to escape a stimulus), or help-seeking behavior (e.g. crying), the operation of positive and negative reinforcement (it is a useful construct in the analysis of animal and infant behavior), or generalized well-functioning and dysfunctioning owing to, for instance, living conditions (as in, for instance, studies of animal welfare [Wiepkema 1990]). The role of emotions in planned behavior pivots around the anticipation of affects. Planning to obtain or avoid an object, or to manifest or suppress a given behavior, is generally thought to be controlled by the anticipation of resulting pleasure and pain (for example, Frank 1988). The two components of affect, the phenomenal and the functional, need not coincide.

Although the qualia of pleasure and pain cannot be analyzed in simpler constituents, the phenomenology of experienced affect allows description. Pleasure and pain are not just sensations of a special sort, in the way that Hume described them. Introspective reports indicate that they are experienced as calls for sustained contact or for ending contact with a stimulus (see Arnold 1960). More substantial are philosophical interpretations: pleasure and pain are one's sense of unimpeded and impeded functioning (Aristotle, *Nicomachean Ethics*, VII, 12), or of one's passage to a higher or lower state of "perfection" in functioning, that is, of the achievement of goals and abilities (Spinoza 1677/1989, 93). The interpretations make it clear that pleasure and pain always have meaning, that is, they point beyond the experience as such.

Affect, a central element in emotional experience, makes it one of enjoyment or of suffering. It also is the central element in orderings of emotional meanings or impact. Most words denoting emotions are rated as having either positive or negative affective valence. In most cluster-analytic studies of frequencies of co-occurrence or of similarity ratings, the words neatly divide into a positive, a negative, and (often) a neutral supercluster (see, for example, Frijda 1973; Shaver, Wu, and Schwartz 1992) or produce a major valence dimension (for example, Russell 1980). The same applies to recalled emotional experiences: affect is almost invariably present and forms the core of a cluster of appraisal features (Frijda et al. 1989). Visual stimuli, too, are easily rated in terms of positive or negative valence (Lang 1995), as are facial expressions (for example, Russell and Bullock 1985). In rating the affective or "connotative" impact of any sort of stimulus, valence usually forms the largest factor (Osgood, May, and Miron 1975).

Affect is also a central element in emotion theory; several theories view it as the process that mediates between stimulus perception and further emotional response, such as behavior or change in action readiness (Frijda 1986; Lang 1995). Emotions arise because one likes or dislikes something. Specific positive or negative emotions tend to vary within the context of a given affective evaluation. Affect arousal (or affective appraisal) is an elementary and automatic process in stimulus processing, sometimes arising even before conscious awareness of categorial stimulus identity (Bargh 1997; Bayens, Eelen, and Van den Bergh 1990; Esteves, Dimberg, and Öhman 1994; Zajonc 1980). Functionally, affect can be interpreted as a generalized signal that dictates a shift in control precedence: it is the process responsible for sustained attention changes, for enhanced approach or avoidance

readiness (Lang 1995), for the activation of more specific behavior systems to deal with the eliciting event, and, in the event, for generalized behavioral disorganization (Hebb 1949). This functional interpretation can be turned around: whenever there is a control shift and/or event-dependent behavioral disorganization, it is meaningful to assume that affect has been aroused. This is to say that one does not need self-report to make meaningful assumptions about affective state.

This analysis of affect underlines its role in well-being. Apart from being one of the latter's ingredients, it affects many functions outside those specifically involved in dealing with the emotional event, as well as those directly involved in such dealing. Enjoyment appears to facilitate activation increase and openness to stimulation (Davitz 1969), and suffering seems to correlate with decreased interest and decreased activation except for coping with the distressing events (for example, Davidson 1992); and both, when extreme, may interfere with optimal task performance (Hebb 1949).

Positive and negative affect are opposites in many ways. They often have opposite behavioral effects (for instance, seeking pleasure and avoiding pain; commanding approach or avoidance), and feelings and objects usually are readily rated on bipolar affective valence scales. It could be argued that pleasure and pain annul or neutralize each other. Opponent process theory (Solomon and Corbit 1974) argues precisely that: negative affect is supposed to arouse positive affect that attenuates the negative affect and begins to dominate when the stimuli evoking negative affect have disappeared; and vice versa. However, neutralization may pertain more to the affective summing-up of one's affective history or prospects over a certain period (the hangover spoiling the after-pleasure of drunkenness; the pleasures of vengeance softening the pains remaining from insult) (Bain 1876) than to actual neutralization of the affects while they occurred. In actual fact, pleasure and pain can coexist at the same moment, and they may do so without annulling each other; masochistic pleasure is a case in point. Simultaneous arousal of both affects leads to complex interactions: the confusing feelings of ambivalence, the experience of conflict, a pungency and excitement added to the pleasure, a sweetness added to the pain, as in nostalgic remembrance. Ambivalence as well as bittersweet experience lead to the hypothesis that pleasure and pain are not the opposite outcomes of one single process, but the outcome of two somewhat independent processes. Neurological and neurochemical evidence (see Ito and Cacioppo, Hoebel, and Shizgal, this volume) supports that hypothesis. This does not preclude the possibility that, as Konorski (1967) has argued, arousal of positive affect reciprocally inhibits readiness for negative affect, and vice versa.

Appraisal

Emotional experience includes appraisal of an object or event. Appraisal as good or bad, pleasant or unpleasant, is sometimes referred to as "primary appraisal" (Lazarus 1991). Appraisal also includes cognitions of various sorts, notably cognitions of why the object or situation is appraised as pleasant or unpleasant and, in particular, of what it does or does not allow the subject to do in dealing with it, and of the resources the subject carries in such dealing (Frijda 1986; Lazarus 1991; Solomon 1993). Conscious appraisals are among the major aspects that distinguish one kind of emotion from another (Frijda 1986; Parkinson 1995); to label one's emotion with a particular word is, to a considerable extent, to label how one has appraised the eliciting event (Davitz 1969; Frijda et al. 1989; Shaver et al. 1987). Fear, for instance, can be described as the experience of a threat that one feels uncertain about being able to cope with (Lazarus 1991; Spinoza 1677/1989). Each emotion concept corresponds to a particular appraisal. The appraisals characterizing major emotions can be understood as patterns of values on a limited number (five to ten) of appraisal dimensions, and several studies have shown that a subject's use of a particular emotion word to label his or her experience can be reasonably well predicted from the appraisal patterns as evident from the subject's responses on relevant questionnaires (Frijda et al. 1989; Scherer 1997). The dimensions are those described earlier in the discussion of the elicitation of emotion, but the evidence on their role in emotion lies primarily in their role as constituents of emotional experience.

Action Readiness

Most noticeable among the emotional phenomena are those that indicate motivation or readiness for changes in interaction with the environment. These motivations or forms of readiness are described by the more or less equivalent notions of "mode of action readiness" (Arnold 1960; Frijda 1986), "action disposition" (Lang 1995), "behavioral system" (Van Hooff 1972), goal (Roseman et al. 1994; Stein and Trabasso 1992), and "reper-

toire of actions appropriate to a recognizable type of . . . event" (Oatley 1992, 208).

The phenomena that lead to these notions include the functional equivalence of different behaviors manifested under particular conditions (for example, threatening, fighting, scolding, and insulting after offense, all manifesting the aim to hurt the offender), the concurrency of different behaviors and facial expressions (Frijda 1986; Plutchik 1980; Van Hooff 1972), self-reports on emotional impulses and changes in impulse (Davitz 1969; Scherer et al. 1986), the functional nature of physiological responses (for example, startle enhancement by unpleasant stimuli suggesting activation of a defensive action disposition [Lang 1995]), and the identification of brain circuits involved in functionally coherent and different emotional responses (Gray 1987; Panksepp 1982). Manifestations of modes of action readiness include overt behaviors, facial or other "expressive" movements, subthreshold activations (as in the startle enhancement by negative stimuli [Lang 1995]), and processes supporting the aimed-for changes in interaction, such as physiological energy mobilization (Obrist 1981), attention deployment (for example, MacLeod, Mathews, and Tata 1986), and cognitive readiness (for example, Keltner, Ellsworth, and Edwards 1993).

Categories of action readiness include affinitive, agonistic, submission, and play behavior systems (Van Hooff 1972) at a higher level of categorization, and "moving toward," "moving away," "moving against," hyperactivation or exuberance, and hypoactivation or apathy at a somewhat lower level (Davitz 1969; Frijda 1986). Verbal emotion categories often differ in terms of implied mode of action readiness (Arnold 1960; Frijda 1986). Self-reports of modes of action readiness indeed predict the use of emotion labels to a significant degree (Frijda et al. 1989; Roseman et al. 1994). The mappings are as would be expected: "moving toward" with affection, "moving away" with fear, "moving against" with anger, hyperactivation with joy and enjoyment, hypoactivation with sadness (Davitz 1969; Frijda et al. 1989; Roseman et al. 1994; Scherer et al. 1986). Determining the most appropriate level of description, and the optimal categories, is a subject of current research (for example, Roseman et al. 1994; Stein and Trabasso 1992). Different categories or levels of description may apply to felt impulses, behavior systems, and neural structures. There is, of course, no guarantee that the optimal categories and levels here correspond to those that best fit verbal emotion labels.

On the other hand, the modes of action readiness more or less characteristic of particular emotion categories can be of rather subtle kinds. Shame appears to involve a submissive behavior tendency (see the behavior repertoire of bending the head and trying to hide [Scheff 1988]); admiration likewise tends to involve a submissive behavior tendency, coupled with approach. Religious feelings as well as love often appear to involve a desire to fuse with the object and lead to actions to promote such fusion.

The phenomena of action readiness indicate that emotions, or at least some emotions, are motivational states. That is to say that they show the properties of equifinality of different behaviors shown under particular conditions, and of persistence under obstacles or interruption (part of what was earlier referred to as control precedence). Some emotions are motivational states in an extended sense, namely, those that involve loss of motivation rather than a particular motivation (as, for example, sadness and despair) or activation increase without a definite aim (for example, joy, diffuse upset, or excitement).

Emotional behavior includes facial expression. It has been proposed that facial expressions correspond to and express emotional experience (Ekman 1994; Izard 1977; Plutchik 1980) and do so universally in similar fashion (Ekman 1994; Izard 1977). However, facial expressions are not ubiquitous accompaniments of emotional states, nor do specific facial expressions invariably accompany specific emotions or emotion classes (Russell 1994; Fridlund 1994, 1997). Facial expression can be considered an emotional response component in its own right, with its own particular determinants. The major interpretations are that it reflects hedonic and activation state and states of activation (Bradley, Greenwald, and Hamm 1993; Russell 1994) and relational action tendencies (Frijda and Tcherkassof 1997; Schlosberg 1954), or that it represents social signals (Fridlund 1994, 1997) that usually serve to influence others in the service of the aims of emotional action readiness (Frijda and Tcherkassof 1997). The feedback from facial expressions may contribute to affect (Adelmann and Zajonc 1989) or to felt emotional intensity, but it is unlikely to differentiate emotional experience to a significant degree (Tourangeau and Ellsworth 1979).

Autonomic Arousal

Autonomic responses in emotions appear to fulfill several functions. They subserve the more active forms of action readiness and parallel the degree of motor preparation or movement (Obrist 1981); they may correspond to efforts to cope with uncontrollable events (Cacioppo et al. 1993; Obrist 1981; Pribram 1981); and they may be involved in attention regulation (Mandler 1984) and inhibition (Pennebaker and Hoover 1986). Different response parameters tend to correlate with different psychological parameters. For instance, peak heart rate has been found to correlate with unpleasantness (Bradley, Greenwald, and Hamm 1993), respiration rate with anticipated or actual muscular effort (Boiten 1996), and skin conductance level with inhibition (Pennebaker and Hoover 1986), anticipated effort (Pecchinenda and Smith 1996), or rated intensity of affect arousal (Bradley, Greenwald, and Hamm 1993).

The relationships found cut across emotion distinctions. Contrary to James's (1884) theorizing, emotions as distinguished in the language are not differentiated by patterns of autonomic response (Philippot 1993; Stemmler 1989). Evidence to the contrary (Levenson, Ekman, and Friesen 1990) is unstable and debatable (Cacioppo et al. 1993), and correlations between emotion conditions and physiological changes found in these studies may be due to muscle activity and resulting respiration changes rather than to emotion variables (Boiten 1996).

It has been proposed that feedback from autonomic arousal is a necessary condition for emotional experience (Hohmann 1966; Mandler 1984; Schachter and Singer 1962). This hypothesis has turned out to be incorrect. Such feedback seems at most to influence ratings of emotion intensity or feelings of excitement (see Reisenzein [1983] for a review of the evidence available until then; see also Bermond et al. 1991). Neither emotional experience as such nor differentiation of emotions thus depends upon autonomic feedback. It is true that self-report studies do yield solid and stable emotion-specific patterns of reported body feelings (Rimé, Phillipot, and Cisamolo 1990). However, these self-reports do not correspond with actual arousal changes (Philippot 1993), probably stem to a large extent from skeletal rather than autonomic feedback, and may be due to social stereotypes rather than actual experience (Rimé et al. 1990).

Autonomic changes form affective stimuli by themselves, however. They may disturb effective behavior during or after the emotion (they may hamper speech and upset fine movements, for instance), and they may on occasion compromise health.

Cognitive Activity Changes

Emotions tend to induce a number of changes in cognitive activity. They may be considered emotion components to the extent that they result from mechanisms forming part of the systems discussed under "action readiness." Findings have been reviewed by Clore, Schwarz, and Conway (1994). The changes include shifts in the control of attention. Evidence has been produced that anxiety increases attention to anxiety-provoking stimuli, thus maintaining the anxiety. (See Williams et. al. [1988] for a review of this evidence until then.) Festinger (1957) investigated emotion-induced belief changes, and Christianson and Loftus (1991) demonstrated the effects of emotional meaning upon remembering. In the context of mood research, recall facilitation and social and other judgment effects have been extensively documented (see Morris, this volume); emotions do not duplicate all of these effects, however (Clore et al. 1994).

Emotions may give rise to intense cognitive activities such as rumination (Rimé 1995), intrusive thoughts (Horowitz 1976), and fantasy (Klinger 1990). These emotion-induced cognitive activities probably have considerable influence upon the further course of the emotion processes. They tend to extend the duration of the processes, causing appraisals to expand and the emotions to feed upon themselves. Such effects have been investigated extensively in the context of depression, where they are among the factors causing self-defeating depression cycles (Coyne 1990). Cycles of a similar sort probably play a role in positive emotions, for instance, by causing unrealistic as well as realistic increases in self-esteem.

EMOTION REGULATION AND EMOTION SIGNIFICANCE

Regulation and Inhibition

Emotions usually are to some degree controlled, either automatically or voluntarily. That is, emotions are usually less intense or vehement than they can be under pathological conditions (for example, after cortical lesions) or during "blind" emotions (blind rage, blind panic, blind desire). Emotional experiences and reactions, as they are felt or observed, generally are the joint product of exciting and inhibitory regulation factors.

Regulation may affect all emotion components.

Automatic regulation of affect is illustrated by numbing and "denial states" after trauma (Horowitz 1976), and automatic regulation of behavior by anxiety-induced freezing (Gray 1987). Regulation of appraisal and emotional impulse in its less automatic forms is discussed as self-regulation and self-control (Salovey, Hsee, and Mayer 1993; Tice and Baumeister 1993) and as "emotion-focused coping" (Lazarus 1991); regulation of expressive behavior has been studied under the heading of "display rules" (Ekman 1994).

Inhibitory emotion regulation is controlled by the anticipation of aversive response consequences of the uncontrolled feelings or behavior (Gray 1987) and is ensured by a specific set of neural circuits in the limbic system that Gray (1987) has named the Behavioral Inhibition System. Control may affect both negative and positive emotions and can be external as well as internal. External consequences include, for instance, social disapproval, retaliation, and loss of behavioral effectiveness (missing your aim when angry, losing precision of finer movements). Internal consequences include guilt feelings and the discomfort of negative affect as such. Emotion regulation thus is not merely a consequence of social norms and conventions.

Inhibition of emotion has its costs. It often steeply enhances autonomic arousal (Gross and Levenson 1993; Pennebaker and Hoover 1986), with ensuing health risks (Pennebaker and Hoover 1986). Most inhibition processes do not follow actual emotion arousal but are anticipatory; thus, their arousal tends to generalize beyond confrontation with the relevant stimuli, with the consequent restriction of the variety of emotions generally and of social interactions. Such restriction has been described as ego-restriction in the neurosis literature, and as a consequence of trauma (Horowitz 1976) and of restraint-demanding sociocultural prescriptions (as among the Ahwad'Ali Bedouins, the Utku Eskimos, the Orissa in India) (Mesquita, Frijda, and Scherer 1997).

Emotion Enhancement

There is enhancing as well as inhibitory emotion regulation. Emotions are enhanced when positive outcomes or their anticipation strengthens emotion beyond what can be accounted for by the affective value of the stimulus conditions as such. Unpleasant emotions as well as pleasant ones may be enhanced, and with social as well as nonsocial motives (Parrott 1993). Positive emotion outcomes include intimidating others by anger, eliciting support and considerateness by sadness and distress, evoking approval and admiration by displays of pride and anger, strengthening social bonds by sharing in joy and grief, and, generally, improving in self-regard and the regard of others. In actual instances of emotion enhancement—for instance, in mass enthusiasm and violence—it is often unclear whether true enhancement or the lifting of inhibitions is involved.

Emotion Anticipation

One of the strategies for emotion regulation is to promote or prevent the occurrence of emotions. The occurrence of emotions can be promoted by seeking occasions on which they can be expected to occur, and it can be prevented by avoiding such occasions. Certain emotions are promoted, for example, by going to suspense and horror movies, watching sports events, climbing mountains, and generally seeking out sensations. Emotions are prevented by closing one's eyes in a horror movie, by engaging in phobic avoidance behavior, and, more importantly, in the dynamics of shame. The force and function of shame is to lead to reticence and conformity (Scheff 1988), which may be the mechanism that ensures individual or cultural restraint and sedate styles of behavior. The importance of emotion anticipation to the regulation of behavior is shown by psychopathic dyscontrol and by the consequences of basal-frontal brain damage, presumably damaging such anticipation (Damasio 1994).

Emotion Significance

Emotion regulation is elicited by the emotional implications of having or manifesting a given emotion under given circumstances. I call the complex of implications of having or showing an emotion that emotion's "significance" (Frijda 1986). Among the implications is that emotions often are the source of other emotions for which having or showing the original emotion is the object. These secondary emotions are also important in their own right. They enter emotional experience, and anticipating them colors one's feelings and modifies the hedonic tone. They are a source of much conflict, ambivalence, pride, and "depth" of feeling.

The significance of an emotion involves evaluation of that emotion or its manifestation, as distinct from the evaluation that is part of the emotion itself. The evaluation may focus on having the emotion, or on the consequences that having or showing it might entail. Parrott (1993) has surveyed the many social and nonsocial motives that may lead to enhancing negative emotions and weakening positive emotions, as well as to weakening negative and enhancing positive ones.

Emotion categories as a whole may have a given significance for the individual or in a given culture. They may have significance with regard to social standards and with regard to the individual's self-image and self-esteem. For instance, sexual desire may be felt to be bad or risky, on the one hand, or to enhance feelings of competence and self-worth, on the other. Anger may be considered unacceptable presumption, except in very special "righteous" circumstances (Stearns and Stearns 1986), or it may be felt as a sign of strength and of one's capacity to stand up for oneself (as among the Ahwad'Ali Bedouins [Abu-Lughod 1986]). Sadness may be felt to be a weak emotion, particularly for men, except when felt upon the death of a family member (as, again, among the Ahwad'Ali). Society may forbid expansive joy, as it does among the Ifaluk in Polynesia (Lutz 1988), and the dangers of envy often make it advisable to suppress manifesting or feeling pride.

In addition, emotions—any emotions—may be valued by a given individual or group as something positive in and of themselves. They can be felt as evidence that one cares, as a sign of being alive, as an index of one's sensitivity or moral standing, as an element of variety in experience, or as a challenge to cope with. Even negative emotions thus often carry a positive hedonic element, the negative affect notwithstanding, and positive emotions may be felt as improper or as threats to equilibrium and independence (Parrott 1993). This multileveled structure of emotional experience explains certain paradoxes in that experience: that pain can be a source of lust (without the pain losing its aversive character); that the absence of emotions may be so painful as to be a reason for suicide; that feeling guilt may be a reason for self-aggrandization. "Significance" may well be one of the major channels by which emotions influence well-being.

INTENSITY, DURATION, AND TEMPORAL DEVELOPMENT

Emotions vary in intensity. The multicomponential nature of emotions makes it evident, however, that "intensity" cannot be a simple concept. The felt intensity of emotional experience may vary independently of the magnitude of autonomic responses, for instance, and within each component domain variables vary with a high degree of independence. Heart rate correlates with skin conductance only to a very modest degree, and how to measure "autonomic arousal" is an unsolved problem (Cacioppo et al. 1993) to such an extent that the very concept may not really be meaningful.

Measuring the intensity of emotions as they are felt offers similar problems. People have little difficulty in rating the intensity of their emotions. However, identical intensity ratings mean different things. Rated emotion intensity appears to be a joint function of several separate felt intensities, notably the strength of felt bodily arousal, the strength of felt action impulse or impulse loss, the frequency of recurrence of the emotion in thought, the magnitude of changes in beliefs about the good or evil nature of the objects or persons involved, and the impact upon long-term behavior (Sonnemans and Frijda 1994). These variables are almost orthogonal and independently contribute to their multiple correlation of .72 with rated overall felt intensity. Emotions differ in the variables that most strongly contribute to that overall intensity. Felt intensity ratings thus only moderately predict felt arousal or any of the other variables, and each of the variables only very weakly predicts any of the others. Prediction of behavior or of any of the physiological parameters from felt intensity is still weaker.

No meaningful unification of the various intensity parameters seems to be possible. When characterizing how intense an emotion is, specification of the aspect or aspects involved appears to be the only way.

What determines emotional intensity, or the various intensities? Apart from the importance of the emotional event—in terms of the amount of harm or benefit implied or the importance of the concerns at stake—several other factors are involved. Sonnemans and Frijda (1995) proposed the following function:

$$E = f(I, A, P, R)$$

In this function, E is emotional intensity; I is event importance; A is appraisal or context (that is, it refers to variables like unpredictability and uncontrollability, which, for instance, may add to distress [Glass and Singer 1972]); P is personality (traits such as propensity for more intense or less intense emotions, or affect intensity [Larsen and Diener 1987], or for particular classes of emotions with

such positive or negative affect [Larsen and Diener 1992]); and R is regulation (regulation efforts decrease felt intensity [Sonnemans and Frijda 1995]). Evidence has indeed been found for the separate influence of each of these parameters upon felt intensity (Sonnemans and Frijda 1995). At the same time, the function is almost certainly incomplete. First, emotion intensity would seem to be dependent upon current mood state; joyful mood almost certainly enhances the impact of joyful events. Second, emotion intensity would seem to depend also upon the individual's history with the type of event involved: his or her adaptation to it (sensitization) or accumulation of successive effects. Emotions obey a "law of change" (Frijda 1988): change in circumstances often counts more than the circumstances as such (see Frederick and Loewenstein, this volume). Third, intensity and event importance both depend upon the context for evaluating the event. Emotions would appear to obey a "law of comparative feeling" (Frijda 1988): emotional intensity is influenced by what or whom the emotional event is compared with. To understand the intensity of regret, for instance, the standard of comparison can be an assessment of how the event might have developed—the influence of the "simulation heuristic," or the persistence of what might have been (Gilovich and Medvec 1995; Landman 1993). Fourth, there is evidence that emotion intensity is nonmonotonically related to the magnitude of some of its determinants, or at least certain of its parameters. At a high magnitude of uncontrollability, for instance, intensity might steeply drop (Brehm 1999).

The duration of an emotion is largely independent of the intensity parameters and overall felt intensity (Sonnemans and Frijda 1994). According to self-reports, emotion durations vary from a few seconds to several days (Scherer et al. 1986; Sonnemans and Frijda 1994). Different emotions have different average or typical durations, anger usually being reported as of short duration, and sadness as quite long. Determining the duration of an emotion presents the conceptual problem of when one emotion ends and another begins; studying emotion duration may call for another level of analysis that takes emotion episodes (Frijda et al. 1991) or emotional transactions (Lazarus 1991) as its units. Apart from that, assessing the duration of an emotion meets the same problems as assessing intensity. Components have different durations. Individual facial expressions last for five seconds or less (Ekman 1992), but cortical arousal, such as that responsible for sleep disturbance, may last for days; of course, the recurrence of the emotion in thought and the persistence of the emotional event may be responsible for such durations. Moreover, because emotions may change over into moods (Frijda et al. 1991), emotion duration self-reports may include the latter. Emotion-induced threshold changes may likewise persist, such as increased or decreased propensity for negative or positive emotions or irritability. Ruminations (Rimé 1995) may indefinitely extend the duration of emotion episodes, whereas adaptation may shorten them (Frederick and Loewenstein, this volume). Little research, however, has been devoted to this aspect. Whatever the precise source, emotional events may influence affect and subjective well-being for a considerable time.

Duration is only one aspect of the time course of emotions. There has also been little work devoted to the temporal dynamics of emotion, specifically, the possible roles of habituation and shifts in adaptation level (Frederick and Loewenstein, this volume), of homeostatic, opponent processes (see Mauro 1992), and of natural time courses. When emotion intensity is set against time, it usually shows a period of onset toward a peak, then a gradual decline; the pattern may repeat several times over one emotion episode (Sonnemans and Frijda 1994). Emotion episodes, moreover, typically involve extended interaction with a person or event that may change the time course. Typically, too, several different emotions may succeed one another or blend into one another during an episode (Oatley and Duncan 1992), depending upon cognitive processes and, of course, the temporal development of the event or sequence of events.

THE SPACE OF EMOTIONS

How can we describe the variety of emotions? What order can be found among them? Answers have been sought through the dimensional, categorial, and multicomponential approaches.

Dimensional Approaches

Emotions all vary along a few major common dimensions. That is, all emotional experiences can be located in a low-dimensional space; this also applies to the emotion concepts represented by emotion words (Russell 1980), facial expressions (Abelson and Sermat 1962; Russell and Bullock 1985), and the affective meaning of various stim-uli (Lang 1993; Osgood, May, and Miron 1975). The dimensions appear from multidimensional analysis of similarity ratings and from factor analyses of multiple ratings of the stimuli involved. Most of the variance in similarities and correlations is explained by two to three dimensions. The two found in almost all studies are affective valence (going from pleasant over neutral to unpleasant) and arousal or activation (running from low to high). A third factor has been labeled "control" (Osgood et al. 1975), or dominance (Russell and Mehrabian 1977). Furthermore, subjects readily produce ratings of emotional stimuli (Lang 1995), facial expressions (Frijda 1969; Schlosberg 1954), and emotion concepts (Russell 1980) along the first two dimensions, and they do this with considerable reliability or inter-observer agreement.

The findings from multidimensional analyses or factor analyses do not provide direct evidence that the two major dimensions represent hedonic value and activation. The analysis provides "circumplex" plots (Russell 1980) that can be described by two dimensions but that do not specify which of those dimensions prevail—that is, which rotation of the axes is best (Larsen and Diener 1992). However, both a hedonic dimension and an activation dimension correlate well with external criteria. For instance, ratings of slides on the pleasantness-unpleasantness dimension correlate with startle modulation, with corrugator and zygomatic muscle activity, and (to a lesser extent) with peak heart rate, and those on the activation dimension correlate with interest ratings, skin conductance, and recall (Bradley et al. 1993; Lang 1995).

The small number of dimensions does explain a considerable amount of variance in similarities and correlations. However, it does not agree well with evidence that more complex information is contained in emotion concepts (Davitz 1969) and in facial expressions. Factor analyses (Frijda 1969) and cluster analyses (Frijda 1973; Shaver et al. 1987) of similarities, for instance, suggest that more information is available. Also, two- and three-dimensional plots find that phenomena or concepts that are clearly different in emotional meaning occupy the same location, for instance, fear and anger. In fact, the descriptions of emotional experiences or of emotion concepts could not be reconstructed from the two- or three-dimensional coordinates.

One could add dimensions to account for the information surplus. However, most of these surplus dimensions would not have meaning in all areas of a multidimensional (even two-dimensional) space, rendering a dimensional model less adequate.

Categorial Views

The space of emotions can also be viewed as consisting of a collection of discrete categories. Discrete categories do not blend into each other; the categorial view asserts that no emotion exists that is midway between fear and anger (without being a blend of them). The categorial approach has its most complete form in the basic emotions view. In that view, there are a limited number of emotions, each representing a class or "family" (Ekman 1992); their members are specifications of the corresponding basic emotion, with regard either to intensity (for example, rage as a high-intensity subclass of anger) or to their antecedent or object (for example, indignation as anger about moral issues). The basic emotions are supposed to partition the space of emotions, exhaustively yielding a fully hierarchical ordering (Johnson-Laird and Oatley 1989; Plutchik 1980). Lists of basic emotions vary considerably from one author to another (Ortony and Turner 1990). Yet, contemporary lists show considerable overlap. They almost always include joy or happiness, sadness or distress, fear, anger, and disgust or aversion; some authors include surprise (Ekman 1992; Plutchik 1980), curiosity or interest (Izard 1977), contempt (Ekman 1992), love or affection (Plutchik 1980; Shaver, Wu, and Schwartz 1992), shame (Izard 1977), or guilt (Izard 1977).

The motivation to identify basic emotions is not only exhaustive ordering, however. Another major reason is the supposition of a biological basis for emotions that includes more specificity than dispositions for hedonic response and activation. Indications for a biological basis might be (1) universality—the emotion exists in all cultures (Ekman 1992; Shaver et al. 1992); (2) adaptive function—the emotion serves a specific fundamental adaptive function and thus has a specific and universal type of antecedent (Ekman 1992; Lazarus 1991); (3) specific neural substrate—the emotion is based in a discrete and identifiable neural system (Gray 1993; Panksepp 1992); (4) early origin—the emotion appears early in evolution and/or ontogeny (Ekman 1992; Izard 1977); (5) specific facial expression—the emotion commands a specific facial expression (Ekman 1992, Izard 1977); and (6) physiological specificity—the emotion has a specific pattern of physiological response, notably an autonomic one.

All criteria are contested (Ortony and Turner 1990; Russell 1991, 1994; Wierzbicka 1992), as is their necessary conjunction and, by consequence, the very notion of basic emotions (Mandler 1984; Ortony and Turner 1990). The relative independence of individual emotion components presents a further problem to the basic emotions view, as it does to categorial views generally (e.g., Ortony and Turner 1990; Scherer 1984), although it is not incompatible with it (Smith and Scott 1997).

However, there is no strict reason why the various criteria should all go together. A universally occurring provision for dealing with a universal contingency does not necessarily command a specific facial expression or physiology. Also, the criticisms notwithstanding, the evidence supporting criteria 1 through 4 is fairly extensive; for instance, I read Russell's (1991) analysis as indicating that most or all of the "basic categories" are found in most or all languages in which they have been examined (Frijda et al. 1995). Also, data on facial expression discriminability suggest a categorial perceptual process (Etcoff and Magee 1992). It is true that the empirical data for the various criteria do not always point to the same set of basic emotions, but this does not represent a strong argument against the basic emotions notion. Determining for which emotion classes there are neural circuits is a matter for ongoing research, a matter of settling upon a level of analysis, and a matter of sticking to a particular and useful conception of basicness to develop the criteria for their selection.

The definition of basic emotions as involving universality and/or biological dispositions does not imply exhaustive hierarchical ordering of all emotion categories that languages distinguish or that phenomenology makes it useful to separate. Detailed proposals for such a hierarchical ordering have been made (notably by Johnson-Laird and Oatley 1989), but an empirical test proved unsatisfactory (Reisenzein 1995). There are emotion categories that distinctly have no stable location in hierarchical analyses; jealousy, for instance, occurs variously under distress (Johnson-Laird and Oatley 1989) and anger (Shaver et al. 1987), and sympathy and love appear variously in a sad or in a happy cluster (Shaver et al. 1992). Other emotions do not fit basic categories because they lack the specificity that would allow location at that level—for instance, "being moved," "upset," or *nguch* (in the Ifaluk language, something like being disturbed [Lutz 1988]).

It should be added that, all discussions about basicness or linguistic/cultural origins notwithstanding, emotion categories are psychologically meaningful entities. They specify scripts (Russell 1991), component patterns (Lazarus 1991), or "intentional structures" (Frijda 1986) and thus carry specific behavioral predictions that go far beyond the dimensional locations. Hope, for instance, can be life-saving in a way that pleasure and activation (a possible circumplex position) cannot; it may stimulate renewed efforts to stay alive (Averill, Catlin, and Chon 1990). Jealousy often involves both fear of loss and efforts to prevent the loss, on the one hand, and desire to punish the rival and one's partner, on the other. Envy involves not only feelings of inferiority (Parrott and Smith 1993) but tendencies to spoil or denigrate the rival's pleasure (Klein 1977; Smith et al. 1994).

Multicomponential Approaches

In the categorial view, emotion types are integrated wholes of the various types of components (Ekman 1992; Izard 1977; Tomkins 1962). This view is difficult to combine with the basic fact about emotions already mentioned—the generally weak correlations between components. That fact has led to the three-systems view of emotions (Lang 1993) or to more general multicomponential conceptions (Ortony and Turner 1990; Scherer 1984). In these conceptions, the various emotion phenomena are not so much unreliable indicants of one underlying emotion process, but results of relatively independent response systems that tend to be activated by one and the same event. The components may vary more or less independently, with only relatively weak constraints on the combinations that can occur.

The components thus define a multidimensional space. Authors who view the components as fully independent interpret verbal emotion concepts as culturally specific linguistic conventions that map onto subspaces but are unlikely to do so in a precise fashion, in part because emotion concepts are fuzzy and emotion instances are centered on prototypes (Fehr and Russell 1984).

However, the space is unlikely to be homogeneous because functional dependencies between components do exist. Notably, appraisal patterns and modes of action readiness are usually conceived as being closely connected (Frijda 1986; Lazarus 1991; Smith and Scott 1997). Thus arises a notion such as "modal emotions" (Scherer 1994), defined as component patterns that occur together frequently and are structured around

components—for instance, the mode of action readiness—that provide a functional link. Also, non-fuzzy emotion categories, and even in some sense basic ones, can be defined as coherent subspaces in the nonhomogeneous space with relatively simple structures.

IN SUMMARY, it seems to me that all three approaches are valid. There is no need to choose among them. Each appears suitable for describing emotion space at a given level in the analysis of emotions. The dimensional conception applies to a global or "strategic" level of the phenomena of emotional experience and behavior (Lang 1993) and treats basic mechanisms that come early in the process of emotion generation. The category conception applies to the level of impulses, motor response types and mechanisms, and forms of adaptation in subject-environment interactions. In principle, a categorial view is compatible with a dimensional one, because a set of categories may usefully be described and ordered by a few dimensions. The multicomponent conception may apply to the level of appraisals and individual motor responses, but at the same time be compatible with patterned subspaces or categories (Smith and Scott 1997), particularly because their subspaces may have fuzzy, prototypelike structures. The only conception that would appear contradictory to the facts is the variant of a basic emotions conception that claims that basic emotions exhaustively and unambiguously subdivide the emotion space. No set of basic emotions does this.

I think that "basic emotions" is a meaningful notion when "basic" is taken in the ontogenetic and phylogenetic sense, and as pointing to biological dispositions. There is evidence for discriminable emotion mechanisms, there exist near-universal emotion categories; there are emotions that appear early in development and emotion names that are used early in development (Shaver et al. 1992); and there are universal emotion elicitors that prototypically correspond to certain action dispositions. However, a set of basic emotions so defined does not exhaust the space of emotions.

FUNCTIONS OF EMOTIONS

Emotions can be seen as provisions to safeguard the individual's concerns. They are instrumental for dealing with emotion-eliciting events or contingencies in several ways.

First, affect and arousal signal that a motivationally relevant event has occurred, and whether it appears relevant in a beneficial or harmful way. This basic function has been emphasized by most current writers. Emotions thereby form one basis for preferences and goal setting.

Second, emotions activate, deactivate, or inhibit behavior. They often involve what Pribram (1981) has called "tonic activation to act," or they involve a mobilization of effort (Pribram 1981) or behavioral inhibition, as in anxiety (Gray 1987); they may on occasion deactivate behavior, for example, when a goal has been achieved. They may function to save energy. In fact, one of the possible functions of a positive emotion like contentment is to suppress energy expenditure and behavioral disruption by negative emotions (Fredrickson 1996). Blass and Smith (1992), for instance, demonstrated that infant crying is suppressed by administration of sweetened water and that the effect is affective, not nutritional.

Third, emotions motivate and activate particular classes of behavior and functioning, aimed at resolving a problematic situation, as in "fight or flight" or calling for help, or at taking advantage of a potentially satisfying one, as in desire (which I include among the emotions because it feels like one and acts like one). The function of activating specific classes of behavior is perhaps clearest in the enjoyment taken in activities and play: attention, activation increase, and play behavior such as laughter (cf. Van Hooff 1972) may lead to full control precedence over fulfilling other tasks or needs or heeding risks (Csikszentmihalyi and Csikszentmihalyi 1988; Zuckerman 1979). Attention arousal (Mandler 1984), enhancement of memory registration (Christanson and Loftus 1991), learning (Esteves et al. 1994), cognitive operations like goal object identification or causal attribution—all are among the activated classes of behavior and functioning.

Finally, emotions function in resetting goal priorities and reevaluating resource allocation to these goals after relevant events. Hebb (1949) interpreted emotions as disruptions that serve to stop ongoing behavior when current input does not fit schemas or expectations, thus facilitating the switch to other behavior. Simon (1967) described emotions as "interrupt systems" triggered by concern-relevant events external to one's current goal or inherent in failure to reach the goal, or as termination signals for ongoing activities. Oatley (1992) described them as provisions to respond to goal- or plan-achievement contingencies, including those that involve successful progress toward one's goal and goal achievement. Similar interpretations of the general function of emotions are given by Frijda (1986) and Mandler (1984). The function of event-dependent resetting of goals is, of course, akin to the resource-dependent resetting of goals that may be a main function of moods (Morris, this volume).

Each of these potentially adaptive effects of emotions may be counteracted by harmful effects of emotional activities. Hence, regulatory, inhibitory provisions are included in the overall emotion system (Gray 1987).

The major function of many emotions lies not so much in dealing with the situation that elicits them, but in dealing with the ecology, that is, with future events of a type similar to the event that elicited the emotion. Examples are indignation and desire for revenge, which often cannot undo an offense but may be instrumental in discouraging its recurrence (Frank 1988; Frijda 1994; Solomon, 1989). Indeed, many emotions function to the advantage of both the individual and society at large by in the long run providing stability in interactions. By signaling to others that they are bound to certain courses of action, certain emotions solve what Frank (1988) has called the "commitment problem."

Promoting interaction with the ecology rather than with the eliciting event may well be one of the main functions of positive emotions. Many positive emotions, such as joy and hope, involve activation that is diffusely directed at the intake of information and becomes available for new initiatives; sympathy and gratitude tend to enhance positive action toward others (Lazarus 1991); and joy induces play behavior that has its function in itself, that is, in exercising competence and interactions.

The main function of several emotions, it would seem, is to motivate behavior that either annuls them or anticipatorily forestalls their occurrence. Grief may lead one to care for the welfare of the persons or objects one is attached to (Averill and Nunley 1988), to seek proximity when this has been lost, or to prevent such loss from occurring (Bowlby 1973). Foreseeing guilt feeling motivates care in dealing with others, as well as repair behavior after harm has been done (Baumeister, Stillwell, and Heatherton 1994). Foreseeing the possibility of shame motivates conformity before shame comes about (Scheff 1988). In fact, it may well be the somewhat complex processes involved in such anticipations that account for the nonrational and asocial behavior of psychopaths and basal-frontal patients (Damasio 1994).

Among the antecedents of emotion I mentioned earlier was unimpeded or impeded functioning. Signaling unimpeded or impeded functioning may well be the primary function of affect, in line with the subjective content of the corresponding feelings. This may be precisely the function of those emotions that arise from unimpeded or impeded functioning when impediments cannot immediately be dealt with or when unimpeded functioning is not self-evident—as when one is trying to transcend one's limits in a particular exploit (Csikszentmihalyi and Csikszentmihalyi 1988). They signal the contingencies with control precedence, so that one spends effort in dealing with the impediment, engages with full vigor and single-mindedness in the unimpeded activity, or seeks objects for the signaled competence elsewhere (White 1959).

Finally, there are exceedingly important functional consequences to emotions, whether or not they are counted among the emotions' functions. These consequences make emotions the spice of life. They are part of what I have called emotional significance and they prompt one's efforts to have or not have the emotions concerned.

Pleasure is pleasant, and pain is painful. Emotions motivate us to seek or avoid occasions that may give rise to them. Emotions also present variety, enhance activation, and produce a sense of being alive. They form the major reason for watching crime movies and sports, listening to music, or going out dancing. Emotions, or at least many emotions, also provide a sense of caring for others and their fate, and of being in touch with one's environment. Emotional emptiness is frequently mentioned as one of the horrors of the state of depersonalization, and as one of the reasons for suicide.

Emotions have powerful effects in shaping and regulating social interactions, even outside the interactions that the emotions are about. One's emotions influence how one appears to others, and thus how these others react in turn. Happiness tends to increase liking, and anger and sadness to decrease it, and these emotions thereby influence the willingness of others to interact (Clark, Pataki, and Carver 1996). These social effects can be of large scope and magnitude. Depressed people tend to estrange other people by being depressed and appearing to call for help, thus increasing their sense of isolation, which reinforces the depression, which initiates a downward spiral

(Coyne 1990). Fear of external dangers leads to a tendency to affiliate (Schachter 1959), whereas social anxiety leads to social withdrawal. Both joy and grief often, in certain cultures, invite close others to join in and share those emotions (Mesquita, Frijda, and Scherer 1997), whereas in other cultures or circumstances grieving persons are avoided.

Beyond that, emotions cement social relationships. That is, emotions are among the reasons for establishing relationships in the first place or breaking them off. A study by Zillmann illustrates this: one of the reasons opposite-gender pairs see horror movies is to establish a particular type of relation on the basis of his strength in facing the horrors and her weakness in seeking support in his arms (Zillmann et al. 1986). At a somewhat more essential level, emotions provide commitment in relationships and evidence of those commitments to the partners or other participants (Frank 1988). Emotional exchange, to a large extent, is what intimate relationships are all about. Both self-disclosure and empathetic perception of the emotions of the other, enable the partners to profit from the change in perspective offered by the other.

CONCLUSION

The preceding analysis of emotions may give rise to a number of inferences as to their role in well-being. There are several possible sources. One's emotions arise from events that are appraised as relevant to one's conditions for well-being, that is, for one's concerns. Momentary well-being and its disturbance are both part of emotional experience, and they are among the many functional consequences of emotions. Emotions directly influence a person's instrumental and social functioning over time periods that may extend far beyond the duration of the emotion proper and of the eliciting interaction.

Furthermore, emotions carry a complex significance, with regard to the emotion incident itself, to self-esteem and the self-image, and to its effects upon others and one's dealings with others. That significance usually has its own hedonic value; it adds pleasurable or painful affect to that which is inherent in the emotion itself.

Emotions may also affect well-being through their functional consequences for one's sense of coherence in the world and one's sense of identity, as well as for social relationships and interactions.

REFERENCES

Abelson, R. B., and Sermat, V. (1962). Multidimensional scaling of facial expressions. *Journal of Experimental Psychology, 63,* 546–664.

Abu-Lughod, L. (1986). *Veiled sentiments.* Berkeley: University of California Press.

Adelmann, P. K., and Zajonc, R. B. (1989). Facial efference and the experience of emotion. *Annual Review of Psychology, 40,* 249–80.

Aristotle. (1941). *Nicomachean ethics.* In *Complete works.* New York: Random House.

Arnold, M. B. (1960). *Emotion and personality.* Vols. 1 and 2. New York: Columbia University Press.

Averill, J. R., Catlin, G., and Chon, K. K. (1990). *Rules of hope.* New York: Springer-Verlag.

Averill, J. R., and Nunley, E. P. (1988) Grief as an emotion and as a disease. *Journal of the Social Issues, 44,* 79–95.

Bain, A. (1876). The gratification derived from the infliction of pain. *Mind, 1,* 429–31.

Bargh, J. A. (1997). The automaticity of everyday life. In R. S. Wyer (Ed.), *Advances in social cognition* (vol. 10, 1–6). Mahwah, N.J.: Erlbaum.

Baumeister, R., Stillwell, A. M., and Heatherton, T. F. (1994). Guilt: An interpersonal approach. *Psychological Bulletin, 115,* 243–67.

Bayens, F., Eelen, P., and Van den Bergh, O. (1990). Contingency awareness in evaluative conditioning: A case for unaware affective-evaluative learning. *Cognition and Emotion, 4,* 3–18.

Bermond, B., Nieuwenhuyse, B., Fasotti, L., and Schuerman, J. (1991). Spinal cord lesions, peripheral feedback, and intensities of emotional feelings. *Cognition and Emotion, 5,* 201–20.

Blass, E. M., and Smith, B. A. (1992). Differential effects of sucrose, fructose, glucose, and lactose on crying in one-to-three-day-old human infants. *Developmental Psychology, 28,* 804–10.

Boiten, F. A. (1996). Autonomic response patterns during voluntary facial action. *Psychophysiology, 33,* 123–31.

Bowlby, J. (1973). *Attachment and loss, vol. 2. Separation: Anxiety and grief.* London: Hogarth Press.

Bradley, M. M., Greenwald, M. K., and Hamm, A. O. (1993). Affective picture processing. In N. Birbaumer and A. Öhman (Eds.), *The structure of emotion* (pp. 48–68). Göttingen: Hogrefe and Huber.

Brehm, J. (1999). The intensity of emotions. *Personality and Social Psychology Review, 3,* 2–22.

Bühler, K. (1930). *Die geistige Entwicklung des Kindes* (The mental development of the child). Jena: Fischer.

Bull, N. (1951). The attitude theory of emotion. *Nervous and Mental Disease Monographs,* no. 81.

Cacioppo, J. T., Klein, D. J., Berntson, G. G., and Hatfield, E. (1993). The psychophysiology of emotion. In M. Lewis and J. Haviland (Eds.), *Handbook of emotions* (pp. 119–43). New York: Guilford.

Carver, C. S., and Scheier, M. F. (1990). Origins and functions of positive and negative affect: A control-process view. *Psychological Bulletin, 97,* 19–35.

Christianson, S.-Å., and Loftus, E. (1991). Remembering emotional events: The fate of detailed information. *Cognition and Emotion, 5,* 81–108.

Clark, M. S., Pataki, S. P., and Carver, V. H. (1996). Some thoughts and findings on self-presentation of emotions in relationships. In G. J. O. Fletcher and J. Fitness (Eds.), *Knowledge structures in close relationships: A social psychological approach* (pp. 247–74). Mahwah, N.J.: Erlbaum.

Clore, G. L., Schwarz, N., and Conway, M. (1994). Cognitive causes and consequences of emotions. In R. R. Wyer and T. K. Srull (Eds.), *Handbook of social cognition* (2nd ed.; vol. 1, pp. 323–417). Hillsdale, N.J.: Erlbaum.

Coyne, J. C. (1990). Interpersonal processes in depression. In G. E. Keitner (Ed.), *Depression and families: Impact and treatment* (pp. 31–53). Washington, D.C.: American Psychiatric Press.

Csikszentmihalyi, M., and Csikszentmihalyi, I. S. (Eds.). (1988). *Optimal experience: Psychological studies of flow in consciousness.* Cambridge: Cambridge University Press.

Damasio, A. (1994). *Descartes' error.* New York: Grosset/Putnam.

Davidson, R. J. (1992). Prolegomenon to the structure of emotion: Gleanings from neuropsychology. *Cognition and Emotion, 6,* 245–68.

Davitz, J. R. (1969). *The language of emotion.* New York: Academic Press.

Ekman, P. (1992). An argument for basic emotions. *Cognition and Emotion, 6,* 169–200.

———. (1994). Strong evidence for universals in facial expression: A reply to Russell's mistaken critique. *Psychological Bulletin, 115,* 268–87.

Esteves, F., Dimberg, U., and Öhman, A. (1994). Automatically elicited fear: Conditioned skin conductance responses to masked facial expressions. *Cognition and Emotion, 8,* 393–414.

Etcoff, N., and Magee, J. J. (1992). Categorial perception of facial expression. *Cognition, 44,* 227–40.

Fehr, B., and Russell, J. A. (1984). Concept of emotion viewed from a prototype perspective. *Journal of Experimental Psychology—General Section 113,* 464–86.

Festinger, L. (1957). *A theory of cognitive dissonance.* Evanston, Ill.: Row, Peterson and Co.

Fox, E. (1996). Selective processing of threatening words in anxiety: The role of awareness. *Cognition and Emotion, 10,* 449–80.

Frank, R. H. (1988). *Passions within reason: The strategic role of the emotions.* New York: Norton.

Fredrickson, B. L. (1996). Psychophysiological functions of positive emotions. In N. H. Frijda (Ed.), *ISRE '96 Proceedings of the ninth conference of the International Society for Research on Emotions* (pp. 92–95). Toronto: ISRE Publications.

Fridlund, A. J. (1994). *Human facial expression: An evolutionary view.* New York: Academic Press.

———. (1997). The new ethology of human facial expressions. In J. A. Russell and J. M. Fernández-Dols (Eds.), *The psychology of facial expression* (pp. 103–32). Cambridge: Cambridge University Press.

Frijda, N. H. (1969). Recognition of emotion. In L. Berkowitz (Ed.), *Advances in experimental social psychology* (vol. 4, pp. 167–223). New York: Academic Press.

———. (1973). The relation between emotion and expression. In M. von Cranach and I. Vine (Eds.), *Social communication and movement* (pp. 325–40). New York: Academic Press.

———. (1986). *The emotions.* Cambridge: Cambridge University Press.

———. (1988). The laws of emotion. *American Psychologist, 43,* 349–58.

———. (1993). The place of appraisal in emotion. *Cognition and Emotion, 7,* 357–88.

———. (1994). The Lex Talionis: On vengeance. In S. H. M. Van Goozen, N. E. Van de Poll, and J. A. Sergeant (Eds.), *Emotions: Essays on emotion theory* (pp. 263–90). Hillsdale, N.J.: Erlbaum.

Frijda, N. H., Kuipers, P., and Terschure, E. (1989). Relations between emotion, appraisal, and emotional action readiness. *Journal of Personality and Social Psychology, 57,* 212–28.

Frijda, N. H., Markam, S., Sato, K., and Wiers, R. (1995). Emotion and emotion words. In J. A. Russell, J. M. Fernández-Dols, A. S. R. Manstead, and J. Wellenkamp (Eds.), *Everyday conceptions of emotion* (pp. 121–44). Dordrecht: Kluwer.

Frijda, N. H., Mesquita, B., Sonnemans, J., and Van Goozen, S. (1991). The duration of affective phenomena, or emotions, sentiments, and passions. In K. Strongman (Ed.), *International review of emotion and motivation* (pp. 187–225). New York: Wiley.

Frijda, N. H., and Tcherkassof, A. (1997). Facial expression and modes of action readiness. In J. A. Russell and J. M. Fernández-Dols (Eds.), *The psychology of facial expression* (pp. 78–102). Cambridge: Cambridge University Press.

Gilovich, T., and Medvec, V. H. (1995). The experience of regret: What, when and why. *Psychological Review, 102,* 379–95.

Glass, D. C., and Singer, J. E. (1972). *Urban stress: Experiments on noise and social stressors.* New York: Academic Press.

Gray, J. A. (1987). *The psychology of fear and stress.* 2nd ed. Cambridge: Cambridge University Press.

———. (1993). Framework for a taxonomy of psychiatric disorder. In S. H. M. Van Goozen, N. E. Van de Poll, and J. A. Sergeant (Eds.), *Emotions: Essays on emotion theory* (pp. 29–60). Hillsdale, N.J.: Erlbaum.

Gross, J. J., and Levenson, R. W. (1993). Emotional suppression: Physiology, self-report, and expressive behavior. *Journal of Personality and Social Psychology, 64,* 970–86.

Hebb, D. O. (1949). *The organization of behavior.* New York: Wiley.

Hess, W. R. (1957). *The functional organization of the diencephalon.* New York: Grune and Stratton.

Hohmann, G. W. (1966). Some effects of spinal cord lesions on experienced emotional feelings. *Psychophysiology 3,* 143–56.

Horowitz, M. J. (1976). *Stress response syndromes.* New York: Aronson.

Izard, C. E. (1977). *Human emotions.* New York: Plenum Press.

James, W. (1884). What is an emotion? *Mind, 9,* 188–205.

Johnson-Laird, P. N., and Oatley, K. (1989). The language of emotions: An analysis of a semantic field. *Cognition and Emotion, 3,* 81–124.

Keltner, D., Ellsworth, P. C., and Edwards, K. (1993). Beyond simple pessimism: Effects of sadness and anger on social perception. *Journal of Personality and Social Psychology, 64,* 740–52.

Klein, M. (1977). *Envy and gratitude and other works, 1946–1963.* New York: Delacorte.

Klinger, E. (1990). *Daydreaming.* Los Angeles: Tarcher.

Konorski, J. (1967). *Integrative activity of the brain: An interdisciplinary approach.* Chicago: University of Chicago Press.

Landman, J. (1993). *Regret: The persistence of the possible.* New York: Oxford University Press.

Lang, P. J. (1984). Cognition in emotion: concept and action. In C. E. Izard, J. Kagan, and R. B. Zajonc (Eds.), *Emotions, cognition and behavior* (pp. 192–226). New York: Cambridge University Press.

———. (1993). The three-system approach to emotion. In N. Birbaumer and A. Öhman (Eds.), *The structure of emotion* (pp. 18–30). Göttingen: Hogrefe and Huber.

———. (1994). The motivational organization of emotion: Affect-reflex connections. In S. H. M. Van Goozen, N. E. Van de Poll, and J. A. Sergeant (Eds.), *Emotions: Essays on emotion theory* (pp. 61–96). Hillsdale, N.J.: Erlbaum.

———. (1995). The emotion probe. *American Psychologist, 50,* 372–85.

Larsen, R. J., and Diener, E. (1987). Affect intensity as an individual differences characteristic: A review. *Journal of Research in Personality, 21,* 1–39.

———. (1992). Promises and problems with the circumplex model of emotion. In M. Clark (Ed.), *Review of personality and social psychology* (vol. 6, pp. 25–59). Beverly Hills: Sage.

Lazarus, R. S. (1991). *Emotion and adaptation.* New York: Oxford University Press.

Levenson, R. W., Ekman, P., and Friesen, W. V. (1990). Voluntary facial action generates emotion-specific autonomic nervous system activation. *Psychophysiology, 27,* 363–84.

Leventhal, L., and Scherer, K. (1987). The relationship of emotion to cognition: A functional approach to a semantic controversy. *Cognition and Emotion, 1,* 3–28.

Lutz, C. (1988). *Unnatural emotions: Everyday senti-*

ments on a Micronesian atoll and their challenge to Western theory. Chicago: University of Chicago Press.

MacLeod, C., Mathews, A., and Tata, P. (1986). Attentional bias in emotional disorders. *Journal of Abnormal Psychology, 95,* 15–20.

Mandler, G. (1984). *Mind and body: The psychology of emotion and stress*. New York: Norton.

Markus, H. R., and Kitayama, S. (1991). Culture and the self: Implications for cognition, emotion, and motivation. *Psychological Review, 98,* 224–53.

Mauro, R. (1992). Affective dynamics: Opponent processes and excitation transfer. In M. Clark (Ed.), *Review of personality and social psychology* (vol. 6, pp. 150–174). Beverly Hills: Sage.

Mauro, R., Sato, K., and Tucker, J. (1992). The role of appraisal in human emotions: A cross-cultural study. *Journal of Personality and Social Psychology, 62,* 301–17.

Mesquita, B., Frijda, N. H., and Scherer, K. R. (1997). Culture and emotion. In P. R. Dasen and T. S. Saraswathi (Eds.), *Handbook of cross-cultural psychology* (vol. 2, pp. 255–98). Boston: Allyn and Bacon.

Meyer, W. U., Niepel, M., Rudolph, U., and Schützwohl, A. (1991). An experimental analysis of surprise. *Cognition and Emotion, 5,* 295–311.

Mowrer, O. H. (1960). *Learning theory and behavior*. New York: Wiley.

Murphy, S. T., and Zajonc, R. B. (1993). Affect, cognition, and awareness: Affective priming with optimal and suboptimal stimulus exposures. *Journal of Personality and Social Psychology, 64,* 723–39.

Oatley, K. (1992). *Best-laid schemes: The psychology of emotions*. Cambridge: Cambridge University Press.

Oatley, K., and Duncan, E. (1992). Incidents of emotion in daily life. In K. Strongman (Ed.), *International review of studies of emotion* (vol. 2, pp. 249–94). Chichester: Wiley.

Obrist, P. A. (1981). *Cardiovascular psychophysiology: A perspective*. New York: Plenum Press.

Öhman, A. (1993). Fear and anxiety as emotional phenomena: Clinical phenomenology, evolutionary perspectives, and information-processing mechanisms. In M. Lewis and J. M. Haviland (Eds.), *Handbook of emotions* (pp. 511–36). New York: Guilford.

Ortony, A., Clore, G., and Collins, A. (1988). *The cognitive structure of emotions*. Cambridge: Cambridge University Press.

Ortony, A., and Turner, T. (1990). What's basic about basic emotions? *Psychological Review, 97,* 315–31.

Osgood, C. E., May, W. H., and Miron, M. S.(1975). *Cross-cultural universals of affective meaning*. Urbana: University of Illinois Press.

Panksepp, J. (1982). Toward a general psychobiological theory of emotions. *Behavioral and Brain Sciences, 5,* 407–67.

Parkinson, B. (1995). *Ideas and realities of emotion*. London: Routledge.

Parrott, W. G. (1993). Beyond hedonism: Motives for inhibiting good moods and for maintaining bad moods. In D. M. Wegner and J. W. Pennebaker (Eds.), *Handbook of mental control* (pp. 278–305). Englewood Cliffs, N.J.: Prentice-Hall.

Parrott, W. G., and Smith, R. H. (1993). Distinguishing the experiences of envy and jealousy. *Journal of Personality and Social Psychology, 64,* 906–20.

Pecchinenda, A., and Smith, C. A. (1996). The affective significance of skin conductance activity during a difficult problem-solving task. *Cognition and Emotion, 10,* 481–503.

Pennebaker, R. W., and Hoover, C. W. (1986). Inhibition and cognition: Toward an understanding of trauma and disease. In R. J. Davidson, G. E. Schwartz, and D. Shapiro (Eds.), *Consciousness and self-regulation* (vol. 4, pp. 107–36). New York: Wiley.

Philippot, P. (1993). Actual psysiological changes and perceived bodily sensations in emotion (Abstract). *Psychophysiology, 30,* 51.

Plutchik, R. (1980). *Emotion: a psychoevolutionary synthesis*. New York: Harper and Row.

Pott, H. (in press). *Rethinking emotion*. New York: Oxford University Press.

Pribram, K. H. (1981). Emotions. In S. B. Filskov and T. J. Boll (Eds.), *Handbook of clinical neuropsychology* (pp. 102–34). New York: Wiley.

Reisenzein, R. (1983). The Schachter theory of emotion: Two decades later. *Psychological Bulletin, 94,* 239–64.

———. (1995). On Oatley and Johnson-Laird's theory of emotion and hierarchical structures in the affective lexicon. *Cognition and Emotion, 9,* 383–416.

Rimé, B. (1995). Mental rumination, social sharing, and the recovery from emotional exposure. In J. W. Pennebaker (Ed.), *Emotion, disclosure, and health* (pp. 271–91). Washington, D.C.: American Psychological Association.

Rimé, B., Philippot, P., and Cisamolo, D. (1990). Social schemata of peripheral changes in emotion. *Journal of Personality and Social Psychology, 59,* 38–49.

Roseman, I. J., Antoniou, A. A., and Jose, P. E. (1996). Appraisal determinants of emotions: Constructing a more accurate and comprehensive theory. *Cognition and Emotion, 10,* 241–78.

Roseman, I. J., Wiest, C., and Swartz, T. S. (1994). Phenomenology, behaviors, and goals differentiate discrete emotions. *Journal of Personality and Social Psychology, 67,* 206–21.

Russell, J. A. (1980). A circumplex model of affect. *Journal of Personality and Social Psychology, 39,* 1161–78.

———. (1991). Culture and the categorization of emotions. *Psychological Bulletin, 110,* 426–50.

———. (1994). Is there universal recognition of emotion from facial expression? A review of the cross-cultural studies. *Psychological Bulletin, 115,* 102–41.

Russell, J. A., and Bullock, M. (1985). Multidimensional scaling of emotional facial expressions: Similarity from preschoolers to adults. *Journal of Personality and Social Psychology, 48,* 1281–88.

Russell, J. A., and Mehrabian, A. (1977). Evidence for a three-factor theory of emotions. *Journal of Research in Personality, 11,* 273–94.

Ryle, G. (1949). *The concept of mind.* London: Hutchinson.

Salovey, P., Hsee, C. K., and Mayer, J. D. (1993). Emotional intelligence and the self-regulation of affect. In D. M. Wegner and J. W. Pennebaker (Eds.), *Handbook of mental control* (pp. 258–77). Englewood Cliffs, N.J.: Prentice-Hall.

Schachter, S. (1959). *The psychology of affiliation.* Stanford, Calif.: Stanford University Press.

Schachter, S., and Singer, J. (1962). Cognitive, social and physiological determinants of emotional state. *Psychological Review, 63,* 379–99.

Scheff, T. J. (1988). Shame and conformity: The deference-emotion system. *American Sociological Review, 53,* 395–406.

Scherer, K. R. (1984). On the nature and function of emotion: A component process approach. In K. R. Scherer, and P. Ekman (Eds.), *Approaches to emotion* (pp. 293–317). Hillsdale, N.J.: Erlbaum.

———. (1988). Criteria for emotion-antecedent appraisal: A review. In V. Hamilton, G. H. Bower, and N. H. Frijda (Eds.), *Cognitive perspectives on emotion and motivation* (pp. 89–126). Dordrecht: Kluwer.

———. (1994). Toward a concept of "modal emotions." In P. Ekman, and R. Davidson (Eds.), *Questions about emotion* (pp. 25–31). Oxford: Oxford University Press.

———. (1997). Profiles of emotion-antecedent appraisal: Testing theoretical predictions across cultures. *Cognition and Emotion, 11,* 113–50.

Scherer, K. R., Walbott, H. G., and Summerfield, A. B. (1986). *Experiencing emotions: A cross-cultural study.* Cambridge: Cambridge University Press.

Schlosberg, H. (1954). Three dimensions of emotion. *Psychological Review 61,* 81–88.

Seligman, M. E. P. (1975). *Helplessness: On depression, development, and death.* San Francisco: Freeman.

Shaver, P., Schwartz, J., Kirson, D., and O'Connor, C. (1987). Emotion knowledge: Further exploration of a prototype approach. *Journal of Personality and Social Behavior, 52,* 1061–86.

Shaver, P., Wu, S., and Schwartz, J. C. (1992). Cross-cultural similarities and differences in emotion and its representation: A prototype approach. In M. Clark (Ed.), *Review of personality and social psychology* (vol. 6, pp. 175–212). Beverly Hills: Sage.

Simon, H. A. (1967). Motivational and emotional controls of cognition. *Psychological Review, 74,* 29–39.

Smith, C. A. (1989). Dimensions of appraisal and physiological response to emotion. *Journal of Personality and Social Psychology, 56,* 339–53.

Smith, C. A., and Ellsworth, P. C. (1985). Patterns of cognitive appraisal in emotion. *Journal of Personality and Social Psychology, 48,* 813–38.

Smith, C. A., and Lazarus, R. S. (1993). Appraisal components, core relational themes, and the emotions. *Cognition and Emotion, 7,* 233–70.

Smith, C. A., and Scott, H. S. (1997). A componential approach to the meaning of facial expressions. In J. A. Russell and J. M. Fernández-Dols (Eds.), *The psychology of facial expression* (pp. 229–54). Cambridge: Cambridge University Press.

Smith, R. H., Parrott, W. G., Ozer, D., and Moniz, A. (1994). Subjective injustice and inferiority as predictors of hostile and depressive feelings in envy. *Personality and Social Psychology Bulletin, 20,* 705–11.

Solomon, R. C. (1989). *A passion for justice.* Reading, Mass.: Addison-Wesley.

———. (1993). *The passions.* 2nd ed. Indianapolis, Ind.: Hackett Publishing.

Solomon, R. L., and Corbit, J. D. (1974). An opponent process theory of motivation: I. Temporal dynamics of affect. *Psychological Review, 81,* 19–145.

Sonnemans, J., and Frijda, N. H. (1994). The structure of subjective emotional intensity. *Cognition and Emotion, 8,* 329–50.

———. (1995). The determinants of subjective emotional intensity. *Cognition and Emotion, 9,* 483–507.

Spinoza, B. (1989). *Ethics.* Translated by G. H. R. Parkinson. London: Everyman's Library. (Originally published in 1677.)

Stearns, C. Z., and Stearns, P. N. (1986). *Anger: The struggle for emotional control in America's history.* Chicago: University of Chicago Press.

Stein, N. L., and Trabasso, T. (1992). The organization of emotional experience: Creating links among emotion, thinking, language, and intentional action. *Cognition and Emotion, 6,* 225–44.

Stemmler, G. (1989). The autonomic differentiation of emotions revisited: Convergent and discriminant validation. *Psychophysiology, 26,* 617–32.

Stenberg, C., Campos, J., and Emde, R. (1983). The facial expression of anger in seven-month-old infants. *Child Development, 54,* 178–84.

Tice, D. M., and Baumeister, R. F. (1993). Controlling anger: Self-induced emotion change. In D. M. Wegner and J. W. Pennebaker (Eds.), *Handbook of mental control* (pp. 393–409). Englewood Cliffs, N.J.: Prentice-Hall.

Tomkins, S. S. (1962). *Affect: Imagery and consciousness. Vol. I, The Positive affects.* New York: Springer-Verlag.

Tourangeau, R., and Ellsworth, P. (1979). The role of facial response in the experience of emotion. *Journal of Personality and Social Psychology, 37,* 1519–31.

Van Hooff, J. A. R. A. M. (1972). A structural analysis of the social behavior of a semi-captive group of chimpanzees. In M. van Cranach and J. Vine (Eds.), *Social communication and movement* (pp. 75–162). New York: Academic Press.

White, R. W. (1959). Motivation reconsidered: The concept of competence. *Psychological Review, 66,* 297–333.

Wiepkema, P. (1990). Stress: Ethological implications. In S. Puglesi-Allegro and A. Polivera (Eds.), *Psychobiology of stress* (pp. 1–13). Dordrecht: Kluwer.

Wierzbicka, A. (1992). Talking about emotions: Semantics, culture, and cognition. *Cognition and Emotion, 6,* 285–319.

Williams, M. G., Watts, F. N., MacLeod, C., and Mathews, A. (1988). *Cognitive psychology and emotional disorders*. Chichester: Wiley.

Wundt, W. (1902). *Grundzüge der pysiologischen Psychologie*. Vol. 3. Leipzig: Engelmann, 5th. Ausgabe.

Zajonc, R. B. (1980). Thinking and feeling: Preferences need no inferences. *American Psychologist, 35,* 151–75.

Zillmann, D., Weaver, J. B., Mundorf, N., and Aust, C. F. (1986). Effects of an opposite-gender companion's affect to horror on distress, delight, and attraction. *Journal of Personality and Social Behavior, 51,* 586–94.

Zuckerman, M. (1979). *Sensation seeking*. Hillsdale, N.J.: Erlbaum.

Part III

Personality and Individual Differences

11 Personality and Subjective Well-Being

Ed Diener and Richard E. Lucas

One of the most consistent and robust findings in the field of subjective well-being (SWB) is that the components of SWB are moderately related to personality. Like personality traits, SWB is consistent across situations and is stable across the life span, even after the occurrence of intervening life events. There appear to be biological influences on SWB: characteristic emotional responses appear early in life, and there are substantial heritability coefficients for the components of SWB. The personality traits that are most consistently and strongly related to SWB are extraversion and neuroticism. Extraversion is moderately correlated with pleasant affect; neuroticism is strongly correlated with unpleasant affect. Other traits (such as optimism and self-esteem) correlate with SWB, but the direction of causality in these relations has not been determined. Temperament models of the personality-SWB relation posit that individuals have biological set-points of emotional experience; individuals have biologically determined emotional reactions to stimuli; or individuals with certain temperaments are able to wrest more rewards from the environment, leading to greater happiness. Congruence models suggest that greater SWB results from the degree to which our personalities fit with our environment. Cognitive theorists believe that the way we process information about rewards and punishments, rather than our biological sensitivities to these stimuli, determines our well-being. Goal theorists posit that our SWB is influenced by our goals, the way we approach our goals, and our success or failure at attaining them. Emotion socialization models suggest that classical conditioning, instrumental learning, and imitation affect characteristic emotional responses to the environment.

THE CONCEPT OF "the good life" varies considerably among individuals. For some, this ideal state is one of wealth and luxury; for others, it is attained through meaningful relationships with friends and family. For still others, the physical comforts of wealth and security are forgone to provide better lives for those in need. These different kinds of Individuals would appear to be quite different in external circumstances, yet they might all share a subjective feeling of well-being.

The term "subjective well-being" (SWB) refers to people's evaluations of their lives. These evaluations include both cognitive judgments of life satisfaction and affective evaluations of moods and emotions. If a person reports that her life is satisfying, that she is experiencing frequent pleasant affect, and that she is infrequently experiencing unpleasant affect, she is said to have high subjective well-being. Although life satisfaction, pleasant affect, and the lack of unpleasant affect often co-occur to some degree within the same individual, these components are separable. Someone who experiences a great deal of pleasant affect, for example, may also experience very little unpleasant affect and be labeled "happy," whereas someone who experiences high levels of both pleasant and unpleasant affect may be labeled "highly emotional." Similarly, an individual who experiences pleasant affect infrequently and experiences unpleasant affect quite often may nevertheless believe the conditions of his life (such as health and income) are excellent and would therefore say that he has high life satisfaction. Thus, although life satisfaction, pleasant affect, and unpleasant affect are related, they are empirically separable and must be studied individually to gain a complete picture of overall subjective well-being (Lucas, Diener, and Suh 1996).

The assessment of SWB offers a challenge to researchers because there are few, if any, external measures of SWB. By definition, SWB refers to well-being from the respondent's own perspective. An onlooker may judge the circumstances of the respondent's life to be unfortunate. Yet, if that respondent reports high levels of life satisfaction, he or she is said to have high SWB. In the assessment of SWB, researchers make a critical assumption about the nature of self-reports of happiness: when an individual says he or she has high SWB, this report reflects (albeit imperfectly) a state with some temporal stability and is not the reflection of a capricious decision resulting from momentary factors only. For example, when someone asks a respondent whether she is satisfied with her life, she should not base her answer solely on the amount of sleep she received the previous night, the amount of work she has to do that day, or the mood she is in at that moment. Although each of these factors may provide information about the status of her life, a report that is completely dependent on such momentary influences would not reflect a stable state of happiness. Instead, for SWB to be a meaningful construct, this judgment should correspond to a subjective state that is at least somewhat stable and that is influenced by factors such as the subject's long-term health, the conditions in which she lives, and the personality traits that govern how she interacts with the world.

Researchers know that the strong form of this hypothesis—that SWB judgments reflect only stable and meaningful conditions of people's lives—is untrue. Momentary factors such as current mood and even current weather conditions can affect judgments of life satisfaction (Schwarz and Strack 1991). Yet in spite of these transitory influences, SWB is moderately stable across situations (Diener and Larsen 1984) and across the life span (Costa and McCrae 1988; Magnus and Diener 1991), suggesting that long-term SWB does exist. Furthermore, it appears that a substantial proportion of stable SWB is due to personality. François La Rochefoucauld stated that "happiness and misery depend as much on temperament as on fortune." Indeed, La Rochefoucauld underestimated the influence of personality on SWB. It appears that pleasant emotions, the experience of unpleasant emotions, and life satisfaction often depend more on temperament than on one's life circumstances or on momentary factors.

EVIDENCE FOR A PERSONALITY–SUBJECTIVE WELL-BEING RELATION

Stability and Consistency of Subjective Well-Being

If personality traits influence levels of subjective well-being, then SWB should behave in ways that are consistent with our knowledge of traits. For example, Costa (1994) reviews evidence that even over a period as long as thirty years, adults are stable in their personalities. If biologically based personality predispositions influence SWB, we expect similar stability over time for SWB. In a longitudi-

nal study using multiple methods of measurement, Magnus and Diener (1991) found that life satisfaction correlated .58 with the same measure administered four years later. Even when life satisfaction at time 1 was self-reported and at the other time was reported by the family and friends of the respondent, the correlation over four years was .52. The use of two measurement sources is important in demonstrating that the stability of SWB is not simply an artifact of consistent response sets, such as acquiescence or social desirability. Furthermore, multi-method analyses provide evidence for the construct validity of SWB. If happiness judgments are decisions based simply on arbitrary and transitory influences, we would expect low convergence with methods across long time intervals and very little convergence with informant ratings of individuals' happiness. The high correlations between self-report and informant report ratings of life satisfaction, even over long time intervals, suggest that the basis for satisfaction judgments is not only consistently used but is substantive enough to be recognized by and communicated to friends and family members.

The affective components of SWB (pleasant and unpleasant affect) also exhibit stability across time. Watson and Walker (1996) found that trait affect scales showed a moderate level of temporal stability when assessed over a six-year interval; Costa and McCrae (1988) found that there were significant stability coefficients (in the .50 range) between the spouse's ratings of the target person's emotions at time 1 and the target person's self-rating six years later. Again, it must be emphasized that these stability coefficients are impressive because they are measured at two times using different methods, and measurement error was not controlled.

The alternative explanation that stability in SWB results totally from stability in people's external conditions is not borne out by studies that have examined changing conditions across the lifetime. Costa, McCrae, and Zonderman (1987), for example, examined both people who lived under relatively stable circumstances and people who lived in more changing conditions, such as in the midst of being divorced or widowed. The high-change group had only slightly lower stability estimates than the low-change group. Similarly, Diener and his colleagues (1993) found that people whose incomes went up, down, or stayed about the same over a ten-year period had approximately the same levels of SWB.

Although it is possible that people experience

stability in external circumstances through stable environmental factors not measured in these studies, researchers consistently find minor effects of external circumstances on SWB. Campbell, Converse, and Rodgers (1976), for example, concluded that all the demographic factors they measured (for example, age, sex, income, race, education, and marital status) together accounted for less than 20 percent of the variance in SWB. Other cross-sectional studies in the United States found that such highly valued resources as wealth (Diener et al. 1993), physical attractiveness (Diener, Wolsic, and Fujita 1995), and even objective health (Okun and George 1984) barely correlated with SWB. Even when the effects of specific life events are examined, personality has a role beyond them. Magnus and Diener (1991) found over a four-year period that time 1 personality predicted time 2 life satisfaction and other measures of subjective well-being beyond the influence of intervening life events.

Thus, longitudinal studies illustrate that SWB, like personality, shows some stability across time. The amount of pleasant affect, unpleasant affect, and life satisfaction an individual experiences in college is likely to remain moderately stable whether he or she gets married or divorced, finds a job or remains unemployed. If this stability is due to characteristic emotional styles, we would also expect consistency across diverse situations. In an experience sampling study that examined cross-situational consistency, Diener and Larsen (1984) found that average levels of pleasant mood in work situations correlated .70 with average levels of pleasant mood in recreation situations. Similarly, mean levels of unpleasant affect in work situations correlated .74 with mean levels of unpleasant affect in recreation situations. Similar levels of consistency for pleasant and unpleasant affect were found across social versus alone situations, and across novel versus typical situations. Mean levels of life satisfaction were even more consistent, with stability coefficients in the .95 range. Therefore, well-being judgments reflect more than just momentary influences—individuals have characteristic emotional responses to their environments that are consistent even when those environments change.

Furthermore, Diener and Larsen's (1984) findings show that the stability of SWB is not an artifact of the global nature of the reports. Kahneman (this volume) points out that global evaluations may be subject to certain biases and may not accurately reflect a summation of more molecular judgments. For example, a person's rating of an entire day may be only slightly related to the ratings of individual moments of that day. Through the use of experience sampling methodology, Diener and Larsen illustrated that SWB is consistent and stable even when measured "on-line."

Evaluations of one's life, whether affective or cognitive, do not result from a purely "bottom-up" process. People do not simply weigh the effects of various external circumstances to arrive at SWB judgments; happiness remains moderately stable in spite of changing circumstances and changing environments. In fact, evaluations of specific events and domains in one's life are colored by one's overall happiness. Kozma (1996) reported that when respondents were asked to rate their satisfaction with various domains in their lives (work, home, relationships), these satisfaction judgments were correlated. If overall happiness was controlled, however, correlations between the different domains were no longer significant. These data suggest a top-down model in which a traitlike construct of overall happiness influences feelings about specific domains. Thus, satisfaction with specific life domains is probably due to specific factors in that domain as well as to a substantial influence from the person's general level of SWB.

Temperament Studies

It is unclear from the above studies whether the positive biases that happy people exhibit result from a lifetime of positive experiences or from an inborn tendency to view the world through rose-colored glasses. Evidence from temperament studies illustrates that characteristic emotional styles emerge early and are likely to have a biological basis. Goldsmith and Campos (1986), for example, believe that some of the earliest individual differences expressed by infants are of an emotional nature. According to Goldsmith and Campos, biologically based emotional reactions emerge early in life, are somewhat stable across time, and provide the building blocks for adult personality dimensions.

Kagan and his colleagues identified a specific manifestation of temperament in the study of inhibited and uninhibited children. Kagan (1994) described two groups of infants who had either an avoidant style to unfamiliar events (inhibited children) or an approach-oriented style (uninhibited children). These emotional styles were hypothesized to be biologically based, resulting from differential excitability of the amygdala and its projections to the motor system, the cingulate and frontal cortex, the hypothalamus, and the sympathetic nervous system (Kagan, Snidman, and Arcus 1992). LaGasse, Gruber, and Lipsitt (1989) were able to predict inhibited behavior by examining sucking in two-day-old newborns, suggesting that these differences are biologically based and do not result from early environment. The effects of this inhibited style are observed early in life, and they persist to some degree at least into the eighth year of childhood. Kagan and Moss (1962) reported that shyness (a characteristic of inhibited children) exhibited in the first three years of life persists into adulthood. Kagan does point out, however, that some of the inhibited children (particularly those in the less extreme groups) do not remain inhibited throughout childhood. Thus, external events and environmental stimuli influence emotional development beyond the effects of early temperament.

It is unclear at this point what determines the extent to which biologically based emotional styles are expressed and maintained throughout childhood. Furthermore, it is not certain whether these early emotional styles correspond to adult personality traits. Rothbart and Ahadi (1994) noted that many early temperamental dimensions are similar to adult personality traits, and Digman and Shmelyov (1996) demonstrated similarities between the childhood temperament and adult personality dimensions.

The existence of early emotional styles suggests an inborn tendency to experience differential amounts of pleasant and unpleasant affect. Additional evidence for the biological basis of SWB comes from Davidson and Fox's (1982) research on frontal cerebral asymmetry. They showed that the fearful behavior exhibited by infants in a laboratory situation is linked to the relative amounts of left frontal versus right frontal cerebral activity that the infants displayed before the testing began. Frontal cerebral asymmetry appears to reflect both current emotional states and a predisposition to experience those states, and the Davidson and Fox data are thus suggestive of early differences in a biological predisposition to experience certain emotions. The implication of this research is that genetic factors may lead to differences in the reactivity of the emotional centers of the brain; these differences, in turn, predispose people to experience greater or lesser degrees of pleasant and unpleasant moods and emotions. These differences possibly represent the basic physiological predispositions to experience higher or lower levels of SWB.

Heritability Studies

Further evidence for a biological basis for SWB comes from research into the heritability of personality characteristics and SWB. In one of the most sophisticated designs, Tellegen and his colleagues (1988) examined monozygotic and dizygotic twins who were reared together and others who were reared apart. Because monozygotic twins share all of their genes, whereas dizygotic twins share on average half of their genes, the effects of genes on personality can be assessed through comparisons of the different sets of twins. Furthermore, comparisons between twins reared apart versus those reared together enable researchers to assess the importance of early family environment, as well as to rule out a number of alternative hypotheses regarding monozygotic and dizygotic twin studies (for example, that monozygotic twins actually have more similar environments than dizygotic twins). Tellegen and his colleagues found that even when monozygotic twins grow up in different homes, they are extremely similar in SWB (as measured by the Multidimensional Personality Questionnaire [MPQ]), whereas dizygotic twins who were raised in the same home were on average far less similar. Twins reared together were not much more similar than twins reared apart. Tellegen and his colleagues estimated that genetics account for about 40 percent of the variability (defined in terms of variance) in pleasant emotionality, 55 percent of the variability in unpleasant emotionality, and 48 percent of the variability in well-being. Shared family environment accounted for almost no variability in unpleasant affect, and just slightly more for pleasant affect (22 percent) and well-being (13 percent).

Twin studies such as these also illustrate an important point about the separability of pleasant and unpleasant emotions—heritability studies suggest that these emotional tendencies arise from different genes with different patterns of heritability. Tellegen and his colleagues (1988) report that the genetic effects for unpleasant affect are, for the most part, additive. That is, the more genes people share, the more likely they will be similar in unpleasant affect. Pleasant emotionality, on the other hand, appears to have a substantial non-additive component. Non-additivity refers to the common sequences of genes necessary for a similar phenotype to occur. The interaction among these genes appears to result in pleasant affect. Thus, identical twins may experience similar amounts of pleasant affect because they have the exact same sequence of genes, whereas siblings who have many of the same genes, but not the exact same sequences, may not be that similar.

To illustrate the differences between additive and non-additive effects of genes, imagine that happiness is completely determined by two genes. If these genes worked in a purely additive manner, people who shared only one gene would be more similar than those who shared none, but less similar than those who shared both: the more genes shared, the more similar the individuals' happiness. If there were a non-additive component, however, people who shared only one gene might be no more similar than those who shared none. In this case, the interaction between the two genes is responsible for the phenotypic similarity, and individuals need to share *both* genes to have similar amounts of happiness.

The importance of heritability studies for SWB is twofold. First, as with studies employing informant report data, it is difficult to explain the results through alternative explanations involving scale response artifacts. It is highly unlikely that monozygotic twins raised apart would have similar scores on SWB scales only because of biases in the way they answer questionnaires. Second, heritability studies point to the substantial biological effects on SWB. Although the degree to which genes are shown to influence SWB vary across methodology (twin studies often show higher heritability coefficients than adoption studies, perhaps owing to the latter's inability to measure non-additive genetic factors), the effects are consistently found. Moreover, heritability studies suggest that pleasant affect and unpleasant affect probably arise from different genes, as evidenced by their different patterns of heritability. Pleasant affect is also more likely to be influenced by shared family environment (Baker et al. 1992), perhaps owing to the sociability component of pleasant affect and its inherent interaction with the environment. Lykken and Tellegen (1996) estimate that when repeated measures of SWB are used, genes account for 80 percent of the stable variance in long-term reports of well-being.

Heritability studies do, however, have limitations. Most notably, heritability coefficients are relative to the influence of environment. For example, if the environment were completely uniform, intelligence would be 100 percent heritable. In a less than ideal educational environment, however, external factors (for example, differences in education) may influence intelligence. Heritability studies conducted within a single culture do not capture the fact that cultural variables may influence SWB. Thus, heritability coefficients are influenced by the degree of variability in the environment of the participants in the study. Furthermore, no studies examining the heritability of SWB have been undertaken using on-line measurements of happiness. Global judgments of SWB may be more or less heritable than the affect and satisfaction one experiences over many individual moments. On the other hand, genes may have additional effects that have not yet been fully measured. Plomin and Neiderhiser (1992), for example, review evidence that suggests that people's genes actually influence their environment. Studies that fail to take this fact into account may underestimate the effects of genes by ignoring the ways in which people shape the world around them.

The preponderance of evidence suggests that there are consistent and stable individual differences in SWB that are, to some degree, inherited. Adoption and twin studies show that adult subjective well-being is in part inherited. Infants and adults show typical emotional reactions that persist over time and across situations. These findings have accumulated from a variety of research paradigms, ranging from temperament studies to heritability studies to more traditional correlational designs. In addition, researchers have not simply relied on global self-report measures but have employed non-self-report techniques, such as informant report ratings of adults and behavioral data in toddlers, as well as on-line experience sampling reports of well-being. The major questions that remain are: Which personality characteristics are related to SWB? And why?

WHICH PERSONALITY ATTRIBUTES ARE CARDINAL?

Big Three and Big Five Models of Personality

One of the primary goals of personality psychology has been to identify major dimensions of personality that can be used to describe and predict individuals' characteristic responses and behaviors. This task has been approached from many different theoretical perspectives, and as a result, there is wide variety in the viewpoints regarding the basic building blocks of personality.

Eysenck (1967, 1981) believes that adult personality results from variation along three biologically based dimensions: extraversion, neuroticism, and psychoticism. Individuals high on extraversion are characterized as sociable, assertive, lively, and sensation-seeking; individuals high on neuroticism are characterized as anxious, depressed, emotional, and having low self-esteem; and individuals high on psychoticism are characterized as aggressive, antisocial, egocentric, and creative (Eysenck 1986). According to Eysenck's "Big Three" model of personality, all major variations in adult personality can be expressed through locations on these three dimensions.

Whereas Eysenck originally derived his model from factor analyses of responses to questionnaire items and has since postulated the psychophysiological process responsible for his dimensions (John 1990), Gray (1981) developed a model of personality in which the psychophysiological processes are central. According to Gray, Eysenck's extraversion and neuroticism dimensions are rotational variants of the underlying dimensions of impulsivity and anxiety. Gray believes that these two dimensions represent the fundamental dimensions of personality (in contrast to extraversion and neuroticism) because they correspond to two separate and independent neural systems. Gray postulates that the behavioral activation system (BAS) is sensitive to cues of reward and nonpunishment and corresponds to the dimension of impulsivity, whereas the behavioral inhibition system (BIS) is sensitive to cues of punishment and nonreward and corresponds to the dimension of anxiety. Eysenck's dimension of extraversion, according to Gray, is the result of the relative strength of the BAS and BIS—individuals who are sensitive to signals of reward (high BAS) are extraverted, whereas those who are sensitive to signals of punishment (high BIS) are introverted. Neuroticism is hypothesized to be an indication of an individual's overall emotionality caused by the summed strength of the BAS and BIS together.

Although Eysenck's and Gray's models differ, the primary dimensions each hypothesizes are theoretically related to the emotional dimensions of pleasant and unpleasant affect. As mentioned earlier, Eysenck's description of the extraverted individual includes such emotional adjectives as "active," "assertive," and "lively," and his description of the neurotic individual includes adjectives such as "anxious" and "depressed." Eysenck's dimensions are theoretically independent, and one can therefore be high in both extraversion and neuroticism. This individual would be considered highly emotional, since he or she would experience much pleasant and unpleasant affect. Figure 11.1 shows the different combinations of extraversion and

neuroticism and the Greek names for the four personality types that result from combinations of pleasant and unpleasant affect.

Gray hypothesizes that the BAS, a system reactive to reward stimuli, is responsible for the production of pleasant affect, whereas the BIS, a system reactive to punishment stimuli, is responsible for the production of unpleasant affect.

Tellegen (1985) emphasized the link between personality and affect in his own model of personality. His factor analyses of the items of the Multidimensional Personality Questionnaire have identified three second-order factors, two of which are explicitly linked to pleasant and unpleasant affect. The first factor, positive emotionality, is associated with MPQ well-being, social potency, and achievement scales. The second factor, negative emotionality, is associated with MPQ stress reaction, alienation, and aggression scales. Although these dimensions are related to Eysenck's extraversion and neuroticism dimensions, respectively, Tellegen believes that they are more closely linked to the rotation described in Gray's BAS-BIS model.

In addition to the above models (in which two dimensions are theoretically related to well-being) proposed by Eysenck, Gray, and Tellegen, personality researchers have focused increasing attention on five-factor models of personality (for reviews, see John [1990] and Goldberg [1993]). Theorists who advocate the "Big Five" system of traits began with the lexical approach to the identification of personality, hypothesizing that all the traits that are useful in describing human behavior are encoded in language, and that the more important a trait is, the more words there are to describe it. By identifying the structure of the personality descriptors, researchers can presumably uncover the structure of personality itself. The results of this endeavor have been strikingly similar across cultures and across different methods of analysis—five factors usually account for the majority of the variance among personality descriptors. Furthermore, research has shown that these "Big Five" factors can account for models that postulate either more or fewer than five factors (Digman 1990).

Although the five factors are given different names in different models, the structure of each of the factors is consistent (John 1990). Costa and McCrae's (1992) labels of extraversion, agreeableness, conscientiousness, neuroticism, and openness to experience will be used in the current discussion to emphasize the similarities of the five-factor structure to the models described. Factors 1 and 4

FIGURE 11.1 The Dimensions of Extraversion and Neuroticism in Eysenck's Model of Personality

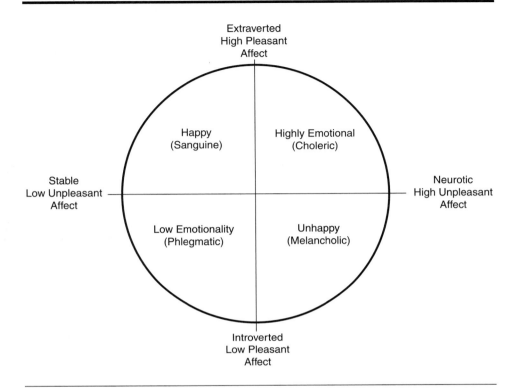

of this five-factor model closely resemble the constructs proposed by Eysenck, Gray, and Tellegen.

Not surprisingly, it is the extraversion and neuroticism personality factors that have been most closely linked to emotion and affect. In an early study, Bradburn (1969) found that sociability (a component of extraversion) was related to pleasant affect, but not to unpleasant affect. Costa and McCrae (1980) extended this finding to modern five-factor conceptions of personality by showing that extraversion relates to pleasant affect (but not unpleasant affect), whereas neuroticism relates to unpleasant affect (but not pleasant affect). Based on these results, Costa and McCrae postulated a model in which extraversion and neuroticism differentially influenced pleasant affect and unpleasant affect, which together compose overall happiness.

The relations between personality and affect have been replicated by even more sophisticated methods. Diener and his colleagues (1992), for example, found that extraversion predicted SWB in a probability sample of Americans. Fujita (1991) found that the correlation between extraversion and pleasant affect was .80 when latent trait methodology was used to control for measurement error, and that neuroticism and unpleasant affect were indistinguishable. Tellegen (1985) found that his higher-order factor of positive emotionality correlated with current pleasant affect and that the higher-order factor of negative emotionality correlated with current unpleasant affect in the range of .40 to .50. These coefficients are impressive considering that current mood—the degree of pleasant and unpleasant emotions an individual feels at a particular moment—can be influenced by many situational factors, yet it still correlates substantially with personality.

The alternative hypothesis that these correlations are due to current mood influences on personality assessment instruments can be ruled out by longitudinal studies on the effects of personality on mood. Costa and McCrae (1980), for example, found that extraversion predicted pleasant affect and neuroticism predicted unpleasant affect over a period of ten years. Similar results were found by

Headey and Wearing (1992) in a longitudinal panel design. Extraversion and neuroticism predicted pleasant affect and unpleasant affect scores a number of years later. Magnus and Diener (1991) found that extraversion and neuroticism scores were able to predict life satisfaction over a four-year period. In fact, personality was a stronger predictor of life satisfaction than were life events.

Given the theoretical links between extraversion and pleasant affect, and between neuroticism and unpleasant affect, it is not surprising that the strongest and most consistent relations between personality and SWB have been found in examinations of these constructs. Other Big Five traits exhibit weaker relations with SWB constructs (Watson and Clark 1992). Agreeableness and conscientiousness are often slightly positively correlated with positive affect and slightly negatively correlated with negative affect, whereas openness to experience is often slightly positively correlated with both pleasant and unpleasant affect. Seidlitz (1993) suggested that the relations between agreeableness, conscientiousness, openness, and SWB are weaker because they are formed by rewards in the environment rather than by biological reactivity per se.

Big Five personality traits such as extraversion and neuroticism have a theoretical link to emotions and affect and consistently correlate in a predictable pattern with pleasant affect, unpleasant affect, and life satisfaction. Although these relations are strong and consistent, examining personality and subjective well-being relations from only a Big Five perspective would be shortsighted. Many researchers (for example, Block 1995; Pervin 1994) remain unconvinced of the validity and utility of Big Five conceptualizations, and many alternative traits and models of personality have been proposed. Although additional traits will be discussed briefly in the next section, some nontrait approaches to personality will be taken up in the discussion of the mechanisms behind the relation between personality and SWB.

Other Traits

Although traits such as self-esteem and optimism are not primarily affective in nature, there is reason to believe that they would influence or be influenced by well-being. Self-esteem theorists, for example, hypothesize that positive evaluations of the self are necessary for positive overall well-being. Scheier and Carver (1985) hypothesize that the trait of dispositional optimism influences well-

being through expectations about the future. Those who believe that positive outcomes for themselves are probable will work for their goals and are more likely to achieve those goals and attain positive outcomes. Lucas, Diener, and Suh (1996) showed that self-esteem and optimism do in fact correlate with measures of SWB such as life satisfaction, pleasant affect, and unpleasant affect. Diener and Diener (1995), however, found that the strength of the relation between self-esteem and life satisfaction does not strongly generalize to collectivist cultures.

As greater numbers of more specific personality traits are considered, two problems regarding the relation between personality and subjective well-being emerge. First, how do researchers identify which personality traits are crucial? There are an indefinite number of traits, and new traits are proposed frequently; therefore, it becomes difficult to determine which of these interrelated traits are actually responsible for SWB.

Second, do personality traits or SWB have causal priority? Just as one's ratings of domains are colored by one's overall happiness (Kozma 1996), perhaps different traits are influenced by a global sense of well-being. According to this model, extraversion, self-esteem, and optimism do not influence happiness; they are related to happiness and to each other because of the influence of happiness on other aspects of life. This theory raises an important chicken-or-egg problem regarding the nature of personality-SWB relations. For example, neurotics have both negative cognitions and negative moods. It is possible that neurotics have a system that is very reactive to negative stimuli, and therefore they experience many unpleasant emotions that lead to negative thoughts. Another possibility, however, is that neurotics tend to concentrate on the undesirable aspects of events and therefore experience greater levels of unpleasant emotions.

Questions regarding the nature of the personality-SWB relationship remain. The body of evidence reviewed here, however, has several implications. Extraversion and neuroticism, in three-factor as well as five-factor models, have theoretical and well-established empirical links to pleasant and unpleasant affect, respectively. These personality traits are able to predict well-being across significant time periods and are in fact stronger predictors than intervening life events. Other more specific, and more cognitive, traits such as self-esteem and optimism have been shown to be related to SWB; however, the number of different traits that exist has not been determined, making a complete understanding of the relations between personality and SWB difficult.

THE PROCESSES INVOLVED—WHY IS PERSONALITY RELATED TO SWB?

At their most basic level of explanation, personality traits provide a useful method for categorizing people and their behaviors. The research reviewed thus far simply categorizes those who are likely to be happy or unhappy—extraverts are more likely than introverts to experience pleasant affect, neurotics are more likely than stable people to experience unpleasant affect, people with high self-esteem are likely to experience higher levels of life satisfaction, and so forth. Yet these correlations do little to explain the processes that underlie the personality-SWB relationship. A more complete scientific understanding will be gained if we can specify the processes that relate traits to SWB.

Temperament Models

Proponents of the temperament model (for example, Eysenck 1967; Gray 1981; Headey and Wearing 1989; Larsen and Ketelaar 1991) postulate a biological determinant of SWB. Headey and Wearing, for example, suggest that a person's baseline level of happiness is decided by his or her temperament. According to their dynamic equilibrium model, extraversion and neuroticism determine a person's baseline level of happiness through the strength of his or her reward and punishment systems. Although events can move people temporarily away from the baseline, their reward and punishment systems will eventually return them to their baseline level. Because of biologically determined "set-points" of reactivity to stimuli, an individual's reward and punishment system adapts to positive or negative stimuli, and the individual thereafter returns to his or her baseline of SWB.

Headey and Wearing (1989) found support for their theory in an Australian panel study. After the occurrence of good and bad events, people returned to previous levels of pleasant and unpleasant affect. Suh, Diener, and Fujita (1996) replicated this finding, illustrating that people adapt to events in surprisingly short periods of time. Even after the occurrence of such severe and life-changing events as becoming a quadriplegic or paraplegic, people are able to adapt (Silver 1980). Mehnert and his colleagues (1990) found support

for an adaptation model by showing that people who acquired disabilities later in life were less satisfied with life than those who acquired their disabilities at birth or in early life, although people with disabilities were less satisfied with their life than were people without disabilities.

Unfortunately, studies such as these cannot determine whether the mechanisms postulated by Headey and Wearing are truly responsible for adaptation effects. Do people adapt because of biological set-points in reactivity, or do they change their goals and use coping strategies? Furthermore, studies that examine only relatively mundane events tell us little about the extent to which people can adapt—although studies of paraplegics and quadriplegics suggest that this ability is quite substantial. (For a more in-depth discussion of the complexities of adaptation, see Frederick and Loewenstein, this volume).

A second temperament explanation of the personality-SWB relation derives from Gray's (1981) theory of differential sensitivity among the BAS and the BIS. According to this model, extraverts are happy because they have a higher sensitivity to reward stimuli. People who are extraverted are more likely to experience pleasant affect when exposed to a reward. Neurotics, on the other hand, are more sensitive to punishment and are therefore more likely to experience unpleasant affect when exposed to a negative stimulus. This model differs from Headey and Wearing's (1989; 1992) in that consistency is the result not of set-points but of characteristic responses to stimuli. In a set-point model, an individual could have an intense reaction to a stimuli, but over time he or she would return to the biological set-point. In a reactivity model, the reactions themselves are governed by personality, and an extravert may be happier than an introvert because the extravert reacts more strongly to positive stimuli than does the introvert.

To test the Gray model, Larsen and Ketelaar (1991) used positive and negative mood manipulations to test sensitivity to positive and negative stimuli. In accordance with their predictions, extraverts were more susceptible to a positive mood manipulation than were introverts, but there was no difference between extraverts and introverts in their susceptibility to a negative mood induction. Conversely, neurotics were more susceptible than stable people to a negative mood induction, but there was no correlation between neuroticism and susceptibility to positive mood induction.

Although this evidence supports Gray's theory of differential sensitivity to reward and punishment cues, neither Gray's model nor Larsen and Ketelaar's data can tell us what form this sensitivity takes. Does the sensitivity of extraverts reflect a greater magnitude response to reward stimuli than introverts have (for example, extraverts respond more positively to the same stimuli than introverts), or do extraverts simply attend to reward cues more than introverts? Derryberry and Reed (1994) provide evidence that the latter explanation can account for differential susceptibility. They used a target detection task to examine biases in attention toward positive and negative stimuli. Extraverts were particularly slow to shift their attention away from positive stimuli, whereas introverts were slow to shift their attention from negative stimuli. These results suggest that extraverts' greater sensitivity to reward stimuli results from differential attention to the positive and negative stimuli in their environment. Studies examining Gray's sensitivity theories have offered some of the most promising insights into the processes underlying the personality-SWB relation.

In addition to direct links between personality and SWB, a number of theorists have postulated indirect mechanisms that lead to greater SWB among people with certain personality traits. Headey and Wearing (1989), for example, found that direct temperamental effects of extraversion and neuroticism could not explain all of the relations between personality and SWB. In examining the role of personality versus life events, Headey and Wearing found that extraverts actually experienced more positive events than introverts did, and that neurotics experienced more negative events than stable individuals did. This finding was replicated by Magnus and his colleagues (1993), who suggested by way of explanation that extraverts may be able to wrest more rewards from their environments or experience more reinforcement for their extraverted behavior. This facility would lead to more positive events, and indirectly to greater SWB. Neurotics, on the other hand, may have greater amounts of anxiety that lead to social failures. This self-defeating behavior could result in lower SWB.

Congruence Models

A quite different process is postulated by those who suggest a person-environment fit is responsible for personality's influence on SWB. This congruence model posits that people experience high SWB only when their personality fits with their environment. This model could explain higher levels of SWB among extraverts, for example, by positing that an extravert is happier in social situations and that involvement in social situations is mandated by the demands of Western society. If she lived in a cloistered nunnery, however, the extravert might be less happy than an introvert. In support of this model, Kette (1991) found that extraverted prisoners were less happy than introverted prisoners, and Diener and his colleagues (1992) found that extraverts live alone less often and more frequently work in social occupations. In another test of the congruence model, Moskowitz and Cote (1995) found that people experience pleasant affect when they engage in behaviors that are concordant with their traits. For example, assertive people experienced unpleasant affect when engaging in agreeable behaviors and pleasant affect when quarreling. Diener, Larsen, and Emmons (1984) found mixed support, however, for a person-environment fit model, since extraverts were happier than introverts whether they lived alone or with others, and whether they worked in social or nonsocial occupations. Similarly, Pavot, Diener, and Fujita (1990) found that extraverts were happier than introverts whether in social or alone situations, and that both extraverts and introverts were happier in social situations than in alone situations. Thus, although people sometimes respond positively when in an environment that is compatible with their personality, the effects of personality on SWB extend beyond that which can be explained by congruence models.

Cognitive Models

In addition to temperament theories that posit differential sensitivity to reward and to punishment, researchers have developed other models that attribute personality's effects on SWB to higher levels of processing. These theorists postulate that the way we process information about rewards and punishments, rather than our biological sensitivities to these stimuli, determines our well-being. An early theory of these cognitive mediational structures is the Pollyanna Principle (Matlin and Gawron 1979). The Pollyanna Principle states that people process pleasant information more accurately and efficiently than less pleasant information. For example: people expose themselves more frequently to pleasant stimuli than to unpleasant stimuli; they recognize pleasant stimuli faster; they judge pleasant stimuli to be more frequent; they use pleasant words more often; they supply a greater number of free associates to pleasant stimuli; they recall pleasant items more accurately; they recall pleasant items earlier in a list; and they process pleasant information more rapidly (Matlin and Gawron, 1979, 411). The general tendency toward positive thoughts would explain why the majority of people report positive levels of SWB (Diener and Diener 1996). Perhaps more importantly for the current topic, individual differences exist in Pollyannaism. Those people who are able to recall more pleasant stimuli are also more likely to report that they are happy. It is possible that differences in accuracy and efficiency of processing pleasant information versus unpleasant information may lead to differential levels of well-being. Moretti and her colleagues (1996), for example, found that positive and negative constructs are differentially accessible for depressed versus nondepressed participants. More specifically, they found that when information was directed toward the self, nondepressed subjects found positive information more informative than negative information, whereas depressed subjects had no such bias.

Lyubomirsky and Ross (1997) showed that high school students waiting to hear about admissions to colleges have differential ratings of schools that rejected them based on their original level of happiness. Happy students were more likely to increase their ratings of schools they eventually chose than were unhappy students, but they were *less* likely to lower ratings of schools that rejected their applications. According to Lyubomirsky and Ross, the happy person's world is one of attractive possibilities, whereas the unhappy person's world is "a place where one has been obliged to choose not between better and best, or even between good and better, but rather between mediocre and bad or even between bad and worse" (in press, 28). The ability to focus on positive information may provide a cognitive strategy to increase well-being, and individual differences in this ability may influence well-being. In the same vein, Lyubomirsky and Tucker (1998) found that although happy and unhappy individuals experience similar life events, they saw them in a more favorable light.

Scheier and Carver's (1985) theory of dispositional optimism also posits that cognitive processes affect well-being. In their model, cognitions affect behaviors, which affect external circumstances and SWB. According to Scheier and Carver, optimism represents a generalized tendency to expect favorable outcomes in life. Presumably, people who believe that their actions will lead to a favorable outcome persist in those actions, whereas those who believe that failure is inevitable withdraw their efforts and disengage themselves from the goals that they set. Scheier and Carver (1993) review evidence showing that optimists maintain higher levels of SWB when faced with stressors.

In addition to the effects of positive thoughts about the future, much research has been undertaken to explore the effects of negative thoughts about the future, the self, and the world. Abramson and her colleagues (Abramson, Metalsky, and Alloy 1989; Abramson, Seligman, and Teasdale 1978), for example, suggest that when people experience a negative event, those who attribute the causes to stable, global, and internal factors are more likely to become depressed than are individuals who do not have such a negative explanatory style. Alloy, Lipman, and Abramson (1992) found that individuals who had these negative biases were more likely to have exhibited a past major depressive disorder than were individuals who did not have these cognitive styles.

It is possible, however, that Abramson and her colleagues, as well as other cognitive theorists, have the causal direction backward. Negative information-processing biases may, as these researchers suggest, lead to unpleasant affect. On the other hand, unpleasant emotions may cause the negative cognitions and negative cognitive biases. The uncertainty of the causal direction is also applicable to optimism. For example, Smith and his colleagues (1989) suggested that the relation between optimism and well-being is mediated by neuroticism. They claim that optimism is simply a weak measure of neuroticism and that correlations between optimism and well-being are eliminated when neuroticism scores are controlled. Others (for example, Marshall et al. 1992) have suggested that optimism is really a combination of extraversion and neuroticism and does not add any information not provided by these more widely studied variables. Although recent data contradict this notion by showing that optimism is not simply a combination of pleasant and unpleasant affect (Lucas, Diener, and Suh 1996), the issue of determining the causal direction of the optimism and unpleasant affect relation has not been resolved.

Goal Models

While our understanding of SWB is enhanced by a knowledge of the relations between traits and happiness, some researchers argue that traits provide a very incomplete picture of personality. Theorists such as Cantor (this volume), Little, Klinger, and Emmons believe that personality comprises not simply traits but also the goals for which individuals typically strive. According to these researchers, we can understand an individual's personality only if we understand the things in life that motivate his or her behaviors. Goals can be examined at a broad level (such as values), at a somewhat narrower level (life tasks), or at an even narrower level (one's current concerns). At each level of understanding, the content of goals, the manner in which goals are approached, and success or failure at attaining goals may have an effect on individuals' well-being.

Emmons (1986), for example, studies personal strivings, which he defines as "the characteristic types of goals that individuals try to achieve through their everyday behavior" (1058). Emmons found that characteristics of individuals' personal strivings predicted the different components of SWB (pleasant affect, negative affect, and life satisfaction) in different ways. For example, pleasant affect was associated with striving value, past fulfillment of strivings, and the degree of effort that the striving required, whereas negative affect was associated with lower perceived probability of success, high conflict between strivings, and ambivalence toward strivings. Life satisfaction was related to striving importance, expectations for success in strivings, and a lack of conflict between different strivings. In fact, the mere presence of important strivings was related to higher life satisfaction.

Whereas Emmons studies the characteristics of the goals themselves, Cantor (1994) believes that personality and individual differences can be understood by focusing on the problem-solving strategies that people use to meet their goals. According to Cantor, an individual's goals are determined by his or her life circumstances and the expectations of the culture, as well as by the individual's more idiosyncratic needs. People can attain their goals in a variety of ways; however, people with high SWB are those who have developed effective strategies for meeting their needs within the constraints of cultural expectations and life circumstances.

Diener and Fujita (1995) used goal theory to explain the counterintuitive finding that resources such as health, wealth, and attractiveness barely correlate with SWB. They posited that resources should affect SWB only when they have an impact on an individual's ability to attain important goals. In accordance with their predictions, Diener and

Fujita found that resources correlate more strongly with SWB when they are relevant to a person's idiographic personal strivings. Having a lot of money most influenced SWB among individuals whose personal strivings included the acquisition of wealth. Furthermore, the degree of congruence of individuals' goals with resources predicted SWB. For example, someone who was rated by friends and family members as having high athletic ability was likely to be happy if excelling at sports was an important striving in his or her life. Resources affect well-being only in interaction with individuals' idiographic goals.

Again, however, the causal priority of goals in the goals-SWB relationship is questionable. For example, it is possible that both an individual's goals and the strategies he or she uses to attain those goals are determined by broader personality traits. The goal of meeting new people may simply be an expression of the broader personality trait of extraversion. Similarly, resources such as assertiveness or sociability may be expressions of personality traits. While Diener and Fujita (1995) found that resources and strivings affected SWB even after controlling for personality traits, this hypothetical link is often left untested. Even the broad goal characteristics that Emmons examines may be subject to personality influences. He found that conflict between goals leads to lower SWB, but as Lyubomirsky and Ross (in press) illustrated, happy people often see their options as a choice between two equally pleasant alternatives, whereas unhappy people view their alternatives much more negatively. Perhaps conflict between goals is a result of low SWB, not the cause. Pavot, Fujita, and Diener (1996), for example, found that congruence between one's actual self and one's ideal self was determined by one's level of neuroticism. The complex relations between personality traits, goals, and resources must be examined more fully with longitudinal and causal modeling designs before definite causal conclusions can be drawn.

Emotion Socialization Models

Research into emotion socialization examines the ways in which processes such as classical conditioning, instrumental learning, and imitation affect emotions (Malatesta et al. 1986). Through socialization, mothers teach infants "how to modulate their feeling states and expressive behavior so as to conform to cultural norms" (Malatesta et al. 1986). In one study, Malatesta and her colleagues (1986) found that from age two and a half months to age seven and a half months, infants showed a linear increase in pleasant affect and a decrease in unpleasant affect. There were corresponding increases in contingent responding to infant interest (pleasant affect) expressions, and decreases in contingent responding to infant pain (unpleasant affect) expressions among maternal responses. Importantly, Malatesta and her colleagues found evidence for learning effects among infants when the data set was examined to establish direction of causality. Differences in socialization of emotions may explain long-term differences in emotion among individuals as well as cultures. Because emotion socialization can be influenced by cultural norms as well as by individual differences among mothers and infants, differences in the amount of affect people express may be explainable through emotion socialization processes.

Whether discussed in terms of traits, goals, or classically conditioned consistencies in behaviors, personality is often the strongest predictor of SWB. Extraversion and neuroticism, as well as narrower traits (such as self-esteem and optimism), are consistently related to the various cognitive and affective forms of SWB. These relations are particularly strong when the data are controlled for measurement error. The presence and characteristics of the goals that individuals work for in their lives are also related to well-being. Furthermore, a number of theories explaining these personality-SWB relations have received empirical support.

1. *Temperament models:* Under *set-point theories,* individuals have emotional set-points to which they return after experiencing positive or negative events. According to *reactivity theories,* individuals differ in their reaction to positive and negative stimuli. *Behavior theories* posit that temperament leads to behaviors that are differentially conducive to SWB.
2. *Congruence models:* People experience high SWB when their personalities fit with the environment.
3. *Cognitive models:* Inborn temperament causes differential propensities to attend and react to positive stimuli, and these thoughts are causes of SWB.
4. *Goal models:* The types of goals for which people strive, the ways in which people attempt to attain their goals, and the success with which these goals are met, all influence SWB.
5. *Emotion socialization models:* Through classical conditioning, instrumental learning, imitation, and so forth, people are taught which emotions are appropriate to feel and express. These socialization processes lead to differences in affect.

Although it has yet to be determined which of these related traits are cardinal in influencing SWB, and considerable research needs to be undertaken to elucidate the mechanisms behind these relations, levels of SWB are clearly related to personality.

STRUCTURE OF WELL-BEING AND PERSONALITY

Thus far, our discussion has focused on the influence of personality on levels of SWB. However, research on the relations between personality and well-being and the causes for these relations provide important information regarding the structure of well-being. Not only do the different components of well-being correlate with personality constructs in distinct ways, but they behave differently over time and across situations. For example, although unpleasant affect and pleasant affect have similar stability coefficients over time (Watson and Walker 1996), Diener and Larsen (1984) present data suggesting that unpleasant affect is more consistent across different types of situations. Similarly, Diener and his colleagues (1996) present data showing that pleasant affect is influenced by cultural norms more than unpleasant affect is. In cultures where it is deemed inappropriate to express pleasant affect, people report lower levels of it; reports of unpleasant affect, on the other hand, are less related to norms. These data, in combination with heredity studies that show that pleasant affect has a stronger shared family environment component, suggest that pleasant affect may be influenced by the environment more than unpleasant affect is. Whereas unpleasant affect may be quite strongly related to biology, pleasant affect may be determined by situational factors and environmental reinforcements in addition to the biological component. Baker and her colleagues (1992) suggest that pleasant affect may be more environmentally influenced because of its more social nature.

An additional structural concern is the degree to which individuals vary on dimensions other than the frequency of different emotions. Larsen and Diener (1987) suggested that an important individual difference in emotional experience is affect intensity—the typical strength of an individual's emotional responsiveness. At one pole of the affect intensity dimension are those people who primarily experience mild emotions and minor fluctuations. At the other pole are those people who experience their emotions strongly, and who are quite variable in their emotions. Larsen and Diener review evidence that the tendency to experience either mild or strong emotions is stable over time. Similarly, Eid and Diener (in press) found that emotional variability is stable over time. Furthermore, whether emotions are assessed individually (for example, pleased, joyful, angry, fearful) or as broad emotional factors (for example, pleasant and unpleasant affect), individuals are consistent in their reactivity.

Affect intensity is uncorrelated with indicators of well-being. Thus, affect intensity reflects the quality rather than the level of SWB that one experiences. Some people may experience mostly contentment and dysphoria but have relatively infrequent episodes of euphoria or despair. Those who experience extreme emotions do not necessarily have different levels of happiness, they just experience their emotions (both pleasant and unpleasant) more intensely.

CONCLUSION

The research reviewed in this chapter provides a strong nomological network for the construct of subjective well-being. Although a number of questions about happiness and its relation to personality remain unanswered, consistent findings have arisen from different lines of research, using varied research methodologies. The major finding is that SWB reports do not completely reflect arbitrary decisions based on temporally unstable factors. Instead, the affective and cognitive components are consistent across time and across situations and can be reliably predicted from a number of personality traits and constructs. Furthermore, the components of SWB are differentially related to different personality traits. Extraversion is moderately correlated with pleasant affect, but only slightly correlated with unpleasant affect; neuroticism is moderately correlated with unpleasant affect, but only slightly correlated with pleasant affect; and goals are more highly related to the cognitive component of SWB than the affective component. This pattern of relations and the variety of research methods used to examine these relations provide evidence for the validity of the SWB construct as well as the instruments used to measure it. Individuals do not fabricate an unreliable judgment of happiness at the time of assessment; rather, SWB ratings reflect a stable and con-

sistent phenomenon that is theoretically and empirically related to personality constructs.

This is not to say that personality is the only factor that influences SWB; we wish only to make the case that the relation is strong and consistent. Lykken and Tellegen (1996) provide the highest estimate of the effects of a person's genes on his or her SWB. Even they, however, estimate this effect to be around 50 percent for immediate SWB and 80 percent for long-term SWB, thus attributing from 20 to 50 percent of the variance in long- and short-term well-being, respectively, to environment (see Argyle, this volume, for a review of environmental influences on SWB). Stones and Kozma (1991) suggest that reports of happiness are due to current status, including events, and a long-term component that is influenced by personality. Schwarz and Strack (1991) review evidence showing that a variety of situational factors can influence how happy people say they are, and Diener and Larsen (1984) found evidence for situational effects on well-being. Although aggregated data illustrate that average levels of SWB are stable across various situations, it is difficult to predict one's happiness at any given moment. Individuals clearly react to momentary stimuli in their environments, and only by aggregating over multiple occasions can this unique variance be eliminated to reveal the effect of personality on SWB scores.

The effects of situations and external circumstances extend beyond individual moments. Mehnert and his colleagues (1990) found that although persons with disabilities who had been injured later in their life were less happy than those who were injured earlier or born with a disability (supporting adaptation theories of well-being), the representative sample of disabled people surveyed was less happy in general than was a representative sample of nondisabled individuals. Thus, although external and demographic factors often have little effect on happiness, important, life-changing events may play a role in overall well-being.

There is much left to learn about the relation between personality and subjective well-being. That this relation exists, however, provides valuable information about the importance and validity of well-being constructs. Temporally unstable factors do not completely control affective and cognitive evaluations of one's life. Rather, these evaluations also reflect characteristic emotional styles that are to some degree inherited, appear early in life, remain stable in adulthood, and generalize across situations and domains. Although the limits of this stability in the face of environmental change are unclear, theories that focus only on external influences on SWB ignore a substantial source of variation in happiness reports.

The influence of genetics and personality suggests a limit on the degree to which policy can increase SWB. Happiness is not determined solely by the resources one has or by the circumstances in which one lives. Changes in the environment, although important for short-term well-being, lose salience over time through processes of adaptation and have small effects on long-term SWB. As a caveat, the findings do leave some room for environmental effects. Factors such as early home environment may influence personality and are possibly amenable to policy interventions. Because of the large impact of personality on SWB, however, as well as factors such as adaptation, SWB cannot be used as the sole measure of quality of life and must be supplemented by social indicators.

REFERENCES

Abramson, L. Y., Metalsky, G. I., and Alloy, L. B. (1989). Hopelessness depression: A theory-based subtype of depression. *Psychological Review, 96,* 358–72.

Abramson, L. Y., Seligman, M. E., and Teasdale, J. D. (1978). Learned helplessness in humans: Critique and reformulation. *Journal of Abnormal Psychology, 87,* 49–74.

Alloy, L. B., Lipman, A. J., and Abramson, L. Y. (1992). Attributional style as a vulnerability factor for depression: Validation by past history of mood disorders. *Cognitive Therapy and Research* (special issue: Cognitive vulnerability to psychological dysfunction), *16,* 391–407.

Baker, L. A., Cesa, I. L., Gatz, M., and Grodsky, A. (1992). Genetic and environmental influences on positive and negative affect: Support for a two-factor theory. *Psychology and Aging, 7,* 158–63.

Block, J. (1995). A contrarian view of the five-factor approach to personality description. *Psychological Bulletin, 117,* 187–215.

Bradburn, N. M. (1969). *The structure of psychological well-being.* Chicago: Aldine.

Campbell, A., Converse, P. E., and Rodgers, W. L. (1976). *The quality of American life.* New York: Russell Sage Foundation.

Cantor, N. (1994). Life task problem solving: Situational affordances and personal needs. *Personality and Social Psychology Bulletin, 20,* 235–43.

Costa, P. T. (1994). Traits through time, or the stability of personality: Observations, evaluations, and a model. Paper presented at the meeting of the American Psychological Association, Los Angeles, (August 12–16).

Costa, P. T., and McCrae, R. R. (1980). Influence of extraversion and neuroticism on subjective well-being: Happy and unhappy people. *Journal of Personality and Social Psychology, 38,* 668–78.

———. (1988). Personality in adulthood: A six-year longitudinal study of self-reports and spouse ratings on the NEO Personality Inventory. *Journal of Personality and Social Psychology, 54,* 853–63.

———. (1992). *Revised NEO Personality Inventory (NEOPI-R) and Five Factor Inventory (NEO-FFI) professional manual.* Odessa, Fla.: Psychological Assessment Resources.

Costa, P. T., McCrae, R. R., and Zonderman, A. (1987). Environmental and dispositional influences on well-being: Longitudinal follow-up of an American national sample. *British Journal of Psychology, 78,* 299–306.

Davidson, R. J., and Fox, N. A. (1982). Asymmetrical brain activity discriminates between positive versus negative affective stimuli in human infants. *Science, 218,* 1235–37.

Derryberry, D., and Reed, M. A. (1994). Temperament and attention: Orienting toward and away from positive and negative signals. *Journal of Personality and Social Psychology, 66,* 1128–39.

Diener, E., and Diener, C. (1996). Most people are happy. *Psychological Science, 7,* 181–85.

Diener, E., and Diener, M. (1995). Cross-cultural correlates of life satisfaction and self-esteem. *Journal of Personality and Social Psychology, 68,* 653–63.

Diener, E., and Fujita, F. (1995). Resources, personal strivings, and subjective well-being: A nomothetic and idiographic approach. *Journal of Personality and Social Psychology, 68,* 926–35.

Diener, E. and Larsen, R. J. (1984). Temporal stability and cross-situational consistency of affective, behavioral, and cognitive responses. *Journal of Personality and Social Psychology, 47,* 580–92.

Diener, E., Larsen, R.J., and Emmons, R. A. (1984). Person x situation interactions: Choice of situations and consequence response models. *Journal of Personality and Social Psychology, 47,* 580–92.

Diener, E., Sandvik, E., Pavot, W., and Fujita, F. (1992). Extraversion and subjective well-being in a U.S. national probability sample. *Journal of Research in Personality, 26,* 205–15.

Diener, E., Sandvik, E., Seidlitz, L., and Diener, M. (1993). The relationship between income and subjective well-being: Relative or absolute? *Social Indicators Research, 28,* 195–223.

Diener, E., Suh, E., Oishi, S., and Shao, L. (1996). Norms for affect: National comparisons. Paper presented at the International Society for Research on Emotion, Victoria University in the University of Toronto, Toronto, August 13–17.

Diener, E., Wolsic, B., and Fujita, F. (1995). Physical attractiveness and subjective well-being. *Journal of Personality and Social Psychology, 69,* 120–29.

Digman, J. M. (1990). Personality structure: Emergence of the five-factor model. *Annual Review of Psychology, 41,* 417–40.

Digman, J. M., and Shmelyov, A. G. (1996). The structure of temperament and personality in Russian children. *Journal of Personality and Social Psychology, 71,* 341–51.

Eid, M., and Diener, E. (in press). An examination of emotional variability controlling for measurement error. *Journal of Personality and Social Psychology.*

Emmons, R. A. (1986). Personal strivings: An approach to personality and subjective well-being. *Journal of Personality and Social Psychology, 51,* 1058–68.

Eysenck, H. J. (1967). *The biological bases of personality.* Springfield, Ill.: Charles C. Thomas.

———. (1986). Models and paradigms in personality research. In A. Angleitner, A. Furnham, and G. Van Heck (Eds.), *Personality psychology in Europe,* vol. 2, *Current trends and controversies* (pp. 213–23). Lisse, The Netherlands: Swets and Zeitlinger.

———. (1981). *A model for personality.* New York: Springer-Verlag.

Fujita, F. (1991). An investigation of the relation between extraversion, neuroticism, positive affect, and negative affect. Master's thesis, University of Illinois.

Goldberg, L. R. (1993). The structure of phenotypic personality traits. *American Psychologist, 48,* 26–34.

Goldsmith, H. H., and Campos, J. J. (1986). Fundamental issues in the study of early temperament: The Denver twin temperament study. In M. E. Lamb, A. L. Brown, and B. Rogoff (Eds.), *Advances in developmental psychology* (pp. 231–83). Hillsdale, N.J.: Erlbaum.

Gray, J. A. (1981). A critique of Eysenck's theory of personality. In H. J. Eysenck (Ed.), *A model for personality* (pp. 246–76). New York: Springer-Verlag.

Headey, B., and Wearing, A. (1989). Personality, life events, and subjective well-being: Toward a dynamic equilibrium model. *Journal of Personality and Social Psychology, 57,* 731–39.

———. (1992). *Understanding happiness: A theory of subjective well-being.* Melbourne: Longman Cheshire.

John, O. P. (1990). The "Big Five" factor taxonomy: Dimensions of personality in the natural language and in questionnaires. In L. A. Pervin (Ed.), *Handbook of personality: Theory and research* (pp. 66–100). New York: Guilford.

Kagan, J. (1994). *Galen's prophecy.* New York: Basic Books.

Kagan, J., and Moss, J. (1962). *Birth to maturity.* New York: Wiley. Reprint, New Haven, Conn.: Yale University Press, 1983.

Kagan, J., Snidman, N., and Arcus, D. M. (1992). Initial reactions to unfamiliarity. *Current Directions in Psychological Science, 1,* 171–74.

Kette, G. (1991). *Haft: Eine socialpsychologische analyse* (Prison: A social psychological analysis). Göttingen: Hogrefe.

Kozma, A. (1996). Top-down and bottom-up approaches to an understanding of subjective well-being. World Conference on Quality of Life, University of Northern British Columbia, Prince George, (August 22–25).

LaGasse, L., Gruber, C., and Lipsitt, L. P. (1989). The infantile expression of avidity in relation to later assessments. In J. S. Reznick (Ed.), *Perspectives on behavioral inhibition* (pp. 159–76). Chicago: University of Chicago Press.

Larsen, R. J., and Diener, E. (1987). Emotional response intensity as an individual difference characteristic. *Journal of Research in Personality, 21,* 1–39.

Larsen, R. J., and Ketelaar, T. (1991). Personality and susceptibility to positive and negative emotional states. *Journal of Personality and Social Psychology, 61,* 132–40.

Lucas, R. E., Diener, E., and Suh, E. (1996). Discriminant validity of well-being measures. *Journal of Personality and Social Psychology, 71,* 616–28.

Lykken, D., and Tellegen, A. (1996). Happiness is a stochastic phenomenon. *Psychological Science, 7,* 186–89.

Lyubomirsky, S., and Ross, L. (in press). Changes in attractiveness of elected, rejected, and precluded alternatives: A comparison of "happy" and "unhappy" individuals. *Journal of Personality and Social Psychology.*

Lyubomirsky, S., and Tucker, K. L. (1998). Implications of individual differences in subjective happiness for perceiving, interpreting, and thinking about life events. *Motivation and Evaluation, 22,* 155–85.

Magnus, K., and Diener, E. (1991). A longitudinal analysis of personality, life events, and subjective well-being. Paper presented at the Sixty-third Annual Meeting of the Midwestern Psychological Association, Chicago (May 2–4).

Magnus, K., Diener, E., Fujita, F., and Pavot, W. (1993). Extraversion and neuroticism as predictors of objective life events: A longitudinal analysis. *Journal of Personality and Social Psychology, 65,* 1046–53.

Malatesta, C. Z., Grigoryev, P., Lamb, C., Albin, M., and Culver, C. (1986). Emotion socialization and expressive development in preterm and full-term infants. *Child Development, 57,* 316–30.

Marshall, G. N., Wortman, C. B., Kusulas, J. W., Hervig, L. K., and Vickers, R. R. (1992). Distinguishing optimism from pessimism: Relations to fundamental dimensions of mood and personality. *Journal of Personality and Social Psychology, 62,* 1067–74.

Matlin, M. W., and Gawron, V. J. (1979). Individual differences in Pollyannaism. *Journal of Personality Assessment, 43,* 411–12.

Mehnert, T., Krauss, H. H., Nadler, R., and Boyd, M. (1990). Correlates of life satisfaction in those with disabling conditions. *Rehabilitation Psychology, 35,* 3–17.

Moretti, M. M., Segal, Z. V., McCann, C. D., Shaw, B. F., Miller, D. T., and Vella, D. (1996). Self-referent versus other-referent information processing in dysphoric, clinically depressed, and remitted depressed subjects. *Personality and Social Psychology Bulletin, 22,* 68–80.

Moskowitz, D. S., and Cote, S. (1995). Do interpersonal traits predict affect? A comparison of three models. *Journal of Personality and Social Psychology, 69,* 915–24.

Okun, M. A., and George, L. K. (1984). Physician- and self-ratings of health, neuroticism, and subjective well-being among men and women. *Personality and Individual Differences, 5,* 533–39.

Pavot, W., Diener, E., and Fujita, F. (1990). Extroversion and happiness. *Personality and Individual Differences, 11,* 1299–1306.

Pavot, W., Fujita, F., and Diener, E. (1996). The relation between self-aspect congruence, personality, and subjective well-being. *Personality and Individual Differences, 22,* 183–91.

Pervin, L. A. (1994). A critical analysis of current trait theory. *Psychological Inquiry, 5,* 103–13.

Plomin, R., and Neiderhiser, J. M. (1992). Genetics and experience. *Current Directions in Psychological Science, 1,* 160–63.

Rothbart, M. K., and Ahadi, S. A. (1994). Temperament and the development of personality. *Journal of Abnormal Psychology* (special issue: Personality and psychopathology), *103,* 55–66.

Scheier, M. F., and Carver, C. S. (1985). Optimism, coping, and health: Assessment and implications of generalized outcome expectancies. *Health Psychology, 4,* 219–47.

———. (1993). On the power of positive thinking: The benefits of being optimistic. *Current Directions in Psychological Science, 2,* 26–30.

Schwarz, N., and Strack, F. (1991). Evaluating one's life: A judgment model of subjective well-being. In F. Strack, M. Argyle, and N. Schwarz (Eds.), *Subjective well-being: An interdisciplinary perspective* (pp. 27–47). New York: Pergamon.

Seidlitz, L. (1993). Agreeableness, conscientiousness, and openness as related to subjective well-being. Paper presented at the sixth meeting of the International Society of the Study of Individual Differences, Baltimore (July 17–21).

Silver, R. L. (1980). Coping with an undesirable life event: A study of early reactions to physical disability. Ph.D. diss., Northwestern University.

Smith, T. W., Pope, M. K., Rhodewalt, F., and Poulton, J. L. (1989). Optimism, neuroticism, coping and symptom reports: An alternative interpretation of the life orientation test. *Journal of Personality and Social Psychology, 56,* 640–48.

Stones, M. J., and Kozma, A. (1991). A magical model of happiness. *Social Indicators Research, 25,* 31–50.

Suh, E., Diener, E., and Fujita, F. (1996). Events and subjective well-being: Only recent events matter. *Journal of Personality and Social Psychology, 70,* 1091–1102.

Tellegen, A. (1985). Structures of mood and personality and their relevance to assessing anxiety, with an emphasis on self-report. In A. H. Tuma and J. D. Maser (Eds.), *Anxiety and the anxiety disorders* (pp. 681–706). Hillsdale, N.J.: Erlbaum.

Tellegen, A., Lykken, D. T., Bouchard, T. J., Wilcox, K. J., Segal, N. L., and Rich, S. (1988). Personality similarity in twins reared apart and together. *Journal of Personality and Social Psychology, 54,* 1031–39.

Watson, D., and Clark, L. A. (1992). On traits and temperament: General and specific factors of emotional experience and their relation to the five-factor model. *Journal of Personality, 60,* 441–76.

Watson, D., and Walker, L. M. (1996). The long-term stability and predictive validity of trait measures of affect. *Journal of Personality and Social Psychology, 70,* 567–77.

12 Life Task Participation and Well-Being: The Importance of Taking Part in Daily Life

Nancy Cantor and Catherine A. Sanderson

This chapter posits that individuals' sustained participation in personally and culturally valued tasks that change across the life course enhances well-being, and in fact that such participation has benefits above and beyond the direct effects of both personal traits (such as extraversion) and tangible resources (such as wealth). First, we show that the type of participation matters, because the strength of the link between participation and well-being depends on the specific tasks on which individuals are working. Specifically, well-being should be enhanced when individuals are able to pursue their distinct personal goals in ways that are intrinsically valued and autonomously chosen, approached at a feasible level, and facilitated in their daily life context. Well-being may also, however, depend on the presence of various social, personal, and tangible resources, which increase individuals' likelihood of participating in various tasks. In the second part of our model, we describe the role of these resources in keeping individuals vigilant as they find new ways to participate and thereby gain well-being, in facilitating intense participation, and in motivating continued participation in the face of threat or frustration. Finally, we show that because changes occur in both the opportunities for participation across the life span and the value various subcultures place on specific types of task pursuit, individuals need to be able to adapt to these changing opportunities in order to experience well-being (for example, by taking on the "right" tasks at the "right" time). Although finding new ways to participate can present a challenge for individuals, it also presents new opportunities for experiencing well-being. (For example, after retirement individuals can replace their occupational participation with social participation.) This model therefore provides a partial counter to adaptation level phenomena (see, for example, Brickman and Campbell's [1971] hedonic treadmill) by suggesting that because individuals are forced to participate in new tasks across the life course, they can experience well-being in different ways. Scholars from a variety of
disciplines, including psychology, sociology, economics, and philosophy, have examined the importance of what individuals are trying to do in their daily lives as critical to well-being (cf. Brickman and Coates 1987; Durkheim 1933; Havighurst 1960; Rubin 1976; Ryff 1993; Sen 1980). This emphasis on the advantages for well-being of taking part in daily life is reflected in Allport's (1937) traditional distinction between the "having" and "doing" side of personality (see also Adler's [1929] style of life and social interest). Individuals need to develop the "doing" side of personality, namely, by being committed to various goals, roles, and activities, perhaps as much as they need to "have" the tangible resources and personal dispositions commonly believed (and often observed) to bring happiness (Cantor 1990, 1994; Snyder 1993). This may in fact be part of the reason why commitments such as marriage, religion, and career involvement are associated with overall life satisfaction (Batson and Ventis 1982; Kessler and Essex 1982). In this chapter, we take a multidimensional perspective on the meaning of valued activities. On the one hand, valued activities can refer to those tasks that are specified by a particular sociocultural context (Erikson 1950; Havighurst 1972), as well as those tasks that individuals find personally rewarding (Emmons 1986; Klinger 1975). In fact, the life-task literature posits that activities that are both culturally specified and personally meaningful are particularly valued (for example, doing the right task at the right time; see Cantor 1990). On the other hand, tasks that are associated with self-directed motives and positive affect are also likely to be valued. For example, Csikszentmihalyi's (1975, 1990) research describes how the pursuit of intrinsically motivating, desired tasks is associated with great satisfaction ("flow") (see also Kasser and Ryan 1993). In this way, valued activities can refer to those tasks that are culturally valued, personally valued, and/or intrinsically rewarding. The opportunity to take part in such valued activities

across the life span has been shown to contribute to well-being above and beyond the effects of "having" various material, personal, and social resources (Harlow and Cantor 1996). Sen's (1980) focus on assessing quality of life and well-being in terms of what a person manages to do or be—the valued functionings he or she can achieve—in leading a life exemplifies this perspective. Furthermore, considerable research has shown that the pursuit and the progression toward valued goals are associated with both psychological and physical well-being (Diener 1984; Emmons 1986). Analyses of advance medical directives by Ditto, Druley, Moore, Danks, and Smucker (1996), for example, have shown that individuals' personal judgments about the quality of a life worth sustaining are influenced substantially by their perceived ability to take part in valued activities ("living the life they want to live"). This functional perspective on well-being and life satisfaction is therefore anchored in what people are doing, trying to do, expected to do, and recovering from doing.

WHY IS PARTICIPATING in valued activities and having and working toward personal goals so important for well-being? On a personal level, commitment to particular goals provides a sense of personal agency and purpose (Cantor 1990). As Brickman describes it, "Happy people know what they want to do and are doing it" (Brickman and Coates 1987, 227). This feeling of confidence in one's beliefs and choices serves to motivate action and involvement in valued life activities. As Csikszentmihalyi's (1975, 1990) research on the state of "flow" illustrates, people experience great satisfaction when they are completely committed to and absorbed in a valued and challenging activity. In fact, reports from chess players, mountain climbers, dancers, surgeons, and composers all describe the sensation of flow as one of life's peak experiences. On the other hand, individuals who are unable to maintain and follow through on commitments experience alienation and anomie (Brickman and Coates 1987). Clinical depression, for example, involves as one facet an inability to commit to and participate in valued life activities and is typically associated with alienation from both activities and relationships.

Participation in valued activities also provides a structure and meaning to daily life (Klinger 1975; Little 1983). The gerontology literature, for example, has shown that participation in various daily social activities, such as entertaining friends and attending social/cultural events, is particularly im-

portant in terms of life satisfaction for retired individuals, who presumably are less able to derive well-being from work-related activity (Hendricks and Hendricks 1986). Similarly, Coyle and her colleagues (Coyle, Lesnik-Emas, and Kinney 1994) found that although leisure participation did not eliminate the decrease in overall well-being for those living with a debilitating injury, it was the greatest predictor of life satisfaction for those with spinal cord injury. This research suggests that the structure and meaning that participation gives to daily life may be most valuable in terms of life satisfaction for those facing newly constrained daily life opportunities, such as those who are recently retired or have incurred limitations on mobility from health crises.

Commitment to goals and tasks may also help individuals cope with various problems in daily life and hence maintain well-being in times of adversity. Lydon's (Lydon and Zanna 1990) value-affirmation approach indicates that individuals who see their current personal projects and goals as value-relevant are more likely to stay committed to them, even in the face of threat or challenge. Adversity may, in fact, serve as a catalyst for commitment (Brickman and Coates 1987) by forcing an individual to search for ways to participate in daily life. Daily life situations that create adverse conditions may actually result in renewed commitment to participation in valued projects and goals. Although letting go of a valued goal that is no longer tenable may be associated with sadness and anger (cf. Carver and Scheier 1990), creating new meaningful goals to work toward can help motivate goal pursuit and increase positive affect. Research with the caregivers of AIDS patients suggests that psychological well-being depends on both relinquishing untenable goals and setting new ones (Folkman and Stein 1996). Well-being emerges from making progress on a task, and hence revising goals to represent more realistic possibilities is an adaptive coping strategy.

Furthermore, commitment and participation also provide for *social* well-being that benefits both individuals and communities (Putnam 1995). Perhaps most important, participation provides social connection with others (Baumeister and Leary 1995; Myers and Diener 1995). This need to belong, namely, to form and maintain strong interpersonal relationships with others, may, in fact, be an essential part of well-being (Baumeister and Leary 1995). Recent writings in evolutionary psychology (Caporael and Brewer 1991), for example, posit that the social group has been a primary survival strategy for humans by providing protection from predators, access to food, and protection from the physical environment. This perspective suggests that sociality, including cooperativeness, group loyalty, and adherence to various norms, may be a fundamental part of human nature (see also Myers, this volume).

Although this focus on social participation and belonging as predictors of well-being may seem counterintuitive given the focus, at least in Western cultures, on individualism, social participation may, in fact, be a vehicle by which people can fulfill various ostensibly self-focused needs. Volunteerism, for example, is one way in which people serve personal needs by participating in society in prosocial and altruistic ways (compare, Wuthnow 1991, "acts of passion"; Snyder 1993). Close to 100 million Americans participate in some type of volunteer activity each year, with nearly 25 million contributing at least five hours per week (Independent Sector 1992). Society obviously benefits from the service of volunteers in many ways, both directly (for example, providing goods and services such as assistance with household chores and free meals to those in need) and indirectly (for example, providing education to the general public and increasing community spirit and civic participation) (Omoto and Snyder 1990; compare, Putnam 1995).

Individuals themselves, however, may also receive a variety of personal rewards for participating in society in this way, including feelings of helpfulness, heightened self-esteem, and friendships (King, Walder, and Pavey 1970; Scheibe 1965). In order to examine the association of individuals' motivations for volunteer service with length of service, Omoto and Snyder (1995) conducted a study with volunteers with an AIDS service organization. Their findings demonstrate that individuals with more self-oriented motivations for volunteering (for example, gaining self-esteem and social support) actually remain in volunteer service for a longer period of time as compared to those with more "purely" other-oriented motivations (for example, helping those who are less fortunate). Apparently, individuals' participation in society through volunteer service is actually a good forum for obtaining self-focused benefits, such as social connectedness and personal agency.

A DYNAMIC MODEL OF PARTICIPATION AND WELL-BEING

In this chapter, we describe a life-span perspective on well-being that posits that individuals' sus-

tained participation in personally and culturally valued tasks that change across the life course enhances well-being, and in fact, such participation benefits individuals above and beyond the direct effects of both personal traits (for example, extraversion) and tangible resources (for example, wealth). First, we show that the type of participation matters, because the strength of the link between participation and well-being depends on the specific tasks on which individuals are working. Specifically, well-being should be enhanced when individuals are able to pursue their distinct personal goals in ways that are intrinsically valued and autonomously chosen, approached at a feasible level, and facilitated in their daily life context (compare, Cantor and Kihlstrom 1987; Emmons 1986; Palys and Little 1983). Well-being may also, however, depend on the presence of various social, personal, and tangible resources that increase individuals' likelihood of participating in various tasks. In the second part of our model, we describe the role of these resources in keeping individuals vigilant about finding new ways to participate and thereby gain well-being, in facilitating intense participation, and in motivating continued participation in the face of threat or frustration. Finally, we show that because not only the opportunities for participation but also the value various subcultures place on specific types of task pursuit change across the life span, individuals need to be able to adapt to these changing opportunities in order to experience well-being (for example, by taking on the "right" tasks at the "right" time). Although finding new ways to participate can present a challenge for individuals, it also presents new opportunities for experiencing well-being. (After retirement, for example, individuals can replace their occupational participation with social participation.) This model therefore provides a partial counter to adaptation level phenomena (Brickman and Campbell's [1971] hedonic treadmill) by suggesting that because individuals are forced to participate in new tasks across the life course, individuals can experience well-being in different ways.

WHAT TYPES OF PARTICIPATION LEAD TO WELL-BEING?

Although we believe that effective functioning and well-being are associated with taking part vigorously in daily life activities, some types of participation may be better than others. After all, individuals need to participate in those tasks that they find personally involving and to approach these tasks in realistic ways that encourage sustained participation (compare, Cantor and Kihlstrom 1987). In this section, we examine the predictors of well-being as a function of what, how, and where individuals choose to participate: what tasks they take on, how they take them on, and where they take them on.

What: Intrinsically Valued, Autonomous, Desired Goals

First of all, individuals who participate in tasks that they find personally rewarding and intrinsically motivating are likely to maintain their interest in participating and thereby experience well-being. In fact, having more autonomous, or self-determined, motives for goal pursuit is associated with general life satisfaction and vitality, as compared to those "controlled" goals that are oriented toward other people's desires (Deci and Ryan 1987; Sheldon and Kasser 1995). Individuals who are actively striving to achieve self-relevant goals are therefore expected to experience greater well-being (Banaji and Prentice 1994; Cantor and Fleeson 1991). As Csikszentmihalyi (1975, 1990) shows, people experience great satisfaction when they are completely involved in a personally valued and desired task (that is, in a state of "flow"). Relatedly, research by Kasser and Ryan (1993) demonstrates that the pursuit of intrinsic goals (for example, personal growth, community contribution) is associated positively with various measures of well-being, whereas the pursuit of extrinsically motivated goals (such as financial success or social recognition) is negatively related to well-being. Although it is likely that some people find goals such as social recognition intrinsically motivating, our broader point is that the link between participation and well-being may be particularly strong for autonomous and intrinsically rewarding goals —whatever they may be. These are the tasks that individuals particularly enjoy and hence are likely to continue to participate in.

Similarly, people who approach rather than avoid their goals may experience greater well-being, in part because it is easier to plan for and participate in a goal than to avoid one (Gollwitzer 1993). Considerable research has examined the distinction between striving to achieve various desired goals and striving to avoid various undesired goals (for example, working toward making friends versus not being lonely) (Higgins et al. 1994). Emmons, Shep-

herd, and Kaiser (1994), for example, found that both college students and community members with a high proportion of avoidance goals had lower physical and psychological well-being, including lower positive moods, less life satisfaction, and more physical symptoms. We believe that this negative association between goal avoidance and well-being is due at least in part to the difficulty individuals have in "actively participating" in avoiding their goals.

How: Realistic Goals

In addition to pursuing particular (personally rewarding) goals, individuals also can approach goals at various levels of specificity, which in turn influence sustained participation and well-being. A number of theories (such as, control theory and action identification theory) posit that goal pursuit may be performed at different levels of specificity, with corresponding degrees of rewardingness and feasibility (see, for example, Little's [1989] "meaningfulness" versus "manageability" trade-off). For example, control theory (Carver and Scheier 1982, 1990) describes low-level goals as focusing concretely on how the action is to be carried out (for example, "memorize twenty French vocabulary words") and higher-level goals as emphasizing broader purposes or implications ("learn French"). Although individuals may have more difficulty working toward and attaining high-level as compared to low-level goals (it is harder to "learn French" than to "memorize twenty vocabulary words"), the pursuit of higher-level goals potentially leads to greater boosts in well-being. Relatedly, Vallacher and Wegner's (1989) action identification theory posits that there are individual differences in the tendency to prefer high over low levels of strivings, and that individuals experience greater satisfaction when their characteristic striving level matches the level of challenge of their daily life tasks (that is, easy tasks and low-level strivings, difficult tasks and high-level strivings). Our model suggests that choosing realistic, feasible goals is particularly important for well-being because those who pursue goals at unmanageable levels may experience frustration and hence stop participating in these tasks.

In addition to selecting goals at an appropriate level of abstraction, individuals who set goals that are congruent with one another may experience well-being. A variety of self theorists have emphasized the importance for well-being of maintaining consistent aspects of the self (compare, Donahue et al. 1993; Lecky 1945). Individuals who attempt to pursue conflicting goals simultaneously (for example, "spend more time with my boyfriend" and "do better in my classes") may experience frustration and could ultimately withdraw from participating in or pursuing either goal (see, for example, Emmons and King's [1988] "action inhibition"). In fact, across a variety of studies goal conflict has been, associated with higher levels of negative affect, neuroticism/depression, increased stress, and lower life satisfaction (Emmons 1986; Sheldon and Kasser 1995), as well as psychosomatic complaints over time (Emmons and King 1988). Similarly, Donahue and her colleagues (1993) found that self-concept differentiation, namely, a fragmentation of the self, was associated with poor emotional adjustment, whereas integration was associated with healthy adjustment. This research suggests the importance for well-being of maintaining complementary personal goals and self-concepts. Such complementarity enables one to avoid action immobilization from goal conflict and also to achieve economies of effort by maximizing the relationship between participation in any one activity and progress on various valued goals.

Where: Goal Pursuit and Daily Life

Finally, and not surprisingly, individuals should be more likely to sustain their participation in those tasks in which they experience greater positive affect and satisfaction, and in turn, these rewarding tasks are likely to be goal-relevant. After all, the daily events of a person's life differ in the extent to which they provide opportunities to pursue personal goals and participate in valued activities, and individuals who participate in goal-relevant daily life situations are likely to experience greater well-being (Buss 1987; Snyder 1981). For example, extraverts, highly sociable individuals, and those high in need for affiliation have greater positive affect in social situations, which are likely to encourage the pursuit of their valued goals (Emmons, Diener, and Larsen 1986; see also Cantor et al. 1991; McAdams and Constantian 1983). Individuals, in fact, go to some lengths to structure their lives in order to find ways of feeling good (Gollwitzer 1993; Mischel, Cantor, and Feldman 1996). This patterning can even be quite specific: Cantor and Sanderson (1998) found that those with predominant intimacy goals in dating spent more time and had greater positive affect in those dating situations particularly conducive to intimacy (such as being alone with the partner) but not in situations in general with their partner (for example, large group situations such as parties). Again, this dis-

tinct patterning makes sense because spending time in goal-relevant situations should encourage sustained participation and hence lead to greater positive affect and well-being.

Relatedly, and as Niedenthal's research indicates (Niedenthal and Mordkoff 1991), some people construct their worlds in ways that allow them to spend time in situations that maximize the fit between themselves and their ideal prototypes. They choose housing, therapists, restaurants, and so on, in ways that fit their ideal self-images. Those who use such decision heuristics as self-prototype matches are, in turn, likely to sustain participation at least in part as an affirmation of themselves and their values (Lydon and Zanna 1990). This research suggests that particular situations, namely, self-concept matching and goal-relevant ones, will be associated with the experience of positive affect, which in turn should lead to continued participation and well-being.

WHAT OPPORTUNITIES ARE THERE FOR SUSTAINED PARTICIPATION?

Of course, participation is not a straightforward matter. Individuals need to have the resources—personal (health, traits, strategies, abilities), social (social network, social support), and material (status, income)—that open doors to participation in valued life activities. In other words, we must ask not just what an individual "has" but what doors are opened for participation by possessing those "goods." These resources can provide access to ways of participating, enable individuals to take advantage of new ways to participate, and encourage persistence in participation in the face of threat or frustration.

Resoures Open Doors to Participate in Valued Activities

The influence of resources on well-being appears to be mediated in part by whether the particular resource enables a person to participate in and work on his/her important life goals; those with the most resources relevant to their goal strivings have the greatest subjective well-being (Diener and Fujita 1995). Wealth, for example, is not strongly associated with well-being: income in the United States is only weakly associated with subjective well-being, and individuals who experience a substantial change in income over a given period of time (in either direction) do not change dramatically in life satisfaction (Diener et al. 1993). The association of resources with subjective well-being is considerably stronger, however, when the resources are relevant to an individual's personal strivings and hence may influence his/her ability to participate in valued life activities (Diener and Fujita 1995). For example, Caspi and Elder (1986) found no association between global satisfaction and the number of formal groups to which middle-class women belonged, but a strong association for working-class women, who may have had fewer opportunities for participation. Similarly, although overall there is no strong correlation between well-being and income in wealthier countries, there is a stronger positive association between income and well-being in the poorest countries, namely, those in which people cannot meet their basic needs and hence wealth may allow one to participate in various tasks and activities that are otherwise closed off (Veenhoven 1991).

Although when people think of personal resources that contribute to well-being they are most likely to think of financial resources, many less obvious resources, such as power and status, may also lead to well-being by strongly enabling sustained participation in valued activities (Bargh et al. 1995; Fiske 1993; Fiske and Depret 1996). Discrepancies in status are, in fact, present in a variety of relationships (such as teacher-student, boss-secretary, therapist-patient), and in these cases the person with the greater power largely controls the agenda for participation. For example, a boss has considerably greater influence over the daily life activities of his/her secretary than the reverse. The resources of power and status may therefore also provide opportunities for experiencing well-being by facilitating participation in valued activities.

Although certain traits, such as extraversion, optimism, and self-esteem, are associated with well-being directly (for example, extraverted individuals report experiencing more positive life events) (see Diener and Lucas, this volume), they may also be associated with well-being indirectly by increasing individuals' ability to participate in valued life activities. Possessing such traits may lead to well-being in part by providing opportunities for participation that, in turn, may allow for goal fulfillment (Diener and Diener 1995). For example, those who are extraverted are likely to approach others with ease, thus increasing opportunities for fulfilling social participation (that is, by providing social contacts with whom they can interact and for whom they can care as well as by whom they can be cared for). Interestingly, the link between self-esteem and well-being is particularly strong in Western cultures (Diener and Diener 1995), perhaps because in many Western cultures self-assertiveness and self-efficacy open doors to participation in valued tasks.

Further, social support from others may be an important resource that enables sustained participation, and hence well-being, in a variety of ways. For example, women with even a single close friend are better able to tolerate various hardships that are otherwise associated with depression for those without such confidants, perhaps because the presence of such a friend provides valuable social participation (Brown and Harris 1978). House and Kahn (1985), in fact, describe four different types of social support (emotional, appraisal, instrumental, informational), which can be differentially beneficial to different people and in different situations: receiving encouragement to continue with a valued goal may facilitate participation in some cases, whereas receiving practical advice about how best to approach a given problem may be most valuable in other cases. Correspondingly, research by Decker and Schulz (1985) with spinal cord patients demonstrates that life satisfaction is positively associated with receiving higher levels of overall social support, presumably at least in part because receiving such assistance enables them to maintain various types of task participation (see also Myers, this volume). Interestingly, this social contact with others (a spouse, children, friends) may be associated with well-being not only directly by providing social support and assistance, but also indirectly by providing individuals with opportunities to *care for others*. As Brickman and Coates (1987) show, individuals sometimes get more out of caring for others than they do out of being cared for, so receiving social support may in fact have its greatest impact on well-being for those in constrained life situations by allowing for reciprocity of such support (and thereby also avoiding resentments from caregivers).

Resources Lead to New Opportunities to Participate

Although individuals need resources in order to have access to various valued activities, they also need resources that enable them to "keep their eyes open" to such opportunities for participation. As Cantor and Kihlstrom (1987) show, social intelligence enables one to utilize effectively various strategies for task pursuit and thereby successfully participate in diverse valued life activities. Such intelligence can include individuals' skills at monitoring emotions, discriminating between various emotions, and using this information to guide action (Mayer and Salovey 1993; Salovey and Mayer 1990). For example, those with more finely tuned skills of emotional intelligence may be particularly vigilant about opportunities to pursue rewarding interpersonal activities and hence be most able to take advantage of such opportunities as they arise. Similarly, Langston's (1994) research demonstrates that individuals differ in their ability to "capitalize on good events," namely, to benefit from positive life events and thereby experience well-being. Individuals with more awareness of and adeptness at managing their social environments may therefore be more successful at noticing and capitalizing on various opportunities for participation. Relatedly, Snyder's (1974, 1979) work on self-monitoring suggests that high self-monitors, namely, those who are particularly adept at adapting themselves to the demands of their environments, may be best able to take advantage of opportunities to participate in various tasks and hence experience greater positive affect.

Individuals may also vary in their ability to engage in flexible goal pursuit, namely, to change the goals they are pursuing in response to personal or situational constraints and opportunities (compare, Brandtstadter and Renner 1990; Gollwitzer 1993; Heckhausen and Schultz 1995; Kuhl 1985). As Heckhausen and Schultz (1993, 1995) indicate, primary control refers to changing one's environment to meet various goals (for example, entering specific daily life situations), whereas secondary control refers to changing internal processes such as goals, expectations, and attributions (cf. Rothbaum, Weisz, and Snyder 1982). Individuals who are able to shift their goals in response to various environmental factors can gain well-being from participating in a variety of valued activities. Older adults, for example, may set more lenient standards for themselves (for example, in terms of health and fitness) that take into account their increasing limitations, and hence they may be able to maintain their participation in valued life activities. (Although the activity may change from jogging to walking, for example, both activities involve participation in exercise.) As described previously, the psychological well-being of caregivers of AIDS patients depends on both relinquishing untenable goals and setting new ones that allow for continued participation (Folkman and Stein 1996). Individuals who are more effective at either

type of control are likely to have an easier time taking part in goal-relevant situations, and hence creating opportunities to participate and thereby increase subjective well-being.

Resources Facilitate Persistence at Valued Tasks in the Face of Difficulty

Although individuals may possess the resources needed to notice and take advantage of opportunities for participation, they also need to be able to maintain a clear focus on their goals in order to continue task participation even in the face of challenging circumstances. As Gollwitzer and colleagues have shown, individuals with specific plans for where, when, and how to pursue a goal (for example, "implementation intentions") are more likely to achieve their goals, perhaps owing in part to an increased ability to cope with various goal-impeding obstacles (Gollwitzer 1993; see also Cantor and Fleeson 1991). Relatedly, Dweck and Leggett (1988) have shown the importance of the use of particular strategies in terms of motivating continued effort at a task following experiences of failure. This research has shown, for example, that individuals who pursue mastery goals in the achievement domain (for example, those with incremental theories of competence who see skills as mutable) persist longer at a task even in the face of failure compared to those who pursue performance goals (for example, those with entity theories who believe that failure is due to lack of ability and unchangeable). Unlike entity theorists, those with incremental theories are able to motivate themselves to maintain perseverance at a task even in the face of poor performance (compare, Deci and Ryan 1987).

Relatedly, research by Norem and her colleagues (for example, Cantor and Norem 1989; Norem and Illingworth 1993) has examined ways in which individuals may effectively anticipate obstacles and prepare for them, so as not to relinquish participation in and persistence at personally important but uncertain tasks (for example, the strategy of defensive pessimism). Interestingly, this research has shown that different strategies lead to persistence and well-being for different people. Specifically, defensive pessimists show better performance when they focus on the possibility (and even probability) of failure, whereas optimists do better when they focus on potential positive outcomes. These findings make sense given the expectations that different individuals place on task performance. Imagine, for example, the difference in terms of well-being of unexpectedly experiencing a task going poorly (for example, failing a test you had expected to do quite well on) versus unexpectedly averting a potential failure (performing well on a test you expected to fail) (Cantor and Norem 1989). In this way, well-being is a function of individuals taking on their valued life tasks with particular strategies. Ironically, given the considerable research on the benefits of optimism (Scheier and Carver 1985), this research indicates that it is not just "being positive" that helps with well-being—in fact, being positive only helps some people (namely, optimists).

Further, the health behavior literature has also shown the importance of training individuals in goal-relevant strategies that enable persistence at valued tasks in the face of difficulty (Miller et al. 1993). Sanderson and Cantor (1995), for example, found that college students who received HIV/AIDS prevention training in their preferred, goal-relevant strategies (namely, interpersonal strategies for condom use for those with intimacy goals and technical strategies for those with identity goals) had greater changes in social-cognitive variables (for example, attitudes toward condoms, intentions to use condoms) and engaged in safer sexual behavior up to one year following the training. Those who received training in goal-relevant skills were more effective at implementing safer sex with their dating partner (usually a difficult challenge) and hence were better able to follow through on their desired goal of participating in safer sexual activity. This research suggests that persistence at a valued task—in this case, the intention to engage in safer sex—is a function of individuals being able to take part in tasks in ways that are in line with their other goals (for example, knowing technical skills so as not to become dependent on a partner).

How Able Are Individuals to Adapt to Changing Opportunities for Participation?

Although we believe that everyone benefits from actively participating in valued tasks, the arenas for participation that produce well-being are likely to change, sometimes dramatically, with age as different life stages emphasize the pursuit of different tasks (Helson, Mitchell, and Moane's [1984] "social clock"). As Erikson's (1950) psychosocial model of development posits, sociocultural contexts both prescribe particular life tasks for individuals to pursue during a given life period and give particular meanings to these tasks, in part by structuring individuals' opportunities to participate in daily life activities (Carstensen 1993; Havighurst 1972; Helson and Moane 1987; Higgins and Eccles-Parsons 1983; Veroff 1983). For example, adolescents are encouraged to work on identity formation and separation from family by the increasing freedoms, responsibilities, and choices accorded to them in their daily lives (Simmons and Blyth 1987; Zirkel and Cantor 1990; Zirkel 1992). By contrast, American society has often eschewed the freedom and leisure time of older adults, pressing for "productive" service after retirement, although providing few avenues for such activity (Atchley 1976; Neugarten and Hagestad 1976). Since people are motivated to fulfill the valued tasks of their community (Winett 1995) and need to take on their valued life tasks in ways that are supported by their subculture, well-being may therefore be a function of taking on the right task at the right time.

This dynamic life-span perspective therefore suggests a partial counter to adaptation level phenomena (Brickman and Campbell's [1971] "hedonic treadmill") in which people quickly adapt to even positive states and hence need new levels of stimulation merely to reach prior levels of subjective well-being. It suggests a counter because the new values and changing opportunities of each life period should provide repeated challenges to keep people striving. As Caspi shows (Caspi and Bem 1990; Caspi, Bem, and Elder 1989), shy boys, for whom shyness may be a distinct liability in the tasks of childhood, may grow into nurturant fathers in adulthood, and these individuals may then experience considerable life satisfaction as adults since nurturance allows them to participate in one of the tasks of adulthood (raising children) in a valued way.

This model also speaks to some of the paradoxes of the well-being literature, such as the short-lived boosts of obtaining valued goods (such as winning a lottery) (Brickman, Coates, and Janoff-Bulman 1978) and the remarkable resilience of subjective well-being in the face of obviously difficult and trying life circumstances (Silver and Wortman 1980). It speaks to these adaptation level phenomena, not by denying the pivotal role of objective goods (such as wealth or health status), but rather by suggesting that what people need most is to be able to continue to participate on a regular, daily basis in valued life tasks, and sometimes objective goods (or the absence of them) alone do not ensure (preclude) beneficial participation. For example, experiencing a positive event such as winning the lottery does not provide continued opportunities for participation, whereas experiencing a negative event such as a debilitating injury may encourage people to search for new ways to participate (for example, joining a support group, spending more time with friends/family). Although finding new ways to participate can present a challenge for individuals, it also presents new opportunities for experiencing well-being and new avenues within which to find pleasure and avert pain.

Taking part in valued life activities may, in fact, have particular importance in terms of life satisfaction for those in newly constrained circumstances, who may have lost familiar opportunities to experience the benefits of commitment to valued activities and goals, including experiencing agency, structure, and social connectedness. Various lifespan theorists such as Carol Ryff (1989) and Kuypers and Bengtson (1990) have emphasized the importance of social integration and participation for the physical and emotional well-being of older adults (see also Myers, this volume), and in fact, satisfaction with social relations and health are more important predictors of well-being in later life than in early adulthood (Herzog, Rogers, and Woodworth 1982). These factors may emerge as particularly strong predictors of well-being in older adulthood precisely because of their influence on individuals' abilities to participate in valued tasks. (For example, participation in valued tasks mediates the association between social life/health satisfaction and well-being.) Harlow and Cantor (1996) found that the association between social life participation and life satisfaction in older adulthood was particularly strong for retirees, who presumably could no longer derive the rewards of participation in work. Although in early adulthood individuals are likely to find opportunities to participate in work/career and family activities and to gain well-being in these ways, as one ages the arenas for engaging in social interaction decrease, and hence the opportunity to participate in such interaction may become more strongly associated with well-being (Carstensen 1993).

Similarly, major life events, such as injury, also provide both challenges and opportunities for participation. In a sample of spinal cord injury patients, greater involvement in daily social and recreational participation was associated with greater life satisfaction, above and beyond the effects of

other related variables, such as education, optimism about work, and marital status (Cantor, Vajk, and Kahneman 1995). Mediational analyses supported the role of many of these more tangible resources, such as occupational and marital status, in facilitating well-being *through* their positive association with participation. These findings indicate that even highly constrained situations can allow for beneficial participation as long as individuals find the right situations in which to participate and have the right tangible resources.

LINGERING RESEARCH ISSUES

Is There a "Right" Way to Participate?

Although this model emphasizes the importance of participation in terms of well-being, it does not specify the "right" or "best" way to participate, and, in fact, the right way to participate may be different for different individuals (depending on what they personally value and find intrinsically rewarding). For example, health professionals place particular emphasis on the link between patients' well-being and "the extent to which they [are] able to maintain reasonable physical, emotional, and intellectual functioning; and the degree to which they retain their ability to participate in valued activities within the family, in the workplace, and in the community" (Wenger and Furberg 1990). However, Ditto's research using the Valued Life Activities Model of Health State Evaluation (Ditto et al. 1996) demonstrates that individuals differ in the extent to which they prioritize or value different functional abilities (such as intellectual functioning, cognitive functioning, physical functioning), and that individuals' perceptions of a potential quality of life (for example, as a blind person) are influenced by the extent to which they imagine that a given condition or state would interfere with their ability to participate in *their* valued life activities. For example, an individual who particularly enjoys cognitive/intellectual activities, such as reading and writing, may experience less of a change in quality of life from a lower limb paralysis than an individual who particularly values physical activities, such as tennis and golf. Ditto and his colleagues' (1996) mediational analyses demonstrate that the link between current states (cognitive, physical, and so on) and well-being is stronger in cases involving personally valued activities. Similarly, a *New York Times Magazine* piece on HIV prevention in the gay community emphasized the importance of focusing on quality of life as opposed to quantity of life (Green 1996). Quality-of-life judgments therefore appear to be influenced by individuals' particular priorities and values, not simply by objective assessment of the debilitation caused by a given state.

Are There Systematic Individual Differences in the Most Valuable Types of Participation?

Presumably, even within a given subculture, some individuals would prefer participation in volunteer organizations, some in religious organizations, and so forth. Research has shown, for example, that different types of social support are more or less helpful for different people (House and Kahn 1985). Correspondingly, does simply taking part in something benefit well-being (for example, could you randomly assign seniors in a nursing home to various groups), or does the activity need to be one that an individual particularly values and for which he/she has a well-developed taste? (Ditto et al. 1996; Snyder 1993.) For example, although Putnam (1995) decried the decrease in various forms of social participation, Pollitt (1996) responded with the retort that no amount of prodding could induce her to wax nostalgic about beer-guzzling bowling leagues as an attractive form of civic participation. This analysis suggests that there are important individual differences in the types of participation that are most rewarding and hence most likely to encourage sustained participation.

What Kind of Participation Is Most Valuable to People?

In this chapter, we have discussed various types of participation (age-graded, social, opportunities for reciprocation, and so on), but it is not yet clear whether individuals need actual participation (direct involvement with others) or whether virtual participation is enough. (Is watching *ER* alone and knowing that many others are watching it really participation?) Even watching television alone can be a valuable form of life participation under some circumstances (Harlow and Cantor 1996; compare, Putnam 1995). Similarly, a growing number of people are participating in valued activities via the Internet. A recent editorial in *Newsweek,* in fact, described the benefits of chat groups on America On-Line as important opportunities for experiencing personal contact (Mott 1996). These types of "virtual participation" may

be particularly important for those in constrained situations (such as retired persons and those with severe disabilities) who do not always have access to more traditional modes of "actual" participation.

How Can We Open Doors for Participation?

As described in our model, individuals need specific resources that provide access to ways of participating and that increase awareness of new opportunities for participation. Public policies therefore need to consider the importance of allowing people to participate in the valued tasks of their community, not just providing objective resources unconnected to opportunities for sustained participation. Affirmative action programs, for example, may lead to well-being by opening doors for participation in various arenas (in schools, jobs, and so on) that have typically been shut for people from particular backgrounds. Interventions that focus on improving well-being but ignore the tasks that individuals participate in on a daily basis (and derive pleasure from) and fail to provide other acceptable and realistic alternative tasks are therefore likely to falter. There may be very little point in striving, for example, to revitalize local PTA participation when growing numbers of single parents and dual-career families are already stretched to the limits with things to do. Similarly, policies that, for example, discourage teen parenthood are likely to be largely ineffective unless they take into account the tasks that go into parenting for these young people at this time in their lives (such as gaining self-esteem, being connected to and valued by others) and then provide alternative ways of letting teenagers pursue these valued tasks. Equally problematic are policies that appear to promote access to opportunity for participation (such as workfare as an alternative to welfare) without doing the work to engage individuals, to train them, and to provide for realistic hopes for sustained participation.

Can People Learn to Maximize Their Participation as Life Circumstances Change?

Although our model suggests that different life stages provide new opportunities for participation, it is not clear how well people take advantage of new opportunity structures. Can individuals gain in emotional intelligence? (Mayer and Salovey 1993; Salovey and Mayer 1990.) Moreover, can individuals be trained to engage more effectively the realistic opportunities around them for participation? (Brandtstadter and Renner 1990.) Future research needs to examine how adept individuals are at finding ways of maximizing their participation, and whether individuals can become more effective at both noticing and taking advantage of such opportunities.

How Can Individuals Experience Present Well-Being as Well as Maintain Future Well-Being?

Although there are certainly experiences that simultaneously allow for positive present and future well-being (such as having a baby or receiving a job promotion), individuals are at times forced to choose between activities that enable present well-being and those that enable future well-being. For example, individuals may experience considerable satisfaction from engaging in unsafe sexual behavior, but this behavior could ultimately lead to low future well-being by limiting their ability to participate in a variety of tasks (owing to an unwanted pregnancy or HIV infection). Various interventions and policies must force individuals to look beyond the rewards of *momentary positive affect* and to focus on the broader issue of *future well-being* (Sen's [1980] "what a person manages to do or be"—the valued functionings he/she can achieve). Health promotion efforts may therefore be most effective when they provide strategies for ensuring future well-being that also allow for positive affect in the present. For example, in research on HIV prevention with college students, Sanderson and Cantor (1995) found that individuals who were trained in goal-relevant strategies for condom use (those strategies that were in line with their predominant dating goals) were more effective in condom use up to one year following the intervention. This research suggests that health promotion interventions may, in fact, be most effective when they provide individuals with ways to experience momentary positive affect (for example, by training them in personally relevant skills for condom use that do not disrupt their present experience) as well as maintain future well-being. Finally, and as described previously, because opportunities for participation change across the life span, individuals who may have difficulty experiencing positive affect at a given point in time can, in fact, experience future well-being (Caspi and Elder 1986). Individuals therefore need to be vigilant about the activities they participate in, in order to be protective of opportunities for experiencing future well-being and life satisfaction.

REFERENCES

Adler, A. (1929). *Problems of neurosis: A book of case histories.* London: Routledge & Kegan Paul.

Allport, G. W. (1937). *Personality: A psychological interpretation.* New York: Holt.

Atchley, R. C. (1976). *The sociology of retirement.* Cambridge, Mass.: Schenkman.

Banaji, M. R., and Prentice, D. A. (1994). The self in social contexts. *Annual Review of Psychology, 45,* 297–332.

Bargh, J. A., Raymond, P., Pryor, J. B., and Strack, F. (1995). Attractiveness of the underling: An automatic power-sex association and its consequences for sexual harassment and aggression. *Journal of Personality and Social Psychology, 68,* 768–81.

Batson, C. D., and Ventis, W. L. (1982). *The religious experience.* New York: Oxford University Press.

Baumeister, R. F., and Leary, M. R. (1995). The need to belong: Desire for interpersonal attachments as a fundamental human motivation. *Psychological Bulletin, 117,* 497–529.

Brandtstadter, J., and Renner, G. (1990). Tenacious goal pursuit and flexible goal adjustment: Explication and age-related analysis of assimilative and accommodative strategies of coping. *Psychology and Aging, 5,* 58–67.

Brickman, P., and Campbell, D. T. (1971). Hedonic relativism and planning the good society. In M. H. Appley (Ed.), *Adaptation level theory: A symposium* (pp. 287–304). New York: Academic Press.

Brickman, P., and Coates, D. (1987). Commitment and mental health. In P. Brickman (Ed.), *Commitment, conflict, and caring* (pp. 222–309). Englewood Cliffs, N.J.: Prentice-Hall.

Brickman, P., Coates, D., and Janoff-Bulman, R. (1978). Lottery winners and accident victims: Is happiness relative? *Journal of Personality and Social Psychology, 36,* 917–27.

Brown, G. W., and Harris, T. (1978). *Social origins of depression: A study of psychiatric disorder in women.* London: Tavistock.

Buss, D. (1987). Selection, evocation, and manipulation. *Journal of Personality and Social Psychology, 53,* 1214–21.

Cantor, N. (1990). From thought to behavior: "Having" and "doing" in the study of personality and cognition. *American Psychologist, 45,* 735–50.

———. (1994). Life task problem-solving: Situational affordances and personal needs. *Personality and Social Psychology Bulletin, 20,* 235–43.

Cantor, N., and Fleeson, W. (1991). Life tasks and self-regulatory processes. *Advances in Motivation and Achievement, 7,* 327–69.

Cantor, N., and Kihlstrom, J. F. (1987). *Personality and social intelligence.* Englewood Cliffs, N.J.: Prentice-Hall.

Cantor, N., and Norem, J. K. (1989). Defensive pessimism and stress and coping. *Social Cognition, 7,* 92–112.

Cantor, N., Norem, J., Langston, C., Zirkel, S., Fleeson, W., and Cook-Flannagan, C. (1991). Life tasks and daily life experiences. *Journal of Personality, 59,* 425–51.

Cantor, N., and Sanderson, C.A. (1998). Social dating goals and the regulation of adolescent dating relationships and sexual behavior: The interaction of goals, strategies, and situations. In J. Heckhausen and C. Dweck (Eds.), *Motivation and self-regulation across the life span* (pp. 185–215). New York: Cambridge University Press.

Cantor, N., Vajk, F., and Kahneman, D. (1995). Participation and well-being. Paper presented at the Seventh Annual American Psychological Society, New York, (June).

Caporael, L. R., and Brewer, M. B. (1991). Reviving evolutionary psychology: Biology meets society. *Journal of Social Issues, 47,* 187–95.

Carstensen, L. L. (1993). Motivation for social contact across the life span: A theory of socioemotional selectivity. In J. E. Jacobs (Ed.), *Developmental perspectives on motivation: Nebraska symposium on motivation* (vol. 40, pp. 209–54). Lincoln: University of Nebraska Press.

Carver, C. S., and Scheier, M. F. (1982). Control theory: A useful conceptual framework for personality-social, clinical, and health psychology. *Psychological Bulletin, 92,* 111–35.

———. (1990). Origins and functions of positive and negative affect: A control-process view. *Psychological Review, 97,* 19–35.

Caspi, A., and Bem, D. J. (1990). Personality continuity and change across the life course. In L. A. Pervin (Ed.), *Handbook of personality: Theory and research* (pp. 549–75). New York: Guilford.

Caspi, A., Bem, D. J., and Elder, G. H., Jr. (1989). Continuities and consequences of interactional styles across the life course. *Journal of Personality, 57,* 375–406.

Caspi, A., and Elder, G. H., Jr. (1986). Life satisfaction in old age: Linking social psychology and history. *Psychology and Aging, 1,* 18–26.

Coyle, C. P., Lesnik-Emas, S., and Kinney, W. B. (1994). Predicting life satisfaction among adults with spinal cord injuries. *Rehabilitation Psychology, 39,* 95–112.

Csikszentmihalyi, M. (1975). *Beyond boredom and anxiety: The experience of play in work and games.* San Francisco: Jossey-Bass.

———. (1990). *Flow: The psychology of optimal experience.* New York: Harper & Row.

Deci, E. L., and Ryan, R. M. (1987). The support of autonomy and the control of behavior. *Journal of Personality and Social Psychology, 53,* 1024–37.

Decker, S. D., and Schulz, R. (1985). Correlates of life satisfaction and depression in middle-aged and elderly spinal cord–injured persons. *American Journal of Occupational Therapy, 39,* 740–45.

Diener, E. (1984). Subjective well-being. *Psychological Bulletin, 95,* 542–75.

Diener, E., and Diener, M. (1995). Cross-cultural correlates of life satisfaction and self-esteem. *Journal of Personality and Social Psychology, 68,* 653–63.

Diener, E., and Fujita, F. (1995). Resources, personal strivings, and subjective well-being: A nomothetic and idiographic approach. *Journal of Personality and Social Psychology, 68,* 926–35.

Diener, E., Sandvik, E., Seidlitz, L., and Diener, M. (1993). The relationship between income and subjective well-being: Relative or absolute? *Social Indicators Research, 28,* 195–223.

Ditto, P. H., Druley, J. A., Moore, K. A., Danks, J. H., and Smucker, W. D. (1996). Fates worse than death: The role of valued life activities in health state evaluations. *Health Psychology, 15,* 332–43.

Donahue, E. M., Robins, R. W., Roberts, B. W., and John, O. P. (1993). The divided self: Concurrent and longitudinal effects of psychological adjustment and social roles on self-concept differentiation. *Journal of Personality and Social Psychology, 64,* 834–46.

Durkheim, E. (1933). *The division of labor in society.* New York: Macmillan.

Dweck, C. S., and Leggett, E. L. (1988). A social-cognitive approach to motivation and personality. *Psychological Review, 95,* 256–73.

Emmons, R. A. (1986). Personal strivings: An approach to personality and subjective well-being. *Journal of Personality and Social Psychology, 47,* 1105–17.

Emmons, R. A., Diener, E., and Larsen, R. J. (1986). Choice and avoidance of everyday situations and affect congruence: Two models of reciprocal interactionism. *Journal of Personality and Social Psychology, 51,* 815–26.

Emmons, R. A., and King, L. A. (1988). Conflict among personal strivings: Immediate and long-term implications for psychological and physical well-being. *Journal of Personality and Social Psychology, 54,* 1040–48.

Emmons, R. A., Shepherd, N. R., and Kaiser, H. A. (1994). Approach and avoidance strivings and psychological and physical well-being. Poster presented at the 102nd Annual Convention of the American Psychological Association, Los Angeles (August).

Erikson, E. H. (1950). *Childhood and society.* New York: Norton.

Fiske, S. T. (1993). Controlling other people: The impact of power on stereotyping. *American Psychologist, 48* (6), 621–28.

Fiske, S. T., and Depret, E. (1996). Control, interdependence, and power: Understanding social cognition and its social context. In W. Stroebe and M. Hewstone (Eds.), *European review of social psychology* (vol. 7, pp. 31–60). New York: Wiley.

Folkman, S., and Stein, N. (1996). A goal-process approach to analyzing narrative memories for AIDS-related stressful events. In N. Stein, P. Ornstein, B. Tversky, and C. Brainerd (Eds.), *Memory for everyday and emotional events* (pp. 113–36). Hillsdale, N.J.: Erlbaum.

Gollwitzer, P. (1993). Goal achievement: The role of intentions. In W. Stroebe and M. Hewstone (Eds.), *European review of social psychology* (vol. 4, pp.141–85). New York: Wiley.

Green, J. (1996, 15 September). Flirting with suicide. *New York Times Magazine*, 39–45, 54–55, 84–85.

Harlow, R. E., and Cantor, N. (1996). Still participating after all these years: A study of life task participation in later life. *Journal of Personality and Social Psychology, 71*, 1235–49.

Havighurst, R. J. (1960). Life beyond family and work. In E. W. Burgess (Ed.), *Aging in Western societies* (pp. 299–353). Chicago: University of Chicago Press.

———. (1972). *Developmental tasks and education.* 3rd ed. New York: McKay.

Heckhausen, J., and Schultz, R. (1993). Optimization by selection and compensation: Balancing primary and secondary control in life-span development. *International Journal of Behavioral Development, 16*, 287–303.

———. (1995). A life-span theory of control. *Psychological Review, 102*, 284–304.

Helson, R., Mitchell, V., and Moane, G. (1984). Personality and patterns of adherence and nonadherence to the social clock. *Journal of Personality and Social Psychology, 46*, 1079–96.

Helson, R., and Moane, G. (1987). Personality change in women from college to midlife. *Journal of Personality and Social Psychology, 53*, 176–86.

Hendricks, J., and Hendricks, C. D. (1986). *Aging in mass society: Myths and realities.* Boston: Little, Brown.

Herzog, A. R., Rogers, W. L., and Woodworth, J. (1982). *Subjective well-being among different age groups.* Ann Arbor: University of Michigan, Survey Research Center.

Higgins, E. T., and Eccles-Parsons, J. E. (1983). Social cognition and the social life of the child: Stages as subcultures. In E. T. Higgins, D. N. Ruble, and W. W. Hartup (Eds.), *Social cognition and social development: A sociocultural perspective* (pp. 15–62). New York: Cambridge University Press.

Higgins, E. T., Roney, C. J. R., Crowe, E., and Hymes, C. (1994). Ideal versus ought predilections for approach and avoidance: Distinct self-regulatory systems. *Journal of Personality and Social Psychology, 66*, 276–86.

House, J. S., and Kahn, R. L. (1985). Measures and concepts of social support. In S. Cohen and S. L. Syme (Eds.), *Social support and health* (pp. 83–108). Orlando, Fla.: Academic Press.

Independent Sector. (1992). *Giving and volunteering in the United States: Findings from a national survey.* Washington, D.C.: Author.

Kasser, T., and Ryan, R. M. (1993). A dark side of the American dream: Correlates of financial success as a central life aspiration. *Journal of Personality and Social Psychology, 65*, 410–22.

Kessler, R. C., and Essex, M. (1982). Marital status and depression: The importance of coping resources. *Social Forces, 61*, 484–505.

King, M., Walder, L., and Pavey, S. (1970). Personality change as a function of volunteer experience in a psychiatric hospital. *Journal of Consulting and Clinical Psychology, 35*, 423–25.

Klinger, F. (1975). Consequences of commitment to a disengagement from incentives. *Psychological Review, 82*, 1–25.

Kuhl, J. (1985). Volitional mediators of cognition-behavior consistency: Self-regulatory processes and action versus state orientation. In J. Kuhl and J. Beckman (Eds.), *Action control from cognition to behavior* (pp. 101–28). New York: Springer-Verlag.

Kuypers, J., and Bengtson, V. L. (1990). Toward understanding health in older families impacted by catastrophic illness. In T. H. Brubaker (Ed.), *Family relationships in later life* (2nd ed., pp. 245–66). Newbury Park, Calif.: Sage.

Langston, C. A. (1994). Capitalizing on and coping with daily-life events: Expressive responses to positive events. *Journal of Personality and Social Psychology, 67*, 1112–25.

Lecky, P. (1945). *Self-consistency: A theory of personality.* New York: Island Press.

Little, B. (1983). Personal projects: A rationale and methods for investigation. *Environment and Behavior, 15*, 273–309.

———. (1989). Personal projects analysis: Trivial pursuits, magnificent obsessions, and the search for coherence. In D. M. Buss and N. Cantor (Eds.), *Personality psychology: Recent trends and emerging directions* (pp. 15–31). New York: Springer-Verlag.

Lydon, J. E., and Zanna, M. P. (1990). Commitment in the face of adversity: A value-affirmation approach. *Journal of Personality and Social Psychology, 58*, 1040–47.

Mayer, J. D., and Salovey, P. (1993). The intelligence of emotional intelligence. *Intelligence, 17*, 433–42.

McAdams, D. P., and Constantian, C. A. (1983). Intimacy and affiliation motives in daily living: An experience sampling analysis. *Journal of Personality and Social Psychology, 45*, 851–61.

Miller, L. C., Bettencourt, B. A., DeBro, S. C., and Hoffman, V. (1993). Negotiating safer sex: Interpersonal dynamics. In J. Pryor and G. Reeder (Eds.), *The social psychology of AIDS infection* (pp. 85–123). Hillsdale, N.J.: Erlbaum.

Mischel, W., Cantor, N., & Feldman, S. (1996). Principles of self-regulation: The nature of willpower and self-control. In E. T. Higgins and A. W. Kruglanski (Eds.), *Social psychology: Handbook of basic principles* (pp. 329–60). New York: Guilford.

Mott, K. (1996, 19 August). Cancer and the Internet. *Newsweek*, 19.

Myers, D. G., and Diener, E. (1995). Who is happy? *Psychological Science, 6*, 10–19.

Neugarten, B. L., and Hagestad, G. O. (1976). Age and the life course. In R. H. Binstock and E. Shanas (Eds.), *Handbook of aging and the social sciences* (pp. 35–55). New York: Van Nostrand Reinhold.

Niedenthal, P. M., and Mordkoff, J. T. (1991). Prototype distancing: A strategy for choosing among threatening situations. *Personality and Social Psychology Bulletin, 17,* 483–93.

Norem, J. K., and Illingworth, K. S. S. (1993). Strategy-dependent effects of reflecting on self and tasks: Some implications of optimism and defensive pessimism. *Journal of Personality and Social Psychology, 65,* 822–35.

Omoto, A. M., and Snyder, M. (1990). Basic research in action: Volunteerism and society's response to AIDS. *Personality and Social Psychology Bulletin, 16,* 152–65.

———. (1995). Sustained helping without obligation: Motivation, longevity of service, and perceived attitudes change among AIDS volunteers. *Journal of Personality and Social Psychology, 68,* 671–86.

Palys, T. S., and Little, B. R. (1983). Perceived life satisfaction and the organization of personal project systems. *Journal of Personality and Social Psychology, 44,* 1221–30.

Pollitt, K. A. (1996). For whom the ball rolls. *The Nation, 262,* 9.

Putnam, R. D. (1995). Bowling alone: America's declining social capital. *Journal of Democracy, 6,* 65–78.

Rothbaum, F., Weisz, J. R., and Snyder, S. S. (1982). Changing the world and changing the self: A two-process model of perceived control. *Journal of Personality and Social Psychology, 42,* 5–37.

Rubin, L. B. (1976). *Worlds of pain: Life in the working-class family.* New York: Basic Books.

Ryff, C. D. (1989). Happiness is everything, or is it? Explorations on the meaning of psychological well-being. *Journal of Personality and Social Psychology, 57,* 1069–81.

———. (1993). Well-being in adult life: Meaning and mechanisms. Paper presented at the 101st Annual Convention of the American Psychological Association, Toronto (August).

Salovey, P., and Mayer, J. D. (1990). Emotional intelligence. *Imagination, Cognition, and Personality, 9,* 185–211.

Sanderson, C. A., and Cantor, N. (1995). Social dating goals in late adolescence: Implications for safer sexual activity. *Journal of Personality and Social Psychology, 68,* 1121–34.

Scheibe, K. E. (1965). College students spend eight weeks in mental hospital: A case report. *Psychotherapy: Theory, Research, and Practice, 2,* 117–20.

Scheier, M. F., and Carver, C. S. (1985). Optimism, coping, and health: Assessment and implications of generalized outcome expectancies. *Health Psychology, 4,* 219–47.

Sen, A. K. (1980). Equality of what? In S. McMurrin (Ed.), *Tanner lectures on human values* (pp. 195–220). Cambridge: Cambridge University Press.

Sheldon, K. M., and Kasser, T. (1995). Coherence and congruence: Two aspects of personality integration. *Journal of Personality and Social Psychology, 68,* 531–43.

Silver, R. L., and Wortman, C. G. (1980). Coping with undesirable life events. In J. Garber and M. E. P. Seligman (Eds.), *Human helplessness: Theory and applications* (pp. 279–375). New York: Academic Press.

Simmons, R. G., and Blyth, D. A. (1987). *Moving into adolescence: The impact of pubertal change and school context.* New York: de Gruyter.

Snyder, M. (1974). The self-monitoring of expressive behavior. *Journal of Personality and Social Psychology, 30,* 526–37.

———. (1979). Self-monitoring processes. In L. Berkowitz (Ed.), *Advances in experimental social psychology* (vol. 12, pp. 85–128). New York: Academic Press.

———. (1981). On the influence of individuals on situations. In N. Cantor and J. Kihlstrom (Eds.), *Personality, cognition, and social interaction* (pp. 309–29). Hillsdale, N.J.: Erlbaum.

———. (1993). Basic research and practical problems: The promise of a "functional" personality and social psychology. *Personality and Social Psychology Bulletin, 19,* 251–64.

Vallacher, R. R., and Wegner, D. M. (1989). Levels of personal agency: Individual variation in action identification. *Journal of Personality and Social Psychology, 57,* 660–71.

Veenhoven, R. (1991). Is happiness relative? *Social Indicators Research, 24,* 1–34.

Veroff, J. (1983). Contextual determinants of personality. *Personality and Social Psychology Bulletin, 9,* 331–44.

Wenger, N. K., and Furberg, C. D. (1990). Cardiovascular disorders. In B. Spilker (Ed.), *Quality of life assessments in clinical trials* (pp. 335–45). New York: Raven Press.

Winett, R. A. (1995). A framework for health promotion and disease programs. *American Psychologist, 50,* 341–50.

Wuthnow, R. (1991). *Acts of compassion: Caring for others and helping ourselves.* Princeton, N.J.: Princeton University Press.

Zirkel, S. (1992). Developing independence in a life transition: Investing the self in the concerns of the day. *Journal of Personality and Social Psychology, 62,* 506–21.

Zirkel, S., and Cantor, N. (1990). Personal construal of life tasks: Those who struggle for independence. *Journal of Personality and Social Psychology, 58,* 172–85.

13 Self-Regulation and Quality of Life: Emotional and Non-Emotional Life Experiences

E. Tory Higgins, Heidi Grant, and James Shah

The hedonic principle that people approach pleasure and avoid pain does not capture the fact that people's life experiences have as much to do with how they regulate pleasure and pain as with the simple fact that they do. Individuals who experience the pleasure of joy and the pain of disappointment do not have the same life experiences as those who experience the pleasure of relaxation and the pain of nervousness. Moreover, there is more to life experience than the pleasures and pains of effective and ineffective self-regulation. Motivational experiences of strategic states, such as feeling eager or cautious, are an important part of life as well. To discover the true nature of approach/avoidance experiences, we need to move beyond the hedonic principle to the principles that underlie the different strategic ways it operates. One such principle is regulatory focus, which distinguishes self-regulation with a promotion focus (accomplishments, aspirations) from self-regulation with a prevention focus (safety, responsibilities). This principle is used to reconsider the nature of emotional and non-emotional life experiences.

IT IS NATURAL to define quality of life in terms of the hedonic principle. After all, the principle that people approach pleasure and avoid pain has been, and continues to be, *the* fundamental motivational principle. It has ancient roots that can be traced at least to Plato's *Protagoras*. In psychology, this principle underlies motivational models from the biological level of analysis distinguishing between the appetitive system involving approach and the aversive system involving avoidance (Gray 1982; Konorski 1967; Lang 1995) to the social level of analysis distinguishing between movements toward desired end-states and away from undesired end-states (Atkinson 1964; Bandura 1986; Carver and Scheier 1981, 1990; Lewin 1935, 1951; McClelland et al. 1953; Roseman 1984; Roseman, Spindel, and Jose 1990). But can we understand the pains and pleasures of emotional experiences through the hedonic principle alone? Indeed, can

we understand quality of life by looking only at the pains and pleasures of emotional experiences?

We propose that to understand emotional and non-emotional life experiences it is useful to consider the self-regulatory processes that underlie them (see also Higgins 1997). The chapter begins by distinguishing between three different self-regulatory principles—*regulatory anticipation, regulatory reference,* and *regulatory focus* (see Higgins 1997). Following this, evidence for the importance of regulatory focus in emotional experiences is reviewed. Next, a model of emotional experiences based on self-regulatory processes is proposed and compared to other models in the literature. Finally, non-emotional life experiences that might also influence quality of life are considered.

SELF-REGULATORY PRINCIPLES

According to the classic perspective on motivation, people approach pleasure and avoid pain. What the literature does not make sufficiently clear is that there are two distinct self-regulatory principles that can be described in this way.

Regulatory Anticipation

The first principle is regulatory anticipation. Based on past experiences of success or failure, people can anticipate future pleasure or future pain. Mowrer (1960), for example, proposed a theory of learning that distinguished between feeling "hope" when anticipating future pleasure and feeling "fear" when anticipating future pain. In his classic theory of achievement motivation, Atkinson (1964) distinguished between self-regulation in relation to "hope of success" and "fear of failure." Kahneman and Tversky's (1979) highly influential "prospect theory" distinguished between looking forward and mentally considering the possibility of experiencing pleasure versus the possibility of experiencing pain.

Regulatory anticipation, it should be noted, is not the same as a specific expectation of a particular outcome. Individuals with the same general anticipation can still have different specific expectations. Moreover, specific expectations can be situationally manipulated, as is commonly done in the achievement motivation literature (Atkinson and Raynor 1974). For example, individuals can be selected who anticipate or fear failure, but their specific expectation of failure will be greater when the task is described as difficult than when it is described as easy. Regulatory anticipation, then, is not expectation per se. Still, it does refer to imagining a future outcome that is pleasurable or painful. In the regulatory anticipation form of the hedonic principle, then, imagining a pleasurable future outcome induces approach motivation while imagining a painful future outcome induces avoidance motivation. Regulatory reference, considered next, involves a different form of the hedonic principle.

Regulatory Reference

Two persons might both imagine romantic love as a desired end-state, but one person might anticipate the pleasure of being in this state while the other anticipates the pain of never being in this state. Two other persons might both imagine being completely alone as an undesired end-state, but one person might anticipate the pain of forever being in this state while the other anticipates the pleasure of never being in this state. The two persons imagining romantic love differ from each other in their regulatory anticipation, as do the two persons imagining being alone. But what about the difference between these two pairs of persons? Each pair has one person anticipating pleasure and another anticipating pain. Thus, the

difference between the pairs does not concern anticipation per se. Rather, it concerns the difference between having a desired end-state versus an undesired end-state as the reference point for self-regulation, independent of whether pleasure or pain is anticipated (see table 13.1).

This distinction between regulatory reference points has been developed most clearly by Carver and Scheier (1981, 1990). Inspired by earlier work on cybernetics and control processes (Miller, Galanter, and Pribram 1960; Powers 1973; Wiener 1948), they distinguish between self-regulatory systems that have positive versus negative reference values. A self-regulatory system with a positive reference value has a desired end-state as the reference point. The system is discrepancy-reducing and involves attempts to move one's (represented) current self state as close as possible to the desired end-state. In contrast, a self-regulatory system with a negative reference value has an undesired end-state as the reference point. This system is discrepancy-amplifying and involves attempts to move the current self state as far away as possible from the undesired end-state.

It should be noted that Carver and Scheier (1981, 1990) suggest that self-regulation with a negative reference value is inherently unstable and relatively rare. Their research, therefore, emphasized self-regulation with a positive reference value. Positive reference values were also emphasized in Miller, Galanter, and Pribram's (1960) famous TOTE model, which involved the execution of operations to reduce existing incongruities or discrepancies to positive reference values. Because most theories and research concern movement toward goals, which are positive reference values, this emphasis is evident throughout the self-regulatory literature (see, for example, Gollwitzer and Bargh 1996; Pervin 1989).

Another reason that self-regulation with a negative reference value has received less attention is

TABLE 13.1   Self-Regulatory Principles Underlying Hedonic Regulation

I. Regulatory anticipation	Avoid anticipated pain	Approach anticipated pleasure
II. Regulatory reference	Avoidance regulation in reference to undesired end-states	Approach regulation in reference to desired end-states
III. Regulatory focus	Prevention Strategically avoid mismatches to desired end-states (and matches to undesired) Ensure correct rejections Ensure against errors of commission	Promotion Strategically approach matches to desired end-states (and mismatches to undesired) Ensure hits Ensure against errors of omission

that several models describe it in terms of behavioral inhibition rather than behavioral production (Atkinson 1964; Gray 1982). That is, these models propose that self-regulation in relation to desired end-states will be reflected in taking action while self-regulation in relation to undesired end-states will be reflected in behavioral suppression. Thus, if one is interested in why people act the way they do, positive reference values will naturally be emphasized. In the classic learning literature as well, behavioral production associated with positive end-states has received greater emphasis than behavioral suppression associated with negative end-states (Estes 1944; Skinner 1953; Thorndike 1935).

Let us consider for a moment, then, just movement toward positive reference values or desired end-states. According to the literature, the critical characteristic of such movement is its direction— *approach*. Consistent with the basic hedonic principle, animal learning/biological models (for example, Gray 1982; Hull 1952; Konorski 1967; Lang 1995; Miller 1944; Mowrer 1960), cybernetic-control models (for example, Carver and Scheier 1990; Powers 1973), and dynamic models (for example, Atkinson 1964; Lewin 1935; McClelland et al. 1953) all highlight the distinction between this basic approach movement toward desired end-states and avoidance movement away from undesired end-states. For example, several models distinguish between the appetitive system involving approach and the aversive system involving avoidance (Gray 1982; Konorski 1967; Lang 1995; Roseman 1984; Roseman et al. 1990). But distinctions between different types of approach in the appetitive system (or between different types of avoidance in the aversive system) have rarely been made. As one example, Gray (1982) explicitly treats approaching "reward" and "nonpunishment" as equivalent. But is this really the case? Let us turn now to the third self-regulatory principle, regulatory focus, which distinguishes between types of approaching desired end-states (as well as between types of avoiding undesired end-states).

Regulatory Focus

If the hedonic principle of approaching pleasure and avoiding pain is truly basic to motivation, one might expect that there would be more than one way in which this principle operates. In particular, one might expect that the principle would operate differently when it serves fundamentally different needs, such as the distinct survival needs of *nurturance* and *security*. Human survival requires ad-

aptation to the surrounding environment, especially the social environment (see Buss 1996). To obtain the nurturance and security they need to survive, children must establish and maintain relationships with caretakers who fulfill these needs by supporting and encouraging them and by protecting and defending them (see Bowlby 1969, 1973). And in order to establish and maintain relationships with their caretakers, children must learn how their appearance and behaviors influence caretakers' responses to them as an object in the world (see Bowlby 1969; Cooley 1902/1964; Mead 1934; Sullivan 1953).

Sometimes caretakers respond to children in ways that are pleasurable to the child and other times they respond in ways that are painful to the child. As the hedonic principle suggests, children must learn how to behave in order to approach pleasure and avoid pain. But what is learned about regulating pleasure and pain can be different for nurturance and security needs. I propose that nurturance-related regulation and security-related regulation differ in *regulatory focus*. Nurturance-related regulation involves a *promotion focus* whereas security-related regulation involves a *prevention focus*. Let us briefly consider how children's experiences of pleasure and pain and what they learn about self-regulation varies when their interactions with caretakers involve a promotion versus a prevention focus (see also Higgins and Loeb, in press).

Consider first caretaker-child interactions that involve a *promotion focus*. The child experiences the pleasure of the "presence of positive outcomes" when the caretaker, for example, hugs and kisses the child for behaving in a desired manner, encourages the child to overcome difficulties, or sets up opportunities for the child to engage in rewarding activities. The caretaker's message to the child is that what matters is attaining accomplishments or fulfilling hopes and aspirations— "This is what I would *ideally* like you to do." A child experiences the pain of the "absence of positive outcomes" when the caretaker, for example, ends a meal when the child throws some food, takes away a toy when the child refuses to share it, stops a story when the child is not paying attention, or acts disappointed in the child for failing to fulfill his or her hopes for the child. Once again the caretaker's message to the child is that what matters is attaining accomplishments or fulfilling hopes and aspirations, but this message is communicated in reference to an undesired state of the child—"This is *not* what I would ideally like you to do." The regulatory focus of the message is the same whether it is in reference to a desired or an undesired end-state, that is, a concern with advancement, growth, accomplishment.

Consider next caretaker-child interactions that involve a *prevention focus*. The child experiences the pleasure of the "absence of negative outcomes" when the caretaker, for example, "child-proofs" the house, trains the child to be alert to potential dangers, or teaches the child to "mind your manners." The caretaker's message to the child is that what matters is ensuring safety, being responsible, and meeting obligations—"This is what I believe you *ought* to do." The child experiences the pain of the "presence of negative outcomes" when the caretaker, for example, behaves roughly with the child to get his or her attention, yells at the child when he or she doesn't listen, criticizes the child when he or she makes a mistake, or punishes the child for being irresponsible. Once again the caretaker's message to the child is that what matters is ensuring safety, being responsible, and meeting obligations, but it is communicated in reference to an undesired state of the child—"This is *not* what I believe you ought to do." The regulatory focus of the message is the same whether it is in reference to a desired or an undesired end-state, that is, a concern with protection, safety, responsibility.

As is evident in this discussion of socialization differences, regulatory focus is independent of regulatory reference. A promotion focus can be taken in reference to either a desired end-state or an undesired end-state, as can a prevention focus. But regulatory focus distinguishes between two different kinds of desired end-states—aspirations and accomplishments (promotion) versus responsibilities and safety (prevention). Regulatory focus theory proposes that the strategic inclination for attaining (or maintaining) desired end-states is different for these two kinds of desired end-states. The strategic inclination is to approach matches to the aspirations and accomplishments of the promotion focus and to avoid mismatches to the responsibilities and safety of the prevention focus. This proposal is supported by the results of several studies (see Higgins, 1997; Higgins et al. 1994).

IN SUM, regulatory anticipation, regulatory reference, and regulatory focus are independent self-regulatory principles underlying approach and avoidance motivations. People approach anticipated pleasures and avoid anticipated pains. Regulatory anticipation of either pleasure or pain can occur in reference to desired end-states to be ap-

proached or in reference to undesired end-states to be avoided. Regulation in reference to desired end-states (or in reference to undesired end-states) can occur with a promotion focus that involves a strategic approach inclination or with a prevention focus that involves a strategic avoidance inclination. Table 13.1 provides a summary of the different ways in which people approach pleasure and avoid pain according to these three distinct principles.

According to regulatory focus theory, people are motivated to approach desired end-states whether those end-states are aspirations and accomplishments or responsibilities and safety. The motivation to approach desired end-states is the same regardless of whether the regulatory focus is promotion or prevention. But as just noted, the strategic inclinations differ. In addition, regulatory focus theory proposes that the pleasurable experience of approach working or the painful experience of approach not working is also different for these two kinds of desired end-states. Let us turn now to which kinds of emotional experiences are predicted by the theory and review some evidence for the predictions.

REGULATORY FOCUS AND EMOTIONAL EXPERIENCES

The different kinds of caretaker-child interactions described earlier concerned different messages to the child about what matters in the world. One aspect of the promotion focus message was about the caretaker's hopes, wishes, and aspirations for the child—*ideals*. One aspect of the prevention focus message was about the caretaker's beliefs about the child's duties, responsibilities, and obligations—*oughts*. Self-discrepancy theory (Higgins 1987, 1989a) was developed specifically to consider how emotional responses to discrepancies between individuals' current states (their represented actual selves) and their desired end-states might be different for ideals and oughts.

The distinction between ideal and ought self-regulation in self-discrepancy theory was initially described in terms of differences in the psychological situations represented by discrepancies and congruencies involving ideal versus ought self-guides (see Higgins 1989a, 1989b). Actual self-congruencies to hopes, wishes, or aspirations represent the presence of positive outcomes, while discrepancies represent the absence of positive outcomes. Thus, the psychological situations involved in ideal self-regulation are the presence and absence of positive outcomes. Whereas the hopes, wishes, and aspirations represented in ideal self-guides function like maximal goals, the duties, obligations, and responsibilities represented in ought self-guides function more like minimal goals that a person must attain (see Brendl and Higgins 1996). Discrepancies to such minimal goals represent the presence of negative outcomes, while congruencies represent the absence of negative outcomes (see Gould 1939; Rotter 1982). Thus, the psychological situations involved in ought self-regulation are the absence and presence of negative outcomes.

If one considers only motivation to approach desired end-states (or the appetitive motive alone), the literature on self-regulation has generally not considered whether different emotions are produced by different ways of approaching desired end-states. Different specific emotions have typically been explained in terms of attributional processes that occur after feedback that there is a discrepancy or failure (Carver and Scheier 1981; Hoffman 1986; Srull and Wyer 1986; Weiner 1982, 1986). When the emotional consequences of just the discrepancy per se are described, usually only general terms have been used, such as negative affect or negative self-evaluation (Bandura 1986; Duval and Wicklund 1972; Carver and Scheier 1981; Mandler 1975).

Discrepancies to different types of desired end-states have been described by various observers, however, and the discrepancies to these different types of desired end-states appear to be associated with different kinds of emotional distress. It has been observed that individuals possessing a discrepancy from their hopes or ideals, or the absence of positive outcomes, tend to experience dejection-related emotions, such as disappointment, dissatisfaction, or sadness (Durkheim 1951; Duval and Wicklund 1972; Horney 1950; James 1890/1948; Kemper 1978; Lazarus 1968; Oatley and Johnson-Laird 1987; Rogers 1961; Roseman 1984; Roseman et al. 1990; Stein and Jewett 1982; Wierzbicka 1972). It has also been observed that individuals possessing a discrepancy from their moral norms, oughts, or safety goals tend to experience agitation-related emotions, such as feeling uneasy, threatened, or afraid (Ausubel 1955; Erikson 1950/1963; Freud 1923/1961; Horney 1939; James 1890/1948; Kemper 1978; Lewis 1979; Oatley and Johnson-Laird 1987; Piers and Singer 1971; Sullivan 1953).

These general observations in the literature, then, suggest that the emotional consequences of discrepancies to ideals versus oughts are distinct. If so, this would support the proposal that emotional experiences when approaching ideals as one type of desired end-state are distinct from emotional experiences when approaching oughts as another type of desired end-state. These observations are not sufficient, however, because the relations between individuals' actual/ideal and actual/ought discrepancies and their dejection-related and agitation-related emotions were not examined in the same study. Moreover, there were no experimental tests of the proposed distinct relations. To fill this void, my colleagues and I have conducted a series of studies to test whether self-regulation in relation to ideals versus oughts as desired end-states produces distinct emotions. Both studies relating chronic discrepancies to chronic emotional experiences and studies relating momentary activation of discrepancies to momentary emotional experiences have been conducted. In addition, we have investigated whether the emotional effects of self-regulation in relation to ideals and oughts vary depending on the strength of individuals' promotion or prevention focus. Finally, we have also examined how situational manipulations of regulatory focus influence emotional experiences. Illustrations of each of these types of studies will be reviewed here.

Chronic Self-Discrepancies and Chronic Emotional Distress

Participants in our studies typically fill out a "Selves Questionnaire" that is included in a general battery of measures handed out six to eight weeks before the dependent measures are collected. The Selves Questionnaire asks respondents to list up to eight or ten attributes for each of a number of different self-states, including the respondent's actual self and the respondent's ideals and oughts from several different standpoints. It is administered in two sections, the first involving the respondent's own standpoint and the second involving the standpoints of the respondent's significant others (for example, mother, father, best friend). The magnitude of self-discrepancy between the actual self and a self-guide is calculated by summing the total number of mismatches and subtracting the total number of matches.

An early study used a latent variable analysis to test the hypothesis that ideal discrepancies predict different emotional problems than do ought discrepancies (Strauman and Higgins 1988). One month after filling out the Selves Questionnaire, undergraduates filled out a battery of depression and social anxiety measures. The only model to provide an acceptable fit to the sample data was the hypothesized causal structure. Consistent with our hypothesis, as the magnitude of participants' actual/*ideal* discrepancies increased, their suffering from depression symptoms increased, while as the magnitude of their actual/*ought* discrepancies increased, their suffering from social anxiety symptoms increased. Actual/ideal discrepancies were not related to social anxiety, and actual/ought discrepancies were not related to depression. Subsequent studies with clinically depressed and anxious persons have also generally found that depression is related to greater actual/ideal discrepancies while anxiety is related to greater actual/ought discrepancies (Scott and O'Hara 1993; Strauman 1989).

Higgins, Vookles, and Tykocinski (1992) investigated the possibility that people suffer from different kinds of depression depending on how their ideals relate to other self-beliefs. In particular, individuals' ideals can be connected to either their beliefs about their potential or capabilities (their "can" selves) or their beliefs about who they actually will be in the future (their "future" selves). Actual self-discrepancies to ideals connected to the can self reflect the negative psychological situation of "chronic failure to meet one's positive potential." This type of ideal discrepancy was hypothesized to be related to *"feeling weak"* as one kind of dejection (where "weak" means "lacking proficiency, potency, or vigor," "ineffective"). In contrast, actual self-discrepancies to ideals connected to the future self reflect the negative psychological situation of "chronically unfulfilled hopes." This type of ideal discrepancy was hypothesized to be related to *"feeling despondent"* as another kind of dejection (where "despondent" means "feeling discouraged and hopeless"). The results of the Higgins et al. (1992) study supported both of these predictions and are generally consistent with the literature distinguishing between different types of depression (for example, Bandura 1986; Blatt, D'Afflitti, and Quinlan 1976).

In another set of studies, Van Hook and Higgins (1988) tested the hypothesis that *conflict between ideals and oughts* would be uniquely related to *confusion-related symptoms* because conflicting goals should produce self-regulatory confusion. Undergraduates who possessed a conflict between their ideals and oughts were compared to a control group of undergraduates who did not, with

levels of actual/ideal and actual/ought discrepancies being controlled. As predicted, participants with a conflict between their ideals and oughts reported experiencing each of the following symptoms more often than participants without a conflict—confusion, muddledness, uncertainty about self and goals, identity confusion, indecision, distractibility, and rebelliousness.

Self-Discrepancy Activation and Momentary Emotional Distress

If ideal and ought self-regulation are motivationally distinct, then it should be possible to activate one or the other of these desired end-states and produce distinct emotions, even for individuals who possess *both* kinds of discrepancies. This hypothesis was tested in a study by Higgins et al. (1986, study 2). Undergraduate participants completed the Selves Questionnaire weeks before the experiment. Individuals who had either *both* types of discrepancies or *neither* type of discrepancy were recruited for the study. The ostensible purpose of the study was to obtain the self-reflections of a youth sample for a life-span developmental study. Half of the participants were randomly assigned to an ideal priming condition in which they described the kind of person they and their parents would *ideally like* them to be and whether there had been any change over the years in these hopes and aspirations for them. The other half of the participants were assigned to an ought priming condition in which they described the kind of person they and their parents believed they *ought* to be and whether there had been any change over the years in these beliefs about their duties and obligations.

The participants filled out a mood questionnaire containing both dejection-related emotions (for example, sad, disappointed, discouraged) and agitation-related emotions (nervous, worried, tense) before and after the priming manipulation. As predicted, individuals with both actual/ideal and actual/ought discrepancies experienced an increase in dejection-related emotions with ideal priming, but an increase in agitation-related emotions with ought priming. The priming had no effect on individuals with neither discrepancy.

In a replication and extension of this study, Strauman and Higgins (1987) tested whether priming just a single desirable attribute contained in either an ideal or an ought would produce a dejection-related or agitation-related emotional syndrome, respectively. Two groups of undergraduate participants were selected on the basis of their responses to the Selves Questionnaire obtained weeks earlier—individuals with predominant actual/ideal discrepancies (that is, individuals with relatively high actual/ideal discrepancies and relatively low actual/ought discrepancies) and individuals with predominant actual/ought discrepancies.

A covert, idiographic priming technique was used to activate self-attributes in a task supposedly investigating the "physiological effects of thinking about other people." The participants were given phrases of the form "An *X* person _____" (where *X* was a trait adjective such as "friendly" or "intelligent") and were asked to complete each sentence as quickly as possible. For each sentence, the subject's total verbalization time and skin conductance amplitude were recorded. The participants also reported their dejection-related and agitation-related emotions at the beginning and at the end of the session.

There were three priming conditions: "nonmatching" priming, in which the trait adjectives were attributes that appeared in the individual's ideal or ought but not in his or her actual self; "mismatching" priming, in which the trait adjectives were attributes that appeared in the individual's ideal or ought and his or her actual self was discrepant from them; and "yoked (mismatching)" priming, in which the trait adjectives were attributes that did not appear in the individual's ideal, ought, or actual self but were the *same* attributes used for some other participant in the "mismatching" priming condition. As predicted, the results showed that in the "mismatching" priming condition *only,* individuals with predominant actual/ideal discrepancies experienced a dejection-related syndrome (increased dejected mood, lowered standardized skin conductance amplitude, decreased total verbalization time), whereas individuals with predominant actual/ought discrepancies experienced an agitation-related syndrome (increased agitated mood, raised standardized skin conductance amplitude, increased total verbalization time).

This research was extended still further by Strauman (1990), who investigated whether presenting goal attributes as retrieval cues would elicit autobiographical memories that varied in their emotional content when the goal was an ideal versus an ought. As in Strauman and Higgins (1987), both "mismatching" priming and "yoked (mismatching)" priming were used. Thus, the attribute cues were always desired end-state attributes involved in a self-discrepancy, but for some participants the attributes concerned their own self-discrepancy whereas for other participants the attributes concerned the self-discrepancy of another participant. The attribute cues also varied in whether they were contained in ideals or oughts as desired end-states. Strauman (1990) found that childhood memories with dejection-related content were more likely to be retrieved spontaneously when the "mismatching" attributes were taken from participants' own ideals than when they were taken from their oughts. Similarly, childhood memories with agitation-related content were more likely to be retrieved when the "mismatching" cues were taken from participants' own oughts than when they were taken from their ideals. The "yoked" ideal and ought attribute cues generally yielded memories with little dejection-related or agitation-related content (less than 5 percent overall).

Strength of Regulatory Focus as Moderator of Emotional Effects of Ideal and Ought Self-Regulation

The psychological literature has suggested that goal strength conceptualized as goal accessibility (for example, Clore 1994) moderates the relation between goal attainment and emotional responses (see also Frijda 1996; Frijda et al. 1992). Although there was little direct support for this hypothesis, evidence that attitude accessibility moderates the relation between attitudes and behavior (Fazio 1986, 1995) prompted Higgins, Shah, and Friedman (1997) to test the possibility that strength of regulatory focus moderates the relation between chronic goal attainment and emotional experiences.

As discussed earlier, ideal goals involve a promotion focus and ought goals involve a prevention focus. Thus, strength of promotion focus increases as strength of ideal goals increases, and strength of prevention focus increases as strength of ought goals increases. As in previous work on attitude accessibility (see Bassili 1995, 1996; Fazio 1986, 1995), ideal and ought strength were conceptualized and operationalized in terms of their accessibility, and accessibility was measured through individuals' response times to inquiries about their ideal and ought attributes. Accessibility is activation potential, and knowledge units with higher activation potentials should produce faster responses to knowledge-related inputs (see Higgins 1996a). A computer measure of actual self, ideal, and ought attributes was developed that was similar to the original Selves Questionnaire. Ideal and ought strength were measured by response latencies in subjects' listing of ideal and ought attributes and extent ratings. Actual/ideal and actual/ought discrepancies were measured by comparing the extent rating of each ideal and ought attribute, respectively, with the extent rating of the actual self for that attribute (see Higgins et al. 1997).

Higgins et al. (1997) hypothesized the following relations between ideal and ought strength, ideal and ought discrepancies, and type of emotional experience: (1) an interaction of ideal strength and actual/ideal discrepancy, such that the correlation between actual/ideal discrepancy and feeling dejected (or actual/ideal congruency and feeling cheerful) would increase as the accessibility of ideals increased; and (2) an interaction of ought strength and actual/ought discrepancy, such that the correlation between actual/ought discrepancy and feeling agitated (or actual/ought congruency and feeling quiescent) would increase as the accessibility of oughts increased. It should be noted that these predictions presume that strength of ideals and oughts as measured by accessibility is relatively independent of magnitude of discrepancies (or congruencies) to ideal and oughts as measured by actual self mismatches and matches. Indeed, Higgins et al. found in each study that these two measures were uncorrelated.

Higgins et al. (1997) conducted three correlational studies. Two studies tested the relation between self-discrepancies (or congruencies) and the frequency with which the undergraduate participants experienced different kinds of emotions during the previous week. A third study tested the relation between self-discrepancies (or congruencies) and the intensity of different kinds of emotions that undergraduate participants experienced before beginning a performance task. All three studies supported the predictions.

These studies support the proposal that strength of regulatory focus, as a motivational variable independent of magnitude of self-discrepancy, moderates the relation between chronic goal attainment and emotional experiences. More generally, they demonstrate that self-regulation in relation to ideals and oughts as desired end-states is distinct. Ideal self-regulation involves a promotion focus; the stronger this focus the stronger are the cheerfulness-related emotions experienced when promotion is working, and the stronger are the dejection-related emotions experienced when promotion is not working. In contrast, ought self-regulation involves a prevention focus; the stronger this focus the stronger are the quiescence-related emotions experienced when prevention is working, and the stronger are the agitation-related emotions experienced when prevention is not working.

Situational Variability in Regulatory Focus and Emotional Experiences

The studies by Higgins et al. (1997) demonstrated that stronger chronic promotion or prevention focus influences the relation between chronic goal attainment and emotional experiences. Higgins et al. hypothesized that similar effects of regulatory focus should also be found for momentary goal attainments and situationally activated regulatory focus. They used a framing technique in a fourth study to manipulate regulatory focus in a manner that kept constant both the actual consequences of attaining or not attaining the goal and the criterion of success and failure. Only the regulatory focus of the instructions varied.

The task involved memorizing trigrams. For the promotion focus, the participants began with five dollars, and the instructions were about gains and non-gains: "If you score above the seventieth percentile, that is, if you remember a lot of letter strings, then you will gain a dollar. However, if you don't score above the seventieth percentile, that is, if you don't remember a lot of letter strings, then you will not gain a dollar." For the prevention focus, the participants began with six dollars and the instructions were about losses and non-losses: "If you score above the seventieth percentile, that is, if you don't forget a lot of letter strings, then you won't lose a dollar. However, if you don't score above the seventieth percentile, that is, if you do forget a lot of letter strings, then you will lose a dollar." Following performance of the task, the participants were given false feedback that they had either succeeded or failed on the task.

It was predicted that feedback-consistent emotional change, that is, increasing positive and decreasing negative emotions following success and decreasing positive and increasing negative emotions following failure, would be different in the promotion-framing versus prevention-framing conditions. Feedback-consistent change on the cheerfulness/dejection dimension should be greater for participants in the promotion-framing than the prevention-framing condition, while feedback-consistent change on the quiescence/agitation dimension should be greater for participants in the prevention-framing than the promotion-framing condition. The results of the study supported both predictions.

Roney, Higgins, and Shah (1995) also found evidence that situational variability in regulatory focus can influence emotional experiences. Undergraduate participants in the first study were told that they would perform two tasks. For everyone the first task was an anagrams task that included both easy anagrams pretested to be solvable by everyone and unsolvable anagrams. The number of easy anagrams included in the task ensured that the participants would ultimately attain the assigned overall goal. All of the participants were told that the second task would be either a computer simulation of the popular *Wheel of Fortune* game or a task called "unvaried repetition," described so as to appear very boring.

Although the performance contingency for playing the fun game rather than the boring game as the second task was the same for everyone, the framing of the contingency was experimentally varied. Half of the participants were given a promotion focus in which they were told that if they solved twenty-two (or more) out of the twenty-five anagrams, they would get to play the *Wheel of Fortune* game; otherwise, they would do the "unvaried repetition" task. The other half of the participants were given a prevention focus in which they were told that if they got four (or more) out of the twenty-five anagrams wrong, they would do the "unvaried repetition" task; otherwise, they would play the *Wheel of Fortune* game. As mentioned earlier, all participants succeeded in the task. The study found that participants with a promotion focus felt more cheerful after attaining the goal compared to participants with a prevention focus, who felt more quiescent.

Undergraduate participants in the second study worked on a set of anagrams that included both solvable anagrams and unsolvable anagrams. Success or failure feedback was given on each trial. Half of the participants received promotion focus feedback, such as, "Right, you got that one," when they solved an anagram, or, "You didn't get that one right," when they did not solve an anagram. The other half of the participants received prevention focus feedback, such as, "You didn't miss that one," when they solved an anagram, and, "No, you missed that one," when they did not solve an anagram. The number of unsolvable anagrams included in the task ensured that all participants ultimately failed to attain the assigned overall goal. The study found that participants

with a promotion focus felt more dejected after failing the goal compared to participants with a prevention focus, who felt more agitated.

These studies demonstrate that regulatory focus can influence the types of emotions that people experience when they succeed or fail on a task. Brendl, Higgins, and Lemm (1995) hypothesized that regulatory focus might also influence people's affective sensitivity to varying amounts of monetary gain or loss. The participants were trained to use sound intensity to indicate the intensity of their emotional response to these varying amounts, thereby obtaining a psychophysical measure of discrimination between different sizes of gains or losses. There were four experimental conditions that varied regulatory focus and the pain versus pleasure of participants' ultimate experience. In one of the conditions, the participants were asked to imagine buying a plane ticket to return home from school on the first day after finals. Their travel agent had told them that the cost of the ticket would vary depending on when they flew. They knew that when they could fly depended on when their finals were over.

Participants in the promotion-framing condition were asked to imagine that they felt hopeful they would be able to take the cheaper flight and receive a $50 savings. Upon checking their finals schedule, they discovered either that they would be able to take the cheaper flight and would feel pleased about saving $50 (the promotion/pleasure condition) or that they would not be able to take that flight and would feel disappointed about not saving $50 (the promotion/pain condition). In the prevention-framing condition, participants were asked to imagine that they felt fearful that they would be forced to take the more expensive flight and be unable to avoid the additional $50 expense. Upon checking their finals schedule, they discovered either that they would not have to take the more expensive flight and would feel relieved about not having to spend an extra $50 (the prevention/pleasure condition) or that they would have to take the more expensive flight and would feel annoyed about having to spend an extra $50 (the prevention/pain condition).

Participants expressed their feelings about the $50 they saved or had to spend extra by matching the tone intensity to the intensity of their feeling. They then imagined different monetary outcomes varying from $17 to $150 and matched the tone intensity to each feeling intensity. The relation between the different monetary outcomes and sound intensities produced a regression line and (positive) slope coefficient for each participant that reflected his or her affective discrimination for increasing gains or increasing losses. Brendl et al. (1995) found that, controlling for the pleasure or pain of the scenario outcome, affective discrimination was reduced (that is, the slope was less positive) when there was a mismatch between individuals' chronic regulatory focus (ideal versus ought self-regulation) and the regulatory focus of their framing condition (promotion versus prevention). Brendl et al. explained this reduction in affective discrimination in terms of promotion focus and prevention focus inhibiting one another when they were simultaneously active. Without such inhibition, a strong regulatory focus increased affective discrimination.

Together, the results of these illustrative studies (as well as other studies not reviewed here) provide strong evidence that chronic or momentary variation in promotion and prevention focus has significant effects on the type and intensity of emotions that people experience. When self-regulation with a promotion focus is working, people experience cheerfulness-related emotions, and when it is not working, they experience dejection-related emotions. In contrast, when self-regulation with a prevention focus is working, people experience quiescence-related emotions, and when it is not working, they experience agitation-related emotions. In addition, for both promotion focus and prevention focus, the intensity of these emotions and their affective discriminability increases as the strength of regulatory focus increases.

To summarize our discussion of regulatory focus to this point, the focus of regulatory promotion is on aspirations and accomplishments, whereas the focus of regulatory prevention is on safety and responsibility. Regulatory promotion and prevention are induced, respectively, by nurturance needs and security needs, socialization of strong ideals and socialization of strong oughts, and situations of gain/non-gain and situations of loss/non-loss. Regulatory promotion yields psychological situations involving the presence or absence of positive outcomes and cheerfulness/dejection-related emotions, whereas regulatory prevention yields psychological situations involving the absence or presence of negative outcomes and quiescence/agitation-related emotions.

Figure 13.1 summarizes the different sets of psychological variables discussed thus far that have distinct relations to promotion focus and prevention focus (as well as some variables to be discussed later). On the input side (left side of figure

13.1), nurturance needs, strong ideals, and situations involving gain/non-gain induce a promotion focus, whereas security needs, strong oughts, and situations involving non-loss/loss induce a prevention focus. On the output side (right side of figure 13.1), a promotion focus yields sensitivity to the presence or absence of positive outcomes and approach as a strategic means, whereas a prevention focus yields sensitivity to the absence or presence of negative outcomes and avoidance as a strategic means. We return later to other distinct effects of regulatory promotion and prevention. In the next section, we extend our consideration of emotional experiences beyond the effects of regulatory focus per se. We propose a self-regulatory model of emotional experiences and compare it to alternative models.

A Self-Regulatory Model of Emotional Experiences

> Our natural way of thinking about these coarser emotions is that the mental perception of some fact excites the mental affection called the emotion, and that this latter state of mind gives rise to the bodily expression. My theory, on the contrary, is that *the bodily changes follow directly the perception of the exciting fact, and that our feeling of the same changes as they occur* is *the emotion.* (James 1890/1948, 375)

James's (1890/1948) well-known theory was that we feel sorry because we cry, and feel afraid because we tremble, rather than that we lose our fortune, feel sorry, and then cry, or that we meet a bear, are frightened, and then tremble. One aspect of James's theory worth highlighting is his proposal that it is our feeling of bodily changes as they occur that *is* the emotion. It is *not* the appraisal or interpretation of the object or event, which James referred to as "our natural way of thinking" about emotions. Perhaps the best-known counter to James's theory that returned to "our natural way of thinking," albeit in a modified manner, was Schachter and Singer's (1962) theory of emotion (see also Schachter 1964). One aspect of their argument is that the physiological experiences underlying different emotions, like anger and euphoria, are often too similar to account for the different emotional experiences. Indeed, it is proposed that a general pattern of sympathetic discharge or physiological arousal is characteristic of emotional states. Such general physiological arousal

FIGURE 13.1   Psychological Variables with Distinct Relations to Promotion Focus and Prevention Focus

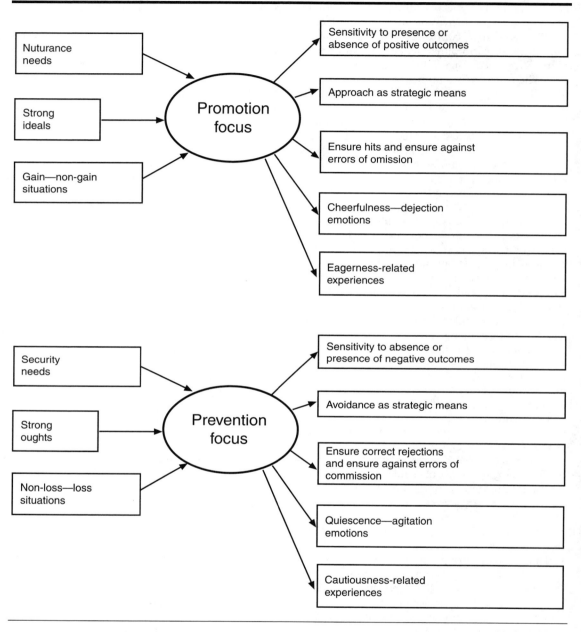

is considered to be a necessary condition of emotional experiences.

Another aspect of their argument is that, although necessary, the physiological arousal is too general across emotional experiences to be sufficient. What produces the different emotions (or no emotion) is the explanation that is available for and appropriate to the bodily state. A non-emotional explanation produces no emotion, an anger-related explanation produces anger, a euphoria-related explanation produces euphoria, and so on. Thus, appropriate cognitions mediate the emotional experience. Other classic approaches to emotion that postulate the mediation of cognitions in emotional experiences include Mandler's (1975) theory of emotion and Lazarus's (1966, 1982) cognitive appraisal model.

Although it might be more interesting to take sides in this long-standing debate (see also Zajonc 1980), we have a third perspective on emotional experiences, one that shares some aspects of each of the other alternatives, as will be seen. Rather than emphasizing either the physiological or the cognitive level of analysis, our perspective emphasizes the motivational role of self-regulation. Consistent with the hedonic principle, this perspective assumes that people prefer some states more than others and that self-regulation supports the occurrence of preferred states over nonpreferred states. But it also assumes that there are different ways in which such self-regulation occurs and that these different ways underlie different emotions.

When self-regulation is working, people experience pleasure, and when it is not working, they experience pain. That is, people's experience of pleasure and pain depends on *self-regulatory effectiveness*. Feedback about success or actual self matches to self-guides produces pleasure, and feedback about failure or actual self mismatches to self-guides produces pain. The notion that feedback about regulation working or not working underlies the basic experience of pleasure and pain, respectively, is common to most appraisal theories as well (for example, Frijda 1986; Ortony, Clore, and Collins 1988; Roseman 1984). But we also propose that the type of pleasure and the type of pain that people experience depends on *which type of self-regulation* is working or not working. For example, self-regulation in relation to a promotion focus on a desired end-state (for example, an aspiration) produces joy when it is working and disappointment when it is not working, while self-regulation in relation to a prevention focus on a desired end-state (such as a responsibility) produces calmness when it is working and nervousness when it is not working (see also Higgins 1996b).

We propose that from one moment to the next, people typically are engaged in self-regulation without feedback about whether it is working or not working. That is, much of people's everyday experiences are ongoing attempts to attain preferred over nonpreferred states without any current feedback about their success at doing so. A person, for example, might have feedback about the means to an end, such as feedback about walking smoothly and quickly down the street, without yet having feedback about the end itself, such as

whether he or she is walking in the right direction. Our position is that these experiences are not themselves emotional, even though they are motivational (cf. Pribram 1984). A student listening carefully to a lecture, for example, could experience his or her effort and concentration without feeling emotional. But when the student receives feedback about success or failure in answering a question posed by the teacher, *then* he or she will experience an emotion.

Other cybernetic-inspired models also postulate that emotions arise from feedback that self-regulation is succeeding or failing (for example, Carver 1996; Pribram 1970). Our basic proposal is that *people engage in different types of self-regulation*. When they receive feedback that a particular type of self-regulation is working or not working, they experience the kind of pleasure or pain associated with that type of self-regulation. Thus, *emotions are the direct experiences of particular types of self-regulatory effectiveness*.

In making this proposal, we need to emphasize some points. The basic distinction between positive and negative emotional experiences in terms of self-regulation working or not working, respectively, is similar to distinctions made by several theories of emotion. This aspect of our proposal is certainly not novel. What is more novel is the notion that specific types of positive emotions and specific types of negative emotions will be experienced directly depending on which type of self-regulatory system is working or not working. For example, people experience sadness when they are engaged in promotion regulation that is not working, whereas they experience nervousness when they are engaged in prevention regulation that is not working. Other than the feedback that the regulation is working or not, no additional information processing (whether conscious *or* unconscious) is necessary for the specific emotions to emerge. Rather, the specificity follows directly from the fact that the person is engaged in a particular type of self-regulation when feedback about its effectiveness is received.

Let us now compare our proposal to other models of emotional experiences.

Appraisal Models of Emotional Experiences

We propose that it is a person's experience of a particular regulatory process working or not working that *is* the emotion. It is not that some event occurs, the event is interpreted along some set of psychological dimensions, and then some specific emotion is produced. We do *not* propose a cognitive model like those that postulate explanations as mediators, such as Schachter and Singer's (1962) theory (described earlier) or Weiner's (1982, 1986) theory of emotions. In Schachter and Singer's model, distinct emotions occur when a person first experiences (or detects) physiological arousal and then explains the bodily state in a specific emotional manner depending on appraisal of a particular situation. In Weiner's model, distinct emotions (excluding happiness and sadness) occur when a person first experiences an outcome such as success or failure and then makes a particular combination of causal attributions for the outcome.

It is true that the feedback in our model of self-regulatory effectiveness can be considered a form of appraisal. But this appraisal alone would produce only pleasure or pain. The distinct emotions occur because it is distinct self-regulatory processes that are experienced as working or not working. All that is necessary for these distinct emotions to be produced is the feedback that the operative self-regulatory process is working or not working. No additional appraisal is required, whether conscious or unconscious.

This is not to say that our model disagrees with "appraisal" models in general. Some models, for example, simply relate patterns of appraisal to specific emotions without claiming that the appraisals produce the emotions (for example, Shaver et al. 1987; Smith and Ellsworth 1985). In addition, the concept of appraisal has been used very broadly. Lazarus (1982), for example, describes appraisal as the emotional meaning of some object or event in the sense of its *significance for well-being*. Moreover, such meaning can inhere in commitments developed over a lifetime. Presumably, regulatory anticipation, regulatory reference, and regulatory focus could all be understood in these terms. In this aspect, then, our model is more like appraisal models than like James's model, which emphasizes bodily changes.

The important point, however, is that the appraisal variables in our model are already in place prior to the feedback that the self-regulation is working or not working. Unlike many appraisal models, ours does not suggest that an event takes place, such as success or failure feedback, and then cognitive appraisal processes (and coping activities) occur that elicit some emotion (Scherer 1988). We are not suggesting that emotions are produced by evaluative judgments of the significance of the ongoing transaction with the environment. Rather, the direct experience of the *particular* self-regulatory process working or not working *is* the emotion.

Our perspective on emotions highlights a basic similarity between all feelings. People say, "I feel hungry," or, "I feel dizzy." We would argue that these feelings involve the direct experience of specific regulatory processes not working. These feelings differ from emotional feelings because the types of self-regulatory processes underlying them are quite different. As Ortony, Clore, and Collins (1988) suggest, emotions concern the state of one's goals, attitudes, or standards rather than the state of one's body. This important and basic dissimilarity is not captured adequately in James's theory of emotions. On the other hand, the basic similarity between all feelings as direct experiences of some specific regulatory process working or not working is not captured adequately in most appraisal models.

Our self-regulatory model of emotional experiences differs from previous appraisal models not only in its general perspective but also in the psychological dimensions that it emphasizes. The one dimension that it certainly shares with most previous appraisal models, and the one they tend to share with one another, is the basic dimension of self-regulatory effectiveness. This dimension has been referred to as situational state by Roseman (1984), that is, whether an event is consistent or inconsistent with personal motives, and as goal conduciveness by Scherer (1988), that is, whether an event blocks or helps achieve an organism's goals. Under a variety of names, it is the basic pleasure and pain dimension in many models (for example, Frijda, Kuipers, and ter Schure 1989; Ortony et al. 1988; Smith and Ellsworth 1985).

There are many psychological dimensions that appear in appraisal models on which our model is currently silent, the most common being agency (caused by self or others) and novelty. On the other hand, relatively little attention has been paid by appraisal models to self-regulatory dimensions. Regulatory anticipation appears to some extent in models that account for "hope" and "fear" in terms of the probability or certainty of a pleasant or unpleasant event, respectively (Frijda et al. 1989; Roseman 1984; Smith and Ellsworth 1985). Regulatory reference has received only limited attention in a few models. Roseman (1984), for example, describes a motivational state dimension distinguishing the motive to obtain reward (appetitive motivation) from the motive to avoid punishment (aversive motivation). This distinction between the appetitive motivational system involving approach and the aversive motivational system involving avoidance is also found in other models (for example, Gray 1982; Konorski 1967; Lang 1995; Mowrer 1960). Frijda's action readiness component of emotions includes a distinction between tendencies to approach versus avoid or flee (see Frijda et al. 1989). Stein and her colleagues (for example, Stein, Liwag, and Wade 1996) distinguish between wanting something (and having or not having it) and not wanting something (and having or not having it).

To our knowledge, regulatory focus as a psychological dimension, *as distinct from regulatory reference,* has not been considered in previous models. It should be noted, however, that one cannot always be certain whether the approach and avoidance being described in previous models concern movement in reference to end-states that would involve regulatory reference or, instead, concern strategic means that would involve regulatory focus. What is clear is that previous models do not distinguish explicitly between regulatory reference and regulatory focus as two separate dimensions. Thus, approaching desired end-states with a promotion focus on aspirations or accomplishments has not been distinguished from approaching desired end-states with a prevention focus on safety or responsibilities. Rather, the distinction is between approaching desired end-states or anticipated pleasure (such as reward) and avoiding undesired end-states or anticipated pain (such as punishment).

Without distinguishing regulatory reference and regulatory focus, one would have to predict that attainment of desired end-states would produce the same emotion for both promotion and prevention, and that non-attainment or loss of desired end-states would produce the same emotion independent of regulatory focus. Indeed, it has been suggested that attaining safety produces "satisfaction" just as attaining reward does, and that the disappearance of safety produces "disappointment" just as losing a reward does (Gray 1982; Mowrer 1960). Our studies have found, however, that feeling satisfied and feeling disappointed are more common emotional responses to self-regulatory promotion working and not working, respectively, than to self-regulatory prevention. The more common emotional responses to self-regulatory prevention working and not working are feeling "calm" or "relaxed" and feeling "tense" or "nervous," respectively.

It is interesting to note that an emotion like feeling calm or relaxed has received relatively little attention in appraisal or learning models of emotion, perhaps because that emotion is perceived as less prototypical of prevention-related emotions than a negative emotion such as fear (see Shaver et al. 1987). Moreover, although fear (as a general uncertainty about a painful future) has received substantial attention, emotions like feeling tense or nervous have received relatively little attention in these models. In contrast, descriptive models of emotional experiences, such as circumplex models, do generally include these emotions. Let us now turn our attention to these models.

Circumplex Models of Emotional Experiences

There have been two basic ways in which these kinds of emotions—feeling calm and relaxed or feeling tense and nervous—have been handled. One kind of model proposes a two-dimensional structure involving valence (that is, pleasure versus pain) as one dimension and arousal or intensity as the other dimension (Larsen and Diener 1985; Russell 1978, 1980). An alternative model proposes a two-dimensional structure involving high versus low negative affect as one dimension and high versus low positive affect as the other dimension (Meyer and Shack 1989; Watson and Tellegen 1985).

There has been fairly good agreement in the literature concerning which emotions tend to co-occur within two-dimensional space. Emotions like feeling calm and relaxed tend to co-occur, and emotions like feeling nervous, tense, or fearful also tend to co-occur and to not co-occur with emotions like feeling calm and relaxed (Meyer and Shack 1989; Russell 1980; Watson and Tellegen 1985). There has not been strong consensus, however, concerning how best to describe the difference between these two types of emotions. It has been noted that there is no a priori correct answer concerning where to place the orthogonal dimensions in a two-dimensional factor analytic solution (Meyer and Shack 1989; Watson, Clark, and Tellegen 1984). And once placed within the space, there is no a priori correct answer concerning how to label the orthogonal dimensions. How, then, should the difference between emotions like feeling calm and relaxed versus feeling nervous and tense be treated?

One solution would be to contrast feeling calm and relaxed as low negative affect emotions with feeling nervous and tense as high negative affect emotions. The problem with this solution is that sadness, gloominess, disappointment, and other dejection-related emotions have also been included within high negative affect emotions (Meyer and Shack 1989; Watson, Clark, and Tellegen 1984) and thus are not clearly distinguished from emotions like feeling nervous, tense, and other agitation-related emotions. But the results of our studies clearly indicate that these two types of emotions have distinct antecedents involving different self-regulatory processes. It might be better to characterize dejection as low positive affect, but this pole of the positive affect dimension is more closely associated with feeling sleepy or tired (see Watson and Tellegen 1985).

Another solution would be to contrast feeling calm and relaxed as pleasant/low-intensity emotions with feeling nervous and tense as painful/high-intensity emotions. The problem here is that low-intensity pleasant emotions such as satisfaction can end up being included with feeling at ease and other emotions like feeling calm and relaxed, and low-intensity unpleasant emotions such as feeling unhappy, disappointed, or dissatisfied can end up being included with feeling worried and other relatively low-intensity unpleasant emotions like nervousness (Russell 1978). Thus, the critical distinction between dejection and agitation-related emotions of low intensity is blurred. But perhaps an even greater problem with distinguishing between different types of emotions in terms of their intensity is that each type can itself vary in intensity. As discussed earlier, cheerfulness-related emotions from attaining promotion goals (chronically or momentarily) and dejection-related emotions from failing to do so, quiescence-related emotions from attaining prevention goals and agitation-related emotions from failing to do so, can all vary in intensity depending on the strength of the goal or standard (see Higgins, Shah, and Friedman 1997).

Thus, intensity varies within types of emotions as well as between emotions. Feeling "worried" means feeling only "slightly afraid," while feeling "terrified" means feeling "extremely afraid." To suggest that the difference between feeling worried and feeling terrified is like the difference between disappointment and terror because both pairs are unpleasant emotions varying in intensity ignores the more important distinction between dejection and agitation. Indeed, we would propose that the difference between feeling worried and feeling disappointed reflects a more fundamental difference in type of self-regulatory process than the difference between feeling worried and feeling terrified, because each member of the latter pair has a prevention focus while the members of the former pair have a prevention focus and a promotion focus, respectively. Let us now consider how our general proposal would handle some other types of emotions.

Types of Emotions as Types of Self-Regulatory Experiences

We propose that the best way to capture the distinctions between feeling calm and relaxed and feeling nervous and tense, and between feeling sad and disappointed and feeling happy and satisfied, is in terms of regulatory focus. As stated earlier, feeling calm and relaxed is the direct experience of prevention focus working, while feeling nervous and tense is the direct experience of this focus not working. Feeling sad and disappointed is the direct experience of promotion focus not working, while feeling happy and satisfied is the direct experience of this focus working. From our self-regulatory perspective, these emotions vary in intensity as a function of the strength of the goal or standard that is or is not attained.

There are, of course, many other emotions not captured by just the variables of self-regulatory effectiveness (working or not working), type of regulatory focus (promotion or prevention), and regulatory strength. It is not our purpose here to provide an exhaustive account of emotional experiences, but it would be useful to consider briefly some other emotional experiences and the self-regulatory processes that might underlie them in order to provide the reader with a better understanding of how a self-regulatory perspective on emotions might work.

It is especially instructive to consider how regulatory reference and regulatory focus underlie emotions because previous models of emotions have not distinguished between these two principles of self-regulation, which involve different kinds of approach and avoidance (see table 13.1). In one set of studies, we presented undergraduates with situations to imagine that varied as a function of regulatory reference (approaching a desired end-state versus avoiding an undesired end-state), regulatory focus (promotion versus prevention), and regulatory effectiveness (self-regulation working versus not working). In one situation, for example, undergraduates were asked to imagine that they want to be the type of person they would consider accomplished—a winner (approaching a desired end-state; promotion focus)—and that their attempts to become this accomplished person do not work out (self-regulation not working). In another situation, they were asked to imagine that they want not to be the type of person they would consider irresponsible—someone dangerous to be (avoiding an undesired end-state; prevention focus)—and that their attempts to avoid becoming this irresponsible person work out (self-regulation working). We controlled regulatory effectiveness by giving the undergraduates positive emotions for situations in which self-regulation was working and negative emotions for situations in which self-regulation was not working. They were asked to rate the extent to which they would feel each emotion.

We found that for some emotions only the regulatory focus of a situation influenced how much participants said they would experience the emotion. For example, the participants reported that they would feel more sad and more disappointed when a promotion focus was not working than when a prevention focus was not working, with the regulatory reference of the situation having no effect. On the other hand, for other emotions only the regulatory reference of the situation influenced how much the participants said they would experience the emotion. For example, the participants reported that they would feel more content and more satisfied when attempts to approach a desired end-state were working than when attempts to avoid an undesired end-state were working, with the regulatory focus of the situation having no effect. Finally, there were some emotions for which both the regulatory focus and the regulatory reference of the situation influenced how much the participants said they would experience the emotion. For example, the participants reported that they would feel more joy when attempts to approach a promotion goal were working than when attempts to avoid a prevention goal were working. The results of our studies clearly indicate that *both* regulatory focus and regulatory reference are important self-regulatory variables underlying people's emotional experiences.

We have found evidence as well in previous research for additional relations between self-regulatory processes and the feelings people experience. Models of emotions typically exclude "feeling confused" because it involves information about one's state of knowledge. Still, we would argue that feeling confused does reflect a direct experience of the state of one's goals or standards. Specifically, Van Hook and Higgins (1988) proposed that feeling confused reflects a self-regulatory conflict. One such conflict is between self-guides. Un-

dergraduates who possessed a conflict between ideals and/or oughts were compared to a control group of undergraduates who did not. (Any difference between these samples in their magnitude of self-discrepancies per se was controlled.) The study found that participants with a self-regulatory conflict experienced a greater frequency of feeling confused, muddled, and indecisive.

Another common emotion is anger. From our self-regulatory perspective, we would predict that people feel angry when they experience a barrier to their self-regulatory movements. A unique feature of this perspective is its ability to distinguish between types of anger as a function of regulatory focus. If the barrier occurs when the regulatory system has a promotion focus, the anger experienced will be a frustration-type anger. In contrast, if the barrier occurs when the regulatory system has a prevention focus, the anger experienced will be a resentment-type anger. Consistent with this proposal, a study by Strauman and Higgins (1988) found that frustration-related anger was uniquely associated with actual/ideal discrepancies (a promotion focus), whereas resentment-related anger was uniquely associated with actual/ought discrepancies (a prevention focus).

This discussion is not intended to provide a general account of emotions. We intend only to illustrate how emotional experiences might be understood as direct experiences of different kinds of self-regulatory processes working or not working. Our position is that an important aspect of quality of life concerns these direct experiences of self-regulatory effectiveness. But we also believe that the pains and pleasures produced by feedback about self-regulatory effectiveness are *not* all there is to subjective well-being. Indeed, we believe that much of our life experiences concern the non-emotional experiences involved in self-regulation independent of feedback about its effectiveness. We briefly consider such non-emotional experiences in the next section.

NON-EMOTIONAL EXPERIENCES OF SELF-REGULATORY PROCESSES

Among social-personality psychologists especially, there has been increasing interest in non-emotional experiences (Clore 1992; Schwarz 1990; Schwarz and Clore 1996; Strack 1992). Elegant studies have demonstrated how experiences of difficulty and effort can strongly influence people's inferences and judgments (Schwarz et al. 1991).

Research on regulatory focus suggests further that how people are motivated could also contribute significantly to their life experiences. To understand how this might be, it is necessary to consider in more detail the motivational differences between a promotion focus and a prevention focus.

A promotion focus is concerned with advancement, growth, accomplishment. Promotion goals are hopes and aspirations, and the strategic inclination is to make progress by approaching matches to the desired end-state. A prevention focus, in contrast, is concerned with security, safety, responsibility. Prevention goals are duties and obligations or even necessities, and the strategic inclination is to be prudent and precautionary and to avoid mismatches to the desired end-state. One would expect, given these differences, that people's self-regulatory states would be different when their focus is promotion versus prevention. The state of people with a promotion focus should be *eagerness* to attain advancement and gains, while the state of people with a prevention focus should be *vigilance* to ensure safety and nonlosses. Being in a state of eagerness constitutes a different life experience than being in a state of vigilance. We propose, then, that individuals with different regulatory focus have different life experiences and therefore have a different quality of life.

To appreciate how life experiences might differ as a function of regulatory focus, let us take a signal detection perspective to consider how a state of eagerness versus a state of vigilance might impact strategic inclinations. From this perspective (Tanner and Swets 1954; Trope and Liberman 1996), individuals in a state of eagerness from a promotion focus should want especially to accomplish "hits" and to avoid errors of omission or "misses" (a failure to accomplish). In contrast, individuals in a state of vigilance from a prevention focus should want especially to attain "correct rejections" and to avoid errors of commission or "false alarms" (making a mistake). A strategy is a pattern of decisions in the acquisition, retention, and utilization of information that serves to ensure certain forms of outcome and to ensure against certain others (Bruner, Goodnow, and Austin 1956). Thus, promotion focus regulation involves a strategic inclination to ensure hits and to ensure against errors of omission, while prevention focus regulation involves a strategic inclination to ensure correct rejections and guard against errors of commission (see table 13.1 and figure 13.1).

How might these different strategic inclinations influence performance? Consider, first, performance on an anagram task. An anagram task requires that the participant find one or more words hidden in a letter string. Success at finding a word would be a correct acceptance, or a "hit," whereas failure to find a word would be an error of omission. On this task, then, the promotion focus individuals should be eager to ensure that they find words ("hits") and do not omit any possible words. This focus would yield high persistence and a strong desire to find words following a failure to find any. In contrast, the prevention focus individuals should be vigilant against forming non-words and want to avoid committing the error of producing them. This orientation might inhibit their ability to find many words and motivate them to quit rather than explicitly commit an error when failure appears likely.

This analysis predicts that when participants experience difficulty on a task, the promotion focus state of eagerness should yield a performance advantage over the prevention focus state of vigilance. Crowe and Higgins (1997) tested this prediction by including specially designed tasks in their study and experimentally manipulating regulatory focus.

As part of a large survey held weeks before the experiment, a questionnaire was given to undergraduate participants in which they expressed their liking for different kinds of activities. Using each participant's idiographic responses, one activity was selected for the experiment that a participant clearly liked and another was selected that the participant clearly disliked. When the participants arrived for the study, they were told that they would first perform a set of initial exercises, one of which was the anagram task, and they would then be assigned a final task. Each participant's liked and disliked activities were described as the two alternative final tasks that they would perform.

Four of the experimental framing conditions were *contingency* conditions in which participants were told that their performance on the set of initial exercises would determine which of the alternative final tasks they worked on at the end of the session. The relation between the initial set of exercises and the final task was described as contingent for everyone, but the framing varied in different conditions as a function of both regulatory focus and valence or regulatory effectiveness, as follows:

1. *Promotion working:* "If you do well on the exercises I'm about to give you, you will get to do (the participant's liked task) instead of the other task."

2. *Promotion not working:* "If you don't do well on the exercises I'm about to give you, you won't get to do (the participant's liked task) but will do the other task instead."

3. *Prevention working:* "As long as you don't do poorly on the exercises I'm about to give you, you won't have to do (the participant's disliked task) but will do the other task instead."

4. *Prevention not working:* "If you do poorly on the exercises I'm about to give you, you will have to do (the participant's disliked task) instead of the other task."

Two different tasks were included in the set of exercises to permit a test of the prediction. One task was an "embedded figures" task in which participants were shown a figure and asked to find it embedded in a more complex figure (see Ruebush 1960). The measure of persistence was whether a participant quit looking for an especially difficult hidden figure before the time limit was up. It was predicted that individuals in a prevention focus would be more likely to quit before the time limit was up in order to avoid committing a mistake, while individuals in a promotion focus would persist longer to prolong the opportunity for a "hit." Another task was a counting-backward task in which an easy sequence was followed by a difficult sequence. It was expected that any performance advantage of the promotion focus would emerge only during the difficult sequence. The results of the study supported both of these predictions. The study also found that the effects of regulatory focus were independent of the valence or regulatory effectiveness of the framing (that is, working versus not working).

Crowe and Higgins (1997) also proposed that the difference between individuals in an eager state from a promotion focus versus those in a vigilant state from a prevention focus would have effects beyond performance. One such effect they predicted was a difference in strategic motivation to generate alternatives. On some tasks, people can produce either few or many alternatives without penalty. On a sorting task, for example, individuals can use the same criterion, such as color, to sort a set of fruits and to sort a set of vegetables, or they can use different criteria, such as color for the fruits and shape for the vegetables. Either strategy is considered correct. The only requirement is that the sorting criterion be consistent within each category across all members of that category. Thus, individuals can reduce the likelihood of making a mistake and still be correct by simplifying the task,

such as sticking to one criterion for both categories. Individuals in a vigilant state from a prevention focus want to avoid errors of commission and thus should be inclined to be repetitive.

This should not be the case, however, for individuals in an eager state from a promotion focus. Sticking to one category means that alternative dimensions or criteria will be omitted during the sorting task. Individuals eager from a promotion focus want to accomplish "hits" and thus should *not* be inclined to use this strategy. Indeed, in a task in which many different alternatives could be produced, one might expect these individuals to be inclined to generate many different alternatives.

This hypothesized difference in strategic inclinations for considering alternatives was also tested by Crowe and Higgins (1997); they included two additional tasks in their set of exercises, both based on tasks used by Mikulincer, Kedem, and Paz (1990). One of these tasks was a sorting task like the one just described. The other task was a characteristic listing task. Participants were presented with the names of furniture objects, such as "desk," "couch," or "bed," and then asked to write down all of the characteristics they could think of for each object.

It was predicted that individuals with a promotion focus, compared to individuals with a prevention focus, would be more fluent in sorting into more subgroups or in listing unique characteristics for different category members because of their stronger strategic inclination to generate many different alternatives when possible. In contrast, individuals with a prevention focus, who are inclined to avoid errors of commission, would be more repetitive in employing sorting criteria across categories or in using specific descriptive terms or words across category members (controlling for fluency). The results supported both of these predictions. Once again, the effects of regulatory focus were independent of the valence or regulatory effectiveness of the framing. (It should be noted that the results for these tasks, as for all the tasks used by Crowe and Higgins [1997], were also independent of the subjects' pre-task mood and change in mood during the experimental session.)

These results support the proposal that individuals who are eager from a promotion focus want to accomplish "hits" and avoid errors of omission, while individuals vigilant from a prevention focus want to attain correct rejections and avoid errors of commission. One might expect that these differences in orientation, and thus life experience, would also be revealed in differences in decision-making biases. Crowe and Higgins (1997) conducted a second study to test this prediction. Specifically, they used a recognition memory task to examine directly signal detection response biases.

This study involved the same basic paradigm as the first study. Participants' previous responses to a questionnaire were used idiographically to select one activity that each participant clearly liked and another he or she clearly disliked. When the participants arrived for the study, they were told that they would first perform a recognition memory task and then be assigned a second task. The liked and the disliked activities previously selected were each described as an alternative second task.

The recognition memory task is a signal detection task that requires participants to make decisions. In signal detection tasks, a signal is either presented or not presented, and a respondent says either "yes" (they detected a signal) or "no" (no signal was detected). There are therefore four possible outcomes for a signal detection trial: (1) a "hit" (saying yes when a signal was presented); (2) a "miss" (saying no when a signal was presented); (3) a "false alarm" (saying yes when there was no signal); and (4) a "correct rejection" (saying no when there was no signal). Signal detection theory per se is silent on motivational determinants of a person's payoff matrix. The principle of regulatory focus, however, does make predictions.

Participants with a promotion focus are in a state of eagerness. This state should induce them to use advancement tactics—that is, to be inclined to approach accomplishments. They want to ensure hits and against errors of omission. These participants, then, should want hits (successfully recognizing a true target) and should not want misses (failing to recognize a true target), producing an inclination to say yes (that is, a "risky" bias). In contrast, participants with a prevention focus are in a state of vigilance. This state should induce them to use precautionary tactics—that is, to be inclined to avoid mistakes. They want to attain correct rejections and avoid errors of commission. These participants, then, should want correct rejections (that is, successfully avoiding a false distractor) and not want false alarms (failing to avoid a false distractor), producing an inclination to say no (that is, a "conservative" bias). In addition, because these individuals are vigilant against errors of commission, they should take more time to respond. Thus, we also predicted that the response latencies would be longer for participants in the prevention focus condition than for those in the promotion focus condition.

Each of these predictions was supported by the results of the study. And once again, the effects of regulatory focus were independent of the valence or regulatory effectiveness of the framing. (In addition, the results were once again independent of the subjects' pre-task mood and change in mood during the experimental session.)

The results of these studies by Crowe and Higgins (1997) demonstrate that it is not only the emotional experiences of individuals that vary as a function of regulatory focus. Non-emotional experiences associated with being eager versus vigilant also vary by regulatory focus. The results of these studies suggest that individuals' experience of eagerness or vigilance not only is a chronic personality variable but also can be situationally induced. Indeed, an experimental study by Friedman and Higgins (1997) found that manipulations of success versus failure on a task produced changes in eagerness experiences for participants in the promotion framing condition and changes in vigilance or cautiousness experiences for participants in the prevention framing condition. Such non-emotional, motivational experiences are states in people's lives that are likely to occur more frequently for some individuals than others, either from personal orientation or from greater exposure to specific kinds of situations. But regardless of the source of these states, they represent an important aspect of people's life experiences.

In sum, it is not only the case, as described earlier, that regulatory promotion yields psychological situations involving the presence or absence of positive outcomes and cheerfulness- or dejection-related emotions, whereas regulatory prevention yields psychological situations involving the absence or presence of negative outcomes and quiescence- or agitation-related emotions. In addition, regulatory promotion yields strategic inclinations to approach matches to desired end-states, ensure hits, and ensure against errors of omission, and it yields the non-emotional, motivational experience of eagerness. In contrast, regulatory prevention yields strategic inclinations to avoid mismatches to desired end-states, ensure correct rejections, and guard against errors of commission, and it yields the non-emotional, motivational experience of vigilance or cautiousness (see figure 13.1).

CONCLUSION

This chapter began by noting that it is natural to define quality of life in terms of the hedonic principle. But the hedonic principle in its classic version does not go far enough. In particular, the hedonic principle does not capture the fact that people's life experiences have as much to do with *how* they regulate pleasure and pain as it does with the simple fact that they do so. Individuals who experience the pleasure of joy and the pain of disappointment do not have the same life experiences as those who experience the pleasure of relaxation and the pain of nervousness. This is not the only limitation of the hedonic principle, however. Specifically, there is more to life experiences than the pleasures and pains of effective and ineffective self-regulation. Motivational experiences of strategic states, such as feeling eager or cautious, are an important part of life as well. For example, happiness from knowing that one has accomplished one's life goals might not be enough for subjective well-being. It might be necessary to remain eager for more "hits." Thus, social policies directed solely at maximizing emotional pleasures might actually undermine quality of life. As has often been noted in classic literature, what makes life worth living is working toward a goal, not simply knowing that it was attained.

REFERENCES

Atkinson, J. W. (1964). *An introduction to motivation.* Princeton, N.J.: D. Van Nostrand.

Atkinson, J. W., and Raynor, J. O. (Eds.). (1974). *Motivation and achievement.* New York: Wiley.

Ausubel, D. P. (1955). Relationships between shame and guilt in the socializing process. *Psychological Review, 62,* 378–90.

Bandura, A. (1986). *Social foundations of thought and action: A social cognitive theory.* Englewood Cliffs, N.J.: Prentice-Hall.

Bassili, J. N. (1995). Response latency and the accessibility of voting intentions: What contributes to accessibility and how it affects vote choice. *Personality and Social Psychology Bulletin, 21,* 686–95.

———. (1996). Meta-judgmental versus operative indices of psychological attributes: The case of measures of attitude strength. *Journal of Personality and Social Psychology, 71,* 637–53.

Blatt, S. J., D'Afflitti, J. P., and Quinlan, D. M. (1976). Experiences of depression in normal young adults. *Journal of Abnormal Psychology, 86,* 203–23.

Bowlby, J. (1969). *Attachment and loss,* vol. 1, *Attachment.* New York: Basic Books.

———. (1973). *Attachment and loss,* vol. 2, *Separation: anxiety and anger.* New York: Basic Books.

Brendl, C. M., and Higgins, E. T. (1996). Principles of judging valence: What makes events positive or negative? In M. P. Zanna (Ed.), *Advances in experimental social psychology* (vol. 28, pp. 95–160). New York: Academic Press.

Brendl, C. M., and Higgins, E. T., and Lemm, K. M. (1995). Sensitivity to varying gains and losses: The role of self-discrepancies and event framing. *Journal of Personality and Social Psychology, 69,* 1028–51.

Bruner, J. S., Goodnow, J. J., and Austin, G. A. (1956). *A study of thinking.* New York: Wiley.

Buss, D. (1996). The evolutionary psychology of human social strategies. In E. T. Higgins and A. W. Kruglanski (Eds.), *Social psychology: Handbook of basic principles* (pp. 3–38). New York: Guilford.

Carver, C. S. (1996). Some ways in which goals differ and some implications of those differences. In P. M. Gollwitzer and J. A. Bargh (Eds.), *The psychology of action: Linking cognition and motivation to behavior* (pp. 645–72). New York: Guilford.

Carver, C. S., and Scheier, M. F. (1981). *Attention and self-regulation: A control-theory approach to human behavior.* New York: Springer-Verlag.

———. (1990). Principles of self-regulation: Action and emotion. In E. T. Higgins and R. M. Sorrentino (Eds.), *Handbook of motivation and cognition: Foundations of social behavior,* (vol. 2, pp. 3–52). New York: Guilford.

Clore, G. L. (1992). Cognitive phenomenology: Feelings and the construction of judgment. In L. L. Martin and A. Tesser (Eds.), *The construction of social judgments* (pp. 133–63). Hillsdale, N.J.: Erlbaum.

———. (1994). Why emotions vary in intensity. In P. Elkman and R. J. Davidson (Eds.), *The nature of emotion: Fundamental questions* (pp. 386–93). Oxford: Oxford University Press.

Cooley, C. H. (1964). *Human nature and the social order.* New York: Schocken Books. (Originally published in 1902)

Crowe, E., and Higgins, E. T. (1997). Regulatory focus and strategic inclinations: Promotion and prevention in decision-making. *Organizational Behavior and Human Decision Processes, 69,* 117–32.

Durkheim, E. (1951). *Suicide: A study in sociology.* New York: Free Press.

Duval, S., and Wicklund, R. A. (1972). *A theory of objective self-awareness.* New York: Academic Press.

Erikson, E. H. (1963). *Childhood and society,* rev. ed. New York: Norton. (Originally published in 1950)

Estes, W. K. (1944). An experimental study of punishment. *Psychological Monographs, 57,* no. 263.

Fazio, R. H. (1986). How do attitudes guide behavior? In R. M. Sorrentino and E. T. Higgins (Eds.), *Handbook of motivation and cognition: Foundations of social behavior* (pp. 204–43). New York: Guilford.

———. (1995). Attitudes as object-evaluation associations: Determinants, consequences, and correlates of attitude accessibility. In R. E. Petty and J. A. Krosnick (Eds.), *Attitude strength: Antecedents and consequences* (pp. 247–82). Mahwah, N.J.: Erlbaum.

Freud, S. (1961). The ego and the id. In J. Strachey (Ed. and Trans.), *Standard edition of the complete psychological works of Sigmund Freud* (vol. 19, pp. 3–66).

London: Hogarth Press. (Originally published in 1923)

Friedman, R., and Higgins, E. T. (1997). *Non-emotional motivational experiences associated with promotion and prevention.* Columbia University. Unpublished paper.

Frijda, N. H. (1986). *The emotions.* New York: Cambridge University Press.

———. (1996). Passions: Emotion and socially consequential behavior. In R. D. Kavanaugh, B. Zimmerberg, and S. Fein (Eds.), *Emotion: Interdisciplinary perspectives* (pp. 1–27). Mahwah, N.J.: Erlbaum.

Frijda, N. H., Kuipers, P., and ter Schure, E. (1989). Relations among emotion, appraisal, and emotional action readiness. *Journal of Personality and Social Psychology, 57,* 212–28.

Frijda, N. H., Ortony, A., Sonnemans, J., and Clore, G. (1992). The complexity of intensity. In M. Clark (Ed.), *Emotion: Review of personality and social psychology* (vol. 13, pp. 60–89). Beverly Hills: Sage.

Gollwitzer, P. M., and Bargh, J. A. (Eds.) (1996). *The psychology of action: Linking cognition and motivation to behavior.* New York: Guilford.

Gould, R. (1939). An experimental analysis of "level of aspiration." *Genetic Psychology Monographs, 21,* 3–115.

Gray, J. A. (1982). *The neuropsychology of anxiety: An enquiry into the functions of the septo-hippocampal system.* New York: Oxford University Press.

Higgins, E. T. (1987). Self-discrepancy: A theory relating self and affect. *Psychological Review, 94,* 319–40.

———. (1989a). Self-discrepancy theory: What patterns of self-beliefs cause people to suffer? In L. Berkowitz (Ed.), *Advances in experimental social psychology* (vol. 22, pp. 93–136). New York: Academic Press.

———. (1989b). Continuities and discontinuities in self-regulatory and self-evaluative processes: A developmental theory relating self and affect. *Journal of Personality, 57,* 407–44.

———. (1996a). Knowledge activation: Accessibility, applicability, and salience. In E. T. Higgins and A. W. Kruglanski (Eds.), *Social psychology: Handbook of basic principles* (pp. 133–68). New York: Guilford.

———. (1996b). Emotional experiences: The pains and pleasures of distinct regulatory systems. In R. D. Kavanaugh, B. Zimmerberg, and S. Fein (Eds.), *Emotion: Interdisciplinary perspectives* (pp. 203–41). Mahwah, N.J.: Erlbaum.

———. (1997). Beyond pleasure and pain. *American Psychologist, 52,* 1280–1300.

Higgins, E. T., Bond, R. N., Klein, R., and Strauman, T. (1986). Self-discrepancies and emotional vulnerability: How magnitude, accessibility, and type of discrepancy influence affect. *Journal of Personality and Social Psychology, 51,* 5–15.

Higgins, E. T., and Loeb, I. (in press). Development of regulatory focus: Promotion and prevention as ways of living. In J. Heckhausen and C. S. Dweck (Eds.), *Motivation and self-regulation across the life span.* London: Cambridge University Press.

Higgins, E. T., Roney, C., Crowe, E., and Hymes, C. (1994). Ideal versus ought predilections for approach and avoidance: Distinct self-regulatory systems. *Journal of Personality and Social Psychology, 66,* 276–86.

Higgins, E. T., Shah, J., and Friedman, R. (1997). Emotional responses to goal attainment: Strength of regulatory focus as moderator. *Journal of Personality and Social Psychology, 72,* 515–25.

Higgins, E. T., and Tykocinski, O. (1992). Self-discrepancies and biographical memory: Personality and cognition at the level of psychological situation. *Personality and Social Psychology Bulletin, 18,* 527–35.

Higgins, E. T., Vookles, J., and Tykocinski, O. (1992). Self and health: How "patterns" of self-beliefs predict types of emotional and physical problems. *Social Cognition, 10,* 125–50.

Hoffman, M. L. (1986). Affect, cognition, and motivation. In R. M. Sorrentino and E. T. Higgins (Eds.), *Handbook of motivation and cognition: Foundations of social behavior* (vol. 1, pp. 244–80). New York: Guilford.

Horney, K. (1939). *New ways in psychoanalysis.* New York: Norton.

———. (1950). *Neurosis and human growth.* New York: Norton.

Hull, C. L. (1952). *A behavior system: An introduction to behavior theory concerning the individual organism.* New Haven, Conn.: Yale University Press.

James, W. (1948). *Psychology.* New York: World Publishing Co. (Originally published in 1890)

Kahneman, D., and Tversky, A. (1979). Prospect theory: An analysis of decision under risk. *Econometrica, 47,* 263–91.

Kemper, T. D. (1978). *A social interactional theory of emotions.* New York: Wiley.

Konorski, J. (1967). *Integrative activity of the brain: An interdisciplinary approach.* Chicago: University of Chicago Press.

Lang, P. J. (1995). The emotion probe: Studies of motivation and attention. *American Psychologist, 50,* 372–85.

Larsen, R. J., and Diener, E. (1985). A multitrait-multimethod examination of affect structure: Hedonic level and emotional intensity. *Personality and Individual Differences, 6,* 631–36.

Lazarus, A. A. (1968). Learning theory and the treatment of depression. *Behavior Research and Therapy, 6,* 83–89.

Lazarus, R. S. (1966). *Psychological stress and the coping process.* New York: McGraw-Hill.

———. (1982). Thoughts on the relations between emotion and cognition. *American Psychologist, 37,* 1019–24.

Lewin, K. (1935). *A dynamic theory of personality.* New York: McGraw-Hill.

———. (1951). *Field theory in social science.* New York: Harper.

Lewis, H. B. (1979). Shame in depression and hysteria.

In C. E. Izard (Ed.), *Emotions in personality and psychopathology* (pp. 371–96). New York: Plenum Press. (Originally published in 1923)

Mandler, G. (1975). *Mind and emotion.* New York: Wiley.

McClelland, D. C., Atkinson, J. W., Clark, R. A., and Lowell, E. L. (1953). *The achievement motive.* New York: Appleton-Century-Crofts.

Mead, G. H. (1934). *Mind, self, and society.* Chicago: University of Chicago Press.

Meyer, G. J., and Shack, J. R. (1989). Structural convergence of mood and personality: Evidence for old and new directions. *Journal of Personality and Social Psychology, 57,* 691–706.

Mikulincer, M., Kedem, P., and Paz, D. (1990). The impact of trait anxiety and situational stress on the categorization of natural objects. *Anxiety Research, 2,* 85–101.

Miller, G. A., Galanter, E., and Pribram, K. H. (1960). *Plans and the structure of behavior.* New York: Holt, Rinehart, and Winston.

Miller, N. E. (1944). Experimental studies of conflict. In J. M. Hunt (Ed.), *Personality and the behavior disorders* (vol. 1, pp. 431–65). New York: Ronald Press.

Mowrer, O. H. (1960). *Learning theory and behavior.* New York: Wiley.

Oatley, K., and Johnson-Laird, P. (1987). Towards a cognitive theory of emotions. *Cognition and Emotion, 1,* 29–50.

Ortony, A., Clore, G. L., and Collins, A. (1988). *The cognitive structure of emotions.* New York: Cambridge University Press.

Pervin, L. A. (Ed.). (1989). *Goal concepts in personality and social psychology.* Hillsdale, N.J.: Erlbaum.

Piers, G., and Singer, M. B. (1971). *Shame and guilt.* New York: Norton.

Powers, W. T. (1973). *Behavior: The control of perception.* Chicago: Aldine.

Pribram, K. H. (1970). Feelings as monitors. In M. B. Arnold (Ed.), *Feelings and emotions.* New York: Academic Press.

———. (1984). Emotion: A neurobehavioral analysis. In K. R. Scherer and P. Ekman (Eds.), *Approaches to emotion* (pp. 13–38). Hillsdale, N.J.: Erlbaum.

Rogers, C. R. (1961). *On becoming a person.* Boston: Houghton Mifflin.

Roney, C. J. R., Higgins, E. T., and Shah, J. (1995). Goals and framing: How outcome focus influences motivation and emotion. *Personality and Social Psychology Bulletin, 21,* 1151–60.

Roseman, I. J. (1984). Cognitive determinants of emotion: A structural theory. *Review of Personality and Social Psychology, 5,* 11–36.

Roseman, I. J., Spindel, M. S., and Jose, P. E. (1990). Appraisals of emotion-eliciting events: Testing a theory of discrete emotions. *Journal of Personality and Social Psychology, 59,* 899–915.

Rotter, J. B. (1982). Some implications of a social learning theory for the practice of psychotherapy. In J. B. Rotter (Ed.), *The development and applications of social learning theory* (pp. 237–62). New York: CBS Educational and Professional Publishing.

Ruebush, B. K. (1960). Interfering and facilitating effects of test anxiety. *Journal of Abnormal and Social Psychology, 60,* 205–12.

Russell, J. A. (1978). Evidence of convergent validity on the dimensions of affect. *Journal of Personality and Social Psychology, 36,* 1152–68.

———. (1980). A circumplex model of affect. *Journal of Personality and Social Psychology, 39,* 1161–78.

Schachter, S. (1964). The interaction of cognitive and physiological determinants of emotional state. In L. Berkowitz (Ed.), *Advances in experimental social psychology* (pp. 49–80). New York: Academic Press.

Schachter, S., and Singer, J. E. (1962). Cognitive, social, and physiological determinants of emotional state. *Psychological Review, 69,* 379–99.

Scherer, K. R. (1988). Criteria for emotion-antecedent appraisal: A review. In V. Hamilton, G. H. Bower, and N. H. Frijda (Eds.), *Cognitive perspectives on emotion and motivation* (pp. 89–126). Norwell, Mass.: Kluwer.

Schwarz, N. (1990). Feelings as information: Informational and motivational functions of affective states. In E. T. Higgins and R. M. Sorrentino (Eds.), *Handbook of motivation and cognition: Foundations of social behavior* (vol. 2, pp. 527–61). New York: Guilford.

Schwarz, N., Bless, H., Strack, F., Klumpp, G., Rittenauer-Schatka, H., and Simons, A. (1991). Ease of retrieval as information: Another look at the availability heuristic. *Journal of Personality and Social Psychology, 61,* 195–202.

Schwarz, N., and Clore, G. L. (1996). Feelings and phenomenal experiences. In E. T. Higgins and A. W. Kruglanski (Eds.), *Social psychology: Handbook of basic principles* (pp. 433–65). New York: Guilford.

Scott, L., and O'Hara, M. W. (1993). Self-discrepancies in clinically anxious and depressed university students. *Journal of Abnormal Psychology, 102,* 282–87.

Shaver, P., Schwartz, J., Kirson, D., and O'Connor, C. (1987). Emotion knowledge: Further exploration of a prototype approach. *Journal of Personality and Social Psychology, 52,* 1061–86.

Skinner, B. F. (1953). *Science and human behavior.* New York: Macmillan.

Smith, C. A., and Ellsworth, P. C. (1985). Patterns of cognitive appraisal in emotion. *Journal of Personality and Social Psychology, 48,* 813–38.

Srull, T. K., and Wyer, R. S. (1986). The role of chronic and temporary goals in social information processing. In R. M. Sorrentino and E. T. Higgins (Eds.), *Handbook of motivation and cognition: Foundations of social behavior* (vol. 1, pp. 503–49). New York: Guilford.

Stein, N. L., and Jewett, J. L. (1982). A conceptual analysis of the meaning of negative emotions: Implications for a theory of development. In C. E. Izard (Ed.), *Measuring emotions in infants and children* (pp. 401–43). New York: Cambridge University Press.

Stein, N. L., Liwag, M. D., and Wade, E. (1996). A

goal-based approach to memory for emotional events: Implications for theories of understanding and socialization. In R. D. Kavanaugh, B. Zimmerberg, and S. Fein (Eds.), *Emotion: Interdisciplinary perspectives* (pp. 91–118). Mahwah, N.J.: Erlbaum.

Strack, F. (1992). The different routes to social judgments: Experiential versus informational strategies. In L. L. Martin and A. Tesser (Eds.), *The construction of social judgments* (pp. 249–75). Hillsdale, N.J.: Erlbaum.

Strauman, T. J. (1989). Self-discrepancies in clinical depression and social phobia: Cognitive structures that underlie emotional disorders? *Journal of Abnormal Psychology, 98,* 14–22.

———. (1990). Self-guides and emotionally significant childhood memories: A study of retrieval efficiency and incidental negative emotional content. *Journal of Personality and Social Psychology, 59,* 869–80.

Strauman, T. J., and Higgins, E. T. (1987). Automatic activation of self-discrepancies and emotional syndromes: When cognitive structures influence affect. *Journal of Personality and Social Psychology, 53,* 1004–14.

———. (1988). Self-discrepancies as predictors of vulnerability to distinct syndromes of chronic emotional distress. *Journal of Personality, 56,* 685–707.

Sullivan, H. S. (1953). *The collected works of Harry Stack Sullivan,* vol. 1, *The interpersonal theory of psychiatry.* Edited by H. S. Perry and M. L. Gawel. New York: Norton.

Tanner, W. P., Jr., and Swets, J. A. (1954). A decision-making theory of visual detection. *Psychological Review, 61,* 401–9.

Thorndike, E. L. (1935). *The psychology of wants, interests, and attitudes.* New York: Appleton-Century-Crofts.

Trope, Y., and Liberman, A. (1996). Social hypothesis testing: Cognitive and motivational mechanisms. In E. T. Higgins and A. W. Kruglanski (Eds.), *Social psychology: Handbook of basic principles* (pp. 239–70). New York: Guilford.

Van Hook, E., and Higgins, E. T. (1988). Self-related problems beyond the self-concept: The motivational consequences of discrepant self-guides. *Journal of Personality and Social Psychology, 55,* 625–33.

Watson, D., Clark, L. A., and Tellegen, A. (1984). Cross-cultural convergence in the structure of mood: A Japanese replication and a comparison with U.S. findings. *Journal of Personality and Social Psychology, 47,* 127–44.

Watson, D., and Tellegen, A. (1985). Toward a consensual structure of mood. *Psychological Bulletin, 98,* 219–35.

Weiner, B. (1982). The emotional consequences of causal attributions. In M. S. Clark and S. T. Fiske (Eds.), *Affect and cognition* (pp. 185–209). Hillsdale, N.J.: Erlbaum.

———. (1986). Attribution, emotion, and action. In R. M. Sorrentino and E. T. Higgins (Eds.), *Handbook of motivation and cognition: Foundations of social behavior* (vol. 1, pp. 281–312). New York: Guilford.

Wiener, N. (1948). *Cybernetics: Control and communication in the animal and the machine.* Cambridge, Mass.: MIT Press.

Wierzbicka, A. (1972). *Semantic primitives.* Frankfurt: Atheneum.

Zajonc, R. B. (1980). Feeling and thinking: Preferences need no inferences. *American Psychologist, 35,* 151–75.

ders; rather, depressive and anxiety disorders are better distinguished by levels of somatic tension (which tend to be higher in anxiety than in mood disorders) and hedonic capacity (which tend to be lower in depressive than in anxiety disorders) (Watson et al. 1995).

Sadness, fear, and worry are the result of undesirable outcomes, or the prospect of undesirable outcomes. For example, worry would be the result of anticipating an accident that would cause the loss of a limb, fear would be the result of perceiving an accident to be imminent (such as when they could see a quickly moving vehicle headed directly toward them), and sadness would be the result of having been in an accident and losing a limb. Individuals may experience excessive sadness, fear, and worry because they experience an extreme number, or an excessive intensity, of undesirable outcomes. Later we describe some of the research documenting a link between stressful conditions and events (what we refer to as environmental factors) and excesses in sadness, fear, and worry. Individuals may also experience excessive sadness, fear, and worry, not because they differ from most other people in terms of the events that occur to them, but because they are especially sensitive to undesirable outcomes. A variety of individual characteristics (what we refer to as intrapersonal factors) are associated with increased sensitivity to the impact of undesirable outcomes. After describing the direct impact of intrapersonal and environmental factors, we describe some of the ways in which interactions among these different factors contribute to excesses in sadness, fear, and worry.

Intrapersonal Factors

Genetic and Other Biological Factors   There is a plethora of evidence that genetic factors play a role in influencing excesses in sadness, fear, and worry. Both adoption and twin studies have found that depressive disorder is genetically influenced (McGuffin et al. 1996; Wender et al. 1986). Several twin studies have found that anxiety disorders are genetically influenced (Kendler et al. 1992a); unfortunately, adoption studies examining anxiety disorders have not been conducted. Consistent with the results of the studies that examined genetic influences on depressive and anxiety disorders, a twin study by Tellegen and his colleagues (1988) found evidence indicating that genes influence levels of negative emotionality (high levels of

which would be expected to be associated with excesses in sadness, fear, and worry). The findings reported by Tellegen and his colleagues are particularly convincing because they were replicated in samples of twins who had been reared apart. By studying twins reared apart, it is possible to rule out the greater relative resemblance of monozygotic (MZ) twins compared to dizygotic (DZ) twins as the result of their having been treated more similarly while they were growing up together. Kendler and his colleagues have conducted genetic multivariate analyses to examine whether high levels of depression and anxiety are influenced by common genetic factors. Based on analyses of a large sample of MZ and DZ twins who had completed questionnaire measures of depression and anxiety, Kendler, Heath, Martin, and Eaves (1987) concluded that genetic factors were not specific to either anxiety or depression, but rather that a common genetic diathesis contributed to both anxiety and depression. Kendler and his colleagues (1995) conducted a twin study examining six psychiatric disorders, including major depressive disorder, panic disorder, and generalized anxiety disorder. They did not find strong evidence of disorder-specific genes, though their results also suggested that multiple genes (albeit not disorder-specific genes) are needed to account for the genetic contributions to these psychiatric disorders.

A large body of evidence has linked different neurotransmitters with excesses in sadness, fear, and worry. Some of the evidence linking neurotransmitters with such excesses comes from drug treatment research. For example, drugs, such as fluoxetine (Prozac), that increase the functional availability of the neurotransmitter serotonin tend to be effective in treating not only depressive disorder but also obsessive-compulsive disorder. Some of the most convincing evidence indicating that neurotransmitters influence excesses in sadness, fear, and worry comes from research using the pharmacological challenge strategy: neurotransmitter levels are manipulated by administering various pharmacological substances or by manipulating the participant's diet. In particular, there is extensive support for the role of norepinephrine and serotonin in the pathogenesis of depressive symptoms. Miller and her colleagues (1996) found that a subset of individuals who had recently had major depressive episodes (but who were currently in remission) experienced a significant increase in depressed mood following a rapid reduction in norepinephrine levels. Other evidence linking functional unavailability of norepinephrine with excesses in sadness include the finding that many antidepressants increase the efficiency of norepinephrine systems in depressed patients (Golden et al. 1988).

Numerous lines of evidence have linked depressive symptoms with deficits in, or functional unavailability of, serotonin. As in the case of norepinephrine, compelling evidence for the role of serotonin in excessive sadness has been generated by manipulating levels of this neurotransmitter. For example, Neumeister and his colleagues (1997) found that reducing serotonin levels in a group of patients diagnosed with seasonal affective disorder (but who were currently in remission) led to a significant number of the patients redeveloping depressive symptoms. Additional evidence supporting a link between serotonin and depression comes from the finding that depressed patients' serotonin receptors have blunted responses to serotonin agonists (Stahl 1994).

Researchers have also noted a relationship between excesses in worry and the neurotransmitters serotonin and norepinephrine (Den Boer and Westernberg 1990). Goddard and his colleagues (1995) used the pharmacological challenge strategy to explore the roles of serotonin and norepinephrine in the genesis of anxious feelings. They found that participants with no history of psychiatric diagnoses reported experiencing significantly more nervousness when the availability of both serotonin and norepinephrine was lowered simultaneously. The striking behavioral effects of these manipulations of serotonergic and noradrenergic function provide evidence for the roles of these neurotransmitters in the pathophysiology of anxious symptoms. However, it should be noted that although pharmacological challenges that alter the functional availability of serotonin and norepinephrine typically alter anxiety levels, the precise pattern of results varies from study to study (Zohar and Insel 1987).

In addition to neurotransmitters, excesses in sadness have been associated with asymmetric patterns of regional brain activation (Heller, Etienne, and Miller 1995). A consistent finding that has emerged is that high levels of sadness are associated with relatively high activity of the right frontal area (Davidson 1992) and with reduced right parietotemporal activation (Tucker and Dawson 1984). Finally, a variety of neuroendocrine disturbances have been implicated in excesses in sadness and anxiety (Ferrier 1994). In particular, there is very strong evidence that overactivity in the hypo-thalamo-pituitary-adrenal (HPA) axis and oversecretion of cortisol is linked to excesses in sadness (Gold et al. 1986).

Schemas   Genes and other biological variables, such as functional neurotransmitter levels, are not the only intrapersonal variables that contribute to excesses in sadness, fear, and worry. Schemas are another intrapersonal factor that can contribute to emotional disturbance. Schemas can be thought of as generalizations about oneself, shaped from past experiences, that serve to organize, encode, retrieve, and evaluate relevant information to a particular domain (Markus 1977). Others have described schemas as cognitive structures made up of self-descriptive traits that are organized in such a way that activation of one trait leads to the activation of other related traits (Higgins, Van Hook, and Dorfman 1988). Schemas are generally enduring, precede the occurrence of stress, and are not dependent on the occurrence of stress for their existence.

One type of schema that has been linked with excesses in sadness, fear, and worry is the self-schema, the most sophisticated treatment of which can be found in self-discrepancy theory (Sullivan 1953). According to self-discrepancy theory, the relations between different types of self-beliefs produce specific emotional vulnerabilities (Higgins 1989). Higgins, Klein, and Strauman (1985) found that individuals who experienced a discrepancy between their ideal selves and their actual selves (that is, who they believed they were) were vulnerable to experiencing dejection-related problems, including sadness. On the other hand, individuals who experienced discrepancies between who they believed they were and the sort of person they (or some other significant person) felt duty-bound to be, were vulnerable to fear, worry, and agitation-related emotion problems.

A type of schema that has been linked to the development and maintenance of depression is the depressogenic schema, or belief (Kovacs and Beck 1978). Depressogenic beliefs are characterized by themes of deprivation, defeat, and loss, which in turn lead to negative views of the self, the world, and the future. Examples of depressogenic beliefs are "I am worthless" and "I am helpless" (Beck 1967). It has frequently been found that depressives are more likely than controls to report having automatic negative thoughts and to have more accessibility to negative constructs (Teasdale et al. 1995). Although anxiogenic beliefs, characterized by themes of danger, catastrophic loss of control, and negative changes in relationships, have been posited to be associated with excesses in fear and worry (Clark and Beck 1988), they have received far less attention than have depressogenic beliefs.

Environmental Factors

Childhood Environment Two types of events in childhood have consistently been found to be associated with excesses in sadness, fear, and worry—parental loss and childhood maltreatment. Parental loss, due to death or separation experienced during childhood, has been linked with major depressive disorder (Kendler et al. 1992b) and with anxiety disorders (Tweed et al. 1989). For example, Bifulco, Harris, and Brown (1992) found that losing one's mother before age seventeen, either by separation or death, doubled the risk of depressive and anxiety disorders.

Numerous investigators have found that childhood physical and sexual abuse are associated with excesses in anxiety and depression (for reviews, see Malinosky-Rummell and Hansen 1993; Polusny and Follette 1995). For example, in a sample of over two thousand randomly selected women from the community of Dunedin, New Zealand, Mullen, Martin, Anderson, Romans, and Herbison (1993) found that the rates of depressive and anxiety disorders were more than twice as high among women who had been sexually abused as they were among women who had not been sexually abused. Using dimensional measures of anxiety and depression in a sample of close to three thousand professional women, Elliott and Briere (1992) found that compared to women who had not been sexually abused, women who had been sexually abused had significantly higher levels of depression and anxiety.

Adult Stress Most of the research examining the impact of stress on psychiatric disturbance has focused on discrete negative life events (such as losing a spouse) that lead to dramatic changes in one's life (Brown and Harris 1978). Although they have not received as much attention as major life events, chronic difficulties (such as poverty and physical illness) and the accumulation of daily hassles (such as driving in traffic) that exceed the individual's capacity to cope have both been found to contribute to psychiatric problems (see also Brown and Harris, 1978; Kanner et al. 1981).

Much of the evidence demonstrating a link between stress and anxiety and mood disorders has examined whether individuals experienced more stressful life events preceding the onset of their emotional disturbance than they had experienced at other points in time. There is strong evidence that depressed individuals experience more stressful life events before the onset of their psychiatric disturbance than they had at earlier points in their life (Paykel and Dowlatshahi 1988); in particular, a marked excess of certain stressors, particularly those involving loss and disappointment, have been found to predict the onset of depression (Brown and Harris 1989). In addition to predicting the onset of depression, life stress increases the probability of individuals relapsing after having recovered from their initial depressive episode (Monroe et al. 1996).

The role of stress in anxiety disorders has received less attention than has the role of stress in mood disorders. Nonetheless, as with depression, the onset of anxiety disorders has been found to be associated with increased levels of stress (Pollard, Pollard, and Corn 1989). The impact of stress on depression and anxiety appears to be linked to several features of the stressor. In particular, the controllability and predictability of the stressor have been associated with the degree to which it contributes to excesses in sadness, fear, and worry (Mineka and Kihlstrom 1978; Seligman 1975). For example, Foa, Zinbarg, and Rothbaum (1992) proposed that stressors characterized by increased levels of uncontrollability and unpredictability are likely to develop excess fear and worry, as indicated by the presence of post-traumatic stress disorder (PTSD).

Interactions The path from etiological factors, such as stressors, genes, and neurotransmitters, to outcomes such as excesses in sadness, fear, and worry is generally indirect and complex. Even the factors already described influence and interact with one another. For example, although individual differences in functional neurotransmitter levels are typically thought of as genetically influenced biological factors, research examining war veterans and victims of childhood abuse suggest that trauma can influence neurotransmitter function (Arora et al. 1993; De Bellis et al. 1994). Similarly, Kendler, Neale, Kessler, Heath, and Eaves (1993) found that the number of stressful life events experienced in the past year in a sample of female twins appeared to be influenced by genetic factors. Thus, what at first glance appears to be a biological factor may be influenced by environmental factors, and what at first glance appears to be an environmental factor may be influenced by genetic factors. Later we describe some of the more important interactions that contribute to the development of excesses in sadness, fear, and worry. In particular, we focus on factors that influence the likelihood of environmental factors contributing to emotional disturbance.

Personal Relevance   The impact of stress depends on the degree to which the outcome is relevant to the most important concerns of the individual (Robins 1990). Individuals who value relationships with others (that is, who have a sociotropic or dependent personality style) are more vulnerable to negative interpersonal life events and are less vulnerable to failures in achievement domains. In contrast, individuals who are self-critical or more achievement-oriented (an autonomous or independent personality style) are vulnerable to a wider range of events that are not confined to achievement-oriented ones (Segal et al. 1992).

Coping   There is a growing body of research that focuses on coping as an important way of understanding how people respond to stress (Lazarus and Folkman 1984). The coping strategies or styles that have received the most attention include: (a) problem-focused or task-oriented coping, in which the individual attempts to engage in problem-solving and other actions with the goal of eliminating or reducing the source of stress; (b) emotion-focused coping, in which the individual does not attempt to eliminate the source of the stress but rather focuses on the experience and communication of emotion, with the goal of changing his or her experience of the stressor; and (c) avoidance coping, in which the individual attempts to distract himself or herself or divert attention away from the stressful situation. In general, problem-focused coping is associated with lower levels of depression, whereas emotion-focused coping is associated with higher levels of depression (Billings and Moos 1985).

The association between coping and anxiety has received less attention than has the association between coping and depression. However, there is some evidence suggesting that elevated levels of fear and worry are associated with lower levels of goal-oriented coping and with higher levels of avoidance coping (Vollrath, Alnaes, and Torgersen 1996). For example, individuals with anxiety disorders, such as obsessive-compulsive disorder and panic disorder with agoraphobia, exhibit an experiential avoidance style that is marked by unhealthy efforts to escape and avoid private experiences (emotions, thoughts) (Hayes et al. 1996).

Social Support   Another important factor that influences whether stress contributes to excesses in negative emotions is how much social support the person has (Sarason, Sarason, and Pierce 1990). For example, Collins, Dunkel-Schetter, Lobel, and Scrimshaw (1993) found that women who were dissatisfied with the prenatal support they received were at greater risk for depressed mood during pregnancy and to six to eight weeks postpartum. In addition, women with fewer prenatal network resources (family, close friends) experienced more postpartum sadness.

Cognitive Processes   Cognitive models of psychopathology emphasize the importance of what individuals attend to, as well as the ways in which they interpret and recall information. These models posit that differences in the ways in which individuals attend to, interpret, and recall information explain why the same environment or stressor can lead to excesses in sadness, fear, and worry in some individuals but not in others. In this section, we describe a variety of cognitive biases and attributional processes, each of which influences whether environmental stressors contribute to excesses in sadness, fear, and worry.

Individuals with excesses in anxiety are biased to attend to threat-related stimuli (Mathews and MacLeod 1994). For example, use of a modified Stroop task (in which the individual is presented with words printed in different colors, and rather than being asked to read the words, they are asked to name the colors in which the words are printed) has shown that highly anxious individuals are slower color-naming threat words than nonthreat words, suggesting that they have difficulty ignoring threat-relevant information (Bryant and Harvey 1995). This bias is especially prominent when negative words are self-descriptive or especially relevant to the individual. For example, individuals with social worries exhibit a high attentional bias toward social threat words, whereas individuals with physical worries exhibit a high attentional bias toward physical threat words (Mogg, Mathews, and Eysenck 1992). Although some research has found that depressives also have attentional biases (McCabe and Gotlib 1995), the findings concerning the association between depression and attentional biases are not as clear or consistent as are the findings concerning the association between anxiety and attentional biases.

Judgment biases have also been found to be associated with excesses in sadness, fear, and worry

(Butler and Mathews 1983). For example, when asked to judge the degree of control that their actions had over an outcome, depressed individuals gave lower, yet more accurate estimates of control than did nondepressed individuals (Alloy and Abramson 1982). Depressives exhibited a similar tendency to provide low (yet accurate) judgments of their own interpersonal performance, in contrast to nondepressed individuals, who tended to overestimate their levels of performance (Cane and Gotlib 1985). Anxious individuals tend to demonstrate judgment biases for negative events that are relevant to their specific fears (McNally and Foa 1987). For example, individuals with generalized social phobia are more likely than nonanxious controls to interpret social events (but not nonsocial events) as more costly and probable (Foa et al. 1996). Individuals suffering from agoraphobia and panic attacks typically interpret bodily sensations as threatening (Clark 1986).

Individuals experiencing excessive sadness exhibit memory biases in which, relative to controls, they are biased to recall negative information. This memory bias is most likely to be detected when the information is self-relevant and when an explicit (direct) test of memory is used, rather than when an implicit (indirect) test of memory is used (Watkins et al. 1992). A memory bias for negative information is also found in nondepressed individuals when negative mood is induced in the laboratory (Teasdale and Russell 1983). Although some studies have found evidence of a memory bias in anxious individuals (Burke and Mathews 1992), the evidence for a memory bias in anxious individuals remains somewhat tenuous (Mineka and Sutton 1992).

In addition to memory biases, individuals who have been diagnosed with anxiety disorders, or who have high levels of fear, exhibit what has been referred to as a covariation bias. Several studies have found that anxious and fearful individuals have a tendency to overestimate the covariation between fear-provoking stimuli and aversive outcomes (Tomarken, Mineka, and Cook 1989). For example, Tomarken, Sutton, and Mineka (1995) showed slides of flowers, mushrooms, damaged electrical outlets, and snakes to individuals with high levels of snake fear, as well as to controls. Each slide presentation was followed by the presentation of a tone, a shock, or nothing. Although the outcome pairings were equal across categories, individuals with high snake fear, but not controls, overestimated the covariation between snake slides and shock, but not between damaged electrical outlets and shock.

Cognitive models of psychopathology have probably devoted more attention to attributional processes than to any other cognitive process. Much of this work was stimulated by the reformulated theory of human helplessness and depression (Abramson, Seligman, and Teasdale 1978). In its most general form, attributional theories posit that the ways in which individuals perceive the causal nature of events (for example, perceiving oneself to have been responsible for an undesirable outcome) predisposes them to being vulnerable to excesses in sadness, fear, and worry. Numerous studies have found evidence of attributional style being associated with elevated levels of sadness and anxiety (Berenbaum et al. 1995). Abramson, Metalsky, and Alloy (1989) argued that the generalized tendency to attribute negative life events to stable, global causes (causes that are perceived to be unchanging and widespread) predisposes individuals to a particular type of depression they called hopelessness depression. Consistent with the predictions made by the hopelessness depression model, Metalsky, Joiner, Hardin, and Abramson (1993) found that a stable global attributional style (measured by a self-report attributional style questionnaire) interacted with a stressor (failure on an examination) to predict enduring depressive symptoms in college students.

Biological and Genetic Factors   There is quite a bit of research pointing to the interactions between stress, genetic and other biological factors, and mood (Carr 1996). For example, True and his colleagues (1993) measured combat exposure and symptoms of post-traumatic stress disorder in a sample of more than four thousand Vietnam veteran twin pairs. They found strong positive correlations between the amount of combat exposure and the presence and severity of PTSD symptoms. However, they also found greater MZ than DZ twin resemblance on measures of PTSD symptoms, indicating that such symptoms were also influenced by genetic factors. Thus, both trauma and genes combined to influence PTSD symptoms.

Cause or Consequence   There are some factors, such as genes and loss of parent during childhood, which can be safely assumed to play causal roles in the development of emotional disturbances. However, a critical issue that has received modest attention but has yet to be resolved is whether the other factors described in this chapter (such as stress, neuroendocrine disturbances, and memory biases) play causal roles or are merely consequences of emotional disturbance. Longitudinal (as opposed to cross-sectional) studies tend to support the notion that the factors we discuss here, such as attributional style, play causal roles (Alloy and Abramson 1997). Unfortunately, even longitudinal studies are often not sufficient to demonstrate causality because many of these factors, such as memory biases and stress, cannot be experimentally manipulated by researchers. Nonetheless, important trends in psychopathology research are the exploration of the possibility of bidirectional influences (such as stress influencing psychopathology, as well as psychopathology influencing stress; see, for example, Daley et al. 1997) and the examination of the associations between hypothesized etiological factors and the initial onset, the course, and the recurrence (following relapse) of psychiatric disturbance (Brown, Harris, and Hepworth 1994).

Guilt and Shame

Guilt and shame are two emotions that have received substantially less attention from psychopathologists than have sadness, fear, and worry. Excessive guilt and shame typically accompany excesses in other negative emotional states. At its extreme, individuals can exhibit delusional levels of guilt. An example of such a delusion is the individual who feels extreme guilt about the assassination of President Kennedy even though he or she could not possibly have had anything to do with it.

Helen Block Lewis (1971) theorized that guilt focuses on specific behaviors ("I did a horrible thing"), whereas shame focuses on the entire self ("I am a horrible person"); a growing body of evidence supports this distinction (Wallbott and Scherer 1995). Guilt appears to be associated with internal attributions for negative outcomes that are less global and stable than are the attributions associated with shame, and thus guilt is less debilitating (Tangney 1993). Excesses in shame and guilt have been observed among individuals who have experienced trauma, including rape victims (Moshe and Schneider 1992), political refugees (Orley 1995), concentration camp survivors (Lifton 1980), and incest survivors (Gold 1986). Survivor guilt, in which the victim feels guilty for being alive when family and friends have perished, has been described by many researchers (Lifton 1980). Since guilt and shame are presumed to be the result, at least in part, of internal attributions for undesirable outcomes, it is surprising that individuals who are clearly innocent victims should feel guilt and shame. One possible explanation for this

phenomenon is that individuals are prone to feel guilt and shame when the type or source of the undesirable event is secret or outside the realm of ordinary experience, thereby making external attributions more difficult.

Excesses in Emotional Arousal and Intensity

Excessive emotional arousal can be pathological. For example, excessive levels of emotional arousal are typically exhibited by individuals in manic episodes. It is worth noting that happiness is not necessarily the only, or even the primary, emotion exhibited by individuals in manic episodes. It is not unusual for individuals in manic episodes to exhibit extreme irritability. In fact, it is not especially uncommon for individuals in manic episodes to report experiencing sad mood (Swann et al. 1997). Mania is best characterized by disturbances in circadian rhythms and activation levels rather than by disturbances in particular moods (Bauer et al. 1991). Thus, the emotional disturbance exhibited by the individual in a manic episode is probably best characterized as excessive emotional arousal. Individuals in manic episodes often act in ways that are dangerous to themselves and others, such as driving their car at one hundred miles per hour or going on a spending spree in which they spend a month's salary in an afternoon, thereby jeopardizing their own well-being as well as that of those around them.

Emotional arousal has been posited to reflect both metabolic and neural activation of two primary motivation systems in the brain, the appetitive system (generally expressed by approach behaviors) and the aversive system (generally expressed by avoidant behaviors) (Lang 1995). In addition to being a phase of bipolar disorder, manic states can be drug-induced (by cocaine, for example). Thus, it is not surprising that manic episodes are associated with dysfunction of neurotransmitters such as dopamine (Joyce, et al. 1995). Additionally, there is abundant evidence that bipolar disorder is influenced by genetic factors (Mendlewicz and Rainer 1977).

Bipolar disorder is not the only psychiatric disturbance associated with excessive levels of emotional arousal or intensity. Individuals with personality disorders, particularly borderline personality disorder, tend to react very intensely to even minor events in their lives, both good and bad. Thus, such individuals can be described as having excessively high levels of what Larsen and Diener (1987) refer to as affect intensity. It is rather common for individuals with borderline personality disorder to have a history of being physically and sexually abused (Zanarini and Frankenburg 1997), and it is possible that such abuse may have predisposed them to developing excessive levels of emotional intensity. Individuals who as adults are exposed to traumatic events, such as a war (a subset of whom will be diagnosed with post-traumatic stress disorder), can also suffer excesses in emotional intensity, especially in anger and fear (Gunderson and Sabo 1993).

Deficits

Most of the attention devoted to psychopathology and emotion has been paid to the sorts of excesses described in the preceding section. However, there is another form of emotional disturbance that is studied by psychopathologists—emotional deficits. More specifically, psychopathologists have noted two types of emotional deficits. Deficits in hedonic capacity, or the ability to experience pleasure, have long been noted among individuals with a variety of psychiatric disturbances. Psychopathologists have also found that some individuals, particularly those who are considered psychopaths, have deficits in fear, guilt, and shame. Unlike emotional excesses, which tend to covary, these two types of emotional deficits appear to be independent.

Pleasure

In our view, one of the most interesting and important, yet understudied, emotional disturbances is a deficit in the ability to experience pleasure. The ability to experience pleasure is often referred to as hedonic capacity, and there is extensive evidence that there are stable individual differences in this characteristic (Chapman, Chapman, and Miller 1982). In extreme cases, individuals do not experience any pleasure whatsoever; psychopathologists typically refer to this phenomenon as anhedonia. When individuals have deficits in their ability to experience pleasure, they are likely to not engage in many activities, since doing so is unlikely to be reinforcing.

It is worth noting that the diminished ability to experience pleasure is not just another way of indicating that someone is sad or depressed. Although they are not completely independent, the distinction between sadness (and negative affect) and the ability to experience pleasure (and positive affect, with which the experience of pleasure is positively correlated) has been demonstrated numerous times (Berenbaum and Connelly 1993). Some individuals who report substantial levels of sadness nevertheless also report being able to experience pleasure, whereas some individuals who do not report being sad report experiencing relatively little pleasure. In fact, the finding that some individuals can report profound sadness yet are capable of experiencing pleasure is central to one of the most important means of subtyping major depressive disorder. The diminished ability to experience pleasure has been described as a central feature of what is typically referred to as melancholic, or endogenomorphic depression (Klein 1974), whereas the capacity to experience pleasure in response to pleasant events is a central feature of what is typically referred to as atypical depression (Quitkin et al. 1990).

The factors that contribute to the diminished experience of pleasure have received surprisingly little attention. There is modest evidence that the ability to experience pleasure is genetically influenced. Dworkin and Saczynski (1984) measured hedonic capacity, using Minnesota Multiphasic Personality Inventory (MMPI) and California Psychological Inventory (CPI) hedonic capacity scales in a nonclinical sample of MZ and DZ twins. Berenbaum, Oltmanns, and Gottesman (1990) measured hedonic capacity using responses to interview questions designed to tap the ability to experience pleasure, in a special sample of MZ and DZ twins in which all of the probands had diagnoses of schizophrenia. (Some of the co-twins also had diagnoses of schizophrenia, some had other psychiatric disturbances, and some did not have any psychiatric disturbance.) In both studies, the MZ twins resembled one another more than did the DZ twins, suggesting that the ability to experience pleasure is genetically influenced. The findings of Tellegen and his colleagues (1988) provide additional evidence suggesting that hedonic capacity is genetically influenced. They found that MZ twins resembled each other more than did DZ twins on a questionnaire measure of positive emotionality (which would be expected to be associated with hedonic capacity). Their findings are especially important because they were replicated in samples of twins who had been reared apart. Interestingly, both Berenbaum, Oltmanns, and Gottesman (1990) and Tellegen and his colleagues (1988) found that DZ twins did not tend to resemble each other (on measures of hedonic capacity and positive emotionality) any more than would be expected by chance. These results are important because they suggest that there are non-additive genetic factors that influence hedonic capacity. More specifically, these results suggest that hedonic capacity may be an emergence trait, that is, a trait that is influenced by configurations of multiple genes (Lykken et al. 1992).

Davidson (1992) has proposed that approach behavior is associated with relative activation levels of the left anterior portion of the brain. Along with some of the empirical findings reported by Davidson and his colleagues, this proposal suggests that left frontal lobe activation is associated with the experience of pleasure. For example, Wheeler, Davidson, and Tomarken (1993) found that higher baseline levels of left frontal activation were associated with higher levels of positive emotional experience (based on self-reported levels of happiness, interest, and amusement) in response to film clips intended to elicit positive emotions. In another study, Ekman, Davidson, and Friesen (1990) examined brain activity when participants were viewing film clips. They found that at those points in time (while viewing positive film clips) when participants were exhibiting Duchenne smiles (which are associated with the spontaneous occurrence of enjoyment), they had elevated levels of left anterior activation.

In addition to left frontal lobe activation, there are theoretical and empirical reasons to expect central dopaminergic activity to be associated with the experience of pleasure. Research on nonhumans has found that dopamine plays an important role in reward (Wise 1982). Theorizing and research examining the role of dopamine in reward and pleasure are not limited to nonhumans. Depue and his colleagues (see, for example, Depue and Iacono 1989) have described a neurological system responsible for approach behavior and reward-seeking that they have called the behavioral facilitation system (BFS). The BFS described by Depue resembles the approach system described earlier by Gray (1970) and later renamed the behavioral activation system (BAS) by Fowles (1980). Both the BFS and BAS have been posited to be associated with dopaminergic activity. To test their hypothesis that dopaminergic activity is associated with the BFS, Depue, Lucian, Arbisis, Collins, and Leon (1994) examined the association between trait levels of positive emotionality (which is associated with the experience of pleasure) and participants' reactivity to a pharmacological challenge in which they ingested a dopamine agonist, bromocriptine. As predicted, these investigators found that physiological reactivity to the dopamine agonist was specifically associated

with positive emotionality. Additional evidence of a role for dopamine in the experience of pleasure comes from research examining levels of the dopamine metabolite homovanillic acid (HVA) in the cerebrospinal fluid (CSF) of individuals with melancholic depression (which is associated with pleasure deficits). Asberg and her colleagues (1984) found that melancholic depressives had lower levels of CSF HVA than did nonpsychiatric controls, and Roy and his colleagues (1985) found that melancholic depressives had lower levels of CSF HVA than did nonmelancholic depressives. Thus, there is converging evidence from human research suggesting that brain dopamine functioning is associated with the experience of pleasure.

Individual differences in the ability to experience pleasure have also been found to be associated with individual differences in information-processing, as measured by performance on cognitive tasks and by evoked response potentials (ERPs) (a psychophysiological index of cortical activity measured following the presentation of a stimulus). For example, Yee and Miller (1994) included a group of anhedonic college students in a study in which P300 ERPs were measured during a memory task. Their examination of participants' P300s led these investigators to conclude that anhedonics differed from controls in both their attentional capacities and in their allocation of attentional resources. In another ERP study, Miller (1996) found that depressives did not exhibit the expected N400 ERP to positive words and hypothesized that these results were due to the depressives being anhedonic. Simons, Fitzgibbons, and Fiorito (1993) described a series of studies in which they compared anhedonic and control participants' self-reported and psychophysiological responses to emotion-eliciting stimuli and instructions. These investigators found consistent evidence that the anhedonic participants processed the emotional stimuli differently than controls; compared to controls, the anhedonic participants were less psychophysiologically reactive to images regardless of whether these images were pleasant or unpleasant. These investigators also found that anhedonic participants reported having less vivid images (for example, picturing a red apple and feeling the prick of a pin) than did controls. Simons, Fitzgibbons, and Fiorito (1993) proposed that anhedonics differ from controls in the ways in which emotion information is represented in memory. More specifically, they proposed that anhedonics have less coherent positive and negative emotion memory prototypes than do non-anhedonics.

Environmental factors are also associated with

the experience of pleasure. In two separate studies, Berenbaum and Connelly (1993) found that stress led to a significant reduction in the experience of pleasure. In their first study, Berenbaum and Connelly (1993) found that ROTC cadets reported experiencing less pleasure while viewing amusing film clips on a day when they had engaged in challenging field training exercises than they did on a control day; in their second study, they found that college students reported enjoying ordinarily pleasurable daily activities less during final exam week than they usually did. In both studies, the effect of stress on hedonic capacity was distinguishable from its effect on negative affect. The most interesting result reported by Berenbaum and Connelly was that the deleterious impact of stress on hedonic capacity was especially pronounced for those individuals with family histories of depression. These results suggest the possibility of a gene-stress interaction influencing the capacity to experience pleasure.

Fear, Guilt, and Shame

Just as some individuals experience little or no pleasure, there are some individuals who experience extremely little, if any, fear, guilt, or shame. It is important to note that although such individuals do not themselves experience this state of affairs as unpleasant, their impact on the well-being of those around them can be striking, as described later in this chapter.

The form of psychopathology with which deficits in the experience of fear, guilt, and shame is most strongly associated is psychopathy. Contemporary views of psychopathy have been strongly influenced by Cleckley's (1941) classic description of a group of individuals who had violated social norms and harmed others yet were not typical criminals. Cleckley developed a list of sixteen criteria that he used to define psychopathy; in addition to antisocial behavior, the list included the absence of nervousness and a lack of remorse or shame. For example, a psychopath would feel no more anxious kidnapping and murdering someone than the average person would feel walking into a grocery store and buying a quart of milk; in addition, the psychopath would feel no remorse or shame about having kidnapped and killed the person. Lykken (1957) was the first person to obtain laboratory evidence of a fear deficit in psychopathy.

The results of family, twin, and adoption studies suggest that psychopathy is genetically influenced

(Cloninger and Gottesman 1987). However, the role of genetic factors in deficits in fear, guilt, and shame is not clear because the studies in this area have varied in the phenotype they have examined (ranging from criminality to antisocial personality disorder) and none have directly examined the role of genetic factors in emotional deficits. A variety of different neurobiological factors have been posited to be associated with psychopathy (Dolan 1994). Although several biochemicals, such as serotonin and monoamine oxidase, have been found to be associated with aggression and impulsivity (Coccaro et al. 1996), their associations with deficits in fear, guilt, and shame remain unclear.

Gray (1970) and Fowles (1980) proposed that psychopathy is caused by an underactive, neurologically based behavioral inhibition system (BIS). Gorenstein and Newman (1980) proposed a septal lesion model to account for the disinhibition seen in psychopathy, and Newman and colleagues (for example, Patterson and Newman 1993) have attempted to clarify how and why information-processing and response biases are linked to disinhibition. Hare and colleagues have proposed that psychopathy is associated with left hemisphere underarousal and with deviant lateralization of language functions (for example, Hare and McPherson 1984). There is growing evidence that psychopathy is associated with deviations in the processing of emotion-relevant and emotion-eliciting stimuli (Day and Wong 1996), and such deficits may be most strongly linked to the emotion-deficit features of psychopathy (Patrick, Bradley, and Lang 1993).

A variety of family and other environmental factors have been found to be associated with antisocial behavior; some of the more consistent predictors of antisocial behavior are child maltreatment, lack of appropriate parental supervision, and poverty (Robins 1966; Yoshikawa 1994). Although much is known about the factors that contribute to antisocial behavior, it is not yet clear which, if any, family and environmental factors contribute to psychopathy and deficits in fear, guilt, and shame. Several studies have found that family and environmental factors interact with genetic or biological factors in influencing antisocial behavior. For example, Cadoret, Yates, Troughton, Woodworth, and Stewart (1995) examined antisocial behavior in a sample of individuals who had been adopted within several days of birth. The biological parents of the adoptees varied in terms of whether they had a history of antisocial behavior. The adoptive families varied in terms of whether they had marital, legal, and/or substance abuse problems. Cadoret and colleagues found that having biological relatives with antisocial histories contributed to elevated rates of antisocial behavior in their adopted offspring, as did being raised in adverse adoptive environments. Most important, there was a significant interaction of genetic and environmental factors, with individuals who had both genetic and environmental risk factors being especially likely to exhibit antisocial problems. Similarly, Raine, Brennan, Mednick, and Mednick (1996) found evidence of an environment-biology interaction: those individuals who had neuromotor deficits during the first year of life and who also grew up in unstable family environments were far more likely to develop antisocial problems than any other group of participants they studied.

DISCONNECTIONS

Although excesses and deficits are the most common and well-known emotional disturbances studied by psychopathologists, another type of disturbance is what we label disconnections. We describe two types of disconnections, affect[4] disconnections and awareness disconnections. The defining characteristic of disconnections is that different parts of the emotion system are disconnected from one another. In some ways, disconnection disturbances appear to resemble the excesses and deficits described earlier. For instance, in the first example of an affect disconnection we provide, that produced by Moebius syndrome, individuals have a deficit in their facial expression of pleasure. However, we consider the emotional disturbance exhibited in Moebius syndrome to be an affect disconnection rather than a pleasure deficit for two reasons: there is a deficit in only one aspect of pleasurable emotion, the production of facial expressions of pleasure; and what we believe is especially noteworthy is that one part of the emotion system (the production of facial expressions of emotion) is disconnected from other parts of the emotion system (such as the subjective experience of emotion).

Affect Disconnections

Neurological conditions that impair the normal production of affect, producing what we label affect disconnection, can have profound effects on well-being. For example, a young girl with Moebius syndrome (which, among other things,

causes paralysis of facial muscles) was described in the July 15, 1996, issue of *People* magazine as having "difficulty eating, for instance, and in pronouncing words. But the most psychologically traumatic result was that she simply could not smile" (54). The inability to smile, even when happy, is an example of what we are calling affect disconnection. There are neurological conditions other than Moebius syndrome that result in affect disconnections. For example, some individuals do not display vocal or facial affect even at times when they report feeling quite happy or sad, whereas other individuals will exhibit intense affect (even weeping or laughing) at times when they report feeling a complete absence of emotion (Black 1982; Ross and Mesulam 1979).

Affect disconnections are also found in individuals with psychiatric disturbance. Laboratory research has found that it is not uncommon for individuals with schizophrenia to have a deficit in the degree to which they exhibit affect, even though they do not differ from control participants in their reported experience of emotion. Such findings suggest that affective flattening in schizophrenia is the result of a disconnection between the production of affect and the other elements of the emotion system (Berenbaum and Oltmanns 1992). It has been proposed that the source of this affect disconnection in schizophrenia is a neuromotor disturbance (Stolar et al. 1994).

Awareness Disconnections

Awareness disconnections are disturbances in which the individual does not have access to, or is not aware of, emotional information, even though the emotion itself may be present. One of the core features of alexithymia is the diminished ability to identify one's own emotional state (Taylor 1984). Since high levels of alexithymia are associated with a variety of disturbances in physical and mental health (Taylor, Bagby, and Parker 1997), we consider alexithymia to be an example of an awareness disconnection.[5] Heiberg and Heiberg (1978) found that dizygotic twins had larger intrapair differences in levels of alexithymia than did monozygotic twins, suggesting that genetic factors contribute to alexithymia. There is some evidence suggesting that alexithymia may be associated with deficits in the functioning of the right hemisphere (Parker, Taylor, and Bagby 1992) and in the interhemispheric transfer of information (Zeitlin et al. 1989). There is also a growing body of evidence linking alexithymia with trauma and other environmental factors, such as rape, military combat, and concentration camp experiences (Zeitlin, McNally, and Cassiday 1993). Berenbaum and James (1994) found that individuals who reported having grown up in environments in which family members were not permitted to act openly and to express their feelings directly, or in which they felt emotionally unsafe, had elevated levels of alexithymia. Berenbaum (1996) found that high levels of alexithymia were associated with a history of being physically and/or sexually abused during childhood.

INDIVIDUAL AND SOCIETAL CONSEQUENCES OF EMOTIONAL DISTURBANCE

The degree of suffering experienced by individuals with emotional disturbances can be remarkably profound. The impact of emotional and psychiatric disturbance is not limited to subjective feelings of well-being. The emotional disturbances we have described, and the psychiatric disorders with which they are associated, also have many negative financial, role-functioning, interpersonal, health, and life-span consequences.[6] Traditionally, the consequences of disturbances in emotion have focused on the individual with the emotional disturbance. However, it is important to recognize that individuals with emotional disturbances often have a profound impact on the levels of well-being and suffering of others around them. Thus, in addition to describing the consequences of emotional disturbance for the individual with the disturbance, we also describe some of the devastating impacts that such individuals have on others.

Individuals with disturbances in emotion experience disruption in all spheres of life. For example, individuals with diagnoses of panic disorder and depression had significantly lower role-functioning in normal daily activities than individuals with chronic medical illness (Sherbourne, Wells, and Judd 1996). Individuals with emotional disturbances have difficulty maintaining steady employment and often do not work at all (Mintz et al. 1992). Disturbances in emotion appear to increase the risk of homelessness.[7] For example, it is estimated that approximately 25 percent of homeless people have mood disorders (Fischer and Breakey 1991). In addition to affecting individuals, emotional disturbance has an impact on society at large. The financial cost to society is staggering. For example, in 1994 the annual financial cost of depression in the United States was estimated at $44 billion (Finklestein 1994). These staggering numbers are the result of numerous factors, including the costs of direct treatment and support, reduced or lost productivity, mortality, and crime.

Research has demonstrated the negative impact that individuals with psychiatric problems, such as depressive disorder, can have on the individuals with whom they interact (Gotlib and Robinson 1982). Therefore, it is not surprising that individuals with disturbances in emotion have poor interpersonal relationships (Fadden, Bebbington, and Kuipers 1987), including marriages characterized by negative affect, tension, and overt hostility (Coyne 1985). Such strains frequently result in anxiety, guilt, and depression in family members (Arey and Warheit 1980).

There is extensive evidence that a variety of psychiatric disturbances contribute to higher rates of physical illness (Hall and Beresford 1984). Some research has examined the links between physical illness and specific emotional disturbances. For example, excessive anger and hostility are associated with poor cardiovascular health (Friedman 1992), and high levels of alexithymia are associated with a variety of medical problems such as diabetes (Abramson et al. 1991) and hypertension (Isaksson, Konarski, and Theorell 1992).

Research has linked a variety of psychiatric disorders, and disturbances in emotion, to higher mortality from natural causes (Berren et al. 1994). It is not just psychiatric disorders that are associated with higher mortality rates. For example, in a prospective, longitudinal study of over two thousand men, those men with elevated levels of alexithymia had a twofold risk of death that could not be accounted for by behavioral or physiological risk factors (Kauhanen et al. 1996).

Suicide is the eighth leading cause of death in the United States, causing roughly the same number of deaths as motor vehicle accidents or HIV infection (U.S. Bureau of the Census 1996). The rate of suicide is probably somewhere between 10 and 15 percent among individuals with major depressive disorder and bipolar disorder (Isometsa 1993). It is not only mood disorders, however, that are associated with suicide. For example, suicide rates of 10 percent or higher have been found among individuals with schizophrenia (Roy 1992), anxiety disorders (Noyes 1991), and alcohol abuse (Frances, Franklin, and Flavin 1987).

Most of the research on suicide has been conducted at the level of diagnostic categories. The little research that has examined specific emotions has found that suicide and suicide attempts are associated with elevated levels of anger (Lehnert, Overholser, and Spirito 1994), anxiety (Keller and

Hanks 1995), guilt (Hendin and Haas 1991), sadness (Apter, Plutchik, and van Praag 1993), and shame (Wandrei 1985).

Disturbances in emotion also affect mortality when disturbed individuals commit homicides. For example, it appears that a disproportionately large number of homicides are committed by individuals with disturbances in emotion (Eronen, Hakola, and Tiihonen 1996). Perhaps the most devastating consequence of disturbances in emotion is mass homicide. It seems quite plausible that leaders such as Stalin, Pol Pot, Hitler, and Idi Amin, who were responsible for sadistic purges and tortures, had emotional disturbances. It would be both simplistic and wrong to argue that disturbances in emotion alone could have motivated scores of brutal leaders and policy-makers to plan mass murders, without acknowledging the complex social, historical, and economic factors that surrounded the rule of these leaders. Nonetheless, a variety of secondary sources (Ferril 1991) lead us to suggest that the beliefs and actions of such brutal leaders can be explained, at least in part, by excesses of anger and deficits in fear, shame, and guilt.

WIDESPREAD IMPLICATIONS FOR WELL-BEING OF PSYCHOPATHOLOGY RESEARCH

Our goal in this final section of the chapter is to summarize briefly what the research on psychopathology and emotion can tell us about well-being in all individuals, not just those with psychiatric disturbance. The first point we wish to make is that virtually all individuals are influenced, directly or indirectly, by the consequences of psychopathology. For example, as noted earlier, the cost of psychiatric disturbance to society (and hence, indirectly, to all members of society)[8] is staggering. Psychiatric disturbance also influences homelessness and crime (including homicide), both of which affect most members of society, regardless of their own psychiatric status. Thus, if societal wealth, homelessness, and crime influence the well-being of most members of society, then we must conclude that the well-being of most members of society is influenced by psychiatric disturbance.

In addition to the indirect effects of psychiatric disturbance, many if not most individuals come into contact with psychiatrically disturbed individuals. There can be little doubt, for example, that individuals who have the misfortune of coming into contact with psychopaths are likely to suffer reductions in their levels of well-being. Psychopaths are not the only individuals with psychiatric disturbance who can affect the well-being of those who interact with them. There is abundant evidence that even brief interactions with psychiatrically disturbed individuals, such as individuals with depressive disorder, lead to higher levels of negative affect (Coyne 1976). There is also abundant evidence indicating that individuals with psychiatric disturbance are prone to induce negative affect in individuals with whom they have ongoing relationships (Hokanson et al. 1989). It should come as no surprise, therefore, that marital distress is associated with depressive and anxiety disorders in one of the partners (McLeod 1994).

Psychopathology research is relevant to the well-being of all individuals not just because of the impact of psychiatric disturbance on well-being, but also because the etiological factors that contribute to psychiatric disturbance influence the well-being of the vast majority of individuals. There are several reasons to expect the link between well-being and the etiological factors described in this chapter to not be limited to a small number of individuals. Epidemiological evidence suggests that approximately one out of every two individuals will develop a diagnosable psychiatric disturbance at some point in their lives (Kessler et al. 1994). Many of the etiological factors described in this chapter are common, and others are ubiquitous. For example, all individuals encounter stress. In fact, interviews with a representative national sample of women in the United States revealed that more than two-thirds of them had been exposed to some sort of trauma at some point in their lives (Resnick et al. 1993). Similarly, all individuals have genes relevant to the functional activity of neurotransmitters such as dopamine and serotonin. A related point is that most of the etiological factors described in this chapter are dimensional rather than being present or absent. For example, it is not the case that individuals do or do not experience stress, but rather that individuals vary in the number and severity of the stressors they encounter. Most, if not all, of the emotional phenomena discussed in this chapter are dimensional. For example, variations in levels of sadness and pleasure are continuous rather than categorical (for example, present versus absent). Thus, it is not just that severe levels of stress are associated with extreme (or disturbed) levels of sadness; the available evidence suggests that the association between stress and sadness is continuous rather than discontinuous. In other words, the more stress an individual experiences, the more sad he or she is likely to feel. Consequently, the level of sadness for all individuals (regardless of whether they have a psychiatric disturbance) should be expected to be associated with the degree of stress they have encountered. Finally, most of the etiological factors described in this chapter can be thought of as bipolar in nature: one pole is associated with emotional disturbance and lower levels of well-being, and the other pole with higher levels of well-being. For example, whereas poor parental supervision, low levels of social support, and biases to attend to and recall unpleasant information are all associated with emotional disturbance and lower levels of well-being, it seems likely that good parental supervision, high levels of social support, and biases to attend to and recall pleasant information are all associated with higher levels of well-being.

Our review of disturbances in emotion revealed several themes that we believe are relevant to understanding well-being in all individuals, not just those with psychiatric disturbance. One observation from psychopathology research that is probably worth attending to when trying to understand well-being is that the absence of pleasure and the presence of distress emotions are not merely two ends of a single bipolar dimension. Individuals can experience profound levels of sadness or anxiety and still be capable of experiencing pleasure. Similarly, there is evidence that some individuals can have deficits in the experience of pleasure yet not report excesses in distress emotions. Furthermore, there is evidence suggesting that pleasure and distress emotions are influenced by different genes and have different neurological correlates. Psychopathology research also reveals that what we are calling distress emotions, such as fear and guilt, are not necessarily negative or bad. In fact, the absence of such emotions can have rather profound deleterious consequences, as demonstrated by individuals with deficits in fear, guilt, and worry, such as psychopaths. Another important finding in the psychopathology literature is that there can be disturbances in emotional arousal and intensity that are independent of the particular emotion being experienced. For example, individuals in manic episodes have heightened levels of emotional arousal, and individuals with personality disorders, such as borderline personality disorder, have a tendency to react quite intensely to all events, regardless of the specific emotion that is elicited. These observations suggest that individuals' levels of well-being are probably influenced not only by the types of emotions they experience and how frequently they experience them, but by the arousal and intensity of their emotions. The results of psychopathology research have also demonstrated that disconnections between different parts of the emotion system can have undesirable consequences. Such findings demonstrate the utility of emotions. For example, those individuals who cannot benefit from their emotional experiences because they are not aware of them (individuals with high levels of alexithymia) tend to have a variety of disturbances in physical and mental health. Thus, well-being in all individuals is probably influenced not just by the types, frequencies, and intensities of the emotions they experience but also by the degree to which they can benefit from their emotional responses in various ways, such as through awareness of their emotions and through social communication of their emotions through facial expressions. Finally, the findings of psychopathology research are useful for reminding well-being researchers of something that is hardly surprising but is easily forgotten or ignored—just as emotional disturbances are multidetermined and influenced by complex interactions over time between different etiological factors, the same is surely true of well-being in all individuals.

Notes

1. Approaching psychopathology through means other than traditional diagnostic categories is hardly novel. See Costello (1992), Hayes, Wilson, Gifford, Follette, and Strosahl (1996), and Persons (1986) for examples of critiques of research that focuses exclusively on traditional diagnostic categories and discussions of how to conceptualize and study psychopathology without focusing on traditional psychiatric disorders.
2. Such inferences should be viewed with caution for a variety of reasons. For example, although the vast majority of individuals who receive a diagnosis of major depressive disorder experience excessive sadness, it is possible to be diagnosed with major depressive disorder without experiencing excessive sadness. Also, no psychiatric disorder is associated exclusively with a single type of emotional disturbance. For example, individuals with major depressive disorder tend to be anxious in addition to being sad, and individuals with anxiety disorders tend to be sad in addition to being anxious.
3. We prefer the term "distress" to the term "negative" because emotions such as fear, guilt, and anger typically are experienced as distressing, and we do not consider them to be inherently negative.
4. We are using the word *affect* as it is typically defined in the field of psychiatry, such as the following definition from the American Psychiatric Association's *Diagnostic and Statistical Manual of Mental Disorders* (1994): "a

pattern of observable behaviors that is the expression of a subjectively experienced feeling state" (763).

5. Dissociation, which is associated with alexithymia (Berenbaum and James 1994), is another type of awareness disconnection. Space limitations prevent us from discussing dissociation.

6. Depending on how well-being is defined, phenomena such as physical health and role-functioning can be considered contributors to well-being, consequences of well-being, or facets of well-being itself.

7. The association between homelessness and psychiatric disturbance is actually rather complex, with each influencing the other.

8. Owing to space limitations, we have not focused on the relevance of psychopathology for well-being at the societal level (the well-being of society as a whole can be distinguished conceptually from the well-being of the sum of the individuals in the society; see Shinn [1990]) but instead have focused exclusively on well-being at the level of the individual.

REFERENCES

Abramson, J., McClelland, D. C., Brown, D., and Kelner, S. (1991). Alexithymic characteristics and metabolic control in diabetic and healthy adults. *Journal of Nervous and Mental Disease, 179,* 490–94.

Abramson, L. Y., Metalsky, G. I., and Alloy, L. B. (1989). Hopelessness depression: A theory-based subtype of depression. *Psychological Review, 96,* 358–72.

Abramson, L. Y., Seligman, M. E. P., and Teasdale, J. (1978). Learned helplessness in humans: Critique and reformulation. *Journal of Abnormal Psychology, 87,* 49–74.

Alloy, L. B., and Abramson, L. Y. (1982). Learned helplessness, depression, and the illusion of control. *Journal of Personality and Social Psychology, 42,* 1114–26.

———. (1997). The Temple-Wisconsin Cognitive Vulnerability to Depression Project: Lifetime prevalence and prospective incidence of axis I psychopathology. Paper presented at the meeting of the Midwestern Psychological Association, Chicago (May).

American Psychiatric Association. (1994). *Diagnostic and statistical manual of mental disorders.* 4th ed. Washington, D.C.: American Psychiatric Association.

Apter, A., Plutchik, R., and van Praag, H. M. (1993). Anxiety, impulsivity, and depressed mood in relation to suicidal and violent behavior. *Acta Psychiatrica Scandinavica, 87,* 1–5.

Arey, S., and Warheit, G. J. (1980). Psychological costs of living with psychiatrically disturbed family members. In L. Robbins, P. Clayton, and J. K. Wing (Eds.), *The social consequences of psychiatric illness* (pp. 158–75). New York: Brunner/Mazel.

Arora, R. C., Fichtner, C. G., O'Connor, F., and Crayton, J. W. (1993). Paroxetine binding in the blood platelets of post-traumatic stress disorder patients. *Life Sciences, 53,* 919–28.

Asberg, M., Bertilsson, L., Martensson, B., Scalia-Tomba, G. P., Thoren, P., and Traskman-Bendz, L.

(1984). CSF monoamine metabolites in melancholia. *Acta Psychiatrica Scandinavica, 69,* 201–19.

Bauer, M. S., Crits-Cristoph, P., Ball, W. A., Dewees, E., McAllister, T., Alahi, P., Cacciola, J., and Whybrow, P. C. (1991). Independent assessment of mania and depressive symptoms by self-rating. *Archives of General Psychiatry, 48,* 807–12.

Beck, A. T. (1967). *Depression: Clinical, experimental, and theoretical aspects.* New York: Harper & Row.

Berenbaum, H. (1992). Posed facial expressions of emotion in schizophrenia and depression. *Psychological Medicine, 22,* 929–37.

———. (1996). Childhood abuse, alexithymia, and personality disorder. *Journal of Psychosomatic Research, 41,* 585–95.

Berenbaum, H., and Connelly, J. (1993). The effect of stress on hedonic capacity. *Journal of Abnormal Psychology, 102,* 474–81.

Berenbaum, H., Fujita, F., and Pfennig, J. (1995). Consistency, specificity, and correlates of negative emotions. *Journal of Personality and Social Psychology, 68,* 342–52.

Berenbaum, H., & James, T. (1994). Correlates and retrospectively reported antecedents of alexithymia. *Psychosomatic Medicine, 56,* 353–59.

Berenbaum, H., and Oltmanns, T. F. (1992). Emotional experience and expression in schizophrenia and depression. *Journal of Abnormal Psychology, 101,* 37–44.

Berenbaum, H., Oltmanns, T. F., & Gottesman, I. I. (1990). Hedonic capacity in schizophrenics and their twins. *Psychological Medicine, 20,* 367–74.

Berren, M. R., Hill, K., Merikle, E., Gonzalez, N. (1994). Serious mental illness and mortality rates. *Hospital and Community Psychiatry, 45,* 604–5.

Bifulco, A., Harris, T., and Brown, G. W. (1992). Mourning or early inadequate care? Reexamining the relationship of maternal loss in childhood with adult depression and anxiety. *Development and Psychopathology, 4,* 433–49.

Billings, A. G., and Moos, R. H. (1985). Life stressors and social resources affect post-treatment outcomes among depressed patients. *Journal of Abnormal Psychology, 94,* 140–53.

Black, D. W. (1982). Pathological laughter: A review of the literature. *Journal of Nervous and Mental Disease, 170,* 67–71.

Brown, G. W., and Harris, T. (1978). *Social origins of depression.* London: Tavistock.

——— (Eds.). (1989). *Life events and illness.* New York: Guilford.

Brown, G. W., Harris, T. O., and Hepworth, C. (1994). Life events and endogenous depression: A puzzle reexamined. *Archives of General Psychiatry, 51,* 525–34.

Bryant, R. A., and Harvey, A. G. (1995). Processing threatening information in post-traumatic stress disorder. *Journal of Abnormal Psychology, 104,* 537–41.

Burke, M., and Mathews, A. M. (1992). Autobiographical memory and clinical anxiety. *Cognition and Emotion, 6,* 23–35.

Butler, G., and Mathews, A. M. (1983). Cognitive processes in anxiety. *Advances in Behaviour Research and Therapy, 5,* 51–62.

Cadoret, R. J., Yates, W. R., Troughton, E., Woodworth, G., and Stewart, M. A. (1995). Genetic-environmental interaction in the genesis of aggressivity and conduct disorders. *Archives of General Psychiatry, 52,* 916–24.

Cane, D. B., and Gotlib, I. H. (1985). Depression and the effects of positive and negative feedback on expectations, evaluations, and performance. *Cognitive Therapy and Research, 9,* 145–60.

Carr, J. (1996). Neuroendocrine and behavioral interaction in exposure treatment of phobic avoidance. *Clinical Psychology Review, 16,* 1–15.

Chapman, L. J., Chapman, J. P., and Miller, E.N. (1982). Reliabilities and intercorrelations of eight measures of proneness to psychosis. *Journal of Consulting and Clinical Psychology, 50,* 187–95.

Clark, D. M. (1986). A cognitive approach to panic. *Behaviour Research and Therapy, 24,* 461–70.

Clark, D. M., and Beck, A. T. (1988). Cognitive approaches. In C. G. Last and M. Hersen (Eds.), *Handbook of anxiety disorders* (pp. 362–85). New York: Pergamon.

Clark, L. A., Watson, D., and Mineka, S. (1994). Temperament, personality, and the mood and anxiety disorders. *Journal of Abnormal Psychology, 103,* 103–16.

Cleckley, H. (1941). *The mask of sanity.* St. Louis: C. V. Mosby.

Cloninger, C. R., and Gottesman, I. I. (1987). Genetic and environmental factors in antisocial behavior disorders. In S. A. Mednick, T. E. Moffitt, and S. A. Stack (Eds.), *The causes of crime: New biological approaches* (pp. 92–109). New York: Cambridge University Press.

Coccaro, E. F., Kavoussi, R. J., Sheline, Y. I., Lish, J. D., and Csernansky, J. G. (1996). Impulsive aggression in personality disorder correlates with tritiated paroxetine binding in the platelet. *Archives of General Psychiatry, 53,* 531–36.

Collins, N., Dunkel-Schetter, C., Lobel, M., and Scrimshaw, S. C. M. (1993). Social support in pregnancy: Psychosocial correlates of birth outcomes and postpartum depression. *Journal of Personality and Social Psychology, 65,* 1243–58.

Costello, C. G. (1992). Research on symptoms versus research on syndromes: Arguments in favor of allocating more research time to the study of symptoms. *British Journal of Psychiatry, 160,* 304–8.

Coyne, J. (1976). Depression and the response of others. *Journal of Abnormal Psychology, 85,* 186–93.

———. (1985). Comment: Studying depressed person's interactions with strangers and spouses. *Journal of Abnormal Psychology, 94,* 231–32.

Daley, S. E., Hammen, C., Burge, D., Davila, J., Paley, B., Lindberg, N., and Herzberg, D. S. (1997). Predictors of the generation of episodic stress: A longitudinal study of late adolescent women. *Journal of Abnormal Psychology, 106,* 251–59.

Davidson, R. J. (1992). Emotion and affective style: Hemispheric substrates. *Psychological Science, 3,* 39–43.

Day, R., and Wong, S. (1996). Anomalous perceptual asymmetries for negative emotional stimuli in the psychopath. *Journal of Abnormal Psychology, 105,* 648–52.

De Bellis, M. D., Lefter, L., Trickett, P. K., and Putnam, F. W., Jr. (1994). Urinary catecholamine excretion in sexually abused girls. *Journal of the American Academy of Child and Adolescent Psychiatry, 33,* 320–27.

Den Boer, J. A., and Westernberg, H. G. M. (1990). Serotonin function in panic disorder: A double blind placebo controlled study with fluoxamine and ritanserin. *Psychopharmacology, 102,* 85–94.

Depue, R. A., and Iacono, W. G. (1989). Neurobehavioral aspects of affective disorders. *Annual Review of Psychology, 40,* 457–92.

Depue, R. A., Lucian, M., Arbisis, P., Collins, P., and Leon, A. (1994). Dopamine and the structure of personality: Relations of agonist-induced dopamine activity to positive emotionality. *Journal of Personality and Social Psychology, 67,* 485–98.

Dolan, M. (1994). Psychopathy: A neurobiological perspective. *British Journal of Psychiatry, 165,* 151–59.

Dworkin, R. H., and Saczynski, K. (1984). Individual differences in hedonic capacity. *Journal of Personality Assessment, 48,* 620–26.

Ekman, P., Davidson, R. J., and Friesen, W. V. (1990). The Duchenne smile: Emotional expression and brain physiology II. *Journal of Personality and Social Psychology, 58,* 342–53.

Elliott, D. M., and Briere, J. (1992). Sexual abuse trauma among professional women: Validating the Trauma Symptom Checklist–40. *Child Abuse and Neglect, 16,* 391–98.

Eronen, M., Hakola, P., and Tiihonen, J. (1996). Mental disorders and homicidal behavior in Finland. *Archives of General Psychiatry, 53,* 497–501.

Fadden, G., Bebbington, P., and Kuipers, L. (1987). Caring and its burdens: A study of the spouses of depressed patients. *British Journal of Psychiatry, 151,* 660–67.

Ferrier, I. N. (1994). Disturbed hypothalamo-pituitary-adrenal axis regulation in depression: Causes and consequences. In S. A. Montgomery and T. Cohn (Eds.), *Psychopharmacology of depression* (pp. 47–56). England: Oxford University Press.

Ferril, A. (1991). *Caligula Emperor of Rome.* London: Thames and Hudson.

Finklestein, S. N. (1994). How much does depression cost society? *Harvard Mental Health Letter, 11,* 8.

Fischer, P. J., and Breakey, W. R. (1991). The epidemiology of alcohol, drug, and mental disorders among homeless persons. *American Psychologist, 46,* 1115–28.

Foa, E. B., Franklin, M. E., Perry, K. J., & Herbert, J. D. (1996). Cognitive biases in generalized social phobia. *Journal of Abnormal Psychology, 105,* 433–39.

Foa, E. B., Zinbarg, R., and Rothbaum, B. O. (1992). Uncontrollability and unpredictability in post-traumatic stress disorder: An animal model. *Psychological Bulletin, 112,* 218–38.

Fowles, D. C. (1980). The three arousal model: Implications of Gray's two-factor learning theory for heart rate, electrodermal activity and psychopathy. *Psychophysiology, 17,* 87–104.

Frances, R. J., Franklin, J., and Flavin, D. K. (1987). Suicide and alcoholism. *American Journal of Alcohol and Drug Abuse, 13,* 327–41.

Friedman H. S. (Ed.) (1992). *Hostility, coping, and health.* Washington: American Psychological Association.

Goddard, A. W., Charney, D. S., Germine, M., Woods, S. W., Heninger, G. R., Krystal, J. H., Goodman, W. K., and Price, L. H. (1995). Effects of tryptophan depletion on responses to yohimbine in healthy human subjects. *Biological Psychiatry, 38,* 74–85.

Gold, E. R. (1986). Long-term effects of sexual victimization in childhood: An attributional approach. *Journal of Consulting and Clinical Psychology, 54,* 471–75.

Gold, P. W., Loriaux, L., Roy, A., Kling, M., Calabrese, J. R., Kellner, C. H., et al. (1986). Responses to corticotropin-releasing hormone in the hypercortisolism of depression and Cushing's disease. *New England Journal of Medicine, 314,* 1329–35.

Golden, R. N., Markey, S. P., Risby, E. D., Cowdrey, R. W., and Potter, W. Z. (1988). Antidepressants reduce whole-body norepinephrine turnover while enhancing 6-hydroxymelatonin output. *Archives of General Psychiatry, 45,* 150–54.

Gorenstein, E. E., and Newman, J. P. (1980). Disinhibitory psychopaths: A new perspective and a model for research. *Psychological Review, 87,* 301–15.

Gotlib, I. H. (1984). Depression and general psychopathology in university students. *Journal of Abnormal Psychology, 93,* 19–30.

Gotlib, I. H., and Robinson, L. A. (1982). Responses to depressed individuals: Discrepancies between self-reports and observer-rated behavior. *Journal of Abnormal Psychology, 91,* 231–40.

Gray, J. A. (1970). The psychophysiological basis of introversion-extraversion. *Behaviour Research and Therapy, 8,* 249–66.

Gunderson, J. G., and Sabo, A. N. (1993). The phenomenological and conceptual interface between borderline personality disorder and PTSD. *American Journal of Psychiatry, 150,* 19–27.

Hall, R. C. and Beresford, T. P. (1984). Physical illness in psychiatric patients: Areas of inquiry. *Psychiatric Medicine, 2,* 401–15.

Hare, R. D., and McPherson, L. M. (1984). Psychopathy and perceptual asymmetry during verbal dichotic listening. *Journal of Abnormal Psychology, 93,* 141–49.

Hayes, S. C., Wilson, K. G., Gifford, E. V., Follette, V. M., and Strosahl, K. (1996). Experiential avoidance and behavioral disorders: A functional dimensional approach to diagnosis and treatment. *Journal of Consulting and Clinical Psychology, 64,* 1152–68.

Heiberg, A. N., and Heiberg, A. (1978). A possible genetic contribution to the alexithymia trait. *Psychotherapy and Psychosomatics, 30,* 205–10.

Heller, W., Etienne, M. A., and Miller, G. A. (1995). Patterns of perceptual asymmetry in depression and anxiety: Implications for neuropsychological models of emotion and psychopathology. *Journal of Abnormal Psychology, 104,* 327–33.

Hendin, H., and Haas, A. P. (1991). Suicide and guilt as manifestations of PTSD in Vietnam combat veterans. *American Journal of Psychiatry, 148,* 586–91.

Higgins, E. T. (1989). Self-discrepancy theory: What patterns of self-beliefs cause people to suffer? In L. Berkowitz (Ed.), *Advances in experimental social psychology* (pp. 93–136). California: Academic Press.

Higgins, E. T., Klein, R., and Strauman, T. (1985). Self-discrepancies: Distinguishing among self-state conflicts, emotional vulnerabilities. In K. M. Yardley and T. M. Honess (Eds.), *Self and identity: Psychological perspectives* (pp. 173–86). New York: Wiley.

Higgins, E. T., Van Hook, E., and Dorfman, D. (1988). Do self-descriptive traits form a self structure? *Social Cognition, 6,* 177–207.

Hokanson, J. E., Rubert, M. P., Welker, R. A., Hollander, G. R., and Hedeen, C. (1989). Interpersonal concomitants and antecedents of depression among college students. *Journal of Abnormal Psychology, 98,* 209–17.

Isaksson, H., Konarski, K., and Theorell, T. (1992). The psychological and social condition of hypertensives resistant to pharmacological treatment. *Social Science Medicine, 35,* 869–75.

Isometsa, E. T. (1993). Course, outcome, and suicide risk in bipolar disorder: A review. *Psychiatrica Fennica, 24,* 113–24.

Joyce, P. R., Fergusson, D. M., Woollard, G., Abbott, R. M., Horwood, L. J., and Upton, J. (1995). Urinary catecholamines and plasma hormones predict mood state in rapid cycling bipolar affective disorder. *Journal of Affective Disorders, 33,* 233–43.

Kanner, A. D., Coyne, J. C., Schafer, C., and Lazarus, R. S. (1981). Comparison of two modes of stress measurement: Daily hassles and uplifts versus major life events. *Journal of Behavioral Medicine, 4,* 1–39.

Kauhanen, J., Kaplan, G. A., Cohen, R. D., Julkunen, J., and Salonen, J. T. (1996). Alexithymia and the risk of death in middle-aged men. *Journal of Psychosomatic Research, 41,* 541–649.

Keller, M. B., and Hanks, D. L. (1995). Anxiety symptom relief in depression treatment outcomes. *Journal of Clinical Psychiatry, 56* (supp. 6), 22–29.

Kendler, K. S., Heath, A. C., Martin, N. G., and Eaves, L. J. (1987). Symptoms of anxiety and symptoms of depression: Same genes, different environments? *Archives of General Psychiatry, 44,* 451–57.

Kendler, K. S., Neale, M. C., Kessler, R. C., Heath, A. C., and Eaves, L. J. (1992a). The genetic epidemiology of phobias in women: The interrelationship of agoraphobia, social phobia, situational phobia, and simple phobia. *Archives of General Psychiatry, 49,* 273–81.

———. (1992b). Childhood parental loss and psychopathology in women. *Archives of General Psychiatry, 49,* 109–16.

———. (1993). A twin study of recent life events and difficulties. *Archives of General Psychiatry, 50,* 789–96.

Kendler, K. S., Walters, E. E., Neale, M. C., Kessler, R. C., Heath, A. C., and Eaves, L. J. (1995). The structure of the genetic and environmental risk factors for six major psychiatric disorders in women. *Archives of General Psychiatry, 52,* 374–83.

Kessler, R. C., McGonagle, K. A., Zhao, S., Nelson, C. B., Hughes, M., Eshleman, S., Wittchen, H. U., and Kendler, K. S. (1994). Lifetime and twelve-month prevalence of *DSM-III-R* psychiatric disorders in the United States. *Archives of General Psychiatry, 51,* 8–19.

Klein, D. F. (1974). Endogenomorphic depression: A conceptual and terminological revision. *Archives of General Psychiatry, 31,* 447–54.

Kovacs, M., and Beck, A. T. (1978). Maladaptive cognitive structures in depression. *American Journal of Psychiatry, 135,* 525–33.

Lang, P. (1995). The emotion probe: Studies of motivation and attention. *American Psychologist, 50,* 372–85.

Larsen, R. J., and Diener, E. (1987). Affect intensity as an individual differences characteristic: A review. *Journal of Research in Personality, 21,* 1–39.

Lazarus, R. S., and Folkman, S. (1984). *Stress, appraisal, and coping.* New York: Springer.

Lehnert, K. L., Overholser, J. C., and Spirito, A. (1994). Internalized and externalized anger in adolescent suicide attempters. *Journal of Adolescent Research, 9,* 105–19.

Lewis, H. B. (1971). *Shame and guilt in neurosis.* New York: International University Press.

Lifton, R. J. (1980). The concept of the survivor. In J. E. Dimsdale (Ed.), *Survivors, victims, and perpetrators: Essays on the Nazi Holocaust* (pp. 113–26). Washington, D.C.: Hemisphere.

Lykken, D. T. (1957). A study of anxiety in the sociopathic personality. *Journal of Abnormal and Social Psychology, 55,* 6–10.

Lykken, D. T., McGue, M., Tellegen, A., and Bouchard, T. J., Jr. (1992). Emergenesis: Genetic traits that may not run in families. *American Psychologist, 47,* 1565–77.

Malinosky-Rummell, R., and Hansen, D. J. (1993). Long-term consequences of childhood physical abuse. *Psychological Bulletin, 114,* 68–79.

Markus, H. (1977). Self-schemata and processing information about the self. *Journal of Personality and Social Psychology, 35,* 63–78.

Maser, J., and Cloninger, C. R. (Eds.). (1990). *Co-morbidity in anxiety and mood disorders.* Washington, D.C.: American Psychiatric Association Press.

Mathews, A., and MacLeod, C. (1994). Cognitive approaches to emotion and emotional disorders. *Annual Review of Psychology, 45,* 25–50.

McCabe, S. B., and Gotlib, I. H. (1995). Selective attention and clinical depression: Performance on a deployment-of-attention task. *Journal of Abnormal Psychology, 104,* 241–45.

McGuffin, P., Katz, R., Watkins, S., and Rutherford, J. (1996). A hospital-based twin register of the heritability of *DSM-IV* unipolar depression. *Archives of General Psychiatry, 53,* 129–36.

McLeod, J. D. (1994). Anxiety disorders and marital quality. *Journal of Abnormal Psychology, 103,* 767–76.

McNally, R. J., and Foa, E. B. (1987). Cognition and agoraphobia: Bias in the interpretation of threat. *Cognitive Therapy and Research, 11* (special issue: *Anxiety: Cognitive factors and the anxiety disorders*), 567–81/567–88.

Mendlewicz, J., and Rainer, J. D. (1977). Adoption study supporting genetic transmission in manic-depressive illness. *Nature, 268,* 327–29.

Metalsky, G. I., Joiner, T. E., Hardin, T. S., and Abramson, L. Y. (1993). Depressive reactions to failure in a naturalistic setting: A test of the hopelessness and self-esteem theories of depression. *Journal of Abnormal Psychology, 102,* 101–9.

Miller, G. A. (1996). How we think about cognition, emotion, and biology in psychopathology. *Psychophysiology, 33,* 615–28.

Miller, H. L., Delgado, P. L., Salomon, R. M., Berman, R., Krystal, J. H., Heninger, G. R., and Charney, D. S. (1996). Clinical and biochemical effects of catecholamine depletion of antidepressant-induced remission of depression. *Archives of General Psychiatry, 53,* 117–28.

Mineka, S., and Kihlstrom, J. F. (1978). Unpredictable and uncontrollable events: A new perspective on experimental neurosis. *Journal of Abnormal Psychology, 87,* 256–71.

Mineka, S., and Sutton, S. K. (1992). Cognitive biases and the emotional disorders. *Psychological Science, 3,* 65–69.

Mintz, J., Mintz, L. I., Arruda, M. J., and Hwang, S. S. (1992). Treatment of depression and the functional capacity to work. *Archives of General Psychiatry, 49,* 761–68.

Mogg, K., Mathews, A. M., and Eysenck, M. (1992). Attentional bias to threat in clinical anxiety. *Cognition and Emotion, 6,* 145–59.

Monroe, S. M., Roberts, J. E., Kupfer, D. J., and Frank, E. (1996). Life stress and treatment course of recurrent depression: II. Postrecovery associations with attrition, symptom course, and recurrence over three years. *Journal of Abnormal Psychology, 105,* 313–28.

Moshe, I., and Schneider, S. (1992). Some psychological reactions of rape victims. *Medicine and Law, 11,* 303–8.

Mulkens, S. A. N., de Jong, P. J., and Merckelbach, H. (1996). Disgust and spider phobia. *Journal of Abnormal Psychology, 105,* 464–68.

Mullen, P. E., Martin, J. L., Anderson, J. C., Romans, S. E., and Herbison, G. P. (1993). Childhood sexual abuse and mental health in adult life. *British Journal of Psychiatry, 163,* 721–32.

Neumeister, A., Praschak-Rieder, N., Hesselmann, B., Rao, M. L., Gluck, J., and Kasper, S. (1997). Effects of tryptophan depletion on drug-free patients with a seasonal affective disorder during a stable response to bright light therapy. *Archives of General Psychiatry, 54,* 133–44.

Noyes, R. (1991). Suicide and panic disorder: A review. *Journal of Affective Disorders, 22,* 1–11.

Orley, J. (1995). Psychological disorders among refugees: Some clinical and epidemiological considerations. In A. J. Marsella, T. Bornemann, S. Ekblad, and J. Orley (Eds.), *Amidst peril and pain: The mental health and well-being of the world's refugees* (pp. 193–206). Washington, D.C.: American Psychological Association.

Parker, J. D. A., Taylor, G. J., and Bagby, R. M. (1992). Relationship between conjugate lateral eye movements and alexithymia. *Psychotherapy and Psychosomatics, 57,* 94–101.

Patrick, C. J., Bradley, M. B., and Lang, P. J. (1993). Emotion in the criminal psychopath: Startle reflex modulation. *Journal of Abnormal Psychology, 102,* 82–92.

Patterson, C. M., and Newman, J. P. (1993). Reflectivity and learning from aversive events: Toward a psychological mechanism for the syndromes of disinhibition. *Psychological Review, 100,* 716–36.

Paykel, E. S., and Dowlatshahi, D. (1988). Life events and mental disorder. In S. Fisher and J. Reason (Eds.), *Handbook of life stress, cognition, and health* (pp. 241–63). New York: Wiley.

Persons, J. B. (1986). The advantages of studying psychological phenomena rather than psychiatric diagnoses. *American Psychologist, 41,* 1252–60.

Pollard, C. A., Pollard, H. J., and Corn, K. J. (1989). Panic onset and major events in the lives of agoraphobics: A test of contiguity. *Journal of Abnormal Psychology, 98,* 318–21.

Polusny, M. A., and Follette, V. M. (1995). Long-term correlates of child sexual abuse: Theory and review of the empirical literature. *Applied and Preventive Psychology, 4,* 143–66.

Quitkin, F. M., McGrath, P. J., Stewart, J. W., Harrison, W., Tricamo, E., Wager, S. G., Ocepek-Welikson, K., Nunes, E., Rabkin, J. G., and Klein, D. F. (1990). Atypical depression, panic attacks, and response to imipramine and phenelzine: A replication. *Archives of General Psychiatry, 47,* 935–41.

Raine, A., Brennan, P., Mednick, B., and Mednick, S. A. (1996). High rates of violence, crime, academic problems, and behavioral problems in males with both early neuromotor deficits and unstable family environments. *Archives of General Psychiatry, 53,* 544–49.

Resnick, H. S., Kilpatrick, D. G., Dansky, B. S., Saunders, B. E., and Best, C. L. (1993). Prevalence of civilian trauma and post-traumatic stress disorder in a representative national sample of women. *Journal of Consulting and Clinical Psychology, 61,* 984–91.

Robins, C. J. (1990). Congruence of personality and life events in depression. *Journal of Abnormal Psychology, 99,* 393–97.

Robins, L. N. (1966). *Deviant children grown up.* Baltimore: Williams & Wilkins.

Ross, E. D., and Mesulam, M. M. (1979). Dominant language functions to the right hemisphere? Prosody and emotional gesturing. *Archives of Neurology, 36,* 144–48.

Roy, A. (1992). Suicide in schizophrenia. *International Review of Psychiatry, 4,* 205–9.

Roy, A., Pickar, D., Linnoila, M., Doran, A. R., Ninan, P., and Paul, S. M. (1985). Cerebrospinal fluid monoamine and monoamine metabolite concentrations in melancholia. *Psychiatry Research, 15,* 281–92.

Russell, J. A. (1983). Pancultural aspects of human conceptual organization of emotion. *Journal of Personality and Social Psychology, 45,* 1281–88.

Sarason, B. R., Sarason, I. G., and Pierce, G. R. (Eds.) (1990). *Social support: An interactional view.* New York: Wiley.

Segal, Z. V., Shaw, B. F., Vella, D. D., and Katz, R. (1992). Cognitive and life stress predictors of relapse in remitted unipolar depressed patients: Test of the congruency hypothesis. *Journal of Abnormal Psychology, 101,* 26–36.

Seligman, M. E. P. (1975). *Helplessness: On depression, development, and death.* San Francisco: Freeman.

Sherbourne, C. D., Wells, K. B., and Judd, L. L. (1996). Functioning and well-being of patients with panic disorder. *American Journal of Psychiatry, 153,* 213–18.

Shinn, M. (1990). Mixing and matching: Levels of conceptualization, measurement, and statistical analysis in community research. In P. Tolan, C. Keys, F. Chertok, and L. Jason (Eds.), *Researching community psychology: Issues of theory and methods* (pp. 111–26). Washington, D.C.: American Psychological Association.

Simons, R. F., Fitzgibbons, L., and Fiorito, E. (1993). Emotion-processing in anhedonia. In N. Birbaumer and A. Ohman (Eds.), *The structure of emotion: Psychophysiological, cognitive, and clinical aspects* (pp. 288–306). Seattle: Hogrefe and Huber.

Stahl, S. (1994). $5HT_{1A}$ receptors and pharmacotherapy: Is serotonin down-regulation linked to the mechanism of action of antidepressant drugs? *Psychopharmacology Bulletin, 30,* 39–43.

Stolar, N., Berenbaum, H., Banich, M. T., and Barch, D. (1994). Neuropsychological correlates of alogia and affective flattening in schizophrenia. *Biological Psychiatry, 35,* 164–72.

Sullivan, H. S. (1953). *The collected works of Harry Stack*

Sullivan, vol. 1. Edited by H. S. Perry & M. S. Gawel. New York: Norton.

Swann, A. C., Bowden, C. L., Morris, D., Calabrese, J. R., Petty, F., Small, J., Dilsaver, S. C., and Davis, J. M. (1997). Depression during mania: Treatment response to lithium or divalproex. *Archives of General Psychiatry, 54,* 37–42.

Tangney, J. P. (1993). Shame and guilt. In C. G. Costello (Ed.), *Symptoms of depression* (pp. 161–80). New York: Wiley.

Taylor, G. J. (1984). Alexithymia: Concept, measurement, and implications for treatment. *American Journal of Psychiatry, 141,* 725–32.

Taylor, G. J., Bagby, R. M., and Parker, J. D. A. (1997). *Disorders of affect regulation: Alexithymia in medical and psychiatric illness.* New York: Cambridge University Press.

Teasdale, J. D., and Russell, M. L. (1983). Differential effects of induced mood on the recall of positive, negative, and neutral words. *British Journal of Clinical Psychology, 22,* 163–71.

Teasdale, J. D., Taylor, M. J., Cooper, Z., Hayhurst, H., and Paykel, E. S. (1995). Depressive thinking: Shifts in construct accessibility or in schematic mental models? *Journal of Abnormal Psychology, 104,* 500–7.

Tellegen, A., Lykken, D. T., Bouchard, T. J., Jr., Wilcox, K. J., Segal, N. L., and Rich, S. (1988). Personality similarity in twins reared apart and together. *Journal of Personality and Social Psychology, 54,* 1031–39.

Thompson, T. (1995). *The beast: A reckoning with depression.* New York: Putnam.

Tomarken, A. J., Mineka, S., and Cook, M. (1989). Fear-relevant selective associations and covariation bias. *Journal of Abnormal Psychology, 98,* 381–94.

Tomarken, A. J., Sutton, S. K., and Mineka, S. (1995). Fear-relevant illusory correlations: What types of associations promote judgmental bias? *Journal of Abnormal Psychology, 104,* 312–26.

True, W. R., Rice, J., Eisen, S. A., Heath, A. C., Goldberg, J., Lyons, M. J., and Nowak, J. (1993). A twin study of genetic and environmental contributions to liability for posttraumatic stress symptoms. *Archives of General Psychiatry, 50,* 257–64.

Tucker, D. M., and Dawson, S. L. (1984). Asymmetric EEG power and coherence as method actors generated emotions. *Biological Psychiatry, 19,* 63–75.

Tweed, J. L., Schoebach, V. J., George, L. K., and Blazer, D. G. (1989). The effects of childhood parental death and divorce on six-month history of anxiety disorders. *British Journal of Psychiatry, 154,* 823–28.

U.S. Bureau of the Census. (1996). *Statistical abstract of the United States.* DHHS publication 0276–4733. Washington, D.C.: U.S. Government Printing Office.

Vollrath, M., Alnaes, R., and Torgersen, S. (1996). Differential effects of coping in mental disorders: A prospective study in psychiatric outpatients. *Journal of Clinical Psychology, 52,* 125–35.

Wallbott, H. G., and Scherer, K. R. (1995). Cultural determinants in experiencing shame and guilt. In J. P. Tangney and K. W. Fischer (Eds.), *Self-conscious emotions: Shame, guilt, embarrassment, and pride* (pp. 143–73). New York: Guilford.

Wandrei, K. E. (1985). Identifying potential suicides among high-risk women. *Social Work, 30,* 511–17.

Watkins, P. C., Mathews, A., Williamson, D. A., and Fuller, R. D. (1992). Mood-congruent memory in depression: Emotional priming or elaboration? *Journal of Abnormal Psychology, 101,* 581–86.

Watson, D., Weber, K., Assenheimer, J. S., Clark, L. A., Strauss, M. E., and McCormick, R. A. (1995). Testing a tripartite model: I. Evaluating the convergent and discriminant validity of anxiety and depression symptom scales. *Journal of Abnormal Psychology, 104,* 3–14.

Wender, P. H., Kety, S. S., Rosenthal, D., Schulsinger, F., Ortmann, J., and Lunde, L. (1986). Psychological disorders in the biological and adoptive relatives of individuals with affective disorders. *Archives of General Psychiatry, 43,* 923–29.

Wheeler, R. F., Davidson, R. J., and Tomarken, A. J. (1993). Frontal brain asymmetry and emotional reactivity: A biological substrate of affective style. *Psychophysiology, 30,* 82–89.

Wise, R. A. (1982). Neuroleptics and operant behavior: The anhedonia hypothesis. *Behavioral and Brain Sciences, 5,* 39–87.

Yee, C. M., and Miller, G. A. (1994). A dual-task analysis of resource allocation in dysthymia and anhedonia. *Journal of Abnormal Psychology, 103,* 625–36.

Yoshikawa, H. (1994). Prevention as cumulative protection: Effects of early family support and education on chronic delinquency and its risks. *Psychological Bulletin, 115,* 28–54.

Zanarini, M. C., and Frankenburg, F. R. (1997). Pathways to the development of borderline personality disorder. *Journal of Personality Disorders, 11,* 93–104.

Zeitlin, D. N., Lane, R. D., O'Leary, D. S., and Schrift, M. J. (1989). Interhemispheric transfer deficit and alexithymia. *American Journal of Psychiatry, 146,* 1434–39.

Zeitlin, S. B., McNally, R. J., and Cassiday, K. L. (1993). Alexithymia in victims of sexual assault: An effect of repeated traumatization? *American Journal of Psychiatry, 150,* 661–63.

Zinbarg, R. E., and Barlow, D. H. (1996). Structure of anxiety and the anxiety disorders: A hierarchical model. *Journal of Abnormal Psychology, 105,* 181–93.

Zohar, J., and Insel, T. R. (1987). Obsessive-compulsive disorder: Psychobiological approaches to diagnosis, treatment, and pathophysiology. *Biological Psychiatry, 22,* 667–87.

15 Personal Control and Well-Being

Christopher Peterson

Personal control refers to the individual's belief that he or she can behave in ways that maximize good outcomes and/or minimize bad outcomes. Because personal control leads the individual to engage the world in a vigorous fashion, outcomes that originally elude control may eventually become controllable. An extensive theoretical and empirical literature links personal control to well-being in a variety of domains. Nevertheless, well-being is overdetermined; personal control enables well-being, but it is neither a necessary nor a sufficient condition.

"PERSONAL CONTROL" refers to the individual's belief that he or she can behave in ways that maximize good outcomes and/or minimize bad outcomes. A belief in personal control may or may not be veridical, but what makes the notion intriguing is its self-fulfilling nature. Because personal control leads the individual to engage the world in a vigorous fashion, outcomes that originally elude control may eventually become controllable.

Psychologists throughout the twentieth century have been interested in various incarnations of the personal control construct. My purpose in this chapter is to review some of this work and in particular its relevance to well-being, an obviously broad notion that can be approached at biological, emotional, cognitive, behavioral, interpersonal, sociocultural, and historical levels. Regardless of the level of analysis, personal control is often linked to well-being, and lack of control to passivity and poor morale, social estrangement, academic and vocational failure, and even illness and untimely death. I refrain from equating personal control and well-being, preferring to regard the former as an enabling condition for the latter (cf. Myers and Diener 1995). Given the consistent yet less than perfect correlation between personal control and well-being, our challenge is to specify when and how this association occurs.

Much of this chapter focuses on research within the *learned helplessness* tradition, a well-known and representative approach to personal control. This line of work began with an interest in the effects of experience with uncontrollable events in a given situation. While it is hardly surprising that animals and people who experience uncontrollability in one setting become passive in that setting, they sometimes generalize the resulting helplessness from that setting to others where outcomes, objectively, can be controlled. The attempts to explain when and why this generalization occurs and to specify failures of human adaptation that are analogous to the helplessness phenomenon have guided research for three decades (Peterson, Maier, and Seligman 1993).

CONTINGENCY LEARNING: THE IMPORTANCE OF CONTROL

Throughout the early part of the twentieth century, stimulus-response (S-R) conceptions of learning dominated psychological theorizing. According to S-R accounts, learning entails the acquisition of particular motor responses in particular situations and the forging of associations between stimuli and responses; the more closely these are linked together in experience (*contiguity*), the more likely learning is to occur. Under the sway of behaviorism, learning was thought to have no central (cognitive) representation. Although this approach was dominant, there were voices of dissent.

Perhaps the strongest argument against S-R views of learning are findings that the associations acquired in conditioning are strengthened not by contiguity per se but rather by *contingency*: the degree to which stimuli provide new information about responses (Rescorla 1968). Traditional S-R conceptions of learning hold that individuals are sensitive only to the temporal conjunction of the response and the reinforcer. In the language of conditional probability, the probability of reinforcement given the occurrence of some response—$P(Rft/R)$—governs all learning.

But animals and people are actually sensitive to all possible variations and combinations of

$P(Rft/R)$ and $P(Rft/no\ R)$. Said another way, individuals are responsive to the correlation between stimulus and response. Whenever the two probabilities are unequal, there is an association between the response and the reinforcer. Here individuals have some *control* over the reinforcer in the sense that they can make its occurrence more versus less likely by enacting or withholding the response, as the case may be. Roughly, the greater the difference between the two probabilities, the greater the degree of control. When the two probabilities are equal for some response, the reinforcer is not associated with it, and the individual is unable to exert any control over the reinforcer, regardless of what is or is not done.

The differences between traditional S-R theory and the contingency view have important implications. S-R theory stresses only temporal contiguity between the response and the reinforcer, viewing the individual as trapped by the momentary co-occurrences of events. If a response is followed by a reinforcer, it is strengthened even if there is no real (causal) relationship between them. And events that occur in the absence of a particular response have no bearing on learning. In contrast, the contingency view of learning proposes that individuals are able to detect cause-effect relationships, separating momentary noncausal relationships from more enduring true ones (Wasserman and Miller 1997).

Learning at its essence becomes the detection of what one can control and what one cannot. This view was foreshadowed by Tolman's (1932) argument decades earlier that learning entails the discovery of "what leads to what." Because learning extends over time, it is sensible to view it in central (cognitive) terms. Although there is disagreement about the fine detail of these central representations, it is clear that control is a critically important psychological process, linked to subsequent motivation, cognition, and emotion. Many theorists in this tradition have opted to regard the representation of contingency learning as an *expectation* in order to explain how it is generalized across situations and projected across time.

COGNATES OF PERSONAL CONTROL

Contemporary interest in personal control began in earnest when contiguity views of learning were melded with a long-standing tradition within personality psychology that focused on individual differences in thoughts and beliefs about one's abilities to predict and direct important life outcomes (Peterson 1992b). The combining of these approaches resulted in a family of theories that can be characterized as transactional, spanning the individual and the environment and being concerned in particular with the interplay between the two. Each theory acknowledges internal and external determinants of behavior. Each accords to cognitions motivational and emotional significance. And each regards control as beneficial because it facilitates well-being.

To be sure, control is an important variable across time and place and species, but it has never been as central to our psychological understanding of human nature as it is now. The centrality of personal control seems to result from a societal emphasis peculiar to the Western world in the late twentieth century (Peterson et al. 1993, ch. 1). Individual choices, individual rights, and individual fulfillments are the watchwords for our era, along with a waning of concern for the common good. Individuals are greatly occupied with what they can and cannot control in their everyday lives; one can characterize this concern as a virtual obsession, matched only by the related pursuit of "feeling good."

As both products and students of what Peterson, Maier, and Seligman (1993) dubbed "the age of personal control," contemporary psychologists have made this defining feature of the Zeitgeist a central topic. There are dozens of theories of personal control, each with an associated body of empirical research. Consider, for example, constructs such as:

- achievement motivation
- desire for control
- dispositional optimism
- effectance motivation
- empowerment
- hardiness
- hope
- illusory control
- internal versus external attributions
- intrinsic motivation
- John Henryism
- learned helplessness
- locus of control
- mindfulness
- perceived freedom
- personal causation
- positive denial
- positive illusions
- power motivation
- psychological reactance
- secondary control

- self-efficacy
- sense of coherence
- striving for superiority
- Type A coronary-prone personality pattern

A survey of the theories that elaborate these constructs is beyond the scope of a single volume, much less a single chapter, so I follow a different strategy here by sketching Peterson and Stunkard's (1989) attempts to discern a family resemblance among the contemporary cognates of personal control (see also Skinner 1995).

Generalizing across constructs like these, Peterson and Stunkard advanced the following composite theory of personal control:

- Personal control subsumes beliefs about how one can interact with the world. It may take the form of believing that one can (a) cause or influence actual outcomes—either their occurrence, their timing, or their extent; (b) choose among outcomes; (c) cope with the consequences of outcomes; and/or (d) understand these outcomes.
- Personal control resides in the transaction between the person and the world: it is not simply a disposition, and it is not simply an objective property of an environment.
- Although personal control may have tacit components, much of what we want to know about personal control can be measured by self-report.
- In a responsive environment (this qualification is critical), personal control is desirable because it encourages emotional, motivational, behavioral, and physiological vigor in the face of demands.
- Personal control can be catalyzed by novel and challenging events and becomes particularly salient in the face of overwhelming aversive events.
- Personal control is thwarted by failure and encouraged by success, although it does not bear a one-to-one relationship to past patterns of success and failure.

Personal control is both a cause and a consequence of the way people respond to their environment. Its relationship to well-being is obvious. Whatever else well-being might be, it does *not* exist apart from the world and what the world affords. Control makes people more than passive recipients of outcomes. It is the psychological process that guides people as they strive to make the world into a more desirable place, even when this goal proves elusive.

LEARNED HELPLESSNESS

Let me now discuss at length the theory of and work in learned helplessness as a good example of both the strengths and weaknesses of research into personal control and its consequences for well-being. Learned helplessness was first described by psychologists studying animal learning. Researchers immobilized a dog and exposed it to a series of electric shocks, painful but not damaging, that could be neither avoided nor escaped. Twenty-four hours later, the dog was placed in a situation in which electric shock could be terminated by a simple response. However, the dog did not make this response; instead, it just sat and passively endured the shock. This behavior was in marked contrast to dogs in a control group that reacted vigorously to the shock and learned readily how to turn it off.

These investigators proposed that the dog had learned to be helpless. In other words, when originally exposed to uncontrollable shock, it learned that nothing it did mattered. The shocks came and went independently of the dog's behaviors. They hypothesized that this learning of response-outcome independence was represented cognitively as an expectation of future helplessness that was generalized to new situations to produce a variety of deficits: motivational, cognitive, and emotional.

The deficits that follow in the wake of uncontrollability have come to be known as the *learned helplessness phenomenon,* and their cognitive explanation as the *learned helplessness model* (Maier and Seligman 1976). Learned helplessness in animals continues to interest experimental psychologists, in large part because it provides an opportunity to investigate the interaction between mind and body (Maier, Watkins, and Fieschner 1994).

The Learned Helplessness Model

The learned helplessness model is very much at odds with the S-R view of learning because it proposes that the helpless animal learns not specific responses but rather general expectations affecting responses across a variety of situations. The helplessness model is a cognitive account of learning, and in the 1960s it was a radical theory in a field long dominated by strict behaviorism.

Accordingly, much of the early interest in learned helplessness stemmed from its clash with the tenets of traditional S-R theories. Alternative accounts of learned helplessness were proposed by theorists who saw no need to invoke mentalistic constructs. Different alternatives were proposed, yet many emphasized an incompatible motor response learned when animals were first exposed to uncontrollable shock. This response was presumably generalized to the second situation, where it interfered with performance at the test task. Said another way, the learned helplessness phenomenon is produced by an inappropriate *response* learned in the original situation rather than an inappropriate *expectation* (of response-outcome independence). For example, perhaps the dogs learned that holding still when shocked somehow decreased pain. If so, then they hold still in the second situation as well, because this response was previously reinforced.

Maier, Seligman, and others conducted a series of studies testing between the learned helplessness model and the incompatible motor response alternatives. In a way, the learned helplessness advocates had an easier time because the helplessness model does not deny the possibility that incompatible motor responses play some role in passivity. Their point was merely that expectations play a role as well. The advocates of incompatible motor responses, in contrast, categorically denied any role of expectations in producing the helplessness phenomenon.

Several lines of research implied that expectations were operative. Perhaps the most compelling argument comes from the so-called *triadic design,* a three-group experimental showing that the uncontrollability of shocks is responsible for ensuing deficits. Animals in one group are exposed to shock that they are able to terminate by making some response. Animals in a second group are yoked to those in the first group, exposed to the identical shocks, the only difference being that animals in the first group control their offset whereas those in the second do not. Animals in a third group are exposed to no shock at all in the original situation. All animals are then given the same test task.

Animals with control over the initial shocks typically show no helplessness when subsequently tested. They act just like animals with no prior exposure to shock. Animals without control become helpless. Whether or not shocks are controllable is not a property of the shocks per se but rather of the relationship between the animal and the shocks. That animals are sensitive to the link between responses and outcomes implies that they must be able to detect and represent the relevant contingencies. A cognitive explanation of this ability is more parsimonious than one phrased in terms of incompatible motor responses.

Also arguing in favor of a cognitive interpretation of helplessness effects are studies showing that an animal can be "immunized" against the debilitating effects of uncontrollability by first exposing it to controllable events. Presumably, the animal

learns during immunization that events can be controlled, and *this* expectation is sustained during exposure to uncontrollable events. Learned helplessness is thus precluded.

Along these same lines, other studies show that learned helplessness deficits can be undone by forcibly exposing a helpless animal to the contingency between behavior and outcome. In other words, the animal is forced to make an appropriate response at the test task, by pushing or pulling it into action. After several such trials, the animal notices that escape is possible and begins to respond on its own. Again, the presumed process at work is a cognitive one. The animal's expectation of response-outcome independence is challenged during the "therapy" experience, and hence learning occurs.

The studies described so far exposed animals to aversive stimuli (shocks). But it is also possible to produce helplessness by providing uncontrollable appetitive stimuli: food or water regardless of responses (Engberg et al. 1972). Here an explanation in terms of incompatible motor responses becomes quite difficult to support. What is gained by holding still in response to food or water? Certainly not the reduction of pain.

Psychologists interested in humans, and particularly human problems, were quick to see the parallels between learned helplessness as produced by uncontrollable events in the laboratory and maladaptive passivity as it exists in the real world. Thus began several lines of research looking at learned helplessness in people.

In one line of work, helplessness in people was produced in the laboratory much as it was in animals, by exposing subjects to uncontrollable events and seeing the effects on their motivation, cognition, and emotion. Unsolvable problems were usually substituted for uncontrollable electric shocks, but the critical aspects of the phenomenon remained: following uncontrollability, people show a variety of deficits.

Other studies further attested to the similarity between the animal phenomenon and what was produced in the human laboratory. Uncontrollable bad events made anxiety and depression more likely. Previous exposure to controllable events immunized people against learned helplessness. Similarly, forcible exposure to contingencies reversed helplessness deficits.

Several aspects of human helplessness differ from animal helplessness. First, uncontrollable bad events seem much more likely than uncontrollable good events to produce helplessness among human beings (Peterson et al. 1993), probably because most people are able to devise coherent accounts for why good things happen to them, even if these explanations are incorrect. So the intriguing phenomenon of appetitive helplessness among animals probably has no reliable counterpart among people, much to the dismay of critics of the welfare system.

A second asymmetry is what can be termed *vicarious helplessness*. Problem-solving difficulties can be produced in people who do not directly experience uncontrollable events if they simply see someone else exposed to uncontrollability (Brown and Inouye 1978). The significance of vicarious helplessness is that it greatly extends the potential ways in which helpless behavior might be produced in the natural world. News stories, for example, often feature uncontrollable events imposed upon other people. The full parameters of this phenomenon have not been investigated, and it is of obvious interest whether we can immunize people against vicarious helplessness or undo its effects via therapy.

A third difference is that small groups of people can be made helpless by exposure to uncontrollable events. In other words, when a group works at an unsolvable problem, it later shows group problem-solving deficits relative to another group with no previous exposure to uncontrollability (Simkin, Lederer, and Seligman 1983). Interestingly, group-level helplessness is not simply a function of individual helplessness produced among group members; it exists at the group level, characterizing group efforts at future tasks but *not* individual efforts. Again, the real-life implications of this phenomenon are intriguing, and future research into this phenomenon seems indicated.

In another line of work, researchers proposed various failures of adaptation as analogous to learned helplessness and investigated the similarity between these failures and learned helplessness on various fronts. Especially popular was Seligman's (1975) proposal that reactive depression and learned helplessness shared critical features: causes, symptoms, consequences, treatments, and preventions.

As these lines of work were pursued, it became clear—in all cases—that the original learned helplessness explanation was an oversimplification when applied to people. Most generally, it failed to account for the range of reactions that people displayed in response to uncontrollable events. Some people indeed showed pervasive deficits, as the model hypothesized, that were general across time and situation, but others did not. Further, failures

of adaptation that the learned helplessness model was supposed to explain, such as depression, were sometimes characterized by a striking loss of self-esteem, about which the model was silent.

The Attributional Reformulation

In an attempt to resolve these discrepancies, Abramson, Seligman, and Teasdale (1978) reformulated the helplessness model as it applied to people. The contrary findings could all be explained by drawing on attribution theory and proposing that when people encounter an uncontrollable (bad) event, they ask themselves why it happened. The nature of their answer sets the parameters for the helplessness that follows. If their causal attribution is stable ("it's going to last forever"), then induced helplessness is long-lasting; if unstable, then it is transient. If their causal attribution is global ("it's going to undermine everything"), then subsequent helplessness is manifest across a variety of situations; if specific, then it is correspondingly circumscribed. Finally, if the causal attribution is internal ("it's all my fault"), the individual's self-esteem drops following uncontrollability; if external, self-esteem is left intact.

These hypotheses form the *attributional reformulation* of helplessness theory. This new theory left the original model in place, because uncontrollable events were still hypothesized to produce deficits when they gave rise to an expectation of response-outcome independence. However, the nature of these deficits was now said to be influenced by the causal attribution offered by the individual.

In some cases, the situation itself provides the explanation made by the person, and the extensive social psychology literature on causal attributions documents many situational influences on the process. In other cases, the person relies on his or her habitual way of making sense of events, what is called one's *explanatory style* (Peterson and Seligman 1984). All things being equal, people tend to offer similar sorts of explanations for disparate bad (or good) events. Accordingly, explanatory style is a distal influence on helplessness and the failures of adaptation that involve helplessness.

According to the attributional reformulation, explanatory style in and of itself is therefore not a cause of problems but rather a risk factor. Given uncontrollable events and the lack of a clear situational demand on the proffered attribution for uncontrollability, explanatory style should influence how the person responds. Helplessness will be long-lasting or transient, widespread or circumscribed, damaging to self-esteem or not, all in accordance with the individual's explanatory style.

Explanatory style as studied by learned helplessness researchers has a specific meaning: the way that people habitually explain the causes of bad events involving themselves along the dimensions of internality, stability, and globality. Explanatory style can be identified only by looking across different explanations; to the degree that individuals are consistent, we can sensibly speak of them as showing a style of explanation. Helplessness theorists expect a degree of consistency across the explanations offered by individuals for different events, that is, these should correlate at above-chance levels. But perfect agreement is not expected, in part because explanatory style is but one of several influences on the actual causal explanations that people offer, and in part because the consistency of one's explanatory style appears to be an individual difference in its own right.

Despite these caveats, explanatory style has been extensively studied. Here is some of what has been learned. Explanatory style seems to take form as a coherent individual difference around eight years of age, when children's cognitive abilities allow them to think in causal terms. Twin studies suggest that explanatory style is moderately heritable (Schulman, Keith, and Seligman 1993), but I hasten to add that there is no reason to believe that there is a specific optimism-pessimism gene. Rather, such characteristics as intelligence, physical prowess, and attractiveness—which are themselves heritable—set the stage for success or failure in a variety of domains, and it is these experiences that lead the individual to entertain optimistic or pessimistic explanations for important outcomes. Early loss, such as death of a parent, or early trauma, such as sexual abuse, makes an individual more pessimistic (Bunce, Larsen, and Peterson 1995). Early success makes an individual more optimistic (Peterson 1990).

Social learning is also implicated in the origins of explanatory style. Studies show convergence between the explanatory styles of parents and their children, although the fine detail of how an explanatory style is transmitted across generations has yet to be explored. I suspect that messages from schoolteachers, peers, and the media about the causes of events are also critical.

However explanatory style is initially forged, it can be highly stable, sometimes over decades (Burns and Seligman 1989). The self-fulfilling nature of explanatory style—and personal control per se—readily explains this stability. Helplessness leads to failure, which strengthens helplessness; control leads to success, which strengthens control. At the same time, explanatory style can and does change in response to ongoing life events. Cognitive therapy, for example, can move explanatory style in an increasingly optimistic direction (Seligman et al. 1988).

Finally, explanatory style has a huge array of correlates. Many of these involve different aspects of well-being. I discuss the most notable of these correlates later in the chapter.

Hopelessness Theory

The attributional reformulation has itself been reformulated by Abramson, Metalsky, and Alloy (1989), who made several modifications to the theory to improve its specific applicability to depression. These theorists hypothesized that a particular subtype of depression, which they identified as hopelessness depression, is immediately caused by the belief that rewards will not occur and/or that punishments will. Other types of depression presumably exist as well, and have different etiologies, such as disordered biochemistry or ruptured social relationships.

According to Abramson et al.'s (1989) *hopelessness theory* of depression, belief in a hopeless future is increased by stable and global explanations for actual bad life events as well as by a high degree of importance attached to these events. These cognitions in turn are influenced by an individual's explanatory style, specifically the habitual tendency to offer stable and global explanations for bad events.

As applied to depression, hopelessness theory differs from the attributional reformulation in several ways. The immediate cause of depression is hopelessness ("the future will be unpleasant") as opposed to helplessness ("nothing I do matters"). In contrast to the attributional reformulation, the importance of bad life events is given an explicit role in hopelessness theory. This emphasis strengthens the link between hopelessness theory and the original learned helplessness model, which was based on the finding that uncontrollable *trauma* (electric shocks) was debilitating. The attributional reformulation treats all uncontrollable events as equally likely to produce helplessness, so long as they are explained in the same way. But this position is unreasonable: traffic lights are uncontrollable and presumably regarded by most commuters as stable and global, yet few would argue that they are depressing. Finally, neither internal causal attributions nor internality of explanatory style is accorded central importance in this new theory, which is consistent with findings showing that low self-esteem is usually not specifically linked to internality (Peterson 1991).

A major contribution of hopelessness theory is its ability to explain why people may show increased perseverance and good moods in the wake of life events: they entertain a belief in a *hopeful* future, presumably because of the operation of mechanisms analogous, yet opposite, to those implicated in the maintenance of a hopeless belief. The original helplessness model and the attributional reformulation do not distinguish between types of nonhelpless responses, yet of course these exist and require an explanation.

Hopelessness theory has not yet been extensively tested, and it is therefore too early to say how different in practice the theory is from its immediate ancestors. For example, hopelessness and helplessness are conceptually distinct, but these cognitions may be so entwined in actual thought that they prove impossible to tease apart. These theories do not compete with each other across the board but rather differ in terms of their emphases on the particular cognitive mechanisms linking uncontrollability and deficits.

Conclusions

Learned helplessness has become a popular line of investigation for at least two reasons (Peterson et al. 1993, ch. 8). One is the development of straightforward measures of explanatory style (see Reivich 1995), notably a self-report questionnaire called the Attributional Style Questionnaire (ASQ) and a flexible content analysis procedure dubbed the Content Analysis of Verbatim Explanations (CAVE) that allows explanatory style to be scored from spontaneous writing or speaking. The downside of these measures is a temptation to neglect the environment in which explanatory style is deployed. Some researchers have treated explanatory style as a decontextualized trait, and this strategy is at best an oversimplification.

The second reason for the popularity of learned helplessness is that the helplessness phenomenon seems analogous to various humans ills involving passivity. Helplessness theory, along with the attributional reformulation and hopelessness theory, suggests a ready explanation of such instances of passivity as well as interventions to prevent or remedy them. Again, there is a downside to the availability of powerful theory: some applications have been promiscuous, overstating the similarity between learned helplessness, on the one hand, and a given failure of adaptation, on the other.

The majority of ostensibly relevant studies have not tested the full helplessness reformulation but only aspects of it. The reformulation and the related hopelessness theory specify a detailed account of the process by which people become helpless. Explanatory style, as noted, is regarded as a risk factor, not an inevitable cause of problems. Presumably, explanatory style is catalyzed by actual bad events, and it is only when explanatory style induces someone to offer a given explanation that passivity follows. Most studies have not investigated these subtleties, which would require at the very least a longitudinal design and an independent assessment of the occurrence of stressful life events.

Instead, studies have usually calculated the synchronous correlation between explanatory style and presumed outcomes, typically finding the predicted correlations. As Peterson and Seligman (1984) noted, these are the least compelling studies vis-à-vis the helplessness reformulation because they are compatible with other possibilities (for example, that the outcome influences attributions and/or that some third variable is responsible for both the outcome and pessimistic attributional style).

The best applications of learned helplessness ideas are to phenomena with three critical features:

1. *Objective noncontingency:* The applied researcher must take into account the contingencies between a person's actions and the outcomes that he or she then experiences. Learned helplessness is present only when there is no contingency between actions and outcomes. Learned helplessness must therefore be distinguished from extinction (when active responses once leading to reinforcement no longer do so) and from learned passivity (when active responses are contingently punished and/or passive responses are contingently reinforced).

2. *Cognitive mediation:* Learned helplessness also involves a characteristic way of perceiving, explaining, and extrapolating contingencies. Both the attributional reformulation and hopelessness theory specify cognitive processes that make helplessness more versus less likely following uncontrollable events. If measures of these processes are not sensibly related to ensuing passivity, then learned helplessness is not present.

3. *Cross-situational generality of passive behavior:* Finally, learned helplessness is shown by passivity in a situation different from the one in which uncontrollability was first encountered. Does the individual give up and fail to initiate actions that might allow him or her to control the situation? It is impossible to argue that learned helplessness is present without the demonstration of passivity in new situations.

Other consequences may also accompany the behavioral deficits that define the learned helplessness phenomenon: cognitive retardation, low self-esteem, sadness, reduced aggression, immunosuppression, and physical illness.

WELL-BEING

With these ideas in mind, consider several lines of work that represent the best applications to date of helplessness ideas to complex failures of human adaptation: depression, physical illness, and poor achievement. In each case, researchers have attempted to demonstrate the critical features of learned helplessness: contingency, cognition, and passivity.

Depression

Let us first see how depression satisfies the three criteria. To start, depression involves passivity; this is part of its very definition. Depression also follows bad events (Lloyd 1980), particularly those that people judge to be uncontrollable. And depression is mediated by cognitions of helplessness, hopelessness, and pessimism. Explanatory style is a consistent correlate of depressive symptoms, as well as a demonstrable risk factor.

Cognitive therapy for depression, which is highly effective, explicitly targets helpless expectations and pessimistic attributions. And research suggests that cognitive therapy may work precisely because it changes these cognitions (Seligman et al. 1988). Improvement in depression goes lockstep with changes in attributions for bad events from internal, stable, and global to external, unstable, and specific. An intriguing possibility is that the encouragement of an optimistic explanatory style may prevent depression (Gillham et al. 1995).

Questions remain about the use of the helplessness model to make sense of depression. One concerns the issue of whether depression is continuous versus discontinuous across its mild and severe forms. Are these essentially the same, differing only in degree, or do mild depression and severe depression differ in kind? The learned helplessness model takes the strong position of continuity, but the other position has its advocates as well.

Another issue concerns the fine detail of the mechanism that leads from helplessness constructs to the symptoms of depression. The typical study in support of the model demonstrates distant links, typically between pessimistic explanatory style and depressive symptoms. What transpires in between? Do expectations of helplessness set off by uncontrollability and influenced by explanatory style bear the sole mediating burden? Some research suggests that people's tendencies to ruminate about bad events and their causes are also important in determining who becomes depressed. Perhaps so, too, are people's tendencies to be self-conscious and to infer negative consequences from setbacks. Further work, with a closer look at mechanisms, is needed to evaluate the specific process hypothesized by the helplessness model.

One more issue about the use of the helplessness model to explain depression comes from laboratory investigations by Alloy and Abramson (1979) showing that nondepressed people perceive more control over events than they actually have. Depressives, in contrast, perceive control realistically, which is to say, without the illusory boost that characterizes nondepressive thinking. This "sadder but wiser" effect is an intriguing one, implying that the helplessness account may be wrong in characterizing depressive cognitions about control as distorted.

Physical Illness

Another popular application of helplessness ideas is to physical illness (Peterson and Bossio 1991). Again, let us ask how the three criteria of learned helplessness have been documented. First, passivity refers not to behavior but to the individual's ability to maintain physical health. Second, research with both animals and people shows that uncontrollable stress foreshadows poor health. However, this research has not always shown that uncontrollability is the critical reason why stressful life events can produce poor health. Third, explanatory style has been found to correlate with such indices of health as duration of symptom reports, physician exams, medical tests, longevity, and survival time following the diagnosis of serious diseases such as cancer. Pessimistic people have worse health than their optimistic counterparts. Many of these correlations have been established in longitudinal studies, where baseline measures of physical health are taken into account.

How strong is the correlation between pessimistic explanatory style and poor health? Most studies report correlation coefficients in the .20 to .30 range, which are moderate in size and typical of correlations in psychological research. At the same time, it is clear that explanatory style is but one influence on physical well-being.

Why does learned helplessness influence health? Several processes have been implicated. There may be an immunological pathway (Kamen-Siegel et al. 1991): animal studies imply that uncontrollable stress can suppress aspects of immune functioning (Visintainer, Volpicelli, and Seligman 1982). However, it should be noted that these findings are highly complex, and one should offer broad generalizations about immune functioning only with the utmost caution.

Another pathway may be emotional. As described, learned helplessness is involved in depression, and epidemiologists have shown that depressed individuals are at increased risk for morbidity and mortality. Perhaps learned helplessness influences health in part because of its role in depression.

A number of studies attest to a behavioral pathway, and my supposition is that behavior is the most important route between helplessness and physical illness. People with a pessimistic explanatory style tend to neglect the basics of health care, and when they fall ill, they tend not to do the sorts of things that might speed recovery. As these failures to promote their health through their actions accumulate, what may result is the observed link between explanatory style and illness. Furthermore, a pessimistic explanatory style puts individuals at risk for untimely death due to accidents or violence, implying that a fatalistic lifestyle plays a role in putting them in the wrong place at the wrong time (Peterson et al. 1998).

A final possibility is that helpless people fall ill because they are socially estranged. Rich and supportive relationships with others are a well-demonstrated correlate of good health. To the degree that helpless people do not partake of social support, poor health is an unsurprising result.

Poor Achievement

Several lines of research have investigated helplessness and its relationship to good or bad performance in such achievement domains as school, work, and sports (Peterson 1990, 1992a; Rettew

and Reivich 1995; Schulman 1995). More so than other venues of life, achievement domains represent situations in which there are right and wrong answers and in which one's efforts indeed matter. School, for example, is a close approximation to the laboratory setting in which learned helplessness was first described and should allow a straightforward generalization of the helplessness model.

With the attributional reformulation, helplessness research converges with the investigations by Weiner (1986) of the attributional determinants of achievement. Weiner began his work in the achievement motivation tradition, to which he then gave a cognitive twist, just as helplessness researchers began in the animal learning tradition, to which they gave the same twist.

Dweck (1975) was among the first researchers to apply helplessness ideas to academic achievement. In her research, she started with children designated as helpless versus mastery-oriented by virtue of their responses to a questionnaire asking about the causes of academic success and failure. Helpless children attributed failure to their lack of ability; when working at problems, they employed ineffective strategies, reported negative feelings, expected to do poorly, and ruminated about irrelevant matters. When these children encountered failure, they fell apart, whereas prior success had little effect on them. Dweck found that attribution retraining—in which students who attribute failure to a lack of ability are taught to attribute it instead to a lack of effort—indeed improved their persistence in the wake of failure.

Another analysis of school failure in learned helplessness terms comes from Butkowsky and Willows (1980), who focused on poor readers. They showed that fifth-grade boys with reading problems expected little success at reading tasks, explained their failures with internal and stable causes, and failed to persist at reading.

Fincham, Hokoda, and Sanders (1989) followed elementary school children for a two-year period, asking their teachers to rate over time the "helplessness" displayed by the children. These ratings proved stable. And initial ratings of helplessness predicted subsequent poor performance at objective achievement tests.

Other studies have shown a link between helplessness constructs and academic outcomes for college students. So Peterson and Barrett (1987) studied first-year students at Virginia Tech, finding that a pessimistic explanatory style predicted poor grades over the year, even when SAT scores were held constant statistically. Also ascertained was the number of times each student in the sample sought out academic advising during the year. As to be expected if they were evidencing learned helplessness, students who explained bad events with internal, stable, and global causes tended not to go to an adviser. In turn, not going to an adviser was associated with poor grades.

The research, then, seems to satisfy two criteria of learned helplessness: passivity and cognition. What about the third criterion? Kennelly and Mount's (1985) study provides pertinent evidence. These researchers studied students in the sixth grade. They devised and administered a measure called the Teacher Contingency Scale that asked students for their perceptions of the degree to which their teachers delivered rewards and punishments on a contingent versus noncontingent fashion. They also measured the students' beliefs about the causes of success and failure, their actual academic performance (grades), and whether or not their teacher saw them as helpless.

Students' perceptions of punishment noncontingency did not relate to other variables, but their perceptions of reward noncontingency were strongly correlated with helplessness on their part. Furthermore, children who thought that academic outcomes were beyond their control were rated by their teachers as helpless. All of these variables predicted actual academic performance.

From a learned helplessness perspective, the piece that does not fit is why only the perceived noncontingency of rewards related to the other variables. Other studies have found the opposite pattern: perceived noncontingency of punishments (but not rewards) predicts poor performance (see, for example, Kennelly and Kinley 1975; Yates, Kennelly, and Cox 1975). Perhaps matters differ from classroom to classroom. Regardless, these studies considered together suggest a good fit between the helplessness model and passivity as shown in the classroom.

A study by Johnson (1981) further implicated the criteria of learned helplessness in poor achievement. She compared three groups of male students between nine and twelve years of age. One group consisted of average students. The second group was composed of chronically failing students. In the third group were students who had been chronic failers but were enrolled in remedial classes. All of the boys completed an attribution questionnaire, a self-concept measure, and an experimental task indexing persistence. In other words, all three criteria of learned helplessness were assessed: history of bad events, cognition, and passivity. All of these variables covaried, as we would expect, along with low self-esteem. All achieved their lowest values among the chronically failing students. Finally, remedial instruction showed some evidence of alleviating learned helplessness.

CONCLUSIONS

Helplessness researchers do not claim that these problems involve only the constructs deemed important by helplessness theory. Depression, physical illness, and poor achievement are obviously overdetermined. As Abramson and her colleagues (1989) implied, there are instances of each explained not at all from the perspective of helplessness and hopelessness. Nonetheless, the case has been made for at least some involvement of the three critical features of learned helplessness in many instances of these phenomena. Questions remain, however, about personal control and well-being.

How Widely Applicable Is the Learned Helplessness Model?

An ongoing puzzle is why learned helplessness ideas appear so applicable. I have focused on the examples of depression, physical illness, and poor achievement, but I also could have described the largely successful use of the helplessness model to explain passivity in response to job stress, unemployment, mental retardation, chronic pain, epilepsy, or crowding (Peterson et al. 1993, ch. 7). What determines whether a given individual who has experienced uncontrollable bad events and thinks about them in pessimistic ways shows any of the possible consequences attributed to helplessness?

It might be that all these outcomes occur to the same individuals, in which case, their problems probably exacerbate one another. Or it might be that other considerations—biological, psychological, and/or social—on which helplessness theory is silent lead an individual in one disastrous direction or another once a state of helplessness is present.

Is Well-Being More Than the Absence of Helplessness?

Almost all of the research on personal control approaches the construct as if it falls along a continuum, from lack of control (helplessness) to control. The two poles—helplessness and control—are treated as simple opposites, and the typical correlational strategies used in research do not allow this juxtaposition to be questioned. But is there more to well-being than just the absence of helplessness? The answer is almost certainly yes. Just as theorists have distinguished between illness, absence of illness, and wellness, it would be productive for theorists in the personal control tradition to make similar distinctions. Well-being has a richer meaning than the simple absence of demoralization and passivity.

In keeping with this idea, some contemporary theorists have described states of enhanced personal control under such rubrics as "learned hopefulness," "learned industriousness," "learned mastery," "learned optimism," "learned relevance," and "learned resourcefulness."

Enhanced personal control presumably leads to increased persistence at problem-solving and sustained good cheer. As is obvious from the labels given to these hypothesized psychological states, they are thought to be the positive versions of learned helplessness. In each case, the state is encouraged by experience with controllable outcomes that leads to an expectation that future outcomes will also be controllable.

My sense is that these states are harder to create than is learned helplessness because of ceiling effects. In other words, most individuals assume as a matter of course that they have control over disparate outcomes, so it is hard to devise experiences that strengthen these already strong expectations. In any event, work here is preliminary and not well integrated within itself or with the much larger literature on helplessness. Nonetheless, constructs like these may someday illuminate what is meant by well-being better than current extrapolations by negation.

Are There Pathologies of Control?

Running through my discussion of personal control is the thesis—supported by dozens of theories and hundreds if not thousands of empirical investigations—that personal control is desirable. Regardless of how well-being is operationalized, a belief in one's own ability to influence outcomes is a consistent correlate of well-being. Several pathways run between personal control and well-being, most notably persistence in the pursuit of one's goals. However, I have also made the point that these conclusions about the benefits of personal control apply only when individuals find themselves in settings in which persistence eventually pays off.

In unresponsive settings, personal control and resulting persistence are not beneficial. Indeed, unrealistic control may be damaging in its own right. Given that people have finite resources, the futile pursuit of any goal means that more attainable goals are neglected or overlooked. And unrealistic personal control may produce additional difficulties: there can be too much of a good thing. Mania is an obvious example of a disorder marked by exaggerated control, but personal control run amok may also be at the root of other psychological problems that seem unrelated until examined in terms of people's beliefs in control.

Risk-Taking   There is an extensive literature concerned with how people perceive their relative risk for specific illnesses or injuries. Researchers ask respondents to provide a percentage estimate that they will someday contract an illness or a comparative rating relative to peers ("less likely," "as likely," "more likely") that they will do so. A robust finding is that people underestimate their risks: the average individual sees himself or herself as below average in risk for a variety of maladies. This phenomenon is usually identified as an *optimistic bias* (Weinstein 1989), and in the present context, it can be described as cohering around unrealistic perceptions of control over one's own well-being. The optimistic bias is justifiably decried because it may lead people to neglect the basics of health promotion and maintenance. For example, several studies have found that individuals who somehow believe that they are immune to contracting AIDS behave precisely in the riskiest of ways (see, for example, Bahr et al. 1993; Perkins et al. 1993).

Personal control facilitates well-being when this belief is at least in principle veridical. What makes control an intriguing psychological variable is precisely that it may be at odds with the initial facts but then that it may be self-fulfilling. If circumstances do not allow personal control to be translated into a good outcome, then this belief leads the individual to pursue impossible and/or dangerous goals.

As Bandura (1986) emphasized, efficacy expectations ("I can perform this behavior") are advantageous only when coupled with veridical outcome expectations ("And this behavior has these consequences"). The optimistic bias in risk perception is the result of incorrect outcome expectations. However, the bias is reduced or eliminated to the degree that individuals have firsthand experience with or extensive knowledge about a given illness or injury and its risk factors. A casual reading of the literature on personal control might lead one to conclude that well-being is all in a person's mind, but thoughts and beliefs must be situated within the person, and the person must be situated within the world.

Hostility   The personal construct theorist George Kelly (1955) proposed that hostility results from an individual's attempt to extort from the world validating evidence for untenable assumptions (constructs). Kelly's proposal is a very general formula, but little is lost when it is recast in terms of mistaken personal control. People who misapprehend the objective contingencies in the environment may become angry when the world fails to work as expected.

Consider research showing that sexually aggressive men tend to misinterpret friendliness on the part of women as a romantic invitation (Malamuth and Brown 1994). Here the objective contingencies in a social interaction are misunderstood, and a man may perceive control over a desired sexual encounter that does not exist. When he acts in accordance with this perception, an assault may result.

Perfectionism   Perfectionism, which can be prominent in obsessive-compulsive personality disorder as well as a problem in its own right, is yet another psychological difficulty marked by an inappropriate belief in personal control. Although perfectionism has numerous determinants, one is the belief that any and all important outcomes can be completely controlled (Slaney and Ashby 1996). Perfectionism becomes a problem in domains where outcomes elude "perfect" control and may exacerbate the related difficulty of procrastination.

Anxiety   Beck and Emery (1985) interpreted the gamut of anxiety disorders as stemming from people's mistaken beliefs about their own fragility. Anxious individuals act as if they were made from spun glass, overly sensitive to what the world may impose upon them. Avoidance and other symptoms of anxiety necessarily follow. Here again we can recast this formula in terms of mistaken beliefs about control, although in this case, it is the external world that is accorded too much causal power.

Paranoia   Along these lines, paranoia often involves the belief that other people, invariably important individuals, are able to exert great control over the details of one's life. Whether we wish to interpret paranoia in classic psychoanalytic terms as projection or more mundanely as a mode of self-enhancement, the role of mistaken control is clear (Kinderman and Bentall 1996).

Is Personal Control a Prerequisite for Well-Being?

Unrelentingly positive expectations may be an inherent part of human nature, one with an evolutionary basis (Tiger 1979). Sometimes unrealistic personal control has no cost, and it is beneficial because it sustains good cheer in the face of otherwise devastating circumstances, such as a positive test result for HIV (Taylor et al. 1992). But can a person have a good quality of life without a pervasive sense of control? I believe the answer is yes. In *Escape from Freedom,* Erich Fromm (1941) argued that citizens may be attracted to totalitarian regimes precisely because they deny freedom of choice and thus relieve individuals from the risk of being wrong. The exercise of personal control can be onerous when choices are too numerous, too complex, or too difficult.

At least some of the choices the modern world presents to a person—such as which long-distance telephone company to patronize—seem to have no differential consequences of any significance. We may exert considerable energy in controlling these but end up too exhausted to attempt to control outcomes that do matter. In these cases, our societal emphasis on personal control leads us to behave in foolish ways. Might video games and the like be the personal control equivalent of crack cocaine, a dangerous activity that capitalizes on usually beneficial tendencies built deeply within us? In any event, a desire to "escape from control" may eventually result, and perhaps it already has in some segments of our society. Attempts to enhance the well-being of people need to consider personal control, among many other factors, but at the same time to avoid assuming that more is necessarily better.

REFERENCES

Abramson, L. Y., Metalsky, G. I., and Alloy, L. B. (1989). Hopelessness depression: A theory-based subtype of depression. *Psychological Review, 96,* 358–72.

Abramson, L. Y., Seligman, M. E. P., and Teasdale, J. D. (1978). Learned helplessness in humans: Critique and reformulation. *Journal of Abnormal Psychology, 87,* 49–74.

Alloy, L. B., and Abramson, L. Y. (1979). Judgment of contingency in depressed and nondepressed students: Sadder but wiser? *Journal of Experimental Psychology: General, 108,* 441–85.

Bahr, G. R., Sikkema, K. J., Kelly, J. A., Fernandez, M. I., Stevenson, L. Y., and Koob, J. J. (1993). Attitudes and characteristics of gay men who remain at continued risk for contracting HIV infection. *International Conference on AIDS, 9,* 697.

Bandura, A. (1986). *Social foundations of thought and action.* Englewood Cliffs, N.J.: Prentice-Hall.

Beck, A. T., and Emery, G. (1985). *Anxiety disorders and phobias: A cognitive perspective.* New York: Basic Books.

Brown, I., and Inouye, D. K. (1978). Learned helplessness through modeling: The role of perceived similarity in competence. *Journal of Personality and Social Psychology, 36,* 900–908.

Bunce, S. C., Larsen, R. J., and Peterson, C. (1995). Life after trauma: Personality and daily life experiences of traumatized people. *Journal of Personality, 63,* 165–68.

Burns, M. O., and Seligman, M. E. P. (1989). Explanatory style across the life span: Evidence for stability over fifty-two years. *Journal of Personality and Social Psychology, 56,* 471–77.

Butkowsky, I. S., and Willows, D. M. (1980). Cognitive-motivational characteristics of children varying in reading ability: Evidence for learned helplessness in readers. *Journal of Educational Psychology, 72,* 471–84.

Dweck, C. S. (1975). The role of expectations and attributions in the alleviation of learned helplessness. *Journal of Personality and Social Psychology, 31,* 674–85.

Engberg, L. A., Hansen, G., Welker, R. L., and Thomas, D. R. (1972). Acquisition of key pecking via autoshaping as a function of prior experience: "Learned laziness"? *Science, 178,* 1002–4.

Fincham, F. D., Hokoda, A., and Sanders, R. (1989). Learned helplessness, test anxiety, and academic achievement. *Child Development, 60,* 138–45.

Fromm, E. (1941). *Escape from freedom.* New York: Rinehart.

Gillham, J. E., Reivich, K. J., Jaycox, L. H., and Seligman, M. E. P. (1995). Prevention of depressive symptoms in schoolchildren: Two-year follow-up. *Psychological Science, 6,* 343–51.

Johnson, D. S. (1981). Naturally acquired learned helplessness: The relationship of school failure to achievement behavior, attributions, and self-concept. *Journal of Educational Psychology, 73,* 174–80.

Kamen-Siegel, L., Rodin, J., Seligman, M. E. P., and Dwyer, J. (1991). Explanatory style and cell-mediated immunity. *Health Psychology, 10,* 229–35.

Kelly, G. A. (1955). *The psychology of personal constructs.* New York: Norton.

Kennelly, K. J., and Kinley, S. (1975). Perceived contingency of teacher-administered reinforcements and academic performance of boys. *Psychology in the Schools, 12,* 449–53.

Kennelly, K. J., and Mount, S. A. (1985). Perceived contingency of reinforcements, helplessness, locus of control, and academic performance. *Psychology in the Schools, 22,* 465–69.

Kinderman, P., and Bentall, R. P. (1996). A new measure of causal locus: The Internal, Personal, and Situational Attributions Questionnaire. *Personality and Individual Differences, 20,* 261–64.

Lloyd, C. (1980). Life events and depressive disorder reviewed: I. Events as predisposing factors. II. Events as precipitating factors. *Archives of General Psychiatry, 37,* 529–48.

Maier, S. F., and Seligman, M. E. P. (1976). Learned helplessness: Theory and evidence. *Journal of Experimental Psychology: General, 105,* 3–46.

Maier, S. F., Watkins, L. R., and Fieshner, M. (1994). Psychoneuroimmunology: The interface between behavior, brain, and immunity. *American Psychologist, 49,* 1004–17.

Malamuth, N. M., and Brown, L. M. (1994). Sexually aggressive men's perceptions of women's communications: Testing three explanations. *Journal of Personality and Social Psychology, 67,* 699–712.

Myers, D. G., and Diener, E. (1995). Who is happy? *Psychological Science, 6,* 10–19.

Perkins, D. O., Leserman, J., Murphy, C., and Evans, D. L. (1993). Psychosocial predictors of high-risk sexual behavior among HIV-negative homosexual men. *AIDS Education and Prevention, 5,* 141–52.

Peterson, C. (1990). Explanatory style in the classroom and on the playing field. In S. Graham and V. S. Folkes (Eds.), *Attribution theory: Applications to achievement, mental health, and interpersonal conflict* (pp. 53–75). Hillsdale, N.J.: Erlbaum.

———. (1991). Meaning and measurement of explanatory style. *Psychological Inquiry, 2,* 1–10.

———. (1992a). Learned helplessness and school problems: A social psychological approach. In F. J. Medway and T. P. Cafferty (Eds.), *School psychology: A social psychological perspective* (pp. 359–76). Hillsdale, N.J.: Erlbaum.

———. (1992b). *Personality* (2nd ed.). Fort Worth: Harcourt Brace Jovanovich.

Peterson, C., and Barrett, L. C. (1987). Explanatory style and academic performance among university freshmen. *Journal of Personality and Social Psychology, 53,* 603–7.

Peterson, C., and Bossio, L. M. (1991). *Health and optimism.* New York: Free Press.

Peterson, C., Maier, S. F., and Seligman, M. E. P. (1993). *Learned helplessness: A theory for the age of personal control.* New York: Oxford University Press.

Peterson, C., and Seligman, M. E. P. (1984). Causal explanations as a risk factor for depression: Theory and evidence. *Psychological Review, 91,* 347–74.

Peterson, C., Seligman, M. E. P., Yurko, K. H., Martin, L. R., and Friedman, H. S. (1998). Catastrophizing and untimely death. *Psychological Science, 9,* 49–52.

Peterson, C., and Stunkard, A. J. (1989). Personal control and health promotion. *Social Science and Medicine, 28,* 819–28.

Reivich, K. (1995). The measurement of explanatory style. In G. M. Buchanan and M. E. P. Seligman (Eds.), *Explanatory style* (pp. 21–47). Hillsdale, N.J.: Erlbaum.

Rescorla, R. A. (1968). Probability of shock in the presence and absence of CS in fear conditioning. *Journal of Comparative and Physiological Psychology, 66,* 1–5.

Rettew, D., and Reivich, K. (1995). Sports and explanatory style. In G. M. Buchanan and M. E. P. Seligman (Eds.), *Explanatory style* (pp. 173–85). Hillsdale, N.J.: Erlbaum.

Schulman, P. (1995). Explanatory style and achievement in school and work. In G. M. Buchanan and M. E. P. Seligman (Eds.), *Explanatory style* (pp. 159–71). Hillsdale, N.J.: Erlbaum.

Schulman, P., Keith, D., and Seligman, M. E. P. (1993). Is optimism heritable? A study of twins. *Behaviour Research and Therapy, 31,* 569–74.

Seligman, M. E. P. (1975). *Helplessness: On depression, development, and death.* San Francisco: Freeman.

Seligman, M. E. P., Castellon, C., Cacciola, J., Schulman, P., Luborsky, L., Ollove, M., and Downing, R. (1988). Explanatory style change during cognitive therapy for unipolar depression. *Journal of Abnormal Psychology, 97,* 13–18.

Simkin, D. K., Lederer, J. P., and Seligman, M. E. P. (1983). Learned helplessness in groups. *Behaviour Research and Therapy, 21,* 613–22.

Skinner, E. A. (1995). *Perceived control, motivation, and coping.* Thousand Oaks, Calif.: Sage.

Slaney, R. B., and Ashby, J. S. (1996). Perfectionism: Study of a criterion group. *Journal of Counseling and Development, 74,* 393–98.

Taylor, S. E., Kemeny, M. E., Aspinwall, L. G., Schneider, S. G., Rodriguez, R., and Herbert, M. (1992). Optimism, coping, psychological distress, and high-risk sexual behavior among men at risk for acquired immunodeficiency syndrome (AIDS). *Journal of Personality and Social Psychology, 63,* 460–73.

Tiger, L. (1979). *Optimism: The biology of hope.* New York: Touchstone.

Tolman, E. C. (1932). *Purposive behavior in animals and men.* New York: Century.

Visintainer, M., Volpicelli, J. R., and Seligman, M. E. P. (1982). Tumor rejection in rats after inescapable or escapable shock. *Science, 216,* 437–39.

Wasserman, E. A., and Miller, R. R. (1997). What's elementary about associative learning? *Annual Review of Psychology, 48,* 573–607.

Weiner, B. (1986). *An attributional theory of motivation and emotion.* New York: Springer-Verlag.

Weinstein, N. D. (1989). Optimistic biases about personal risks. *Science, 246,* 1232–33.

Yates, R., Kennelly, K. J., and Cox, S. H. (1975). Perceived contingency of parental reinforcements, parent-child relations, and locus of control. *Psychological Reports, 36,* 139–46.

16 Hedonic Adaptation

Shane Frederick and George Loewenstein

Hedonic adaptation refers to a reduction in the affective intensity of favorable and unfavorable circumstances. This chapter discusses the purposes, underlying mechanisms, and most common functional representations of hedonic adaptation. We then examine some of the methodological problems that hamper research in this area and review the literature on adaptation in four negative domains, (noise, imprisonment, bereavement, and disability) and four positive domains (foods, erotic images, increases in wealth, and improvements in appearance produced by cosmetic surgery). Following this review, we discuss several circumstances that promote or impede hedonic adaptation. We conclude by discussing the dark side of hedonic adaptation—the negative consequences for individuals and society.

Those surgical operations in the field, the sickening butchery that shook even the toughest of the natives, had gradually deadened our sensibilities; we were no longer able to judge the horror of it all. . . blood flowing and spurting, the unbearable smell from suppurating wounds—all this left us unmoved.
—Maurice Herzog, *Annapurna* (1952)

MOST OF US are familiar with striking examples of people who seem to be adapting well to circumstances that are extremely adverse. We may have seen footage of malnourished children playing happily in garbage dumps or know of severely handicapped people who maintain a cheerful disposition in spite of their disabilities. However, counterexamples come to mind as well: people who seem perpetually miserable, or those who were "never quite the same" after experiencing some devastating event. This chapter examines both the extent and limits of *hedonic adaptation*—processes that attenuate the long-term emotional or hedonic impact of favorable and unfavorable circumstances.

HEDONIC ADAPTATION

Adaptation, in its broadest sense, refers to any action, process, or mechanism that reduces the effects (perceptual, physiological, attentional, motivational, hedonic, and so on) of a constant or repeated stimulus.[1] Adaptation can occur at several different levels—from overt behaviors that reduce exposure to a stimulus, to molecular changes at the cellular level that diminish the perceived or experienced intensity of an objective stimulus. For example, stepping from a dark building into sunshine induces a variety of behavioral and physiological responses to the increased light level—turning away from the sun, squinting, pupil contraction, photochemical changes in the retina, and neural changes in the areas of the brain that process the retinal signal. Counterparts to these processes occur when we step back into the building. Although there are limits to what these adaptive processes can achieve (as indicated by our need for welding helmets and night vision goggles), they do allow us to see normally over luminance intensities that vary by a factor of over one million.[2]

Hedonic adaptation is adaptation to stimuli that are affectively relevant. It relies on many of the same processes that underlie other types of adaptation and is often derivative of these processes. For example, hedonic adaptation to a foul odor is a direct consequence of sensory adaptation because an odor that is perceived as less intense will be experienced as less unpleasant. Similarly, hedonic adaptation to paraplegia may result in part from physiological adaptations, such as increases in upper body muscle mass, that enable paraplegics to manipulate their wheelchairs more effectively. However, many hedonic stimuli are cognitive rather than sensory. Thus, many of the processes involved in hedonic adaptation involve cognitive changes—in interests, values, goals, attention, or characterization of a situation. For example, the effects of diminished mobility accompanying paraplegia will be less important if one develops new interests that do not demand as much mobility, such as playing Scrabble instead of tennis.[3] Hedonic adaptation may also involve consciously directing one's attention away from troubling thoughts or engaging in activities likely to direct attention elsewhere, such as playing sports or keeping busy at work. This strategy may diminish at least the "quantity" of saddening cognitions, if not their intensity, when they do intrude into consciousness. Hedonic adaptation may also be facilitated by cognitive transformations of situations—for example, by interpreting a tragedy as a "learning experience" (see, for example, Janoff-Bulman and Wortman 1977). Finally, neurochemical processes within the brain may work to oppose persistent intense negative or positive affect (Solomon and Corbit 1974) by desensitizing overstimulated hedonic circuitry. For example, continual high-level cocaine or amphetamine use may diminish the functioning of reward pathways in the brain (see, for example, Cassens et al. 1981; Wise and Munn 1995).

Functions of Hedonic Adaptation

Adaptive processes serve two important functions. First, they *protect* organisms by reducing the internal impact of external stimuli. (For example, sweating causes evaporative cooling, which reduces or negates the increase in body temperature that would otherwise accompany an increase in ambient temperature.) Second, they *enhance perception* by heightening the signal value of changes from the baseline level.[4] The types of adaptive processes involved in visual perception illustrate this function. When we first walk indoors from the afternoon sun, we have difficulty seeing and would have difficulty judging which of two dark rooms is darker. After we have been inside for a while, however, the adaptive processes that have restored our vision have also restored our sensitivity to luminance changes at the new, lower light level—enabling us to detect, for example, a single lightbulb burning out in an auditorium lit by hundreds.

Hedonic adaptation may serve similar protective and perception-enhancing functions. Hedonic states (hunger, thirst, pain, sleepiness, sexual excitement, and so on) are necessary because they direct attention to high-priority needs and provide the motivation to engage in behaviors that satisfy those needs and to avoid behaviors that compromise them (Cabanac 1979; Damasio 1994; Pribram 1984, 2). However, persistent strong hedonic states (for example, fear or stress) can have destructive physiological concomitants, such as ulcers, circulatory disease, and viral infections (see Sapolsky, this volume). Thus, hedonic adaptation may help to protect us from these effects.

Hedonic adaptation may also increase our sensitivity to, and motivation to make, local changes in our objective circumstances. To illustrate this second function of hedonic adaptation, consider a man who has been incarcerated. The prisoner's situation is illustrated in figures 16.1 and 16.2, which specify hedonic intensity in terms of a Prospect Theory value function (Kahneman and Tversky 1979), in which utility is determined by the difference between the prisoner's current state and the state to which he has adapted. Before he has adapted to his incarceration (see figure 16.1), he is miserable in his seven-foot cell. At this time, the difference in value between a seven-foot cell and a nine-foot cell seems insignificant, and he would have little motivation for acquiring the larger cell. However, after the prisoner has adapted (see figure 16.2), not only is he happier, but the difference in hedonic value between the small and large cells is much greater, and the prisoner would, correspondingly, be increasingly motivated to secure the larger cell.

Because the persistence of an aversive state is an indication that it cannot be changed, hedonic adaptation may prevent the continued expenditure of energy in futile attempts to change the unchangeable and redirect motivation to changes that can be made. To paraphrase a famous aphorism, hedonic adaptation "provides the serenity to accept the things one cannot change, the courage to change the things one can, and the wisdom to know the difference."

Shifting Adaptation Levels Versus Desensitization

Although we have used the term "adaptation" broadly to denote anything that reduces the subjective intensity of a given stimulus, it is important to distinguish between adaptive processes that diminish subjective intensity by altering the stimulus level that is experienced as neutral (*shifting adaptation levels*) and adaptive processes that diminish the subjective intensity of the stimulus generally (*desensitization*). Both processes diminish the subjective intensity of a given stimulus, but shifting adaptation levels preserve or enhance sensitivity to stimulus differences, whereas desensitization diminishes such sensitivity.

A shifting adaptation level is illustrated by the prisoner example as described earlier. The conditions initially experienced as intensely negative are later experienced as hedonically neutral (V_0 [7-ft. cell] < 0, whereas V_t [7-ft. cell] $= 0$), and as the prisoner's hedonic state improves, he also becomes *more* sensitive to stimulus differences ([V_t (9-ft.

Figure 16.1   Prisoner's Situation Prior to Adapting to Incarceration

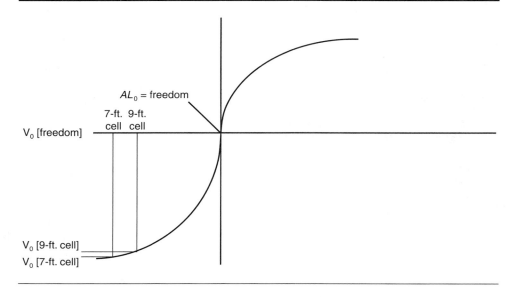

cell) − V_t (7-ft. cell)] > [V_0 (9-ft. cell) − V_0 (7-ft. cell)]). Desensitization, in contrast, involves a change in the shape, rather than the position, of the response function (see figure 16.3). Like a shifting adaptation level, the hedonic intensity de-

creases over time (V_0 [7-ft. cell] < V_t [7-ft. cell]), but unlike shifting adaptation levels, the prisoner's sensitivity to change also decreases ([V_t (7-ft. cell) − V_t (7ft. cell)] < [V_0 (9-ft. cell) − V_0 (7-ft. cell)]). People who are hedonically desensitized—

Figure 16.2   Prisoner's Situation Following Adaptation to Incarceration

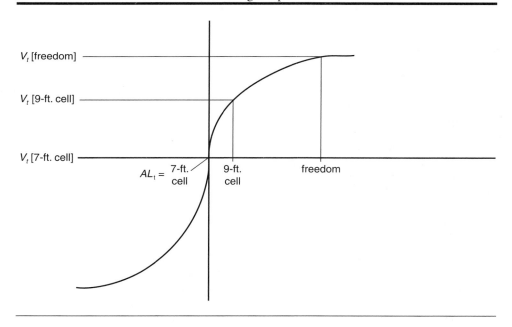

FIGURE 16.3   Sensitization and Desensitization

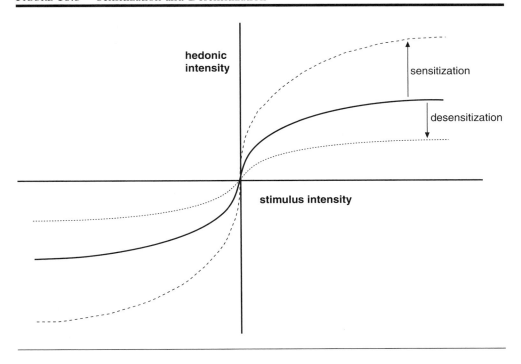

that is, "hardened," "jaded," "jaundiced"—are typically unmotivated to make any kind of change, whether local or global.[5]

Adaptation Versus Sensitization

Adaptation is not the only possible response to ongoing stimuli. Sometimes the hedonic intensity of a constant stimulus *increases* over time—a process called "sensitization" (Groves and Thompson 1973). The increasing irritation produced by exposure to a disliked roommate is a familiar example. Sensitization is rarely discussed in the literature but has been observed for some painful and other intense stimuli (Thompson et al. 1973). Sensitization to pleasurable stimuli might be illustrated by the alleged increasing pleasure from successive experiences with marijuana, or high-quality wine, food, and culture.[6] The "mere exposure effect" (Zajonc 1968) is another example of sensitization because it is an *increasing* hedonic response to repetition of stimuli that are initially hedonically neutral—such as pictures of male faces (Zajonc 1968) or Pakistani folk music (Heingartner and

Hall 1974).[7] One might also consider mood-dependent memory as a form of sensitization, because a depressed mood cues negative thoughts, which intensify the depressed mood, which, in turn, cues further negative thoughts, and so on (Bower 1981).

Modeling the Functional Form of Adaptation

Helson (1947, 1948, 1964) was one of the first to propose a quantitative model of adaptation. His model was an attempt to characterize formally the effect of past stimuli on the subjective experience of a current stimulus. He introduced the notion of an adaptation level (*AL*)—the level of a stimulus that elicits no response (or, in the context of *hedonic* adaptation, the level that is affectively neutral). Helson proposed that *AL* is the average of past stimulus levels (X = stimulus level, and t = time):[8]

$$AL_t = \frac{1}{t} \sum_{\tau = 0}^{t} X_\tau \qquad (16.1)$$

He further proposed that an individual's hedonic state (u) at any time (t) is a function of the difference between the current stimulus level, X_t, and *AL*:

$$u_t = f(X_t - AL_t), \qquad (16.2)$$

where $f(0) = 0$, and $f' \geq 0$, as is true of the value function in figures 16.1, 16.2, and 16.3. Because *AL* gradually converges to the value of any constant stimulus level, X_t, the absolute difference between X_t and *AL*, gradually diminishes over time, as does the absolute value of u_t, which is a function of this difference. Thus, Helson's model captures the essence of adaptation—that persistent bad things gradually become less aversive, and persistent good things gradually become progressively less pleasurable.

Helson's specific formulation has, however, been criticized on a number of grounds. Sarris (1967) demonstrated (in the context of judgments of the heaviness of hefted weights) that extreme stimulus levels do not influence *AL* as much as Helson's theory predicts. Parducci (1968) found that judgments are influenced by factors other than the mean stimulus level and proposed "range-frequency" theory as an alternative to Helson's theory. Range-frequency theory postulates that judgments of perceptual stimuli (lengths of lines, heaviness of weights) and hedonic stimuli (odors or rewards of money) are jointly determined by two separate contextual features—the position and the rank of a stimulus within the stimuli included in some judgmental context. Suppose, for example, that a traveling salesman earns $0, $95, $100, $100, and $90, respectively, on each of his first five days of work. The range principle alone would cause $90 to be evaluated favorably because $90 exceeds the midpoint of the stimulus range ($50). The frequency principle alone would cause $90 to be experienced negatively because it ranks below the median stimuli ($95). The aggregate judgment will depend on the relative importance of these two principles (see Parducci 1995).

Helson's and Parducci's models of adaptation share a common shortcoming—they do not explicitly account for the role of time. For example, although both theories imply that the judged quality of a dinner will be influenced by the quality of past dinners, they make no explicit distinction between the effects of a fancy dinner experienced last week and one enjoyed last year.[9] Intuitively, it seems far more likely that recent events will have a larger impact on one's *AL* than events that are more remote in time.

A formulation that does explicitly include the temporal component and has been widely used to model adaptive processes (See for example, Hardie, Johnson, and Fader 1993; March 1988; Ryder and Heal 1973) is:

$$AL_t = \alpha X_{t-1} + (1 - \alpha)AL_{t-1}, \qquad (16.3)$$

with $1 \geq 0$. The α parameter determines the speed of adaptation. If $\alpha = 1$, then the adaptation level is equal to the last period's stimulus level, so that the individual's hedonic state will depend solely on the difference in stimulus level between the last period and the current period. If $\alpha = 0$, then the adaptation level will not be influenced by past stimulus levels at all. Equation 16.3 can be rewritten as:

$$AL_t - AL_{t-1} = \alpha(X_{t-1} - AL_{t-1}), \quad (16.4)$$

which highlights the equation's implicit assumption that the change in the adaptation level from one time period to the next is proportional to the difference between the last period's stimulus level and the last period's adaptation level. By applying equation 16.3 recursively, it is also possible to show that the adaptation level at any point in time can be represented by a weighted average of past stimulus levels, with recently experienced stimuli receiving greater weight than those experienced in the more distant past.[10]

To illustrate some of the implications of this formulation, assume that f is the identity function, that $\alpha = 0.5$, and that X represents the objective level of some positive stimulus occurring on seven consecutive days (for example, number of encyclopedias sold, hours of sunshine, minutes of attention from one's spouse).

	Mon.	Tue.	Wed.	Thu.	Fri.	Sat.	Sun.
X	3	5	12	4	5	5	5
AL	3[a]	3	4	8	6	5.5	5.25
u	0	+2	+8	−4	−1	−0.5	−0.25

Notes: X = stimulus level; AL = adaptation level; u = hedonic state.

[a]For simplicity, we assume that the stimulus level had been constant at a level of 3 in the past.

This example illustrates two principal features of most models of hedonic adaptation: (1) the affective intensity and valence of a given stimulus level depend on past stimuli (note that Tuesday is a good day, and Friday is a bad day, though the objective circumstances are the same on both days); and (2) the affective intensity of a constant stimulus diminishes over time (note that the experience of receiving five units of X gets better [less bad] from Friday to Sunday).

Several authors have proposed modifications to the "weighted average" model of adaptation level formation. Some have argued, for example, that satisfaction with income depends not just on the absolute improvement over past levels but on the *rate* of improvement over time (Frank 1992; Hsee and Abelson 1991; Hsee, Abelson, and Salovey 1991; Loewenstein and Sicherman 1991). Strahilevitz and Loewenstein (1998) have proposed that hedonic adaptation to improvements is faster than hedonic adaptation to deteriorations, an asymmetry that implies a separate, larger α parameter for gains than for losses.

It is difficult, however, to formally represent all of the factors that determine the influence of a stimulus on adaptation level. Certain extreme or memorable events may have a much greater influence on adaptation level than most variants of the models discussed here would predict. For example, the memory of a single romantic encounter with Mr. or Ms. Perfect may forever diminish the satisfaction of subsequent interactions with Mr. or Ms. Ordinary—even if that single encounter happened ten years ago and even if it has been succeeded by scores of lesser experiences. Parducci (1995) reports that the memoirs of Russian émigrés who lost their wealth fleeing the 1917 revolution suggest that they felt impoverished for the remainder of their lives because they continued to judge their later material circumstances against the wealth level they had enjoyed many years before, rather than against some average of their lifetime wealth (much less against a weighted average that emphasized the recent past). Conversely, even very recent events may not influence our reference points if they do not seem relevant to some judgmental context.[11] For example, a Christmas bonus probably does not reduce our satisfaction with our normal monthly salary in January, and resort owners are probably not disappointed by the usual marked drop in attendance following Labor Day. These complexities pose serious challenges to theories of adaptation that attempt to model the impact of past stimuli as a simple function of their magnitude and recency.

Is an Average Stimulus Hedonically Neutral?

According to a popular joke, sex is like pizza: when it is good, it is really good, and when it is bad, it is still pretty good. This captures an important point that models of adaptation often miss: many experiences are inherently pleasant and do not require a positive comparison to make them so (see Kahneman, this volume). An encyclopedia salesman who likes his job can have a pleasant day in spite of average sales, just as an average pizza can taste good.

A simple way of modifying adaptation models to account for this obvious truth is to add a positive or negative constant ($u_t = c + f[X_t - AL_t]$) to reflect the "inherent" goodness or badness of an experience—that is, the amount of pleasure or pain one receives from an "average" experience (when $X_t = AL_t$). This would reflect the fact that certain experiences continue to be pleasurable even when the current level is at, or even below, AL. Experiences like pizza and sex that have a large intrinsic pleasantness component would require a large constant term, whereas a smaller constant would apply to experiences such as an exam score, where experience is evaluated primarily by comparative standards. This would capture the intuition that it takes a very bad pizza to make the experience unpleasant, but only a slightly lower grade than you are used to getting to spoil a grade that is good by other standards.[12]

The Influence of Future Stimuli

Although adaptation level is typically assumed to be a function of past stimuli, it may also depend on anticipation of future stimulus levels—a process called "feedforward." Feedforward was dramatically illustrated by Siegel and his colleagues (Siegel et al. 1982; Siegel, Krank, and Hinson 1988). Rats injected with gradually increasing doses of heroin came to tolerate dosages that would have been lethal to them at the outset of the study. However, the resistance to heroin was observed only when the injection was administered at a regular time in a regular location. The identical dose of heroin administered at an unexpected time or in a new location was often fatal. Apparently, the rats' adaptive response to the heroin was not triggered solely by ingestion of the drug, but also by cues that became associated with, and therefore predictive of, imminent heroin use. Feedforward processes have also been implicated as an important process underlying human drug addiction (for reviews of this literature, see Laibson 1997; Loewenstein 1996).

Feedforward seems to apply to hedonic phenomena as well. Van Praag and his colleagues (for example, van Praag 1977; van Praag and van der Sar 1988) found that the income people view as "sufficient" depends, in part, on their expectations for the future.[13] There is also evidence that the final days of a prison sentence are often regarded as the most frustrating—suggesting that prisoners are "adapting" prematurely to the anticipated joys of freedom (Bukstel and Kilmann 1980, 482). Such adaptation may be responsible for the frequently noted anomaly that escape attempts are often made near the end of a prison sentences.[14] Feedforward processes may also help explain the paradoxical observation that revolutions tend to occur just after conditions begin to *improve*—the "revolution of rising expectations" (Gurr 1970). Initial improvements may produce expectations of future improvement and create frustration when the anticipated improvements do not occur or are not realized quickly enough.

Multiple Reference Points

The literature on sensory and perceptual adaptation has commonly assumed that the adaptation level in a particular domain can be characterized by a single summary number. As Helson (1947) comments, "For every excitation-response configuration, there is assumed a stimulus which represents the pooled effect of all the stimuli to which the organism may be said to be attuned or adapted" (2). The assumption of a single adaptation level may be reasonable for many types of adaptation. For example, the adaptation level of spiciness marking the boundary between too spicy and too bland may be accurately modeled by a single number representing the average spiciness of the foods one is used to consuming. In other contexts, however, the effect of past stimuli cannot be summarized so simply. Consider the case of an individual who earned $20,000 annually for her first six years on the job, got a promotion that raised her salary to $50,000, then was transferred two years later to a different department where she earned $40,000. What is her adaptation level income? It is possible that she compares her current salary to a single adaptation level lying somewhere between $20,000 and $50,000. It seems more likely, however, that she has two different adaptation levels—one at $20,000 and the other at $50,000—that are invoked in different situations and both of which contribute to her satisfaction or dissatisfaction with her current salary.[15] Although the issue of multiple reference points has been raised (see, for example, Boles and Messick 1995; Kahneman 1992; Schweitzer 1995; Strahilevitz and Loewens-

tein 1998), their formation and relative weighting has not been investigated empirically.

MEASUREMENT ISSUES

A comprehensive treatment of the literature on hedonic adaptation is impossible without considering the many methodological problems that plague this line of research.

Scale Norming

The literature on perceptual adaptation has hosted a long-standing debate about whether adaptation is "real" or simply a matter of relabeling. Stevens (1958), for example, argues that some of the evidence Helson cites to support his adaptation level theory merely illustrates the judgmental relativity of labels and not "adaptation" in its conventional sense (see also Krantz and Campbell 1961). For example, when a given weight is called "very heavy" in the context of lighter weights and "very light" in the context of heavier weights, it seems more plausible that a different label is being given to the same (or a similar) perception than that the perception itself is changing.[16]

Similar issues plague research on hedonic adaptation because answers to questions about well-being inherently confound respondents' "true" happiness with their semantic conventions, reference groups, and other factors that influence their interpretation of the response scale on which well-being is reported. When asked for judgments of well-being (for example, "How happy are you on a scale from 0 to 100?"), respondents must usually decide for themselves what the endpoints of the response scale represent. Thus, one person may interpret 100 as the highest level of happiness they have thus far experienced, another may interpret it as the highest level of happiness they can imagine experiencing on earth, and a third might interpret it as a hypothetical state of ideal, heavenly bliss. Similarly, one person might interpret 0 as the absence of salient good feelings, while another may reserve that label to represent the most intolerable hell imaginable.

An obvious problem arises if factors that affect respondents' "true" happiness also affect their use of scales. Suppose, for example, that a sample of quadriplegics and control subjects both rate their happiness as 80 on a 100-point scale. This number may accurately represent the true happiness levels of the two groups. However, it may also overstate the happiness of the quadriplegics if they implicitly rate their own happiness relative to that of other quadriplegics (who may be much less happy than the control group)[17] or elevate their current rating to reflect the contrast to their extreme despair immediately following the onset of their disability, or if they have adopted lower standards for the intensity of positive affect that warrants the rating 80. All of these forms of norming could lead researchers to overestimate the degree of adaptation to paralysis.

Some researchers (for example, Diener et al. 1985) have suggested that *frequency* measures of affect (the proportion of time an individual feels "good" or "bad") may be less susceptible to scale norming than *intensity* measures (how happy the individual is at a given time, or how happy he or she is overall). Evidence from some judgmental domains suggests that contextual effects do not influence the judged *valence* (positive versus negative) of a stimulus even if they do influence the absolute value of the judgment. In other words, contextual factors may make things more or less good or more or less bad, but they do not make bad experiences good or good experiences bad. (Changing the context of reference may turn a -7 into a -2 but will not turn a -2 into a $+2$.) Kicking someone's dog is not rated positively even if it is evaluated in the context of very severe crimes (Parducci 1968), and losing fifty dollars in a card game is not considered good even if you usually lose more (Marsh and Parducci 1978).

However, frequency measures have their own problems. First, valence does not capture everything one might want to know about affect. A person who experiences extreme highs and shallow lows clearly enjoys a higher quality of life than one who experiences the opposite, even if the two individuals spend identical proportions of time on the positive and negative sides of the hedonic ledger. Second, it is not obvious that even the valence of well-being judgments is immune to scale-norming effects. If you ask someone whether she is having a good day, she must still decide where to make the division between good and bad, and this choice may be affected by the distribution of recent experiences that set the context for that judgment. Thus, a "no" response from a newlywed might indicate a more positive level of affect than a "yes" response from a person receiving chemotherapy.

There have been occasional attempts to avoid the problems created by scale norming by supplementing verbal responses with physiological or behavioral measures that should be immune to such effects. For example, Krupat (1974) found that prior exposure to threat not only lowered subjects' ratings of the "threateningness" of a given situation but also reduced their galvanic skin conductance (a physiological measure of experienced threat)—suggesting that the difference in ratings was not purely a semantic phenomenon. Dar, Ariely, and Frenk (1995) used both verbal and behavioral measures of pain in veterans who had suffered injuries of varying severities in the past: *pain threshold*—the length of time the subject could hold his index finger in hot (48 degrees Celsius) water before he classified the sensation as painful—and *pain tolerance*—the length of time before he pulled his finger out of the water. The authors found that veterans with more severe past injuries not only held their finger in longer before classifying the sensation as painful (10.1 seconds versus 4.7 seconds) but also held their finger in longer before terminating the experiment (58 seconds versus 27 seconds).[18] This is compelling, but not conclusive, evidence that the veterans with more severe prior injuries actually felt less pain. It is possible that the more severely injured veterans not only had different semantic standards for the intensity of sensation that warrants the label "pain" but also had different standards about how much pain they should be willing to endure.

Not all studies, however, have observed parallel results between physiological and self-report measures. For example, Paulus, McCain, and Cox (1973) reported a positive relation between prisoner density and palmar sweat (a physiological measure of stress), but not between density and subjective appraisals of crowding. Ostfeld and his colleagues (1987) found that prisoner density was correlated with blood pressure, but not with measures of anxiety, hostility, or depression. Zisook, Shuchter, and Lyons (1987) observed a dramatic decrease in tearfulness in the first year following the death of a spouse, but no significant decline in reported depression. Divergence between measures that are intended to measure the same construct may indicate the presence of measurement error or bias, or it could point to the existence of multiple independent dimensions of hedonic status.

Context and Demand Effects

Some judgments requested from subjects in adaptation studies are vulnerable to social-desirability effects. Adaptation may be overreported if subjects feel pressured to exaggerate how much they benefited from some intervention like a support group

(Conway and Ross 1984). Conversely, adaptation may be underreported if subjects fear appearing callous if they truthfully report substantial or complete emotional recovery from some negative event, such as the death of a spouse. Indeed, many psychiatrists have considered the lack of affective reaction to some negative event as a disorder. For example, Wortman and Silver (1989) cite an Institute of Medicine report by Osterweis, Solomon, and Green (1984) that stated: "The absence of grief phenomena following bereavement represents some form of personality pathology. . . . Professional help may be warranted for persons who show no evidence of having begun grieving" (18). They also cited an article by Siller (1969) that maintained: "[When] a newly disabled person does not seem to be particularly depressed, this should be a matter of concern. [The person] should be depressed because something relatively significant has happened, and not to respond as such is denial" (292).

Furthermore, apart from demand effects, simply asking respondents about a particular event may temporarily raise its prominence.[19] This problem is noted by Lehman, Wortman, and Williams (1987) in a paper about the long-term effects of losing a spouse or child in a motor vehicle crash: "The most serious threat to the validity of these findings concerns the possibility that respondents' distress scores were artificially inflated because . . . by contacting respondents and requesting an interview, we raised a series of troubling issues that are not normally on their minds"(228).

Asking about a troubling event may not only raise its prominence but actually induce negative affect, a possibility that raises ethical as well as methodological issues.

Threats to Internal Validity

Interpretation of study results from most empirical research on hedonic adaptation is nonexperimental, and, thus, subject to the problem of confounds. *Retrospective* studies (in which people are asked to report their current subject state and to recall past states) are problematic because recollections are notoriously inaccurate and may reflect the individual's implicit theories about change processes rather than a veridical recollection of prior hedonic states (Ross 1989).[20] *Cross-sectional* studies (which compare the affect of people who have been exposed to a particular stimulus with that of those who have not) suffer from the difficulty of matching the exposed and nonexposed

subgroups. For example, Janal and his colleagues (1994) found that habitual joggers displayed a higher pain threshold for cold than nonjogging control subjects. They noted, however, that this relative insensitivity could suggest either that jogging produces adaptation to pain or that people who are more tolerant of discomfort are likely to select jogging as their form of exercise.[21] *Longitudinal* studies (which compare the affect of people at different points in time) are confounded by the problem of *history* (other events that occur during the observed time period), *maturation* (effects that result from the aging of the observed population), and *regression* to the mean if study participants are selected based on an extreme value of some hedonic measure (such as being counseled for depression).

Measurement Ambiguities Created by a Nonconstant Stimulus

Adaptation is well defined only when a response diminishes or remains the same despite constant or increasing stimulus level; sensitization is well defined only when a response increases or stays the same despite a constant or decreasing stimulus level. It is difficult to determine whether adaptation or sensitization has occurred in situations in which both the stimulus and response levels move in the same direction. For example, suppose the amperage of an electric shock delivered to an experimental subject is increased over a series of trials, and the behavioral or subjective response measure also increases—the subject yells louder, jumps higher, or exhibits a greater elevation in blood pressure. It isn't clear whether this observation supports adaptation (the response increase was less than it would have been without adaptation), sensitization (the response increased more than would be expected from the stimulus increase), or neither (the response increase was commensurate with the stimulus increase). For another example, suppose that the concentration of some atmospheric pollutant doubles, and the subjective rating of air quality decreases from a 4 to a 3 (on a 5-point scale), or the average time spent outdoors decreased by twenty minutes. Would the changes in these dependent variables indicate adaptation or sensitization to the increased air pollution? (Of course, whether we choose to label the change in the dependent variable "adaptation" or "sensitization" may be less important than an evaluation of whether the effects are "big" or "small" relative to our expectations, or relative to the effects wrought by other changes.)

Is It Possible to "Adapt to Depression"?

A second source of conceptual ambiguity regarding hedonic adaptation is illustrated by a colleague's comment that people "can't adapt to depression," a speculation that struck us as strange, after some reflection. Because depression is itself a subjective state, it is difficult to interpret what adapting to depression could mean—that a person doesn't feel bad when he feels bad? The concept of adapting to pain also seems problematic, though less so. While it still seems unusual to say, "Although I'm still experiencing intense pain, I've completely adapted to it," the statement may make sense if one separates the experience of pain into *sensory* and *affective* components, as many pain researchers have done (Ahles, Blanchard, and Leventhal 1983; Fernandez and Turk 1992; Leventhal et al. 1979; Leventhal et al. 1989; Price, Harkins, and Baker 1987). For example, in a study by Price, Harkins, and Baker (1987), subjects experiencing pain separately rated its sensory and affective components using two visual analog scales whose endpoints were either "the *most intense sensation* imaginable" (the sensory component) or "the *most unpleasant feeling* imaginable" (the affective component). By considering the components of pain separately, one could interpret "adapting to pain" as a reduction in intensity of the affective component, despite a constant or increasing sensory component.[22]

RESEARCH ON ADAPTATION IN SPECIFIC DOMAINS

We now turn to a review of the literature on hedonic adaptation to specific experiences and conditions, both undesirable (such as noise) and desirable (such as an increase in income). Our review is limited by the shortage of high-quality empirical studies.[23] We discuss only the small subset of domains where it seemed possible to draw at least tentative conclusions about the extent of hedonic adaptation.

Undesirable Experiences

Noise   Few studies have observed adaptation to noise, and some have even found sensitization (for a discussion, see Weinstein 1982). Weinstein (1978) interviewed first-year college students about their reactions to dormitory noise in the first few weeks of the school year and again at the end of the year. Reported annoyance *increased* significantly. In a study on highway noise, Weinstein (1982) interviewed a panel of residents four months and sixteen months after the highway was opened. Reported irritation remained constant, and residents became *increasingly* pessimistic about their ability to adjust to the noise (the proportion who said they would *not* be able to adjust increased from 30 to 52 percent). Perhaps more tellingly, in two control groups interviewed only once, fewer than one-third of residents interviewed at $t =$ four months spontaneously mentioned highway noise as something they disliked about the neighborhood, compared to over half of those interviewed at $t =$ sixteen months. Jonsson and Sörensen (1973) had earlier found comparable results, in a similar study. Cohen and his colleagues (1980, 1981) found little evidence of adaptation to aircraft noise among Los Angeles schoolchildren. Children in noisy schools did more poorly on a cognitive task and had shorter attention spans and higher systolic and diastolic blood pressure than those from matched control schools. Neither longitudinal nor cross-sectional analyses suggested that the differences in these outcomes diminished over time, with the exception of systolic blood pressure, where the differences between noisy and quiet schools did decrease slightly.

Incarceration   Although incarceration is *designed* to be unpleasant, most of the research on adjustment to prison life points to considerable adaptation following a difficult initial adjustment period.[24] In a study of British prisoners, Flanagan (1980) observed generally successful long-term adjustment (although prisoners reported that specific stressors, such as the loss of relationships with people outside the prison, became increasingly difficult to deal with as time passed). In a sample of inmates whose sentences varied from one month to ten years, Wormith (1984) observed significant improvement over time in deviance, attitude, and personality measures. Mackenzie and Goodstein (1985) recorded similar results. Zamble and Proporino (1990) and Zamble (1992) reported declining dysphoria, a reduction in stress-related problems such as sleep disturbances, and decreasing boredom over the course of prison sentences.

Even inmates placed in solitary confinement for long periods adapt to their circumstances. Deaton and his colleagues (1977) report that American soldiers placed in solitary confinement during the Vietnam War (for up to six years) were highly successful in devising effective coping mechanisms. Suedfeld and his colleagues (1982) observed similarly successful adaptation to solitary confinement in civilian prisons. Indeed, some found it difficult to adjust to *release* from solitary confinement.

Although there appears to be considerable hedonic adaptation to imprisonment throughout most of the prison term, evidence suggests that prisoners find their incarceration less tolerable as they approach the end of their sentence—presumably because they begin to compare the circumstances of incarceration with the freedom they are beginning to anticipate (see section on *feedforward*). Bukstel and Kilmann (1980) reviewed thirty-one studies of adaptation to prison and concluded that the hedonic response to incarceration shows a curvilinear pattern over time, with long-term improvement in functioning followed by a short-term deterioration near the end of the sentence.

Disability/Disease   Several studies have observed substantial adaptation to disability. The most famous is Brickman, Coates, and Janoff-Bulman's (1978) "Lottery Winners and Accident Victims: Is Happiness Relative?" Accident victims (those who had become paraplegic or quadriplegic as a result of an accident within the last year) rated their happiness as 2.96 on a 5-point scale (above the midpoint)—a result that is widely interpreted as evidence for remarkable adaptation to extreme misfortune.[25] Other researchers have come to similar conclusions. Schulz and Decker (1985) interviewed one hundred middle-aged and elderly paraplegics and quadriplegics and found that reported well-being levels were only slightly lower than population means of nondisabled people of similar age.[26] Wortman and Silver (1987) found that quadriplegics reported no greater frequency of negative affect than control respondents. In a review of several empirical studies, Tyc (1992) found "no difference in quality of life or psychiatric symptomatology" in young patients who had lost limbs to cancer compared with those who had not.[27] In a review of studies examining adaptation to burn injuries, Patterson and his colleagues (1993) reported similarly high levels of psychosocial adaptation by one year after the accident.

There is less evidence of adaptation to chronic or progressive diseases such as chronic rheumatoid arthritis (Smith and Wallston 1992), multiple sclerosis (Antonak and Livneh 1995), and other degenerative disorders (Livneh and Antonak 1994).

However, the progressive deterioration associated with these diseases makes it difficult to measure the degree of adaptation (see the section on *nonconstant stimulus*). The progression of multiple sclerosis, for example, typically leads to increasing numbness, paralysis, spasticity, fatigue, vertigo, problems in bladder control, sexual dysfunction, difficulty in communication, cognitive deterioration, and visual impairments (Antonak and Livneh 1995). Thus, in contrast to paralysis victims, whose condition is likely to remain constant over time, sufferers of such debilitating diseases must cope not only with the disabilities resulting from the cumulative deterioration they have thus far suffered but with new impairments as their disease progresses. Even maintaining a constant hedonic state in the face of these deteriorating conditions would be impressive evidence of hedonic adaptation. Thus, the hedonic deterioration that is commonly observed does not provide evidence that adaptive processes are not occurring—only that they are not occurring fast enough to keep pace with the progression of the disease.

Loss (Bereavement)   Studies of bereavement have generally found that those who lose a child or spouse experience intense and prolonged grief (Dyregrov 1990; Lehman et al. 1987; Sanders 1980; Weiss 1987), and that such dramatic effects are much rarer in those losing friends, colleagues, parents, or siblings who live in different households (Weiss 1988; Stroebe, Stroebe, and Hansson 1993). Kaprio, Koskenvuo, and Rita (1987) noted that in the week following the death of a spouse, suicide rates are elevated almost tenfold for women, and almost seventyfold for men. Wortman and her colleagues (1992) found that it took almost one decade before widows and widowers approached a control group's scores on life satisfaction, and nearly two decades before differences in depression were no longer significant.

While intense and prolonged grief is common, it is not universal. Wortman and Silver (1989, 1990) review evidence suggesting that a substantial minority of individuals do not experience extreme grief at all. For example, Wortman and Silver (1987) found that about 30 percent of parents who had lost a child to sudden infant death syndrome (SIDS) showed no significant depression at any time following the infant's death. In the same article, these authors contest the widely held belief that the absence of grief shortly after a death is a sign of repression or denial. They found, instead, that the absence of grief shortly after the loss is a positive indicator of long-term well-being, and that "delayed grief" is, in fact, fairly uncommon.

Similarly, there is little evidence supporting the widespread belief that recovery from (adaptation to) bereavement proceeds in "stages." Considerable variability is observed with respect to the types of emotions that are experienced, their sequence, and their intensity at various times (Silver and Wortman 1980; Wortman et al. 1993). While there are clearly large individual differences in styles of coping with bereavement, some of the variability observed among people may be due to the situational aspects of the loss. For example, grief seems to be particularly long-lasting if the loss is unexpected (Lehman et al. 1987; Wortman and Silver 1987). We return to this issue when we discuss forewarning as a moderator of adaptation.

Desirable Experiences

Just as adaptive processes reduce the impact of negative changes, they may also diminish the pleasure of positive events or improving circumstances. In this section, we review evidence of adaptation (or lack of adaptation) to two favorable changes, increases in wealth and improved appearance following cosmetic surgery, and to the repetition of hedonically positive stimuli—erotic images and foods.

Increases in Income   Few studies have examined the relation between wealth levels and happiness within individuals across time. However, hedonic adaptation is suggested by the following findings. First, Brickman, Coates, and Janoff-Bulman (1978) studied twenty-two state lottery winners who had won between $50,000 and $1,000,000 within the previous year. These lottery winners reported only slightly higher levels of life satisfaction than a control group (4.0 versus 3.8 on a 5-point scale).[28] Second, at least within the United States, there is only a small positive correlation between wealth and reported happiness. Diener and his colleagues (1993) estimated the correlation at 0.12. Third, several studies have observed no change in well-being in a country as its real income increases over time (Campbell 1981; Duncan 1975; Easterlin 1974, 1995). For example, between 1958 and 1987, real per capita income in Japan rose fivefold, while subjective judgments of happiness did not increase (Easterlin 1995). Fourth, though moderately strong correlations between wealth and well-being have been found between countries (Veenhoven 1991; Diener et al. 1993; Diener, Diener, and Diener 1995), wealth per se does not appear to be driving the correlation. For example, Diener, Diener, and Diener (1995) conducted a massive cross-sectional study of reported well-being in one hundred thousand people from fifty-five different countries whose per capita income ranged from $120 (Tanzania) to $32,790 (Switzerland). Although measures of per capita wealth and average reported well-being were highly correlated (0.58), controlling for human rights eliminated the correlation. Fifth, Clark (1996) presents evidence from British data that job satisfaction is strongly related to *changes* in a worker's pay, but not to *levels* of pay.

Scitovsky (1976) has even suggested that wealth may undermine happiness. He argues that pleasure results from incomplete and intermittent satisfaction of desires, and that the continuous comforts made possible by substantial wealth may remove the conditions necessary for this experience. While consistent with the popular conception of the "poor little rich girl," this speculation is inconsistent with the positive, albeit small, correlation between wealth and happiness that is observed in cross-sectional empirical studies.

Cosmetic Surgery   The small number of longitudinal studies of people who have received cosmetic surgery have generally not observed adaptation to increased attractiveness. The vast majority of patients report satisfaction with the results of cosmetic operations (Wengle 1986),[29] which does not appear to decrease over time. In a study of nine hundred cosmetic and plastic surgery patients, Reich (1982) found that satisfaction increased from 70 percent at three months after the operation to 85 percent four years later. Young, Nemecek, and Nemecek (1994) found that reported satisfaction remained constant. Beale and his colleagues (1985) did, however, observe a slight decrease.[30]

In addition to satisfaction with the surgery itself, several studies have indicated an overall improvement in psychological health or life satisfaction as a whole. Ohlsen, Ponten, and Hamburt (1978) noted that twenty-five of seventy-one women in their study were receiving psychiatric treatment prior to a breast augmentation procedure, whereas only three continued to do so after the operation. Klassen and his colleagues (1996) also found substantial reductions in psychiatric symptomatology among people receiving plastic surgery. Cole and his colleagues (1994) reported that 73 percent of their patients reported a higher quality of life after cosmetic surgery, compared to only 6 percent who reported a lower quality of life. The largest gains were for cosmetic breast surgery (both reductions and enlargements), with slightly smaller gains for abdominoplasty (tummy tucks) and only slight gains for rhinoplasty (nose jobs). All of these studies should be treated with caution, however, because of the likelihood of strong demand effects in reporting satisfaction with cosmetic surgery.[31]

Sexually Arousing Stimuli   The evidence regarding adaptation to sexually arousing stimuli is mixed. O'Donohue and Geer (1985) and Koukounas and Over (1993) found that male sexual arousal (as measured by penile tumescence and subjective report) diminished with repeated presentation of erotic slides. Meuwissen and Over (1990) found similar results for female sexual arousal to fantasy and sexual films. However, Smith and Over (1987) found no decline in physiological or subjective arousal for male subjects who were instructed to imagine the same sexual fantasy in eighteen repeated trials, and Laan and Everaerd (1995) found no evidence of reduction in genital arousal for females repeatedly presented with erotic slides—in fact, arousal increased somewhat over the ten trials despite returning to baseline levels during interstimulus intervals.[32]

Foods   Most adults enjoy every day at least one substance they once found aversive, such as coffee, beer, tobacco, chili peppers, and other strong spices (Rozin and Schiller 1980). Thus, for some foods, repeated exposure not only reduces initial subjective unpleasantness (adaptation) but later continues to increase subjective pleasantness (sensitization). Torrence (1958) found that previous consumption of pemmican (dried meat) by military aircrewmen led to increased liking when it was later eaten during a survival exercise, even among the minority who initially found the taste pleasant. Stevenson and Yeomans (1995) found that the hedonic quality of the burning sensation of capsaicin (the hot compound in chili peppers) was enhanced by repeated exposure. Crandall (1984) gave the employees of a remote Alaskan fish cannery access to cake doughnuts not normally available in their diet on thirteen occasions during a twenty-nine-day period. He found a significant rise in consumption of doughnuts over time, which suggests increased liking. Repeated exposure has also been found to increase liking for unfamiliar tropical fruit juices (Pliner 1982), novel fruits and cheeses (Birch and Marlin 1982), low-salt foods (Beauchamp, Bertino, and Engelman 1983), and plain yogurt (Kahneman and Snell 1990).

The hedonic effects of repeated consumption may, of course, depend on the interval between consumption events—one may like kiwi fruit more and more every year, but not enjoy the fifth kiwi fruit consumed at dinner as much as the first. There has been little research on the duration of "sensory-specific satiety" (Rolls et al. 1981) for different types of foods. Thus, conclusions about the temporal dynamics of affect may depend on the length of the interval between successive consumptions. For example, Kahneman and Snell (1990) found that people who consumed a small serving of their chosen flavor of ice cream over eight consecutive *days* liked it less over time. Perhaps an opposite effect would be found if the servings were consumed over eight consecutive *weeks*.[33]

Explaining Domain-Specific Differences in Hedonic Adaptation

What distinguishes the things people can and cannot adapt to hedonically? Why can people adapt to prison but not to noise? Why are the pleasures of increased income fleeting, while the pleasures of foods and erotic stimuli are sustained despite repeated exposure? Part of the answer may lie in evolutionary pressures. We should not expect much adaptation to stimuli that are necessary for continued survival and reproduction (for example, food and sex), nor to stimuli that strongly compromise survival (for example, harmful chemicals, very hot or cold temperatures).[34]

Beyond this broad generalization, we may look for specific features of situations and stimuli that can help to explain differences in the degree of hedonic adaptation across different domains. For example, the failure to adapt to highway noise may reflect its high temporal variability. Perhaps people could adapt to a constant loud drone, but not to occasional random bursts of noise from motorcycles with sawed-off mufflers. In the following section, we discuss some of the moderators of adaptation.

MODERATORS OF ADAPTATION

Social Support

Social contact with other people who have had similar experiences is generally found to facilitate hedonic adaptation. In their study of bereavement over the death of a spouse or child, Wortman and Lehman (1985) found that contact with a similar other was frequently mentioned as *the* most helpful factor in assuaging grief, and it was never mentioned as unhelpful. Mullan (1992) found similar results. Regarding adaptation to limb loss, Parkes (1972) argues: "It is only when [handicapped persons] meets someone more seriously mutilated than [themselves] who appears to be coping well and cheerfully with his disability that it becomes possible for [them] to look to the future in an optimistic and realistic manner."[35]

People who have not had similar experiences, however, often give inadequate or inappropriate support. For example, Walker, MacBride, and Vachon (1977) concluded that even intimate friends of widows did not support their need to mourn for more than a few days after the death, and Shuchter and Zisook (1993) cite the intolerance of family members to the bereaved one's continuing grief as a major impediment to successful coping with bereavement. Maddison and Walker (1967) reported that bereaved widows were often encouraged by friends to begin thinking about remarriage within a few *weeks* of the husband's death. Similarly, Hughes, Good, and Candell (1993) found that the psychological adjustment of recent divorcees was impeded when friends continually offered advice. Afflictions and disabilities with no obvious manifestations (such as chronic fatigue syndrome) pose special problems as well, because sufferers are likely to face performance expectations that exceed their abilities (see Tyc 1992).

Advance Notice

Studies on forewarning of and anticipatory grief over a loved one's death generally indicate that it improves affect and functioning after bereavement (though for a more equivocal interpretation of the evidence, see Stroebe and Stroebe 1987; and Hill, Thompson, and Gallagher 1988). In a review of the literature on the effects of forewarning on coping with the death of a husband, O'Bryant (1991) concluded: "No investigation of conjugal bereavement . . . has found that adjustment to widowhood was poorer when the spouse had been forewarned" (229). In a study of the bereavement of people who had cared for spouses or parents with progressive dementia, Mullan (1992) states: "The progressive decline of the impaired family member . . . affords ample opportunity to prepare psychologically for the death"; moreover, "many of these

caregivers reported that they had already experienced the loss of the person for whom they were caring, and the greater the sense of loss during caregiving, the lower the depression during bereavement" (681). Parkes and Weiss (1983) found that those who had "short forewarning" (less than two weeks' notice) that their spouse was going to die seemed less able to put the death behind them than those who had had a longer warning period, and a large body of evidence reviewed by Lehman, Wortman, and Williams (1987) is also consistent with the conclusion that preadaptation occurs, or that the anticipation of loss accelerates the adaptation process.[36]

However, the benefits of advance notice of a negative outcome must be balanced against the aversiveness of waiting for that outcome to take place. Even if advance notice does improve post-outcome well-being, its *overall* effect on well-being is ambiguous since receipt of the bad news may diminish the well-being of the person between the time the notice is received and the time the event actually occurs. Thus, the improved post-outcome adaptation doesn't necessarily compensate for the earlier onset of misery associated with advance warning. In some cases, however, the net effect seems clear. For example, in the study by Parkes and Weiss (1983), the tremendous reduction in long-term suffering associated with advance notice of widowhood would seem to more than compensate for the reduction in affect from receiving the bad news somewhat sooner.

When forewarning does improve post-loss well-being, how does it do it? Does it produce a type of *preadaptation,* or accelerate the process of post-loss adaptation? In principle, these processes could be discriminated by a longitudinal study of people who suffered a loss either with or without prewarning.[37] If forewarning advances the time course of adaptation (that is, if there is preadaptation), as illustrated by figure 16.4, the immediate post-loss state would be more favorable among those who had forewarning. If forewarning accelerates the process of adaptation, however, as depicted in figure 16.5, then hedonic ratings would be similar immediately after the event but would improve more quickly.

Curiously, advance warning seems to predict worse outcomes in other domains. Lazarus (1968) reviews evidence suggesting that subjects who were given a longer advance warning that they would watch a gruesome film clip (about genital subincision or wood-shop accidents) displayed more stress during the film (as measured by skin conductance) than subjects who received no such

FIGURE 16.4   Hedonic Impact of Forewarning If It *Advances the Start* of Adaptation

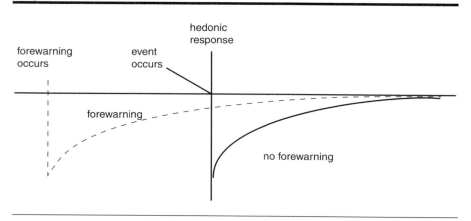

advance warning. He concludes: "Very clearly, when the anticipatory times involved are relatively brief, a longer period of anticipation results in a more marked stress reaction" (236). Breznitz (1967) made a similar observation, which he called the "incubation of threat." Subjects were told they would receive a severe electric shock after either three, six, or twelve minutes. Those facing a longer time interval had faster heart rates immediately preceding the shock.

Sapolsky (this volume) reports evidence from animal research suggesting that the effect of advance warning may depend on the interval prior to the aversive event. If two groups of rats are exposed to a random pattern of electric shock, but one is shown a warning light that flashes ten seconds before the shock, the rats receiving the warning exhibit lower stress and lower incidence of stress-related disease than the rats who receive no such warning. However, flashing the warning signal a half-hour before the shock produces the opposite pattern—the warned rat displays greater amounts of stress and stress-related disease than the non-warned rats. These results make intuitive sense if one assumes that forewarning decreases the aversiveness of the event itself but increases the stressfulness of the waiting period. Thus, the hedonically optimal forewarning period may be one that is long enough to allow for the mobilization of defenses, but no longer.

FIGURE 16.5   Hedonic Impact of Forewarning If It *Accelerates the Rate* of Adaptation

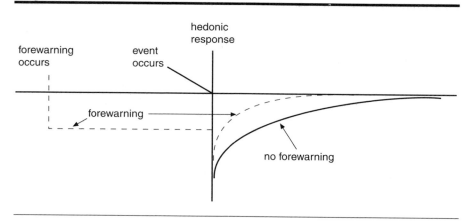

Uncertainty

Although folk wisdom often stresses the importance of maintaining hope in the face of some likely negative outcome, many researchers have suggested that successful adaptation to an adverse outcome is actually *impeded* by the possibility of relief. Herrmann and Wortman (1985), for example, draw a sharp distinction between stressors that "confront victims with a life situation that is fundamentally altered" (168), such as the loss of their spouse or permanent paralysis, and more ambiguous situations, such as that of a couple who continue to fail to conceive a child for some unknown reason and who must continually decide between abandoning their hope to conceive a child and intensifying their efforts at conception—perhaps by seeking out new medical specialists or procedures. The authors suggest that the latter type of situation poses special difficulties for adaptation.

Successful hedonic adaptation may require a person to "take a hit"—to recognize, admit, and confront some loss. Even a small possibility that such actions will later prove to be premature or unnecessary may prevent people from undertaking them. Consistent with this argument, it is commonly reported that concrete proof of a missing person's death (such as physical remains) has a large, long-term, positive impact on the coping of family members, and that, likewise, adaptation is poor for relatives of people who die without leaving concrete evidence of their demise—such as soldiers missing in action, the people who "disappeared" from their homes during the dictatorships in Argentina and Chile, or the victims of "ethnic cleansing" in Bosnia.[38]

The notion that someone who is 100 percent sure that something bad has happened is better off than someone who is 95 percent sure may seem counterintuitive. However, a small remaining hope may impede the onset of adaptive processes that could eventually return one to normal hedonic levels. Indeed, there is substantial evidence suggesting such a pattern. Moulton and his colleagues (1991) examined the impact of HIV testing in a sample of homosexual men and found that those testing positive showed less hopelessness and distress than did a cohort of non-notified controls (who agreed to be tested but did not wish to be notified). A similar pattern has been observed in studies examining the impact of notification of Huntington's disease test results (Brandt et al.

1989; Wiggins et al. 1992). Those receiving adverse test results eventually had better hedonic outcomes than those who were not tested or those who received an uninformative test result. Sapolsky (this volume) reports that "During the blitz of London, there was more of an increase in ulcer rates in the suburbs, which were bombed only intermittently, than in the city center, which was bombed like clockwork each night." Schelling (1984) reports that addicts suffer less withdrawal pain when there is absolutely no possibility of obtaining the drug.

Adaptation to imprisonment provides further anecdotal evidence for the conjecture that uncertainty impedes hedonic adaptation. Sapsford (1978) claims that uncertainty about the length of their sentence is a source of misery for prisoners with a life sentence but also a chance of parole. Scitovsky (1976) cites Farber (1944) to the effect that "prisoners who had hopes of parole suffered much more than those who knew they would never be released" (57). Roberts and Jackson (1991) cite the case of a man released from prison after serving thirty-seven years under an indeterminate sentence on the grounds that his continued imprisonment under these circumstances constituted cruel and unusual punishment. The stress of uncertainty may be particularly acute for inmates on death row who cling to the small possibility of repeal. Thus, successful adaptation to death row may, paradoxically, involve giving up hope (Gallemore and Panton 1972, 170).[39]

Reminders, Distractions, and Intrusive Thoughts

Shuchter and Zisook (1993) comment that the bereaved find themselves trapped in a world of continuous threats because of the triggers that cue painful thoughts and memories. For example, among parents who have recently lost an infant, the mere sight of other babies often stimulates intense grieving (Cornwell, Nurcombe, and Stevens 1977). The powerful influences of reminders raises two issues for hedonic adaptation. First, does successful adaptation involve avoiding painful cues, or confronting them, or some of each (for example, by deliberately confronting grief-inducing cues in a supportive setting but otherwise avoiding them)? Second, if cues cannot easily be avoided (as in the case of marital sex triggering memories of prior incest or rape), how can the emotional consequences be minimized?

Attributions

Attribution theory predicts that (1) people will attempt to assign responsibility for adverse events, and (2) those who hold themselves responsible will feel worse than those who do not (see, for example, Weiner 1982). The evidence we reviewed on both of these points, however, was mixed. Taylor (1983) found that 95 percent of a sample of women diagnosed with breast cancer did try to make some attribution for its occurrence, such as stress, taking birth control pills, living near a chemical dump, hereditary factors, or diet. However, Downey, Silver, and Wortman (1990) found that nearly half of the mothers in their study who lost their babies to SIDS were unconcerned about assigning responsibility. Similarly, studies have found that less than half of all victims of accidents that led to severe burns (Kiecolt-Glaser and Williams 1987) or physical disabilities (Silver 1982) said they ever asked themselves, "Why me?"

Regarding the second point, Wortman (1976), Janoff-Bulman (1979), and Tennen and Affleck (1990) have all argued that external attributions do not always facilitate coping. Janoff-Bulman and Wortman (1977) found that victims of severe accidents who blamed themselves for the accident were coping more successfully eight to twelve months afterward than those who did not, and that victims who blamed other *people* (as opposed to some nonspecific external cause) displayed especially low coping scores. The authors postulate that self-blame may help to maintain a sense of personal control. However, Sapolsky (this volume) comments on the negative effects of rigidly maintaining an internal locus of control: "It is beneficial for individuals to interpret themselves as being in control only if they live in relatively benign environments. . . . Such an attitude may be considered pathological when it occurs in poor people with limited opportunities. . . . In such a setting, an internal locus of control, where one habitually decides that those insurmountable odds could have been surmounted if only they had worked harder, is highly maladaptive."[40]

Perception of "Silver Linings"

The desire to explain an event is closely related to the desire to find "meaning" in an experience or to identify some positive consequence of it (a "silver lining"). In a study of seventy-eight women with breast cancer, Taylor (1983) found that over half reported that the cancer experience had caused them to reappraise their lives in a favorable way. Similarly, ten of the twenty-nine accident victims in Janoff-Bulman and Wortman's (1977) study believed that God had intentionally (and benevolently!) selected them for victimization. However, in a study of people paralyzed in auto accidents, Lehman, Wortman, and Williams (1987) report that three-fourths of their subjects were unable to find any meaning in their loss.

From his experience in Auschwitz, Frankl (1963) concluded that the ability to find meaning and purpose in their suffering was essential for the survival of concentration camp prisoners. Less anecdotally, Taylor (1983) found that women who found positive meaning in their breast cancer exhibited "significantly better psychological adjustment" (1163). Affleck and his colleagues (1987) found that men who perceived benefits from a heart attack were less likely to have a subsequent attack and exhibited lower morbidity eight years later. Of course, the causal direction between meaning-making and adaptation may run in either or both directions. It is also possible that adaptation and meaning-making are spuriously correlated through their common relation to a third factor, such as innate happiness, which causes people to both adjust successfully to their new condition and find meaning in it.

Counterfactuals

Counterfactuals—mental representations of things that were not actually experienced—can sometimes influence the evaluation of (or adaptation to) a situation in the same way that actual experiences do. Thus, salient positive counterfactuals ("Things could have turned out so much better") should increase one's reference point and reduce well-being, and salient negative counterfactuals ("There but for the grace of God go I") should reduce one's reference point and improve well-being. Deliberate attempts to enhance affect by generating negative counterfactuals are not typically very effective, however. We cannot usually make ourselves happy by simply imagining more unfortunate individuals or more unpleasant situations. To influence our hedonic state, counterfactuals must be *plausible*, not just *possible*, alternatives to reality (see Kahneman and Miller 1986).[41]

Conclusions

Limits of Adaptation

The literature on adaptation has led some to the view that long-run happiness and life satisfaction do not depend much on one's objective circumstances (Lykken and Telligen 1996). However, anyone who has experienced extended periods of happiness in certain environments and unhappiness in others should be skeptical of this extreme conclusion. There are other reasons for skepticism as well. First, as our review suggests, adaptation is not observed in all domains, and there may even be some domains where *sensitization* is the rule. Both of us can think of ongoing features of our environments, such as a good or bad roommate, that were *increasing* sources of either pleasure or pain. Second, as argued earlier, some of the results indicating dramatic adaptation may be partly due to scale norming. Third, satisfaction with a particular outcome or outcome level is often influenced by social norms, social comparisons, and other salient referents that do not necessarily converge to our average experience. For example, if a person aspires to earn as much as his neighbor, the difference between his income and his aspiration level income may increase over time. Conversely, a prosperous individual who grew up in poverty may remain perpetually delighted with her luxurious lifestyle if her memory of her early days remains salient throughout her life. Fourth, and most obviously, some things are just inherently good or bad—they occupy only one side of a natural and immutable "zero point" (see Kahneman, this volume).

Costs of Adaptation

Although hedonic adaptation confers enormous benefits by reducing the subjective effects of adverse conditions, it has associated costs as well. The most obvious cost of hedonic adaptation is that it occurs for goods as well as bads, creating what Brickman and Campbell (1971) have called the "hedonic treadmill"—the tendency for transitory satisfactions to eventually give way to indifference or even dissatisfaction. Scitovsky (1976) comments that "the attainment of a goal seems, when the moment of triumph is over, almost like a let-down" (62). Adaptation to pleasurable experiences may also be responsible for destructive

addictions, which are due in part to the decreasing pleasure from a given level of a good or activity and in part to the displeasure (craving) when consumption of the good or activity ceases (see, for example, Koob et al. 1989; Loewenstein 1996).

Second, the low sensitivity to differences in stimulus levels far from the adaptation level and the high sensitivity to differences near the adaptation level (see figures 16.1 and 16.2) may degrade the quality of decision-making, considering the experienced value of the relevant outcomes. For example, from the vantage point of a $10,000-a-year graduate fellowship, the difference between a $60,000 or $65,000 starting salary may seem inconsequential and not even worth asking about, much less bargaining over. Yet just a few years later, when the student is a faculty member earning $60,000, she may be willing to pack up, move, and sever friendships to earn $5,000 more somewhere else.

Third, adaptation may erode our aesthetic standards. Dubos (1965) comments on adaptation to urban life:

> This very adaptability enables [us] to become adjusted to conditions and habits which will eventually destroy the values most characteristic of human life. Millions . . . are so well adjusted to the urban and industrial environment that they no longer mind the stench of automobile exhaust, or the ugliness generated by the urban sprawl; they regard it as normal to be trapped in automobile traffic; to spend much of a sunny afternoon on concrete highways among the dreariness of anonymous and amorphous streams of motor cars. (278–79)

Fourth, adaptation may work against moral values. In his book *Nazi Doctors,* Robert J. Lifton (1990) describes a process whereby German doctors (who had taken the Hippocratic oath to do no harm) were gradually transformed into active killers. Doctors were first asked to be present when euthanasia took place, then to add their signature to a document, then to supervise a mercy killing, and so on, until they actually administered the lethal injections to "eugenically undesirable" persons. The famous Milgram experiment provides another example. Subjects were not asked to administer a potentially lethal shock immediately but were given a series of requests to increase the voltage slightly. Having just administered a one-hundred-volt shock to someone, it may be difficult to justify stopping at that particular level rather than complying with the experimenter's request to increase the voltage to 105.

Fifth, adaptation may reduce our empathy toward others in different situations. People indignantly wonder: How can Donald Trump be so rapacious when he already has so many millions? Why is that academic, already so renowned, greedy for still more recognition and so reluctant to acknowledge the contributions of collaborators? How could a few misplaced items provoke such an impassioned response from our spouse when the apartment seems so immaculate by our former standards? All of these examples suggest the difficulty of empathizing with the motivations and behaviors of others who have adapted to situations different from our own.

Sixth, just as adaptation causes us to fail to understand the behavior of others, it may cause us to mispredict our own emotions or behavior under different future circumstances. For example, untenured academics overestimate how happy they will be if they get tenure or how unhappy they will be if they fail to get tenure (Gilbert et al. 1997). People also typically underestimate how attached they will become to objects that are not currently in their possession (Loewenstein and Adler 1995). Errors in predicting one's own feelings and behavior are the focus of Loewenstein and Schkade's chapter (this volume).

Final Comments

Existing research permits few general conclusions about hedonic adaptation. We have made an attempt to summarize results that recur in the small subset of rigorous studies and to at least broach some of the issues that remain unresolved. Clearly, more research is required in specific domains and on specific moderators of hedonic adaptation. However, perhaps the single most pressing need is for richer and more diverse measures of hedonic states. Along with subjective self-reports of sensation or affect, researchers should make greater use of alternative hedonic indicators, including: global measures of functioning, such as employment status, frequency of hospital visits, and quantity of psychiatric help sought; behavioral measures, such as tearfulness or facial expressions (see, for example, Husted Medvec, Madey, and Gilovich 1995), gross physiological correlates such as blood pressure; specific neurological correlates such as the relative activation between brain regions (for example, negative affect seems to be associated with activation of the right frontal hemisphere, whereas

positive affect seems to be associated with activation of the left frontal hemisphere—see Ito and Cacioppo, this volume); and performance in affect-mediated memory and decision-making tasks (see, for example, Arkes, Herren, and Isen 1988).[42]

Assuming that future research provides a deeper understanding of hedonic adaptation, is it likely that such information would cause people to conduct their lives differently? Would they stop wearing seatbelts with the assurance that they would get used to being paralyzed? Would they exploit an embezzlement opportunity knowing that prison wouldn't be all that bad in the long run? We suspect not. However, perhaps a few would be saved from the misery of renting a noisy apartment they would never have gotten used to.

We are grateful for comments and suggestions from Robyn Dawes, Tonya Engstler-Schooler, Baruch Fischhoff, Donna Harsch, Daniel Kahneman, Susan Nolan-Hoeksema, and Daniel Read, and for financial support from the Center for Integrated Study of the Human Dimensions of Global Change at Carnegie-Mellon University (NSF grant #SBR-9521914).

NOTES

1. Calling any behavior that reduces the effect of a stimulus an "adaptation" may be using the term too loosely. Suppose that a person who moves to a hot climate reports that she has gotten used to the heat. Does that report constitute evidence of adaptation if we know that she now wears lighter clothes, has purchased an air conditioner, and ventures outdoors less during the middle of the day? Is it correct to say that she has "adapted" to the heat or merely that she limited her exposure to it? Similarly, suppose a bereaved man destroys all pictures of a deceased loved one and moves to a different city to avoid contact with friends who might trigger disturbing memories. If those steps do, in fact, reduce emotional pain, would it be correct to say that he has successfully "adapted" to his bereavement?

2. Adaptation is the primary biological property differentiating physics and *psycho*physics (Shepard 1981). Compare how a thermometer and a human hand register temperature. Mercury has an invariant and unique response—its volume is always the same at fifty-five degrees, and always different at other temperatures. It does not matter whether the mercury was previously stored in an oven or an ice bath, or whether it was stored in either place for hours or days or years. Mercury has no memory for previous states. Humans and other organisms do not behave this way. Our subjective experience of, and response to, a stimulus depends on more than its current physical intensity; it also depends on the strength, duration, and recency of previously experienced stimuli. Our experience of fifty-five-degree water is neither *invariant*

(fifty-five *feels* warmer to a hand previously immersed in ice water than to one previously immersed in hot water) nor *constant* (fifty-five feels different upon initial immersion than it does later) nor *unique* (fifty-five might feel the same to a hand previously immersed in ice water, as eighty does to a hand previously immersed in hot water).

3. Warr, Jackson, and Banks (1988) make a distinction between *resigned* adaptation and *constructive* adaptation. Resigned adaptation involves passive acceptance of one's condition, or reducing one's aspirations. Constructive adaptation, on the other hand, involves active attempts to mitigate one's loss or the adoption of different, but equally ambitious goals.

4. Our eyes (just one of our five senses) can transmit between 1.6 and 3 million bits of information per second, thousands of times more information than our brains can process (Scitovsky 1976, 52). Thus, some mechanism must act as an informational filter to select which perceptual information is processed. Adaptation serves this role by relegating constant stimuli to the perceptual background and focusing attention on rapid changes in stimulus levels—perceptual signals most likely to require a behavioral response.

5. For other examples of desensitization, imagine a commercial fisherman who develops thick calluses on his hands. Such calluses are an adaptation because they reduce the abrasive and lacerating effects of fishing nets and fish spines. However, the calluses will probably also cause a long-term reduction in overall tactile sensitivity, such as the ability to discriminate between different qualities of silk. Similarly, the destruction of cochlear cilia caused by continued exposure to loud noises may reduce the aversiveness of those loud noises but may also reduce sensitivity to changes in noise level at normal volumes (for example, when a baby's cry upstairs is added to the volume of a television show downstairs). Cometto-Muniz and Cain (1992) provide another example of desensitization. They found that exposure to airborne irritants like cigarette smoke increases mucus production, which physically impedes the transfer of molecules of airborne irritants from the air to the free nerve endings. This reduces the subjective intensity of airborne irritants, but it also reduces perceptual sensitivity to (and therefore the hedonic effect of) subtly pleasant smells. Linz and his colleagues (Linz, Donnerstein, and Penrod 1984, 1988; Linz, Donnerstein, and Adams 1989) have argued that repeated exposure to graphic sexual violence, such as "slasher" films, causes a type of emotional desensitization. They present evidence suggesting that viewers not only become less physiologically aroused and emotionally responsive while watching such films but less sympathetic to victims of violence in other, unrelated contexts.

6. Despite reports of high-level pleasures from connoisseurs, there is little empirical evidence that total pleasure is increased. The refinement in the tastes of connoisseurs may increase their ability to discriminate and the pleasure they derive from small positive differences. However, such refinement may also increase the aversiveness of negative differences. Moreover, a greater proportion of experiences may fall short of the connoisseur's ever-increasing standards. It would be interesting to investigate this issue using objective measures of pleasure such as facial encoding.

7. Berlyne (1970) offered a possible explanation for the apparent conflict between the adaptation literature, which suggests that repeated exposure *reduces* the affective intensity of stimuli, and the "mere exposure" effect, which shows the opposite. He speculated that repetition of "simple" stimuli decreases liking and repetition of "complex" stimuli increases liking. Rozin and Vollmecke (1986) made a similar observation: "On the basis of the data on food and other research on exposure effects . . . it seems that exposure is more likely to enhance liking when it occurs at moderate frequency, and when the stimuli are novel, relatively complex, or both. For many novel items, there may be enhanced liking at moderate levels of exposure, followed by decreased liking when exposure becomes more frequent" (449). However, stimulus "complexity" is difficult to measure, or even define, for many hedonically relevant stimuli like tastes or smells (Bornstein 1989).

8. In Helson's model, *AL* is the *arithmetic* mean of the psychological values or the *geometric* mean of the objective stimulus level, because it was assumed that the psychological magnitudes are a logarithmic function of the objective, physical stimulus magnitudes.

9. Parducci (1995) does posit that stimuli experienced in the distant past drop out of the judgmental context, though the model does not explicitly suggest the rate or degree to which they do.

10. For the multiple-period case, the formula can be simplified to:

$$AL_t = \sum_{\tau = -\infty}^{t} \alpha(1 - \alpha)^{t-\tau} x_\tau. \qquad (16.5)$$

11. Brown (1953) found that the effects of previous stimuli on subjects' assessments of weights were influenced much more when those stimuli were normal-looking laboratory brass weights than when they were metal trays of equal mass.

12. It is not clear that even this modification would be adequate, because the formulation still implies that introducing sufficiently excellent pizza into one's consumption history could render the experience of average pizza unpleasant. Note that if $f(X_t - AL_t)$ is a monotonically decreasing function of *AL,* and *AL* is a weighted average of previous stimulus levels, $X_{t-n} \cdots X_{t-1}$, introducing a sufficiently extreme experience would raise *AL* enough to make the entire expression $(c + f[X_t - AL_t])$ negative.

13. Van Praag and his colleagues have conducted some of the most careful studies focusing on the functional form of hedonic adaptation. In the late 1960s, van Praag developed a survey item that asked respondents to state the weekly, monthly, or yearly incomes they associated with six different descriptors: "very bad," "bad," "insufficient," "sufficient," "good," and "very good." Van Praag defined the individual's adaptation level income as the midpoint of the interval between insufficient and sufficient. He and his colleagues have conducted several studies to determine how the adaptation level income changes over time as a function of past, current, and anticipated income. His estimates based on British data suggest that the current period's reference point is an additive function of these three variables, with a weight of .16 for last year's income, .75 for this year's income, and .09 for next year's (anticipated) income. However, he notes, weight on the future is almost certainly underestimated owing to er-

rors in variables, since he estimates the equation using *actual* future income (identified by the researcher after the fact) as a proxy for *expected* future income.

14. The second author has collected a large amount of data on escape attempts in different states in an attempt to test this anomaly. The data proved extremely difficult to analyze owing to a combination of reporting irregularities, statistical complications, and other problems. However, conversations with wardens revealed that they had not, in general, noticed any pattern of late-stage escape attempts. Several did mention, though, that prisoners often attempt to escape after parole applications they had expected to be affirmed are rejected, a phenomenon that is consistent with a type of anticipatory adaptation.

15. Unless utility is a linear function of income, single and multiple reference points yield different utilities. With a single reference point formulation, $u = f(\$40,000 - [\alpha\ \$20,000 + (1-\alpha)\ \$50,000])$, where α designates the weighting of the two referents in determining the average reference value. With a multiple reference point formulation, $u = \alpha\ f(\$40,000 - \$20,000) + (1 - \alpha)\ f(\$40,000 - \$50,000)$, where α designates the fraction of time or attention devoted to each referent.

16. This criticism is not applied to all of the phenomena Helson cites in support of his theory. Stevens does not, for example, take issue with Helson's earlier work on changes in visual perceptions of color, which he admits as "real" adaptation. In other cases, like the judged darkness of different shades of gray, both real adaptation and semantic norming may be occurring.

17. Of course, such social comparisons may have real hedonic consequences as well as influencing how people interpret response scales.

18. All but one of the sixteen subjects who had previously suffered severe injuries held their finger in the water for the entire experiment (sixty seconds), whereas none of the other twenty-four subjects did so.

19. A similar focusing effect may occur when people predict the hedonic impact of future events. Simply asking people about how an event would affect their well-being seems temporarily to raise its prominence, leading to an overprediction of its actual impact (Loewenstein and Frederick 1997; Schkade and Kahneman 1998).

20. For example, Ross (1989) cited a study in which people who completed a weight-loss program remembered themselves as having been heavier at the outset of the program than they actually were, enabling them to maintain the (mistaken) belief that the program had been effective. Likewise, women's memories of menstrual pain bear little resemblance to their actual prior pain ratings. Instead, the pain ratings appear to be reconstructed from implicit (and inaccurate) theories about menstrual pain (McFarland, Ross, and DeCourville 1989).

21. The authors did not, however, find differences in tolerance with respect to other types of pain.

22. The set of experiential components we choose to call pain are themselves a subset of the aggregate experience. People who are congenitally unable to feel pain can nevertheless *detect* that they are being burned, pinched, or pricked—they simply do not experience those sensations as unpleasant (Cabanac 1971).

23. To illustrate some of the problems with the literature on adaptation, we excerpt some lamentably characteristic passages below, without attribution:

- "Problems relating to deprivation of liberty . . . were ranked as the most severe problems among the American long-term prisoners."
- "Parents generally suffer mood disturbances after the death of an infant. Depression and sadness is a very common reaction."
- "Major life changes . . . make demands that are larger and broader than those made by smaller ones."
- "High self-esteem may contribute to the sense of personal confidence."
- "Knowing that one experiences a positive event . . . yields the knowledge that something good has happened."
- "Enhanced motivation is associated with greater persistence at tasks."
- "Almost all children of divorce regard their childhood and adolescence as having taken place in the shadow of divorce."
- "Each individual is constrained in his or her actions by capability constraints."
- "When the processes of recovery are blocked, the result is a failure to recover."
- "Research on depression among people with Parkinson's disease . . . suggest that between 4 percent and 90 percent of this population are clinically depressed."

24. The fact that the initial shock of imprisonment gives way to substantial adaptation is evident from the statistic that 50 percent of suicides in prisons occur within the first twenty-four hours of imprisonment (Hayes 1983).

25. The evidence of hedonic adaptation in the paper is not overwhelming—paraplegics rate their happiness as 2.96 on a 5-point scale, compared to 3.82 for a control group. This seems to be a substantial difference, especially considering the tendency for subjects to avoid extreme response categories (Poulton 1989).

26. However, the authors noted that one of the respondents "frequently cried during the interview, and asked the interviewer to get a gun and kill him."

27. Caine (1973) did not find similarly successful adaptation among adult amputees, however. Perhaps adults suffer more "phantom limb" pain (Katz and Melzack 1990), which may be difficult to adapt to.

28. The authors suggested that the ecstasy accompanying the lottery win may have created a high reference point against which the rest of the winner's life then compared unfavorably. They noted that the lottery winners rated everyday activities (for example, eating breakfast, reading a magazine) as less pleasurable than did control subjects. The potential costs of intense positive affect are also discussed by Parducci (1984), Diener and his colleagues (1991), and Tversky and Griffin (1991).

29. Over 95 percent of rhinoplasty (nose job) patients were satisfied with the results (Klabunde and Falces 1964). The short-term postoperative satisfaction rate of women receiving breast enlargements ranges from 72 percent (Beale et al. 1985) to 86 percent (Young et al. 1994) to 89 percent (Ohlsen, Ponten, and Hambert 1978).

30. As noted by the authors, the reduced satisfaction may have been due to objective changes in the shape or softness of the breasts.

31. Beale and his colleagues (1985) comment on the strong demand effects to report satisfaction with the results of breast enlargements: "The women who have

complied with an augmentation mammaplasty have suffered; they have gone through laborious interviews, waited for years, and finally they have taken the risk of being operated on. All this is done by free choice and many times against the advice of relatives and doctors. Against this background, it seems impossible to admit to the interviewer, or even to oneself, that the operation was a failure" (484).

32. Laan and Everaerd (1995) noted an interesting contradiction—that evidence of adaptation to sexual stimuli has been used to explain both *inhibited* and *extreme* sexuality (*inhibited* because repeated behavior ceases to be sufficiently arousing, and *extreme* because people engage in increasingly intense sexual activities to maintain prior levels of gratification).

   For both males and females, the literature consistently found that arousal diminished more slowly to varied or novel stimuli than to constant stimuli (the same slide repeatedly viewed). In fact, novelty may not only diminish the effects of adaptation but reverse them. Consider, for example, the "Coolidge effect," which refers to the tendency for new sexual partners to restore the sex drive of previously satiated male animals (Bolles 1975; Dewsbury 1981).

33. Because rapidly repeated consumption of a specific food temporarily reduces its subjective pleasantness compared to other foods, access to a wide variety of foods serves to maintain the pleasantness of continued consumption. Indeed, increasing food variety has been shown to increase caloric intake in rats, cats, and humans (Rolls et al. 1981) and may partly explain the higher rates of obesity in cultures where a wide variety of foods are readily available (Rolls et al. 1981).

34. Indeed, Cometto-Muniz and Cain (1992) found very little sensory adaptation to pungent, harmful chemicals.

35. The recent rapid growth of specialized "support groups" may reflect a growing belief in the benefits of social contact with people who are experiencing similar problems. However, people's self-reports that they have been helped by a group are notoriously invalid measures of their actual hedonic change (see Ross 1989). For example, a recent study by Helgeson and her colleagues (1997) compared the effectiveness of two types of support interventions for women who had undergone breast surgery—an education program and a support group—against a control condition in which women were simply referred to their general practitioner. Although there was no difference in self-reported satisfaction with the two interventions, women who participated in the support group actually came out worse on a variety of psychological and health measures than either the education or control groups at a six-month follow-up.

36. Preadaptation may occur for divorce as well as death. Melichar and Chiriboga (1988) found that the psychological adjustment among women who initiated divorce was positively correlated with the time since their (private) decision to seek divorce, holding constant the time since the physical separation.

37. In practice, however, it is probably exceedingly difficult to separate the effect of forewarning from the effects of other attributes that correlate with forewarning and may themselves influence grief. For example, most of the deaths with no forewarning are likely to occur from homicides and auto accidents, whereas deaths with long forewarning are primarily from diseases such as cancer. If the group with no forewarning is adapting more poorly, it could be because of the lack of forewarning or because of the particular characteristics of deaths accompanied by little or no warning—for example, their violence or their "preventability."

38. The difficulty of adapting to loss in the face of uncertainty is evident in two passages from Sebastian Junger's best-seller *The Perfect Storm*, which is about a storm that cost the lives of men on the fishing boat Andrea Gail. As Sebastian recounts,

   If the men on the Andrea Gail had simply died and the bodies were lying in state somewhere, their loved ones could make their goodbyes and get on with their lives. But they didn't die, they disappeared off the face of the earth and, strictly speaking, it's just a matter of faith that these men will never return. Such faith takes work, it takes effort. The People of Gloucester must willfully extract these men from their lives and banish them to another world. (273)

   Writing about the wife of one of the missing men who was lost at sea in the same storm, Sebastian relates "After almost a month, Marianne Smith is able to start absorbing the loss of her husband. As long as the planes are going out she holds on to some shred of hope, and that keeps her in a ghastly kind of limbo." (283)

39. Uncertainty seems to impede adaptive behaviors in less weighty domains as well. For example, people seem far more reluctant to replace an item they have misplaced than one they have broken, even for items that cost only a few dollars and which exhaustive searches have failed to locate. It is very difficult to accept the fact that the ice cream scoop is "gone" if we do not know where it has gone to and this somehow seems to block or greatly delay the adaptive behavior of buying a new one.

40. Weiss (1971a, 1971b) found that laboratory rats who sit and endure electric shocks do not show as many stress symptoms as those who try, unsuccessfully, to avoid the shocks—thus obtaining feedback that their coping responses have been ineffective.

41. On this point, Parducci (1995, 179) comments: "Reminding well-fed children that the starving waifs of Africa would be grateful for the food they refuse to eat will not improve its taste. The well-fed child can hardly believe that he or she could just as well be among the starving. But knowing full well how freezing it would be outside, the same child might derive enhanced pleasure from snuggling beneath a down comforter on a cold winter night. There would have been ample experience with cold, perhaps as recently as when first slipping down between the cold sheets."

42. These ideas for alternative measures of happiness were stimulated by a discussion with Jonathan Schooler.

REFERENCES

Affleck, G., Tennen, H., Croog, S., and Levine, S. (1987). Causal attribution, perceived benefits, and morbidity after a heart attack: An eight-year study. *Journal of Consulting and Clinical Psychology, 55,* 29–35.

Ahles, T. A., Blanchard, E. B., and Leventhal, H. (1983). Cognitive control of pain: Attention to the sensory aspects of the cold pressor stimulus. *Cognitive Therapy and Research, 7,* 159–77.

Antonak, R. F., and Livneh, H. (1995). Psychosocial adaptation to disability and its investigation among persons with multiple sclerosis. *Social Science and Medicine, 40,* 1099–1108.

Arkes, H. R., Herren, L. T., and Isen, A. M. (1988). The role of potential loss in the influence of affect on risk-taking behavior. *Organizational Behavior and Human Decision Processes, 47,* 181–93.

Beale, S., Hambert, G., Lisper, H., Ohlsen, L., and Palm, B. (1985). Augmentation mammaplasty: The surgical and psychological effects of the operation and prediction of the result. *Annals of Plastic Surgery 14* (6), 473–93.

Beauchamp, G. K., Bertino, M., and Engelman, K. (1983). Modification of salt taste. *Annals of Internal Medicine, 98* (2), 763–69.

Berlyne, D. E. (1970). Novelty, complexity, and hedonic value. *Perception and Psychophysics, 8,* 279–86.

Birch, L. L., and Marlin, D. W. (1982). "I don't like it; I never tried it": Effects of exposure on two-year-old children's food preferences. *Appetite, 3,* 353–60.

Boles, T. L., and Messick, D. M. (1995). A reverse outcome bias: The influence of multiple reference points on the evaluation of outcomes and decisions. *Organizational Behavior and Human Decision Processes, 61,* 262–75.

Bolles, R. C. (1975). *The theory of motivation.* 2nd ed. New York: Harper and Row.

Bornstein, R. (1989). Exposure and affect: Overview and meta-analysis of research, 1968–1987. *Psychological Bulletin, 106* (2), 265–89.

Bower, G. H. (1981). Emotional mood and memory. *American Psychologist, 36,* 129–48.

Brandt, J., Quaid, K. A., Folstein, S. E., Garber, P., et al. (1989). Presymptomatic diagnosis of delayed-onset disease with linked DNA markers: The experience in Huntington's disease. *Journal of the American Medical Association, 261,* 3108–14.

Breznitz, S. (1967). Incubation of threat: Duration of anticipation and false alarm as determinants of the fear reaction to an unavoidable frightening event. *Journal of Experimental Research in Personality, 2,* 173–79.

Brickman, P., and Campbell, D. (1971). Hedonic relativism and planning the good society. In M. H. Appley (Ed.), *Adaptation-level theory: A symposium* (pp. 287–302). New York. Academic Press.

Brickman, P., Coates, D. and Janoff-Bulman, R. (1978). Lottery winners and accident victims: Is happiness relative? *Journal of Personality and Social Psychology, 36* (8), 917–27.

Brown, D. R. (1953). Stimulus similarity and the anchoring of subjective scales. *American Journal of Psychology, 66,* 199–214.

Bukstel, L. H., and Kilmann, P. R. (1980). Psychological effects of imprisonment on confined individuals. *Psychological Bulletin, 88* (2), 469–93.

Cabanac, M. (1979). Sensory pleasure. *Quarterly Review of Biology, 54* (1), 1–29.

Caine, D. (1973). Psychological considerations affecting rehabilitation after amputation. *Medical Journal of Australia, 2,* 818–21.

Campbell, A. 1981. *The sense of well-being in America: Recent patterns and trends.* New York: McGraw-Hill.

Cassens, G., Actor, C., Kling, M., and Schildkraut, J. J. (1981). Amphetamine withdrawal: Effects on threshold of intracranial reinforcement. *Psychopharmacology, 73,* 318–22.

Clark, A. E. (1996). Are wages habit-forming? OECD working paper. DEELSA.

Cohen, S., Evans, G. W., Krantz, D. S., and Stokols, D. (1980). Physiological, motivational, and cognitive effects of aircraft noise on children: Moving from the laboratory to the field. *American Psychologist, 35,* 231–43.

Cohen, S., Evans, G. W., Krantz, D. S., Stokols, D., and Kelly, S. (1981). Aircraft noise and children: Longitudinal and cross-sectional evidence on adaptation to noise and the effectiveness of noise abatement. *Journal of Personality and Social Psychology, 40* (2), 331–45.

Cole, R. P., Shakespeare, V., Shakespeare, P., and Hobby, J. A. E. (1994). Measuring outcome in low-priority plastic surgery patients using quality-of-life indices. *British Journal of Plastic Surgery, 47,* 117–21.

Cometto-Muniz, J. E., and Cain, W. S. (1992). Sensory irritation: Relation to indoor air pollution. In W. G. Tucker, B. P. Leaderer, L. Molhave, and W. S. Cain (Eds.), *Sources of indoor air contaminants: Characterizing emissions and health impacts. Annals of the New York Academy of Sciences* (vol. 641). New York: New York Academy of Sciences.

Conway, M., and Ross, M. (1984). Getting what you want by revising what you had. *Journal of Personality and Social Psychology, 47,* 738–48.

Cornwell, J., Nurcombe, B., and Stevens, L. (1977). Family response to loss of a child by sudden infant death syndrome. *Medical Journal of Australia, 1,* 656–58.

Crandall, C. (1984). The liking of foods as a result of exposure: Eating doughnuts in Alaska. *Journal of Social Psychology, 125* (2), 187–94.

Damasio, A. R. (1994). *Descartes' error: Emotion, reason, and the human brain.* New York. Putnam.

Dar, R., Ariely, D., and Frenk, H. (1995). The effect of past injury on pain threshold and tolerance. *Pain, 60,* 189–93.

Deaton, J. E., Berg, S. W., Richlin, M., and Litrownick, A. J. (1977). Coping activities in solitary confinement of U.S. Navy POWs in Vietnam. *Journal of Applied Social Psychology, 7,* 239–56.

Dewsbury, D. (1981). Effects of novelty on copulatory behavior: The Coolidge effect and related phenomena. *Psychological Bulletin, 89,* 464–82.

Diener, E., Colvin, R., Pavot, W., and Allman, A. (1991). The psychic costs of intense positive affect. *Journal of Personality and Social Psychology, 61* (3), 492–503.

Diener, E., Diener, M., and Diener, C. (1995). Factors predicting the subjective well-being of nations. *Journal of Personality and Social Psychology, 69* (5), 851–64.

Diener, E., and Fujita, F. (1996). Social comparisons and subjective well-being. In B. Buunk and R. Gibbons (Eds.), *Health, coping, and social comparison.* Hillsdale, N.J.: Erlbaum.

Diener, E., Larsen, R. J., Levine, S., and Emmons, R. A. (1985). Frequency and intensity: The underlying dimensions of positive and negative affect. *Journal of Personality and Social Psychology, 48,* 1253–65.

Diener, E., Sandvik, E., Seidlitz, L., and Diener, M. (1993). The relationship between income and subjective well-being: Relative or absolute? *Social Indicators Research, 28,* 195–223.

Downey, G., and Silver, R. C., and Wortman, C. B. (1990). Reconsidering the attribution-adjustment relation following a major negative event: Coping with the loss of a child. *Journal of Personality and Social Psychology, 59,* 925–40.

Dubos, R. (1965). *Man adapting.* New Haven, Conn.: Yale University Press.

Duncan, O. T. (1975). Does money buy satisfaction? *Social Indicators Research, 2,* 267–74.

Dyregrov, A. (1990). Parental reactions to the loss of an infant child: A review. *Scandinavian Journal of Psychology, 31,* 266–80.

Easterlin, R. A. (1974). Does economic growth improve the human lot? Some empirical evidence. In P. A. David and M. W. Reder (Eds.), *Nations and households in economic growth* (pp. 89–125). New York: Academic Press.

———. (1995). Will raising the incomes of all increase the happiness of all? *Journal of Economic Behavior and Organization, 27,* 35–47.

Farber, M. L. (1944). Suffering and the time perspective of the prisoner. *University of Iowa Studies in Child Welfare, 20,* 155–227.

Fernandez, E., and Turk, D. C. (1992). Sensory and affective components of pain: Separation and synthesis. *Psychological Bulletin, 112* (2), 205–7.

Flanagan, T. J. (1980). The pains of long-term imprisonment. *British Journal of Criminology, 20,* 148–56.

Frank, R. H. (1992). Frames of reference and the intertemporal wage profile. In G. Loewenstein and J. Elster (Eds.), *Choice over Time* (pp. 371–82). New York: Russell Sage Foundation.

Frankl, V. E. (1963). *Man's search for meaning.* New York: Washington Square Press.

Gallemore, J. L., and Panton, J. H. (1972). Inmate responses to lengthy death row confinement. *American Journal of Psychiatry, 129,* 167–72.

Gilbert, D. T., Pinel, E. C., Wilson, T. D., and Blumberg, S. J. (1997). Affective forecasting and durability bias: The problem of the invisible shield. Working paper. Cambridge, Mass.: Department of Psychology, Harvard University.

Groves, P. M., and Thompson, R. F. (1973). A dual-process theory of habituation: Neural mechanisms. In H. V. S. Peeke and M. J. Herz (Eds.), *Habituation* (vol. 2, pp. 175–205). New York: Academic Press.

Gurr, T. (1970). *Why men rebel.* Princeton, N.J.: Princeton University Press.

Hardie, B. G. S., Johnson, E. J., and Fader, P. S. (1993).

Modeling loss aversion and reference dependence effects on brand choice. *Marketing Science, 12,* 378–94.

Hayes, L. M. (1983). "And darkness closed in": A national study of jail suicides. *Criminal Justice and Behavior, 10,* 461–84.

Heingartner, A., and Hall, J. V. (1974). Affective consequences in adults and children of repeated exposure to auditory stimuli. *Journal of Personality and Social Psychology, 29* (6), 719–23.

Helgeson, V. S., Cohen, S., Schulz, R., and Yasko, J. (1997). Effects of education and peer discussion group interventions on six-month adjustment to stage I and II breast cancer. Working paper. Pittsburgh: Department of Psychology, Carnegie-Mellon University.

Helson, H. (1947). Adaptation level as frame of reference for prediction of psychophysical data. *American Journal of Psychology, 60* (1), 1–29.

———. (1948). Adaptation level as a basis for a quantitative theory of frames of reference. *Psychological Review, 55* (6), 297–313.

———. (1964). *Adaptation-level theory: An experimental and systematic approach to behavior.* New York: Harper and Row.

Herrman, C., and Wortman, C. (1985). Action control and the coping process. In J. Kuhl and J. Beckman (Eds.), *Action control: From cognition to behavior* (pp. 151–80). New York: Springer-Verlag.

Hill, C. D., Thompson, L. W., and Gallagher, D. (1988). The role of anticipatory bereavement in older women's adjustment to widowhood. *The Gerontologist, 28* (6), 792–96.

Hsee, C. K., and Abelson, R. P. (1991). The velocity relation: Satisfaction as a function of the first derivative of outcome over time. *Journal of Personality and Social Psychology, 60,* 341–47.

Hsee, C. K., Abelson, R. P., and Salovey, P. (1991). The relative weighting of position and velocity in satisfaction. *Psychological Science, 2,* 363–66.

Hughes, R., Good, E. S., and Candell, K. (1993). A longitudinal study of the effects of social support on the psychological adjustment of divorced mothers. *Journal of Divorce and Remarriage, 19* (1), 37–56.

Husted Medvec, V., Madey, S., and Gilovich, T. (1995). When less is more: Counterfactual thinking and satisfaction among Olympic medalists. *Journal of Personality and Social Psychology, 69,* 603–10.

Janal, M. N., Glusman, M., Kuhl, J. P., and Clark, W. C. (1994). Are runners stoical?: An examination of pain sensitivity in habitual runners and normally active controls. *Pain, 58,* 109–16.

Janoff-Bulman, R. (1979). Characterological versus behavioral self-blame: Inquiries into depression and rape. *Journal of Personality and Social Psychology, 37,* 1798–1809.

Janoff-Bulman, R., and Wortman, C. (1977). Attributions of blame and coping in the "real world": Severe accident victims react to their lot. *Journal of Personality and Social Psychology, 35* (5), 351–63.

Jonsson, E., and Sörensen, S. (1973). Adaptation to community noise: A case study. *Journal of Sound and Vibration, 26,* 571–75.

Junger, S. (1997). *The perfect storm.* New York: Harper-Collins.

Kahneman, D. (1992). Reference points, anchors, norms, and mixed feelings. *Organizational Behavior and Human Decision Processes, 51,* 296–312.

Kahneman, D., and Miller, D. T. (1986). Norm theory: Comparing reality to its alternatives. *Psychological Review, 93* (2), 136–53.

Kahneman, D., and Snell, J. (1990). Predicting utility. In R. Hogarth (Ed.), *Insights in decision making: A tribute to Hillel J. Einhorn* (pp. 295–310). Chicago: University of Chicago Press.

Kahneman, D., and Tversky, A. (1979). Prospect theory: An analysis of decision under risk. *Econometrica, 47,* 263–91.

Kaprio, J., Koskenvuo, M., and Rita, H. (1987). Mortality after bereavement: A prospective study of 95,647 widowed persons. *American Journal of Public Health, 77,* 283–87.

Katz, J., and Melzack, R. (1990). Pain "memories" in phantom limbs: Review and clinical observations. *Pain, 43,* 319–36.

Kiecolt-Glaser, J. K., and Williams, D. A. (1987). Self-blame, compliance, and distress among burn patients. *Journal of Personality and Social Psychology, 53,* 187–93.

Klabunde, E. H., and Falces, E. (1964). Incidence of complications in cosmetic rhinoplasties. *Plastic and Reconstructive Surgery, 34* (2), 192–6.

Klassen, A., Jenkinson, C., Fitzpatrick, R., and Goodacre, T. (1996). Patients' health-related quality of life before and after aesthetic surgery. *British Journal of Plastic Surgery, 49,* 433–38.

Koob, G. F., Stinus, L., Le Moal, M., and Bloom, F. E. (1989). Opponent process theory of motivation: Neurobiological evidence from studies of opiate dependence. *Neuroscience and Biobehavioral Reviews, 13,* 135–40.

Koukounas, E., and Over, R. (1993). Habituation and dishabituation of male sexual arousal. *Behaviour Research and Therapy, 31* (6), 575–85.

Krantz, D. L., and Campbell, D. T. (1961). Separating perceptual and linguistic effects of context shifts upon absolute judgments. *Journal of Experimental Psychology, 62* (1), 35–42.

Krupat, E. (1974). Context as a determinant of perceived threat: The role of prior experience. *Journal of Personality and Social Psychology, 29* (6), 731–36.

Laan, E., and Everaerd, W. (1995). Habituation of female sexual arousal to slides and film. *Archives of Sexual Behavior, 24* (5), 517–41.

Laibson, D. I. (1997). A cue-theory of consumption. Working paper. Cambridge, Mass.: Economics Department, Harvard University.

Lazarus, R. (1968). Emotions and adaptation: Conceptual and empirical relations. *Nebraska Symposium on Motivation, 16,* 175–266.

Lehman, D. R., Wortman, C. B., and Williams, A. F. (1987). Long-term effects of losing a spouse or child in a motor vehicle crash. *Journal of Personality and Social Psychology, 52* (1), 218–31.

Leventhal, E. A., Leventhal, H., Shacham, S., and Easterling, D. V. (1989). Active coping reduces reports of pain from childbirth. *Journal of Consulting and Clinical Psychology, 57,* 365–71.

Leventhal, H., Brown, D., Shacham, S., and Enquist, G. (1979). Effect of preparatory information about sensations, threat of pain, and attention on cold pressor distress. *Journal of Personality and Social Psychology, 37,* 688–714.

Lifton, R. J. (1990). *The Nazi doctors: Medical killings and the psychology of genocide.* New York: Basic Books.

Linz, D., Donnerstein, E., and Adams, S. M. (1989). Physiological desensitization and judgments about female victims of violence. *Human Communication Research, 15* (4), 509–22.

Linz, D., Donnerstein, E., and Penrod, S. (1984). The effects of multiple exposures to filmed violence against women. *Journal of Communication, 34,* 130–47.

———. (1988). The effects of long-term exposure to violent and sexually degrading depictions of women. *Journal of Personality and Social Psychology, 55,* 758–68.

Livneh, H., and Antonak, R. (1994). Review of research on psychosocial adaptation to neuromuscular disorders: I. Cerebral palsy, muscular dystrophy, and Parkinson's disease. *Journal of Social Behavior and Personality, 9* (5), 201–30.

Loewenstein, G. (1996). A visceral account of addiction. In J. Elster and O. J. Skog (Eds.), *Getting hooked: Rationality and addiction* (pp. 235–64). Cambridge: Cambridge University Press.

Loewenstein, G., and Adler, D. (1995). A bias in the prediction of tastes. *Economic Journal, 105,* 929–37.

Loewenstein, G., and Frederick, S. (1997). Predicting reactions to environmental change. In M. Bazerman, D. Messick, A. Tenbrunsel, and K. Wade-Benzoni (Eds.), *Psychological perspectives on the environment* (pp. 52–72). New York: Russell Sage Foundation.

Loewenstein, G., and Sicherman, N. (1991). Do workers prefer increasing wage profiles? *Journal of Labor Economics, 9,* 67–84.

Lykken, D., and Telligen, A. (1996). Happiness is a stochastic phenomenon. *Psychological Science, 7,* 186–89.

Mackenzie, D. L., and Goodstein, L. 1985. Long term impacts and characteristics of long term offenders. *Criminal Justice and Behavior, 13,* 427–47.

Maddison, D., and Walker, W. (1967). Factors affecting the outcome of conjugal bereavement. *British Journal of Psychiatry, 113,* 1057–67.

March, J. G. (1988). Variable risk preferences and adaptive aspirations. *Journal of Economic Behavior and Organization, 9,* 5–24.

Marsh, H. W., and Parducci, A. (1978). Natural anchoring at the neutral point of category rating scales. *Journal of Experimental Social Psychology, 14,* 193–204.

McFarland, C., Ross, M., and DeCourville, N. (1989). Women's theories of menstruation and biases in recall of menstrual symptoms. *Journal of Personality and Social Psychology, 57,* 522–31.

Melichar, J. F., and Chiriboga, D. A. (1988). Significance of time in adjustment to marital separation. *American Journal of Orthopsychiatry, 58* (2), 221–27.

Meuwissen, I., and Over, R. (1990). Habituation and dishabituation of female sexual arousal. *Behaviour Research and Therapy, 28,* 217–26.

Moulton, J. M., Stempel, R. R., Bacchetti, P., Temoshok, L., and Moss, A. M. (1991). Results of a one-year longitudinal study of HIV antibody test notification from the San Francisco General Hospital cohort. *Journal of AIDS, 4,* 787–94.

Mullan, J. T. (1992). The bereaved caregiver: A prospective study of changes in well-being. *The Gerontologist, 32* (5), 673–83.

O'Bryant, S. L. (1991). Forewarning of a husband's death: Does it make a difference for older widows? *Omega Journal of Death and Dying, 22,* 227–39.

O'Donohue, W. T., and Geer, J. H. (1985). The habituation of sexual arousal. *Archives of Sexual Behavior, 14,* 233–46.

Ohlsen, L., Ponten, B., and Hambert, G. (1978). Augmentation mammaplasty: A surgical and psychiatric evaluation of the results. *Annals of Plastic Surgery, 2* (1), 42–52.

Osterweis, M., Solomon, F., and Green, M. (Eds.). (1984). *Bereavement: Reactions, consequences, and care.* Washington, D.C.: National Academy Press.

Ostfeld, A., Kasl, S., D'Atri, D., and Fitzgerald, E. (1987). *Stress, crowding, and blood pressure in prison.* Hillsdale, N.J.: Erlbaum.

Parducci, A. (1968). The relativism of absolute judgments. *Scientific American, 219,* 84–90.

———. (1984). Value judgments: Toward a relational theory of happiness. In J. R. Eiser (Ed.), *Attitudinal judgment* (pp. 3–21). New York. Springer-Verlag.

———. (1995). *Happiness, pleasure, and judgment: The contextual theory and its applications.* Hove, Eng.: Erlbaum.

Parkes, C. M. (1972). Components of the reaction to loss of a limb, spouse, or home. *Journal of Psychosomatic Research, 16,* 343–49.

Parkes, C. M., and Weiss, R. S. (1983). *Recovery from bereavement.* New York: Basic Books.

Patterson, D. R., Everett, J. J., Bombardier, C. H., Questad, K. A., Lee, V. K., and Marvin, J. A. (1993). Psychological effects of severe burn injuries. *Psychological Bulletin, 113,* 362–78.

Paulus, P., McCain, G., and Cox, V. (1973). A note on the use of prisons as environments for investigation of crowding. *Bulletin of the Psychonomic Society, 6,* 427–28.

Pliner, P. (1982). The effects of mere exposure on liking for edible substances. *Appetite, 3,* 283–90.

Poulton, E. C. (1989). *Bias in quantifying judgments.* Hove, Eng.: Erlbaum.

Pribram, K. H. (1984). Emotion: A neurobehavioral analysis. In K. R. Scherer and P. Ekman (Eds.), *Approaches to emotion* (pp. 13–38). Hillsdale, N.J.: Erlbaum.

Price, D., Harkins, S., and Baker, C. (1987). Sensory-affective relationships among different types of clinical and experimental pain. *Pain, 28,* 297–307.

Reich, J. (1982). The interface of plastic surgery and psychiatry. *Clinics in Plastic Surgery, 9* (3), 367.

Roberts, J. V., and Jackson, M. (1991). Boats against the current: A note on the effects of imprisonment. *Law and Human Behavior, 15,* 557–65.

Rolls, B., Rowe, E., Rolls, E., Kingston, B., Megson, A., and Gunary, R. (1981). Variety in a meal enhances food intake in man. *Physiology and Behavior, 26,* 215–21.

Ross, M. (1989). Relation of implicit theories to the construction of personal histories. *Psychological Review, 96,* 341–57.

Rozin, P., and Schiller, D. (1980). The nature and acquisition of a preference for chili pepper by humans. *Motivation and Emotion, 4* (1), 77–101.

Rozin, P., and Vollmecke, T. A. (1986). Food likes and dislikes. *Annual Review of Nutrition, 6,* 433–56.

Ryder, H. E., and Heal, G. M. (1973). Optimal growth with intertemporally dependent preferences. *Review of Economic Studies, 40,* 1–33.

Sanders, C. M. (1980). A comparison of adult bereavement in the death of a spouse, child, and parent. *Omega Journal of Death and Dying, 10,* 303–22.

Sapsford, R. J. (1978). Life-sentence prisoners: Psychological changes during sentence. *British Journal of Criminology, 18,* 128–45.

Sarris, V. (1967). Adaptation-level theory: Two critical experiments on Helson's weighted-average model. *American Journal of Psychology, 80* (3), 331–44.

Schelling, T. (1984). Self-command in practice, in policy, and in a theory of rational choice. *American Economic Review, 74,* 1–11.

Schkade, D., and Kahneman, D. (1998). Does living in California make people happy? A focusing illusion in judgments of life satisfaction. *Psychological Science, 9,* 340–46.

Schulz, R., and Decker, S. (1985). Long-term adjustment to physical disability: The role of social support, perceived control, and self-blame. *Journal of Personality and Social Psychology, 48* (5), 1162–72.

Schweitzer, M. (1995). Multiple reference points, framing, and the status quo bias in health care financing decisions. *Organizational Behavior and Human Decision Processes, 63,* 69–72.

Scitovsky, T. (1976). *The joyless economy: The psychology of human satisfaction.* New York: Oxford University Press.

Shepard, R. (1981). Psychological relations and psychophysical scales: On the status of "direct" psychophysical measurement. *Journal of Mathematical Psychology, 24,* 21–57.

Shuchter, S. R., and Zisook, S. (1993). The course of normal grief. In M. Stroebe, W. Stroebe, and R. Hansson (Eds.), *Handbook of bereavement: Theory, research, and intervention* (pp. 23–43). Cambridge: Cambridge University Press.

Siegel, S., Hinson, R. E., Krank, M. D., and McCully, J. (1982). Heroin "overdose" death: Contribution of drug-associated environmental cues. *Science, 23,* 436–37.

Siegel, S., Krank, M. D., and Hinson, R. E. (1988). Anticipation of pharmacological and nonpharmacological events: Classical conditioning and addictive behavior. In S. Peele (Ed.), *Visions of Addiction.* Lexington, Mass.: Lexington Books.

Siller, J. (1969). Psychological situation of the disabled with spinal cord injuries. *Rehabilitation Literature, 30,* 290–96.

Silver, R. L. (1982). Coping with an undesirable life event: A study of early reactions to physical disability. Ph.D. diss. Northwestern University, Evanston, Ill.

Silver, R. L., and Wortman, C. B. (1980). Coping with undesirable life events. In J. Garber and M. E. P. Seligman (Eds.), *Human helplessness: Theory and applications* (pp. 279–340). New York: Academic Press.

Smith, C. A., and Wallston, K. A. (1992). Adaptation in patients with chronic rheumatoid arthritis: Application of a general model. *Health Psychology, 11* (3), 151–62.

Smith, D., and Over, R. (1987). Does fantasy-induced sexual arousal habituate? *Behaviour Research and Therapy, 25* (6), 477–85.

Solomon, R. L., and Corbit, J. D. (1974). An opponent-process theory of motivation: I. Temporal dynamics of affect. *Psychological Review, 81* (2), 119–45.

Stevens, S. (1958). Adaptation-level versus the relativity of judgment. *American Journal of Psychology, 71* (4), 633–46.

Stevenson, R. J., and Yeomans, M. R. (1995). Does exposure enhance liking for the chili burn? *Appetite, 24,* 107–20.

Strahilevitz, M., and Loewenstein, G. (1998). The effect of ownership history on the valuation of objects. *Journal of Consumer Research, 25,* 276–89.

Stroebe, M., Stroebe, W., and Hansson, R. (Eds.). (1993). *Handbook of bereavement: Theory, research, and intervention.* Cambridge: Cambridge University Press.

Stroebe, W., and Stroebe, M. (1987). *Bereavement and health.* New York: Cambridge University Press.

Suedfeld, P., Ramirez, C., Deaton, J., and Baker-Brown, G. (1982). Reactions and attributes of prisoners in solitary confinement. *Criminal Justice and Behavior, 9,* 303–40.

Taylor, S. (1983). Adjustment to threatening life events: A theory of cognitive adaptation. *American Psychologist, 38,* 1161–73.

Tennen, H., and Affleck, G. (1990). Blaming others for threatening events. *Psychological Bulletin, 107,* 209–32.

Thompson, R. F., Groves, P. M., Teyler, T. J., and Roemer, R. A. (1973). In H. V. S. Peeke and M. J. Herz (Eds.), *Habituation* (vol. 1, pp. 239–71). New York: Academic Press.

Torrence, E. (1958). Sensitization versus adaptation in preparation for emergencies: Prior experience with an emergency ration and its acceptability in a simulated survival situation. *Journal of Applied Psychology, 42* (1), 63–67.

Tversky, A., and Griffin, D. (1991). Endowment and contrast in judgments of well-being. In F. Strack, M. Arguyle, and N. Schwartz (Eds.), *Subjective well-being: An interdisciplinary perspective* (vol. 21, pp. 101–18). Oxford: Pergamon Press.

Tyc, V. L. (1992). Psychosocial adaptation of children and adolescents with limb deficiencies: A review. *Clinical Psychology Review, 2,* 275–91.

van Praag, B. (1977). The welfare function of income in Belgium: An empirical investigation. *European Economic Review,* 337–69.

van Praag, B. M. S., and van der Sar, N. L. (1988). Empirical uses of subjective measures of well-being. *Human Resources, 23,* 193–210.

Veenhoven, R. (1991). Is happiness relative? *Social Indicators Research, 24,* 1–34.

Walker, K. N., MacBride, A., and Vachon, M. L. S. (1977). Social support networks and the crisis of bereavement. *Social Science and Medicine, 11,* 35–41.

Warr, P., Jackson, P., and Banks, M. (1988). Unemployment and mental health: Some British studies. *Journal of Social Issues, 44* (4), 47–68.

Weiner, B. (1982). The emotional consequences of causal attributions. In M. S. Clark and S. T. Fiske (Eds.), *Affect and cognition: The seventeenth annual Carnegie symposium on cognition* (pp. 185–210). Hillsdale, N.J.: Erlbaum.

Weinstein, N. D. (1978). Individual differences in reactions to noise: A longitudinal study in a college dormitory. *Journal of Applied Psychology, 63,* 458–66.

———. (1982). Community noise problems: Evidence against adaptation. *Journal of Environmental Psychology, 2,* 87–97.

Weiss, J. M. (1971a). Effects of coping behavior in different warning signal conditions on stress pathology in rats. *Journal of Comparative and Physiological Psychology, 77,* 1–13.

———. (1971b). Effects of punishing the coping response (conflict) on stress pathology in rats. *Journal of Comparative and Physiological Psychology, 77,* 14–21.

Weiss, R. S. (1987). Principles underlying a manual for parents whose children were killed by a drunk driver. *American Journal of Orthopsychiatry, 57,* 431–40.

———. (1988). Loss and recovery. *Journal of Social Issues, 44* (3), 37–52.

Wengle, H. (1986). The psychology of cosmetic surgery: A critical overview of the literature 1960–1982. Part I. *Annals of Plastic Surgery, 16* (5), 435–43.

Wiggins, S., Whyte, P. Huggins, M., Adam, S., et al. (1992). The psychological consequences of predictive testing for Huntington's disease. *New England Journal of Medicine, 327,* 1401–5.

Wise, R. A., and Munn, E. (1995). Withdrawal from chronic amphetamine elevates baseline intracranial self-stimulation thresholds. *Psychopharmacology, 117,* 130–36.

Wormith, J. S. (1984). The controversy over the effects of long-term imprisonment. *Canadian Journal of Criminology, 26,* 423–37.

Wortman, C. B. (1976). Causal attributions and personal control. In J. H. Harvey, W. J. Ickes, and R. F. Kidd (Eds.), *New directions in attribution research* (vol. 1, pp. 23–51). Hillsdale, N.J.: Erlbaum.

Wortman, C. B., Kessler, R., Bolger, N., House, J. (1992). The time course of adjustment to widowhood: Evidence from a national probability sample. Unpublished manuscript, Duke University.

Wortman, C., and Lehman, D. (1985). Reactions to victims of life crises: Support attempts that fail. In I. G. Sarason and B. R. Sarason (Eds.), *Social support: Theory, research, and applications* (pp. 463–89). The Hague: Nijhof.

Wortman, C., and Silver, R. (1987). Coping with irrevocable loss. In *Cataclysms, crises and catastrophes: Psychology in action.* Master lecture series (vol. 6, pp. 189–235). Washington, D.C.: American Psychological Association.

———. (1989). The myths of coping with loss. *Journal of Consulting and Clinical Psychology, 57,* 349–57.

———. (1990). Successful mastery of bereavement and widowhood: A life course perspective. In P. B. Baltes and M. M. Baltes (Eds.), *Successful aging: Perspectives from the behavioral sciences* (pp. 225–64). New York: Cambridge University Press.

Wortman, C. B., Silver, R. C., and Kessler, R. C. (1993). The meaning of loss and adjustment to bereavement. In M. Stroebe, W. Stroebe, and R. Hansson (Eds.), *Handbook of bereavement: Theory, research, and intervention* (pp. 349–66). Cambridge: Cambridge University Press.

Young, V. L., Nemecek, J. R., and Nemecek, D. A. (1994). The efficacy of breast augmentation: Breast size increase, patient satisfaction, and psychological effects. *Plastic and Reconstructive Surgery, 94* (7), 958–69.

Zajonc, R. (1968). Attitudinal effects of mere exposure. *Journal of Personality and Social Psychology Monograph Supplement, 9* (2), 2:1–32.

Zamble, E. (1992). Behavior and adaptation in long-term prison inmates: Descriptive longitudinal results. *Criminal Justice and Behavior, 19,* 409–25.

Zamble, E., and Proporino, F. (1990). Coping, imprisonment, and rehabilitation: Some data and their implications. *Criminal Justice and Behavior, 17,* 53–70.

Zisook, S., Shuchter, S., and Lyons, L. (1987). Adjustment to widowhood. In S. Zisook (Ed.), *Biopsychosocial aspects of bereavement* (pp. 51–74). Washington, D.C.: American Psychiatric Association Press.

17 Gender Differences in Well-Being

Susan Nolen-Hoeksema and Cheryl L. Rusting

This chapter reviews the evidence for gender differences in well-being and the major explanations for these gender differences that have been offered. Gender differences are consistently found in several moods and behaviors, including sadness, fear/anxiety, antisocial personality disorder and conduct disorder, and substance abuse and dependence. Gender differences are also found, although less consistently, in angry moods, everyday aggressive behavior, hostility, and positive moods. Explanations for these gender differences are quite diverse, and evidence for the various biological, personality, and social context explanations are reviewed. Although some explanations are better supported than others, most of them focus on negative moods and behaviors and cannot account for gender differences in positive mood. The chapter concludes with recommendations for future research examining gender differences in well-being.

GENDER DIFFERENCES are commonly found in measures of psychological well-being. In this chapter, we review the evidence for gender differences in major psychopathology and everyday moods and behaviors. We review evidence for gender differences in both negative moods and disorders and positive moods and behaviors. We also note when gender differences are consistent across measurement methods, cultures, and age groups, and when they are not. Then we examine the evidence for the various biological, personality, and social context explanations that have been offered for these gender differences. We conclude by highlighting the explanations that have received the most empirical support and by making recommendations for future research.

NEGATIVE MOODS AND RELATED BEHAVIORS

Negative moods and behaviors can be divided into two categories: internalizing problems and externalizing problems. The internalizing psychopathologies include depression and anxiety disorders, and the everyday internalizing moods include sadness, fear or nervousness, and shame or guilt. The externalizing psychopathologies include inappropriate aggression and substance abuse, and the primary externalizing mood is anger. We will first consider gender differences in internalizing problems, then turn to gender differences in externalizing problems.

Internalizing Disorders

All of the studies of psychological disorders reviewed in this section use structured clinical interviews to determine the prevalence of disorders in random samples of the population. The structured clinical interview is the most widely accepted method for measuring psychological disorders. Trained interviewers administer a standard set of questions to respondents, and the respondents' answers are used to determine whether the respondent should be diagnosed with a disorder. The gender differences obtained in these studies also tend to be consistent with studies using other measurement methods, including self-reports and diagnoses of people seeking treatment.

In the most recent and comprehensive nationwide study of mental disorders in the United States, women showed higher rates than men for all of the mood and anxiety disorders, with the exception of manic episodes (Kessler et al. 1994). Similar gender differences in depressive and anxiety disorders have been found in many previous studies (Nolen-Hoeksema 1995a; Yonkers and Girguis 1995). Although gender differences in mania are typically not found, there is some evidence for a gender difference among people with manic-depression (referred to as bipolar disorder in the *DSM-IV*) (American Psychiatric Association 1994). Women are more likely than men to have severe episodes of depression and milder episodes of mania, whereas men are more likely than women to have severe episodes of mania and milder episodes of depression (Nolen-Hoeksema 1995a). Thus, women's greater proneness to depression compared to men's obtains even in manic-depression.

There is some cross-cultural variation in these gender differences, with fewer differences found in "less modern" cultures (Nolen-Hoeksema 1990). For example, in a study of the Old Order Amish of central Pennsylvania, who have a traditional eighteenth-century agrarian lifestyle focused around the church and family, the overall prevalence of depression was much lower than in the general U.S. population, and no gender differences in the prevalence of depression were found (Egeland and Hostetter 1983). Additionally, gender differences in depression are often smaller in magnitude in developing countries than in developed countries.

Within the United States, the differences between ethnic and racial groups in the prevalence of internalizing disorders and the distribution of these disorders by gender vary from study to study (see Nolen-Hoeksema 1995a). Although most studies find that women are more prone to depression and anxiety across ethnic and racial groups, several studies find that this gender difference is smaller in ethnic minority groups than in Caucasians, in large part because ethnic minority men have higher rates of depression and anxiety than Caucasian men (Blazer et al. 1994).

There are also some gender differences in the developmental course of internalizing disorders. Gender differences in depression and anxiety tend to emerge in early adolescence and continue into adulthood (Angold and Worthman 1993; Nolen-Hoeksema and Girgus 1994). Girls show a dramatic escalation in the prevalence of these disorders somewhere between the ages of eleven and fifteen, whereas boys show little significant increase in these disorders after childhood. By about age eighteen, the large gender differences in these disorders seen in adult populations are established.

In sum, women have a higher prevalence than men of depressive and anxiety disorders, and these gender differences tend to be found across most ethnic and racial groups in the United States. These gender differences may be lower in "less modern" cultures. Finally, gender differences tend to emerge in early adolescence and continue into adulthood.

Everyday Internalizing Moods and Behaviors

Two different measurement methods have been used in studies of everyday moods and behaviors—self-reports of subjective experience and observa-tions of emotional expression. For some moods and behaviors, these two measurement methods have yielded similar results, and for others they have not.

Experience Studies using self-report measures of emotional experience have yielded fairly consistent gender differences in internally focused negative emotions. Brody and Hall (1993) suggest that women generally exceed men on self-reports of intropunitive emotions (shame, guilt, sadness, fear, and anxiety), and most of the self-report literature supports this conjecture. A number of studies asking participants to rate their experiences of different emotions have found gender differences in the experiences of sadness and fear (or anxiety), with women reporting more sadness and fear than men (Allen and Haccoun 1976; Balswick and Avertt 1977; Brody, Hay, and Vandewater 1990; Croake, Myers, and Singh 1987; Dillon, Wolf, and Katz 1985; Highlen and Gilles 1978; Highlen and Johnston 1979; Kirkpatrick 1984; McDaniel and Richards 1990; Scherer, Wallbott, and Summerfield 1986; Stapley and Haviland 1989). Two meta-analyses of gender differences in reported anxiety have confirmed this pattern, showing that women score higher on self-report anxiety measures than do men (Feingold 1994; Hall 1984). Women also report experiencing more shame and guilt than do men, in samples of both adults (Tangney 1990) and adolescents (Stapley and Haviland 1989). Thus, the findings from self-report studies of emotion have yielded a consistent pattern: women report experiencing more frequent and intense internally focused emotions than men.

Expression Studies investigating the *expression* of negative internally focused emotions have yielded results very similar to those obtained in studies of emotional experience. In studies that have measured the self-report of emotional expressiveness, women report expressing fear and sadness more than do men (Blier and Blier-Wilson 1989; Brody 1993; Dosser, Boswick, and Halverson 1983; Grossman and Wood 1993).

Some studies have used observational techniques to measure emotional expressiveness by recording physiological or facial expressions during exposure to emotionally arousing slides or films. In one study, for example, men and women viewed a sad film while observers measured their responsiveness (Choti et al. 1987). Women not only cried more than men during the film but also exhibited stronger correlations between sadness and crying than did men. In another study, men and women watched positive, negative, and neutral slides while their electromyographic (EMG) activity was recorded (Grossman and Wood 1993). The finding that women showed a stronger EMG response than men during the negative slides suggests that women were especially emotionally reactive to negative emotional material. In the same study, women reported more intense and more frequent expressions of fear and sadness, an indication that they may have been reacting to such material in the negative slides. Taken together, the results of these studies suggest that women express more fear and sadness than do men.

In sum, women report greater experience and expression of internally focused negative moods, such as fear/anxiety, sadness, and guilt. These gender differences are obtained in both self-report and observational studies. In addition, women appear to be better than men at communicating and recognizing internally focused moods and behaviors.

Externalizing Disorders

The externalizing disorders, including antisocial personality disorder and substance use disorders, are diagnosed much more often in males than females. Structured clinical interviews with members of the general population show that, among adults, antisocial personality disorder is diagnosed four to five times more often, and substance abuse is diagnosed twice as often, in men than in women (Kessler et al. 1994). The greater rate of externalizing disorders in men occurs across ethnic and racial groups in the United States, and across cultures outside of the United States (Helzer and Canino 1992). These gender differences tend to emerge very early in life: greater tendencies toward aggressive behavior in males than females was found even in preschoolers (Loeber 1990).

Everyday Externalizing Moods and Behaviors

The everyday externalizing moods and behaviors are primarily anger and aggression. Studies investigating gender differences in the experience and expression of these moods yield a complex pattern of results. This complexity is linked partially to the different measurement methods used in these studies.

Experience　The literature on gender differences in everyday experiences of externally focused nega-

tive emotions has yielded inconsistent findings. Some studies of self-reported anger have found that men report more frequent anger than women (Biaggio 1980; Doyle and Biaggio 1981), whereas others have failed to find significant gender differences (Allen and Haccoun 1976; Averill 1982; Wintre, Polivy, and Murray 1990). On self-report measures of trait anger or hostility, gender differences are typically found, with men having higher hostility levels than women (Biaggio 1980; Novaco 1975; Scherwitz et al. 1991). Similar results are found for contempt, with men reporting more contempt than women (Stapley and Haviland 1989). However, Averill (1982) conducted an investigation of everyday experiences of anger and found that women experienced anger in daily life about as much as did men. Averill concluded that men and women do not differ markedly in their everyday experience of anger. The existence of gender differences in anger experience is thus far from clear.

One explanation for these inconsistent findings is that contextual factors may influence gender differences in anger experience, and that gender differences in emotional experience are situationally specific (Blier and Blier-Wilson 1989; Brody 1993; Brody, Lovas, and Hay 1995; Dosser et al. 1983; van Goozen et al. 1994). In an investigation of these contextual factors, van Goozen and colleagues (1994) found gender differences in the factors that elicit anger. Women were more likely than men to report that they would be angry as a result of impolite treatment and frustrations, rather than as a result of their own incompetence (manipulated by giving negative performance feedback). Women were more likely than men to feel sad or shameful (instead of angry) when given negative performance feedback. Stapley and Haviland (1989) found a similar contextual effect, where men felt angry in response to situations where their achievement was thwarted, whereas women felt angry in response to situations where they felt interpersonally slighted or frustrated. Thus, men and women may feel angry equally often, but in response to different eliciting circumstances.

Expression　Aggression can be thought of as a behavioral manifestation of angry feelings. Many experimental studies of aggression have shown that men are more aggressive than women (for reviews, see Eagly and Steffen 1986; Frodi, Macaulay, and Thorne 1977; Hyde 1984; White 1983). Self-reports of anger expression follow a similar pattern, with women reporting less expression of anger than men (Biaggio 1989). As with the emotion of anger, gender differences in aggression appear to depend on certain contextual factors. One of these factors is whether the aggression was provoked or not; unprovoked men are more aggressive than women, but when provoked, men and women show equally aggressive responses (for a review, see Bettencourt and Miller 1996). Another factor is the type of aggressive response—for example, physical aggression is more appropriate for men, but verbal aggression is more appropriate for women (Deaux and Major 1988; Eagly and Steffen 1986).

Some research has demonstrated that women experience more conflict than men over anger expression and that they tend to downplay anger and aggression (Egerton 1988; Frodi 1978); this tendency could be a contributing factor to the lower incidence of anger expression by women than by men. Frodi (1978) noted that verbalization of feelings (on a thought-listing task) about a research partner who had provoked the subject's anger tended to have different consequences for each gender. Women instructed to write down their thoughts downplayed anger and aggression, whereas men "tended to preoccupy themselves with thoughts of anger" (347).

Although many studies of aggression and anger expression have indicated that women express less anger than men, this research has not always provided consistent results. Biaggio (1989) conducted two studies to determine whether men and women react differently to anger-arousing incidents. In the first study, college students were asked to record their behavioral responses to anger-provoking incidents over the course of two weeks; these responses were then categorized by raters. Men reported more anger-arousing incidents and responded with more physical and verbal antagonism then did women. In the second study, students were brought into the laboratory and their behavioral reactions to experimentally induced provocation were recorded. No gender differences in behavioral reactions to provocation were observed. Thus, gender differences were obtained when anger was measured by self-report, but not when anger reactions were observed experimentally.

In sum, the literature on gender differences in externally focused moods and behaviors yields a complex and sometimes inconsistent pattern of results. Some studies of self-reported anger have found that men report greater anger than women,

but other studies do not find significant gender differences. Gender differences in anger experience and expression may depend on contextual factors and eliciting circumstances. Studies of the expression indicate that women feel conflict over and tend to downplay the expression of anger and aggression, whereas men do not. These findings may depend, however, on whether expression is measured by self-report or observation.

POSITIVE MOODS

Mania is the only psychological disorder that might be considered a disorder of positive mood, and as noted, some studies have found that among people with manic-depression, women experience more severe depressed moods and milder manic episodes, whereas men experience more severe manic episodes and milder depressive episodes. There is a larger literature, however, on gender differences in the experience and expression of everyday positive moods.

A number of studies have found that women report experiencing greater happiness and more intense positive emotions than do men (Cameron 1975; Diener, Sandvik, and Larsen 1985; Fujita, Diener, and Sandvik 1991; Grossman and Wood, 1993; Wood, Rhodes, and Whelan 1989). Others, however, have found either no difference (Diener 1984; Gurin, Veroff, and Feld 1960; Larson 1978) or greater happiness for men than women (Harring, Stock, and Okun 1984). Wood, Rhodes, and Whelan (1989) attempted to resolve this debate in a meta-analysis of studies reporting tests for gender differences in positive well-being. They concluded that women report experiencing more happiness than men. Marriage was associated with increased well-being for both genders, but this relationship was stronger for women than for men, suggesting that positive well-being may be explained in terms of social roles. Thus, contextual factors (such as marriage) may be important in whether such gender differences in positive moods are obtained.

The literature on the expression of positive emotions has consistently shown that women *express* positive emotions more than men. On self-report measures, women report expressing positive emotions (including love, happiness, and joy) more than do men (Allen and Haccoun 1976; Balswick and Avertt 1977; Dosser et al. 1983; Grossman and Wood 1993). Observational studies of nonverbal behavior have found similar results, with women displaying expressions of positive emotions more often than men (Hall 1978, 1984, 1987). Hall's (1978, 1984, 1987) reviews of the literature on nonverbal expression suggest that women consistently express more positive emotion through smiling and laughing than do men, except in childhood, when differences have not yet emerged. In addition, women have more expressive faces, gaze more, employ smaller approach distances, and are approached closer by others. Thus, the literature on gender differences in the expression of positive emotions has fairly consistently shown that women express more positive emotions than do men.

Summary

Gender differences in both internalizing disorders and everyday internalizing moods and behaviors are consistently found, with women experiencing more of these than men. There also are consistent gender differences in externalizing disorders, with men experiencing more than women. Gender differences in everyday externalizing moods and behaviors are somewhat less consistent. Men may self-report more anger and hostility and act more aggressively, compared to women, but the strength and even the direction of these gender differences appear to vary by context. Similarly, context appears to be important in determining the gender differences in positive moods, but there is a trend toward women reporting greater experience and expression of positive moods than men.

EXPLANATIONS FOR GENDER DIFFERENCES IN MOODS AND BEHAVIORS

A host of different explanations for gender differences mood and behavior has been offered. Almost all these explanations have focused on the negative moods and behaviors; the gender differences in positive moods and behaviors have been largely ignored. Moreover, most of the explanations for gender differences in negative moods and behaviors cannot account for gender differences in positive mood and life satisfaction.

In the remainder of this chapter, we review the biological, personality, and social context explanations that have been offered for gender differences in moods and behaviors. Although we cannot provide an exhaustive review of all possible explanations in each of these categories, we review the most researched ones. The reader may wish to con-

sult Seeman (1995) and Nolen-Hoeksema (1990) for comprehensive reviews of these literatures.

Biological Explanations

Biological explanations for gender differences in negative moods and behaviors have attributed these differences to two sources: hormonal influences and sex-linked genetic predispositions.

Hormones   Most of the biological explanations for gender differences in psychopathology and mood have focused on hormones. Women's greater vulnerability to depression and anxiety has been tied to estrogen and progesterone. The main fuel for this idea comes from the belief that women are more prone to depression and anxiety during the premenstrual period of the menstrual cycle, the postpartum period, menopause, and puberty. These are times when levels of estrogen and progesterone change dramatically. Given how strongly people tend to believe that women's moods are influenced by their hormones, it is remarkable how little evidence there is for this belief.

Let us consider the premenstrual period first. Early research suggested that the majority of women are regularly incapacitated by depression, anxiety, and physical discomfort during their premenstrual periods (Reid and Yen 1981). However, many of these early studies relied on the faulty method of asking women to complete retrospective questionnaires about their premenstrual mood experience. The information women provide on these retrospective questionnaires often bears little resemblance to their actual experience of mood across the menstrual cycle. For example, in one study, women completed daily mood ratings but did not know that the study was investigating the relationship between mood and the menstrual cycle. At the end of the study, the same women were asked to report, retrospectively, on their moods during the different phases of their most recent menstrual cycle. On the retrospective questionnaire, the women reported having experienced significantly more negative symptoms during their premenstrual period than during any other period in their last cycle. However, the daily mood ratings of these same women showed no relationship between cycle phase and actual mood experience (Abplanap, Hasket, and Rose 1979; see also Parlee 1994; Schnurr, Hurt, and Stout 1994).

More recent studies have found that it is possible to identify a small group of women who frequently report increases in depressive symptoms during the premenstrual phase (Endicott 1994). Since these women also tend to have a history of frequent major depressive episodes not connected to the menstrual cycle, perhaps they have a general vulnerability to depression rather than a specific vulnerability to premenstrual depression (Parry 1994). This pattern has generated some controversy. Many researchers argue that severe negative mood during the premenstrual period should not be given a separate diagnosis, such as premenstrual dysphoric disorder, but should be considered only an exacerbation of major depression or an anxiety disorder. Others argue that we should recognize premenstrual dysphoria separately with its own diagnosis, because it is different from dysphoria that has no link with the menstrual cycle, and that it should be studied separately (Gold and Severino 1994).

Similarly, women with a history of or general vulnerability to depression or anxiety may become depressed or anxious during the postpartum period (the first couple of months after giving birth). However, studies comparing postpartum women and matched nonpostpartum women find no evidence for differences in the rates of depression and anxiety between these two groups (O'Hara and Swain 1996). Even for women who do become seriously depressed during the postpartum period, there is no evidence that their depressions are linked to specific hormone imbalances (Gitlin and Pasnau 1989; Whiffen 1992). On the other hand, postpartum depressions are most often linked to severe environmental stress, such as financial strain, marital difficulties, or lack of social support (O'Hara and Swain 1996). Another clue that environmental factors rather than hormonal changes contribute to postpartum depression is that adoptive mothers and natural fathers also are at increased risk for depression following the arrival of a new baby (Rees and Lutkins 1971).

The belief that women are more prone to depression during the menopause was so strong among clinicians that, twenty years ago, there was a separate diagnostic category in the *DSM* for menopausal depression. Several subsequent studies have found, however, that women are no more likely to show depression around the time of menopause than at any other time in their lives (Matthews et al. 1990).

Finally, let's consider puberty. As discussed, girls' rates of depression and anxiety escalate dramatically in early adolescence, but boys' rates do not. The increase in girls' depression and anxiety does not, however, seem to be directly tied to the hormonal changes of puberty (Brooks-Gunn and Warren 1989; Paikoff, Brooks-Gunn, and Warren 1991; Sussman, Dom, and Chrousos 1991; Sussman et al. 1987). Instead, the observable physical changes of adolescence may be more closely linked to emotional development because girls appear to value the physical changes that accompany puberty much less than do boys. In particular, girls dislike the weight they gain in fat, and their loss of the long, lithe look that is idealized in modern fashions. Boys, in contrast, value the increase in muscle mass and other pubertal changes occurring in their bodies (Dornbusch et al. 1984). These changes affect girls' and boys' self-esteem differently. Body dissatisfaction appears to be more closely related to low self-esteem and depression in girls than in boys (Allgood-Merten, Lewinsohn, and Hops 1990).

Girls who mature much earlier than their peers seem especially at risk for depression and anxiety during puberty. Girls whose bodies are changing long before their friends' bodies have higher rates of depression and anxiety than girls who mature later in adolescence (Hayward, Killen, and Taylor 1994). There are at least three possible reasons for this group's increased risk. First, they have the worst body image of any group of girls, and this may contribute to their vulnerability to depression and anxiety. Second, these girls seem to become involved in mature dating relationships at a very young age, and they date older boys and become sexually active earlier than their peers. These relationships may be difficult for many girls to cope with and may contribute to depression and other emotional problems. Third, because they are becoming sexually mature at a younger age, these girls may be more vulnerable to sexual assault and abuse than girls who mature later, and as we discuss shortly, sexual abuse contributes to an increased risk for depression (Hayward et al. 1994).

In sum, the notion that women's higher rates of internalizing disorders are tied to their hormones has not been well supported. There does not seem to be as great an increase in risk for depression during periods of hormonal change as commonly believed. Even though some women do experience depression or anxiety during periods of hormonal change, there is no consistent evidence for a particular hormonal or biochemical abnormality that distinguishes them from women who do not experience such depressions.

Before closing this section on hormones, we note the popular theory that men are more prone to aggressive behavior than women owing to their higher levels of the hormone testosterone. Although it is clear that high levels of testosterone are associated with aggressive behavior in animals, few studies of this association have been conducted with humans. One study of fifty-eight boys between fifteen and seventeen years of age (Olweus et al. 1980) found that boys who were prone to verbal and physical aggression in response to provocation, and who were impatient and irritable, had higher blood levels of testosterone.

Although some children may have a biological predisposition to act aggressively, they are unlikely to develop conduct disorders unless they are also exposed to environments that promote antisocial behavior (Rutter et al. 1990). Studies of children who develop conduct disorders find that they come from families in which parents frequently ignore the child, and that when the child transgresses in some way, the parents lash out at the child violently (Loeber et al. 1993). That these parents are more likely to give boys severe physical punishments than girls may partially account for the higher rate of conduct disturbances in boys (Lytton and Romney 1991). Thus, even if hormones influence aggressive tendencies, the environment also plays a role in the development of aggressive behavior.

Genetics   Although genetics probably do play a role in determining individuals' vulnerability to depression and anxiety, there is presently little evidence that gender differences in these internalizing problems are genetically caused (Blehar and Oren 1995). Genetic studies of aggressive behavior problems, such as antisocial personality disorder or conduct disorder, have focused almost exclusively on boys and men, making it impossible to determine whether the gender difference in these externalizing problems is genetically based.

Men may carry a greater genetic vulnerability than women to certain kinds of substance use disorders, especially alcoholism. In a study of 356 twins, the concordance rate for alcohol abuse or dependence among the male twins was .76 for the monozygotic (MZ) twins and .53 for the same-sex dizygotic (DZ) twins, but the concordance rates among the female twins were .38 for the MZ twins and .42 for the same-sex DZ twins (McGue, Pickens, and Svikis 1992). This pattern of findings suggests that alcohol dependence includes a heritable component for men but not for women. In addition, among the male twins, evidence of heritability was strong only for early-onset alcoholism (onset of first symptoms before age twenty), but not for later-onset alcoholism. These findings suggest that genetics may play a strong role in early-onset male alcoholism.

Summary   There is little evidence to date that the gender differences in depression, anxiety, or aggressive behavior are linked to hormonal differences or are genetically caused, although the research testing this hypothesis is sparse. Some studies do suggest that males have a greater genetic vulnerability to alcoholism than females, particularly early-onset alcoholism.

Personality Explanations

The personality explanations for gender differences in mood and behavior have focused on a variety of traits, behavioral styles, cognitive styles, and coping styles that may lead men and women to experience and express moods and behaviors differently. Although many personality characteristics have been linked to gender differences in mood and behavior, we focus on the most discussed and researched ones in the literature.

Affect Intensity   Perhaps the only theory that has been used to explain gender differences in both positive and negative moods is the affect intensity theory. Larsen and Diener (1987) defined affect intensity as an individual difference characteristic involving one's intensity of response to emotional stimulation. The construct refers to both positive and negative emotional experiences. Individuals high on affect intensity tend to experience high levels of both positive and negative emotional intensity.

Fujita, Diener, and Sandvik (1991) suggest that women are higher on affect intensity than men, and that this may reconcile the paradoxical findings that females report more negative emotion but also more happiness than males. In their study, they used four different measurement methods (self-report, peer report, daily mood report, and memory performance) to create valence and emotional intensity scores. Women were as happy as men, with no gender difference on the valence scale. However, women scored significantly higher than men on the emotional intensity scale, which measures the intensity of both positive and negative emotions. Gender accounted for more variance in affect intensity (over 13 percent) than in valence (less than 1 percent). They concluded that women's more intense positive emotions balance their intense negative emotions.

Other studies have also supported the notion

that women are higher in affect intensity (both positive and negative) than men. Diener, Sandvik, and Larsen (1985) reported gender differences in self-reported affect intensity across the life span and found that women scored higher on measures of affect intensity than did men. Schwartz, Brown, and Ahern (1980) asked male and female participants to imagine happy, sad, angry, and fearful situations and then had them rate their emotional reactions. They found that women reported more intense experiences of emotion during the imagery than did men. In addition, they measured facial EMG patterns and found that women showed an increased magnitude of facial EMG response during the emotional imagery. Thus, the increased affect intensity of women (as compared to men) has been obtained across many measurement procedures.

Type A Personality The Type A personality has been defined as the constellation of several characteristics: (1) a sense of time urgency, (2) competitive achievement striving, and (3) a high level of aggressiveness and/or free-floating hostility (Rosenman and Friedman 1974). We can consider gender differences in the extent to which men and women differ in Type A personality, as well as the extent to which these differences may predict different health outcomes for men and women. For example, Type A personality is thought to be more common in men than women. If so, then this constellation of behaviors could explain gender differences in the experience and expression of externalizing moods and behaviors, such as anger and hostility, because these emotions are a significant part of the Type A behavior pattern.

Type A behavior is also considered a risk factor for coronary heart disease (see, for example, Booth-Kewley and Friedman 1987; Cooper, Detre, and Weiss 1981; Matthews and Haynes 1986). In an older review of the literature, Waldron (1976) concluded that gender differences in this behavior pattern contribute to men's higher rates of coronary heart disease. However, a recent review of the Type A literature found no gender differences in scores on Type A personality (Lyness 1993). Men and women do not differ in level of Type A personality; rather, they appear to have different behavioral and health outcomes related to Type A personality. Type A personality in men is fairly consistently related to cardiovascular responses to stressful challenges or competition, whereas Type A personality in women appears to be related to measures of daily stress and tension (Baker et al.

1984; Matthews and Haynes 1986). The pattern of relationships between Type A personality and measures of stress also differs for men and women (Kelly and Houston 1985).

These findings have led some researchers to suggest that Type A personality is expressed differently for men and women. In one study, Type A men showed elevated cardiovascular responses during a challenging response time task, but Type A women showed elevated responses during a verbally challenging interaction (MacDougall, Dembrowski, and Krantz 1981). In another study, McCann and colleagues (1987) had participants complete several Type A behavior measures, factor-analyzed these measures, and then compared correlations between the scales for men and women. They found that women showed strong correlations between Type A personality and guilt, whereas men showed strong correlations between Type A personality and suspiciousness. The authors suggest that Type A personality for men involves a competitive orientation toward life, in which others are seen as rivals not to be trusted. In contrast, Type A personality for women might bring up accompanying feelings of guilt and anxiety over anger expression (Frodi et al. 1977). These findings suggest that gender differences in Type A behavior depend on the situational context in which such behavior is measured, and that the expression of Type A behaviors is likely to be accompanied by different emotional experiences for men and women.

Investment in Relationships A popular personality theory is that women are often overinvested in relationships and do not have an autonomous sense of self. As a result, they are thought to be more vulnerable than men to the vicissitudes of relationships and more likely to have a sense of helplessness and low self-esteem, both of which make them more prone to internalizing problems (Chevron, Quinlan, and Blatt 1978; Gilligan 1982; Jack 1991). Unfortunately, "investment in relationships" has been defined loosely. Because this term has been defined in various ways across studies, the investment explanation has not been tested adequately (see Nolen-Hoeksema 1990; Nolen-Hoeksema and Girgus 1994).

Self-report studies find that women and girls do describe themselves as more concerned with relationships than do boys and men (Allgood-Merten et al. 1990; Levit 1991). However, there is little evidence that this self-reported greater concern with relationships in females is linked to a greater vulnerability to internalizing problems. For example, high scores on questionnaire measures of communality and concern for others do not tend to be correlated with higher levels of depression or anxiety in either men or women (see, for example, Allgood-Merten et al. 1990).

Several investigator have been interested in gender differences in a particular form of dependency, referred to by Jack (1991) as "silencing the self" and by Helgeson (1994) as "unmitigated communion." Jack (1991) and Hegelson (1994) both argue that females are more likely than males to silence their own wants and needs in the relationships in favor of maintaining a positive emotional tone in relationships, and to feel too responsible for the quality of the relationship. This leads females to have less power and obtain less benefit from relationships. In recent studies using measures to tap "feeling too responsible for relationships" or "unmitigated communion," adolescent girls have scored higher on such measures than adolescent boys (Aube, Fichman, Saltaris, and Koestner in press; Blatt et al. 1993; Luthar and Blatt 1993). In addition, Aube et al. (in press) found that gender differences in "feeling too responsible" were not present in seventh and eighth graders, but significant in ninth, tenth, and eleventh graders, in support of an emergence of this difficulty in girls in adolescence. In turn, both girls and boys who score high on these measures of over-responsibility and interpersonal concern are more likely to have depressive symptoms (for example, Saragovi et al. 1997).

Are girls more reactive to interpersonal stressors than boys, as might be suggested by theories that say girls are more concerned with relationships than boys? Again, the literature provides mixed answers to this question. A few studies have found that girls are more likely than boys to show depressive symptoms in response to social stressors—conflict with and rejections by others (Leadbeater, Blatt, and Quinlan 1995; Moran and Echenrode 1991).

Similarly, the adult literature provides evidence both for and against the hypothesis that women respond more negatively to interpersonal stressors than men (see Nolen-Hoeksema 1990). Although some studies suggests that women are more likely than men to experience elevations in depressive symptoms in reponse to "social network stressors"—negative events in the lives of others (Kessler and McLeod 1984; Wethington et al. 1987), we found no evidence that women were more reactive than men to negative events in the lives of others in a recent study of over 1,100 randomly selected adults (Nolen-Hoeksema and Larson 1999).

Yet, some studies suggest that the absence of good interpersonal relationships is more detrimental to the well-being of males than females. For example, studies of children find that low popularity with peers is more highly correlated with depressive symptoms in boys than in girls (Nottelmann 1987). Among adults, there is some evidence that men's emotional health is more at risk than women's when a close relationship ends. Men more often react to the breakup of an intimate relationship or the death of their spouse with long-term depression and physical illness than do women (Bernard 1972; Hill, Rubin, and Peplau 1976; Stroebe and Stroebe 1983). Finally, whereas married men clearly are at lower risk for depression than unmarried men, marriage does not afford the same protection against depression for women (Nolen-Hoeksema 1990). Thus, it seems that men's emotional well-being is more closely tied than women's to whether they are in a close relationship.

It might be argued that women's well-being is not tied to the mere presence or absence of a relationship in their lives, but to the quality of their relationships. According to this perspective, women are more vulnerable than men to distress when close others do not affirm or value them, because they base their self-image on their close relationships. Again, however, the evidence in favor of this hypothesis is mixed. Vanfossen (1981) found that lack of affirmation from one's partner was associated with higher depressive symptoms in both full-time homemakers and employed husbands, but not in employed wives. Nolen-Hoeksema and Larson (1999) found that affirmation and intimacy in one's primary relationship was related to depressive symptoms equally strongly for women and men.

Dispositional Empathy   A related personality explanation focuses on basic gender differences in empathy toward others. Eisenberg and colleagues (1991) define empathy as "an emotional reaction that is based on the apprehension of another's emotional state or condition, and that involves feelings of concern and sorrow for the other person" (776). Dispositional empathy therefore refers to a stable tendency to respond vicariously to other people's emotional states. One theory that has been used to explain the higher incidence of negative emotions in women than men is that women are higher in dispositional empathy than men, making them more susceptible to the negative emotional experiences of others. In a review of the literature, Eisenberg and Lennon (1983) concluded that women have relatively high levels of dispositional empathy compared to men. When empathy was measured by self-report, the gender difference was strong. When empathy was operationalized behaviorally (for example, crying in response to emotionally provocative stimuli), the gender difference was moderate but still significant.

Subsequent studies have obtained similar results. Gore, Aseltine, and Colten (1993) surveyed male and female adolescents regarding feelings of distress and interpersonal caring. They found that there was indeed a gender difference in reported distress (girls were more distressed than boys), and that girls' high interpersonal caring and involvement in others' problems accounted for 25 percent of the gender difference in distress. Girls who were involved in others' problems or those having a strong interpersonal caring orientation (high empathy) had elevated depressed mood. Boys did not show this pattern of results. Kessler, McLeod, and Wethington (1985) found a similar result for adults. Women felt distressed following a negative event in the life of a loved one, whereas men were unaffected by such events.

Women not only report greater reactivity to others' emotional experiences but also evidence stronger reactions to emotion interactions when observed in the laboratory. For example, Eisenberg and colleagues (1991) showed men and women a sympathy-provoking film and found that women showed higher levels of emotional facial responding during the film than did men. In addition, women have been found to cry more in response to the characters in a sadness-inducing film, a response that was also associated with high dispositional empathy (Choti et al. 1987).

A large number of studies have investigated gender differences in the ability to communicate or recognize facial expressions of emotion. These studies have been extensively reviewed by Hall (1978, 1984, 1987), who concluded that women are better than men in identifying emotions from facial expressions and at expressing emotions via nonverbal communication. This gender difference may be especially strong for internally focused emotions, such as fear and sadness. In one study, professional actors posed facial expressions, and participants were asked to identify them (Wallbott 1988). The results indicated that female actors were better than males in communicating fear and

sadness, and that people were better able to recognize fear and sadness when they were communicated by female actors than when they were communicated by male actors. Women thus appear to be better than men at expressing and communicating internally focused negative emotions such as fear and sadness.

A few studies have found that men are superior to women in identifying expressions of anger (Rotter and Rotter 1988; Wagner, MacDonald, and Manstead 1986; Wallbott 1988). Others, however, have failed to find evidence for this gender difference (see, for example, Duhaney and McKelvie 1993). Although inconsistent, these findings indicate that anger may be the only facial emotion for which men sometimes show superior decoding skills.

The literature appears to support consistently the notion that women are higher in dispositional empathy than men, with the possible exception of anger-related emotions. This increased empathy may help to explain why women experience internally focused emotions (such as sadness, anxiety, guilt, and so on) more than men; they may be more emotionally involved than men in others' problems and respond in kind to others' emotions. However, it may also be the case that dispositional empathy does not necessarily predispose one to respond in kind to another person's emotions. The relationship between interpersonal caring and distress (Gore et al. 1993; Kessler et al. 1985) may be mediated by high investment in relationships, rather than being a direct effect of emotional involvement or empathy.

Attributional Styles   Yet another popular explanation for why women are more prone than men to internalizing problems is that women's tendency to explain the negative events that happen to them in a pessimistic, self-defeating style leads them to develop depressive symptoms (Abramson, Seligman, and Teasdale 1978; Peterson and Seligman 1984). Most of the evidence regarding gender differences in attributional or explanatory style comes from studies of the causal attributions children or adults make for achievement-related successes and failures, and their subsequent tendencies toward helplessness or mastery orientation. Meta-analyses of the literature on sex differences in attributions for events have shown that the evidence for such differences is mixed at best (Frieze et al. 1982; Sohn 1982). In a recent study of a representative sample of adults ranging in age from twenty-five to seventy-five, Nolen-Hoeksema and Jackson (1996) found no gender differences in scores on a standard measure of attributional style for any of the adult age groups. Thus, gender differences in attributional style cannot explain gender differences in depression or other internalizing disorders.

Coping Styles   People use a variety of strategies to regulate their negative moods. Some strategies are more effective than others at reducing negative moods, and the apparent gender differences in the use of particular strategies may partially account for gender differences in internalizing and externalizing disorders.

Mood regulation strategies that involve passively focusing on the negative mood appear to maintain and exacerbate the mood, whereas strategies that involve using pleasant activities to distract oneself from the mood tend to interrupt or shorten the mood (Ellis and Ashbrook 1988; Ingram 1990; Lewinsohn et al. 1985; Musson and Alloy 1988; Pyszczynski and Greenberg 1987; Smith and Greenberg 1981). Much of the research on mood regulation strategies has focused on depressed mood. For example, inducing depressed people to focus on their depressed moods and the meanings and consequences of these moods worsens the depressed mood, whereas distracting depressed people from their moods temporarily lifts their mood (Fennell and Teasdale 1984; Gibbons et al. 1985; Lyubomirsky and Nolen-Hoeksema 1993, 1995; Morrow and Nolen-Hoeksema 1990; Nolen-Hoeksema 1991). Similarly, depressed people who spontaneously engage in self-focused, ruminative responses to their moods show longer and more severe periods of depression than those who do not ruminate (Bromberger and Matthews 1996; Carver, Scheier, and Weintraub 1989; Ingram et al. 1987; Nolen-Hoeksema and Morrow 1991; Nolen-Hoeksema, Morrow, and Fredrickson 1993; Nolen-Hoeksema, Parker, and Larson 1994; Pyszczynski, Holt, and Greenberg 1987; Wood et al. 1990). Women are more likely than men to engage in self-focused, ruminative responses to depressed mood; in turn, this tendency to ruminate is associated with longer and more severe periods of depressed mood in women than in men (Allgood-Merten et al. 1990; Blanchard-Fields, Sulsky, and Robinson-Whelen 1991; Butler and Nolen-Hoeksema 1994; Ingram et al. 1987; Nolen-Hoeksema 1995b; Nolen-Hoeksema et al. 1994; Nolen-Hoeksema and Larson 1999; Wood et al. 1990).

Other research on ruminative and distracting mood regulation strategies has focused either on anxiety or on general negative mood (Catanzaro and Mearns 1990; Thayer, Newman, and McClain 1994). For example, Thayer and colleagues (1994) reported that active distracting strategies that divert attention to something other than negative mood were among the most successful for reducing tension and anxiety, and that men were more likely to use these strategies than women. Women, on the other hand, were likely to use more passive ruminative strategies, such as discussing the emotion-provoking event with others or expressing the emotion by crying or screaming.

It is not the case that women are more prone than men to focus on all types of negative mood. In a series of laboratory studies of responses to angry mood, Rusting and Nolen-Hoeksema (1998) found that when women were induced to feel angry, they were more likely to choose to distract themselves from their angry mood rather than to focus on their mood. When women were in a neutral mood, however, they overwhelmingly chose to focus on their emotional state. In contrast, men tended to choose distraction over emotion-focusing, both when they were in an angry mood and when they were in a neutral mood.

The distractions men choose when in a negative mood may often be benign or pleasant, such as exercising. However, men also seem more likely than women to choose maladaptive distractions. In particular, men are more likely than women to use alcohol to cope with stressful events and negative moods. Because men who use alcohol to cope have a heavier alcohol intake and more alcohol-related problems, their tendency to use alcohol to cope may help to explain the higher rate of alcohol-related disorders in men compared to women (Cooper, Russell, and George 1988; Cooper et al. 1992).

Summary   Although there is some evidence for gender differences in affect intensity and Type A behavior patterns, we question whether these gender differences explain gender differences in moods or simply represent another way of measuring gender differences in moods. The evidence that women's greater investment in relationships explains their higher rates of internalizing problems is building; the evidence for a link between greater dispositional empathy and internalizing problems in women is greater. There is little evidence that gender differences in attributional style contribute to gender differences in mood and behavior. Finally, gender differences in coping may help to account for gender differences in both internalizing and externalizing problems.

Social Context Explanations

The final set of explanations we review considers the different social contexts of men's and women's lives, which result from differences in the status, roles, and social expectations of men and women.

Abuse   The most compelling social explanation for women's higher rates of depression and anxiety is that women's lower social status puts them at high risk for physical and sexual abuse, and these experiences often lead to internalizing problems. Women are much more likely than men to be the victims of rape, incest, battering, or sexual harassment (Browne 1993; Koss 1993). The rates of these types of violence against women are staggering. Most studies of rape estimate that between 14 and 25 percent of women will be raped in their lives, most often before the age of thirty (Koss 1993). One in eight women report that they have been physically assaulted by their husband in the last year, and 1.8 million women report having been severely assaulted (punched, kicked, choked, threatened with a gun or knife) (Nolen-Hoeksema 1990). In turn, survivors of physical and sexual assault show high rates of major depression and anxiety disorders (Kendall-Tackett, Williams, and Finkelhor 1993). For example, Burnam and colleagues (1988) found that assault survivors were twice as likely as people who had not been assaulted to have a diagnosable depressive disorder or anxiety disorder at some time after the assault. Cutler and Nolen-Hoeksema (1991) estimated that up to 35 percent of the difference in rates of depression between women and men may be attributable to the higher rates of childhood sexual abuse in females compared to males. (Other forms of abuse were not examined in that study.) Thus, the higher rates of internalizing disorders in women compared to men are likely to be due, at least in part, to the higher prevalence of sexual abuse of women compared to men, and the resulting internalizing problems of sexual abuse survivors.

Balance of Power in Relationships   Even when women escape physical and sexual abuse in the context of heterosexual relationships, they tend to hold less power over important decisions in the daily lives of their families than men (for a review, see Nolen-Hoeksema 1990). Several theorists have suggested that the inequities of power in heterosexual relationships leave women feeling helpless and devalued and contribute to their higher rates of internalizing disorders (Gove and Herb 1974).

Many studies conducted in the United States suggest that married women in traditional relationships are at higher risk for depression than unmarried women or women who spurn traditional sex roles (McGrath et al. 1990). In contrast, married men have much lower rates of depression than unmarried women, and men who conform to the masculine sex role have lower rates of depression than men who spurn the masculine sex role. Although some studies suggest that men and women are both happier when married than not married (see, for example, Wood et al. 1989), married women report higher levels of depression than married men. It appears that traditional marriages and sex roles are good for men but not for women in terms of risk for depression. This effect may occur only in mainstream U.S. culture, however. Among the Old Order Amish within the United States, and in other "traditional" cultures outside the United States, there are no gender differences in internalizing problems (Egeland and Hostetter 1983).

Another variation on balance-of-power explanations is the role-overload explanation for women's internalizing problems (Gove and Herb 1974). According to this explanation, women's internalizing problems are due to the fact that women fill more roles in their daily lives than men, and their multiple roles overload them and put them at risk for distress. Women do tend to put more time into filling multiple roles than do men, but the number of different roles is not usually associated with depressive symptoms. For example, Nolen-Hoeksema and Jackson (1996) found that women worked about the same number of hours per week in the paid workforce as men but put many more hours per week into housework and caregiving of children and elderly family members. When the number of hours per week across all these roles were added together, women worked significantly more hours than did men. However, the number of hours per week across roles was not strongly associated with depressive symptoms in either men or women. Other researchers have also found that multiple roles actually protect women (and men) against emotional health problems rather than contributing to more emotional health problems (Kandel, Davies, and Raveis 1985; Repetti and Crosby 1984). Thus, we conclude that there is little evidence that role overload accounts for women's greater rates of internalizing problems.

Gender Roles   Gender roles are the sets of behaviors, concerns, and personality characteristics into which males and females are socialized. Several researchers have suggested that gender differences in emotional experience and expressiveness stem from the emotional roles men and women are expected to fill (Brody 1993; Brody and Hall 1993; Eagly 1987; Eagly and Wood 1991; Grossman and Wood 1993; Wood et al. 1989). The female gender role involves being emotionally expressive, concerned with emotional feelings, and emotionally unstable (Broverman et al. 1972; Ruble 1983). The male gender role involves being inexpressive and emotionally stable. Thus, women are expected to be more sensitive and emotionally expressive than men.

Grossman and Wood (1993) have suggested that men's and women's enactment of these roles leads to gender differences in emotional well-being. Because women's roles involve sensitivity to the needs of others and emotional expressiveness, whereas men's roles involve toning down emotional responsiveness, men and women are likely to develop different emotional skills and attitudes. These skills and attitudes, in conjunction with gender role expectations, are thought to lead to gender differences in emotional experience and expressiveness. In support of this theory, Grossman and Wood demonstrated that the extent to which women believed in gender role stereotypes was related to self-reported emotional experience and expressiveness.

It has been argued that different standards exist for what constitutes appropriate emotional behavior in men and women, with anger in particular being evaluated more negatively for women than men (Shields 1987). Eagly and Steffen (1986) conducted a meta-analytic review of gender differences in aggressive behavior, using a social role framework for explaining such gender differences. They suggested that gender differences in aggression reflect differences in normative expectations that society holds for men and women. They noted, "The male gender role includes norms encouraging many forms of aggression. . . . The traditional female gender role places little emphasis on aggressiveness" (310). Accordingly, they argued, men tend to be more aggressive than women,

unless contextual features make gender role considerations less salient. The idea that contextual factors play a role in making gender roles salient provides some explanation for the inconsistent findings regarding gender differences in externally focused negative emotions (anger).

Women are additionally expected to express positive emotions in social situations. For example, in one study, men and women imagined themselves expressing positive emotions to another person, and then they reported their expectations about the other person's reactions to them (Graham, Gentry, and Green 1981). Both men and women expected to receive favorable reactions from others, but only women expected others to respond more negatively toward them if they failed to express positive emotions. In a similar study, men and women rated the costs and rewards for a character (in a story) expressing positive emotions (Stoppard and Grunchy 1993). Women expected more rewards and fewer costs when positive emotion was expressed toward another person, but not when positive emotion was expressed toward the self. Men expected more rewards and fewer costs in both other-directed and self-directed contexts. The authors interpreted this finding as evidence for a gender norm in which women are particularly required to respond with positive emotion toward others.

A number of studies have been conducted using children and their parents as participants in order to investigate how gender roles are socialized. These studies provide evidence for the early emergence of gender-role consistent behavior and suggest some ways in which such behaviors may be "passed on" from parents. For example, there is some evidence indicating that mothers' facial expressions with daughters are more frequent and more varied than with sons during the first year of life (Malatesta et al. 1989). There is also evidence suggesting that mothers talk about emotional experiences more with daughters than with sons, and girls may come to talk more about emotions than boys as they grow older (Adams et al. 1995; Dunn, Bretherton, and Munn 1987; Fivush 1991; Kuebli, Butler, and Fivush 1995; Kuebli and Fivush 1992; Zahn-Waxler, Cole, and Barrett 1991). Fivush (1991) had mothers discuss past events related to happiness, sadness, anger, and fear with their children and then coded these conversations for several characteristics. The results indicated that mothers talked for a longer amount of time about sadness, and more often emphasized the causes of sadness, with daughters than with sons. In contrast, conversations about anger were longer with sons than with daughters, and mothers accepted retaliation as an appropriate response to anger with sons but not with daughters. Kuebli and Fivush (1992) similarly recorded parents' conversations with their children about past events and found that mothers and fathers both used a greater variety of emotion words, and more often mentioned sad events, with daughters than with sons. Two later studies found similar results and additionally demonstrated that girls began talking more about emotion and about a greater variety of emotions than boys one and a half years following the initial conversational assessment (Adams et al. 1995; Kuebli et al. 1995).

Taken together, the literature on gender roles for emotional experience and expression suggests that women are expected to be more emotionally unstable than men, to express sadness, fear, and positive emotion more than men, and to express anger less than men. The research reviewed in this section suggests that men and women take on these roles to some extent, and that early parent-child interactions play a role in the process of learning and adopting gender roles.

Stereotypes Brody and Hall (1993) have reviewed much of the literature on gender stereotypes relating to emotional experience and expression. The data they review suggest that individuals hold clear stereotypes about the emotional experiences of men and women. Women are thought to be more expressive of emotions, especially sadness and fear, and men are thought to be more expressive of anger. Brody and Hall note that these stereotypes may become self-fulfilling prophecies that influence gender differences in expressed emotion.

A number of studies have provided evidence for the existence of these stereotypes. For example, Grossman and Wood (1993) had participants make stereotypic judgments of the "typical man" and the "typical woman." They found that the typical woman was believed to experience emotions more intensely than the typical man, with the exception of anger. Fabes and Martin (1991) asked participants to judge the frequency with which they thought men and women typically experienced a variety of emotions. Women were thought to express more love, sadness, and fear than men. Men were thought to express more anger than women. Similar results have been obtained for preschoolers, who believe that girls are more likely than boys to feel sad, whereas boys are more likely than girls to feel angry (Birnbaum

1983; Birnbaum, Nosanchuk, and Croll 1980; Birnbaum and Chemelski 1984). The stereotype that women express more emotions than men, with the exception of anger, is therefore quite prevalent. Sadness and fear are considered female responses; anger and aggressiveness are considered male responses (Shields 1984).

Gender stereotypes concerning the *experience* of emotions are sometimes found to be less strong than gender stereotypes concerning the *expression* of emotions. For example, Fabes and Martin (1991) found strong evidence for gender stereotypes concerning the expression of love, sadness, fear, and anger, but they found evidence for gender stereotypes only for the experience of love (and not for sadness, fear, or anger). These findings suggest that people's stereotypes about gender differences in emotion may apply primarily to outward emotional expression and not necessarily to inner emotional experience. This distinction could possibly account for some of the conflict women feel over expressing anger, and for gender differences in the regulation of the expression of anger and aggression.

CONCLUSIONS

Gender is an important variable in studies of psychological well-being. Consistent gender differences are found in several moods and behaviors, including sadness, anxiety or fear, antisocial personality disorder and conduct disorder, and substance abuse and dependence. Gender differences are also found, although less consistently, in angry moods, everyday aggressive behavior, hostility, and positive moods.

Despite the growing popularity of biological explanations for gender differences in moods and behaviors, we found little evidence for these explanations. Some of the personality explanations appear better supported, especially explanations focusing on affect intensity, Type A personality, dispositional empathy, and coping styles. All of these explanations focus on negative moods and behaviors, however, and they cannot account for the gender differences in positive mood. In addition, with each of these explanations, we are left with the question of where the gender differences in personality come from—are they rooted in biological differences between males and females or in differences in their social context?

Several of the social context explanations seem to be useful in understanding gender differences in negative moods and behaviors. The much greater rate of physical and sexual abuse of women is likely to play a role in their higher rates of internalizing disorders compared to men. One can ask why the experience of abuse does not lead to externalizing problems in women as well. It may be because gender roles and stereotypes lead women into internalizing problems because internalizing problems are expected and reinforced for women while externalizing problems are not. On the other hand, men who face severe stress may be led by gender roles and stereotypes down the pathway toward externalizing problems rather than internalizing problems. Finally, gender roles and stereotypes may shape women's expression, and perhaps their experience, of positive moods as well as negative moods.

In closing, we wish to provide an integrative model of how these factors may influence each other over time to create the gender differences in well-being. We suggest that being socialized to experience and express the internalizing (but not the externalizing) moods and behaviors, and to be sensitive to others' emotions, leads girls and women to become more emotionally expressive than men (except perhaps for anger), to report higher levels of affect, to develop internalizing rather than externalizing coping strategies, and to develop dispositional empathy. In addition, frequent experiences with uncontrollable events or the threat of these events may make some women develop the belief that they cannot do anything to change their lives and thus to develop internalizing ways of coping with distress. When these personality traits interact with new experiences of negative events—including the kinds of uncontrollable events that appear more common in women's than men's lives (such as sexual abuse)—or with negative events in the lives of people close to them, women may be prone to express intense affect over these events and to cope with that affect in internalizing patterns that contribute to depression, anxiety, shame, and guilt.

In contrast, males are socialized not to experience or express affect as intensely as females and are not encouraged, as females are, to be sensitive to others' emotions. They are allowed to express externalizing emotions and behaviors more than females, however. In addition, males may experience fewer uncontrollable traumas and have more mastery experiences than females throughout their lives. As a result, males develop lower levels of affect intensity, more externalizing than internalizing ways of responding to distress, and lower levels

of dispositional empathy. When negative life events do happen to men or their loved ones, they may be less likely than women to experience intense distress and more likely to cope with the distress they do experience with externalizing coping behaviors that put them at risk for externalizing disorders.

Given the strength of stereotypes and self-expectations about gender differences in the moods and related behaviors, experimental and observational studies have clear advantages over self-report and correlational studies. All studies in this area, however, must contend with the fact that a fundamental component of mood is the subjective experience of the mood. We therefore encourage multimethod programs of research using self-reports, experimental, and observational methods to explore the viability of existing and newly proposed explanations for gender differences in psychological well-being.

REFERENCES

Abplanap, J. M., Haskett, R. F., and Rose, R. M. (1979). Psychoendocrinology of the menstrual cycle: I. Enjoyment of daily activities and moods. *Psychosomatic Medicine, 41,* 587–604.

Abramson, L. Y., Seligman, M. E. P., and Teasdale, J. (1978). Learned helplessness in humans: Critique and reformulation. *Journal of Abnormal Psychology, 87,* 49–74.

Adams, S., Kuebli, J., Boyle, P. A., and Fivush, R. (1995). Gender differences in parent-child conversations about past emotions: A longitudinal investigation. *Sex Roles, 33,* 309–23.

Allen, J. G., and Haccoun, D. M. (1976). Sex differences in emotionality: A multidimensional approach. *Human Relations, 29,* 711–22.

Allgood-Merten, B., Lewinsohn, P. M., and Hops, H. (1990). Sex differences and adolescent depression. *Journal of Abnormal Psychology, 99,* 55–63.

American Psychiatric Association. (1994). *The Diagnostic and Statistical Manual of the American Psychiatric Association.* 4th ed. Washington, D.C.: American Psychiatric Association Press.

Angold, A., and Worthman, C. W. (1993). Puberty onset of gender differences in rates of depression: A developmental, epidemiological, and neuroendocrine perspective. *Journal of Affective Disorders, 29,* 145–58.

Aube, J., Fichman, L., Saltaris, C., and Koestner, R. (in press). Why are adolescent girls more distressed than boys? Toward and integrated social-developmental model. *Journal of Personality and Social Psychology.*

Averill, J. R. (1982). *Anger and aggression: An essay on emotion.* New York: Springer-Verlag.

Baker, L. J., Dearborn, M., Hastings, J. E., and Hamberger, K. (1984). Type A behavior in women: A review. *Health Psychology, 2,* 477–97.

Balswick, J., and Avertt, C. P. (1977). Differences in expressiveness: Gender, interpersonal orientation, and perceived parental expressiveness as contributing factors. *Journal of Marriage and the Family, 39,* 121–27.

Bernard, J. (1972). *The future of marriage.* New York: Bantam Books.

Bettencourt, B. A., and Miller, N. (1996). Gender differences in aggression as a function of provocation: A meta-analysis. *Psychological Bulletin, 119,* 422–47.

Biaggio, M. K. (1980). Assessment of anger arousal. *Journal of Personality Assessment, 44,* 289–98.

———. (1989). Sex differences in behavioral reactions to provocation of anger. *Psychological Reports, 64,* 23–26.

Birnbaum, D. W. (1983). Preschoolers' stereotypes about sex differences in emotionality: A reaffirmation. *Journal of Genetic Psychology, 143,* 139–40.

Birnbaum, D. W., and Chemelski, B. E. (1984). Preschoolers' inferences about gender and emotion: The mediation of emotionality stereotypes. *Sex Roles, 10,* 505–11.

Birnbaum, D. W., Nosanchuk, T. A., and Croll, W. L. (1980). Children's stereotypes about sex differences in emotionality. *Sex Roles, 6,* 435–43.

Blanchard-Fields, F., Sulsky, L., and Robinson-Whelen, S. (1991). Moderating effects of age and context on the relationship between gender, sex role differences, and coping. *Sex Roles, 25,* 645–60.

Blatt, S. J., Hart, B., Quinlan, D. M., Leadbeater, B., and Auerbach, J. (1993). Interpersonal and self-critical dysphoria and behavioral problems in adolescents. *Journal of Youth and Adolescence, 22,* 253–269.

Blazer, D. G., Kessler, R. C., McGonagle, K. A., and Swartz, M. S. (1994). The prevalence and distribution of major depression in a national community sample: The National Comorbidity Survey. *American Journal of Psychiatry, 151,* 979–86.

Blehar, M. C., and Oren, D. A. (1995). Women's increased vulnerability to mood disorders: Integrating psychobiology and epidemiology. *Depression, 3,* 3–12.

Blier, M. J., and Blier-Wilson, L. A. (1989). Gender differences in self-rated emotional expressiveness. *Sex Roles, 21,* 287–95.

Booth-Kewley, S., and Friedman, H. S. (1987). Psychological predictors of heart disease: A quantitative review. *Psychological Bulletin, 101,* 343–62.

Brody, L. R. (1993). On understanding gender differences in the expression of emotion: Gender roles, socialization, and language. In S. Ablon, D. Brown, E. Khantzian, and J. Mack (Eds.), *Human feelings: Explorations in affect development and meaning* (pp. 87–121). New York: Analytic Press.

Brody, L. R., and Hall, J. A. (1993). Gender and emotion. In M. Lewis and J. M. Haviland (Eds.), *Handbook of emotions* (pp. 447–60). New York: Guilford.

Brody, L. R., Hay, D., and Vandewater, E. (1990). Gender, gender role identity, and children's reported feelings toward the same and opposite sex. *Sex Roles, 3,* 363–87.

Brody, L. R., Lovas, G. S., and Hay, D. H. (1995). Gender differences in anger and fear as a function of situational context. *Sex Roles, 32,* 47–78.

Bromberger, J. T., and Matthews, K. A. (1996). A "feminine" model of vulnerability to depressive symptoms: A longitudinal investigation of middle-aged women. *Journal of Personality and Social Psychology, 70,* 591–98.

Brooks-Gunn, J., and Warren, M. P. (1989). Biological contributions to affective expression in young adolescent girls. *Child Development, 60,* 372–85.

Broverman, I. K., Vogel, S. R., Broverman, D. M., Clarkson, F. E., and Rosenkrantz, P. S. (1972). Sex-role stereotypes: A current appraisal. *Journal of Social Issues, 28,* 59–78.

Browne, A. (1993). Violence against women by male partners: Prevalence, outcomes, and policy implications. *American Psychologist, 48,* 1077–87.

Burnam, M. A., Stein, J. A., Golding, J. M., Siegel, J. M., Sorensen, S. G., Forsythe, A. B., and Telles, C. A. (1988). Sexual assault and mental disorders in a community population. *Journal of Consulting and Clinical Psychology, 56,* 843–50.

Butler, L. D., and Nolen-Hoeksema, S. (1994). Gender differences in depressed mood in a college sample. *Sex Roles, 30,* 331–46.

Cameron, P. (1975). Mood as an indicant of happiness: Age, sex, social class, and situational differences. *Journal of Gerontology, 30,* 216–24.

Carver, C. S., Scheier, M. F., and Weintraub, J. K. (1989). Assessing coping strategies: A theoretically based approach. *Journal of Personality and Social Psychology, 56,* 267–83.

Catanzaro, S. J., and Mearns, J. (1990). Measuring general expectancies for negative mood regulation: Initial scale development and implications. *Journal of Personality Assessment, 54,* 546–63.

Chevron, E. S., Quinlan, D. M., and Blatt, S. J. (1978). Sex roles and gender differences in the expression of depression. *Journal of Abnormal Psychology, 87,* 680–83.

Choti, S. E., Marston, A. R., Holston, S. G., and Hart, J. T. (1987). Gender and personality variables in film-induced sadness and crying. *Journal of Social and Clinical Psychology, 5,* 535–44.

Cooper, M. L., Russell, M., and George, W. H. (1988). Coping, expectancies, and alcohol abuse: A test of social learning formulations. *Journal of Abnormal Psychology, 97,* 218–30.

Cooper, M. L., Russell, M., Skinner, J. B., and Windle, M. (1992). Development and validation of a three-dimensional measure of drinking motives. *Psychological Assessment, 4,* 123–32.

Cooper, T., Detre, T., and Weiss, S. M. (1981). Coronary-prone behavior and coronary heart disease: A review. *Circulation, 63,* 1199–1215.

Croake, J. W., Myers, K. M., and Singh, A. (1987). Demographic features of adult fears. *International Journal of Social Psychiatry, 33,* 285–93.

Cutler, S. E., and Nolen-Hoeksema, S. (1991). Accounting for sex differences in depression through female victimization: Childhood sexual abuse. *Sex Roles, 24,* 425–38.

Deaux, K., and Major, B. (1988). Putting gender into context: An interactive model of gender-related behavior. *Psychological Review, 94,* 369–89.

Diener, E. (1984). Subjective well-being. *Psychological Bulletin, 95,* 542–75.

Diener, E., Sandvik, E., and Larsen, R. J. (1985). Age and sex effects for emotional intensity. *Developmental Psychology, 21,* 542–46.

Dillon, K. M., Wolf, E., and Katz, H. (1985). Sex roles, gender, and fear. *Journal of Psychology, 119,* 355–59.

Dornbusch, S. M., Carlsmith, J. M., Duncan, P. D., Gross, R. T., Martin, J. A., Ritter, P. L., and Siegel-Gorelick, B. (1984). Sexual maturation, social class, and the desire to be thin among adolescent females. *Development and Behavioral Pediatrics, 5,* 308–14.

Dosser, D. A., Boswick, J. O., and Halverson, C. F. (1983). Situational content of emotional expressions. *Journal of Counseling Psychology, 30,* 375–87.

Doyle, M. A., and Biaggio, M. K. (1981). Expression of anger as a function of assertiveness and sex. *Journal of Clinical Psychology, 37,* 154–57.

Duhaney, A., and McKelvie, S. J. (1993). Gender differences in accuracy of identification and rated intensity of facial expressions. *Perceptual and Motor Skills, 76,* 716–18.

Dunn, J., Bretherton, I., and Munn, P. (1987). Conversations about feeling states between mothers and their children. *Developmental Psychology, 23,* 132–39.

Eagly, A. H. (1987). *Sex differences in social behavior: A social-role interpretation.* Hillsdale, N.J.: Erlbaum.

Eagly, A. H., and Steffen, V. J. (1986). Gender and aggressive behavior: A meta-analytic review of the social psychological literature. *Psychological Bulletin, 100,* 309–30.

Eagly, A. H., and Wood, W. (1991). Explaining sex differences in social behavior: A meta-analytic perspective. *Personality and Social Psychology Bulletin, 17,* 306–15.

Egeland, J. A., and Hostetter, S. M. (1983). Amish study I: Affective disorders among the Amish, 1976–1980. *American Journal of Psychiatry, 140,* 56–61.

Egerton, M. (1988). Passionate women and passionate men: Sex differences in accounting for angry and weeping episodes. *British Journal of Social Psychology, 27,* 51–66.

Eisenberg, N., Fabes, R. A., Schaller, M., Miller, P. A., Carlo, G., Poulin, R., Shea, C., and Shell, R. (1991). Personality and the socialization correlates of vicarious emotional responding. *Journal of Personality and Social Psychology, 61,* 459–71.

Eisenberg, N., and Lennon, R. (1983). Sex differences in empathy and related constructs. *Psychological Bulletin, 94,* 100–31.

Ellis, H. C., and Ashbrook, P. W. (1988). Resource allocation model of the effects of depressed mood states on memory. In K. Fiedler and J. Forgas (Eds.), *Affect, cognition, and social behavior* (pp. 1–21). Toronto: Hogrefe.

Endicott, J. (1994). Differential diagnoses and comorbidity. In J. H. Gold and S. K. Severino (Eds.), *Premenstrual dysphorias* (pp. 3–17). Washington, D.C.: American Psychiatric Association Press.

Fabes, R. A., and Martin, C. J. (1991). Gender and age stereotypes of emotionality. *Personality and Social Psychology Bulletin, 17,* 532–40.

Feingold, A. (1994). Gender differences in personality: A meta-analysis. *Psychological Bulletin, 116,* 429–56.

Fennell, M. J. V., and Teasdale, J. D. (1984). Effects of distraction on thinking and affect in depressed patients. *British Journal of Clinical Psychology, 23,* 65–66.

Fivush, R. (1991). Gender and emotion in mother-child conversations about the past. *Journal of Narrative and Life History, 1,* 325–41.

Frieze, I. H., Whitley, B., Hanusa, B., and McHugh, M. (1982). Assessing the theoretical models for sex differences in causal attributions for success and failure. *Sex Roles, 3,* 333–43.

Frodi, A. (1978). Experiential and physiological responses associated with anger and aggression in women and men. *Journal of Research in Personality, 12,* 335–49.

Frodi, A., Macaulay, J., and Thorne, P. R. (1977). Are women always less aggressive than men? A review of the experimental literature. *Psychological Bulletin, 84,* 634–60.

Fujita, F., Diener, E., and Sandvik, E. (1991). Gender differences in negative affect and well-being: The case for emotional intensity. *Journal of Personality and Social Psychology, 61,* 427–34.

Gibbons, F. X., Smith, T. W., Ingram, R. E., Pearce, K., Brehm, S. S., and Schroeder, D. (1985). Self-awareness and self-confrontation: Effects of self-focused attention on members of a clinical population. *Journal of Personality and Social Psychology, 48,* 662–75.

Gilligan, C. (1982). *In a different voice: Psychological theory and women's development.* Cambridge, Mass.: Harvard University Press.

Gitlin, M. J., and Pasnau, R. O. (1989). Psychiatric syndromes linked to reproductive function in women: A review of current knowledge. *American Journal of Psychiatry, 146,* 1413–22.

Gold, J. H., and Severino, S. K. (Eds.). (1994). *Premenstrual dysphorias.* Washington, D.C.: American Psychiatric Association Press.

Gore, S., Aseltine, R. H., and Colten, M. E. (1993). Gender, social-relational involvement, and depression. *Journal of Research on Adolescence, 3,* 101–25.

Gove, W., and Herb, T. (1974). Stress and mental illness

among the young: A comparison of the sexes. *Social Forces, 53,* 256–65.

Graham, J. W., Gentry, K. W., and Green, J. (1981). The self-presentational nature of emotional expression: Some evidence. *Personality and Social Psychology Bulletin, 7,* 467–74.

Grossman, M., and Wood, W. (1993). Sex differences in intensity of emotional experience: A social role interpretation. *Journal of Personality and Social Psychology, 65,* 1010–22.

Gurin, G., Veroff, J., and Feld, S. (1960). *Americans view their mental health: A nationwide interview survey.* New York: Basic Books.

Hall, J. A. (1978). Gender effects in decoding nonverbal cues. *Psychological Bulletin, 85,* 845–57.

———. (1984). *Nonverbal sex differences: Communication accuracy and expressive style.* Baltimore: Johns Hopkins University Press.

———. (1987). On explaining gender differences: The case of nonverbal communication. *Review of Personality and Social Psychology, 7,* 177–200.

Harring, M. J., Stock, W. A., and Okun, M. A. (1984). A research synthesis of gender and social class as correlates of subjective well-being. *Human Relations, 37,* 645–57.

Hayward, C., Killen, J., and Taylor, C. B. (1994). Timing of puberty and the onset of psychiatric symptoms. Paper presented at the annual meeting of the Society for Research on Adolescence, San Diego (May 1994).

Helgeson, V. S. (1994). Relation of agency and communion to well-being: Evidence and potential explanations. *Psychological Bulletin, 116,* 412–28.

Helzer, J. E., and Canino, G. J. (1992). *Alcoholism in North Americ, Europe, and Asia.* New York: Oxford University Press.

Highlen, P. S., and Gilles, S. F. (1978). Effects of situational factors, sex, and attitude on affective self-disclosure with acquaintances. *Journal of Counseling Psychology, 25,* 270–76.

Highlen, P. S., and Johnston, B. (1979). Effects of situational variables on affective self-disclosure with acquaintances. *Journal of Counseling Psychology, 26,* 255–58.

Hill, C. T., Rubin, Z., and Peplau, L. A. (1976). Breakups before marriage: The end of 103 affairs. *Journal of Social Issues, 32,* 147–91.

Hyde, J. S. (1984). How large are gender differences in aggression? A developmental meta-analysis. *Developmental Psychology, 20,* 722–36.

Ingram, R. E. (1990). Self-focused attention in clinical disorders: Review and a conceptual model. *Psychological Bulletin, 107,* 156–76.

Ingram, R. E., Lumry, A. B., Cruet, D., and Sieber, W. (1987). Attentional processes in depressive disorders. *Cognitive Therapy and Research, 11,* 351–60.

Jack, D. C. (1991). *Silencing the self: Women and depression.* New York: Harper Perennial.

Kandel, D. B., Davies, M., and Raveis, V. H. (1985). The stressfulness of daily social roles for women: Marital, occupational, and household roles. *Journal of Health and Social Behavior, 26,* 64–78.

Kelly, K. E., and Houston, B. K. (1985). Type A behavior in employed women: Relation to work, marital, and leisure variables, social support, stress, tension, and health. *Journal of Personality and Social Psychology, 48,* 1067–79.

Kendall-Tackett, K., Williams, L., and Finkelhor, D. (1993). Impact of sexual abuse on children: A review and synthesis of recent empirical studies. *Psychological Bulletin, 113,* 164–80.

Kessler, R. C., McGonagle, K. A., Zhao, S., Nelson, C. B., Hughes, M., Eshleman, S., Wittchen, H., and Kendler, K. S. (1994). Lifetime and Twelve-month prevalence of *DSM-III-R* psychiatric disorders in the United States: Results from the National Comorbidity Study. *Archives of General Psychiatry, 51,* 8–19.

Kessler, R. C., and McLeod, J. D. (1984). Sex differences in vulnerability to undesirable life events. *American Sociological Review, 49,* 620–31.

Kessler, R. C., McLeod, J. D., and Wethington, E. (1985). The costs of caring: A perspective on the relationships between sex and psychological distress. In I. G. Sarason and B. R. Sarason (Eds.), *Social support: Theory, research, and applications* (pp. 491–506). Dordrecht: Nijhoff.

Kirkpatrick, D. R. (1984). Age, gender, and patterns of common intense fear among adults. *Behavior Research and Therapy, 22,* 141–50.

Koss, M. P. (1993). Rape: Scope, impact, interventions, and public policy responses. *American Psychologist, 48,* 1062–69.

Kuebli, J., Butler, S., and Fivush, R. (1995). Mother-child talk about past emotions: Relations of maternal language and child gender over time. *Cognition and Emotion, 9,* 265–83.

Kuebli, J., and Fivush, R. (1992). Gender differences in parent-child conversations about past emotions. *Sex Roles, 27,* 683–98.

Larsen, R. J., and Diener, E. (1987). Affect intensity as an individual difference characteristic: A review. *Journal of Research in Personality, 21,* 1–39.

Larson, R. (1978). Thirty years of research on the subjective well-being of older Americans. *Journal of Gerontology, 33,* 109–25.

Leadbeater, B. J., Blatt, S. J., and Quinlan, D. M. (1995). Gender-linked vulnerabilities to depressive symptoms, stress, and problem behaviors in adolescents. *Journal of Research on Adolescence, 5,* 1–29.

Levit, D. B. (1991). Gender differences in ego defenses in adolescence: Sex roles as one way to understand the differences. *Journal of Personality and Social Psychology, 61,* 992–99.

Lewinsohn, P. M., Hoberman, H., Teri, L., and Hautzinger, M. (1985). An integrative theory of depression. In S. Reiss and R. Bootzin (Eds.), *Theoretical issues in behavior therapy* (pp. 331–59). New York: Academic Press.

Loeber, R. (1990). Development and risk factors of juvenile antisocial behavior and delinquency. *Clinical Psychology Review, 10,* 1–41.

Loeber, R., Wung, P., Keenan, K., Giroux, B., Stouthamer-Loeber, M., Kammen, W. B. V., and Maughan, B. (1993). Developmental pathways in disruptive child behavior. *Development and Psychopathology, 5,* 103–33.

Luthar, S. S. and Blatt, S. (1993). Dependent and self-critical depressive experiences among inner-city adolescents. *Journal of Personality, 61,* 365–386.

Lyness, S. A. (1993). Predictors of differences between Type A and B individuals in heart rate and blood pressure reactivity. *Psychological Bulletin, 114,* 266–95.

Lytton, H., and Romney, D. M. (1991). Parents' differential socialization of boys and girls: A meta-analysis. *Psychological Bulletin, 109,* 267–96.

Lyubomirsky, S., and Nolen-Hoeksema, S. (1993). Self-perpetuating properties of depressive rumination. *Journal of Personality and Social Psychology, 65,* 339–49.

———. (1995). Effects of self-focused rumination on negative thinking and interpersonal problem-solving. *Journal of Personality and Social Psychology, 69,* 176–90.

MacDougall, J. M., Dembrowski, T. M., and Krantz, D. S. (1981). Effects of types of challenge on pressor and heart rate responses in Type A and Type B women. *Psychophysiology, 18,* 1–9.

Malatesta, C. Z., Culver, C., Tesman, J., and Shepard, B. (1989). The development of emotion expression during the first two years of life. *Monographs of the Society for Research in Child Development, 50* (serial no. 219).

Matthews, K. A., and Haynes, S. G. (1986). Type A behavior and coronary risk: Update and critical evaluation. *American Journal of Epidemiology, 123,* 923–60.

Matthews, K. A., Wing, R. R., Kuller, L. H., Costello, E. J., and Caggiula, A. W. (1990). Influences of natural menopause on psychological characteristics and symptoms of middle-aged healthy women. *Journal of Consulting and Clinical Psychology, 58,* 345–51.

McCann, B., Woolfolk, R. L., Lehrer, P. M., and Schwarcz, L. (1987). Gender differences in the relationship between hostility and the Type A behavior pattern. *Journal of Personality Assessment, 51,* 355–66.

McDaniel, D. M., and Richards, R. C. (1990). Coping with dysphoria: Gender differences in college students. *Journal of Clinical Psychology, 46,* 896–99.

McGrath, E., Keita, G. P., Strickland, B. R., and Russo, N. F. (1990). *Women and depression: Risk factors and treatment issues.* Washington, D.C.: American Psychological Association.

McGue, M., Pickens, R. W., and Svikis, D. S. (1992). Sex and age effects on the inheritance of alcohol problems: A twin study. *Journal of Abnormal Psychology, 101,* 3–17.

Moran, P. B. and Eckenrode, J. (1991). Gender differences in the costs and benefits of peer relationships during adolescence. *Journal of Adolescent Research, 6,* 396–409.

Morrow, J., and Nolen-Hoeksema, S. (1990). Effects of responses to depression on the remediation of depressive affect. *Journal of Personality and Social Psychology, 58,* 519–27.

Musson, R. F., and Alloy, L. B. (1988). Depression and self-directed attention. In L. B. Alloy (Ed.), *Cognitive processes in depression* (pp. 193–220). New York: Guilford.

Nolen-Hoeksema, S. (1990). *Sex differences in depression.* Stanford, Calif.: Stanford University Press.

———. (1991). Responses to depression and their effects on the duration of depressive episodes. *Journal of Abnormal Psychology, 100,* 569–82.

———. (1995a). Epidemiology and theories of sex differences in depression. In M. Seeman (Ed.), *Gender and psychopathology* (pp. 63–87). Washington, D.C.: American Psychiatric Association Press.

———. (1995b). Gender differences in coping with depression across the life span. *Depression, 3,* 81–90.

Nolen-Hoeksema, S., and Girgus, J. S. (1994). The emergence of gender differences in depression during adolescence. *Psychological Bulletin, 115,* 424–43.

Nolen-Hoeksema, S., and Jackson, B. (1996). Ruminative coping and gender differences in depression. Paper presented at the annual meeting of the American Psychological Association, Toronto (August 1996).

Nolen-Hoeksema, S. and Larson, J. (1999). A dynamic model of the gender difference in depressive symptoms. Manuscript submitted for publication.

Nolen-Hoeksema, S., and Morrow, J. (1991). A prospective study of depression and distress following a natural disaster: The 1989 Loma Prieta earthquake. *Journal of Personality and Social Psychology, 61,* 105–21.

Nolen-Hoeksema, S., Morrow, J., and Fredrickson, B.L. (1993). Response styles and the duration of depressed moods. *Journal of Abnormal Psychology, 102,* 20–28.

Nolen-Hoeksema, S., Parker, L., and Larson, J. (1994). Ruminative coping with depressed mood following loss. *Journal of Personality and Social Psychology, 67,* 92–104.

Nottelmann, E. D. (1987). Competence and self-esteem during transition from childhood to adolescence. *Developmental Psychology, 23,* 441–50.

Novaco, R. W. (1975). *Anger control: The development and evaluation of an experimental treatment.* Lexington, Mass.: Lexington Books.

O'Hara, M. W., and Swain, A. M. (1996). Rates and risk of postpartum depression—a meta-analysis. *International Review of Psychiatry, 8,* 37–54.

Olweus, D., Mattsson, A., Schalling, D., and Low, H. (1980). Testosterone, aggression, physical, and personality dimensions in normal adolescent males. *Psychosomatic Medicine, 42,* 253–69.

Paikoff, R. L., Brooks-Gunn, J., and Warren, M. P. (1991). Effects of girls' hormonal status on depressive and aggressive symptoms over the course of one year. *Journal of Youth and Adolescence, 20,* 191–215.

Parlee, M. B. (1994). Commentary on the literature review. In J. H. Gold and S. K. Severino, (Eds.), *Premenstrual dysphorias* (pp. 149–67). Washington, D.C.: American Psychiatric Association Press.

Parry, B. L. (1994). Biological correlates of premenstrual complaints. In J. H. Gold and S. K. Severino (Eds.), *Premenstrual dysphorias* (pp. 47–66). Washington, D.C.: American Psychiatric Association Press.

Peterson, C., and Seligman, M. E. P. (1984). Causal explanations as a risk factor for depression: Theory and evidence. *Psychological Review, 91,* 347–74.

Pyszczynski, T., and Greenberg, J. (1987). Self-regulatory perseveration and the depressive self-focusing style: A self-awareness theory of reactive depression. *Psychological Bulletin, 201,* 122–38.

Pyszczynski, T., Holt, K., and Greenberg, J. (1987). Depression, self-focused attention, and expectancies for positive and negative future life events for self and others. *Journal of Personality and Social Psychology, 52,* 994–1001.

Rees, W. D., and Lutkins, S. G. (1971). Parental depression before and after childbirth: An assessment with the Beck Depression Inventory. *Journal of the Royal College of General Practitioners, 21,* 26–31.

Reid, R. L., and Yen, S. S. C. (1981). Premenstrual syndrome. *American Journal of Obstetrics and Gynecology, 1,* 85–104.

Repetti, R. L., and Crosby, F. (1984). Women and depression: Exploring the adult role explanation. *Journal of Social and Clinical Psychology, 2,* 57–70.

Rosenman, R. H., and Friedman, M. (1974). Neurogenic factors in the pathogenesis of coronary heart disease. *Medical Clinics of North America, 58,* 269–79.

Rotter, N. G., and Rotter, G. S. (1988). Sex differences in the encoding and decoding of negative facial emotions. *Journal of Nonverbal Behavior, 12,* 139–48.

Ruble, T. (1983). Sex stereotypes: Issues of change in the 1970s. *Sex Roles, 9,* 397–402.

Rusting, C. L., and Nolen-Hoeksema, S. (1998). Regulating responses to anger: Effects of rumination and distraction on angry mood. *Journal of Personality and Social Psychology, 74,* 790–803.

Rutter, M., Macdonald, H., LeCouteur, A., and Harrington, R. (1990). Genetic factors in child psychiatric disorders: II. Empirical findings. *Journal of Child Psychology and Psychiatry and Allied Disciplines, 31,* 39–83.

Saragovi, C., Koestner, R., Di Dio, L., Aube, J. (1997). Agency, communion, and well-being: Extending Helgeson's (1994) model. *Journal of Personality and Social Psychology, 73,* 593–609.

Scherer, K. R., Wallbott, H. G., and Summerfield, A. B. (1986). *Experiencing emotion: A cross-cultural study.* New York: Cambridge University Press.

Scherwitz, L., Perkins, L., Chesney, M., and Hughes, G. (1991). Cook-Medley Hostility Scale and subsets: Relationship to demographic and psychosocial characteristics in young adults in the CARDIA study. *Psychosomatic Medicine, 53,* 36–49.

Schnurr, P. P., Hurt, S. W., and Stout, A. L. (1994). Consequences of methodological decisions in the diagnosis of late luteal phase dysphoric disorder. In J. H. Gold and S. K. Severino (Eds.), *Premenstrual dysphorias* (pp. 19–46). Washington, D.C.: American Psychiatric Association Press.

Schwartz, G. E., Brown, S., and Ahern, G. L. (1980). Facial muscle patterning and subjective experience during affective imagery: Sex differences. *Psychophysiology, 17,* 75–82.

Seeman, M. V. (Ed.). (1995). *Gender and psychopathology.* Washington, D.C.: American Psychiatric Association Press.

Shields, S. A. (1984). Distinguishing between emotion and non-emotion: Judgments about experience. *Motivation and Emotion, 8,* 355–69.

———. (1987). Women, men, and the dilemma of emotion. *Review of Personality and Social Psychology, 7,* 229–50.

Smith, T. W., and Greenberg, J. (1981). Depression and self-focused attention. *Motivation and Emotion, 5,* 323–32.

Sohn, D. (1982). Sex differences in achievement self-attributions: An effect-size analysis. *Sex Roles, 8,* 345–57.

Stapley, J. C., and Haviland, J. M. (1989). Beyond depression: Gender differences in normal adolescents' emotional experiences. *Sex Roles, 20,* 295–308.

Stoppard, J. M., and Grunchy, C. G. (1993). Gender, context, and expression of positive emotion. *Personality and Social Psychology Bulletin, 19,* 143–50.

Stroebe, M. S., and Stroebe, W. (1983). Who suffers more?: Sex differences in health risks of the widowed. *Psychological Bulletin, 93,* 279–301.

Sussman, E. J., Dom, L. D., and Chrousos, G. P. (1991). Negative affect and hormone levels in young adolescents: Concurrent and predictive perspectives. *Journal of Youth and Adolescence, 20,* 167–90.

Sussman, E. J., Nottelmann, E. D., Inoff-Germain, G. E., Dom, L. D., and Chrousos, G. P. (1987). Hormonal influences on aspects of psychological development during adolescence. *Journal of Adolescent Health Care, 8,* 492–504.

Tangney, J. P. (1990). Assessing individual differences in proneness to shame and guilt: Development of the Self-Conscious Affect and Attribution Inventory. *Journal of Personality and Social Psychology, 59,* 102–11.

Thayer, R. E., Newman, J. R., and McClain, T. M. (1994). Self-regulation of mood: Strategies for changing a bad mood, raising energy, and reducing tension. *Journal of Personality and Social Psychology, 67,* 910–25.

Vanfossen, B. E. (1981). Sex differences in the mental health effects of spouse support and equality. *Journal of Health and Social Behavior, 22,* 130–43.

Van Goozen, S., Frijda, N., Kindt, M., and van de Poll, N. E. (1994). Anger proneness in women: Development and validation of the Anger Situation Questionnaire. *Aggressive Behavior, 20,* 79–100.

Wagner, H. L., MacDonald, C. J., and Manstead, A. S. R. (1986). Communication of individual emotions by spontaneous facial expressions. *Journal of Personality and Social Psychology, 50*, 737–43.

Waldron, I. (1976). Why do women live longer than men? *Social Science and Medicine, 10*, 349–62.

Wallbott, H. G. (1988). Big girls don't frown, big boys don't cry—Gender differences of professional actors in communicating emotions via facial expression. *Journal of Nonverbal Behavior, 12*, 98–106.

Wethington, E. McLeod, J., and Kessler, R. C. (1987). The importance of life events for explaining sex differences in psyological distress. In R. C. Barnett (Ed.), *Gender and stress* (pp. 144–54). New York: Free Press.

Whiffen, V. E. (1992). Is postpartum depression a distinct diagnosis? *Clinical Psychology Review, 12*, 485–508.

White, J. W. (1983). Sex and gender issues in aggression research. In R. G. Green and I. Donnerstein (Eds.), *Aggression: Theoretical and empirical reviews* (vol. 2, pp. 1–26). New York: Academic Press.

Wintre, M. G., Polivy, J., and Murray, M. (1990). Self-predictions of emotional response patterns: Age, sex, and situational determinants. *Child Development, 61*, 1124–33.

Wood, J. V., Saltzberg, J. A., Neale, J. M., Stone, A. A., and Rachmiel, T. B. (1990). Self-focused attention, coping responses, and distressed mood in everyday life. *Journal of Personality and Social Psychology, 58*, 1027–36.

Wood, W., Rhodes, N., and Whelan, M. (1989). Sex differences in positive well-being: A consideration of emotional style and marital status. *Psychological Bulletin, 106*, 249–64.

Yonkers, K. A., and Girguis, G. (1995). Gender differences in the prevalence and expression of anxiety disorders. In M. V. Seeman (Ed.), *Gender and psychopathology* (pp. 113–30). Washington, D.C.: American Psychiatric Association Press.

Zahn-Waxler, C., Cole, P., and Barrett, K. (1991). Guilt and empathy: Sex differences and implications for the development of depression. In J. Garber and K. Dodge (Eds.), *The development of emotion regulation and disregulation*. Cambridge Studies in Social and Emotional Development. New York: Cambridge University Press.

Part IV

The Social Context

18 Causes and Correlates of Happiness

Michael Argyle

This chapter examines the correlations of demographic and other environmental factors with happiness and, where possible, their independent and causal effects. Age has a small positive effect on some aspects of happiness because of a declining goal-achievement gap. Education is correlated with positive affect, mainly through the impact of education on income and occupational status, especially in third world countries. Social class is similarly correlated for the same reasons but also because class affects leisure and health. Income has complex and generally weak effects on happiness. Cross-sectional studies find a small positive effect but only at the lower end of the income scale; money is spent by the poor on more important goods like food. The increased prosperity for all during recent years has had no effect, but declining prosperity causes reduced happiness. Winning lotteries is more a cause of disruption than of happiness. Comparisons with the incomes of others are important in wage negotiations and more important than absolute income values. Social relationships are a major source of well-being. Marriage has the strongest effect, with the married being on average the most happy, the divorced and separated least. Social support also benefits mental and physical health. Ethnic minority groups are less happy, but this effect is very small after controlling for income, education, and occupation. Unemployment is a major cause of unhappiness, independent of reduced income, but the retired, even though they are "unemployed," are, if anything, happier than those at work. Leisure is an important cause of happiness because it is under voluntary control. Sport and exercise, social clubs, music and voluntary work all show strong positive effects. Television watching is very popular but produces a very weak though positive state. Religion, especially church attendance, has overall a small positive effect, but this is stronger for the elderly and members of some churches. This is due to the very close support of church communities and the relation experienced with God, and optimism. The frequency of life events correlates with happiness; their intensity has a weaker effect, though some major life events like falling in love, while disruptive, have a big impact. Mood induction experiments show that happiness can be enhanced experimentally, though it may not last for long. Competencies like intelligence and physical attractiveness have very weak positive correlations. Social skill does better, since it produces improved social relationships. Some policy implications are that less emphasis should be placed on income by governments, apart from that of the very poor, and more emphasis should be placed on employment, leisure facilities, and sustaining marriage and other relationships, which could be accomplished through education. It is concluded that demographic and environmental variables have some strong effects on happiness. Marriage, employment, and leisure are important, especially for certain groups, and their absence and loss is a major source of unhappiness.

THERE IS AN immense amount of information about the effects of the demographic variables of age, sex, occupation, and the rest, which are normally included as the causes and correlates of happiness in social surveys. These surveys started with Cantril's (1965) study of 23,875 people in 11 countries, the studies by Bradburn (1969) and Campbell, Converse, and Rodgers (1976) in the United States, and Inglehart's (1990) analysis of Eurobarometer surveys for 16 countries, averaged over a number of years, usually 1980 to 1986, with a total of 163,538 respondents. Veenhoven and colleagues (1994) later presented the findings of 603 such studies from 69 countries. These surveys constitute a massive source of information about the causes and correlates of happiness.

It is found that these demographic variables all correlate with subjective well-being. We will see how strong the relationships are, how far they vary between populations, whether they hold up when the others are controlled, how far the relationships are causal, and how they can be explained. Andrews and Withey (1976) concluded that these relationships were all fairly weak and accounted for less than 10 percent of the variance between them. Diener (1984) suggested 15 percent. Inglehart (1990) was surprised at these small effects and suggested it was because happiness depends on the goal-achievement gap and aspirations over time, so that it is only changes that have much impact on happiness. In pointing out that happiness differences between countries were much larger, he suggested that there is less pressure for the aspirations of whole populations to adjust.

When other, usually demographic, variables have been controlled, the effect of other variables falls, often expressed by beta weights, but all have survived such controls. The question of the direction of causation is more difficult. Many of the findings are basically correlational, that is cross-sectional; for example, it is found that happy people have more friends. But is this because having more friends makes people happy or vice versa? Where possible, we will cite studies that have produced evidence of causation, the main methods being (1) experiments—for example, persuading some subjects to take more exercise for a period; (2) quasi-experimental designs—for example, following up individuals who have lost their jobs or become bereaved; (3) panel studies of those who have experienced a change, such as their salary becoming larger or smaller; and (4) multiple regression designs in which changes in happiness are predicted from variables measured at time 1.

Age

Many surveys of happiness or satisfaction have found a small increase in happiness with age, with a correlation of about .10, as in Cantril's (1965) survey of fourteen nations. Job satisfaction has a slightly stronger relation with age, and a positive relation is found whenever satisfaction or other cognitive measures are used (Schmotkin 1990). However, if more affective measures are used, happiness increases with age, most clearly for positive affect but to a lesser extent for negative affect, too (Bradburn 1969; Diener and Suh, in press). If more specialized aspects of subjective well-being are assessed, some of them increase with age, others decline. Cantril found that older people are more satisfied with their past and current life, but less satisfied with their future prospects. Ryff (1995) found that environmental mastery and autonomy increased with age, but that purpose in life and personal growth declined.

Some of these apparent effects of age are reduced or disappear when controls are applied, for example, for health or education. Schmotkin (1990) in Israel found that the increase in cognitive satisfaction did not survive controls, while a decline in affect did. On the other hand, Inglehart (1990), with the Eurobarometer surveys, found that the effect of age on increasing satisfaction was greater after controls had been applied for the lower rates of marriage, education, and income for older people.

Direction of causation is not really a problem here, since happiness cannot affect age. Since happy people live a little longer, however, there could be a small tendency for the old to be happier for this reason.

In several studies it has been found that while men become happier with age, women become less happy. Spreitzer and Snyder (1974), in an American study, found a very strong effect, while the much larger World Values Study Group survey (1994) in forty-three nations found a smaller effect in the same direction.

Is the apparent effect of age on happiness causal? Happiness cannot affect age, but the relation could be due to cohort differences: older people are on average less educated and may have lower expectations, be more easily satisfied, or be more concerned with basic survival (Felton 1987). The characteristics of successive waves of immigrants to Israel, for example, may explain apparent age differences. Longitudinal studies are needed to settle this issue.

The effects of age on happiness are small, but they still require explanation. In some ways older people are objectively worse off in that they tend to be in worse health, after retirement they often have lower incomes, and fewer are still married. Despite all this, they are more satisfied. Campbell, Converse, and Rodgers (1976) found evidence that the old have lower aspirations, and more than this, the goal-achievement gap is smaller. This fits with Inglehart's (1990) ideas about adjustment of aspirations. The old, for example, expect to be out of a job and possibly widowed; bereavement has a far greater effect on young widows (Stroebe and Stroebe 1987). Older individuals have had time to adapt to their condition; older workers may also have managed to adjust the work situation to their needs, for example, by changing their job or conditions of work (Argyle 1989).

Finally, there is some increase in religious activity and beliefs with increasing age; as we will see later, religion is more important for the happiness of the elderly.

EDUCATION

Many surveys have correlated educational level with measures of happiness, either using number of years of education received or the level attained (for example, high school, college). In all such studies, a small positive correlation has been found, of the order of .10 (Cantril 1965). When positive and negative affect have been assessed separately, there has been a clear relation with positive affect, but none with negative affect (Bradburn 1969). Moreover, different results have been obtained in different parts of the world. The effect of education is weakest in the United States, and it has become weaker over time (for a comparison of surveys repeated in 1957 and 1978, see Campbell [1981]). In 1957, 44 percent of college graduates said they were very happy, compared with 23 percent of those with no high school, while in 1978 the corresponding percentages were 33 and 28 percent. The effects of education in most European countries are also quite small, and it is also weak in Japan and Singapore. However, education has more effect in Austria, South Korea, Mexico, Yugoslavia, the Philippines, and Nigeria (Veenhoven et al. 1994). This suggests that the key variable is national wealth—education has more effect in poorer countries.

Education is closely linked to income and to occupational status; indeed, it can be a cause of both. However, Witter and his colleagues (1984) found in a meta-analysis that education contributed to subjective well-being primarily by affecting occupation, but not income, and that it had a rather small effect apart from this. Does education have any effect on happiness independently of income and job status? When income is held constant, the effect of education is reduced but is still present (Diener et al. 1993). The effect of education is stronger for those with low incomes (Campbell 1981). If occupational status is also controlled, the effect of education either becomes very small or disappears completely (Glenn and Weaver 1979). However, in some studies education has been found to have a negative effect, if income is held constant, because education creates expectations of higher income (Clark and Oswald 1996).

Could education be caused by happiness? It is possible that happiness, through its components of optimism and self-esteem, could enhance success in education, but this has not so far been shown.

The main explanation for the effect of education on happiness is that it affects income and occupational status, both of which, we will see, are causes of happiness. The additional effects of education may be due to the social status conveyed by education; this could explain the relatively strong effects in Third World Countries—the surveys here were controlled for income in some cases, but not for occupational status. Education may affect those with low incomes in the United States by creating wider interests and hence other sources of happiness, especially through enhanced leisure interests. This could explain why the effect of education is on positive affect. On the other hand, education may raise aspirations, thus increasing the goal-achievement gap.

SOCIAL CLASS

Social class is the level in society at which an individual is accepted; this is a function of occupational status and also of income, education, area of residence, and lifestyle. In British studies, class is usually measured from occupation alone, but in the United States account has been taken of income and education as well. A meta-analysis of sixty-five effects from thirty-four American studies found that such composite measures of social class correlated on average .20 with happiness, but that occupational status alone, with the other variables controlled, had a beta weight of .11 (Haring, Stock, and Okun 1984). This correlation has been smaller in the more recent American studies. Veroff, Douvan, and Kulka (1981) found that in 1967, 46 percent of professional-class Americans were very happy compared with 28 percent of unskilled laborers; in 1976, however, this difference had almost disappeared. Where positive and negative affect have been measured separately, the effect of class is much greater on positive affect; the relationship is also stronger in economically depressed areas and for older people in those areas (Bradburn 1969). When social class is assessed by asking people to rate themselves, there is a correlation with happiness of about .25 to .30 in American and European studies.

Correlations, or similar measures of strength of

relationship, are much stronger in some countries; for example, for objective social class the correlations are: Israel .55, Nigeria .52, Philippines .44, India .42, and Brazil .38 (Cantril 1965). This suggests that class has more effect on happiness in countries that are highly stratified, that is, where there is great inequality of incomes. Happiness and satisfaction are particularly high for those who think they are of high social class: in India, for example, 58 percent of them said they were very happy, compared with 18 percent of the upper-middle class and 1 percent of the lowest. In Australia, on the other hand, the corresponding percentages were 58 percent, 47 percent, and 33 percent (Leisure Development Centre 1980); Australia has much greater equality and a smaller income distribution than India.

There could be a reverse causation effect, whereby happy people are more socially mobile. This might be more possible in countries with more social mobility, but as just shown, the effects are actually greater in countries like India and Brazil where there is less social mobility, suggesting that this direction of causation is not important.

As the meta-analysis by Haring, Stock, and Okun (1984) showed, there is still an effect of occupational status after income and education have been controlled, though the effect is reduced to about half the original effect size. If self-perceptions of class are used, the beta weights after controlling for other measures are still about .15 to .20 (Veenhoven et al. 1994).

What is the explanation for the effect of social class on happiness? The overall effect, including the effect of income and education, is easy to explain: there is a multiple effect of better jobs, housing, relationships, and leisure. We show later that there are massive class differences in leisure— middle-class individuals engage in much more active leisure, belong to twice as many clubs, take much more exercise, take more holidays and outings, read more, have more social life, and pursue more hobbies. Working-class people just watch more television. Middle-class marriages are happier and last longer; they are more successful, partly because young middle-class couples marry later and are more likely to have a place of their own, while working-class couples often marry very young and when the girl is pregnant, and have to live with in-laws (Argyle 1994). Middle-class people have more friends, but working-class people see more of their kin because they live nearer. However, relatives are less important as a source of happiness. In addition, there may be a sheer social

status effect: the greater respect received from others can contribute to self-esteem (Argyle 1994). The separate effect of occupational status may be due to greater job satisfaction of those who do more interesting work.

INCOME

Many studies have looked at the relation between income and measures of happiness. In the Euro-barometer surveys, 86 percent of those in the upper quartile of incomes were satisfied or very satisfied, compared with 72 percent of the lowest quartile. In American studies the correlation has usually been quite small. Haring, Stock, and Okun (1984) did a meta-analysis of 154 effect sizes from 85 studies and found an average correlation of .17. Diener and his colleagues (1993) reported surveys carried out in 1971 to 1975 with 6,913 respondents and in 1981 to 1984 with 4,942. The results are shown in Figures 18.1 and 18.2.

It can be seen that the relation is curvilinear, with a much stronger relation at the lower end of the income scale. There may be an additional effect at the top end, too; Diener, Horwitz, and Emmons (1985) found that forty-nine individuals who were earning over $10 million a year were happy 77 percent of the time, compared with 62 percent of the time for a comparison group. There

FIGURE 18.1   Income and Well-Being in the United States, 1971 to 1975

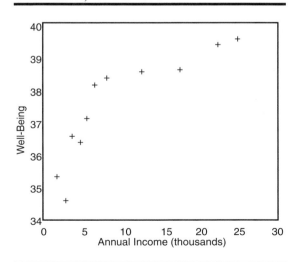

Source: Diener et al. (1993), figure 1. Reprinted with kind permission from Kluwer Academic Publishers.

FIGURE 18.2   Income and Well-Being in the
United States, 1981 to 1984

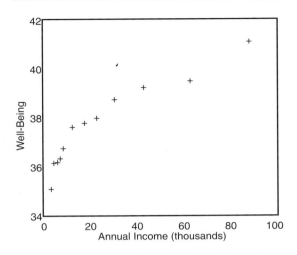

Source: Diener et al. (1993), figure 2. Reprinted with kind permission from Kluwer Academic Publishers.

is a problem with the "happy poor," who are apparently satisfied with their lot. This has been interpreted as a state of adaptation and learned helplessness produced by long experience of being unable to do anything about it (Olson and Schober 1993). The reason for the rather weak effect of income in the United States may be that many Americans are above the level at which income affects happiness. The relation is stronger in some poorer countries, such as India and the Philippines.

There is a stronger relation for reported satisfaction with income, subjective poverty, having a satisfactory standard of living, and so forth, and even in North American studies the correlations with happiness are typically .40. They are even stronger for poor countries, such as Tanzania (.68) and Jordan (.51) (Veenhoven et al. 1994). These correlations fall to rather smaller beta weights after controls have been applied; however, controlling for education and occupation may be misleading, since together with wealth they make up the variable of social class.

Similar findings are obtained if the average incomes and happiness of whole nations are compared. The most extensive analysis of this kind was by Diener, Diener, and Diener (1995), who compared several measures of income—for example, gross national product and purchasing power—and of happiness for fifty-five countries. In this study, a stronger correlation of .50 or above was found for all combinations of the measures used, considerably above the usual within-country findings.

We turn to studies that have produced evidence of causality. Bradburn (1969) found slightly greater happiness scores for families whose chief wage earner had received a pay raise in the past year compared with those who had received a pay cut. In another American study, Diener and his colleagues (1993) compared the happiness of individuals whose salaries had increased or decreased over a ten-year period; they found nonsignificant changes in the opposite direction to that predicted.

Inglehart (1990) found that 85 percent of those who said that their financial situation was "a lot better" were satisfied, compared with 57 percent of those who said it was "a lot worse." There has been more interest in the possible effects of national changes in income. Inkeles and Diamond (1986) compared individuals of the same occupational status and found a correlation of .60 between their well-being and national economic growth. When particular countries are examined, the evidence is mixed. In the United States, average personal income has risen from $4,000 in 1970 to $16,000 in 1990 (in 1990 dollars), but there has been no change in average happiness or satisfaction (Myers and Diener 1996). On the other hand, there was a fall in the percentage who said they were "very happy" in Belgium between 1978 and 1983, of 40 percent to 20 percent, during the time of a fall in income (Inglehart and Rabier 1986). There was a smaller fall in European happiness during the depression of 1980 to 1982, and similar changes have been found in Brazil, Ireland, and Japan (Veenhoven 1989). The lack of response to prosperity in America may be due to rising expectations and an American optimistic belief that things will keep on improving. The small long-term effects of income may be due to adaptation, that is, people become accustomed to a particular level of prosperity.

Another possible source of causal information on the effects of income on happiness comes from the study of lottery winners. Overall it is found that after the initial joy there is little effect on happiness, and some winners experience major disruption of their lives, with distinctly negative consequences; for example, in a British study, 70 percent gave up their jobs, thus losing their job satisfaction and workmates (Smith and Razzell 1975). They move to a different house but are not socially acceptable to their new neighbors; they may have an identity problem, not knowing where they now belong. One of many press interviews with winners of the British National Lottery was of interest. A twenty-four-year-old woman won £1,375,000; she bought a car but couldn't drive, she bought a lot of clothes and had to put them into storage, she went to an expensive restaurant but decided that she preferred fish fingers. She was still unemployed and had the same empty and unsatisfying life. I think that analysis of lottery winners is not a good way to study the effects of money on happiness, since the effects are mainly of disruption rather than of riches.

Insofar as income has some effect on happiness, what is the explanation? There is no problem in explaining this: richer people have a higher standard of living, better food, housing, transport, education, and leisure, access to medicine—resulting in better health, even better mental health and a more competent personality (through being able to afford therapy)—and the higher self-esteem resulting from the respect given to the rich. The rich are in better health, partly through better access to medicine, but also through better health behavior, though in Britain the very rich drink too much (Blaxter 1990). Money is good for marriage, since it enables the newly wedded to have a place of their own instead of living with one of the families, and marriage is a major source of happiness. The problem is in explaining why the relation with income is so weak, at least in within-country studies, for all except the quite poor. The leveling-off effect shown in figure 18.1 may occur simply because money makes a greater difference to the quality of life when it is spent on food, housing, and other necessities than when it is spent on larger cars, works of art, antiques, or jewelry.

People do enjoy having possessions, but those who score high on materialism scales are found to be less happy than others. These scales have items about believing that possessions are necessary for happiness, the importance of possessions, and envy (Belk, 1984). The reason may be that these people are really seeking nonmaterial goals such as personal fulfillment or the meaning of life and are disappointed when material things fail to provide them (Dittmar 1992).

A widely held explanation for the weak effects of money is that it is relative income rather than, or as well as, actual income, that makes people happy. Several surveys have found that reports of having more or less income than others correlates quite strongly (for example, .34) with satisfaction and happiness (Mitchell 1972). Evidence that relative income may be more important than actual income comes from research based on Michalos's (1980) "Michigan model," or goal-achievement gap model, whereby happiness is said to be due to the gap between aspirations and achievements, and this gap is due to comparisons with both "average folks" and one's own past life (see figure 18.3).

The gap is found to be a better predictor of overall satisfaction than satisfaction with the various domains (Michalos 1986). While the goal-achievement gap for income is usually found to predict overall well-being, this is not always the case, and Taylor (1982) found that the theory works only for realistic aspirations, or those under one's own control. Several studies have found that comparison with the past is important; Schwarz and Strack (1991) found that asking people to think of negative past events put them in a better mood. How about comparisons with others? Runciman (1966) found that better-paid manual workers in Britain were more satisfied with their pay than nonmanual workers who earned the same amount—they had different comparison groups. Comparisons seem to be very important as a source of satisfaction with wages. Berkowitz and his colleagues (1987), in a survey in Wisconsin, found that the strongest predictor of pay satisfaction was current inequity ($-.49$). Clark and Oswald (1996) used a different design: "comparison incomes" were calculated for ten thousand British workers, that is, the average incomes of those with the same jobs, education, and so on. They found that while income had little effect on satisfaction, comparison income had a correlation of $-.25$ to $-.30$; in other words, the lower their comparison income, the more satisfied employees were. Similar findings were obtained in an American study by

FIGURE 18.3   Satisfaction with Life as a Whole: The Goal-Achievement Gap Model

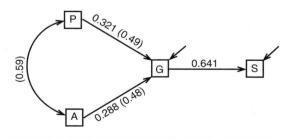

Source: Michalos (1980) (shows regression coefficients; zero-order correlations are in brackets).

Leicht and Shepelak (1994) with 4,567 employees; pay satisfaction was greater if there were procedures for ensuring fair incomes. Clark and Oswald also found that satisfaction with pay was less if the spouse or other household members earned more, confirming a comparison effect.

Average happiness is greater in those countries where dispersion of incomes is less—the opportunity for unfavorable comparisons for many would be reduced (Diener et al. 1995).

While Clark and Oswald (1996) found that education had the predicted negative effect on satisfaction, when pay was held constant, Diener and his colleagues (1993) did not find this, nor did they find that being black had a positive effect (since it would lower it); there were small differences in the opposite to the predicted direction. In another analysis, the happiness of those living in poor areas was not greater, nor that of those in richer areas less (with respondents' income constant), following the same line of argument.

Women are paid less than men, even when they are doing the same kinds of work, and are satisfied with smaller earnings. This is because they compare their pay with that of other women and feel entitled to less pay than men (Jackson 1989). However, when they do the same work as men, they start to compare their pay with that of men and are no longer satisfied with lower wages (Loscocco and Spitze 1991). And the young and better-educated, professionals, and those in male-dominated work places do not show greater pay satisfaction; these are the jobs for which there are less likely to be gender differences in pay expectations (Clark 1996).

It looks as if comparisons are most important for pay, especially when employees know exactly what they and members of other groups of workers are paid. This is very important in wage disputes; Brown (1978) found that industrial workers would choose a lower salary if doing so allowed them to receive more than a rival group.

MARRIAGE

Marriage has often been found to be one of the strongest correlates of happiness and well-being (Glenn and Weaver 1979). People who are married or who are living together are on average happier, and in better mental and physical health, than those who live alone, never married, or are widowed, divorced, or separated. In the Eurobarometer surveys in sixteen countries in 1975 to 1979,

clear differences were found between the different marital states. These results are shown in table 18.1; very similar findings have been found in other and more recent studies.

Many other surveys have found that the married are happier than the unmarried; Haring-Hidore and his colleagues (1985) did a meta-analysis of fifty-eight American studies and found an overall correlation of .14; the effect was stronger for younger couples. Many other studies have found that the married are happier than those in any of the unmarried categories (Veenhoven et al. 1994). And within these categories, those who are cohabiting, "living as married," are usually found to be happier than the single, and a little less happy than the married (table 18.1; Nock 1995). Their rate of breaking up is twice as high as that of the married in Britain, and three times as high in Sweden (Watt 1994). Satisfaction with marriage also predicts general happiness or satisfaction. Despite these benefits, marriage is the relationship that is the greatest source of conflict (Argyle and Furnham 1983). Violence is not uncommon, and divorce is increasingly common; it is a complex and intense, relationship, quite different from friendship, for example, and it has more powerful effects.

The married are also in better mental health; Brown and Harris (1978) in London found that for women who had experienced stressful life events, 10 percent of those who had a supportive partner were depressed, compared with 41 percent of those who did not. The death of a spouse is a major source of depression; in one study 42 percent of widows were found to be in the mild-to-severe range of the Beck Depression Inventory, compared with 10 percent of the married (Stroebe and Stroebe 1987). It has often been assumed in stress research that being widowed is the worst thing that can happen; however, health research finds that being divorced or separated has a

TABLE 18.1   Marriage and Satisfaction

	Men	*Women*
Married	79	81
Living as married	73	75
Single	74	75
Widowed	72	70
Divorced	65	66
Separated	67	57

Source: Inglehart 1990.
Note: Percentages include "satisfied" and "very satisfied."

greater effect on rates of death from heart disease in particular, as well as a range of other illnesses; it literally produces broken hearts (Lynch 1977).

The positive effects of marriage are still found after controls for age, sex, income, and so forth; Glenn and Weaver (1979) averaged several U.S. national surveys and found beta weights of .16 for males and .21 for females. Other studies have found that marriage does a little more for the happiness of women (Wood, Rhodes, and Whelan 1989; see table 18.1), though marriage does more for the physical and mental health of men (Gove 1972). Men are more distressed and made more ill by bereavement, but women suffer more from divorce. Quality of marriage is an additional factor predicting happiness (Russell and Wells 1994). Having children has a rather small effect on marital satisfaction and happiness. Overall the effect is negative (Glenn and Weaver, 1979); it is also curvilinear, two to three children being best, and the

effect depends on stage in the family life cycle. Figure 18.4 shows how marital happiness varies with the point in the life cycle of the family.

The honeymoon (1) and empty nest (2) periods are best; the time when there are children under five (3) and when they are adolescents (5) are the worst for marital satisfaction (Walker 1977). Nevertheless children are a major source of satisfaction, as well as stress, to their parents. In particular, they are sources of affection and fun (Hoffman and Manis 1982). Later they are a source of social support. In Third World countries, where children are a major source of labor, it might be expected that the more the better.

Are the effects of marriage causal, or could they be explained by happy people being more likely to get married? The fact that over 90 percent of people get married argues against the latter explanation. Hughes and Gove (1981) could not find any differences in preexisting psychological tendencies

FIGURE 18.4   Marital Satisfaction by Stage of Family Life Cycle

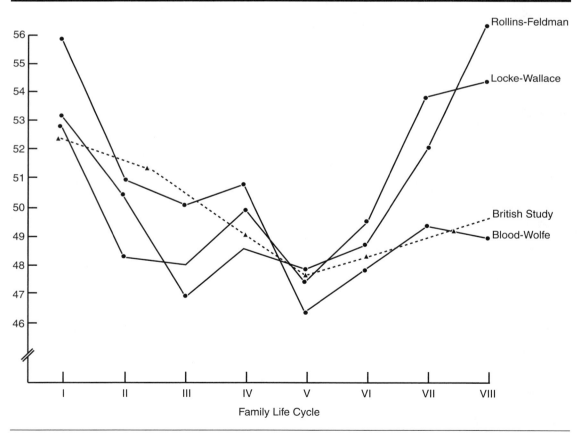

Source: Walker (1977); Rollins and Cannon (1974); *Women's Own* (1974). Reprinted with permission from the Academic Press Ltd.

between those who lived alone and others, but Mastekaasa (1992) found that individuals who were in poor health were less likely to marry during the next four years. Being divorced may be partly caused by the unhappiness or related characteristics of those involved, but being widowed can be assumed to be mainly due to other causes.

Marriages are happier under certain conditions, and this helps to explain some of the other demographic effects we have described. Middle-class marriages are more successful, as we have seen. Marriage is a greater source of positive affect when couples are young and in love; passionate love is later replaced by companionate love, a source of satisfaction rather than joy. The effect of bereavement is much greater for younger people (Stroebe and Stroebe 1987). Religious couples stay together longer because of the teachings and social support of churches. And couples stay together longer if they have enjoyable leisure to share (Argyle and Henderson 1985).

What is the explanation for the benefits of marriage? Marriage is the greatest source of social support for most people, more than friends or kin, including emotional and material support and companionship (Argyle and Furnham 1983, see figure 18.5). For those who are married, the spouse is involved in and instrumental to a wide range of other satisfactions, including sex and leisure. Being in love is the greatest source of positive emotions. Marriage is good for health partly because it results in better health behavior—married people drink and smoke less, have a better diet, and do what the doctor orders. In addition, their immune systems are activated, an effect that has been found with health behavior held constant (Kennedy, Kiecolt-Glaser, and Glaser 1990). Marriage is a kind of biological cooperative whose members look after one another and receive mental health benefits, too, as the result of being able to confide in and discuss problems with a sympathetic listener. Women are better at such listening than men, which explains why men benefit more from marriage in terms of having lower rates of depression (Vanfossen 1981).

Marriage is the relationship that has the most influence on happiness, but there are other relationships that affect happiness, and also health and mental health, by providing "social support." The main forms that social support takes are material help, emotional support, and companionship (Argyle and Furnham 1983). If all

FIGURE 18.5   Relationships Plotted on the Satisfaction Dimensions

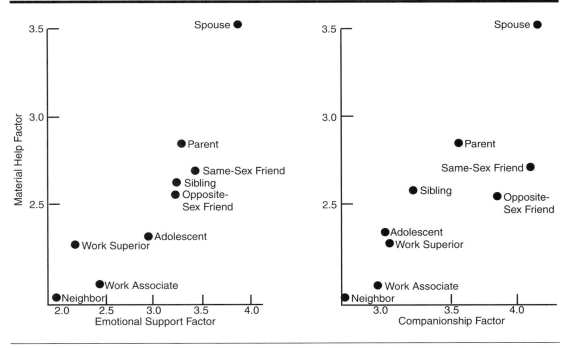

Source: Argyle and Furnham (1983). Copyrighted 1983 by the National Council on Family Relations, 3989 Central Ave. NE, Suite 550, Minneapolis, MN 55421.

kinds of social support are combined, a social support factor is found to have a strong correlation with happiness, for example, of .50 (Austrom 1984). Berkman and Syme (1979) followed up seven thousand people over nine years and found that more of those with the stronger support networks were still alive at the end of the study.

Different relationships work in somewhat different ways. Marriage is the most intimate, and has the strongest effects, though also the most conflict, as we have seen. (For more on marriage, see Myers, this volume.) Friends are primarily a source of companionship; they share in leisure activities, especially for middle-class people, and are a major source of positive moods. We discuss friends later in the context of life events and activities. Workmates are an important source of help with work problems and also of companionship at work. Kin are an enduring source of major help when needed; neighbors are the weakest source of support, though they are a source of frequent minor help. Neighbors and kin are more important in working-class communities (Argyle and Henderson 1985).

ETHNICITY

There have been many American studies in which the happiness of blacks and whites has been compared. Blacks are always found to be less happy; Campbell and his colleagues (1976) found that 18 percent of blacks said they were very happy compared with 32 percent of whites; these were averages of four surveys between 1957 and 1972. Similar results have been obtained in other countries. In South Africa, the happiest were whites, followed by Indians, coloreds, and blacks (Moller 1989). In the Netherlands, the happiest were the Dutch, followed by Moroccans, Surinams, and Turks (Verkuyten 1986).

The lower happiness of ethnic minorities is mainly due to their lower incomes, education, and job status. When these variables are controlled, the effect of ethnicity is reduced, in some studies to nothing, but typically to a beta weight of about .07 or less (Veenhoven et al. 1994). There are some other interactions. The effect of ethnicity on happiness is greater for those of higher occupational status, education, or income: while black farmworkers were little different in happiness from white ones, the happiness of educated and professional blacks in the United States declined between 1946 and 1966 (Manning-Gibbs 1972). However, this pattern was not confirmed in a later study by Diener and his colleagues (1993). In several studies, there was little black-white difference for older individuals.

It has usually been found that black Americans have lower self-esteem than whites; Campbell, Converse, and Rodgers (1976) found that 32 percent of blacks and 50 percent of whites had high self-esteem, but this has not always been found. And black children have often been found to have higher self-esteem than white children. This effect is stronger for children who go to segregated schools. Bachman (1970) found that black children in segregated schools had self-esteem that was .50 of a standard deviation higher than that of whites; for those in integrated schools it was .30 higher.

The main explanation for the lower happiness and self-esteem of members of ethnic minorities is that they have lower incomes, less education, and less skilled jobs. The effect of ethnicity when these have been controlled is quite small. Lower happiness may be the result of lower status in society; this is suggested by how precisely the ordering of average happiness levels for different groups in South Africa and the Netherlands follows the social status of the groups concerned. The high self-esteem of black American children is an interesting exception; it can partly be explained for children at segregated schools, who would rarely meet whites. It is known that low-status groups often select groups for self-comparison which avoid unfavorable comparisons (Argyle 1994). The low and falling happiness of high-status blacks in the United States has been ascribed to rising expectations that were not fulfilled.

International comparisons show that Africa, India, and Asia have low average happiness scores. These can partly be explained in terms of national differences in average income, income dispersion, and political freedom (Diener et al. 1995). There may be residual effects of race or culture when such factors have been controlled. It was widely believed by writers and observers in West Africa in the 1960s that there was a "happy African personality," but so far no survey evidence has been able to show this.

EMPLOYMENT

The benefits of employment for happiness are shown from studies of the unemployed and the retired. The level of unemployment in the modern world is very high, between 7 and 15 percent in most industrialized countries. The unemployed in nearly all countries are much less happy than those at work. Inglehart (1990) found that 61 percent of the unemployed were satisfied, compared with 78 percent of manual workers. In an American study, 10 to 12 percent of the unemployed described themselves as very happy, compared with 30 percent of the general population (Campbell et al. 1976). A British study found the corresponding figures of 27 percent and 38 percent (Fogarty 1985). In a meta-analysis, Haring, Okun, and Stock (1984) found an overall relationship of .18. Other studies have found that several aspects of happiness are affected by employment status, especially positive affect, satisfaction, self-esteem, apathy, and satisfaction with money, health, and housing. The unemployed are often very bored and don't know what to do with their time. The mental health of the unemployed is worse, with higher rates of depression, suicide, and alcoholism in particular. Their health is also worse, and their death rate higher (Argyle 1989).

Unemployment affects some sections of the population more than others. The effects are worse when there is a high level of employment, so that being without work is seen as personal failure (Kelvin and Jarrett 1985). Palisi (1987) pooled American data for the years 1972 to 1983 to make up a total of 15,320; those with a history of unemployment were less happy. This effect was stronger for blacks than for whites, especially for urban and more educated blacks, for whom the correlation was typically − .29 to − .33, and the beta weights about − .20. Rural blacks were not so affected. The effect is also greater after a longer period of unemployment; for those who are more committed to work (Jackson et al. 1983); for men; for the single; and for working-class individuals (Veenhoven et al. 1994). And while the effects are similar in most countries, in Spain there is little effect, perhaps, as has been suggested, because the Protestant work ethic is low in that country (Alvaro and Marsh 1989). The effects of unemployment are greater if there is little social support from family; Cobb and Kasl (1977) found that factory closure produced more cases of arthritis or raised cholesterol for those who did not have a supportive spouse.

When controls are applied for income, the effects are reduced but remain (Campbell et al. 1976). Controls for education, family support, and so forth, reduce the effects further, but they still remain in most studies.

The retired are also not working, though for a different reason. However, they are not unhappy; in fact, they are on average happier than those at work. Campbell, Converse, and Rodgers (1976) found that people over sixty-five were one-quarter of a standard deviation above the population mean in subjective well-being. Warr and Payne (1982), in Britain, found that 36 percent of retired men felt very pleased with things all the time, compared with 23 percent of those still at work. On the other hand, the retired can also feel bored, lonely, and useless; they experience a loss of self-image. There may be a temporary fall in mental health, but after this there is little difference in mental health. There is little effect on health, though some retire early because of poor health (Kasl 1980). People are happier in retirement if it was voluntary; if they are in good health; if they have not suffered much fall in income; and if they have active interests and activities, for example, in voluntary work, leisure groups, or adult education (Argyle 1996).

Housewives are another group who are not employed. There is no clear or consistent difference between their happiness and that of women at work, though there are a lot of complex interactions with the nature of work and family.

Are the links between employment and well-being causal? One way of studying this is to look at longitudinal studies of workers before and after they lose their jobs, for example, by plant closure. In a British study of the closure of a steelworks, those who had not found jobs six months later scored 2.3 on Bradburn's positive affect scale, compared with 3.05 for those who had (Warr 1978). In a similar American study, plant closure led to increased cholesterol and blood pressure after the announcement of closure, but before work had stopped (Cobb and Kasl 1977). Another method was used by Banks and Jackson (1982), who studied two thousand school leavers in Leeds, before they left school and at two yearly intervals afterward, on the General Health Questionnaire. Those who did not find jobs became less mentally well over the next one and two years, while those who did find jobs became better; however, those who got jobs had slightly higher scores for general mental disturbance in the first place. This shows that the main direction of causation was from employment to mental health, but that there is a little reverse causation as well.

What is the explanation of all this? The main explanation is that the unemployed are financially worse off; when this is controlled, the effects are weaker. There is also an effect of self-esteem, as is shown by the fact that the retired are generally happy, and unemployment has less effect when unemployment is normal. There is probably an effect of commitment to work—the effects are worse for older, white males and for those with high work involvement scores. Work is more central to men than it is to most women. The effects of job loss are partly mediated by poor health, owing to poor diet, high levels of smoking and drinking, and other poor health behavior. These findings show the partly hidden benefits of work, for example, in structuring time and providing social life and self-image (see Warr, this volume).

LEISURE

In a survey of 8,622 people in ten European countries, life satisfaction had a higher correlation with nonwork satisfaction (average .68) than with work satisfaction (average .52) in all countries. The reverse was found in Japan (Near and Rechner 1993). However, nonwork satisfaction would include the effects of religion and social relationships, which we treat separately here.

In the surveys reviewed by Veenhoven and his colleagues (1994), happiness was found to be correlated with leisure satisfaction, and level of leisure activities typically at .40, and after controls for employment, social class, and so forth, the correlation between happiness and leisure activities fell to about .20. The correlation with leisure was greatest for those not working—the unemployed or the retired, the old, those of greater wealth or social class, and the married without children at home (Zuma 1989).

Better information about the causal effect of leisure on happiness can be derived from longitudinal studies. Glancy, Willits, and Farrell (1986) followed up 1,521 high school children for twenty-four years and found that adolescent leisure predicted adult life satisfaction, with a number of controls applied. Headey, Holmstrom, and Wearing (1985) followed up a sample of six hundred Australians at two-year intervals, using LISREL analysis, and found that enjoyable activities with friends (in other words, leisure) and at work predicted increases in subjective well-being. Stronger evidence on causation is provided by a number of experiments on the effects of sport and other kinds of leisure. Sport is a reliable form of positive mood induction: Thayer (1989) found that a ten-minute brisk walk produced more positive feelings

and more energy for up to two hours afterward. More substantial courses of exercise, such as aerobics, for eight to ten weeks, two to four times a week, have been found to increase happiness and to reduce clinical depression and anxiety (Biddle and Mutrie 1991). However, these experiments can be criticized on the grounds that not all potential subjects agree to do such exercise. Steptoe, Kimbell, and Basford (1996) have carried out experiments that are not open to this criticism; they found that periods of exercise led to reduced depression and anxiety for some hours afterward, and that during this period stressful tasks had less effect on heart rate and blood pressure.

Looking at more specific kinds of leisure, we have seen that *sport and exercise* are effective, partly owing to the release of endorphins, but also because of the social interaction with others and perhaps the experience of success, of self-efficacy. A lot of leisure activities are done in *groups,* such as social clubs, choirs, and teams, and this is a source of happiness, especially for extraverts. Additional factors are the mood-inducing nature of the activities, such as dancing and music, and also the social support and social integration. Indeed, it is possible to fulfill a variety of social needs through such activities—for intimacy, public performance, cooperation, and so on (Argyle 1996). It has been argued by Csikszentmihalyi and Csikszentmihalyi (1988) that the greatest satisfaction comes from activities where *challenges* are met by skills, producing a state of "flow." They found that this happened in various kinds of serious and demanding leisure activities, but it has been found that most people prefer activities in which the challenge is not too great. In any case, more flow is experienced at work. Leisure is more satisfying, however, when there is some commitment, some use of skill, some kind of achievement.

The most popular form of leisure in the modern world, however, is *watching television*, an activity that requires no skill or commitment. Heavy television watchers are less happy than others, probably because they do not have anything better to do. However, television watching does provide positive and relaxing pleasure, at a very low level of arousal ("somewhere between being awake and asleep" Kubey and Csikszentmihalyi, 1990), and soap opera watchers feel they have a group of imaginary friends (Argyle 1996). *Holidays* are also a source of happiness, relaxation, and good health. Rubenstein (1980), in a survey of a large number of readers of *Psychology Today,* found that while on vacation 3 percent had headaches compared with

21 percent when not on holiday, with similar differences for being tired, irritable, or constipated. On the other hand, "workaholics" are happier when they can get back to work. A quite different kind of leisure, which fits the Csikszentmihalyi model better perhaps, is *voluntary work*, which is a source of great satisfaction, as shown in table 18.2. In the study by Argyle (1996), volunteer and charity work were found to generate high levels of joy, exceeded only by dancing.

A number of demographic differences in the use of leisure can be used to explain some of the other findings. We saw that individuals of higher *social class* engage in more active leisure, while working-class people watch much more television. The greater leisure of the first group is partly due to *wealth*, to having cars and more money for activities and baby-sitters, but also to *education*, which is the source of many leisure interests. Indeed, many leisure interests are acquired in the course of education—for example, music, art, sport, and reading—but even more through the leisure activities provided in educational institutions, which compete in persuading students to join. Another demographic factor is age: the old and the retired have more time for leisure, but participation in many forms of leisure falls off with age, especially sport and exercise, other physically active leisure, and outings; the main activities that remain are walking, gardening, hobbies, social clubs, and television. The *unemployed* also have more time

for leisure, but do even less than the old and the retired. They do much less exercise and all kinds of positive leisure but spend much more time watching television, drink more, and spend more time with friends. Their low level of leisure partly explains their low level of happiness. Experiments in which young unemployed persons have been provided with sports training and facilities have had very positive effects (Kay, cited by Glyptis 1989).

RELIGION

Many surveys have found that happiness is greater for those who are more religious, however this is assessed, though the effect is often small. Inglehart (1990), in a survey of 163,000 in fourteen European countries, found, for example, that 84 percent of those who went to church once a week said they were very satisfied with life, compared with 77 percent of those who never went. In a meta-analysis of twenty-eight American studies, Witter, Okun, and Haring (1985) found that the effect of religion is positive, of modest strength, and strongest for church attendance. There is a clear effect for having a sense of meaning and purpose.

The studies reviewed by Veenhoven and his colleagues (1994) found that the effect was stronger

TABLE 18.2   The Benefits of Volunteering

	Very important (%)	*Fairly important* (%)	*Not very important* (%)	*Not important at all* (%)	*Don't know* (%)
I meet people and make friends through it.	48	37	11	4	0
It's the satisfaction of seeing the results.	67	26	5	2	1
It gives me the chance to do things that I'm good at.	33	36	24	7	—
It makes me feel less selfish as a person.	29	33	24	13	2
I really enjoy it.	72	21	6	2	—
It's part of my religious belief or philosophy of life to give help.	44	22	9	23	2
It broadens my experience of life.	39	36	15	9	1
It gives me a sense of personal achievement.	47	31	16	6	—
It gives me the chance to learn new skills.	25	22	29	23	1
It gives me a position in the community.	12	16	33	38	1
It gets me "out of myself."	35	30	19	15	1
It gives me the chance to get a recognized qualification.	3	7	15	74	1

Source: Lynn and Smith (1991). Reprinted with permission from the authors.

in American than in European surveys, and that the effect was stronger for older people, blacks, women, and Protestants compared with Catholics. The effect is strongest for satisfaction with religion (for example, $r = .50$ for Andrews and Withey [1976]), followed by church attendance (typically $r = .15$ to $.20$), and weaker for membership or beliefs. Those who have had religious experiences are happier: Greeley (1975) found a correlation of .60 between reporting having been "bathed in light" and positive affect. Psychic experiences, such as experiences of ESP or talking to the dead, had no such effect.

A number of studies have carried out multiple regressions to see how far the effects of religion can be explained by other variables. When demographic controls are applied—for age, class, and education—the beta weight for religion falls to about .15; when controls for social contacts are also applied, it drops to about .10 (Halman et al. 1987). We shall see shortly that social support is probably one of the main ways in which religion affects happiness.

Does religion cause happiness or vice versa? There is little clear evidence on this point, but two sources of evidence suggest that religion can affect happiness. Chiriboga (1982) found that church attendance predicted happiness fifteen years later in elderly individuals ($r = .28$ for males, non significant for females). Secondly, religious experiences

produce enhanced happiness up to six months later, even when these experiences are induced by drugs (Pahnke 1966). Religious conversion has similar effects; those affected are often in a state of anxiety and distress before the event and feel at peace afterward; such conversions are in large part due to social pressures, though personality factors also play a part (Beit-Hallahmi and Argyle, 1997).

If religion does affect happiness, what is the explanation? The main factor seems to be the very strong social support churches give to their members. In an early study, Moberg and Taves (1965) used a measure of subjective well-being with a sample of 1,343 elderly people in Minnesota. Some of the results are shown in table 18.3; it can be seen that the benefits of church are greatest for those who are single, old, retired, or in poor health.

In a survey of 310,000 Australian church members, 24 percent said that their closest friends belonged to their church, and another 46 percent had close friends in it. The figures were greater for Pentecostal and other small churches (Kaldor et al. 1984). It is not clear why churches are so supportive; perhaps the ideology of love requires such an atmosphere, which may also arise from the intimacy and self-disclosure in house groups or the experience of shared rituals. The social support received from the church community predicts subjective well-being, especially of the old, after other

TABLE 18.3   Happiness and Church Membership

	Church leaders (%)	Other church members (%)	Non-church members (%)
Married	15	15	12
Widowed	15	11	7
Single	12	8	5
Sixty-five to seventy	18	14	10
Seventy-one to seventy-nine	15	12	7
Eighty or over	13	8	6
Fully employed	18	18	17
Partly employed	16	16	13
Fully retired	15	12	7
Health (self-rated)			
Excellent	17	14	13
Good	15	14	11
Fair	17	6	8
More active in religious organizations than in fifties	16	13	9
Less active	14	11	7

Source: Moberg and Taves (1965).

works in a similar way and also has a small correlation with happiness (figure 18.6).

Social skills are much more important. Argyle and Lu (1990) found that extraverts are happy because of their greater assertiveness skills, which mediated the extraversion-happiness relation.

Further studies found that happiness is also related to cooperativeness, leadership, and heterosexual skills (Argyle, Martin, and Lu 1995). Social skills lead to happiness because they lead to the desired relationships with others. At the lower end of the happiness dimension, lonely people are often depressed, and they are lonely because of their lack of social skills. Individuals who are unrewarding, poor at verbal or nonverbal communication, or otherwise socially incompetent, are likely to be socially rejected and to become isolated and unable to find companionship or social support (Sarason and Sarason 1985). Extraverts have more social skills, and this is one reason for their happiness (Argyle and Lu 1990).

Health can be regarded as a kind of competence, since it functions in a similar way. A meta-analysis found an overall correlation between health and happiness of .32 (Okun et al. 1984). This is stronger for women and when subjective measures of health are used. But does health influence happiness or vice versa? In fact, both directions of causation have been found, sometimes both in the same study (Feist et al. 1995). However, it is clear that health can affect happiness: Brief et al. (1993), using an objective measure of health, found that it predicted satisfaction and the absence of negative affect but failed to predict positive affect. Health affects happiness partly because those in good health simply feel subjectively better, partly because they are able to do more of the things that they want to do, and partly because they are more socially and physically active.

POLICY IMPLICATIONS

Do these results have any implications for how happiness could be enhanced in the world? Of course, some demographic variables, like age and ethnicity, we can do nothing about, but others can be changed. Governments often behave as if increasing incomes and the standard of living is their main policy, though we have seen that income is a fairly minor predictor of happiness, has almost no effect for the richest half of the population, and has no historical effect at all. Increasing the incomes of the very poor and of very poor countries is, however, worth doing from this point of view.

Employment is a much more important factor, in that the lack of employment is a major cause of unhappiness. It is less serious when the overall level is high, and it may become less serious if the Protestant work ethic declines. Meanwhile, the effects of unemployment could be alleviated by policies of work-sharing, working shorter hours or having shorter working lives, and workfare, which requires the unemployed to earn their welfare benefits. Enhanced leisure is another solution; providing sports training and facilities for young unemployed persons had a very positive effect on morale. A minority of the unemployed are happier than when they were working since they have found more interesting things to do (Fryer and Payne 1984). The long-term future of work is almost certainly that there is going to be less and less of it as the result of computers and automation, so that the development of serious and satisfying leisure is most important (Argyle 1996).

We have seen that leisure is not only an important source of happiness but one that is to a large extent under an individual's control. Limitations on access to leisure include lack of facilities, although governments already do a great deal to provide sporting, cultural, educational, and other facilities. Lack of skills is another limitation; people will not pursue leisure interests unless they have acquired the interest and the skills in the first place. Lack of money is less important, since a great deal of leisure is either free or very cheap (Argyle 1996).

Marriage and other close relationships are a major cause of happiness, and the breakup of marriages a major source of unhappiness, for the time being at least, often forever for at least one partner

FIGURE 18.6   The Extraversion-Happiness Relation

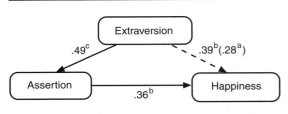

Source: Reprinted from Argyle and Lu (1990) with permission from Elsevier Science.
[a] Reduced correlation between extraversion and later happiness with assertion controlled.
[b] Correlation between extraversion and later happiness.
[c] Correlation between extraversion and later assertiveness.

and for the children. Anything that can be done to strengthen the institution of marriage seems desirable. Friendship is another important source of happiness, but there are many who lack friends because of their lack of social skills.

Education is a positive source of happiness, but it could do more. Already education is a source of leisure interests. It could also be a greater source of social skills training, so that people could more easily make friends and stay married. Education could also help with health behavior; the uneducated have much worse health behavior, suggesting that education may be part of the answer.

CONCLUSIONS

Andrews and Withey (1976) may have been right with their estimate that 10 percent of the variance in levels of happiness is due to demographic factors; Diener (1984) might be closer with 15 percent. Later research has confirmed that all demographic variables affect happiness, but that most of the effects are small. However, they all hold up after controls have been applied, and they are mostly causal. In this chapter, we have taken account of some further, mainly environmental, variables that account for quite a lot more variance, including religion, leisure activities, life events, and personal competencies. Another environmental variable, work, is discussed by Warr in another chapter. These sources of happiness are not negligible: the strongest effects are due to marriage, employment, occupational status, leisure, and the "competencies" of health and social skills. The effects are much stronger for certain groups, for example, the effect of income on the poor, and religion on the old; the unemployed are often very unhappy, as are the separated and divorced. Some of the findings can be explained in terms of other variables cited here, such as class differences in leisure and marriage.

REFERENCES

Agnew, R. (1984). The effect of appearance on personality and behaviour: Are the beautiful really good? *Youth and Society, 15*, 285–303.

Alvaro, J. L., and Marsh, C. (1989). A cross-cultural perspective on the social and psychological distress caused by unemployment: A comparison of Spain and the United Kingdom. Complutense University (Madrid). Unpublished paper.

Andrews, F. M., and Withey, S. B. (1976). *Social indicators of well-being*. New York: Plenum.

Argyle, M. (1976). Personality and social behaviour. In R. Harre (Ed.), *Personality* (pp. 145–88). Oxford: Blackwell.

———. (1989). *The social psychology of work*. 2nd Ed. London: Penguin.

———. (1994). *The psychology of social class*. London: Routledge.

———. (1996). *The social psychology of leisure*. London: Penguin.

Argyle, M., and Furnham, A. (1983). Sources of satisfaction and conflict in long-term relationships. *Journal of Marriage and the Family, 45*, 481–93.

Argyle, M., and Henderson, M. (1985). *The anatomy of relationships*. Harmondsworth: Penguin.

Argyle, M., and Lu, L. (1990). The happiness of extraverts. *Personality and Individual Differences, 11*, 1011–17.

Argyle, M., Martin, M., and Lu, L. (1995). Testing for stress and happiness: The role of social and cognitive factors. In C. D. Spielberger and I. G. Sarason (Eds.), *Stress and emotion* (pp. 173–87). Washington: Taylor and Francis.

Austrom, D. R. (1984). *The consequences of being single*. New York: Peter Lang.

Bachman, J. G. (1970). *Youth in transition*, vol. 2, *The impact of family background and intelligence on tenth-grade boys*. Ann Arbor: Survey Research Center, University of Michigan.

Banks, M. H., and Jackson, P. R. (1982). Unemployment and risk of minor psychiatric disorder in young people: Cross-sectional and longitudinal evidence. *Psychological Medicine, 12*, 789–98.

Beit-Hallahmi, B., and Argyle, M. (1997). *The psychology of religious behaviour, belief, and experience*. London: Routledge and Kegan Paul.

Belk, R. W. (1984). Three scales to measure constructs related to materialism: Reliability, validity, and relationships to measures of happiness. In T. C. Kinnear (Ed.) *Advances in Consumer Research* (vol. 11, 291–97).

Berkman, L. F., and Syme, S. L. (1979). Social networks, host resistance, and mortality: A nine-year follow-up of Alameda County residents. *American Journal of Epidemiology, 109*, 186–204.

Berkowitz, L., Fraser, C., Treasure, F. P., and Cochran, S. (1987). Pay, equity, job qualifications, and comparisons in pay satisfaction. *Journal of Applied Psychology, 72*, 544–51.

Biddle, S., and Mutrie, N. (1991). *Psychology of physical activity and exercise*. London: Springer/Tavistock/Routledge.

Blaxter, M. (1990). *Health and lifestyle*. London: Tavistock/Routledge.

Bradburn, N. M. (1969). *The structure of psychological well-being*. Chicago: Aldine.

Brief, A. P., Butcher, A. H., George, J. M., and Link, K. E. (1993). Integrating bottom-up and top-down theories of subjective well-being: The case of health. *Journal of Personality and Social Psychology, 64,* 646–53.

Brown, G. W., and Harris, T. (1978). *Social origins of depression.* London: Tavistock.

Brown, R. (1978). Divided we fall: An analysis of relations between sections of a factory workforce. in H. Tajfel (Ed.), *Differentiation between social groups* (pp. 395–429). London: Academic Press.

Campbell, A. (1981). *The sense of well-being in America.* New York: McGraw-Hill.

Campbell, A., Converse, P. E., and Rodgers, W. L. (1976). *The quality of American life.* New York: Sage.

Cantril, H. (1965). *The Pattern of Human Concerns.* New Brunswick, N.J.: Rutgers University Press.

Chiriboga, D. A. (1982). Consistency in adult functioning: The influence of social stress. *Aging and Society, 2,* 7–29.

Clark, A. E. (1996). L'utilité est-elle relative? Analyse a l'aide de données sur les ménages. *Economie et Prevision, 121,* 151–64.

Clark, A. E., and Oswald, A. J. (1996). Satisfaction and comparison income. Discussion paper 419. Department of Economics, Essex University.

Cobb, S., and Kasl, S. V. (1977). *Termination: The consequences of job loss.* Cincinnati: U.S. Department of Health, Education, and Welfare.

Csikszentmihalyi, M., and Csikszentmihalyi, S. S. (1988). *Optimal experience.* Cambridge: Cambridge University Press.

Cutler, N. E. (1976). Membership of different kinds of voluntary associations and psychological well-being. *Gerontologist, 16,* 335–39.

Diener, E. (1984). Subjective well-being. *Psychological Bulletin, 95,* 542–75.

Diener, E., Diener, M., and Diener, C. (1995). Factors predicting the subjective well-being of nations. *Journal of Personality and Social Psychology, 69,* 851–64.

Diener, E., Horwitz, J., and Emmons, R. A. (1985). Happiness of the very wealthy. *Social Indicators Research, 16,* 263–74.

Diener, E., Sandvik, E., and Pavot, W. (1991). Happiness is the frequency, not the intensity, of positive versus negative affect. In F. Strack, M. Argyle, and N. Schwarz (Eds.), *Subjective well-being* (pp. 119–39). Oxford: Pergamon.

Diener, E., Sandvik, E., Seidlitz, L., and Diener, M. (1993). The relationship between income and subjective well-being: Relative or absolute? *Social Indicators Research, 28,* 195–223.

Diener, E., and Suh, E. (in press). Subjective well-being and age: An international analysis. *Annual Review of Gerontology and Geriatrics, 17.*

Dittmar, H. (1992). *The social psychology of material possessions.* Hemel Hempstead: Harvester Wheatsheaf.

Ellison, C. G. (1991). Religious involvement and subjective well-being. *Journal of Health and Social Behavior, 32,* 80–99.

Feist, G. J., Bodner, T. E., Jacobs, J. F., Miles, M., et al. (1995). Integrating top-down structural models of subjective well-being: A longitudinal investigation. *Journal of Personality and Social Psychology, 68,* 138–50.

Felton, B. J. (1987). Cohort variations in happiness: Some hypotheses and exploratory analyses. *International Journal of Aging and Human Development, 25,* 27–42.

Fogarty, M. (1985). British attitudes to work. In M. Abrams, D. Gerard, and M. Timms (Eds.), *Values and social change in Britain* (pp. 173–200). London: Macmillan.

Fryer, D., and Payne, R. (1984). Proactive behaviour in unemployment. *Leisure Studies, 3,* 273–95.

Glancy, M., Willits, F. K., and Farrell, P. (1986). Adolescent activities and adult success and happiness. *Sociology and Social Research, 70,* 242–70.

Glenn, N. D., and Weaver, C. N. (1979). A multivariate, multisurvey study of marital happiness. *Journal of Marriage and the Family, 40,* 269–82.

———. (1981). Education's effect on psychological well-being. *Public Opinion Quarterly, 45,* 22–39.

Glyptis, S. (1989). *Leisure and unemployment.* Milton Keynes: Open University Press.

Gove, W. R. (1972). The relationship between sex roles, marital status, and mental illness. *Social Forces, 51,* 34–44.

Greeley, A. M. (1975). *The sociology of the paranormal.* London: Sage.

Halman, L., Heunks, F., DeMoor, R., and Zanders, H. (1987). *Traditie, secularisatie en individualisering.* Tilburg: Tilburg University Press.

Haring, M. J., Okun, M. A., and Stock, W. A. (1984). A quantitative synthesis of literature on work status and subjective well-being. *Journal of Vocational Behavior, 25,* 316–24.

Haring, M. J., Stock, W. A., and Okun, M. A. (1984). A research synthesis of gender and social class as correlates of subjective well-being. *Human Relations, 37,* 645–57.

Haring-Hidore, M., Stock, W. A., Okun, M. A., and Witter, R. A. (1985). Marital status and subjective well-being: A research synthesis. *Journal of Marriage and the Family, 47,* 947–53.

Headey, B. W., Holmstrom, E. L., and Wearing, J. H. (1985). Models of well-being and ill-being. *Social indicators Research, 17,* 211–34.

Hoffman, L. W., and Manis, J. D. (1982). The value of children in the United States. In F. I. Nye (Ed.), *Family relationships* (pp. 143–70). Beverly Hills: Sage.

Hughes, M., and Gove, W. R. (1981). Living alone, social integration, and mental health. *American Journal of Sociology, 87,* 48–74.

Inglehart, R. (1990). *Culture shift in advanced industrial society.* Princeton, N.J.: Princeton University Press.

Inglehart, R., and Rabier, J.-R. (1986). Aspirations adapt to situations—But why are the Belgians so much happier than the French? In F. M. Andrews

(Ed.), *Research on the quality of life* (pp. 1–56). Ann Arbor: Survey Research Center, University of Michigan.

Inkeles, A., and Diamond, L. (1986). Personal development and national development: A cross-cultural perspective. In A. Szalai and F. M. Andrews (Eds.), *The quality of life: Comparative studies* (pp. 73–109). Ann Arbor: Institute for Social Research, University of Michigan.

Jackson, L. A. (1989). Relative deprivation and the gender wage gap. *Journal of Social Issues, 45,* 117–33.

Jackson, P. R., et al. (1983). Unemployment and psychological distress in young people: The moderating role of employee commitment. *Journal of Applied Psychology, 68,* 52.

Jarvis, G. K., and Northcott, H. C. (1987). Religion and differences in morbidity and mortality. *Social Science and Medicine, 25,* 813–24.

Kaldor, P. (1984). *Winds of change.* Anzea, New South Wales: Homebush.

Kanner, A. D., Coyne, J. C., Schaefer, C., and Lazarus, R. S. (1981). Comparison of two methods of stress measurement: Hassles and uplifts versus major life events. *Journal of Behavioral Medicine, 4,* 1–39.

Kasl, S. V. (1980). The impact of retirement. In C. L. Cooper and R. Payne (Eds.), *Current concerns in occupational stress* (pp. 137–86). Chichester: Wiley.

Kelvin, P., and Jarrett, J. (1985). *The social psychological effects of unemployment.* Cambridge: Cambridge University Press.

Kennedy, S., Kiecolt-Glaser, J. K., and Glaser, R. (1990). Social support, stress, and the immune system. In B. R. Sarason, I. G. Sarason, and G. R. Pierce (Eds.), *Social support: An interactional view* (pp. 253–66). New York: Wiley.

Kirkpatrick, L. A. (1992). An attachment-theory approach to the psychology of religion. *International Journal for the Psychology of Religion, 2,* 3–28.

Kozma, A., Stone, S., Stones, M. J., Hannah, T. E., and McNeil, K. (1990). Long- and short-term affective states in happiness: Model, paradigm, and experimental evidence. *Social Indicators Research, 22,* 119–38.

Kubey, R., and Csikszentmihalyi, M. (1990). *Leisure and the quality of life.* Hillsdale, N.J.: Erlbaum.

Larson, R. (1990). The solitary side of life: An examination of the time people spend alone from childhood to old age. *Developmental Review, 10,* 155–83.

Leicht, K. T., and Shepelak, N. (1994). Organizational justice and satisfaction with economic rewards. *Research in Social Stratification and Mobility, 13,* 175–202.

Leisure Development Centre. (1980). *A thirteen-country survey of values.* Tokyo: Leisure Development Center.

Lewinsohn, P. M., and Macphillamy, D. J. (1974). The relationship between age and engagement in pleasant activities. *Journal of Gerontology, 29,* 290–4.

Lewinsohn, P. M., Sullivan, J. M., and Grosscup, S. J. (1982). Behavioral therapy: Clinical applications. In A. J. Rush (Ed.), *Short-term therapies for depression* (pp. 50–87). New York: Guilford.

Loscocco, K. A., and Spitze, G. (1991). The organizational context of women's and men's pay satisfaction. *Social Science Quarterly, 72,* 3–19.

Lynn, P., and Smith, J. D. (1991). *Voluntary action research.* London: Volunteer Centre.

Lynch, J. J. (1977). *The broken heart.* New York: Basic Books.

MacPhillamy, D. J., and Lewinsohn, P. M. (1976). *Manual for the pleasant events schedule.* Eugene: University of Oregon.

Manning-Gibbs, B. A. (1972). Relative deprivation and self-reported happiness of blacks. Ph.D. thesis, University of Texas at Austin. Cited in Veenhoven et al. (1994).

Mastekaasa, A. (1992). Marital status and subjective well-being: A changing relationship? *Social Indicators Research, 29,* 249–89.

Michalos, A. C. (1980). Satisfaction and happiness. *Social Indicators Research, 8,* 385–422.

———. (1986). Job satisfaction, marital satisfaction, and the quality of life: A review and a preview. In F. M. Andrews (Ed.), *Research on the quality of life* (pp. 57–83). Ann Arbor: Institute for Social Research, University of Michigan.

Mitchell, R. E. (1972). *Levels of emotional strain in Southeast Asian cities.* Taipei: Orient Cultural Service. Cited in Veenhoven et al. (1994).

Moberg, D. O., and Taves, M. J. (1965). Church participation and adjustment in old age. In A. M. Rose and W. A. Peterson (Eds.), *Older people and their social world* (pp. 113–24). Philadelphia: F. A. Davis.

Moller, V. (1989). Can't get no satisfaction. *Indicator South Africa, 7,* 43–46. Cited by Veenhoven et al. (1994).

Myers, D. G., and Diener, E. (1996). The pursuit of happiness. *Scientific American* (May), 54–56.

Near, J. P., and Rechner, P. L. (1993). Cross-cultural variations in predictors of life satisfaction: An historical view of differences among West European countries. *Social Indicators Research, 29,* 109–21.

Nock, S. L. (1995). A comparison of marriages and cohabiting relationships. *Journal of Family Issues, 16,* 53–76.

Okun, M. A., Stock, W. A., Haring, M. J., and Witter, R. A. (1984). The social activity/subjective well-being relation: A quantitative synthesis. *Research on Aging, 6,* 45–65.

Olson, G. I., and Schober, B. I. (1993). The satisfied poor. *Social Indicators Research, 28,* 173–93.

Pahnke, W. H. (1966). Drugs and mysticism. *International Journal of Parapsychology, 8,* 295–314.

Palisi, B. J. (1987). Effects of urbanism, race, and class on happiness and physical health. *Sociological Spectrum, 7,* 271–95.

Pollner, M. (1989). Divine relations, social relations, and well-being. *Journal of Health and Social Behavior, 30,* 92–104.

Reich, J. W., and Zautra, J. (1981). Life events and personal causation: Some relationships with satisfaction and distress. *Journal of Personality and Social Psychology, 41,* 1002–12.

Rollins, B. C., and Cannon, R. L. (1974). Marital satisfaction over the family life cycle. *Journal of Marriage and the Family, 36,* 271–82.

Rubenstein, C. (1980). Vacations. *Psychology Today, 13,* May, 62–76.

Runciman, W. G. (1966). *Relative deprivation and social justice.* London: Routledge and Kegan Paul.

Russell, R. J. H., and Wells, P. A. (1994). Predictors of happiness in married couples. *Personality and Individual Differences, 17,* 313–21.

Ryff, C. D. (1995). Psychological well-being in adult life. *Current Directions in Psychological Science, 4,* 99–104.

Sarason, I. G., and Sarason, R. B. (Eds.). (1985). *Social support: Theory, research, and applications.* Dordrecht: Nijhoff.

Scherer, K. R., Walbott, H. G., and Summerfield, A. B. (1986). *Experiencing emotion.* Cambridge: Cambridge University Press.

Schmotkin, D. (1990). Subjective well-being as a function of age and gender: A multivariate look for differentiated trends. *Social Indicators Research, 22,* 201–30.

Schwarz, N., and Strack, F. (1991). Evaluating one's life: A judgment model of subjective well-being. In F. Strack, M. Argyle, and N. Schwarz (Eds.), *Subjective well-being* (pp. 27–47). Oxford: Pergamon.

Smith, S., and Razzell, P. (1975). *The pools winners.* London: Caliban Books.

Spreitzer, E., and Snyder, E. E. (1974). Correlates of life satisfaction among the aged. *Journal of Gerontology, 29,* 454–58.

Steptoe, A., Kimbell, J., and Basford, P. (1996). Exercise and the experience and appraisal of daily stressors: A naturalistic study. *Journal of Behavioral Medicine, 21,* 363–74.

Stroebe, W., and Stroebe, M. S. (1987). *Bereavement and health.* Cambridge: Cambridge University Press.

Taylor, M. C. (1982). Improved conditions, rising expectations, and dissatisfaction: A test of the past/present relative deprivation hypothesis. *Social Psychology Quarterly, 45,* 24–33.

Thayer, R. E. (1989). *The biopsychology of mood and emotion.* New York: Oxford University Press.

Turner, V. W. (1969). *The ritual process.* London: Routledge and Kegan Paul.

Vanfossen, B. E. (1981). Sex differences in the mental health effects of spouse support and equity. *Journal of Health and Social Behavior, 22,* 130–43.

Veenhoven, R. (Ed.). (1989). *Did the crisis really hurt?* Rotterdam: Rotterdam University Press.

Veenhoven, R., and coworkers (1994). *World database of happiness: Correlates of happiness.* Rotterdam: Erasmus University.

Verkuyten, M. (1986). The impact of ethnic and sex differences on happiness among adolescents in the Netherlands. *Journal of Social Psychology, 126,* 259–60.

Veroff, J., Douvan, B., and Kulka, R. A. (1981). *The inner American.* New York: Basic Books.

Walker, C. (1977). Some variations in marital satisfaction. In R. Chester and J. Peel (Eds.), *Equalities and inequalities in family life* (pp. 127–39). London: Academic Press.

Warr, P. (1978). A study of psychological well-being. *British Journal of Psychology, 69,* 111–21.

Warr, P., and Payne, R. (1982). Experience of strain and pleasure among British adults. *Social Science and Medicine, 16,* 498–516.

Watt, E. (1994). *For better for worse.* Cambridge: Relationships Foundation.

Witter, R. A., Okun, M. A., Stock, W. A., and Haring, M. J. (1984). Education and subjective well-being: A meta-analysis. *Educational Evaluation and Policy Analysis, 6,* 165–73.

Women's Own. (1974). A questionnaire. October 12, 1974.

Wood, W., Rhodes, N., and Whelan, M. (1989). Sex differences in positive well-being: A consideration of emotional style and marital status. *Psychological Bulletin, 106,* 249–64.

World Values Study Group (1994). *World Values Survey, 1981–1984 and 1990–1993.* Inter-University Consortium for Political and Social Research (ICPSR) version (computer file). Ann Arbor: Institute for Social Research, University of Michigan.

Zuma. (1989). *Wohlfahrtsurveys 1978–1988.* Mannheim: Zentrum fur Umfrageforschung Mannheim. Cited in Veenhoven et al. (1994).

19 Close Relationships and Quality of Life

David G. Myers

As social animals, we humans have a powerful urge to belong—to feel attached to others in close relationships. Our human connections bind infants protectively to their caregivers and enhanced our ancestors' survival. When needs for close relationships are met, through supportive friendships or marriage, people enjoy better physical and emotional quality of life. Cultural and gender variations in social connectedness reveal both benefits and costs of Western individualism. As individualism has increased, and the bonds of marriage and informal networks have decreased, concern has grown for the well-being of children and civil society. Communitarians therefore argue for policies that balance individualism with community, and personal rights with social responsibilities.

I get by with a little help from my friends.
> —John Lennon and Paul McCartney,
> *Sgt. Pepper's Lonely Hearts Club Band,* 1967

Do CLOSE, supportive, intimate human connections enhance quality of life? Western cultures offer mixed messages.

On the one hand, we fret over supposedly addictive, dysfunctional relationships. Pop psychology books warn us against the yoke of "codependent" connections, marked by too much support and loyalty to a troubled partner at the cost of one's own self-fulfillment. Recognizing that the "chains" of marriage and the "shackles" of commitment can put us in "bondage," we are advised to give priority to enhancing our own identity and self-expression. "The only question which matters," declared Carl Rogers (quoted by Wallach and Wallach 1985), "is, 'Am I living in a way which is deeply satisfying to me, and which truly expresses me?'"

On the other hand, we yearn to be liked and loved. Asked, "What missing element would bring you happiness?" the most frequent answer is, "Love" (Freedman 1978). When college students were asked, "What would make you happy—winning millions in the lottery, achieving fame/ prestige in your career, enjoying physical pleasures (sex, food, drink), or falling (or staying) in love with your ideal mate?" 78 percent picked love as their first choice (Pettijohn and Pettijohn 1996).

THE HUMAN NEED TO BELONG

We humans feel motivated to eat, to drink, to have sex, and to achieve. But being what Aristotle called "the social animal," we also have a need to belong, to feel connected with others in enduring, close relationships. Roy Baumeister and Mark Leary (1995) identify functions of this basic human motive.

Aiding Survival

Social bonds boosted our ancestors' survival rate. For both children and adults, bonding was adaptive. By keeping children close to their caregivers, attachments served as a powerful survival impulse. As adults, those who formed attachments were more likely to come together to reproduce and to stay together to nurture their offspring to maturity. Groups shared food, provided mates, and helped care for children.

Survival also was enhanced by group members' cooperation. In solo combat, our ancestors were not the toughest predators. But as hunters they learned that six hands were better than two. Those who foraged in groups also gained protection from predators and enemies. There was strength in numbers. If, indeed, those who felt a need to belong survived and reproduced most successfully, their genes would in time predominate. The inevitable result: an innately social creature.

Wanting to Belong

The need to belong colors our thoughts and emotions. People spend much time thinking about their actual and hoped-for relationships. When relationships form, we often feel joy. Falling in mutual love, people have been known to get cheek-aches from their irrepressible grin. Asked, "What is necessary for your happiness?" or, "What is it that makes your life meaningful?" most people mention—before anything else—satisfying close relationships with family, friends, or romantic partners (Berscheid 1985).

Short-term, superficial relationships alone do not satisfy. Prostitutes report having many physically intimate interactions with interesting people and without the yoke of ongoing obligations. Yet such interactions do not satisfy, prompting a quest for more lasting bonds, sometimes even self-destructive ties to procurers (McLeod 1982). When brothel rules aim to maximize brief contacts and prevent long-term relationships, many prostitutes object, preferring lengthier and repeated contacts, even at the cost of reduced earnings (Symanski 1980).

Because of our pan-human quest for enduring, close relationships, new social bonds are typically marked by celebration. When we marry, have a child, gain a new job, or join a fraternity, sorority, or religious community, we mark the event with food, ritual, or parties.

People in every human society belong to groups and prefer and favor "us" over "them." Thus, in the classic Robbers Cave study, previously unacquainted boys assigned to a group quickly developed strong group loyalty and identification—and antagonism toward those randomly assigned to other groups (Sherif 1966). In experiments, even trivial definitions of groups—for instance, those who favor one abstract painter over another—have led to group identification and in-group biases when dividing up money (Tajfel 1981; Wilder 1981). When facing common predicaments or working for superordinate goals, the sense of belonging becomes all the stronger.

Increasing Social Acceptance

Much of our social behavior aims to increase our belonging—our social acceptance and inclusion. To avoid rejection, we generally conform to group standards and seek to make favorable impressions. To win friendship and esteem, we monitor our behavior, hoping to create the right impressions. Seeking love and belonging, we spend billions on clothes, cosmetics, and diet and fitness aids—all motivated by our quest for acceptance. In cultures where the decline of arranged marriages and the possibility of divorce make romantic attachment more dependent on attractiveness, more billions are spent on becoming and staying attractive.

Like sexual motivation, which fuels both love and exploitation, the need to belong feeds both deep attachments and menacing threats. Out of our need to define a "we" come loving families, faithful friendships, fraternal organizations, and team spirit, but also teen gangs, isolationist cults, ethnic hostilities, and fanatic nationalism. So it goes with all basic motives that have multiple and strong effects on how we think, feel, and act. It therefore "seems safe to conclude," say Baumeister and Leary, "that human beings are fundamentally and pervasively motivated by a need to belong" (522).

Maintaining Relationships

People resist breaking social bonds (Hazan and Shaver 1994). For most of us, familiarity breeds liking, not contempt. Thrown together at school, at summer camp, on a cross-country bus tour, people resist the group's dissolution. Hoping to maintain the relationships, they promise to call, to write, to come back for reunions. Parting, they feel distress. At the end of a mere vacation cruise, people may hug their waiter or cry when saying good-bye forever to their cabin attendant. Attachments can even keep people in abusive relationships; the fear of being alone may seem worse than the pain of emotional or physical abuse.

When something threatens or dissolves our social ties, negative emotions overwhelm us. Exile, imprisonment, and solitary confinement are progressively more severe forms of punishment. Recently bereaved people often feel that life is empty and pointless. Those denied others' acceptance and inclusion may feel depressed. Anxiety, jealousy, loneliness, and guilt all involve threatened disruptions of our need to belong.

ATTACHMENT

Our infant dependency strengthens our human bonds. Soon after birth we exhibit various social responses—love, fear, anger. But the first and greatest of these is love. As babies we almost immediately prefer familiar faces and voices. We coo and smile when our parents give us attention. By eight months, we crawl after mother or father and typically let out a wail when separated from them. Reunited, we cling.

Deprived of familiar attachments—sometimes

in barren institutions, sometimes locked away at home under conditions of extreme neglect—children may become withdrawn, frightened, silent. Those abandoned in Romanian orphanages were said to "look frighteningly like Harlow's [socially deprived] monkeys" (Blakeslee 1995). After studying the mental health of homeless children for the World Health Organization, John Bowlby (1980) reflected: "Intimate attachments to other human beings are the hub around which a person's life revolves, not only when he is an infant or a toddler or a schoolchild but throughout his adolescence and his years of maturity as well, and on into old age. From these intimate attachments a person draws his strength and enjoyment of life" (442).

Passionate Attachments

Researchers have compared the nature of attachment and love in various close relationships—between parents and children, same-sex friends, and spouses or lovers (Davis 1985; Maxwell 1985; Sternberg and Grajek 1984). Some elements are common to all loving attachments: mutual understanding, giving and receiving support, valuing and enjoying being with the loved one. Passionate love is, however, spiced with some added features: physical affection, an expectation of exclusiveness, and an intense fascination with the loved one.

Passionate love is not just for lovers. Phillip Shaver, Cindy Hazan, and Donna Bradshaw (1988) note that year-old infants display a passionate attachment to their parents. Much like young adult lovers, they welcome physical affection, feel distress when separated, express intense affection when reunited, and take great pleasure in the significant other's attention and approval.

Attachment Styles

Some babies, when placed in a strange situation (usually a laboratory playroom), show *secure attachment*. They play comfortably in their mother's presence, happily exploring the strange environment. If she leaves, they get distressed; when she returns, they run to her, hold her, then relax and return to exploring and playing. Other infants show the anxiousness and ambivalence of *insecure attachment*. In the strange situation, they are more likely to cling anxiously to their mother. If she leaves, they cry; when she returns, they may be indifferent or even hostile. Still others show *avoidant attachment*. Although internally aroused, they reveal little distress during separation or attachment upon reunion (Ainsworth 1973, 1989).

Some researchers attribute these varying attachment styles to parental responsiveness. Sensitive, responsive mothers—mothers who engender a sense of basic trust in the world's reliability—typically have securely attached infants, observed Mary Ainsworth (1979) and Erik Erikson (1963). Other researchers believe attachment styles may reflect inherited temperament. Regardless, early attachment styles do seem to lay a foundation for future relationships.

Shaver and Hazan (1993, 1994) and others (Feeney and Noller 1990; Simpson, Rholes, and Nelligan 1992) have explored adult versions of the infant attachment styles. *Secure* individuals find it easy to get close to others and don't fret about getting too dependent or being abandoned. As lovers they enjoy sexuality within the context of a continuing relationship. *Anxious-ambivalent* individuals are less trusting and therefore more possessive and jealous. They may break up repeatedly with the same person. *Avoidant* individuals fear closeness and therefore become less invested in relationships and more likely to leave them. They also are more likely to engage in one-night stands of sex without love. Kim Bartholomew and Leonard Horowitz (1991) note that avoidant individuals may be either *fearful* ("I am uncomfortable getting close to others") or *dismissing* ("It is very important to me to feel independent and self-sufficient").

CLOSE RELATIONSHIPS AND HEALTH

We can easily imagine why close relationships might contribute to illness. Relationships are often fraught with stress, especially in crowded living conditions lacking privacy (Evans et al. 1989). "Hell is others," wrote Jean-Paul Sartre. Peter Warr and Roy Payne (1982) asked a representative sample of British adults what, if anything, had emotionally strained them the day before. "Family" was the most frequent answer. Even when well meaning, family intrusions can be stressful. And stress contributes to heart disease, hypertension, and a suppressed immune system.

On balance, however, close relationships more often contribute to health and happiness. Asked what prompted the previous day's times of pleasure, the same British sample, by an even larger margin, again answered, "Family." For most of us, family relationships provide not only our greatest heartaches but also our greatest comfort and joy.

Moreover, seven massive investigations, each

following thousands of people for several years, reveal that close relationships affect health. Compared with those having few social ties, people are less likely to die prematurely if supported by close relationships with friends, family, fellow church members, coworkers, or members of other support groups (Cohen 1988; House, Landis, and Umberson 1988; Nelson 1988). "Woe to one who is alone and falls and does not have another to help," observed the writer of Ecclesiastes. Some examples:

- A review commissioned by the National Academy of Sciences revealed that broken social ties among people recently widowed, fired, or divorced correlate with increased vulnerability to disease (Dohrenwend et al. 1982). A Finnish study of ninety-six thousand widowed people confirmed the phenomenon: their risk of death doubled in the week following their partner's death (Kaprio et al. 1987). The National Academy of Sciences (1984) reported that the grief and depression that follow the death of a spouse decrease immune defenses (which helps explain the increase in disease among those recently widowed).
- One study followed leukemia patients preparing to undergo bone marrow transplants. Two years later only 20 percent of those who said they had little social support from their family or friends were still alive. Among those who felt strong emotional support, the two-year survival rate was 54 percent (Colon et al. 1991).
- A study of 1,234 heart attack patients found that the rate of a recurring attack within six months nearly doubled among those living alone (Case et al. 1992).
- A study of 1,965 heart disease patients revealed a five-year survival rate of 82 percent among those who were married or had a confidant, but only 50 percent among those did not have such support (Williams et al. 1992).
- A seventy-year study following 1,528 high–IQ score California children found that those whose parents did not divorce during their childhood outlived children of divorce by about four years (Friedman et al. 1995).

There are several possible reasons for the link between health and social support. Perhaps people with strong social ties eat better and exercise more because their partners guide and goad them into healthier living. Perhaps they smoke and drink less; that would help explain the repeated finding that religiously active people enjoy better health (Idler and Kasl 1992; Levin and Vanderpool 1987). If close relationships help us evaluate and overcome stressful events, such as social rejection, then perhaps they bolster immune functioning. When wounded by someone's dislike or by the loss of a

job, a friend's advice, assistance, and reassurance may be good medicine (Cutrona 1986; Rook 1987). Given lots of social support, spouses of cancer patients exhibit stronger immune functioning (Baron et al. 1990).

Close relationships also provide the opportunity to confide painful feelings. In one study, James Pennebaker and Robin O'Heeron (1984) contacted the surviving spouses of people who had committed suicide or died in car accidents. Those who had borne their grief alone had more health problems than those who had openly expressed it.

In a simulated confessional, Pennebaker asked volunteers to share with a hidden experimenter some upsetting events that had been preying on their minds. He asked some of the volunteers to describe a trivial event before they divulged the troubling one. Physiological measures revealed that their bodies remained tense the whole time they talked about the trivial event; they relaxed only when they later confided the cause of their turmoil. Even writing about personal traumas in a diary can help. When volunteers in other experiments did this, they had fewer health problems during the ensuing four to six months (Pennebaker 1990). As one subject explained, "Although I have not talked with anyone about what I wrote, I was finally able to deal with it, work through the pain instead of trying to block it out. Now it doesn't hurt to think about it."

If suppressed, traumas can affect physical health. James Pennebaker, Steven B. Barger, and John Tiebout (1989) also invited thirty-three Holocaust survivors to spend two hours recalling their experiences. Many did so in intimate detail never before disclosed. Most watched and showed family and friends a videotape of their recollections in the weeks following. Those who were most self-disclosing had the most improved health fourteen months later. Although talking about a stressful event can temporarily arouse people, it calms them in the long run (Mendolia and Kleck 1993).

CLOSE RELATIONSHIPS AND SUBJECTIVE WELL-BEING

Being attached to friends and partners with whom we can share intimate thoughts has two effects, observed Francis Bacon in his 1625 essay "Of Friendship": "It redoubleth joys, and cutteth griefs in half." Bacon would not be surprised by observed correlations between close relationships and psychological well-being.

Friendships and Well-Being

"Looking over the last six months, who are the people with whom you discussed matters important to you?" Compared to those who could name no such intimate when queried by the National Opinion Research Center (Burt 1986), those who named five or more such friends were 60 percent more likely to feel "very happy."

Other findings confirm the correlation between social support and well-being:

- The happiest university students are those who feel satisfied with their love life (Emmons et al. 1983).
- Those who enjoy close relationships cope better with various stresses, including bereavement, rape, job loss, and illness (Abbey and Andrews 1985; Perlman and Rook 1987).
- Compared to army soldiers in large, conventional units, with changing memberships, those on stable, cohesive, twelve-person A-teams experience greater social support, better physical and mental health, and more career satisfaction (Manning and Fullerton 1988).
- People report greater well-being if their friends and families support their goals by frequently expressing interest and offering help and encouragement (Israel and Antonucci 1987; Ruehlman and Wolchik 1988).
- Among eight hundred alumni of Hobart and William Smith Colleges surveyed by Wesley Perkins (1991),

those with "Yuppie" values—who preferred a high income and occupational success and prestige to having very close friends and a close marriage—were twice as likely as their former classmates to describe themselves as "fairly" or "very" *un*happy.

Marriage and Well-Being

For more than nine in ten people worldwide, reports the United Nations' *Demographic Yearbook,* one eventual example of a close relationship is marriage. So, given our need to belong and the resulting link between friendship and happiness, does marriage predict greater happiness? Or is there more happiness in pleasure-seeking independence than under the "yoke" of marriage?

A mountain of data reveal that most people are happier attached than unattached. Survey after survey of many tens of thousands of Europeans and Americans has produced a consistent result: compared to those single or widowed, and especially compared to those divorced or separated, married people report being happier and more satisfied with life (Gove, Style, and Hughes 1990; Inglehart 1990). During the 1970s and 1980s in the United States, for example, 24 percent of never-married adults, but 48 percent of married adults, reported being "very happy" (figure 19.1). Pooling data from national surveys of 20,800 people in

FIGURE 19.1   Marital Status and Happiness

Source: Data from 31,901 participants in the General Social Survey, National Opinion Research Center, 1972 to 1994.

nineteen countries, Arne Mastekaasa (1994) confirmed the correlation between marital status and happiness. Compared to other demographic predictors, such as age, gender, or income, the marriage predictor looms large (Inglehart 1990; Myers 1993). Moreover, unmarried people are at increased risk of depression (figure 19.2).

Is marriage, as is so often supposed, more strongly associated with men's happiness than women's? Do "Guys Wed for Better; Wives for Worse," as *USA Today* headlined (1 October 1993), based on one small study? Given women's greater contribution to household work and to supportive nurturing, we might expect so. From this standpoint, marriage is a better deal for men. However, the married versus never-married happiness gap has been only slightly greater among American men than women (Gove et al. 1990). Moreover, in European surveys, and in a statistical digest of ninety-three other studies, this happiness gap is virtually identical for men and women (Inglehart 1990; Wood, Rhodes, and Whelan 1989). Although a bad marriage can be more depressing to a woman than to her more emotionally numbed husband, the myth that single women are happier than married women can be laid to rest. Throughout the Western world, married people of both sexes report more happiness than those never married, divorced, or separated.

However, more important than being married is the quality of the marriage. People who say their marriage is satisfying—who find themselves still in love with their partner—rarely report being unhappy, discontented with life, or depressed. Fortunately, most married people *do* declare their marriages happy ones. In the United States almost two-thirds say their marriage is "very happy." Three out of four say their spouse is their best friend. Four out of five people say they would marry the same person again (Greeley 1991). The consequence? Most such people feel quite happy with life as a whole.

But why are married people generally happier? Does marriage promote happiness? Or does happiness promote marriage? Are happy people more appealing as marriage partners? Do grouchy or depressed people more often stay single or suffer divorce? Certainly, happy people are more fun to be with. They are more outgoing, trusting, compassionate, and focused on others (Veenhoven 1988). Unhappy people are more often socially rejected. Misery may love company, but research on the social consequences of depression reveals that company does not love misery. An unhappy (and therefore self-focused, irritable, and withdrawn) spouse or roommate is no fun to be around (Gotlib 1992; Segrin and Dillard 1992). For these reasons, positive, happy people more readily form happy relationships.

FIGURE 19.2   Marital Status and Rate of Depression

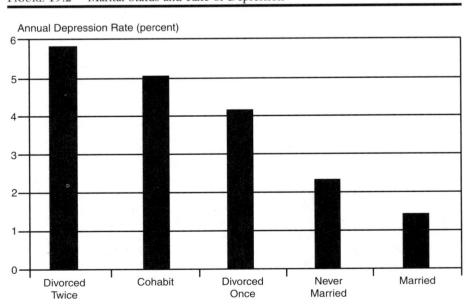

Source: Robins and Regier 1991, 72.

Yet "the prevailing opinion of researchers," reports the sociologist Arne Mastekaasa (1995), is that the association between marriage and well-being is "mainly due" to the beneficial effects of marriage. Consider: if the happiest people marry sooner and more often, then as people age (and progressively less happy people move into marriage), the average happiness of both married and never-married people should decline. (The older, less happy newlyweds would pull down the average happiness of married people, leaving the unhappiest people in the unmarried group.) But the data do not support this prediction. This suggests that marital intimacy, commitment, and support really do—for most people—pay emotional dividends.

There are at least two reasons why marriage might enhance happiness. The first one is prosaic. Marriage offers the roles of spouse and parent, which can provide additional sources of self-esteem (Crosby 1987). True, multiple roles can multiply stress. One's circuits sometimes overload. Yet each role provides rewards, status, avenues to enrichment, and escape from stress faced in other parts of one's life. When one's personal identity stands on several legs, it more easily holds up under the loss of any one of them. If I mess up at work, well, I can tell myself, I'm still a good husband and father, and in the final analysis, these parts of me are what matter most.

Second, married people are more likely to enjoy an enduring, supportive, intimate relationship and are less likely to suffer loneliness. No wonder male students survived UCLA Medical School with less stress and anxiety if married (Coombs 1991). A good marriage gives each partner a dependable companion, a lover, and a friend.

A good marriage is typically marked by *equity* and *intimacy*. When equity exists—when both partners freely give and receive, and when they share decision-making—their chances for sustained and satisfying companionate love are good (Gray-Little and Burks 1983; Van Yperen and Buunk 1990). Mutually sharing self and possessions, giving and getting emotional support, promoting and caring about one another's welfare, are at the core of every type of loving relationship (Sternberg and Grajek 1984). It's true for lovers, for intimate friends, even for parent and child.

A strong friendship or marriage also involves self-disclosure, a mutual revealing of intimate details about likes and dislikes, dreams and worries, proud and shameful moments (Berg and McQuinn 1988; Hendrick et al. 1988; Sprecher 1987). As a relationship deepens, self-disclosure

increases. As one person reveals a little, the other reciprocates, the first person reveals more, and on and on, as friends or lovers move to deeper intimacy. "When I am with my friend," reflected Seneca, "methinks I am alone, and as much at liberty to speak anything as to think it." At its best, marriage is such a friendship, sealed by commitment. Given reciprocated intimacy and mutually supportive equity, the odds favor enduring love—and happiness.

HUMAN CONNECTIONS ACROSS CULTURES

So, beginning with our infant attachments, we humans have a deep need to belong. With those needs met, through supportive friendships or marriage, we enjoy better physical and emotional quality of life. Consider, then, some curious variations in social connectedness.

Industrialized Western cultures typically value individualism. They give more priority to self-reliance and personal well-being than to social identity. Western books and movies often celebrate rugged individuals who seek their own fulfillment rather than fulfilling others' expectations. Individualism flourishes under conditions of affluence, mobility, urbanism, and exposure to mass media (Triandis et al. 1993). Across time and place, individualism rises as economies become more market-oriented. "Changes in the nature and organization of work under capitalism in Western industrial societies have produced a long-term shift from communal to market values and an accompanying rise of individualism," contends Margaret Mooney Marini (1990). As competition increases and production shifts from families to factories, moral restraints and religious outlooks associated with communal life subside. So do communal values such as trust and sharing.

Asian and Third World cultures place a greater value on collectivism. They give more priority to the goals and welfare of their groups—family, clan, work group. Books and movies often celebrate those who, despite temptations to self-indulgence, remember who they are and do their social duty. When Kobe, Japan, was struck by the devastating 1995 earthquake, Western reporters were struck by the absence of looting and the orderly way in which people lined up for relief supplies—"as if they were waiting for a bus." Collectivism flourishes where people face shared threats such as famine, where families are large, and where life requires cooperation, as when building canals or harvesting and storing food. In Australia, for example, Aboriginal people tend to value collectivism, while non-Aboriginal people value individualism (Fogarty and White 1994).

Without discounting individual differences within cultures, cross-cultural psychologists such as Harry Triandis, Richard Brislin, and C. Harry Hui (1988; Triandis 1994) have shown how a culture's individualism or collectivism affects self-concept and social relations.

Self-Concept

Shorn of their social connections—separated from family, friends, and work group—individualists retain their identity, their sense of "me." Thus, individualists feel free to leave jobs, homes, churches, and extended families in search of better opportunities for themselves. As adolescents they struggle to separate from parents and define their own personal sense of self. "Get in touch with yourself, accept yourself, be true to yourself," they hear from their culture's individualistic advice givers. The therapist Fritz Perls (1973) epitomized the individualism of Western popular psychology: "I do my thing, and you do your thing. I am not in this world to live up to your expectations. And, you are not in this world to live up to mine" (70). Popular songs and sayings express such individualism: "I gotta be me"; "I did it my way"; "Do your own thing"; "If it feels good, do it"; "It's not my bag"; "Seek your own bliss"; "I owe it to myself."

In collectivist cultures, where communal solidarity is prized, such words would seldom be spoken. For collectivists, social networks provide one's bearings and help define who one is. Extended families are close-knit. One's family name may even be written first to emphasize one's social identity (Hui Harry). Self-reliance means not "doing one's own thing" but "being responsible" (Triandis et al. 1993). Compared to U.S. magazine ads, Korean magazine ads are less likely to appeal to individual interests ("She's got a style all her own") and more likely to appeal to collective interests ("We have a way of bringing people closer together") (Han and Shavitt 1994). Rather than the squeaky wheel getting the grease, "the nail that stands out gets pounded down."

Social Relations

Collectivists may have fewer relationships, but they are deeper and longer-lasting. Compared to North American students, university students in Hong Kong talk during a day with fewer people for longer periods (Wheeler et al. 1989). In the United States, feeling good is linked with disengaged positive feelings—for example, feeling proud, an emotion that Westerners often feel (Kitayama, Markus, and Matsumoto 1995). In Japan, feeling good more often links with feeling interpersonally engaged (for example, having friendly feelings). In collectivist cultures, employer-employee relations are marked by mutual loyalty. Valuing social solidarity, people seek to maintain harmony by showing respect and allowing others to save face. They avoid confrontation, blunt honesty, and boasting. Instead, they stay away from touchy topics, defer to others, and display a self-effacing humility (Kitayama and Markus, in press). People do favors for one another and remember who has done favors for them. For collectivists, no one is an island. The self is not independent but *inter*dependent. What matters is less "me" than "we."

Because social identity is so important, collectivists are, however, somewhat quicker to prejudge people by their groups. In their culture, they explain, it *helps* to know people's group identities—"tell me a person's family, schooling, and employment, and you tell me a lot about the person." In Japan, people exchange cards when first meeting—cards that tell their social identity (name, occupation, address). Individualists warn against stereotyping and prefer not to judge people by their backgrounds and affiliations: "Everyone's an individual, so you shouldn't make assumptions just from knowing a person's sex, race, or background." Individualists do prejudge people but often by obvious personal attributes, such as physical attractiveness (Dion, Pak, and Dion 1990). And they more often attribute someone's behavior to their disposition, as when attributing a violent act to a "very bad temper" rather than a personal conflict or rivalry (Morris and Peng 1994).

Each cultural tradition offers benefits, for a price. In competitive, individualist cultures, people enjoy more personal freedom, take greater pride in their own achievements, and are less restricted by others' prejudgments. They also enjoy more privacy, behave more spontaneously, and feel freer to move about and choose their own lifestyles. Innovation and creativity are celebrated. Human rights are respected. Such may help explain Ed, Marissa, and Carol Diener's (1995) finding that people in individualistic cultures report greater happiness. When individualists pursue their own ends, and all goes well, life can seem rewarding.

For such benefits, the price is more frequent loneliness, more divorce, more homicide, and more stress-related disease (Popenoe 1993; Triandis et al. 1988). "Rampant individualism," suggests Martin Seligman (1988), helps explain a huge increase in rates of depression in Western countries, resulting partly from the "meaninglessness" that occurs when there is no "attachment to something larger than the lonely self" (55). When things go not so well, and social support is lacking, life can seem less than rewarding.

Gender and Close Relationships

The cultural difference between individualism and collectivism parallels a gender difference between independence and social connectedness. Without denying individual differences, the psychologists Nancy Chodorow (1978, 1989), Jean Baker Miller (1986), and Carol Gilligan and her colleagues (1982, 1990) contend that women more than men give priority to relationships.

The difference surfaces in childhood. Boys strive for independence; they define their identity in separation from the caregiver, usually their mother. Girls value interdependence; they define their identity through their social connections. Boys' play often involves group activity. But girls' play occurs in smaller groups, with less aggression, more sharing, more imitation of relationships, and more intimate discussion (Lever 1978).

Adult relationships extend this gender difference. In conversation, men more often focus on tasks, women on relationships. In groups, men contribute more task-oriented behaviors, such as giving information; women contribute more positive social-emotional behaviors, such as giving help or showing support (Eagly 1987). Women spend more time caring for both preschoolers and aging parents (Eagly and Crowley 1986). They buy most birthday gifts and greeting cards (DeStefano and Colasanto 1990; Hallmark 1990). In most of the U.S. caregiving professions—such as social worker, teacher, and nurse—women outnumber men. Among first-year college students, five in ten males and seven in ten females say it is *very* important to "help others who are in difficulty" (Astin et al. 1995). Women's greater social concern helps explain why, in survey after survey, American women are more likely than men to support Democratic Party candidates and to oppose military initiatives (*American Enterprise*, 1991).

When surveyed, women are also far more likely to describe themselves as having empathy—being able to rejoice with those who rejoice and weep with those who weep. To a lesser extent, the empathy difference extends to laboratory studies, in which women are more likely to cry or report feeling distressed at another's distress (Eisenberg and Lennon 1983). Shown slides or told stories, girls, too, react with more empathy (Hunt 1990). The gender empathy difference helps explain why, compared to friendships with men, both men and women report friendships with women to be more intimate, enjoyable, and nurturing (Rubin 1985; Sapadin 1988). When they want empathy and understanding, someone to whom they can disclose their joys and hurts, both men and women usually turn to women.

HUMAN CONNECTIONS ACROSS TIME

Since 1960 individualism has strengthened and supportive social connections have weakened. These trends are evident in the weakening of marriage bonds and of informal networks. Although the trends cross Western cultures, I will focus on my own country as a case example.

The Decline of Marriage

Americans are marrying later and divorcing more often. The Census Bureau reports that the typical man isn't marrying until age 26.7 (up from 22.8 in 1960), and the typical woman not until age 24.5 (up from 20.3 in 1960).

Second, people are divorcing more often—at double the 1960 rate. "We are living longer, but loving more briefly," quips Os Guiness (1993, 309). Although the divorce rate has now leveled off, this does not signify a renewal of marital stability, note sociologist Sara McLanahan and Census Bureau researcher Lynne Casper (1994). The divorce rate almost had to level off, given increased cohabitation, increased age at first marriage, and the passage of the baby boom generation through their most divorce-prone years. The high plateau on which divorce continues, combined with the decline of marriage, means that currently divorced people are a still-increasing number of the population (from 2.9 million in 1960 to 17.6 million in 1995). From 1960 to 1995, the percentage of divorced adults quadrupled from 2.3 to 9.2 percent. "The scale of marital breakdowns in the West since 1960 has no historical precedent that I know of, and seems unique," reports the Princeton University family historian Lawrence Stone (1989). "There has been nothing like it for the last two thousand years, and probably longer." Moreover, this is not just an increase in bad marriages ending, but in marriages going bad. If it were the former, today's surviving or remarried couples should be happier rather than slightly *un*happier, as survey data indicate (Glenn 1996).

Third, we are marrying less. This trend, combined with delayed and broken marriages, has produced an increasing proportion of single adults—from 25 percent in 1960 to 39 percent in 1995. With 74.9 million singles (59 percent of whom have never married), there has been an understandable boom in singles bars, singles ministries, singles housing, and singles cruises. With so many more singles—more than twice as many as in 1960—the stigma associated with being single has lessened. Yesterday's "spinster" is today's single professional woman.

People are also delaying remarriage. From the late 1960s to the early 1980s, the proportion of women who remarried within a year after the end of their first marriage plunged from 33 percent to 16 percent (London 1991).

Waning Networks

Like the bonds of marriage, informal bonds have weakened. Face-to-face interactions are waning, thanks partly to the conveniences afforded by drive-through food pickups, ATM machines, and E-mail. People visit one another less, belong to fewer groups, and more often live alone (House 1986). In 1940, 8 percent of American households involved people living alone. Today 25 percent do. The Census Bureau predicts (in a 3 May 1996 release) that by 2010, 27 percent will live alone.

Although Americans still join voluntary groups and volunteer in large numbers, participation is dwindling in Scouting, Red Cross, Jaycees, women's clubs, and fraternal lodges (Grossman and Leroux 1995). PTA membership dropped from twelve million in 1964 to seven million in 1993. We are even bowling more often apart from groups. Since 1980, reports Robert Putnam (1995), the number of bowlers has risen 10 percent, but participation in bowling leagues has dropped 40 percent.

Trust has declined sharply from 1960, when 58 percent told National Opinion Research Center interviewers that they felt people generally could be trusted, to 1994, when slightly more than one-third said the same. In 1994, 69 percent of Americans responding to a Gallup poll (1994) agreed that "these days a person doesn't really know whom he can count on." Prudential Insurance Company, once "the rock" you could count on, now wants to help you "be your own rock." High school seniors' sense of trust has similarly declined (figure 19.3).

Voting, the elementary act of citizenship, also has declined. Compare the 63 percent of eligible American voters who went to the polls in 1960 to the percentage voting in the next presidential election. All in all, note Ron Grossman and Charles Leroux (1995), today's more individualistic twenty- and thirty-somethings are half as likely as their grandparents were to join face-to-face groups, trust others, and vote. This dramatic decline in civic engagement has occurred despite a doubled proportion of high school graduates. Consider: (1) Highly educated people are more likely to be trusting and engaged in civic groups; (2) more people today are highly educated; yet (3) civic involvement has declined sharply (Putnam 1996). Clearly, some social toxin—something powerful enough to overwhelm our increasing education—is corroding America's civic life.

Over the last half-century, parents have become more likely to prize independence and self-reliance in their children, and less concerned with obedience (Alwin 1990; Remley 1988). The pollster Daniel Yankelovich (1994) has observed that the children-cum-adults of the 1990s place a lower value on self-sacrifice, on sexual restraint, and on what we owe others out of moral obligation. "Civilization is an exercise in self-restraint," noted William Butler Yeats. Radical individualism, say its critics, undermines both restraint and concern for future generations.

Another price tag on individualism, argues Martin Seligman (1991), is increased risk of depression, which has risen with individualism and is higher in individualist countries. Seligman attributes the current epidemic of depression to a cultural shift away from the "minimal self" of Yankee culture, which was concerned less with feelings than with behavior, less with freedom than with duty, and less with passions than with virtues. "I believe our epidemic of depression is a creature of [today's] maximal self." With the maximization of the individual self has come a "diminished sense of community and loss of higher purpose. These together proved rich soil for depression to grow in." Having forgone commitments to things larger

FIGURE 19.3   Declining Trust

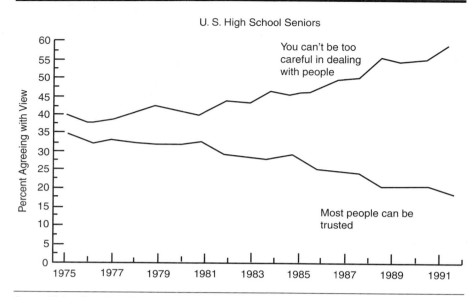

U. S. High School Seniors

Source: University of Michigan's annual *Monitoring the Future Survey* of U.S. high school seniors, as reported by Bronfenbrenner et al., 1996, 2. Reprinted with permission of the Free Press, a division of Simon & Schuster, Inc.

than self (God, country, family), "where can we now turn for identity, for purpose, and for hope? When we need spiritual furniture, we look around and see that all the comfortable leather sofas and stuffed chairs have been removed and all that's left to sit on is a small, frail folder chair: the self" (284–85).And if success is to be attributed to the individual self, then so is failure. If my career falls short of expectations, my marriage is a disappointment, or my children are flawed, well, who else is to blame? For shame. I should have tried harder, dreamed bigger, thought smarter. Psychologically speaking, the individualist self is ultimately, for better or worse, alone.

Yet we must also remember the complementary truth. There is also a brighter side to individualism. Individualistic countries, as we have noted, exhibit greater respect for individual human rights, more personal freedom, higher levels of individual self-esteem, and (when relationships and work is going well) greater happiness.

Individualism and the American Family

Individualism is up, and family integrity is down. Is there a connection between these two trends?

If individualism corrodes family commitments, we should first expect to see that rising individual-

ism correlates with family decline over time—which it does. Individualism is, however, restrained by our collectivist urges, including our need to belong. Thus, there is always a tension between, on the one side, the value we put on self-fulfillment—we insist on our rights, cherish personal freedom, and value self—and, on the other side, the value we put on commitments—our sense of responsibility, our view of permanence as a virtue, our belief that love is not just a feeling but a binding obligation. Over time the balance has shifted toward prizing fulfillment over commitment, rights over responsibilities, wants over oughts. Rather than view the self as "the servant of the marriage," notes Roy Baumeister (1991), "today people feel that marriage should serve the self" (7). In 1951 only 51 percent of Americans agreed that "parents who don't get along should not stay together because there are children in the family." In 1985, 82 percent agreed (Glenn 1991). And by 1994 only 15 percent agreed that "parents should stay together even if they don't get along" (*American Enterprise*, 1995).

Marriage is less often idealized as self-sacrificial love, as a union for the sake of love's children, or as an enduring mutual commitment. Bernard Farber (1987) sees the culture shifting toward "permanent availability"—with adults, regardless of marital status, continuing to compare their marriage with perceived alternatives. The idea that a continual openness to a more satisfying partner would increase satisfaction and happiness ignores "the fact that the freedom of one spouse to leave the marriage at will is the other spouse's insecurity," notes Norval Glenn (1996). And "without a reasonable degree of security, it is unlikely that a spouse will commit fully to the marriage and make the sacrifices and investments needed to make it succeed." Glenn (1993) also is concerned that with increased individualism "the social metric in America has shifted from child well-being to adult well-being" (10).

If individualism corrodes family commitments, we should also expect to see greater individualism linked with weaker family bonds across cultures—and we do. The United States is both the world's most individualistic and most divorce-prone nation. Britain is somewhat less individualistic and has barely half the divorce rate. (Ronald Reagan could divorce, remarry, and become president, but it is not a given that Prince Charles can divorce, remarry, and become king.) Divorce rates tend to be even lower in collectivist cultures such as Japan (Census Bureau 1995, table 1366; Triandis 1994). Collectivists demand less romance and personal fulfillment in marriage, thus putting the marriage relationship under less pressure (Dion and Dion 1993; Hatfield and Sprecher 1995). In one survey, "keeping romance alive" was rated as important to a good marriage by 78 percent of American women and 29 percent of Japanese women (*American Enterprise*, 1992).

If individualism corrodes family commitments we should, finally, expect to see greater individualism correlate with weaker attachments across individuals—and once again, we do. The more people view self-actualization rather than child-rearing as the purpose of partnership, the more likely they are to divorce (Hall 1996). Compared to those who marry, those who cohabit have a greater desire to maintain their autonomy and a lesser need for attachment (Cunningham and Antil 1994). Individualists feel more frustration with their marriages: they criticize their partners more severely and express less marital happiness (Scanzoni et al. 1989).

Declining Civility

Coincident with the weakening of family bonds and social networks have been some additional favorable and not-so-favorable trends. Since 1960 overt racial and gender prejudice is down and equal opportunities are up—another of individualism's benefits. Disposable (inflation-adjusted) per-person income has doubled, as has the number of cars per person, the frequency of eating out, and other indicators of growing affluence (Myers 1999). Educational levels, life expectancy, and computer-enhanced technologies similarly suggest improving quality of life.

Had Rip Van Winkle fallen asleep in 1960 and awakened in 1996, would he feel pleased with other social trends? Here are the facts of life that would greet him (Myers 2000). Since 1960:

- Since 1976 child abuse and neglect reports quintupled to more than 3.1 million annually.
- Teen sexual activity has doubled, with accompanying increases in sexually transmitted diseases.
- The 5 percent of babies born to unmarried parents in 1960 has increased more than sixfold to 32 percent. Increasingly, in all ethnic groups, children are having children and men are fathering children with little commitment to mother or child.
- In 1960 just over one in ten children did not live with two parents. Today three in ten do not, and most of these rarely see their biological fathers.
- While the over-sixty-five poverty rate has plummeted from 35 to 11 percent in 1997, thanks to shifting resources from children toward older adults, children's poverty dropped during the 1960s, then rose after 1970 from 15 to 20 percent.

Edward Zigler and Elizabeth Gilman (1990) report a consensus among researchers: "In the past thirty years of monitoring the indicators of child well-being, never have the indicators looked so negative." Urie Bronfenbrenner (quoted by Clinton 1995) paints the trends starkly: "The present state of children and families in the United States represents the greatest domestic problem our nation has faced since the founding of the Republic. It is sapping our very roots."

Moreover, family decline since 1960 has been accompanied by other social trends:

- a tripled teen suicide rate
- a quadrupled rate of reported rapes
- a quintupled juvenile violent crime
- soaring depression rates

Are these indicators of social recession interconnected? We know that poverty, school dropout, juvenile violence, and other forms of social and emotional pathology are more common in father-absent homes. For example, the Bureau of Justice Statistics has reported that seven in ten hard-core delinquents in correctional facilities did not consistently live with both parents while growing up. From this, David Lykken (1994) has computed that the sons of single parents are at seven times greater risk of incarceration than sons reared by two biological parents. Is increased single- and step-parenting and the decline in father care a mere correlate of children's diminishing quality of life, or is it causal?

Although children's responses to family breakup are diverse (some benefit from escaping a traumatic situation), Mavis Hetherington and her colleagues (Hetherington, Stanley-Hagan, and Anderson 1989; Hetherington and Clingempeel 1992) conclude that divorce places "children at increased risk for developing social, psychological, behavioral and academic problems." Two studies that control for many covarying circumstances implicate family breakup. Knowing that intact and divided families can differ in many ways, Census Bureau researchers studying more than seventeen thousand children for the National Center for Health Statistics (Dawson 1991) controlled for parental education, race, and income. Still, children of divided parents were about twice as likely to experience a variety of social, psychological, or academic problems (such as being suspended from school or needing psychological counseling).

To glimpse divorce effects, the sociologist Andrew Cherlin and his colleagues (Cherlin et al. 1991; Cherlin, Kiernan, and Chase-Lansdale 1995) compared children before and after divorce. This monumental study began when researchers interviewed 17,414 women—the mothers of 98 percent of all British children born during the first full week of March 1958. Cherlin and his coworkers studied these children as seven-year-olds and again as eleven-, sixteen-, and twenty-three-year-olds, knowing that some would experience parental divorce. For example when the children had reached age twenty-three, the intrepid researchers traced and interviewed 12,537 of the original sample, enabling them to compare those who at age seven had been living with two biological parents and whose parents divorced by age sixteen with those whose parents did not divorce by that time. Their finding: those whose parents had divorced experienced more problems.

Summing up dozens of studies, Patrick Davies and Mark Cummings (1994) note: "Destructive forms of marital conflict undermine children's feelings of emotional security" (405). So, are children's postdivorce problems influenced solely by the preexisting marital conflict (divorce or no), or also by the marriage breakup? Controlling for predivorce family problems did *not* weaken the divorce effect, report Cherlin and his colleagues. Even after adjusting for emotional problems and school achievement at age seven, the odds of scoring above the clinical cutoff for psychopathology were 39 percent greater among sixteen-year-olds whose parents had divorced in the intervening years. By launching children into "negative life trajectories through adolescence into adulthood," divorce predicted problems that were unexplained by predivorce family problems (Chase-Lansdale, Cherlin, and Kiernan 1995). Curiously, a parental death (which can feel less rejecting and involves less conflict) had "a substantially weaker effect." For a child, death and divorce are not psychological equivalents.

POLICY IMPLICATIONS: COMMUNITARIAN INDIVIDUALISM

We humans have a basic need to belong, to feel attached. Close, supportive, committed relationships boost our chances for physical and subjective well-being. Yet family connections and civic networks have waned since 1960, with accompanying increases in incivility and decreases in children's well-being. Three decades after Martin Luther King Jr. implored us "to choose between chaos and community," one senses a seismic shift in our national dialogue.

- The sociologists Robert Bellah (1985), Amitai Etzioni (1993), and Philip Selznick (1992) challenge contemporary individualism and remind us of the importance of social ties and social norms.
- The Harvard legal scholar Mary Ann Glendon's *Rights Talk* (1991) illuminates the price we pay for translating every political dispute into the language of individual entitlement.
- The Democratic Leadership Council and its research affiliate, the Progressive Policy Institute, seek alternatives to the individualism of both Reagan conservatism and classical liberalism. President Clinton is elected with talk of a "New Covenant" of mutual responsibility between the government and the governed, between what society gives individuals and what individuals give back in voluntary service.
- Charles Colson (1989) warns that the restraints on America's individualism "have all but collapsed" (36) and that the time has come to "reassert a sense of shared destiny as an antidote to radical individualism" (178).

The message common to these varied voices is this: *As the collapse of communism shows the failure of extreme collectivism, so the American social recession shows the failure of extreme individualism.* "Most civilizations die from within," observes John Gardner (1993), founder of Common Cause and a former cabinet secretary, "and are conquered less often by traitors within the gate than by traitors within the heart—loss of belief, corruption and disintegration of shared purposes."

Sharing such concerns, Gardner and several dozen other prominent citizens (including John Anderson, Betty Friedan, Elliot Richardson, Lester Thurow, and Daniel Yankelovich) have signed on to a "communitarian platform" that "recognizes that the preservation of individual liberty depends on the active maintenance of the institutions of civil society" and that a "fragile social ecology" supports the family and community life that is essential to civility. Communitarians see themselves as a third way alternative to libertarianism and collectivism. "Democratic communitarianism is based on the value of the sacredness of the individual, which is common to most of the great religions and philosophies of the world," explains Bellah (1995–96). But it also "affirms the central value of solidarity . . . that we become who we are through our relationships." Agreeing that "it takes a village to raise a child," communitarians remind us of what it takes to raise a village.

Listen to communitarians talk about European-style child benefits, extended parental leaves, flexible working hours, campaign finance reform, and ideas for "fostering the commons," and you'll swear they are liberals. Listen to them talk about marital commitments, divorce reform, father care, and character education, and you'll swear they are conservatives. In fact, communitarians see themselves as a third alternative to the liberal-conservative polarity. Their aim, expressed with appreciation for both individual rights and committed relationships, is to protect essential freedoms by balancing rights with responsibilities, individualism with community, liberty with fraternity.

Parts of this chapter are adapted from my books *The Pursuit of Happiness, Psychology,* and *Social Psychology.*

REFERENCES

Abbey, A., and Andrews, F. M. (1985). Modeling the psychological determinants of life quality. *Social Indicators Research, 16,* 1–34.

———. (1979). Infant-mother attachment. *American Psychologist, 34,* 932–37.

Ainsworth, M. D. S. (1973). The development of infant-mother attachment. In B. Caldwell and H. Ricciuti (Eds.), *Review of child development research* (vol. 3). Chicago: University of Chicago Press.

———. (1979). Infant-mother attachment. *American Psychologist, 34,* 932–37.

———. (1989). Attachments beyond infancy. *American Psychologist, 44,* 709–16.

Alwin, D. F. (1990). Historical changes in parental orientations to children. In N. Mandell (Ed.), *Sociological studies of child development* (vol. 3). Greenwich, Conn.: JAI Press.

American Enterprise. (1991). Women and the use of force. March-April, 85–86.

———. (1992). Women, men, marriages, and ministers. January-February, 106.

———. (1995). 1992 Yankelovich Clancy Shulman survey for *Time* and CNN; 1994 National Opinion Research Center survey. July-August, 104.

Astin, A. W., Sax, L. J., Korn, W. S., and Mahoney, K. M. (1995). *The American freshman: National norms for fall, 1995.* Los Angeles: UCLA Higher Education Research Institute.

Baron, R. S., Cutrona, C. E., Hicklin, D., Russell, D. W., and Lubaroff, D. M. (1990). Social support and immune function among spouses of cancer patients. *Journal of Personality and Social Psychology, 59,* 344–52.

Bartholomew, K., and Horowitz, L. (1991). Attachment styles among young adults: A test of a four-category model. *Journal of Personality and Social Psychology, 61,* 226–44.

Baumeister, R. F. (1991). *Escaping the self: Alcoholism, spirituality, masochism, and other flights from the burden of selfhood.* New York: Basic Books.

Baumeister, R. F., and Leary, M. R. (1995). The need to belong: Desire for interpersonal attachment as a fundamental human motivation. *Psychological Bulletin, 117,* 497–529.

Bellah, R. N. (1985). *Habits of the heart: individualism and commitment in American life.* Berkeley: University of California Press.

———. (1995–96). Community properly understood: A defense of "democratic communitarianism." *The Responsive Community* (Winter): 49–54.

Berg, J. H., and McQuinn, R. D. (1988). Loneliness and aspects of social support networks. Unpublished manuscript, University of Mississippi.

Berscheid, E. (1985). Interpersonal attraction. In G. Lindzey and E. Aronson (Eds.), *The handbook of social psychology.* New York: Random House.

Blakeslee, S. (1995). In brain's early growth, timetable may be crucial. *New York Times,* August 29, C1, C2.

Bowlby, J. (1980). *Attachment and loss,* vol. 3, *Loss, sadness, and depression.* New York: Basic Books.

Bronfenbrenner, U., McClelland, P., Wethington, E., Moen, P., and Ceci, S. J. (1996). *The state of Americans.* New York: Free Press.

Burt, R. S. (1986). *Strangers, friends, and happiness.* GSS Technical Report 72. Chicago: National Opinion Research Center, University of Chicago.

Case, R. B., Moss, A. J., Case, N., McDermott, M., and Eberly, S. (1992). Living alone after myocardial infarction: Impact on prognosis. *Journal of the American Medical Association, 267,* 515–19.

Census Bureau (1995). *Statistical abstract of the United States 1995.* Washington, D.C.: U.S. Government Printing Office.

Chase-Lansdale, P. L., Cherlin, A. J., and Kiernan, K. E. (1995). The long-term effects of parental divorce on the mental health of young adults: A developmental perspective. *Child Development, 66,* 1614–34.

Cherlin, A. J., Furstenberg, F. F., Jr., Chase-Lansdale, P. L., Kiernan, K. E., Robins, P. K., Morrison, D. R., and Teitler, J. O. (1991). Longitudinal studies of effects of divorce on children in Great Britain and the United States. *Science, 252,* 1386–89.

Cherlin, A. J., Kiernan, K. E., and Chase-Lansdale, P. L. (1995). Parental divorce in childhood and demographic outcomes in young adulthood. *Demography, 32,* 299–316.

Chodorow, N. J. (1978). *The reproduction of mothering: Psychoanalysis and the sociology of gender.* Berkeley: University of California Press.

———. (1989). *Feminism and psychoanalytic theory.* New Haven, Conn.: Yale University Press.

Clinton, H. R. (1995). *It takes a village.* New York: Simon & Schuster.

Cohen, S. (1988). Psychosocial models of the role of social support in the etiology of physical disease. *Health Psychology, 7,* 269–97.

Colon, E. A., Callies, A. L., Popkin, M. K., and McGlave, P. B. (1991). Depressed mood and other variables related to bone marrow transplantation survival in acute leukemia. *Psychosomatics, 32,* 420–25.

Colson, C. (1989). *Against the night: Living in the new dark ages.* Ann Arbor, Mich.: Servant Publications.

Coombs, R. H. (1991). Marital status and personal well-being: A literature review. *Family Relations, 40* (January): 97–102.

Crosby, F. J. (Ed.). (1987). *Spouse, parent, worker: On gender and multiple roles.* New Haven, Conn.: Yale University Press.

Cunningham, J. D., and Antil, J. K. (1994). Cohabitation and marriage: Retrospective and predictive comparisons. *Journal of Social and Personal Relationships, 11,* 77–93.

Cutrona, C. E. (1986). Behavioral manifestations of social support: A microanalytic investigation. *Journal of Personality and Social Psychology, 51,* 201–8.

Davies, P. T., and Cummings, E. M. (1994). Marital conflict and child adjustment: An emotional security hypothesis. *Psychological Bulletin, 116,* 387–411.

Davis, K. E. (1985). Near and dear: Friendship and love compared. *Psychology Today* (February): 22–30.

Dawson, D. A. (1991). *Family structure and children's health: United States, 1988.* Department of Health

and Human Services publication 91–1506. *Vital and Health Statistics,* series 10, no. 178. Washington, D.C.: National Center for Health Statistics.

DeStefano, L., and Colasanto, D. (1990). Unlike 1975, today most Americans think men have it better. *Gallup Poll Monthly,* no. 293 (February): 25–36.

Diener, E., Diener, M., and Diener, C. (1995). Factors predicting the subjective well-being of nations. *Journal of Personality and Social Psychology, 69,* 851–64.

Dion, K. K., and Dion, K. L. (1993). Individualistic and collectivistic perspectives on gender and the cultural context of love and intimacy. *Journal of Social Issues, 49,* 53–69.

Dion, K. K., Pak, A. W.-P., and Dion, K. L. (1990). Stereotyping physical attractiveness: A sociocultural perspective. *Journal of Cross-cultural Psychology, 21,* 378–98.

Dohrenwend, B., Pearlin, L., Clayton, P., Hamburg, B., Dohrenwend, B. P., Riley, M., and Rose, R. (1982). Report on stress and life events. In G. R. Elliott and C. Eisdorfer (Eds.), *Stress and human health: Analysis and implications of research* (A study by the Institute of Medicine/National Academy of Sciences). New York: Springer-Verlag.

Eagly, A. H. (1987). *Sex differences in social behavior: A social-role interpretation.* Hillsdale, N.J.: Erlbaum.

Eagly, A. H., and Crowley, M. (1986). Gender and helping behavior: A meta-analytic review of the social psychological literature. *Psychological Bulletin, 100,* 283–308.

Eisenberg, N., and Lennon, R. (1983). Sex differences in empathy and related capacities. *Psychological Bulletin, 94,* 100–31.

Emmons, R., et al. (1983). Factors predicting satisfaction judgments: A comparative examination. Paper presented at the Midwestern Psychological Association Convention, Chicago (May).

Erikson, E. H. (1963). *Childhood and society.* New York: Norton.

Etzioni, A. (1991). The community in an age of individualism (interview). *The Futurist* (May-June): 35–39.

———. (1993). *The spirit of community.* New York: Crown.

Evans, G. W., Palsane, M. N., Lepore, S. J., and Martin, J. (1989). Residential density and psychological health: The mediating effects of social support. *Journal of Personality and Social Psychology, 57,* 994–99.

Farber, B. (1987). The future of the American family: A dialectical account. *Journal of Family Issues, 8,* 431–33.

Feeney, J. A., and Noller, P. (1990). Attachment style as a predictor of adult romantic relationships. *Journal of Personality and Social Psychology, 58,* 281–91.

Fogarty, G. J., and White, C. (1994). Differences between values of Australian Aboriginal and non-Aboriginal students. *Journal of Cross-cultural Psychology, 25,* 394–408.

Freedman, J. (1978). *Happy people.* New York: Harcourt Brace Jovanovich.

Friedman, H. S., Tucker, J. S., Schwartz, J. E., Tomlinson-Keasey, C., Martin, L. R., Wingard, D. L., and Criqui, M. H. (1995). Psychosocial and behavioral predictors of longevity: The aging and death of the "Termites." *American Psychologist, 50,* 69–78.

Gallup Poll Monthly. (1994). Gallup poll (July): 35.

Gardner, J. W. (1993). Rebirth of a nation. Address to the Forum Club of Houston, February 17.

Gilligan, C. (1982). *In a different voice: Psychological theory and women's development.* Cambridge, Mass.: Harvard University Press.

Gilligan, C., Lyons, N. P., and Hanmer, T. J. (Eds.). (1990). *Making connections: The relational worlds of adolescent girls at Emma Willard School.* Cambridge, Mass.: Harvard University Press.

Glendon, M. A. (1991). *Rights talk: the impoverishment of political discourse.* New York: Free Press.

Glenn, N. D. (1991). *The family values of Americans.* New York: Institute for American Values.

———. (1993). Letter to the editor. *Atlantic* (July): 10.

———. (1996). Values, attitudes, and the state of American marriage. In D. Popenoe, J. B. Elshtain, and D. Blankenhorn (Eds.), *Promises to keep: Decline and renewal of marriage in America.* Lanham, Md.: Rowman and Littlefield.

Gotlib, I. H. (1992). Interpersonal and cognitive aspects of depression. *Current Directions in Psychological Science, 1,* 149–54.

Gove, W. R., Style, C. B., and Hughes, M. (1990). The effect of marriage on the well-being of adults: A theoretical analysis. *Journal of Family Issues, 11,* 4–35.

Gray-Little, B., and Burks, N. (1983). Power and satisfaction in marriage: A review and critique. *Psychological Bulletin, 93,* 513–38.

Greeley, A. (1991). *Faithful attraction.* New York: Tor Books.

Grossman, R., and Leroux, C. (1995). Nation of strangers: A new silence. *Chicago Tribune,* December 29, 1, 8–9.

Guiness, O. (1993). *The American hour: A time of reckoning and the once and future role of faith.* New York: Free Press.

Hall, D. R. (1996). Marriage as a pure relationship: Exploring the link between premarital cohabitation and divorce in Canada. *Journal of Comparative Family Studies, 27,* 1–12.

Hallmark Cards (1990). Odds and trends. *Time,* Fall special issue on women, *136,* 26.

Han, S.-P., and Shavitt, S. (1994). Persuasion and culture: Advertising appeals in individualistic and collectivistic societies. *Journal of Experimental Social Psychology, 30,* 326–50.

Hatfield, E., and Sprecher, S. (1995). Men's and women's preferences in marital partners in the United States, Russia, and Japan. *Journal of Cross-cultural Psychology, 26,* 728–50.

Hazan, C., and Shaver, P. R. (1994). Attachment as an organizational framework for research on close relationships. *Psychological Inquiry, 5,* 1–22.

Hendrick, S. S., Hendrick, C., and Adler, N. L. (1988).

Romantic relationships: Love, satisfaction, and staying together. *Journal of Personality and Social Psychology, 54,* 980–88.

Hetherington, E. M., and Clingempeel, W. G. (1992). Coping with marital transitions: A family systems perspective. *Society for Research in Child Development Monographs, 57,* 1–242.

Hetherington, E. M., Stanley-Hagan, M., and Anderson, E. R. (1989). Marital transitions: A child's perspective. *American Psychologist, 44,* 303–12.

House, J. S. (1986). Social support and the quality and quantity of life. In F. M. Andrews (Ed.), *Research on the quality of life.* Ann Arbor: University of Michigan Press.

House, J. S., Landis, K. R., and Umberson, D. (1988). Social relationships and health. *Science, 241,* 540–45.

Hunt, M. (1990). *The compassionate beast: What science is discovering about the humane side of humankind.* New York: Morrow.

Idler, E. I., and Kasl, S. V. (1992). Religion, disability, depression, and the timing of death. *American Journal of Sociology, 97,* 1052–79.

Inglehart, R. (1990). *Culture shift in advanced industrial society.* Princeton, N.J.: Princeton University Press.

Israel, B. A., and Antonucci, T. C. (1987). Social network characteristics and psychological well-being: A replication and extension. *Health Education Quarterly, 14,* 461–81.

Kaprio, J., Koskenvuo, M., and Rita, H. (1987). Mortality after bereavement: A prospective study of 95,647 widowed persons. *American Journal of Public Health, 77,* 283–87.

Kitayama, S., and Markus, H. R. (in press). Construal of the self as cultural frame: Implications for internationalizing psychology. In J. D'Arms, R. G. Hastie, S. E. Hoelscher, and H. K. Jacobson (Eds.), *Becoming more international and global: Challenges for American higher education.* Ann Arbor: University of Michigan Press.

Kitayama, S., Markus, H. R., and Matsumoto, H. (1995). Culture, self, and emotion: A cultural perspective on "self-conscious" emotions. In J. P. Tangney and K. W. Fisher (Eds.), *Self-conscious emotions: The psychology of shame, guilt, embarrassment, and pride: Empirical studies of self-conscious emotions* (pp. 439–64). New York: Guilford.

Lever, J. (1978). Sex differences in the complexity of children's play and games. *American Sociological Review, 43,* 471–83.

Levin, J. S., and Vanderpool, H. Y. (1987). Is frequent religious attendance really conducive to better health?: Toward an epidemiology of religion. *Social Science and Medicine, 14,* 589–600.

London, K. A. (1991). Cohabitation, marriage, marital dissolution, and remarriage: United States, 1988. Data from National Center for Health Statistics, *National Survey of Family Growth: Vital and health statistics: Advance data.* Report 194 (January 4).

Lykken, D. T. (1994). On the causes of crime and violence: A reply to Aber and Rappaport. *Applied and Preventive Psychology, 3,* 55–58.

Manning, F. J., and Fullerton, T. D. (1988). Health and well-being in highly cohesive units of the U.S. Army. *Journal of Applied Social Psychology, 18,* 503–19.

Marini, M. M. (1990). The rise of individualism in advanced industrial societies. Paper presented at the Population Association of America annual meeting.

Mastekaasa, A. (1994). Marital status, distress, and well-being: An international comparison. *Journal of Comparative Family Studies, 25,* 183–206.

———. (1995). Age variations in the suicide rates and self-reported subjective well-being of married and never-married persons. *Journal of Community and Applied Social Psychology, 5,* 21–39.

Maxwell, G. M. (1985). Behaviour of lovers: Measuring the closeness of relationships. *Journal of Personality and Social Psychology, 2,* 215–38.

McLanahan, S., and Casper, L. (1994). The American family in 1990: Growing diversity and inequality. Princeton University. Unpublished paper.

McLeod, E. (1982). *Women working: Prostitution today.* London: Croom Helm.

Mendolia, M., and Kleck, R. E. (1993). Effects of talking about a stressful event on arousal: Does what we talk about make a difference? *Journal of Personality and Social Psychology, 64,* 283–92.

Miller, J. B. (1986). *Toward a new psychology of women.* 2nd ed. Boston: Beacon Press.

Morris, M. W., and Peng, K. (1994). Culture and cause: American and Chinese attributions for social and physical events. *Journal of Personality and Social Psychology, 67,* 949–71.

Myers, D. G. (1993). *The pursuit of happiness.* New York: Avon.

———. (2000). *The American paradox.* New Haven: Yale University Press.

National Academy of Sciences. (1984). *Bereavement: Reactions, consequences, and cure.* Washington, D.C.: National Academy Press.

Nelson, N. (1988). A meta-analysis of the life-event/health paradigm: The influence of social support. Ph.D. diss., Temple University.

Pennebaker, J. (1990). *Opening up: The healing power of confiding in others.* New York: Morrow.

Pennebaker, J. W., Barger, S. D., and Tiebout, J. (1989). Disclosure of traumas and health among Holocaust survivors. *Psychosomatic Medicine, 51,* 577–89.

Pennebaker, J. W., and O'Heeron, R. C. (1984). Confiding in others and illness rate among spouses of suicide and accidental death victims. *Journal of Abnormal Psychology, 93,* 473–76.

Perkins, H. W. (1991). Religious commitment, Yuppie values, and well-being in post-collegiate life. *Review of Religious Research, 32,* 244–51.

Perlman, D., and Rook, K. S. (1987). Social support, social deficits, and the family: Toward the enhancement of well-being. In S. Oskamp (Ed.), *Family processes and problems: Social psychological aspects.* Newbury Park, Calif.: Sage.

Perls, F. S. (1973). *Ego, hunger, and aggression: The beginning of Gestalt therapy.* New York: Random House, 1969.

Pettijohn, T. F., II, and Pettijohn, T. F. (1996). Perceived happiness of college students measured by Maslow's hierarchy of needs. *Psychological Reports, 79,* 759–62.

Popenoe, D. (1993). The evolution of marriage and the problem of stepfamilies: A biosocial perspective. Paper presented at the National Symposium on Stepfamilies, Pennsylvania State University.

Putnam, R. D. (1995). Bowling alone: America's declining social capital. *Journal of Democracy, 6,* 65–78.

———. (1996). The strange disappearance of civic America. *American Prospect* (Winter): 34–48.

Remley, A. (1988). From obedience to independence. *Psychology Today* (October): 56–59.

Robins, L., and Regier, D. (1991). *Psychiatric disorders in America.* New York: Free Press.

Rook, K. S. (1987). Social support versus companionship: Effects on life stress, loneliness, and evaluations by others. *Journal of Personality and Social Psychology, 52,* 1132–47.

Rubin, L. B. (1985). *Just friends: The role of friendship in our lives.* New York: Harper and Row.

Ruehlman, L. S., and Wolchik, S. A. (1988). Personal goals and interpersonal support and hindrance as factors in psychological distress and well-being. *Journal of Personality and Social Psychology, 55,* 293–301.

Sapadin, L. A. (1988). Friendship and gender: Perspectives of professional men and women. *Journal of Social and Personal Relationships, 5,* 387–403.

Sax, L., Astin, A. W., Korn, W. S., and Mahoney, K. M. (1995). *The American Freshman: National Norms for Fall 1995.* Washington, D.C.: American Council on Education.

Scanzoni, J., Polonko, K., Teachman, J., and Thompson, L. (1989). *The sexual bond: Rethinking families and close relationships.* Newbury Park, Calif.: Sage.

Segrin, C., and Dillard, J. P. (1992). The interactional theory of depression: A meta-analysis of the research literature. *Journal of Social and Clinical Psychology, 11,* 43–70.

Seligman, M. E. P. (1988). Boomer blues. *Psychology Today* (October): 50–55.

———. (1991). *Learned optimism.* New York: Knopf.

Selznick, P. A. (1992). *The moral commonwealth: Social theory and the promise of community.* Berkeley: University of California Press.

Shaver, P. R., and Hazan, C. (1993). Adult romantic attachment: Theory and evidence. In D. Perlman and W. Jones (Eds.), *Advances in personal relationships* (vol. 4). Greenwich, Conn.: JAI.

———. (1994). Attachment. In A. L. Weber and J. H. Harvey (Eds.), *Perspectives on close relationships.* Boston: Allyn and Bacon.

Shaver, P., Hazan, C., and Bradshaw, D. (1988). Love as attachment: The integration of three behavioral systems. In R. J. Sternberg and M. L. Barnes (Eds.), *The psychology of love*. New Haven, Conn.: Yale University Press.

Sherif, M. (1966). *In common predicament: Social psychology of intergroup conflict and cooperation*. Boston: Houghton Mifflin.

Simpson, J. A., Rholes, W. S., and Nelligan, J. S. (1992). Support seeking and support giving within couples in an anxiety-provoking situation: The role of attachment styles. *Journal of Personality and Social Psychology, 62,* 434–46.

Sprecher, S. (1987). The effects of self-disclosure given and received on affection for an intimate partner and stability of the relationship. *Journal of Personality and Social Psychology, 4,* 115–27.

Sternberg, R. J., and Grajek, S. (1984). The nature of love. *Journal of Personality and Social Psychology, 47,* 312–29.

Stone, L. (1989). The road to polygamy. *New York Review of Books,* March 2, 12–15.

Symanski, R. (1980). Prostitution in Nevada. In E. Muga (Ed.), *Studies in prostitution*. Nairobi: Kenya Literature Bureau.

Tajfel, H. (1981). *Human groups and social categories: Studies in social psychology*. London: Cambridge University Press.

Triandis, H. C. (1994). *Culture and social behavior*. New York: McGraw-Hill.

Triandis, H. C., Bontempo, R., Villareal, M. J., Asai, M., and Lucca, N. (1988). Individualism and collectivism: Cross-cultural perspectives on self-ingroup relationships. *Journal of Personality and Social Psychology, 54,* 323–38.

Triandis, H. C., Brislin, R., and Hui, C. H. (1988). Cross-cultural training across the individualism-collectivism divide. *International Journal of Intercultural Relations, 12,* 269–89.

Triandis, H. C., McCusker, C., Betancourt, H., Iwao, S., Leung, K., Salazar, J. M., Setiadi, B., Sinha, J. B. P., Touzard, H., and Zaleski, Z. (1993). An etic-emic analysis of individualism and collectivism. *Journal of Cross-cultural Psychology, 24,* 366–83.

Van Yperen, N. W., and Buunk, B. P. (1990). A longitudinal study of equity and satisfaction in intimate relationships. *European Journal of Social Psychology, 20,* 287–309.

Veenhoven, R. (1988). The utility of happiness. *Social Indicators Research, 20,* 333–54.

Wallach, M. A., and Wallach, L. (1985). How psychology sanctions the cult of the self. *Washington Monthly* (February): 46–56.

Warr, P., and Payne, R. (1982). Experiences of strain and pleasure among British adults. *Social Science and Medicine, 16,* 1691–97.

Wheeler, L., Reis, H. T., and Bond, M. H. (1989). Collectivism-Individualism in Everyday Social Life: The Middle Kingdom and the Melting Pot. *Journal of Personality and Social Psychology, 57,* 79–86.

Wilder, D. A. (1981). Perceiving persons as a group: Categorization and intergroup relations. In D. L. Hamilton (Ed.), *Cognitive processes in stereotyping and intergroup behavior*. Hillsdale, N.J.: Erlbaum.

Williams, R. B., Barefoot, J. C., Califf, R. M., Haney, T. L., Saunders, W. B., Pryor, D. B., Hlatky, M. A., Siegler, I. C., and Mark, D. B. (1992). Prognostic importance of social and economic resources among medically treated patients with angiographically documented coronary artery disease. *Journal of the American Medical Association, 267,* 520–24.

Wood, W., Rhodes, N., and Whelan, M. (1989). Sex differences in positive well-being: A consideration of emotional style and marital status. *Psychological Bulletin, 106,* 249–64.

Yankelovich, D. (1994). The affluence affect. In H. J. Aaron, T. Mann, and T. Taylor (Eds.), *Values and public policy*. Washington, D.C.: Brookings Institution.

Zigler, E. F., and Gilman, E. P. (1990). An agenda for the 1990s: Supporting families. In D. Blankenhorn, S. Bayme, and J. B. Elshtain (Eds.), *Rebuilding the nest: A new commitment to the American family*. Milwaukee: Family Service America.

20 Well-Being and the Workplace

Peter Warr

Paid employment has a substantial impact on the well-being of most adults. This chapter examines the nature of employee well-being and the key features of jobs and people that affect well-being. The proposed framework distinguishes between feelings that are context-specific (for instance, satisfaction with one's job) and those that are context-free (for example, life satisfaction). Three principal axes for the measurement of both forms of well-being are described, ranging from displeasure to pleasure, from anxiety to comfort, and from depression to enthusiasm. Ten key job features have been found to be associated with these axes of employee well-being. Stable personality dispositions, in terms of trait negative affectivity and trait positive affectivity, are also shown to be important, as are sociodemographic features such as age and gender. The research reviewed indicates that greater employee well-being is significantly associated with better job performance, lower absenteeism, reduced probability of leaving an employer, and the occurrence of more discretionary work behaviors. However, well-being is only one influence on these measures; other organizational and individual factors also have substantial impact.

PAID EMPLOYMENT is central to the functioning of societies and to the mental health of individuals. The majority of adults spend a large part of their life at work, and they are affected by it in multiple and sometimes conflicting ways. "Work" is usually defined in part as an activity directed to valued goals beyond enjoyment of the activity itself. (Not that work cannot be enjoyed, but immediate enjoyment is not part of the definition.) Definitions also often include a suggestion that it is a required activity and that it involves the expenditure of effort.

People work in a range of settings. The focus here is on *paid* work, although many of the issues raised also apply to nonpaid activities: housework, voluntary work, do-it-yourself work, and so on. Paid work is often "full-time": the job takes up on average between thirty-five and forty hours a week, but traveling to and from a place of employ-

ment on average adds a further 10 percent or so (Szalai 1972). "Part-time" jobs, of course, vary in their duration, but thirty hours a week is often taken as their upper limit for statistical and survey purposes.

Men have traditionally sought paid employment throughout most of their adult lives, whereas labor market participation by women has often declined after the age of about thirty. However, recent years have seen a marked increase in the number of women remaining in paid employment rather than leaving work because of family responsibilities. For example, some 60 percent of U.S. women of conventional employment age are now economically active (Fullerton 1995). In 1950 women constituted only 33 percent of the U.S. labor force, whereas today they represent around 45 percent. For the same age range in Europe as a whole, around 50 percent of women are economically active, making up 42 percent of the workforce (European Commission 1996); in the United Kingdom, those percentages are 70 and 48 percent, respectively. Many women are employed part-time (more so in Europe than in the United States), and most of those prefer part-time to full-time work. For example, in the United Kingdom around 80 percent of part-time women employees report that they do not want a full-time job, with most indicating that they prefer to have time for domestic and family activities (Office of National Statistics 1996).

Men are less likely than women to be employed on a part-time basis, both through preference and because of aspects of national welfare schemes. (Welfare legislation has typically been designed with the full-time worker in mind.) The majority of men who work part-time are at the extremes of the labor-force age range, being either students or workers moving into retirement (Delsen 1995).

The labor-force participation rate for older men has declined in recent years in many countries, so that the proportion of men who may be termed "retired" has increased accordingly. However, for many men retirement does not mean a complete cessation of paid employment; it is often partial, especially at relatively young ages. Between one-quarter and one-half of retired people take up at some point either full-time or (more often) part-time work, possibly on a temporary or intermittent basis (see, for example, Myers 1991).

Other labor-market developments include a shift to more short-term and temporary jobs, although these are less common in the United States than in Europe (Delsen 1995). Self-employment has also increased in recent years, partly because of the difficulty experienced by some people in finding an employed position (for instance, if displaced from the declining number of manufacturing jobs), and partly because self-employment provides a second job for some temporary or part-time workers. These changes have been accompanied by downward shifts in many people's career expectations, as uncertainty and frequent moves between employers become increasingly common (see, for example, Hall and Mirvis 1995).

It is clear that most adults want to be in paid employment, report high satisfaction with their job, and wish to avoid unemployment. Conversely, some individuals experience considerable stress in their job, and that can affect their behavior in important ways. National estimates of stress-related absence from work are somewhat unreliable, but it is generally accepted that such absence costs the U.S. economy many tens of billions of dollars each year. At the level of individuals, Manning, Jackson, and Fusilier (1996) observed that more workplace stressors and reported job stress were significantly associated with greater subsequent doctor's and hospital outpatient costs within two companies' health care schemes.

THE NATURE OF WELL-BEING

Especially when examining one particular domain, such as the workplace, it is important to distinguish between specific forms of well-being and more general feelings about one's life. The more limited form of primary concern in this chapter is "job-specific" well-being—people's feelings about themselves in relation to their job. "Context-free" well-being has a broader focus, covering feelings in any setting. Both forms of well-being are located within the broader concept of "mental health." This notion also includes features like positive self-regard, competence, aspiration, au-

tonomy, and integrated functioning (Warr, 1987, 1997; Compton et al. 1996).

Well-being of all kinds is often viewed along a single dimension—roughly, from feeling bad to feeling good. Such a dimension can, of course, capture important feelings, but it is preferable to think in terms of a two-dimensional framework of the kind set out in figure 20.1. Such a framework has been substantiated in many investigations (for example, Matthews, Jones, and Chamberlain 1990; Thayer 1989; Watson, Clark, and Tellegen 1988), which have pointed to the importance of two independent dimensions of feeling, here labeled "pleasure" and "arousal."

We may describe a person's well-being in terms of its location relative to those two dimensions (representing the *content* of feelings) and its distance from the midpoint of the figure (such that a more distant location indicates a greater *intensity*). A particular degree of pleasure or displeasure may be accompanied by high or low levels of mental arousal, and a particular quantity of mental arousal (sometimes referred to as "activation") may be either pleasurable or unpleasurable.

Within this framework, three principal axes of measurement are illustrated in figure 20.2. In view of the central importance of feelings of low or high pleasure, the first axis measures this horizontal dimension alone. The other two axes take account of mental arousal as well as pleasure by running diagonally between opposite quadrants through the midpoint of the figure. The arousal dimension on its own is not considered to reflect well-being, and its end points are therefore left unlabeled.

In thinking about job-specific or context-free well-being, we may thus consider three main axes (Daniels and Guppy 1994; Lucas, Diener, and Suh 1996). First is displeasure-to-pleasure, the positive pole of which is often examined as satisfaction or happiness. Those broad concepts are usually examined without attention to a person's level of mental arousal, whereas the other two axes are differentiated in that respect. The second axis runs from anxiety to comfort. Feelings of anxiety combine low pleasure with high mental arousal, whereas comfort is illustrated as low-arousal pleasure. Third is the axis from depression to enthusiasm. Feelings of enthusiasm and positive motivation are in the top-right quadrant, and depression and sadness (low pleasure and low mental arousal) are at the other end of the axis. A person may be characterized in terms of his or her location on each of the three axes, which are, of course, intercorrelated because of the central

FIGURE 20.1   A Two-Dimensional View of Well-Being

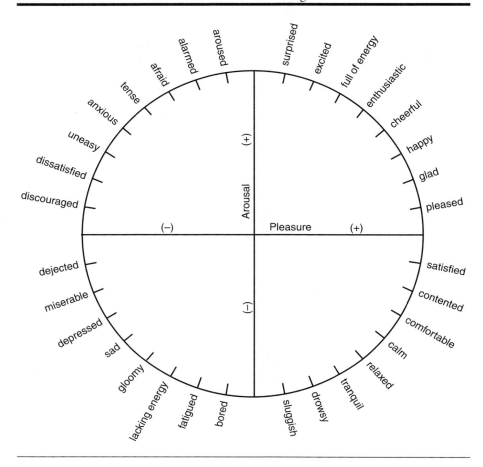

importance of feelings of pleasure (the horizontal dimension).

Despite that general intercorrelation, the three axes have different associations with certain other variables. For example, the level of a person's job is linked in a different manner with job-specific anxiety and depression. People in higher-level jobs report significantly *less* job-related depression than those in lower-level jobs, but also significantly *more* job-related anxiety (Birdi, Warr, and Oswald 1995; Warr 1990b, 1992). That pattern of well-being seems likely also to be found among self-employed individuals relative to those employed in an organization. It may be interpreted in terms of the dimension of mental arousal: people in higher-level positions (and the self-employed?) experience greater arousal on both the diagonal axes in figure 20.2.

The notions of positive and negative affect introduced by Bradburn (1969) have some similarity to the second and third axes. Bradburn's scale to

measure positive affect included items located in the top-right quadrant of figure 20.2 ("particularly excited," "on top of the world," and so on), but he tapped negative affect through items that appear to reflect both end-points 2a and 3a in the figure ("upset," "restless," "bored," "depressed," "lonely"). Bradburn's measures are significantly correlated in the expected manner with later scales tapping the two axes in figure 20.2 (Watson, Clark, and Tellegen 1988).

Links Between Job-Specific and Context-Free Well-Being

What is known about the association between a person's job-specific well-being and his or her more general well-being? With respect to axis 1 (pleasure), this has been examined through measures of overall job satisfaction and life satisfaction; the correlation between these is on average found

FIGURE 20.2   Three Axes for the Measurement of Well-Being

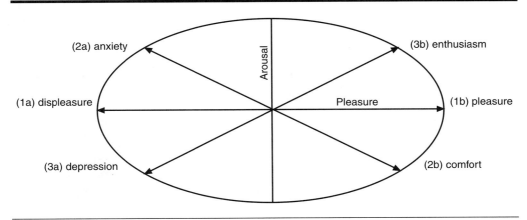

to be about .35 (Tait, Padgett, and Baldwin 1989). Some overlap is, of course, in part logically necessary, since feelings about a job are themselves one component of wider life satisfaction.

Research has sought to identify the pattern of causality in this relationship: does job satisfaction cause life satisfaction, or vice versa? (The role of continuing personality dispositions will be considered later.) A longitudinal investigation by Judge and Watanabe (1993) indicated that the pattern was one of mutual influence, but that the impact of life satisfaction on job satisfaction was greater than in the other direction (see also Judge and Locke 1993). A person's overall well-being has a strong impact on his or her job-specific well-being, and job well-being also affects general feelings.

These overlaps have been examined in terms of the "spillover" from job to home and from home to work. For example, in a study of male employees, Piotrkowski (1978) described cases of positive spillover, husbands who enjoyed their work and experienced feelings of self-enhancement from the working day; they came home cheerful and both emotionally and interpersonally available to their families. On the other hand, some husbands were tired, irritable, and emotionally nonresponsive after a day's work, and family members had to work hard to engage them in domestic and social activities. Taking the reverse perspective, Crouter (1984) focused particularly on family-to-work spillover. She showed that both positive and negative influences from family experience were widespread, particularly for mothers of young children. Reciprocal relationships between work and family life have been emphasized in the model presented by Frone, Yardley, and Markel (1997).

It is likely that the relations between job-specific and context-free well-being vary between individuals and across situations, within the framework of an overall positive and reciprocal association. For example, Bamundo and Kopelman (1980) found that the association was stronger for high-income, better-educated, and self-employed individuals; Thompson, Kopelman, and Schriesheim (1992) replicated this finding for self- versus organizational employment. Examining findings reported over a period of forty years, Tait and her colleagues (1989) looked at differences between men and women. Prior to 1974, the correlation between job satisfaction and life satisfaction for women was quite low (.16), but thereafter it increased to the level found for men (.31). This increase may be due to the greater centrality of paid employment for women in more recent years.

General differences (for men and women together) might also be expected between employees with relatively high or low personal involvement in their paid work. This possibility has been studied by Steiner and Truxillo (1989), who hypothesized, and found, that measures of job satisfaction and life satisfaction were more strongly intercorrelated among people with higher work involvement than among others.

Components of Job Satisfaction

The nature and degree of people's satisfaction with their jobs (the job-specific form of axis 1 in figure 20.2) have been examined in thousands of research investigations. In some cases, especially in nationwide surveys, a single question has been asked, such as, "All in all, how satisfied would you say you are with your job?" However, in most settings multiple-item questionnaires have been used to obtain more reliable estimates.

Just as the focus of job-specific satisfaction is narrower than that of context-free satisfaction, so may we identify within job satisfaction itself several levels of specificity. The most general construct is "overall job satisfaction"—the extent to which a person is satisfied with his or her job as a whole. More focused "facet-specific" satisfactions derive from different aspects of a job, such as pay, colleagues, supervisors, working conditions, job security, promotion prospects, the company, and the nature of the work undertaken. Different facet-specific satisfactions tend to be positively intercorrelated, and satisfaction with one (the nature of the work undertaken) is particularly closely associated with other facet-specific satisfactions and with overall job satisfaction.

At an intermediate level of abstractness is the distinction between "intrinsic" and "extrinsic" satisfaction. "Intrinsic" job satisfaction covers satisfaction with features inherent in the conduct of the work itself: opportunity for personal control or for the utilization of skills, amount of task variety, and so on. "Extrinsic" job satisfaction concerns aspects of a job that form the background to the work activities themselves: satisfaction with pay, working conditions, job security, industrial relations procedures, and so on. Intrinsic and extrinsic satisfaction scores are positively intercorrelated, but the conceptual distinction between them is sometimes important, as will be illustrated later.

Job Stress and Job-Related Burnout

Although the three axes of figure 20.2 are conceptually and operationally distinguishable, some investigators have combined elements from more than one of them into overall measures of well-being. For example, much research has examined the feelings of stress that arise from certain job features (usually referred to as "stressors" in the environment). Stress is often measured in terms of generalized distress (either job-specific or context-free), combining the two negative forms of well-being identified as end-points 2a and 3a in figure 20.2 (both anxiety and depression). A minority of stress studies have also examined psychosomatic symptoms (in terms of reported sleeplessness, headaches, and similar problems) or physiological variables such as heart rate, blood pressure, and catecholamine levels (for example, Kahn and Byosiere 1992).

One particular form of job stress has been studied within the concept of job-related "burnout" (Maslach and Jackson 1981), which has been viewed as an adverse reaction by workers involved in close interactions with clients in the helping professions, although it may also occur in other areas of work (see Cordes and Dougherty 1993). Burnout contains three job-specific dimensions, usually labeled as emotional exhaustion, depersonalization (felt distance from others), and reduced personal accomplishment. The content of measures of the principal component, emotional exhaustion, defines burnout clearly as an example of job-related stress (covering feelings of strain, being used up, fatigued, and working too hard). Studies of burnout and stress are illustrated later in the chapter.

ENVIRONMENTAL DETERMINANTS OF WELL-BEING

Much research has investigated links between specific aspects of a person's work environment and his or her well-being, usually that which is job-specific rather than context-free. Different investigators have examined different job characteristics, and the classification suggested by Warr (1987, 1994) seeks to embrace all main factors.[1] The following list cites the suggested key features of work (item 8 has been recently added). For each feature, a principal label is accompanied by other terms that are commonly used in the employment-related literature. Jobs differ in the degree to which they are characterized by each feature, and those variations give rise to differences in job-related well-being.

1. *Opportunity for personal control:* Employee discretion, decision latitude, autonomy, absence of close supervision, self-determination, participation in decision-making, freedom of choice.
2. *Opportunity for skill use:* Skill utilization, utilization of valued abilities, required skills.
3. *Externally generated goals:* Job demands, task demands, quantitative or qualitative workload, attentional demand, demands relative to resources, role responsibility, conflicting demands, role conflict, work-family conflict, normative requirements.
4. *Variety:* Variation in job content and location, non-repetitive work, skill variety, task variety.
5. *Environmental clarity:* Information about the consequences of behavior, task feedback; information about the future, absence of job future ambiguity,

absence of job insecurity; information about required behavior, low role ambiguity.

6. *Availability of money:* Income level, amount of pay, financial resources.

7. *Physical security:* Absence of danger, good working conditions, ergonomically adequate equipment, safe levels of temperature and noise.

8. *Supportive supervision:* Leader consideration, boss support, supportive management, effective leadership.

9. *Opportunity for interpersonal contact:* Quantity of interaction, contact with others, social density, adequate privacy; quality of interaction, good relationships with others, social support, good communications.

10. *Valued social position:* Wider evaluations of a job's status in society, social rank, occupational prestige; more localized evaluations of in-company status or job importance; personal evaluations of task significance, valued role incumbency, contributions made to others, meaningfulness of job, self-respect from job.

Job Features and Job-Specific Well-Being

Variables within each of these ten features have been shown to be significantly associated with the three axes of job-specific well-being illustrated in figure 20.2. Higher job-feature values are accompanied by greater job-specific well-being, at least up to moderate levels of the feature. Beyond moderate levels, increases in item 3 (externally generated goals, yielding overload) are associated with *lower* well-being, but the existence of such a curvilinear pattern for other features remains in dispute (see later discussion). Warr (1987) has summarized dozens of empirical studies demonstrating the importance of the features, and later evidence is illustrated in the publications cited in the appendix to this chapter.

Some job features are more predictive of one form of well-being than of others. For example, a very high level of job demands (item 3) is more strongly associated with low job-specific well-being on axis 2 (anxiety-to-comfort) than on the third axis (depression-to-enthusiasm); however, for very low opportunity for personal control (item 1), the opposite is the case (Warr 1990a). Correlations of job demands and control opportunity with job-specific anxiety (axis 2) and overall job satisfaction (axis 1) also show that differentiated pattern; demands are associated more with anxiety, and control opportunity is correlated more with satisfaction (Spector and O'Connell 1994). Stronger associations with job-related depression-enthusiasm than with anxiety-comfort have been reported for items 1, 2, 4, 5, and 10 by Sevastos, Smith, and Cordery (1992). Conversely, job demands are associated more with the emotional exhaustion component of job-related burnout than are social support and team cohesion (Lee and Ashforth 1996).

Although most research has been cross-sectional, correlating job features and well-being at a single point in time, causal interpretation has been supported by longitudinal studies showing that changes in job conditions lead to changes in well-being. For instance, Martin and Wall (1989) studied machine operators as they moved between roles with different levels of demand, finding predicted changes in job-related anxiety and depression. In Campion and McClelland's (1993) study, overall job satisfaction increased significantly after clerical workers' jobs were enlarged to increase skill utilization and knowledge demands.

It is clear that the ten job features operate in various combinations to affect a worker's well-being. For instance, the aggregate measure of job content used by Campion and McClelland (1993) was correlated .63 with overall job satisfaction. But in what way do the features combine—additively or synergistically? There have been suggestions that features such as job demands and personal control (items 3 and 1, respectively) are related to employee well-being through a synergistically interactive combination (see, for example, Karasek 1979). Jobs that combine very high demands with very low opportunity for control are known to be particularly harmful. The interactive suggestion is that together they are significantly *more* harmful than would be expected from an additive combination. Although a few studies have observed such an interaction (for example, Wall et al. 1996), the usual empirical finding is of mere additivity (see, for example, Agho, Mueller, and Price 1993; Kasl 1996; Warr 1990a). Jobs with low values on several of the key job features are indeed associated with very low job-specific well-being, but that appears to be attributable to a linear compounding effect, not to a super-additive process.

What about the specific pattern of single associations? Most investigators have examined only linear correlations between job features and well-being, although it might be expected that too much (as well as too little) of a feature is often undesirable (Warr 1987). That is clear for externally generated goals (item 3): both underload and overload have been found to be associated with lower well-being. In several other cases, extremely high levels of a feature are also likely to become unpleasantly coercive rather than providing the opportunities for personal gain that prevail at moderate levels. These features are opportunity for personal control (item 1), opportunity for skill use (item 2), variety (item 4), environmental clarity (item 5), and opportunity for interpersonal contact (item 9). All of these features carry the possibility of "having too much of a good thing." Similarly, extremely high levels of one feature are likely to be associated with other characteristics that are themselves undesirable; for example, managers' unremittingly high control opportunities (item 1) tend also to result in relentless overload (item 3).

There is some evidence for such nonlinear associations between job features and well-being, but so far it is rather limited. Karasek (1979), Warr (1990a), and De Jonge and Schaufeli (1998) have demonstrated significant curvilinearity for job demands: job-specific well-being scores were low with least demand, increased (cross-sectionally) with moderate demand, and then declined again at particularly high levels of demand. The same pattern in opportunities for personal control has been observed in laboratory situations by Burger (1989) and among employees by de Jonge and Schaufeli (1998). Curvilinearity was also found by Xie and Johns (1995) for a general measure of job features 1, 2, 4, 5, and 10, relative to employees' feelings of job-related emotional exhaustion.

Research into all kinds of environmental sources of well-being faces a general uncertainty: should an environmental feature be defined by the target person or by some independent method? Most research into job features has obtained assessments from the person whose well-being is being studied; strictly speaking, one should usually refer to "self-reported" job characteristics. Reliance on target persons' perceptions of job features seems likely to inflate the correlation between those features and their well-being—for example, because a person's well-being can influence how he or she views the job. That reverse effect was demonstrated by Mathieu, Hofmann, and Farr (1993) in an examination of alternative structural models. However, the analyses pointed to a reciprocal pattern, with job perceptions influencing job satisfaction as well as vice versa.

It might be thought that a preferable approach is to obtain independent measures of job features, through ratings made by people whose well-being is not being investigated. Studies using both self-ratings and other-ratings of job features have revealed that the two forms of assessment are substantially intercorrelated, and that they yield a similar pattern of associations with well-being scores, but that associations of well-being with other-ratings are smaller than with self-ratings (Melamed et al. 1995; Spector, Dwyer, and Jex 1988; Spector and Jex 1991; Warr 1987, 110–11; Xie and Johns 1995). However, judgments about jobs made by other people are not necessarily valid or appropriate. Other raters often have limited time for observation, may not understand key elements of a job, and do not always agree among themselves. In some studies, job *titles* have been rated rather than specific jobs held by specific individuals; those general characterizations can be very different from the job as experienced by individual workers.

Furthermore, there are theoretical arguments for measuring "reality" through the perceptions of a target person, since it is the personal meaning of a job feature that we would expect to influence well-being, and personal meanings vary between people in the same job. For example, two individuals may have different perceptions of a job's opportunity for control or opportunity for skill use because they are attuned to different aspects of the same environment. It appears that, although self-reports of job content enhance the size of correlations with employee well-being (because of the reciprocal effect), self-ratings have a particular value. Conversely, other people's assessment of job features may reduce the impact of judgmental bias but also underestimate those correlations (because of raters' imperfect information about the job in general and about personal meanings as viewed by individual job-holders).

Irrespective of this measurement issue, it is clear that the ten key job features can influence employee well-being. That impact derives, of course, from the absolute level of a job feature, but it is also likely that well-being is in part determined by relative judgments. Feelings and attitudes of all kinds are in part based on social comparison processes, so that evaluations are affected by perceptions of other people's situations and rewards as well as by absolute levels of a feature in one's own setting (Schwarz and Strack, this volume). For example, normative evaluations are often based on socially constructed views of what feelings are "reasonable" in a particular situation. Furthermore, if other people in jobs similar to one's own report substantially higher opportunities of a certain kind, experienced *relative* deprivation may impair job satisfaction irrespective of an absolute level.

Although this idea is extremely plausible, it is difficult to demonstrate systematically, since measurements of person-specific comparison levels cannot usually be obtained. Progress has been made in relation to income level (item 6): it is possible to generate an appropriate comparison level for each individual in terms of average population values associated with specific personal and job attributes. Clark and Oswald (1996) demonstrated that this comparison level (an econometrically predicted "going rate" for each person's job and demographic characteristics) had a significantly negative impact on predicted levels of overall job satisfaction (despite control for actual income): the more a person's income was "out of line," the less satisfied he or she was with the job, irrespective of actual income. A similar pattern is expected for other job characteristics, but this has not yet been shown.

Job Features and Context-Free Well-Being

What about the wider impact of jobs outside work? Do job features affect *context-free* well-being? The strong correlation reported earlier between job satisfaction (known to be affected by job content) and life satisfaction suggests that they do, and some research has examined the association between specific job features and context-free well-being. Significant linkages of that kind have been demonstrated by, for instance, Adelmann (1987) (for general happiness), Chay (1993) (for context-free distress), Dooley, Rook, and Catalano (1987) (for context-free distress), Kalimo and Vuori (1991) (for context-free distress), Loscocco and Spitze (1990) (for general happiness and context-free distress), Lowe and Northcutt (1988) (for context-free depression), Martin and Wall (1989) (for context-free distress), Melamed and his colleagues (1995) (for context-free distress), Parasuraman, Purohit, and Godshalk (1996) (for overall life stress), Pugliesi (1995) (for active forms of happiness), and Roxburgh (1996) (for context-free distress). Causal interpretation is supported by longitudinal studies of employees moving between jobs. Changes in context-free well-being have been reported by Barnett and her colleagues (1995) (for a measure combining context-free anxiety and depression), Karasek (1979) (for context-free depression), and Martin and Wall (1989) (for context-free general distress).

Is the association of job features with *context-free* well-being direct or indirect? Job characteristics might influence both job-specific and context-free well-being directly, or a job might have its direct effect only on job-specific feelings; these might subsequently spill over into wider well-being. This question has been addressed through techniques of statistical path analysis, and it appears that the major path is through job well-being itself (Kelloway and Barling 1991; Pugliesi 1995). The effect of a job on wider forms of well-being is principally indirect, being mediated by its impact on job-specific well-being. Associated with this mediated process, findings suggest that the impact of job features is greater on job-specific well-being than on context-free well-being; by definition, the latter is also open to influence from other domains of a person's life, such as family relationships or physical health.

Job and non-job features have been examined together in studies of work-family conflict (a particular form of demands—item 3 in the present framework). Research has consistently confirmed that difficulty in meeting the demands of both roles is associated with low scores on several aspects of job-specific and context-free well-being (Frone et al. 1997; Rice, Frone, and McFarlin 1992). The negative impacts appear to be similar for both men and women (Frone, Russell, and Barnes 1996; Frone, Russell, and Cooper 1992), and to be reduced if people have opportunities to control time allocation, organize child care, and so on (Thomas and Ganster 1995). Work-family conflict is experienced more strongly by employees who have greater job involvement (Adams, King, and King 1996).

A MODEL OF EMPLOYEE WELL-BEING AND ITS DETERMINANTS

The pattern of findings outlined so far may be viewed in terms of the schematic model shown in figure 20.3. At the center are two boxes containing the three axes of job-specific and context-free well-being. The horizontal double-headed arrow between those boxes represents the bidirectional causality identified earlier; feelings at work and feelings outside work influence each other in a mutual fashion. At the top of the figure are boxes representing features of job and non-job environments. The two downward-pointing arrows suggest that these environments have a bearing on job-specific and context-free well-being—directly in their own domain, but also indirectly influencing the other form of well-being, as shown by the horizontal arrow between the two central boxes.

However, the environment is only one of the sources of a person's feelings. It is also essential

FIGURE 20.3   A Model of Employee Well-Being and Its Determinants

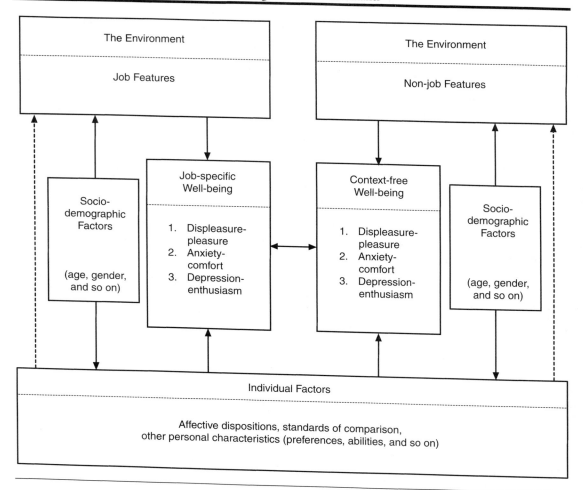

to include in the model certain individual factors that can also influence well-being—affective dispositions, standards of comparison, and other personal characteristics (see the box at the bottom of figure 20.3). It is suggested that sociodemographic characteristics (at the sides of the figure) influence both environmental and individual factors, through which they may be associated with well-being.

INDIVIDUAL DETERMINANTS OF WELL-BEING

Two main affective dispositions (at the bottom of figure 20.3) have been described as negative affectivity (NA) and positive affectivity (PA). These personality traits reflect pervasive individual differences in emotional style and feelings about one

self, and both have a general influence on emotional responses to features and events in the environment. Scores on measures of the two dispositions are negatively correlated with each other (averaging about $-.25$; see Cropanzano, James, and Konovsky 1993; Elliott, Chartrand, and Harkins 1994; George 1989; Munz et al. 1996; Watson and Pennebaker 1989; Watson and Slack 1993; Watson and Walker 1996).

The personality trait of negative affectivity embraces a broad range of aversive emotional states, such that people with high negative affectivity are more likely than others to experience raised levels of distress and dissatisfaction in any circumstances (Watson and Clark 1984). High-NA individuals tend to focus on the negative side of themselves and the world in general; they scan the environment for impending trouble, and they experience anxiety about what they see. On the other hand, low-NA individuals are more likely to feel secure and be satisfied with their environments. Questionnaire items representing high negative affectivity include self-descriptions as nervous, worrying, and overly sensitive (see, for example, Levin and Stokes 1989; Watson and Slack 1993).

On the other hand, the continuing trait of positive affectivity is seen in high levels of energy, excitement, and enthusiasm. High-PA individuals tend to lead more active lives than low-PA people and to view their environments in a more positive fashion. Questionnaire items to tap positive affectivity cover a person's tendency to feelings of happiness and enthusiasm, raised energy, and interest in life.

In general, personality "traits" are liable to be reflected in a person's "state" when he or she is in a trait-relevant situation. Well-being experienced at one point in time is a form of "state," and the second and third well-being axes in figure 20.2 are in practice state measures of trait negative affectivity and trait positive affectivity, respectively; the content of the constructs remains the same between trait and state, but the time frame is different. In other words, we would expect that high-trait-NA persons are in a more anxious state than others when in work situations (that is, to exhibit lower job-specific well-being on axis 2 in figure 20.2), and that high-PA individuals are likely to have raised job-related scores on axis 3. Are these trait-state expectations supported by research findings?

Affective Dispositions and Job-Specific Well-Being

Consider first studies of job-specific well-being. It is clear that trait negative affectivity is significantly predictive of low job well-being on axis 2 (anxiety-to-comfort). For example, Brief and his colleagues (1988) found a correlation of .57 between trait NA and a measure of negative affect at work during the previous week. George (1989) recorded a value of .34 using a more comprehensive measure of personality. Elliott, Chartrand, and Harkins (1994) examined correlations between trait NA and reports of recent emotional distress at work, finding a median value of .45.

Studies of positive affectivity and the third axis of job-related well-being (depression-to-enthusiasm) also show that trait PA is significantly associated with short-term feelings of that kind in a job setting (see, for example, George 1989). However, the association between trait and state is specific to its own axis of well-being (either axis 2 or axis 3 in

figure 20.2). For example, George (1989) found that, although the correlation between trait NA and job well-being on axis 2 (the relevant axis, anxiety-to-comfort) was .34, the coefficient was only −.03 for axis 3 (depression-to-enthusiasm).

Several investigations have examined people's overall job satisfaction (axis 1) as a function of these dispositional measures. In keeping with its intermediate position as the horizontal axis in figure 20.2, this form of job-specific well-being is expected to be moderately positively correlated with trait PA and moderately negatively correlated with negative affectivity. Median values are in fact .33 from five studies of positive affectivity, and −.26 from nine studies of negative affectivity (Agho et al. 1993; Brief et al. 1988; Chen and Spector 1991; Cropanzano et al. 1993; Jex and Spector 1996; Levin and Stokes 1989; Munz et al. 1996; Schaubroeck, Ganster, and Fox 1992; Watson and Slack 1993; Williams, Gavin, and Williams 1996). However, the strength of this association differs between intrinsic and extrinsic satisfactions. In research into specific facet satisfactions, trait PA and trait NA have been found to be more highly associated with (intrinsic) satisfaction with the nature of work undertaken (medians of .36 and −.28, respectively) than with (extrinsic) satisfactions with pay (medians of .16 and −.12), promotion (.22 and −.14), supervision (.14 and −.20), or coworkers (medians of .08 and −.21 for PA and NA, respectively) (Judge and Locke 1993; Necowitz and Roznowski 1994; Schaubroeck, Ganster, and Kemmerer 1996; Watson and Slack 1993). That difference is linked to the fact that intrinsic forms of satisfaction are more closely associated with overall job satisfaction than are extrinsic forms (see earlier discussion).

There is thus sound empirical support for the short vertical arrow in figure 20.3 from affective dispositions (in the bottom box) to job-specific well-being, especially its more intrinsic aspects. Furthermore, some studies have examined both the upward arrow to job-specific well-being and the downward arrow from job features, finding in multivariate analyses that both sets of features contribute significantly to well-being (see, for example, Agho et al. 1993; Watson and Slack 1993). In a comparison of independent contributions, Levin and Stokes (1989) showed that the impact of job characteristics on job satisfaction was stronger than that of trait negative affectivity.

People's feelings about their work are thus a function of both the work itself and their own personality. Other individual factors shown at the bottom of figure 20.3 include personal standards

of comparison. As pointed out earlier, people select other individuals and groups (as well as their
previous selves) in order to evaluate emotionally
significant information that is ambiguous. These
comparison standards are likely to derive in part
from personal choice of referent. Other influential
individual factors include stable preferences for
certain kinds of activity, as well as specific ability
levels that influence those preferences (and also
the kind of work a person takes up). Well-being in
any situation is affected by people's attitudes toward task content (at least at extreme levels) and
their ability to undertake the task.

The importance of these cross-situational individual factors suggests that job satisfaction and
other indicators of job-related well-being should
be relatively stable across time. That is indeed the
case. For example, Staw and Ross (1985) showed
that, for people remaining with the same employer
across either two or five years, test-retest correlations for overall job satisfaction were .47 and .37,
respectively. For employees who changed both
their occupation and their employer over those
periods, correlations were lower (demonstrating
the impact of environmental factors) but remained
as high as .33 and .19, respectively; similar patterns were reported by Gerhart (1987) and Schaubroeck, Ganster, and Kemmerer (1996).

This long-term stability of job satisfaction was
further examined by Arvey and his colleagues
(1989), who raised the question of whether variations in satisfaction might in part be inherited.
They reported data from thirty-four pairs of monozygotic twins who had been reared apart, concluding that approximately 30 percent of variance
in overall job satisfaction was attributable to genetic factors. This conclusion was supported in a
much larger investigation by Arvey and his colleagues (1994), with more than twenty-two hundred pairs of monozygotic and dizygotic twins.
For a range of methodological reasons, the precise
magnitude of the effect of heredity is open to dispute (see Cropanzano and James 1990), but there
appears to be some genetic influence on job satisfaction, presumably through inherited aspects of
broader personality dispositions and of ability
levels affecting job attainments and preferences.

Affective Dispositions and
Context-Free Well-Being

What about the relationship between individual
factors and wider forms of well-being (the right-
hand central box in figure 20.3)? Significant asso-

ciations between context-free well-being and affec-
tive dispositions have often been demonstrated
(Warr, Barter, and Brownbridge 1983; Diener and
Lucas, this volume).

In a study of reactions to job insecurity, Roskies,
Louis-Guerin, and Fournier (1993) reported correlations of .66 and −.53 between current generalized distress and personality-scale indicators of
NA and PA, respectively. Costa and McCrae
(1980) examined the two continuing dispositions
in terms of trait neuroticism and extraversion.
They found significant correlations between trait
neuroticism and recent negative affect, and between trait extraversion and recent positive affect.
(However, as with job-specific well-being, the correlations were negligible between each aspect of
personality and the *other* index of recent affect; see
also Watson and Clark [1992].) The differentiated
pattern was also found longitudinally in predictions from the two personality dispositions measured ten years previously; Watson and Walker
(1996) reported a similar pattern over seven years.
Recognizing that common-method variance
(through self-reports of both personality and well-
being) might inflate the associations, Costa and
McRae (1984) examined personality ratings made
by spouses. Significant associations between context-free well-being and spouse-rated personality,
as well as the differentiated pattern between PA
and NA, were confirmed.

Some researchers have viewed individuals in
terms of their "hardiness," a tendency to act positively and proactively in the face of environmental
challenges (Kobasa 1979). Much research has
shown that hardier individuals are likely to report
less depression and other negative forms of context-free well-being. However, low hardiness is in
practice very similar to raised negative affectivity
(Funk 1992), and findings about that variable may
be interpreted in the more general terms presented
here. In a similar fashion, traits such as "dispositional optimism" (Jex and Spector 1996; Scheier
and Carver 1985) may be viewed as a form of positive affectivity, with probable correlates of the
kind described earlier.

INDIVIDUAL FACTORS AND THE
ENVIRONMENT

Many of the relationships indicated in figure 20.3
between well-being, environmental features, and
individual factors are thus empirically supported.
We have discussed the continuous lines in the fig-

ure, representing probable causal influences, but not the two vertical dotted lines at the left-hand and right-hand sides of the figure: upward from individual factors to job features and non-job features. These lines are dotted rather than continuous to indicate that they should be interpreted primarily in terms of perceptual and behavioral influences rather than the causal impacts suggested in other cases.

The perceptual effect has mainly been investigated in terms of trait negative affectivity rather than trait positive affectivity. Consistent with the fact that high-NA people are anxious and prone to scan their environment for potentially threatening features, it has often been shown that negative affectivity is associated with perceptions of more unpleasant characteristics in jobs and elsewhere (see, for example, Brief et al. 1988; Burke, Brief, and George 1993; Chen and Spector 1991; Elliott et al. 1994; Levin and Stokes 1989; Spector and O'Connell 1994). Conversely, high-PA workers perceive more social support in their work settings than do low-PA people (Chay 1993).[2]

The dotted lines in figure 20.3 also point to behavioral possibilities. Continuing personal attributes are likely to have a causal impact on behavior, which in turn affects well-being. People tend to seek out situations that reflect and support their personal characteristics. For instance, a significant association between positive affectivity and time spent in social recreation (Diener, Larsen, and Emmons 1984) illustrates how this aspect of personality may influence the settings a person enters or within which he or she remains. Furthermore, high-NA people may generate more stressors in their environment than do low-NA individuals, consistent with the finding that neuroticism was associated across a four-year period with greater experience of objective negative life events (Magnus et al. 1993). More longitudinal research is needed to explore these possible sequential forms of influence and to substantiate other possibilities associated with the two dotted lines in figure 20.3.

SOCIODEMOGRAPHIC FEATURES AND JOB-SPECIFIC WELL-BEING

Figure 20.3 also suggests that sociodemographic features (age, gender, ethnic group, geographical region, and so on) can affect employee well-being, through their impact on environmental and individual factors. Consideration of all these sociodemographic features is not appropriate within the focus of this chapter, but age and gender effects on *job-specific* well-being will be reviewed briefly. (Context-free well-being relative to age and to gender is examined by Diener and Suh [1997] and Nolen-Hoeksema and Rusting [this volume], respectively.)

It is regularly found that older workers report significantly higher job-specific well-being on the three axes of figure 20.2 (Birdi et al. 1995; Pugliesi 1995; Warr 1992). In addition, there is evidence that in certain circumstances very young employees report higher well-being than those in their late twenties; a curvilinear association with age is sometimes present (Clark, Oswald, and Warr 1996). Several reasons have been suggested for greater job-related well-being at older ages. For example, older people tend to move into more attractive jobs, they come to value differently certain job features, and their standards of comparison may be reduced across time (Warr 1997). In addition, improved *context-free* well-being at older ages is likely to enhance job-specific well-being through the mutual influence summarized earlier.

Job-specific well-being scores have also been examined separately for men and women. Findings have varied between studies, associated with small samples, differing measures, and differing proportions of full-time and part-time workers. However, large-scale surveys have shown consistently that there are no gender differences in the United States in overall job satisfaction (see, for example, Pugliesi 1995; Weaver 1980); conversely, in the United Kingdom, women report significantly greater job satisfaction than men (Clark 1996). The reason for that difference between the countries is not yet clear.

What about the influence of specific job features? Are they similar for men and women? Associations with overall job satisfaction often appear to be the same, but opportunity for personal control has been found to have more impact for men (Mottaz 1986; Pugliesi 1995), and the presence of supportive supervision to be associated more with job satisfaction for women (Mottaz 1986). That pattern was observed by Piltch and her colleagues (1994) in relation to context-free distress, but no gender differences in the impact of specific job features were found by Kalimo and Vuori (1991). Roxburgh's (1996) study of context-free distress indicated that women were more adversely affected by high job demands and low variety, but no difference was present in respect of social support. In view of the limited and conflicting evidence, it is not possible to reach an overall conclusion about possible gender differences in the impact of specific job features.

The fact that women are at least as satisfied with their jobs as men is surprising, since on average women are in lower-quality employment (in terms of the ten key job features) than are men. Possible explanations may be found in the individual factors box of figure 20.3. For example, it is possible that many women have lower standards of comparison, that is, they expect less from their jobs (Clark 1996). Or they may not be as concerned as men with aspects such as high pay, good security, or opportunity for personal control (Mottaz 1986).

Contrary to findings for well-being axis 1, scores on the emotional exhaustion component of job-related burnout (covering both the other axes) have been shown to vary in the opposite direction: women report significantly more emotional exhaustion than men (Kauppinen-Toropainen, Kandolin, and Mutanen 1983; Maslach and Jackson 1981). Interpretation of that finding is made difficult by the fact that male and female jobs were not identical in the groups studied; it is desirable to compare men and women who are employed in the same roles.

WELL-BEING AND WORK BEHAVIOR

What about the associations of well-being with behavior in a job? It is sometimes suggested that employees with greater well-being behave differently from those with lower well-being.

Even if such a difference were found, the direction of causality would remain unclear. It would not necessarily be the case that, say, high job satisfaction causes a particular form of behavior, for example, good work performance. The opposite might be true: good performers might be more satisfied as a result of their effective performance. Alternatively, a third factor (or several of them) might bring about both high performance and high satisfaction. For instance, particular equipment characteristics or managerial styles might enhance both performance and satisfaction. Note also that behavior is determined by a range of different factors (organizational policies, management practices, group pressures, individual abilities, available options, and so on), so that the maximum possible correlation with well-being alone is expected to be much less than 1.00.

Recognizing the causal ambiguity of such correlations, what is known about the behavioral correlates of employee well-being? Four types of behavior will be considered: performance in the job, absence from work, staff turnover, and discretionary activities.

Performance in the Job

Iaffaldano and Muchinsky (1985) provided a meta-analysis of previous studies of job performance (usually indexed through supervisor ratings) and job satisfaction (axis 1 in figure 20.2). They found that overall job satisfaction was positively associated with performance to a significant degree (the average observed correlation was .25). Stronger associations were found for intrinsic satisfaction than extrinsic satisfaction.

Petty, McGee, and Cavender (1984) reported very similar findings (the average correlation was .23) but also noted that the association of overall job satisfaction with rated performance was stronger for managerial and professional employees than for others (average correlations of .31 and .15, respectively). In subsequent studies, Shore and Martin (1989) recorded a median correlation of .25 for two samples of white-collar workers, and Podsakoff, MacKenzie, and Bommer (1996) estimated from a meta-analysis a population value of .24.

Ostroff (1992) examined this association at the level of entire organizations, predicting that those with more satisfied employees would be more productive than others. In a study of 298 schools, standardized measures of academic performance, administrative efficiency, and student behavior were found to be significantly associated with teachers' overall job satisfaction (an average coefficient of .28). This pattern was retained after statistical controls were introduced for differences between the schools in student characteristics and available resources. Standardized observational procedures were applied by Robertson and his colleagues (1995) in a study of nurses' delivery of geriatric health care; strong differences were found in the quality of care between wards with nurses whose overall job satisfaction was either high or low.

What about axis 2, measuring anxiety-to-comfort job-specific feelings? It seems likely that employees who report more job anxiety might be experiencing difficulty in coping with job demands and thus would be liable to perform relatively less effectively; a negative association between job-related anxiety and job performance is thus probable. Very few investigations have examined this question, but Jamal (1984) found that higher levels of job-related tension were associated with lower supervisory ratings (a median correlation of −.35). Spector and his colleagues (1988) reported a correlation of −.16.

An alternative hypothesis is that lower performances occur on either side of a possible optimal amount of challenge. It may be the case that the relationship between job tension and performance is one of an inverted U, such that moderate demands are linked to raised but manageable job-related tension and also to high performance, but that both lower and higher levels of tension (and of job demands) are accompanied by lower performance. Anderson (1976) suggested that this was the case in data from a sample of small-business owners, but the possibility remains in need of more substantial examination.

The third axis of job-specific well-being in figure 20.2 ranges from depression to enthusiasm. It appears likely that employees with positive feelings of this active kind will be among the more productive, but few relevant studies have been reported. George (1991) found a correlation of .26 with supervisors' ratings of salespeople's helpful customer behavior; however, the correlation with actual sales performance was only .10. Motowidlo, Packard, and Manning (1986) examined the association between nurses' job-related depression and ratings by supervisors and coworkers of their interpersonal effectiveness (sensitivity to patients, cooperation, warmth, and so on) and of their cognitive/motivational effectiveness (concentration, perseverance, and so on). In both bivariate and multivariate analyses, job-related depression was significantly associated with lower effectiveness of both kinds.

Absence from Work

Another index of employee performance is absenteeism (or its converse, work attendance). Such behavior is determined by a range of factors. In addition to sickness itself, social and family pressures can affect decisions to attend work (see, for example, Brooke and Price 1989). Organizational influences include specific policies to encourage attendance, support from a supervisor (Tharenou 1993), and, more broadly, the "absence culture" of the workplace (Martocchio 1994)—norms and sanctions (informal as well as formal) about reasonable levels of absence. Although employee well-being at work might be expected to be linked to absenteeism, other factors are clearly also important.

Absenteeism is conventionally measured in two different ways, through the Time-Lost Index and the Frequency Index. The Time-Lost Index is computed as the total duration of absence during a specified period, perhaps expressed as a proportion of the total time examined; and the Frequency Index is the number of separate incidents of absence in a specified period, regardless of their duration. The Time-Lost Index, which gives greater emphasis to long periods of absence, is considered primarily to represent *involuntary* responses to incapacitating sickness. On the other hand, the Frequency Index, in which a single day's absence is given the same weight as, say, a three-month absence, is widely thought to describe more *voluntary* choices to take time off work for brief periods of time.

How do the three aspects of job-specific well-being correlate with these two indices of absenteeism? We might expect the Frequency Index (with its emphasis on possibly voluntary behavior) to be predicted more by well-being, but as with job performance, the causes underlying any observed association are complex and multidirectional.

In a meta-analysis of previous studies, Farrell and Stamm (1988) found that overall job satisfaction (axis 1 in figure 20.2) on average correlated only −.10 with the Frequency Index and −.13 with the Time-Lost Index. Hackett (1989) obtained similar findings but found that job satisfaction is associated with absence frequency more for women than for men; he suggested that this difference arises from many women's greater family responsibilities. Melamed and his colleagues (1995) reported a correlation of −.11 between satisfaction with work content and a Frequency Index of absence specifically associated with reported sickness.

The average correlations of job-related anxiety (axis 2) with the Frequency Index and the Time-Lost Index were .11 and .18, respectively, in Farrell and Stamm's (1988) analysis. The Frequency Index of absenteeism was also examined by Jamal (1984) and Spector, Dwyer, and Jex (1988), who reported correlations with job-related anxiety of .25 (median value) and .15, respectively. Note that raised anxiety may sometimes be a consequence of high levels of absence deriving from ill health, although causal influences from well-being to absences can also be envisaged.

It might be expected that higher well-being on the third axis of job-specific well-being (depression-to-enthusiasm) is accompanied by less time off work. George (1989) examined positive feelings of this kind and observed a correlation of $-.28$ with the number of single-day absences (thought to indicate voluntary time off work). In the review by Farrell and Stamm (1988), measures of job involvement (emphasizing active interest in one's role, as in positive forms of axis 3) were on average correlated $-.28$ with the Frequency Index of absenteeism. It thus appears (although evidence is limited) that this third aspect of job-specific well-being is more predictive of voluntary absenteeism than are the other two measurement axes.

Staff Turnover

A third behavioral measure that we might expect to be related to job-specific well-being is whether people remain with their current employer. The average correlation between absence and subsequent turnover has been estimated at .33 (Mitra, Jenkins, and Gupta 1992), and affective precursors of the two forms of behavior no doubt overlap in many ways. The average correlation between overall job satisfaction and employee turnover was $-.23$ and $-.16$ in the meta-analyses by Carsten and Spector (1987) and Hom and his colleagues (1992), respectively. However, additional factors influence turnover decisions, especially the availability of suitable alternative employment; job satisfaction better predicts actual turnover when local unemployment is lower (Carsten and Spector 1987; Hom et al. 1992).

Some investigators have asked about people's future plans, finding that intentions to leave are predicted by overall job satisfaction (axis 1 in figure 20.2) (see, for example, George and Jones 1996; Hom et al. 1992; Zaccaro and Stone 1988) and by job-specific anxiety (axis 2) (see, for example, Spector et al. 1988). Lee and Ashforth (1996) reported an average correlation between job-related emotional exhaustion (the main component of burnout) and turnover intention of .37. Intentions are themselves strongly intercorrelated with actual turnover (.38 and .33 on average in the reviews by Carsten and Spector [1987] and Hom et al. [1992]).

Discretionary Activities

A fourth issue concerns work behaviors that are specifically discretionary (rather than prescribed as enforceable requirements). In practice, the distinction between the two types of activity is somewhat fuzzy, and employers tend to encourage a wider view of prescribed behavior than is held by some employees. However, it might generally be expected that employee well-being is particularly associated with behaviors that are voluntary, within the discretion of the individual, rather than closely determined by job requirements or technological constraints. Three possibilities may be considered.

One form of discretionary behavior is *voluntary overtime*. Many jobs offer the possibility of undertaking unpaid work outside the required hours, and employees' job-specific well-being may be predictive of such behavior. This was found to be the case in a study of schoolteachers: overall job satisfaction was correlated .25 with the amount of additional (unpaid) time devoted to work-related activities (Gechman and Wiener 1975).

Several investigators have examined a second form of discretionary behavior at work, *prosocial activity*, also referred to as "organizational citizenship behavior," or "contextual performance" (outside a prescribed main task). Such behaviors include providing assistance to colleagues, being friendly, volunteering to undertake needed tasks, adhering closely to specified rules, and making suggestions to improve effectiveness. It is established that overall job satisfaction is significantly associated with this type of discretionary ("extrarole") behavior as rated by a boss or colleagues (see, for example, McNeely and Meglino 1994; Motowidlo 1984; Smith, Organ, and Near 1983). In a meta-analytic review, Organ and Ryan (1995) reported average correlations with ratings of behavior made by other people of .25. George (1991, 1996) has suggested that this association is due to more satisfied employees experiencing more positive short-term mood (similar to quadrant 3b in figure 20.2), which she showed to be linked to discretionary behaviors.

Finally, forms of *adaptive behavior* are increasingly valued in organizations that have to face intense market pressure and rapid technological change. Are aspects of employee well-being likely to influence this type of discretionary activity, seen in a willingness to take steps to acquire new skills and knowledge? This possibility has been raised by Karasek and Theorell (1990). They suggest that job-related stress is created by the combination of low discretion and high demands (items 1 and 3 on the list of key job features), and that anxiety accumulated across time in turn inhibits new learning. This has two possible consequences for stressed employees: they may become less able to handle a current situation, and also less likely to change their approach in the face of new requirements. A vicious cycle is thus created. On the other hand, high demands coupled with high discretion are thought to enhance well-being, inhibiting the potential harmful impact of work overload and bringing together feelings of personal mastery and an interest in facing new challenges and acquiring new skills and knowledge. There is at present no direct evidence for this possible link between employee well-being and openness to new experiences, but the idea appears plausible.

Initial information has been provided by Birdi, Gardner, and Warr (1998) in a study of manufacturing employees. Overall job satisfaction was found to be greater among those who were more active in required training activities and in work-based development activities (undertaking personal projects, serving on working groups, and so on). This positive association remained significant after statistical control for demographic variables (such as age and education level), which were themselves predictive of participation in these forms of new activity. However, from this cross-sectional investigation alone we cannot determine whether greater well-being promoted learning, learning activities enhanced well-being, or both effects occurred.

ISSUES FOR FUTURE RESEARCH

Progress in the field covered by this chapter has been considerable in recent years, and substantial knowledge has been gained. However, there is a need for further investigation into many of the issues outlined here: the linearity or curvilinearity of associations between job features and well-being; the forms of combination of job features; the specific processes through which each job feature influences well-being; and the different behavioral outcomes of the three aspects of well-being.

However, the overarching need in this field is for more comprehensive investigations. Research has typically focused on narrow questions, avoiding an overview of the kind suggested in figure 20.3. It is now particularly desirable to seek to combine within single studies several elements of that model. For instance, how might sociodemographic factors combine with individual factors and job features to influence the well-being of employees? Which of the several possible causal factors is particularly significant relative to the others? Longitudinal investigations have a special place in such a program.

Two additional issues require examination. Viewing the model in dynamic terms, one can envisage a cyclical operation of all the elements across time. That raises issues beyond the immediate time period: what are the *long-term* effects (on psychiatric ill health, physiological condition, or the pace of psychological aging) of extended periods of low well-being arising from poor jobs? Second, recent shifts in the labor market have increased the proportions of self-employed, temporary, and part-time employees. Such jobs have both positive and negative features, and these deserve to be examined in relation to the aspects of well-being outlined here.

A final issue of overriding practical importance concerns the optimization of employees' performance in addition to their well-being. Enhancement of one of these aspects can sometimes impair progress in the other. As an extreme case, one can envisage the creation of very high well-being in a company to the detriment of effectiveness. This may lead to a failure to meet competitive challenges, so that all jobs are lost (leading to a large and widespread decrease in well-being). Recognizing that desirable outcomes of well-being and effectiveness can conflict, future investigations need to expand their perspective and consider the simultaneous attainment of these objectives. It seems likely that this development will involve a more explicit consideration of both short-term processes and those that extend over longer periods; temporary states of high or low well-being must coexist with a longer-term maintenance of effective performance.

APPENDIX

Cited here are illustrative recent studies that have indicated that the ten key job features are associated with employees' job-specific well-being. See Warr (1987) for a comprehensive review of earlier investigations.

1. *Opportunity for personal control:* Agho, Mueller, and Price (1993); Fried (1991); Kelloway and Barling (1991); Sevastos, Smith, and Cordery (1992); Spector, Dwyer, and Jex (1988); Spector and O'Connell (1994); Wall and colleagues (1996); Warr (1990a, 1990b); Xie and Johns (1995).

2. *Opportunity for skill use:* Campion and McClelland (1993); Sevastos, Smith, and Cordery (1992); Warr (1990b).

3. *Externally generated goals:* Campion and McClelland (1993); Kelloway and Barling (1991); Martin and Wall (1989); Netemeyer, Johnston, and Burton (1990); Spector, Dwyer, and Jex (1988); Spector and O'Connell (1994); Wall and colleagues (1996); Warr (1990a, 1990b); Williams, Gavin, and Williams (1996).

4. *Variety:* Agho, Mueller, and Price (1993); Fried (1991); Kelloway and Barling (1991); Sevastos, Smith, and Cordery (1992); Warr (1990b); Xie and Johns (1995).

5. *Environmental clarity:* Agho, Mueller, and Price (1993); Fried (1991); Kelloway and Barling (1991); Landeweerd and Boumans (1994); Sevastos, Smith, and Cordery (1992); Spector, Dwyer, and Jex (1988); Spector and O'Connell (1994); Williams, Gavin, and Williams (1996); Xie and Johns (1995).

6. *Availability of money:* Agho, Mueller, and Price (1993).

7. *Physical security:* Campion (1988); Oldham and Fried (1987); Zaccaro and Stone (1988).

8. *Supportive supervision:* Agho, Mueller, and Price (1993); Landeweerd and Boumans (1994); Miles, Patrick, and King (1996); Mottaz (1986).

9. *Opportunity for interpersonal contact:* Agho, Mueller, and Price (1993); Chay (1993); Kelloway and Barling (1991); Warr (1990b).

10. *Valued social position:* Agho, Mueller, and Price (1993); Sevastos, Smith, and Cordery (1992); Xie and Johns (1995).

NOTES

1. The classification was developed to cover a wide range of settings of nonemployment as well as employment. The focus in this chapter is on the latter.

2. Given that trait NA is associated both with perceptions of a more negative environment and with lower state well-being, it is possible that this continuing disposition acts also to inflate the magnitude of observed correlations between self-reported job characteristics and well-being (Burke et al. 1993). Recent research tends toward the conclusion that this effect is small or nonexistent (Elliott et al. 1994; Jex and Spector 1996; Munz et al. 1996; Schonfeld 1996), but the issue remains in need of further study.

REFERENCES

Adams, G. A., King, L. A., and King, D. W. (1996). Relationships of job and family involvement, family social support, and work-family conflict with job and life satisfaction. *Journal of Applied Psychology, 81,* 411–20.

Adelmann, P. K. (1987). Occupational complexity, control, and personal income: Their relation to psychological well-being in men and women. *Journal of Applied Psychology, 72,* 529–37.

Agho, A. O., Mueller, C. W., and Price, J. L. (1993). Determinants of employee job satisfaction: An empirical test of a causal model. *Human Relations, 46,* 1007–27.

Anderson, C. R. (1976). Coping behaviors as intervening mechanisms in the inverted-U stress-performance relationship. *Journal of Applied Psychology, 61,* 30–34.

Arvey, R. D., Bouchard, T. J., Segal, N. L., and Abraham L. M. (1989). Job satisfaction: Environmental and genetic components. *Journal of Applied Psychology, 74,* 187–92.

Arvey, R. D., McCall, B. P., Bouchard, T. J., Taubman, P., and Cavanaugh, M. A. (1994). Genetic influences on job satisfaction and work values. *Personality and Individual Differences, 17,* 21–33.

Bamundo, P. J., and Kopelman, R. E. (1980). The moderating effects of occupation, age, and urbanization on the relationship between job satisfaction and life satisfaction. *Journal of Vocational Behavior, 17,* 106–23.

Barnett, R. C., Raudenbush, S. W., Brennan, R. T., Pleck, J. H., and Marshall, N. L. (1995). Changes in job and marital experiences and change in psychological distress: A longitudinal study of dual-earner couples. *Journal of Personality and Social Psychology, 69,* 839–50.

Birdi, K. S., Gardner, C. R., and Warr, P. B. (1998). Correlates and perceived outcomes of four types of employee development activity. *Journal of Applied Psychology, 82,* 845–57

Birdi, K. S., Warr, P. B., and Oswald, A. (1995). Age differences in three components of employee well-being. *Applied Psychology, 44,* 345–73.

Bradburn, N. M. (1969). *The structure of psychological well-being.* Chicago: Aldine.

Brief, A. P., Burke, M. J., George, J. M., Robinson, B. S., and Webster, J. (1988). Should negative affectivity remain an unmeasured variable in the study of job stress? *Journal of Applied Psychology, 73,* 193–98.

Brooke, P. P., and Price, J. L. (1989). The determinants of absenteeism: An empirical test of a causal model. *Journal of Occupational Psychology, 62,* 1–19.

Burger, J. M. (1989). Negative reactions to increases in perceived personal control. *Journal of Personality and Social Psychology, 56,* 246–56.

Burke, M. J., Brief, A. P., and George, J. M. (1993). The role of negative affectivity in understanding relations between self-reports of stressors and strains: A comment on the applied psychology literature. *Journal of Applied Psychology, 78,* 402–12.

Campion, M. A. (1988). Interdisciplinary approaches to job design: A constructive replication with extensions. *Journal of Applied Psychology, 73,* 467–81.

Campion, M. A., and McClelland, C. L. (1993). Follow-up and extension of the interdisciplinary costs and benefits of enlarged jobs. *Journal of Applied Psychology, 78,* 339–51.

Carsten, J. M., and Spector, P. E. (1987). Unemployment, job satisfaction, and employee turnover: A meta-analytic test of the Muchinsky model. *Journal of Applied Psychology, 72,* 374–81.

Chay, Y. W. (1993). Social support, individual differences and well-being: A study of small-business entrepreneurs and employees. *Journal of Occupational and Organizational Psychology, 66,* 285–302.

Chen, P. Y., and Spector, P. E. (1991). Negative affectivity as the underlying cause of correlations between stressors and strains. *Journal of Applied Psychology, 76,* 398–407.

Clark, A. E. (1996). Job satisfaction in Britain. *British Journal of Industrial Relations, 34,* 189–217.

Clark, A. E., and Oswald, A. J. (1996). Satisfaction and comparison income. *Journal of Public Economics, 61,* 359–81.

Clark, A. E., Oswald, A., and Warr, P. B. (1996). Is job satisfaction U-shaped in age? *Journal of Occupational and Organizational Psychology, 69,* 57–82.

Compton, W. C., Smith, M. L., Cornish, K. A., and Qualls, D. L. (1996). Factor structure of mental health measures. *Journal of Personality and Social Psychology, 71,* 406–13.

Cordes C. L., and Dougherty, T. W. (1993). A review and integration of research on job burnout. *Academy of Management Review, 18,* 621–56.

Costa, P. T., and McCrae, R. R. (1980). Influence of extraversion and neuroticism on subjective well-being: Happy and unhappy people. *Journal of Personality and Social Psychology, 38,* 668–78.

———. (1984). Personality as a lifelong determinant of well-being. In C. Z. Malatesta and C. E. Izard (Eds.), *Emotion in adult development* (pp. 141–55). Beverly Hills: Sage.

Cropanzano, R., and James, K. (1990). Some methodological considerations for the behavioral genetic analysis of work attitudes. *Journal of Applied Psychology, 75,* 433–39.

Cropanzano, R., James, K., and Konovsky, M. A. (1993). Dispositional affectivity as a predictor of work attitudes and job performance. *Journal of Organizational Behavior, 14,* 595–606.

Crouter, A. C. (1984). Spillover from family to work: The neglected side of the work-family interface. *Human Relations, 37,* 425–42.

Daniels, K., and Guppy, A. (1994). Relationships between aspects of work-related psychological well-being. *Journal of Psychology, 128,* 691–94.

De Jonge, J., and Schaufeli, W. B. (1998). Job characteristics and employee well-being: A test of Warr's Vitamin Model in health-care workers using structural equation modelling. *Journal of Organizational Behavior, 19,* 387–407.

Delsen, L. (1995). *Atypical employment: An inter-national perspective.* Amsterdam: Wolters-Noordhoff.

Diener, E., Larsen, R. J., and Emmons, R. A. (1984). Person *x* situation interactions: Choice of situations and congruence response models. *Journal of Personality and Social Psychology, 47,* 580–92.

Diener, E., and Suh, E. (1997). Subjective well-being and age: An international analysis. In K. W. Schaie and M. P. Lawton (Eds.), *Annual review of gerontology and geriatrics* (vol. 17, pp. 304–24). New York: Springer-Verlag.

Dooley, D., Rook, K., and Catalano, R. (1987). Job and non-job stressors and their moderators. *Journal of Occupational Psychology, 60,* 115–32.

Elliott, T. R., Chartrand, J. M., and Harkins, S. W. (1994). Negative affectivity, emotional distress, and the cognitive appraisal of occupational stress. *Journal of Vocational Behavior, 45,* 185–201.

European Commission. (1996). *Employment in Europe.* Luxembourg: Office for Official Publications of the European Communities.

Farrell, D., and Stamm, C. L. (1988). Meta-analysis of the correlates of employee absence. *Human Relations, 41,* 211–27.

Fried, Y. (1991). Meta-analytic comparison of the Job Diagnostic Survey and Job Characteristics Inventory as correlates of work satisfaction and performance. *Journal of Applied Psychology, 76,* 690–97.

Frone, M. R., Russell, M., and Barnes, G. M. (1996). Work-family conflict, gender, and health-related outcomes: A study of employed parents in two community samples. *Journal of Occupational Health Psychology, 1,* 57–69.

Frone, M. R., Russell, M., and Cooper, L. M. (1992). Antecedents and outcomes of work-family conflict: Testing a model of the work-family interface. *Journal of Applied Psychology, 77,* 65–78.

Frone, M. R., Yardley, J. K., and Markel, K. S. (1997). Developing and testing an integrative model of the work-family interface. *Journal of Vocational Behavior, 50,* 145–67.

Fullerton, H. N. (1995). The 2005 labor force. *Monthly Labor Review, 118*(11), 29–44.

Funk, S. C. (1992). Hardiness: A review of theory and research. *Health Psychology, 11,* 335–45.

Gechman, A. S., and Wiener, Y. (1975). Job involvement and satisfaction as related to mental health and personal time devoted to work. *Journal of Applied Psychology, 60,* 521–23.

George, J. M. (1989). Mood and absence. *Journal of Applied Psychology, 74,* 317–24.

———. (1991). State or trait: Effects of positive mood on prosocial behaviors at work. *Journal of Applied Psychology, 76,* 299–307.

———. (1996). Trait and state affect. In K. R. Murphy (Ed.), *Individual differences and behavior in organizations* (pp. 145–71). San Francisco: Jossey-Bass.

George, J. M., and Jones, G. R. (1996). The experience of work and turnover intentions: Interactive effects of value attainment, job satisfaction, and positive mood. *Journal of Applied Psychology, 81,* 318–25.

Gerhart, B. (1987). How important are dispositional factors as determinants of job satisfaction?: Implications for job design and other personnel programs. *Journal of Applied Psychology, 72,* 366–73.

Hackett, R. D. (1989). Work attitudes and employee absenteeism: A synthesis of the literature. *Journal of Occupational Psychology, 62,* 235–48.

Hall, D. T., and Mirvis, P. H. (1995). The new career contract: Developing the whole person at midlife and beyond. *Journal of Vocational Behavior, 47,* 269–89.

Hom, P. W., Caranikas-Walker, F., Prussia, G. E., and Griffeth, R. W. (1992). A meta-analytical structural equations analysis of a model of employee turnover. *Journal of Applied Psychology, 77,* 890–909.

Iaffaldano, M. T., and Muchinsky, P. M. (1985). Job satisfaction and job performance: A meta-analysis. *Psychological Bulletin, 97,* 251–73.

Jamal, M. (1984). Job stress and job performance controversy: An empirical assessment. *Organizational Behavior and Human Performance, 33,* 1–21.

Jex, S. M., and Spector, P. E. (1996). The impact of negative affectivity on stressor-strain relations: A replication and extension. *Work and Stress, 10,* 36–45.

Judge, T. A., and Locke, E. A. (1993). Effect of dysfunctional thought processes on subjective well-being and job satisfaction. *Journal of Applied Psychology, 78,* 475–90.

Judge, T. A., and Watanabe, S. (1993). Another look at the job satisfaction–life satisfaction relationship. *Journal of Applied Psychology, 78,* 939–48.

Kahn, R. L., and Byosiere, P. (1992). Stress in organizations. In M. D. Dunnette and L. M. Heugh (Eds.), *Handbook of industrial and organizational psychology* (vol. 3, pp. 571–650). Palo Alto, Calif.: Consulting Psychologists Press.

Kalimo, R., and Vuori, J. (1991). Work factors and health: The predictive role of pre-employment experiences. *Journal of Occupational Psychology, 64,* 97–115.

Karasek, R. A. (1979). Job demands, job decision latitude, and mental strain: Implications for job design. *Administrative Science Quarterly, 24,* 285–308.

Karasek, R. A., and Theorell, T. (1990). *Healthy work.* New York: Basic Books.

Kasl, S. V. (1996). The influence of the work environment on cardiovascular health: A historical, conceptual, and methodological perspective. *Journal of Occupational Health Psychology, 1,* 42–56.

Kauppinen-Toropainen, K., Kandolin, I., and Mutanen, P. (1983). Job dissatisfaction and work-related exhaustion in male and female work. *Journal of Occupational Behaviour, 4,* 193–207.

Kelloway, E. K., and Barling, J. (1991). Job characteristics, role stress and mental health. *Journal of Occupational Psychology, 64,* 291–304.

Kobasa, S. C. (1979). Stressful life events, personality, and health: An enquiry into hardiness. *Journal of Personality and Social Psychology, 37,* 1–11.

Landeweerd, J. A., and Boumans, N. P. G. (1994). The effect of work dimensions and need for autonomy on nurses' work satisfaction and health. *Journal of Occupational and Organizational Psychology, 67,* 207–17.

Lee, R. T., and Ashforth, B. E. (1996). A meta-analytic examination of the correlates of the three dimensions of job burnout. *Journal of Applied Psychology, 81,* 123–33.

Levin, I., and Stokes, J. P. (1989). Dispositional approach to job satisfaction: Role of negative affectivity. *Journal of Applied Psychology, 74,* 752–58.

Loscocco, K. A., and Spitze, G. (1990). Working conditions, social support, and the well-being of male and female factory workers. *Journal of Health and Social Behavior, 31,* 313–27.

Lowe, G. S., and Northcutt, H. C. (1988). The impact of working conditions, social roles, and personal characteristics on gender differences in distress. *Work and Occupations, 15,* 55–77.

Lucas, R. E., Diener, E., and Suh, E. (1996). Discriminant validity of well-being measures. *Journal of Personality and Social Psychology, 71,* 616–28.

Magnus, K., Diener, E., Fujita, F., and Pavot, W. (1993). Extraversion and neuroticism as predictors of objective life events: A longitudinal analysis. *Journal of Personality and Social Psychology, 65,* 1046–53.

Manning, M. R., Jackson, C. N., and Fusilier, M. R. (1996). Occupational stress, social support, and the costs of health care. *Academy of Management Journal, 39,* 738–50.

Martin, R., and Wall, T. D. (1989). Attentional demand and cost responsibility as stressors in shopfloor jobs. *Academy of Management Journal, 32,* 69–86.

Martocchio, J. J. (1994). The effects of absence culture on individual absence. *Human Relations, 47,* 243–62.

Maslach, C., and Jackson, S. E. (1981). The measurement of experienced burnout. *Journal of Occupational Behaviour, 2,* 99–113.

Mathieu, J. E., Hofmann, D. A., and Farr, J. L. (1993). Job perception–job satisfaction relations: An empirical comparison of three competing theories. *Organizational Behavior and Human Decision Processes, 56,* 370–87.

Matthews, G., Jones, D. M., and Chamberlain, A. G. (1990). Defining the measurement of mood: The UWIST mood adjective checklist. *British Journal of Psychology, 81,* 17–42.

McNeely, B. L., and Meglino, B. M. (1994). The role of dispositional and situational antecedents in prosocial organizational behavior: An examination of the intended beneficiaries of prosocial behavior. *Journal of Applied Psychology, 79,* 836–44.

Melamed, S., Ben-Avi, I., Luz, J., and Green, M. S. (1995). Objective and subjective work monotony: Effects on job satisfaction, psychological distress, and absenteeism in blue-collar workers. *Journal of Applied Psychology, 80,* 29–42.

Miles, E. W., Patrick, S. L., and King, W. C. (1996). Job level as a systemic variable in predicting the relationship between supervisory communication and job satisfaction. *Journal of Occupational and Organizational Psychology, 69,* 277–92.

Mitra, A., Jenkins, G. D., and Gupta, N. (1992). A meta-analytic review of the relationship between absence and turnover. *Journal of Applied Psychology, 77,* 879–89.

Motowidlo, S. J. (1984). Does job satisfaction lead to consideration and personal sensitivity? *Academy of Management Journal, 27,* 910–15.

Motowidlo, S. J., Packard, J. S., and Manning, J. S. (1986). Occupational stress: Its causes and consequences for job performance. *Journal of Applied Psychology, 71,* 618–29.

Mottaz, C. (1986). Gender differences in work satisfaction, work-related rewards and values, and the determinants of work satisfaction. *Human Relations, 39,* 359–76.

Munz, D. C., Huelsman, T. J., Konold, T. R., and McKinney, J. J. (1996). Are there methodological and substantive roles for affectivity in Job Diagnostic Survey relationships? *Journal of Applied Psychology, 81,* 795–805.

Myers, D. A. (1991). Work after cessation of a career job. *Journal of Gerontology, 46,* S93–102.

Necowitz, L. B., and Roznowski, M. (1994). Negative affectivity and job satisfaction: Cognitive processes underlying the relationship and effects on employee behaviors. *Journal of Vocational Behavior, 45,* 270–94.

Netemeyer, R. G., Johnston, M. W., and Burton, S. (1990). Analysis of role conflict and role ambiguity in a structural equations framework. *Journal of Applied Psychology, 75,* 148–57.

Office of National Statistics. (1996). Full-time and part-time workers. *Labour Force Quarterly Bulletin, 18,* 8–9.

Oldham, G. R., and Fried, Y. (1987). Employee reactions to workspace characteristics. *Journal of Applied Psychology, 72,* 75–80.

Organ, D. W., and Ryan, K. (1995). A meta-analytic review of attitudinal and dispositional predictors of organizational citizenship behavior. *Personnel Psychology, 48,* 775–802.

Ostroff, C. (1992). The relationship between satisfaction, attitudes, and performance: An organizational level analysis. *Journal of Applied Psychology, 77,* 963–74.

Parasuraman, S., Purohit, Y. S., and Godshalk, V. M. (1996). Work and family variables, entrepreneurial career success, and psychological well-being. *Journal of Vocational Behavior, 48,* 275–300.

Petty, M. M., McGee, G. W., and Cavender, J. W. (1984). A meta-analysis of the relationship between individual job satisfaction and individual performance. *Academy of Management Review, 9,* 712–21.

Piltch, C. A., Walsh, D. C., Mangione, T. W., and Jennings, S. E. (1994). Gender, work, and mental distress in an industrial labor force. In G. P. Keita and J. J. Hurrell (Eds.), *Job stress in a changing work-force* (pp. 39–54). Washington, D.C.: American Psychological Association.

Piotrkowski, C. S. (1978). *Work and the family system.* New York: Free Press.

Podsakoff, P. M., MacKenzie, S. B., and Bommer, W. H. (1996). Meta-analysis of the relationships between Kerr and Jermier's substitutes for leadership and employee job attitudes, role perceptions, and performance. *Journal of Applied Psychology, 81,* 380–99.

Pugliesi, K. (1995). Work and well-being: Gender influences on the psychological consequences of employment. *Journal of Health and Social Behavior, 36,* 57–71.

Rice, R. W., Frone, M. R., and McFarlin, D. B. (1992). Work-nonwork conflict and the perceived quality of life. *Journal of Organizational Behavior, 13,* 155–68.

Robertson, A., Gilloran, A., McGlew, T., McKee, K., McInley, A., and Wight, D. (1995). Nurses' job satisfaction and the quality of care received by patients in psychogeriatric words. *International Journal of Geriatric Psychiatry, 10,* 575–84.

Roskies, E., Louis-Guerin, C., and Fournier, C. (1993). Coping with job insecurity: How does personality make a difference? *Journal of Organizational Behavior, 14,* 616–30.

Roxburgh, S. (1996). Gender differences in work and well-being: Effects of exposure and vulnerability. *Journal of Health and Social Behavior, 37,* 265–77.

Schaubroeck, J., Ganster, D. C., and Fox, M. L. (1992). Dispositional affect and work-related stress. *Journal of Applied Psychology, 77,* 322–35.

Schaubroeck, J., Ganster, D. C., and Kemmerer, B. (1996). Does trait affect promote job attitude stability? *Journal of Organizational Behavior, 17,* 191–96.

Scheier, M. F., and Carver, C. S. (1985). Optimism, coping, and health: Assessment and implications of generalized outcome expectancies. *Health Psychology, 4,* 219–47.

Schonfeld, I. S. (1996). Relation of negative affectivity to self-reports of job stressors and psychological outcomes. *Journal of Occupational Health Psychology, 1,* 397–412.

Sevastos, P., Smith, L., and Cordery, J. L. (1992). Evidence on the reliability and construct validity of Warr's (1990) well-being and mental health measures. *Journal of Occupational and Organizational Psychology, 65,* 33–49.

Shore, L. M., and Martin, H. J. (1989). Job satisfaction and organizational commitment in relation to work performance and turnover intentions. *Human Relations, 42,* 625–38.

Smith, C. A., Organ, D. W., and Near, J. P. (1983). Organizational citizenship behavior: Its nature and antecedents. *Journal of Applied Psychology, 68,* 653–63.

Spector, P. E., Dwyer, D. J., and Jex, S. M. (1988). Relation of job stressors to affective, health, and performance outcomes: A comparison of multiple data sources. *Journal of Applied Psychology, 73,* 11–19.

Spector, P. E., and Jex, S. M. (1991). Relations of job characteristics from multiple data sources with employee affect, absence, turnover intentions, and health. *Journal of Applied Psychology, 76,* 46–53.

Spector, P. E., and O'Connell, B. J. (1994). The contribution of personality traits, negative affectivity, locus of control and Type A to the subsequent reports of job stressors and job strains. *Journal of Occupational and Organizational Psychology, 67,* 1–11.

Staw, B. M., and Ross, J. (1985). Stability in the midst of change: A dispositional approach to job attitudes. *Journal of Applied Psychology, 70,* 469–80.

Steiner, D. D., and Truxillo, D. M. (1989). An improved test of the disaggregation hypothesis of job and life satisfaction. *Journal of Occupational Psychology, 62,* 33–39.

Szalai, A. (Ed.). (1972). *The use of time: Daily activities of urban and suburban populations in twelve countries.* The Hague: Mouton.

Tait, M., Padgett, M. Y., and Baldwin, T. T. (1989). Job and life satisfaction: A re-evaluation of the strength of the relationship and gender effects as a function of the date of the study. *Journal of Applied Psychology, 74,* 502–7.

Tharenou, P. (1993). A test of reciprocal causality for absenteeism. *Journal of Organizational Behavior, 14,* 193–210.

Thayer, R. E. (1989). *The biopsychology of mood and arousal.* Oxford: Oxford University Press.

Thomas, L. T., and Ganster, D. C. (1995). Impact of family–supportive work variables on work-family conflict and strain: A control perspective. *Journal of Applied Psychology, 80,* 6–15.

Thompson, C. A., Kopelman, R. E., and Schriesheim, C. A. (1992). Putting all one's eggs in the same basket: A comparison of commitment and satisfaction among self- and organizationally employed men. *Journal of Applied Psychology, 77,* 738–43.

Wall, T. D., Jackson, P. R., Mullarkey, S., and Parker, S. K. (1996). The demands-control model of job strain: A more specific test. *Journal of Occupational and Organizational Psychology, 69,* 153–66.

Warr, P. B. (1987). *Work, unemployment, and mental health.* Oxford: Oxford University Press.

———. (1990a). Decision latitude, job demands, and employee well-being. *Work and Stress, 4,* 285–94.

———. (1990b). The measurement of well-being and other aspects of mental health. *Journal of Occupational Psychology, 63,* 193–210.

———. (1992). Age and occupational well-being. *Psychology and Aging, 7,* 37–45.

———. (1994). A conceptual framework for the study of work and mental health. *Work and Stress, 8,* 84–97.

———. (1997). Age, work, and mental health. In K. W. Schaie and C. Schooler (Eds.), *The impact of work on older individuals* (pp. 252–96). New York: Springer-Verlag.

Warr, P. B., Barter, J., and Brownbridge, G. (1983). On the independence of positive and negative well-being. *Journal of Personality and Social Psychology, 44,* 644–51.

Watson, D., and Clark, L. A. (1984). Negative affectivity: The disposition to experience aversive emotional states. *Psychological Bulletin, 96,* 465–90.

———. (1992). On traits and temperament: General and specific factors of emotional experience and their relation to the five-factor model. *Journal of Personality, 60,* 441–76.

Watson, D., Clark, L. A., and Tellegen, A. (1988). Development and validation of brief measures of positive and negative affect: The PANAS scales. *Journal of Personality and Social Psychology, 54,* 1063–70.

Watson, D., and Pennebaker, J. W. (1989). Health complaints, stress, and distress: Exploring the central role of negative affectivity. *Psychological Review, 96,* 234–54.

Watson, D., and Slack, A. K. (1993). General factors of affective temperament and their relation to job satisfaction over time. *Organizational Behavior and Human Decision Process, 54,* 181–202.

Watson, D., and Walker, L. M. (1996). The long-term stability and predictive validity of trait measures of affect. *Journal of Personality and Social Psychology, 70,* 567–77.

Weaver, C. N. (1980). Job satisfaction in the United States in the 1970s. *Journal of Applied Psychology, 65,* 364–67.

Williams, L. J., Gavin, M. B., and Williams, M. L. (1996). Measurement and non-measurement processes with negative affectivity and employee attitudes. *Journal of Applied Psychology, 81,* 88–101.

Xie, J. L., and Johns, G. (1995). Job scope and stress: Can job scope be too high? *Academy of Management Journal, 38,* 1288–1309.

Zaccaro, S. J., and Stone, E. F. (1988). Incremental validity of an empirically based measure of job characteristics. *Journal of Applied Psychology, 73,* 245–52.

21 The Measurement of Welfare and Well-Being: The Leyden Approach

Bernard M. S. van Praag and Paul Frijters

This chapter focuses on the measurement of individual welfare derived from income, known as the Leyden approach. The approach, initiated by van Praag (1971), is one of the few attempts to measure welfare that has been developed within the economic discipline. The method is based on the Income Evaluation Question, which is intended to get an idea of the individual's norms on income: respondents are asked what they consider to be a "good" income and a "bad" income. The answers to these questions may be used to get an insight into the effects of family size and climate on individual welfare. The influence of past incomes and anticipated incomes on current welfare is also considered. The method is generalized toward the measurement of other norms. We also consider how a social standard may be derived from individual norms. Finally, we address the question of how welfare is related to well-being. By measuring both concepts, it can be shown that they are different. The combination of both measures makes it possible to distinguish between the monetary costs and the nonmonetary benefits of choices, such as having children.

THE UTILITY CONCEPT is a key concept in economics. It is well known that modern economics is a discipline with numerous subfields, but nearly all relevant problems have to do with people and people's choice behavior. Individuals have limited resources and opportunities and therefore must choose between alternatives. An efficient way to describe the choice problem is to attach a *utility value* to these alternatives, for example, U_1, U_2, $U_3, \ldots, U_i, \ldots$ and to postulate that an individual chooses the alternative that has the highest utility value for him. For example, if there is a choice set $\{1,2,3, \ldots i, \ldots\}$, then the choice behavior is described mathematically by

$$\max_{i = 1,2,3, \ldots} U_i$$

The implication of this description is that we could predict the individual's choice behavior by knowing his utility values U_1, U_2, $U_3. \ldots$. In empirical reality, it is the other way around. We do not know the values of U, but we can observe the choice process. If an individual consistently chooses alternative 1, economists generally infer that U_1 is larger than U_2, $U_3. \ldots$. If we then remove alternative 1 from the choice set and 2 is chosen consistently, we know that $U_1 > U_2$ and that U_2 is larger than other U values. In this way, it is possible to find the preference ordering of the alternatives and also to establish inequality relations between the U values. However, we are unable to say whether U_2 is a *little* smaller than U_1 or if U_2 is *much* smaller than U_1. In short, by observing choices we get an *ordinal* utility ordering.

The choice model may be extended in two ways. First, we can consider a set of alternatives that is infinite. Alternatives can be described by a continuous variable x or by more than one variable, for example, $(x_1, x_2, \ldots x_n) = \mathbf{x}$. Then the utility values are denoted by the ordinal utility function $U(\mathbf{x})$. Second, we may assume that each decision maker z has his own utility ordering. In that case, the ordinal utility function reads $U(\mathbf{x}; z)$ where z may incorporate individually varying parameters such as age, gender, income, social class, and so on. We notice that this ordinal function is of the *decision utility* type in the terminology of Kahneman, Wakker, and Sarin (1997). It is needed to make decisions and is empirically established by observations of choice decisions.[1]

The traditional example of choice behavior in economics is the *purchasing* behavior of consumers. The model starts from a utility function

$$U(x; z)$$

where x stands for quantities of commodities purchased and z for characteristics describing the individual's circumstances (for example, age, gender). The consumer is faced by prices $p_1, \ldots p_n$

for goods x_1 to x_n. If he has income y, his choice set is described by:

$$p_1 x_1 + \ldots + p_n x_n \leq y$$

Any commodity bundle $(x_1, x_2, \ldots x_n)$ violating the constraint is too expensive for him. The behavioral model explains behavior by assuming that individuals maximize $U(.;z)$ with respect to the feasible commodity bundle x subject to the freedom given by the choice set.

Edgeworth (1881) called $U(.)$ the utility function; Pareto (1904) called it the ophelimity function. Edgeworth more or less implicitly assumed that U could be measured in a direct way. Samuelson (1945) therefore stated that "Edgeworth considered utility to be as real as his morning jam" (206). Edgeworth interpreted U as *experienced utility*, that is, a cardinal measure of the joy that the individual derives from the commodity bundle. Pareto became aware of the fact that it could be difficult to establish the individual's utility function over goods. For the description of the consumer choice process, an *experienced utility* function appeared to be unnecessary. Actually, it is a choice between alternatives that can be described by an *ordinal* utility function, as described earlier. If $U(.)$ is an ordinal utility function, any other utility function that assigns the *same ordering* of utility to the alternatives is also a utility function describing that same choice process. For example, if $U_1 > U_2 > U_3 > 0$ describes the choice process between alternatives and 1, 2, 3, then $\bar{U}_1 = \sqrt{U_1} > \bar{U}_2 = \sqrt{U_2} > \bar{U}_3 = \sqrt{U_3}$ will describe the same process. Hence, there is a whole equivalence class of *ordinal* utility functions describing the same preference structure.

It is an error to assume that Pareto denied the existence of meaningful cardinal utility measurement or the possibility of measuring it, but he pointed to the fact that utility in the cardinal sense could not be measured by observing consumer behavior, and moreover that it was unnecessary to do so for consumer studies.

Robbins (1932), who had a tremendous influence on economics, was the first to proclaim that utility was immeasurable and that it was more or less a scientific folly to endeavor to measure it. At the very least, it should be left to psychologists.

Other economists, such as Pigou (1948) and the Nobel laureates Tinbergen (1991) and Frisch (1932), have certainly been of a different opinion.

However, the ordinal line has been continued by Arrow (1951) and Debreu (1959), who were able to include decisions over time and/or under uncertainty in this ordinal framework. They assumed a preference ranking described by a utility function on the dated commodity space. Behavior is subject to a budget constraint where the consumption of goods and the prices of those goods are differentiated according to the date of consumption.

Similarly, they incorporated uncertainty by distinguishing states of nature s varying over S and commodities available only if s prevails. Commodities are then available *contingent* on the status of nature, which is a priori not known to an individual. It can be shown that the model describes consumer choice behavior, but it is also clear that this model leads to a decision problem with an unworkable number of dimensions. Its realism as a positive behavioral model is not significant, and it has never been used, according to our knowledge, in empirical work, except in very simplified versions.

In practice, economists are frequently confronted by problems where more is needed than the ordinal concept (see also Ng 1997).

One such problem concerns decision-making under *uncertainty,* which is the basis for insurance theory, investment and saving behavior. Also, decisions that have to do with different *time* periods, such as saving and investment decisions, need more than the ordinal concept. The objective function in such models is usually simplified to an additive form such as $\Sigma_t w_t U_t$ or $\Sigma p_s U_s$ where U_t stands for *instantaneous* period utilities and w_t for time-discounting weights, and where U_s stands for state-contingent utility and p_s for the (real or perceived) chance that state s occurs. Evidently, time-state mixtures and continuous generalizations are easy to think of.

There are two points of interest in these objective functions. The basic ingredient is a utility function U that is no longer ordinal. We cannot change the individual form at will according to a monotonous transformation. More specifically, maximizing $\Sigma_t w_t \varphi(U_t)$ will yield an optimum that varies with $\varphi(.)$, except if φ is a positive linear transformation (that is, $\varphi(.) = \alpha U + \beta$ with $\alpha > 0$). The utility concept in these kinds of problems is what economists call a *cardinal* utility function. It is a much smaller class that allows only for positive linear transformations.

Most mainstream economists have a very uneasy feeling about cardinal utility functions. This uneasiness seems to be based on the Anglo-American dogmatism against cardinality instilled by Robbins. However, most actual studies conducted by economists start with very general "ordinal formulations" but after a while present a structural specification that nine times out of ten turns out to be of the cardinal type (see also van Praag 1968). These cardinal utility functions are still of the decision utility type. They are instrumental to the description of *decision* processes.

There is a second class of problems for which economists need cardinal utility functions: normative problems. The first example of such problems arises if we try to look for optimal (re)distributions. Notably in income taxation, a progressive tax schedule (richer individuals pay relatively more tax than poorer individuals) is advocated so that the rich man suffers as much as the poor man. Such comparisons are impossible without a cardinal and interpersonally comparable utility function. Obviously, these utility functions are of the *experienced* utility type.

A second example is provided by equity measures: the concepts of a just income distribution and poverty and the evaluation of income inequality. It is evident that nearly all of these measures are based on a cardinal concept of experienced income utility, though this is rarely mentioned explicitly (compare, Atkinson 1970).

A third field where interpersonally comparable and cardinal utility is needed concerns all types of cost-benefit analyses, in which specific measures, such as building a bridge, deregulating markets, establishing a health insurance program, or controlling noise pollution by an airport, have to be evaluated. In these cases, some citizens will profit and others will lose. Those benefits and costs may be partially translated in monetary amounts, but money means different things for different people. For example, when a policy means a loss of $100 to a poor man and a gain of $10,000 to a rich man, it is not at all evident that the policy should be realized. The only way to make a decision is to create a balance in terms of comparable utility gains and losses.

The situation in economics is succinctly and wittily summarized by Wansbeek and Kapteyn (1983):

> Utility seems to be to economists what the Lord is to theologians. Economists talk about utility all the time, but do not seem to have hope of ever observing it this side of heaven. In micro-economic theory, almost every model is built on utility functions of some kind. In empirical work little attempt is made to measure this all-pervasive concept. The concept is considered to be so esoteric as to defy direct measurement by mortals. Still, in a different role, viz., of non-economists, the same mortals are the sole possessors of utility functions and can do incredible things with it. (249)

By detaching economics from the psychology of "feelings," economists have found it difficult to have anything relevant to say on a whole range of issues. In the next section of this chapter, we review an attempt made by economists to measure utility functions using the evaluations given by individuals themselves. Before we do so, however, we first discuss the approaches taken in general to utility function in the economic literature. We divide the approaches that have been taken concerning the problem of utility functions into five distinct approaches.

GENERAL APPROACHES TO CARDINAL UTILITY TAKEN BY ECONOMISTS

The first approach to cardinal utility, which is by far the most popular in the economic profession, is not to measure utility at all but to simply assume a functional form of the utility function for the theoretical or empirical problem at hand. We ignore this approach in the remainder of this chapter.

Economists who use the second approach, of whom perhaps the best known are Christensen, Jorgenson, and Lau (1975) and Jorgenson and Slesnick (1984), have taken an axiomatic approach to utility functions. They specify the conditions they believe a utility function should satisfy and then derive (a shape of) the utility function that fits these requirements.[2] After inferring the level of utility that individuals enjoy from their observed behavior, they use it to make normative statements. This approach is not elaborated here because utility levels are not directly measured but essentially assumed. Moreover, if this method has validity, it yields a cardinal decision utility.

Economists who take the third approach use subjective and objective indicators of the work and living conditions of individuals to define a measure of utility. This large group is subdivided into three groups: one group is concerned with poor individuals, another with the quality of life of nations, another with the quality of life of individuals.

The empirical literature on poverty centers on the material resources available to individuals (Townsend 1979, 1993; Sen 1987; Ravallion 1994). The standard approach is to define households as poor if their household income falls below a certain cutoff point. This cutoff point can be defined in several ways. For instance, in the "basic needs" approach, the cutoff point is calculated from the expenditures needed to buy a basket of commodities that the researcher considers vital for individuals. In the "relative needs" approach, the cutoff point is defined as a certain percentage of the average or median income in a country. It is clear that neither approach, which together form the bulk of the poverty literature, actually measures utility functions, but that they are based on the *assumption* that the utility of individuals whose income is below the cutoff point is in some sense "low." Callan and Nolan (1991) and Frijters and van Praag (1995) provide a more detailed review of the normative issues involved in poverty measurement.

Other literature examines the "quality of life" of nations. In this literature (Kurian 1984; Maasoumi 1989; Nussbaum and Sen 1992; Sen 1987), economics attempt to rank countries with respect to the quality of life.[3] The quality of life is usually defined as a weighted average of specific country statistics. The statistics used include, for instance, the literacy level of the entire population, the literacy level of women, infant mortality rates, income levels per head, life expectancies of men and women, indicators of political stability, energy consumption per capita, average household size, the number of persons per physician, levels of civil liberties, and so on. It is clear that these variables may be very important for the utility levels of individuals and nations; however, the utility levels themselves are *not* measured by these variables. An obvious problem is then, how should these statistics be weighted? Does the quality of life increase more when the female literacy level increases by 1 percent or when the civil liberty index improves by 1 percent? It is clear that if one does not want to use the evaluations of individuals themselves as a weighting method, the opinions of the researcher become the deciding criterion. The problem of how to weight these different variables into a composite quality-of-life index is, not surprisingly, the main source of dispute in this literature. For an empirical analysis of some of the weighting methods employed, see Hirschberg, Maasoumi, and Slottje (1991).

Some of the works of Clark and Oswald also belong to the third category. In their 1994 paper, Clark and Oswald define "unhappiness" by aggregating the answers to the following twelve questions:

1. Have you been able to concentrate on whatever you are doing?

2. . . . lost much sleep over worry?
3. . . . felt that you are playing a useful part in things?
4. . . . felt capable of making decisions about things?
5. . . . felt constantly under strain?
6. . . . felt you couldn't overcome your difficulties?
7. . . . been able to enjoy your normal day-to-day activities?
8. . . . been able to face your problems?
9. . . . been feeling unhappy and depressed?
10. . . . been losing confidence in yourself?
11. . . . been thinking of yourself as a worthless person?
12. . . . been feeling reasonably happy, all things considered?

The variable "unhappiness" ranges from 0 to 12, with 12 denoting the maximum level of unhappiness and 0 a complete lack of unhappiness. Although some of these questions could arguably be seen as a measure of utility, such as questions 9 and 12, the simple aggregate of all twelve questions cannot be seen as a direct measurement of utility: utility is an evaluation of an individual of his circumstances. Although "losing a lot of sleep" or "being under strain" may either affect utility or be affected *by* utility, these factors do not directly measure a utility level for they are not an evaluation of "losing sleep" or "being under strain." This measure of happiness may correlate perfectly with the experienced utility of individuals and may hence be as useful as any other measure of experienced utility. Nevertheless, it remains an *indirect* measure of experienced utility that is useful only if "losing sleep" and "being under strain" correlate with experienced utility (which seems very likely). Hence, it is a measure of the quality of life entirely on its own. Clark and Oswald (1994) seem to acknowledge this by arguing that the individual scores are "more accurately" described as "mental stress" scores. Other individual measures of an individual's quality of life that are based on aggregations of individual circumstances also fall into this category.

A fourth approach is to estimate decision utility functions by performing probability-choice experiments on individuals: When individuals must choose between either a certain outcome Y or a lottery in which fate decides whether they will receive an outcome less than Y or an outcome greater than Y, individuals will reveal the relative attractiveness of the sure Y versus the proposed lottery. The main problem is this line of research has been that individuals are not good at using probabilities: they overestimate small probabilities and underestimate large probabilities, as was first demonstrated by the Allais paradox (see Allais and

FIGURE 21.1   A Value Function of Income

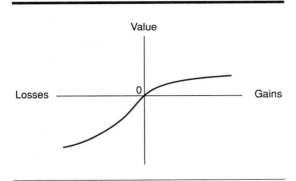

Hagen 1979). This means that an individual's choice of a lottery is the result of a combination of the individual's valuation of the outcomes and his or her perception of the probability of the outcomes. Following the theoretical advances by Kahneman and Tversky (1979) and Wakker and Tversky (1993), Kahneman, Knetsch, and Thaler (1991) have managed to isolate the effect of gains and losses on the individual's evaluation of outcomes. We will ignore the results on probabilities and focus on the value function they find. The shape of the value function suggested by the choice experiments of Kahneman and his colleagues (1991) is sketched in figure 21.1.

The main feature of this function is that losses are found to have a greater impact than gains. A second characteristic of this value function, leveling off at either end of the loss or gain scale, implies decreasing marginal value of losses and gains, as well as a convex-concave shape (also suggested by Markowitz [1952] and van Praag [1968]).

Finally, the fifth approach, initiated by the Leyden group, is to assume that individuals are able to describe their utility level by means of *verbal* qualifications. The rest of this chapter will be devoted to discussing the efforts of economists who belong to this group. There are other economists, of course, who use verbal qualifiers as measures of experienced utility (for example, Clark 1996; Clark and Oswald 1996; Dow and Juster 1985; Easterlin 1974; Heywood, Siebert, and Wei 1997; Levy-Garboua and Montmarquette 1997; and Gershuny and Halpin 1995).

UTILITY MEASUREMENT BASED ON VERBAL QUALIFIERS: THE LEYDEN APPROACH

In this section, we discuss an economic line of research that tries to operationalize the concept of experienced utility. It originated at Leyden University in the Netherlands in the early 1970s. Its main contributors are Bernard van Praag, Ari Kapteyn, Paul Wansbeek, Aldi Hagenaars, Edwin Van der Sar, Erik Plug, and Paul Frijters. It is known in the literature as the Leyden approach (or school). For psychologists, the ideas in this approach may not appear alien, but for most economists they were and still are. Most economists still believe that cardinal experienced utility is unmeasurable and that any measurement should be based on observed decision behavior. Consequently, the Leyden approach has met with stiff opposition, disbelief, and outright hostility. The most outspoken example of this attitude is found in an article by Seidl (1994) in the *European Economic Review* in which he criticizes van Praag (1968).[4]

Although van Praag (1968) served as a theoretical basis, the ensuing literature on the Leyden approach started with van Praag (1971) and is mainly empirical and data-oriented. The Leyden approach focuses primarily on the evaluation of *income*, although in later work the focus was extended. We also speak of utility of income, income satisfaction, or, in other words, economic *welfare*. We drop the adjective "economic" from now on, but when we use the term "welfare," we have welfare derived from income in mind. This concept is narrower than the concept of well-being that includes feelings associated with factors unconnected to income or purchasing power. Later we shall consider well-being and its relationship with welfare in greater detail.

The Leyden approach is based on two assumptions. The first is that individuals are able to evaluate income levels in general, and their own income in particular, in terms of "good," "bad," "sufficient," and so on. We call these terms *verbal qualifiers*. The second assumption is that verbal labels can be translated in a meaningful way into a numerical evaluation on a bounded scale, for example [0,1]. We shall consider both steps of the measurement procedure in detail.

If we are interested in how a specific income level is evaluated, there are two ways to gather information. The first and most natural way is to propose a sequence of income levels and to ask for their verbal qualifications. An example of this type of question follows:

Here is a list of income levels per month, after tax: please evaluate these amounts using verbal qualifications, such as "very bad," "bad," "insufficient," "sufficient," "good," "very good":

$2,000
$4,000
$6,000
$8,000
$10,000

It is obvious that someone who earns $20,000 a month would be unable to make a distinction between most of these levels. All the incomes are insufficient or worse for him. Therefore, instead of staring with income levels, we can also supply the verbal qualifications as *stimuli* and ask the respondent which income level corresponds with the verbal label. This leads to the so-called Income Evaluation Question (IEQ):

While keeping prices constant, what after-tax total monthly income would you consider for your family to be:

very bad _____	$_____
bad _____	$_____
sufficient _____	$_____
insufficient _____	$_____
good _____	$_____
very good _____	$_____

This question appears to have been successful in anonymous mail-questionnaires, although it has also been posed orally with success. Theoretically, finding a continuous relationship between income and utility would require an infinite number of levels, but in practice between four and nine levels have been and can be used. We discuss here the format used most often, the six-level format.

The question is now, how do we derive a welfare function from the answers to this question? Or more precisely, how do we translate the verbal labels into numbers on a [0,1] scale? Following van Praag (1971), we make an assumption about the way individuals answer the question. We assume that respondents try to provide information to the interviewer about the shape of their welfare function. The most accurate way for individuals to provide information then depends on the accuracy criterion. Van Praag (1971) and Kapteyn (1977) show that, for a broad class of intuitively plausible criterion functions, the best way for a respondent to provide information is to choose the answers in such a way that each of the six levels corresponds to a jump of $1/6$. This is the so-called Equal Quantile Assumption (EQA). It implies that

$$U \text{ (very bad)} = U \text{ (first interval)} = 1/12$$
$$U \text{ (bad)} = U \text{ (second interval)} = 3/12$$

. . .
. . .
$$U \text{ (very good)} = U \text{ (last interval)} = 11/12$$

It may be surmised that, even if the verbal descriptions are somewhat vague, the respondent will tend to interpret the question as if it were an equal partition. Only if the verbal labels are ambiguous, are practically equal, or strongly suggest an unequal partition should we no longer expect this effect.

If the number of verbal labels is k, the general formula for the welfare corresponding to the ith verbal label is obviously $\frac{2i-1}{2k}$. This reasoning and the EQA assumption are very similar to the thesis developed by Parducci (see, for example, Parducci 1995). It is obvious that this translation of verbal labels into numbers is a linch pin in this measurement procedure. Although it has been subject to criticism by some economists, experimental psychologists do not find much to criticize: it is a type of Thurstonian measurement. If we do not accept this or any translation into figures, it is obvious that a meaningful analysis of the response is severely hampered, although not impossible (see later discussion).

In van Praag (1991), an experiment is described in which five labels were supplied and 364 respondents were asked to "translate" these verbal labels into a [0,100]-scale. Similarly, the same labels had to be linked with line segments. Both the numbers between [0,100] and the lengths of the line segments were re-scaled onto a [0,1] mapping. We present the average results for 364 respondents in table 21.1.

TABLE 21.1   Translation into Numbers and Line Segments

Numbers	Empirical Mean	Standard Deviation	Theoretical Prediction
Very bad	$\bar{v}_1 = 0.0892$	0.0927	0.1
Bad	$\bar{v}_2 = 0.2013$	0.1234	0.3
Not bad, not good	$\bar{v}_3 = 0.4719$	0.1117	0.5
Good	$\bar{v}_4 = 0.6682$	0.1169	0.7
Very good	$\bar{v}_5 = 0.8655$	0.0941	0.9
Line segments			
Very bad	$\bar{w}_1 = 0.0734$	0.0556	0.1
Bad	$\bar{w}_2 = 0.1799$	0.0934	0.3
Not good, not bad	$\bar{w}_3 = 0.4008$	0.1056	0.5
Good	$\bar{w}_4 = 0.5980$	0.1158	0.7
Very Good	$\bar{w}_5 = 0.8230$	0.1195	0.9

Source: van Praag (1991).

For the "numbers" case, one can see that all averages fall within a one σ–interval of their theoretical prediction. This also holds for all levels for the line segments, except one. It is intriguing that the averages are all *below* their theoretical prediction. Perhaps this is due to the order in which the verbal labels were supplied. We think, but do not know, that the bias would have been the other way around if the order in which the verbal labels were supplied was reversed. When we regress the translation of the verbal labels into numbers by individual i, say, $v_{i,n}$, onto the translation of the verbal label into a line segment, say, $w_{i,n}$, we find

$$v_{i,n} = 0.056 + 0.974 w_{i,n}$$
$$\quad\quad (0.005)\ (0.010)$$

$$R^2 = 0.848$$

for 364*5 observations, where we did not account for the fact that the five level disturbances per individual will be strongly correlated. The fit is, however, remarkably good. From table 21.1 and this regression, we can draw some tentative conclusions:

1. A verbal label sequence seems to be understood in a similar way by different respondents, irrespective of the context of the individual respondent.
2. A verbal label sequence may be translated on a numerical scale or on a line scale: in both cases the translations are uniform over individuals.
3. Translations via various translation mechanisms (lines and figures) are consistent with each other. That is, we seem to be measuring the same thing whether we use line segments or numbers.
4. The verbal labels are translated on a bounded scale roughly in accordance with the Equal Quantile Assumption.

An interesting point is that these results were found in a context-free setting, that is, the respondents did not know which concept they were evaluating.

A final point of critique is whether the verbal labels "good," "bad," and so on, convey the same feeling to every respondent. If not, we falsely assume that individuals derive the same degree of joy from their income when describing the same verbal label. Actually, this is a question of psycholinguistics. Generally, the basic idea of language is that frequently used words will have the same meaning and emotional connotation for the members of a language community. It is the main tool of communication between people. Hence, we must assume that verbal labels like "good," "bad,"

and so on, mean approximately the same thing to all respondents sharing the same language.

The Shape of the Welfare Function

For each respondent we now have six income levels connected to six utility levels. The shape of the function can be inferred from these six combinations. Many functions can be fitted using these six points. In van Praag (1968), it was argued on theoretical grounds that it would be a lognormal distribution function. We use a distribution function because we assume boundedness of the utility function: there is a worst and a best position in terms of welfare (satisfaction). It is also known that the Von Neumann–Morgenstern model requires a bounded utility function (see Savage 1954).

Van Herwaarden and Kapteyn (1981) showed that the points of the welfare function, which were found empirically, best fitted a lognormal curve within the class of distribution functions. The logarithmic function did slightly better, but it is not bounded. Also, the logarithmic function is not borne out by the choice experiments of Kahneman, Knetsch, and Thaler (1991) and others: the marginal effect of greater losses is found to decrease, whereas the logarithmic function would imply that they should increase.

The lognormal function is defined as

$$\Lambda\,(y;\,\mu,\,\sigma) = N\,(\ln y;\,\mu,\,\sigma)$$
$$= N\,(\frac{\ln y - \mu}{\sigma};\,0,\,1)$$

where $N\,(.;0,1)$ stands for the standard lognormal distribution function. The lognormal function is sketched in figure 21.2. Notice the resemblance to the shape suggested by the experiments of Kahne-

FIGURE 21.2 The Welfare Function of Income

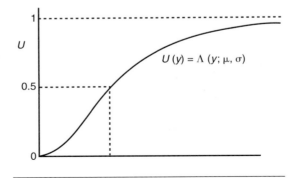

ian, Knetsch, and Thaler (1991): in both cases the function is S-shaped. Also, it is generally the case that losses to an individual have a greater effect than gains.[5]

The parameter μ is interpreted by realizing that $\Lambda\,(e^{\mu};\,\mu,\,\sigma) = 0.5$. Hence, the income level e^{μ} is halfway between the worst and the best situation.

There are two interesting aspects of this function. First, the function is not concave for all income levels, but convex for low incomes. This runs counter to mainstream economic assumptions. In economics, it is conventional wisdom that the utility function of income is always concave. This is known as the so-called Law of Decreasing Marginal Utility, also known as Gossen's first law. It has always been based on introspection. Concavity implies that individuals are risk-averse, but scientific experiments with insurance and gambling behavior show that this is not always true; it therefore follows that a utility function may be convex in certain regions.[6]

The second point of interest about the lognormal utility function consists of the two parameters μ and σ, which may *vary individually*. Two functions with different μ and equal σ are sketched in figure 21.3. In figure 21.4, two functions are sketched with different σ and equal μ.

One can see that as μ increases, the individual needs more income to reach the same welfare level. For instance, in order to reach the welfare level 0.5, person A with $\mu_A = \ln(4,000)$ needs $4,000 per month, while B needs $6,000 per month to reach the same welfare level. If the welfare levels of individuals A and B are to be equal for other welfare levels (if σ is equal for both persons), it should hold that

$$\ln y_A - \mu_A = \ln y_B - \mu_B$$

FIGURE 21.3   Welfare Function of Income with Different $\mu_A\ \mu_B$ (σ Constant)

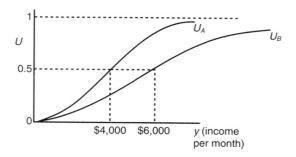

FIGURE 21.4   Welfare Function of Income with Different $\sigma_A\ \sigma_B$ (μ Constant)

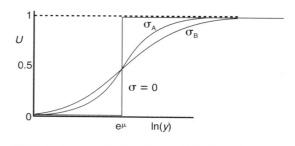

Hence, for any welfare level, income levels are equivalent to A and B if

$$\ln \frac{y_A}{y_B} = \mu_A - \mu_B$$

and therefore

$$\frac{y_A}{y_B} = e^{\mu_A - \mu_B} = \frac{4,000}{6,000}$$

Hence, a change in μ implies a proportional shift of the welfare function. One of our main preoccupations in the remaining section is to discover why individual's μ-values differ.

The parameter σ defines the slope of the welfare function.

In figure 21.4, two functions are sketched with $\sigma_A < \sigma_B$. If $\sigma = 0$, we get the limiting case where individuals are completely unsatisfied with any income until their income reaches e^{μ}, and where they are completely satisfied if income exceeds e^{μ}. It is the welfare function of a hermit. The parameter σ is called the *welfare sensitivity* of the individual.

The parameters μ and σ are estimated for each individual by

$$\hat{\mu} = \frac{1}{6} \Sigma \ln c_j \text{ and } \hat{\sigma} = \frac{1}{5} \Sigma (\ln c_j - \mu)^2$$

where $c_1, \ldots c_6$ stand for the six income levels reported in the IEQ.

The Definition of Income

In the usual IEQ version, the income concept is after-tax *monthly* household income. In some versions income *per year* has also been used and/or *before-tax* income (see Dubnoff, Vaughan, and Lancaster 1981). The choice of the definition should be adapted to what is well known to the individual. Hence, an entrepreneur who knows his annual income better than his monthly income should be questioned in terms of his annual income, while a civil servant who is paid monthly should be approached in terms of his monthly income.

THE EXPLANATION OF THE WELFARE FUNCTION

In mainstream literature, it is always assumed that the utility function of income is the same for all individuals. A major finding of our empirical research, although intuitively completely plausible, is that individual welfare functions differ between individuals. When differences are found, the imminent question is whether such differences are structural and can be correlated with observable variables. In our case, this means that we try to "explain" the variable μ by other factors, varying by individual and/or environment. In the studies, it appeared that μ could be explained to a large extent.[7] The parameter σ posed much more of a problem. We shall therefore concentrate on the explanation of μ and assume that σ is constant.

We recall that μ determines the position of $U(y)$. If μ increases, the individual becomes less satisfied with the same amount of income. In other words $U(y;\mu)$ is decreasing in μ. The first determinant that naturally comes to mind is the size of the family to be supported from the income. Income needs are probably also determined by the actual circumstances of the individual, for instance, as reflected by the individual's current income y_c. We therefore expect that needs will increase with family size (denoted by fs) and with current income y_c. Hence, fs and y_c are parameters in the individual welfare function. In van Praag (1971) and van Praag and Kapteyn (1973), the following simple relation has been found

$$\mu_i = \text{constant} + \beta_1 \ln fs_i + \beta_2 \ln y_{i,c}$$

In van Praag and Kapteyn (1973), the following (approximate values) were found: $\beta_1 = 0.1$ and $\beta_2 = 0.6$, $R^2 = 0.6$, where fs_i denotes the number of individuals living in the household of respondent i, and $y_{i,c}$ denotes the current household income of i.

Since then, the IEQ has been posed in many countries, and similar results have been found. We give an example drawn from a study on poverty by van Praag, Hagenaars, and Van Weeren (1982), based on a 1979 EUROSTAT survey of eight European countries. Moreover, we add values for

Russia estimated by Frijters and van Praag (1995). In table 21.2, we present the regression estimates for the nine countries using the equation

$$\mu_i = \beta_0 + \beta_1 \ln fs_i + \beta_2 \ln y_{i,c} + f(X_i) + u_i$$

where X denotes a number of variables used in the regression that we do not show (including age, education, employment levels, and gender), and u_i denotes the normally distributed error term. All coefficients are highly significant.

The variables vary over the nine countries, but not dramatically. The value of β_1, of course, depends on the national family allowance system. If the family allowance is high and compensates for the additional child costs, we may expect a β_1 of about zero. On the other hand, in poor countries with a less liberal system, β_1 may be rather high. This is indeed what we observe: the highest coefficient of β_1 is for Russia (in 1995), where family allowances and child support are virtually nonexistent.

It is not surprising that the satisfaction derived from a specific income level depends on the size of the household. Somewhat more surprising, especially for most economists, is that income satisfaction for any income level, not only for an individual's own current income, depends on an individual's own current income. It implies that two individuals A and B with current incomes $y_{A,c}$ and $y_{B,c}$ will evaluate any income differently. More precisely, the following is usually true:

$$U(y_B; fs, y_B) \neq U(y_B; fs, y_A)$$

That is, B evaluates his own income differently than A would evaluate the income of B. It is obvious that this fact is very relevant for the evaluation of social inequality, for the theory of a fair income distribution, and for the evaluation of social welfare. The outcomes of such normative eval-

TABLE 21.2   Estimates of Welfare Parameters for Nine Countries

	β_1	β_2	N	R^2
Belgium	0.097	0.433	1272	0.695
Denmark	0.075	0.631	1972	0.829
France	0.059	0.505	2052	0.676
West Germany	0.112	0.583	1574	0.693
Great Britain	0.115	0.364	1183	0.575
Ireland	0.169	0.455	1733	0.636
Italy	0.156	0.381	1911	0.510
The Netherlands	0.100	0.537	1933	0.664
Russia (1995)	0.250	0.501	1444	0.501

Source: van Praag, Hagenaars, and Van Weeren (1982).

uations depend on the income norm of the evaluations. Actually, U_A (y; fs_A, $y_{A,c}$) describes the norms of A with respect to what equals a "bad"/"good" income and all levels in between.

A person's income may increase, for example, from $y_c^{(1)}$ to $y_c^{(2)}$. The evaluation of this change will be evaluated *differently* before the change and after the change, or, as economists say, *ex ante* and *ex post*. The ex ante evaluation of future income is U_A ($y_c^{(2)}$; fs, $y_c^{(1)}$), while the ex post evaluation is U_A ($y_c^{(2)}$; fs, $y_c^{(2)}$). We sketch the difference between the ex ante and ex post welfare function in figure 21.5.

Due to the fact that μ increases with the income change, the welfare function shifts to the right. The effect of this is that the ex post evaluation of both $y_c^{(1)}$ and $y_c^{(2)}$ falls compared to the corresponding ex ante evaluations. It can be seen, and also shown, that the ex ante welfare gain is larger than the ex post gain. As a consequence, the ex ante evaluation is exaggerated when reconsidered later on, or to put it differently, the income increase will be a disappointment in retrospect. The value of the coefficient β_2 is crucial in this context. If $\beta_2 = 0$, the curve will not shift to the right and the whole income increase will be translated as a welfare increase. In that case, ex ante and ex post evaluations are equal.

On the other hand, if $\beta_2 = 1$, perceived welfare will not increase at all. This can be seen by examining

$$\ln y_c - \mu = \ln y_c - \beta_0 - \beta_1 \ln fs - 1.00$$
$$\ln y_c = - \beta_0 - \beta_1 \ln fs$$

In this case, the subjective ex post welfare evaluation does not depend on actual income. Evidently, this is a pathological case that has not been found in reality. The anticipated welfare increase would end with a complete deception.

The phenomenon of a shifting welfare function arising from a partial adaptation of income norms to changing current incomes is what Brickman and Campbell (1971) called the hedonic "treadmill." Van Praag (1971) introduced the term "preference drift" for the same phenomenon.

If all individuals have their own norms with regard to income levels, which depend on their own circumstances, it is justified to ask whether it is possible to construct *social standards* with respect to what is a "good" income, a "bad" income, and so on. This is possible in a certain sense. We define a social standard for a "good" income, say $\bar{y}_{good}$, as that level of income that is evaluated to be "good" by an individual with that current income. If "good" income corresponds with a welfare value of 0.7 on a [0,1] scale, it implies that $\bar{y}_{good}$ is the solution to the equation

$$U (\bar{y}_{good}; fs, \bar{y}_{good}) = 0.7$$

Using lognormality and our estimate of μ, it is possible to show that

$$U (\bar{y}_{good}; fs, \bar{y}_{good}) = \Lambda \bar{y}_{good};$$
$$\frac{\beta_0 + \beta_1 \ln fs}{1 - \beta_2}, \frac{\sigma}{1 - \beta_2})$$

Similarly, we can obtain a social standard income for each possible welfare level, sketched in figure 21.6.

We call the ensuing welfare function of the social standard income levels, which is also lognormal, a *social standard function*. We know that someone with $\bar{y}_{0.4}^*$ current income will evaluate his own income by 0.4. This analysis is frequently used to define a *subjective poverty* line as $\bar{y}_{0.4}^*$ for poverty and $\bar{y}_{0.5}^*$ as near-poverty. Notice that this line varies as a function of family size. Hence, there is a two-person household poverty line, a

FIGURE 21.6   The Social Standard Welfare Function

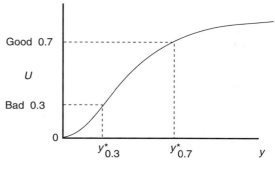

FIGURE 21.5   The Welfare Gain on Income Increase

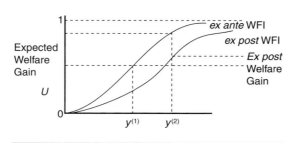

three-person poverty line, and so on. The social standard function is an obvious tool for social policy and the evaluation of income redistribution and tax policy.

From a social-psychological viewpoint, it is very interesting to compare the welfare sensitivity of the *individual* welfare function σ with the corresponding slope parameter of the social standard function $\frac{\sigma}{1 - \beta_2}$. If $0 < \beta_2 < 1$, the latter function is less steep than its individual counterpart. In other words, the larger the preference drift β_2, or in psychological terms, the stronger the working of the hedonic treadmill, the flatter the social standard curve will be compared to the individual welfare function.

Obviously, the difference between the two functions explains why a person with moderate income, for instance, $40,000 a year, thinks that someone with $100,000 is rich, while the rich person himself with $100,000 does not perceive himself to be rich. In the same way, people with $20,000 do not feel as poor as the observer earning $40,000 thinks they would.

The explanation of μ by individual variables and the stability of these explanations over samples (see also van Praag and Van der Sar 1988) may be seen as indirect evidence for the validity of the Welfare Function of Income (WFI). The measured concept may be explained to a certain extent by individual circumstances in a plausible way. One of the more recent additions is a quadratic part in age. It is seen that financial needs are greatest at the age of about forty.

However, the explanation of μ may be useful for *policy* purposes as well. If we find that the welfare derived from income depends on family size, this gives a natural clue to the question what *family allowance* would keep the family at the same household level if family size is increased from two to three by having a child. The welfare a household derives from income is

$$U_{ind} = \Lambda \, (y_{i,c}; \text{constant} + 0.1 \ln fs_i + 0.6 \ln y_{i,c}, \sigma)$$

In order to keep welfare constant if fs increases from 2 to 3, we should add $0.1 \ln (\frac{3}{2})$ to $\ln y_{i,c}$ or multiply $y_{i,c}$ by $(\frac{3}{2})^{0.1}$.

However, in the long run, this increase will not be enough to compensate the family for an increase in family size, as current income $y_{i,c}$ increases and hence μ. Therefore, we need a second increase of $0.1 \ln (\frac{3}{2}) * 0.6$, and so forth. The total increase necessary to compensate the household equals

$$0.1 \ln \left(\frac{3}{2} \right) [1 + 0.6 + 0.6^2 + \ldots]$$

$$= \frac{0.1 \ln (\frac{3}{2})}{1 - 0.6}$$

and this is precisely what the social standard welfare function would prescribe. Here we encounter a dynamic aspect, viz., that the individual welfare function is *anchored* on the individual's own current income. That is the meaning of preference drift. People adapt their norms to the present situation.

Parts of this analysis are also possible on the separate c_i levels without any reference to a cardinal utility function (see van Praag and Van der Sar 1988).

DYNAMICS

In the previous section, we described how the need parameter μ could be explained by variables such as family size and current income y_c. The latter effect is now refined by supposing that μ depends not only on *present* income but also on income in the past and income that is anticipated in the future. It follows that in the μ-equation we replace y_c by $\ldots y_{-2}, y_{-1}, y_0, \hat{y}_1, \hat{y}_2, \ldots$ whereby y_0 denotes current income, y_{-2}, y_{-1} denotes incomes one or two years in the past, and $\hat{y}_1$ stands for anticipated future income in one year's time. All experienced and anticipated incomes contribute to the formation of our present norm on incomes. In its simplest form, the μ-equation looks like

$$\mu_i = \beta_0 + \beta_1 \ln fs_i + \beta_2 \left(\sum_{t = -\infty}^{+\infty} w_t \ln y_{i,t} \right)$$

where i refers to respondent i.

The coefficients $\ldots w_{-2}, w_{-1}, w_0, w_1, w_2 \ldots$ are weights that add up to one, whereby the weight w_0 denotes the weight of the present income, and $w_p = \sum_{t=-\infty}^{-1} w_t$ and $w_f = \sum_{t=1}^{\infty} w_t$ denote the weight of all past incomes and anticipated future incomes, respectively. Van Praag and Van Weeren (1983, 1988) estimated the parameters of this model on Dutch panel data. The main question concerns how the distribution of time weights will look. They regressed θ_i on the incomes of the three years in which the panel was held. For the second wave they found

$$\mu_i = 3.04 + 0.10 \ln fs_i + 0.68(0.16 \ln y_{i,t-1}$$
$$+ 0.75 \ln y_{i,t} + 0.09 \ln y_{i,t+1})$$
$$\bar{R}^2 = 0.69$$
$$N = 645$$

where all coefficients are significant. The results tell us that current income has the greatest time weight, which implies that the time-weight distribution peaks near the present. Also, incomes in the past carry more time weight than incomes in the future, which suggests that on aggregate the time-weight distribution peaks just before the present. Of course, this is an aggregate relationship that will differ for individuals of different ages and education profiles. For a more complete analysis, more incomes than the three available were needed. Therefore, van Praag and Van Weeren (1988) used econometric techniques to *estimate* the incomes that were further back than one year (. . . y_{-3}, y_{-2}). They also estimated incomes further than one year in the future (y_2, y_3 . . .). With the use of this complete income stream, they looked somewhat further at the shape of the time-weight distribution.[8] In general, they found the time-weight distribution to have the shape of a normal curve. More specifically, the time-weight distribution may be characterized by a mode parameter, μ_τ, and a dispersion parameter, σ_τ. The empirically estimated shapes of the time-weight distribution are presented in figure 21.7 for three age brackets: thirty, fifty, and seventy.

The most interesting points are that:

- The time-weight distribution varies for different ages.
- The distribution is not symmetric around the present.
- The time weights of the past are greatest for young and old people.
- The middle-aged bracket derives its norm mostly from the present and the anticipated future.

FIGURE 21.7   Time-Discounting Density Functions for Various Ages

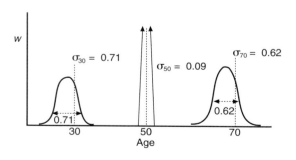

- The dispersion of the distribution varies considerably over different ages. In midlife, the time weights are extremely concentrated.

The mode and symmetry point of the time-weight distribution is at μ_τ. We call it the *time focus* of the individual. It shifts from more than one year in the past (-1.3), at twenty, to almost half a year in the future (0.45), at fifty, while it shifts back to the past (-0.43) for the age of seventy.

The change of σ_τ is also interesting. We call σ_τ the *time span* of the individual. It is rather long for young individuals and shortens when people approach midlife. The time span is intimately related to the *velocity of time* as it is perceived by the individual. The midlife has a narrow time horizon, which implies that the individual lives "day by day." The velocity of middle-aged time is high. For young and old people, the time horizon is wider, and hence the velocity of time is lower. We call the reciprocal of σ_τ, that is, $\frac{1}{\sigma_\tau}$, the *subjective velocity of time*.

In table 21.3, we present the relevant figures for several age classes. It is seen that the subjective velocity of time $\frac{1}{\sigma_\tau}$ increases by a factor $\frac{1.44}{0.09} \approx 15$ up to midlife, and then falls by a factor 6 at age seventy, and still more at later ages.

The time-weight distribution is clearly important for individuals because it determines the speed of adaptation of the income norms of the individual when faced with changing circumstances. This may be the case for individuals who become jobless and then become dependent on social benefits. The adaptation process may be a reason to smooth the path of the income reduction over time, in order to smooth the decline in welfare.

Another potential application is to evaluate the impact of inflation and accelerating inflation on the income norms and the satisfaction level derived from income. These applications are discussed in greater detail in van Praag and Van Weeren (1988).

TABLE 21.3   Values of μ_τ, σ_τ, w_P, w_O, w_F

Age	μ_τ	σ_τ	w_P	w_O	w_F
20	-1.32	1.44	0.72	0.18	0.10
30	-0.32	0.71	0.40	0.48	0.12
40	0.27	0.26	0.00	0.81	0.19
50	0.45	0.09	0.00	0.70	0.30
60	0.22	0.21	0.00	0.91	0.09
70	-0.43	0.62	0.46	0.48	0.07

The research on the time-weight distribution has not been repeated since 1988. Therefore, this must be seen as a first attempt and the results have to be considered with care. It may be that other models would yield other results. This method of obtaining time weights is based on a simple household survey and is very cheap compared to experimental laboratory experiments.

The estimates of time weights are exclusively based on the analysis of income norms. The memory and anticipation weights from norms on other subjects—for instance, on fashion, housing, or ethics—may be determined by other variables and have different time-weight distributions. There is a great need for more research in this area and for cooperation with psychologists.

METHODOLOGICAL DISCUSSION

The approach outlined above for measuring individual norms on income has been expanded to other aspects such as age and education by van Praag, Dubnoff, and Van der Sar (1988). More specifically, individuals were asked to connect age levels to subjective labels in the following Age Evaluation Question (AEQ):

When I think of other adults, I consider people to be

. . . *young*, if they are younger than _____ years old
. . . *somewhat young*, if they are about __ years old
. . . *middle aged*, if they are about _____ years old
. . . *somewhat old*, if they are about _____ years old
. . . *old*, if they are older than _____ years old

Similar to the analysis of the IEQ, it is possible to analyze the age norms of respondents, for ex-

ample, by explaining the answers by means of regression analysis. In van Praag, Dubnoff, and Van der Sar (1988), this is done level by level for the Boston data set. Letting a_i ($i = 1 \ldots 5$) be the respondents' age levels, they consider the equation

$$\ln a_i = \alpha_{0,i} + \alpha_{1,i} \ln age + \alpha_{2,i} \ln schooling + \alpha_{3,i} \ln fs + \alpha_{4,i} D_{gender}$$

where they assume that what is considered "young" or "old" depends on the age of the respondent, the number of years of schooling, the size of the family, and the gender of the respondent. The results of the regressions are presented in table 21.4.

From a statistical point of view, most coefficients are significant and follow a definite pattern. Our evaluation is that there is a strong systematic pattern that indicates that there is no confusion in connotation. The fraction of the variance explained, as measured by R^2, is poor in comparison to that of the IEQ but is certainly not below standard for samples of microdata of this size (≈ 500). However, it implies that there are more individual factors that were not covered in the survey than in the case of income standards, and they must be added to the systematic structure.

With respect to the interpretation of the coefficients, we make the following observations. The older the respondent is, the higher his age standards. It follows that if A is 10 percent older than B, he will have an age standard for "younger" that is about 3 percent higher (0.319*10 percent). Or in other words, if someone aged twenty finds himself "somewhat young," an older person will find him still "young." For the age standards of "old," there is much less divergence between respondents of different ages.

We see that schooling has a strong impact on the definition of "young"; people tend to stay

TABLE 21.4   Regression Equations for the Age Standards ($N = 538$)

	Constant	Age	Education	Family Size	Gender	R^2
Young	1.414	0.319	0.180	0.069	0.027	0.091
	(0.270)*	(0.043)	(0.067)	(0.026)	(0.030)	
Somewhat young	2.329	0.266	0.045	0.056	0.019	0.135
	(0.183)	(0.029)	(0.045)	(0.018)	(0.020)	
Middle-aged	3.160	0.177	0.014	0.016	0.048	0.163
	(0.115)	(0.018)	(0.028)	(0.011)	(0.013)	
Somewhat old	3.740	0.117	0.018	0.003	0.047	0.132
	(0.095)	(0.015)	(0.023)	(0.009)	(0.011)	
Old	4.243	0.058	0.067	0.003	0.048	0.071
	(0.099)	(0.016)	(0.025)	(0.010)	(0.011)	

Source: van Praag, Dubnoff, and Van der Sar (1988).
*Standard deviations in parentheses.

"young" longer. The impact of a large family on age standards is also evident. In such families, youngsters are considered to be children longer.

The social implications of these tendencies are not imminent. However, culturally it might be of interest that, in Western countries, where the level of education has been increasing for decades, the concept of adulthood has become identified with an increase in age. Finally, the gender of the respondent also plays a role. If the respondent is female, the age standards are somewhat higher than for males, which implies that females tend to diminish the impact of age slightly. Except for the female tendency to stay and look young as long as possible, the gender difference also conforms to the longevity of women compared to men.

Again we see that "young" does not mean the same thing to young people as to old people. We can derive a general age a_i^* standard by setting a_i^* = age, yielding

$$\ln a_i^* = \frac{1}{1 - \alpha_{1,i}}$$
$$[\alpha_{0,i} + \alpha_{2,i}\ln schooling + \alpha_{3,i}\ln fs + \alpha_{4,i}D_{gender}]$$

The resulting age standards are tabulated in table 21.5.

Similarly to the Age Evaluation Question, individuals were asked which education level they thought was "very educated," "uneducated," and so on. By explaining the answers to this Education Evaluation Question (EEQ), Van der Sar (1991) was able to measure an individual norm on education as well. The interested reader is referred to Van der Sar (1991) for a full discussion of the AEQ, EEQ, and related questions.

Individual Norms and General Standards

The evidence described earlier suggests that people have *subjective norms* concerning various concepts. These norms will differ among individuals. They are measured by questions such as the IEQ, AEQ, and EEQ, which supply us with numerical levels related to verbal labels or other symbols.

These questions may be posed theoretically in two ways: one may supply the label as stimulus and ask for an amount as a reply, or one may supply an amount as stimulus and ask for a label as a reply. The first way has been selected as the most practical when there are many different respondents with differing norms. It is also somewhat more informative, as people can space their answers.

In addition, we have *evaluations* by individuals of their *own situation*. This is done by fitting their own situation on their own norm. For instance, an individual i with current income y_c evaluates his own income by $U_i (y_c; y_c, fs)$.

A final point is whether we may in some sense speak of general or social objective standards in contrast to individual subjective norms. Each individual may have an idea about what he thinks is a "bad" or a "good" income, but is there also a way to give content to a social norm with respect to what is a "good" income and what is a "bad" income? This question is especially pertinent when we think of a socially acceptable definition of poverty, or eligibility for social assistance. A second example is the general standard for being "old," which is relevant for fixing the retirement age. A general standard may be derived from the individual standards by calculating the income level, age, education, and so on, where people evaluate their *own* income, age, and so on, as "bad," "good," or "young," "old."

Political applications of the IEQ are not extensively dealt with in this chapter, but we mention applications to poverty measurement (Goedhart et al. 1977; van Praag, Hagenaars, and Van Weeren 1982; Hagenaars 1986; Plug et al. 1996; van Praag and Flik 1992; Frijters and van Praag 1995; Colasanto, Kapteyn, and Van der Gaag 1983; Stanovnik 1992). Further applications concern income inequality (van Praag 1977), household equivalence scales (Kapteyn and van Praag 1976; Kapteyn 1994; van Praag and Warnaar 1997), and climate equivalence scales (Frijters and van Praag 1998; van Praag 1988).

In this method, there is a strong anchor effect. The answer of the respondent depends very strongly on his own situation. One may attempt to avoid this, for example, by asking "Thinking about an *average* family with two children, what does it

TABLE 21.5   General Age Standards

	General Standards	
	Male Respondents	Female Respondents
Young	17.69	18.41
Somewhat young	30.16	30.95
Middle-aged	49.54	52.50
Somewhat old	65.73	69.31
Old	75.06	78.91

Source: van Praag, Dubnoff, and Van der Sar (1988).

need per month for an adequate living?" (compare, Rainwater 1971). While avoiding the anchor effect of one's own situation, this question introduces a new problem: what is regarded as an average family will depend on the reference weighting system of the respondent. We can at least deal with the anchor effect of the individual's situation, as we know the respondent's own situation, but we do not know what the respondent considers to be an average family. The usefulness of this question thus depends on whether it is reasonable to assume that there is common agreement about what constitutes an average family. In heterogeneous populations, such agreement will be absent.

Obviously, the method works only to evaluate one-dimensional situations where numbers may be assigned and where a natural ordering is manifest.

The described IEQ method breaks down when the society is only partly monetized. In that case, welfare cannot be characterized on the one-dimensional income scale. An ingenious way out of this problem has been suggested by Pradhan and Ravallion (1998). Their approach is to ask for evaluations of consumption levels instead of evaluations of income levels.

At present, welfare functions have been measured in nearly all EC countries, the United States, Hungary, Slovenia, Poland, and Russia. In almost all cases, except in the United States, the samples were fairly large-scale, ranging from one thousand respondents to over twenty thousand. Panel data are scarce; the Dutch Socio-Economic Panel carried the question for a number of years, while at present a Russian large-scale household panel includes the question as well (see Frijters and van Praag 1995).

FUTURE DIRECTIONS: WELL-BEING *AND* WELFARE

Traditionally, economists identify welfare (or even happiness) with income. However, it is well known and also fully recognized by other disciplines that there is more between heaven and earth than income and everything that can be bought with income.

This calls for an operational distinction between economic *welfare* and *well-being*. Welfare is the evaluation assigned by the individual to income or, more generally, to the contribution to his well-being from those goods and services that he can buy with money.

Next to material resources, other aspects determine the quality of our life. We can think of our health, the relationship with our partner and family and friends, the quality of our work (job satisfaction), our political freedom, our physical environment, and so on. We shall call this comprehensive concept *well-being* or quality of life (see Nussbaum and Sen [1992] for philosophical discussions about this concept).

It is empirically possible for most individuals to evaluate their life as a whole. A well-known example is the following question devised by Cantril (1965): "Here is a ladder with ten steps which denote the 'ladder of life.' The bottom step stands for the worst possible life. If you climb up and arrive at the tenth step, you arrive at the best possible life. Can you indicate where you are at the moment?" Other questions that are very similar to Cantril's question ask individuals to denote how *satisfied* or how *happy* they are with their life as a whole. The concept of well-being is thus very similar to that of life satisfaction or happiness, and we will not discuss the differences.

These questions are a standard module in many psychosociological surveys, and respondents have no difficulty responding. See Veenhoven (1996) and Diener and Suh (1997) for reviews of the psychological literature on well-being. It is also obvious that responding to these questions is tantamount to evaluating one's life situation on a bounded numerical scale between 0 and 10.

In fact, we have here a measurement method that *defines* the well-being concept in an operational way. We notice that what we measure is an evaluation of the individual's actual situation. Hence, it is not an "individual norm," as measured by the IEQ, where six qualitative labels are linked to income levels, yielding an "income norm." The Cantril question provides us with a *social standard* on well-being.

We assume again, as is always done implicitly, that the respondents' answers are comparable, in the sense that individuals evaluating their lives with the same grade, such as a 5 or an 8, are equally unhappy or happy. The main questions are:

- What determines well-being?
- What are the differences between welfare and well-being?

Plug and van Praag (1995) and Plug (1997), analyzed these two questions on a large sample (1991) of about six thousand Dutch married couples, with the husband younger than sixty-five years of age. They hypothesized that well-being, to be denoted by W, depends on various contributing factors and determinants. Some of these factors are objective ones, like family size, income, age, and religion. Other variables are called "problem intensities." They relate to the intensity with which an individual "has problems" with his health, job, marriage, physical environment, and so on.[9] Formally we write

$$W = W(P, z)$$

where P stands for a vector of problem areas, and z for a number of objective variables. Problem intensities, such as $P_{health}, P_{job} \ldots$, are operationalized by asking individuals "many/few/no problem" questions. An example of such a question is: "Have you had problems in the last three months with your health?" (no/a little/some/serious?). The outcomes are on a numerical scale.[10] Plug and van Praag (1995) found the estimates presented in table 21.6.

The first column refers to the explanation of well-being, while the second column refers to the explanation of μ by the *same* variables. The first nine variables stand for problems with health, with partner, with job, with sleep, with alcohol and drugs, with family, sexual problems, problems with parents, and the evaluation of the neighborhood. These variables reach their highest value when there are no problems. "Religion" stands for the intensity of religious feelings where the highest value corresponds to "nonreligious." The IEQ measures welfare, while the Cantril question measures the broader concept of life satisfaction or well-being.

The main difference between welfare and well-being is that "problem" variables hardly affect the evaluation of income but do, however, affect well-being.

The second question is also answered at the same time. Welfare and well-being are different concepts, where welfare is dependent only on a small subset of the set of variables that influence well-being. The size and sign of the effect is also different.

To illustrate the relevance of the results, Plug and van Praag (1995) estimated the optimum number of children, as family size appears quad-

TABLE 21.6   Estimation Results of w and μ

	w	μ
Health	0.08	−0.00
	(11.43)	(−1.11)
Partner	0.04	−0.01
	(3.62)	(−1.13)
Job	0.07	−0.01
	(9.57)	(−1.67)
Sleep	0.07	0.00
	(8.90)	(0.55)
Alcohol/drugs	0.04	−0.01
	(4.27)	(−1.22)
Family	0.07	−0.01
	(7.92)	(−2.61)
Sexuality	0.03	0.00
	(3.50)	(0.86)
Parents	0.05	−0.01
	(6.53)	(−2.16)
Neighborhood	0.08	0.00
	(13.61)	(0.26)
Religion	0.02	−0.01
	(4.00)	(−3.54)
ln y	0.12	0.55
	(5.13)	(41.49)
ln fs	−0.81	−0.34
	(−3.60)	(−2.66)
ln y ln fs	0.09	0.03
	(4.13)	(2.44)
$\ln^2 fs$	−0.06	0.03
	(−3.36)	(2.49)
ln age	−2.14	1.10
	(−5.88)	(5.27)
$\ln^2 age$	0.30	−0.14
	(4.13)	(−4.82)
Dummy-job	−0.10	0.01
	(−5.07)	(−0.57)
Constant	3.10	2.24
	(4.72)	(5.93)
R^2	0.24	0.61

Source: van Praag and Plug (1995).

ratically in W. This optimum number of children depends on such factors as income. Table 21.7 was derived for the Netherlands. It shows that the optimum number of children is zero for a family with an annual after-tax income of NLG20,418. For a family with an annual income of NLG51,451, two children are the optimum family size.

TABLE 21.7   The Optimum Family Size for Specific Income Levels

$fs = 1$	$fs = 2$	$fs = 3$	$fs = 4$	$fs = 5$	$fs = 6$
8,103	20,418	35,060	51,451	69,280	88,346

Note: Family income is measured in Dutch guilders (NLG2 is about $1.00).

An especially promising path is the *combination* of more than one satisfaction measure. We will explain this idea with a specific example from van Praag and Plug (1995).

We consider again the social standard function of income as derived earlier, which we denote by $\bar{U}(y;fs)$ and where we ignore other variables. We know already that $\bar{U}$ decreases with the number of children. More specifically, it is possible to assess the monetary value of the "welfare cost of additional children." Assuming that a representative couple has two children and an annual income of $50,000, their welfare will be $\bar{U}(50;4)$. Assume now that the couple has another child, which causes $\bar{U}$ to change to $\bar{U}(50;5)$. The welfare decline may be compensated by an income increase $\Delta^{U}y$ such that

$$\bar{U}(50 + \Delta^{U}y; 5) = \bar{U}(50; 4)$$

We call $\Delta^{U}y$ the *shadow price* of the additional child, which is the monetary amount needed to keep a household on the same welfare level.[11] Notice that this depends on the rank order of the child and that the shadow price will depend on income.

On the other hand, we have the well-being measure W, based on the Cantril question, yielding a well-being function

$$W(y, fs)$$

again ignoring all other variables. Given our estimates of the previous table, W is strongly quadratic in fs, implying that well-being initially increases with family size up to a certain point, thereafter falling with increasing family size. This *nonmonotonic* behavior points to the fact that an extra child may be wanted for its non-economic contribution. It is a gain for well-being while at the same time a loss in terms of welfare. Hence, there are *nonmonetary* benefits of having children and monetary costs. The W function captures both and increases with family size if the benefits outweigh the costs, and decreases if the costs outweigh the benefits. There is equality at the optimum family size.

Considering $W(y,fs)$, we may calculate the *shadow well-being* price of an additional child $\Delta^{W}y$, by solving

$$W(y, fs) = W(y + \Delta^{W}y, fs + \Delta fs)$$

Here $\Delta^{W}y$ is the monetary counter value of this difference:

$$\Delta^{W}y = Benefits - Costs$$

We call it the shadow price with respect to well-being. It is positive if we welcome a child and neg-

ative if the opposite holds. From the calculation on U, we obtained an estimate of the cost

$$\Delta^{U}y = Costs$$

Adding $\Delta^{W}y$ and $\Delta^{U}y$ yields the monetary value of benefits.

The benefits may be considerable, as witnessed by the fact that childless couples try to adopt children or are willing to undergo expensive medical treatment. The benefits of children as calculated for Dutch families in 1991 are shown in table 21.8

We see that the value of the (nonmonetary) benefits of the first child is negative at a low income level. The benefit of the first child becomes positive for incomes above NLG20,000. For the second child, the benefits remain negative until an income of about NLG40,000. For the third and fourth children, the benefits remain negative for even longer. With respect to costs, there is no ambiguity: costs are always positive. However, the cost of each additional child decreases. As we can see, these nonmonetary benefits are substantial and increase strongly with income.

At this stage, we warn that the study is in the beginning stage and that not too much value should be assigned to this or other results without replication. However, the path seems promising. A future step is to estimate the substitution and trade-off between variables and the calculation of

TABLE 21.8 Money Value of Nonmonetary Child Benefits

	One Breadwinner			
Income*	First Child	Second Child	Third Child	Fourth Child
20,000	−262	−838	−1,005	−1,039
30,000	1,114	−236	−748	−959
40,000	2,911	651	−279	−713
50,000	5,023	1,749	348	−341
60,000	7,383	3,018	1,100	130
	Two Breadwinners			
Income	First Child	Second Child	Third Child	Fourth Child
20,000	−726	−1,153	−1,240	−1,223
30,000	419	−708	−1,100	−1,236
40,000	1,983	22	−747	−1,082
50,000	3,871	964	−237	−802
60,000	5,990	2,074	399	−423

Source: van Praag and Plug (1995)
*Family income is measured in Dutch guilders (NLG2 is about $1.00).

monetary values of health increases, family increases, education, marriage quality, and so on.

See Frijters (1998) for other applications and extensions of Leyden methodology on welfare and satisfaction.

CONCLUSIONS

The work originating from Leyden School has tried to operationalize the concepts of welfare, well-being, and so on, which are considered immeasurable and esoteric by most of the economic profession. With rather simple and inexpensive questions in large-scale surveys, considerable information has been found on feelings. At least the feelings of welfare and well-being may be "explained" by objectively measurable variables and by partial satisfaction measures with respect to aspects of life. The information is helpful for quantifying memory and anticipation weights.[12] The potential policy applications are plentiful. We briefly described its use to calculate family equivalence scales. A rather recent development is the combination of the welfare and well-being measurements, which makes it possible to identify the costs and benefits of various choices. We demonstrated this for the option of choosing to have children.

The apparatus developed thus far is not typically restricted to economic problems but can also be used by psychologists, sociologists, and political scientists. Its use in health economics seems straightforward.

The story, we hope, is not finished but only in the early stages. The main empirical restriction is that the data sets are scattered and almost never contain the IEQ, sound economic information (consumption, income, job characteristics), and "soft" information on feelings on several aspects of life, such as the Cantril question. In this respect, the United States, where so much effort is given to research, is conspicuously absent.

NOTES

1. Decision utility as defined by Kahneman, Wakker, and Sarin (1997) may be ordinal or cardinal.
2. See also van Praag (1968) for an attempt to find a functional form of the utility function with the use of axioms and secondary assumptions.
3. The "quality-of-life" concept is very broad and interpreted by some to mean the same thing as happiness (Veenhoven 1996) or average satisfaction (Dow and

Juster 1985). We discuss here the interpretation we believe most *economists* in this field use.
4. A reply was given by van Praag and Kapteyn (1994).
5. One particular feature of the value function found by Kahneman, Knetsch, and Thaler (1991) cannot be replicated: they find a value function that changes direction abruptly at the reference position. The number of levels used in our measure is simply too small to find such a jump in direction.
6. A variable of much economic interest, Pratt's (1964) measure of relative risk aversion (or Frisch flexibility), can be directly calculated as

$$\frac{\partial \ln u}{\partial \ln y} = -\frac{1}{2\sigma^2}(\ln y - \mu) - 1$$

It varies from highly positive for small y to very negative for large y.
7. An explanation does not necessarily mean a one-way causal relationship.
8. The likely result of using estimates for some incomes is that the effect of income different from the present income will be underestimated. The qualitative results should, however, remain the same.
9. Plug and van Praag (1995) name the extent to which individuals are free of a problem, a "partial satisfaction." However, given that this term may be confusing, we use here the term "problem intensities."
10. For estimation purposes, they prefer to transform W and P from their bounded scale into $(-\infty, +\infty)$. It might be feared that people will center in the middle and that extreme answers will be rare. To solve both problems, the *empirical* distribution functions $\tilde{F}$ of the W and P values are calculated, and the value $\tilde{F}$ is assigned to the various levels instead of the original ones. Then they transform $\tilde{F}$ again by taking the inverse standard normal, which means that instead of W and P, $\bar{W} = N^{-1}(\tilde{F}_w(W); 0, 1)$ and $\bar{P} = N^{-1}(\tilde{F}_p(P); 0, 1)$ are utilized. The transformations do no intrinsic harm, but they are used only to get more response differentiation and a stretching on $(-\infty, +\infty)$. From now on, we will drop the tildes.
11. The "cost of children" will at least include the expenditures on an additional child. Future research looks at whether it also includes the monetary shadow value of time spent on a child.
12. In van Praag (1981), Kapteyn (1977), Van der Sar (1991), Van de Stadt, Kapteyn, and Van de Geer (1985), Kapteyn, van Praag, and van Heerwaarden (1976), and van Praag, Kapteyn, and van Heerwaarden (1979) the IEQ was also used for the extraction of information on the social reference mechanism, as the answers to the IEQ are influenced by social reference groups. This application was not dealt with in this chapter.

REFERENCES

Allais, M., and Hagen, O. (1979). *Expected utility hypothesis and the Allais paradox*. Dordrecht: Reidel.
Arrow, K. (1951). *Social choice and individual values*. New York: Wiley.
Atkinson, A. B. (1970). On the measurement of inequality. *Journal of Economic Theory*, 2, 244–63.

Brickman, P., and Campbell, D. T. (1971). Hedonic relativism and planning the good society. In M. H. Appley (Ed.), *Adaptation-level theory: A Symposium* (pp. 287–304). New York: Academic Press.

Callan, T., and Nolan, B. (1991). Concepts of poverty and the poverty line. *Journal of Economic Surveys, 5,* 243–61.

Cantril, H. (1965). *The pattern of human concerns.* New Brunwick, N.J.: Rutgers University Press.

Christensen, L. R., Jorgenson, D. W., and Lau, L. J. (1975). Transcendental logarithmic utility functions. *American Economic Review, 65,* 367–83.

Clark, A. E. (1996). Job satisfaction in Britain. *British Journal of Industrial Relations, 34,* 189–217.

Clark, A. E., and Oswald, A. J. (1994). Unhappiness and unemployment. *Economic Journal, 104,* 648–59.

———. (1996). Satisfaction and comparison income. *Journal of Public Economics, 61,* 359–81.

Colosanto, D., Kapteyn, A., and Van der Gaag, J. (1983). Two subjective definitions of poverty: Results from the Wisconsin basic needs study. *Journal of Human Resources, 28,* 127–38.

Debreu, G. (1959). *Theory of value.* New Haven, Conn.: Yale University Press.

Diener, E., and Suh, E. (1997). Measuring quality of life: Economic, social, and subjective indicators. *Social Indicators Research, 40,* 189–216.

Dow, G. K., and Juster, F. T. (1985). Goods, time, and well-being: The joint dependency problem. In F. T. Juster and F. P. Stafford (Eds.), *Time, goods, and well-being.* Ann Arbor, Mich.: Institute of Social Research.

Dubnoff, D., Vaughan, D., and Lancaster, C. (1981). Income satisfaction measures in equivalence scale applications. *Proceedings of the Social Statistics Section, American Statistical Association,* 348–52.

Easterlin, R. (1974). Does economic growth improve the human lot? Some empirical evidence. In P. David and R. Reder (Eds.), *Nations and households in economic growth: Essays in honor of Moses Abramovitz* (pp. 89–125). New York: Academic Press.

———. (1995). Will raising the incomes of all increase the happiness of all? *Journal of Economic Behavior and Organization, 27,* 35–47.

Edgeworth, F. Y. (1881). *Mathematical psychics.* London: Kegan Paul.

Frijters, P. (1998). Explorations of welfare and satisfaction. Ph.D. diss. University of Amsterdam.

Frijters, P., and van Praag, B. M. S. (1995). Estimates of poverty ratios and equivalence scales for Russia and parts of the former USSR. *Tinbergen Discussion Papers,* 95–149.

———. (1998). Climate equivalence scales and the effect of climate change on Russian welfare and well-being. *Climate Change, 39,* 61–81.

Frisch, R. (1932). *New methods of measuring marginal utility.* Tübingen: Mohr.

Gershuny J., and Halpin, B. (1995). Time use, quality of life, and process benefit. In A. Offer (Ed.), *In pursuit of the quality of life* (pp. 188–210). Oxford: Clarendon Press.

Goedhart, T., Halberstadt, V., Kapteyn, A., and van Praag, B. M. S. (1977). The poverty line: Concepts and measurement. *Journal of Human Resources, 12,* 503–20.

Hagenaars, A. J. M. (1986). *The perception of poverty.* Amsterdam: North-Holland.

Heywood, J. S., Siebert, W. S., and Wei, X. (1997). Are union jobs worse? Are government jobs better? University of Birmingham. Unpublished paper.

Hirschberg, J. G., Maasoumi, E., and Slottje, D. J. (1991). Cluster analysis for measuring welfare and quality of life across countries. *Journal of Econometrics, 50,* 131–50.

Jorgenson, D. W., and Slesnick, D. T. (1984). Aggregate consumer behavior and the measurement of inequality. *Review of Economic Studies, 166,* 369–92.

Kahneman, D., Knetsch, J., and Thaler, R. (1991). The endowment effect, loss aversion, and status quo bias. *Journal of Economic Perspectives, 5,* 193–206.

Kahneman, D., and Tversky, A. (1979). Prospect theory: An analysis of decision under risk. *Econometrica, 47,* 263–91.

Kahneman, D., Wakker, P. P., and Sarin, R. (1997). Back to Bentham? Explorations of experienced utility. *Quarterly Journal of Economics* (May) 375–405.

Kapteyn, A. (1977). A theory of preference formation. Ph.D. diss., Leyden University.

———. (1994). The measurement of household cost functions: Revealed preference versus subjective measures. *Journal of Population Economics, 7,* 333–50.

Kapteyn, A., and van Praag, B. M. S. (1976). A new approach to the construction of equivalence scales. *European Economic Review, 7,* 313–35.

Kapteyn, A., van Praag, B. M. S., and Van Heerwaarden, F. G. (1976). Individual welfare functions and social reference spaces. Report 76.01. Economic Institute, Leyden University.

Kurian, G. T. (1984). *The new book of world rankings,* London: Macmillan.

Levy-Garboua, L., and Montmarquette, L. C. (1997). Reported job satisfaction: What does it mean? Cahier de Recherche 1. University of Paris.

Maasoumi, E. (1989). Composite indices of income and other developmental indicators: A general approach. *Research on Economic Inequality, 1,* 269–86.

Markowitz, H. M. (1952). The utility of wealth. *Journal of Political Economy, 60,* 51–58.

Ng, Y. K. (1997). A case for happiness, cardinalism, and interpersonal comparability. *Economic Journal, 107,* 1848–58.

Nussbaum, M., and Sen, A. K. (Eds.). (1992). *The quality of life.* Oxford: Clarendon Press.

Parducci, A. (1995). *Happiness, pleasure, and judgment: The contextual theory and its applications.* Mahwah, N.J.: Erlbaum.

Pareto, V. (1904). *Manuel d'economic politique.* Paris: Girard.

Pigou, A. C. (1948). *The economics of welfare.* 4th ed. London: Macmillan.

Plug, E. J. S. (1997). Leyden welfare and beyond. Ph.D. diss. University of Amsterdam.

Plug, E. J. S., Krausse, P., van Praag, B. M. S., and Wagner, G. G. (1996). The measurement of poverty: Exemplified by the German case. In N. Ott and G. G. Wagner (Eds.), *Income inequality and poverty in Eastern and Western Europe* (pp. 69–90). Heidelberg: Springer.

Plug, E. J. S., and van Praag, B. M. S. (1995). Family equivalence scales within a narrow and broad welfare context. *Journal of Income Distribution, 4,* 171–86.

Pradhan, M., and Ravallion, M. (1998). Measuring poverty using qualitative perceptions of welfare. *World Bank Policy Research Working Paper, NR 20-11.*

Pratt, J. W. (1964). Risk aversion in the small and in the large. *Econometrica, 32,* 122–26.

Rainwater, L. (1971). Interim report on explorations of social status, living standards, and family life styles. Cambridge Mass.: Joint Center for Urban Studies of the Massachusetts Institute of Technology and Harvard University. Unpublished paper.

Ravallion, M. (1994). *Poverty comparisons.* Fundamentals in Pure and Applied Economics 56. Chur, Switzerland: Harwood Academic Press.

Robbins, K. (1932). *An essay on the nature and significance of economic science.* London: Macmillan.

Samuelson, P. A. (1945). *Foundations of economic science.* Cambridge Mass.: Harvard University Press.

Savage, L. J. (1954). *The foundations of statistics.* New York: Wiley.

Seidl, C. (1994). How sensible is the Leyden individual welfare function of income? *European Economic Review, 38,* 1633–59.

Sen, A. K. (1987). *The standard of living.* Tanner Lectures. Cambridge: Cambridge University Press.

Stanovnik, T. (1992). Perception of poverty and income satisfaction. *Journal of Economic Psychology, 13,* 57–69.

Tinbergen, J. (1991). On the measurement of welfare. *Journal of Econometrics, 50,* 7–13.

Townsend, P. (1979). *Poverty in the United Kingdom.* Harmondsworth: Penguin.

———. (1993). *The analysis of poverty.* London: Harvester/Wheatsheaf.

Van der Sar, N. L. (1991). Applied utility analysis. Ph.D. diss. Erasmus University, Rotterdam, Haveka (Alblasserdam).

Van de Stadt, H., Kapteyn, A., and Van de Geer, S. (1985). The relativity of utility: Evidence from panel data. *Review of Economics and Statistics, 67,* 179–87.

van Herwaarden, F. G., and Kapteyn, A. (1981). Empirical comparison of the shape of welfare functions. *European Economic Review, 15,* 261–86.

van Praag, B. M. S. (1968). Individual welfare functions and consumer behavior: A theory of rational irrationality. Ph.D. diss. University of Amsterdam.

———. (1971). The welfare function of income in Belgium: An empirical investigation. *European Economic Review, 2,* 337–69.

———. (1977). The perception of welfare inequality. *European Economic Review, 10,* 189–207.

———. (1981). Reflections on the theory of individual welfare functions. Report 81.14. Center for Research in Public Economics, Leyden University. *Proceedings of the American Statistical Association.*

———. (1988). Climate equivalence scales: An application of a general method. *European Economic Review, 32*(4), 1019–24.

———. (1991). Ordinal and cardinal utility: An integration of the two dimensions of the welfare concept. *Journal of Econometrics, 50,* 69–89.

van Praag, B. M. S., Dubnoff, S., and Van der Sar, N. L. (1988). On the measurement and explanation of standards with respect to income, age, and education. *Journal of Economic Psychology, 9,* 481–98.

van Praag, B. M. S., and Flik, R. J. (1992). Poverty lines and equivalence scales: A theoretical and empirical investigation. Poverty Measurement for Economies in Transition in Eastern Europe, International Scientific Conference, Warsaw, October 7–9. Polish Statistical Association, Central Statistical Office.

van Praag, B. M. S., Hagenaars, A., and Van Weeren, J. (1982). Poverty in Europe. *Review of Income and Wealth, 28,* 345–59.

van Praag, B. M. S., and Kapteyn, A. (1973). Further evidence on the individual welfare function of income: An empirical investigation in the Netherlands. *European Economic Review, 4,* 33–62.

———. (1994). How sensible is the Leyden individual welfare function of income? A reply. *European Economic Review, 38,* 1817–25.

van Praag, B. M. S., Kapteyn, A., and Van Herwaarden, F. G. (1979). The definition and measurement of social reference spaces. *Netherlands Journal of Sociology, 15,* 13–25.

van Praag, B. M. S., and Plug, E. J. S. (1995). New developments in the measurement of welfare and well-being. Tinbergen Discussion Paper 95–60. University of Amsterdam.

van Praag, B. M. S., and Van der Sar, N. L. (1988). Household cost functions and equivalence scales. *Journal of Human Resources, 23,* 193–210.

van Praag, B. M. S., and Van Weeren, J. (1983). Some panel-data evidence on the time-discounting mechanism in the formation of value judgments on income with applications to social security and income policy. Report 83.22. Center for Research in Public Economics, Leyden University.

———. (1988). Memory and anticipation processes and their significance for social security and income inequality. In S. Maital (Ed.), *Applied behavioral economics* (pp. 731–51). Brighton: Wheatsheaf Books.

van Praag, B. M. S., and Warnaar, M. (1997). The cost

of children and the effect of demographic variables on consumer demand. In M. R. Rosenzweig and O. Stark (Eds.), *The handbook of population and family economics* (pp. 241–72). Amsterdam: North Holland.

Veenhoven, R. (1996). Happy life expectancy: A comprehensive measure of quality of life in nations. *Social Indicators Research, 39,* 1–58.

Wakker, P. P., and Tversky, A. (1993). An axiomatization of cumulative prospect theory. *Journal of Risk and Uncertainty, 7,* 147–76.

Wansbeek, T., and Kapteyn, A. (1983). Tackling hard questions by means of soft methods: The use of individual welfare functions in socioeconomic policy. *Kyklos, 36,* 249–69.

22 National Differences in Subjective Well-Being

Ed Diener and Eunkook Mark Suh

There are substantial differences between nations in reported subjective well-being (SWB). Although surveys of subjective well-being face methodological challenges, the existing data suggest that the measures have a degree of validity and that the between-nation differences are substantive. People in wealthy nations tend to report greater SWB than people in poor nations. The causal factors relating wealth to well-being, however, are not yet understood. The wealth of nations strongly correlates with human rights, equality between people, the fulfillment of basic biological needs, and individualism. Because of the high intercorrelations between these predictor variables and wealth, their separate effects on SWB have not yet been isolated. Another variable that correlates with higher SWB in nations is political stability and a related variable, interpersonal trust. Individualism is a cultural variable that correlates across nations with both higher reported SWB and higher suicide rates. Possible reasons for these divergent outcomes of individualism are discussed. Individualists believe that happiness is more important than do collectivists, who emphasize other values such as "harmony" and "respect." Furthermore, reports of SWB are highest in those nations where it is thought to be important. Interestingly, when making life satisfaction judgments, individualists are more likely than collectivists to weight their moods and emotions and less likely to consult norms about how appropriate it is to be satisfied. Furthermore, people in Latin cultures prize pleasant affect and denigrate unpleasant affect, whereas people in the Confucian cultures of the Pacific Rim appear to place less emphasis on pleasant affect and are more accepting of unpleasant emotions. The major approaches to the psychological understanding of the differences in SWB between societies are the innate needs approach, the theory of goal striving, models of emotion socialization, and genetic explanations. Policy implications of the national differences in SWB are discussed briefly.

FOR MILLENNIA THINKERS have discussed the quality of human existence—what makes a desirable society and individual life. Philosophers such as Thomas Aquinas concentrated on the individual and defined the quality of human life in terms of virtue, closeness to God, and other personal qualities. Other scholars such as Confucius focused on the quality of life of a society, stressing relationships between people. In modern times scientists measure the quality of life and approach this task from several directions. Economists assess the amount of goods and services produced by a society as a reflection of quality of life. Their assumption is that if a society produces abundant goods and services, people will select those that they most want and therefore are likely to create a desirable life. Human needs are most likely to be fulfilled in a society that produces many goods and services, and therefore well-being or utility will be heightened in a nation with greater productivity. Other researchers, especially scientists working in the social indicators tradition, have enumerated other felicitous qualities of a society beyond goods and services and devised methods to measure them. For example, in addition to products and services, the good society should have low crime, a long life expectancy, respect for human rights, and an equitable distribution of resources. In this approach, scientists attempt to compare societies based on indices that summarize a variety of important social indicators (see, for example, Diener 1995).

A third approach to defining and measuring quality of life is in terms of subjective well-being (SWB)—how individuals evaluate their lives, both in terms of satisfaction judgments and in terms of affective reactions (moods and emotions). In this tradition, the individual with a desirable life is satisfied and experiences frequent pleasant emotions and infrequent unpleasant emotions. The ideal society is defined as one in which all people are happy and satisfied and experience an abundance of pleasure. Furthermore, more specific variables, such as trust, self-esteem, absence of pain, and satisfaction with one's work and with one's marriage, can also be added to the list of subjective indicators.

We need subjective, economic, and social indicators to appraise the full range of quality of life of a society because the strengths and weaknesses of these approaches are complementary (Diener and Suh 1997). This chapter, however, concentrates on subjective measures of well-being in comparing the quality of life of nations. Measurement validity in this area is sufficient to derive a few broad inferences, but improvements in methodology are needed before we can gain strong conclusions.

Although measures of SWB are available other than the self-report responses of survey respondents, this methodology is the source of data for most researchers. Probability sample measurement of SWB in nations was begun in 1946. Since that time, there have been several studies that obtained probability samples in many nations (for example, Cantril 1965; World Values Study Group, 1994; Eurobarometer 1991). In addition, studies based on narrower samples, such as college students (for example, Suh et al., in press; Michalos 1991), have been conducted. Finally, the results of surveys conducted within nations can be compared across countries when comparable measures were used. A summary of the results of 916 national surveys is available in Veenhoven (1993).

Table 22.1 presents mean levels of reported SWB from forty-one nations based on responses to the World Value Survey II (World Values Study Group, 1994). Three components of SWB are shown: life satisfaction, pleasant affect, and unpleasant affect. The life satisfaction score is based on respondents' answers to the question "All things considered, how satisfied are you with your life as a whole these days?" using a number from 1 (dissatisfied) to 10 (satisfied). Although in smaller studies, such as Diener and his colleagues' life satisfaction inventory (Pavot and Diener 1993b), life satisfaction measures are often based on multi-item scales, for reasons of expediency the typical life satisfaction measure in large-scale surveys is based only on a single item. Bradburn's (1969) Affect Balance Scale has five questions that assess pleasant emotions and five questions that assess unpleasant moods. For example, respondents answer whether, during the past few weeks, they felt "on top of the world/feeling that life is wonderful," and "depressed or very unhappy." The positive affect score is based on the number of items from 0 to 5 that the respondent answers affirmatively, and the negative affect scale is scored in an identical manner.

Three of the major components of SWB are life satisfaction, the presence of frequent pleasant affect, and infrequent unpleasant affect. As can be seen in table 1, mean levels of these three types of SWB differed substantially across countries. For instance, average levels of life satisfaction varied from approximately 5.0 in Bulgaria to about 8.4 in Switzerland. Similarly, hedonic balance (pleasant affect minus unpleasant affect) also varied substantially between societies. For example, respondents reported nearly an equal number of pleasant and unpleasant emotional experiences in Russia, whereas in Sweden participants responded affirmatively to many more pleasant affect than unpleasant affect items. In colloquial terms, the citizens of Sweden appear to be happier than those of Russia because respondents in the latter society do not experience a relative abundance of pleasant emotions.

It can also be seen that nations appeared to be more emotional than others—that is, their citizens reported high levels of both types of affect. For example, the citizens of Turkey and Japan had about the same life satisfaction scores, but Turks reported much higher levels of both pleasant and unpleasant affect. The mean levels of life satisfaction correlate with hedonic balance across nations, although measures seemed to provide some complementary information because the correlation between them is not perfect ($r = .73$). As yet, we have few insights into factors that might influence one type of SWB but not another type. We will return to the question of what might cause the differences between nations in SWB.

Finally, it should be noted that all means in table 1 are above the neutral points of the scales. That is, although average levels of happiness across nations, they tend to start at neutral. For example, on Bradburn's (1969) Affect Balance Scale, all nations report more positive than negative affect. In an article titled "Most People Are Happy," Diener and C. Diener (1996a) note that in most nations and even in very disadvantaged groups the majority of people report SWB in the moderately positive range, although scores at the highest end are rare. Diener and Diener did note, however, that in previous surveys there were some values below neutrality in a few very poor societies. Diener and M. Diener (1995) also found that the majority of respondents in virtually every country were above the midpoint of the scale on both life satisfaction and happiness. In addition, they found that in all nations respondents scored in the positive zone for satisfaction with friends and with family, but that in some societies respondents fell below the neutral point of the scale when it came to financial satisfaction.

TABLE 22.1   Subjective Well-Being Values of Nation

Nation	Life Satisfaction	Hedonic Balance	Positive Affect	Negative Affect
Bulgaria	5.03	.91	1.93	1.01
Russia	5.37	.29	1.69	1.41
Belarus	5.52	.77	2.12	1.35
Latvia	5.70	.92	2.00	1.08
Romania	5.88	.71	2.34	1.63
Estonia	6.00	.76	2.05	1.28
Lithuania	6.01	.60	1.86	1.26
Hungary	6.03	.85	1.96	1.11
India	6.21	.33	1.41	1.09
South Africa	6.22	1.15	2.59	1.44
Slovenia	6.29	1.53	2.33	.80
Czech Repul	6.30	.76	1.84	1.08
Nigeria	6.40	1.56	2.92	1.36
Turkey	6.41	.59	3.09	2.50
Japan	6.53	.39	1.12	.72
Poland	6.64	1.24	2.45	1.21
South…any	6.69			
Eas'	6.72	1.25	3.05	1.80
Fr	6.76	1.33	2.34	1.01
ɡal	7.05	1.26	2.34	1.08
	7.10	1.33	2.27	.94
ι Germany	7.13	.70	1.59	.89
ıy	7.22	1.43	3.23	1.79
·rgentina	7.24	1.21	2.04	.84
Brazil	7.25	1.26	2.45	1.19
Mexico	7.39	1.18	2.85	1.68
Britain	7.41	1.38	2.68	1.30
Chile	7.48	1.64	2.89	1.25
Belgium	7.55	1.03	2.78	1.75
Finland	7.67	1.54	2.46	.93
Norway	7.68	1.18	2.33	1.15
United States	7.68	1.59	2.54	.95
Austria	7.71	2.21	3.49	1.27
Netherlands	7.74	1.77	2.90	1.13
Ireland	7.84	1.81	2.91	1.10
Canada	7.87	1.99	2.89	.90
Sweden	7.88	2.31	3.47	1.15
Iceland	7.97	2.90	3.63	.73
Denmark	8.02	2.50	3.29	.78
Switzerland	8.16	1.90	2.83	.93
	8.39	1.14	1.39	.24

Source: World Values Study Group (1994).
Note: Values are weighted to achieve probability samples of nations, and respondents with apparent data errors were dropped before analyses.

METHODOLOGICAL ISSUES

Measurement

Before proceeding with an analysis of the survey results, several methodological issues should be discussed. The first, and most obvious, is whether the SWB surveys are valid. A situation in which a researcher asks respondents questions about life satisfaction may seem rife with possibilities for measurement artifacts. Although a thorough discussion of the measurement of SWB is beyond the scope of this chapter, further discussion can be found in Andrews and Robinson (1992), Diener (1994), Diener and his colleagues (1997), Larsen,

Diener, and Emmons (1985), Sandvik, Diener, and Seidlitz (1993), and Schwarz and Strack (this volume).

When self-reports of well-being are correlated with other methods of measurement, they show adequate convergent validity. They covary with ratings made by family and friends, with interviewer ratings, with amount of smiling in an interview, and with the number of positive versus negative memories people recall (see, for example, Sandvik et al. 1993). In a few international studies, there are more than self-report measures available to examine the SWB differences between nations. For example, Balatsky and Diener (1993) found not only that Russian students reported much lower levels of well-being than U.S. respondents, but also that they scored lower on an event memory measure of SWB. In this measure participants were to recall as many positive events as they could in a defined period, and then as many negative events as they could in a separate time period; Russian students recalled relatively fewer pleasing events than American respondents. This finding served to support the self-report conclusions of the study and cast doubt on artifactual explanations of the results.

In a study in the areas that were formerly West and East Berlin, Oettingen and Seligman (1990) examined the relation of facial expressions and posture to happiness and unhappiness, as well as optimistic versus pessimistic accounts of events in newspapers. Raters coded facial expression (smiling versus frowning), posture (slumped versus erect), and laughing and gesturing in working-class men in pubs. They found that West Berliners smiled more, exhibited an upright and open posture more frequently, laughed more, and gestured purposefully more often. Consistent with these differences, the authors found that the newspaper explanations of good and bad events differed strongly between the two areas. West Berlin newspapers described the causes of good events in more global and stable terms compared to East Berlin papers, whereas the latter publications described negative events in more global terms. As can be seen in table 22.1, the behavioral and cognitive differences described by Oettingen and Seligman are mirrored in the self-reported SWB of West and East Germans.

The validity of SWB reports is also attested to by the fact that self-reports of SWB correlate with other measures as predicted, for example, with measures of self-esteem, optimism, self-efficacy, and depression. Furthermore, measures of SWB

show temporal reliability even over a period of several years, although some change in SWB is evident over time, as would be expected. In addition, in the international data, different surveys converge in terms of their conclusions about the SWB of nations. For example, Diener, Diener, and Diener (1995) reported an average Pearson correlation of .71 between the mean levels of SWB reported for nations in three different international surveys.

Finally, measures of SWB are often not strongly influenced by people's current moods, by their habitual use of numbers in responding to scales, by their propensity to be humble, or by their tendency to avoid extremes on the scale (Diener et al. 1991; Diener, Suh, et al. 1995; Oishi et al. 1996; Pavot and Diener 1993a). Veenhoven (1993), Inglehart and Rabier (1986), and Shao (1993) present evidence that language translation is unlikely to have a large impact on the measures. Veenhoven also reviews data that suggest that differences in the desirability of SWB concepts or familiarity with them are not responsible for reported nation differences. Thus, self-report measures of SWB possess some validity, and this conclusion is supported by the reliable correlates of international differences in SWB reports that we review later.

Despite the evidence for validity, SWB measures are not without shortcomings. For example, Schwarz and Clore (1983) showed that respondents' current mood can sometimes affect their evaluation of longer time periods of their life. Schwarz and Strack (this volume) found that different information may be weighted in life satisfaction judgments, depending on how the questions are asked and on the factors that are salient to the respondent at the moment. Furthermore, some researchers (for example, Cutler, Bunce, and Larsen 1996; Levine 1997; Thomas and Diener 1990) have found that people recalling their moods over long periods of time experience systematic memory biases. Thus, momentary situational factors can add error to the measurement of long-term SWB. Indeed, life satisfaction judgments probably always include some variance that is due to immediate situational influences.

There is also the potential problem that people might try to make a favorable impression by reporting high SWB. We examined this artifact by comparing the responses of individuals who are randomly assigned to report their responses in an interview situation versus in an anonymous questionnaire. Replicating King and Buchwald (1982), we found in several samples of college students that the method of reporting responses did not influence the mean level of SWB reported. However, Sudman, Greeley, and Pinto (1967) found that people reported greater happiness in an in-person interview than in a self-administered questionnaire. Moum (1996) found that younger people reported less depression in interviews compared to self-administered questionnaires, whereas older respondents did not show this bias. Thus, it appears that some groups of people may report being happier or less happy depending on the social pressures of the situation. Such impression management can produce spurious differences in mean levels of well-being.

Our broad conclusion about the assessment of SWB is that although the SWB measures have a degree of validity and are often not as contaminated as popular lore might suggest, they can be influenced by measurement artifacts and momentary situational factors. Thus, strong conclusions can be gained only when measurement artifacts are assessed and controlled, and when several different types of measurement methods are employed and lead to the same conclusions. Unfortunately, a strong multimethod database for SWB does not exist across countries. International data sets using non-self-report measures of SWB are quite limited in number and should be expanded in the future. In addition, on-line measures should be used in which people record their moods when they are signaled at random moments. The major advantages of this methodology would be reducing memory biases and allowing the researcher to determine in which situations people are happier and less happy. Thus, on-line measures of mood in international studies would yield firmer statements about country and situational differences in SWB. The conclusions we derive later in this chapter are limited by the fact that the strongest level of measurement is not yet available for international comparison of well-being.

A final methodological point is that most of the discussion on national differences of SWB in this chapter is based on national mean scores of SWB measures. Although the validity of the SWB measures documented at the individual level provides a launch pad for studying aggregated mean national differences in SWB, it should be noted that the underlying reasons for the SWB differences observed at the national level and at the individual level may be different in some cases. The explanatory factors that are important at the international level may not necessarily be the most significant determinants of the outcomes observed within nations. Similarly, data supporting the validity of SWB measures at the individual level do not conclusively demonstrate that the measures are valid when making cross-nation comparisons. Because of the limited amount of between-nation data available, however, we attempt in this chapter to merge the findings obtained from both the national and the individual levels in understanding the SWB differences across nations.

Nations as Units of Analysis

Another methodological issue is whether nations are a meaningful level of analysis in light of the fact that there are huge differences between the people within nations, as well as obvious similarities between certain nations. Some countries are quite heterogeneous. Indeed, individual differences within nations are often larger than the differences between nations. Thus, a question arises as to whether nations are meaningful units of analysis.

There are several reasons to believe that countries provide one justifiable way of examining differences in SWB. In the first place, Inglehart and Rabier (1986) noted that nationality is a strong predictor of SWB. This suggests that nationality captures important influences on SWB. Furthermore, they point out, "there is striking continuity" in the relative rankings of countries over time, suggesting that the influences that nationality summarizes are stable.

Another way to answer the question of whether nations are meaningful units for the analysis of SWB is to examine whether nations retain the same relative positions when various subgroupings are compared across nations. We therefore computed separate means for men and for women for each nation, and the resulting correlation between these figures was .97. In other words, the nation means for men are almost perfectly predictable from the means for women. Similarly, we computed the mean SWB of different age groups in each nation (in four generational groups: twenty to thirty-nine, forty to fifty-nine, sixty to seventy-nine, and eighty to ninety-nine). If one examines the correlation matrix across these different age groups based on nation means, the lowest correlation for any two groups is $r = .65$ (between the youngest group and the oldest group). The mean correlation between all of the age groups is .93. What these analyses reveal is that there is a degree of homogeneity of SWB within nations that makes countries a justifiable unit of analysis. People of different ages and sexes within nations tend to report similar levels of SWB, suggesting that there are common nationwide influences on SWB.

Of course, means for nations also average out meaningful information on subcultures and other groups within nations—we lose information when we use simplifying numbers such as means. Anthropologists frequently argue for a cultural parsing in which ever narrower subgroupings are described because they differ in systematic ways. Thus, we will analyze both differences between and within nations in SWB because both types of analyses may reveal important information. The analyses of nation means is justified, however, based on the fact that certain factors have some influence on the majority of people within a nation. Although analyses of cultural subgroupings within nations is also desirable, such analyses are beyond the scope of this chapter.

Scale Structure Invariance

A third methodological issue is concerned with the structural invariance of SWB measures across cultures. That is, items of scales must cohere in the same way in different nations before the scores on these scales can be meaningfully compared. Without structural invariance across nations, the scales might have a different meaning in different countries. The limited amount of work on measures that are used in international studies is encouraging. For example, Balatsky and Diener (1993) found that the Satisfaction with Life Scale formed a single factor in the Soviet Union, just as it does in the United States and in the People's Republic of China (Shao 1993). Similarly, the affect adjectives of Watson, Clark, and Tellegen's (1988) Positive Affect Negative Affect Schedule (PANAS), designed to measure separately pleasant and unpleasant affect, form two clear factors in Japan, China, and the United States (Shao 1993; Watson, Clark, and Tellegen 1984). Indeed, one of the most replicable findings across studies is that pleasant and unpleasant affect form two separate factors. This finding suggests that two neural systems might underlie the two types of affect, and it strongly indicates the need to measure pleasures and pains independently. The separability of pleasant and unpleasant affect indicates that nations should be compared on both types of affect, and that the two usually should not be conflated onto one dimension. Unfortunately, many international researchers use only a global well-being scale and

do not separately assess pleasant and unpleasant affect.

THE NATIONAL CORRELATES OF SWB

Wealth and Economic Development

One of the most replicable predictors of the SWB of nations is economic wealth. Diener, Diener, and Diener (1995) found a correlation of .58 between the gross domestic product per capita of fifty-five nations and their level of SWB. The correlation between per capita purchasing power parity in nations (thus controlling for differences in cost of living) and SWB was $r = .61$. Veenhoven (1991) reported an even higher correlation of .84 between the wealth of nations and their reported well-being and showed that the low relation between income and SWB reported by Easterlin (1974) was an error. Gallup (1976) and Inglehart (1990) also reported relatively strong correlations between national wealth and life satisfaction.

Figure 22.1 shows the relation between the per capita purchasing power of nations and several types of SWB, based on data from forty-one nations in the World Value Survey II. The purchasing power parity figures reflect the percentage of consumption power the citizens of a nation possess compared to people in the United States. The zero-order correlation between the mean life satisfaction level and mean purchasing power across nations is .69 in this data set, and the correlations of purchasing power with pleasant and unpleasant affect were .28 and -.41, respectively. As can be seen, SWB increases with income, although there is no increase between the third and the highest-income quartile groups. In accord with the data shown in figure 1, Veenhoven (1991) suggested that SWB shows a curvilinear relation with income, with the highest-income nations not differing. In contrast, Diener, Diener, and Diener (1995) did not find a leveling off of SWB in the richest nations. Thus, wealth may count most in poorer nations and have a decreasing effect in wealthier countries, but the evidence is inconsistent on this point.

Why is higher income in nations related to SWB? Diener and Diener (1996b) found that virtually all social indicators, with only a few exceptions, are more positive in wealthier nations. Thus, for example, in richer countries there is more schooling, more food and clean drinking water, a greater respect for human rights, more doctors per

FIGURE 22.1   National Income and Mean Subjective Well-Being

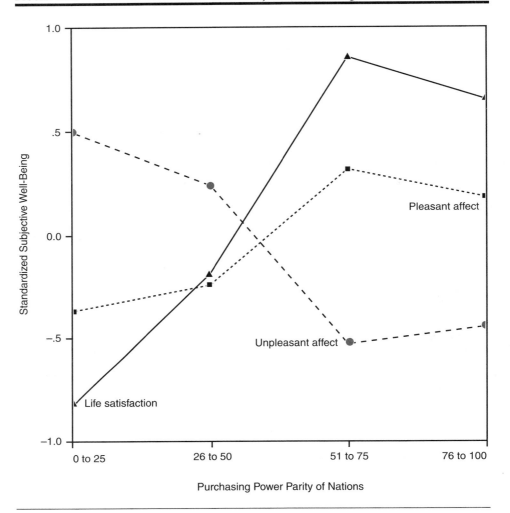

capita, greater income equality, more parity between the sexes, greater longevity, and so forth. If we examine the relation between these other factors and SWB, we also find strong positive correlations. For example, Cantril (1965) aggregated eleven measures such as literacy, urbanization, energy consumption, and newspaper circulation, as well as GNP per capita, and found that this index correlated .67 with the level of reported satisfaction with one's current life across fourteen nations. In a larger sample of fifty-five nations, Diener, Diener, and Diener (1995) found that human rights indicators correlated .48 with mean levels of reported SWB, and that an equality index correlated .48 with SWB. Veenhoven (1996) also found

a strong relation between equality and SWB. Diener, Diener, and Diener reported that the degree to which nations could fulfill basic biological needs (as assessed through longevity, low infant mortality, available calories, availability of sanitary facilities, and percentage of the population with clean drinking water) correlated .52 with the mean SWB of nations.

Why Does Economic Development Correlate with SWB?   Given that so many desirable characteristics covary with the wealth of nations, it is unsurprising that the income of nations correlates strongly with well-being. This leaves us, however, with the question of the causal pathways by which wealth may enhance feelings of well-being. Is it luxury goods and services, human rights, greater equality, or the fulfillment of basic needs that leads to greater well-being? Unfortunately, we are unable to disentangle the various potential national factors that cause SWB from the available data. The predictor variables are too highly correlated, and the sample sizes of nations too small, to control meaningfully one variable when examining the predictive power of others. For example, Diener, Diener, and Diener (1995) reported that income correlated with human rights and with the equality within nations .80 and .84, respectively. With sample sizes of nations that rarely exceed forty in number, the effects of such overlapping variables cannot be statistically disentangled. Thus, one cannot be certain from the available data whether the wealth of nations increases SWB through the greater products and services it provides or through other correlates of wealth such as human rights and greater equality. Indeed, it might even be that greater SWB leads to greater wealth—the correlations do not indicate causal direction. An important course for future researchers is to tease apart the causal influence on SWB of the variables that tend to change together during industrial development, using larger samples and longitudinal designs.

Some clues about the processes connecting the wealth of nations and well-being can perhaps be attained by examining satisfaction with different life domains in rich and poor nations. In the World Value Survey II we found that people in wealthy nations were significantly more satisfied with their home life and job. In our international student sample, we found that respondents in wealthier nations were more satisfied with their freedom and friends. Thus, economic development seems to have broad effects that spread beyond material life. However, this finding leaves open two interesting alternative explanations of the positive effects of living in wealthy nations: (1) people are more satisfied with other areas because of a spreading effect from satisfaction with their material lives, or (2) wealthier nations have additional characteristics, such as equality, that directly lead to higher satisfaction in nonmaterial areas. At this point, we do not have sufficient data to determine which of these explanations is correct.

In contrast to the findings between nations, SWB has not changed substantially over time in many highly industrialized nations, despite the fact that wealth has risen dramatically. The United States exemplifies this interesting trend. Samuelson (1995) describes the enormous increases in wealth in the United States since World War II. Yet SWB has not increased (Diener and Suh 1997). Samuelson maintains that people have come to expect more and more, and that therefore the improvement in material conditions has not led to greater feelings of well-being. Similarly, rapid economic growth in countries such as Japan and France has been accompanied by a virtually flat line for SWB.

The fact that changes in wealth in many affluent nations have not been accompanied by changes in SWB, despite the strong correlation between income and SWB at the international level, may be interpreted in several ways. First, it might be that after basic biological needs are met, further increases in wealth in relatively affluent nations do not enhance well-being. Another possibility is that concomitant factors of national income, such as equality, personal freedom, and human rights, are the prime underlying causes of SWB. Although such societal characteristics may differ significantly between poor and wealthy nations, these conditions may have not improved dramatically during the recent history of the wealthiest nations. It is also possible that wealthy nations are the happiest because they set the standard against which poorer nations compare themselves, but increases in income in the wealthiest nations produces no net increase in happiness because the standard continually rises for the citizens of the richest countries as their income rises.

Individualism Versus Collectivism

Another factor that correlates highly with national wealth is a cultural variable called "individualism." Hofstede (1980) proposed a broad cultural dimension labeled individualism-collectivism, and this dimension, also related to independence-interdependence, has been described in depth by others (for example, Markus and Kitayama 1991; Triandis 1995). Cultures differ in whether they give priority to the individual or to the group. In individualistic cultures such as the United States, there is an emphasis on a person's internal feelings and thoughts, and the individual is afforded relatively more freedom. In collectivistic cultures, priority is given to the in-group (usually a person's family and friends), and a sharp distinction is drawn between the in-group and others. Furthermore, the person's role and relationships to others are seen as central in defining who she or he is; collectivists therefore have less freedom of expression and often subordinate their private feelings to the group. Because individualism-collectivism appears to be an important cultural dimension, we examined the well-being of nations based on where they stand on this continuum.

Diener, Diener, and Diener (1995) found a strong correlation of $r = .77$ between the individualism of nations and their SWB. In the World Value Survey II and our international college student data set, we obtained correlations of .55 and .54, respectively, with mean life satisfaction. In controlling first individualism and then income in their mutual relation to SWB, we obtained different outcomes in different samples, with a flip-flop in which variable was deemed a better predictor. Because individualism and the wealth of nations correlate .80 (Diener, Diener, and Diener 1995), it is not surprising that their influence is difficult to disentangle. Thus, it seems impossible with existing data to reach a firm statistical conclusion about which factor is more important.

Another interesting finding is that SWB appears to be a more salient concept for individualists. For example, if one examines the percentage of people in the World Value Survey II who said they had never thought about whether they were happy or satisfied, this percentage is higher in collectivistic nations. Similarly, in our international college student sample, individualists reported that SWB was significantly more important to them than collectivists said it was. The latter group may emphasize duty and obligation over personal "happiness." Thus, the value one places on SWB differs across cultures (Triandis 1995).

Not only does SWB differ in importance for individualists versus collectivists, but people in different cultures are likely to judge their life satisfaction in different ways (Suh et al. 1998). Individualists tend to weight their personal emotional experiences heavily, whereas collectivists emphasize interpersonal factors when they construct life satisfaction judgments. For instance, cultural norms that dictate the correct and appropriate level of SWB influence a person's life satisfaction judgment in collectivist cultures, but not in individualist cultures. Thus, it is not only that people differently weight various domains such as marriage or work when making a life satisfaction judgment, but that they also turn more toward either internal or external information in constructing their responses.

Such cultural differences in the relative emphasis on personal attributes (such as private emotions) versus collective concerns (social ties, for example)

may yield SWB reports that seem paradoxical at a first glance. For instance, although individualist nations report higher levels of SWB than collectivist nations, suicide is committed more often in the former societies. As a result, reported SWB and suicide correlate positively across nations! If we examine marriage, a similar pattern emerges. Individualists report that they are more satisfied with their home lives, yet they get divorced at a much greater rate than collectivists.

The explanation for this paradox might be the costs and benefits of personal freedom. In collectivist nations, there is greater social support because of the strong extended family. Such support can serve as a buffer during times of stress, and therefore suicide rates are lower. The same extended family that offers support in the collectivist culture also serves to limit personal freedom. Thus, as a trade-off for strong social support in difficult times, the collectivist is less able to follow his or her own personal desires and is less likely to experience high life satisfaction in good times. Furthermore, it may also be that in individualistic nations people are more likely to commit suicide if they are not happy because being happy is thought to be an important goal. In contrast, in collectivistic societies, suicide rates may be lower because people believe that one's obligations to one's family are more important than personal happiness. Thus, depression or other unpleasant subjective states may not be seen as sufficient justification for taking one's own life.

Similarly, the paradox that marriage satisfaction is higher where divorce rates are higher is explained by the greater freedom within individualistic societies. If their marriage is not rewarding, it is easier for individualists to obtain a divorce. Those who remain married are thus more likely to be satisfied with their marriages in an individualistic country. In contrast, in a collectivist society there are strong pressures to remain married, and therefore those who stay married are on average less likely to be happy with the relationship. In fact, disappearance of emotional rewards (love) in a marital relationship is a much weaker justification for divorce in collectivist than in individualist cultures (Levine et al. 1995).

In sum, individualism-collectivism appears to be a fascinating cultural dimension that relates to SWB in several ways. First, individualists chronically pay more attention to their own opinions and feelings because of the freedom in these cultures. Therefore, SWB is more salient to individualists—they can use their evaluation of their own

SWB when making life decisions. For collectivists, whose life may be largely dictated by cultural scripts and the decisions of others, a conscious appraisal of personal SWB may not be as relevant because there are fewer life choices. Other values such as interpersonal harmony, duty, and respect are likely to be more important than individual happiness.

The second reason that the individualism-collectivism dimension is fascinating is that individualists report greater well-being. The higher SWB report of individualist nations may be due to both economic and cultural reasons. The high correlation between income and individualism at the national level indicates that the objective quality-of-life conditions in individualist nations are better than those of the collectivist societies. Thus, members of individualist cultures on the average may be happier than citizens of collectivist nations in part because of the relatively affluent life conditions of their society. At a psychological level, individualist cultural values provide more personal freedom, which may lead to higher SWB when life is going well. However, because of the lack of strong connection to extended groups, adverse life experiences may also lead to more severe negative consequences (such as suicide) in individualist societies. Furthermore, social pathology may be greater in individualistic nations, where there are fewer family pressures constraining one's behavior.

Research at the individual level teaches us that optimal psychological well-being requires a balance between one's orientation toward the self and toward others (see, for example, Helgeson, 1994). An upcoming task for studies of individualism and collectivism is to delineate and prevent the negative consequences for SWB that may result from an excessive emphasis on either the self or the group within the two contrasting cultural systems.

Other Cultural Factors

Although the economic development of a nation is a good predictor of the mean SWB of that country, it obviously is not the only factor. Looking at Japan, it is evident that variables other than income and its concomitants must influence well-being because the average SWB reported in this nation is lower than is predicted by its wealth. Japan is an outlier in the low-SWB direction; Chile is a high outlier, where more elevated SWB is reported than would be predicted from its income.

What additional national characteristics might influence SWB?

Inglehart and Rabier (1986) point out that across countries SWB seems to covary with interpersonal trust. They note that the French and Italians report low levels of trust and also lower levels of SWB than one would predict based on their incomes. Inglehart (1990) maintains that interpersonal trust and life satisfaction are related cultural variables that predispose nations to stable forms of government: "Life satisfaction, political satisfaction, interpersonal trust, high rates of political discussion, and support for the existing order all tend to go together" (41). Moreover, "democratic institutions seem to depend on enduring cultural traits, such as life satisfaction and interpersonal trust, more than on relatively fluctuating variables, such as political satisfaction" (33). If one examines the life satisfaction data of table 1, the former Communist nations of Eastern Europe stand out for their low levels of life satisfaction compared to the incomes of these nations. Perhaps the instability in these nations led to low levels of SWB. However, it might also be that low levels of SWB were brought on by a relative lack of economic progress and thus led to the political instability. It is interesting to note that the level of life satisfaction in the Dominican Republic at a time of tremendous political upheaval (in 1962, between the dictator Trujillo's assassination and prior to the overthrow of the constitutional government) was the lowest level of a measure of SWB ever recorded for any group (1.6 on a 0-to-10 scale). Thus, SWB and political stability seem to be closely related, but the causal arrow between the two might go in either or both directions.

Cultural norms to some extent dictate what emotions are desirable. The citizens of some cultures believe that life satisfaction and pleasant affect are more desirable than do people in other cultures, whereas others emphasize the relative appropriateness of unpleasant emotions. Table 22.2 shows norms, based on our international college student sample, for how desirable and appropriate it is to experience pleasant and unpleasant emotions. As can be seen, nations differ substantially in how appropriate they consider these various forms of SWB to be.

It can be seen that in the Latin nations, such as Colombia, there is a tendency to view pleasant emotions as desirable, and unpleasant emotions as relatively inappropriate. In contrast, in Confucian cultures, such as China, there tends to be relatively more acceptance of unpleasant emotions and rela-

TABLE 22.2   Norms for the Experience of Subjective Well-Being

Nation	Life Satisfaction	Pleasant Affect	Unpleasant Affect
China	4.00	4.47	4.00
Tanzania	4.43	5.07	3.83
Bahrain	4.74	5.66	3.87
Nepal	4.78	5.06	3.81
Zimbabwe	4.80	5.76	3.33
Thailand	4.92	5.44	3.13
Korea	4.98	5.91	4.10
Hong Kong	5.07	4.99	3.23
Ghana	5.11	5.14	2.88
Nigeria	5.11	5.50	3.06
Japan	5.14	6.10	4.11
India	5.15	5.37	3.38
Guam	5.28	5.04	3.71
Turkey	5.29	6.03	4.04
Indonesia	5.33	5.94	4.24
Pakistan	5.49	5.68	3.34
Lithuania	5.54	5.66	3.04
Argentina	5.55	6.10	2.95
Estonia	5.59	5.91	3.15
South Africa	5.69	5.91	3.37
Singapore	5.72	5.83	3.48
Slovenia	5.76	6.22	3.92
Peru	5.77	5.96	2.83
United States	5.77	6.15	3.52
Greece	5.80	6.38	3.15
Germany	5.81	6.06	3.88
Brazil	5.82	5.93	2.60
Denmark	5.82	6.06	4.17
Taiwan	5.83	5.60	3.65
Italy	5.89	5.98	3.38
Portugal	5.91	6.10	2.75
Austria	5.92	5.91	3.76
Finland	5.93	6.20	4.01
Hugary	5.97	6.21	4.32
Netherlands	6.00	5.97	3.67
Puerto Rico	6.12	6.24	2.30
Norway	6.12	6.11	3.18
Egypt	6.14	5.26	2.84
Spain	6.20	5.96	2.94
Colombia	6.20	6.30	2.52
Australia	6.23	6.25	3.71

Source: International College Student Data (1995).
Notes: Life satisfaction is the mean response for the ideal level of the five items of the Satisfaction with Life Scale (7-point scale). Affect values range from 1 (extremely inappropriate) to 4 (neutral) to 7 (extremely appropriate).

tively less acceptance of pleasant emotions. These normative differences are also evident in life satisfaction. For life satisfaction, respondents were asked how the ideal person would respond to five items on a seven-point scale. In China the ideal level of life satisfaction was considered to be neutrality—neither satisfied nor dissatisfied. In contrast, in Spain, Colombia, and Australia respondents viewed the ideal as strong satisfaction with life.

The differences in norms corresponded to differences in the reported experience of pleasant affect. However, unpleasant affect norms and reported experience did not correlate (Diener et al. 1996). We also found that the mean ideal level for satisfaction with life correlated .73 with the mean reported life satisfaction across nations. When the effects of income were controlled in the norm and reported life satisfaction correlation, the figure remained strongly significant at $r = .68$. Thus, although the causal direction between norms and well-being is uncertain, there were high correlations between reported norms and reports of pleasant affect and life satisfaction. In sum, cultural norms appear to be promising candidates for factors that influence SWB beyond wealth.

Noncorrelates

Certain other variables do not correlate with the SWB of nations. For example, Diener, Diener, and Diener (1995) reported that the homogeneity of nations (in terms of ethnicity, religion, and language) does not correlate with reports of well-being, despite the fact that people in homogeneous nations are less likely to be in conflict with others over religion, politics, or values. Measures of ethnic diversity and separatist movements (degree to which portions of the population want to form their own nation) were inversely correlated with SWB, but not significantly so. An unpublished finding is that population density also did not correlate with SWB. However, population is spread very unevenly in most nations, so research examining population density only within urban areas may provide a more meaningful analysis than the overall density figures we used.

Conclusion

The variables that most clearly correlate with SWB across nations are related to industrial development. The meeting of basic needs, individualism, human rights, equality, and per capita income are all variables that correlate with SWB but also correlate strongly with each other. In those nations where people are socialized to trust others, to be warm and sociable, and to not worry excessively, levels of SWB are also higher. Thus far, little research has been conducted to explore the interrelation of these variables. Cultural norms governing the experience of life satisfaction and emotions also correlate, beyond the effects of income, with reported levels of life satisfaction and pleasant emotions. A related finding is that cultures differ in the degree to which they value SWB. Finally, although wealthier nations tend to be happier, increases in income in the wealthiest nations have not been accompanied by increases in SWB.

WITHIN-NATION FINDINGS

Despite the fact that there are consistencies in the well-being of different groups in countries, the within-nation differences are also informative (see also Argyle, this volume). Moller (1996) found in South African university students that only 27 percent of blacks scored above the midpoint of the life satisfaction scale, whereas 58 percent of whites did so. Cantril (1965) systematically studied educational, income, and urban/rural differences in probability samples of fourteen nations. In most nations, poor people were less satisfied than high-income individuals, as were people with less education compared to those with more. On the average, age and sex differences were small within nations. However, there were exceptions, such as Nigeria, where older people were more satisfied than the young adult group. In the United States, rich people on average reported higher SWB than poor people, although the difference was not great. However, there were much larger differences in SWB between the rich and the poor in Brazil, the Dominican Republic, Israel, and the Philippines. Diener and Suh (1999) reported on the well-being of different age groups in many nations. They found that in many nations life satisfaction goes upward very slightly with age, despite the higher rates of widowhood and lower incomes among the elderly. However, Diener and Suh also found that pleasant affect decreases with age in most nations.

It is not just that groups within nations may differ in their mean levels of SWB, but also that different factors predict SWB in different nations. Inglehart and Rabier (1986) point out that value differences between countries lead to differences in how people seek happiness and therefore can change the variables linked to it. For example, one finding from Cantril's landmark study is that satisfaction with national issues predicted SWB in some nations but not in others. Andrews and Withey (1976) replicated Cantril's finding that

satisfaction with national affairs was virtually unrelated to personal life satisfaction in the United States. In contrast, in Nigeria and Cuba satisfaction with national and personal affairs was correlated in the neighborhood of .40. Thus, in the United States people can be satisfied with their lives and still be dissatisfied with the government and with other institutions, whereas in nations that more recently achieved independence, personal satisfaction is tied more to one's view of the nation.

Diener and Diener (1995) found that self-esteem was a stronger predictor of life satisfaction in individualistic nations than in collectivistic ones. Apparently individualists must think highly of themselves before they can be satisfied, whereas for collectivists positive feelings about oneself appear not to be critical to SWB. In sum, the correlates of SWB differ to some degree between cultures. This finding suggests that what causes SWB depends at least to some degree on people's goals and values.

PSYCHOLOGICAL PROCESSES

What are the psychological processes responsible for the variation in SWB between nations? There are several explanations for the similarities and differences in the SWB of nations—one emphasizing the fulfillment of inborn needs, one rooted in the attainment of goals, one based on the socialization of emotions and norms regarding pleasure and pain, and one focusing on genetic differences between groups.

The Innate Needs Approach

Veenhoven (1996) argues that SWB rests on "inborn reactions to situations that are good or bad for human survival" (25). People have organic, social, and self-actualization needs, and Veenhoven asserts that they will be happy when these needs are met. Veenhoven argues that income correlates with SWB across countries primarily because in some of the poorest nations inborn needs related to basic biological drives such as hunger and thirst cannot be met. In the wealthiest nations, in contrast, greater amounts of wealth over time do not increase the fulfillment of already satiated inborn drives, and therefore SWB does not rise as wealth increases further. In Veenhoven's approach, it is not that all innate needs are fully achieved in wealthy societies, but rather that the material needs that money can buy are met for most people. In these societies, only development in other directions, such as social relationships or self-actualization, can enhance SWB further.

Veenhoven's (1996) approach is similar to that developed by Deci, Ryan, and their colleagues (Ryan et al. 1996), who maintain that some activities are intrinsically rewarding to people. Intrinsically pleasing activities that relate to the needs for autonomy, competence, and relatedness are likely to lead to long-term feelings of well-being. In contrast, extrinsically motivated activities are imposed on the person by others or are sought as means to other ends. According to Deci, Kasser, and their colleagues, the quests for money, fame, and physical attractiveness are often extrinsically motivated (Kasser and Ryan 1993). Like Veenhoven, Deci, Ryan, and their colleagues tie SWB to performing intrinsically rewarding behaviors. It follows that national variations in SWB resulting from differences in wealth, according to the innate needs approach, are due to differences in the fulfillment of basic needs and to the pursuit of intrinsic interests.

Yet a third theorist who falls in the needs traditions is Scitovsky (1976), who maintained that feelings of well-being come both from comforts and the absence of pain and from an optimal level of stimulation. Because we adapt to comforts, he maintained that some deprivation is needed to continue to enjoy life. We can experience pleasure, according to Scitovsky, only if we first experience some need. In this view, wealthy societies may inadvertently deprive people of pleasures because they satiate needs and never allow deprivation to occur. Furthermore, according to Scitovsky, people require an optimal level of arousal for maximal well-being, and pleasure is derived from moving toward this optimal level. People need the right amount of mental and physical stimulation for maximal well-being, and too much or too little can cause unhappiness. Thus, the ideal society is one in which deprivation and comforts are in fine balance, and arousal-producing stimulation is at the optimum level.

Finally, Hobfoll, Lilly, and Jackson (1992) argue that moods are a reflection of a person's resources in relation to the demands made on him or her. Although resources are often physical in nature, they can also be based on social relationships and personal characteristics such as intelligence. If a person has inadequate resources to meet the demands of his or her environment, stress and negative emotions will occur. If resources are plentiful and increasing, the person will experience positive affect. In a manner similar to prospect theory (Kahneman and Tversky 1984), resource loss is seen as more powerful than the gain of resources. Hobfoll and his colleagues describe resources in terms of the demands made by the environment. Therefore, happiness will come from having adequate resources to meet the demands of the physical and social environments, and the good society will be one in which demands and resources are carefully balanced. In a complementary view of resources, Diener and Fujita (1995) view the individual as taking a more active role by selecting the goals for which resources are necessary.

The innate needs approaches share the assumption that there are some universal causes of SWB. At a concrete level, the fulfillment of needs may vary, but at a more abstract level, there may be universals. For example, an eighty-year-old lady might enjoy her family, whereas a teenager might not. However, both may need social relationships in order to be happy.

A view that in some respects is contrary to the inborn needs approach is offered by Edgerton (1992), who argues that sick societies can result if they do not limit and socialize humans' instincts. For example, if men are allowed to follow their sexual instincts, they may fight constantly over nubile women. According to Edgerton, if needs are unrestricted, they may lead to a conflictual and unhappy society. In this view, the society with high well-being is one that channels and socializes innate human needs.

In the innate needs approach, nations differ in happiness to the extent that they satisfy inborn needs. If a scientist adheres to the innate needs approach, the challenge is to uncover those needs that are common across all conditions and cultures. In contrast to the innate needs approach, the goals approach described in the next section suggests that the causes of happiness differ from person to person.

The Goals Approach

In the goals approach, people are thought to gain pleasure from moving toward their goals, and from achieving them, and are believed to suffer when they fail to make progress toward their goals. Extreme displeasure may occur, according to the goals approach, either when one realizes that it is impossible to reach one's important goals or when one finds that one is moving further away from one's goals.

The goals approach recognizes that innate needs can influence SWB because biological needs frequently influence people's goals. Humans are likely to have goals related to obtaining food and shelter, interacting with loved ones, and finding a secure source of income. In addition, people's values are likely to influence their goals. For example, some people may value physical attractiveness more than other people do, and for the former group possessing comeliness is more likely to be related to SWB. The goals approach also recognizes the importance of relative standards. For example, what other people possess may influence one's goals, and what one already has is likely to influence one's goals. However, the goals approach suggests that factors such as social comparison will not influence SWB unless they influence the goals people set for themselves.

Once goals are achieved, people are likely to set new goals, and achieving the old goal loses its power to enhance SWB. Furthermore, people are likely to alter their goals when the conditions of their lives change. If a person, for example, becomes a paraplegic, she may give up the goal of being an Olympic gymnast and pursue nonathletic goals instead. The athlete will adapt to the disability only to the extent that she sets new goals for herself. If she continues to harbor dreams of athletic fame, happiness will elude her.

The goals approach accounts for the fact that people achieve life satisfaction in different ways. In this approach, SWB depends not solely on universal needs but also on the particular goals of individuals. Which goals are selected by individuals depend on biological needs, cultural imperatives, the person's life stage (see Cantor and Sanderson, this volume), and his or her learning history.

Diener and Fujita (1995) demonstrated that varying resources predicted SWB for different people, depending on their particular goals. This finding suggests that factors such as physical attractiveness or material goods will be most related to SWB for individuals who strive after these assets. Similarly, we found that the correlates of SWB differed across nations. Diener and M. Diener (1995) found that financial satisfaction was a stronger predictor of life satisfaction in poor nations than in wealthy ones, and that self-esteem was a stronger predictor of life satisfaction in individualistic than in collectivistic nations. In the goals approach, wealthy nations are presumed to be happier because people throughout the world frequently have material goals that are best met where income is high. Similarly, individualistic nations may

have higher SWB because people in them are freer to pursue their own goals.

The goals approach is not necessarily incompatible with the innate needs approach. For example, in the goals approach, one can posit that innate drives such as hunger and sex often influence people's goals. However, according to the goals approach, it is possible that some individuals will develop goals that run counter to innate needs; for these individuals, it would be the achievement of the goals rather than the needs that determines emotional happiness. The goals approach suggests that people are happier if they live in a society that generates goals that people are capable of moving toward and achieving. Furthermore, the goals approach specifies that people will be unhappy where the culture fosters incompatible goals, that is, where people cannot reach some goals without simultaneously failing to reach others. Similarly, when a culture fosters goals that deprive people of pleasure or cause suffering, conflicts are likely to arise between contradictory motives.

The Emotion Socialization Approach

The socialization hypothesis states that there are cultural influences on the experience of emotions and pleasure and pain that affect people's level of SWB. Although pleasant and unpleasant affect consistently form two separate factors across cultures, the relative emphasis and value attached to these emotions may be partly shaped through socialization processes. For example, in certain cultures, people may be socialized to avoid an unpleasant emotion such as anger. If people constantly avoid anger-provoking situations, they will be less likely to interpret situations in a way that produces anger. In the long run, the experience and expression of anger may become less intense and less frequent. Thus, in nations where negative affect is discouraged, individuals might from an early age be taught strategies for avoiding it. As mentioned, Latin nations deplore negative emotions compared to the Confucian nations of the Pacific Rim, where they are viewed as neutral. Similarly, different religious cultural traditions teach that suffering either is something to be avoided or has redemptive and transformative value (Glicksman 1995).

In some cultures, there appears to be more encouragement of pleasant affect. Children may be encouraged to smile and laugh and to seek out fun situations. Individuals may be taught that seeking pleasurable situations is a good thing, and they may be taught to identify a feeling of arousal in a positive way. Our international data indicate that there are substantial differences in the value that people place on happiness, and these variations may reflect deeply held values that in turn influence how much pleasure is experienced.

According to the emotion socialization approach, differences between nations and cultures in SWB may result at least in part from the value that cultures place on various unpleasant and pleasant emotions, and on pleasure and pain. These values in turn influence the manner in which individuals are socialized, a process that then influences their levels of SWB. People may value pleasure and seek it out, or they may believe that suffering has value and do less to avoid it. In the socialization approach, variations in SWB may result from the differential importance afforded to SWB in different cultures.

The Genetic Differences Approach

Finally, it is possible that genetic differences between ethnic groups might explain differences in SWB. For example, East Asian and Navajo infants are less reactive than their Euro-American counterparts (Edgerton 1992), suggesting possible temperament differences between the groups. Although it is possible that genetics can explain SWB differences between nations, cultural and economic differences can also provide reasonable explanations for the same data. Thus, it is premature to accept such explanations, although genetics does provide a viable explanation for some of the variability between nations in SWB. If individual differences within cultures are largely inheritable, it is conceivable that differences between groups might at least in part be due to genetic differences between the populations.

Conclusion

The four theoretical approaches have not been tested rigorously. For example, the study of immigrant groups moving from one region to another (including successive immigrant generations) would shed light on the genetic hypothesis, but such research has not been conducted. How the socialization of emotion correlates with SWB has barely been empirically explored. A systematic comparison of the innate needs and goals approaches has not been carried out. Thus, future work in the area should focus on exploring the psychological

and biological causes of national differences in SWB.

POLICY IMPLICATIONS

The efforts of policy-makers to improve the quality of life are not well placed when only the economy or social indicators such as crime and infant mortality are measured. If only objective indicators are collected, valuable information is lost about how people evaluate and weight the conditions of their lives. Subjective indicators can summarize how people feel about aspects of their lives, weighted by how important these factors are to them. Although subjective indicators should not substitute for measures of external conditions, they serve as a useful complement in assessing and improving the quality of life of societies.

If policy-makers are to use SWB indicators effectively, they will be best served by a variety of indicators. Although a global indicator of SWB analogous to GNP might be useful, more specific indicators are beneficial as well. Certainly both positive and negative indicators are necessary to assess the overall feeling tone of a nation. Furthermore, global measures are unlikely to be sufficient for the policy-makers' needs because so many different factors influence global SWB. Thus, more specific indicators, such as people's satisfaction with their job, their frequency of worry about unemployment, and their fear of crime, will probably be more useful to policy-makers, especially when collected longitudinally.

In terms of substantive findings, it is clear that material well-being correlates with the SWB of citizens. We do not fully understand whether this is because wealthy societies are able to meet the innate material needs of citizens or because people the world over have come to desire a high level of material wealth and they are better able to meet this goal if they live in a wealthy nation. We also do not know whether wealth has its effect through intangibles such as greater human rights, democracy, and equality rather than through physical comforts.

An intriguing idea that bears repeating is Inglehart's (1990) hypothesis that a widespread feeling of well-being is necessary for democracy to prosper. Thus, stable and democratic governments may thrive best when their citizens are happy. In times of distress and unhappiness, people may be more likely to turn to dictators to cure their ills.

Policy-makers who intend to improve the lot of

their society should be aware of the influence of adaptation and expectancies. Although people may be happier if they live under improved conditions, the influence is likely to be large at first and then taper off. Expectancies can outstrip reality even when an economy is growing rapidly—with a net loss in SWB. Thus, specific living conditions sought by policy-makers should be desirable as an end in themselves, because they may not always produce increases in happiness. Subjective well-being is desirable, but other values must also be respected. There is little in the SWB findings, however, to support the notion that economic development leads to unhappiness.

REFERENCES

Andrews, F. M., and Robinson, J. P. (1992). Measures of subjective well-being. In J. P. Robinson, P. R. Shaver, and L. S. Wrightsman (Eds.), *Measures of personality and social psychological attitudes* (pp. 61–114). San Diego: Academic Press.

Andrews, F. M., and Withey, S. B. (1976). *Social indicators of well-being: America's perception of life quality.* New York: Plenum.

Balatsky, G., and Diener, E. (1993). Subjective well-being among Russian students. *Social Indicators Research, 28,* 225–43.

Bradburn, N. M. (1969). *The structure of psychological well-being.* Chicago: Aldine.

Cantril, H. (1965). *The pattern of human concerns.* New Brunswick, N.J.: Rutgers University Press.

Cutler, S. E., Bunce, S. C., and Larsen, R. J. (1996). Repressive coping style and its relation to daily emotional experience and remembered emotional experience. *Journal of Personality, 64,* 379–405.

Diener, E. (1994). Assessing subjective well-being: Progress and opportunities. *Social Indicators Research, 31,* 103–57.

———. (1995). A value-based index for measuring national quality of life. *Social Indicators Research, 36,* 107–27.

Diener, E., and Diener, C. (1996a). Most people are happy. *Psychological Science, 7,* 181–85.

———. (1996b). The wealth of nations revisited: Income and quality of life. *Social Indicators Research, 36,* 275–86.

Diener, E., and Diener, M. (1995). Cross-cultural correlates of life satisfaction and self-esteem. *Journal of Personality and Social Psychology, 68,* 653–63.

Diener, E., Diener, M. and Diener, C. (1995). Factors predicting the subjective well-being of nations. *Journal of Personality and Social Psychology, 69,* 851–64.

Diener, E., and Fujita, F. (1995). Resources, personal strivings, and subjective well-being: A nomothetic and ideographic approach. *Journal of Personality and Social Psychology, 68,* 926–35.

Diener, E., Sandvik, E., Pavot, W., and Gallagher, D. (1991). Response artifacts in the measurement of subjective well-being. *Social Indicators Research, 24,* 35–56.

Diener, E., and Suh, E. (1997). Measuring quality of life: Economic, social, and subjective indicators. *Social Indicators Research, 40,* 189–216.

Diener, E., and Suh, E. (1999). Subjective well-being and age: An international analysis. In K. W. Schaie and M. P. Lawton (Eds.), *Annual Review of Gerontology and Geriatrics, 17.*

Diener, E., Suh, E., Lucas, R., and Smith, H. (1997). Subjective well-being: Three decades of progress—1967 to 1997. University of Illinois at Urbana-Champaign. Unpublished paper.

Diener, E., Suh, E., Shao, L., and Oishi, S. (1996). Norms for affect: National comparisons. Paper presented at the ninth conference of the International Society for Research on Emotions, Toronto (August 13–17).

Diener, E., Suh, E., Smith, H., and Shao, L. (1995). National differences in reported subjective well-being: Why do they occur? *Social Indicators Research, 34,* 7–32.

Easterlin, R. A. (1974). Does economic growth improve the human lot?: Some empirical evidence. In P. A. David and W. R. Levin (Eds.), *Nations and households in economic growth* (pp. 98–125). Stanford, Calif.: Stanford University Press.

Edgerton, R. (1992). *Sick societies: Challenging the myth of primitive harmony.* New York: Free Press.

Eurobarometer. (1991). *Trends 74–90 B1: The public opinion in the E. C.* Brussels: Commission of the European Community.

Gallup, G. H. (1976). Human needs and satisfactions: A global survey. *Public Opinion Quarterly, 40,* 459–67.

Glicksman, A. (1995). Cultural issues in aging. Paper presented at the National Academy of Elder Law Attorneys, Symposium on Elder Law, New York (May).

Helgeson, V. S. (1994). Relation of agency and communion to well-being: Evidence and potential explanations. *Psychological Bulletin, 116,* 412–28.

Hobfoll, S. E., Lilly, R. S., and Jackson, A. P. (1992). Conservation of social resources and the self. In H. O. F. Veiel and U. Baumann (Eds.), *The meaning and measurement of social support.* Washington, D.C.: Hemisphere.

Hofstede, G. (1980). *Culture's consequences: International differences in work-related values.* Beverly Hills: Sage.

Inglehart, R. (1990). *Culture shift in advanced industrial society.* Princeton, N.J.: Princeton University Press.

Inglehart, R., and Rabier, J. R. (1986). Aspirations adapt to situations—but why are the Belgians so much happier than the French? In F. M. Andrews (Ed.), *Research on the quality of life* (pp. 1–56). Ann Arbor: Institute for Social Research, University of Michigan.

Kahneman, D., and Tversky, A. (1984). Choices, values, and frames. *American Psychologist, 39,* 341–50.

Kasser, T., and Ryan, R. M. (1993). A dark side of the American dream: Correlates of financial success as a central life aspiration. *Journal of Personality and Social Psychology, 65,* 410–22.

King, D. A., and Buchwald, A. M. (1982). Sex differences in subclinical depression: Administration of the Beck Depression Inventory in public and private disclosure situations. *Journal of Personality and Social Psychology, 42,* 963–69.

Larsen, R. J., Diener, E., and Emmons, R. A. (1985). An evaluation of subjective well-being measures. *Social Indicators Research, 17,* 1–18.

Levine, L. (1997). Reconstructing memory for emotions. *Journal of Experimental Psychology: General, 126,* 165–77.

Levine, R., Sato, S., Hashimoto, T., and Verma, J. (1995). Love and marriage in eleven cultures. *Journal of Cross-cultural Psychology, 26,* 554–71.

Markus, H. R., and Kitayama, S. (1991). Culture and the self: Implications for cognition, emotion, and motivation. *Psychological Review, 98,* 224–53.

Michalos, A. C. (1991). *Global report on student well-being.* New York: Springer-Verlag.

Moller, V. (1996). Life satisfaction and expectations for the future in a sample of university students: A research note. *South African Journal of Sociology, 27,* 16–26.

Moum, T. (1996). Mode of administration and interviewer effects in self-reported symptoms of anxiety and depression. University of Norway, Oslo. Unpublished paper.

Oettingen, G., and Seligman, M. E. P. (1990). Pessimism and behavioral signs of depression in East versus West Berlin. *European Journal of Social Psychology, 20,* 207–20.

Oishi, S., Diener, E., Eid, M., and Suh, E. (1996). An analysis of response artifacts across nations: The case of subjective well-being. University of Illinois at Urbana-Champaign. Unpublished paper.

Pavot, W., and Diener, E. (1993a). The affective and cognitive context of self-reported measures of subjective well-being. *Social Indicators Research, 28,* 1–20.

———. (1993b). Review of the Satisfaction with Life Scale. *Psychological Assessment, 5,* 164–72.

Ryan, R. M., Sheldon, K. M., Kasser, T., and Deci, E. L. (1996). All goals are not created equal: An organismic perspective on the nature of goals and their regulation. In P. M. Gollwitzer and J. A. Bargh (Eds.), *The psychology of action: Linking cognition and motivation to behavior* (pp. 1–26). New York: Guilford.

Samuelson, R. J. (1995). *The good life and its discontents.* New York: Random House.

Sandvik, E., Diener, E., and Seidlitz, L. (1993). Subjective well-being: The convergence and stability of self-report and non-self-report measures. *Journal of Personality, 61,* 317–42.

Schwarz, N., and Clore, G. L. (1983). Mood, misattribution, and judgments of well-being: Informative and directive functions of affective states. *Journal of Personality and Social Psychology, 45,* 513–23.

Scitovsky, T. (1976). *The joyless economy.* Oxford: Oxford University Press.

Shao, L. (1993). Multilanguage comparability of life satisfaction and happiness measures in mainland Chinese and American students. Master's thesis, University of Illinois at Urbana-Champaign.

Sudman, S., Greeley, A. M., and Pinto, L. J. (1967). The use of self-administered questionnaires. In S. Sudman (Ed.), *Reducing the cost of surveys* (pp. 46–57). Chicago: Aldine.

Suh, E., Diener, E., Oishi, S., and Triandis, H. C. (1998). The shifting basis of life satisfaction judgments across cultures: Emotions versus norms. *Journal of Personality and Social Psychology, 74,* 482–93.

Thomas, D., and Diener, E. (1990). Memory accuracy in the recall of emotions. *Journal of Personality and Social Psychology, 59,* 291–97.

Triandis, H. C. (1995). *Individualism and collectivism.* Boulder, Colo.: Westview Press.

Veenhoven, R. (1991). Is happiness relative? *Social Indicators Research, 24,* 1–34.

———. (1993). *Happiness in nations: Subjective appreciation of life in fifty-six nations, 1946–1992.* Rotterdam: Risbo.

———. (1996). The study of life satisfaction. In W. Saris, R. Veenhoven, A. C. Scherpenzeel, and B. Bunting. (Eds.), *A comparative study of satisfaction with life in Europe* (pp. 11–48). Budapest: Eotvos University Press.

Watson, D., Clark, L. A., and Tellegen, A. (1984). Cross-cultural convergence in the structure of mood: A Japanese replication and a comparison with U.S. findings. *Journal of Personality and Social Psychology, 47,* 127–44.

———. (1988). Development and validation of brief measures of positive and negative affect: The PANAS scale. *Journal of Personality and Social Psychology, 54,* 1063–70.

World Values Study Group (1994). *World Values Survey, 1981–1984 and 1990–1993.* Inter-University Consortium for Political and Social Research (ICPSR) version (computer file). Ann Arbor: Institute for Social Research, University of Michigan.

Part V

Biological Perspectives

23 The Physiology and Pathophysiology of Unhappiness

Robert M. Sapolsky

Stress physiology, as applied to the average vertebrate, is the study of the defenses mobilized by the body in response to physical challenges—being chased by a predator when injured, or sprinting after a meal when starving. In contrast, humans have the cognitive sophistication to activate habitually the identical stress response for purely psychological or social reasons—worries about mortgages, relationships and the thinning ozone layer. While activation of the stress response is critical for surviving pursuit by a lion, it is pathogenic when mobilized chronically, and many Westernized diseases are caused or worsened by overactive stress responses. How do psychological and social factors—such as unhappiness—activate the stress response? Broadly, for the same physical stressor, an organism is more likely to have a stress response if it lacks outlets for frustration, social support, control, or predictability. Social status also modulates the stress response. Many studies of social primates suggest that low-ranking individuals have chronically activated stress responses and are more prone to stress-related diseases. This tendency probably reflects their being subject to higher rates of both physical and psychological stressors than are dominant individuals. However, in primates, social subordinance is not always associated with such maladaptive physiology; it is not just rank that influences physiology, but also the sort of society in which the rank occurs, and the individual's experience of rank and society. These same principles can be applied to interpreting social status and patterns of diseases in humans. Particular emphasis is placed on the extensive literature on the health risks of low socioeconomic status (SES), which are interpreted in the context of the psychological stressors associated with low SES. Personality and temperament also modulate the stress response; for example, primates with a "hot reactor" temperament have an overactivated stress response, as do humans with major depression, anxiety disorders, Type A personality, or repressive personality. Finally, social status and personality can interact in a critical manner—specifically, an inner locus of control can be highly adaptive in one position in society but highly predictive of cardiovascular disease in another.

IMAGINE THAT AN earnest young wildebeest, in the early stages of its Ph.D. program in psychobiology, has finally selected a thesis project. The ambitious ungulate plans to study the physiological correlates of social behavior of the primate *Homo sapiens*. Thanks to anesthetic dartings of groups of tourists that frequent the savanna, a study population is outfitted with telemetry devices, remote blood collection systems, and ambulatory EKG monitors. All is going well, and a degree seems conceivable for this scholarly wildebeest when an inexplicable set of data appears—on certain occasions, specifically in the afternoons when the humans lounge in the shade of their camp, pairs of them perform a strange behavior. Two males, for example, might begin these odd, ritualized interactions, and as they do, blood pressure quickly soars, heart rate increases dramatically, muscle tension rises, as does caloric expenditure, and androgenic steroid hormones pour into the circulation. The wildebeest knows precisely what the physiology implies, namely, an intense male-male dispute. The physiological profile is identical to when two male wildebeest contest for females in heat, as they lunge at each other. Yet the two humans do nothing more than sit in close proximity, decrease their rates of vocalization and eye contact, and, occasionally, do nothing more physically taxing than move a small piece of wood.

A startling aspect of human psychobiology: people who care about such things get physiologically aroused during chess matches, and get aroused in ways that make them indistinguishable from animals having territorial disputes (Leedy and DuBeck 1971). The poor wildebeest has just discovered a startling fact about humans, one that makes no sense to virtually any other animal (particularly those comprising its dissertation committee): humans mobilize the same physiology as any other animal, but for reasons unrelated to physical demands.

This chapter is concerned with another circumstance in which humans mobilize a common set of physiological responses, but for novel reasons. For most species, this system signals either a physical insult or the imminent threat of one. For humans, in contrast, it far more frequently signals a state of unhappiness, of psychological or social unease.

The *stress response* is a set of hormonal and neural events that are fairly stereotyped among vertebrates. This phylogenetic conservation implies a vital role in physiology, namely, saving your neck during a crisis. For most species, the stress response mediates adaptation to threats to *homeostasis*. This term, coined by the physiologist Walter Cannon early in the century, and a cornerstone of our ninth-grade biology education, refers to a sense of physiologic equilibrium where body temperature, acidity, blood glucose level state, and so on, are all in balance and ideal. A *stressor* can be something in the environment that disrupts homeostatic balance, and the stress response represents the adaptations that help reestablish homeostasis. For most species, such disruptions can be anything but subtle—starvation, injury, an attack by a predator, combat with a conspecific—nature bloody in tooth and claw. In that context, the stress response represents the adaptations that help save your life.[1]

In some cases, a stressor can also be the *anticipation* that one is just about to be thrown out of balance. Thus, a wildebeest, seeing a lion charging toward it, may immediately mobilize the stress response—increasing its heart rate and blood pressure, diverting energy to its muscles—even though it has not yet been torn asunder. And in the same way, a lion may mobilize its stress response in anticipation of a threat to allostasis, such as having to sprint after a meal. Stress responses in anticipation of the immediacy of a physical stressor are obviously adaptive, insofar as they give the organism a head start in physiologically coping.

Among humans, however, the stress response is mobilized in ways unimaginable in the rest of the animal kingdom. When scanning the cloudless skies and the parched soil during a drought, a subsistence farmer in the developing world might mobilize the stress response in the knowledge that, months later, his children will be starving, even though their current nutritional state is perfectly adequate. When scanning a calendar, an overextended American might mobilize a stress response with the realization that 15 April is just around the corner, even though this individual is not being menaced by carnivores at the moment. And virtually all humans at some sleepless point at night will mobilize the stress response after recognizing that their time on this earth is horribly finite. Humans can activate the typical vertebrate stress response in anticipation of physical stressors that are extremely displaced in time. This is made possible by a vast extension of the cognitive skills that allow a wildebeest to react in alarm at the sight of a rapidly approaching lion, allowing us instead to fret over challenges long in the future. Moreover, humans can readily activate the identical stress response for purely psychological or social reasons, when there are *no* conceivable physical challenges. This requires features of thought and emotion that are shared with only a handful of other species, and that are possessed by them to a far lesser extent. Experiments will be discussed in which stress responses in rats can be triggered by purely psychological manipulations, or in which a primate's endocrine profile reflects his cognitive assessment of his role in his society. Nonetheless, no rat or primate is ever going to understand why these humans get stressed by blind dates, promotions, public speaking, or traffic jams.

The centerpiece of stress physiology is our human ability to mobilize the system for psychological or social reasons. The centerpiece of stress *patho*physiology is the mostly human province of increased likelihood of disease owing to *chronic* mobilization of the stress response. Stressors for most animals are typically short-term and physical, since either the crisis or the animal is soon over with. Wildebeests do not have thirty-year sprints from lions, but we can be stressed with thirty-year mortgages, and it is the chronicity of the stress response that increases the risk of disease (for reasons to be explained later). This chapter reviews the physiology and pathophysiology of the stress response, focusing on features that are most central to understanding humans and their psychological stressors. Why bother? Perhaps monitoring the stress response is a particularly accurate way of detecting the emotive state of an individual. This is precisely what is being done in studies with non-human primates. Animal care laws commendably mandate that attention be paid to the "psychological well-being" of laboratory primates, generating the nontrivial task of determining when that state has been achieved. In the absence of the extensive observation that would be required of each animal, a reasonable solution is to decide that animals that have elevated circulating levels of stress-responsive hormones probably do not have a psychological sense of well-being. However, this approach is not particularly needed for humans. In general, you do not need to monitor a dozen different hormones in someone's bloodstream to know that they are unhappy (nor, as will be discussed later, is that likely to actually tell you much).

The important reason for studying stress physiology is its relevance to disease. Few of us will die of bubonic plague, malnutrition, or dengue fever—infectious disease and diseases of poor nutrition or hygiene have mostly been vanquished in Western societies. Instead, we die of diseases of slow accumulation of damage—the gradual blockage of blood vessels that can cause heart or cerebrovascular disease; the slow derangement of metabolism of adult-onset diabetes; the repeated challenge and ultimate defeat of immune defenses that is cancer. Lifestyle, emotional temperament, and psychological factors have virtually nothing to do with how a body manages exposure to a massive and rapidly acting insult such as cholera, but they have much to do with the progression of some of our most common Western diseases. Insofar as chronic unhappiness, anxiety, and depression can cause sustained overactivation of the stress response, they increase the risk of some of these diseases. Humans are unique in the extent to which they can mobilize the stress response for sustained, psychological reasons, and Westernized humans are unique in living well enough and long enough to pay the price for this.

In the first part of this chapter, I review the physiology of the stress response, and how stress-related disease occurs. I recognize that readers are not physiologists, and that they do not wish to become one; to make this section more user-friendly, it closes with a summary, to which the faint-hearted can skip immediately; moreover, I give only broad references to reviews of the subject. Following that, I review how psychological, social, and personality factors can modulate or cause the stress response.

THE PHYSIOLOGY OF THE STRESS RESPONSE AND THE EMERGENCE OF STRESS-RELATED DISEASE

As noted, varied stressors trigger a fairly stereotyped set of endocrine and neural responses, known as the stress response. At the heart of this is the activation of the sympathetic nervous system (a division of the autonomic, or involuntary, nervous system). This leads to the secretion into the bloodstream of the hormones adrenaline and noradrenaline (also known as epinephrine and norepinephrine), which mediate the classic "fight or flight" syndrome. Of equal importance is the secretion during stress of other hormones called glucocorticoids. These steroids come from the adrenal gland, with the human version being cortisol (also known as hydrocortisone). Stress also stimulates the secretion of additional hormones, such as beta-endorphin, glucagon, prolactin, and vasopressin (reviewed in chapter 2 of Sapolsky 1998).

The stress response inhibits other endocrine and neural systems. There is decreased secretion of insulin, of hormones related to sexual behavior and reproduction, and of hormones related to growth and tissue repair, as well as inhibition of the parasympathetic nervous system. While the sympathetic activation mediates arousal, parasympathetic activation works in opposition, having a calming, vegetative effect (see Sapolsky 1998, ch. 2).

Remarkably, the actions of this daunting array of hormones make sense when one considers the physiological needs of a prey species desperately trying to evade a predator, or those of that predator desperately trying to obtain a meal. For both animals, this crisis requires the immediate mobilization of energy into the bloodstream and its subsequent diversion to exercising muscle; this would be a singularly inauspicious time to be depositing energy into fat cells for a project for next spring. As such, during stress, energy storage is blocked and previously stored energy is liberated into the bloodstream and diverted to muscle. These steps are accomplished by the inhibition of insulin secretion and of parasympathetic tone, and by the activation of the sympathetic nervous system, glucocorticoids, and glucagon (which were named for their ability to mobilize energy by increasing circulating levels of glucose) (reviewed in Munck, Guyre, and Holbrook 1984). It is also adaptive to deliver those nutrients to muscle as rapidly as possible, and sympathetic hormones plus glucocorticoids increase heart rate and blood pressure.

During a crisis, it is also useful to inhibit any physiological processes that are unessential, wasteful drains on resources. As such, the stress response also involves triaging a variety of functions. Digestion is inhibited (including the inhibition of salivary secretion, accounting for our dry mouths when we are nervous); for the hungry predator, digestion is irrelevant, while for the prey, the energy being mobilized comes from glycogen stored in the liver (rather than from glucose in the gut), and this is no time for the slow and costly process of digestion. Growth, inflammation, and tissue repair are also deferred for later. In addition, reproductive physiology is inhibited; a desperate sprint across the savanna is no time to ovulate. As another feature of the stress response, immune function is inhibited, because of the danger of overactivation of immunity (to the point of autoimmune disease) during stressors (an idea first hypothesized by Munck et al. [1984] and heavily supported by both experimental and clinical data). Finally, during certain types of stressors, pain perception is blunted (the phenomenon of stress-induced analgesia, where someone in the middle of combat might be unaware of being injured) (reviewed by Terman et al. 1984).

Collectively, these steps are vital for surviving a physical stressor, as demonstrated by a handful of rare diseases in which components of the stress response fail. For example, in Addison's disease, sufferers are depleted of glucocorticoids, while in Shy-Drager syndrome, it is the sympathetic nervous system that is impaired. In both cases, individuals are extremely fragile if untreated, and a variety of physical stressors can prove fatal.

Yet sustained overactivation of this same stress response (most typically, for psychological reasons) can be pathogenic. To be more precise, it is not that stress makes you sick, but that it increases the likelihood of contracting a disease that makes you sick.

When the pathogenic potential of stress was first recognized in the 1930s (Selye 1936), an explanation emerged that is now considered wrong. In the face of a short-term stressor, as just described, the stress response is mobilized and a state of adaptation, a reestablishment of allostatic balance, can be achieved. As conceptualized back then, prolonged stress causes a state of exhaustion—literally, the body is depleted of hormones such as glucocorticoids, epinephrine, or norepinephrine, and disease occurs because the external stressor now pummels the body unopposed (see Selye 1971). In this scenario, stress-related disease arises because the defending army of the stress response runs out of ammunition.

As a first demonstration that this cannot be the explanation for stress pathophysiology, purely psychological stressors (in which there is no external insult to pummel the body, should defenses fail) are pathogenic when prolonged. Moreover, it is exceedingly rare that chronic stress of any sort leads to the hypothesized exhaustion stage, where stores of stress hormones are depleted. The facets of the stress response just outlined, though generally costly and inefficient, are essential for surviving an acute crisis. When those same facets are chronically activated, they exact a price; in effect, stress-related disease arises not because the army runs out of ammunition, but because the rest of the economy is bankrupted by the size of the defense budget. This principle applies to numerous organismal systems. As outlined, when running at full speed during a physical stressor, it is adaptive to divert energy to muscle. Yet if you mobilize the same metabolic stress response chronically when worrying about the ozone layer, there is atrophy of storage tissues, fatigue, and increased risk of adult-onset diabetes (or worsening of preexisting cases) (see Surwit, Ross, and Feingloss 1991). Moreover, while increasing blood pressure in order to sprint away from a predator is adaptive, doing the same repeatedly in the face of daily traffic jams places significant wear and tear on blood vessels.

The triaging of nonessential tasks also becomes damaging when prolonged. Repeated inhibition of blood flow to the stomach (part of the inhibition of digestion) increases the risk of certain types of ulcers (probably unrelated to the recently discovered ulcerogenic bacteria) (see Yabana and Yachi 1988). Prolonged stress also wreaks havoc with reproduction. In females, cycles become irregular or cease altogether, implantation of fertilized eggs become less likely owing to thinning of the uterine lining, and the risk of miscarriage increases. In males, prolonged stress decreases testosterone concentrations and, of even more functional significance, causes impotency or premature ejaculation (reviewed in Sapolsky 1991).

Continuing this theme, we cannot constantly defer long-term building and repair in our bodies without paying a price. In young organisms, chronic stress disrupts growth. At an extreme, growth can cease entirely, despite adequate food intake. Such cases have been given a number of labels, including failure to thrive, stress dwarfism, or psychogenic or psychosocial dwarfism (see Green, Campbell, and David 1984). Remarkably, removal of the child from the stressful environment typically reinstates growth.

Finally, insofar as stress is immunosuppressive, tremendous attention has been focused on the possibility that chronic stress increases vulnerability to infectious disease and cancer. This forms a cornerstone of the nascent discipline of psychoneuroimmunology (Ader, Felten, and Cohen 1991). It appears that stress does indeed increase the risk of some relatively minor infectious diseases (for example, the common cold). Far more attention has been focused, however, on possible links between chronic stress and cancer; a careful reading of the literature indicates that any such links are quite weak (and inflated in many circles) (reviewed in Sapolsky 1998, ch. 8). Finally, the immensely complicated relations between chronic stress and autoimmune disease are beyond the scope of this chapter.

In summary, various physical and psychological stressors trigger the fairly stereotyped stress response, which includes secretion of the adrenal steroid hormones called glucocorticoids, activation of the "flight or fight" sympathetic nervous system (leading to the secretion of epinephrine and norepinephrine), and inhibition of secretion of hormones related to growth and sex. Collectively, these responses are adaptive during an acute physical crisis, such as a sprint across the savanna—energy is mobilized from storage sites and delivered to exercising muscle, cardiovascular tone is enhanced to accelerate such nutrient delivery, and anything unessential to surviving the immediate crisis—digestion, reproduction, growth, tissue repair, immunity—is deferred until a more auspicious time. However, if these same responses are prolonged, there is increased risk of disease, or worsening of preexisting disease, mainly because these responses themselves are sufficiently costly to become damaging themselves eventually. Thus, with prolonged stress, there is often worsening of metabolic diseases such as adult-onset diabetes (owing to chronic mobilization of energy stores), hypertension (owing to the cardiovascular effects of the stress response), certain types of ulcers (owing to the inhibition of digestion), amenorrhea and impotency (owing to the inhibition of reproduction), stress dwarfism (owing to the inhibition of growth), and there is also sufficient suppression of immunity to increase the risk of some infectious diseases.

While it is highly maladaptive if an organism cannot mobilize the stress response during an acute physical challenge, it can be just as deleterious if the system is activated for too long, as is often the case with the psychological stressors in the lives of humans. From a physiological standpoint, the most commonly accepted indices of such overactivation involve elevated resting levels of glucocorticoids or of the hormones of the sympathetic nervous system (epinephrine and norepinephrine).

PSYCHOLOGICAL MODULATORS OF THE STRESS RESPONSE

The two central concepts of this chapter are that (1) while most animals activate the stress response because of an acute physical challenge to physiological equilibrium, or the impending threat of such a challenge, humans tend to activate the stress response for purely psychological or social reasons, and that (2) chronic activation of the stress response (as often happens with humans for those nonphysical reasons) can increase the risk of certain diseases, or worsen certain preexisting diseases. The preceding section detailed how the adaptive features of the short-term stress response turn into maladaptive pathophysiology when chronic. In this section, I focus on what is perhaps the most important question in this chapter: What features make psychological stressors stressful? We might initially assume that answering this question involves rather imprecise, nonquantitative, psychological approaches (and the use of the term "psychological" by most stress physiologists—who earn their livings by making precise measurements of how the extent of insults like blood volume loss, hypothermia, or hypoglycemia trigger the stress response—is most definitely pejorative). However, some rigorous and clear-cut paradigms have emerged (reviewed in Levine, Coe, and Wiener 1989; Weiss 1968). It is worth reviewing them here—if in a somewhat simplified or schematized form.

In one scenario, two rats are in adjacent cages and receive, for example, mild electric shocks through an electrified floor grid. Critically, both animals receive the same shocks, of equal intensity, at precisely the same times; by all of the rules of now-classic stress physiology, their bodies would be challenged to identical extents. The sole difference would be some psychological variable manipulated in one of the rats. The endpoint would then be a measure of the stress response (for example, blood pressure, heart rate, glucocorticoid or epinephrine levels in the bloodstream), or a measure of a stress-related disease (such as the incidence of stress ulcers). This approach has provided extremely clear demonstrations of the psychological variables that modulate the stress response.

The first critical variable is whether an organism has *outlets* for the frustration caused by a physical stressor. Expose two rats to the identical shocks, and there will be less of a stress response and less risk of a stress-related disease in the one with access to a running wheel or a bar of wood to gnaw. This has been generalized to other paradigms and species, producing the general observation that a physical stressor is more pathogenic when an individual lacks outlets or sources of displacement. These studies form the scientific rationale for the stress management emphasis on outlets like hobbies or exercise.

These studies gave some insight into another, less adaptive coping response in many humans: a rat being shocked is buffered from the stress response if it is allowed to be polydipsic or polyphagic—stress can trigger overeating or drinking. Finally, these studies showed another, even more disquieting coping response—a rat exposed to shocks has less of a stress response if it can attack another rat. The tendency of organisms to reduce stress by displacing aggression onto other individuals is at the heart of the stress management caveat that you shouldn't avoid getting ulcers by giving them to others. And it might give us some insight into the links between socioeconomic stress and increased rates of spousal or child abuse (discussed in Lenington 1981).

The classic yoked-rat paradigm revealed a second psychological variable. Expose two rats to a pattern of electric shocks; in one cage, however, there is a warning light that, ten seconds before each shock, signals the impending stressor. The rat receiving *predictive information* has less chance of a stress response or a stress-related disease. This finding, too, has generalized across paradigms and species (including humans exposed to loud noises with or without a prior warning; see, for example, Brier et al. 1987) and shows that under circumstances of certain inevitable stressors, it is protective to know how bad and how long the stressor will be, and when it starts. When asking a dentist whether some painful drilling is almost finished, all of us take more comfort from the answer, "I just need to drill *X* more times and we're done," than from hearing, "Hmm, hard to say with these things, could be a few more seconds, could be hours, I remember a patient once. . . ."

Predictability protects for two reasons. First, by revealing when the stressor is coming, and how bad it will be, it helps shape the type of coping response mobilized. This can be detected with physiological measures with the demonstration that predictive information decreases the size of the stress response *during* the stressor. For example, an individual undergoes a surgical procedure and is given some predictive information—the first postsurgical day will involve a fair amount of pain, the second day only some minor discomfort. Most people would find that information helpful in planning their coping outlets: plan to watch the four distracting action movies on video during the first day; wait until the second day to peruse that collection of delicate haikus.

The second way in which predictive information helps is perhaps even more important. By signaling when a stressor is impending, the absence of that signal indicates when an organism can relax (termed the "safety-signal hypothesis" by Seligman 1975). The rat without the warning light might always be a half-second away from a shock. This can be detected with physiological measures with the demonstration that predictive information makes for a faster recovery of the stress response *after* the abatement of the stressor—the organism knows that it is over with until the next warning.

The relevance of predictability in explaining patterns of human stressors is obvious. The simplest demonstration is that students hate pop quizzes. The more important arenas are considerably more complicated. As will be discussed later, predictability works only in certain circumstances. Another psychological variable is critical. Expose two rats, once again, to the same shocks. One rat has been trained in an active avoidance task. Specifically, that rat has learned to repeatedly press a lever to decrease the likelihood of receiving shocks. Even if that lever has been disconnected and the rat receives the same number of shocks as does its yoked neighbor, it has less of a stress response. The same physical stressor can be less pathogenic when the individual has a sense of *control*. Identical studies have been done with humans exposed to aversive noise, with or without access to a (placebo) lever. The relevance of this variable to real-life circumstances is obvious and underlies stress management advice to find footholds of control in stressful circumstances. A striking example of this is seen in the person working as a secretary for a temporary agency who, when asked if it isn't stressful to be constantly thrown into a new setting and often required to deal with difficult, demanding individuals, replies, "Not at all—if it's too much of a drag, I'm out of there." In fact, you know that this person rarely actually walks off a job.

It should be clear that control and predictability are closely related concepts. (And as will also be discussed later, an increased sense of control does not always protect against stress either.) Some investigators have conceptualized them under the umbrella of *novelty:* lack of control or predictability augments the stress response insofar as events turn out to be discrepant from expectations, increasing the demands for vigilance on an organism's part as it tries to discern and master whatever new rules are in effect (Levine et al. 1989).

The power of novelty as a stressor is shown with an extremely informative study by Goldman, Coover, and Levine (1973). A rat is maintained on an interval-reinforcement schedule, and it must lever-press to receive pellets of food. Over the course of any ten-minute period, an average of twenty lever presses are needed per food pellet, with the requirement fluctuating randomly between fifteen and twenty-five lever presses. The animal has settled into this reinforcement schedule when a change is made. Specifically, the average of twenty lever presses per food pellet is maintained, but the variability is increased, now ranging from ten to thirty lever presses. Note that the animal is fed the exact same amount as before, but it simply has less predictability or control over outcome; this triggers a physiological stress response. The key in this study is that the stress response occurs in the context of food reward, rather than of aversive shocks. Prior studies showed that psychological factors could modulate the response to physical stressors. This study demonstrates that psychological factors can trigger the stress response in the absence of any physical stressor, even in a rat. One can even see evidence of an increased stress response in a context where there was more novelty but *less* actual physical challenge—during the London blitz there was more of an increase in ulcer rates in the suburbs, which were bombed only intermittently, than in the city center, which was bombed like clockwork each night (Stewart and Winser 1942).

Another important psychological variable is your *perception of events as improving or worsening*. A version of this can be shown with two rats. On one day one rat receives fifty shocks, the other ten. The next day both receive twenty-five. Once again, by the rules of classic stress physiology, their bodies are now being exposed to identical physical challenges and should mobilize identical stress responses. However, the rat that has been shifted from ten to twenty-five shocks is far more reactive—its life is getting worse, in contrast to that of its yoked conspecific.

A similar finding emerged from some of my own work with male baboons in East Africa (Sapolsky 1992). These animals live in linear dominance hierarchies that are often quite stable and unchanging. (Number 5 in the hierarchy, for ex-

ample, consistently dominates number 6 and is consistently subordinated to number 4.) Periods of instability (for instance, 5 still dominates 6, but barely, winning perhaps 51 percent of their interactions rather than 95 percent of them) should be stressful, because of their unpredictability. However, I observed very different glucocorticoid concentrations in baboons, depending on whether instability occurred with animals below or above them in the hierarchy. This is logical: unstable interactions with subordinates signaled to the baboon that he was about to drop in the hierarchy— and were associated with elevated glucocorticoid levels. In contrast, equivalent rates of unstable interactions with dominant baboons did not signal a stressor but instead a promotion—and was not associated with elevated glucocorticoid levels. Thus, it is not just the external stressor that regulates the stress response, but its interpretation. We can see the same principle at work in humans. Imagine a corporation where the mail-room clerk, because of superb work, is given a raise from minimum wage to $50,000 a year, while the senior vice president, because of lackluster work, is punished with the equivalent salary. Both have equal ability to buy items that will buffer them from allostatic challenge—yet you know who will be making angry calls about a new job from the cellular phone in the BMW.

A final psychological variable also modulates the stress response and is most readily demonstrated with primates. Place a monkey in a new, empty cage, and it will have a stress response. Place it in there and fill the space with strange monkeys, and the stress response worsens. Place it in there with a group of familiar friends, and the stress response is blunted (Levine et al. 1989). Allowing the animals to sit in contact or to groom mitigates the stress response even further. This finding generalizes across paradigms and species as well. It is protective to have someone to lean on.

Why *sociality* should protect in a nonhuman primate is complex and appears to incorporate some of the variables raised previously. One function of sociality is to modulate the novelty of the situation—the novelty of a new cage setting is decreased when it is filled with known individuals. Sociality also provides outlets for frustration, such as grooming another individual. It also signals that life is improving in that, even in this novel new cage, there is at least a friend who can be relied upon to groom you.

These issues contribute to one of the most important observations in behavioral medicine. When considering the mortality and morbidity rates across a wide variety of diseases, an enormous risk factor in a human is social isolation (House, Landis, and Umberson 1988). For example, it is socially isolated parents (often those who are divorced or widowed), following the loss of an adult child, who are significantly at risk of death in the following year (Levav et al. 1988). Are these relationships simply due to some confounds? For example, a socially isolated individual won't be reminded to take daily medicine or is more likely to eat a half-cooked, unnutritious meal out of a can. Careful work has shown these relationships to hold even after controlling for those factors (Berkman 1983; House et al. 1988). For social primates, such as we are, isolation appears to be an aching and potent stressor.

Collectively, these studies demonstrate that for the same physical stressor, a stress response and stress-related disease become more likely if the individual lacks outlets for frustration, lacks a sense of control or predictability, perceives events as worsening, and lacks social affiliation. Moreover, these psychological factors can generate a stress response even in the absence of a physical stressor. As noted, many stress management techniques involve manipulating some of these psychological variables. The next section briefly reviews the considerable complexity in such an approach.

SOME CAVEATS IN UNDERSTANDING PSYCHOLOGICAL MODIFIERS OF THE STRESS RESPONSE

One might come away from the preceding section concluding that an optimal strategy for reducing psychological stress is to maximize a sense of predictability, control, outlets, and so on. The relationship is more subtle than that, and if these variables are manipulated incorrectly, they can actually worsen the stress response.

A first example will make sense to denizens of singles bars—social support and affiliation are helpful only insofar as they are real. A particularly powerful example of this comes from psychoimmunology: while marriage constitutes one version of protective affiliation, a bad marriage is associated with immune suppression (Kiecolt-Glaser et al. 1987).

These issues are more subtle with the variable of predictability. Consider a circumstance in which a stressor is inevitable. When is it protective to be informed that it will occur? One important param-

eter is time course (see Natelson, Dubois, and Sodetz 1977; Weiss 1972). Giving a rat a warning signal ten seconds before a shock is protective. In contrast, a warning a quarter of a second before is not—there is no opportunity for the preparation prior to the stressor or the relaxation with the implied signaling of no impending stressor. Even more important, giving the signal a half-hour before the stressor worsens the stress response. This makes considerable sense; would you find it to be stress-reducing, for example, to be informed that a dozen years hence you will lose a limb in a horrible accident?

Predictive information helps only with intermediate time lags between the signal and stressor. It is also helpful only when it signals the onset of moderately common stressors. Predictability about a rare (and remember, inevitable) stressor that no one is worrying about anyway is of little help—few of us would derive comfort from being told exactly when a meteor will crash into our garage. Conversely, information about extremely common stressors is also of little help: we are already taking their occurrence for granted.

The previous section emphasized that predictive information helps in part because it aids the individual in planning coping strategies. As such, information will not be helpful when individuals are in no position to cope. For example, most health professionals would probably agree that it is not wise to inform an accident victim that no other members of the family survived when that individual is still barely holding on to life in intensive care. This example taps into subtle ideas in stress management concerning the uses of denial, to be considered later (also see Lazarus 1983).

The studies in the preceding section demonstrated that, in some cases, a sense of control is protective, independent of whether the individual actually has any control. This is not always the case, however. Some of our greatest acts of compassion involve minimizing an individual's sense of control when true disaster has struck: no one could have stopped the car in time, the way she darted out; it wouldn't have mattered even if you had gotten him to the doctor two months ago. And some of our most brutal acts involve artificially elevating a sense of control in victims to make them responsible for their victimization: what does she expect if she's going to dress that way; of course they're going to be persecuted if they refuse to assimilate. In general, a sense of control aids in coping with minor or moderate stressors by encouraging individuals to focus on how much worse things would have been if they hadn't been in charge. In contrast, a sense of control worsens outcome when the stressor is major: the individual focuses on how much better things could have been, and on how it is his or her fault that things turned out as they did. You do not want individuals to feel as if they could have controlled the uncontrollable.

Thus, predictability and control help only within certain narrow parameters and can even worsen outcomes when outside those bounds. As will be seen in the coming sections, this idea is extremely applicable when considering stress response and stress-related diseases in the context of social status and personality.

INDIVIDUAL DIFFERENCES IN THE STRESS RESPONSE AND SOCIAL STATUS

What does an individual's position in society have to do with the stress response and proclivity toward stress-related disease? There is ample evidence that social status is relevant to understanding individual differences in both physical and psychological components of the stress system.

Most work in this area has been done with animals. Since the discernment of pecking orders in chickens, scientists have recognized the role of dominance hierarchies in many species. The most common and simplistic such system is a fairly linear hierarchy in which high rank is attained initially through aggression and maintained thereafter through the threat of it. In this scenario, dominance carries with it numerous perks, including preferential access to contested resources and sources of social support and the ability to displace aggression onto subordinates when frustrated. As will be seen, this is but one version of a dominance system, but one that monopolized early thinking on the subject because it is seen among rats and among the males of some of the more frequently studied Old World primates.

When considering dominance systems like these, it is easy to generate some predictions as to who will have the most active stress responses and stress-related disease—subordinates. Under the most ideal ecological circumstances, these are the animals who spend the most time and effort to obtain their calories, and during times of famine, these are the first to be hungry. In many social systems, it is subordinates who are most subject to predation or to attack owing to displacement aggression from higher-ranking individuals in their group.

Subordinance also carries considerable psychological stress. The frequent inability of low-ranking animals to predict or control access to resources generates psychological stress and has physical costs as well. In addition to the physical injury that may result from random displaced aggression, there is the psychological stress of the lack of predictability. Finally, subordinates are often limited in their access to social support (for example, being groomed) or to outlets for frustration (such as displacement aggression).

A fairly consistent literature demonstrates that in stable versions of such dominance hierarchies (as seen in rats, macaque monkeys, baboons, and a large number of other species), the predictions above are borne out (reviewed in Sapolsky 1993a). When compared to dominant individuals, subordinates (1) secrete elevated levels of glucocorticoids and overactivate the sympathetic nervous system under basal, nonstressed circumstances; (2) are more prone to cardiovascular disease; (3) if female, have significantly higher rates of anovulatory cycles and lower estradiol levels; if male, have testicular systems that are more readily suppressed during stress; and (4) are immunosuppressed and may be more prone to infectious diseases. These findings, derived from studies of animals in cages, in seminatural outdoor enclosures, as well as in the wild, seem quite logical and suggest that social rank is an important determinant of the stress response and of vulnerability to stress-related disease. However, there are numerous complications that must be considered before considering stress physiology and human social status.

A first important qualifier is that it is not just one's rank that is important, but the sort of society in which it exists. I alluded earlier to one example, indicating that not all species have dominance systems in which high rank is achieved through aggressive success, after which dominant individuals rule a stable and linear hierarchy through bluff and intimidation and garner the perks of office. One exception to this occurs in those same species (for example, male baboons or rhesus monkeys) when the hierarchy is unstable. In the wild, this is rare, occurring after the death or transfer of some key individual; in captive populations, instability is the norm during the first months when animals are formed into a group and must establish their dyadic dominance relations. Whether in the wild or in captivity, periods of instability are marked by high rates of aggression, frequent reversals of dyadic relations that change the direction of dominance, rapid formation and collapse of coalitions, reduced rates of sociality—in other words, these are times when high-ranking animals, who are at the center of the most intense competition within the shifting hierarchy, undergo particularly high rates of physical stressors over which they have little control or predictability, and with fewer outlets or sources of support. At such times, it is dominant animals, rather than the usual subordinates, who have the highest basal levels of glucocorticoids (Sapolsky 1993b). Therefore, social dominance is associated with an optimal stress response only when dominance is associated with the psychological advantages of stability. The theme of the importance of not only rank but the sort of society in which it exists is shown in a very different type of dominance system. Numerous New World monkeys (such as marmosets and tamarins) and mongooses are "cooperative breeders" whose social units are extended and cooperative families. Among macaques, subordination is brought about through aggression and harassment. In contrast, a subordinate marmoset female is typically a younger relative waiting her turn and helping older relatives with child care in the interim; in these species, subordinance is not associated with high rates of being the target of displaced aggression. Importantly, among these animals, subordinance is not associated with elevated glucocorticoid levels (Abbott et al., in press).

The rank/physiology relationship is also sensitive to the particular experience of being a dominant or subordinate individual in the particular (macaque, baboon, marmoset, mongoose) group. Among rhesus monkeys and baboons, for example, the usual pattern of elevated glucocorticoid levels in subordinates is less pronounced if they happen to live in a troop with either atypically high rates of reconciliative behaviors or low rates of displacement aggression by dominant males (Gust et al. 1993; Sapolsky 1986). This latter case was based on my studies of male baboons in the Serengeti. Among these animals, subordinates are subject to the highest rates of displacement aggression and have the highest basal glucocorticoid concentrations. During the 1984 East African drought, these baboons, while not starving, devoted all of their day to foraging. Rates of displacement aggression declined markedly, as did the hypercortisolism of the subordinates. Thus, ironically, for those low-ranking animals, an ecological stressor protected them from a greater social stressor.

A second caveat to emerge from the more sub-tle animal studies is that stress-related physiology is influenced not just by rank and by the society in which that rank occurs, but by the personal experience of both of these factors. I have discussed one example of this already—times of social instability among baboon males are not particularly stressful for those rising in the hierarchy during the tumult, independent of the number of unpredictable, dominance interactions that they participate in.

As another example, among female macaques, the severity of basal hypercortisolism varies as a function of how often animals are subject to dominance or aggressive interactions and how often they are given affiliative support (Gust et al. 1993). A similar relationship was observed among female baboons between the rate of being subject to aggression and the extent of suppression of circulating white blood cell counts (Alberts, Altmann, and Sapolsky 1992). Moreover, among young macaques placed in peer groups after separation from their mothers, the smallest decline in antibody levels occurred in animals with the highest rates of social contact (Laudenslager 1994). As another example of the importance of personal experience, in a group of wolves, and of macaques, the highest glucocorticoid concentrations occurred in animals whose ranks were most unstable (the beta male among the wolves, and recent transfer animals among the macaques) (McLeod et al. 1996; Van Schaik 1991). Another example comes from orangutans, among whom dominant males are big muscular beasts with conspicuous secondary sexual characteristics (such as dramatic cheek flanges). In contrast, subordinate males are either slender individuals (lacking the secondary sexual characteristics) or in a transitional state between this gracile form and the more robust one. Both types of subordinate males are reproductively active; the gracile individuals do their mating covertly, and the transitional animals more overtly challenge dominant males for access to females. Not surprisingly, it is the latter type of subordinate individual who has the chronically elevated stress hormone levels (Maggioncalda 1995).

These studies show that there is not a monolithic relationship between social rank and the pathogenicity of the stress response. Instead, absolutely opposite physiologic correlates of rank can occur, depending on the societal and personal context of that rank.

One can readily predict that these subtleties should apply with a vengeance to human "rank" and the stress response. Some investigators have been inspired by the fact that rank differences among animals of some species often emerge from aggressive interactions, and they have examined physiological differences between winners and losers of athletic events (see, for example, Elias 1981). I find these to be of limited use. Aggression is only one of many factors that play a role in establishing and maintaining dominance in animals; I suspect that we learn even less in humans by studying aggressive interactions that are rare and highly symbolic. (For example, it is not common for weekend tennis matches to determine one's access to adequate calories.)

Other studies have focused on more permeating systems of status in humans, such as different ranks in the military, or different positions in hierarchical workplaces. Some investigators have considered the most salient feature of differential rank in animals to be differential access to contested resources and have drawn parallels between that and differential income in humans as a function of occupational status. Again, I question the value of this, since differences in your place in the corporate hierarchy may influence your ability to obtain a large-screen television, but not to obtain sufficient calories.

Others have emphasized the idea that, among animals, the most important thing about different ranks is that they have different psychological implications. These investigators (see, for example, Rose and Fogg 1993) have attributed some of the high rates of stress-related disease in certain occupations (such as air traffic controllers, middle-level management, bus drivers) to a psychological milieu in which there is a high degree of demand and responsibility with little autonomy. This seems quite valid to me, so long as one factors in the ability of humans to belong to multiple hierarchies simultaneously, with some being more psychologically meaningful than others; thus, a "low-ranking" individual in some workplace may be deriving most of his sense of hierarchical status from the fact that he is, nonetheless, an elder of his church. Furthermore, the human capacity for rationalization, internalization of standards, and so on, greatly confounds the impact of any ranking system.

In many ways, it seems to be that the most meaningful way that a Westernized human can be "low-ranking" is by being of low socioeconomic status (SES). One would assume this to be one of the surest ways of being chronically stressed. Low SES involves increased exposure to a variety of physical stressors, ranging from greater demands for physical labor and greater risk of injury in the workplace to, at the more depressing extremes of our unequal society, decreased access to appropriate nutrition. Moreover, low SES involves vastly increased exposure to psychological stressors—low levels of control or predictability about employment, housing, and so on; limited time and funds for protective outlets (hobbies, vacations); decreased access to many sources of social support (reflecting the time demands of second jobs).

This predicts that low SES individuals should have chronically elevated stress responses. To my knowledge, this has not been examined in any systematic way. However, there is a literature concerning another consequence of low SES: the extraordinarily powerful link between low SES and adverse health—which could be interpreted in part as reflecting physical and psychological stressors.

A large number of studies from an array of Western nations have demonstrated that SES (as measured by income, occupation, housing, or, most reliably, educational level) powerfully predicts risk of various diseases, prognoses, the likelihood of successful aging, and life expectancy (see, for example, Kitagawa and Hauser 1973; Marmot, Kogevinas, and Elston 1987). This constitutes, arguably, the single most consistent finding in health psychology. Not surprisingly, droves of investigators have sought to understand its bases. The most immediate explanation is a factor quite unique in discussions of stress, physiology, and social status in animals, namely, differential access to medical care. Obviously, individuals who cannot afford regular checkups, preventative measures, or the best of care when sick will have illnesses that are detected later and treated less effectively. However, differential access cannot be the sole, or even a major explanation for the SES gradient in health (and is in fact a relatively minor factor). First, there are strong SES gradients for diseases whose incidences could not be decreased by improved medical access (such as diabetes) (Pincus and Callahan 1995). Even more strikingly, the SES gradient still occurs in countries with universal health coverage and equal access to medical care (Diderichsen 1990; Kunst and Mackenbach 1994).

Other investigators have emphasized another relatively unique human feature, that low SES is associated with higher rates of risk factors for disease, such as smoking, alcohol abuse, or increased fat and cholesterol intake. Multivariate analyses, however, have demonstrated the persistence of robust health gradients even after controlling for these factors (Adler et al. 1993; Feldman 1989).

Some investigators have explored the impact of variables more related to the animal studies, namely, differential exposure to physical stressors revolving around nutrition and adequate shelter. Remarkably, SES gradients exist (albeit, often to a considerably lesser extent) even after controlling for those factors. In one notable example, the health and life expectancy of elderly nuns was significantly predicted by SES differences at adolescence, despite an intervening half-century during which all subjects shared diet, health care, and living conditions (Snowdon, Ostwald, and Kane 1989).

Because of these findings, some researchers believe that a significant proportion of the SES gradient is attributable to many of the psychological factors related to stress (Adler et al. 1993; Antonovsky 1968; Pincus and Callahan 1995). This is reinforced by the finding that diseases that are not particularly stress-related (such as cancer, as discussed earlier) show the shallowest SES gradients, while those that are most stress-related (such as psychiatric disorders) show the most dramatic SES gradients (Pincus, Callahan, and Burkhauser 1987). This section allows for one conclusion that strikes me as rather ironic. Early observations concerning dominance hierarchies in animals suggested that social subordinance is associated with overactivated stress responses and increased risk of certain stress-related diseases. Subsequent studies showed some support for this, but with far more qualifiers than originally anticipated (particularly with primates), reflecting the importance of the type of society and the personal experience of both the society and the rank. This stands as a testimonial to the social and psychological complexities of nonhuman primates. Similarly, the nature of SES in Western societies suggested that low SES is associated with increased risk of certain stress-related diseases as well. This has been borne out dramatically and, most important, is consistent despite variations in the type of society and the personal experience of both the society and low SES. It strikes me that either humans are less complex than related species, or that with the invention of societal stratification, humans have come up with a form of subordination whose impact is unprecedented in the primate world.

INDIVIDUAL DIFFERENCES IN THE STRESS RESPONSE AND PERSONALITY

An understanding of rank, the society in which it occurs, and the personal experience of both gives considerable information as to what physical and psychological stressors an individual is exposed to. Just as important is whether an individual accurately perceives the stressors and sources of coping. In this regard, individual differences in temperament and personality are critical to understanding differences in the stress response in both humans and primates.

One temperamental style among primates is associated with elevated basal glucocorticoid secretion and increased risk of stress-related disease (for example, atherosclerosis). Among macaques, these are the animals who are most behaviorally and physiologically reactive to novelty (Suomi 1987). Among baboon males, and after controlling for rank, these are the individuals who are least adept at distinguishing between threatening and merely neutral interactions with rivals—for them, everything constitutes a provocation (Ray and Sapolsky 1992; Sapolsky and Ray 1989). This style of animal has been called a "hot reactor," a term akin to many used in the Type A literature (see discussion later in this chapter). I think this temperamental type can also be understood in the context of predictability—these animals are particularly poor at discerning the predictive information that should discriminate stressful from nonstressful circumstances, and thus they must be atypically vigilant and aroused.

A second cluster of temperamental traits also predicts elevated glucocorticoid levels among these baboons, after controlling for rank. These are the animals who are the least adept at inserting a degree of control during stressors (for example, when overtly threatened by a rival, they are least likely to be the ones to start the inevitable fight) and are least capable of behaviorally distinguishing between good and bad outcomes of fights (Ray and Sapolsky 1992; Sapolsky and Ray 1989). Again, this can be framed psychologically—these animals either do not attempt coping responses that would give them control, cannot recognize their efficacy when it happens, or cannot determine whether a situation is improving or worsening.

Finally, elevated glucocorticoid levels occur in male baboons with the lowest levels of affiliative behaviors such as grooming, sitting in contact with others, or playing with infants (Ray and Sapolsky 1992). Again, this is after controlling for social rank.

Similar themes emerge from studies linking certain human personality types with overly active stress responses. One example involves individuals with anxiety disorders, who can be viewed as attempting defensive coping responses that are overactivated—they perceive the world as filled with endless challenges that demand searches for safety. In contrast, major depressive disorder has been conceptualized as reflecting "learned helplessness": the individual perceives the world to be full of stressful challenges but feels incapable of managing coping responses (Seligman 1975). Both disorders can be viewed as cases of stress responses that are discrepant with the stressor. Importantly, both also involve chronic overactivation of the stress response; anxiety is most closely aligned with moderately elevated sympathetic tone, and depression with elevated basal levels of glucocorticoids (APA Taskforce 1987; Gulley and Nemeroff 1993; Lundberg and Frankenhaeuser 1980; Sapolsky and Plotsky 1990).

One of the more carefully studied links between personality and stress-related disease concerns Type A personality and cardiovascular disease. As originally conceptualized, Type A individuals were competitive, overachieving, time-pressured, impatient, and hostile. At present, there remains considerable debate as to whether it is the hostility or the time-pressured features of this disorder that are most critical to the cardiovascular disease risk (Matthews and Haynes 1986; Williams 1991). These are individuals who respond to minor social provocations as if they were far from minor, and frustrations are typically interpreted as being personally motivated. This is the epitome of "hot reacting," and laboratory studies indicate that for the same small frustration, Type A individuals have the largest and most prolonged sympathetic arousal. When played out over a lifetime of mobilizing stress responses during situations that others view as no big deal, a price is paid in terms of heart disease risk.

Some recent work has revealed an additional and surprising personality type associated with elevated glucocorticoid levels, namely, repressive personalities (Brown et al. 1996). By definition, these people are neither depressed nor anxious. Instead, they have an emotionally controlled style: they dot their i's and cross their t's, strive for structured, predictable lives without surprises, and are relatively emotionally inexpressive. Personality tests show repressive individuals to have a strong need for social conformity, a discomfort with ambiguity (for example, on questionnaires they disproportionately endorse statements with words such as *never* or *always*), and a tendency to repress negative emotions. Studies have shown that forcing healthy volunteers to repress the expression of emotional responses to stressful stimuli exaggerates the physiological responses (Gross and Levenson 1997), suggesting that this is what occurs chronically in repressive individuals. A lesson of depressives, anxious individuals, and Type A individuals seems to be the danger of stress responses that do not match the magnitude of the stressor. In the face of contentment and a high level of functioning, repressives appear to teach the lesson that sometimes it can be quite stressful to construct a world in which there are no stressors.

A final point is quite important for the purposes of this chapter. There is considerable individual variation in these links between personality and physiology. For example, not all anxious individuals have elevated sympathetic tone, and not all Type A's are hypertensive. As the most carefully documented example, elevated glucocorticoid levels are seen in only half of depressives, and its manifestations are often quite subtle. Thus, while there are many ways to be unhappy (for example, by being hypervigilant and anxious, or by having a sense of helpless depression), they do not always manifest in a reliable physiological marker. Again, one does not study these links between unhappiness and physiology in order to develop a more scientific way of proving that someone is unhappy; it is not only unnecessary but probably unlikely to work. Instead, one studies these links in order to gain insights into the mechanisms by which emotional states (including unhappiness) might have pathologic consequences.

THE INTERACTIONS BETWEEN SOCIAL STATUS AND PERSONALITY, AND SOME CONCLUDING WARNINGS

In the section on modulators of the stress response, I emphasized the importance of basic psychological factors such as control and predictability. Following that, I emphasized the narrow parameters in which they worked, and the potential dangers of their simplistic applications. In the subsequent sections on the relevance of social status, temperament, and personality to the stress response, I heavily interpreted findings in those areas in the context of those basic psychological factors. It is important now to further interpret those findings in the context of the narrow parameters in which those factors work. One striking example should make this point.

In the face of a singular stressor, when does a sense of control protect against stress? As discussed, emphasizing or even inflating a sense of control helps when stressors are of only minor severity, but is detrimental for catastrophic stressors.

Similarly, when is it beneficial for individuals to have an attributional style in which they habitually interpret themselves as being in control? The obvious extension of the dictum just noted is that such a style works only for individuals whose world is generally benign. When one considers the benign world of comfortably middle-class individuals, that tendency is referred to as an "internal locus of control" and is highly predictive of success, identifying the go-getters, the self-starters, the proverbial captains of their fates with their hands on the rudder. These individuals view their successes as mostly arising from the force and competence of their own efforts.

Yet the same attributional style is so maladaptive in a different setting that it has its own pathologic label. "John Henryism" refers to the folk hero who tried to outrace a steam drill tunneling through a mountain. Hammering with a six-foot-long steel drill, John Henry did the impossible, beating the machine, only to fall dead from the effort. As defined, John Henryism is a predisposition to approach stressful situations with a maximal amount of personal effort. On questionnaires, John Henrys endorse statements such as "When things don't go the way I want them to, it just makes me work even harder," or, "Once I make up my mind to do something, I stay with it until the job is completely done." With enough effort and determination, they feel as if they can regulate all outcomes—the epitome of an inner locus of control.

In a privileged, meritocratic world, these are ideal traits. Yet they define a pathology when they occur in poor people with limited opportunities, in a setting where prejudice reigns. Here, an inner locus of control, which drives you habitually to decide that those insurmountable odds could have been surmounted if only you had worked even harder, is maladaptive; John Henryism is highly predictive of hypertension and cardiovascular disease when it appears among working-class African Americans—but not particularly among working-class whites, or middle-class African Americans (James 1994). Low SES seems to predispose toward some stress-related diseases in a tremendous range of settings. It appears that it particularly does so for the subset of individuals who, while in a low SES position in part because of some of the more brutal aspects of society, have decided it is all just a matter of insufficient will on their parts. The links between social status or personality and patterns of physiology or pathophysiology are not monolithic but reflect subtle, context-dependent interactions. Thus, the application of stress management techniques cannot be monolithic either, and in fact such techniques can be disastrous if applied incorrectly. This is a conclusion with moral implications as well as scientific ones, as emphasized by the late Aaron Antonovsky in his critique of the "well-being" movement (Antonovsky 1994). Explorations of the mind-body interface as it applies to health—the realm of stress management techniques, the well-being movement, and holistic medicine—have produced some impressive findings, suggesting that a reframing of the way in which stressors are viewed can be highly salutary. This brings to mind the old parable about the difference between heaven and hell. In heaven, as the story goes, all of eternity is spent in the intensive study of the holy books. In contrast, hell consists of all of eternity spent in the intensive study of the holy books. To some extent, our personalities and the coping techniques that we mobilize alter our perception of the world, determining whether the same events constitute heaven or hell.

But, Antonovsky noted, it is a moral failure to consider these mind-body relations outside their larger societal context. Many of the hells we are able to finesse into heavens are the minor stressors afflicting the relatively well-off in society. What if we blithely counsel the same optimistic conclusion to those whose stressors are enormous? What of well-being movement gurus such as the Yale surgeon Bernie Siegel (1986) who, writing about terminal disease, opines, "There are no incurable diseases, only incurable people"? (99). What of the clinician who applies the standard middle-class approaches of psychotherapy in working with the homeless? This not only denies the pains of the individual suffering but props up the worst of the status quo. When the individual has the perceptual potential to turn all hells into heavens, there is no imperative to change the world, and one need only rouse oneself from eating peeled grapes while reclining on a sedan chair to point out to victims whose fault it is if they are unhappy. In studying the physiology of how we respond to unhappiness, we have learned many means for modulating the hellishness of numerous types of psychological stressors that may fill many of our everyday lives. But when faced with the truly brutal stressors that life brings so disproportionately to some, it is both bad science and morally unacceptable to preach as an outsider about the techniques for transforming hells into heavens. There is probably little that an outsider can do for people in such cruel circumstances other than to validate the tragedy of their situation and to aid them in their means of denial.

NOTE

1. "Homeostasis," as used classically, typically refers to the body's continuous small adjustments needed to keep any given physiological measure in balance. A newer, fancier term, "allostasis," has been introduced to refer to the integrated balancing of large, interrelated physiological systems in the face of an ever-changing environment (Sterling and Eyer 1988). As such, "homeostasis" is a term most relevant to understanding how your body maintains, for example, the same blood pressure over any given five-minute period. In contrast, "allostasis" is a term more relevant to understanding how all sorts of things in your body have very different setpoints when you are sleeping deeply in the middle of the night than when you are alert and active at noon. As such, a wildebeest with its innards ripped open and dragging in the dust after a lion's attack might better be thought of as being allostatically challenged than homeostatically challenged (a distinction that even it would appreciate).

REFERENCES

Abbott, D., Saltzman, W., Schultz-Darken, N., and Smith, T. (in press). Specific neuroendocrine mechanisms not involving generalized stress mediate social regulation of female reproduction in cooperatively breeding marmoset monkeys. In C. Carter, B. Kirkpatrick, and I. Lederhendler (Eds.), *The integrative neurobiology of affiliation. Annual Proceedings of the New York Academy of Science.*

Ader, R., Felten, D., and Cohen, N. (1991). *Psychoneuroimmunology.* 2nd ed. San Diego: Academic Press.

Adler, N., Boyce, T., Chesney, M., Folkman, S., Syme, S. (1993). Socioeconomic inequalities in health: No easy solution. *Journal of the American Medical Association, 269,* 3140–54.

Alberts, S., Altmann, J., and Sapolsky, R. (1992). Behavioral, endocrine, and immunological correlates of immigration by an aggressive male into a natural primate group. *Hormonal Behavior, 26,* 167–73.

Antonovsky, A. (1968). Social class and the major cardiovascular diseases. *Journal of Chronic Diseases, 21,* 65–89.

———. (1994). A sociological critique of the "well-being" movement. *Advances, 10,* 6–21.

APA Task Force on Laboratory Tests in Psychiatry. (1987). The dexamethasone suppression test: An overview of its current status in psychiatry. *American Journal of Psychiatry, 144,* 1253–68.

Berkman, L. (1983). *Health and ways of living: Findings from the Alameda County study.* New York: Oxford University Press.

Brier, A., Albus, M., Pickar, D., Zahn, T., Wolkowitz, O., and Paul, S. (1987). Controllable and uncontrollable stress in humans: Alterations in mood and neuroendocrine and psychophysiological function. *American Journal of Psychiatry, 144,* 11–16.

Brown, L., Tomarken, A., Orth, D., Loosen, P., Kalin, N., and Davidson, R. (1996). Individual differences in repressive-defensiveness predict basal salivary cortisol levels. *Journal of Personality and Social Psychology, 70,* 362–68.

Diderichsen, F. (1990). Health and social inequities in Sweden. *Social Science Medicine, 31,* 359–67.

Elias, M. (1981). Cortisol, testosterone, and testosterone-binding globulin responses to competitive fighting in human males. *Aggressive Behavior, 215,* 7–15.

Feldman, J. (1989). National trends in education differentials in mortality. *American Journal of Epidemiology, 129,* 919–25.

Goldman, L., Coover, G., and Levine, S. (1973). Bidirectional effects of reinforcement shifts on pituitary-adrenal activity. *Physiology and Behavior, 10,* 209–18.

Green, W., Campbell, M., and David, R. (1984). Psychosocial dwarfism: A critical review of the evidence. *Journal of the American Academy of Child Psychiatry, 23,* 1–11.

Gross, J., and Levenson, R. (1997). Hiding feelings: The acute effects of inhibiting negative and positive emotion. *Journal of Abnormal Psychology, 106,* 95–103.

Gulley, L., and Nemeroff, C. (1993). The neurobiological basis of mixed depression-anxiety states. *Journal of Clinic Psychiatry, 54,* 16–21.

Gust, D., Gordon, T., Hambright, K., and Wilson, M. (1993). Relationship between social factors and pituitary-adrenocortical activity in female rhesus monkeys (Macaca mulatta). *Hormones and Behavior, 27,* 318–27.

House, J., Landis, K., and Umberson, D. (1988). Social relationships and health. *Science, 241,* 540–45.

James, S. (1994). John Henryism and the health of African-Americans. *Culture, Medicine, and Psychiatry, 18,* 163–88.

Kiecolt-Glaser, J., Fisher, L., Ogrocki, P., Stout, J., Speicher, C., and Glaser, R. (1987). Marital quality, marital disruption, and immune function. *Psychosomatic Medicine, 49,* 13–22.

Kitagawa, E., and Hauser, P. (1973). *Differential mortality in the United States: A study of socioeconomic epidemiology.* Cambridge, Mass.: Harvard University Press.

Kunst, A., and Mackenbach, J. (1994). Size of mortality differences associated with educational level in nine industrialized countries. *American Journal of Public Health, 84,* 932–53.

Laudenslager, M. (1994). Research perspectives in psychoimmunology. *Psychoneuroendocrinology, 19,* 751–63.

Lazarus, R. (1983). The costs and benefits of denial. In

S. Breznitz (Ed.), *The denial of stress* (pp. 1–18). New York: International Universities Press.

Leedy, C., and DuBeck, L. (1971). Physiological changes during tournament chess. *Chess Life and Review, 1,* 708–12.

Lenington, S. (1981). Child abuse: The limits of sociobiology. *Ethology and Sociobiology, 2,* 17–28.

Levav, I., Friedlander, Y., Kark, J., and Peritz, E. (1988). An epidemiological study of mortality among bereaved parents. *New England Journal of Medicine, 319,* 457–63.

Levine, S., Coe, C., and Wiener, S. (1989). The psychoneuroendocrinology of stress: A psychobiological perspective. In S. Levine and R. Brush (Eds.), *Psychoendocrinology.* New York: Academic Press.

Lundberg, U., and Frankenhaeuser, M. (1980). Pituitary-adrenal and sympathetic-adrenal correlates of distress and effort. *Journal of Psychosomatic Research, 24,* 125–35.

Maggioncalda, A. (1995). Testicular hormone and gonadotropin profiles of developing and developmentally arrested adolescent male orangutans. *American Journal of Physical Anthropology Supplement, 20,* 140.

Marmot, M., Kogevinas, M., and Elston, M. (1987). Social/economic status and disease. *Annual Review of Public Health, 8,* 111–32.

Matthews, K., and Haynes, S. (1986). Type A behavior pattern and coronary disease risk. *American Journal of Epidemiology, 123,* 923–36.

McLeod, P., Moger, W., Ryon, J., Gadbois, S., and Fentress, J. (1996). The relation between urinary cortisol levels and social behaviour in captive timber wolves. *Canadian Journal of Zoology, 74,* 209–16.

Munck, A., Guyre, P., and Holbrook, N. (1984). Physiological actions of glucocorticoids in stress and their relation to pharmacological actions. *Endocrine Reviews, 5,* 25–40.

Natelson, B., Dubois, A., and Sodetz, F. (1977). Effect of multiple stress procedures on monkey gastro-duodenal mucosa, serum gastrin and hydrogen ion kinetics. *American Journal of Digestive Diseases, 22,* 888–96.

Pincus, T., and Callahan, L. (1995). What explains the association between socioeconomic status and health: Primarily medical access of mind-body variables? *Advances, 11,* 4–23.

Pincus, T., Callahan, L., and Burkhauser, R. (1987). Most chronic diseases are reported more frequently by individuals with fewer than 12 years of formal education in the age 18–64 United States population. *Journal of Chronic Diseases, 40,* 865–73.

Ray, J., and Sapolsky, R. (1992). Styles of male social behavior and their endocrine correlates among high-ranking baboons. *American Journal of Primatology, 28,* 231–38.

Rose, R., and Fogg, L. (1993). Definition of a responder: Analysis of behavior, cardiovascular, and endocrine responses to varied workload in air traffic controllers. *Psychosomatic Medicine, 55,* 325–31.

Sapolsky, R. (1986). Endocrine and behavioral correlates of drought in the wild baboon. *American Journal of Primatology, 11,* 217.

———. (1991). Testicular function, social rank and personality among wild baboons. *Psychoneuroendocrinology, 16,* 281–86.

———. (1992). Cortisol concentrations and the social significance of rank instability among wild baboons. *Psychoneuroendocrinology, 17,* 701–7.

———. (1993a). Endocrinology alfresco: Psychoendocrine studies of wild baboons. *Recent Progress in Hormone Research, 48,* 437–59.

———. (1993b). The physiology of dominance in stable versus unstable social hierarchies. In W. Mason and S. Mendoza (Eds.), *Primate social conflict* (pp. 171–204). Albany: State University of New York Press.

———. (1994). *Why zebras don't get ulcers: A guide to stress, stress-related diseases, and coping.* 2d. ed. New York: W. H. Freeman.

———. (1998). The physiological and pathophysiological implications of social stress in mammals. In B. McEwen (Ed.), *Handbook of physiology: Endocrinology.* Washington: American Physiological Society.

Sapolsky, R., and Plotsky, P. (1990). Hypercortisolism and its possible neural bases. *Biological Psychiatry, 27,* 937–46.

Sapolsky, R., and Ray, J. (1989). Styles of dominance and their physiological correlates among wild baboons. *American Journal of Primatology, 18,* 1–11.

Seligman, M. (1975). *Helplessness: On depression, development, and death.* San Francisco: W. H. Freeman.

Selye, H. (1936). A syndrome produced by diverse nocuous agents. *Nature, 138,* 32–35.

———. (1971). *Hormones and resistance.* New York: Springer-Verlag.

Siegel, B. (1986). Love, medicine, and miracles. New York: Harper and Row.

Snowdon, D., Ostwald, S., and Kane, R. (1989). Education, survival, and independence in elderly Catholic sisters 1936–1988. *American Journal of Epidemiology, 120,* 999–1005.

Sterling, P., and Eyer, J. (1988). Allostasis: A new paradigm to explain arousal pathology. In S. Fisher and J. Reason (Ed.), *Handbook of life stress, cognition, and health* (pp. 21–40). New York: Wiley.

Stewart, D., and Winser, D. (1942). Incidence of perforated peptic ulcer: Effect of heavy air-raids. *The Lancet,* February 28, 259–60.

Suomi, S. (1987). Genetic and maternal contributions to individual differences in rhesus monkey biobehavioral development. In N. Krasnegor, E. Blass, M. Hofer, and W. Smotherman (Eds.), *Perinatal development: A psychobiological perspective* (pp. 118–41). New York: Academic Press.

Surwit, R., Ross, S., and Feingloss, M. (1991). Stress, behavior, and glucose control in diabetes mellitus. In

P. McCabe, N. Schneidermann, T. Field, and J. Skyler (Eds.), *Stress, coping, and disease* (pp. 37–48). Hillsdale, N.J.: Erlbaum.

Terman, G., Shavit, Y., Lewis, J., Cannon, J., and Liebeskind, J. (1984). Intrinsic mechanisms of pain inhibition: Activation by stress. *Science, 226,* 1270–75.

Van Schaik, C. (1991). A pilot study of the social correlates of levels of urinary cortisol, prolactin, and testosterone in wild long-tailed macaques (Macaca fascicularis). *Primates, 32,* 345–50.

Weiss, J. (1968). Effects of coping response on stress. *Journal of Comparative Physiological Psychology, 65,* 251–64.

———. (1972). Psychological factors in stress and disease. *Scientific American, 226,* 104–10.

Williams, R. (1991). A relook at personality types and coronary heart disease. *Progress in Cardiology, 4* (October): 683–94.

Yabana, T., and Yachi, A. (1988). Stress-induced vascular damage and ulcer. *Digestive Disease Science, 33,* 751–59.

24 The Psychophysiology of Utility Appraisals

Tiffany A. Ito and John T. Cacioppo

The psychophysiological evidence on utility has several implications. The spatial topography of event-related brain potentials (ERPs) suggests that the computation of utility is performed by neural sources that are at least partially independent of those underlying discriminative appraisals (for example, stimulus identification). ERP and cortical asymmetry data suggest distinctive currency functions for positivity and negativity. These currency functions represent multifarious appetitive and aversive inputs, respectively, along common metrics. Research further suggests a positivity offset and a negativity bias in these currency functions. A bipolar model in which positive and negative evaluative processes are treated invariantly as reciprocally related along a whole continuum does not provide as parsimonious an account of the data as does a bivariate (positivity x negativity) model of evaluative space. The likelihood of observing the reciprocal activation of positivity and negativity increases as one moves down the neuraxis. Thus, the reciprocal activation of positivity and negativity is more likely to be observed in startle eyeblink modulation and facial electromyography. Autonomic nervous system activity appears to vary more as a function of the level of activation than of the valence of emotions, with the possible exception that negative stimuli tend to be more activating than positive stimuli. The greater likelihood of reciprocal relations between positivity and negativity as one moves from the calculation of utility to action based on utility appraisals is consistent with the physical constraints on behavioral manifestations to bivalent actions (approach-withdrawal) and on the role of the somatic and autonomic nervous system in carrying out the results of utility calculations to achieve these actions.

To SURVIVE, all species must be able to differentiate and respond appropriately to harmful and hospitable stimuli. The human brain and body have therefore been shaped by natural selection to calculate utility and respond accordingly. Evaluative decisions and responses are so critical that organisms have rudimentary reflexes for categorizing and approaching or withdrawing from certain classes of stimuli, and for providing metabolic support for these actions. A remarkable feature of humans is the extent to which the evaluations relevant to well-being are shaped by learning and cognition (for a similar point, see Sapolsky, this volume).

The processes subserving the evaluation of utility are also physiological processes and cannot be understood fully without considering the structural and functional aspects of the physical substrates. Noninvasive investigations of the physiological operations associated with evaluative processes provide an important window through which to view these processes without disturbing them. The purpose of this chapter is to review evidence from psychophysiology on the nature of these evaluative processes. We begin with psychophysiological evidence consistent with the data from brain stimulation presented by Shizgal (this volume) indicating that the neural circuitry involved in computing the utility of a stimulus (evaluative processing) diverges from the circuitry involved in identification and discrimination (nonevaluative processing).

EVENT-RELATED BRAIN POTENTIALS

When an individual appraises a stimulus, the associated neural units produce electrical potentials that can be recorded at the scalp. These event-related brain potentials (ERPs) are typically small relative to ongoing electroencephalographic (EEG) activity and therefore are not apparent on any single trial. Signal processing procedures such as digital filtering and ensemble averaging have made it possible to extract these ERPs from spontaneous EEG activity, which is not time-locked to the presentation of a known stimulus. The topographical features of the ERPs are referred to as components. Classification of the components usually involves the identification of peaks and troughs in the wave form, characteristic latencies of the peaks and troughs, and their spatial distributions. Such components are assumed to reflect one or more information-processing operations, and the amplitude of a component is thought to reflect the extent to which a specific operation is engaged (for reviews, see Coles, Gratton, and Fabiani 1990; Coles et al. 1986).

A large literature demonstrates that one of the components—commonly referred to as a P300 because it is a positive potential that peaks around 300 milliseconds following the presentation of a stimulus—can be used to examine nonevaluative (such as physical or semantic) categorization processes. In a typical study, ERPs are recorded as participants are exposed to a long sequence of simple stimuli from at least two different classes, such as a high-pitched and a low-pitched tone. Participants may be required to count the number of stimuli presented from one of the two classes, and stimuli from one class are presented much less frequently than are stimuli from the other. Results have shown that the rare (oddball) stimuli evoke a larger positive potential than the frequent stimuli, and that this P300 tends to be largest over midline central and parietal scalp sites (Donchin and Coles 1988; Donchin et al. 1986; Gehring et al. 1992; Johnson 1993). Factors that influence categorization processes (for example, the probability that a stimulus from a given class will appear, the task-relevance of a stimulus, or simple versus difficult discriminations) also influence the P300, while factors that influence an individual's ability to choose or execute a response to a stimulus (for example, whether the person is instructed to respond to a stimulus on the left side of a display screen with the right or left hand) affect the behavioral response but have much less effect on the P300 (McCarthy and Donchin 1981). Accordingly, the P300 has been used to investigate nonevaluative categorizations independently of behavioral responses.

Drawing upon this literature, we developed a paradigm using ERPs to investigate evaluative processes independent of behavioral responses (Cacioppo, Crites, and Gardner 1996; Crites and Cacioppo 1996). In the first such study, Cacioppo, Crites, Berntson, and Coles (1993) recorded ERPs as participants were exposed to series of positive and negative stimuli (foods, for example). To maximize the likelihood that participants were categorizing the stimuli along evaluative dimensions, the stimuli were presented within sequences of six, and participants were asked to count silently the number of positive (or negative, counterbalanced) stimuli that appeared in each sequence. The majority of the stimuli within each sequence were drawn from a single evaluative category (for example, all positive or all negative). In some sequences, all six stimuli were drawn from this same evaluative category, but in others, one of the six stimuli was drawn from the other evaluative category (for example, a positive food embedded within a sequence of negative foods). This made it possible to record the ERPs associated with the appraisal of evaluatively consistent and evaluatively inconsistent target stimuli. We found a larger-amplitude late positive potential (LPP—a P300-like component) with a mean latency of approximately 650 ms to evaluatively inconsistent stimuli (for example, a negative stimulus embedded in a sequence of positive stimuli) than to evaluatively consistent stimuli (for example, a positive stimulus embedded in a sequence of positive stimuli). This LPP enhancement was found whether the evaluatively inconsistent stimulus was positive or negative. Furthermore, the LPP enhancement was obtained when the evaluative category of the targets was determined using each participant's own idiosyncratic attitude ratings of the targets (for example, food, universities [study 1]) and when the evaluative category of the targets was determined using prior normative ratings (positive and negative personality traits [study 2]). Subsequent studies demonstrated that the LPP amplitudes associated with evaluative processes are maximal over central-parietal regions, vary as a function of the degree of evaluative inconsistency (for example, LPP amplitudes are larger to extremely negative than moderately negative stimuli embedded in a sequence of positive stimuli), and vary more as a function of evaluative categorizations than response selection or execution (Cacioppo et al. 1994; Crites et al. 1995).

Thus, ERPs have been used to investigate evaluative and nonevaluative processes independent of behavioral responses. Evaluative appraisals in our paradigm produce an LPP component that is largest to categorically inconsistent stimuli, maximal over central-parietal scalp sites, and relatively insensitive to response operations. These are the same characteristics found for the P300 component in studies of nonevaluative processes in the oddball paradigm. Consistent with the hypothesis that the neural circuitry involved in computing the utility of a stimulus diverges from the circuitry involved in identification and discrimination, differences in the ERPs observed during evaluative and nonevaluative appraisals have also been found

(Cacioppo et al. 1996; Crites and Cacioppo 1996). Specifically, investigations of the spatial distribution of the LPP amplitudes across the scalp have revealed a right lateralization of evaluative categorizations (Cacioppo et al. 1996). For instance, the LPP recorded at right-scalp sites (F4, C4, P4) are larger than those recorded at homologous sites over the left hemisphere (F3, C3, P3) when participants are attending to the utility of the stimuli (for instance, judging whether a stimulus is positive or negative).[1] The spatial distribution of the LPP associated with nonevaluative categorizations, in contrast, appears more symmetrical. In an illustrative study, the words *pleasant* and *unpleasant* were embedded within sequences of other positive and negative adjectives (Cacioppo et al. 1996, Study 5). Participants were given the nonevaluative task of determining whether the word *pleasant* or *unpleasant* had been shown. Under these task instructions, analysis of standardized LPP amplitudes at lateral scalp sites revealed a symmetrical distribution.

As this study demonstrates, right lateralization is unlikely to be an artifact of the paradigm or of the affective nature of the stimuli used in these experiments. Rather, it is suggestive of an orientation of neural generators toward the right hemisphere or a right hemispheric engagement in evaluative categorizations. To address more directly the specificity of right lateralization to evaluative processes, Crites and Cacioppo (1996) manipulated the type of task (evaluative or nonevaluative categorization) within the same study. They recorded ERPs as participants viewed words that could be categorized with respect to both an evaluative (positive or negative) and a nonevaluative (vegetable or nonvegetable) dimension. The researchers instructed the participants to either categorize each food as positive or negative or to categorize them as vegetable or nonvegetable. Analyses of standardized LPP amplitudes at lateral scalp sites revealed right lateralization among those performing the evaluative appraisals but not among those performing the nonevaluative ones. Thus, even when viewing identical stimuli and performing similar tasks, the neural activity associated with evaluative categorizations can be differentiated from the neural activity associated with nonevaluative categorizations.

These results do not mean that the neural and psychological processes underlying the two processes are completely dissimilar. In fact, analyses of the midline sites in Crites and Cacioppo (1996) revealed main effects of categorical inconsistency within both task types. Evaluatively inconsistent foods produced an enhanced LPP compared to evaluatively consistent foods among those performing the evaluative task. Similarly, categorically inconsistent pictures (for instance, a vegetable embedded within sequences of nonvegetables) produced an enhanced LPP relative to categorically consistent foods (for instance, a nonvegetable embedded within sequences of nonvegetables) among those performing the nonevaluative task. Moreover, the LPP in both task conditions had a central-parietal distribution. Similar results have been obtained by Cacioppo et al. (1996). These similarities support the notion that evaluative and nonevaluative appraisals rely on a number of common information-processing operations. The asymmetrical distribution of the LPP associated with evaluative categorizations further suggests that the calculation of utility is associated with the activation of additional neural generators, possibly located in or oriented toward the right hemisphere.

Evaluative Processes: The Bivariate Model of Evaluative Space

In humans, evaluative discriminations have traditionally been conceptualized as bipolar (hostile-hospitable) and measured using bipolar scales to gauge the net affective predisposition toward a stimulus. Such an approach treats positive and negative evaluative processes (and the resulting affective states and judgments of utility) as equivalent, reciprocally activated, and interchangeable. Even though physical constraints may restrict behavioral manifestations of utility calculations to bivalent actions (approach-withdrawal), early behavioral theorists recognized that approach and withdrawal were behavioral manifestations that could come from distinguishable motivational substrates (Miller 1951, 1961). Conflict theory was enriched by conceptualizing approach and withdrawal separately, investigating their unique antecedents and consequences, and examining the psychological constraints that led typically to the reciprocal activation of approach and withdrawal tendencies (Berntson, Boysen, and Cacioppo 1993; Lang, Bradley, and Cuthbert 1992). The assessment of utility may similarly benefit from expanding the principle of reciprocal evaluative activation to accommodate the distinguishable activation of positive and negative evaluative processes, the investigation of their unique antecedents and consequences, and the examination of the psychological and physiological constraints that produce their reciprocal activation.

We proposed an evolutionary model of evaluative processes in which a stimulus may vary in terms of the strength of positive evaluative activation (positivity) and the strength of negative evaluative activation (negativity) that it evokes (Cacioppo and Berntson 1994; Cacioppo, Gardner, and Berntson 1997). Specifically, the model posits that positive and negative evaluative processes are distinguishable (stochastically and functionally independent), are characterized by distinct activation functions (positivity offset and negativity bias principles), are related differentially to ambivalence (corollary of ambivalence asymmetries), have distinguishable antecedents (heteroscedacity principle), and tend to gravitate from a bivariate toward a bipolar structure when the underlying beliefs are the target of deliberation or a guide for behavior (principle of motivational certainty). The model also posits the existence of modes, or multiple combinations, of evaluative activation (Cacioppo et al. 1997).

Modes of Evaluative Activation   Whereas a bipolar model allows only for reciprocal activation between positivity and negativity, the bivariate model posits multiple modes of activation of the motivational substrates: (1) reciprocal activation occurs when a stimulus has opposing effects on the activation of positivity and negativity, (2) uncoupled activation occurs when a stimulus affects only positive or only negative evaluative activation, and (3) nonreciprocal activation occurs when a stimulus increases (or decreases) the activation of both positivity and negativity (Cacioppo and Berntson 1994). Thus, the bivariate model of evaluative space does not reject reciprocal activation but rather subsumes it as one of the three possible modes of activation and explores the antecedents for each mode of evaluative activation.

Evidence for the existence of multiple modes of evaluative activation has been observed across all levels of analysis (see review by Cacioppo and Berntson 1994). For instance, Hoebel (this volume) reviews evidence that food restriction alters the neurochemical effects underlying approach behavior in an uncoupled fashion, while morphine has reciprocal effects on the neurochemical processes underlying approach and withdrawal behavior. The separable activation of positivity and negativity at the verbal level is evident in a study by Goldstein and Strube (1994) in which self-reported positive and negative affect were collected from students at the beginning and end of three consecutive class periods. Whereas a bipolar model would predict reciprocal activation of positive and negative affect, as evidenced by negative within-participant correlations between the intensity of positive and negative reactions on a particular day, the reactions were in fact uncorrelated. Moreover, exam feedback activated positivity and negativity differently. Students who scored above the mean on the exam showed an increase in positive affect relative to their beginning-of-class level, whereas their level of negative affect remained unchanged within the class period. Similarly, students who scored below the mean on the exam showed an increase in negative affect, but no change in positive affect within the class period.

Activation Functions for Positivity and Negativity

As suggested by Shizgal (this volume), the complexities of stimuli and events in the world, while seemingly incomparable, nevertheless become expressed on a common motivational metric. According to the bivariate model, the common metric governing approach/withdrawal is the consequence of two intervening metrics, the activation function for positivity (appetition) and the activation function for negativity (aversion). The activation functions for positivity and negativity can be thought of as currency functions (Shizgal, this volume): the value of separate and multifarious appetitive inputs is expressed on a common scale of positivity, and the value of diverse aversive inputs is expressed on a common scale of negativity. Low activation of positivity and negativity by a stimulus reflects neutrality or indifference, whereas high activation of positivity and negativity reflects conflict or ambivalence.

The currency functions for truly bipolar constructs, such as for hot and cold, are essentially identical in form: the rate at which an element cools is essentially the same rate at which heat dissipates. Hot and cold are endpoints on a bipolar continuum, and the functions for these endpoints are equal and reciprocal. The currency functions for positivity and negativity appear to differ in several noteworthy respects.

Positivity Offset   Research on approach/withdrawal conflict provided early evidence for what we have termed a "positivity offset." As is illustrated in figure 24.1, the positivity offset is the tendency for there to be a weak positive (approach) motivational output at zero input (that is, an intercept difference). As a consequence of the positivity offset, the motivation to approach is stronger than the motivation to avoid at distances far from the goal (that is, at low levels of evaluative activation). What might be the possible evolutionary significance of the positivity offset? Without a positivity offset, an organism in a neutral environment may be unmotivated to approach novel objects, stimuli, or contexts. The neophobic response to foreign stimuli that characterizes most species permits an initial period of observation. With a positivity offset, however, an organism facing neutral or unfamiliar (nonvalenced) stimuli would be weakly motivated to approach and, with the quick habituation of the initial fear response (the diminution of the evoked negativity by foreign stimuli or startling events), to engage in exploratory behavior. Such a tendency may have important survival value, at least at the level of a species.

Negativity Bias   The slope for the avoidance gradient was found to be steeper than the slope for the approach gradient in Miller's (1951, 1961) research on conflict behavior. This difference illustrates the negativity bias, a second difference in the currency functions of positivity and negativity: with each unit of activation, the change in negative motivational output is larger than the change in positive motivational output (see figure 24.1). Thus, the positivity offset can be conceived as relative activation of positivity even in the absence of any hedonic input, and the negativity bias refers to the finding that the increase in motivational output per quantum of activation tends to be greater for negativity than for positivity. Exploratory behavior can provide useful information about an organism's environment, but it can also place the organism in the proximity of hostile stimuli. Because it is more difficult to reverse the consequences of an injurious or fatal assault than an opportunity unpursued, the process of natural selection may have resulted in distinguishable motivational organizations for positivity and negativity with the propensity to react more strongly to negative than positive stimuli. The negativity bias, which underlies a stronger responsiveness to proximate negative than proximate positive or neutral events, may therefore be a complementary, adaptive motivational organization that complements the positivity offset. Species with a positivity offset *and* a negativity bias enjoy the benefits of exploratory behavior and the self-preservative benefits of a predisposition to avoid or withdraw from threatening events. The negative bias may be especially relevant to understanding assessments of utility by accounting for what has been called loss aversion (Kahneman and Tversky 1984). Observing that losses loom larger than gains, Kahneman and Tversky have argued that the value function relating negative events to subjective value has a steeper slope than the one relating positive events to subjective value. That is, they have hypothesized a steeper slope for the currency function for negative as opposed to positive inputs.

ERP Studies of Currency Functions   The LPP component has also been used to examine the currency functions for positive and negative evaluative categorization processes. To assess operation of negativity bias, Ito, Larsen, Smith, and Cacioppo (1998) presented participants with neutral, positive, and negative pictures. The researchers presented neutral pictures most frequently in all sequences of stimuli. In some sequences, a single positive or negative picture was presented. The positive and negative pictures were thus both evaluatively inconsistent with the surrounding stimuli. Consistent with prior research, evaluatively inconsistent stimuli were associated with a larger LPP. That is, both positive and negative pictures were associated with larger LPPs than neutral pictures. The data also reveal evidence of the negativity bias such that LPPs were larger to negative than equally probable, evaluatively extreme, and arousing positive pictures. A reexamination of the investigation by Crites and his colleagues (1995) similarly reveals larger LPP amplitudes to negative stimuli embedded in a series of positive stimuli (M = 8.93 millivolts) as compared to positive stimuli embedded in a series of negative stimuli (M = 6.70 millivolts). Because the degree of evaluative consistency and inconsistency was equivalent for positive and negative targets in Crites et al. (1995), the larger LPPs evoked by negative stimuli are consistent with the notion that the currency function for negativity is steeper than the currency function for positivity.

EEG ASYMMETRY

In addition to distinguishing between positive and negative motivational substrates, positive and negative currency functions, and modes of evaluative activation, the bivariate model assumes that the motivational systems are instantiated in only partially overlapping brain mechanisms (Cacioppo et al. 1997). As discussed by Hoebel (this volume),

FIGURE 24.1   The Bivariate Evaluative Plane and Its Associated Preference Surface

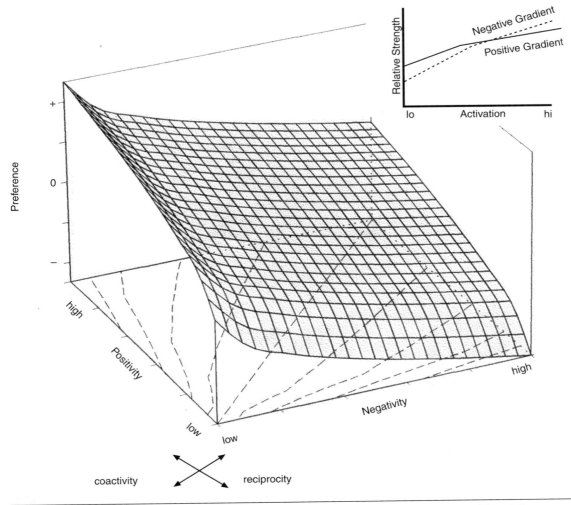

Source: Adapted from Cacioppo and Berntson (1994). Copyright 1994 by the American Psychological Association.
Notes: The surface represents the behavioral disposition of an individual toward (+) or away from (−) the target stimulus. Preference is expressed in relative units. The point on the surface overlying the left axis intersection represents the maximally positive disposition evoked by the target stimulus, and the point on the surface overlying the right axis intersection represents the maximally negative disposition toward the target stimulus. The inset superimposes the strength of the activation of positive and negative motivational forces as a function of movements along the coactivity diagonal. Note that the predictions depicted in this inset mirror those for approach-avoidance conflict in Miller's theory of conflict (see Miller 1959, figure 5).

positivity and negativity may be distinguishable with respect to the neurotransmitters primarily associated with each. Accumbens dopamine has been implicated in rewarding behavior, whereas acetylcholine has been associated with aversive states. Similarly, the research reviewed by Shizgal (this volume) implicates midbrain dopaminergic pathways that project from the ventral tegmental area to the nucleus accumbens in the rewarding effects of brain stimulation. In psychophysiology, research on cerebral asymmetry at rest suggests that right frontal hemispheric activation reflects a predisposition to respond negatively, while left frontal hemispheric activation reflects a predisposition to respond positively.

Speculation relating hemispheric asymmetry to

affective reactions was originally spurred by clinical observations linking depressive symptomology to left-hemisphere damage. Particularly compelling evidence was provided by Robinson and his colleagues (Robinson et al. 1984; Robinson and Downhill 1995), who used computerized tomography to link stroke-related lesion location with the severity and valence of affective symptomology. The severity of post-stroke depression was positively related to lesion proximity to the left frontal pole, but negatively related to lesion proximity to the right frontal pole.

These clinical observations are supported by experimental research suggesting that stable individual differences in activation of left and right anterior cortical areas result in a predisposition to experience approach-related positive affective states and withdrawal-related negative affective states, respectively. Davidson and his colleagues (Davidson 1992; Davidson and Tomarken 1989) have integrated these findings into a diathesis-stress model linking individual differences in anterior cortical asymmetry to dispositional affective tendencies. An important feature of this model is the requirement of an affective elicitor. That is, differences as a function of cerebral asymmetry are expected only when a "stress," or affective challenge, is experienced.

In studies illustrative of this body of research, emotionally evocative film clips served as the affective challenge, and self-reported reactions to the films were related to anterior cortical activity that was measured prior to film exposure (Wheeler, Davidson, and Tomarken 1993; Tomarken, Davidson, and Henriques 1990). In these studies, as in much of the research in this area, cortical asymmetry was quantified using scalp EEG recordings. The dependent measure of interest in these and other studies was power in the alpha band (8–13 hertz), which is inversely related to hemispheric activation (Shagass 1972). Measures of alpha power at midfrontal and anterior temporal regions show high internal consistency (across eight one-minute recording periods), as indicated by alpha coefficients in the .81–.94 range (Tomarken et al. 1992). Individual patterns of asymmetry in these regions also appear relatively stable over time, as evidenced by test-retest correlations between .66 and .72 over a three-week period (with asymmetry computed as log right—log left alpha power, such that higher scores indicate greater activation in the left hemisphere). Consistent with the diathesis stress model, relative left anterior cortical asymmetry in the resting EEG was positively correlated

with intensity of positive reactions reported to positive film clips, but negatively correlated with intensity of negative reactions in response to negative film clips. Importantly, this relationship between asymmetry and affective responses is valence-dependent, and not simply a function of greater affective reactivity associated with one or the other hemispheres. That is, global reactivity, computed as the sum of the positive reactions to the positive films and the negative reactions to the negative films, was uncorrelated with cerebral asymmetry.

Differences in temperament as a function of cortical asymmetry are also apparent in children. For example, behaviorally inhibited toddlers tend to show relative right midfrontal activation, whereas their uninhibited counterparts display relative left midfrontal activation (Davidson 1993). Participants in this study were classified based on behavior in a peer play session at thirty-one months of age. Resting EEG was assessed five months later.[2] Among the criteria used to determine behavioral inhibition were time spent in close proximity to the mother, latency to touch first toy, latency to first utterance, and other behaviors related to exploration in a novel environment. A similar relation between anterior cortical asymmetry and childhood temperament was observed in infants as young as ten months (Davidson and Fox 1989), with maternal separation serving as the affective challenge. Those children who cried during the sixty-second separation had greater relative right-hemisphere activation in a resting EEG period that preceded the separation, whereas infants who did not cry showed relative left-hemisphere activation.

The studies reviewed thus far have sought to relate cortical asymmetry to phasic differences in the tendency to *activate* either approach- or withdrawal-related motivation. It is also possible to classify affective states as resulting from a hypoactivation of one of these systems. Depression, in particular, may result from a hypoactivation of approach-related motivation. This characterization of depression is supported by differences in resting EEG asymmetry recorded from clinically depressed and control participants (Henriques and Davidson 1991). Whereas the two groups did not differ in right midfrontal activation, the clinically depressed participants showed decreased left midfrontal activation relative to controls. Similar results have been obtained with currently normothymic participants with a history of depression (Henriques and Davidson 1990). It is important to note that in this latter study, previously depressed and control participants did not differ in their current self-reported mood, a result that has been interpreted to mean that left-hemisphere hypoactivation renders individuals vulnerable to depressive episodes. Similarly, the studies comparing resting EEG asymmetry to reactions elicited by emotionally evocative films in nondepressed populations reveal relations between left-hemisphere activation and positive affective states and right-hemisphere activation and negative affective states, even when the effects of baseline mood are statistically removed (Tomarken et al. 1990; Wheeler et al. 1993).

Phasic shifts in cortical asymmetry have also been observed during the actual experience of affective reactions. Davidson and his colleagues (Davidson et al. 1990) have recorded EEG during the presentation of film clips chosen to elicit the approach-related positive states of amusement and happiness and the withdrawal-related state of disgust. Surreptitious video recording of the participants as they watched the films allowed for off-line coding of facial expressions. EEG epochs corresponding to the facial expressions of either happiness or disgust were retained for analysis. Disgust as compared to happy expressions was associated with greater activation over right midfrontal and anterior temporal regions, similar activation over left midfrontal regions, and less activation over left anterior temporal regions. Analyses conducted across all artifact-free EEG data (that is, including those times in which a facial expression was not present), failed to reveal any relation of positive and negative film clips and cerebral asymmetry. Thus, it appears that only emotional experiences strong enough to produce overt facial expressions are associated with concomitant cortical asymmetry.

Early work in this area implicitly assumed that positivity and negativity were reciprocally activated. Theoretically, positive affect and negative affect were conceptualized as a single continuum along which anterior cortical activation was lateralized (Davidson et al. 1990). Methodologically, cerebral asymmetry was measured as the difference between log alpha power in the right and left hemispheres (for an exception, see Wheeler et al. 1993), a computation that implies a single continuum of activation. As evidence suggesting separable motivational systems has grown within cerebral asymmetry research (Sutton and Davidson 1997) and other areas of neurophysiology (for example, Gray 1982, 1987; Hoebel, this volume), theoretical accounts of cerebral asymmetry have similarly evolved, and now explicitly incorporate

separable systems. Recent research by Sutton and Davidson (1997) nicely integrates the assumption of separable motivational systems with Davidson's diathesis stress model. In this study, resting EEG asymmetries were compared to scores on Carver and White's (1994) Behavioral Approach System/Behavioral Inhibition System measure. The latter is a self-report instrument designed to assess individual differences in the tendency to approach or withdraw, respectively, and to experience concomitant affective states (see also Gray 1982). Consistent with the notion that positivity and negativity are separable systems differentially associated with left- and right-hemispheric activation, respectively, greater relative left asymmetry at midfrontal electrode sites was positively correlated with behavioral activation system scores and negatively correlated with behavioral inhibition system scores.

Whereas theoretical conceptualizations of cortical asymmetry have moved from a purely bipolar and reciprocal model to one consistent with the bivariate model, the implicitly bipolar practice of measuring cortical asymmetry as a difference score (log alpha power in the right hemisphere minus log alpha power in the left) remains, owing to methodological considerations. Specifically, difference scores are preferred to site-specific resting EEG activation (for example, raw power or power density) because of concerns with skull thickness and volume conduction from homologous sites (Wheeler et al. 1993); difference scores have been adopted as the best method for removing common variance due to these non-neurogenic sources. Unfortunately, multiple modes of evaluative activation can manifest as the same asymmetry difference score. For example, an asymmetry score indicative of relative left activation could be produced by left-hemisphere hyperactivation (such as with uncoupled activation of the positive system), right-hemisphere hypoactivation (such as with uncoupled activation of the negative system), or some combination of right hyperactivation and left hypoactivation (such as with reciprocal activation of the positive and negative systems). Likewise, an individual with low levels of activation within both the positive and negative systems could produce the same difference score as an individual with extremely high activation of both systems. In the former case, the pattern of activation indicates neutrality, whereas the latter case is indicative of ambivalence. (For a more general discussion of the shortcomings of bipolar scales in measuring bivariate motivational systems, see Cacioppo and Berntson 1994.)

Methods for removing the effects of skull thickness and volume conduction at homologous sites have been developed but have not yet gained widespread use. When they have been used, they reveal evidence interpretable by the multiple modes of evaluative activation specified by the bivariate model. Wheeler, Davidson, and Tomarken (1993) employed a regression technique for statistically removing from a given site whole head power and power at its homologous site. Correlations between these computed power scores and ratings of positive reactions to positive films and negative reactions to negative films were then obtained. The EEG scores were derived from resting EEG periods that were recorded prior to exposure to the films. Negative affect ratings in response to the negative film clips were predicted only by right frontal activation, but positive affect ratings in response to the positive film clips were predicted both by left frontal activation and inversely by right frontal activation. One possible interpretation of these results is that the negative film clips in this study elicited relatively uncoupled activation of the negative motivational system, whereas the positive film clips produced reciprocal activation of both the positive and negative systems.

In sum, research on cortical asymmetry is consistent with the bivariate model in suggesting two separable motivational systems. As we noted in our discussion of how asymmetry is measured, there are theoretical limitations to using an inherently bipolar difference score to express relative activation between the hemispheres. As new methods for quantifying resting EEG within a hemisphere are developed, it will be interesting to assess questions related to how and when different modes of evaluative activation (reciprocal, uncoupled, and coactivated) are observed. Interestingly, the anterior cortical asymmetry reviewed in this section and the right-lateralized ERPs reviewed in the previous section appear to index different facets of affect (see Cacioppo et al. 1996). For instance, cerebral EEG asymmetries are associated with a predisposition to respond positively or negatively, whereas lateralized ERPs are associated with the perception and categorization of affective information.

We suggested at the outset of this chapter that the human brain and body have been shaped by natural selection to calculate utility and to respond accordingly. Thus far, we have focused on processes underlying or associated with the calculation of utility. In the next section, we turn to studies of a rudimentary protective reflex—the startle-blink reflex.

STARTLE EYEBLINK MODULATION

Imagine you have just watched a very scary film and, on leaving the theater, you hear a loud bang. A common reaction in such instances is to show a startle response. Your heart jumps, your eyes snap shut, and your shoulders hunch forward in a protective pose. Now imagine you have watched a very funny film rather than a scary film. The loud bang still elicits a startle response, but its intensity is likely lessened. One of the most reliably elicited components of this startle response is the blinking of the eye. Serving as a means of protecting the eyes from potential harm, this component of the startle reflex is sensitive to both attentional and affective processes (Anthony 1985). It is the latter area of research on which we will focus here. Specifically, relative to neutral states, negative states tend to potentiate startle eyeblink, whereas positive states tend to inhibit it (Lang, Bradley, and Cuthbert 1990).

Startle modulation has been studied most frequently using color pictures to induce affective states, and brief, intense, unexpected acoustic events to elicit the startle reflex. In an illustrative study, Vrana, Spence, and Lang (1988) had participants view a series of positive, negative, and neutral slides for six thousand milliseconds each. The slides were selected from the International Affective Picture System (IAPS) (Center for the Study of Emotion and Attention 1995), a set of nearly 500 color images used widely in emotion research in general, and in startle reflex research in particular. Normative ratings from college-aged samples for self-reported bipolar valence and arousal are available for the IAPS images and were used to select slides in the study conducted by Vrana and his colleagues. The positive and negative slides were equated for mean arousal, and both valent categories were more arousing than the neutral slides. An unsignaled 50-millisecond burst of 95-decibel white noise was presented binaurally through headphones during presentation of a subset of slides at either 500, 2,500, or 4,500 milliseconds after slide onset. Participants were instructed to attend to the slides and ignore noises in their headphones. The magnitude of the blink response, measured by miniature electrodes placed over the periocular (orbicularis oculi) muscle under one of the eyes, revealed a significant inverse relation between blink magnitude and valence of the affective foreground. Specifically, blinks elicited during the presentation of negative slides were augmented relative to those elicited during neutral slides. By contrast, blinks elicited during positive slides were inhibited relative to the neutral slides.

Startle eyeblink modulation has been obtained when the affective foreground is elicited by a wide range of stimuli, including films (Jansen and Frijda 1994), hedonic odors (see for example, Ehrlichman et al. 1995), stimuli classically conditioned to have hedonic relevance (Lipp, Sheridan, and Siddle 1994), facial expressions (Balaban 1995), and imagery (Cook et al. 1991), as well as slides. Affective modulation also generalizes beyond acoustic startle probes and has been obtained using tactile (Hawk and Cook 1997) and visual probes (Bradley, Cuthbert, and Lang 1990).

Lang and his colleagues (Lang et al., 1990, 1992; Lang, 1995) have explained startle eyeblink modulation as a function of affective foreground in terms of motivational priming. This notion presumes two motivational systems, one appetitive and concerned with rewarding stimuli that results in a currency function we have termed positivity, and the other aversive and concerned with defensive responses that results in a currency function we have termed negativity. Affective stimuli are thought to prime associations, representations, and action programs linked with one or the other system. Such priming is thought to increase the likelihood and potential strength of responding of the activated system while simultaneously decreasing the likelihood and potential strength of responding for the non-engaged system (that is, reciprocal activation). A negative stimulus that precedes a startle probe is therefore thought to activate the aversive system. The subsequent match between the already primed aversive system and the defensive startle reflex results in potentiation of startle eyeblinks. By contrast, a positive affective foreground results in a mismatch between the valence of the affective foreground and the reflexive response, resulting in inhibition of startle eyeblinks.

The motivational matching hypothesis, like the bivariate model, assumes two separate valent systems (Lang 1995), but because positive affective states tend to attenuate, and negative affective states tend to accentuate, the amplitude of a startle blink, startle eyeblink modulation has been interpreted as supporting a bipolar organization of affect (Lang et al. 1992). Such results, however, are also consistent with the bivariate model. For instance, positivity and negativity could be operating in an independent and uncoupled manner, with each exerting an opposite effect on the startle eyeblink. This would give the appearance of recip-rocal activation at the behavioral level even if it were the effects on the startle eyeblink rather than the activation of positivity and negativity that were reciprocal. Alternatively, Witvliet and Vrana (1995) have argued that startle eyeblink modulation varies as a function of negativity per se rather than valence (positivity-negativity). This explanation is consistent with the tendency toward reciprocity of positivity and negativity observed at lower levels of the neuraxis, such as at the level of the spinal reflexes (Berntson et al. 1993).

Furthermore, the bivariate model subsumes reciprocal activation but additionally posits a steeper gradient for withdrawal than approach. If there is a negativity bias in psychophysiological responding, negative foregrounds may modulate startle eyeblinks more strongly than positive foregrounds. Consistent with this reasoning, several investigators have reported that negative foregrounds enhance startle blinks while positive foregrounds produce blinks comparable in amplitude to those associated with neutral foregrounds (for example, Bradley, Cuthbert, and Lang 1996; Cuthbert, Bradley, and Lang 1996; Ehrlichman et al. 1995; Hawk and Cook 1997; Jansen and Frijda 1994; Miltner et al. 1994; Vrana 1995). These results suggest that whereas activation of the negative motivational system reliably potentiates the defensive startle response, activation of the positive motivational system may less consistently inhibit the startle reflex.

Interestingly, stimuli that are not arousing or that elicit weak affective reactions do not reliably modulate the amplitude of startle eyeblinks (Lang et al. 1992). These stimuli, however, have been found to affect incipient expressive movements in the face, as measured by facial electromyography (EMG). We turn to this research next.

FACIAL ELECTROMYOGRAPHY

Contemporary developments viewing facial expression as a marker of emotion can be traced to Tomkins's (1962) ascription of an instrumental role to facial movement and feedback in the experience of emotion and to his suggestion that high-speed filming be used to perform microscopic analyses of facial expressions and emotion. These proposals led to important methodological advances in the coding of facial expressions (Ekman and Friesen 1978; Izard 1971, 1977). Building on this foundation, investigators over the past three decades have provided provocative evidence that:

At least a subset of discrete emotions have been associated with distinct, overt facial expressions; the induction of states in which individuals report positive and negative emotions are associated with distinctive facial actions; and displays similar to those of the adult can be found in neonates and the congenitally blind (Ekman 1973, 1982, 1994; Ekman and Friesen 1978; Ekman et al. 1987; Izard 1971, 1977, 1994; Steiner 1979). Many emotional and affect-laden information processes are not accompanied by visually perceptible facial actions, however, and this has limited the utility of analyses of facial actions in emotions. Furthermore, although observers across cultures attribute the same emotional meaning to the expressions of happiness, sadness, fear, anger, surprise, and disgust, these attributions are not perfect (Russell 1994). Complicating research in this area, the specific emotion that is evoked (or the sequence or blend of emotions that are evoked) by a stimulus may vary across individuals and cultures. Finally, individuals can invoke display rules to mask or hide the emotion they are feeling, and observers can confuse the meaning of expressions (on fear and surprise, for example, see Ekman 1973; cf. Cacioppo, Bush, and Tassinary 1992). For these reasons, the coding of overt facial expressions can be a less than perfect measure of affective state (Cacioppo et al. 1988).

Use of facial EMG to investigate emotions began in the 1970s. As Rinn (1984) noted, overt facial expressions are the result of varied and specific movements of the facial skin and connective tissue caused by the contraction of facial muscles. These movements create folds, lines, and wrinkles in the skin and the movement of facial landmarks, such as the brows and corners of the mouth. Although muscle activation must occur if these facial actions are to be achieved, muscle action potentials in the face can occur in the absence of any overt facial action if the activation of the muscle(s) is weak or very transient or if the overt response is aborted sufficiently early in the facial action. Facial EMG activity has therefore been especially useful in studies of emotions or emotional processes that are so weak that facial action coding is insensitive (Cacioppo and Petty 1982; Cacioppo, Tassinary, and Fridlund 1990; Schwartz et al. 1976).

Schwartz and his colleagues demonstrated the usefulness of monitoring EMG activity over the brow (corrugator supercilii), cheek (zygomaticus major), and perioral (depressor anguli oris) muscle regions in studies of emotional imagery. For instance, Schwartz and his colleagues (1976) asked participants to imagine positive or negative events in their lives. Results revealed that people showed more EMG activity over the brow region and less over the cheek and perioral regions when imagining sad as compared to happy events. Cacioppo and Petty (1979) found that measures of EMG activity over the cheek and brow muscle regions similarly distinguished individuals who were anticipating and who subsequently were exposed to proattitudinal and counterattitudinal communications even though overt facial expressions were rare, did not differentiate these conditions, and were excluded prior to analyses.

Subsequent research on facial EMG confirmed that: (1) EMG activity over the brow (corrugator supercilii) muscle region is lower and EMG activity over the cheek (zygomaticus major) and periocular (orbicularis oculi) muscle regions is higher when mild positive than when mild negative emotions are evoked, whereas (2) EMG activity over the forehead (medial frontalis, lateral frontalis) and perioral (orbicularis oris, depressor anguli oris) muscle regions does not consistently differentiate mild positive emotions from mild negative ones (Bush et al. 1989; Cacioppo et al. 1992; Cacioppo et al. 1986; Cacioppo et al. 1988; Lang 1995; Dimberg, 1986, 1988; Englis, Vaughan, and Lanzetta 1982; Greenwald, Cook, and Lang 1989; McCanne and Anderson 1987; McHugo et al. 1985). In studies of facial EMG, too, positive and negative affective stimuli tend to have opposing effects on facial EMG activity over the cheek and brow regions, with these opposing effects more apparent at the group (nomethetic) level than individual (idiographic) level of analysis.

Research on the effects of discrete emotions on facial EMG activity also suggests that incipient expressive actions differentiate only positive from negative states. In an especially comprehensive study of facial EMG activity in discrete emotions, for instance, Brown and Schwartz (1980) paced sixty participants through forty-eight imagery conditions designed to elicit happiness, sadness, fear, and anger at three levels of intensity while EMG activity was recorded over the brow, cheek, forehead, and jaw muscle regions. Results revealed that fear, anger, and sadness imagery was associated with higher EMG activity over the brow muscle regions than happiness imagery. EMG activity over the cheek region was highest during happiness imagery but was also elevated during fear imagery, and to a lesser extent during anger imagery. Whether these latter elevations reflect some participants engaging in miserable or distress smiling

(Ekman, Friesen, and Ancoli 1980), cross-talk from other muscles of the middle and lower facial regions, or the putative phylogenetic origin of smiling and laughter in primitive agonistic displays (Andrew 1963; van Hooff, 1972) is unclear. Increasing emotional intensity led to increased EMG activity, particularly over the brow muscle regions during sadness, anger, and fear imagery, and over the cheek muscle region during happiness imagery. Again, EMG activity over the jaw and forehead muscle regions did not vary significantly (see also Brown and Schwartz 1980; Hess et al. 1992; Schwartz et al., 1976; Cacioppo et al., in press). Thus, facial EMG activity during low-intensity emotions appears to be more closely associated with the activation of positivity and negativity than of discrete emotions.

Facial EMG responses have also been found to be more predictive of the extent of positivity or negativity than of discrete emotional experiences during conversation. For instance, Cacioppo and his colleagues (1988) interviewed fifteen undergraduate women about themselves while facial EMG and audiovisual recordings were obtained. Afterwards, participants were asked to describe what they had been thinking during specific segments of the interview marked by distinctive EMG responses over the brow (corrugator supercilii) muscle region in the context of ongoing but stable levels of activity elsewhere in the face. Analyses of the videotapes indicated that observers could not differentiate the recorded segments associated with different emotions. Nevertheless, relatively low levels of EMG activity over the brow muscle region marked feelings of merriment and warmheartedness, whereas relatively high levels of EMG activity over this region marked feelings of fear, sadness, disgust, tension, irritation, and contempt. That is, increased EMG activity over the brow muscle region was associated with lower reports of positive emotions and higher reports of negative emotions. Further differentiation based on facial EMG activity over this region was not reliable.

AUTONOMIC ACTIVITY

As our review of the psychophysiology of evaluative and affective processes indicates, research on rostral brain areas suggests a bivariate organization of positivity and negativity. Moving lower in the neuraxis, the research on the startle eyeblink and facial EMG suggests a greater tendency toward reciprocity between positivity and negativity. Such patterning makes sense when one recognizes the physical constraints that restrict behavioral manifestations of utility calculations to bivalent actions (approach-withdrawal) and the role of the somatic nervous system in carrying out the results of utility calculations to achieve these actions. The autonomic nervous system, in turn, serves to maintain homeostasis and to provide the metabolic support for approach and withdrawal. That is, the autonomic nervous system provides the necessary physiological adjustments and adaptations for humans to enjoy a free and independent existence. Accordingly, the final area of research we review here, that of autonomic nervous system activity, supports the notion that the autonomic nervous system is primarily responsive to the metabolic demands associated with or expected in response to an emotional challenge (Cacioppo et al., in press).

Much of the research on autonomic nervous system activity and affective responses has been influenced by James's (1884) proposal that peripheral physiological changes are antecedents rather than consequents of the perception of emotional experience. James's theorizing generated a great deal of interest in determining not only whether somatovisceral reactions precede emotional experience but also whether discrete emotions are associated with unique patterns of physiological activity. The autonomic nervous system has been the area where many researchers have focused their search for emotion-specific patterning.

Unfortunately, the early research on autonomic activity and affective reactions was characterized by a lack of replicability and consistency. For example, heart rate responses have differentiated pleasant from unpleasant stimuli, but the direction of the effect has been inconsistent. Significantly greater heart-rate deceleration has been reported to pleasant as compared to unpleasant pictorial stimuli (Cacioppo and Sandman 1978; Greenwald, Cook, and Lang 1989; Hubert and de Jong-Meyer 1991; Winton, Putnam, and Krauss 1984). By contrast, imagery of negatively valent material has been associated with greater heart-rate acceleration (Jones and Johnson 1980; Vrana, Cuthbert, and Lang 1989; Vrana and Lang 1990). Studies of pupillary responses were also initially encouraging, with early reports of pupillary dilation to pleasant visual stimuli (Hess and Polt 1960) and pupillary constriction to unpleasant visual stimuli (Hess 1965). Attempts to replicate this effect have often failed, especially when precautions have been taken to control for possible methodological artifacts, such as differences in luminance and visual fixation, and potential confounding psychological variables, such as orienting, mental effort, fatigue, and arousal (Stern and Dunham 1990). Furthermore, subsequent reexamination of Hess and Polt's original data revealed that much of the support for the hypothesis was attributable to atypical responses from one particular participant (Skinner 1980). Also problematic is the failure to obtain a significant relationship between pupillary response and affective state when auditory, olfactory, or tactile stimuli are used (Goldwater 1972). Thus, as with heart rate, the cumulative evidence indicates that pupillary responses do not reliably differentiate emotional states.

Ekman, Levenson, and their colleagues (Ekman, Levenson, and Friesen 1983; Levenson 1988) have also attributed much of the inconsistency in prior results to various methodological problems, including the failure to verify independently that an emotional state has been aroused (for instance, through self-report or behavioral observation) and the recording of physiological measures too long before or after the likely onset and offset of the emotion. They have also noted conceptual shortcomings, such as an inattention to which specific emotion is aroused and to the duration of its arousal. Furthermore, they argued that differentiation requires simultaneous examination of a number of indices of autonomic nervous system activity. Ekman, Levenson, and their colleagues argued that emotion-specific autonomic differentiation would be obtained if methodological shortcomings such as these were eliminated. They first presented evidence of this in an influential paper in 1983 (Ekman et al. 1983). Heart rate, left- and right-hand finger temperature, skin resistance, and forearm flexor muscle tension were recorded during the manipulation of the emotional states of anger, fear, sadness, happiness, surprise, and disgust. One method for evoking emotions involved a directed facial action task in which a participant was induced to form a facial expression associated with a discrete emotion through muscle-by-muscle contraction instructions that omitted any reference to the emotional state. For example, a participant may have been told to pull the eyebrows down and together, raise the upper eyelid, push the lower lip up, and press the lips together. These instructions correspond to the facial expression associated with anger. Autonomic responses recorded during the contraction of an emotional expression were compared to times when a control (nonemotional) expression was posed. Physiological data from a posed expression were analyzed only if inspection of a video record indicated that the desired expression had been achieved. Using the directed facial action task, Ekman, Levenson, and Friesen (1983) reported that (1) heart rate was higher in anger, fear, and sadness than in happiness, disgust, and surprise, and (2) anger could be further differentiated from fear and sadness by its higher finger temperature.

Emotion was also evoked in this experiment with an imagery task in which participants were asked to relive a past emotional experience for thirty seconds. Participants reported the strength of any feelings aroused during the imagery period, and data were retained for analysis only if the strength of the target emotion was at or above the scale midpoint (of a nine-point scale), and no other emotion of similar strength was reported. Physiological responses during a relived emotion period were compared to a non-imagery resting baseline, revealing higher skin resistance during sadness than in fear, anger, or disgust. Together, the results from the two emotion induction techniques generated considerable enthusiasm for the idea of emotion-specific autonomic patterning, especially because emotions of the same valence (such as anger and fear) appeared distinguishable. Similar results were obtained by Levenson, Ekman, and Friesen (1990) using the directed facial action task, leading these researchers to propose that each discrete emotion is associated with an innate affect program whose role is to coordinate changes in the organism's biological states. These changes are directed at supporting the behavioral adaptations and motor programs most likely associated with a particular emotion (such as fleeing in the case of fear) and can be recorded as emotion-specific changes in autonomic nervous system activity (Levenson et al. 1990).

There is now a large body of research relevant to this hypothesis, and several comprehensive reviews have been performed on it (Cacioppo, Klein, Berntson, and Hatfield 1993, Cacioppo et al., in press; Zajonc and McIntosh 1992). Rather than duplicating those efforts here, we will only summarize some of the major findings. Interested readers are encouraged to refer to these reviews for greater detail. These reviews reveal that whereas some reliable autonomic differentiation has been obtained across studies, the results are far from singular in suggesting the presence of emotion-specific autonomic patterning. Cacioppo and his colleagues (in press) conducted a meta-analysis of seventeen separate studies providing data relevant to the question of whether emotion-specific autonomic patterning exists. Studies were included in the review only if they contrasted the effects of at least two discrete emotions on two or more autonomic measures. These criteria yielded nearly eight hundred separate effect sizes involving twenty measures. (Age of participants was also included as a moderator in the analysis, but we will not discuss those effects here.)

Heart rate reliably differentiated several emotions in the meta-analysis. In fact, heart rate provided the strongest evidence for emotion-specific differentiation. Consistent with Ekman, Levenson, and Friesen (1983), greater heart-rate acceleration was obtained with anger, fear, and sadness as compared to disgust. There was also a tendency for happiness to be associated with greater heart-rate acceleration than disgust. However, disgust was associated with the same heart-rate response as control conditions; indeed, disgust did not differ from control on any autonomic measure. Heart-rate responses in the meta-analysis were also found to be larger in (1) anger than happiness, (2) fear than happiness (which also differed on finger pulse volume), (3) fear than sadness (which differed also on respiration rate), (4) anger than surprise, (5) sadness than surprise, and (6) happiness than surprise.

Emotion-specific differentiation for measures other than heart rate was less reliable in the meta-analysis. Diastolic blood pressure did differentiate anger from sadness and happiness, and in turn sadness from happiness (which also differed on the measure of systolic blood pressure), but did not differentiate fear from sadness or happiness. Skin conductance level increased less in happiness than disgust, and less in surprise than disgust, but as noted earlier, disgust did not differ from control conditions in terms of any autonomic response. Fear was associated with greater increases in skin conductance level than surprise, and greater increases in nonspecific skin conductance responses and smaller increases in skin conductance level than sadness in the meta-analysis. There was little support for replicable autonomic differences in pair-wise comparisons of the emotions on the measures of bodily tension, facial temperature, respiration amplitude, inspiration volume, or cardiac stroke volume, and too little data were available on several other measures—such as systolic time intervals, finger pulse volume, pulse transit time, and body movement—to allow strong conclusions (Cacioppo et al., in press; see also Zajonc and McIntosh 1992).

In sum, a review of relevant research reveals only equivocal support for emotion-specific autonomic differentiation. Moreover, a study by Boiten (1996) suggests that at least some of the autonomic differentiation of emotions that is obtained is an artifact of effort-related changes in respiration. Boiten used the directed facial action task to elicit facial expressions of anger, fear, sadness, disgust, and happiness, as well as a nonemotional control expression. Heart-rate results replicated the pattern obtained by Ekman, Levenson, and Friesen (1983) and Levenson, Ekman, and Friesen (1990). Specifically, larger heart-rate increases were observed with anger, fear, and sadness as compared to disgust and surprise. Importantly, however, both respiratory changes and self-report ratings of difficulty in posing an expression covaried with the heart-rate changes. Participants reported that anger, fear, and sadness were the most difficult expressions to pose. These same expressions were also associated with larger respiratory changes than the easier-to-pose emotional expressions and the nonemotional expression. It is therefore not clear whether emotion-specific heart-rate differentiation during posed facial expressions is in fact indicative of innate and emotion-specific affect programs (compare, Levenson et al. 1990).

Several reviews have also noted the failure of imagery to reliably produce differentiation (Cacioppo et al., in press; Zajonc and McIntosh 1992); this is also problematic for the idea of emotion-specific patterning. The imagery data instead suggest that autonomic nervous activity is primarily responsive to the metabolic demands associated with or expected in response to an emotional challenge (Cacioppo et al., in press; Lang et al. 1990). Imagery would be expected to produce few such demands, explaining the general lack of autonomic reactivity associated with this emotion-eliciting procedure. The notion that autonomic nervous system activity is mobilized in response to perceived or expected metabolic demands is consistent with a distinction made by Lang and his colleagues (1990) between strategic and tactical aspects of emotions. Strategies are viewed as underlying organizations that direct actions in the pursuit of broad goals. The dimensions of valence (appetitive or aversive) and intensity are viewed by Lang as strategic aspects of emotion. Tactics, by comparison, are specific, context-bound patterns of action. Affective reactions can be organized into a finite set of discrete emotions, but tactical demands vary among situations, making it possible for the same emotion to be associated with a range of behavior. For example, Lang et al. (1990)

note that the behaviors associated with fear can range from freezing to vigilance to flight. This tactical variability may account for the absence of reliable emotion-specific autonomic patterning. Taken together, the failure of imagery to produce autonomic differentiation, the lack of reliability of emotion-specific patterning on most measures of autonomic nervous system activity, and the possibility that differences in effort are responsible for heart-rate differentiation during the directed facial action task, all suggest that autonomic activity reflects strategic aspects of emotion.

CONCLUSION

As the varied perspectives represented in this volume suggest, the study of utility can be informed from a wide range of viewpoints. The psychophysiological research reviewed in this chapter suggests the following conclusions about utility. First, the computation of utility appears to be performed by neural sources that are at least partially independent from sources associated with discriminative (such as stimulus identification) decisions. This conclusion is supported by the right lateralization of ERPs associated with evaluative but not with nonevaluative categorizations. A similar position is proposed by Shizgal (this volume). Given the importance of utility assessments, it is not at all surprising that specialized neural substrates may have evolved to perform them. The ERP research demonstrating a negativity bias also suggests the existence of separate currency functions for positivity and negativity. These currency functions serve to represent multifarious appetitive and aversive inputs, respectively, along common metrics that can then be used in computations of utility. The phenomenon of loss aversion (Kahneman and Tversky 1984) is one demonstration of how the currency functions may influence decisions about utility. The negativity bias predicts that negative features of a situation will, ceteris paribus, have a larger impact than equally strong positive features.

Associations between cortical asymmetry and affective reactivity are similarly consistent with the notion of separable positive and negative currency functions. In particular, the tendency for left- and right-hemisphere activation to be associated with a predisposition to respond positively or negatively, respectively, suggest that the neural substrates associated with computing the positive and negative significance of stimuli are instantiated in at least partially separable brain mechanisms. We should

note that whereas the EEG and ERP research are each consistent with the separability of positive and negative motivational substrates, these two lines of research most likely assess different aspects of affective and evaluative processing. The former body of research concerns the relative amount of spontaneous alpha activity in the two hemispheres at rest and relates this to the experience of certain affective states, or to the predisposition to experience these states. These relations between EEG and affective reactivity have been obtained primarily in frontal and anterior temporal areas. The right-lateralized LPP is, by contrast, an event-related component of the EEG and has been observed not only at frontal but also at central and parietal sites. Rather than reflecting a predisposition to experience certain affective states, the LPP reflects moment-to-moment evaluative categorizations of people, objects, opportunities, and events.

Three other conclusions are suggested by our review: (1) the magnitude of the startle eyeblink, a defensive reflex, is potentiated by negative affective states and, perhaps to a lesser extent, is attenuated by positive affective states; (2) facial EMG activity over the cheek (zygomaticus major) and periocular (orbicularis oculi) muscle regions varies as a function of positivity, whereas EMG activity over the brow (corrugator supercilii) muscle region varies as a function of negativity; and (3) autonomic activation differs primarily as a function of the energetic (for example, metabolic, action) components of affective states. Thus, research on ERPs and EEG, which reflects evaluative processes at higher levels of the neuraxis, suggests a bivariate organization of positivity and negativity, whereas research on the startle eyeblink and facial EMG, which reflects response processes, suggests a greater tendency toward reciprocity between positivity and negativity. The greater likelihood of finding reciprocal relationships between positivity and negativity as one moves from the calculation of utility to action based on utility appraisals is consistent with the physical constraints that restrict behavioral manifestations to bivalent actions (approach-withdrawal) and the role of the somatic nervous system in carrying out the results of utility calculations to achieve these actions. The autonomic nervous system, in turn, serves to maintain homeostasis and to provide the metabolic support for approach and withdrawal. Accordingly, the autonomic nervous system is primarily responsive to the metabolic demands associated with or expected in response to an emotional challenge.

These findings also clearly demonstrate that a

bipolar model in which positive and negative evaluative processes are assumed to be necessarily reciprocally related is insufficient to accommodate the extant research. Instead, the psychophysiological research on affective and evaluative processes is understandable from within a bivariate model of evaluative activation (Cacioppo and Berntson 1994). Among the assumptions of the model are the separability of the positive and negative motivational substrates, and the specification of distinct activation functions for positivity and negativity (for example, the positivity offset and negativity bias). The ERP and EEG research we have reviewed is consistent with these aspects of the model. An additional feature of the model is its ability to accommodate all the modes of evaluative activation observed in the psychophysiological research. According to the bivariate model, three modes of evaluative activation are possible: (1) reciprocal activation, in which a stimulus has opposing effects on the activation of positivity and negativity; (2) uncoupled activation, in which a stimulus affects only positive or only negative evaluative activation; and (3) nonreciprocal activation, in which a stimulus increases (or decreases) the activation of both positivity and negativity. The tendency to move from separability of positivity and negativity to reciprocity as one moves lower in the neuraxis is therefore understandable from within the bivariate model. As we have noted, physical constraints may restrict behavioral manifestations to bivalent actions (approach-withdrawal), but we believe that the assessment of utility will benefit from recognizing the separability of positivity and negativity, examining their unique antecedents and consequents, and understanding when and why various modes of evaluative activation are observed.

NOTES

1. These topographic analyses are performed on amplitudes that are standardized to remove differences in the absolute amplitude of the P300 across experimental conditions (McCarthy and Wood 1985). Such a standardization allows changes in scalp topography to be interpreted as reflecting changes in the location or combination of neural sources generating a signal and rules out the possibility that a change in topography is simply reflecting differences in intensity of activity across conditions (Johnson 1993; Ruchkin et al. 1995).
2. Power in lower-frequency bands (for example, less than 12 hertz) is thought to be the precursor of adult alpha activity for toddlers and infants (Davidson 1993; Davidson and Fox 1989) and is used as the inverse marker of cortical asymmetry in studies with children.

REFERENCES

Andrew, R. J. (1963). The origin and evolution of the calls and facial expressions of the primates. *Behavior, 20,* 1–109.

Anthony, B.J. (1985). In the blink of the eye: Implications of reflex modification for information processes. In P. K. Ackles, J. R. Jennings, and M. G. H. Coles (Eds.), *Advances in psychophysiology* (vol. 1, pp. 167–218). Greenwich, Conn.: JAI Press.

Balaban, M. T. (1995). Affective influences on startle in five-month-old infants: Reactions to facial expressions of emotions. *Child Development, 66,* 28–36.

Berntson, G. G., Boysen, S. T., and Cacioppo, J. T. (1993). Neurobehavioral organization and the cardinal principle of evaluative bivalence. *Annals of the New York Academy of Sciences, 702,* 75–102.

Boiten, F. (1996). Autonomic response patterns during voluntary facial action. *Psychophysiology, 33,* 123–31.

Bradley, M. M., Cuthbert, B. N., and Lang, P. J. (1990). Startle reflex modification: Emotion or attention? *Psychophysiology, 27,* 513–22.

———. (1996). Lateralized startle probes in the study of emotion. *Psychophysiology, 33,* 156–61.

Brown, S. L., and Schwartz, G. E. (1980). Relationships between facial electromyography and subjective experience during affective imagery. *Biological Psychology, 11,* 49–62.

Bush, L. K., Barr, C. L., McHugo, G. J., and Lanzetta, J. T. (1989). The effects of facial control and facial mimicry on subjective reactions to comedy routines. *Motivation and Emotion, 13,* 31–52.

Cacioppo, J. T., and Berntson, G. G. (1994). Relationship between attitudes and evaluative space: A critical review, with emphasis on the separability of positive and negative substrates. *Psychological Bulletin, 115,* 401–23.

Cacioppo, J. T., Berntson, G. G., Klein, D. J., and Poehlmann, K. M. (in press). The psychophysiology of emotion across the lifespan. *Annual Review of Gerontology and Geriatrics, 17.*

Cacioppo, J. T., Bush, L. K., and Tassinary, L. G. (1992). Microexpressive facial actions as a function of affective stimuli: Replication and extension. *Personality and Social Psychology Bulletin, 18,* 515–26.

Cacioppo, J. T., Crites, S. L., Jr., Berntson, G. G., and Coles, M. G. H. (1993). If attitudes affect how stimuli are processed, should they not affect the event-related brain potential? *Psychological Science, 4,* 108–12.

Cacioppo, J. T., Crites, S. L., Jr., and Gardner, W. L. (1996). Attitudes to the right: Evaluative processing is associated with lateralized late positive event-related brain potentials. *Personality and Social Psychology Bulletin, 22,* 1205–19.

Cacioppo, J. T., Crites, S. L., Jr., Gardner, W. L., and Berntson, G. G. (1994). Bioelectrical echoes from evaluative categorizations: I. A late positive brain potential that varies as a function of trait negativity and extremity. *Journal of Personality and Social Psychology, 67,* 115–25.

Cacioppo, J. T., Gardner, W. L., and Berntson, G. G. (1997). Beyond bipolar conceptualizations and measures: The case of attitudes and evaluative space. *Personality and Social Psychology Review, 1,* 3–25.

Cacioppo, J. T., Klein, D. J., Berntson, G. G., and Hatfield, E. (1993). The psychophysiology of emotion. In R. Lewis and J. M. Haviland (Eds.), *The handbook of emotion* (pp. 119–42). New York: Guilford.

Cacioppo, J. T., Martzke, J. S., Petty, R. E., and Tassinary, L. G. (1988). Specific forms of facial EMG response index emotions during an interview: From Darwin to the continuous flow hypothesis of affect-laden information processing. *Journal of Personality and Social Psychology, 54,* 592–604.

Cacioppo, J. T., and Petty, R. E. (1979). Attitudes and cognitive response: An electrophysiological approach. *Journal of Personality and Social Psychology, 37,* 2181–99.

———. (1982). A biosocial model of attitude change: Signs, symptoms, and undetected physiological responses. In J. T. Cacioppo and R. E. Petty (Eds.), *Perspectives in cardiovascular psychophysiology* (pp. 151–88). New York: Guilford.

Cacioppo, J. T., Petty, R. E., Losch, M. E., and Kim, H. S. (1986). Electromyographic activity over facial muscle regions can differentiate the valence and intensity of affective reactions. *Journal of Personality and Social Psychology, 50,* 260–68.

Cacioppo, J. T., and Sandman, C. A. (1978). Physiological differentiation of sensory and cognitive tasks as a function of warning, processing demands, and reported unpleasantness. *Biological Psychology, 6,* 181–92.

Cacioppo, J. T., Tassinary, L. G., and Fridlund, A. J. (1990). The skeletomotor system. In J. T. Cacioppo and L. G. Tassinary (Eds.), *Principles of psychophysiology: Physical, social, and inferential elements* (pp. 325–84). New York: Cambridge University Press.

Carver, C. S., and White, T. L. (1994). Behavioral inhibition, behavioral activation, and affective responses to impending reward and punishment: The BIS/BAS Scales. *Journal of Personality and Social Psychology, 67,* 319–33.

Center for the Study of Emotion and Attention. (1995). *The International Affective Picture System: Photographic slides.* Gainesville, Fla.: Center for Research in Psychophysiology, University of Florida.

Coles, M. G. H., Gratton, G., and Fabiani, M. (1990). Event-related brain potentials. In J. T. Cacioppo and L. G. Tassinary (Eds.), *Principles of psychophysiology: Physical, social, and inferential elements* (pp. 413–55). Cambridge: Cambridge University Press.

Coles, M. G. H., Gratton, G., Kramer, A. F., and Miller, G. A. (1986). Principles of signal acquisition and analysis. In M. G. H. Coles, E. Donchin, and S. W. Porges (Eds.), *Psychophysiology: Systems, processes, and applications* (pp. 183–226). New York: Guilford.

Cook, E. W., Hawk, L. W., Jr., Davis, T. L., and Stevenson, V. E. (1991). Affective individual differences and startle reflex modulation. *Journal of Abnormal Psychology, 100,* 5–13.

Crites, S. L., Jr., and Cacioppo, J. T. (1996). Electrocortical differentiation of evaluative and nonevaluative categorizations. *Psychological Science, 7,* 318–21.

Crites, S. L., Jr., Cacioppo, J. T., Gardner, W. L., and Berntson, G. G. (1995). Bioelectrical echoes from evaluative categorizations: II. A late positive brain potential that varies as a function of attitude registration rather than attitude report. *Journal of Personality and Social Psychology, 68,* 997–1013.

Cuthbert, B. N., Bradley, M. M., and Lang, P. J. (1996). Probing picture perception: Activation and emotion. *Psychophysiology, 33,* 103–11.

Davidson, R. J. (1992). Anterior cerebral asymmetry and the nature of emotion. *Brain and Cognition, 20,* 125–51.

———. (1993). Childhood temperament and cerebral asymmetry: A neurobiological substrate of behavioral inhibition. In K. H. Rubin and J. B. Asendorpf (Eds.), *Social withdrawal, inhibition, and shyness in childhood* (pp. 31–48). Hillsdale, N.J.: Erlbaum.

Davidson, R. J., Ekman, P., Saron, C. D., Senulis, J. A., and Friesen, W. V. (1990). Approach-withdrawal and cerebral asymmetry: I. Emotional expression and brain physiology *Journal of Personality and Social Psychology, 58,* 330–41.

Davidson, R. J., and Fox, N. A. (1989). Frontal brain asymmetry predicts infants' response to maternal separation. *Journal of Abnormal Psychology, 98,* 127–31.

Davidson, R. J., and Tomarken, A. J. (1989). Laterality and emotion: An electrophysiological approach. In F. Boller and J. Grafman (Eds.), *Handbook of neuropsychology* (vol. 3, pp. 419–41). New York: Elsevier.

Dimberg, U. (1986). Facial reactions to fear-relevant and fear-irrelevant stimuli. *Biological Psychology, 23,* 153–61.

———. (1988). Facial electromyography and the experience of emotion. *Journal of Psychophysiology, 2,* 277–82.

Donchin, E., and Coles, M. G. H. (1988). Is the P300 component a manifestation of context updating? *Behavioral and Brain Sciences, 11,* 357–74.

Donchin, E., Karis, D., Bashore, T. R., Coles, M. G. H., and Gratton, G. (1986). Cognitive psychophysiology and human information processing. In M. G. H. Coles, E. Donchin, and S. W. Porges (Eds.), *Psychophysiology: Systems, processes, and applications* (pp. 244–67). New York: Guilford.

Ehrlichman, H., Brown, S., Zhu, J., and Warrenburg, S. (1995). Startle reflex modulation during exposure to pleasant and unpleasant odors. *Psychophysiology, 32,* 150–54.

Ekman, P. (1973). Cross-cultural studies of facial expression. *Darwin and facial expression: A century of research in review.* New York: Academic Press.

———. (1982). *Emotion in the human face.* (2d ed.) New York: Cambridge University Press.

———. (1994). Strong evidence for universals in facial expressions: A reply to Russell's mistaken critique. *Psychological Bulletin, 115,* 268–87.

Ekman, P., and Friesen, W. V. (1978). *The facial action coding system: A technique for the measurement of facial movement.* Palo Alto, Calif.: Consulting Psychologists Press.

Ekman, P., Friesen, W. V., and Ancoli, S. (1980). Facial signs of emotional experience. *Journal of Personality and Social Psychology, 39,* 1125–34.

Ekman, P., Friesen, W. V., O'Sullivan, M., Chan, A., Diacoyanni-Tarlatzis, I., Heider, K., Krause, R., LeCompte, W. A., Pitcairn, T., Ricci-Bitti, P. E., Scherer, K., Tomita, M., and Tzavaras, A. (1987). Universals and cultural differences in the judgments of facial expressions of emotion. *Journal of Personality and Social Psychology, 53,* 712–17.

Ekman, P., Levenson, R. W., and Friesen, W. V. (1983). Autonomic nervous system activity distinguishes among emotions. *Science, 221,* 1208–10.

Englis, B. G., Vaughan, K. B., and Lanzetta, J. T. (1982). Conditioning of counterempathetic emotional responses. *Journal of Experimental Social Psychology, 38,* 375–91.

Gehring, W. J., Gratton, G., Coles, M. G. H., and Donchin, E. (1992). Probability effects on stimulus evaluation and response processes. *Journal of Experimental Psychology: Human Perception and Performance, 18,* 198–216.

Goldstein, M. D., and Strube, M. J. (1994). Independence revisited: The relation between positive and negative affect in a naturalistic setting. *Journal of Personality and Social Psychology, 20,* 57–64.

Goldwater, B. C. (1972). Psychological significance of pupillary movements. *Psychological Bulletin, 77,* 340–55.

Gray, J. A. (1982). *The neuropsychology of anxiety: An inquiry into the functions of the septo-hippocampal systems.* Oxford: Oxford University Press.

———. (1987). *The psychology of fear and stress.* 2nd ed. Cambridge: Cambridge University Press.

Greenwald, M. K., Cook, E. W., III, and Lang, P. J. (1989). Affective judgment and psychophysiological response: Dimensional covariation in the evaluation of pictorial stimuli. *Journal of Psychophysiology, 3,* 51–64.

Hawk, L. W., and Cook, E. W. (1997). Affective modulation of tactile startle. *Psychophysiology, 34,* 23–31.

Henriques, J. B., and Davidson, R. J. (1990). Regional brain electrical asymmetries discriminate between previously depressed and healthy controls. *Journal of Abnormal Psychology, 99,* 22–31.

———. (1991). Left frontal hypoactivation in depression. *Journal of Abnormal Psychology, 100,* 535–45.

Hess, E. H. (1965). Attitude and pupil size. *Scientific American, 212,* 46–54.

Hess, E. H., and Polt, J. M. (1960). Pupil size as related to interest value of visual stimuli. *Science, 132,* 349–50.

Hess, U., Kappas, A., McHugo, G. J., Lanzetta, J. T., and Kleck, R. E. (1992). The facilitative effect of facial expression on the self-generation of emotion. *International Journal of Psychophysiology, 12,* 251–65.

Hubert, W., and de Jong-Meyer, R. (1991). Autonomic, neuroendocrine, and subjective responses to emotion-inducing film stimuli. *International Journal of Psychophysiology, 11,* 131–40.

Ito, T. A., Larsen, J. T., Smith, N. K., and Cacioppo, J. T. (1998). Negative information weighs more heavily on the brain: The negativity bias in evaluative categorizations. *Journal of Personality and Social Psychology, 75,* 887–900.

Izard, C. E. (1971). *The face of emotion.* New York: Appleton-Century-Crofts.

———. (1977). *Human emotions.* New York: Academic Press.

———. (1994). Innate and universal facial expressions: Evidence from developmental and cross-cultural research. *Psychological Bulletin, 115,* 288–99.

James, W. (1884). What is an emotion? *Mind, 9,* 188–205.

Jansen, D. M., and Frijda, N. H. (1994). Modulation of the acoustic startle response by film-induced fear and sexual arousal. *Psychophysiology, 31,* 565–71.

Johnson, R., Jr. (1993). On the neural generators of the P300 component of the event-related potential. *Psychophysiology, 30,* 90–97.

Jones, G. E., and Johnson, H. J. (1980). Heart rate and somatic concomitants of mental imagery. *Psychophysiology, 17,* 339–47.

Kahneman, D., and Tversky, A. (1984). Choices, values, and frames. *American Psychologist, 39,* 341–50.

Lang, P. J. (1995). The emotion probe: Studies of motivation and attention. *American Psychologist, 50,* 372–85.

Lang, P. J., Bradley, M. M., and Cuthbert, B. N. (1990). Emotion, attention, and the startle reflex. *Psychological Review, 97,* 377–95.

———. (1992). A motivational analysis of emotion: Reflex-cortex connections. *Psychological Science, 3,* 44–49.

Levenson, R. W. (1988). Emotion and the autonomic nervous system: A prospectus for research on autonomic specificity. In H. L. Wagner (Ed.), *Social psychophysiology and emotion: Theory and clinical applications* (pp. 17–42). London: Wiley.

Levenson, R. W., Ekman, P., and Friesen, W. V. (1990). Voluntary facial action generates emotion-specific autonomic nervous system activity. *Psychophysiology, 27,* 363–84.

Lipp, O. V., Sheridan, J., and Siddle, D. A. T. (1994). Human blink startle during aversive and nonaversive Pavlovian conditioning. *Journal of Experimental Psychology: Animal Behavior Processes, 20,* 380–89.

McCanne, T. R., and Anderson, J. A. (1987). Emotional responding following experimental manipulation of facial electromyographic activity. *Journal of Personality and Social Psychology, 52,* 759–68.

McCarthy, G., and Donchin, E. (1981). A metric for thought: A comparison of P300 latency and reaction time. *Science, 211,* 77–80.

McCarthy, G., and Wood, C. C. (1985). Scalp distributions of event-related potentials: An ambiguity associated with analysis of variance models. *Electroencephalography and Clinical Neurophysiology, 62,* 203–8.

McHugo, G., Lanzetta, J. T., Sullivan, D. G., Masters, R. D., and Englis, B. G. (1985). Emotional reactions to a political leader's expressive displays. *Journal of Personality and Social Psychology, 49,* 1513–29.

Miller, N. E. (1951). Comments on theoretical methods illustrated by the development of a theory of conflict theory. *Journal of Personality, 20,* 82–100.

———. (1959). Liberalization of basic S-R concepts: Extensions to conflict behavior, motivation, and social learning. In S. Koch (Ed.), *Psychology: A study of science,* study 1 (pp. 198–292). New York: McGraw-Hill.

———. (1961). Some recent studies on conflict behavior and drugs. *American Psychologist, 16,* 12–24.

Miltner, W., Matjak, M. Braun, C., Diekman, H., and Brody, S. (1994). Emotional qualities of odors and their influence on the startle reflex in humans. *Psychophysiology, 31,* 107–10.

Rinn, W. E. (1984). The neuropsychology of facial expression: A review of the neurological and psychological mechanisms for producing facial expressions. *Psychological Bulletin, 95,* 52–77.

Robinson, R. G., and Downhill, J. E. (1995). Lateralization of psychopathology in response to focal brain injury. In R. J. Davidson and K. Hugdahl (Eds.), *Brain asymmetry* (pp. 693–711). Cambridge, Mass.: MIT Press.

Robinson, R. G., Kubos, K. L., Starr, L. B., Rao, K., and Price, T. R. (1984). Mood disorders in stroke patients. *Brain, 107,* 81–93.

Ruchkin, D. S., Canoune, H. L., Johnson, R., Jr., and Ritter, W. (1995). Working memory and preparation elicit different patterns of slow wave event-related brain potentials. *Psychophysiology, 32,* 399–410.

Russell, J. A. (1994). Is there universal recognition of emotion from facial expressions? A review of the cross-cultural studies. *Psychological Bulletin, 115,* 102–41.

Schwartz, G. E., Fair, P. L., Salt, P., Mandel, M. R., and Klerman, G. L. (1976). Facial muscle patterning to affective imagery in depressed and nondepressed subjects. *Science, 192,* 489–91.

Shagass, C. (1972). Electrical activity of the brain. In N. S. Greenfield and R. A. Sternbach (Eds.), *Handbook of psychophysiology* (pp. 263–328). New York: Holt, Rinehart and Winston.

Skinner, N. F. (1980). The Hess et al. study of pupillary activity in heterosexual and homosexual males: A reevaluation. *Perceptual and Motor Skills, 51,* 844.

Steiner, J. E. (1979). Human facial expression in response to taste and smell stimulation. *Advances in Child Development and Behavior, 13,* 237–95.

Stern, J. A., and Dunham, D. N. (1990). The ocular system. In J. T. Cacioppo and L. G. Tassinary (Eds.), *Principles of psychophysiology: Physical, social, and inferential elements* (pp. 513–53). Cambridge: Cambridge University Press.

Sutton, S. K., and Davidson, R. J. (1997). Prefrontal brain asymmetry: A biological substrate of the behavioral approach and inhibition systems. *Psychological Science, 8,* 204–10.

Tomarken, A. J., Davidson, R. J., and Henriques, J. B. (1990). Resting frontal asymmetry predicts affective responses to films. *Journal of Personality and Social Psychology, 59,* 791–801.

Tomarken, A. J., Davidson, R. J., Wheeler, R. E., and Kinney, L. (1992). Psychometric properties of resting anterior EEG asymmetry: Temporal stability and internal consistency. *Psychophysiology, 29,* 576–92.

Tomkins, S. S. (1962). *Affect, imagery, and consciousness,* vol. 1, *The positive affects.* New York: Springer-Verlag.

van Hooff, J. A. R. A. M. (1972). A comparative approach to the phylogeny of laughter and smiling. In R. Hinde (Ed.), *Non-verbal communication* (pp. 129–79). London: Cambridge University Press.

Vrana, S. R. (1995). Emotional modulation of skin conductance and eyeblink responses to a startle probe. *Psychophysiology, 32,* 351–57.

Vrana, S. R., Cuthbert, B. N., and Lang, P. J. (1989). Processing fearful and and neutral sentences: Memory and hear rate change. *Cognition and Emotion, 3,* 179–95.

Vrana, S. R., and Lang, P. J. (1990). Fear imagery an the startle-probe reflex. *Journal of Abnormal Psychology, 99,* 181–89.

Vrana, S. R., Spence, E. L., and Lang, P. J. (1988). The startle probe response: A new measure of emotion? *Journal of Abnormal Psychology, 97,* 487–91.

Wheeler, R. E., Davidson, R. J., and Tomarken, A. J. (1993). Frontal brain asymmetry and emotional reactivity: A biological substrate of affective style. *Psychophysiology, 30,* 82–89.

Winton, W. M., Putnam, L. E., Krauss, R. M. (1984). Facial and autonomic manifestations of the dimensional structure of emotion. *Journal of Experimental Social Psychology, 20,* 195–216.

Witvliet, C. V., and Vrana, S. R. (1995). Psychophysiological responses as indices of affective dimensions. *Psychophysiology, 32,* 436–43.

Zajonc, R. B., and McIntosh, D. N. (1992). Emotions research: Some promising questions and some questionable promises. *Psychological Science, 3,* 70–74.

in future situations in which the sights, sounds, or smells of the predator are detected. But the price we pay for this efficiency is substantial. We often develop fears and anxieties that are not very useful. And these, like their more beneficial counterparts, are very difficult to get rid of. When we pair a tone with a shock, we are tapping into this evolutionarily old learning system that underlies both adaptive and maladaptive aspects of human behavior.

Fear conditioning may not tell us all we need to know about all aspects of fear, or all aspects of anxiety disorders, but it is an excellent starting point. Furthermore, many of the other fear assessment procedures, such as the various forms of avoidance conditioning, crucially involve an initial phase of fear conditioning that then provides motivational impetus for the later stages of instrumental avoidance learning (see, for example, Dollard and Miller 1950; Mowrer 1939). Some fear assessment procedures do not require learning (for example, open field, the elevated maze, or light avoidance tasks), but these are somewhat less amenable to a neural systems analysis than fear conditioning, owing mainly to the fact that the stimulus situation is often poorly defined in these procedures.

BASIC NEURAL SYSTEMS INVOLVED IN FEAR CONDITIONING

Significant progress has been made over the past two decades in elucidating the neural circuits underlying fear conditioning (for reviews, see Davis 1992; Kapp et al. 1992; LeDoux 1995, 1996; Maren and Fanselow 1996). Most of this work has been performed in rats and has focused on the processing of a simple auditory CS, such as a pure tone (a single-frequency acoustic signal), that is paired with a US consisting of a mild electric shock to the feet. For this reason, we focus here on the circuits in the rat brain involved in auditory fear conditioning. Nonetheless, many of the auditory findings also apply to other sensory modalities, and the results from rat studies apply to other animals, including birds, dogs, cats, mice, monkeys, and humans (for a summary, see LeDoux 1996). The basic circuits and mechanisms thus seem to have been conserved throughout much of the evolutionary history of vertebrates.

The centerpiece of the fear conditioning system is the amygdala, a small region located in the temporal lobe. It is essential for the acquisition of conditioned fear as well as for the expression of innate and learned fear responses (see Blanchard and Blanchard 1972; Davis 1992; Kapp et al. 1992; LeDoux 1996). It is generally believed that through the process of conditioning, the CS acquires the capacity to access and trigger the hardwired fear response network organized by the amygdala and its output connections to the brain stem, producing a cascade of innate defensive reactions. It is thus important to understand how information about the CS is transmitted to, and processed by, the amygdala and to determine the cellular mechanisms in the amygdala that underlie the changes in processing during learning.

Auditory CS information is transmitted from the ear, through auditory pathways of the brain stem, to the auditory relay nucleus in the thalamus, the medial geniculate body (MGB) (LeDoux, Sakaguchi, and Reis 1984). The signal is then relayed to the amygdala by way of two parallel pathways (figure 25.2). A direct monosynaptic projection originates in a particular subset of nuclei of the auditory thalamus (LeDoux, Farb, and Ruggiero 1990). A second, indirect pathway conveys information from all areas of the auditory thalamus to the auditory cortex. Several cortico-cortical pathways then transmit auditory information to the amygdala (Mascagni, McDonald, and Coleman 1993; Romanski and LeDoux 1993). Both the direct and

FIGURE 25.2   Dual Pathways to the Amygdala in Fear Conditioning

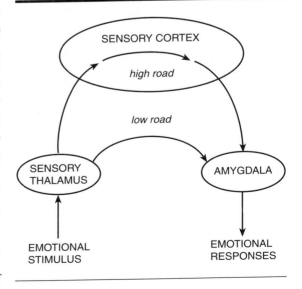

indirect pathways terminate in the lateral nucleus of the amygdala (LA) (LeDoux, Cicchetti et al. 1990; Mascagni et al. 1993; Romanski and LeDoux 1993; Turner and Herkenham 1991), often converging on single neurons (Li, Stutzmann, and LeDoux 1996). Experimental manipulations that disrupt normal functioning of LA—such as permanent lesions (LeDoux, Cicchetti et al. 1990), temporary inactivation of the region (Helmstetter and Bellgowan 1994; Muller et al. 1997), or pharmacological blockade of excitatory amino-acid receptors (Fanselow and Kim 1994; Gerwitz and Davis 1997; Maren, Aharonov et al. 1996; Miserendino et al. 1990)—interfere with fear conditioning.

Although the auditory cortex is not required for the acquisition of conditioned fear to a simple auditory stimulus (Armony, Servan-Schreiber, Romanski et al. 1997; Romanski and LeDoux 1992), processing of the CS by cells in the auditory cortex is modified as a result of its pairing with the US (Quirk, Armony, and LeDoux 1997; Weinberger 1995). In situations involving more complex stimuli that must be discriminated, recognized, and/or categorized, the auditory cortex may be an essential link to the amygdala (see, for example, Cranford and Igarashi 1977; Whitfield 1980).

What are the advantages of the parallel processing capabilities of this system? First, the existence of a subcortical pathway allows the amygdala to detect threatening stimuli in the environment quickly, in the absence of a complete and time-consuming analysis of the stimulus. This quick and dirty processing route may confer an evolutionary advantage to the species. Second, the rapid subcortical pathway may function to "prime" the amygdala to evaluate subsequent information received along the cortical pathway (LeDoux 1996; Li et al. 1996). For example, a loud noise may be sufficient to alert the amygdala, at the cellular level, to prepare to respond to a dangerous predator lurking nearby, but defensive reactions may not be fully mobilized until the auditory cortex analyzes the location, frequency, and intensity of the noise to determine specifically the nature and extent of this potentially threatening auditory signal. The convergence of the subcortical and cortical pathways on single neurons in the lateral nucleus (Li et al. 1996) provides a means by which the integration could take place. Third, recent computational modeling studies show that the subcortical pathway can function as an interrupt device (Simon 1967) that enables the cortex, by way of amygdalo-cortical projections, to shift attention to dangerous stimuli that occur outside the focus of attention (see Armony, Servan-Schreiber, Cohen et al. 1997).

Information processed by the lateral nucleus is then transmitted via intra-amygdala connections (Pitkänen et al. 1995; Pitkänen, Savander, and LeDoux 1997; Savander, LeDoux, and Pitkänen 1996, 1997) to the basal and accessory basal nuclei, where it is integrated with other incoming information and further transmitted to the central nucleus (figure 25.2). The central nucleus is the main output system of the amygdala. Damage to the central amygdala interferes with the acquisition and expression of all conditioned responses, whereas lesions of areas that the central amygdala projects to interferes with individual responses, like blood pressure changes or freezing behavior or hormone release, but not all of these (see, for example, LeDoux et al. 1988; van der Kar et al. 1991).

Most of the work described so far has involved rodents. However, recent studies have shown that damage to the human amygdala interferes with fear conditioning (Bechara et al. 1995; LaBar et al. 1995) and that activation of the human amygdala occurs during conditioning, as demonstrated with functional magnetic resonance imaging (fMRI) (LaBar et al. 1998).

The amygdala is thus the key to the fear conditioning system. It is the region that receives information about external stimuli, interprets the significance of the stimulus, and initiates defensive responses in a wide variety of species, including ours.

FEARFUL SITUATIONS

Whether a stimulus signals danger, and thus elicits fear reactions, may depend on the situation (context) in which it occurs. For example, the sight of a bear in the zoo poses little threat to us, but seeing the same bear while we are walking in the woods would make us run away in fear. Furthermore, contexts may themselves acquire aversive value through prior experiences. If we are mugged, we will most likely feel uneasy when we return to the scene of the crime.

The relationship between environmental situations and fear responses can be investigated in the laboratory through contextual fear conditioning: when a rat is conditioned to expect a foot shock in the presence of a tone CS, it will also exhibit fear reactions to the chamber where the conditioning took place, even in the absence of the CS (Kim and Fanselow 1992; Phillips and LeDoux 1992). Recent studies have shown that the formation and consolidation of contextual fear associations depend on the hippocampus. Lesions of the hippocampus made prior to training interfere with the acquisition of conditioned responses to the context without having any effect on the conditioning to the CS (Phillips and LeDoux 1992, 1994; Selden et al. 1991). Furthermore, hippocampal lesions made after training interfere with the retention of contextual fear association (Kim and Fanselow 1992). This selective retrograde amnesia for contextual fear, however, is temporally graded: lesions made more than two weeks after conditioning have no effect (Kim and Fanselow 1992). These findings are consistent with human studies (Squire, Slater, and Chace 1975) and computational models (Alvarez and Squire 1994; Gluck and Myers 1993; McClelland, McNaughton, and O'Reilly 1995) that suggest a time-limited contribution of the hippocampus in the formation and consolidation of explicit memories. The role of the hippocampus in the evaluation of contextual cues in fear conditioning is also consistent with current theories of spatial, configural, and relational processing in the hippocampus (Cohen and Eichenbaum 1993; O'Keefe and Nadel 1978; Sutherland and Rudy 1989).

The exact way in which contextual information coded in the hippocampus interacts with the emotional system is still unclear. Bidirectional projections between the hippocampal formation and the amygdala (Amaral et al. 1992; Canteras and Swanson 1992; Ottersen 1981) provide anatomical channels through which the attachment of emotional value to context may take place. The fibers from the hippocampus to the amygdala terminate extensively in the basal and accessory basal nuclei, and to a much lesser extent in the lateral nucleus, suggesting why lesions of the lateral have little effect on context conditioning, but lesions of the basal and/or accessory basal seem to be disruptive (Majidishad, Pelli, and LeDoux 1996; Maren, Aharonov, and Fanselow 1996).

GETTING RID OF FEAR

Fear responses tend to be very persistent. This tendency can be extremely helpful for survival, because it allows us to keep a record of all previously encountered threatening experiences and thus allows us to respond quickly to similar situations in the future. Nonetheless, it is also important to be able to learn that a stimulus no longer signals danger. Otherwise, unnecessary fear responses will be elicited by innocuous stimuli and may become a liability, interfering with other important routine tasks. In humans, the inability to inhibit unwarranted fear responses can have devastating consequences, as observed in phobias, post-traumatic stress disorder, generalized anxiety disorder, and other anxiety disorders.

In laboratory experiments, learned fear responses can be reduced (extinguished) by repeatedly presenting the CS without the US. It is important to note, however, that extinction of conditioned fear responses is not a passive forgetting of the CS-US association, but an active process, possibly involving a new learning (Bouton and Swartzentruber 1991). In fact, CS-elicited responses can be spontaneously reinstated following an unrelated traumatic experience (Jacobs and Nadel 1985; Pavlov 1927; Rescorla and Heth 1975).

Experimental observations in fear conditioning studies suggest that neocortical areas, particularly the prefrontal cortex, are involved in the extinction process. Lesions of the ventromedial and medial orbital prefrontal cortex retard the extinction of behavioral responses to the CS (Morgan, Romanski, and LeDoux 1993; Morgan and LeDoux 1995; but see Gerwitz and Davis 1997). These findings complement electrophysiological studies showing that neurons within the orbitofrontal cortex are particularly sensitive to changes in stimulus-reward associations (Rolls 1996; Thorpe, Rolls, and Maddison 1983). Lesions of sensory areas of the cortex also retard extinction (LeDoux, Romanski, and Xagoraris 1989; Teich et al. 1989), and neurons in the auditory cortex exhibit extinction-resistant changes to an auditory CS (Quirk et al. 1997). Thus, the medial prefrontal cortex, possibly in conjunction with other neocortical regions, may be involved in regulating amygdala responses to stimuli based on their current affective value. These findings suggest that fear disorders may be related to a malfunction of the prefrontal cortex that makes it difficult for patients to extinguish fears they have acquired (Armony and LeDoux 1997; LeDoux 1996; Morgan et al. 1993; Morgan and LeDoux 1995). Recent studies have shown that stress has the same effects as lesions of the medial prefrontal cortex (fear exaggeration) (Conrad et al. 1997; Corodimas et al. 1994). Given that stress is a common occurrence in psychiatric patients, and that stress can induce functional changes in the prefrontal cortex, it is possible that the exaggeration of fear in anxiety disorders results from stress-induced alterations in the medial prefrontal region.

AN EMOTIONAL HUB

The amygdala can be thought of as the hub in a wheel of fear. The centerpiece of the fear system, it receives inputs from many cortical and subcortical regions. It can be activated by processes occurring in any of these regions, by way of these various connections. Figure 25.3 illustrates some of the relevant pathways. However, many others, especially those going from the amygdala back to the cortex, are not shown. These actually outnumber the projections from the cortex to the amygdala and suggest that it may be easier for the amygdala to control the cortex than for the cortex to control the amygdala. This may be why psychotherapy to reduce fear and anxiety is such a difficult and prolonged process.

EMOTIONAL ACTION

The defensive responses we've considered so far are hard-wired reactions to danger signals. Evolution's gifts to us, they provide a first line of defense against danger. Some animals rely mainly on these responses. But mammals, especially humans, are able to make the transition from reaction to action. This is one of the benefits of the forebrain expansion that characterizes mammalian evolution.

Considerably less is understood about the brain mechanisms of emotional action than reaction, owing in part to the fact that emotional actions come in many varieties and are limited only by the ingenuity of the actor. For example, once we are freezing and expressing physiological responses to a dangerous stimulus, the rest is up to us. On the basis of our expectations about what is likely to happen next and our past experiences in similar situations, we make a plan about what to do. We become instruments of action.

Instrumental responses in situations of danger are often studied using avoidance conditioning procedures. Avoidance is a multi-stage learning process (Mowrer and Lamoreaux 1946). First, conditioned fear responses are acquired. Then the CS becomes a signal that is used to initiate responses that prevent encounters with the US. Finally, once avoidance responses are learned, animals no longer show the characteristic signs of fear (Rescorla and Solomon 1967). They know what to do to avoid the danger and simply perform the response in a habitual way. Consistent with this is

FIGURE 25.3   The Amygdala: The Hub in a Wheel of Fear

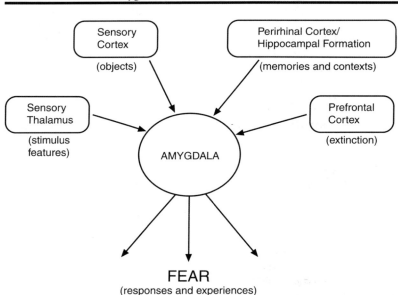

the fact that the amygdala is required for avoidance learning (for the fear conditioning part) but not for the expression of well-trained avoidance responses (the instrumental part) (Parent, Tomaz, and McGaugh 1992). The involvement of an instrumental component in some aversive learning tasks may explain why these are not dependent on the amygdala for long-term storage (McGaugh et al. 1995; Packard et al. 1995).

Because avoidance learning involves fear conditioning, at least initially, it is subject to all the factors that influence fear conditioning and conditioned fear responding. However, because avoidance learning involves more than simple fear conditioning, it is to be expected that avoidance is subject to influences that have little or no effect on conditioned fear. Much more work is needed to understand how fear and avoidance interact, and thus how emotional actions emerge out of emotional reactions. It seems, from what we know so far, that like other habit systems (Mishkin, Malamut, and Bachevalier 1984), interactions between the amygdala, basal ganglia, and neocortex are important in avoidance (Everitt and Robbins 1992; Gray 1987; Killcross, Robbins, and Everitt 1997) (see figure 25.4).

SO WHAT ABOUT FEELINGS?

Consciousness is an important part of the study of emotion and other mental processes. Our hypothesis is that the mechanisms of consciousness are the same for emotional and non-emotional subjective states and that what distinguishes these states is the brain system that consciousness is aware of at the time.

We are far from solving what consciousness is, but a number of theorists have proposed that it has something to do with working memory, a serially organized mental workspace where things can be compared and contrasted and mentally manipulated (Johnson-Laird 1988; Kihlstrom 1984; Schacter 1989; Shallice 1988). Working memory allows us, for example, to compare an immediately present visual stimulus with information stored in long-term (explicit) memory about stimuli with similar shapes and colors or stimuli found in similar locations.

A variety of studies of humans and nonhuman primates point to involvement of the prefrontal cortex, especially the dorsolateral prefrontal areas, in working memory processes (Baddeley and Della Sala 1996; Fuster 1989; Goldman-Rakic 1987). Immediately present stimuli and stored representations are integrated in working memory by way of interactions between prefrontal areas, sensory processing systems (which serve as short-term memory buffers as well as perceptual processors), and the long-term explicit (declarative) memory system involving the hippocampus and related areas of the temporal lobe. Recently the notion has arisen that working memory may involve interactions between several prefrontal areas, including the anterior cingulate and orbital cortical regions,

FIGURE 25.4   Emotional Action Versus Reaction

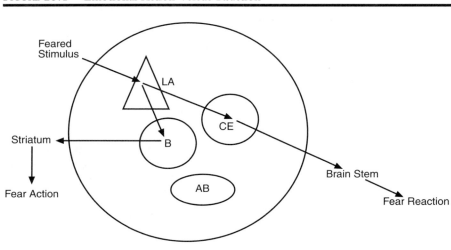

as well as the dorsolateral prefrontal cortex (D'Esposito et al. 1996; Gaffan et al. 1993).

Now suppose that the stimulus is affectively charged, say a trigger of fear. The same sorts of processes are called upon as for stimuli without emotional implications, but in addition, working memory becomes aware of the fact that the fear system of the brain has been activated. We propose that this additional information, when added to perceptual and mnemonic information about the object or event, is the condition for the subjective experience of an emotional state of fear.

But what is the information that is added to working memory when the fear system is activated? As noted earlier, the amygdala projects to many cortical areas, even some that it does not receive inputs from. It can thus influence the operation of perceptual and short-term memory processes, as well as processes in higher-order areas. Although the amygdala does not have extensive connections with the dorsolateral prefrontal cortex, it does communicate with the anterior cingulate and orbital cortex, two other components of the working memory network. But in addition, the amygdala projects to nonspecific systems involved in the regulation of cortical arousal. And the amygdala controls bodily responses (behavioral, autonomic, endocrine), which then provide feedback that can influence cortical processing indirectly. Thus, working memory receives a greater number of inputs, and receives inputs of a greater variety, in the presence of an emotional stimulus than in the presence of other stimuli. These extra inputs may just be what is required to add affective

charge to working memory representations, and thus to turn subjective experiences into emotional experiences (see figure 25.5).

Though described in terms of the fear system, the present hypothesis about feelings is a general one that applies to any emotion. That is, an emotional feeling results when working memory is occupied with the fact that an emotion system of the brain is active. The difference between an emotional state and other states of consciousness, then, is not due to different underlying mechanisms that give rise to the qualitatively different subjective experiences. Instead, there is one mechanism of consciousness, and it can be occupied by either mundane events or emotionally charged ones. If this view is correct, we might expect to make progress in understanding the basis of the subjective states we call joy and suffering by figuring out which brain systems are feeding working memory when people are in such states. While neurobiology has not solved the problem of feelings, it has at least given us a way to think about how our most personal states might emerge from the organization of synaptic pathways in the brain.

REFERENCES

Alvarez, P., and Squire, L. R. (1994). Memory consolidation and the medial temporal lobe: A simple network model. *Proceedings of the National Academy of Sciences, USA, 91,* 7041–45.

Amaral, D. G., Price, J. L., Pitkänen, A., and Carmichael, S. T. (1992). Anatomical organization of the primate amygdaloid complex. In J. P. Aggleton (Ed.), *The amygdala: Neurobiological aspects of emotion, memory, and mental dysfunction* (pp. 1–66). New York: Wiley-Liss.

Armony, J. L., and LeDoux, J. E. (1997). How the brain processes emotional information. *Annals of the New York Academy of Sciences, 821,* 259–70.

Armony, J. L., Servan-Schreiber, D., Cohen, J. D., and LeDoux, J. E. (1997). Computational modeling of emotion: Explorations through the anatomy and physiology of fear conditioning. *Trends in Cognitive Sciences, 1,* 28–34.

Armony, J. L., Servan-Schreiber, D., Romanski, L. M., Cohen, J. D., and LeDoux, J. E. (1997). Stimulus generalization of fear responses: Effects of auditory cortex lesions in a computational model and in rats. *Cerebral Cortex, 7,* 157–65.

Baddeley, A., and Della Sala, S. (1996). Working memory and executive control. *Philosophical Transactions of the Royal Society B, 351,* 1397–1404.

Bechara, A., Tranel, D., Damasio, H., Adolphs, R., Rockland, C., and Damasio, A. R. (1995). Double

FIGURE 25.5   How Feelings Come About

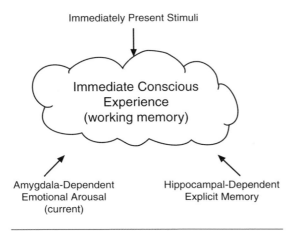

dissociation of conditioning and declarative knowledge relative to the amygdala and hippocampus in humans. *Science, 269,* 1115–18.

Blanchard, C. D., and Blanchard, R. J. (1972). Innate and conditioned reactions to threat in rats with amygdaloid lesions. *Journal of Comparative Physiological Psychology, 81,* 281–90.

Blanchard, R. J., and Blanchard, D. C. (1969). Passive and active reactions to fear-eliciting stimuli. *Journal of Comparative Physiological Psychology, 68,* 129–35.

Bolles, R. C., and Fanselow, M. S. (1980). A perceptual-defensive-recuperative model of fear and pain. *Behavioral and Brain Sciences, 3,* 291–323.

Bouton, M. E., and Bolles, R. C. (1980). Conditioned fear assessed by freezing and by the suppression of three different baselines. *Animal Learning and Behavior, 8,* 429–34.

Bouton, M. E., and Swartzentruber, D. (1991). Sources of relapse after extinction in Pavlovian and instrumental learning. *Clinical Psychology Review, 11,* 123–40.

Canteras, N. S., and Swanson, L. W. (1992). Projections of the ventral subiculum to the amygdala, septum, and hypothalamus: A PHAL anterograde tract-tracing study in the rat. *Journal of Comparative Neurology, 324,* 180–94.

Cohen, N. J., and Eichenbaum, H. (1993). *Memory, amnesia, and the hippocampal system.* Cambridge, Mass.: MIT Press.

Conrad, C. D., Magariños, A. M., LeDoux, J. E., and McEwen, B. S. (1997). Chronic restraint stress enhanced contextual and cued fear conditioning in rats. *Society for Neuroscience Abstracts, 718*(4), 718.

Corodimas, K. P., LeDoux, J. E., Gold, P. W., and Schulkin, J. (1994). Corticosterone potentiation of learned fear. *Annals of the New York Academy of Sciences, 746,* 392–93.

Cranford, J. L., and Igarashi, M. (1977). Effects of auditory cortex lesions on temporal summation in cats. *Brain Research, 136,* 559–64.

Davis, M. (1992). The role of the amygdala in conditioned fear. In J. P. Aggleton (Ed.), *The amygdala: Neurobiological aspects of emotion, memory, and mental dysfunction* (pp. 255–306). New York: Wiley-Liss.

D'Esposito, M., Detre, J. A., et al. (1996). The neural basis of the central executive system of working memory. *Nature, 378,* 279–81.

Dollard, J. C., and Miller, N. E. (1950). *Personality and psychotherapy.* New York: McGraw-Hill.

Estes, W. K., and Skinner, B. F. (1941). Some quantitative properties of anxiety. *Journal of Experimental Psychology, 29,* 390–400.

Everitt, B. J., and Robbins, T. W. (1992). Amygdala-ventral striatal interactions and reward-related processes. In J. P. Aggleton (Ed.), *The amygdala: Neurobiological aspects of emotion, memory, and mental dysfunction* (pp. 401–29). New York: Wiley-Liss.

Fanselow, M. S., and Kim, J. J. (1994). Acquisition of contextual Pavlovian fear conditioning is blocked by application of an NMDA receptor antagonist D,L-2–amino-5–phosphonovaleric acid to the basolateral amygdala. *Behavioral Neuroscience, 108,* 210–12.

Fuster, J. M. (1989). *The prefrontal cortex.* New York: Raven.

Gaffan, D., Murray, E. A., et al. (1993). Interaction of the amygdala with the frontal lobe in reward memory. *European Journal of Neuroscience, 5,* 968–75.

Gerwitz, J. C., and Davis, M. (1997). Second-order fear conditioning prevented by blocking NMDA receptors in amygdala. *Nature, 388,* 471–73.

Gluck, M. A., and Myers, C. E. (1993). Hippocampal mediation of stimulus representation: A computational theory. *Hippocampus, 3,* 491–516.

Goldman-Rakic, P. S. (1987). Circuitry of primate prefrontal cortex and regulation of behavior by representational memory. In F. Plum (Ed.), *Handbook of physiology: The nervous system* (vol. 5, pp. 373–417). Bethesda, Md.: American Physiological Society.

Gray, J. A. (1987). *The psychology of fear and stress.* Vol. 2. New York: Cambridge University Press.

Helmstetter, F. J., and Bellgowan, P. S. (1994). Effects of muscimol applied to the basolateral amygdala on acquisition and expression of contextual fear conditioning in rats. *Behavioral Neuroscience, 108,* 1005–9.

Jacobs, W. J., and Nadel, L. (1985). Stress-induced recovery of fears and phobias. *Psychological Review, 92,* 512–31.

James, W. (1884). What is emotion? *Mind, 9,* 188–205.

Johnson-Laird, P. N. (1988). *The computer and the mind: An introduction to cognitive science.* Cambridge, Mass.: Harvard University Press.

Kapp, B. S., Whalen, P. J., Supple, W. F., and Pascoe, J. P. (1992). Amygdaloid contributions to conditioned arousal and sensory information processing. In J. P. Aggleton (Ed.), *The amygdala: Neurobiological aspects of emotion, memory, and mental dysfunction* (pp. 229–54). New York: Wiley-Liss.

Kihlstrom, J. F. (1984). Conscious, subconscious, unconscious: A cognitive perspective. In K. S. Bowers and D. Meichenbaum (Eds.), *The unconscious reconsidered* (pp. 149–211). New York: Wiley.

Killcross, S., Robbins, T. W., and Everitt, B. J. (1997). Different types of fear-conditioned behavior mediated by separate nuclei within amygdala. *Nature, 388,* 377–80.

Kim, J. J., and Fanselow, M. S. (1992). Modality-specific retrograde amnesia of fear. *Science, 256,* 675–77.

LaBar, K. S., Gatenby, J. C., Gore, J. C., LeDoux, J. E., Phelps, E. A. (1998). Human amygdala activation during conditioned fear acquisition and extinction: a mixed-trial fMRI study. *Neuron, 20,* 937–45.

LaBar, K. S., LeDoux, J. E., Spencer, D. D., and Phelps, E. A. (1995). Impaired fear conditioning following unilateral temporal lobectomy in humans. *Journal of Neuroscience, 15,* 6846–55.

LeDoux, J. E.(1994). Emotion, memory, and the brain. *Scientific American, 270,* 32–39.

———. (1995). Emotion: Clues from the brain. *Annual Review of Psychology, 46,* 209–35.

————. (1996). *The emotional brain.* New York: Simon & Schuster.

LeDoux, J. E., Cicchetti, P., Xagoraris, A., and Romanski, L. M. (1990). The lateral amygdaloid nucleus: Sensory interface of the amygdala in fear conditioning. *Journal of Neuroscience, 10,* 1062–69.

LeDoux, J. E., Farb, C. F., and Ruggiero, D. A. (1990). Topographic organization of neurons in the acoustic thalamus that project to the amygdala. *Journal of Neuroscience, 10,* 1043–54.

LeDoux, J. E., Iwata, J., Cicchetti, P., and Reis, D. J. (1988). Different projections of the central amygdaloid nucleus mediate autonomic and behavioral correlates of conditioned fear. *Journal of Neuroscience, 8,* 2517–29.

LeDoux, J. E., Romanski, L. M., and Xagoraris, A. E. (1989). Indelibility of subcortical emotional memories. *Journal of Cognitive Neuroscience, 1,* 238–43.

LeDoux, J. E., Sakaguchi, A., and Reis, D. J. (1984). Subcortical efferent projections of the medial geniculate nucleus mediate emotional responses conditioned by acoustic stimuli. *Journal of Neuroscience, 4,* 683–98.

Li, X. F., Stutzmann, G. E., and LeDoux, J. L. (1996). Convergent but temporally separated inputs to lateral amygdala neurons from the auditory thalamus and auditory cortex use different postsynaptic receptors: *In vivo* intracellular and extracellular recordings in fear conditioning pathways. *Learning and Memory, 3,* 229–42.

Majidishad, P., Pelli, D. G., and LeDoux, J. E. (1996). Disruption of fear conditioning to contextual stimuli but not to a tone by lesions of the accessory basal nucleus of the amygdala. *Society for Neuroscience Abstracts, 22,* 1116.

Manderscheid, R. W., and Sonnenschein, M. A. (1994). *Mental health, United States, 1994.* Rockville, Md.: U.S. Department of Public Health and Human Services.

Maren, S., Aharonov, G., and Fanselow, M. S. (1996). Retrograde abolition of conditional fear after excitotoxic lesions in the basolateral amygdala of rats. *Behavioral Neuroscience, 110,* 718–26.

Maren, S., Aharonov, G., Stote, D. L., and Fanselow, M. S. (1996). N-methyl-d-aspartate receptors in the basolateral amygdala are required for both acquisition and expression of the conditional fear in rats. *Behavioral Neuroscience, 110,* 1365–74.

Maren, S., and Fanselow, M. S. (1996). The amygdala and fear conditioning: Has the nut been cracked? *Neuron, 16,* 237–40.

Marks, I. (1987). *Fears, phobias, and rituals: Panic, anxiety, and their disorders.* New York: Oxford University Press.

Mascagni, F., McDonald, A. J., and Coleman, J. R. (1993). Corticoamygdaloid and corticocortical projections of the rat temporal cortex: A phaseolus vulgaris leucoagglutinin study. *Neuroscience, 57,* 697–715.

McAllister, W. R., and McAllister, D. E. (1971). Behavioral measurement of conditioned fear. In F. R. Brush (Ed.), *Aversive conditioning and learning* (pp. 105–79). New York: Academic Press.

McClelland, J. L., McNaughton, B. L., and O'Reilly, R. C. (1995). Why there are complementary learning systems in the hippocampus and neocortex: Insights from the successes and failures of connectionist models of learning and memory. *Psychological Review, 102,* 419–57.

McGaugh, J. L., Mesches, M. H., Cahill, L., Parent, M. B., Coleman-Mesches, K., and Salinas, J. A. (1995). Involvement of the amygdala in the regulation of memory storage. In J. L. McGaugh, F. Bermudez-Rattoni, and R. A. Prado-Alcala (Eds.), *Plasticity in the central nervous system* (pp. 18–39). Mahwah, N.J.: Erlbaum.

Miserendino, M. J. D., Sananes, C. B., Melia, K. R., and Davis, M. (1990). Blocking of acquisition but not expression of conditioned fear—potentiated startle by NMDA antagonists in the amygdala. *Nature, 345,* 716–18.

Mishkin, M., Malamut, B., and Bachevalier, J. (1984). Memories and habits: Two neural systems. In J. L. McGaugh, G. Lynch, and N. M. Weinberger (Eds.), *The neurobiology of learning and memory.* New York: Guilford.

Morgan, M., and LeDoux, J. E. (1995). Differential contribution of dorsal and ventral medial prefrontal cortex to the acquisition and extinction of conditioned fear. *Behavioral Neuroscience, 109,* 681–88.

Morgan, M. A., Romanski, L. M., and LeDoux, J. E. (1993). Extinction of emotional learning: Contribution of medial prefrontal cortex. *Neuroscience Letters, 163,* 109–13.

Mowrer, O. H. (1939). A stimulus-response analysis of anxiety and its role as a reinforcing agent. *Psychological Review, 46,* 553–65.

Mowrer, O. H., and Lamoreaux, R. R. (1946). Fear as an intervening variable in avoidance conditioning. *Journal of Comparative Psychology, 39,* 29–50.

Muller, J., Corodimas, K. P., Fridel, Z., and LeDoux, J. E. (1997). Functional inactivation of the lateral and basal nuclei of the amygdala by muscimol infusion prevents fear conditioning to an explicit CS and to contextual stimuli. *Behavioral Neuroscience, 111,* 683–91.

Ohman, A. (1992). Fear and anxiety as emotional phenomena: Clinical, phenomenological, and evolutionary perspectives, and information-processing mechanisms. In M. Lewis and J. M. Haviland (Eds.), *Handbook of the emotions* (pp. 511–36). New York: Guilford.

O'Keefe, J., and Nadel, L. (1978). *The hippocampus as a cognitive map.* Oxford: Clarendon Press.

Ottersen, O. P. (1981). The afferent connections of the amygdala of the rat as studied with retrograde transport of horseradish peroxidase. In Y. Ben-Ari (Ed.), *The amygdaloid complex* (pp. 91–104). New York: Elsevier/North-Holland Biomedical Press.

come. Whereas remembered utility returns the overall "goodness" of the last meal we ate at a particular restaurant, predicted utility reflects our expectation of how much we will enjoy a visit to that restaurant today.

RELATIONSHIP OF BSR TO DIFFERENT VARIANTS OF UTILITY

How is the ongoing neural activity driven by rewarding electrical stimulation related to instantaneous utility? According to the proposal advanced by Conover and Shizgal (1994a), the rewarding stimulation achieves its grip over ongoing behavior by simulating the real-time effect of a natural reward on the evaluative system, that is, by driving instantaneous utility to positive values. I propose that this signal can steer behavior in the absence of awareness but does not do so invariably. Through the allocation of attentional resources, the instantaneous utility signal can gain access to working memory and may be manifested in human experience as pleasure or suffering. Thus, the dual meaning imparted to instantaneous utility by Kahneman, Wakker, and Sarin (1997) has been retained, but the link between the action component and the hedonic component is weakened, with the action component treated as the more fundamental. Some advantages of allowing the instantaneous utility signal to impinge on awareness are discussed later.

In the vignette at the beginning of this chapter, the behavior of the rat depends on whether or not it has received sufficiently rewarding stimulation in the goal box on preceding trials. Thus, the rat appears to have recorded the utility of the stimulation received previously. We will see shortly that there is a striking similarity in the ways that the instantaneous utilities of BSR in rats and certain temporally extended experiences in humans are translated into remembered utilities.

Records of payoff are inherently multidimensional and may well be derived from multiple modes of processing. I argue later that what Kahneman, Wakker, and Sarin (1997) call remembered utility captures the reinforcer's subjective "intensity," which is but one of several components of such records. The evaluative channel that assesses intensity is complemented by a stopwatch timer that delivers assessments of encounter rate and delay and by perceptual mechanisms that can return estimates of amount (for instance, the mass of an acorn) and kind (for instance, food versus water).

Information about kind can be used to determine the degree to which one reinforcer can substitute for another. A key tenet of behavioral economics is that substitutability determines whether and how much behavioral allocation will shift from one reinforcer to another in the face of price changes. Moreover, it can be argued that the elasticity of demand for a particular kind of resource depends on additional information of perceptual origin: the environmental distribution of that resource in the environment.

In this view, decision utilities are derived from a combination of perceptual, timing, and evaluative data. If BSR indeed reflects meaningful signals in the evaluative and timing systems in the absence of meaningful perceptual information, then performance for BSR should respond differently to economic constraints than performance for natural reinforcers. The literature reviewed here is interpreted to support this contention and to suggest that comparisons between performance for BSR and for natural reinforcers shed light on the psychological resources involved in computing decision utilities.

In the opening vignette, the start-box stimulation produces an aftereffect that potentiates behavior aimed at procuring additional reward. If the rat has been given a free "taste" of the stimulation at the start of the trial, it will show more pronounced anticipatory behaviors prior to the removal of the barrier and will run down the alley faster once allowed to enter. This is reminiscent of the way that savoring a particularly tasty hors d'oeuvre at a reception can incite visual search for the waiter and vigorous pursuit once he reappears. Just as the anticipatory search and the pursuit of the waiter depend on the expectation that the supply of hors d'oeuvres has not yet been exhausted, the anticipatory behavior of the rat in the start box depends on the expectation that stimulation will be available in the goal box. Such expectations may be related to the predicted utilities discussed by Kahneman, Wakker, and Sarin (1997) in that anticipation of a future event influences present choices.

In order to be manifested in behavior, a decision utility must be processed by a selection rule. "Choose the largest" will be assumed as the rule. The question of how the resulting decisions are translated into action is beyond the scope of this chapter; the reader is referred to Gallistel's *Organization of Action* (1980) for a fine introduction to this topic.

In the following sections, the relationship between BSR and the variants of utility proposed by

Kahneman, Wakker, and Sarin (1997) is discussed in detail. Exploration of this relationship casts BSR data in a new light and suggests new directions for future research.

BSR Basics

Some basic characteristics of the electrical stimulus and the neural circuitry responsible for its rewarding effect must be described before developing the arguments linking BSR to different variants of utility. The stimuli used in most modern BSR experiments consist of trains of short-duration current pulses. With pulse duration held constant, the strength of a train is determined by pulse amplitude (current) and frequency. The greater the current, the larger the number of neurons directly stimulated by the electrode. Over the ranges of frequencies used in most studies, each directly stimulated neuron can be assumed to fire once per pulse. Thus, as depicted in figure 26.1, each pulse produces a synchronous volley of nerve impulses (action potentials) in the population of directly stimulated cells that give rise to the rewarding effect, and the aggregate firing rate of this population is determined by the stimulation current and frequency. It is highly unlikely that this population of neurons responds in such a synchronous manner to any natural stimulus, yet the artificial stimulation does mimic some of the properties of a natural reinforcer. As discussed later, this provides a clue as to how information is represented in the neural system underlying the rewarding effect.

The Counter Model

The firings of the directly stimulated neurons appear to be translated into the rewarding effect in a surprisingly simple manner. With the duration of a stimulation train held constant, the strength of the rewarding effect appears to depend only on the aggregate rate of firing in this population of directly stimulated cells. According to this "counter model" (Gallistel 1978; Gallistel, Shizgal, and Yeomans 1981; Simmons and Gallistel 1994), it matters not whether one hundred directly stimulated neurons fire ten times each during a particular time window or whether twenty neurons fire fifty times each. The rewarding impact of the stimulation will be the same provided that aggregate impulse flow is constant. If activity elicited in these neurons by natural stimuli is integrated in the same manner, then the synchronous firings triggered by the artificial stimulation should produce the same effect as an equivalent number of asynchronous firings triggered by a natural stimulus.

The counter model is shown in figure 26.1. The directly stimulated neurons responsible for the rewarding effect are depicted as providing input to an "integrator" that combines the effects of incoming action potentials over time and space. The output of the integrator is determined by the aggregate rate of firing at its input. It is argued here

FIGURE 26.1   The Counter Model of Spatio-Temporal Integration in the Neural Circuitry Subserving Brain Stimulation Reward

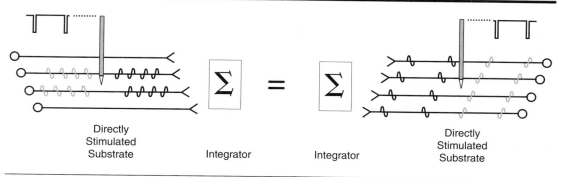

Directly Stimulated Substrate   Integrator   Integrator   Directly Stimulated Substrate

Notes: Action potentials elicited in the directly activated neurons responsible for BSR impinge on a neural circuit that integrates their effects over time and space. The output of this integrator is determined by the aggregate rate of firing during a fixed time window. Thus, firing two neurons four times each produces the same output as firing four neurons twice each. (In addition to triggering action potentials that propagate to the synaptic terminals, the stimulation also triggers action potentials that propagate "backward" toward the cell body. These "antidromic" action potentials, shown in gray, have no behavioral effect unless they invade another axonal branch.)

that this output is the sole determinant of the instantaneous utility of the stimulation and that the remembered utility of the stimulation is derived from certain "exemplar values" (Schreiber and Kahneman 1997) of its instantaneous utility.

INSTANTANEOUS UTILITY, RESISTANCE TO INTERRUPTION, AND BSR

At many brain sites, BSR is accompanied by aversive side effects, which are due to the activation of different neurons than the ones responsible for the rewarding effect (Bielajew and Shizgal 1980; Bower and Miller 1958; Shizgal and Matthews 1977). By judicious selection of stimulation site, current, frequency, and temporal pattern, the aversive side effects can be minimized. When such precautions are taken, the rat will readily press a lever to initiate a long-duration train of stimulation but will not press a second lever that turns off the stimulation (Shizgal and Matthews 1977). If the experimenter interrupts such a train, the rat will immediately rush over to the lever and reinitiate the stimulation. This suggests that if given the opportunity, the rat would strive to prevent interruption of such stimulation. If so, it should prove possible to measure the action component of instantaneous utility in real time by assessing the commitment of the rat to keeping the current flowing.

To my knowledge, such an experiment has not been done. A promising way to perform it would be to use the temptation of an alternative reward to assess the rat's commitment to the ongoing stimulation. At different times during the delivery of a long train, a choice would be offered between two options: continuation of the train, or immediate cessation of the train coupled with delivery of an alternative reward. The strength of the alternative reward required to tempt the rat to terminate the long train would provide a measure of the instantaneous utility of the ongoing stimulation at the moment of choice. In principle, such a measure would provide a direct test of the prediction that both the remembered utility of the stimulation and its instantaneous utility are derived from the output of one and the same integrator.

INSTANTANEOUS UTILITY, HEDONIC EXPERIENCE, AND BSR

We experience pleasure and pain as powerful, adaptive influences on our behavior. As Bentham put it so memorably (1789/1996): "Nature has placed mankind under the governance of two sovereign masters, pain and pleasure. It is for them alone to point out what we ought to do, as well as to determine what we shall do" (11). Bentham's assertion that pleasure and pain *direct* action may ring so true to our experience as to lead us to the converse view: that action *reflects* hedonic state. If pleasure and pain lead us to seek out or maintain contact with a pleasurable stimulus and to avoid or interrupt contact with a painful one, then is it not justified to infer these experiences from observation of the acts they promote? It is in this sense that the description of BSR sites as "pleasure areas" has had an intuitive appeal to many. If the rat is willing to work so hard to initiate the electrical stimulation, then must not the stimulation be pleasurable?

In my view, the answer to both questions is no, not necessarily. I will argue that the two components of instantaneous utility can coincide, but that they need not do so invariably. Thus, the link between hedonic experience and the control of action is less direct in the account presented here than in Bentham's original formulation or in modern developments of Bentham's position (Cabanac 1992). I speculate later on what may be gained by supplementing the action-oriented component of instantaneous utility with a hedonic response.

To turn Bentham's formulation around and to infer pleasure and pain from behavior is to make a strong assumption: that actions such as resistance to interruption of a stimulus or attempts to escape from it cannot be produced in the absence of a hedonic response, that is, without the express consent of the "sovereign." ("It is for them *alone . . .* to determine what we shall do.") By labeling a state as pleasurable or painful, we imply that we are aware of it; "unconscious pleasure" and "unconscious suffering" are oxymorons. If so, asserting that a hedonic response is a necessary condition for resistance to interruption or escape is tantamount to stating that such actions cannot be produced in the absence of awareness.

Bentham's position does not stand up well in the face of a large body of psychological research and theory that treats much of the foundation of perception, thought, emotion, and action as hidden from awareness (Baars 1988; LeDoux 1996; Nisbett and Wilson 1977). In such views, consciousness depends on the serial operation of a limited-capacity process. Rather than forcing all signals vying for the control of action to pass through this processing bottleneck, much of the task of real-time control is assigned to a collection of specialized lower-level processors operating in parallel and in the absence of awareness (Baars 1988). If so, the hedonic and action-oriented components of instantaneous utility are dissociable, and we cannot necessarily infer the hedonic content of experience on the basis of behavioral observation alone.

In human subjects, we can address the relationship between hedonic experience and the control of action empirically, using methods for concurrent measurement of self-ratings and behavior. For example, ratings of the sign and intensity of hedonic experience can be collected while observing whether the subject maintains or breaks off contact with a stimulus. It is not surprising that strong correlations have been noted in such studies between subjective hedonic ratings and measures of choice (Cabanac and LeBlanc 1983). However, dissociations have been noted as well. For example, in a study of heroin addicts self-administering morphine, low doses of the drug were vigorously self-administered despite subjective ratings of zero on both a monetary value scale and a Lickert scale of liking; a saline solution received similar subjective ratings but was not self-administered (Lamb et al. 1991). It is interesting to note that increasing the dose of morphine brought the subjective ratings into accord with the behavioral measure. Thus, self-ratings of hedonic response could coincide with action but did not do so invariably. (The reader is referred to the chapter in this volume by Berridge for an alternative interpretation of these data.)

In contrast to the tools available for studying the relationship between hedonic experience and action in humans, we do not have well-validated and general means for measuring enjoyment and suffering in nonhuman animals. Although it should prove possible, as proposed earlier, to measure the rat's resistance to interruption of the stimulation, we cannot be sure how the rat feels while the current is flowing. Nonetheless, I will propose that the relationship between the control of ongoing behavior and processes that contribute to awareness in humans could be investigated by neurobiological means in nonhuman subjects.

In the view elaborated here, which borrows from proposals by Ledoux (1996), the output of the neural process that determines whether an action will be continued or terminated (the "continue/stop signal"—the action-oriented component of instantaneous utility) is not isomorphic with pleasure or suffering but will be manifested in awareness as a hedonic response if the continue/

stop signal gains access to working memory. This access is gated by attention and will be most likely to occur when the action-oriented signal and associated stimuli attain high values. Nonetheless, sufficient allocation of attention might allow weaker signals to trigger a hedonic response, and strong signals might fail to do so in the absence of attention, for example, when events are highly predictable and behavioral responses are highly practiced. When the continue/stop signal does succeed in breaching the waterline of awareness, it can marshal further attentional resources and direct planning while coordinating the activity of processes that operate beyond the margins of conscious experience.

To develop the argument, let us assume that we were given the task of designing a robot that simulates the behavior of a rat. Ongoing action is controlled by a continue/stop signal derived from real-time information about external stimuli and from the state of the internal environment. For example, when body temperature is low and a warm microenvironment is encountered, the continue/stop signal will have a positive value, thus promoting continued contact with the heat source and a return to thermal homeostasis; when internal temperature is too high, the same thermal stimulus will drive the continue/stop signal to negative values and termination of contact. This adjustment of the neutral point as a function of internal state reflects Cabanac's concept of alliesthesia (Cabanac 1971).

The sensory and evaluative mechanisms that generate the continue/stop signal should allow the robot to simulate certain adaptive responses of a rat to ongoing sensory stimulation. However, the robot would need additional circuitry in order to mimic abilities that figure prominently in cognitively oriented accounts of goal-directed behavior, such as resolving conflicts between multiple goal-related stimuli by means of selective allocation of attention, navigating in space using stored representations, and planning a route leading from the current state to a higher-valued one. In an influential treatment of animal navigation (Gallistel 1990), an egocentric spatial representation of the current environment is constructed from successively encountered stimuli and then translated into geocentric coordinates using stored information about the position of vantage points and angles of view. Essential to such tasks is a readily accessible ("working") memory store, in which critical information is held on-line. Working memory also plays an essential role in models that find efficient routes to goals (Gallistel 1990; Johnson-Laird 1988; Miller, Galanter, and Pribram 1960); access to this limited-capacity store is gated by attention. If we were to incorporate attention, working memory, and a route-finding mechanism in our robot, would it be advantageous to allow the continue/stop signal to interact with them, and if so, how?

For help in addressing this question, let us enlist the assistance of a wise student of behavior, the novelist Joseph Heller. In *Catch-22* (1961), Heller explores the relationship between instantaneous utility and the control of action. Heller's antihero, Yossarian, is a World War II bombardier surrounded by suffering, death, and destruction. Desperate to survive his military service, Yossarian refuses to accept that things are as they ought to be. During a philosophical argument about the failings of the Supreme Being, Yossarian complains: "Why in the world did He ever create pain? . . . Why couldn't He have used a doorbell instead to notify us, or one of his celestial choirs? Or a system of blue-and-red neon tubes right in the middle of each person's forehead. Any jukebox manufacturer worth his salt could have done that. Why couldn't He?" (184).

Yossarian wants to believe that the protective function of pain could be fulfilled by a warning signal that is merely informative. But what would confer upon such a signal the ability to capture attention, wrest control of planning, and coordinate the multiple processes controlling action? Sadly for Yossarian and his flak-riddled comrades, the insistent unpleasantness of pain is a highly effective means of achieving these ends. Gladly for the rest of us, so, too, is the shock of intense pleasure.

With our response to Yossarian in mind, let us return to our robotic rat and implement a key improvement. We will now arrange things so that the continue/stop signal can access working memory and influence the allocation of attention. The continue/stop signal will attain large negative values in response to ongoing or imminent tissue damage; focusing attention on such a signal would tend to promote it to the top of the planning agenda and reduce the odds that competing stimuli would divert scarce cognitive resources from the task of terminating the noxious input. In contrast, the continue/stop signal will register large positive values in response to contact with potentially beneficial stimuli such as food sources or locations that promote maintenance of thermal neutrality. The likelihood of interrupting contact with

the beneficial input would be reduced by allowing it to draw attention away from competing stimuli. Temporarily suppressing planning might also help "lock in" contact with an input that is driving the continue/stop signal to large positive values.

Working memory and attentional control of its input are regarded as key components of the foundation for awareness in humans (Baars 1988; Johnson-Laird 1988; LeDoux 1996). Thus, if this sketch were generalized from our robotic rat to ourselves, we should predict that extremes of instantaneous utility (strong continue/stop signals) would tend to be reflected in our experience as well as in our behavior. Stimuli that produce weaker excursions of instantaneous utility might, nonetheless, exercise behavioral control, but as in the case of the low doses of morphine self-administered by the addicts, such stimuli are less likely to be manifested in awareness.

It has been argued that consciousness enables the "broadcasting" of information throughout the cognitive architecture to the many specialized processors that operate beyond the margins of awareness (Baars 1988). If so, expressing the continue/stop signal in awareness as pleasure or pain would help marshal and coordinate the activity of multiple cognitive processes in mounting a highly integrated response to the eliciting stimuli.

I propose later that direct electrical stimulation of certain brain regions can mimic the effect of a naturally occurring stimulus on the neural circuitry that computes instantaneous utility. If so, the argument developed earlier predicts that such stimulation will be able to drive instantaneous utility to levels that can impinge on awareness in humans. Indeed, when direct electrical stimulation has been delivered to some of the brain regions homologous to sites where BSR is obtained in rats, its effect has been described by human subjects as pleasurable (Heath 1964).

By means of electrophysiological recordings, the activity of neurons implicated in working memory is monitored routinely in nonhuman animals (Goldman-Rakic 1996; Watanabe 1996), and the modulating effects of attention can be observed (Treue and Maunsell 1996). Thus, it may prove possible to determine, by conventional neurobiological means, whether instantaneous utility signals can capture attentional resources and gain access to working memory. Research on BSR could play a crucial role in such experiments by identifying neural circuitry subserving instantaneous utility and by providing a potent means of controlling it.

Instantaneous utility is a property of the moment, and thus, this discussion has been focused on real-time processing. Let us now turn to a process that bridges the present and the future: translation of instantaneous utility into a stored record. The bulk of the research carried out on BSR has probed such records.

TRANSFORMATION OF INSTANTANEOUS UTILITY INTO REMEMBERED UTILITY

In the portrayal of Kahneman and his colleagues, remembered utility is derived from a temporal profile of instantaneous utility (Kahneman, Wakker, and Sarin 1997). The continuously fluctuating value of instantaneous utility during a temporally extended experience is compressed into a single remembered utility on which future decision weights can be based. Imagine, for example, that upon pressing the lever in the goal box, the rat receives a prolonged train of stimulation that waxes and wanes in strength over several minutes (see, for example, Lepore and Franklin 1992), much as the level of a drug in the bloodstream rises and falls following administration. How does the rat compress this temporally extended experience over time so as to derive a single decision utility that can weight future choices?

One way to derive a single remembered utility from a temporally extended experience is to compute the temporal integral or the average of the entire sequence of instantaneous utilities. Kahneman and his colleagues propose a very different and much simpler strategy. Their human subjects appear to extract two key values from the temporal profile: the peak instantaneous utility and the instantaneous utility at the end of the experience. Some intermediate value, such as the average of the peak and end values, is then used as the remembered utility (Kahneman et al. 1993; Redelmeier and Kahneman 1996). Only in unusual circumstances would the peak-end rule be expected to generate a result radically different from the outcome of temporal integration. However, a simple rule of thumb, such as peak-end averaging, should be executed more quickly than retrospective temporal integration, while consuming fewer mnemonic and computational resources.

If the peak-end heuristic is employed, then remembered utility should be insensitive to variations in the duration of the temporally extended experience. This prediction has been confirmed in both experimental and observational studies carried out with human subjects (Fredrickson and

Kahneman 1993; Kahneman et al. 1993; Redelmeier and Kahneman 1996). For example, in retrospective evaluations of colonoscopy procedures that varied in duration from four to sixty-seven minutes, aversiveness was not correlated with duration but was strongly correlated with real-time ratings of both peak pain and pain at the end of the procedure (Redelmeier and Kahneman 1996). Such insensitivity to duration has been called "duration neglect" (Fredrickson and Kahneman 1993).

Duration neglect has also been observed in the case of BSR (Gallistel 1978; Mark and Gallistel 1993; Shizgal and Matthews 1977). Based on available data, figure 26.2 depicts the simulated growth of instantaneous utility as a stimulation train is prolonged. The x-axis of the three-dimensional graph represents the aggregate firing rate produced by the stimulation in the neurons responsible for the rewarding effect; the higher the current or the frequency, the higher the aggregate firing rate. At each firing rate, the level of instantaneous utility climbs as the duration of the train is increased, eventually approaching asymptote. This saturation occurs quickly at high firing rates and more slowly at low ones (Mason and Milner 1986). Duration neglect would be manifested by indifferent choice between two trains of the same strength (trains that produce the same aggregate firing rate) but different durations. This would be the case for values lying on the "plateau" of the depicted surface. Indeed, if the output of one and the same integrator were responsible for both the instantaneous and remembered utility of the stimulation, then the surface in figure 26.2 would describe the contribution of aggregate firing rate and duration not only to measures of choice but also to measures of the resistance to the interruption of ongoing stimulation.

The translation of the instantaneous value of the stimulation-induced signal into a remembered utility has been modeled previously as the recording of the peak value (measuring the height of the plateau in figure 26.2) (Gallistel 1978; Gallistel et al. 1981). However, Kahneman's peak-end model makes the same prediction as a peak model in response to a steady, prolonged input (because the peak height is the same as the height at the end). Thus, further work is required to see which model works best in the case of BSR. Indeed, if the instantaneous utility at the end of an experience is particularly important in assessing aversive states that one wishes to terminate, the value at the be-

FIGURE 26.2 BSR: Computing Instantaneous Utility

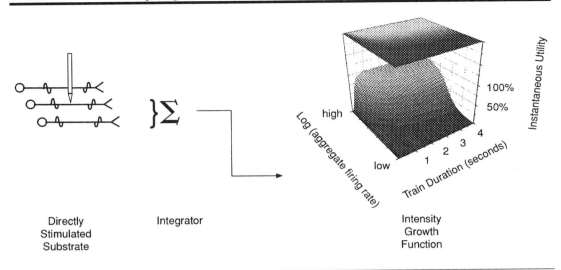

Directly Stimulated Substrate

Integrator

Intensity Growth Function

Notes: This figure shows the growth of instantaneous utility as a function of stimulation strength and duration. The stronger the stimulation, the higher the aggregate rate of firing in the directly stimulated neurons responsible for the rewarding effect. Three relationships are depicted by the three-dimensional graph. With aggregate firing rate held constant, instantaneous utility climbs as the duration of the input is prolonged, eventually leveling off. This leveling-off is responsible for the "duration neglect" that has been reported in BSR experiments (Gallistel 1978; Mark and Gallistel 1993; Shizgal and Matthews 1977). With duration held constant, instantaneous utility climbs steeply as the aggregate firing rate is increased and then levels off. A logistic growth function has been used to simulate this effect. The third relationship is depicted in the projected contour map. The outlines of successive horizontal sections through the three-dimensional structure have been projected onto this plane. Each contour line gives the combinations of aggregate firing rate and train duration that raise instantaneous utility to a given "altitude." The contour lines follow the hyperbolic form first described by Gallistel (1978). Changing the altitude at which the cross-section is taken shifts the curve along the axis representing the logarithm of the firing rate but does not change the curvature. Plotting the growth of instantaneous utility as a function of both aggregate firing rate and train duration illustrates an important consequence of the parallelism of the contour lines: the rate at which instantaneous utility grows with train duration increases as a function of aggregate firing rate. At high aggregate firing rates, instantaneous utility approaches asymptote very quickly; at low firing rates, much more time is required for instantaneous utility to level off. Results consistent with this relationship have been reported by Mason and Milner (1986).

ginning may have a large bearing on the assessment of states that one wishes to initiate. Regardless of the relative contributions of beginnings and ends, the available data do suggest that the decision utility of BSR is computed in the spirit of the proposal by Kahneman and his colleagues (1993; Kahneman, Wakker, and Sarin 1997). Rather than computing the temporal integral of instantaneous utility, the rat seems to apply a simple rule to a single exemplar value or a limited set thereof, thus showing profound neglect of duration. Determining the values that serve as the exemplars of instantaneous utility during different states, and the rules used to combine these exemplars, is an important goal for future research.

In figure 26.2, the signal responsible for BSR is portrayed as a unidimensional quantity that fluctuates in intensity over time as a function of aggregate firing rate and duration. In the following sections, the notion that a unidimensional signal is responsible for BSR is developed and the relationship of this signal to gustatory reward and the evaluative system is discussed.

RELATIONSHIP BETWEEN THE UTILITY OF BSR AND GUSTATORY STIMULI

A currency function expresses the value of different inputs on a common scale. Animals behave as if they routinely compute currency functions because they make orderly choices between complex, mutually exclusive alternatives, such as returning to the shelter of a nest or visiting a habitual foraging site. Each of these alternatives has multiple attributes germane to physiological regulation and risk. For example, these two options differ in the probability of finding food and water, losing body heat, and encountering a predator. Choosing the more valuable option requires that the multi-dimensional representations be "boiled down" to a single common dimension (McFarland and Sibley 1975), a common scale of utility.

In the experiments to be reviewed, the choices made by rats that had been offered various reinforcers were recorded. By definition, these choices reflect the decision utilities of the available outcomes. In a later section, I discuss the translation of remembered utility into decision utility. For now, let us assume that remembered utility was the only determinant of decision utility that varied in the experiments to be reviewed; hence, we can "see through" the translation process. Given this assumption and the portrayal provided earlier of how remembered utility is computed from instantaneous utility, the observed choices of the rats can be seen to reflect underlying changes in instantaneous utility.

To determine whether rats use a common currency to evaluate rewarding LH stimulation and a sucrose solution, Conover and I performed two types of experiments. First, we placed the rewarding LH stimulation in competition with the sucrose by presenting our subjects with a forced choice between them (Conover and Shizgal 1994a). The strength of the BSR was varied across trials. Not surprisingly, the rats chose the sucrose in preference to the BSR when the strength of the electrical stimulation was below the threshold required to support responding in the absence of the sucrose. When the strength of the LH stimulation was set somewhat above this threshold, the rats continued to prefer the sucrose. In other words, the presence of the sucrose caused the rats to forgo trains of BSR for which they had worked rather vigorously in the absence of the gustatory stimulus. However, once the electrical stimulation was sufficiently strong, BSR was chosen exclusively in preference to the sucrose. Thus, the rats behaved as if they had selected the larger of two payoffs evaluated on a common scale.

In a subsequent experiment, we offered the rats a choice between BSR alone and a compound reward consisting of an intraoral infusion of sucrose and an equally preferred train of BSR. Five of the six rats preferred the compound reward to its electrical component alone. Thus, the effects of LH stimulation and sucrose summate in the computation of utility. Summation is possible only when the inputs share a common property that is registered by the system of measurement. Given the

arguments and assumptions laid out earlier, the common property registered by our system of measurement, behavioral choice, is the ability to drive instantaneous utility to positive values.

The competition and summation experiments demonstrate that the LH stimulation and the sucrose have something important in common, much as Hoebel and others had proposed (Hoebel 1969). However, two subsequent experiments demonstrate important differences between the gustatory and electrical rewards.

In one experiment (Conover, Woodside, and Shizgal 1994), we increased the utility of a gustatory stimulus, a sodium chloride solution, by depleting the subjects of sodium. In the second experiment (Conover and Shizgal 1994b), we decreased the utility of another gustatory stimulus, a sucrose solution, by allowing large quantities of this solution to accumulate in the gut. We reasoned that if the LH stimulation re-creates the experience normally produced by a rewarding tastant, then manipulations that alter the utility of a tastant should have a similar effect on the BSR. The findings did not support such a hypothesis. Depleting the rats of sodium by administering a diuretic dramatically increased the utility of the saline solution without producing any observable change in the utility of BSR. Allowing large quantities of a sucrose solution to accumulate in the gut dramatically reduced the utility of this solution, in some cases rendering it aversive. However, the same manipulation either failed to alter BSR or produced a much smaller reduction in the utility of the electrical reward than in the utility of the gustatory reward.

Our results suggest that although a common signal represents the instantaneous utilities of the gustatory and electrical rewards, the LH electrode accesses the neural circuitry that computes this signal downstream from the point where gustatory stimuli are weighted by physiological feedback. Two models of how this could be arranged are shown in figure 26.3. Routing physiological feedback to act at the inputs to the circuitry that computes the currency enables behavior to contribute to the specificity of regulation. This can be seen by considering the alternative, a system where a currency function returns the relative utilities of sucrose and saline on a common scale and physiological feedback operates uniquely on the output values. In such a system, changes in sodium balance would alter the utility of both saline and sucrose solutions, as would feedback from the gut following accumulation of a sucrose load. In con-

FIGURE 26.3   Two Schemes for Combining the Rewarding Effects of LH Stimulation and Gustatory Stimuli

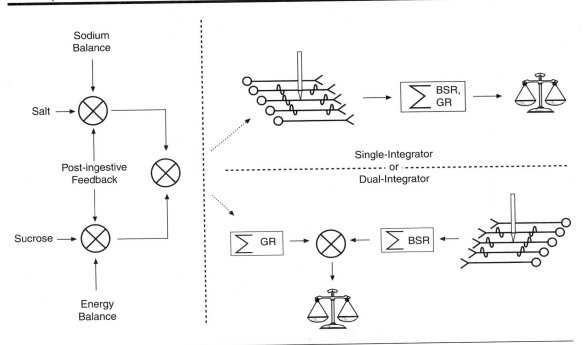

Notes: On the basis of experiments by Conover and his colleagues (Conover and Shizgal 1994b; Conover et al. 1994), signals that give rise to gustatory reward are weighted by physiological feedback prior to their combination with the signals that give rise to BSR. In the upper right panel, the two rewards are combined by passing the gustatory reward through the population of neurons from which the stimulating electrode samples. Thus, the postsynaptic effects of the gustatory and electrical rewards are integrated by a common circuit. In the lower panel, the gustatory and electrical reward signals are integrated separately before they are combined and relayed to the choice mechanism (adapted from Shizgal and Conover [1996]). Reprinted with the permission of Cambridge University Press.

trast, if physiological feedback weights the inputs to the currency function, then the relative utilities of saline and sucrose solutions can be adjusted independently, thus biasing consumption in response to physiological needs.

UNIDIMENSIONAL VERSUS MULTIDIMENSIONAL CODING

In typical BSR experiments, neurons are excited within a relatively large region surrounding the electrode tip (Yeomans 1990). The argument advanced by Shizgal and Conover (1996)—the rewarding effect of BSR is tied to the output of a currency function—addresses the question of how electrical stimulation of a large population of cells could mimic a naturally occurring signal. Multiple coding dimensions are required to cap-

ture information about stimulus quality. If only a single dimension were available, then changes in quality would be indistinguishable from changes in intensity. This is why we see the world monochromatically under dim illumination, when only a single class of photoreceptors is activated. To represent multiple dimensions of information, some form of spatiotemporal coding is required. For example, the cells activated by the stimulus might be divided into multiple subpopulations, each sensitive to a particular quality ("labeled-line coding"), or a unitary population might produce different temporal patterns of activity in response to different stimulus qualities. In either extreme case, or in mixtures thereof, it is unlikely that gross electrical stimulation would mimic the multidimensional code. Neurons that do not normally fire in concert would be activated simultaneously, and all the directly stimulated cells would fire with the same, rigid, stimulation-induced periodicity.

In contrast, the electrical stimulation could mimic the effect of a naturally occurring stimulus if activity in the stimulated system represented only a single dimension of information. In such a system, an aggregate rate code suffices. In such a code, it matters neither which neuron fires nor when, but only how many firings are produced by the entire population. The spatially contiguous and temporally synchronous firing evoked by the electrode could produce the same number of firings in a system using an aggregate rate code as the spatially discontinuous and temporally asynchronous firing that is likely to be evoked by a natural stimulus. Thus the stimulation-induced activity would mimic the effect of the natural stimulus. Indeed, in studies of motion perception in unanesthetized monkeys, microstimulation of a population of neurons that appear to use aggregate firing rate to code a single perceptual dimension, the direction of visual motion, can mimic the effect of adding correlated motion to the elements of a visual stimulus (Newsome and Salzman 1993).

As discussed earlier (see the section on BSR basics), there is strong evidence that the decision utility of BSR and, by inference, its remembered and instantaneous utility are derived from aggregate firing rate. An aggregate code is well suited to represent values in a common currency since, by definition, these values are arrayed along a single dimension. Thus, values derived from an aggregate code could be used to compare and combine the contributions to instantaneous utility of a draught of sucrose, a draught of saline, or a train of BSR.

THE EVALUATIVE, PERCEPTUAL, AND TIMING CHANNELS

Inevitably, information is lost in boiling down a multidimensional representation of a stimulus to obtain a currency value. For example, one cannot recover the temperature, sweetness, or texture of a gustatory stimulus from a currency value representing its instantaneous utility. However, the information lost due to the collapsing of multiple dimensions is essential for identifying the stimulus and distinguishing it from others. Thus, the circuitry that computes instantaneous utility must diverge from the perceptual circuitry subserving identification and discrimination. This divergence makes it possible to distinguish between the many

different objects and outcomes that may share the same utility. Similarly, in order to predict the time when the reinforcer will next be available, it is important to segregate information about when a reinforcer was encountered from information in the perceptual and evaluative channels. Thus, as depicted in figure 26.4, information about reinforcers must be processed in at least three different ways.

In this view, the perceptual channel tells the animal what and where the stimulus is, the evaluative channel returns the instantaneous utility of the stimulus, and the timer predicts when the reinforcer will next be available. Gross electrical stimulation of the evaluative channel could produce a meaningful signal if, as I have argued, information is encoded in the stimulated stage by the aggregate rate of firing. In contrast, gross electrical stimulation is unlikely to produce a meaningful, multidimensional signal in the perceptual channel because of the nature of the coding required. What about the response of the timer? It stands to reason that transitions in the state of many different channels would be accessible to the timer as "events." If so, an abrupt change in the activity of the evaluative channel, such as the stimulation-induced perturbation responsible for BSR, may provide a sufficient input to support measurement of temporal intervals.

The perceptual channel is constructed to return facts about the world. Thus, it is equipped with constancies and normalization procedures that minimize the impact of changes in external or internal state on identification and discrimination. Of course, these constancies and normalization procedures are imperfect, and bandwidth limitations make it impossible for perception to be veridical. For example, subjective response varies nonlinearly with changes in the strength of sensory stimuli, and it is possible to trick the perceptual system into producing illusions. Nonetheless, the system does a remarkably good job at estimating objective physical properties such as size, shape, distance, and reflectance.

The interval timer also appears to be designed to capture data about objective events. In scalar expectancy theory (Gibbon 1977), the subjective measure of a temporal interval is a noisy scalar transform of the objective interval. Although the interval timer is less accurate than the circadian oscillator, it is highly flexible, operating over a huge temporal range and accommodating concurrent timing of multiple intervals with arbitrary stop and start times (Gibbon et al. 1997).

FIGURE 26.4   The Parallel Channels That Process Information About Goal Objects in Real Time

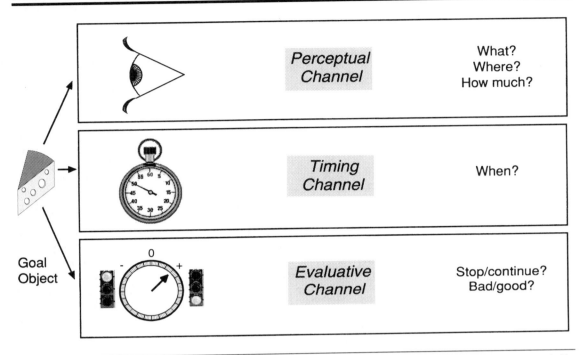

Notes: The perceptual channel returns the identity, location, and amount of the goal object, whereas a stopwatch-like channel marks the time when the goal object was encountered. The evaluative channel steers ongoing behavior so as to maintain or terminate contact with the goal object. Given sufficient allocation of attention and working memory, the output of the evaluative channel may be manifested in hedonic experience as pleasure or suffering.

In contrast to the perceptual and timing channels, the evaluative channel operates without even a pretense of objectivity. External objects do not have an inherent worth independent of present physiological and ecological conditions. For example, both the sign and magnitude of the instantaneous utility signal produced by a given stimulus can change as a function of physiological state (Cabanac 1971); thus, a cool stimulus applied to the skin can be refreshing when one is overheated and unpleasant when one is hypothermic. The evaluative channel is constructed, not to return objective properties of stimuli, but rather to return a subjective estimate of the current significance of these properties.

In contemporary accounts of sensory information processing, the perceptual "channel" is often treated as a community of neural modules, each specialized to extract information of a particular kind, such as color, form, movement, depth, and texture. The evaluative channel can also be regarded as a specialized neural module charged with the task of deriving another, more subjective kind of information from the flow of sensation. It is not clear whether this module is also composed of a set of specialized processors, perhaps each linked to a given modality or combination thereof. If so, the outputs of all the evaluative processors that influence an ongoing course of action would have to be combined in order to compute instantaneous utility. (The continue/stop signal has only one degree of freedom.) Thus, the output of the evaluative system is treated here as unitary.

The circuitry responsible for interval timing would appear to constitute yet another module. Formal models of this stopwatch-like device have been developed and tested extensively in behavioral studies. Components of one such model, based on the scalar expectancy theory of timing (Church 1984; Gibbon 1977, 1995), have been linked to the activity of pharmacologically and anatomically characterized neural populations (Gibbon et al. 1997; Meck 1996).

Natural reinforcers are processed by the perceptual, evaluative, and timing channels. In the following sections, the notion of remembered utility is generalized to reflect this parallel processing of information about reinforcers, and the roles of each of these channels in computing different dimensions of payoff are discussed.

SUBJECTIVE DIMENSIONS OF PAYOFF

According to the view developed here, changes in the strength of the stimulation delivered in BSR experiments (for example, changes in frequency or current) alter the aggregate firing rate of neurons that give rise to instantaneous utility. As shown in figure 26.5, a stored record of this response to the change in stimulus strength is derived by applying a heuristic, such as the peak-end rule, to exemplar values of instantaneous utility, such as the beginning, peak, and end. Variables controlling the strength of natural reinforcers, such as the concentration of a sucrose solution or the temperature of an air current, are viewed as acting analogously, with the exception that the impact of these variables is weighted by physiological state. Kahneman and his colleagues (Kahneman et al. 1997; Schreiber and Kahneman 1997) have used the term "remembered utility" to refer to the stored record derived from exemplar values of instantaneous utility. In the remaining discussion, I sub-

stitute the term "subjective intensity of the payoff" for remembered utility in labeling the stored appraisal of the variables that contribute to stimulus strength.

Why introduce yet another term? I do this because decision utilities reflect not only the output of the evaluative channel subserving instantaneous utility but also the outputs of the timing and perceptual channels. Thus, the effects of reinforcers on future choices depend not only on their strength but also on their rate, delay, amount, and kind. The notion of remembered utility proposed by Kahneman, Wakker, and Sarin (1997) and developed by Schreiber and Kahneman (1997) is tied to the intensity dimension alone. A more general means of describing recorded payoffs is required if we are to capture the multidimensional contribution of reinforcers to decision utility.

To illustrate the need for a multidimensional treatment of reinforcement, consider the interaction of the rate and strength of reinforcement. Using preference tests, it can be shown that rats prefer highly concentrated solutions to less concentrated ones (Young 1967). This difference in the intensity of the payoff can be offset by a compensatory change in its rate (Heyman and Monaghan 1994): the allocation of time or responding

FIGURE 26.5   BSR: Computing Subjective Intensity

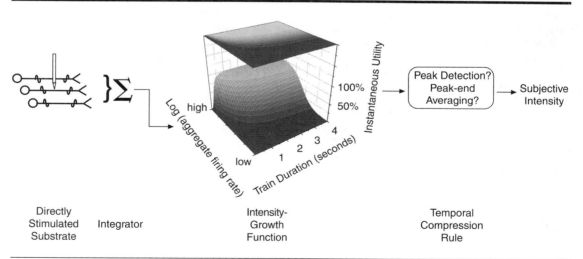

Notes. Shown here is "representation by exemplar" (Schreiber and Kahneman 1997) in computing the subjective intensity of BSR. The quantity recorded in memory (the subjective intensity) is derived from exemplar values of instantaneous utility, such as the peak (Gallistel 1978; Gallistel et al. 1981) or the peak and end (Kahneman et al. 1993; Redelmeier and Kahneman 1996). These exemplar values are independent of the temporal integral of instantaneous utility. Thus, subjects working for BSR manifest duration neglect: once instantaneous utility has reached the plateau of the plotted surface, further increases in duration fail to increase the remembered subjective intensity.

to the two solutions can be equated by making the less concentrated solution available more frequently than the highly concentrated one. The same relationship between stimulus strength and rate of reinforcement in determining behavioral allocation seems to hold when BSR, rather than a natural goal object, serves as the reinforcer (Hamilton, Stellar, and Hart 1985). Similarly, weaker trains of stimulation are preferred equally to stronger trains when the rate at which the weaker trains are available is sufficiently high (Gallistel 1991).

That both the rate and strength of reinforcers contribute to payoff suggests that the stored record of the reinforcer is multidimensional. The perceptual, timing, and evaluative channels not only process information about reinforcers in parallel but also record their outputs in parallel. Payoff is then computed by combining the contents of the multidimensional record. In this view, illustrated in figure 26.6, subjective intensity is the dimension of the stored record derived from the output of the evaluative channel. An output of the timing channel constitutes the second dimension. The na-

ture of this stored quantity is a matter of debate. In one well-formulated proposal, this temporal dimension of the stored record contains a noisy measure of the inter-reinforcer interval (the inverse of reinforcement rate) (Gibbon 1995). For convenience of phrasing, I use the term "subjective rate of payoff" to refer to this dimension of the stored record, leaving open the possibility that the stored quantity is not a rate per se but rather a measure from which a rate could be derived, such as an inter-reinforcement interval.

In addition to subjective rate, the timer provides another quantity that contributes to subjective payoff: the delay between the reinforced response and the delivery of the reinforcer. Payoff appears to decline hyperbolically as the presentation of the reinforcer is delayed (Commons et al. 1987; Mazur 1986; Myerson and Green 1995). This relationship appears to hold for BSR as well as for natural reinforcers (Mazur, Stellar, and Waraczynski 1987).

The treatment of BSR presented here implies that a record consisting of a subjective intensity

FIGURE 26.6   Recording the Output of the Parallel Information-Processing Channels

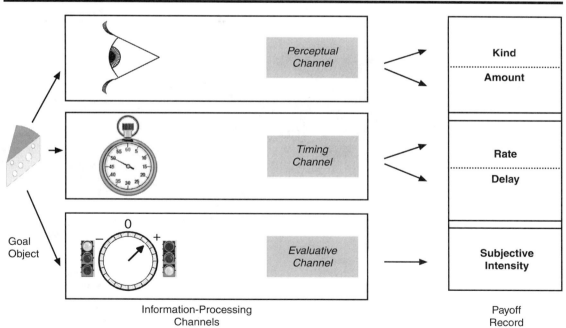

Notes: Stored information from all three channels contributes to payoff. Information derived from the perceptual channel indicates kind ("Is the goal object a source of food, water, or salt?") as well as amount. Estimates of the encounter rate and the delay between a successful response and delivery of a reinforcer are derived from the output of the stopwatch timer. The evaluative channel contributes an estimate of subjective intensity (see figure 26.4) to the payoff record.

and the subjective weighting of rate and delay is sufficient for computing a payoff on which a decision utility can be based. However, in the case of natural stimuli, additional dimensions contribute to payoff. For example, reinforcers, such as food pellets, may vary in mass. It stands to reason that the amount of a natural reinforcer would be recovered from perceptual information such as size and heft, and that unlike the estimation of intensity, the estimation of amount would be stable in the face of changes in physiological state. For example, one would hope that hunger would not alter one's judgments about the size of the fruit on a tree. Thus, an additional dimension of remembered payoff, the subjective weighting of amount, is likely to be returned by the perceptual channel. If BSR is not accompanied by a meaningful signal in the perceptual channel, then the information in this cell of the payoff record is likely to be absent or indecipherable.

The contribution of payoff to decision utility would appear to involve at least two stages of processing. First, a stored record is obtained by mapping physical dimensions such as strength, rate, delay, and amount into corresponding subjective

ones. Decision utility would appear to reflect the result of performing a combinatorial operation on the quantities in the stored record of payoff. Accounts of matching, to be discussed in the next section, tend to treat the combinatorial operation in question as multiplication (Baum and Rachlin 1969; Davison and McCarthy 1988). Figure 26.7 depicts multiplicative combination of intensity and rate in computing the subjective payoff provided by a train of rewarding stimulation.

MATCHING: TRANSLATION OF SUBJECTIVE PAYOFF INTO DECISION UTILITY

Imagine a pair of exquisite but idiosyncratically managed restaurants. The quality of the cuisine may be truly outstanding, and the philanthropic proprietors demand no remuneration other than the commitment of time by the diners. Each restaurant is open a certain number of times per month on the average, a rate that may or may not differ from the accessibility of the competing establishment. Although the average rate at which each restaurant opens is constant over time, the

FIGURE 26.7   BSR: Computing Subjective Payoff

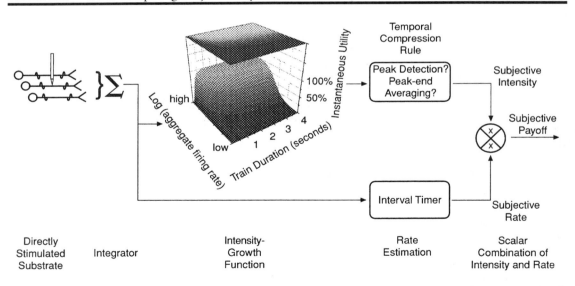

Notes: The left-hand portion of the figure, reproduced from figures 26.1 and 26.2, shows how the instantaneous utility of the rewarding stimulation is derived from the aggregate firing rate in the directly stimulated stage of the underlying neural circuit. Via the principle of representation by exemplar, instantaneous utility is transformed into the subjective intensity of the payoff, one of the dimensions of the stored record of subjective payoff. Two possible rules for carrying out this transformation are shown: peak-end averaging and peak detection. A second dimension of the stored record, the subjective rate of payoff, is provided by an interval timer. On the basis of research on operant matching, the combinatorial operation for combining these two dimensions is shown as multiplication.

interval between openings varies randomly. Openings are unannounced, thus keeping the clientele guessing as to the date and time when they can gain entry. Sometimes a client arrives to find the chosen restaurant already open; on other occasions, the restaurant is closed at the time of arrival, and the client may either wait until the restaurant opens or leave. Once a seat at a table has been secured, the diners face a delay until the serving of the first course, an interval that may differ in the two establishments. Finally, both chefs are experimenting with different portion sizes; currently, one leans toward "cuisine minceure," and the other toward the fashion of a Chicago steak house.

The matching law was formulated to describe the allocation of behavior in experimental settings roughly analogous to the competing restaurants. Lest the reader find the capricious scheduling too bizarre to take seriously, I should point out that the unpredictable availability of a reinforcer might well seem more realistic to people living in the manner of our ancestors. The traditional Inuit hunter did not expect a seal to visit a particular breathing hole in the ice at any designated time, yet he derived an estimate of the average frequency of visits and allocated his time accordingly.

In the terminology of operant conditioning, the diners in this example are presented with concurrent variable-interval schedules of reinforcement. According to the strict form of the matching law (Davison and McCarthy 1988; de Villiers 1977; Herrnstein 1961; Herrnstein 1970; Williams 1988), they will allocate their time and visits in proportion to the relative payoffs provided by the two restaurants. These payoffs are calculated by multiplicative combination of the subjective intensity (the "goodness" of the food) with the subjective weightings of the rate of opening, delay of meal onset, and portion size. In the terms employed here, the matching law translates the multidimensional records of subjective payoffs into decision utilities. Under the strict form of the matching law, relative decision utility is proportional to relative subjective payoff.

The subject performing on concurrent variable-interval schedules can be portrayed as repeatedly flipping a biased coin, with the bias reflecting the relative payoffs provided by the two reinforcers (Gibbon 1995; Heyman 1988; Heyman and Goodman 1998). If so, the relative payoffs will be reflected in the relative allocations of time to the two schedules. Given strict matching and multiplicative combination of subjective intensity and rate, the ratio of the subjective intensities of two reinforcers can then be calculated from the observed ratios of reinforcement rates and time allocation. This logic was used by Miller (1976) to measure, in pigeons, the relative intensity of the payoffs provided by three different types of seeds, and by Gallistel and his students (Gallistel 1991; Leon and Gallistel 1992; Simmons and Gallistel 1994) to measure how the subjective intensity of BSR grows as a function of the strength of electrical stimulation in rats. Gallistel's group found that as the stimulation strength rises above threshold, the subjective intensity of the payoff climbs steeply, initially approximating a power function; the growth eventually slows and levels off as stimulation strength is increased to ever higher levels. In figures 26.2, 26.5, 26.7 and 26.8, the growth of BSR as a function of the aggregate rate of stimulation-induced firing is modeled as a logistic, thus capturing the steep initial rise, the later deceleration, and the eventual leveling-off.

Knowing the form and parameters of the intensity-growth function could serve as a powerful constraint in interpreting recordings of neural activity. For example, if one wished to argue that a particular population of neurons encodes the intensity of the payoff produced by the rewarding stimulation, one would have to demonstrate that some attribute of activity in this population corresponds to the form and parameters of the intensity-growth function.

BEYOND STRICT MATCHING: CONTRIBUTION OF ECONOMIC CONSTRAINTS TO DECISION UTILITY

The discussion of matching was confined to cases in which the two competing reinforcers are of the same kind (for example, food) and where the reinforcers are available outside the test environment. When reinforcers of different kinds are pitted against each other in choice experiments or when a natural reinforcer is available uniquely in the test environment, the strict form of the matching law may no longer account gracefully for the translation of subjective payoffs into decision utility. Two additional pieces of information appear to contribute to the computation of decision utility: the category to which the reinforcer belongs (its kind) and the environmental distribution of the reinforcer. The role of the perceptual channel in providing this information is highlighted by experiments in which BSR competes with natural reinforcers.

FIGURE 26.8   Computing Behavioral Allocation

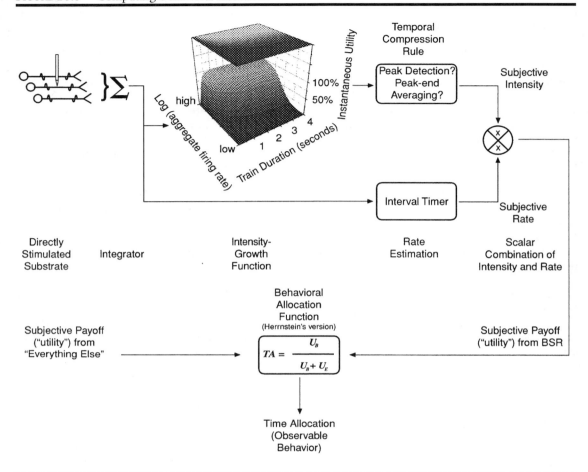

Notes. According to Herrnstein's (1970) treatment of operant performance for a single experimenter-controlled reinforcer, the payoff obtained by working for the experimenter-controlled reinforcer is compared to the payoff from competing activities such as grooming, exploring, and resting ("everything else"). The allocation of behavior to the experimenter-controlled reinforcer is determined by the payoff it provides as a proportion of the sum of all payoffs available in the test environment. This view of behavioral allocation runs into difficulty when the subject works for an essential natural reinforcer unavailable outside the test environment or when the subject chooses between two natural reinforcers of different kinds. However, neither of these restrictions apply in the case of BSR.

The needs addressed by behavioral means are many and varied. Thus, humans and other animals seek "goods" of different kinds. If a sufficiently broad time frame is adopted, choices between alternatives are rarely constrained to single decisions between mutually exclusive options. Under such circumstances, the problem of adaptive choice is to select the best "bundle" of goods rather than the single item with the highest value in a common currency. Research in behavioral economics suggests that when available goods are not of the same kind, calculating the utility of the bundle usually requires an operation more complex than simply summing the utilities of the individual items (Kagel, Battalio, and Green 1995; Rachlin et al. 1976; Rachlin, Kagel, and Battalio 1980).

The relationships between the items in the bundle can be arrayed on a continuum. At one extreme are goods that are entirely substitutable, like two brands of cola to an indifferent consumer. At the other extreme are goods that are complements, such as bicycle frames and bicycle wheels, or left shoes and right shoes. In the case of perfect substitutes, the utility of the bundle is simply the sum of the utilities of the constituent goods. In contrast, the more complementary the constituents, the less each is worth individually in comparison with the utility of the bundle.

The distinction between substitutes and complements has profound behavioral implications. For example, if the relative prices of two highly substitutable goods are changed and the budget of the consumer is adjusted so as to make possible the purchase of the same quantities as had been acquired at the former prices, consumption shifts toward the cheaper good. In contrast, complementary goods tend to be consumed in a fixed ratio that is insensitive to changes in relative price.

When substitutability is taken into account, the simple form of the matching law no longer suffices. For example, responding for the reinforcer on the richer of two schedules will increase when the schedule for a perfect substitute is made leaner (increasing its "price"), as the matching law predicts. However, responding on the richer schedule will decrease when the schedule for a perfect complement is made leaner. Rachlin, Kagel, and Battalio (1980) have shown how a generalization of the simple form of the matching law can be interpreted to incorporate substitutability. Each of the ratios reflecting the subjective weighting of rate, delay, amount, and strength is first raised to an exponent before scalar combination. For perfect substitutes, the exponent is one, and the equation reduces to the simple form of the matching law. According to this modification to the matching law, the translation of subjective payoff into decision utility depends on the substitutability of the reinforcers.

Substitutability of BSR and Natural Reinforcers

Results of an experiment carried out by Green and Rachlin (1991) to measure the substitutability of rewarding LH stimulation, food, and water can be interpreted in terms of the role of the perceptual channel in computing decision utility. As expected, they found that food and water were poor substitutes. Nonetheless, BSR was highly substitutable for both food and water.

Presumably, dry food and water are poor substitutes because they fulfill non-overlapping physiological needs. If so, does the high substitutability of BSR with both food and water imply that the signal injected by the electrode mimics signals specific to both energy balance and fluid balance? If this were the case, one would expect that BSR would be less substitutable for food and water than for itself. This is not what Green and Rachlin found. BSR triggered by one lever was about as substitutable for BSR triggered by the other lever as for food or water.

One interpretation suggested by Green and Rachlin is that BSR acts as a "general" reinforcer. This is reminiscent of the coding argument advanced by Shizgal and Conover (1996). We proposed that any activity produced by the rewarding stimulation in the perceptual system would tend to be "noisy" and unlikely to mimic the signature of a naturally occurring goal object. Moreover, our results suggest that the rewarding stimulation acts downstream from the point where physiological feedback weights gustatory rewards. Thus, there may well be no way for the rat to determine the regulatory system or the class of goal object to which the stimulation is germane. However, our data suggest that the evaluative channel produces a unidimensional currency signal in response to rewarding brain stimulation, a sucrose solution, and a saline solution. If this were also the case for water and for the food employed by Green and Rachlin, then these goods would also substitute well for BSR. In contrast, food and water would register distinct signals in the perceptual channel, making it possible to incorporate the identity and, hence, the low substitutability of these two reinforcers when computing the relative decision utilities of the activities that produce these two goods.

Elasticity of Demand for BSR and Natural Reinforcers

Most experiments that employ food reinforcement are conducted under the conditions of an "open economy": food is made available during the relatively short test sessions and is also available during at least some of the much longer period the subject spends in its home cage. Often the body weight of the subjects is maintained at some proportion of the free-feeding value. Thus, the supplementary food given to the subjects in the home environment can bring total intake to a fixed level when added to what was earned in the test environment. In such circumstances, "demand" (the number of reinforcers earned in the test environment) is said to be highly "elastic," changing steeply in response to variations in "price" (the number of responses required to obtain a single reinforcement). For example, the higher the cost of food in the experimental situation, the less food the animal earns there (Hursh 1980). In contrast, when the economy is "closed," and the reinforcer is available uniquely in the test environment, demand for food becomes highly *in*elastic over an appreciable range of prices (Collier et al. 1986; Hursh 1980). When the subject must fend for itself, without the benefit of supplements, response rates tend to increase with price so that consumption is largely defended.

Although it is tempting to attribute the inelastic demand observed in a closed economy to an accumulating effect of deprivation, the data do not fit this hypothesis gracefully. Over the range of prices within which demand remains highly inelastic in such experiments, subjects can maintain their body weight or even increase it (Collier 1983). If so, some aspect of the economic circumstances appears to be altering the translation of subjective payoff into decision utility.

According to the single-operant version of the matching law (Herrnstein 1970), subjects presented with a single experimenter-supplied reinforcer choose between working for it and performing alternative activities, such as taking the opportunity to groom, rest, or explore. Herrnstein's formulation predicts that increasing the price of the experimenter-supplied reinforcer will shift the allocation of behavior away from that reinforcer and toward "everything else." The effect of price on performance for food in a closed economy violates this form of the matching law: contrary to prediction, relative allocation of behavior to natural reinforcers is no longer proportional to relative payoff.

The situation is different in the case of BSR. In the great majority of BSR experiments, the economy is closed; no stimulation is available in the home cage. Yet demand for BSR is highly elastic; the larger the number of responses required to earn a reinforcement, or the more stringent the limit on maximum consumption per unit time, the lower the allocation of behavior to responding for BSR (Druhan, Levy, and Shizgal 1993; Fouriezos, Emdin, and Beaudoin 1996; Hamilton et al. 1985). Thus, as Hursh and Natelson (1981) have demonstrated, closing the economy produces very different changes in performance for BSR and food: demand for BSR remains highly elastic, whereas demand for food is highly inelastic.

The effect of closing the economy on responding for food and water reinforcement has been interpreted to suggest that the subject learns the relative availability of the reinforcer in the different environments to which it is exposed (Collier 1983), much as optimal-foraging theorists have postulated (Charnov 1976; Stephens and Krebs 1986). Such a representation would appear to store information from the perceptual channel in a spatial or spatiotemporal context (e.g., food is available in the test chamber, but not in the home cage) and to contribute, along with the subjective weightings of rate, delay, amount, and strength, to determining decision utility. The situation for BSR seems far simpler: demand for BSR appears unaffected by whether or not the economy is open (although direct experimental confirmation of this prediction is lacking). Perhaps this is so because the "noisy" signal produced by rewarding brain stimulation in the perceptual channel cannot be attributed to a particular natural reinforcer.

EXPECTANCY

In the fanciful scenario described earlier, the prospective diners could not predict the time when either of the restaurants would next open. Although the availability of resources in the natural world may also be unpredictable, there are circumstances in which events occur in reliable sequences. For example, after a flower has been drained by a hummingbird, the nectar tends to accumulate at a characteristic rate, and the bird adjusts the timing of its return accordingly (Gallistel 1990). Subjects working on fixed-interval schedules of reinforcement in laboratory experiments manifest a pause in responding after delivery of the reinforcer; responding then resumes as the time to the next scheduled delivery of reinforcement approaches (Gibbon 1977). In such circumstances, decision utility is adjusted dynamically to reflect information provided by the interval timer concerning the scheduling of reinforcement. The probability that the animal will direct its behavior toward the goal shifts from low to high as the predicted time of reinforcement approaches. This adjustment in behavior is anticipatory, and thus the animal can be said to have formed an expectation of future payoff.

In scalar expectancy theory, the average level of expectancy is increased by a large recent payoff (Gibbon 1977). It stands to reason that this increase might be specific to the expectancy of future payoffs of the same kind as the large, recent one. This proposal is in the spirit of Loewenstein's (1996) treatment of the focusing effects produced by sensations and states that have large instantaneous utilities. Such sensations and states are portrayed as "crowding out" consideration of alternative reinforcers.

With this view of expectancy in mind, let us return to the vignette at the beginning of this chapter. Toward the end of the rat's confinement in the start box, it approaches the barrier blocking access to the alley. Such behavior is much more pronounced on trials when stimulation is delivered in the start box than on trials when it is not; on the trials preceded by stimulation, the rat not only approaches the barrier but makes frenzied attempts to climb over it. This potentiation of anticipatory acts cannot be due simply to stimulation-induced arousal because the same start-box stimulation fails to galvanize behavior when the rat has learned that additional stimulation is no longer available in the goal box. Rather, the experience of a large, recent payoff seems to rescale expectancy (Sax and Gallistel 1990), boosting its magnitude at each point in time as the delay to accessing the alley elapses. However, when the rat has learned that reinforcement is no longer available in the goal box, there is, in effect, no expectancy for the start-box stimulation to rescale, and the rat's behavior in the start box becomes nonchalant.

The effect of a large, recent payoff on decision utility is illustrated by two experiments in which thirsty rats chose between BSR and water (Deutsch, Adams, and Metzner 1964; Wasserman, Gomita, and Gallistel 1982). Shortly following delivery of pretrial stimulation, the rats chose BSR in preference to water. When the pretrial stimulation was omitted, the preference reversed, and the rats opted for the water instead of the BSR. The pretrial stimulation was very similar to the stimulation offered as a reward. In contrast, the stimulation is unlikely to have mimicked the perceptual experience produced by the water (see the section on unidimensional versus multidimensional coding). According to the argument sketched out earlier, the expectancy boosted by the large pretrial payoff will be directed at the reward with the neural signature most similar to that of the pretrial stimulation. This augmented expectancy would boost the decision utility of BSR, thus biasing choice. It would be interesting to determine whether pretrial exposure to water would produce a complementary effect. More generally, the dependence of decision utility on the interaction between the experience, expectation, and recording of payoffs deserves additional attention. Rewarding brain stimulation may prove to be a valuable tool for investigating such interactions.

CONCLUSION

Vigorous efforts are under way to identify the components of the neural circuitry responsible for BSR. Although the quarry has long proved elusive, new methods for visualizing candidate neurons (Arvanitogiannis, Flores, Pfaus, and Shizgal 1996; Arvanitogiannis, Flores, and Shizgal 1997; Flores, Arvanitogiannis, and Shizgal 1997) and for measuring the behavioral effects of drugs and lesions (Arvanitogiannis, Waraczynski, and Shizgal 1996; Shizgal, Conover, and Arvanitogiannis 1996) offer hope for better hunting. Once these cells are found, we will have new questions to ask them as a result of this attempt to align conceptions of utility that have grown out of the study of BSR and natural reinforcers in laboratory animals with ideas derived from the study of evaluation and choice in humans. It will be particularly interesting to test the hypothesis that the neurons responsible for the signal recorded as the subjective intensity of the payoff also give rise to the instantaneous utility of the stimulation. By recording from these neurons in awake, behaving subjects, it should prove possible to test many of the hypotheses discussed here concerning the role of these cells in the computation of utility. Among these hypotheses is the proposal that the output of the directly activated neurons underlying BSR can gain access to working memory under attentional control. Investigating this hypothesis could shed light on how signals fundamental to the experience of pleasure gain access to awareness.

The author is grateful to Andreas Arvanitogiannis, Kent Berridge, Kent Conover, Randy Gallistel, Bart Hoebel, Daniel Kahneman, and Roy Wise for their helpful comments and to the Fonds pour la Formation de Chercheurs et l'Aide à la Recherche du Québec (grants ER–0124 and CE–0103), the Medical Research Council of Canada (grant MT–8037), and the Natural Sciences and Engineering Research Council of Canada (grant A0308) for research support.

REFERENCES

Arvanitogiannis, A., Flores, C., Pfaus, J. G., and Shizgal, P. (1996). Increased ipsilateral expression of Fos following lateral hypothalamic self-stimulation. *Brain Research, 720,* 148–54.

Arvanitogiannis, A., Flores, C., and Shizgal, P. (1997). Fos-like immunoreactivity in the caudal diencephalon and brain stem following lateral hypothalamic self-stimulation. *Behavioural Brain Research, 88*(2), 275–79.

Arvanitogiannis, A., Waraczynski, M., and Shizgal, P. (1996). Effects of excitotoxic lesions of the basal forebrain on MFB self-stimulation. *Physiology and Behavior, 59*(4/5), 795–806.

Baars, B. J. (1988). *A cognitive theory of consciousness.* Cambridge: Cambridge University Press.

Baum, W. M., and Rachlin, H. (1969). Choice as time allocation. *Journal of the Experimental Analysis of Behavior, 12,* 861–74.

Bentham, J. (1996). *An introduction to the principles of morals and legislation.* Oxford: Clarendon Press. (Originally published in 1789)

Bielajew, C., and Shizgal, P. (1980). Dissociation of the substrates for medial forebrain bundle self-stimulation and stimulation-escape using a two-electrode stimulation technique. *Physiology and Behavior, 25,* 707–11.

Bishop, M. P., Elder, S. T., and Heath, R. G. (1963). Intracranial self-stimulation in man. *Science, 140,* 394–96.

Bower, G. H., and Miller, N. E. (1958). Rewarding and punishing effects from stimulating the same place in the rat's brain. *Journal of Comparative and Physiological Psychology, 51,* 669–74.

Boyd, E. S., and Gardiner, L. C. (1962). Positive and negative reinforcement from intracranial stimulation of a teleost. *Science, 136,* 648–49.

Cabanac, M. (1971). Physiological role of pleasure. *Science, 173,* 1103–7.

———. (1992). Pleasure: The common currency. *Journal of Theoretical Biology, 155,* 173–200.

Cabanac, M., and LeBlanc, J. (1983). Physiological conflict in humans: Fatigue versus cold discomfort. *American Journal of Physiology, 244,* R621–28.

Charnov, E. L. (1976). Optimal foraging: The marginal value theorem. *Theoretical Population Biology, 9,* 129–36.

Church, R. M. (1984). Properties of the internal clock. In J. Gibbon and L. Allan (Eds.), *Timing and time perception* (vol. 423, pp. 566–82). New York: New York Academy of Sciences.

Collier, G. H. (1983). Life in a closed economy: The ecology of learning and motivation. In M. D. Zeller and P. Harzem (Eds.), *Advances in analysis of behaviour* (vol. 3, pp. 223–74). New York: Wiley.

Collier, G. H., Johnson, D. F., Hill, W. L., and Kaufman, L. W. (1986). The economics of the law of effect. *Journal of the Experimental Analysis of Behavior, 46,* 113–36.

Commons, M. L., Mazur, J. E., Nevin, J. A., and Rachlin, H. (Eds.). (1987). *Quantitative analysis of behavior: The effects of delay.* Vol. 5. Cambridge, Mass.: Ballinger.

Conover, K. L., and Shizgal, P. (1994a). Competition and summation between rewarding effects of sucrose and lateral hypothalamic stimulation in the rat. *Behavioral Neuroscience, 108*(3), 537–48.

———. (1994b). Differential effects of post-ingestive feedback on the reward value of sucrose and lateral hypothalamic stimulation in the rat. *Behavioral Neuroscience, 108*(3), 559–72.

Conover, K. L., Woodside, B., and Shizgal, P. (1994). Effects of sodium depletion on competition and summation between rewarding effects of salt and lateral hypothalamic stimulation in the rat. *Behavioral Neuroscience, 108*(3), 549–58.

Davison, M., and McCarthy, D. (1988). *The matching law.* Hillsdale, N.J.: Erlbaum.

De Villiers, P. (1977). Choice in concurrent schedules and a quantitative formulation of the law of effect. In W. K. Honig and J. E. R. Staddon (Eds.), *Handbook of operant behavior* (pp. 233–87). Englewood Cliffs, N.J.: Prentice-Hall.

Deutsch, J. A., Adams, D. W., and Metzner, R. J. (1964). Choice of intracranial stimulation as a function of delay between stimulations and strength of competing drive. *Journal of Comparative and Physiological Psychology, 57,* 241–43.

Distel, H. (1978). Behavior and electrical brain stimulation in the green iguana (*Iguana iguana L.*): II. Stimulation effects. *Experimental Brain Research, 31*(3), 353–67.

Druhan, J. P., Levy, M., and Shizgal, P. (1993). Effects of varying reinforcement schedule, reward current, and pretrial priming stimulation on discrete-trial performance for brain stimulation reward. *Psychobiology, 21*(1), 37–42.

Edmonds, D. E., and Gallistel, C. R. (1974). Parametric analysis of brain stimulation reward in the rat: III. Effect of performance variables on the reward summation function. *Journal of Comparative and Physiological Psychology, 87,* 876–83.

Flores, C., Arvanitogiannis, A., and Shizgal, P. (1997). Fos-like immunoreactivity in forebrain regions following self-stimulation of the lateral hypothalamus and the ventral tegmental area. *Behavioural Brain Research, 87*(2), 239–51.

Fouriezos, G., Emdin, K., and Beaudoin, L. (1996). Intermittent rewards raise self-stimulation thresholds. *Behavioural Brain Research, 74,* 57–64.

Frank, R. A., and Stutz, R. M. (1984). Self-deprivation: A review. *Psychological Bulletin, 96*(2), 384–93.

Fredrickson, B. L., and Kahneman, D. (1993). Duration neglect in retrospective evaluations of affective episodes. *Journal of Personality and Social Psychology, 65*(1), 45–55.

Gallistel, C. R. (1978). Self-stimulation in the rat: Quantitative characteristics of the reward pathway. *Journal of Comparative and Physiological Psychology, 92,* 977–98.

———. (1980). *The organization of action: A new synthesis.* Hillsdale, N.J.: Erlbaum.

———. (1990). *The organization of learning.* Cambridge, Mass.: MIT Press.

———. (1991). Measuring the subjective magnitude of brain stimulation reward by titration with rate of reward. *Behavioral Neuroscience, 105*(6), 913–25.

Gallistel, C. R., Shizgal, P., and Yeomans, J. S. (1981). A portrait of the substrate for self-stimulation. *Psychological Review, 88,* 228–73.

Gibbon, J. (1977). Scalar expectancy theory and Weber's law in animal timing. *Psychological Review, 84*(3), 279–325.

———. (1995). Dynamics of time matching: Arousal makes better seem worse. *Psychonomic Bulletin and Review, 2*(2), 208–15.

Gibbon, J., Church, R. M., Fairhurst, S., and Kacelnik, A. (1988). Scalar expectancy theory and choice between delayed rewards. *Psychological Review, 95*(1), 102–14.

Gibbon, J., Malapani, C., Dale, C. L., and Gallistel, C. (1997). Towards a neurobiology of temporal cognition: Advances and challenges. *Current Opinion in Neurobiology, 7*(2), 170–84.

Goldman-Rakic, P. S. (1996). Regional and cellular fractionation of working memory. *Proceedings of the National Academy of Sciences, USA, 93,* 13473–80.

Green, L., and Rachlin, H. (1991). Economic substitutability of electrical brain stimulation, food, and water. *Journal of the Experimental Analysis of Behavior, 55,* 133–43.

Hamilton, A. L., Stellar, J. R., and Hart, E. B. (1985). Reward, performance, and the response strength method in self-stimulating rats: Validation and neuroleptics. *Physiology and Behavior, 35,* 897–904.

Heath, R. G. (1964). Pleasure response of human subjects to direct stimulation of the brain: Physiologic and psychodynamic considerations. In R. G. Heath (Ed.), *The role of pleasure in behavior* (pp. 219–43). New York: Harper & Row.

Heller, J. (1961). *Catch-22* (17th printing, 1966). New York: Dell.

Herrnstein, R. J. (1961). Relative and absolute strength of response as a function of frequency of reinforcement. *Journal of the Experimental Analysis of Behavior, 4,* 267–72.

———. (1970). On the law of effect. *Journal of the Experimental Analysis of Behavior, 13*(2), 243–66.

Heyman, G. (1988). How drugs affect cells and reinforcement affects behavior: Formal analogies. In M. L. Commons, R. M. Church, J. R. Stellar, and A. R. Wagner (Eds.), *Biological determinants of reinforcement* (vol. 7, pp. 157–82). Hillsdale, N.J.: Erlbaum.

Heyman, G. H., and Goodman, J. B. (1998). Matching as an elementary behavioral principle: A Markov analysis of preference in concurrent choice procedures. Harvard University. Unpublished paper.

Heyman, G. M., and Monaghan, M. M. (1994). Reinforcer magnitude (sucrose concentration) and the matching law theory of response strength. *Journal of the Experimental Analysis of Behavior, 61,* 505–16.

Hoebel, B. G. (1969). Feeding and self-stimulation. *Annals of the New York Academy of Sciences, 157,* 758–78.

Hursh, S. R. (1980). Economic concepts for the analysis of behavior. *Journal of the Experimental Analysis of Behavior, 34,* 219–38.

Hursh, S. R., and Natelson, B. H. (1981). Electrical brain stimulation and food reinforcement dissociated by demand elasticity. *Physiology and Behavior, 26,* 509–15.

Johnson-Laird, P. N. (1988). *The computer and the mind.* Cambridge, Mass.: Harvard University Press.

Kagel, J. K., Battalio, R. C., and Green, L. (1995). *Economic choice theory: An experimental model of animal behavior.* Cambridge: Cambridge University Press.

Kahneman, D. (1994). New challenges to the rationality assumption. *Journal of Institutional and Theoretical Economics, 150*(1), 18–36.

Kahneman, D., Fredrickson, B. L., Schreiber, C. A., and Redelmeier, D. A. (1993). When more pain is preferred to less: Adding a better end. *Psychological Science, 4*(6), 401–5.

Kahneman, D., Wakker, P. P., and Sarin, R. (1997). Back to Bentham? Explorations of experienced utility. *Quarterly Journal of Economics, 112*(2), 375–405.

Lamb, R. J., Preston, K. L., Schindler, C. W., Meisch, R. A., Davis, F., Katz, J. L., Henningfield, J. E., and Goldberg, S. R. (1991). The reinforcing and subjective effects of morphine in post-addicts: A dose-response study. *Journal of Pharmacology and Experimental Therapeutics, 259*(3), 1165–73.

LeDoux, J. (1996). *The emotional brain.* New York: Simon & Schuster.

Leon, M., and Gallistel, C. R. (1992). The function relating the subjective magnitude of brain stimulation reward to stimulation strength varies with site of stimulation. *Behavioural Brain Research, 52,* 183–93.

Lepore, M., and Franklin, K. B. J. (1992). Modelling drug kinetics with brain stimulation: Dopamine antagonists increase self-stimulation. *Pharmacology, Biochemistry, and Behavior, 41,* 489–96.

Lilly, J. C., and Miller, A. M. (1962). Operant conditioning of the bottlenose dolphin with electrical stimulation of the brain. *Journal of Comparative and Physiological Psychology, 55,* 73–79.

Loewenstein, G. (1996). Out of control: Visceral influences on behavior. *Organizational Behavior and Human Decision Processes, 65*(3), 272–92.

Macfarlane, D. B. (1954). McGill opens vast new research field with brain "pleasure area" discovery. *Montreal Star,* March 12, 1–2.

Mark, T. A., and Gallistel, C. R. (1993). Subjective reward magnitude of medial forebrain stimulation as a function of train duration and pulse frequency. *Behavioral Neuroscience, 107*(2), 389–401.

Mason, P., and Milner, P. (1986). Temporal characteristics of electrical self-stimulation reward: Fatigue rather than adaptation. *Physiology and Behavior, 36,* 857–60.

Mazur, J. E. (1986). Choice between single and multiple delayed reinforcers. *Journal of the Experimental Analysis of Behavior, 46,* 67–78.

Mazur, J. E., Stellar, J. R., and Waraczynski, M. (1987). Self-control choice with electrical stimulation of the brain. *Behavioural Processes, 15,* 143–53.

McFarland, D. J., and Sibley, R. M. (1975). The behavioural final common path. *Philosophical Transactions of the Royal Society of London B, 270,* 265–93.

Meck, W. H. (1996). Neuropharmacology of timing and time perception. *Cognitive Brain Research, 3,* 227–42.

Miller, G. A., Galanter, E., and Pribram, K. H. (1960). *Plans and the structure of behavior.* New York: Holt, Rinehart and Winston.

Miller, H. L. (1976). Matching-based hedonic scaling in the pigeon. *Journal of the Experimental Analysis of Behavior, 26,* 335–47.

Morgan, C. W., and Mogenson, G. J. (1966). Preference of water-deprived rats for stimulation of the lateral hypothalamus and water. *Psychonomic Science, 6,* 337–38.

Myerson, J., and Green, L. (1995). Discounting of delayed rewards: Models of individual choice. *Journal of the Experimental Analysis of Behavior, 64,* 263–76.

Newsome, W. T., and Salzman, C. D. (1993). The neuronal basis of motion perception. *Ciba Foundation Symposium, 174,* 217–46.

Nisbett, R. E., and Wilson, T. D. (1977). Telling more than we can know: Verbal reports on mental processes. *Psychological Review, 84*(3), 231–59.

Olds, J. (1956). Pleasure centers in the brain. *Scientific American, 195,* 105–16.

———. (1958). Self-stimulation of the brain. *Science, 127,* 315–24.

Olds, J., and Milner, P. M. (1954). Positive reinforcement produced by electrical stimulation of septal area and other regions of rat brain. *Journal of Comparative and Physiological Psychology, 47,* 419–27.

Pfaffmann, C., Norgren, R., and Grill, H. J. (1977). Sensory affect and motivation. *Annals of the New York Academy of Sciences, 290,* 18–34.

Porter, R. W., Conrad, D. G., and Brady, J. V. (1959). Some neural and behavioral correlates of electrical self-stimulation of the limbic system. *Journal of the Experimental Analysis of Behavior, 2,* 43–55.

Rachlin, H., Green, L., Kagel, J. H., and Battalio, R. C. (1976). Economic demand theory and psychological studies of choice. In G. H. Bower (Ed.), *The psychology of learning and motivation* (vol. 10, pp. 129–54). New York: Academic Press.

Rachlin, H., Kagel, J. H., and Battalio, R. C. (1980). Substitutability in time allocation. *Psychological Review, 87,* 355–74.

Redelmeier, D. A., and Kahneman, D. (1996). Patients' memories of painful medical procedures: Real-time and retrospective evaluations of two minimally invasive treatments. *Pain, 66,* 3–8.

Roberts, W. W. (1958). Both rewarding and punishing effects from stimulation of posterior hypothalamus of cat with same electrode at same intensity. *Journal of Comparative and Physiological Psychology, 51,* 400–7.

Routtenberg, A., and Lindy, J. (1965). Effects of the availability of rewarding septal and hypothalamic stimulation on bar pressing for food under conditions of deprivation. *Journal of Comparative and Physiological Psychology, 60*(2), 158–61.

Sax, L., and Gallistel, C. R. (1990). Characteristics of spatiotemporal integration in the priming and rewarding effects of medial forebrain bundle stimulation. *Behavioral Neuroscience, 105,* 884–900.

Schreiber, C. A., and Kahneman, D. (1997). Determinants of the remembered utility of aversive sounds. University of California, Berkeley. Unpublished paper.

Shizgal, P. (1997). Neural basis of utility estimation. *Current Opinion in Neurobiology, 7*(2), 198–208.

Shizgal, P., and Conover, K. (1996). On the neural computation of utility. *Current Directions in Psychological Science, 5*(2), 37–43.

Shizgal, P., Conover, K., and Arvanitogiannis, A. (1996). Performance for brain stimulation reward as a function of the rate and magnitude of reinforcement. *Society for Neuroscience Abstracts, 22*(1), 686.

Shizgal, P., and Matthews, G. (1977). Electrical stimulation of the rat diencephalon: Differential effects of interrupted stimulation on on- and off-responding. *Brain Research, 129,* 319–33.

Shizgal, P., and Murray, B. (1989). Neuronal basis of intracranial self-stimulation. In J. M. Liebman and S. J. Cooper (Eds.), *The neuropharmacological basis of reward* (pp. 106–63). Oxford: Oxford University Press.

Simmons, J. M., and Gallistel, C. R. (1994). Saturation of subjective reward magnitude as a function of current and pulse frequency. *Behavioral Neuroscience, 108,* 151–60.

Stephens, D. W., and Krebs, J. R. (1986). *Foraging theory.* Princeton, N.J.: Princeton University Press.

Treue, S., and Maunsell, J. H. R. (1996). Attentional modulation of visual motion processing in cortical areas MT and MST. *Nature, 382,* 539–41.

Wasserman, E. M., Gomita, Y., and Gallistel, C. R. (1982). Pimozide blocks reinforcement but not priming from MFB stimulation in the rat. *Pharmacology Biochemistry and Behavior, 17,* 783–87.

Watanabe, M. (1996). Reward expectancy in primate prefrontal neurons. *Nature, 382,* 629–32.

Williams, B. A. (1988). Reinforcement, choice, and response strength. In R. C. Atkinson, R. J. Herrnstein, G. Lindzey, and R. D. Luce (Eds.), *Stevens's handbook of experimental psychology: Learning and cognition* (2nd ed., vol. 2, pp. 167–244). New York: Wiley.

Wise, R. A. (1996). Addictive drugs and brain stimulation reward. *Annual Review of Neuroscience, 19,* 319–40.

Yeomans, J. S. (1988). Mechanisms of brain-stimulation reward. In A. E. Epstein and A. R. Morrison (Eds.), *Progress in psychobiology and physiological psychology* (vol. 13, pp. 227–65). New York: Academic Press.

———. (1990). *Principles of brain stimulation.* New York: Oxford University Press.

Young, P. T. (1967). Palatability: The hedonic response to foodstuffs. In Code, C. F., Heidel, W., et al. (Eds.), *Handbook of physiology* (vol. 1, pp. 353–66). Washington D.C.: American Physiological Society.

Zajonc, R. B. (1980). Feeling and thinking: Preferences need no inference. *American Psychologist, 35*(2), 151–75.

27 Pleasure, Pain, Desire, and Dread: Hidden Core Processes of Emotion

Kent C. Berridge

Elemental emotional states, such as simple pleasures, pains, desires, and fears, may seem irreducible, but they are not. Each contains dissociable psychological components, or core processes. This chapter explores dissociation of components within elemental emotion, the relations between components, and their embodiment in brain systems. The core processes of emotion and motivation are essentially unconscious and not directly represented in subjective emotional feelings. For example, the subjective experience of an emotion itself may be split apart into dissociable subjective components under a variety of circumstances. Core processes of emotion that underlie subjective experience can be further separated from subjective emotional feelings and occur without conscious awareness under limited conditions. For positive emotional states, core processes of "liking" and "wanting" are psychologically dissociable from each other. "Liking" corresponds to a basic sensory pleasure or hedonic activation. "Wanting" corresponds to a different core process, the attribution of incentive salience to stimuli or events. Core processes of "liking" and "wanting" are mediated by different neural systems in the brain. "Liking" may be activated without "wanting" through brain manipulations. Conversely, "wanting" can be activated without "liking." The phenomenon of "wanting" without "liking" has special relevance for understanding the causes of addiction. Negative emotions involving fear and pain also are dissociable into core processes. Some of the core processes of fear and anxiety may overlap with those of positive desires. In other words, positive and negative emotions may share psychological building blocks (such as incentive salience) even though the final emotions are experienced as opposite.

A COGENT CASE can be made that the quality of life depends partly on the fulfillment of cultural themes of life *meaning*, such as personal goals or relationships (Cantor, Acker, and Cook-Flannagan 1992; Cantor et al. 1991; Ellsworth 1994; Roney, Higgins, and Shah 1995). The quality of life is not reducible to its mere quantity of pleasures and pains but includes purposeful, aesthetic, and moral considerations, too. Life is still a series of pleasures and pains, however, some large and some small, and hedonic states determine at least one important aspect of life's quality. Any appraisal of the quality of life requires consideration of its affective tone. Since cultural appraisals of life meaning are relatively resistant to biopsychological analysis, I restrict myself here to the hedonic analysis of basic emotions.

I argue that even the simplest emotions, as we experience them, are not as elemental or irreducible as they seem. They contain multiple core processes. The nature of these core processes of emotion is not evident to conscious awareness and may not fit into traditional psychological categories. Evidence for these propositions is drawn both from the cognitive and social psychology of subjective emotion (Fischman and Foltin 1992; Hilgard 1986; Kahneman et al. 1993; Murphy and Zajonc 1993; Zajonc 1980) and from the affective neuroscience of emotional processes in the brain (Berridge 1996; Davidson and Sutton 1995; LeDoux 1996; Panksepp 1991).

DISSOCIATION OF EMOTION INTO UNCONSCIOUS CORE COMPONENTS

Our conscious experience of emotion might be likened to the glimmering surface of a pond. We see only the surface of our own emotion. Below the surface lie objects and creatures within the pond—core emotional processes and their antecedents. Cognitive mechanisms of conscious perception must translate an event into active declarative representations in order to be subjectively perceived, representing the event, as the pond's surface represents what is below. What we know of the pond is what we see from above. But the view from above is distorted by ripples in the surface—nuances of the translation process—and by reflected light from above—the modulating influence of cognitive expectation and appraisal. What is below the surface of our experience of the quality of life?

What defines an emotion, for many psychologists as well as for most other people, is its conscious *feeling*. It is almost impossible to conceive of emotion in any other way. Most would agree with the view expressed by the psychologist Phoebe Ellsworth: "I have always found the idea of unconscious emotions extremely difficult to think about . . . [as] in most definitions of emotion . . . a subjective experience of feeling is an essential component" (1995, 214).

Emotion is nearly unique among psychological categories to the degree that we judge subjective experience of feelings to be an essential component. Unconscious motivations, memories, and even perceptions may be granted, but an unconscious emotion is more difficult to imagine. For memory, we are not conscious of the vast array of declarative memories that may nonetheless be called up at another time, and we have procedural memories that are resistant to introspection. Unconscious perception is somewhat more problematic, and its existence was once a point of contention in psychology (Eriksen 1960). But there have been many demonstrations that events too brief to be consciously perceived may nonetheless have clear psychological consequences, including on subsequent emotional ratings (Kunst-Wilson and Zajonc 1980; Lazarus and McCleary 1951; Moreland and Zajonc 1977; Murphy and Zajonc 1993; Winkielman, Zajonc, and Schwarz 1997; Zajonc 1980). Dramatic demonstrations of unconscious perception have been provided by human patients after neurological damage. For example, a person experiencing the phenomenon of "blindsight" reports no conscious visual sensation in a portion of visual space after damage to the visual area of the occipital cortex. Yet the same person may be able to "guess" the identity of presented visual objects (Gazzaniga, Fendrich, and Wessinger 1994; Weiskrantz 1986, 1996). A similar phenomenon can be reproduced in normal subjects using brief presentations of visual stimuli (Kolb and Braun 1995). But unconscious emotion is less readily accepted. What do we mean by it? How can a process be emotional if it cannot be felt?

Perhaps one reason we find it easier to accept unconscious cognition than unconscious emotion is simply the weight of empirical evidence that forces us to posit unconscious memory or perception; similar phenomena are rare or missing for unconscious emotion. It takes brute demonstra-

tions to compel us to believe in unconscious psychological processes, and we have those in abundance for memory and perception.

Brute demonstrations of unconscious emotion are less common, less forceful, and so less able to compel assent. Most demonstrations of unconscious processes in emotion have focused on showing that people may be unaware of the events that caused their emotion, rather than unaware of the emotions themselves (Murphy and Zajonc 1993; Nisbett and Wilson 1978; Wilson and Schooler 1991; Winkielman et al. 1997; Zajonc 1980). However, demonstrations of unconscious emotional processes do exist, and they are examined later in the chapter.

Dissociation

The concept of "dissociation" among psychological components provides a useful tool for thinking about emotion (Hilgard 1986). Although dissociation as a concept originated far earlier, the work of Hilgard and his colleagues in the 1960s and 1970s may be said to have revived it for mainstream psychology (see Hilgard 1986 for review). Dissociation in this context means the breaking apart of what seems to be an indissoluble whole into components that diverge under special conditions.

Hypnosis provides the most impressive of Hilgard's dissociation examples, which he and his colleagues called "hidden observer" phenomena, reproducible in approximately 5 percent of hypnotically susceptible individuals (Hilgard 1986). "Hidden observer" refers to the "covert" reporting of an event by a person under deep hypnosis even though the person is subjectively unaware of the event (often having received hypnotic instruction not to perceive it). In such incidents, a person may accurately be said both to be completely unaware of the event (to the extent they deny conscious registration of it) and to have cognitively evaluated it (to the extent they can describe it in detail). For example, in one case "hypnotic deafness" was induced by prior suggestion. Afterward the subject reported with apparent sincerity that he heard nothing during this period. Yet when addressed during the hypnotic deafness state with the suggestion that "perhaps there is some part of you that is hearing" and asked to respond if that were true, the subject lifted his hand. Later he reported remembering the action but not having heard the request, and he was unable to explain his own action (Hilgard 1986). In other cases, hypnotic analgesia has been induced prior to dental or medical procedures that would ordinarily be quite painful. It is difficult to imagine feigning anesthesia in the face of such procedures. Yet although the subjects reported little or no subjective pain, covert behavioral measures using the hidden observer approach revealed normal pain ratings. One seems compelled to conclude that the subjects' reports are massively deceptive, impaired by a memory deficit of a magnitude that defies belief, or instances of cognitively processed pain that fails to reach consciousness. However difficult to conceive, the option of unconscious emotion may become more plausible than the alternatives.

Dissociation of such magnitude, by definition, is a deviation from our ordinary experience. But although this evidence is often startlingly counterintuitive, it comes from an impeccable source and must be considered. If true, it serves to show what is *possible* in the realm of psychological dissociation.

Dissociation Between Emotional Experience and Remembered or Predicted Emotion

Kahneman and his colleagues have drawn on Bentham to apply the term "utility" to depict qualitative outcomes (Kahneman 1994; Kahneman et al. 1993; Kahneman and Snell 1992), and the utility concept has also been used profitably in behavioral neuroscience studies of reward (Shizgal and Conover 1996; Shizgal, this volume). Utility comes in several types. Kahneman (1994), for example, distinguishes between *instant experienced* utility, *decision* utility, and *predicted/retrospective* utility (figure 27.1). Experienced utility is the outcome's

hedonic value—the degree to which it is *liked* or *disliked.*[1] Decision utility is the degree to which the outcome is *wanted* or *unwanted,* manifest in decisions to get it, lose it, keep it, or avoid it. Predicted utility and retrospective utility are *expectations* or *memories* about the value of an outcome at another time.

For a coherent and rational mind, the three types of utility might be expected to correlate closely. If an event was pleasant, it should be remembered as pleasant, expected to be pleasant, and desired again. But it appears that the three types of utility often diverge for outcomes in real life (Kahneman 1994; Tversky and Kahneman 1986). Decision utility, the degree to which one wants a particular outcome, may be increased or decreased without changing the outcome itself (experienced utility). For example, mere *possession* of a mildly good outcome, such as a free gift mug, increases the decision utility assigned to it: loss has more impact than gain on decision utility, even for the same object (Kahneman, Knetsch, and Thaler 1990). Still, one might argue that this is not necessarily dissociation between wanting and liking (decision utility and experienced utility): perhaps a mug in the hand is not only wanted more but is also *liked* more than one on the shelf?

Dissociation of Belief from Wanting/Liking

Other dissociations cannot be explained away in this manner. Some come from experiments on predicted pleasure and remembered pain in which experienced hedonic utility is assessed and compared to future or past decision utility ratings. For example, Kahneman and Snell (1992) asked subjects to predict what would happen to their liking and

FIGURE 27.1   Reward Value

Expected/ Remembered Utility	Decision Utility	Instant Experienced Utility
Beliefs about value	Wants	Likes

Notes: Three types of utility, corresponding to beliefs about value, wants based on value, and the hedonic value of actual experience. For a given outcome, these three types of utility might be expected to covary together for a rational individual who had experienced the outcome.

wanting ratings for a palatable ice cream if they ate a small portion of it every day for a week. Then the subjects ate the ice cream over a week and rated it each day. Most subjects predicted that their liking/wanting ratings would decline over the week, and they did. But subjects markedly overestimated the magnitude of their decline, doubling it in their predictions (Kahneman and Snell 1992). Their predictions seemed to be guided by the true belief that a monotonous diet reduces preference for a food (LeMagnen 1967; Rolls et al. 1981). But their cognitive belief was apparently stronger than the truth itself, and they misjudged the magnitude of the change. In a second study, Kahneman and Snell asked subjects to taste a spoonful of marginally palatable unflavored yogurt, to rate their liking of it, and to predict how much they would like it and want to eat a full-sized serving of it at home the next day, and then a week later after eating it every day. Again, most subjects predicted a long-term decline over the course of a week. They also predicted they would begin the week (the next day) at the same liking/wanting level they gave in the "spoonful taste test." They were wrong on both counts: they rated each full-sized serving as more unpleasant than they had found the spoonful, and it was their dislike for the unflavored yogurt that declined over time. The inaccuracy of their prediction is striking, since it applies to a relatively commonplace experience: getting used to a new food (figure 27.2).

Memories for pleasures and pains are as vulnerable to distortion as predictions. For example, Thomas and Diener (1990) found that subjects' memories of their emotions of the past several weeks tended to overestimate the intensity of emotional events, as compared with their previous daily reports of the events themselves. They also found that emotion frequency tended to be confused with emotion intensity in memory. Recalled intensity ratings for a type of emotion were often biased by its frequency, especially for negative emotions.

Dissociation of Disliking from Decisions

Decision utility (wanting) and predicted utility (beliefs) can be decoupled from experienced utility (liking) on the basis of memory distortion. In a dramatic example, subjects were asked to rate two painful procedures, which induced pain by submersion of the hand in ice-cold water (Kahneman et al. 1993). Later they chose the "least aversive" one to repeat based on their memory of each. Fascinatingly, subjects could be induced to choose the more painful procedure (measured by their own on-line ratings) if that procedure happened to include a decrement at the end (figure 27.3). A similar dissociation between pain reported on-line and remembered later was found in a painful real-life medical procedure (Redelmeier and Kahneman 1996).

People may be no more accurate in their memories for pleasure than they are in remembering pain. If one asks subjects to report hedonic ratings during a meal, as they pass from hungry to full, they report that the food becomes less palatable. This change of hedonic experience due to physiological factors has been labeled "alliesthesia" (Cabanac 1971). Similar palatability decrements after a meal have been detected in animal studies using electrophysiological or behavioral measures of affective expression to taste, indicating that alliesthesia is shared across species (Berridge 1991; Cabanac and Lafrance 1990; Rolls et al. 1986). Yet despite the fundamental nature of this phenomenon, when people are asked to remember *why* they typically stop eating at the end of a meal, they virtually never report reduced palatability as a reason and may even deny it if it is suggested as a

FIGURE 27.2   Dissociated Reward Value

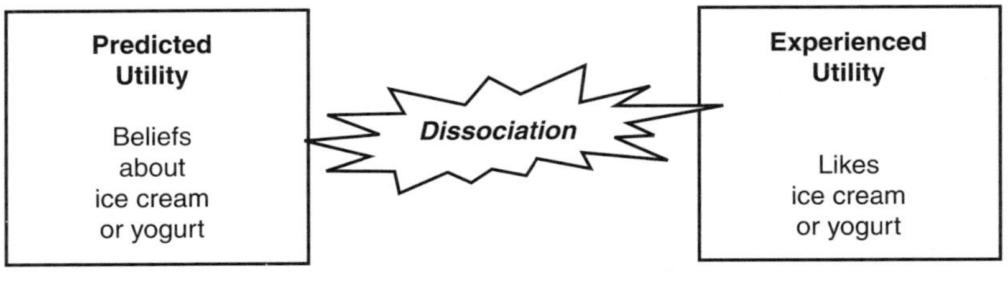

Notes: Dissociation of predicted utility (beliefs about future emotion) from actual subsequent utility (liking ratings for ice cream or yogurt; based on Kahneman and Snell [1992]).

FIGURE 27.3   Dissociated Pain

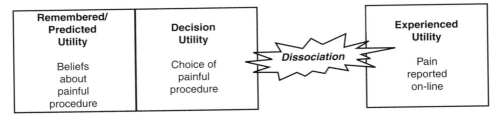

Notes: Dissociation of choice and belief about a painful experience from the actual experience itself, due to the distortion of memory for pain (based on Kahneman et al. 1993). Alliesthesia (change in food palatability as a function of satiety and repetition) provides a similar dissociation for pleasure (based on Mook and Votaw 1992).

potential explanation (Mook and Votaw 1992). Although the hedonic decline is quite apparent in on-line subjective ratings, it seems not to be sufficiently noticeable in memory to be explicitly recalled.

Dissociation of Consciousness from Core Process

The studies above reflect dissociation between the *beliefs* (predictions and memories) people hold about their wants and likes—together with decisions based on those beliefs—from the actual emotional *experience* of events when they occur. As a general rule regarding such dissociations, instant experienced utility (pleasures and pains) seems readily dissociated from remembered utility (memories of pleasure and pain), from expected utility (predictions of future pleasure or pain), and from decision utility (decisions between outcomes that will produce pleasure or pain). Typically, remembered utility, expected utility, and decision utility all cohere together (decisions are usually congruent with past memory and future expectations about particular outcomes), but all of these can be dissociated individually and as a group from experienced utility (the actual experience of the outcome itself).[2] But we can go a step further and actually break apart the instant experienced utility of a particular outcome into dissociated components. It is possible to dissociate *subjective experience* of an event from the underlying *core processes* that constitute wants and likes for that immediate event. The example of hypnotic covert pain from Hilgard, described earlier, is a nice ex-

FIGURE 27.4   Painful Event in Hypnosis

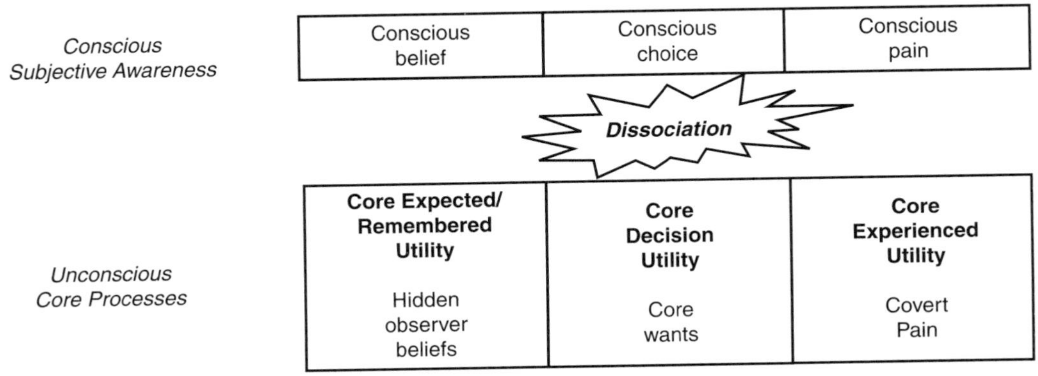

Conscious Subjective Awareness	Conscious belief	Conscious choice	Conscious pain
		Dissociation	
Unconscious Core Processes	**Core Expected/ Remembered Utility** Hidden observer beliefs	**Core Decision Utility** Core wants	**Core Experienced Utility** Covert Pain

Notes: Hypnotic dissociation of conscious awareness of pain from underlying core processes of the emotion for all types of utility. Hypnotic analgesia reduces the subjective awareness of pain as an experienced event, and therefore decisions and beliefs based on subjective pain. But underlying processes of pain, detected by hidden observer measures, persist. (Description of hypnotic analgesia based on Hilgard [1986]).

emplar of an unconscious emotional core process. It is "pain" in a sense—but not in the usual sense of conscious feeling.

For ordinary people, it may be possible to identify unconscious aspects of emotion even without hypnosis. There are several levels of evidence (in order of increasing strength for unconscious emotion): emotions triggered by unconscious perception; unconscious changes of emotion; and instances where emotion itself is unconscious. The first level consists of demonstrations that it is possible to manipulate conscious aesthetic ratings of a conscious stimulus by prior exposure to events too brief to be consciously perceived, such as by a four-millisecond tachistoscopic presentation of a smiling or scowling face (Murphy, Monahan, and Zajonc 1995; Murphy and Zajonc 1993; Winkielman et al. 1997). These demonstrate unconscious affective processing, at least in the sense that subjects remain unaware of what caused their affective rating. However, it is not clear in such cases whether subjects are completely unaware of the emotion itself or merely unaware of the manipulating event. In support of true unconscious emotion, Winkielman, Zajonc, and Schwarz (1997) found that even when subjects' affective evaluations were altered by prior subliminal presentation of a face, the subjects denied afterward that they had had an emotional experience at the time of the subliminal presentation. Still, it is conceivable that a conscious emotion occurred but was not remembered.

A second, slightly stronger, level of evidence consists of cases in which a conscious emotion is changed, but the *change* in that emotional state seems not to be consciously perceived. For example, in a study of fear, Arntz (1993) asked women who suffered from a spider phobia to perform a series of progressively more difficult actions: to walk toward a spider that was captive in a jar, to touch the jar, to open it, to use a pencil to touch the spider, to dump the spider in an open sink, to touch the spider by hand, and to let it walk on their hand. The women could refuse at any point. They were asked to report their subjective fear or anxiety at each step. Before the test, the women were given either a dose of naltrexone (an opioid antagonist drug that blocks brain receptors for endorphin and enkephalin neurotransmitters) or a placebo, without being told which they received. The high dose of naltrexone markedly inhibited approach to the spider. After receiving it, women refused at an earlier stage (usually before using the pencil to touch the spider) compared to when they received the placebo (usually after touching

the spider with the pencil). But subjective reports of fear were *not* significantly increased at *any* stage by naltrexone (though there was a nonsignificant trend toward elevated means). As Arntz notes, this is not entirely conclusive, as a different measure of subjective fear might have detected an effect of the opioid blocker on subjective fear, and the behavioral and subjective measures were obtained in different groups. But oral report is a legitimate measure—and by it these women were not aware of any naltrexone-induced change in fear.

Unconscious Emotion and Motivation

The strongest level of evidence for unconscious emotional processes comes from instances in which the emotion itself—not merely a change in it—is inaccessible to subjective awareness. Not only is unconscious emotion hard to define conceptually, but it is also hard to detect empirically. We can't expect to find lots of instances. But if we find any instances that stand up to close scrutiny, we must recognize them as phenomena of key importance. By their existence, they would radically change the range of psychological entities that must be considered in theories of emotion.

EEG Evidence for Unconscious Emotional Responses

One source of evidence for unconscious emotional responses may come from EEG studies of reaction to subliminal words. For example, Shevrin and colleagues examined classically conditioned fear, instilled by pairing a brief, subliminally presented picture with electric shock (Wong, Shevrin, and Williams 1994). They found that subliminal presentation of the conditioned stimulus came to elicit a distinctive EEG component, even when the subject failed to detect the presentation of anything at all, and they interpreted their results to mean that a conditioned fear response can be elicited entirely outside of conscious awareness. In a related study, Shevrin and colleagues (1992) presented phobic patients with lists of emotional words from various categories. The words were presented tachistoscopically, either too briefly to be perceived consciously (one millisecond) or just long enough to register consciously (thirty to forty milliseconds). One category of emotional words *evoked a more rapid high-frequency EEG response when presented in the subliminal mode* than when the words remained onscreen long enough to register consciously. Words from this emotionally laden category appeared more effective at evoking an emotional EEG response—in other words, when the patient remained unaware of what had been presented.

Behavioral Evidence of Unconscious Liking and Wanting for Drugs

Evidence for unconscious emotional processes may also be found in human behavior, without using tachistoscopic procedures. A striking example comes from studies of apparently unconscious self-administration by drug addicts (Fischman and Foltin 1992; Lamb et al. 1991). For example, in a study by Fischman and her colleagues, recovering addicts were invited to the laboratory, where they were comfortably seated (Fischman 1989; Fischman and Foltin, 1992). Intravenous lines were inserted into their veins. The subjects could obtain either of two intravenous infusions, depending on which of two buttons they pressed. On a particular day, one intravenous infusion might contain a high dose of cocaine while the other contained a low dose of cocaine. On another day, one might be saline solution without any drug while the other contained cocaine. Or—for all the subjects knew—both lines might contain merely saline. Each time the addict pressed one of the buttons, it turned on a light and delivered a pulse of its particular infusion. The subjects were free to try the solutions and to administer each to themselves as they chose.

At moderate to high doses (eight to fifty milligrams of cocaine), subjects described the subjective effects as pleasant and typical of cocaine, and they reliably pressed the button that would obtain the highest available dose. But at the lowest dose of cocaine tested (four milligrams), a remarkable dissociation occurred between "self-administration" and subjective effects. At this very low dose, the subjects reported that they had received only saline, and that the solution contained no cocaine. Indeed, no cardiovascular responses were observed, supporting the subjects' mistaken contention that the infusion was drug-free. But the four-milligram dose was not below threshold by all measures. According to the cumulative record of button pushing over the two- to four-hour session, the addicts *chose and pressed the button that delivered four milligrams of cocaine far more often than the button for saline*, even while they were unable to detect consciously a difference between the two infusions. As Fischman (1992) recounted: "If you want to know what the subjects *say* about

their self-administration of these low doses, they tell me that they were not choosing cocaine over placebo. They often insist that they were sampling equally from each of the two choice options and both were placebo. On the other hand if you look at the *data* from that session you see that they were choosing the low dose [over saline]" (179).

If we apply the terminology of Kahneman and his colleagues, Fischman's drug users had zero utility (experienced, decision, and predictive) for the lowest cocaine dose, according to their own subjective report. In ordinary terms, they did not like it, did not want it, and did not even believe that cocaine was available. But there was another sense, manifest in their actions, in which they simultaneously did "want," and perhaps "liked," the watered-down drug reward. They worked for it and selectively strove to gain it.

Such stark dissociation between awareness and behavior is rare, but this finding is not a single isolated fluke. Another study by Lamb and his colleagues (1991) of hospitalized addicts who received morphine injections in return for button pressing found similar results. In that study, heroin addicts received an injection of the same dose of morphine or of saline each day, Monday through Friday. The weekly dose changed unpredictably: each Monday brought its own adventure. After each injection, the subjects reported their subjective experience of the drug. Did they like it? How much drug had they been given? How much would they pay for it if it were sold on the street? Lamb and his colleagues were concerned especially with what happened on Thursdays and Fridays, after the addicts had several days' experience with a particular injection. On these days, the subjects had to "earn" their injection, if they wanted it, by pushing a lever three thousand times within forty-five minutes. The subjects did indeed work hard for every injection that contained any morphine at all. For the saline, they refused to work reliably. In their subjective reports, they described the morphine injections as "quite good," "contained drug," "worth paying money for," and so on—all except for the lowest dose of morphine (3.75 milligrams), which they described as equivalent to saline: worthless and empty, despite the fact that they had worked as hard for it as for any of the other morphine doses.

Drug addicts who work to obtain a threshold dose that they cannot subjectively detect, while unaware that they have preferentially chosen it, or who repeatedly press a bar to regain an experience they rate as "worthless," have something in com-

FIGURE 27.5   Unconscious Drug Reward

Conscious Subjective Awareness	Conscious belief: No drug	No conscious preference	No conscious pleasure

Dissociation

Unconscious Core Processes	**Core Predicted Utility** Detect drug-lever relation	**Core Decision Utility** Work to obtain drug ("Want")	**Core Experienced Utility** Unconscious drug reward ("Like")

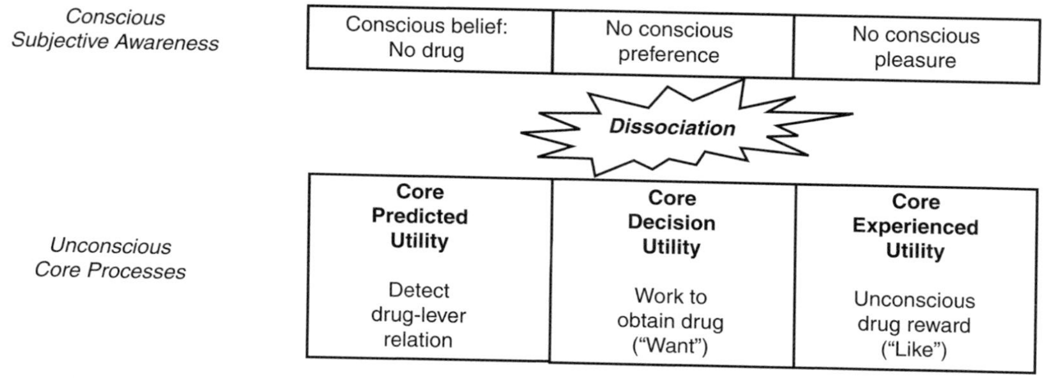

Notes: Dissociation of conscious drug-related emotion from the underlying unconscious core processes of "liking" and "wanting," based on the descriptions of Fischman and Foltin (1992) and Lamb et al. (1991). The dissociation of awareness from core processes applies to all three types of utility and is revealed in the behavior of addicts seeking a "below threshold" dose of cocaine or morphine. Although they may not be subjectively aware of the drug, they may nonetheless show behavioral evidence that they "like" it, "want" it, and act on their belief of how to get it.

mon with Hilgard's hypnotic subjects. The hypnotic subjects' hidden observers reported covert pain, while the subjects themselves reported they felt no subjective pain. Both cases give behavioral evidence of the existence of an emotional/motivational state that the conscious individuals deny having (figure 27.5).

Unfortunately for those who would study unconscious emotional processes, dramatic dissociations between subjective experience and objective emotional responses so far are limited to special cases such as hypnosis, subliminally brief events, and addicts exposed to threshold doses of drugs. Even these instances provide only sparse information, since investigators are not often theoretically prepared to deal with the dissociations they find between subjective report and behavioral manifestations of emotion. Further studies are needed. But while rare, the instances of unconscious emotional responses collected so far have an important consequence for psychological theory if we accept them as real. They contradict the idea that emotions are necessarily conscious states.

Summary

People often are not accurately aware of what they will like or want in the future, or of what they have liked or wanted in the past. There may even be special moments in which people are unaware of their own "likes," "dislikes," and "wants."

These dissociations indicate that emotional core processes are separable from the conscious experience we ordinarily think of as the entire emotion. Even those who believe that emotion is conscious by definition would probably accept that these examples reveal something that is crucial to an understanding of emotion. But although these instances of dissociation point to the existence of unconscious emotional processes, they tell us nothing about the nature of those processes.

MEASURING "LIKING" AND "WANTING" IN CREATURES THAT DON'T SPEAK

How can one study emotional core processes that are not accessible to conscious awareness? Psychologists typically measure emotions by asking people to say how they feel. But verbal reports of feelings may miss the very core processes we wish to examine. To explore psychological processes unrevealed in verbal report we also need measures that don't depend on introspection. These measures may be physiological or behavioral. What is necessary is a distinct relation between any measure we choose and underlying emotional processes.

Traditional psychological studies of emotion have focused on adult subjects who can describe their feelings. Human infants prior to language, or animals incapable of language, would be regarded by many to be poor subjects for studying emotion precisely because they cannot put their feelings into words. But this disadvantage vanishes if we switch our focus of interest to core processes of emotion. Lack of language is not a problem if the process of interest is essentially separate from subjective introspection and verbal report. Infants and animals may in fact be the best subjects for studying some basic aspects of core processes of emotion precisely because of their relative freedom from the many cultural factors that influence construction, expression, or inhibition of adult emotional reactions (Ellsworth 1994; Markus and Kitayama 1991; Ortony and Turner 1990).

Measurement of infant emotion poses a knotty problem to the psychologist but has perhaps been viewed as a more straightforward task, at least in certain respects, by countless generations of parents. Emotional processes find one expression in vocal and behavioral affective reactions. Crying, smiling, and other affective reactions that involve distinct patterns of facial and body responses can often give insight into underlying psychological states (Ekman 1992; James 1884). Even mildly emotional events, such as a pleasantly sweet taste or an unpleasantly strong bitter or salty taste, evoke distinctive affective reactions from human infants (Steiner 1973, 1974; Steiner 1979, figure 6).

The idea that emotions are revealed in behavioral affective reactions as well as in subjective reports is by no means new. Ribot (1897) wrote a century ago: "Every kind of emotion ought to be considered in this way: all that is objectively expressed by movements of the face and body, by vaso-motor, respiratory, and secretory disturbances, is expressed subjectively by correlative states of consciousness, classed by external observations according to their qualities. It is a single occurrence expressed in two languages" (112). Perhaps the reader will have concluded after all that an emotion is not necessarily a single unitary psychological process. But the two languages, objective affective movements/physiological reactions and subjective states/verbal reports, still both express something important about underlying emotional processes (LeDoux 1996; Panksepp 1991, 1992).

It is important to stress the limits of the case being made for the usefulness of affective reactions in the study of emotional processes. There is no implication of a one-to-one relation between affective expression and emotion as an experienced event. Affective expressions can be counterfeited or suppressed, especially by humans. Cultures may construct different configurations of emotional reaction. Many emotions may have no distinctive nonverbal expression. A single emotional reaction may occur in more than one emotional context. But these reservations merely define the border of our interpretive framework for studies of affective reaction. They do not rule out the usefulness of behavioral reactions for the study of emotional core processes.

Affective Reaction and Emotion in Animals

To the extent that we grant emotion to animals, our basis for doing so is likely to be precisely the same as for granting emotion to human infants: their affective reactions strike us in some ways as similar to our own (Darwin 1872; James 1884). Even theorists who believe that human emotions are primarily constructed from social and cultural frameworks still grant that animals share at least some emotions in common with us, based on their facial and other affective reactions to events: "So, for example, one may feel confident in attributing anger and fear to chimpanzees, cats, dogs, and even rats" (Ortony and Turner 1990, 321). The question for a social construction theorist is *which* emotions are shared and which are not.

From a "subcomponents of emotion" perspective, the real question is not *which* emotions we share with animals. Fear itself may not be a unitary phenomenon, to be considered simply present or absent. Even a simple pain or a simple pleasure may be different across species, across different people, and even across different occasions for a single person. This is because it contains multiple core components that may vary in balance. The real questions are: What core processes of emotion, taken as subcomponents, exist in animals, and how similar are they to our own emotional core processes? What is their psychological nature? What are their neural substrates and causes? Core processes of emotion may be shared with creatures that don't speak—infants and animals—even if the final emotion, as a composite event or subjective experience, is quite different in them than in us.

How can a core process of emotion be recognized? *Primarily by features that it shares with ordinary conscious emotion.* Even if unconscious, core processes of emotion must evaluate whether something is good or bad. They must respond qualitatively to the positive or negative nature of an event. They may be specific to a particular emotional category, such as fear, or to a particular

FIGURE 27.6   Facial Display of Hedonic Impact

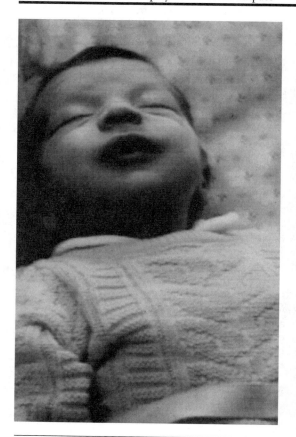 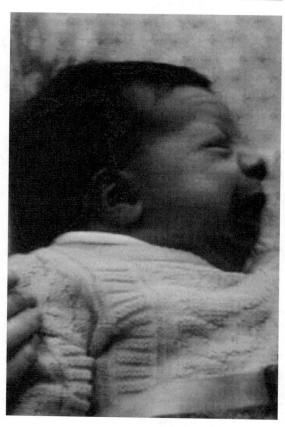

Notes: Affective expressions of a three-week infant to a sweet taste (left) and to an intensely salty taste. Observations collected by Harris, Booth, and Berridge; photo from Berridge (1996) following Steiner (1973).

type of encounter, such as a loved offspring, a painful injury, or a desired food. That minimal definition is all we have with which to begin. Beyond this, the identifying features of emotional core processes must be established on the basis of evidence. Rather than assert definitions a priori, we must look to experimental results for more detail about the defining features of emotional core processes. That is the goal of the remaining sections.

Conscious Emotion Versus Core Processes of "Emotion"

Despite shared features, there *is* an important difference between emotion as a subjective event and the core processes of emotion that may occur independent of subjective awareness and are revealed through behavioral or physiological measures. One is a conscious emotion, the other is not. It makes sense to distinguish between unconscious emotional core processes and conscious emotional experience, and not to call them by the same name. Perhaps we could agree to use unmodified words such as wants, likes, pains, and fears to denote the subjective emotional feelings. We distinguish these—with quotation marks—from mere "wants," "likes," "fears," "pains," and other unconscious core emotional processes, which, though behavior reveals them to exist and they share features with their subjective states, are not fully worthy of the traditional name (Berridge and Robinson 1995; Berridge 1996).

Core Processes of Positive Emotion in Animals

As conscious entities, we know what we mean by reward: something that is both liked and wanted. In our conscious experience of positive emotions, we want the things we like, and we like the things we want. Liking and wanting seem so closely entwined that we might almost regard the words as referring to the same basic emotion. But the underlying core processes of positive emotion may not fit into this familiar psychological category of reward. Instead, affective neuroscience studies indicate they can be broken apart into dissociable components. As a first approximation, these core processes can be called "liking" versus "wanting," although we will see that the actual processes may diverge from what is ordinarily meant by these familiar words.

Ever since the discovery that rats would learn to electrically stimulate an electrode implanted in "pleasure centers" in their brains, animal research on the brain substrates for pleasure and reward has been predicated on the postulate that animals, like us, often seek to repeat pleasurable events (Olds 1956; Olds and Milner 1954). The pleasure was inferred, correctly or not, from the observation that animals sought the stimulation. The brain mechanisms of positive emotion have been studied largely by posing questions to animals about the "decision utility" of emotional states. Whether a brain system mediates an animal's "liking" for a reward, in other words, has been approached primarily by answering the related question of whether it "wants" the reward: whether it will work to gain the reward. This approach has revealed many insights into the brain systems whose activation is rewarding in their own right, and that mediate the value of natural rewards such as food or sex (Fibiger, Phillips, and Brown 1992; Gallistel 1994; Hoebel 1988; Olds 1977; Panksepp 1991; Phillips et al. 1992; Shizgal 1997, this volume; Shizgal and Conover 1996; Smith 1995; Valenstein 1976; Wise 1989, 1996; Yeomans 1989). But it rests on the indirect inference of "liking" from "wanting."

Affective Expression of "Emotion"

A more direct measure of "emotion" such as "liking" is through affective reaction patterns. Animal affective reactions are often less intuitively obvious to us than our own. Yet many can be recognized. Chimpanzees and other primates, for example, show affective expressions to pleasant sweet tastes or unpleasant bitter ones that are in many ways similar to those of a human infant (Steiner and Glaser 1995; Steiner et al. 1999). Given a sweet drink of sugar water, the chimpanzee smacks its lips and reaches for more. Given a bitter drink, it screws up its face into a grimace and gape. Animals other than primates have affective expressions less like ours. But even so apparently unpromising a subject as the rat, an omnivore like us that prefers sweet and fatty foods and dislikes bitter ones, emits distinctive facial and body affective expressions that mirror human and primate affective reactions to tastes (Grill and Berridge 1985; Grill and Norgren 1978b). Sweet tastes elicit a hedonic pattern of reactions such as tongue protrusions—sort of a licking of lips—paw licking, and related movements (figure 27.7). Bitter tastes elicit an aversive pattern of different expressions such as gapes, headshakes, and frantic wiping of the mouth.

There are several reasons to believe that affective reactions of rats to food reflect core processes of emotion similar to those of human pleasure and displeasure (Berridge 1996). One is that they share some expressive movements with equivalent human emotional expressions (such as gape to bitterness). Another is that they fluctuate in similar ways as human subjective pleasure as circumstances change. Human emotional ratings of food pleasure or displeasure can be altered by physiological factors such as hunger or satiety and by psychological factors such as learned aversions or food preferences (Cabanac 1979; Rozin and Schulkin 1990). The affective reaction of rats to taste can be altered by the same sets of physiological and psychological factors. The changes in the animal behavior match the changes in human reports of subjective pleasure (Berridge 1996; Grill and Berridge 1985).

For example, an extremely salty taste such as seawater is ordinarily perceived as unpleasant by humans, and it elicits aversive patterns from rats. But salt elicits hedonic patterns if a rat is in a physiological state of sodium depletion, which produces salt appetite (Berridge et al. 1984; Schulkin 1991), a state in which humans would also find salt to be more pleasant (Beauchamp et al. 1990). A milder enhancement of food palatability similarly accompanies ordinary hunger and is evident in both human reports and animal affective reactions (Berridge 1991; Cabanac 1979; Cabanac and Lafrance 1990). In the opposite direction, pleasure can be changed to distaste. For example, humans often form aversions to the taste of novel foods that have been accompanied by visceral illness (Rozin and Schulkin 1990). They subsequently find the food to be subjectively unpalatable despite having liked it before. Similarly, a rat that emits a hedonic pattern to a novel sweet taste that is followed by visceral illness will switch to

FIGURE 27.7   Animal Display of Hedonic Impact

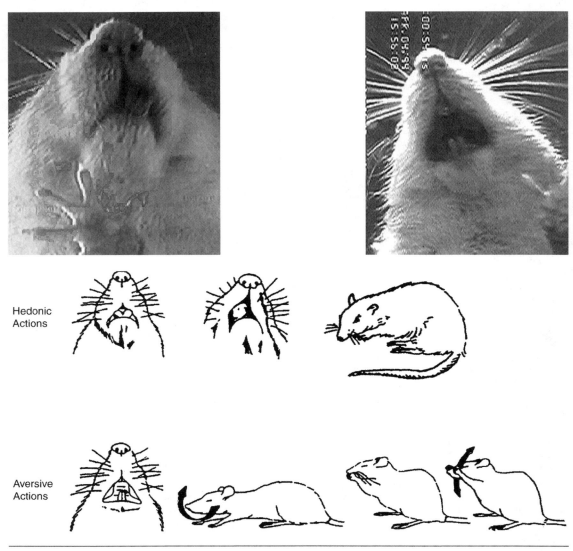

Notes: Affective expressions of rats to sweet and bitter tastes. Hedonic "liking" patterns include tongue protrusion to a sweet taste (left photograph), lateral tongue protrusion, and paw lick (drawing). Aversive "disliking" patterns include gape (right photograph), headshake, face wash, and forelimb flail (drawing). Drawing after Grill and Norgren (1978a).

aversive expressions to future presentations (Grill and Norgren 1978a).

The correspondence between human subjective pleasure or displeasure and animal/infant affective reactions suggests that they share a core process of hedonic or aversive evaluation (Berridge 1996). This correspondence need not imply that the conscious experience of emotion is also the same. Sometimes it is plausible that they correspond: in the case of an ordinary human infant or adult chimpanzee, many observers might be willing to grant conscious emotions similar to our own. Some might extend this to a rat. But sometimes it is implausible to posit consciousness as an accompaniment to the core emotional processes reflected in affective reactions. For example, anencephalic human infants, who have been born without any forebrain at all, still show both positive and negative affective reactions to presentation of sweet and bitter tastes during their brief lives (Steiner 1973). Similarly, "decerebrate" rats that possess only a brain stem and no forebrain retain a basic capacity to show positive and negative reactions appropriately to sweet and bitter tastes (Grill and Norgren 1978a; Grill and Norgren 1978c). Few would be willing to posit any conscious experience recognizable to us to an anencephalic infant or a decerebrate rat. Still, core processes of evaluation demonstrably exist in such creatures, although they are simpler in behavioral manifestations than the corresponding processes in their full-brained counterparts (Grill and Berridge 1985). Behavioral reactions provide windows into core processes of "wanting" and "liking" that are basically independent of whether the core process is accompanied by subjective emotional experience.

Neural Systems of "Liking" and "Disliking"

Core processes of emotion can be powerfully altered by manipulations of the brain. These can be done painlessly on rats in which the necessary

preparations are made while they are anesthetized. Brain manipulations typically change both "liking" and "wanting" core processes of reward together (figure 27.8). One example comes from brain lesions that produce "aphagia"—the pathological failure to eat. The most famous brain region related to appetite and food reward is the lateral hypothalamus and adjacent zones, where lesions have long been known to abolish normal feeding (Teitelbaum and Epstein 1962). Aphagia can lead to starvation unless the individual is artificially fed. (That is always done in contemporary studies.)

Food is not merely "unwanted" after such lesions, it is also "disliked." The aphagia is driven by a dramatic emotional shift. If a normally delicious sweet food is placed in the mouth of the rat, it elicits the complete set of aversive reactions normally reserved for bitter tastes (Cromwell and Berridge 1993; Schallert and Whishaw 1978; Stellar, Brooks, and Mills 1979; Teitelbaum and Epstein 1962). By mapping the brain region involved, my former student Howard Cromwell discovered that the location where neuron destruction produces the emotional shift is actually outside the hypothal-

FIGURE 27.8   Brain Substrates of Food "Liking"

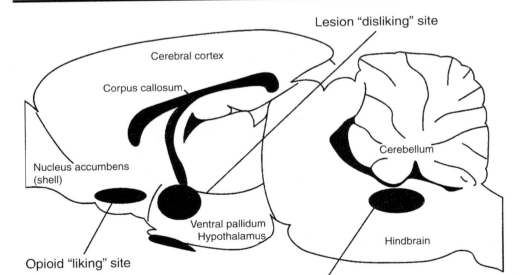

Notes: Brain substrates of food "liking." These include the ventral pallidum site, where damage produces "disliking" or aversion even for sweet tastes; the shell of the nucleus accumbens site, where opioid stimulation by morphine enhances food "liking," and the brain-stem region, where benzodiazepine/GABA stimulation also enhances food liking. Each manipulation of "liking" changes food "wanting" secondarily. See Berridge (1996) for review. Brain atlas based on Paxinos and Watson (1996).

amus, within a structure immediately above and in front of it called the ventral pallidum (Cromwell and Berridge 1993). This is the only site in the brain, as far as I know, where a small lesion can reverse the emotional response to an event from "liking" to "disliking." In a rat brain, it is roughly the size and shape of a dried pea. In the human brain, its size might presumably be closer to that of a larger fresh pea.

Neurotransmitters of "Liking"

Drugs can be potent emotional stimuli. Taking recreational drugs that stimulate brain neurotransmitter systems (cocaine, heroin, etc.) is perhaps the only direct physiological manipulation of the brain that people in substantial numbers are willing to practice on themselves. Pharmacological manipulations of the brain can change "liking" and "wanting" together, just as brain lesions can. But the special feature of some drugs is to shift emotion in the *positive* direction, activating the "liking" and "wanting" components of reward themselves and potentiating the hedonic impact of other events.

Appetite, or "wanting" for food, can be enhanced by a number of drugs, administered either directly to the brain or systemically to the entire body. For example, eating is stimulated by drugs that activate opioid neurotransmitter receptors, such as morphine (Gosnell 1987; Stanley, Lanthier, and Leibowitz 1989). Eating is also stimulated by drugs, such as diazepam (Valium), that facilitate gamma-amino-butyric-acid (GABA) neurotransmission by activating benzodiazepine receptors that are attached to GABA receptors (Berridge and Peciña 1995; Cooper, Higgs, and Clifton 1995). The effects have been best documented in animal studies but appear to occur for humans, too (Drewnowski et al. 1995; Kelly et al. 1992).

Hedonic "liking" for food also can be facilitated by opioid and benzodiazepine drugs. In animals, opioid and benzodiazepine drugs potently enhance hedonic reaction patterns to sweet tastes (Berridge and Treit 1986; Doyle, Berridge, and Gosnell 1993; Gray and Cooper 1995; Parker 1995; Parker et al. 1992). Human subjective palatability ratings are also changed by drugs relevant to opioid neurotransmitter receptors (Drewnowski et al. 1995).

Hedonic enhancement of "liking" occurs even if the opioid or benzodiazepine drugs are delivered directly to the brain of rats by microinjection (Berridge and Peciña 1995; Peciña and Berridge 1995,

1996a). In such a study, the drug is dissolved in a droplet almost too small to be seen by the naked eye, and the tiny droplet flows painlessly into the desired structure of the brain. The droplet is delivered through a permanent microinjection cannula that was implanted on an earlier day while the rat was anesthetized. Minutes after the microinjection, a sweet or other-tasting solution is infused into the rat's mouth, typically for a minute or so, and elicits enhanced hedonic reactions that can be videotaped for later slow-motion analysis (Berridge and Peciña 1995).

Microinjection "mapping" studies have helped identify particular hedonic regions of the brain where benzodiazepine and opioid drugs enhance the emotional response to foods (see figure 27.8). They have showed that neural systems of hedonic processing are distributed throughout the entire extent of the brain, from front to back. For example, an opioid drug like morphine appears to be most effective at enhancing "liking" and "wanting" for food in a small paired region near the base of the front of the brain, called the shell of the nucleus accumbens (Peciña and Berridge 1996b). The left and right members of this pair of sites are shaped a bit like short celery stalks, running lengthwise through the brain (front to back), with their inner concave surfaces facing each other. Microinjections of morphine into the sites enhance hedonic reactions to sweet taste and elicit feeding, whereas injections in nearby surrounding regions fail to do so (Peciña and Berridge 1996b).

By contrast, neural systems responsible for "liking" and consequent "wanting" enhancement by benzodiazepine drugs are contained in the posterior hindbrain. If forebrain systems are disconnected by decerebration, leaving the brain stem to make basic evaluations on its own, a benzodiazepine drug still potentiates positive reactions made by the decerebrate rat to sweet tastes (Berridge 1988). Also, microinjections of a benzodiazepine drug into an ordinary rat's brain elicit more feeding and enhance hedonic reactions to taste more effectively when placed in brain-stem sites than when placed in the forebrain (Higgs and Cooper 1994; Peciña and Berridge 1996a).

Brain systems of food "liking" are thus distributed throughout the entire length of the brain, perhaps as a vertically arranged set of layers. Ordinarily, the layers function together as a single system in a hierarchical fashion (Grill and Berridge 1985). If upper layers are stripped away, the lower ones continue to operate at least to a degree. The core processes of isolated lower substrates still share some evaluative features with ordinary emo-

FIGURE 27.9   Conceptual Dissociation of Decision Utility from Experienced Utility by Manipulation of Dopamine Brain Systems

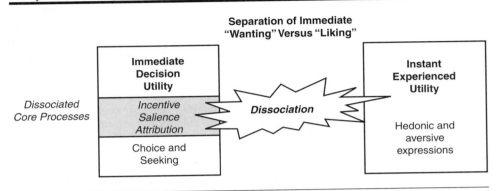

tion, though the features are fewer and less flexible than when all layers are present, and they almost certainly do not include consciousness. If affect can be "free-floating," as pleasure not assigned to a particular object, it may be in part because the neural instantiation of "liking" is distributed widely, including brain-stem systems incapable of representing events as targets. By contrast, "wanting" may always have an object of desire. And "wanting" is mediated by forebrain systems tied to representations of objects and events.

"Wanting" Without "Liking"

In contrast to the brain manipulations that simultaneously change "liking" and "wanting" together, there is a different group of brain manipulations whose effect is selective to "wanting" alone (figures 27.9 and 27.10). These change "wanting" as measured by instrumental goal-directed behavior and voluntary eating—they cause individuals either to seek out food and other rewards and to consume them, or to abandon rewarded tasks and

FIGURE 27.10   Brain Substrates of "Wanting"

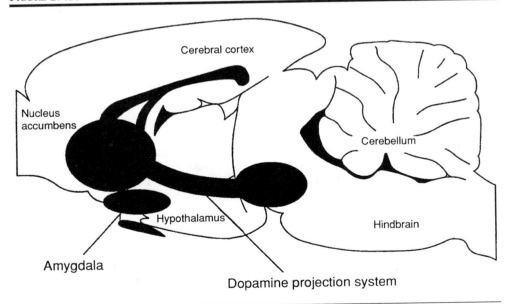

Notes: Sites include the ascending dopamine projection from midbrain to nucleus accumbens, where stimulation induces "wanting" without "liking," and where lesions eliminate decision utility without impairing experienced utility or predicted utility, and the amygdala nuclei, where lesions disrupt the elicitation of fear or reward by particular stimuli (see Berridge 1996).

refuse food when given it. But they do *not* change "liking" for that food reward, as measured by hedonic or aversive expressions, in the same individuals. This group of brain manipulations includes hypothalamic stimulation, drugs that act on dopamine receptors or on dopamine release, and 6-hydroxydopamine lesions that selectively destroy neurons that contain dopamine. All of these act on the massive projections of dopamine neurons that stretch from the midbrain to the forebrain, often called the mesolimbic or mesoaccumbens dopamine system (see Hoebel, this volume; Shizgal, this volume). This neural system appears to be a neural common denominator or substrate shared in common by most manipulations that alter "wanting" without changing "liking."

Even hypothalamic stimulation, a potent motivational elicitor, acts in part via this same ascending neural system. Brief pulses of hypothalamic stimulation can be a powerful reward—animals and people will work in order to get them (Hoebel 1976; Olds and Milner 1954; Sem-Jacobsen 1976; Shizgal and Conover 1996; Shizgal, this volume). If stimulation is given freely, especially in sustained bursts, it also has motivating properties. Free stimulation of the lateral hypothalamus can motivate animals or people to eat or to engage in sex, aggression, or another behavior (Glickman and Schiff 1967; Sem-Jacobsen 1976; Valenstein 1976). Which behavior is elicited depends in part on preexisting features of the individual, in part on the electrode placement and other stimulation parameters, and in part on the type of experiences the individual has had previously with hypothalamic stimulation (Valenstein 1976). Dopamine neurons appear to be a crucial link in the chain of causal events responsible for the motivational and rewarding effects of hypothalamic stimulation (Hoebel 1988; Valenstein 1976; Wise 1996; Yeomans 1989).

An early interpretation had been that electrode-induced motivation could be explained by the electrode-induced reward (Hoebel 1988; Olds 1977; Olds and Milner 1954; Wise 1982a). In other words, the pleasure of food, sex, and so on, might be enhanced while the stimulation was on, and that could be a reason the motivated behavior was displayed during stimulation. In a contemporary version of this hypothesis, Shizgal (this volume) suggests that a rewarding electrode evokes high "instantaneous utility," the same psychological concept of instant experienced utility developed by Kahneman and his colleagues (Kahneman 1994; Kahneman, this volume; Kahneman et al.

1997). Instantaneous utility in this sense means the hedonic intensity of the event and also its capacity to generate action to instigate the event (and to resist interruption). Instantaneous utility thus consists of a single global evaluation of current reward intensity, which encompasses both hedonic evaluation and goal-directed action (Shizgal, this volume).

If global enhancement of instant experienced utility were the full story, such brain stimulation should elicit both "wanting" and "liking" for a reward, just as opiate and benzodiazepine microinjections do. But Elliot Valenstein and I have found evidence that "liking" and "wanting" are probably not both activated by brain stimulation of the lateral hypothalamus that evoked eating (Berridge and Valenstein 1991). In our study, rats were allowed to eat or not as they chose during hypothalamic stimulation. Stimulation-induced motivation becomes increasingly stronger with repeated experiences, and after receiving a half-hour of this for several days, many rats became "reliable stimulation-bound eaters." Those rats began to eat as soon as the hypothalamic electrode was turned on, and they stopped eating when the stimulation went off. Once it was clear that stimulation made these rats "want" food, they were tested to see whether the stimulation also made them "like" it more. In order to do that, their affective reactions were videotaped as a sugary solution was infused into their mouths. As the infusion continued, hypothalamic stimulation was turned on for fifteen seconds at a time, interspersed with equal pauses when it was turned off. The sugar infusion remained steady whether stimulation was on or off (since otherwise the rats would have consumed more when the stimulation was on, making it difficult to compare "liking" across the two conditions). Our results surprisingly contradicted the hypothesis that hypothalamic stimulation made rats "want" food by making them "like" it more. Hypothalamic stimulation never enhanced hedonic reactions of rats to sweetness, even though it made the same rats eat avidly. On the contrary, hypothalamic stimulation elevated *aversive* reactions to sweet solutions. Hypothalamic stimulation appeared to make rats "*dislike*" sweetness somewhat rather than "like" it more, but it still made them "want" to eat despite their enhanced "dislike." Cooling the hypothalamus rather than electrically stimulating it can also induce a similar phenomenon of "wanting" food without "liking" it (Berridge and Zajonc 1991; incidentally supporting a hypothesis proposed by Zajonc that focal brain temperature changes may cause fluctuations in an aspect of positive emotion; see, for example, Zajonc, Murphy, and Inglehart 1989).

Selective Suppression of "Wanting" by Drugs

The mirror image of "wanting" without "liking," namely "liking" without "wanting," can be obtained by suppressing brain dopamine systems. Drugs that block receptors for dopamine, such as haloperidol or pimozide, suppress the incentive value of many rewards (Smith 1995; Wise 1982b, 1994; Yeomans 1989). Such drugs cause animals to refuse to work, whether the reward is food, hypothalamic stimulation, cocaine, or something else. Although the drugs produce motor impairment, too, many investigators believe the reduced willingness to work reflects a distinct motivational deficit. In other words, they reduce the decision utility or "wanting" for such rewards.

But perhaps surprisingly, such drugs do not shift "liking" for the same rewards. Studies of affective taste reactivity aimed at measuring the "liking" for a palatable taste have converged upon the conclusion that dopamine-blocking drugs leave hedonic processes unchanged (Peciña, Berridge, and Parker, 1997; Treit and Berridge 1990). Dopamine receptor blockers fail to shift hedonic expressions to a sweet food or to replace them with aversive reactions, even though they reduce the motivation to eat.

Eliminating "Wanting" for Still "Liked" Rewards

The most dramatic dissociation of "wanting" from "liking" is to eliminate one while preserving the other. Decision utility ("wanting") can be abolished—not merely reduced—while preserving experienced utility ("liking") unchanged, by selective neurochemical lesions that destroy the dopamine system. Many of the aphagia and adipsia symptoms of lateral hypothalamic lesions can be reproduced by microinjections of the neurotoxin 6-hydroxydopamine. In these experiments, the chemical neurotoxin is delivered directly to dopamine neurons while a rat is anesthetized. If particular procedures are followed, the neurotoxin destroys neurons that release dopamine as their neurotransmitter, but it leaves all other neurons healthy. These lesions produce movement deficits, but the aphagia of dopamine disruption cannot be fully explained on the basis of impaired movement alone (Smith 1995). After recovery from their op-

eration, rats that have had 6-hydroxydopamine lesions seem uninterested in food, water, or any other reward. Even if surrounded by mountains of tasty food, they will voluntarily starve to death unless someone regularly feeds them by intubation, even though they seem able to make the limited movements needed to eat.

Such absolute indifference to reward might be explained if the neurotoxin rendered the brain unable to have any reward experience: complete anhedonia. But the rats do not appear to be anhedonic. Despite showing no "wants" whatsoever, rats with 6-hydroxydopamine lesions seem to have normal "likes." We've found that if tastes are infused into their mouths, such rats show normal hedonic reactions to sweet tastes and normal aversive reactions to bitter ones (Berridge and Robinson 1998; Berridge, Venier, and Robinson 1989). These rats are even capable of adjusting their *expected* utility value for particular food by learning about its consequences; that is, they can acquire new "likes" or "dislikes." For example, they learn taste aversions in a normal fashion when a new taste comes to predict visceral illness. If presented with a novel sweet taste, these rats show hedonic reactions, as normal rats do. But if the initial sweet taste is then followed associatively on several occasions by visceral illness, induced by injection of lithium chloride, then rats with dopamine lesions respond to it with aversive reactions on future encounters (Berridge and Robinson, 1998). Taste aversion conditioning switches the *experienced* utility ("liking") of the taste to aversive—reflected by affective expressions—via a change in its *expected* utility or predicted value derived from past associative learning. Both experienced and expected utility apparently remain normal after dopamine loss. Only *decision* utility, or "wanting," appears to be destroyed by the dopamine lesion—reflected by normal intake, preference, instrumental commerce with rewards, and so on—whereas "liking" remains perfectly normal and intact.

The Nature of "Wanting": Attribution of Incentive Salience

I have argued that there is a fracture line of separation between the psychological core processes of "liking" and "wanting." However closely tied together liking and wanting seem in our conscious lives, they are essentially different core processes, with different neural substrates. But what is the *nature* of an unconscious core process such as "wanting"? The word "wanting" is a convenient label to highlight the dissociation, but it does not tell us much about defining properties.

My colleagues and I have suggested that "wanting" is best viewed as a kind of hybrid core process that combines motivational, associative, and perceptual features. This process transforms the representation within the brain of external stimuli and events. The transformation, which is altered by dopamine manipulations, imbues forebrain representations of objects and events with *incentive salience*. Attribution of incentive salience enables an event to grab attention and to be perceived as attractive, making it a sought-after incentive in its own right (Berridge 1989, 1996; Berridge and Valenstein 1991; Robinson and Berridge 1993).

We posit incentive salience attribution to be one step in a three-step process of reward (figure 27.11), after hedonic activation and the association of an outside event with hedonic activation (Berridge 1996; Berridge and Valenstein 1991; Robinson and Berridge 1993). Incentive salience attribution is mediated in part by neural activity in dopamine-accumbens brain systems, activity that is triggered by subsequent encounters with incentive stimuli or by their cognitive representations. Although stimulus-linked, incentive salience is not merely *sensory* salience. It also enables the attributed stimulus or its representation to elicit approach and to become the target of desire and goal-directed strategies. When translated into conscious awareness, incentive salience may give rise to a subjective experience of wanting or craving. But the core process can occur independently of consciousness—as we saw in the examples described earlier of addicts unconsciously seeking drugs (Berridge 1996; Fischman and Foltin 1992; Lamb et al. 1991). That means its properties may in some ways be studied most directly via behavioral and neurophysiological measures (Berridge 1996; Phillips et al. 1992; Robinson and Berridge 1993).

Perceptual Transformation Aspects of Incentive Salience

The brain structures most strongly linked to incentive salience attributions are those that receive extensive dopamine projections: neostriatum and nucleus accumbens, amygdala, and frontal cortex. These are not primary "sensory" brain structures, but they nonetheless receive massive sensory inputs from the cortex and other sources (Lidsky, Manetto, and Schneider 1985). The motivational effects of hypothalamic stimulation, which act in part via these neurons (Yeomans 1989), depend strongly on the sensory qualities of available targets (Valenstein 1976). The sensory-embedded nature of stimulation-elicited motivation is so marked that a visual signal for food may be effective in motivating behavior when seen through the eye that relays directly to the stimulated side of the brain, but not when seen through the other eye (Beagley and Holley 1977).

Viewed by the use of neurophysiological techniques that monitor neural activation, many neurons in the nucleus accumbens and neostriatum, as well as some dopamine neurons that project to them, are activated by sensory stimuli—especially if the stimuli have important motivational significance, such as the sight of a tasty morsel that the animal expects to receive (Aosaki, Graybiel, and Kimura 1994; Phillips et al. 1993; Schultz, Dayan, and Montague 1997). I believe the activation of a subset of these neurons in the nucleus accumbens and related sites reflects the attribution of incentive salience to the perceived stimulus. Presumably memories or cognitive representations of incentive events might achieve activation of the same neurons, even in the absence of the physical stimulus. The psychological core process of "wanting" may thus be embodied in identifiable neural events (see Berridge and Robinson [1998] for more discussion of the neural mediation of incentive salience).

It is worth noting that the nature of this core "wanting" process spans traditional psychological categories, such as emotion and perception, and perhaps other categories, too. Incentive salience is a psychological "building block" whose identity would not be anticipated by existing theories of emotion or motivation. Its psychological importance has been revealed by biopsychological manipulations of the brain and observation of their effects on behavior.

Addiction and Sensitization: Dissociated Wanting Run Amok

The hypothesis of incentive salience or "wanting," separate from "liking" and mediated in part by dopamine neural projections, has special application to understanding drug addiction (Berridge and Robinson 1995; Robinson and Berridge 1993). For an addict, drugs of abuse have enormous decision utility. They are powerfully wanted and sought—often at great risk and great cost. The question is, why? Of course, drugs may have been pleasant to an addict in the past, and they can also alleviate withdrawal symptoms. But drug pleasure and withdrawal are probably not sufficient explanations for addiction. Euphoric drugs are sought

FIGURE 27.11   Three Stages of Normal Reward—Incentive Salience Model

Stage 1. Hedonic Activation by Unconditioned Stimulus

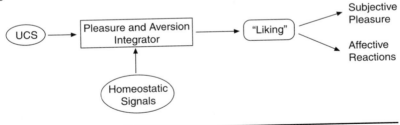

Stage 2. Associative Learning (Conditioned Stimulus–Unconditioned Stimulus trace)

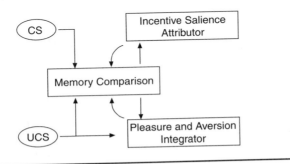

Stage 3. Incentive Salience to Conditioned Stimulus

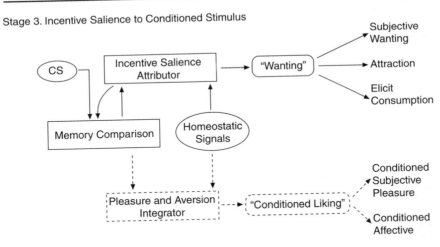

Notes: (1) Hedonic pleasure ("liking") acts as the normal trigger for reward. Hedonic neural systems activate the associative and incentive salience steps. "Liking" by itself is free-floating and not sufficient to motivate goal-directed behavior. (2) Associative learning systems are needed to correlate the representation of external objects and events (conditioned stimuli) with hedonic activation. Associative neural systems are separate from those of "liking" and "wanting." (3) Incentive salience is subsequently attributed to conditioned stimuli or their representations by dopamine-related systems, making these stimuli attractive and "wanted." The attributed stimulus acts as an incentive to elicit action and direct motivated behavior.

by addicts even when the available dose is so low or so poor in quality that it can't be expected to give much pleasure. Some addictive drugs, such as nicotine, are not especially euphoric even for people who are addicted. Life for an addict cannot be described as a series of overwhelming pleasures, even when drugs can be had. Hence, pleasure often is not a compelling explanation of addiction.

Similarly, the avoidance of painful withdrawal does not fully explain addiction. Even after an addict has successfully finished withdrawal, addiction often remains a problem. Relapse is a common fate for the graduates of detoxification programs, and addicts who do give up their drug may attest that the struggle did not end with the last pang of withdrawal. Neither pleasure seeking nor pain avoidance provide a fully satisfactory explanation of addiction, even combined (for more discussion of their explanatory inadequacy, see Robinson and Berridge 1993). In other words, the decision utility of a drug for an addict may have strength beyond both its experienced utility or predicted utility. Why?

There may be a straightforward reason. Many addictive drugs, such as cocaine, amphetamine, heroin, and their synthetic derivatives, produce *neural sensitization* of brain dopamine systems if the drug is taken repeatedly (Robinson and Becker 1986). The baseline activity rate of a sensitized neural system may be normal, but the neurons are hyper-reactive to a triggering stimulus. Sensitized hyper-responding is elicited by another dose of the drug itself but also appears to involve associative learning about stimuli and contexts that have been paired with the drug (Anagnostaras and Robinson 1996; Robinson and Berridge 1993). The associative focus of sensitized incentive salience on drug stimuli and the act of drug taking may be the reason an addict's intense "wanting" is directed specifically toward drugs. Once induced, neural sensitization lasts for a long time—much longer than withdrawal symptoms—and possibly for a lifetime (Paulson, Camp, and Robinson 1991).

My colleague Terry Robinson and I have suggested an *incentive-sensitization theory* of addiction, which incorporates these points. It hypothesizes that neural sensitization of dopamine-related systems occurs in addicts, and that it is responsible for the compulsive nature of drug use in addiction (Berridge and Robinson 1995; Robinson and Berridge 1993). Neural sensitization of incentive salience systems, coupled with associative control of its expression, causes excessive attribution of incentive salience to the act of taking drugs, and to

drug-related stimuli and contexts. Drugs become excessively and compulsively "wanted," irrespective of whether they are "liked," and irrespective of whether withdrawal is happening. Addicts, by this view, are much like a rat under hypothalamic stimulation: forced to "want" whether or not they "like" drugs. Paradoxically, if this incentive-sensitization theory of addiction is true, it means that psychological therapies are likely to remain the most effective treatments for addiction for some time. Medication holds less hope, at least for now, because neural sensitization is not reversible by any known physiological or pharmacological means.

Summary

Behavioral affective reactions provide a means of studying core processes of emotion that are not accessible by subjective report. Our biopsychological studies indicate that simple positive emotion has separable core processes of "liking" and "wanting." These psychological components appear to be mediated by different brain systems. The core processes of "wanting" and "liking" typically cohere, but they can be dissociated from each other, as well as from conscious awareness, under some conditions. The compulsive craving of drugs in addiction may be caused by the neural sensitization of the dissociated "wanting" component of incentive salience. For addicts, this may cause drug craving independently of drug pleasure or withdrawal. "Wanting" thus takes on a life of its own and becomes focused on drugs. Whether this account of drug addiction applies also to other types of addictions remains for now an open and unexplored question.

DISSOCIATION OF CORE PROCESSES OF NEGATIVE EMOTION: PAIN, FEAR, AND ANXIETY

Negative states such as pain and fear seem totally different to conscious awareness from positive liking and wanting. But these psychological polar opposites share more in common than one might expect. For example, although we have focused on the role of ascending dopamine systems in positive "wanting," dopamine systems also are needed for at least some types of avoidance behavior motivated by conditioned fear (Salamone 1994).

At the most abstract level, liking versus wanting might be equivalent to a distinction between an immediate feeling versus doing something about it (and the feeling that accompanies anticipatory doing). Bolles and Fanselow (1980) once suggested that a similar relationship holds between pain and fear. Pain is an affective state, an unconditioned response, a type of experienced utility. Fear or anxiety might be viewed in part as a conditioned or anticipatory response to pain, a type of decision utility similar to the relation of wanting to liking.

In this final section of the chapter, I wish to directly compare positive emotion and negative emotion. My goal is to demonstrate two similarities between them. First, simple negative emotions such as fear can be broken apart into dissociated psychological core processes, just as positive emotions can. This is seen most clearly after brain manipulations. Second, one of the component core processes of negative emotion may overlap to a surprising degree with the core process of "wanting" in positive emotion.

The Anatomy of Fear and Anxiety

A set of fearful affective reactions are evoked from rats by presentation of a sound or other stimulus that predicts a painful event, such as startle, tense freezing, or elevation of heart rate and blood pressure (Davis 1992; LeDoux 1992, this volume; Maren and Fanselow 1996). Conditioned fear reactions are eliminated by several types of brain lesions. Some lesions are relatively uninteresting from the emotional point of view because they simply eliminate sites of auditory processing: the inferior colliculus of the midbrain brain stem, or the medial geniculate nucleus of the thalamus. Other sites in which lesions block conditioned fear are psychologically more interesting, and chief among these is the amygdala.

The neural signal for a sound ascends the brain in two directions relevant to fear from the auditory relay of the thalamus. One goes to the auditory cerebral cortex, and the other to the basolateral complex of the amygdala. Lesions of the auditory neocortex block "old" fears that were conditioned to a sound before the lesion was made (LeDoux 1992). But *new* fearful conditioned reactions to sound can still be acquired based on new learning. One interpretation of this observation has been that fear *ordinarily* is learned through a neocortical pathway but can be diverted to a secondary route after brain damage. A different interpretation would be that cortical sensory lesions change the brain's encoding and *perception* of the stimulus and hence disrupt recognition of sounds previ-

ously experienced before the lesion. In either case, fear responses can still be acquired after sensory cortex lesions.

Lesions of the amygdala disrupt the acquisition of new fears, as well as "old" fear to previously trained sounds or places (Davis 1992; Killcross, Robbins, and Everitt 1997; LeDoux 1996, this volume; Maren and Fanselow 1996). They do this even though the neocortex may remain perfectly intact. The same disruption can be produced if the lesion is made smaller and limited to only a portion of the amygdala: either the *basolateral complex* (which receives most of the auditory input from the medial geniculate of the thalamus mentioned earlier) or the *central nucleus* of the amygdala (to which the basolateral nucleus in turn sends its own information). Either lesion disrupts fear conditioning nearly as much as both together. Lesions of the amygdala disrupt many types of fear conditioning in animals and humans (Bechara et al. 1995; LeDoux 1996, this volume; Scott et al. 1997). Thus, at first sight, the amygdala might be taken to mediate the emotion of fear.

Anxiety

Unfamiliar situations can evoke anxiety, which is often viewed as similar to fear, but more diffuse, and is also linked to the amygdala. Ordinary rats and mice, for example, tend to be shy of new places, as expressed by their tendency to avoid elevated and exposed places. These avoidance tendencies are often reduced by amygdala lesions (Davis 1992). Many human children are shy of new situations, too. Individual human children markedly differ in the degree to which unfamiliar situations evoke anxiety and inhibition, and these differences may persist in later life (Kagan and Snidman 1991; Schwartz, Snidman, and Kagan 1996). The persistence of individual human differences in global reactivity, especially to stressful situations, from the earliest months of life through many years later has led Kagan and his colleagues to suggest that these differences may reflect stable underlying neurobiological variations (related to their amygdala) between children.

It has been argued that agitated, or melancholic, depression, which is often accompanied by anxiety, involves a similar brain dysfunction. Jay Schulkin has suggested an explanation that posits the amygdala to be chronically overactivated in such patients, owing to elevation of the glucocorticoid stress hormones that stimulate it (Schulkin 1994). Animal experiments show that corticotropin releasing factor in the amygdala enhances fearful reactions (Schulkin, McEwen, and Gold 1994). Schulkin posits that constant stimulation of this amygdala system in humans who are prone to melancholic depression (for reasons that are not yet clear) may cause their elevated levels of continual vigilance, anxiety, and fear.

Dissociations of Fear: Not a Unitary Emotion?

Taken at face value, the considerations discussed in the preceding section could lead one to conclude that the amygdala generates fearful states as elemental emotions. But it would be too simple to equate amygdala activation with fear. Closer examination shows that fear is not eliminated as a unitary state by amygdala damage. Instead the emotion is fractionated, appearing in some situations but not in others.

For instance, monkeys that fail to show fearful reactions to many frightening events after bilateral amygdala lesions nonetheless still show fear to especially strong stimuli (Kling and Brothers 1992). After the conditioned fear of rats is "eliminated" by amygdala lesions, it can still be reinstated by additional retraining (Kim and Davis 1993). In a striking series of dissociations, Treit and his colleagues found that amygdala lesions suppressed rats' avoidance of a shock-associated object but *failed* to suppress their avoidance of high open platforms (Treit, Pesold, and Rotzinger 1993). To suppress the latter, lesions needed to be made in a different forebrain structure, the septum. A further dissociation between *subtypes of fear* was found when microinjections of a benzodiazepine tranquilizer, midazolam, were placed in particular subnuclei of the amygdala itself. Microinjections limited to the central nucleus suppressed object avoidance but not elevated platform avoidance, whereas basolateral nucleus microinjections produced the opposite pattern of suppression (Pesold and Treit 1995).

Why is fear or anxiety suppressed in some situations but not in others? One possibility is that there are qualitatively distinct subtypes of fear and anxiety, each mediated by its own neural system. Several authors have suggested that such dissociations reflect the elimination of some subtypes of fear but not others, or that they may eliminate essential fear while leaving more elaborate cognitive or behavior reactions to danger (Kagan and Schulkin 1995; Killcross et al. 1997; LeDoux 1996). However, it is difficult to specify the psychological features of the different fear subtypes (beyond merely describing the situations in which fear re-

sponses do or do not occur after brain damage) or to say why, for example, fearful freezing or startle should reflect "real fear" more essentially than fearful escape or avoidance measures. An alternative to positing multiple subtypes of fear, and trying to define which is lost after brain damage, is to entertain the possibility that lesions of amygdala nuclei do not result in loss of *any* subtype of fear as a distinct psychological category. *Instead, they may alter other psychological core processes that are not fear but ordinarily help trigger it in particular situations.* The nature of these psychological processes, of course, remains to be elucidated, but there are clues about their features in existing evidence.

Human Case Study of Fear After Amygdala Lesions

A glimpse into the nature of these psychological processes comes from studies of human patients who have suffered brain damage. Adolphs, Tranel, Damasio, and Damasio (1995), for example, describe the case of a woman who lost most of her right and left amygdala owing to a genetic disease that induced calcification of brain tissue. When asked to identify the emotional expression of facial portraits, she failed to describe fearful ones as "afraid." She successfully identified happy, angry, disgusted, sad, and, to some extent, surprised facial expressions. Expressions that ordinary control subjects considered to be fearful, this woman instead described as surprised or angry. The woman never assigned high ratings of the adjective "afraid" to any faces. (Although she gave her highest ratings in this category to appropriately fearful ones, her fear ratings were far below normal.)

Further insight into her mental condition was provided by her facility at drawing cartoon characters. Her renderings of happy, sad, surprised, disgusted, and angry faces were quite lifelike—so good that most readers could probably correctly assign the intended state to each cartoon (figure 27.12). When asked to draw someone who was afraid, by contrast, she at first failed to comply. When the request was repeated, she drew a figure that conveyed almost no sense at all of a fearful state: a childlike figure crawling on all fours, whose only resemblance to fear was that the figure's hair was stiff and standing on end. Asked about her relatively poor drawing, she replied that "*she did not know what an afraid face would look like*" (5887, original italics).

It seems noteworthy that the artist did not say

FIGURE 27.12   Depiction of Emotion After Amygdala Damage

Source: Reproduced with permission from Adolphs, Tranel, Damasio, and Damasio (1995, 5888).
Notes: Emotional expressions drawn by a woman who had bilateral amygdala lesions due to disease. Note that all emotions are fairly well depicted except for "afraid."

that she did not know what fear was. Fear—as a constructed category of emotion—still made enough sense to her to talk about it. Neither did she claim that she had drawn a good rendering of fear. She was not oblivious to her deficit. Clearly, this deficit was in some way especially related to the recognition and expression of fear. But the possibility that the patient "does not experience fear in a normal way," as the authors suggest (5887), may not be equivalent to a categorical lack of fear. It is certainly not a lack of the construct of fear as a global category of emotional appraisal. Rather, her deficit applies specifically to the interface between fear and the outside world: emotional recognition of the particular events that others would perceive as frightening, expression of fear through facial and other affective reactions, and recognition of fearful affective displays by others.

A related case is that of a woman who lost her amygdala on both sides owing to surgery for epilepsy (Scott et al. 1997). Afterward, she was markedly impaired at recognizing vocal emotion in speech that was deliberately intended to sound fearful, angry, happy, sad, or disgusted. The patient was especially poor at recognizing fearful or angry tones of voice, though she was marginally impaired also at recognizing happy and sad intonations. When asked to identify nonspeech vocal expressions of emotion, such as a fearful scream, a happy laugh, sad sobbing, disgusted retching, or an angry growl, she was often wrong only for the sounds intended to convey fear or anger. However, the patient's difficulty in abstracting information from the sound of a voice was not limited strictly to emotion. She also had trouble recognizing the identity of a voice, indicating an impairment of perceptual recognition that extended beyond emotion. Thus it would be difficult to conclude that her deficit was specific to fear, or even simply to emotion.

Summary

Fearful and anxious emotional reactions to situations unquestionably involve amygdala function. But it appears that the amygdala mediates neither "fear" nor "anxiety" as pure psychological categories. Some aspects of fear and anxiety persist after amygdala damage. Further, some of the fear-related deficits seem to be more closely linked to specific perceptual or representational aspects than to loss of fear as an emotional category.

BEYOND FEAR: PARTICIPATION OF A RELATED CORE PROCESS IN POSITIVE EMOTION

Just as fear may not be totally lost as a unitary emotional category after brain damage, but rather distorted, other emotions are often similarly distorted. Amygdala lesions alter many reactions to emotionally *positive* events. Indeed, the original Kluver-Bucy syndrome included "hyper-orality" (attempts to eat atypical objects) and "hypersexuality" (attempts to mate with atypical targets) among the consequences of losing the amygdala and other temporal lobe structures in monkeys (Kluver and Bucy 1939). Animals after amygdala damage sometimes err in the opposite direction. For example, they fail to engage in sexually motivated tasks that an intact rat would perform (Everitt 1990). They also fail to select particular nutrients to eat that would be good for them under particular circumstances, such as salt when they are deficient in body sodium (Schulkin, Marini, and Epstein 1989). Ordinary rats will avidly drink a very salty solution after they are depleted of physiological sodium by a drug. (A similar salt appetite can occur in humans who have lost excessive amounts of sodium in perspiration or who have been on a completely salt-free diet for a prolonged time) (Schulkin 1991). Lesions of the central amygdala block the willingness of rats to ingest salt when they are sodium-deficient (Seeley et al. 1993). They fail to consume salt even though they still seek food and water, and even though they would "like" the taste of salt (they would emit enhanced hedonic reactions) if they did taste it (Galaverna et al. 1993). These observations suggest that even relatively "innate" emotional reactions to positive "key stimuli," such as the taste of salt during sodium appetite, are vulnerable to the same types of amygdala damage that dissociate fear.

Emotional responses that require explicit *learning* appear even more vulnerable to amygdala damage. For example, lateral amygdala lesions prevent a rat from learning to return to a place where it has obtained drug reward before (Hiroi and White 1991). In a "conditioned reinforcement" task, lesions of the basolateral amygdala abolish the value of learned rewards. Ordinary rats will work for conditioned stimulus (a light or sound) that has been paired either with food or with a sexual partner, but amygdala lesions eliminate such conditioned reinforcement (Everitt 1990; Everitt and Robbins 1992). The rats will still work for an unconditioned reward (food or sex itself), but no longer for a learned reward. One interpretation of this has been that amygdala lesions disrupt an aspect of *reward learning* (Everitt and Robbins 1992). Reward learning, coupled with fear learning, could be expanded to a category of general emotional learning (Davidson and Sutton 1995).

Although emotional learning as a psychological category does seem to bear a special relationship to this brain system, it still does not fit perfectly. The thrust of my argument is that no familiar category will fit. The human failure to recognize facial expression, voice intonation, or voice identity (but retaining the capacity to discuss emotions, which is surely as dependent on learning as the impaired functions are), or the rat failure to drink salt while in a state of sodium depletion (but retaining normal food and water intake and even salt alliesthesia), will not fit without force into the category of emotional learning. Of course, the amygdala nuclei no doubt mediate many functions, and some consequences could be explained by loss of other functions in addition to emotional learning. But most troublesome for an emotional learning hypothesis are the observations that amygdala lesions never really eliminate the capacity for learned emotion at all. Some evidence for this has already been discussed. In addition, even in experiments in which some aspects of emotional learning are lost, as when conditioned reward is disrupted, animals may still show other aspects of having learned an association to the reward. For example, when a sound that has been paired with a food reward is presented to rats that have basolateral amygdala

lesions, the rats immediately run to their empty food dish, as normal rats would (Everitt and Robbins 1992; Hatfield et al. 1996). Both the sound and the food dish are merely conditioned stimuli. The rat's response to them in the absence of real food suggests that learned stimuli still trigger a reward association of some sort.

One more traditional psychological category, namely, attention, has been suggested as an amygdala function to explain why animals might retain reward learning yet not show all appropriate behavior to conditioned stimuli (Gallagher and Holland 1994). This idea is based on the finding that central nucleus lesions of the amygdala block orienting or attending reactions to conditioned stimuli for reward, while preserving other reward-related learning. Ordinary rats will turn to look at or listen to a conditioned stimulus light or sound that has been paired with reward, but after being given central amygdala lesions, rats do not (Gallagher, Graham, and Holland 1990; Hatfield et al. 1996). The same lesion disrupts "unblocking," the normal propensity to increase learning about a conditioned stimulus whose predictive value is suddenly enhanced by a change in its paired unconditioned stimulus (Holland and Gallagher 1993). Such failure has been interpreted as a failure to attend to stimulus relations. However, it is difficult to account for many phenomena with an attention deficit hypothesis. For example, although the lesion disrupts unblocking in classical conditioning, it does not disrupt blocking (failing to learn about a conditioned stimulus if the un-

FIGURE 27.13   Dissociation of Fear by Amygdala Damage

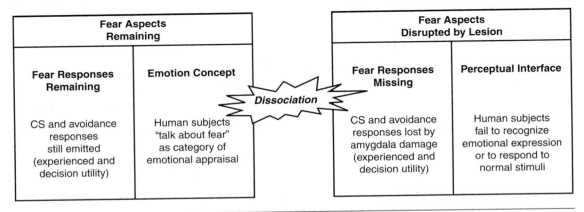

Notes: Dissociation of fear by amygdala damage. Many fearful behavioral and autonomic responses of animals are disrupted, but others persist (as may be true for positive emotional responses too). Similarly, humans fail to recognize fearful stimuli or expressions after damage, but can still talk coherently about fear as an emotional category.

conditioned stimulus is already predicted) (Holland and Gallagher 1993). It is difficult to devise a plausible account on that basis for why unblocking but not blocking should be disrupted by an attention deficit. Holland and Gallagher (1993) note that blocking prevents the growth of an association whereas unblocking produces it, but even this difference does not translate immediately into an explanation.

Alternatives to Traditional Psychological Categories

The evidence reviewed earlier suggests that the amygdala nuclei may not, after all, mediate "fear" or "reward" or "emotion" or "emotional learning" or "attention" as distinct psychological categories, or any group of these as traditional psychological categories. This may tell us something important. We need to devise new psychological core processes that will better account for the phenomena. Perhaps the general conclusion to be taken from this discussion is that the real core processes of emotion, revealed by biopsychological studies of brain-behavior relations, simply will not fit into traditional psychological categories. Fortunately, again, the phenomena give clues about the properties of the real core processes.

Overlap of Fear and Anxiety Core Process with "Wanting"

A possibility that seems to me to merit further examination is that some of the emotional deficits related to amygdala damage may reflect an interaction with the incentive salience attribution system of "wanting" discussed earlier. The amygdala receives ascending dopamine projections, and the behavioral effects of amygdala lesions are modulated by dopamine manipulations of the nucleus accumbens. For example, some of the reward learning deficits produced by amygdala lesions are reversed by microinjection of amphetamine into the nucleus accumbens (Cador et al. 1991). Could some of the consequences of amygdala lesions involve changes in the attribution of incentive salience to stimuli? Not in the same way as dopamine lesions do. It is clear that, unlike the dopamine/accumbens system, the amygdala is not needed for the *generation* of incentive salience attributions. Amygdala lesions do not produce global deficits of "wanting" that follow suppression of dopamine neurotransmission. Both humans and rats continue to eat and drink and to

seek out many incentives after amygdala damage, seeking some perhaps more than they ordinarily would. But the amygdala might still participate in the *targeted focusing* of incentive salience attributions on particular stimuli rather than on others. Loss of such a function would produce behavioral deficits that combine emotional, motivational, associative learning, and perceptual aspects, as amygdala lesions appear to do. For example, rats that fail to consume salt when they have a sodium deficiency, but eat and drink normally otherwise, might fail specifically to focus incentive salience on salt-related stimuli under appropriate conditions.

"Wanting" Versus "Fear"

Incentive salience by its very name entails a positive state. How could an incentive process be reconciled with an amygdala or dopamine/accumbens role in fear? Despite their differences, there are points of overlap between the core processes of "wanting" and "fear." From the psychological point of view, both are a form of decision utility: they elicit a decision to engage or avoid based on an event's potential for pleasure or pain. From the neural point of view, brain manipulations of the dopamine/accumbens system that alter "wanting" for positive incentives can also alter fearful reactions or avoidance of danger (Robinson and Berridge 1993; Salamone 1994), just as manipulations of the amygdala do.

That positive incentives and negative fear may tap into similar psychological core processes mediated by the same brain systems poses a challenge for the construction of biopsychological hypotheses. What sort of core process could be relevant to both desire and dread? There are several possibilities that could join "wanting" and "fear" together in the same dopamine/amygdala system (Robinson and Berridge 1993). In some cases, a positive incentive could masquerade as an aversive task: individuals in a fearful situation may "want" to escape to safety. But even in a situation in which the motivation is entirely aversive, a process related to incentive salience could be at work. For example, different dopamine/accumbens/amygdala subsystems might mediate "wanting" and "fear" as distinct processes: "incentive salience" versus "aversive salience." Alternatively, the two psychological functions might be combined together into a single "generic" motivational salience attributed by the dopamine/accumbens/amygdala system, while positive/negative valence could be set by other factors. For example, determination of whether motivational salience would be rewarding or frightening could arise either from within the dopamine/accumbens/amygdala system itself, such as from the intensity of dopamine activation (for example, moderate levels of activation causing attraction, but very high levels becoming frightening), or from outside by the co-activation of separate neural systems. This possibility converges with Kagan's and Schulkin's view of inhibited children and agitated depressed patients as hyper-responsive to events of many kinds owing to a putatively hyperactive amygdala system (Kagan and Snidman 1991; Schulkin 1994).

My speculation concerning potential interaction in positive and negative emotion is not intended as a finished hypothesis but rather is meant simply as a starting point to highlight the kinds of issues involved. The real goal is to identify adequate core psychological processes that can legitimately be mapped onto emotional phenomena and the consequences of brain manipulations.

Summary

Amygdala lesions dissociate aspects of positive emotion in the same way that they dissociate aspects of fear and anxiety, perhaps indicating disruption of a shared underlying core process. In each case, some aspects of the emotion are distorted while others are preserved. Just as the manipulations of brain dopamine systems unexpectedly dissociate emotional reward into "liking" and "wanting" categories, the consequences of amygdala damage seem to cross traditional psychological boundaries of emotion, motivation, learning, perception, and attention, while not entirely disrupting any of the psychological subcategories that have so far been proposed. Reconsideration of our categories of psychological organization may help match the phenomena to their causes.

CONCLUSION

The dissociations of emotional processes discussed in this chapter illustrate the composite nature of seemingly simple positive and negative emotions. The fracture lines that dissociate core psychological components are not apparent in everyday life, and the nature of those core components is not evident to conscious awareness. Information about psychological core processes comes from studies of unconscious emotional reactions and studies of brain-behavior relations. These suggest that even

the simplest emotional experience can be dissociated into components. Some components are essentially unconscious: core processes of "emotion" that may ordinarily help cause subjective emotional feelings but are not themselves accessible to awareness. For positive emotional states, these seem to include separable core processes of "wanting" and of "liking," which are mediated by different brain systems. Particular core processes of positive emotion, such as the incentive salience attribution process denoted by "wanting," may also be components of "fear" and "anxiety."

Dissociation between conscious emotional feelings and unconscious core processes of emotion becomes obvious only under unusual circumstances. It requires hypnosis, addiction, tachistoscopic presentation, or brain manipulations in order to provide compelling demonstrations. The reason for this is that our conscious experience of an emotion and the core processes that constitute it are generally integrated in ordinary life. Experienced utility, decision utility, and predicted/remembered utility do typically covary together. Similarly, hedonic and action-inducing properties of pleasure or pain (instant experienced utility, as conceived by Kahneman [this volume] and Shizgal [this volume]) typically cohere. Most rewards that are liked are also wanted. Most pains are feared. It has been adaptive for these components to work closely together to achieve life goals. But their identity as components allows them to dissociate under some conditions. For psychologists who wish to understand the process and structure underlying hedonic life quality, the dissociation of core components that *can* occur is as important as the association that usually *does*.

More and more we are learning that emotions, like other psychological processes, are actually made up of separate components, many of which are excluded from conscious experience. The perceived unity of an emotional event arises from integration by the systems that generate conscious experience, whose representation of core processes involves distortion and omission. It seems clear that our understanding will be advanced when we parse psychological phenomena into meaningful categories that reflect the nature of evolved components, and when we learn the rules that relate components to each other and to conscious experience.

I thank Phoebe Ellsworth, Daniel Kahneman, Stephen Maren, Susana Peciña, Jay Schulkin, Peter Shizgal, Terry Robinson, Jacob Steiner, and Elliot

Valenstein for their helpful comments on earlier versions of this chapter. I also thank Ralph Adolphs and his colleagues, and the *Journal of Neuroscience*, for permission to reproduce the drawings by their patient.

NOTES

1. Instant experienced utility, as it is currently conceived by Kahneman and his colleagues, is slightly more complicated than I have indicated here (Kahneman, this volume; Kahneman, Wakker, and Sarin 1997). Instant experienced utility for Kahneman also includes an action tendency, manifest as action to acquire an immediately available incentive and to resist interruptions of that goal-directed action, in addition to the hedonic experience of the incentive. Decision utility, by contrast, involves a decision to act or choose between more distant incentives, not immediately present. For instant experienced utility, the two connotations of resistance to interruption and hedonic experience are presumed to be different manifestations of the same underlying process. This dual-property sense of instant utility has been adopted for biopsychological analyses of brain stimulation reward by Shizgal (Shizgal 1997; Shizgal, this volume), who views the resistance to interruption by a self-administering rat as tantamount to the hedonic intensity of a brain stimulation reward.

   I focus only on the hedonic value component of instant experienced utility, not on the connotation of action tendency or resistance to interruption included by Kahneman and by Shizgal, because evidence shows the hedonic evaluation of an incentive to be dissociable by brain manipulations from the persistence of the incentive-directed action. These dissociations suggest that the hedonic experience connotation of instant experienced utility may not reflect the same process as the action persistence connotation. In that case, the hedonic evaluation of experienced utility corresponds closely to what I call "liking," whereas the action persistence included by Kahneman and by Shizgal corresponds more closely to "wanting," sharing some properties in common with decision utility.

   To avoid confusion, I use "experienced utility" only to refer to the hedonic evaluation of an incentive ("liking"), and use "decision utility" to refer to decisions to acquire, choose, and persistently pursue the incentive ("wanting"). This is meant to allow transition between the two frameworks. While respecting the definition of these utility terms as given by their authors, it seems reasonable to suppose that they will continue to evolve as concepts in psychology generally do.

2. Although there may be cases in which choice between future outcomes (decision utility) diverges from predictions of future hedonic value (expected utility). For example, people may choose a variety of foods for future consumption that are different from the choices they would make when the occasions arrived; the choices can be made to converge more closely, however, if they are asked to predict explicitly their future likings before making their choice (Kahneman 1994; Simonson 1990). Such cases of dissociation between choice and predic-

tions perhaps occur only when individuals choose without bothering to think through a prediction of future value, or when their choices for the future are guided by criteria that go beyond hedonic maximization (Kahneman, this volume). Both situations differ from the type of dissociation discussed here, in which generated forms of hedonic utility (experienced, decision, expected/remembered) have discrepant values for the same event.

REFERENCES

Adolphs, R., Tranel, D., Damasio, H., and Damasio, A. R. (1995). Fear and the human amygdala. *Journal of Neuroscience, 15,* 5879–91.

Anagnostaras, S. G., and Robinson, T. E. (1996). Sensitization to the psychomotor stimulant effects of amphetamine: Modulation by associative learning. *Behavioral Neuroscience, 110*(6), 1397–1414.

Aosaki, T., Graybiel, A. M., and Kimura, M. (1994). Effect of the nigrostriatal dopamine system on acquired neural responses in the striatum of behaving monkeys. *Science, 265*(5170), 412–15.

Arntz, A. (1993). Endorphins stimulate approach behaviour, but do not reduce subjective fear: A pilot study. *Behaviour Research and Therapy, 31*(4), 403–5.

Beagley, W. K., and Holley, T. L. (1977). Hypothalamic stimulation facilitates contralateral visual control of a learned response. *Science, 196*(4287), 321–23.

Beauchamp, G. K., Bertino, M., Burke, D., and Engelman, K. (1990). Experimental sodium depletion and salt taste in normal human volunteers. *American Journal of Clinical Nutrition, 51*(5), 881–89.

Bechara, A., Tranel, A., Damasio, H., Adolphs, R., Rockland, C., and Damasio, A. R. (1995). Double dissociation of conditioning and declarative knowledge relative to the amygdala and hippocampus in humans. *Science, 269,* 1115–18.

Berridge, K. C. (1988). Brainstem systems mediate the enhancement of palatability by chlordiazepoxide. *Brain Research, 447*(2), 262–68.

———. (1989). Substantia nigra 6-OHDA lesions mimic striatopallidal disruption of syntactic grooming chains: A neural systems analysis of sequence control. *Psychobiology, 17,* 377–85.

———. (1991). Modulation of taste affect by hunger, caloric satiety, and sensory-specific satiety in the rat. *Appetite, 16*(2), 103–20.

———. (1996). Food reward: Brain substrates of wanting and liking. *Neuroscience and Biobehavioral Reviews, 20*(1), 1–25.

Berridge, K. C., Flynn, F. W., Schulkin, J., and Grill, H. J. (1984). Sodium depletion enhances salt palatability in rats. *Behavioral Neuroscience 98*(4), 652–60.

Berridge, K. C., and Peciña, S. (1995). Benzodiazepines, appetite, and taste palatability. *Neuroscience and Biobehavioral Reviews, 19,* 121–31.

Berridge, K. C., and Robinson, T. F. (1995). The mind of an addicted brain: Sensitization of wanting versus liking. *Current Directions in Psychological Science, 4,* 71–76.

———. (1998). The role of dopamine in reward: Hedonics, reward learning, or incentive salience? *Brain Research Reviews, 28,* 309–69.

Berridge, K. C., and Treit, D. (1986). Chlordiazepoxide directly enhances positive ingestive reactions in rats. *Pharmacology, Biochemistry, and Behavior, 24*(2), 217–21.

Berridge, K. C., and Valenstein, E. S. (1991). What psychological process mediates feeding evoked by electrical stimulation of the lateral hypothalamus? *Behavioral Neuroscience, 105*(1), 3–14.

Berridge, K. C., Venier, I. L., and Robinson, T. E. (1989). Taste reactivity analysis of 6-hydroxydopamine-induced aphagia: Implications for arousal and anhedonia hypotheses of dopamine function. *Behavioral Neuroscience, 103*(1), 36–45.

Berridge, K. C., and Zajonc, R. B. (1991). Hypothalamic cooling elicits eating: Differential effects on motivation and emotion. *Psychological Science, 2,* 184–89.

Bolles, R. C., and Fanselow, M. S. (1980). A perceptual-defensive-recuperative model of fear and pain. *Behavioral and Brain Sciences, 3,* 291–323.

Cabanac, M. (1971). Physiological role of pleasure. *Science, 173*(2), 1103–7.

———. (1979). Sensory pleasure. *Quarterly Review of Biology, 54*(1), 1–29.

Cabanac, M., and Lafrance, L. (1990). Postingestive alliesthesia: The rat tells the same story. *Physiology and Behavior, 47*(3), 539–43.

Cador, M., Robbins, T. W., Everitt, B. J., Simon, H., Le Moal, M., and Stinus, L. (1991). Limbic-striatal interactions in reward-related processes: Modulation by the dopaminergic system. In P. Willner and J. Scheel-Kruger (Eds.), *The mesolimbic dopamine system: From motivation to action* (pp. 225–50). New York: Wiley.

Cantor, N., Acker, M., and Cook-Flannagan, C. (1992). Conflict and preoccupation in the intimacy life task. *Journal of Personality and Social Psychology, 63,* 644–55.

Cantor, N., Norem, J., Langston, C., and Zirkel, S. (1991). Life tasks and daily life experience. *Journal of Personality, 59,* 425–51.

Cooper, S. J., Higgs, S., and Clifton, P. G. (1995). Behavioral and neural mechanisms for benzodiazepine-induced hyperphagia. *Appetite, 24*(1), 78–79.

Cromwell, H. C., and Berridge, K. C. (1993). Where does damage lead to enhanced food aversion: The ventral pallidum/substantia innominata or lateral hypothalamus? *Brain Research, 624*(1–2), 1–10. (Published erratum appears in *Brain Research, 642*(1–2): 355)

Darwin, C. (1872). *The expression of the emotions in man and animals.* London: J. Murray.

Davidson, R. J., and Sutton, S. K. (1995). Affective neuroscience: The emergence of a discipline. *Current Opinions in Neurobiology, 5*(2), 217–24.

Davis, M. (1992). The amygdala and conditioned fear. In J. P. Aggleton (Ed.), *The amygdala: Neurobiological aspects of emotion, memory, and mental dysfunction* (pp. 255–306). New York: Wiley.

Doyle, T. G., Berridge, K. C., and Gosnell, B. A. (1993). Morphine enhances hedonic taste palatability in rats. *Pharmacology, Biochemistry, and Behavior, 46,* 745–49.

Drewnowski, A., Krahn, D. D., Demitrack, M. A., Nairn, K., and Gosnell, B. A. (1995). Naloxone, an opiate blocker, reduces the consumption of sweet high-fat foods in obese and lean female binge eaters. *American Journal of Clinical Nutrition, 61*(6), 1206–12.

Ekman, P. (1992). An argument for basic emotions. *Cognition and Emotion, 6,* 169–200.

Ellsworth, P. C. (1994). Sense, culture, and sensibility. In H. Markus and S. Kitayama (Eds.), *Emotion and culture: Empirical studies of mutual influence* (pp. 23–50). Washington, D.C.: American Psychological Association.

———. (1995). The right way to study emotion. *Psychological Inquiry, 6,* 213–16.

Eriksen, C. W. (1960). Discrimination and learning without awareness: A methodological survey and evaluation. *Psychological Review, 67,* 279–300.

Everitt, B. J. (1990). Sexual motivation: A neural and behavioural analysis of the mechanisms underlying appetitive and copulatory responses of male rats. *Neuroscience and Biobehavioral Reviews, 14*(2), 217–32.

Everitt, B. J., and Robbins, T. W. (1992). Amygdala-ventral striatal interactions and reward-related processes. In J. P. Aggleton (Ed.), *The amygdala: Neurobiological aspects of emotion, memory, and mental dysfunction* (pp. 401–29). New York: Wiley.

Fibiger, H. C., Phillips, A. G., and Brown, E. E. (1992). The neurobiology of cocaine-induced reinforcement. *Ciba Foundation Symposium, 166,* 96–111 (discussion 111–24).

Fischman, M. W. (1989). Relationship between self-reported drug effects and their reinforcing effects: Studies with stimulant drugs. *NIDA Research Monographs, 92,* 211–30.

Fischman, M. W., and Foltin, R. W. (1992). Self-administration of cocaine by humans: A laboratory perspective. In G. R. Bock and J. Whelan (Eds.), *Cocaine: Scientific and social dimensions* (vol. 166, pp. 165–80). Chichester, Eng.: Wiley.

Galaverna, O. G., Seeley, R. J., Berridge, K. C., Grill, H. J., Epstein, A. N., and Schulkin, J. (1993). Lesions of the central nucleus of the amygdala: I. Effects on taste reactivity, taste aversion learning, and sodium appetite. *Behavioral Brain Research, 59*(1–2), 11–17.

Gallagher, M., Graham, P. W., and Holland, P. C. (1990). The amygdala central nucleus and appetitive Pavlovian conditioning: Lesions impair one class of conditioned behavior. *Journal of Neuroscience, 10*(6), 1906–11.

Gallagher, M., and Holland, P. C. (1994). The amygdala complex: Multiple roles in associative learning and attention. *Proceedings of the National Academy of Science, USA, 91*(25), 11771–76.

Gallistel, C. R. (1994). Foraging for brain stimulation: Toward a neurobiology of computation. *Cognition, 50* (1–3), 151–70.

Gazzaniga, M. S., Fendrich, R., and Wessinger, C. M. (1994). Blindsight reconsidered. *Current Directions in Psychological Science, 3,* 93–96.

Glickman, S. E., and Schiff, B. B. (1967). A biological theory of reinforcement. *Psychological Review, 74,* 81–109.

Gosnell, B. A. (1987). Central structures involved in opioid-induced feeding. *Federation Proceedings, 46* (1), 163–67.

Gray, R. W., and Cooper, S. J. (1995). Benzodiazepines and palatability: Taste reactivity in normal ingestion. *Physiology and Behavior, 58*(5), 853–59.

Grill, H. J., and Berridge, K. C. (1985). Taste reactivity as a measure of the neural control of palatability. In J. M. Sprague and A. N. Epstein (Eds.), *Progress in psychobiology and physiological psychology* (vol. 11, pp. 1–61). Orlando, Fla.: Academic Press.

Grill, H. J., and Norgren, R. (1978a). Chronically decerebrate rats demonstrate satiation but not bait shyness. *Science, 201*(4352), 267–69.

———. (1978b). The taste reactivity test: I. Mimetic responses to gustatory stimuli in neurologically normal rats. *Brain Research, 143*(2), 263–79.

———. (1978c). The taste reactivity test: II. Mimetic responses to gustatory stimuli in chronic thalamic and chronic decerebrate rats. *Brain Research, 143*(2), 281–97.

Hatfield, T., Han, J. S., Conley, M., Gallagher, M., and Holland, P. (1996). Neurotoxic lesions of basolateral, but not central, amygdala interfere with Pavlovian second-order conditioning and reinforcer devaluation effects. *Journal of Neuroscience, 16*(16), 5256–65.

Higgs, S., and Cooper, S. J. (1994). Microinjection of the benzodiazepine agonist midazolam into the parabrachial nucleus of the rat results in a hyperphagia. *Appetite, 23*(3), 307–8.

Hilgard, E. R. (1986). *Divided consciousness: Multiple controls in human thought and action.* New York: Wiley.

Hiroi, N., and White, N. M. (1991). The lateral nucleus of the amygdala mediates expression of the amphetamine-produced conditioned place preference. *Journal of Neuroscience, 11*(7), 2107–16.

Hoebel, B. G. (1976). Brain-stimulation reward in relation to behavior. In A. Waquier and E. T. Rolls (Eds.), *Brain-stimulation reward* (pp. 335–72). New York: Elsevier.

———. (1988). Neuroscience and motivation: Pathways and peptides that define motivational systems. In R. C. Atkinson, R.J. Herrnstein, G. Lindzey, and R.D. Luce (Eds.), *Stevens's handbook of experimental psychology* (2nd ed., vol. 1, pp. 547–626). New York: Wiley.

Holland, P. C., and Gallagher, M. (1993). Effects of

amygdala central nucleus lesions on blocking and unblocking. *Behavioral Neuroscience, 107*(2), 235–45.

James, W. (1884). What is an emotion? *Mind, 9,* 188–205.

Kagan, J., and Schulkin, J. (1995). On the concepts of fear. *Harvard Review of Psychiatry, 3,* 231–34.

Kagan, J., and Snidman, N. (1991). Infant predictors of uninhibited profiles. *Psychological Science, 2,* 40–44.

Kahneman, D. (1994). New challenges to the rationality assumption. *Journal of Institutional and Theoretical Economics, 150,* 18–36.

Kahneman, D., Fredrickson, B. L., Schreiber, C. A., and Redelmeier, D. A. (1993). When more pain is preferred to less: Adding a better end. *Psychological Science, 4,* 401–5.

Kahneman, D., Knetsch, J., and Thaler, R. (1990). Experimental tests of the endowment effect and the Coase theorem. *Journal of Political Economy, 98,* 1325–48.

Kahneman, D., and Snell, J. (1992). Predicting a changing taste. *Journal of Behavioral Decision Making, 5,* 187–200.

Kahneman, D., Wakker, P. P., and Sarin, R. (1997). Back to Bentham? Explorations of experienced utility. *Quarterly Journal of Economics, 112,* 375–405.

Kelly, T. H., Foltin, R. W., King, L., and Fischman, M. W. (1992). Behavioral response to diazepam in a residential laboratory. *Biological Psychiatry, 31*(8), 808–22.

Killcross, S., Robbins, T. W., and Everitt, B. J. (1997). Different types of fear-conditioned behaviour mediated by separate nuclei within amygdala. *Nature, 388* (6640), 377–80.

Kim, M., and Davis, M. (1993). Electrolytic lesions of the amygdala block acquisition and expression of fear-potentiated startle even with extensive training but do not prevent reacquisition. *Behavioral Neuroscience, 107*(4), 580–95.

Kling, A. S., and Brothers, L. A. (1992). The amygdala and social behavior. In J. P. Aggleton (Ed.), *The amygdala: Neurobiological aspects of emotion, memory, and mental dysfunction* (pp. 353–77). New York: Wiley.

Kluver, H., and Bucy, P. C. (1939). Preliminary analysis of the temporal lobes in monkeys. *Archives of Neurology and Psychiatry, 42,* 979–1000.

Kolb, F. C., and Braun, J. (1995). Blindsight in normal observers. *Nature, 377*(6547), 336–38 (see comments).

Kunst-Wilson, W. R., and Zajonc, R. B. (1980). Affective discrimination of stimuli that cannot be recognized. *Science, 207*(4430), 557–58.

Lamb, R. J., Preston, K. L., Schindler, C. W., Meisch, R. A., Davis, F., Katz, J. L., Henningfield, J. E., and Goldberg, S. R. (1991). The reinforcing and subjective effects of morphine in post-addicts: A dose-response study. *Journal of Pharmacology and Experimental Therapies, 259*(3), 1165–73.

Lazarus, R., and McCleary, R. (1951). Autonomic dis-

get food. The answer is neural activity somewhere in the brain. By looking at the brain of a rat, we can find the neural circuit that underlies the economics of foraging and eating.

When this brain system is excessively activated by sweet food or powerful drugs, it can lead to abuse and even addiction. When this system is underactive, signs of depression ensue. The neural system I will describe not only provides the cause of normal work, it can also be pushed into a cycle of excessive enjoyment and abnormal suffering, as seen in addiction. These extremes are having an enormous impact on health and the economy.

THE LAWS OF PLEASURE AND REINFORCEMENT

From Bentham to Skinner, reward has been a foundation topic for economists and psychologists. Bentham went the route of attributing behavior to the pleasure principle, the Law of *Affect,* which states that people maximize pleasure (Bentham 1789). Skinner exhorted us to avoid terms like pleasure as "explanatory fictions." He advocated understanding human behavior according to the reinforcement principle, Thorndike's Law of *Effect,* which states that behavior is shaped by its effects (Skinner 1953). Bentham's study of pleasure is the study of hedonics, happiness, joy, and other such expressions of good feelings when people engage in eating, mating, altruism, and profit taking. There is also pleasure in relief from pain and suffering. The study of reinforcement, on the other hand, is the study of responses that are followed by stimuli that increase the probability that the person will emit the response over again. Measurement of reinforcement in terms of behavior does not depend on language and can therefore be studied in animals as well as people. We simply measure preferences when animals are given a choice, and we record changes in the frequency of their responses when they work.

THE NEURAL CORRELATES OF PLEASURE AND REINFORCEMENT: THE GO/STOP DECISION

To study pleasure, modern neuroscience has developed brain imaging techniques, such as MRI and PET, that can be used to reveal areas of intense neural activity during enjoyable feelings. For example, when a cocaine addict lies with his head in a PET scanner and thinks about smoking crack with his beloved crack pipe, he has feelings of craving that are memories of the drug-induced high and a longing for the cocaine rush. At the same time he evidences a significant change in neural activity in at least two important brain areas known as the amygdala and nucleus accumbens (Grant et al. 1996; Volkow, Wang, and Fowler 1997). The amygdala is an area implicated in fearful memories (LeDoux, this volume), and, according to the brain imaging studies, also involved in pleasurable memories. The nucleus accumbens (NAc) is an extension of the amygdala that translates the emotions into action by reinforcing actions that reduce fear and get pleasure. This is sketched in figure 28.1, a simplified side view of the brain.

This chapter focuses on the NAc as a crucial brain region for go/stop decisions and then extends its role to drug dependence, at one extreme, and depression, at the other. One way to explore the behavior reinforcement mechanism is to record the electrical activity of single neurons in a monkey when it tastes a rewarding food. For example, when a monkey tastes sweet fruit juice or sees the familiar juice container, neurons are active in the amygdala (Rolls 1995). Neurons also respond in the cortical region, which recognizes tastes for what they are: orange, grapefruit, mango, banana. Most intriguing are the neurons in the prefrontal cortex, the highest and most recently evolved part of the brain. Some neurons there respond to the palatable taste but do so in proportion to the monkey's hunger or need for fruit juice. The prefrontal cortex is informed about the monkey's need (metabolic state) by neural inputs from brain regions that monitor blood sugar utilization, fat stores, protein sufficiency, and body temperature. When there is no need for nutrition, the fruit taste causes less activity in the prefrontal cortex, and the monkey does not reach out for the juice. Thus, the monkey's decision, whether or not to reach for it, is encoded, in part, in the prefrontal cortex. This cortical decision about eating is conveyed to the nucleus accumbens that can initiate and reinforce behavior. (In figure 28.1, note the cortical choice decisions projecting to the stimulus-response reinforcement region.) The part of the nucleus accumbens we are studying also receives input from emotional memory (amygdala), taste recognition (sensory cortex), and place memory in a cognitive map (hippocampus). Thus, the nucleus accumbens is a major sensory-motor interface that integrates sensory recognition and need decisions, with emotional memory and place memory and then activates response output—basically

Figure 28.1   A Schematic Side View of the Brain

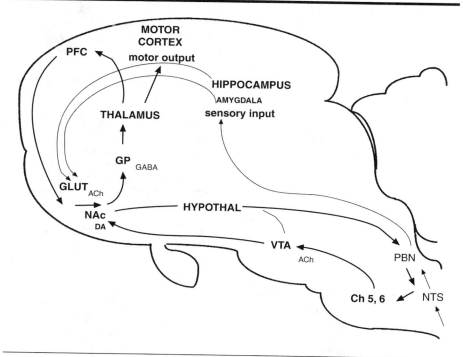

Notes: Starting in the lower right corner of the figure, taste and other chemosensory signals from the hypothalamus, tongue, and gut enter brain stem nuclei (in the nucleus tractus solitarius(NTS) and parabrachial nucleus (PBN). Brain stem output projects indirectly to the taste sensory cortex and prefrontal cortex (PFC). In the amygdala and hippocampus, taste information is combined with other sense modalities (sights, sounds, locations, and codes for safe nutrition versus toxic foods). The arrows from the hippocampus (for example, place memory), amygdala (for example, emotion memory), and prefrontal cortex (for example, complex choice memory) represent highly processed sensory information that goes to the nucleus accumbens (NAc). The NAc is a sensory-motor interface in the loop, drawn in bold lines from PFC to NAc and back to the PFC with commands branching off to the motor cortex. The acetylcholine(ACh) neurons in the NAc may act as gates between sensory signals and motor action outputs. These "gates" are modulated by dopamine (DA), along with norepinephrine, serotonin, and opioid peptides (not shown, but discussed in the text). The medial and lateral hypothalamus help control the NAc via the loops shown (hypothalamus to the NAc). By this route, feeding signals control the DA/ACh balance in the NAc to reinforce or inhibit "voluntary" instrumental behavior. A more detailed version of this figure is given in a recent review (Leibowitz and Hoebel 1998). GLUT refers to the neurotransmitter glutamate for sensory inputs to the NAc. GABA is the neurotransmitter for NAc outputs.

a "go" or "stop" decision (Hoebel 1988, 1997; Mogenson et al. 1980; Robbins and Everitt 1996; Rolls 1995).

The Neural Reinforcement System: Positive Feedback That Says "Do It Again"

In order for behavior to be reinforced, that is, for behavior to be repeated, the system must be informed as to whether the outcome was good.

There is a special input to the nucleus accumbens for the purpose of reinforcing successful responses. One can think of the process as literally reinforcing the stimulus-response connections (synapses) that were active at the time when success occurred. Thus, if a response leads to stimuli associated with food, sex, or profit, the currently active connections are reinforced by an input that is often referred to as the reward system. It uses dopamine as its neurotransmitter in the nucleus accumbens. Berridge (this volume) points out that reward can be subdivided into concepts of wanting versus liking. There is evidence for dopamine involvement in both (Koob and Bloom 1998; Phillips et al. 1992; Salamone and Snyder 1997; Vaccarino 1996; Wise et al. 1995), so I will simply refer to this dopamine system as the "reinforcement system," where reinforcement is operationally defined as the function of increasing the force or frequency of a preceding response (Skinner 1953). In order to find out when dopamine neurons generate nerve impulses, we can once again turn to nonhuman primates.

An electrode can be used to record from dopamine cells in the midbrain of monkeys while they reach for food and eat it. (In figure 28.1, see the midbrain dopamine cells.) These nerve cells are active when novel food is ingested. The nerve impulses then travel up the nerve axons and release dopamine in many forebrain sites, notably the nucleus accumbens, as shown in figure 28.1. Recording from these cells in a primate can reveal exactly what makes the cells fire (Schultz, Dayan, and Montague 1997). Not only do they respond when the monkey first tastes the food, but they soon respond instead as the monkey recognizes signals that food is available. Presumably the dopamine that is released causes reinforcement of the neural connections between the anticipatory signals and the reaching movements that procure the food. Thus, signals (environmental signs and symbols) take on meaning by association with a primary reinforcer such as food.

Turning from monkeys, which forage, to people, who go shopping, we can now assume that signs along the way become learned stimuli for the activation of dopamine neurons in the midbrain. A sign that says "Coca-Cola," or the money to buy it, becomes associated with food, and then it too can elicit approach responses and release dopamine. These learned stimuli increase the frequency of responses in the chain of behavior that procures the primary reinforcer. In this example, the reward is extraordinary since it contains refined sugar from Hawaii and caffeine imported from Colombia. People in wealthy countries can afford extraordinary reinforcers compared to those typically available to our ancestral primates. This can lead to problems, which I discuss further on.

There is another technique for studying the "reward" or reinforcement system that has fascinated every astounded witness. This is electrical self-stimulation of the brain (Hoebel 1988; Olds and Milner 1954). People, monkeys, or rats will stimulate themselves with an electrode that is permanently implanted in the correct brain locus. For example, laboratory rats will self-stimulate three thousand times an hour for half-second bursts of brain stimulation with an electrode in the hypothalamus. This is part of the appetite control system described earlier. Rats will also self-stimulate the system for sexual appetite. In the feeding system, electrical stimulation turned on continuously for a minute can elicit appetite, shown by immediate eating when palatable food is nearby. In the sex system, immediate copulation is elicited if a willing partner is nearby. And in both cases, if the electricity that generates nerve impulses comes on for only half a second (instead of a minute), then the animal ignores the food, ignores its mate, and does whatever it has learned to do to get more of the stimulation. Thus, rats will dance a jig or press a switch three thousand times an hour. Why? Apparently the neural effect of the self-stimulation is like food or sex. You can think of it as "electric food" or "electric sex" in the sense that it activates the reinforcement system directly. As you probably guessed, electrical self-stimulation of the hypothalamus activates a pathway that releases dopamine (Yeomans, Mathur, and Tampakeras 1993). (See the path from the hypothalamus to the accumbens in figure 28.1.)

The frequency of self-stimulation at the feeding-reward electrode will slow down if the animal eats a big meal that reduces appetite (Hoebel 1979). At the copulation electrode, ejaculation diminishes the appetite for self-stimulation. But in the absence of natural forms of inhibitory feedback, the animal just goes on enjoying the brain stimulation. As you would expect, the rat never gets satiated and will self-stimulate all day and all night.

This raises a question as to whether there is a common neural reinforcement system underlying natural eating and mating. Perhaps it is also at the root of unnatural self-stimulation, drug abuse, and obsessive-compulsive behavior. If so, then the economics of buying food, finding a mate, and obtaining psychoactive drugs is based on the economics of stimulating various parts of this neural circuit for stimulus-response reinforcement (Shizgal, this volume).

Extreme cases are often useful for understanding ordinary cases. Extremes in psychology are like a magnifying glass that makes a phenomenon bigger than life. Addiction is a good example of a "magnifying glass" for economics and psychology. Addiction allows us to see the processes of reinforcement at work. However, enlarging a phenomenon makes it easy to lose sight of its context. Therefore, after taking a close look at drug addiction, we will step back to see whether addiction acts in the same system as natural eating. Our hypothesis is that eating and addiction involve neural activity in one and the same system for behavioral reinforcement.

People who work for money to buy food do not need to know about these mechanisms of reinforcement, any more than they need to know the mechanisms of gravity to walk. But the mechanisms of reinforcement are always at work. If we knew them, we could explain judgments of utility, explain illogical behavior, shed light on mental disorders, treat the mentally ill, discover why some rewards are interchangeable, and find out how neutral stimuli become associated with rewards. The mechanisms of reinforcement are as important to economics and psychology as the mechanisms of gravity are to a physicist. It is in the very nature of these fields to analyze the basis of response reinforcement. We await only the discovery of tools for measurement and a scientific theory to guide us. New methods and the beginnings of a theory are becoming available. The results are intriguing for not only psychology and economics but the legal system as well.

AN ANIMAL WITH DEPLETED DOPAMINE: A SAILBOAT WITHOUT A SAIL

If the dopamine pathway from the midbrain to the accumbens is part of a basic reinforcement system, then damage to this system should impair motivated behavior. However, this can be difficult to prove because there are two closely related dopamine pathways that emanate from the midbrain. Parkinson's disease patients are missing dopamine neurons in a path that is necessary for initiating stereotyped movements used, for example, in walking. When dopamine is depleted, people neglect sensory input and tend to do nothing, unless the stimulation is very strong or someone helps them get started (as in the movie *Awakenings*). They suffer from sensory neglect and motor inanition. Nearby, in the path to the accumbens, dopamine is needed for initiating new, complex movements, such as bar-pressing for food. Apparently dopamine facilitates the transfer of neural information from the sensory inputs to the motor outputs in both systems. The constellation of symptoms depends on exactly which of the dopamine systems is impaired.

In rats it is possible to deplete dopamine in the various dopamine terminal areas, separately, to find out what dopamine does. A drug that kills the dopamine neurons can be injected locally in the accumbens. When dopamine is selectively depleted just in the accumbens, the animal can still walk, eat, and even bar-press for food if the bar-press response is already well learned, but it will neither work hard nor overcome obstacles to obtain food (Cousins and Salamone 1994; Maldonado-Irizarry and Kelley 1995). They refuse to self-inject intravenous cocaine, in part because cocaine acts directly on the dopamine nerve terminals; so with the accumbens dopamine nerves gone, cocaine is no longer as reinforcing (Caine and Koob 1994).

Another technique is to block dopamine. When dopamine is normally released, it diffuses through the fluids in the neural junction (synapse) and throughout the immediate brain area. It binds to specialized protein molecules that serve as dopamine receptors on neighboring neurons. Dopamine can activate the receptors and cause a reaction in the next neurons in the circuit. Local injection of a drug that binds to the receptors, without activating them, prevents dopamine from binding. This is functionally similar to the selective depletion of dopamine but has the great advantage that the effect is temporary. The effect is graded according to the dose, and it can be selective for different subtypes of receptors. Dopamine blockers cause a temporary disruption of the system. The dopamine-impaired animals show abnormal motivation in sensitive tests (Ettenberg 1989; Wise 1982). For example, they treat sugar as less sweet than usual (Smith 1995). With dopamine receptors blocked, the good things in life have little effect. The animal does not react to the reinforcers that usually propel it through life, and it is "lost at sea."

AN ANIMAL WITH TOO MUCH DOPAMINE: DRIVEN TO EXCESS

Psychostimulants are drugs that increase synaptic dopamine. The most powerful ones are drugs that are abused, such as methamphetamine ("speed"), crack cocaine, and phencyclidine ("angel dust"). People who overdose on these drugs show magnified effects of dopamine, including hyperactivity, abnormal cognitions, sensory inputs that come from they know not where (it is enough to make them paranoid), and overall psychotic behavior typical of a schizophrenic. Rats on speed race around the cage, press the food lever repeatedly just for the sound of it, and distrust other rats (Ellison and Eison 1983). They generally act the opposite of a dopamine-depleted rat. Everything is reinforcing when there is too much dopamine. Depending on the psychostimulant dose, a person or animal goes from peppy to manic to psychotic.

The next question is: What normally releases dopamine in normal amounts in normal people and normal animals? The evidence suggests that dopamine is paramount in the neural circuit that generates the pay for work. What do we have to do to get it?

MICRODIALYSIS FOR MEASURING DOPAMINE IN THE BRAIN

To measure dopamine during normal behavior, hypodermic needle tubing is prepared with a cellulose tip to form a microdialysis probe that can be lowered into the accumbens. The surgery is done while the animal is anesthetized. Once the probe is in place and the animal is fully recovered, dopamine that is diffusing through the nearby fluids does a random walk right through the porous cellulose and is gently flushed out by a tiny stream of fluid inside the probe. The amount of dopamine exiting the probe is proportional to what was released nearby in the brain. The exact amount is measured by analytical chemistry. The animal cannot feel the microdialysis probe and behaves normally. We monitor the dopamine that comes out in twenty-minute intervals.

Microdialysis in normal rats proves that dopamine is released in the accumbens when the animal eats (Hoebel et al. 1989; Hoebel, Leibowitz, and Hernandez 1992). In some circumstances, dopamine is released by signals of forthcoming food before the animal starts eating (Phillips et al. 1992), just like the anticipatory dopamine cell activity mentioned earlier in the monkey experiment (Schultz, Daylan, and Montague 1997). Microdialysis with probes in different parts of the accumbens has parceled the accumbens into subregions (Maldonado-Irizarry, Swanson, and Kelley 1995). Eating releases dopamine in a particular region of the accumbens, where the normal sequence of events would go something like this. First, sensory stimuli related to food enter the accumbens from higher processing centers such as the amygdala, hippocampus, and cortex (see figure 28.1). This information arrives via neurons that release the neurotransmitter glutamate. The accumbens output makes the animal perform a response such as picking up food, going to the grocery store, or pressing a food lever (Kelley and Delfs

1991). The resultant food is eaten and releases additional dopamine. This theoretically reinforces the sensory motor connections that led to eating. Thus, the animal will live to eat again.

Sexual behavior is another natural way to get dopamine in the accumbens. Control tests show that it is not just the exercise but the anticipatory stimuli and copulation that does it. Foreplay, not the orgasm, releases the most dopamine (Damsma et al. 1992; Pfaus et al. 1995).

We know that eating can release dopamine, but how do we know that dopamine reinforces instrumental behavior? As amazing as it sounds, if dopamine is injected as a reinforcer for bar-pressing, the animal will bar-press to self-inject the dopamine directly into its nucleus accumbens. Rats will also self-inject amphetamine into their accumbens, because it releases dopamine (Guerin et al. 1984; Hoebel et al. 1983).

As discussed earlier, an electrode implanted in the hypothalamus can activate the reinforcement circuit and support electrical self-stimulation, which releases dopamine in the accumbens. The earlier discussion suggested that self-stimulation of feeding sites or sex sites is analogous to eating and copulation (Hoebel 1976). It appears that dopamine reinforces a variety of innately successful acts that stimulate the reinforcement circuit via the hypothalamus (Shizgal, this volume; Wise 1982).

Since escape from pain is also reinforcing, one might wonder if that, too, releases dopamine. To test this idea, we stimulated a part of the hypothalamus that is aversive (Rada, Mark, and Hoebel 1998). Aversive stimulation decreased dopamine slightly. But when the rat was allowed to press a lever to turn the stimulation off for five seconds at a time, dopamine dramatically increased. Learned escape is what Skinner (1953) considered as evidence of negative reinforcement. It releases dopamine just as well as positive reinforcement with food, sex, or self-stimulation. Thus dopamine apparently facilitates repetition of escape as well as approach.

CAN PEOPLE LEARN TO RELEASE DOPAMINE?

Recall that memories of smoking crack caused neural activity in the accumbens and other brain sites of an addict (Volkow et al. 1997). Clearly the addicted person could activate the accumbens by imaging something pleasurable. He had, in some sense, learned to activate the accumbens. Similarly using rats, we first trained them to associate intragastric feeding with the taste of a novel flavor. Then we brought the food to mind by squirting the flavor onto the tongue. The reminder released dopamine in the accumbens (Mark et al. 1996). This must be how people develop learned food preferences and cultural cuisine.

Conversely, we paired the taste of saccharin with poison-induced nausea. Later, saccharin was squirted on the tongue to remind the animal of nausea. As a result, this taste caused a decrease in dopamine release (Mark, Blander, and Hoebel 1991). This is clearly part of the neural mechanism underlying conditioned taste aversions. Such aversions, which can last a lifetime, help protect us from being poisoned (Garcia, Ervin, and Koelling 1966).

Other examples confirm that learning can alter the release of dopamine (Kelley and Delfs 1991). The most dramatic is the monkey experiment again. When recording neural activity in dopamine cells, the cells fired first during eating, but when the monkey discovered that a sound (the proverbial dinner bell) predicted food, the cells started to fire in advance of eating and in advance of reaching for food (Schultz, Dylan, and Montague 1997). They fired when the sound came on. From Pavlov's classic work, we know that the monkey probably started salivating as well as reaching out for the food. Given the evidence that dopamine cells can be conditioned to become active in rats and monkeys, we can be sure it works in people. Thus, people can learn to release dopamine. Dopamine in turn has something to do with making us remember and repeat what we have learned.

ACETYLCHOLINE IN THE ACCUMBENS: EVIDENCE FOR INHIBITION OF BEHAVIOR

We hypothesize that acetylcholine neurons within the accumbens play a major role in stopping behavior. They may act as gates that keep incoming sensory signals from getting through to the response mechanisms. Evidence in support of this idea comes from a conditioned taste aversion experiment. The taste that reminded the animal of nausea increased the release of acetylcholine (Mark et al. 1996). This response is just the opposite of what happens with dopamine.

Release of acetylcholine when a rat is reminded of nausea is not just a coincidence. A chemical was infused into the accumbens to protect acetylcholine from enzymatic destruction, thereby increasing acetylcholine in the synapses. This procedure was carried out on rats while they consumed saccharin. Normally rats would drink great quantities of saccharin solution, but after the taste was paired with high levels of acetylcholine in the accumbens, they lost their preference (Taylor et al. 1992). They avoided saccharin. This suggests that the acetylcholine in the accumbens can *cause* aversion. This phenomenon may be analogous, or perhaps even homologous, to aversion induced by nausea.

A normal meal is defined by starting and stopping a bout of eating. Dopamine seems to help start a meal by increasing approach responses. Acetylcholine, on the other hand, may help in the termination of meals. Microdialysis showed an increase in acetylcholine release when eating slowed down (Mark et al. 1992). Again, both correlation and cause were demonstrated. When acetylcholine was experimentally made to increase, it caused the inhibition of an ongoing meal. As a control, the animals continued to drink water even though they stopped eating. We surmise that a little acetylcholine simply retards eating and gradually stops a meal, but a large amount of acetylcholine can create a lasting taste aversion. Thus, using satiety and taste aversion as our model, part of the answer to the question "What stops behavior?" is acetylcholine in the accumbens.

THE HYPOTHALAMUS: CONTROLLING THE DOPAMINE/ACETYLCHOLINE BALANCE

The next research question focused on discovering the distant site that controls dopamine and acetylcholine. Since we are dealing with a subregion of the accumbens that is specialized for eating, it is logical that dopamine and acetylcholine would be controlled by a site that controls appetite. It is well known that eating is initiated and terminated by neurochemicals in the hypothalamus. For example, *carbohydrate* appetite is initiated by neuropeptide Y acting in concert with norepinephrine and other factors that promote carbohydrate utilization. Another peptide, galanin, works with norepinephrine to make rats eat preferred foods, particularly *fats*. To round out the story, *protein* intake is caused by a peptide that promotes growth (Leibowitz and Hoebel 1998). Carbohydrates, fats, and protein are the three staples of any diet. We find that injecting galanin or norepinephrine in the hypothalamus causes not only eating but also a predictable change in dopamine and acetylcholine in the accumbens (Hoebel

1997; Hoebel et al. 1996). Dopamine release rises, and acetylcholine falls. According to our theory, the dopamine facilitates and reinforces responses for food, and the fall in acetylcholine disinhibits this behavior. Thus, the hypothalamus controls behavior, in part, by controlling dopamine and acetylcholine in the accumbens.

CONTROLLING DOPAMINE ARTIFICIALLY WITH DRUGS

In terms of "dopamine economics," it makes sense to take drugs that release dopamine. There are plenty of choices. The psychostimulants—amphetamine, cocaine, and phencyclidine—have already been mentioned. Others include the opiates, heroin and morphine, which act both in the dopamine cell region of the midbrain and in the dopamine terminal region of the accumbens. Another way to get dopamine is with nicotine from cigarettes. Nicotine stimulates both the cells and the terminals of dopamine neurons. This dual action gives a "double dose" of dopamine. Marijuana acts indirectly to activate the opioid system, which, in turn, activates the dopamine system. Alcohol in liquor and caffeine in coffee also yield dopamine in the accumbens (Hoebel et al. 1989; Tanda, Pontieri, and Di Chiara 1997). We can save ourselves the trouble of working for food by taking these drugs. They are often more expensive than food, but they clearly give a rush of dopamine that is more effective.

Drugs may be more effective for several reasons. They act in many brain sites at once. Some of them also act on more than one neurochemical system. For example, cocaine gives both dopamine reinforcement effects and serotonin antidepressant effects. Multiple sites and multiple actions can lead to wanted or unwanted side effects. One side effect of the psychostimulants is appetite suppression, via the hypothalamus (Leibowitz and Hoebel 1998). Opiates, on the other hand, tend to prolong meals. Body weight changes can ensue, and this can affect drug taking. The interaction between body weight and drug abuse is very interesting.

WEIGHT LOSS AND DOPAMINE DEPLETION

Everyone knows that dieting or semistarvation leads to weight loss that promotes eating. Electrical self-stimulation is also enhanced by weight loss (Carr 1996; McClelland and Hoebel 1991). Even drug self-administration is augmented in underweight rats, monkeys, and people (Carroll, France, and Meisch 1979). Low dopamine may be an "economic" reason for this increase in eating, self-stimulation, and drug abuse. When synaptic dopamine is scarce, animals seem to work for it.

Weight loss in rats decreases the release of dopamine. This was indicated by low basal dopamine in microdialysis samples from the accumbens of rats that were given restricted food until they were at about 80 percent of their normal weight (Pothos, Creese, and Hoebel 1995). Dopamine levels were down to as much as half what is normally detected. We speculate that underweight animals and people may eat more to release stored-up dopamine and restore accustomed levels in the synapses. Drugs of abuse would do it faster. It is conceivable that this is one reason people sometimes take more of these drugs when they lose weight. Thus dopamine-releasing behavior may be potentiated when body weight is relatively low. This would help to explain food binges, alcohol binges, and preference for fast-acting crack cocaine in people who have been dieting. Moreover eating sweet foods can alter the economics of working for drugs (Rodefer and Carroll 1996).

Abstaining from drug abuse can cause dopamine to decrease dramatically (Pothos et al. 1991; Rossetti et al. 1992). Drug withdrawal may thus create a need for dopamine, a need that can be met by taking more of the drug. Indeed, rats barpressing for intravenous cocaine took the drug in a pattern that maintained dopamine at a high level by restoring it whenever it dropped to a trigger point (Wise et al. 1995). Thus, animals work for dopamine when it is relatively scarce and highly effective.

During the initial "cold turkey" period of drug withdrawal, the tendency to work for dopamine may be counteracted by a rise in acetylcholine release. We gave rats morphine daily for a week and then precipitated withdrawal with a drug that blocks the brain's opiate receptors. The animals showed physical signs of withdrawal. Morphine addicts say this is a very unhappy, unpleasant state. The accumbens is involved in the aversive state of withdrawal (Koob, Wall, and Bloom 1989). During withdrawal in rats, not only did dopamine decrease but acetylcholine release increased (Rada et al. 1991b). The conditioned aversion studies suggest that this high level of accumbens acetylcholine is related to stopping behavior and perhaps to the aversive aspects of drug withdrawal. To get rid of the withdrawal symptoms, a person may turn to some other drug or some other source of dopamine.

HOW DOES DOPAMINE BECOME ADDICTIVE?

A review of the literature indicates that intermittent bingeing on drugs releases too much dopamine and somehow contributes to addiction (Koob and Le Moal 1997). The actual mechanism of addiction is not fully known (Nestler and Aghajanian 1997). The effect is more noticeable in animals and people with a familial tendency to addictive disorders. Alcohol-preferring strains of rats and mice have been selectively bred for study (Overstreet, Rezvani, and Janowsky 1992). Researchers are trying to find out what is different about their brains. For one thing, they may have genetically low dopamine and serotonin levels, which might tend to make them prone to depression and excessive alcohol intake.

It is sometimes claimed, according to the "gateway theory," that one addictive drug leads to another. Rats and mice do not like the taste of cocaine. When we gave alcohol-preferring mice the experience of drinking alcohol or nicotine (legal drugs), they could then—and only then—be weaned over to drinking cocaine, too (an illegal drug).

There are three main steps to becoming addicted. The first is behavioral augmentation: the person or animal increases intake of the drug. This can occur through a combination of adaptation to the aversive side effects and changes in the reinforcing effects. Second is the withdrawal phase in which abstaining from the drug can cause symptoms that are very unpleasant in people and physically obvious even in rats. Third is the craving phase, which can last for years and is characterized by a strong appetite for the drug that leads to loss of control and relapse into more drug taking. There must be a long-term neural change that creates the loss of control that is the hallmark of addiction. The change is somewhere in the reinforcement circuit. This is indicated by several things that happen during the course of addiction.

1. Almost all drugs of abuse increase accumbens dopamine (Hoebel et al. 1992; Tanda et al. 1997).
2. As a rat becomes *sensitized* to morphine by successive injections, the acetylcholine response diminishes, and other neurochemical changes occur in the accumbens (Rada et al. 1991b).

3. During *withdrawal,* dopamine release decreases and acetylcholine increases in the accumbens (Rada et al. 1991b).
4. During *craving,* the animal is probably driven by the incentive motivational aspects of learned dopamine release triggered by memories (Robinson and Berridge 1993).

THE ADDICTIVE POTENTIAL OF WORKING FOR FOOD

After studying the role of dopamine in working for food, then in working for drugs, and then in addiction, we came to the realization that food might be addictive itself. Having found that food and drugs are somewhat interchangeable and have a common basis in dopamine function, there are two main possibilities to explain addiction. Either drugs act powerfully and abnormally to stimulate the system and cause addiction as an aberration that has nothing to do with eating, or the system evolved in nature to produce addiction to natural products, including food. The two possibilities are not mutually exclusive. Addiction to cocaine may confer a selective advantage on high-mountain Peruvian Indians. Drinking coffee may have survival value for long-distance truck drivers. Abuse of sedatives such as heroin, marijuana, and alcohol is harder to explain except as a pharmacological aberration. However, suppose the opioid system is normally activated by eating, and eating evolved as an addiction.

To find evidence for this, we noted in the literature that sweet taste or morphine prolongs a meal and that this effect is blocked by opiate antagonists such as naloxone (Gosnell and Levine 1996; Nader and van der Kooy 1994). Eating palatable food can be a pain killer by releasing endogenous opioids (Kanarek et al. 1991). Moreover, repeated weight loss sensitizes animals and increases opiate-induced eating (Hagan and Moss 1991; Specker, Lac, and Carroll 1994), and weight loss enhances self-stimulation via opioids (Carr 1996). All these links between eating and "the brain's own morphine" make one wonder whether people could become addicted to foods that release opioids. If so, this would explain the addictive potential of heroin, marijuana, and alcohol via opioid systems that are normally involved in eating.

The first step in the search for food addiction was to have rats binge on sugar. For this they were deprived for twelve hours, including the four hours of breakfast time. Then they were given chow supplemented with a graduated cylinder full of delicious 25 percent glucose, which they consumed avidly. This cycle of bingeing was kept up for a week, during which their intake increased. As a test for withdrawal, the food and glucose were removed for a day. Physical symptoms were teeth chattering, paw fanning, and head shaking. Naloxone made it worse; morphine or sugar made it better. Binge eating caused significant changes in opioid receptor binding in certain areas of the brain, notably the accumbens (Colantuoni et al. 1997). We are still looking for more signs that binge eating is related to addiction. As for craving, this is difficult to measure in rats but has been assessed in women with binge eating disorder. Binge eaters score high on feelings of loss of control (Stunkard et al. 1996). Some people with binge eating disorder or bulimia also have a tendency toward depression.

THE RELATIONSHIP BETWEEN DEPRESSION AND ADDICTION

When animals are in withdrawal from morphine, they act depressed. This is shown by their relative lack of effort to find a way out of a swim tank. They give up easily and just tread water. This is related to a drop in dopamine release in the accumbens (Rossetti et al. 1993). To the extent that addiction leaves people "low," depressed, and unhappy, it is logical that they self-medicate by taking more of the drug or palatable food such as ice cream and cake. In addition, they may crave the drug or food months later when imagining the "high." Addiction is perpetuated in both ways: (1) seeking escape from the aversive or depressing aftereffects, and (2) seeking the positive effects (Koob and Le Moal 1997; Rada et al. 1991a, 1991b). Thus, addiction is perpetuated by both positive and negative reinforcement, both of which can release dopamine, as explained earlier.

TREATING DEPRESSION

Serotonergic drugs are famous for their ability to bring people out of depression. Prozac is the best-known example. Binge eating symptoms such as loss of control can also be treated with serotonergic drugs (Stunkard et al. 1996). How do these drugs work? The answer is complex, but one part of it relates to our study of why people work. Recall that acetylcholine is released in the accumbens during morphine withdrawal, and that acetylcholine can inhibit behavior. Prozac (fluoxetine) injected directly into the accumbens lowered acetylcholine in normal rats (Rada, Mark, and Hoebel 1993), and it forestalled behavioral depression in the swim test. The effect of Prozac could be due to this inhibition of acetylcholine release or potentiation of the dopamine system, or both.

Another way to treat depression is to release dopamine with mild drugs such as caffeine, if one does not mind the possibility of becoming addicted to caffeine. The same is true of nicotine, which is motivating but addicting. Other drugs such as amphetamine or cocaine may also reverse depression temporarily, but later withdrawal will exacerbate it and may lead to addiction to an illegal substance. Theoretically it would work to combine a mild, legal dopaminergic drug such as phentermine with a serotonergic drug such as Prozac. We are currently testing this combination and find it can reduce cocaine self-administration in rats.

A GENERAL THEORY OF MOTIVATION

The studies cited in this chapter suggest a general theory of behavior reinforcement and motivation. The following theoretical construct is a partial answer to the question of why people work. Dopamine release in the appropriate parts of the accumbens facilitates a response to neural inputs that initiate eating. These inputs are triggered by stimuli coming into the accumbens via glutamate neurons from the amygdala, hippocampus, and cortex. When the animal eats novel food that provides needed calories or particular nutrients, this eating releases dopamine and reinforces the stimulus inputs and response outputs associated with that success. The process can be thwarted by acetylcholine release when the animal becomes full, fat, nauseous, or otherwise sated. The balance of positive feedback, involving dopamine, and negative feedback, involving acetylcholine, determines when we work for food and how much we eat. This balance, in turn, contributes to body weight regulation (Hoebel 1997).

The hypothalamus is largely responsible for integrating environmental and physiological stimuli related to energy needs. The hypothalamus uses this information to influence hormones, behavior, and cognition. On the hormonal side, the hypothalamus uses the integrated information to regulate the release of pancreatic insulin and adrenal glucocorticoids for utilization and storage of energy-rich calories. On the behavioral side, the hypothalamus controls feeding reflexes in the brain stem and helps control eating by influencing the balance between dopamine and acetylcholine in the accumbens. With regard to cognition, the hypothalamus informs the prefrontal cortex about the animal's need state, thereby influencing the cortical reaction to tastes and plans for foraging (Leibowitz and Hoebel 1998; Rolls 1996).

This chapter has outlined the process of hypothalamic control of the economic decisions a person must make. Peptides that evolved eons ago, such as galanin, neuropeptide Y (NPY), and growth hormone releasing peptide, have coded functions in hypothalamic systems that control fat, carbohydrate, and protein intake via brain systems. These behaviorally coded peptides also control metabolism via hormonal systems. Hormones such as insulin and leptin reflect body fat and can enter the hypothalamus to regulate galanin and NPY expression. For example, a lack of body fat would lead to low insulin and low leptin. This deficit would foster the expression of galanin. The subsequent release of dopamine and decrease in acetylcholine in the accumbens prompts the animal to eat. Eating fat can also release galanin, thus releasing accumbens dopamine to reinforce more eating. This positive feedback would continue until short-term satiety signals or a long-term increase in circulating insulin and leptin gradually inhibit galanin production and by this negative feedback slow the rate of eating (Leibowitz and Hoebel 1998).

While the animal is underweight, it is particularly susceptible to anything that potentiates dopaminergic function, including palatable opioid-releasing foods and drugs of abuse. Opioid peptides have evolved, in part, to suppress pain and thus foster approach behavior for hunting and foraging. Palatable food releases opioids that suppress discomfort and prolong eating. Many drugs of abuse act by increasing synaptic dopamine directly or via opioid receptors. These drugs essentially bypass or override the hypothalamic negative feedback systems. When this happens, the animal's behavior is reinforced without normal satiety, especially when underweight (Gosnell and Levine 1996; Pothos, Creese, and Hoebel 1995).

We have proposed that bingeing on palatable food can be addictive. This natural form of addiction forms the neural basis of drug addiction. It is even conceivable that infants become addicted to mother's milk by virtue of milk's dopamine and opioid-releasing properties. Infants may learn to associate other maternal stimuli with nursing and thus develop an addiction—love, if you will—for both milk and mother. To help the process along, milk itself contains opioid peptides.

Withdrawal for an addicted person, or even an addicted rat, gives evidence of behavioral depression. Along with depressed behavior may come depressed mood. According to our theory, these symptoms of depression are related to low dopamine, combined with high acetylcholine release, in the accumbens. To treat the depression, one can take action with the help of cognitive therapy, or one can take drugs that raise dopamine and inhibit acetylcholine release.

There are a variety of pharmacological treatments for addiction. For example, methadone is a long-acting opiate that is a passable substitute for heroin or morphine. Naltrexone is a long-acting opiate blocker that is useful in treating alcoholism (O'Brien, Volpicelli, and Volpicelli 1996). Prozac is a serotonergic drug that will reduce cocaine intake in rats (Carroll et al. 1990) but is not very effective in the doses given to people. A noradrenergic drug, such as clonidine, can help bring dopamine/acetylcholine into balance (Pothos et al. 1991). Many dopaminergic pharmaceuticals are being tested. Perhaps a new generation of therapeutic drugs based on the hypothalamic peptides will have better results. Since these peptides evolved in the control of feeding, and drug abuse acts in part via the feeding system, it is reasonable to suggest that satiety peptides, or antagonists of the feeding peptides, will someday prove effective in helping people control their craving for addictive substances.

THE MEANING FOR PSYCHOLOGY, ECONOMICS, AND LAW

Super-sweet milk products, foods containing caffeine, drinks containing alcohol, and cigarettes provide a ready source of legal dopamine-releasing products. Unfortunately, rich foods and caffeine drinks in restaurants and vending machines in every workplace tempt people to binge on fat and sugar, and bingeing leads to obesity or eating disorders. Obesity increases the risk of cardiovascular disease and diabetes. Alcohol can damage the brain and liver and lead to fatal accidents. Cigarettes cause lung cancer. Illegal drugs are also a costly problem beyond calculation. Thus, much of society's effort and tax dollars are spent in the cause of managing addictions of one sort or another.

It should be evident from this chapter that drug abuse is a special type of illness. I have argued that it is an outgrowth of a natural addictive process. It stems from being able to buy substances that excessively stimulate the behavior reinforcement system in the adult. The fact that people put themselves in harm's way in order to binge on foods and drugs demonstrates the power of the process. The problem is compounded by the gateway from legal to illegal drugs that is based on the interchangeability of dopamine-enhancing substances. Social pressure to be very thin is another contributing factor.

Breaking the law to get drugs is a symptom of the illness. Society has a choice of imprisoning those who break the law or treating their illness, or both. Susceptibility to relapse can last a lifetime. Any "recovered" alcoholic will vouch for this. Binge eaters say their problem is the worst of all. They cannot swear off food, the way one may learn to say no to drugs. For society as a whole, the enforcement of drug laws and the imprisonment of addicts extracts a terrible cost. For all these reasons, it makes sense to find treatments and offer them to those in need before they end up in the hospital or in prison. Follow-up treatment is also important to prevent relapse.

The behavior reinforcement system described in this chapter is the neural substrate of both healthy and unhealthy responses. It is the reason people work. Research to understand how this system functions will contribute to effective psychological and medical treatment for addictive illness and thereby contribute to an effective health system and economic order. The alternative is an overburdened health system, an overburdened penal system, and a major subcurrent of economic disorder. One could say the economy itself will continue to have an "illness" until addiction is understood and treated in the brain, where it happens.

Even when treatments are found, many people will prefer to be addicted. Some people can control their addictions. Some use drugs of abuse to self-medicate depression. And not all addictions are bad. But for those who lose control, pharmacological therapy, cognitive therapy, and behavior therapy should be available.

This chapter has illustrated an approach that studies both human patients and animal models. For the treatment of depression, this approach gave us effective cognitive therapy and the discovery of Prozac. Measures to prevent depression before it starts by training students to think constructively are being tried in the classroom with long-term success (Gillham et al. 1995). The economic benefits will be considerable. For the treatment of substance abuse, this combined approach to psychology and neuroscience will eventually lead to discovery of psychological therapy, pharmacological therapy, and early prevention.

CONCLUSION

The brain contains a sensory-motor interface where environmental stimuli and internally generated plans are translated into action. These action patterns constitute work. We take as an example the energy regulation system that controls the work involved in foraging and eating. Dopamine released in the nucleus accumbens helps reinforce responses that are successful in acquiring good food. If the dopamine system is impaired, then ability to work is compromised. Conversely, excess dopamine function can cause hyperactivity and mania. Learning how to release dopamine is the essence of learning to work.

Acetylcholine in the accumbens can do the opposite of dopamine by inhibiting response output. In excess, this inhibition may lead to pathological loss of reinforcement and behavioral depression. An energy-control network in the hypothalamus has circuits that use coded brain/body peptides to control appetite and eating—in part, by managing dopamine and acetylcholine release in the accumbens. Drugs that potentiate dopamine directly, such as amphetamine, cocaine, and nicotine, or indirectly, such as heroin, alcohol, and marijuana, have the effect of artificially manipulating dopamine/acetylcholine balance.

Substance abuse can lead to addiction with a cycle of bingeing, withdrawal, and craving. Means to influence this system are urgently needed. The situation calls for a fair economic system of rewards, sound psychological principles for therapy and education, and pharmaceuticals to correct inborn or acquired errors. These approaches can be used together to maintain a healthy balance in this neural substrate of behavior reinforcement.

The recent research reported in this chapter was supported by U.S. Public Health Service grants NS 30697 and DA 10608.

REFERENCES

Bentham, J. (1948). *An introduction to the principles of morals and legislations.* Oxford: Blackwell. (Originally published 1789)

Caine, S. B., and Koob, G. F. (1994). Effects of mesolimbic dopamine depletion on responding maintained by cocaine and food. *Journal of Experimental Analysis of Behavior, 61,* 213–221.

Carr, K. D. (1996). Opioid receptor subtypes and stimulation-induced feeding. In S. J. Cooper and P. G. Clifton (Eds.), *Drug receptor subtypes and ingestive behavior* (pp. 167–92). San Diego: Academic Press.

Carroll, M. E., France, C. P., and Meisch, R. A. (1979). Food deprivation increases oral and intravenous drug intake in rats. *Science, 205,* 319–21.

Carroll, M. E., Lac, S. T., Asencio, M., and Kragh, R. (1990). Fluoxetine reduces intravenous cocaine self-administration in rats. *Pharmacology, Biochemistry, and Behavior, 35,* 237–44.

Colantuoni, C., McCarthy, J., Gibbs, G., Searls, E., Alisharan, S., and Hoebel, B. G. (1997). Repeatedly restricted food access combined with highly palatable diet leads to opiate-like withdrawal symptoms during food deprivation in rats. *Society for Neuroscience Abstracts, 23,* 517.

Cousins, M. S., and Salamone, J. D. (1994). Nucleus accumbens dopamine depletions in rats affect relative response allocation in a novel cost/benefit procedure. *Pharmacology, Biochemistry, and Behavior, 49,* 85–91.

Damsma, G., Wenkstern, D., Pfaus, J. G., Phillips, A. G., and Fibiger, H. C. (1992). Sexual behavior increases dopamine transmission in the nucleus accumbens and striatum of male rats: Comparison with novelty and locomotion. *Behavioral Neuroscience, 1,* 181–91.

Ellison, G. D., and Eison, M. S. (1983). Continuous amphetamine intoxication: An animal model of the acute psychotic episode. *Psychological Medicine, 13,* 751–61.

Ettenberg, A. (1989). Dopamine, neuroleptics, and reinforced behavior. *Neuroscience and Biobehavioral Reviews, 13,* 105–11.

Garcia, J., Ervin, R., and Koelling, R. (1966). Learning with prolonged delay of reinforcement. *Psychonomic Science, 5,* 121–22.

Gillham, J. E., Revich, K. J., Jaycox, L. H., and Seligman, M. E. P. (1995). Prevention depression in schoolchildren: Two-year follow-up. *Psychological Science, 6,* 342–51.

Gosnell, B. A., and Levine, A. S. (1996). Stimulation of ingestive behaviour by preferential and selective opioid agonists. In S. J. Cooper and P. G. Clifton (Eds.), *Drug receptor subtypes and ingestive behavior* (pp. 147–66). San Diego: Academic Press.

Grant, S., London, E. D., Newlin, D. B., Villemagne, V. L., Xiang, L., Contoreggi, C., Phillips, R. L., Kimes, A. S., and Margolin, A. (1996). Activation of memory circuits during cue-elicited cocaine craving. *Proceedings of the National Academy of Science, 93,* 12040–45.

Guerin, B., Goeders, N. E., Dworkin, S. I., and Smith, J. E. (1984). Intracranial self-administration of dopamine into the nucleus accumbens. *Society for Neuroscience Abstracts, 10,* 1072.

Hagan, M. M., and Moss, D. E. (1991). An animal model of bulimia nervosa: Opioid sensitivity to fasting episodes. *Pharmacology Biochemistry and Behavior, 39*(2), 421–22.

Hoebel, B. G. (1976). Brain-stimulation reward and aversion in relation to behavior. In A. Wauquier and E. T. Rolls (Eds.), *Brain-stimulation reward* (pp. 335–72). Amsterdam: Elsevier/North-Holland.

———. (1979). Hypothalamic self-stimulation and stimulation escape in relation to feeding and mating. *Federation Proceedings, 38,* 2454–61.

———. (1988). Neuroscience and motivations: Pathways and peptides that define motivation. In R. C. Atkinson, R. J. Herrnstein, G. Lindzey, and R. D. Luce (Eds.), *Stevens' handbook of experimental psychology* (pp. 547–625). New York: Wiley.

———. (1997). Neuroscience and appetitive behavior research: Twenty-five years. *Appetite, 29,* 119–33.

Hoebel, B. G., Hernandez, L., Mark, G. P., and Pothos, E. (1992). Microdialysis in the study of psychostimulants and the neural substrate for reinforcement: Focus on dopamine and serotonin. In J. Frascella and R. Brown (Eds.), *Neurobiological approaches to brain-behavior interaction, NIDA Research Monograph, 124,* 1–34.

Hoebel, B. G., Hernandez, L., Schwartz, D. H., Mark, G. P., Hunter, G. A. (1989). Microdialysis studies of brain norepinephrine, serotonin, and dopamine release during ingestive behavior: Theoretical and clinical implications. In L. H. Schneider, S. J. Cooper, and K. A. Halmi (Eds.), *The psychobiology of human eating disorders* (pp. 171–93). New York: New York Academy of Sciences.

Hoebel, B. G., Leibowitz, S. F., and Hernandez, L. (1992). Neurochemistry of anorexia and bulimia. In H. Anderson (Ed.), *The biology of feast and famine: Relevance to eating disorders* (pp. 21–45). London: Oxford University Press.

Hoebel, B. G., Monaco, A. P., and Hernandez, L., Aulisi, E. F., Stanley, B. G., and Lenard, L. (1983). Self-injection of amphetamine directly into the brain. *Psychopharmacology, 81,* 158–63.

Hoebel, B. G., Rada, P., Mark, G. P., Parada, M., Puig De Parada, M., Pothos, E., and Hernandez, L. (1996). Hypothalamic control of accumbens dopamine: A system for feeding reinforcement. In G. Gray and D. Ryan (Eds.), *Molecular and genetic aspects of obesity* (pp. 263–80). Baton Rouge: Louisiana State University Press.

Kanarek, R. B., White, E. S., Biegen, M. T., Marks-Kaufman, R. (1991). Dietary influences on morphine-induced analgesia in rats. *Pharmacology Biochemistry and Behavior, 38,* 681–84.

Kelley, A. E., and Delfs, J. M. (1991). Dopamine and conditioned reinforcement. *Psychopharmacology, 103,* 187–96.

Koob, G. F., and Bloom, F. E. (1998). Cellular and molecular mechanisms of drug dependence. *Science, 242,* 715–21.

Koob, G. F., and Le Moal, M. (1997). Drug abuse: Hedonic homeostatic dysregulation. *Science, 278,* 52–58.

Koob, G. F., Wall, T. L., and Bloom, F. E. (1989). Nucleus accumbens as a substrate for the aversive stimulus effects of opiate withdrawal. *Psychopharmacology, 98,* 530–34.

Leibowitz, S. F., and Hoebel, B. G. (1998). Behavioral neuroscience of obesity. In G. A. Bray, C. Bouchard, and W. P. T. James (Eds.), *Handbook of obesity* (pp. 315–58). New York: Marcel Dekker.

Maldonado-Irizarry, C. S., and Kelley, A. E. (1995). Excitotoxic lesions of the core and shell subregions of the nucleus accumbens differentially disrupt body weight regulation and motor activity in rats. *Brain Research Bulletin, 38*(6), 551–59.

Maldonado-Irizarry, C. S., Swanson, C. J., and Kelley, A. E. (1995). Glutamate receptors in the nucleus accumbens shell control feeding behavior via the lateral hypothalamus. *Journal of Neuroscience, 15,* 6779–88.

Mark, G. P., Blander, D. S., and Hoebel, B. G. (1991). A conditioned stimulus decreases extracellular dopamine in the nucleus accumbens after the development of a learned taste aversion. *Brain Research, 551,* 308–10.

Mark, G. P., Rada, P., Pothos, E., and Hoebel, B. G. (1992). Effects of feeding and drinking on acetylcholine release in the nucleus accumbens, striatum, and hippocampus of freely behaving rats. *Journal of Neurochemistry, 58,* 2269–74.

Mark, G. P., Smith, S. E., Mark, G. P., Rada, P. V., and Hoebel, B. G. (1996). An appetitively conditioned taste elicits a preferential increase in mesolimbic dopamine release. *Pharmacology, Biochemistry, and Behavior, 48,* 461–60.

Mark, G. P., Weinberg, J. B., Rada, P., and Hoebel, B. G. (1995). Extracellular acetylcholine is increased in the nucleus accumbens following the presentation of an aversively conditioned taste stimulus. *Brain Research, 688,* 184–88.

McClelland, R. C., and Hoebel, B. G. (1991). d-Fenfluramine and self-stimulation: Loss of fenfluramine effect on underweight rats. *Brain Research Bulletin, 27,* 341–45.

Mogenson, G. J., Jones, D. L., and Yim, C. Y. (1980). From motivation to action: Fundamental interface between the limbic system and the motor system. *Progress in Neurobiology, 14,* 69–97.

Nader, K. and van der Kooy, D. (1994). The motivation produced by morphine and food is isomorphic: Approaches to specific motivational stimuli are learned. *Psychobiology, 22,* 68–76.

Nestler, E. J., and Aghajanian, G. K. (1997). Molecular and cellular basis of addiction. *Science, 278,* 58–63.

O'Brien, C. P., Volpicelli, L. A., and Volpicelli, J. R. (1996). Naltrexone in the treatment of alcoholism: A clinical review. *Alcohol 13*(1), 35–39.

Olds, J. and Milner, P. (1954). Positive reinforcement produced by electrical stimulation of septal area and others regions of rat brain. *Journal of Comparative and Physiological Psychology, 47,* 419–27.

Overstreet, D. H., Rezvani, A. H., and Janowsky, D. S. (1992). Genetic animal models of depression and ethanol preference provide support for cholinergic and serotonergic involvement in depression and alcoholism. *Biological Psychiatry, 31,* 919–36.

Pfaus, J. G., Damsma, G., Wenkstern, D. Fibiger, H. C. (1995). Sexual activity increases dopamine transmission in the nucleus accumbens and striatum of female rats. *Brain Research, 693,* 21–30.

Phillips, A. G., Blaha, C. D., Pfaus, J. G., and Blackburn, J. R. (1992). Neurobiological correlates of positive emotional states: Dopamine, anticipation, and reward. In *International review of studies on emotions* (pp. 31–50). New York: Wiley.

Pothos, E., Rada, P. Mark, G. P., and Hoebel, B. G. (1991). Dopamine microdialysis in the nucleus accumbens during acute and chronic morphine, naloxone-precipitated withdrawal and clonidine treatment. *Brain Research, 466,* 348–50.

Pothos, E., Creese, I., and Hoebel, B. G. (1995). Restructureed eating with weight loss selectively decreases extracellular dopamine in the nucleus accumbens and alters dopamine response to amphetamine, morphine, and food intake. *Journal of Neuroscience, 15,* 6640–50.

Rada, P., Mark, G., and Hoebel, B. G. (1993). In vivo modulation of acetylcholine in the nucleus accumbens of freely moving rats: I. Inhibition by serotonin. *Brain Research, 619,* 98–104.

———. (1998). Dopamine release in the nucleus accumbens by hypothalamic stimulation-escape behavior. *Brain Research, 782,* 228–34.

Rada, P., Mark, G., Pothos, E., and Hoebel, B. G. (1991a). Systemic morphine simultaneously decreases extracellular acetylcholine and increases dopamine in the nucleus accumbens of freely moving rats. *Neuropharmacology, 30,* 1133–36.

Rada, P., Pothos, E., Mark, G., and Hoebel, B. G. (1991b). Microdialysis evidence that acetylcholine in the nucleus accumbens is involved in morphine withdrawal and its treatment with clonidine. *Brain Research, 561,* 354–56.

Robbins, T., Everitt, B. (1996). Neurobehavioural mechanisms of reward and motivation. *Current Opinion in Neurobiology, 6,* 228–36.

Robinson, T. E., and Berridge, K. C. (1993). The neural basis of drug craving: An incentive-sensitization theory of addiction. *Brain Research Reviews, 18,* 247–91.

Rodefer, J. S., and Carroll, M. E. (1996). Progressive ratio and behavioral economic evaluation of the reinforcing efficiency of orally delivered phencyclidine and ethanol in monkeys: Effects of feeding conditions. *Psychopharmacology, 128,* 265–73.

Rolls, E. T. (1995). Central taste anatomy and neurophysiology. In R. L. Doty (Ed.), *Handbook of olfaction and gustation* (pp. 549–73). New York: Marcel Dekker.

———. (1996). The orbitofrontal cortex. *Philosophical Transactions of the Royal Society of London B Biological Science, 351*(1346), 1433–43.

Rossetti, Z. L., Lai, M., Hmaidan, Y., and Gessa, G. L. (1993). Depletion of mesolimbic dopamine during behavioral despair: Partial reversal by chronic imipramine. *European Journal of Pharmacology 242*(3), 313–15.

Rossetti, Z. L., Melis, F., Carboni, S., Diana, M., and Gessa, G. L. (1992). Alcohol withdrawal in rats is associated with a marked fall in extraneuronal dopamine. *Alcoholism: Clinical and Experimental Research, 16*, 529–32.

Salamone, J. D., and Snyder, B. J. (1997). Behavioral functions of nucleus accumbens dopamine: Empirical and conceptual problems with the anhedonia hypothesis. *Neuroscience and Behavioral Reviews, 21*, 341–59.

Schultz, W., Dayan, P., and Montague, P. R. (1997). A neural substrate of prediction and reward. *Science, 275*, 1593–99.

Skinner, B. G. (1953). *Science and human behavior.* New York: Macmillan.

Smith, G. P. (1995). Dopamine and food reward. In S. Fluharty and A. M. Morrison (Eds.), *Progress in psychobiology and physiological psychology* (pp. 83–144). New York: Academic Press.

Specker, S. M., Lac, S. T., and Carroll, M. E. (1994). Food deprivation history and cocaine self-administration: An animal model of binge eating. *Pharmacology, Biochemistry, and Behavior, 48*, 1025–29.

Stunkard, A. J., Berkowitz, R. J., Tanrikut, C., Reiss, E., and Young, L. (1996). d-Fenfluramine treatment of binge eating disorder. *Obesity Research 3(suppl. 3),* 341s.

Tanda, G., Pontieri, F. E., and Di Chiara, G. (1997). Cannabinoid and heroin activation of mesolimbic dopamine transmission by a common mu-1 opioid receptor mechanism. *Science, 276*, 2048–50.

Taylor, K. M., Davidson, K., Mark, G. P., Rada, P., and Hoebel, B. G. (1992). Conditioned taste aversion induced by increased acetylcholine in the nucleus accumbens. *Society for Neuroscience Abstracts, 18*, 1066.

Vaccarino, F. J. (1996). Dopamine-opioid mechanisms in ingestion. In S. J. Cooper and P. G. Clifton (Eds.), *Drug receptor subtypes and ingestive behavior* (pp. 219–32). San Diego: Academic Press.

Volkow, N. D., Wang, G. J., Fowler, J. S. (1997). Imaging studies of cocaine in the human brain and studies of the cocaine addict. *Annals of the New York Academy of Sciences, 820*, 41–45.

Wise, R. A. (1982). Common neural basis of brain stimulation reward, drug reward, and food reward. In B. G. Hoebel and D. Novin (Eds.), *The neural basis of feeding and reward* (pp. 445–54). Brunswick, Maine: Haer Institute.

———. (1996). Neurobiology of addiction. *Current Opinion in Neurobiology, 6*(2), 243–51.

Wise, R. A., Newton, P., Leeb, K., Burnette, B., Pocock, D., and Justice, J. B., Jr. (1995). Fluctuations in nucleus accumbens dopamine concentration during intravenous cocaine self-administration in rats. *Psychpharmacology, 120*(1), 10–20.

Yeomans, J. S., Mathur, A., and Tampakeras, M. (1993). Rewarding brain stimulation: Role of tegmental cholinergic neurons that activate dopamine neurons. *Behavioral Neuroscience, 107*, 1077–87.

Contributors

DANIEL KAHNEMAN is Eugene Higgins Professor of Psychology and professor of public affairs at Princeton University.

ED DIENER is professor of psychology at the University of Illinois, Urbana-Champaign.

NORBERT SCHWARZ is professor of psychology at the University of Michigan, Ann Arbor, and senior research scientist at the Survey Research Center and the Research Center for Group Dynamics of Michigan's Institute for Social Research.

MICHAEL ARGYLE is professor emeritus of psychology at Oxford Brookes University and reader emeritus in social psychology at Oxford University.

JORGE ARMONY is Kinross Fellow in Cognitive Neuroscience in the Wellcome Department of Cognitive Neurology at the Institute of Neurology, London.

HOWARD BERENBAUM is professor of psychology and psychiatry at the University of Illinois, Urbana-Champaign.

KENT C. BERRIDGE is professor of psychology at the University of Michigan, Ann Arbor.

IAN A. BRODKIN is assistant clinical professor in the Department of Anesthesiology at the University of British Columbia.

JOHN T. CACIOPPO is professor of psychology at the University of Chicago.

NANCY CANTOR is provost and executive vice-president and professor of psychology at the University of Michigan, Ann Arbor.

ANURADHA F. CHAWLA is doctoral candidate in industrial/organizational psychology at the University of Guelph.

MARTIN W. DEVRIES is professor of social psychiatry at Maastricht University in the Netherlands and is scientific director of the International Institute for Psycho-Social and Socio-Ecological Research (IPSER).

ERIC EICH is professor of cognitive psychology at the University of British Columbia.

SHANE FREDERICK is doctoral candidate in social and decision sciences at Carnegie Mellon University.

BARBARA L. FREDRICKSON is assistant professor of psychology at the University of Michigan, Ann Arbor.

NICO H. FRIJDA is professor emeritus at Amsterdam University.

PAUL FRIJTERS is senior research associate in economics at the Free University, Amsterdam.

JOSE GOMEZ is doctoral candidate in psychology at the University of Illinois, Urbana-Champaign.

HEIDI GRANT is doctoral candidate in the Department of Psychology at Columbia University.

E. TORY HIGGINS is professor of psychology in the Department of Psychology at Columbia University

BARTLEY G. HOEBEL is professor in the Psychology Department at Princeton University.

TIFFANY A. ITO is assistant professor of psychology at the University of Colorado.

MICHAEL KUBOVY is professor of psychology at the University of Virginia.

RANDY J. LARSEN is Stuckenberg Professor of Human Values and Moral Development in the Psychology Department of Washington University in St. Louis.

HUYNH-NHU LE is postdoctoral fellow in psychiatry at the University of California, San Francisco.

JOSEPH LEDOUX is Henry and Lucy Moses Professor of Science in the Center for Neural Science and Department of Psychology at New York University.

GEORGE LOEWENSTEIN is professor of economics and psychology at Carnegie Mellon University.

RICHARD E. LUCAS is doctoral candidate in psychology at the University of Illinois, Urbana-Champaign.

GREGORY P. MARK is assistant professor in the Department of Behavioral Neuroscience at Oregon Health Sciences University, Portland.

WILLIAM N. MORRIS is professor of psychology at Dartmouth College.

DAVID G. MYERS is John Dirk Werkman Professor of Psychology at Hope College.

SUSAN NOLEN-HOEKSEMA is professor of psychology and director of the Gender and Mental Health Program at the University of Michigan, Ann Arbor.

CHRISTOPHER PETERSON is professor of psychology and director of clinical training at the University of Michigan, Ann Arbor.

EMMANUEL N. POTHOS is associate research scientist in the Department of Neurology at Columbia University.

PEDRO V. RADA is professor in the Department of Physiology at the School of Medicine, University of Los Andes, Merida, Venezuela.

CHITRA RAGHAVAN is postdoctoral fellow in psychiatry at Yale University.

JOHN L. REEVES is director of Behavioral Medical Services in the Pain Center at Cedars-Sinai Medical Center, Los Angeles.

PAUL ROZIN is Edmund J. and Louise W. Kahn Professor for Faculty Excellence in the Department of Psychology at the University of Pennsylvania.

CHERYL L. RUSTING is assistant professor of psychology at the State University of New York, Buffalo.

CATHERINE A. SANDERSON is assistant professor of psychology at Amherst College.

ROBERT M. SAPOLSKY is professor of biological sciences and neuroscience at Stanford University and research associate at the Institute of Primate Research, National Museums of Kenya.

DAVID SCHKADE is professor of management and the William T. Spriegel Fellow at the University of Texas, Austin.

JAMES SHAH is assistant professor in the Department of Psychology at the University of Wisconsin, Madison.

SAUL S. SHIFFMAN is professor of psychology at the University of Pittsburgh.

PETER SHIZGAL is professor of psychiatry and director of the Center for Studies in Behavioral Neurobiology at Concordia University.

ARTHUR A. STONE is professor of psychiatry at the State University of New York, Stony Brook, and is vice-chair for research in the Department of Psychiatry.

FRITZ STRACK is professor of psychology at the University of Wuerzburg, Germany.

EUNKOOK MARK SUH is doctoral candidate is psychology at the University of Illinois, Urbana-Champaign.

BERNARD M. S. VAN PRAAG is professor of applied economic research at the University of Amsterdam and managing director of the Foundation for Economic Research of the University of Amsterdam.

LAURA VERNON is doctoral candidate in psychology at the University of Illinois, Urbana-Champaign.

PETER WARR is research professor at the Institute of Work Psychology, University of Sheffield, United Kingdom.

Index

Numbers in **boldface** refer to tables and figures.

Inkeles, A., 357
innate needs approach to well-being, 445–46
insecure attachment, 376
insecurity, job, 402
instant utility: brain stimulation reward, 502, 503, 505–11; vs. decision utility, 18–19; definition, 4, 5; and dissociation with emotions, 527–30; and evaluation by changes, 15–16; nonverbal measurement of, 532–44; and reinforcement, 560–61; and temporal integration, 5–7
integrated pleasure, 112, 113
integration, affective, 4, 5–7
intelligence, 368
intensity of emotion: and adaptation, 308; and duration of utility, 6; excesses in, 274–75; vs. frequency, 309; gender differences in, 336–37; growth of, 517; measurement issues, 199–200; and personality, 225–26; regulation of, 258; and self-focused attention, 176
intentional state, emotion as, 191
interactions, and psychopathology, 271–72. *See also* relationships
interdependence, 381, 382
interindividual comparisons, 70–74
internal consistency estimates, 43
internal context, and food, 117–18
internalizing disorders, 330–31, 335. *See also* anxiety; depression
internal locus of control, 466
internal validity, threats to, 310–11
International Association for the Study of Pain (IASP), 155
international implications of environmental factors on well-being, 355–56, 362. *See also* cross-cultural analysis
Internet, and valued activity participation, 239
interpersonal relations. *See* relationships
interview methods, 26
intimacy in marriage, 380
intraindividual comparisons, 62–70
intrapersonal factors, 12, 269–71. *See also* individual factors
intrinsically valued goals, 124, 233, 446
introversion, 221–22. *See also* personality
intuitive theories, 94–96
Isen, Alice M., 170, 171, 172, 174, 175
Ito, Tiffany A., 470–88
Izard, C. E., 46

Jack, D. C., 338
Jackson, A. P., 446
Jackson, B., 339–40, 341
Jackson, C. N., 393
Jackson, M., 317
Jackson, P. R., 363
Jacobsen, Edith, 170
Jamal, M., 405
James, T., 279
James, William, 197, 253, 481, 489
Jamison, Kay, 169
Jamison, R. N., 164–65
Jamner, L., 35
Janal, M. N., 310
Janoff-Bulman, R., 13, 16, 89, 165, 312, 313, 318
Jenson, M. P., 161
Jex, S. M., 405
jobs, 355–56, 362–64, 369. *See also* workplace
job-specific vs. context-free well-being, 394–95, 399

John Henryism, 466
Johns, G., 398
Johnson, D. S., 297
Johnson, E. J., 175
Johnston, V. S., 142–43
Joiner, T. E., 273
Jolly, A., 148
Jonsson, E., 311
Jorgenson, D. W., 415
The Joyless Economy (Scitovsky), 13
joy of verification, 147
Judge, T. A., 395
judgments: and adaptation, 306, 310, 320; affective consequences of comparison, 12–13; biases in, 21–22, 89, 96, 272–73; economic considerations, 424–25; interindividual comparisons, 70–74; intraindividual comparisons, 62–70; measurement of value, 308–9; methodological implications, 79–81; model for, 77–79; and mood, 55–56, 74–77, 79, 170, 174–76, 177; neurological factors in, 7–9; vs. perception, 11–13; and subjective well-being, x. *See also* utility

Kagan, J., 215, 216, 545, 551
Kagel, J. H., 519
Kahn, R. L., 235
Kahneman, Daniel, 3–25, 5, 9, 16, 19, 20, 47, 87, 88–89, 89–90, 97, 112, 113, 137, 140, 215, 244–45, 314, 315, 413, 417, 419–20, 474, 502, 503, 504, 508, 509, 514, 527, 528, 531, 540, 551
Kaiser, H. A., 233
Kalimo, R., 403
Kamarck, T. W., 36
Kaniasty, K., 179–80
Kanouse, D. E., 94
Kant, Immanuel, 127, 190
Kaprio, J., 312
Kapteyn, Ari, 415, 417, 418, 419, 421
Karasek, R. A., 398, 406
Karoly, P., 161
Kasl, S. V., 363
Kasper, S., 178
Kasser, T., 233, 446
Katz, David, 20, 118
Kavanagh, J. D., 175, 185
Kedem, P., 261
Keefe, F. J., 162
Kelly, George, 299
Kemmerer, B., 402
Kendler, K. S., 269
Kennelly, K. J., 297
Kent, Gerry, 91
Kessler, R. C., 339
Ketelaar, T., 55, 221
Kette, G., 222
Kihlstrom, J. F., 235–36
Kilmann, P. R., 312
Kimbell, J., 364
King, D. A., 437
King, Martin Luther, Jr., 386
kinship ties, 362, 376–77, 384–86, 422–23. *See also* children; marriage
Kishchuck, N., 62
Klassen, A., 313
Klein, R., 270
Kleinginna, P. R. and A. M., 41
Kleinmuntz, D. N., 99